The 1999-2000   Official PFA

FOOTBALLERS
FACTFILE

Edited by
Barry J Hugman

Assistant Editor
Roy Grant

Photographs by
Colorsport

Queen Anne Press

First published in Great Britain in 1999 by
Queen Anne Press
a division of Lennard Associates Limited
Mackerye End, Harpenden
Hertfordshire AL5 5DR

A CIP catalogue record for this book
is available from the British Library

ISBN 1 85291 607 9

PFA Awards photograph on p 352: Allsport UK

Typeset and designed by
Typecast (Artwork & Design)
8 Mudford Road
Yeovil, Somerset BA21 4AA

Printed and bound in Great Britain by
Butler & Tanner, London and Frome

Acknowledgements

Now into its fifth year, the Factfile continues to expand and reach out, not only as a media tool, and invaluable to those in the game, but as a part-work which, in due course, will cover the season-by-season record of every player's complete career and should be of interest to all who follow this great game of ours. As a book with a heavy workload, I would once again like to express my thanks to **Gordon Taylor**, the chief executive, and all those at the PFA, including **Brendon Batson** and **Garry Nelson**, who are genuinely supporting and helping to establish the Factfile. Their help is much appreciated.

Also, I am exceedingly grateful to all those at the Football League, such as **Debbie Birch**, and **Louise Standing**, and **Mike Foster**, **Adrian Cook**, and **Jonathan Hargreaves** at the Premiership, for their help in establishing good, solid, and reliable information, especially regarding player appearance stats. That gratitude also extends to **Sandy Bryson** of the Scottish FA.

On the international front, I was lucky to have the help and co-operation of **David Barber** (English FA), **Brendan McKenna** (FA of Ireland), **Ceri Stennett** (official FA of Wales statistician), and **Marshall Gillespie** (editor of the Northern Ireland Football Yearbook). Having co-ordinated this exercise, **Roy Grant** (assistant editor), along with **Andy Shute**, also gave his time to numerous other tasks, including keeping note of all player appearances, subs, and goals for each club on a weekly basis. And, as in previous years, I was happy to call upon **Mick Featherstone**, who helped Roy collate heights, weights, birthplaces, birthdates, and double checked the statistical input. Others who gave of their time were **Dick Barton**, **Alan Platt**, **Jenny Hugman**, and many Football League and Premiership staff members up and down the country.

For the fifth year, **Jonathan Ticehurst**, managing director of Windsor Insurance Brokers' Sports Division, has thrown his weight behind the Factfile, both financially and vocally. His and Windsor's support, as with the British Boxing Board of Control Yearbook, is greatly appreciated.

For details provided on players, I have listed below, in alphabetical order, the names of the "team", without whose help this book would not have been possible to produce. Once again, I thank every one of them for all the hard work they put in.

Audrey Adams *(Watford):* Producer and statistician for BBC Radio Sport and a Watford supporter since the days of Cliff Holton, Audrey is also the club statistician for the *Ultimate Football Guide.*

Steve Adamson *(Scarborough):* A 41-year-old postman who has supported Scarborough for 30 years, and previously edited the club programme, Yore Publications published his official club history last November. With Boro relegated last season, and now in the Conference, we wish Steve well for the future and thank him for all of the hard work he has done on behalf of the *Factfile.*

Geoff Allman *(Walsall):* A university lecturer by trade, he saw his first ever game in February 1944, Walsall versus Wolves. Has written for Walsall's programme for over 30 seasons and, at one time or another, has provided articles for more than half of the clubs currently in the Premiership and Football League. Geoff is also a Methodist local preacher and press officer.

Stuart Basson *(Chesterfield):* Saw his 1998 *Who's Who, Lucky Whites and Spireites,* become Yore Publications fastest-selling book to date. A contributor to the *Factfile* since its inception, Stuart hopes to complete a Chesterfield FC history in the next couple of years, and is starting work on a broader history of football in north-east Derbyshire.

Ian Bates *(Bradford):* Has followed City since 1951 and refereed in amateur football up until 1995-96. A member of the AFS, this is the first publication that Ian has been involved in.

David Batters *(York City):* A supporter since 1948, he is the club historian, a contributor to the programme and author of *York City: The Complete Record 1922-1990.* Also commentates on matches at York Hospital.

Harry Berry *(Blackburn Rovers):* Author of the club centenary history, *A Century of Soccer* and other books on Rovers, and co-author of the *Preston North End* history, along with several books on athletics.

Eddie Brennan *(Sunderland):* A season ticket holder at the Stadium of Light, and a contributor to the *Carling Ultimate Football Guide,* Eddie has been a regular supporter since 1976.

Jonathan Brewer *(Plymouth Argyle):* Currently the Argyle statistician for the *Ultimate Football Guide,* Jonathan also writes articles for the *Pasty News,* a publication run by the London branch of the supporters' club.

Jim Brown *(Coventry City):* The club's official statistician and contributor to the programme, he also pens a column for the local newspaper answering readers' queries.

Trevor Bugg *(Hull City):* A supporter of the Tigers for 30 years, Trevor is a major contributor to Hull City's much respected matchday programme.

Graham Caton *(Bournemouth):* Into his fifth year with the *Factfile,* Graham is a committed Cherries' supporter who has always enjoyed collating facts and figures relating to the club.

Wallace Chadwick *(Burnley):* A supporter for over 30 years, he has seen all the extremes in the period from the great days of the '60s, including the championship of all four divisions and a narrow escape from relegation to the Conference. Wallace is a regular contributor to the Clarets' programme.

Dennis Chapman *(Manchester City):* Now retired, Dennis has followed City since 1937-38. Has worked on several publications, including the *FA Carling Premier League: The Players* and the *Ultimate Football Guide.* Possesses possibly the largest collection of City programmes, the earliest being 1902-03. Has been a life member of the Association of Football Statisticians since 1980.

Paul Clayton *(Charlton Athletic):* Paul wrote a regular feature in the Charlton programme for several seasons, and still contributes to other publications connected with the club, including supplying the statistics for the *Ultimate Football Guide,* which he has done for the last 12 years. Is also a season ticket holder at the Valley despite living in Wiltshire, and is a member of the AFS.

Grant Coleby *(Exeter City):* A member of both Exeter City's Supporters' Club and the Association of Football Statisticians, Grant has been the official contributor to the Factfile since its inception.

Eddie Collins *(Nottingham Forest):* A Forest supporter since 1956, and a member of the Associated Football Statisticians, this is the first publication he has been involved in.

David Copping *(Barnsley):* The writer of the past meetings column in the Barnsley programme for the last eight seasons, he also commentated live hospital broadcasts from Oakwell between 1978 and 1991 and has since narrated for the club videos.

Frank Coumbe *(Brentford):* Has not missed a competitive Brentford home match since December 1977, and has been the Brentford statistician for the *Ultimate Football Guide* for 15 years.

Ken Craig *(Colchester United):* Ken, who continues to produce the monthly newsletter, *U's from 'ome,* for all United fans living away from home, has just celebrated 25 years of supporting the club. He is now looking forward to the next 25 years!

Peter Cullen *(Bury):* A life-long Bury supporter, Peter is 39 years old and now works full time at his beloved club as the ticket office manager and programme editor. He is also the club's official historian and a collector of all things connected with the Shakers.

John Curtis *(Scunthorpe United):* A life-long Scunthorpe fan who has seen all of United's league matches, home and away, for the past seven seasons, John is currently deputy sports editor of the *Scunthorpe Evening Telegraph,* and a former editor of the matchday programme for four years.

Carol Dalziel *(Tranmere Rovers):* A Tranmere supporter for 30 years, Carol operates the club's electronic scoreboard on match days, and contributes regularly to the programme. She also acts as the supporters' liaison officer.

Denise Dann *(Aston Villa):* In her own words, Denise is a mad,

crazy Villa supporter, who follows them up and down the country without fail. Her only previous football work was to help me with the club's profiles required for the *Premier League: The Players* publication. She is helped by her husband, Paul.

Gareth Davies (*Wrexham*): Assists in the much acclaimed club programme, the editor of which, **Geraint Parry**, also helped on heights and weights, etc, for this publication. Gareth has written and published the *Coast of Soccer Memories*, the centenary history of the *North Wales Coast FA (1995)*, and co-authored with Ian Garland the *Who's Who of Welsh International Soccer Players (1991)*. Also heavily involved in Wrexham, *A Complete Record 1872-1992*, written by Peter Jones. Currently researching *Wrexham FC's Who's Who* at the moment, he still finds time to compile the club section for the *Ultimate Football Guide*.

David Downs (*Reading*): David has been a Reading supporter for 50 years, and played in the last-ever match at Elm Park, for a veteran's XI, camping overnight in the centre circle before the pitch was ploughed up. After retiring from a teaching career, he has now been appointed as education and welfare officer at Reading FC's Academy. His most recent publication is *Keep it on the Island*, the story of football in Jersey.

Ray Driscoll (*Chelsea*): A life-long Blues' fan, born and bred two miles away from Stamford Bridge – he still has to pinch himself to make sure that he has not dreamed the last three seasons at Chelsea, although he was saddened by the departure of Ruud Gullit. Is a contributor to many football books, and also wrote articles for the *Euro '96* programmes.

Mark Evans (*Leeds United*): Has supported United for over 30 years and describes his association with the club as one of the loves of his life. The Leeds' statistician for the *Ultimate Football Guide* for nearly nine years, he was also involved in my two editions of the *FA Carling Premiership: The Players*.

Keith Evemy (*Fulham*): A regular supporter, both home and away, since 1943, Keith missed Fulham's only previous post-war honour, the Second Division championship in 1948-49, being away on military service. Has contributed to the club programme for more than 20 years, and last season's success was the sweeter for having waited so long.

Colin Faiers (*Cambridge United*): A 39-year-old chartered accountant, Colin, a fan for over 29 years, is the recognised club statistician and currently writes the historical features for the programme.

Harold Finch (*Crewe Alexandra*): The club's historian and a supporter for over 60 years, Harold has been the programme editor for more than 40 of them. A one-club man, he has travelled extensively to watch them play.

Mick Ford and **Richard Lindsey** (*Millwall*): Mick has been a life-long supporter of Millwall from childhood, through army service, and now back in civilian life 46 years later. Brought up in the New Den area, but now living in Worcester, he goes to all the home games and most of the away fixtures, and has a formidable collection of memorabilia which he adds to when attending many programme fairs right across the country. And, as a full badge licence holder, he likes to cast an eye over the team performance. Meanwhile, his Factfile partner, Richard, the author of *Millwall: The Complete Record*, continues to help estaablish the Millwall FC Museum at the New Den.

Dave Goody (*Southend United*): United historian, statistician and collector, he co-authored *Southend United: The Official History of the Blues* and is a regular contributor to the programme.

Frank Grande (*Northampton Town*): Author of *The Cobblers, A History of Northampton Town FC* and a *Who's Who* on the club, he has now written a fourth book titled *The Centenery History of Northampton Town*. Has contributed a regular column to the club programme for the past 19 seasons.

Roy Grant (*Oxford United*): Formerly assistant secretary at Oxford United, as well as being the club programme editor and statistician, he also handled the clubline telephone service. In the past, a contributor to the *Official Football League Yearbook*, he currently contributes to the *Ultimate Football Guide and Factfile*. Has supported United from boyhood.

Michael Green (*Bolton Wanderers*): Despite being a fanatical

Newcastle United supporter, Michael covers Bolton for the Factfile and his excellent efforts are much appreciated. Having a yearning to get involved in the area of freelance journalism, preferably concerning football or popular entertainment (music, films etc), he hopes to go full time sooner or later.

Don Hales and **Raymond Hugman** (*Luton Town*): An Events Director at *Winning Business*, a sales management magazine, Don has contributed to *World Soccer, Team Talk*, and the *Ultimate Football Guide*, as well as compiling the obituary column for the AFS booklet. This year, Don was helped by my cousin, Raymond, who is looking to build himself a career in writing.

Roger Harrison (*Blackpool*): Life-long supporter who has seen the Pool play every other league side both home and away, and joint programme editor and club statistician, Roger also contributes to other publications, including *Rothmans* and the *Ultimate Football Guide*.

Richard and **Janey Hayhoe** (*Tottenham Hotspur*): Now the proud parents of Holly (a future Spurs' fan), Janey and Richard were again happy to put the club's biographies together for the *Factfile* despite their exta duties. With George Graham now in charge at White Hart Lane, things can only get better.

Ron Hockings (*International football*): Has now published five books involving the history of Chelsea, European and South American Cups. *The Nations of Europe*, currently available in two volumes, includes every line-up for all the European countries' matches up until 1993, with volume three envisaged being ready shortly and has recently completed *90 Years of the "Blues"*, the statistical history of Chelsea. Provided all the international appearances for non-British teams in this year's *Factfile*.

Mike Jay (*Bristol Rovers*): As the club's official historian and programme contributor, Mike has had three books published on Bristol Rovers, namely *The Complete Record (1883-1987), Pirates in Profile: A Who's Who of Players 1920-1994*, and *Bristol Rovers FC Images of England Photographic History 1999*.

Colin Jones (*Swansea City*): A fan since the early 1960s and a contributor to the club programme during the last six years. Played non-league football, before being involved in training and coaching.

Andrew Kirkham (*Sheffield United*): A Blades' supporter since 1953, and a regular contributor to the club programme and handbook since 1984, Andrew is a member of the AFS and 92 club. Was also a contributor to *Sheffield United: The First 100 Years*.

Gordon Lawton (*Oldham Athletic*): Employed as the public relations officer at the club and Athletic's official photographer. Other publications contributed to, include *Carling Premiership: The Players, Rothmans Yearbook, Ultimate Football Guide* and *News of the World* annual.

Geoffrey Lea (*Wigan Athletic*): Editor of the matchday programme, Geoff has been an Athletic supporter for over 25 years, first watching the club during their non-league days. And, as the matchday reporter for Clubcall, he has worked for local radio stations following the club's progress. Is also the club statistician for the *Ultimate Football Guide*.

Bob Lonkhurst (*Arsenal*): A life-long Gunners' supporter, having had trials with the club as a 16-year-old goalie, Bob is a regular visitor to Highbury, and has a keen interest in the youth team. Is also a successful boxing author, with a large collection of boxiana, being a contributor to two magazines and the author of *Man of Courage*, the story of the ring legend, Tommy Farr. Pat Rice, the former Arsenal star, also helped out with information.

John Lovis (*Torquay United*): A supporter since 1955, and a regular contributor to the club programme, he is also United's statistician for the *Ultimate Football Guide*.

Gordon Macey (*Queens Park Rangers*): Gordon has been following QPR for nearly 40 years and is now recognised as the club's official historian and statistician. A life-long member of the AFS, and the author of the successful *Complete Record of Queens Park Rangers* published by Breedens, his third book on the club was published in August 1999. His "daytime" job involves a large amount of overseas travel, which gives him the opportunity to watch football (and ice hockey) in a number of different countries.

Steve McGhee (*Derby County*): A collector of Derby

memorabilia and a fan since 1969. Earlier involved in a bi-monthly historical magazine on County, he currently compiles the club section for the *Ultimate Football Guide*.

Richard Mackey *(Swindon Town)*: Having supported the club from boyhood, Richard joined Town as the marketing and press officer on leaving Cardiff University with a BA (Hons) in 1977. Has recently moved to the Carling Premier League, and will be managing the press office.

John Maguire *(Manchester United)*: Working on several sports related booklets during the course of the year, John would like to dedicate this piece to *Sportspages* in Manchester for their continued support; to Don Hales for suggesting his name to Barry Hugman when the *Factfile* was in its infancy; to his family who happily tolerate the ever-growing pile of newspaper cuttings; and, finally, to Les Olive who gave him so much encouragement to write about all things United many moons ago. Is a member of the Association of Football Statisticians.

John Martin *(Chester City)*: Has supported Chester City for over 30 years, and is the club statistician for both the *Rothmans Yearbook* and *Ultimate Football Guide*, as well as supplying data to various other programmes. A contributor to the matchday programme for 20 years, including the role of programme editor for ten years – winning the "Third Division Programme of the Year" award in 1993-94 when he was at the helm.

Wade Martin *(Stoke City)*: For many years a major contributor to the club programme, as well as writing *A Potters Tale* and the *Master Potters'* series of books.

Tony Matthews *(West Bromwich Albion)*: Official statistician and curator of Albion, his publications include, *the complete records of Aston Villa, Birmingham City, WBA, Wolves, Walsall and Stoke City*. Has also compiled *Who 's Whos* on the first four clubs listed above, plus Manchester United, and currently contributes to several programmes.

Paul Morant *(Leyton Orient)*: Paul, a 29-year-old insurance messenger who works in the City of London, has been supporting Orient for 21 years, and travels to all games, whether home or away – even attending reserve and youth-team matches where possible.

Ian Nannestad *(Lincoln City)*: A past contributor to the Imps' programme and co-author of the *Who's Who of Lincoln City, 1892-1994* publication.

Adrian & Caroline Newnham and **Tim Carder** *(Brighton & Hove Albion)*: Both Adrian and Caroline were heavily involved in the recent campaigns to "Bring home the Albion" and to gain support for a new stadium at Falmer, near Brighton. They completed the *Factfile* biographies begun by Roger Harris, who died suddenly in April. Roger was a life-long supporter of Albion and took an immense interest in the history of the club and, indeed, in football in general. An active member of the AFS, who co-authored *Seagulls! The Story of Brighton & Hove Albion FC*, and *Albion A-Z: A Who's Who of Brighton & Hove Albion* with Tim Carder, he was a founding member of the Albion Collectors and Historians' Society, again with Tim, and will be sadly missed by those who knew him. When Roger passed away, Tim, a respected local historian who is also chairman of the Brighton Supporters' Club, organised what needed to be done to bring the *Factfile* up to speed, and for that I thank him. He continues to work tirelessly to bring home the Albion.

John Northcutt *(West Ham United)*: Has supported the Hammers since 1959 and is the co-author of West Ham books, *The Complete Record* and the *Illustrated History*. A regular contributor to the club programme and the club adviser to the *Ultimate Football Guide*.

Richard Owen *(Portsmouth)*: A life-long supporter and official club historian for Portsmouth, Richard co-published the *Pictorial History of Pompey* in 1998, and then compiled a separate book with every team picture since 1898. A regular contributor to the club programme for the last 21 years, he has missed only a handful of away matches in the past 23 years and seen Pompey on 103 league grounds. Is an avid programme collector too, having an almost complete collection of post-war Portsmouth home and away issues.

Richard Partington *(Stockport County)*: As sports editor of the award-winning *Stockport Express* newspaper, Richard covers the club's fortunes, home and away, for the only paper in the Greater Manchester region solely devoted to County.

Brian Pead *(Liverpool)*: Brian, who can be reached on 0181 302 6446, has authored several books on Liverpool FC, hundreds of articles, and is the writer for BBC's Extra Time, involving Liverpool's matches.

Steve Peart and **Dave Finch** *(Wycombe Wanderers)*: A former programme editor of the club and a supporter for over 20 years, Steve put together the player profiles, while the club statistics were supplied by Dave, the official Wycombe statistician. Both were authors of *Wycombe Wanderers 1887-1996 – The Official History*, published in 1996.

Steve Phillips *(Rochdale)*: A Dale fan of over 30 years standing, he is the club's official statistician and author of *The Survivors: The Story of Rochdale AFC*.

Terry Phillips *(Cardiff City)*: Chief soccer writer for the *South Wales Echo* since 1994, and a sports journalist for 28 years – *Kent Evening Post* (1970-1977), *Derby Evening Telegraph* (1977-1986), *Gloucester Citizen* (1986-1994) – Terry has previously covered clubs at all levels, including Brian Clough's Nottingham Forest, Derby County, Gillingham, and Gloucester City.

Andrew Pinfield *(Halifax Town)*: Andrew is a life-long supporter of Halifax who follows the Shaymen home and away without fail. He is also the club's commercial manager and programme editor.

Kevan Platt *(Norwich City)*: Kevin has supported the Canaries for over 30 years and has been employed by the club in various full-time capacities since 1980, witnessing at first hand the enormous swings in fortune during that period. Currently City's programme editor and press officer, he also co-edits the official handbook, and is a keen statistician, keeping detailed records of all the club's representative sides. Now the club secretary, despite his official role, he remains a fan, and can still be witnessed leaping to his feet in celebration when surrounded by the gathered media within the press box.

David Prentice *(Everton)*: Everton correspondent for the *Liverpool Echo* since 1993 and author of a club history five years earlier, when he was reporting both Everton and Liverpool for the *Daily Post*, he completed his Mersey set when reporting on Tranmere Rovers for three years from 1990.

Chris Pugsley *(Macclesfield Town)*: Currently Macclesfield's official statistician, he was the supporters' club shop manager from 1990-1993, and was the supporters' vice chairman during 1992-93. Resigned from the committee to work with the parent club as first team kit man from October 1993, and edited the matchday programme from 1995-1997. Has missed very few games, home or away, since Town joined the Conference in 1987.

Mike Purkiss *(Crystal Palace)*: Having supported Palace since 1950 and produced stats on them since 1960, Mike is the author of the *Complete History of Crystal Palace, 1905-1989*, the club statistician for the *Ultimate Football Guide*, and contributed to *Premier League: The Players*.

Mike Renshaw *(Sheffield Wednesday)*: Has followed Wednesday for over 40 years and is a great supporter of European soccer. Currently produces the club section for the *Ultimate Football Guide*.

Robert Ringsell and **Christine Jennison** *(Wimbledon)*: Robert (brother), who works for the DDVLA and is due to marry Lisa (also a Wimbledon fan), has supported the Dons from boyhood, and rarely misses a match. Christine (sister), who first watched the Dons over 25 years ago, is enjoying bringing up two Wimbledon-mad boys to follow in the family tradition. Sat on an FA Premier supporters' panel at the end of 1998.

Mick Robinson *(Peterborough United)*: Another life-long fan, for a number of years Mick has contributed to the club programme and was the joint editor of the *Official Peterborough History*. Also the club statistician for the *Ultimate Football Guide*.

Phil Sherwin *(Port Vale)*: As Vale's statistician, Phil works on a number of other publications and has contributed to the club programme for 18 years. A fan since 1968, he follows them home and away.

Derrick Slasor *(Middlesbrough)*: First saw the Boro play in

December 1946 and, as Managing Director of Trapezium Transport Services, is well known in the area for sponsoring various club activities.

Mike Slater (*Wolverhampton Wanderers*): Mike has attended over 1,000 Wolves' matches and, in 1988, wrote and published a book on their history called *Molineux Memories*. From 1989 to 1995 he compiled the annual *Brain of Wolves' Quiz*, prior to producing a booklet containing all the club's competitive results. Is currently writing the questions for the Wolves' quiz, revived this year.

Andrew Sleight (*Barnet*): Andrew enjoyed his inaugural season at Underhill in his role of press officer and editor of the matchday programme, having followed the Bees for ten years. His most memorable moment during 1998-99 was the last-minute victory at home against Leyton Orient, while his worst was undeniably the 9-1 home defeat at the hands of Peterborough.

Gordon Small (*Hartlepool United*): Having supported United since October 1965, experiencing two promotions, two relegations, and several close calls, with 1998-99 being another to add to the list, Gordon is currently the club statistician for the *Ultimate Football Guide*. He also brought out the *Definitive Hartlepool United FC* book last year.

Dave Smith (*Leicester City*): A regular columnist in the programme, co-author of *Fossils & Foxes* and the *Foxes Alphabet*, he assists with several other club handbooks.

Gerry Somerton (*Rotherham United*): The deputy sports editor of the *Rotherham Advertiser*, and co-editor of the club matchday programme, Gerry was the author of the official history of Rotherham United, *Now We Are United*, a book which sold out within months of its issue. Also covers United's games on a party-time basis for BBC Radio Sheffield, and with more than 50 years experience of watching his team he is recognised as being the club's historian.

Paul Stead (*Huddersfield Town*): A life-long supporter of his hometown team, Huddersfield, and a regular spectator at the McAlpine Stadium, Paul recently surpassed 700 games watching the Terriers. He also contributes to the *Ultimate Football Guide*.

David Steele (*Carlisle United*): A regular contributor to the club programme for several years now, his current interest is in tracking down ex-United players.

Richard Stocken (*Shrewsbury Town*): A supporter for over 40 years and a collector of club programmes and memorabilia, Richard is an annual contributor to the *Ultimate Football Guide* and other publications.

Bill Swann (*Newcastle United*): A supporter since the Jackie Milburn days of the early 1950s, and a long-term shareholder in the club along with his wife and three children, Bill is a keen collector of memorabilia connected with the club. A member of the AFS, he assisted in the production of the club's volume in the *Complete Record* series, and this is his fourth year as a contributor to the *Factfile*. His 13-year-old son Richard, also a United fanatic, supplied much of the "anorack" information in the player biographies.

Alan Tait (*Scottish clubs*): A regular contributor to Tony Brown's ultimate *Scottish League* book, and a compiler of statistics appertaining to that country, Alan is currently working on a project, probably still several years down the road, that will give line-ups for all Scottish League matches since 1890.

Colin Tattum (*Birmingham City*): Colin has reported the fortunes of Birmingham City and west midland's clubs for the *Birmingham Evening Mail* and *Sports Argus* newspapers for almost a decade. A native of the second city, he also covers the national side.

Paul Taylor (*Mansfield Town*): A Mansfield supporter for over 30 years, Paul has contributed to many publications over the last few years, and co-authored the *Stag's Centenary History* with the late Jack Retter, which was published two years ago. Recently deceased, Jack first saw Town play over 60 years ago and, as a contributor to the *Factfile*, will be missed. Rest in Peace.

Richard and **Sarah Taylor** (*Notts County*): Richard (father) is a member of the AFS, and a life-long fan in a family of County

supporters; while Sarah (daughter) is a young student who has been an avid follower of the team for over ten years, and rarely misses a game.

Les Triggs (*Grimsby Town*): Became involved with the statistical side of the club when asked to assist with Town's centenary exhibition in 1978. A retired librarian, Les, who first saw the Mariners in a wartime league match, is the co-author of the Grimsby Town volume in the *Complete Record* series and has been club statistician to the *Ultimate Football Guide* since its inception.

Roger Triggs (*Gillingham*): Has written three books on the club, *Gillingham FC - A Chronology 1893-1984*, *Priestfield Profiles 1950-1988* and the centenary publication, *Home of the Shouting Men*, which he co-authored with Andy Bradley. Also a feature writer in the programme since 1975.

Frank Tweddle (*Darlington*): The club's official historian and statistician, Frank has contributed to the Darlington programme for the last 24 seasons. A supporter for over 40 years, and a member of the 92 club, he is the author of *Darlington's Centenary History* published in 1983, and the *Definitive Darlington 1885-1999*. Is also a member of the AFS, and produces work for various other football magazines.

Paul Voller (*Ipswich Town*): A Town supporter since 1963-64, Paul works at the ground on matchdays and is a member of the supporters' management committee. Other publications worked on include the *FA Carling Premier League: The Players* and the *Ultimate Football Guide*.

Tony Woodburn and **Martin Atherton** (*Preston North End*): Both North End fans for over 30 years, Tony (statistics) and Martin (text) provide statistical and historical information on the club for the permanent Preston North End collection being established at the National Football Museum at Deepdale, as well as writing for the club programme and, of course, the *Factfile*. Tony is a member of the Association of Football Statisticians, the 92 club, and the Scottish 38 club, whilst Martin is the principal researcher for the University of Central Lancashire's Deaf United project, investigating the history, social, and cultural aspects of deaf football in Britain.

David Woods and **Tony Ticktum** (*Bristol City*): A BSc Hons (OU) graduate, David has been a regular City supporter since March 1958, and a shareholder since 1973. Is presently working on a 32-year record of the club for Desert Island Books, having been previously involved with three other books on City as well as writing regular articles in both the Bristol City and Bristol Rovers' programmes. A member of the 92 club. and a life member of the Association of Football Statisticians, his other interests include rugby, tennis, cricket, badminton, speedway, geology, history, photography, and reading. Played for his school at rugby, but helped form Bristol Casuals FC in 1966 when they became one of the founder members of the Bristol and District Sunday Football League. Tony has been a committed City fan since September 1945, and as a shareholder and season ticket holder, he vows to continue supporting his favourite club no matter what. Won cup and league medals during his National Service days in Germany, as well as playing in Bristol amateur soccer in the 1950s.

Richard (Dick) Wright (*Southampton*): A Saints' supporter who, after having a relatively comfortable time of it in 1997-98 when the club finished 12th, was sweating on the top line right down to the last game of last season as they fought off relegation. President of the local football club he helped to found in 1983, Dick is planning to come out of retirement to help run the club's newly-formed second adult team next season. The club, Goldsworth Park Rangers FC, is proud that it can offer football for boys from six years old to adult, half the latter squad having played for the club for ten years or more.

Finally, on the production side of the book, my thanks go to Jean Bastin, of Typecast (Artwork & Design), for her patience and diligent work on the typesetting and design, which again went far beyond the call of normal duty and was much appreciated. She was ably supported by Nina Whatmore (Orchard Design).

Forewords

Once again I am extremely pleased to give the PFA's full endorsement and recommendation to Footballers' Factfile. I consider it the finest work of its kind, and one that presents a comprehensive coverage on statistics and profiles for every one of the 2,000 plus members of the PFA who played in first-team football throughout the Premier League and Football League in England and Wales during 1998-99.

The publication has been sponsored by Windsor Insurance Brokers, the key figures in our industry with regard to the protection of players against injury, and written by Barry Hugman, whose record in this field is unsurpassed. Barry has a team of over 90 people who provide him with the invaluable aspects of local information that gives this book such credibility, and makes it a must for every enthusiast, administrator, and commentator on our great game. It will occupy the most prominent position on my desk.

Gordon Taylor,
Chief Executive, The Professional Footballers' Association.

The Footballers' Factfile goes from strength to strength as the years go by. Barry Hugman and his research team are to be congratulated, yet again, on this season's publication, which I see on the desk or in the bookcase of almost everybody connected with the game today.

The Windsor Insurance Group continues its close association with professional football that was first established over 25 years ago. Together, with the Professional Footballers' Association, we manage the Players' Permanent Disablement Fund, by which every registered player in the English leagues receives an insurance benefit if his career is ended through injury or sickness. The level of benefit is continually reviewed and was increased significantly fairly recently .

Our close links with the Professional Footballers' Association, and the clubs, leagues, and national associations, give us a unique position from which we can offer advice on insurance-related matters to all in football. And, we are more than happy to continue to support and again lend our name as sponsors to this excellent publication.

Jonathan Ticehurst,
Managing Director of the Sports Division, Windsor Insurance Brokers Limited.

Editorial Introduction

Following on from last year's edition, the Factfile portrays the statistical career record of every FA Carling Premiership and Nationwide League player who made an appearance in 1998-99, whether it be in league football, the Football League (Worthington Cup), FA Cup (Sponsored by AXA), Charity Shield, European Cup, European Cup Winners' Cup, UEFA Cup, Auto Windscreens Shield, or in the Play Offs. Not included are Inter-Toto Cup or Welsh Cup matches. It goes beyond mere statistics, however, with a write up on all of the 2,300 plus players involved, and also records faithfully last season's playing records separately by club.

The work falls into three sections, all inter-relating. Firstly, the main core, PFA Footballers' Factfile: A-Z (pages 9 to 332); secondly, Where Did They Go? (pages 333 to 336); lists all players shown in the previous edition of the Factfile who either moved on or did not play in 1989-99; and thirdly, FA Carling Premiership and Nationwide League Clubs: Summary of Appearances and Goals for 1998-99 (pages 337 to 351). Below is an explanation on how to follow the PFA Footballers' Factfile.

As the title suggests, all players are listed in alphabetical order and are shown by Surnames first, followed by full Christian names, with the one the player is commonly known by shown in **bold.** Any abbreviation or pseudonym is bracketed.

Birthplace/date: You will note that several players who would be predominately classified as British, were born in places like Germany and India, for example. My book, Football League Players' Records, which covers every man who has played league football since the war, has, in the past, used the family domicile as a more realistic "birthplace". But, for our purposes here, I have reverted to that which has been officially recorded.

Height and Weight: Listed in feet and inches, and stones and pounds, respectively. It must be remembered that a player's weight can frequently change and, on that basis, the recorded data should be used as a guide only, especially as they would have been weighed several times during the season.

Club Honours: Those shown, cover careers from the Conference and FA Trophy upwards. For abbreviations, read:- European Honours: EC (European Cup), ESC (European Super Cup), ECWC (European Cup Winners' Cup). English Honours: FAC (FA Cup), FLC (Football League Cup), CS (Charity Shield), FMC (Full Members Cup, which takes in the Simod and Zenith Data sponsorships), AMC (Associated Members Cup - Freight Rover, Sherpa Van, Leyland DAF, Autoglass and Auto Windscreens), AIC (Anglo-Italian Cup), GMVC (GM Vauxhall Conference), FAT (FA Trophy), FAYC (FA Youth Cup). Scottish Honours: SPD (Scottish Premier Division), S Div 1/2 (Scottish Leagues), SC (Scottish Cup), SLC (Scottish League Cup). Welsh Honours: WC (Welsh Cup). Please note that medals awarded to P/FL, FLC, and AMC winners relate to players who have appeared in 25%, or over, of matches, while FAC, EC, and ECWC winners medals are for all-named finalists, including unused subs. For our purposes, however, Charity Shield winners' medals refer to men who either played or came on as a sub. Honours applicable to players coming in from abroad are not shown, but the position will be reviewed in future editions.

International Honours: For abbreviations, read:- E (England), NI (Northern Ireland), S (Scotland), W (Wales) and Ei (Republic of Ireland). Under 21 through to full internationals give total appearances (inclusive of subs), while schoolboy (U16s and U18s) and youth representatives are just listed. The cut off date used for appearances was 12 July.

Player Descriptions: Gives position and playing strengths and, in keeping the work topical, a few words on how their season went in 1998-99. This takes into account, in a positive fashion, key performances, along with value to the team, injuries, honours, and other points of interest, etc. To allow for play off and international input to be included, and the publication date to be maintained, the cut-off date used was 12 July. Transfers, however, are shown as stop press if they took place after 18 May, the cut-off date used by the Football and Premier Leagues to produce the close season retained and free transfer lists. The decision was taken on the grounds that the May/June Registration and Transfer booklets would not be available until after going to press.

Career Records: Full appearances, plus substitutes and goals, are given for all Carling Premiership and Nationwide League games and, if a player who is in the book has played in any of the senior Scottish Leagues, his appearances with the club in question will also be recorded. Other information given, includes the origination of players (clubs in the non-leagues, junior football, or from abroad), registered signing dates (if a player signs permanently following a loan spell, for our purposes, we have shown the initial date as being the point of temporary transfer. Also, loan transfers are only recorded if an appearance is made), transfer fees (these are the figures that have been reported in newspapers and magazines and should only be used as a guide to a player's valuation), and a breakdown of matches by P/FL (Premiership and Football League), PL (Premier League), FL (Football League), FLC (Football League Cup), FAC (FA Cup), and Others. Other matches will take in the Play Offs, Anglo-Italian Cup, Auto Windscreens Shield, Charity Shield, and any major European competition. All of these matches are lumped together for reasons of saving space. Scottish appearances for players on loan to P/FL clubs in 1998-99 are shown at the point of transfer and do not include games following their return to Scotland.

Career statistics are depicted as
Appearances + Substitutes/Goals

Whether you wish to analyse someone for your fantasy football team selection or would like to know more about a little-known player appearing in the lower reaches of the game, the *PFA Footballers' Factfile* should provide you with the answer.

Barry J. Hugman, Editor, PFA Footballers' Factfile

ABBEY Nathanael (Nathan)
Born: Islington, 11 July 1978
Height: 6'1" Weight: 12.0
Despite a lack of games at Luton, with Kelvin Davis performing admirably as the first-choice 'keeper in 1998-99 Nathan was again asked to be patient. However, when called upon, apart from a 3-0 home defeat at the hands of Walsall in the Auto Windscreens Shield, the promising young goalie did well in league wins at Burnley and Millwall, being beaten just once before somewhat surprisingly released during the summer. Both confident and assured, he looks to stay in the league.
Luton T (From trainee on on 2/5/96) FLC 2 FLC 1 Others 1

ABLETT Gary Ian
Born: Liverpool, 19 November 1965
Height: 6'1" Weight: 12.7
Club Honours: Div 1 '88, '90; CS '88, '95; FAC '89; '95
International Honours: E: B-1; U21-1
Handed the Birmingham captaincy following Steve Bruce's departure from the club, Gary proved to be a reliable and consistent leader in the heart of the City defence throughout 1998-99, again reading play impressively. Although being left out in October, he was quickly restored to play a key part in getting the Blues into the top four. Unfortunately, on 6 February, a day after agreeing a new one-year contract verbally, he suffered medial and cruciate knee-ligament damage and was ruled out of action for the remainder of the campaign. The club owners, under pressure not to abandon him, promised a new contract that will take him through to October, when he is expected to be fit and in a position to re-negotiate terms.
Liverpool (From apprentice on 19/11/83) FL 103+6/1 FLC 10+1 FAC 16+2 Others 9
Derby Co (Loaned on 25/1/85) FL 3+3 Others 2
Hull C (Loaned on 10/9/86) FL 5
Everton (£750,000 on 14/1/92) F/PL 128/5 FLC 12 FAC 12/1 Others 4
Sheffield U (Loaned on 1/3/96) FL 12
Birmingham C (£390,000 on 21/6/96) FL 96+8/1 FLC 13 FAC 7/1

ABOU Samassi
Born: Gagnoa, Ivory Coast, 4 August 1973
Height: 6'0" Weight: 11.6
International Honours: Ivory Coast
After impressing a lot of people in the previous campaign, the talented Ivory Coast international was used sparingly up front at West Ham in 1998-99, making just three appearances before being loaned to Ipswich at the beginning of December as cover for David Johnson, who was having a knee

operation. Very skilful, and a forward who likes to run at defenders, it took a couple of games at Town for him to get the feel of things and he opened his scoring account in the 2-1 win at Sheffield United. He then combined well with Richard Naylor for his two goals at Portsmouth before returning to Upton Park. Contracted until the end of 1999-2000, it is difficult to see where he goes from here.
West Ham U (£300,000 from Cannes on on 3/11/97) PL 14+8/5 FLC 2+1/1 FAC 3+3
Ipswich T (Loaned on 3/12/98) FL 5/1

ABRAHAMS Paul
Born: Colchester, 31 October 1973
Height: 5'10" Weight: 11.3
Paul started last season in good form at Colchester and was soon amongst the goals, playing as the wide man in a front three. Injury soon intervened, however, and the rest of the campaign saw him making only spasmodic appearances between regular spells out of action, during which he went on the transfer list at his own request. Finished with three goals in all, from 16 starts and a further 15 substitute appearances, and scored the winner against Ipswich in Tony Adcock's testimonial game before being released during the summer.
Colchester U (From trainee on on 11/8/92) FL 30+25/8 FLC 2+3 FAC 4/2 Others 3/2
Brentford (£30,000 on on 9/3/95) FL 26+9/8 FLC 1+2 Others 1
Colchester U (Loaned on on 29/12/95) FL 8/2 Others 1
Colchester U (£20,000 on on 23/10/96) FL 56+25/16 FLC 4/1 FAC 2+1 Others 7+1/2

ACHTERBERG John
Born: Utrecht, Holland, 8 July 1971
Height: 6'1" Weight: 13.8
Signed on a free transfer from Eindhoven last September to provide goalkeeping cover for Tranmere after the sale of Steve Simonsen to Everton, John soon found himself in first-team action when Danny Coyne was sidelined through injury. A proficient custodian who possesses good handling skills and positional know-how, he was dropped in mid term but returned in March to turn in several impressive displays as the season drew to a close, ending it as Rovers' undisputed first-choice 'keeper.
Tranmere Rov (Free from Eindhoven FC on 22/9/98) FL 24 FLC 1

ADAMS Neil James
Born: Stoke, 23 November 1965
Height: 5'8" Weight: 10.12
Club Honours: Div 1 '87, Div 2 '91
International Honours: E: U21-1
For the second season in succession, Neil suffered the misfortune of sustaining several injuries which forced him to sit out large parts of Norwich's 1998-99 campaign, breaking a collar bone at Swansea in August and a foot against Stockport in February. When in the team, he continued to supply a stream of crosses from the right flank, using

his ability to deliver the early cross with telling effect, but, unfortunately, missed the first spot kick of his career, the unlucky 13th, in the early season Worthington Cup-tie at Swansea. Was released during the summer.
Stoke C (Signed on 1/7/85) FL 31+1/4 FLC 3 FAC 1 Others 3
Everton (£150,000 on 7/7/86) FL 17+3 FLC 4+1/1 Others 5+1
Oldham Ath (Loaned on 11/1/89) FL 9
Oldham Ath (£100,000 on 21/6/89) F/PL 93+36/23 FLC 13+2/1 FAC 10+2/2 Others 1+1
Norwich C (£250,000 on 17/2/94) P/FL 164+18/25 FLC 16+1/4 FAC 7/1

ADAMS Stephen (Steve) Marc
Born: Plymouth, 25 September 1980
Height: 6'0" Weight: 11.10
As the captain of Plymouth's youth team, and still a trainee, Steve gained some vital experience last season when coming off the bench after 36 minutes of the FA Cup replay at Kidderminster, replacing first-team skipper, Mick Heathcote, against Brentford in the Auto Windscreens Shield. A footballing centre half who likes to get the ball to feet and come through the midfield, he has been working on his strength and aggression, and has got stronger, especially in the air.
Plymouth Arg (Trainee) Others 0+1

Tony Adams

ADAMS Tony Alexander
Born: Romford, 10 October 1966
Height: 6'3" Weight: 13.11
Club Honours: Div 1 '89, '91; PL '98; FLC '87, '93; FAC '93, '98; ECWC '94
International Honours: E: 57; B-4; U21-5; Yth
Long-serving Arsenal captain whose 1998-99 season was disrupted by a series of back and ankle injuries which caused him to miss a number of games at both club and international level. Despite this, his incredible drive and determination helped him to return to fitness and make an essential contribution to the soundest

defence in the Premiership. A commanding, passionate, and influential figure, he is a natural leader at the highest level. Again proved to be extremely solid both on the ground and in the air, and he continued to get forward whenever he could. His height and strength made him very dangerous at set pieces, where he was always likely to score or create goals, and within a period of ten days he scored crucial goals in the home victories over Manchester United and Panathinaikos. Despite his injury problems, he was still an automatic choice for England. Off the field he was a tremendous motivator and, following Arsenal's defeat by Manchester United in the FA Cup semi-final replay, he quickly roused a number of his dejected team mates.

Arsenal (From apprentice on 30/1/84) F/PL 443+4/31 FLC 58+1/5 FAC 45+1/5 Others 36/4

ADAMSON Christopher (Chris)
Born: Ashington, 4 November 1978
Height: 5'1" Weight: 11.0
A broken right arm sustained by their regular custodian, Ian Bowling, after the transfer deadline, forced Mansfield to ask the Nationwide League for special dispensation to bring West Bromwich's third-choice goalkeeper to Field Mill for the final two matches of the season. The agile Baggies youngster was soon a hit with the fans after a confident display in his debut at Shrewsbury, and the following week he showed off his shot-stopping ability at home to promoted Cardiff.

West Bromwich A (From trainee on 2/7/97) FL 3
Mansfield T (Loaned on 30/4/99) FL 2

ADCOCK Anthony (Tony) Charles
Born: Bethnal Green, 27 February 1963
Height: 6'0" Weight: 11.9
As Colchester's veteran goal-grabber supreme, Tony enjoyed a fully-deserved testimonial year in 1998-99, the highlight of which was a 1-0 win over a full-strength Ipswich team in his testimonial match. Unfortunately, his season did not go as well as his big night, as he fought against a series of injuries throughout the campaign, his only goal being the late consolation in the FA Cup humiliation at Bedlington. With the club record of league goals remaining tantalisingly just out of reach, he finished on loan to Heybridge Swifts, where his younger brother was a regular goalscorer, before hanging up his boots at Layer Road – the end of a legend.

Colchester U (From apprentice on 31/3/81) FL 192+18/98 FLC 16+1/5 FAC 12+2/3 Others 9/6
Manchester C (£75,000 on 1/6/87) FL 12+3/5 FLC 2+1/1 FAC 2 Others 2/3
Northampton T (£85,000 on 25/1/88) FL 72/30 FLC 6/3 FAC 1 Others 4/1
Bradford C (£190,000 on 6/10/89) FL 33+5/6 FLC 1 FAC 0+1 Others 2
Northampton T (£75,000 on 11/1/91) FL 34+1/10 FLC 1 FAC 2 Others 2/1
Peterborough U (£35,000 on 30/12/91) FL 107+4/35 FLC 8+1/3 FAC 5/1 Others 3+2
Luton T (£20,000 on 4/8/94) FL 0+2 FAC 0+1
Colchester U (Free on 3/8/95) FL 86+22/28 FLC 5+4/2 FAC 4+3/1 Others 10+1/6

ADEBOLA Bamberdele (Dele)
Born: Lagos, Nigeria, 23 June 1975
Height: 6'3" Weight: 12.8
Dele made a blistering start to 1998-99, scoring five goals in five games for Birmingham, his pace, power and sheer strength making him a fearsome opponent. Despite a calf injury suffered in September, he battled on when he should have been resting until coming good again in the New Year. Two goals against West Bromwich in a 4-0 win at St Andrews in March, Blues' biggest success over their local rivals in 51 years, took him to 16 in the scoring charts before he pulled a hamstring. Good in the air and a natural left footer, he came back to help in the play-off push.

Crewe Alex (From trainee on 21/6/93) FL 98+26/39 FLC 4+3/2 FAC 8+2/3 Others 10+1/2
Birmingham C (£1,000,000 on 6/2/98) FL 49+7/20 FLC 4/2 FAC 1/1 Others 1+1/1

AGGREY James (Jimmy) Emmanuel
Born: Hammersmith, 26 October 1978
Height: 6'3" Weight: 13.6
Released by Fulham during the 1998 close season after being unable to get a first-team game, Jimmy went north of the border with Airdrie before signing for Torquay in October. A no-nonsense, lanky defender who signed initially on a non-contract basis during a desperate injury crisis, after an impressive baptism he was handed a long-term contract. Had a particularly outstanding game at Plymouth and if he can put some finishing touches to his distribution, the Londoner will definitely play a big part in United's defence in the coming term.

Fulham (Free from Chelsea juniors on 2/7/97)
Airdrieonians (Free on 30/6/98)
Torquay U (Free on 22/10/98) FL 22+3 FAC 2 Others 1

AGNEW Stephen (Steve) Mark
Born: Shipley, 9 November 1965
Height: 5'10" Weight: 11.9
Club Honours: Div 1 '96
Released by Sunderland during the 1998 close season, the experienced midfielder was, at times, troubled by injuries and was not able to fully establish himself in the York side in 1998-99. His highlight being two excellent goals scored in a 3-3 draw at Fulham in September but, although showing an obvious creative ability, he suffered from inconsistency and was placed on the transfer list in the closing weeks of the campaign.

Barnsley (From apprentice on 10/11/83) FL 186+8/29 FLC 13/3 FAC 20/4 Others 6+1
Blackburn Rov (£700,000 on 25/6/91) FL 2 FLC 2
Portsmouth (Loaned on 21/11/92) FL 3+2 Others 2
Leicester C (£250,000 on 9/2/93) F/PL 52+4/4 FLC 4+1 FAC 2 Others 2
Sunderland (£250,000 on 11/1/95) P/FL 56+7/9 FLC 4 FAC 2+1/1
York C (Free on 10/7/98) FL 19+1/2 FLC 1 FAC 3

AGOGO Manuel (Junior)
Born: Accra, Ghana, 1 August 1979
Height: 5'10" Weight: 11.7
A broken foot in a pre-season game meant

that this pacy young striker never got into Sheffield Wednesday manager Danny Wilson's plans for 1998-99. Despite the Owls' lack of goals, Junior only managed a couple of substitute appearances up to March, which was very poor reward for an enthusiastic youngster. He certainly needs to build more awareness and confidence into his play but, of course, can only achieve this by playing regularly. 1999-2000 will be an important season for him and he must hope for an injury-free run in which to impress.

Sheffield Wed (Signed from Willesden Constontaine on 8/10/96) PL 0+2 FAC 0+1

AINSWORTH Gareth
Born: Blackburn, 10 May 1973
Height: 5'9" Weight: 12.5
Began last season with Port Vale and starred on their right wing before moving to Wimbledon in November. A strong, pacy runner who never gives up, and Vale's leading scorer when he left, he virtually won games against Norwich and Bristol City on his own prior to leaving. Earlier, Vale had turned down an offer of £1.5 million from Leeds during George Graham's reign. After making his debut for the Dons in the 1-0 win at Nottingham Forest, unfortunately his season was then dogged by a groin injury, and with only five league starts and three subs' appearances behind him he has not yet had the opportunity to show his full capabilities in the Premiership.

Preston NE (Signed from Northwich Vic, via Blackburn Rov YTS, on 21/1/92) FL 2+3 Others 1/1
Cambridge U (Free on 17/8/92) FL 1+3/1 FLC 0+1
Preston NE (Free on 23/12/92) FL 76+6/12 FLC 3+2 FAC 3+1 Others 8+1/1
Lincoln C (£25,000 on 31/10/95) FL 83/37 FLC 8/3 FAC 2 Others 4/1
Port Vale (£500,000 on 12/9/97) FL 53+2/10 FLC 2/1 FAC 2
Wimbledon (£2,000,000 on 3/11/98) PL 5+3

AISTON Samuel (Sam) James
Born: Newcastle, 21 November 1976
Height: 6'1" Weight: 12.10
Club Honours: Div 1 '96
International Honours: E: Sch
A tall, skilful left winger, Sam made only two subs' appearances for Sunderland last term, returning to Chester on loan in November after a successful spell at the club a couple of seasons ago. With chances at the Stadium of Light limited, he arrived at the Deva and made a total of 11 league appearances on the wide left before being forced to return to the north east after sustaining an injury at Plymouth in February. Although his pace and direct approach made him a favourite with City fans once again, it remains to be seen whether he can break into the Premiership newcomers' side on a regular basis.

Sunderland (Free from Newcastle U juniors on 14/7/95) P/FL 5+15 FLC 0+2 FAC 0+2
Chester C (Loaned on 21/2/97) FL 14 FLC 1 Others 2
Chester C (Loaned on 27/11/98) FL 11 Others 1

AKINBIYI Adeola (Ade) Peter
Born: Greenwich, 10 October 1974
Height: 6'1" Weight: 12.9
Having arrived at Ashton Gate from Gillingham during the 1998 close season and becoming Bristol City's record signing, Ade endeared himself to the fans in 1998-99 with his total commitment in every game, during a difficult campaign. For a player with such a high workrate, his goalscoring was exceptional, his tremendous pace and strength making him a big asset to the club. The former Norwich striker scored many vital goals, including the classic finish in the home game against Swindon, and the two he got in the home game with Grimsby.
Norwich C (From trainee on 5/2/93) P/FL 22+27/3 FLC 2+4/2 FAC 1+2 Others 0+1
Hereford U (Loaned on 21/1/94) FL 3+1/2
Brighton & Hove A (Loaned on 24/11/94) FL 7/4
Gillingham (£250,000 on 13/1/97) FL 63+28 FLC 2 FAC 2/1 Others 0+1
Bristol C (£1,200,000 on 28/5/98) FL 44/19 FLC 4/4 FAC 1

ALBERT Philippe
Born: Bouillon, Belgium, 10 August 1967
Height: 6'3" Weight: 13.7
Club Honours: Div 2 '99
International Honours: Belgium: 41
Philippe is a cultured, left-sided player with the ideal physique for a central defender and a fine first touch on the ball. Elegant with a strong attacking flair, his passing ability enables him to quickly turn defence into attack, and he also enjoys carrying the ball forward himself to join his front men and seek opportunities to exploit his powerful left-footed shooting. He began last season on Newcastle's bench and started in each of new manager Ruud Gullit's first three games. Thereafter, his opportunities were limited to three substitute appearances and in January he rejoined his former manager, Kevin Keegan, at Fulham, on loan until the end of the campaign, with a view to a permanent move. Playing an important part in Fulham's promotion, winning a Second Division championship medal, he appeared in central defence, left-wing back, and central midfield, his headed goal against Wigan being the catalyst to a vital win in April.
Newcastle U (£2,650,000 from Anderlecht, via Charleroi and Mechelen, on 10/8/94) PL 87+9/8 FLC 11+1/2 FAC 7+1/1 Others 19+3/1
Fulham (Loaned on 25/1/99) FL 12+1/2

ALCIDE Colin James
Born: Huddersfield, 14 April 1972
Height: 6'2" Weight: 13.10
Having failed in a bid to bring Wigan's Graeme Jones to the club, Hull fought off stiff competition from Colchester and Plymouth to add this big, abrasive Lincoln striker to their attack last February. Then, having made his considerable presence felt at Boothferry, Colin was ordered by the Football League to return to Sincil Bank (played in the visit to Fulham) after a month at Hull due to an alleged lapse in the agreed payment. That sorted, he returned four days later, showing his commitment to the City cause by turning down a chance to join the

St Lucia World Cup squad in April. Holds the ball up well and has a very good touch for such a big man.
Lincoln C (£15,000 from Emley on 5/12/95) FL 105+16/27 FLC 7+2/2 FAC 3+3/2 Others 3+1
Hull C (Loaned on 4/2/99) FL 5/1
Hull C (£50,000 on 10/3/99) FL 12/2

ALDRIDGE Martin James
Born: Northampton, 6 December 1974
Height: 5'11" Weight: 12.1
Released by Oxford during the 1998 close season, the striker made such a good impression while on trial at Blackpool, scoring a hat trick at Goole, that he signed for the Seasiders prior to the start of 1998-99. Despite picking up an injury against Scunthorpe in the Worthington Cup, two games into the new campaign, he came back strongly to become the club's top scorer before he was forced to have a hernia operation in December. A "sniffer" of goalscoring chances, he came back in February but suffered some reaction and was forced to miss more games. Also has a good long throw.
Northampton T (From trainee on 27/8/93) FL 50+20/17 FLC 1+2 FAC 1+1/1 Others 5+2/4
Oxford C (Free on 22/12/95) FL 46+26/19 FLC 8+4/3 FAC 2+2
Southend U (Loaned on 23/2/98) FL 7+4/1
Blackpool (Free on 3/8/98) FL 19+3/7 FLC 2/2 FAC 1/1

ALEXANDER Graham
Born: Coventry, 10 October 1971
Height: 5'10" Weight: 12.7
Playing in Luton's opening 23 games of 1998-99 – scoring five times, four of them being penalties – until being forced to carry a hamstring problem, Graham came back strongly in nine starts before signing for Preston in March's transfer deadline week. Making an impressive debut at right back for North End, against Northampton, he proved to be quick, decisive in the tackle, a precise passer, and a striker of accurate, powerful free kicks around the penalty area. He will also no doubt be looking for an opportunity to show off his skills in midfield this term.
Scunthorpe U (From trainee on 20/3/90) FL 149+10/18 FLC 11+1/2 FAC 12/1 Others 13+3/3
Luton T (£100,000 on 8/7/95) FL 146+4/15 FLC 17/2 FAC 6+1 Others 6+2
Preston NE (£50,000 on 25/3/99) FL 10 Others 2

ALEXANDERSSON Niclas
Born: Halmstad, Sweden, 29 December 1971
Height: 6'2" Weight: 11.8
International Honours: Sweden: 30
Missed all the pre-season and the first couple of months of 1998-99, recovering from the injury from the previous campaign. However, he came back strongly to claim his place almost immediately on the right-hand side of midfield, where his attacking strengths had been sorely missed, and seemed to have recovered all of his skill and verve. He also reclaimed his place in a very successful Swedish international side, and just needs to improve on his goalscoring prowess to become the complete modern-day midfielder.

Sheffield Wed (£750,000 from Gothenburg, via Halmstad, on 9/12/97) PL 36+2/3 FLC 0+1 FAC 5/1

ALJOFREE Hasney
Born: Manchester, 11 July 1978
Height: 6'0" Weight: 12.1
International Honours: E: Yth
Although a promising left back, Hasney found it difficult to break into the Bolton side in 1998-99, due to the fact that quality players such as Mike Whitlow, Robbie Elliott, and Jimmy Phillips were all vying for the same position. His one and only league start came in the 2-0 defeat at QPR in November, and other first-team opportunities were limited to a handful of substitute appearances. Although a consistent performer for the reserve team, one would have expected the England youth international to have figured more prominently than he did. Composed and comfortable on the ball, he is sure to challenge strongly in 1999-2000.
Bolton W (From trainee on 2/7/96) P/FL 3+3 FLC 1

ALLAN Derek Thomas
Born: Irvine, 24 December 1974
Height: 6'0" Weight: 12.1
International Honours: S: Yth
Steady Brighton defender, able to play at centre half or right back. Very quick and a ball winner, he also likes to get forward, and scored only his second league goal with a left-foot scorcher at Cambridge. Was transfer listed in November 1998 whilst, ironically, enjoying probably his best spell with the club, and was released during the summer.
Ayr U (Trainee) SL 5
Southampton (£75,000 on 16/3/93) PL 0+1
Brighton & Hove A (Free on 28/3/96) FL 77+3/2 FLC 3 FAC 1 Others 2+1

ALLARDYCE Craig Samuel
Born: Bolton, 9 June 1975
Height: 6'3" Weight: 13.7
Released by Chesterfield at the end of 1997-98, having been on non-contract forms, the tall central defender arrived at Peterborough immediately prior to the start of last season and made four starts before departing for non-league Welling United. The son of Sam, the Notts County manager, Craig came back into the league with Mansfield in mid December and forced his way into the side during March, making six appearances, until losing his place to Mark Peters due to him being suspended. Out of contract during the summer, at the time of going to press the club had offered him terms of re-engagement.
Preston NE (From trainee on 16/7/93) FL 0+1 (Free to Macclesfield T on 16/4/94)
Blackpool (Free from Northwich Vic on 20/9/94) FL 0+1 (Freed on 23/11/96)
Chesterfield (Free from Chorley on 26/3/98) FL 0+1
Peterborough U (Free on 6/8/98) FL 3 (Free to Welling U on 5/11/98)
Mansfield T (Free on 22/12/98) FL 6

ALLEN Bradley James
Born: Romford, 13 September 1971
Height: 5'8" Weight: 11.0
International Honours: E: U21-8; Yth

1998-99 was another disappointing season for Bradley, who failed to make a Premiership appearance for Charlton despite scoring regularly when playing for the reserve side. Making a solitary first-team appearance when he came on as substitute against Queens Park Rangers in the Worthington Cup at the Valley in September, the striker showed that he was still a model professional who worked extremely hard at his game. After suffering bad luck with injuries he was eventually loaned out to Colchester in February, where he suffered a back injury which brought his campaign to a halt. Was released during the summer.

Queens Park R (From juniors on 30/9/88) F/PL 56+25/27 FLC 5+2/5 FAC 3+2 Others 1
Charlton Ath (£400,000 on 28/3/96) FL 30+10/9 FLC 3+1/2 FAC 0+2 Others 1+1
Colchester U (Loaned on 24/2/99) FL 4/1

ALLEN Christopher (Chris) Anthony
Born: Oxford, 18 November 1972
Height: 5'11" Weight: 12.2
International Honours: E: U21-2

Unable to get a game at Nottingham Forest, Chris made seven appearances for Cardiff during a loan spell last October and was disappointing. Bluebirds' fans expected more from the speed king. After all he was with a Premiership club. Freed by Forest in March, he signed a short-term contract with Port Vale and made an excellent start when heading a goal on his debut against Stockport, but generally only lived up to his promise in short bursts. Blotted his copybook when turning up late for a game against Grimsby and was subsequently dropped and, despite returning occasionally, he was released during the summer.

Oxford U (From trainee on 14/5/91) FL 110+40/12 FLC 11+2/4 FAC 5+5/1 Others 5+3
Nottingham F (Loaned on 24/2/96) PL 1+2/1
Nottingham F (£300,000 on 3/7/96) F/PL 17+8 FLC 2/1 FAC 1/1
Luton T (Loaned on 28/11/97) FL 14/1
Cardiff C (Loaned on 22/10/98) FL 3+1 Others 1
Port Vale (Free on 8/3/99) FL 2+3/1

ALLEN Graham
Born: Bolton, 8 April 1977
Height: 6'1" Weight: 12.8
International Honours: E: Yth

Making a permanent move to Tranmere from Everton in August 1998, after a successful loan spell playing at right back, Graham proved himself to be accomplished in both attack and defence, ever eager to support his colleagues up front, but equally sound at the back. He was often enterprising and always consistent, but his uncompromising style of play led to eight yellow cards by the end of the season. Perhaps underrated at the start of his Rovers' career, he nonetheless scored five goals and picked up four "Man of the Match" awards.

Everton (From trainee on 10/12/94) PL 2+4
Tranmere Rov (Free on 28/8/98) FL 41/5 FLC 2 FAC 1

Graham Allen

ALLEN Rory William
Born: Beckenham, 17 October 1977
Height: 5'11" Weight: 11.2
Club Honours: FLC '99
International Honours: E: U21-3

A natural striker who made his way to becoming a regular on the Tottenham subs' bench in 1998-99, as cover for Chris Armstrong, Steffan Iversen, and Les Ferdinand, he was always enthusiastic and, with the ability to deliver under pressure, he became a more mature player as his understanding of the game grew. While developing into an excellent team player, he has only a short way to go now to break through into regular first-team football and will benefit greatly from the experience and quality being built in the squad at White Hart Lane.

Tottenham H (From trainee on 28/3/96) PL 10+11/2 FLC 3+3/2 FAC 1
Luton T (Loaned on 26/3/98) FL 8/6

ALLISON Wayne Anthony
Born: Huddersfield, 16 October 1968
Height: 6'1" Weight: 12.6
Club Honours: Div 2 '96

A big front man, Wayne served Huddersfield well in 1998-99, working his socks off throughout the campaign and, in battling away, he was often given little protection by referees, finishing matches battered and bruised. Although unselfish, winning many aerial challenges and holding up play for others, just like his strike partner, Marcus Stewart, he found the net with regularity. Soon into double figures, the determined striker scored many of his goals with classic headers. Always ready to help in defence when the going gets tough, he captained the side for the last few weeks following the injury to Barry Horne.

Halifax T (From trainee on 6/7/87) FL 74+10/23 FLC 3/2 FAC 4+1/2 Others 8+1/3

Watford (£250,000 on 26/7/89) FL 6+1
Bristol C (£300,000 on 9/8/90) FL 149+46/48 FLC 4+5/2 FAC 12+1/5 Others 6+2/2
Swindon T (£475,000 on 22/7/95) FL 98+3/31 FLC 9/3 FAC 7/2 Others 3
Huddersfield T (£800,000 on 11/11/97) FL 71/15 FLC 3/2 FAC 6/2

ALLOTT Mark Stephen
Born: Manchester, 3 October 1977
Height: 5'11" Weight: 12.6

Starting 1998-99 at Oldham as the first-choice strike partner for Adrian Littlejohn up front, when the latter left for Bury in mid November so did some of Mark's confidence. However, he is still learning the game, and with his ability to hold the ball up well for others, along with his pace, there are still high hopes for him at the club. Scored two goals when coming off the bench, the one at Reading being the equaliser.

Oldham Ath (From trainee on 14/10/95) FL 42+26/10 FLC 2+1/1 FAC 3+4 Others 0+1

ALLOU Anoh Bernard
Born: Ivory Coast, 19 June 1975
Height: 5'8" Weight: 10.4

Signed on a free transfer from the Japanese club, Grampus 8, last March, the young Frenchman was given a four-year contract by Ron Atkinson, then manager at Nottingham Forest. A midfielder, who likes to play out wide from where he can reach the front men, made his Premiership debut when coming off the bench in a 2-2 draw against Liverpool at the City Ground. Having begun his career with Paris St Germain, and with 24 French U21 caps under his belt, despite interest from elsewhere, Bernard opted to join Forest and will now be playing in the First Division this coming season.

Nottingham F (Free from Grampus 8 on 22/3/99) PL 0+2

ALLSOP Daniel (Danny)
Born: Australia, 10 August 1978
Height: 6'1" Weight: 12.0

Signed from Port Melbourne Sharks in the summer of 1998, the well-built, strong-running Australian striker made his Manchester City debut against Blackpool on the opening day of last season, coming on as a late substitute. In the next game, in the Football League Cup at Notts County, he again came on as a late substitute, scoring the second goal in the 90th minute. His confidence showed as he took the ball some distance out, drew the 'keeper, and slotted the ball home with great flair. On the fringe of a regular place, he spent the campaign mainly being used as a substitute but, at the same time, scored his share of goals. He also scored two hat tricks in successive games for the reserves, a feat last done by a City reserve player in September 1913.

Manchester C (£10,000 from Port Melbourne on 7/8/98) FL 3+21/4 FLC 0+3/1 Others 1+1/1

ALOISI John
Born: Australia, 5 February 1976
Height: 6'0" Weight: 12.13
International Honours: Australia: 10

Having scored 12 goals in his first season, 1997-98, when playing alongside various partners in 1998-99 his strike rate in a struggling Portsmouth side was remarkable, and saw him net seven in the first seven games before he was sold far below his real value to Coventry in December. As the First Division's leading goalscorer, scoring 17 league and cup goals for Pompey, his first appearance in a Sky Blues' shirt was from the bench at Highfield Road against Derby. After marking his second subs' appearance with an equaliser against Tottenham, his real impact came in March when, in successive games, he scored twice in City's first ever league win at Aston Villa, was sent off at home to Charlton, and then struck a superb right-footed goal against Blackburn. Also scored in a 2-2 home draw against Leeds on the final day of the campaign.

Portsmouth (£300,000 from Cremonese on 8/8/97) FL 55+5/26 FLC 6/3 FAC 1
Coventry C (£650,000 on 18/12/98) PL 7+9/5 FAC 0+2

John Aloisi

ALSAKER Paal Christian
Born: Stord, Norway, 6 November 1973
Height: 5'9" Weight: 10.9
A Norwegian right-sided midfielder who had caught the attention of Barcelona while playing for Estonian side, Floria Talin, before agreeing to join Stockport in August 1998, he arrived at the club on a free transfer under the Bosman ruling and made his debut in the opening home game of last season against Norwich. Just one more appearance followed (against Hull City in the Worthington Cup) before he was relegated to the reserves and released in October, returning home to Norway.
Stockport Co (Free from Flora Tallin on 10/8/98) FL 1 FLC 1

ALSFORD Julian
Born: Poole, 24 December 1972
Height: 6'2" Weight: 13.7
An efficient stopper, Julian joined Barnet

last September on loan in a bid to kick-start a career that had been stagnating at Dundee United, making his debut at Exeter and featuring alongside fellow debutant, Mark Arber, in the centre of the back line. Although enjoying some good displays, most notably at home against Rotherham, and in the clash with Torquay where he netted his only goal, the return of Greg Heald to the side after injury indicated that his services were surplus to requirements and he went back to Scotland in December. Released in February, he returned to Chester for the remainder of the campaign and did well before leaving for Hong Kong.
Watford (From trainee on 30/4/91) FL 9+4/1 FLC 1 Others 2
Chester C (Free on 11/8/94) FL 136+5/6 FLC 8+1 FAC 8 Others 8
Dundee U (Free on 27/3/98) SL 3
Barnet (Loaned on 17/9/98) FL 9/1 FAC 1 Others 1
Chester C (Free on 5/2/99) FL 9+1/1

ALSOP Julian Mark
Born: Nuneaton, 28 May 1973
Height: 6'4" Weight: 14.0
As well as establishing himself as one of Swansea's front-line strikers, Julian became a firm favourite with the supporters during last season for his hard work in either setting up or converting chances in the opposition penalty area. An extremely difficult striker to handle in that part of the pitch because of his physical presence and strength in aerial challenges, he was respected by his opponents as being one of the best headers of the ball in the Third Division.
Bristol Rov (£15,000 from Halesowen on 14/2/97) FL 20+13/4 FLC 2/1 FAC 1/1 Others 2
Swansea C (Loaned on 20/1/98) FL 5/2
Swansea C (£30,000 on 12/3/98) FL 44+4/11 FLC 2 FAC 4+1/1 Others 4

AMPADU Patrick Kwame
Born: Bradford, 20 December 1970
Height: 5'10" Weight: 11.10
Club Honours: AMC '94
International Honours: Ei: U21-4; Yth
After joining from Swansea during the summer of 1998, Kwame was a Leyton Orient first-team regular at the start of last season but his campaign was interrupted by injuries. When fit, he was one of the best passers in the Third Division, being an excellent outlet for the defenders and a good supplier for the strikers. Not only will he be looking to regain full fitness, but he will be looking to become an integral part of the side in 1999-2000.
Arsenal (From trainee on 19/11/88) FL 0+2
Plymouth Arg (Loaned on 31/10/90) FL 6/1 Others 1
West Bromwich A (£50,000 on 24/6/91) FL 27+22/4 FLC 6+1 FAC 1 Others 5/1
Swansea C (£15,000 on 16/2/94) FL 128+19/12 FLC 8+1/1 FAC 5+1/1 Others 16/1
Leyton Orient (Free on 30/7/98) FL 26+3/1 FLC 4 FAC 2+1

AMSALEM David
Born: Israel, 4 September 1971
Height: 6'1" Weight: 12.6
International Honours: Israel: 1
An experienced Israeli international, David became 'Terry Venables' first cash signing

for Crystal Palace at the start of 1998-99, when arriving from Beitar Jerusalem. Sent off in Vienna in the Austria versus Israel game, the tall, commanding and versatile defender joined Palace following the transfer of Dean Gordon to Middlesbrough and made his first-team debut at Selhurst Park when coming off the bench in an extra-time 2-1 Worthington Cup win over Torquay. A huge disappointment, he completed just three matches in all before injuries and loss of form saw him out of contention in January.
Crystal Palace (£800,000 from Beitar Jerusalem on 11/8/98) FL 6+4 FLC 1+1

ANDERSEN Braastrup (Bo)
Born: Slagelse, Denmark, 26 March 1976
Height: 6'0" Weight: 13.10
A much heralded signing from Lyngby last December, Bo had to wait a long time before being given his chance by Bristol City. The Danish U21 international goalkeeper finally made his first-team debut, at Barnsley in March, and could not be faulted despite a 2-0 defeat. A regular from then on, keeping clean sheets in his next two games, City are hoping he will continue to prove to be as good as his reputation suggests. Prior to moving to Ashton Gate, it was reported that a European club had earlier been prepared to offer £1 million for his services.
Bristol C (£190,000 from Lyngby on 4/12/98) FL 10

Soren Andersen

ANDERSEN Soren
Born: Aarhus, Denmark, 31 January 1970
Height: 5'9" Weight: 11.8
International Honours: Denmark: 10
Signed in the 1998 close season from Aalborg BK, the Danish international striker started 1998-99 with a bang, scoring two goals in his first game, against Oxford, and then a wonderful equaliser in the televised match at Sunderland. However, he found himself the subject of much controversy when played in a wide midfield role by

coach Benny Lennartsson, a move which most fans found hard to understand. Showed his class with some of the goals he scored, and would have undoubtedly got more had he been played in his rightful position on a more regular basis.

Bristol C (£410,000 from Aalborg BK, via Vejle, AGF, Royal Vallecano and Norrkoping on 17/7/98) FL 26+13/10 FLC 2+1/1 FAC 1

ANDERSON Ijah Massai
Born: Hackney, 30 December 1975
Height: 5'8" Weight: 10.6
Club Honours: Div 3 '99

An attacking Brentford left back with good crossing ability, Ijah is also sound in defence as well. Returned to action at the start of last season, following a broken leg, he soon saw off the challenge of Paul Watson for the number three shirt, capping a fine campaign with a 20 yarder at Chester in April for his only goal of 1998-99. Won a Third Division championship medal as Bees were promoted at their first attempt.

Southend U (Free from Tottenham H juniors on 2/8/94)
Brentford (Free on 31/7/95) FL 123+3/4 FLC 13/1 FAC 4+3 Others 6+1

Ijah Anderson

ANDERSSON Andreas Claes
Born: Osterhoninge, Sweden, 10 April 1974
Height: 6'1" Weight: 13.0
International Honours: Sweden: 23

Andreas is a Swedish international attacker brought to Newcastle by Kenny Dalglish to provide a foil for Alan Shearer, although he declared a preference for playing just behind the front line rather than as an out-and-out striker. His close control, mobility, and unselfishness created space up front for his attacking colleagues but, although a prolific scorer in his homeland, he did not find the net as frequently as expected in the Premiership. He began last season as first choice alongside Alan Shearer, securing a

point with a goal at Chelsea in the second game, and was a revelation in the Euro 2000 qualifier playing for Sweden against England in September, when he scored and turned in a "Man of the Match" performance. However, his campaign was then disrupted when he fell ill with glandular fever. He returned to the side in late 1998, but then lost his place early in January, following which he made only one further appearance, plus two from the bench.

Newcastle U (£3,600,000 from AC Milan, via Tidaholm, Degafors and IFK Gothenburg, on 29/1/98) PL 21+6/4 FAC 3+1 Others 1

ANDERTON Darren Robert
Born: Southampton, 3 March 1972
Height: 6'1" Weight: 12.5
Club Honours: FLC '99
International Honours: E: 27; B-1; U21-12; Yth

By Darren's own high standards last season, on the back of a successful World Cup performance in France, was particularly satisfying. The pacy midfield playmaker experienced a campaign free from injury and demonstrated much of the form which had made him such a favourite at White Hart Lane. Playing now in a more central midfield role, and looking fit and enthusiastic in each game, he has developed the ability to keep possession, despite challenges from opponents. He has also developed a much improved ability to win the ball back from competitors and looked gritty when in the challenge. A good footballing brain, coupled with a tremendous capacity to accurately cross the ball were further enhanced by the new responsibility as penalty taker and master of driving free kicks. All this adding to the maturity of a player who, if free from injury, will be at the forefront of Tottenham's challenge for honours in 1999-2000. His penchant to score fabulous goals was best demonstrated in the FA Cup fifth round replay at home to Leeds in February, when his 30-yard drive put Tottenham on their way to a victory which would lead to the quarter final of the FA Cup and put Darren in the reckoning for goal of the season. Maintaining his regular England spot, he will be looking forward eagerly to the coming challenge of Europe. Won a Football League Cup winners medal following the 1-0 Wembley win over Leicester.

Portsmouth (From trainee on 5/2/90) FL 53+9/7 FLC 3+2/1 FAC 7+1/5 Others 2
Tottenham H (£1,750,000 on 3/6/92) PL 162+17/25 FLC 20/4 FAC 20+1/4

ANDREASSEN Svein Are
Born: Hadsel, Norway, 3 July 1968
Height: 6'0" Weight: 12.10

A tall, well-built Norwegian midfielder whose month's loan to Portsmouth on Christmas Eve resulted in one muddy FA Cup appearance – a successful giant-killing result over Nottingham Forest – and two appearances as a substitute in league matches before he returned home. Alan Ball was not impressed and Svein left bemoaning that the club had not given him further

opportunities. He could read the game well but appeared to lack fitness.

Portsmouth (Loaned from Lillestrom, via Sogndal, on 24/12/98) FL 0+2 FAC 1

ANDREASSON Marcus
Born: Sweden, 13 July 1978
Height: 6'4" Weight: 12.2

A Swedish national, the 19-year-old athletic defender made a favourable impression after a pre-season trial and made his league debut for Bristol Rovers in their opening match of 1998-99, at Burnley. Unfortunately, in his third match he suffered a mystery knee injury which required surgery and meant him missing seven months, before he was able to return to action in April, being used initially as an emergency striker in the Easter Monday draw with Northampton. His height and pace are his strongest assets and much is hoped from him after his early experience of English football.

Bristol Rov (Free from Osters IF on on 28/7/98) FL 4+1 FLC 2

ANDREWS Benjamin (Ben) Phillip
Born: Burton, 18 November 1980
Height: 6'0" Weight: 12.10

19-year-old versatile Brighton defender. After one appearance as a substitute, when he came on to bolster the attack at Carlisle on the opening day of last season, Ben suffered a cruciate ligament injury and was expected to miss the whole of the campaign. However, he resumed training in February and, after a couple of appearances in the youth side, manager Micky Adams offered him a new one-year contract. Gives himself plenty of time on the ball and is good in the air.

Brighton & Hove A (From trainee on 26/3/98) FL 2+2

ANDREWS Bradley James
Born: Bristol, 8 December 1979
Height: 5'11" Weight: 11.0

A natural left-footed winger, Bradley joined his home town club, Bristol Rovers, last March after being released by Norwich, and made his league debut in a thrilling 3-3 match at Walsall. A good crosser of the ball, he kept his place in the next two games, both at the Memorial Stadium, against Wycombe and Notts County. He was substituted in both games and failed to pick up a win bonus before being excluded from the team and being released during the summer.

Norwich C (From trainee on 6/7/98)
Bristol Rov (Free on 19/3/99) FL 3

ANDREWS Wayne Michael Hill
Born: Paddington, 25 November 1977
Height: 5'9" Weight: 11.6

Unable to get a game at Watford in 1998-99, Wayne was loaned out to Cambridge (October) and Peterborough (February) to get match practice following an injury. Having made a limited impression in two games for Cambridge he returned to Watford, but then had an immediate impact when scoring four goals in his first loan appearance for Peterborough, in a 5-2 home win over Barnet. Unfortunately, injuries saw him in and out of the side, making nine more

appearances (and one more goal) before going back to Vicarage Road and being released during the summer.

Watford (From trainee on 5/7/96) FL 16+12/4 FLC 3+2/1 FAC 0+2 Others 2/1
Cambridge U (Loaned on 2/10/98) FL 1+1
Peterborough U (Loaned on 5/2/99) FL 8+2/5

ANELKA Nicolas
Born: Versailles, France, 27 March 1979
Height: 6'0" Weight: 12.3
Club Honours: PL '98; FAC '98; CS '98
International Honours: France: 7

A quality striker with with a tremendous amount of natural pace, and having a wonderfully controlled touch, Nicolas became a regular first-team member at Arsenal in 1998-99, showing a remarkable improvement from the previous season due mainly to being much stronger. As a result, his confidence grew dramatically and he proved extremely difficult to knock off the ball. Although possessing excellent distribution skills, he was always willing to attack defenders in order to create his own scoring opportunities. Scored a number of crucial goals in closely fought matches, but none more important than his last-gasp equaliser against Middlesbrough in November. Also notched a fine hat trick against Leicester, linking particularly well with Dennis Bergkamp. His development was sensational, and two crucial strikes for France against England at Wembley demonstrated that he has a promising international career ahead of him. Not surprisingly he was recognised by his peers as the PFA's "Young Player of the Year" and also took his place in the award-winning Premiership side.

Arsenal (£500,000 + from Paris St Germain on 6/3/97) PL 50+15/23 FLC 3 FAC 13+1/3 Others 7+1/2

ANGEL Mark
Born: Newcastle, 23 August 1975
Height: 5'10" Weight: 11.10

A tricky West Bromwich winger, who loves to cut inside a defender and fire in a shot from any distance, Mark was signed from Oxford during the 1998 close season. At home on either flank, although preferring the right, and a player who likes to dribble with the ball, unfortunately his chances were restricted to only a handful of first-team outings during 1998-99, and even then he appeared mainly as a second-half substitute.

Sunderland (From Walker Central on 31/12/93)
Oxford U (Free on 9/8/95) FL 40+33/4 FLC 4+4 FAC 4+2 Others 2+1/1
West Bromwich A (Free on 2/7/98) FL 4+18/1 FLC 0+1 FAC 0+1

ANGELL Brett Ashley Mark
Born: Marlborough, 20 August 1968
Height: 6'2" Weight: 13.11

Big Brett topped Stockport's scoring charts for the third consecutive season in 1998-99, maintaining his impressive record as a regular goalgetter in the First Division. Not the most mobile of centre forwards, he more than makes up for his lack of pace with outstanding aerial ability and the poacher's instinct of being in the right place at the

right time. His goalscoring prowess was crucial in Stockport's bid to avoid relegation, particularly as the side struggled to find goals from other sources.

Portsmouth (From trainee on 1/8/86)
Derby Co (£40,000 from Cheltenham T on 19/2/88)
Stockport Co (£33,000 on 20/10/88) FL 60+10/28 FLC 3 FAC 3/1 Others 8/4
Southend U (£100,000 on 2/8/90) FL 109+6/47 FLC 7+1/4 FAC 3/2 Others 9+1/10
Everton (£500,000 on 17/1/94) PL 16+4/1 FLC 0+1
Sunderland (£600,000 on 23/3/95) FL 10 FLC 1/1
Sheffield U (Loaned on 30/1/96) FL 6/2
West Bromwich A (Loaned on 28/3/96) FL 0+3
Stockport Co (£120,000 on 19/8/96) FL 117+4/50 FLC 14+2/6 FAC 7/4 Others 4+1/1

Brett Angell

ANSAH Andrew (Andy)
Born: Lewisham, 19 March 1969
Height: 5'7" Weight: 10.7

Despite being better known as a forward, the lively south Londoner spent most of last season playing in midfield for Brighton's reserves. A willing runner who causes problems for defences with his constant movement, he had a short lay off after undergoing a cartilage operation in October, but first-team chances were limited and he was often used as a substitute. Was released by Micky Adams at the end of 1998-99.

Brentford (Free from Dorking on 21/3/89) FL 3+5/2 FLC 0+1
Southend U (Free on 29/3/90) FL 141+16/33 FLC 7+2 FAC 4 Others 7+3/5
Brentford (Loaned on 4/11/94) FL 2+1/1 Others 2/1
Brentford (Loaned on 15/11/95) FL 6/1 Others 1
Peterborough U (Free on 15/3/96) FL 0+2/1
Gillingham (Free on 28/3/96) FL 0+2
Leyton Orient (Free on 19/12/96) FL 0+2 (Free to Hayes on 1/2/97)
Brighton & Hove A (Free from Heybridge Swifts on 7/11/97) FL 10+15/3 FAC 0+1 Others 1+1

ANSELIN Cedric
Born: Lens, France, 24 July 1977
Height: 5'9" Weight: 11.4

Signed from Bordeaux on loan last March for the rest of the 1998-99 season, this technically proficient right-sided midfield player was keen to make an impression on Norwich's boss, Bruce Rioch, in that period, making his debut in the 1-0 victory at Grimsby. A former French U20 international, he had played in both legs of the 1996-97 UEFA Cup final for Bordeaux against Bayern Munich. With his first touch and passing skills being excellent, it was interesting to watch him trying to adjust to the more physical demands of English football.

Norwich C (Loaned from Bordeaux on 25/3/99) FL 7/1

ANTHONY Graham John
Born: South Shields, 9 August 1975
Height: 5'8" Weight: 10.8

In his first full season at Carlisle, Graham featured in just over half the club's matches. An excellent passer of the ball, it fell to him to supply the creative spark in a midfield that was often fully stretched on more defensive duties. Nevertheless, he turned in some fine performances, especially early on when he set up several goals. He never quite scored himself though, his closest effort being a 25-yard shot at Hull that rattled the bar.

Sheffield U (From trainee on 7/7/93) FL 0+3 FLC 1 Others 2
Scarborough (Loaned on 1/3/96) FL 2
Swindon T (Free on 26/3/97) FL 3
Plymouth Arg (Free on 7/8/97) FL 5 FLC 2
Carlisle U (Free on 26/11/97) FL 46+5/2 FLC 1 Others 4+1/1

ANTHROBUS Stephen (Steve) Anthony
Born: Lewisham, 10 November 1968
Height: 6'2" Weight: 13.0

An experienced Crewe player who leads the line well and is good in the air, Steve found it difficult to maintain a first-team place in 1998-99, but was still very popular with the fans. Came into the side at Bury for his first outing during the campaign, and opened his goals account when scoring twice in a 5-2 defeat at Bristol City, five appearances later. Then, after rising above the West Bromwich defence to head home the equaliser in a 1-1 home draw in early December, there were just two more starts and three from the bench before he was released during the summer. Can also play in the centre of defence if necessary.

Millwall (From juniors on 4/8/86) FL 19+2/4 FLC 3 Others 1
Wimbledon (£150,000 on 16/2/90) F/PL 27+1 FLC 1 FAC 2
Peterborough U (Loaned on 21/1/94) FL 2
Chester C (Loaned on 26/8/94) FL 7
Shrewsbury T (£25,000 on 8/8/95) FL 60+12/16 FLC 4+1 FAC 5+3/1 Others 7+2/1
Crewe Alex (£75,000 on 24/3/97) FL 53+8/9 FLC 2+1

APPLEBY Matthew (Matty) Wilfred
Born: Middlesbrough, 16 April 1972
Height: 5'8" Weight: 11.12

Matty had a season in 1998-99 in which he

was not a Barnsley regular when it started, but became one when manager John Hendrie wanted a ball-playing sweeper. His strengths were being able to read a situation and then getting into position to deal with it. A player who likes to link up with both midfield and the attack, and is comfortable on the ball, the second half of the campaign saw him miss games due to injuries to his pelvis and hamstring.

Newcastle U (From trainee on 4/5/90) F/PL 18+2 FLC 2+1 FAC 2 Others 2+2
Darlington (Loaned on 25/11/93) FL 10/1 Others 1
Darlington (Free on 15/6/94) FL 77+2/7 FLC 2 FAC 4 Others 8/3
Barnsley (£200,000 on 19/7/96) F/PL 81+3 FLC 7+1 FAC 5+2

APPLEBY Richard (Richie) Dean
Born: Middlesbrough, 18 September 1975
Height: 5'9" Weight: 11.4
International Honours: E: Yth
An exciting Swansea winger when on song, Richie is capable of teasing and tormenting the best of defenders. Suffered with groin and hamstring problems midway through last season, which, unfortunately for him, saw him sidelined from the exciting FA Cup games against West Ham and Derby, especially after scoring the match winner against Stoke in the second round. Sent off at Southend in March, a likely lengthy ban was overruled by the Welsh FA during an appeal.

Newcastle U (From trainee on 12/8/93) Others 2
Ipswich T (Free on 12/12/95) FL 0+3 Others 1
Swansea C (Free on 16/8/96) FL 77+8/7 FLC 3+1 FAC 3+1/2 Others 2+2/1

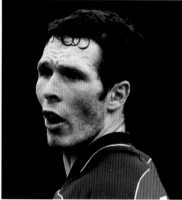
Michael Appleton

APPLETON Michael Antony
Born: Salford, 4 December 1975
Height: 5'9" Weight: 12.4
Preston's record signing had his 1998-99 season blighted by injuries after scoring North End's first goal of the season versus York. Sent off in the next match at Luton, a superb match-winning goal at Oldham demonstrated his dribbling skills, but was followed by an ankle operation in November. The powerful midfielder never seemed to fully recover, and a foot injury on his return to the first-team finally identified the problem. After having special insoles

made for his boots, he finally returned to regular action from March, mainly as a substitute, where he was able to use his tackling and distribution to great effect.
Manchester U (From trainee on 1/7/94) FLC 1+1
Lincoln C (Loaned on 15/9/95) FL 4 Others 1
Grimsby T (Loaned on 17/1/97) FL 10/3
Preston NE (£500,000 on 8/8/97) FL 44+19/4 FLC 4+1 FAC 5+1/1 Others 4+1/1

ARBER Mark Andrew
Born: Johannesburg, South Africa, 9 October 1977
Height: 6'1" Weight: 12.11
Another graduate from Tottenham's revered youth system, Mark initially signed for Barnet on loan last September and enjoyed his first taste of league football in the match at Exeter. He rapidly won over the Bees' fans with his no-nonsense style of play at the back and, also proved equally comfortable when bringing the ball into the attacking half of the field. Arriving on a permanent basis following another month on loan, he proved a real asset to the team on the left side of the central defensive trio. Utilised in the role of left back when the club experimented with a flat back-four formation, his debut goal was a thumping header at Swansea in December, and he scored a classic effort at Hartlepool in January. Still in the formative stages of a career that contains plenty of promise, John Still, Barnet's manager, is well aware that he has the ability to perform at a higher level and he will, no doubt, use the 1999-2000 season to showcase his vast array of talents.
Tottenham H (From trainee on 27/3/96)
Barnet (£75,000 on 18/9/98) FL 35/2 Others 1

ARDLEY Neal Christopher
Born: Epsom, 1 September 1972
Height: 5'11" Weight: 11.9
International Honours: E: U21-10
An attacking Wimbledon midfielder, very much involved in set pieces, and a superb crosser of the ball, the former England U21 international scored a memorable goal against Portsmouth in the Worthington Cup with a thunderous shot from 25 yards. He also scored two more in the same competition, both against Birmingham. Having a good understanding with Kenny Cunningham on the right-hand side, often tracking back to defence, he is a skilful player, and very much part of the Dons' playmaking and dead-ball operations. Was unfortunate to miss the final six games after suffering a recurrence of an earlier toenail injury.
Wimbledon (From trainee on 29/7/91) F/PL 139+23/10 FLC 18+3/5 FAC 21+2/1

ARENDSE Andre
Born: Capetown, South Africa, 27 June 1967
Height: 6'4" Weight: 11.5
International Honours: South Africa: 27
Due to the outstanding form of Northern Ireland 'keeper, Maik Taylor, Andre's only first-team appearance for Fulham last season was in the Auto Windscreens Shield match at Torquay, when Fulham fielded a

complete reserve side and lost 2-1. A regular in the Combination side, Andre is a tall, imposing figure and a very good shot stopper.
Fulham (Signed from Capetown Spurs on 7/8/97) FL 6 FLC 2 FAC 1 Others 1

ARMSTRONG Alun
Born: Gateshead, 22 February 1975
Height: 6'1" Weight: 11.13
Club Honours: Div 1 '98
Alun will remember his first season in the Premiership with Middlesbrough more for his lack of action than because of it. Up to the end of last March, the determined young striker had enjoyed only three minutes of football, courtesy to his various injuries, and his frustration was apparent to everyone. The goalscoring ability that had seen him bang in seven goals in his first 11 Boro outings augured well for the future and his examination at the highest level had been eagerly awaited. His popularity was fully endorsed by the fans who raised the biggest cheer of the night when he took the field as sub in the 87th minute against long-time adversaries, Nottingham Forest. Almost back to full fitness his appearances off the bench were very selective by coaches who were anxious to preserve his talents with a clean bill of health for the coming campaign.
Newcastle U (From trainee on 1/10/93)
Stockport Co (£50,000 on 23/6/94) FL 151+8/48 FLC 22/8 FAC 10+1/5 Others 7
Middlesbrough (£1,500,000 on 16/2/98) P/FL 7+10/8

Chris Armstrong

ARMSTRONG Christopher (Chris) Peter
Born: Newcastle, 19 June 1971
Height: 6'0" Weight: 13.3
Club Honours: Div 1 '94; FLC '99
International Honours: E: B-1
Athletic with great ability in the air, Chris had a promising return to form with the

arrival of George Graham at Tottenham in 1998-99. A final tally of 12 goals for the season made him the club's top scorer, a hat trick in the 4-1 win over Everton in December underlining exactly what he is capable of when fully fit and benefiting from a run of first-team action. He also added the ability to create in the middle of the field to his game, along with a defensive side, which delighted new boss Graham and earned Chris a surprise call up as attacking cover for an injury-wrecked England squad for the Euro 2000 qualifier against Poland at Wembley. Yet another of the squad rumoured to be exiting in the summer, should that be the case he will attract interest from a host of clubs. However, the Tottenham fans hope that their leading goalscorer continues at White Hart Lane as a valuable member of the squad.

Wrexham (Free from Llay Welfare on 3/3/89) FL 40+20/13 FLC 2+1 FAC 0+1 Others 5+1/3
Millwall (£50,000 on 16/8/91) FL 11+17/5 FLC 3+1/2 FAC 0+1 Others 0+1
Crystal Palace (£1,000,000 on 1/9/92) F/PL 118/45 FLC 8/6 FAC 8/5 Others 2/1
Tottenham H (£4,500,000 on 30/6/95) PL 85+16/32 FLC 13/10 FAC 9+3/4

ARMSTRONG Steven Craig
Born: South Shields, 23 May 1975
Height: 5'11" Weight: 12.10
Finally got his chance of a first-team place at Nottingham Forest in 1998-99 after a patient wait and did not look out of place in the Premiership. Primarily regarded as a left back, he made most of his appearances in the centre of the defence and impressed enough to be called up by England as an over-age player for the U21 squad. Also able to play in midfield, he became Huddersfield's most expensive defender when they signed him last February, and he immediately came in for the game at Wolves. Following that up with an outstanding performance at the McAlpine against Bolton, and scoring a great goal, he certainly looked the part as a central defender who was commanding and comfortable on the ball. Selected as "Man of the Match" against Birmingham, he missed just one game due to suspension and looks to be an outstanding buy.

Nottingham F (From trainee on 2/6/92) P/FL 24+16 FLC 6+2/2 FAC 1
Burnley (Loaned on 29/12/94) FL 4
Bristol Rov (Loaned on 8/1/96) FL 4
Bristol Rov (Loaned on 28/3/96) FL 9+1
Gillingham (Loaned on 18/10/96) FL 10 FLC 2 Others 1
Watford (Loaned on 24/1/97) FL 3
Watford (Loaned on 14/3/97) FL 12
Huddersfield T (£750,000 on 26/2/99) FL 13/1

ARMSTRONG Gordon Ian
Born: Newcastle, 15 July 1967
Height: 6'0" Weight: 12.11
Club Honours: Div 3 '88
Burnley's captain joined in August 1998 from manager Stan Ternent's former club, Bury, and scored on his debut at Walsall. In many ways the archetypal Ternent player, Gordon was sometimes more effective than a leader of the side than in his own performances, though he was perhaps

hindered to some extent by the lack of a settled role as the team was constantly changed. During last season, he appeared in midfield, in central defence, as a sweeper, and, perhaps most effectively, at left back.

Sunderland (From apprentice on 10/7/85) FL 331+18/50 FLC 25+4/3 FAC 19/4 Others 18+1/4
Bristol C (Loaned on 24/8/95) FL 6
Northampton T (Loaned on 5/1/96) FL 4/1 Others 1
Bury (Free on 16/7/96) FL 49+22/4 FLC 5+2/2 FAC 2+1 Others 1+1
Burnley (Free on 27/8/98) FL 40/1

ARMSTRONG Paul George
Born: Dublin, 5 October 1978
Height: 5'10" Weight: 10.12
International Honours: Ei: U21-2
Impressing in the right-wing back role when he returned to the Brighton side last December, Paul scored his first senior goal against Chester in January when he converted a penalty in the fourth minute of injury time to earn a 1-1 draw in front of the Sky TV cameras. Was awarded a one-year extension to his contract by Brian Horton just before the manager departed to join Port Vale, and also scored in the next game (Jeff Wood's first in charge) against Scarborough. Gained further international honours when coming on as substitute for the Republic of Ireland U21s against Sweden.

Brighton & Hove A (From trainee on 10/7/97) FL 33+15/2 FAC 1 Others 1

ARNOTT Andrew (Andy) John
Born: Chatham, 18 October 1973
Height: 6'1" Weight: 13.2
Having made an impressive debut for Brighton in the away win at Barnet last October, this versatile player, who was signed from Fulham a few days earlier was immediately awarded a two-and-a-half-year contract. Scored his first goal in two years in the 3-1 victory over the eventual champions, Brentford, on Boxing Day and concluded his scoring for the season two games later in the 1-1 draw at Torquay. Able to play in defence, midfield, and up front, he is a veritable danger at set pieces.

Gillingham (From trainee on 13/5/91) FL 50+23/12 FLC 2+3 FAC 10+2/1 Others 3+2
Leyton Orient (£15,000 on 25/1/96) FL 47+3/6 FLC 2 FAC 2 Others 1
Fulham (£23,000 on 17/6/97) FL 0+1 Others 0+2
Brighton & Hove A (£20,000 on 23/10/98) FL 27/2 FAC 1 Others 1

ARPHEXAD Pegguy Michel
Born: Abymes, Guadeloupe, 18 May 1973
Height: 6'2" Weight: 13.5
The Leicester goalkeeper had few chances to take the field as understudy to Kasey Keller in 1998-99, but whenever he did he always looked both confident and competent. He twice had to come off the substitutes' bench to replace Keller, at Old Trafford on the opening day, when Kasey injured a knee, and later in the win at Wimbledon when back trouble was the cause. Was also involved in the opening round victory over Chesterfield that signalled the start of the Foxes' run to Wembley and is widely regarded as a most important member of Martin O'Neill's

squad. Out of contract during the summer, the club will be looking for him to sign their offer of re-engagement.

Leicester C (Free from Lens on 20/8/97) PL 8+2 FLC 1

ASABA Carl Edward
Born: London, 28 January 1973
Height: 6'2" Weight: 13.4
Signed from Reading, Gillingham paid out a club record fee to secure his services late last August and it was no surprise that the team's performances improved on his arrival. A strong-running front runner, who finished last season as the top scorer, he was dismissed during the home match against Colchester in February and was given a four-match ban. Following statements from supporters, including fans, the ban was quashed by an FA committee.

Brentford (Free from Dulwich Hamlet on 9/8/94) FL 49+5/25 FLC 5 FAC 4 Others 7/2
Colchester U (Loaned on 16/2/95) FL 9+3/2
Reading (£800,000 on 7/8/97) FL 31+2/8 FLC 7+2/4 FAC 3/1
Gillingham (£600,000 on 28/8/98) FL 40+1/20 FAC 1 Others 7/2

ASHBEE Ian
Born: Birmingham, 6 September 1976
Height: 6'1" Weight: 13.7
International Honours: E: Yth
An ever reliable member of the Cambridge squad in 1998-99, Ian once again proved to be an extremely versatile player who could slot into the team as a midfielder, and also played at full back. He even had an outstanding game when selected as an emergency centre half. Possessing a fierce shot, and scoring some memorable goals for the club, he is possibly at his best when attacking opposing defenders. Aggressive and hard working, he puts the team first.

Derby Co (From trainee on 9/11/94) FL 1
Cambridge U (Free on 13/12/96) FL 68+8/5 FLC 2 FAC 6 Others 3+1

ASHBY Barry John
Born: Park Royal, 21 November 1970
Height: 6'2" Weight: 13.8
Club Honours: FAYC '89
Barry became an important member of Gillingham's defence during last season, and was missed when he had to serve bans for two dismissals that he incurred during the course of the campaign. Steady, reliable, and good in aerial combat, on Bank Holiday Monday in April he scored his first ever goal for the club in an important 2-0 victory at Wycombe.

Watford (From trainee on 1/12/88) FL 101+13/3 FLC 6 FAC 4 Others 3/1
Brentford (Signed on 22/3/94) FL 119+2/4 FLC 11 FAC 9/1 Others 11+1
Gillingham (£140,000 on 8/8/97) FL 81/1 FLC 3 FAC 3 Others 5

ASHCROFT Lee
Born: Preston, 7 September 1972
Height: 5'10" Weight: 11.10
International Honours: E: U21-1
A record signing for Grimsby from Preston at the start of 1998-99, to remedy the Mariners' lack of fire power, Lee had a couple of lengthy spells out of the side due

to injury, which made it difficult for him to establish himself, being unable to find the touch that made him North End's leading scorer. A versatile player, with the ability to perform either up front or in a central midfield position, it is likely that a more prolonged spell in the side this coming season will find him rediscovering his old skill in front of goal.

Preston NE (From trainee on 16/7/91) FL 78+13/13 FLC 3 FAC 5 Others 6+2/1
West Bromwich A (£250,000 on 1/8/93) FL 66+24/17 FLC 2+3 FAC 3+1/1 Others 8+3
Notts Co (Loaned on 28/3/96) FL 4+2
Preston NE (£150,000 on 5/9/96) FL 63+1/22 FLC 4 FAC 5/5 Others 2+1
Grimsby T (£500,000 on 12/8/98) FL 21+6/3 FLC 2/1

ASHTON Jonathan (Jon) Frank
Born: Plymouth, 4 August 1979
Height: 5'11" Weight: 12.0

One of the most improved players on the Plymouth staff, Jon started 1998-99 as a squad member, but initially due to injuries and then his own good form he established himself at right back after making his first start for the club at Rotherham. With a great attitude, he has really worked hard to improve his all-round game, being athletic, quick, and determined to win the ball.

Plymouth Arg (From trainee on 29/7/97) FL 22+5 FLC 0+2 FAC 4 Others 1

Jon Ashton

ASKEY John Colin
Born: Stoke, 4 November 1964
Height: 6'0" Weight: 12.2
Club Honours: GMVC '95, '97; FAT '96
International Honours: E: SP-1

As the longest serving player at Macclesfield, John was moved from his usual midfield winger role last season, to that of a front man, usually just behind the other striker. He quickly established this position with a double strike against Stoke in the Worthington Cup first round, first leg. However, relegated to the bench for a spell in mid season when the manager experimented with a single-striker system,

he gained his place back in January after the team reverted to the 4-4-2 formation, and was a regular starter from then on.

Macclesfield T (Free from Milton U during 1987-88) FL 68+9/10 FLC 6/2 FAC 4/1 Others 1

ASPIN Neil
Born: Gateshead, 12 April 1965
Height: 6'0" Weight: 13.10
Club Honours: AMC '93

Once again, Neil proved to be a solid presence in Port Vale's back four and, as usual, gave his all for the cause in 1998-99. He often popped up to clear a goalbound effort with any part of his anatomy but sometimes let his enthusiasm get carried away, resulting in a couple of sendings off, both of which were for second bookable offences. Completed ten years with the Vale and was rewarded with a well deserved testimonial against Leicester, before being released during the summer.

Leeds U (From apprentice on 6/10/82) FL 203+4/5 FLC 9/1 FAC 17 Others 11
Port Vale (£200,000 on 28/7/89) FL 343+5/3 FLC 20 FAC 24 Others 18

ASPINALL Warren
Born: Wigan, 13 September 1967
Height: 5'9" Weight: 12.8
Club Honours: AMC '85, '97; Div 3 '99
International Honours: E: Yth

Having started the first 22 games of Brentford's 1998-99 campaign prior to being replaced by Gavin Mahon, Warren

made only a few further appearances before joining Colchester in February, initially on loan. A vastly experienced, combative midfielder, brought by Mick Wadsworth to add experience and a competitive edge to the relegation struggle, he very quickly won the supporters over with a series of never-say-die performances, beginning with a fierce battle at Gillingham, where he had to play in several positions as his colleagues succumbed to injury. A regular in the side after arriving, he ended the season with three vital goals to his name – a flying header to beat Preston, a late penalty to see off Notts County, and another pressure spot kick at Northampton. Is a firm fans' favourite. Won a Third Division championship medal during his stay with the Bees.

Wigan Ath (From apprentice on 31/8/85) FL 21+12/10 FLC 1 FAC 2+3/2 Others 1+5/2
Everton (£150,000 on 4/2/86) FL 0+7 FLC 0+1 Others 0+2
Wigan Ath (Loaned on 6/2/86) FL 18/12 Others 2/2
Aston Villa (£300,000 on 19/2/87) FL 40+4/14 FLC 4/2 FAC 1+1
Portsmouth (£315,000 on 26/8/88) FL 97+35/21 FLC 8+3/3 FAC 4+5/2 Others 6+1/2
Bournemouth (Loaned on 27/8/93) FL 4+2/1
Swansea C (Loaned on 14/10/93) FL 5 Others 1
Bournemouth (£20,000 on 31/12/93) FL 26+1/8 FLC 4 FAC 1 Others 1
Carlisle U (Free on 8/3/95) FL 99+8/12 FLC 8/3 FAC 6 Others 10+1/1
Brentford (£50,000 on 21/11/97) FL 41+2/5 FLC 4 FAC 1+1 Others 2
Colchester U (Free on 9/2/99) FL 15/3

Warren Aspinall

ATHERTON Peter
Born: Orrell, 6 April 1970
Height: 5'11" Weight: 13.12
International Honours: E: U21-1; Sch
As Sheffield Wednesday's club captain and a strong, resolute character, Peter enjoyed a good season in 1998-99 back in his preferred defensive role, albeit at full back. Having enjoyed a good spell in a holding midfield role the previous campaign, he adapted well to the switch. Not spectacular, in fact he is easily ignored by the casual observer, but regular supporters appreciate his great value to team morale. For such a tough-tackling player, he stays remarkably free from injury and always gives his all to the side.
Wigan Ath (From trainee on 12/2/88) FL 145+4/1 FLC 8 FAC 7 Others 12+1
Coventry C (£300,000 on 23/8/91) F/PL 113+1 FLC 4 FAC 2
Sheffield Wed (£800,000 on 1/6/94) PL 179/8 FLC 13 FAC 14

ATKINS Mark Nigel
Born: Doncaster, 14 August 1968
Height: 6'0" Weight: 13.2
Club Honours: PL '95
International Honours: E: Sch
A good all-rounder, and a useful member of the Wolves' squad who can play in several different positions, he came on as a sub in the second match of 1998-99, but was playing for the reserves when he sustained suspected medial knee-ligament damage. Thankfully, it was not as bad as first feared and his first start was at Portsmouth on 17 October, and the next nearly a month later. In December, he came in at right back and did well, replacing the unavailable Kevin Muscat, who eventually came in at left back, for a total of 15 matches. He was very steady and reliable during this period, yet at Queens Park Rangers he was sent off for an uncharacteristic action and missed three matches through suspension, before being released during the summer.
Scunthorpe U (From juniors on 9/7/86) FL 45+5/2 FLC 3+1 FAC 5 Others 6+1
Blackburn Rov (£45,000 on 16/6/88) F/PL 224+33/35 FLC 20+2/4 FAC 11+3 Others 17+2/1
Wolverhampton W (£1,000,000 on 21/9/95) FL 115+11/8 FLC 12+1/2 FAC 11+1 Others 2/1

ATKINSON Brian
Born: Darlington, 19 January 1971
Height: 5'10" Weight: 12.5
International Honours: E: U21-6
Only missing a handful of games in his third full season with Darlington in 1998-99, after struggling with injuries in his first two, the fully fit Brian was a major influence on the left-hand side of midfield with his tenacity and ability to keep the ball under pressure. Out of contract during the summer, he scored only twice, but one was a vital penalty against Burnley in the FA Cup.
Sunderland (From trainee on 21/7/89) FL 119+22/4 FLC 8+2 FAC 13/2 Others 2+3
Carlisle U (Loaned on 19/1/96) FL 2 Others 1
Darlington (Free on 10/8/96) FL 96+9/6 FLC 7 FAC 6+1/2 Others 4/1

ATKINSON Graeme
Born: Hull, 11 November 1971
Height: 5'8" Weight: 11.3
Club Honours: Div 3 '96
A cultured left back with a powerful shot, who was originally released by Brighton in May 1998, but re-signed as cover for Stuart Tuck last August, playing eight times before being freed for the second time in five months and signing non-contract forms for Scunthorpe in early November. After appearing briefly as a sub he was on his way again, this time to Scarborough in mid February, where he showed up as an experienced and composed left back. Giving a "Man of the Match" display on his debut, a 2-1 win over Swansea, he was ever present from then until the close of the season, before being released in the summer.
Hull C (From trainee on 6/5/90) FL 129+20/23 FLC 6+3/2 FAC 4+1/1 Others 9
Preston NE (Signed on 7/10/94) FL 63+16/6 FLC 5/1 FAC 2+1 Others 5/2
Rochdale (Loaned on 12/12/97) FL 5+1
Brighton & Hove A (Free on 5/3/98) FL 16 FLC 1
Scunthorpe U (Free on 2/11/98) FL 0+1
Scarborough (Free on 18/2/99) FL 15/1

ATKINSON Patrick (Paddy) Darren
Born: Singapore, 22 May 1970
Height: 5'9" Weight: 11.6
Formerly with York, having been freed during the 1998 close season he joined neighbouring Scarborough in time for the start of 1998-99. A skilful defender who likes to attack, and who also showed his versatility with a couple of outings in midfield in April, unfortunately, he suffered an injury-hit campaign before being released in the summer after the club was relegated to the Conference.
Hartlepool U (Free from Sheffield U juniors on 23/8/88) FL 9+12/3 FLC 0+1 FAC 2 Others 1+1 (Free to Gateshead during 1990 close season)
York C (Free from Workington, via Newcastle Blue Star and Barrow on 17/11/95) FL 36+5 FAC 3+1 Others 4+1
Scarborough (Free on 6/8/98) FL 23+4 FLC 2 FAC 2 Others 1

AUSTIN Dean Barry
Born: Hemel Hempstead, 26 April 1970
Height: 5'11" Weight: 12.4
Freed by Spurs during the 1998 close season, Dean, who had been under Terry Venables at White Hart Lane, joined up with his former manager once more when arriving at Crystal Palace in time for the beginning of 1998-99. Started in the opener at home to Bolton, but never found his true form until the mass exodus of players from Selhurst in March. At his best a right-sided defender who enjoys coming out with the ball to attack the opposition, he scored his first goal for seven years in a 1-0 win at Norwich. Determination and speed are among his other abilities.
Southend U (£12,000 from St Albans C on 22/3/90) FL 96/2 FLC 4/1 FAC 2 Others 7
Tottenham H (£375,000 on 4/6/92) PL 117+7 FLC 7+2 FAC 16+1
Crystal Palace (Free on 8/7/98) FL 17+3/1 FLC 4

AUSTIN Kevin Levi
Born: Hackney, 12 February 1973
Height: 6'0" Weight: 14.0
Kevin's speed and strength at the back made him a vital player in Lincoln's 1998-99 campaign. He missed only seven matches, all either through injury or suspension, with his highlight of the season coming when he netted the winner in the home game against Manchester City – his first goal in more than 100 appearances for the Imps. In rejecting a £400,000 move to Bristol City, he finished the campaign out of contract after turning down the club's new offer. Stop Press: Reported to have signed for Barnsley in early July.
Leyton Orient (Free from Saffron Walden on 19/8/93) FL 101+8/3 FLC 4/1 FAC 6 Others 7
Lincoln C (£30,000 on 31/7/96) FL 128+1/1 FLC 9 FAC 6 Others 4

AVDIU Kemajl
Born: Kosovo, 22 December 1976
Height: 5'10" Weight: 11.7
A Serbian-born striker who took out Swedish citizenship, but played with FC Esbjerg in Denmark before trying his luck last season in England, he spent pre-season on trial at Sheffield United but was not taken on and arrived at Bury in September. After impressing in the Shakers' Lancashire League and Pontins League sides, Kemajl – nicknamed "Kemo" – was given a 12-month professional contract in October by Neil Warnock. Impressing everyone with his exciting pace, he went on to earn six substitute appearances in the senior side, although he did not make the starting line up. Scored his first senior goal in English football in a 2-1 away defeat at Portsmouth in February and, despite scoring 12 goals in the reserve team, he was allowed to join Partick Thistle on loan in March for match practice.
Bury (Free from Esbjerg on 28/8/98) FL 0+6/1
Partick Thistle (Loaned on 30/3/99) SL 6/1

AWFORD Andrew (Andy) Terence
Born: Worcester, 14 July 1972
Height: 5'10" Weight: 12.0
International Honours: E: U21-9; Yth; Sch
Solid, dependable defender, whose 39 appearances in the number six shirt for Portsmouth last season were reliable, honest, and with 100 per-cent effort. The son of former Worcester City full back, Terry, Andy's consistently good passing and reading of the game helped balance an erratic season for his only club as he looks forward to a testimonial year in 1999-2000, having surpassed 250 games and scored the second league goal of his career in March 1999 – an impressive header which gave the side a valuable win over Sheffield United at Fratton Park. His unflappable manner, and hard concentration throughout a toiling campaign saw him become a popular favourite among supporters, and he is still only 26 years of age.
Portsmouth (From trainee on 24/7/89) FL 263+14/2 FLC 27+1 FAC 16 Others 12

We're a big supporter in all sorts of arenas.

At The Royal Bank of Scotland we're delighted to give our continued support to a wide variety of sporting events throughout the U.K.

The Royal Bank of Scotland

B

BAARDSEN Espen
Born: San Rafael, USA, 7 December 1977
Height: 6'5" Weight: 13.13
Club Honours: FLC '99
International Honours: Norway: 2
Making his first appearance of last season for Tottenham as early as 29 August, at home to Everton, Espen demonstrated just how much he had grown into a first-class 'keeper. Strong and confident in the air, his best performances came in the games against Newcastle in October and Arsenal in November when, despite being up against some of the prolific goalscorers in the Premiership, he kept remarkable clean sheets in both games. As each game of his 17-match run went by, the confidence and capability of the 22-year old visibly grew, along with a calmness under pressure not usually associated with such raw talent. With that in mind it was no surprise to find top Premiership teams enquiring as to the availability of the young 'keeper, who gave Spurs' fans a real lift by signing a long-term deal in November, thus demonstrating his commitment to the club and disappointing many rival Premiership clubs in doing so.
Tottenham H (Free from San Francisco All Blacks on 16/7/96) PL 22+1 FLC 3 FAC 2+1

BABAYARO Celestine
Born: Kaduna, Nigeria, 29 August 1978
Height: 5'8" Weight: 11.0
Club Honours: FLC '98; ESC '98
International Honours: Nigeria: 11
Celestine recovered from his serious foot injury to play a significant part in Nigeria's World Cup campaign in 1998 and, at long last fully fit, figure prominently in Chelsea's first-team plans. He began last season playing on the left of midfield, forming a good partnership with Graeme Le Saux, and showed his versatility by filling in left back while Graeme was suspended. "Baba" won a European Super Cup winners' medal against Real Madrid and opened his goalscoring account with goals against Newcastle and West Ham, which secured 1-1 Premiership draws for the Blues. Later in the campaign, he tucked away a nicely-angled drive against Valerenga and a firmly struck volley against Derby in the final league game, both of which were celebrated with his customary somersault! Is a strong-running, athletic and aggressive player, who loves to get forward to whip over dangerous crosses for the front men, and had a very satisfactory first full season, to impress the fans with his wholehearted displays.
Chelsea (£2,250,000 from Anderlecht on 20/6/97) PL 34+2/3 FLC 4+1 FAC 4+1 Others 9+2/1

BABB Philip (Phil) Andrew
Born: Lambeth, 30 November 1970
Height: 6'0" Weight: 12.3
Club Honours: FLC '95
International Honours: Ei: 29; B-1
Many Liverpool supporters maintain that the Republic of Ireland international defender has never quite fulfilled their expectations. After a brilliant World Cup in 1994, Liverpool bought him to Anfield and in his initial season he looked like the answer to the club's defensive prayers. However, as his Pool career has unfolded he has come under much pressure from the expectant fans, and has proved a particularly enigmatic character. On his day, a defender of some style who is solid in the tackle and constructive in distribution, but, in and out of the team in 1998-99 and often played out of position, he failed to settle. Performed well in what was possibly the club's best result of the campaign, a 2-0 fight back to draw at home to Manchester United.
Millwall (From trainee on 25/4/89)
Bradford C (Free on 10/8/90) FL 73+7/14 FLC 5+1 FAC 3 Others 3+1
Coventry C (£500,000 on 21/7/92) PL 70+7/3 FLC 5/1 FAC 2
Liverpool (£3,600,000 on 1/9/94) PL 124+4/1 FLC 16 FAC 12 Others 12+2

BACQUE Herve
Born: Bordeaux, France, 13 July 1976
Height: 5'9" Weight: 11.8
After arriving at Luton on trial from AS Monaco, and scoring goals in two pre-season friendlies, against Coventry and Arsenal, Herve signed up in time for 1998-99 to get underway, coming straight into the first team to make his debut in a 1-0 win at Wycombe. A centre forward with flair and skill, and a tremendous right foot, his only doubt was whether he would adapt favourably to an English winter. Although his ability to thread in precise through balls was displayed on several occasions, most of his appearances were from the subs' bench, and dissatisfied with his lot at Kenilworth Road the Frenchman left the club on 21 January, bound for Motherwell.
Luton T (Free from AS Monaco on 7/8/98) FL 2+5 FLC 1+2 Others 1

BADDELEY Lee Matthew
Born: Cardiff, 12 July 1974
Height: 6'1" Weight: 12.7
International Honours: W: U21-2; Yth
Exeter's Lee missed the start of last season after having had a hernia operation, and following this he suffered from a long-standing hamstring injury. As such, he never really established himself in the side, although when selected for the first team he equipped himself well and never let the side down. Released during the summer, he is a central defender who can be relied upon in aerial battles and on the ground.
Cardiff C (From trainee on 13/8/91) FL 112+21/1 FLC 4+2 FAC 8 Others 24
Exeter C (Free on 6/2/97) FL 60+6/1 FAC 3 Others 0+1

BAGSHAW Paul John
Born: Sheffield, 25 September 1979
Height: 5'10" Weight: 12.2
An attacking midfielder who came through Barnsley's junior ranks and was a regular in the reserves last season, he made his first-team debut as a sub in the Worthington Cup at Reading and impressed. A player who has the ability to beat defenders on both sides and is an adequate finisher inside the box, he was loaned to Carlisle during transfer deadline week and featured in a striking role in the last month of the campaign. Proving to be a hard worker whose best match was perhaps his debut against Torquay, his last three appearances were all from the substitutes' bench.
Barnsley (From trainee on 1/7/97) FL 0+1 FLC 0+1
Carlisle U (Loaned on 25/3/99) FL 5+4

BAIANO Francesco
Born: Naples, Italy, 24 February 1968
Height: 5'7" Weight: 10.7
International Honours: Italy: 2
The former Italian international, and an attacking midfielder, after a highly successful 1997-98 at Derby he found 1998-99 more of a struggle as a lack of confidence led to him being in and out of the side during the first half. Injury to Lars Bohinen gave him a longer run, but the highlight of his campaign were two goals in the FA Cup replay against Huddersfield that earned County a place in the quarter finals. Suffered a groin strain towards the close of the campaign, just as he seemed to have reclaimed his place, Francesco must be hoping for a return to his previous consistency as well as a better goals to appearances ratio this coming term. Has excellent passing skills and control.
Derby Co (£1,500,000 from Fiorentina, via Napoli, Empoli, Parma, Avelino and Foggia, on 8/8/97) PL 47+8/16 FLC 4 FAC 5/3

BAILEY Alan
Born: Macclesfield, 1 November 1978
Height: 5'9" Weight: 11.12
One of the many promising youngsters at Manchester City, having been there since the age of 11, he has received a sound grounding in the reserves. Not a big man for a striker but one who relies on a quick approach, holding the ball up and speed being his top assets, Alan made his first-team debut in the Auto Windscreens Shield game against Mansfield last season. Was loaned out to Macclesfield during January and February and scored his first league goal to help Town beat Colchester in the last minute.
Manchester C (From trainee on 2/7/97) Others 0+1
Macclesfield T (Loaned on 29/1/99) FL 5+5/1

BAILEY John Andrew
Born: Lambeth, 6 May 1969
Height: 5'8" Weight: 10.8
John's wholehearted approach to the game at Bournemouth has seen him become a firm favourite with the Cherries' crowd. Unfortunately, 1998-99 was brought to a premature end for him through injury in March, although he began to come back to fitness towards the end of the campaign, managing a couple of appearances before the close. Able to play either on the right or in central midfield, he is a tireless worker and a tigerish tackler who will give you 100 per cent for the full 90 minutes.
Bournemouth (£40,000 from Enfield on 5/7/95) FL 136+12/6 FLC 11+1 FAC 9+1 Others 11+1/1

BAILEY Mark
Born: Stoke, 12 August 1976
Height: 5'8" Weight: 10.12
Following his regular appearances the previous term, Mark's hard-running style earned him a place in the Rochdale midfield in early season games during 1998-99, and he netted his first career goal when claiming the winner against Shrewsbury. Subsequently, he had to settle mostly for a place on the bench until a niggling injury ruled him out of the squad altogether, before reappearing for a few games towards the end of the campaign at right back. Was released during the summer.
Stoke C (From trainee on 12/7/94)
Rochdale (Free on 10/10/96) FL 49+18/1 FLC 3+1 FAC 1 Others 4

BAIRD Andrew (Andy) Crawford
Born: East Kilbride, 18 January 1979
Height: 5'10" Weight: 12.6
Very talented striker in his first full season at Wycombe as a senior player. By mid 1998-99, he had firmly established himself as first choice, despite his young years, being the first striker to make the grade from the junior ranks at the club for many years. His debut goal summed up his style of play when, coming on as a sub at home to Macclesfield, he quickly latched on to a defensive mistake, strongly held off a defender, and coolly finished with his left foot. Andy can score with either foot, his looping headed goal at Macclesfield being masterly, and he scored a spectacular goal at home to Northampton, beating several players before scoring with a fierce shot from the edge of the box. He bravely had to play with a foot injury early on before an operation put him out for six weeks in December. With the presence of mind to spin quickly off defenders, good first touch, and the ability to take long passes comfortably on the volley, a number of clubs were interested in signing him and a large offer from Portsmouth was turned down before the new manager, Lawrie Sanchez, persuaded him to stay at Wycombe until the summer of 2002.
Wycombe W (From trainee on 18/3/98) FL 25+5/6 FLC 0+2 FAC 3/1 Others 1

BAKAYOKO Ibrahima
Born: Seguela, Ivory Coast, 31 December 1976
Height: 5'11" Weight: 12.10
International Honours: Ivory Coast: 17
A compact and pacy striker, Ibrahima arrived at Goodison from Montpellier (France) last October with an impressive reputation, but found it difficult to live up to the advance publicity. Previously on trial with Arsenal, Everton paid handsomely for his services, but he struggled to come swiftly to terms with the English Premiership. However, his strength of character was clear. He demanded a penalty in his third match at Middlesbrough, missed it, but then went on to score his first goal in English football. Still a youngster, he showed flashes of unpredictable star quality, not least with a stunning free kick in the FA

Cup at Bristol City, but generally struggled to settle. Stop Press: Joined Marseilles on 22 June for a reported fee of £4 million.
Everton (£4,500,000 from Montpellier on 9/10/98) PL 17+6/4 FLC 2/1 FAC 1+2/2

Ibrahima Bakayoko

BAKER Joseph (Joe) Philip
Born: London, 19 April 1977
Height: 5'8" Weight: 10.4
Although Joe did not start any league games for Leyton Orient last season he still proved, when he appeared as a substitute, what a crowd favourite he is, his driving runs at tiring defenders causing havoc. A wide player, who gets to the line to cross and packs a potent shot in his boots, he will be looking to regain a first-team place this season.
Leyton Orient (Free from Charlton Ath juniors on 24/5/95) FL 23+52/3 FLC 1+4/2 FAC 0+3 Others 2+3

BAKER David Paul
Born: Newcastle, 5 January 1963
Height: 6'1" Weight: 14.2
Out of competitive football for more than a year, this vastly experienced and powerful striker has been desperately unlucky with injuries, having suffered two broken legs and a fractured ankle in a matter of months. In the 1998 close season he turned down the chance to become Torquay's player/manager but, as Hartlepool's player/coach, he looked to be surplus to requirements when Mick Tait vacated the manager's office last January. Always determined to resume his playing career, however, he went on trial to Plymouth, but was then surprisingly recalled to Pool's first-team squad, often being utilised as a late substitute. He proved a great success, most importantly scoring a close-range goal to secure a valuable 1-0 win at Shrewsbury. At the veteran stage, many fans will be sorry that he has been released, although there was talk that he will be granted a testimonial this coming term.

Southampton (£4,000 from Bishop Auckland on 1/7/84)
Carlisle U (Free on 2/7/85) FL 66+5/11 FLC 4/1 FAC 3 Others 2+1
Hartlepool U (Free on 31/7/87) FL 192+5/67 FLC 12/4 FAC 16/6 Others 16/5
Motherwell (£77,500 on 1/8/92) SL 5+4/1 SLC 1
Gillingham (£40,000 on 7/1/93) FL 58+4/16 FAC 5/1 Others 2
York C (£15,000 on 1/10/94) FL 36+12/18 FLC 2+2/2 FAC 3 Others 5+1/1
Torquay U (£25,000 on 19/1/96) FL 30/8 FLC 2/3
Scunthorpe U (£15,000 on 4/10/96) FL 21/9 FAC 3/5 Others 2
Hartlepool U (Signed on 27/3/97) FL 25+10/9 FLC 2/1 Others 0+1

BAKER Steven (Steve) Richard
Born: Pontefract, 8 September 1978
Height: 5'10" Weight: 11.11
International Honours: Ei: U21-4
A highly thought of young Middlesbrough professional who came through the ranks from trainee, local lad Steve actually made his debut in October 1997, eventually winning his Premiership chance over two years later at Coventry last April. A stylish full back, quick and strong in the tackle, he is one of the reasons that the reserves had such a successful season in 1998-99, and confidently expects his call up to first-team duty to lead to a permanent squad place. Continued to play for the Republic of Ireland U21 side, making two appearances.
Middlesbrough (From trainee on 24/7/97) P/FL 6+2 FLC 2+2 FAC 0+1

BALDRY Simon Jonathan
Born: Huddersfield, 12 February 1976
Height: 5'10" Weight: 11.6
Starting last season on loan at Bury in early September, he made a handful of subs' appearances for the Shakers but generally struggled to make an impression there prior to returning to Huddersfield. Back at the McAlpine, he shone with defence-splitting displays in the reserves until first-team football eventually arrived with a late call up for the big FA Cup-tie against Derby. Always willing to use his pace to take defenders on, and crossing accurately, he remained in the side for a few games before becoming more involved from the subs' bench. Later, on regaining his place, he turned in excellent performances against Sunderland and Bradford, looking good whether it was in an attacking role or a defensive one.
Huddersfield T (From trainee on 14/7/94) FL 39+27/3 FLC 3+2 FAC 1+1 Others 1+2/1
Bury (Loaned on 8/9/98) FL 0+5

BALL Kevin Anthony
Born: Hastings, 12 November 1964
Height: 5'10" Weight: 12.6
Club Honours: Div 1 '96, '99
As the Sunderland skipper and midfield driving force, "Bally" led the Wearsiders to the First Division championship in 1998-99, for the second time. As usual, Kevin's combative style meant that he picked up his fair share of bookings last term, but his ability to play the holding role in midfield gave the team vital stability and allowed his fellow midfielders to get forward. He also

weighed in with two vital goals during the campaign, particularly away at West Bromwich in October, when his winner completed a remarkable fight back by a team who had been 2-0 down at half time. Regularly seen encouraging the home crowd to get behind the side, hopefully, his richly-deserved testimonial in July against Sampdoria would have seen a packed Stadium of Light paying tribute to one of Sunderland's most popular players of all time.

Portsmouth (Free from Coventry C juniors on 6/10/82) FL 96+9/4 FLC 8+1 FAC 8 Others 6
Sunderland (£350,000 on 16/7/90) P/FL 323+5/21 FLC 23+2/3 FAC 16 Others 7/2

BALL Michael John
Born: Liverpool, 2 October 1979
Height: 5'10" Weight: 11.2
International Honours: E: U21-5; Yth; Sch
An outstandingly talented young Everton left back, Michael capped his first full season in the Premiership with a surprise call up to a full England squad for the friendly international in Hungary, and also represented the U21 side. And, if his performances did not quite meet the exacting standards he set for himself during the second half of 1998-99, he still remains one of the brightest of the Premiership's young guns. Sharp tackling, quick, good in the air, and possessing composure well in advance of his years, he is equally at home in central defence, left back, or midfield. He also proved a composed penalty taker, converting three of his four efforts during the campaign. The player he succeeded at Goodison, Andy Hinchcliffe, tipped him for full international recognition more than a year ago, and the youngster looks more than capable of fulfilling the prediction. Having also attracted plenty of unsettling publicity that he could be on his way to Manchester United for £5 million, as a childhood Evertonian he has simply taken all the speculation in his ice-cool stride.

Everton (From trainee on 17/10/96) PL 59+8/4 FLC 4+2 FAC 4

BALMER Stuart Murray
Born: Falkirk, 20 September 1969
Height: 6'0" Weight: 12.11
Club Honours: AMC '99
International Honours: S: Yth; Sch
Recruited from Charlton in the middle of last September, Stuart quickly established himself at the heart of Wigan's defence. A dominant centre back who leads by example, only enforced absences forced him out of action in a season which saw him mark his 250th Football League game. Scored his only league goal in the 3-3 away draw at Northampton Town. Was a member of the side that beat Millwall at Wembley in the Auto Windscreens Shield.

Glasgow C (From juniors in 1987)
Charlton Ath (£120,000 on 24/8/90) FL 201+26/8 FLC 15 FAC 9+1 Others 11+1
Wigan Ath (£200,000 on 18/9/98) FL 36/1 FLC 1 FAC 3 Others 7/1

BANGER Nicholas (Nicky) Lee
Born: Southampton, 25 February 1971
Height: 5'9" Weight: 11.6

Nicky spent most of the second half of last season at Oxford in a wide midfield role, having started off in a striking position. After being involved in the first ten games of the campaign, he picked up a shoulder injury just as he was establishing himself and, after returning, it was sometime before he won back a regular place, two goals at Portsmouth over the Christmas period helping him with that. Finished the campaign with five goals, only one of them coming at the Manor Ground, but hit a great free kick to win the game at Sheffield United – in injury time! Was released during the summer.

Southampton (From trainee on 25/4/89) F/PL 18+37/8 FLC 2+2/3 FAC 0+2 Others 1
Oldham Ath (£250,000 on 4/10/94) FL 44+20/10 FLC 6/1 FAC 2+1 Others 0+1
Oxford U (Free on 24/7/97) FL 40+20/8 FLC 6+1/1 FAC 3

BANKS Steven (Steve)
Born: Hillingdon, 9 February 1972
Height: 6'0" Weight: 13.2
Due to leave Blackpool at the end of last season under the Bosman ruling, Steve joined Bolton just prior to the transfer deadline and brought with him an ever-growing reputation as a quality goalkeeper (no less a player than Peter Schmeichel had reportedly spoken of Steve as being the best goalkeeper outside of the Premiership). Celtic had supposedly offered somewhere in the region of £1 million for him at the beginning of the season. Their loss was certainly Wanderers' gain as he went straight into the side to make his debut in the 0-0 draw away at Oxford, where he pulled off a string of world-class saves and won himself the "Man of the Match" award. He followed that up with a number of assured performances in the Bolton goal and the fee paid for his services is already beginning to look like one of the bargains of the decade. Although originally signed due to a goalkeeper crisis at the club, it looks as though he may well have made the number-one shirt his own.

West Ham U (From trainee on 24/3/90) Others 1
Gillingham (Free on 25/3/93) FL 67 FAC 7 Others 2
Blackpool (£60,000 on 18/8/95) FL 150 FLC 13 FAC 8 Others 10
Bolton W (£50,000 on 25/3/99) FL 9 Others 3

BARACLOUGH Ian Robert
Born: Leicester, 4 December 1970
Height: 6'1" Weight: 12.2
Club Honours: Div 3 '98
International Honours: E: Yth
A Queens Park Rangers wing back who operates on the left-hand side, he was a permanent fixture in the first team last season, missing few league matches. After being sent off in first game, Ian made the number three shirt his own and proved to be a steady player who got on with his game and made a number of successful attacking forays forward. Finally broke his goal scoring duck with a splendid free kick against Huddersfield at Easter.

Leicester C (From trainee on 15/12/88) FAC 1 Others 0+1
Wigan Ath (Loaned on 22/3/90) FL 8+1/2

Grimsby T (Loaned on 21/12/90) FL 1+3
Grimsby T (Free on 13/8/91) FL 1
Lincoln C (Free on 21/8/92) FL 68+5/10 FLC 7/1 FAC 4 Others 7
Mansfield T (Free on 6/6/94) FL 47/5 FLC 7 FAC 4 Others 4
Notts Co (Signed on 13/10/95) FL 107+4/10 FLC 5+1/1 FAC 5 Others 1
Queens Park R (£50,000 on 19/3/98) FL 49+2/1 FLC 4 FAC 1

BARCLAY Dominic Alexander
Born: Bristol, 5 September 1976
Height: 5'11" Weight: 11.9
Released by Bristol City during the 1998 close season, Dominic started 1998-99 at Macclesfield as a regular on the bench until he got his chance to prove himself as the first-choice striker during a goal drought in September, following injuries to the first-team squad. He made his mark in his full outing, at Oldham, with a superb ten-yard drive into the back of the net. However, he lost his place when two on-loan strikers were brought in and played for the reserves for most of the remaining part of the campaign, being one of the top scorers. Was loaned to Kettering in the Conference on transfer deadline day with a view to a permanent deal, prior to being released in the summer.

Bristol C (From trainee on 3/7/95) FL 2+10 FLC 0+1 FAC 0+1
Macclesfield T (Free on 15/7/98) FL 3+6/1 FLC 1+2

BARDSLEY David John
Born: Manchester, 11 September 1964
Height: 5'10" Weight: 12.2
International Honours: E: 2; Yth
Freed by Queens Park Rangers during the summer of 1998, David returned to the club where it all started for him – Blackpool. Originally a full back, he played most of last season as a sweeper, using his vast expertise to help the defence. He also showed that he had lost none of his ability to hit long, accurate passes down the flanks.

Blackpool (From apprentice on 5/11/82) FL 45 FLC 2/1 FAC 2
Watford (£150,000 on 23/11/83) FL 97+3/7 FLC 6/1 FAC 13+1/1 Others 1
Oxford U (£265,000 on 18/9/87) FL 74/7 FLC 12 FAC 5 Others 3
Queens Park R (£500,000 on 15/9/89) F/PL 252+1/4 FLC 20/1 FAC 19 Others 3/1
Blackpool (Free on 3/7/98) FL 29 FLC 3 Others 1

BARKER Richard (Richie) Ian
Born: Sheffield, 30 May 1975
Height: 6'0" Weight: 13.5
International Honours: E: Yth; Sch
The centre forward was the butt of Brighton fans' frustration at first, but pulled them around with a series of bustling, whole-hearted displays in 1998-99, which then earned him the nickname "The Bear". Linking up well with Rod Thomas and Gary Hart, and scoring both goals to cap an excellent display in the 2-1 win at Peterborough last December, he performed better with wingers in the side and suffered when Thomas missed the last four months of the season through injury. Offered a new contract by manager Micky Adams, Richie

was nominated as the Third Division "Player of the Month" for December by *Match Magazine* and went on to finish joint-top scorer with 12 goals.

Sheffield Wed (From trainee on 27/7/93) (Free to Linfield on 22/8/96)
Doncaster Rov (Loaned on 29/9/95) FL 5+1 Others 0+1
Brighton & Hove A (Free on 19/12/97) FL 48+12/12 FLC 1+1/1 FAC 1/1 Others 1

BARKER Simon
Born: Farnworth, 4 November 1964
Height: 5'9" Weight: 11.7
Club Honours: FMC '87
International Honours: E: U21-4

Released by Queens Park Rangers early on in 1998-99, this dependable Port Vale midfielder originally arrived at the club on trial before securing a full-time contract. Using his experience well to hold together the centre of the park, he received an excellent welcome when he returned to his old club, and celebrated the occasion by scoring his first Vale goal, following it up soon afterwards when converting a penalty against Bury. Obviously not as quick as he used to be, but still possesses an excellent football brain. Out of contract during the summer, at the time of going to press the club were known to have made an offer of re-engagement.

Blackburn Rov (From apprentice on 6/11/82) FL 180+2/35 FLC 11/4 FAC 12 Others 8/2
Queens Park R (£400,000 on 20/7/88) F/PL 291+24/33 FLC 29+2/5 FAC 22+1/3 Others 7
Port Vale (Free on 11/9/98) FL 23+4/2

BARLOW Andrew (Andy) John
Born: Oldham, 24 November 1965
Height: 5'8" Weight: 11.1
Club Honours: Div 2 '91

Andy lost his left-back place at Rochdale to new signing, Dean Stokes, at the start of last season, but reappeared when the latter was injured. He then only lasted four games, and even when he got back into the side again at the end of the year a string of knocks led to him failing to finish the 90 minutes on several occasions. However, Dale's switch to a formation with three central defenders and wing backs allowed him more opportunity to utilise his attacking skills. His first goal for the club came in the last minute of the campaign when he netted the equaliser at Brighton. Was released during the summer.

Oldham Ath (From juniors on 31/7/84) F/PL 245+16/5 FLC 22 FAC 19 Others 6
Bradford C (Loaned on 1/11/93) FL 2
Blackpool (Free on 13/7/95) FL 77+3/2 FLC 4+2 FAC 4 Others 6
Rochdale (Free on 7/7/97) FL 60+7/1 FLC 1 FAC 1+1 Others 2

BARLOW Martin David
Born: Barnstaple, 25 June 1971
Height: 5'7" Weight: 10.3

The last campaign was Martin's testimonial year at Plymouth, despite only being 28 years of age. He was again extremely consistent in his midfield berth and achieved more appearances than any other member of the squad. His neat control and passing set up numerous chances for his colleagues and,

although not renowned for his goalscoring, scored one of the best goals seen at Home Park, a "Van Basten" effort against Shrewsbury.

Plymouth Arg (From trainee on 1/7/89) FL 276+31/24 FLC 9+1/2 FAC 17 Others 17+1

BARLOW Stuart
Born: Liverpool, 16 July 1968
Height: 5'10" Weight: 11.0
Club Honours: AMC '99

Enjoying his best goalscoring season in his career in 1998-99, and finishing top scorer at Wigan with 26 goals, Stuart's tremendous acceleration and ball control proved to be a constant menace to all defenders. An excellent opportunist who is never afraid to go for goal, his strike at home to Manchester City in the play offs was the last to be scored by an Athletic player at Springfield Park. Prior to that, his goal at Wrexham was voted by the supporters as "The Away Goal of the Season", and he ended a memorable campaign by finishing runner up in the "Player of the Year" awards. Was a member of the side that beat Millwall 1-0 at Wembley to win the Auto Windscreens Shield.

Everton (Free from Sherwood Park on 6/6/90) F/PL 24+47/10 FLC 3+5/1 FAC 4+3/2 Others 0+2
Rotherham U (Loaned on 11/92) Others 0+1
Oldham Ath (£450,000 on 20/11/95) FL 78+15/31 FLC 5+1 FAC 6+1/1 Others 1
Wigan Ath (£45,000 on 26/3/98) FL 48+2/22 FLC 2/1 FAC 2/1 Others 8+1/5

BARMBY Nicholas (Nick) Jonathan
Born: Hull, 11 February 1974
Height: 5'7" Weight: 11.3
International Honours: E: 10; B-2; U21-4; Yth; Sch

Following a fitful start to last season, during which he suffered a recurrence of a long-standing groin injury, Nick bounced back to hit a rich vein of form for Everton early in the year, operating from either the centre of midfield or wide on the left, and weighing in with a number of invaluable goals. Previously believed to be most effective when behind two strikers, he displayed the best form of his Toffees' career on the left of midfield. Quick and technically gifted, with a razor sharp footballing brain, he is still a hugely popular figure amongst Goodison supporters.

Tottenham H (From trainee on 9/4/91) PL 81+6/20 FLC 7+1/2 FAC 12+1/5
Middlesbrough (£5,250,000 on 8/8/95) PL 42/8 FLC 4/1 FAC 3/1
Everton (£5,750,000 on 2/11/96) PL 68+11/9 FLC 2+2/3 FAC 7/2

BARNARD Darren Sean
Born: Rintein, Germany, 30 November 1971
Height: 5'9" Weight: 12.3
International Honours: E: Sch. W: 6

An excellent crosser of the ball, as in the previous campaign he gave Barnsley natural balance on the left-hand side in 1998-99. And, as well as being a dead-ball expert he also scored spectacular goals in open play. Having turned down the chance to move to Southampton in November, he injured his ankle in mid January, which put him out of

action for a number of months. A Welsh international who has had experience of Premiership football with Chelsea and Barnsley, he will be hoping to get back to that level as soon as it is possible, hopefully with the Tykes.

Chelsea (£50,000 from Wokingham T on 25/7/90) F/PL 18+11/2 FLC 1+1 FAC 1+1
Reading (Loaned on 18/11/94) FL 3+1
Bristol C (£175,000 on 6/10/95) FL 77+1/15 FLC 4/1 FAC 6 Others 6/1
Barnsley (£750,000 on 8/8/97) P/FL 59+2/6 FLC 9/1 FAC 6/2

BARNARD Mark
Born: Sheffield, 27 November 1975
Height: 5'11" Weight: 11.10

Mark ended his fourth season at Darlington out of the team after the arrival of Paul Heckingbottom on transfer deadline day last March. A strong-running, overlapping full back, he hit two goals from his surging runs, the first being the last-minute winner against Burnley in the FA Cup, after two seasons without a goal. One of three players still at the club who appeared at Wembley in the 1996 play-off final, he was released during the summer and joined non-league Doncaster on 8 July.

Rotherham U (From trainee on 13/7/94) (Free to Worksop T during 1995 close season)
Darlington (Free on 27/9/95) FL 131+12/4 FLC 9 FAC 8+1/1 Others 7

BARNES John Charles Bryan
Born: Jamaica, 7 November 1963
Height: 5'11" Weight: 12.7
Club Honours: FAYC '82; Div 1 '88, '90; FAC '89; CS '88, '89, FLC '95
International Honours: E: 79; U21-3

Now approaching the latter stages of a distinguished career, John still retains a deft touch on the ball, shrewd distribution skills, and an eye for goal. His cool head and positional awareness enable him to find space and time even in the hectic midfield of a Premiership game. Coming on as a substitute for Newcastle in the opening game of last season, at home to Charlton, he strained a hamstring and had to be substituted himself. Following his recovery, he made only occasional appearances on the bench without being called upon to play, but remained a respected and valuable member of the club's staff by appearing regularly in the reserve side, where he used his considerable experience and know-how to help nurture the young talent being developed there. Aspiring to move into management when his playing days are over, he was linked with the Blackburn manager vacancy following the departure of Roy Hodgson. In February, he joined Charlton on a free transfer until the end of the campaign to assist in their fight for Premiership survival. Used mainly as a sub at the Valley, when coming on he usually made a difference, especially when working well with Mark Kinsella in the heart of midfield. Was appointed MBE in October for services to football, and his social awareness and responsibility were demonstrated when he visited Burundi in June 1998 as an unofficial ambassador for

Christian Aid. Released at the end of the season, he became part of the Glasgow Celtic "dream ticket" under Kenny Dalglish.
Watford (Free from Sudbury Court on 14/7/81) FL 232+1/65 FLC 21/7 FAC 31/11 Others 7
Liverpool (£900,000 on 19/6/87) F/PL 310+4/84 FLC 26/3 FAC 51/16 Others 16/5
Newcastle U (Free on 14/8/97) PL 22+5/6 FLC 3 FAC 3+2 Others 5/1
Charlton Ath (Free on 10/2/99) PL 2+10

BARNES Kevin
Born: Fleetwood, 12 September 1975
Height: 6'0" Weight: 12.5
A well-built striker who has been around the north west non-league scene for a while, having a good goalscoring record first with Fleetwood and then Lancaster City, Kevin trialled with Blackpool last March before joining the club as a part timer until the end of the season. Making his first-team debut at home to Stoke, he was substituted in two starts and came off the bench in another couple of games.
Blackpool (Free from Lancaster C on 5/3/99) FL 2+2

BARNES Paul Lance
Born: Leicester, 16 November 1967
Height: 5'11" Weight: 13.6
For most of 1998-99, Paul had to be content with a place on the Huddersfield subs' bench, the patient striker only starting two games but, still firmly in the manager's mind, an offer to take him to Bury was turned down in November. Despite having to settle for a bit-part role because of the form of the other front men at Town, he came off the bench to delight the supporters with a goal against Bradford. Finally, the Bury manager, Neil Warnock, got his man in mid March in an attempt to cure the club's lack of goal power, only to be thwarted when the new signing picked up a hamstring injury at Oxford and failed to start the next four games, before coming back for the last match of the campaign.
Notts Co (From apprentice on 16/11/85) FL 36+17/14 FAC 0+1 Others 4+6/5
Stoke C (£30,000 on 23/3/90) FL 10+14/3 FLC 0+2 Others 3+1/2
Chesterfield (Loaned on 8/11/90) FL 1 FAC 1/1
York C (£50,000 on 15/7/92) FL 147+1/76 FLC 10/5 FAC 5 Others 16/4
Birmingham C (£350,000 on 4/3/96) FL 15/7
Burnley (£350,000 + on 6/9/96) FL 63+2/30 FLC 5 FAC 5/1
Huddersfield T (Signed on 16/1/98) FL 13+17/2 FLC 0+3 FAC 1+1
Bury (£40,000 on 15/3/99) FL 6+2

BARNES Philip (Phil) Kenneth
Born: Sheffield, 2 March 1979
Height: 6'1" Weight: 11.1
Still only a youngster as far as goalkeepers go, Phil again had to wait in the wings at Blackpool as first Steve Banks and then Tony Caig performed consistently well. Continued to show promise, performing well in the reserves, he stepped up for just one senior game in 1998-99, a 2-2 draw at Colchester. Has good, safe hands and shot-stopping ability.
Rotherham U (From trainee on 25/6/97) FL 2
Blackpool (£100,000 on 22/7/97) FL 2 Others 1

BARNES Steven (Steve) Leslie
Born: Harrow, 5 January 1976
Height: 5'4" Weight: 10.9
Released by Birmingham, Barnet fought off the attention of several clubs to secure the signature of Steve last October and it appeared to be the ideal location for him to kick-start his career. However, ill fortune and a change in the team's formation meant that his first-team opportunities were rare. Having made his debut as a substitute in the home clash with Brighton, he then started in the role of left-wing back against Torquay at Underhill, beginning the match in scintillating form and delivering an array of accurate crosses into the penalty area. He also exhibited great pace and close control but, after a clash with United's Andy Gurney when they were both given their marching orders, it consequently proved to be a major blow to his progression. His next substantial taste of action was against Carlisle in March, when he replaced Stevie Searle in the formative stages of the game. Consequently awarded the "Man of the Match" award, despite his diminutive stature he has already shown glimpses of being a potential match winner and, with a regular slot in the line-up, he has the ability to evolve into a useful component in the team.
Birmingham C (£75,000 from Welling U on 9/10/95) FL 0+3 FLC 0+1 Others 0+1
Brighton & Hove A (Loaned on 23/1/98) FL 12
Barnet (Free on 22/10/98) FL 3+9

BARNESS Anthony
Born: Lewisham, 25 March 1973
Height: 5'10" Weight: 13.1
Anthony only made a handful of appearances for Charlton in 1998-99, all as a substitute when the abundance of defenders at the Valley. Although predominately right footed, he is equally comfortable in either full-back spot, and can also play in midfield, where he appeared in several games for the reserve side. Likes to get forward and frequently makes runs into the opposition penalty area, often resulting in a shot at goal. Can be relied upon to do a professional job whenever brought into the side.
Charlton Ath (From trainee on 6/3/91) FL 21+6/1 FLC 2 FAC 3 Others 1+1/1
Chelsea (£350,000 on 8/9/92) PL 12+2 FLC 2 Others 2+1
Middlesbrough (Loaned on 12/8/93) Others 1
Southend U (Loaned on 2/2/96) FL 5
Charlton Ath (£165,000 on 8/8/96) P/FL 66+11/3 FLC 5 FAC 2+1 Others 1+1

BARNETT David (Dave) Kwame
Born: London, 16 April 1967
Height: 6'1" Weight: 13.12
Club Honours: AMC '95; Div 2 '95
Rugged central defender with Port Vale who operated a "they shall not pass" attitude in 1998-99. Played in the majority of games, missing a few due to suspension for bookings and one sending off at Oxford, but always gave everything before losing his place at Easter after a defeat at Bristol City ended with accusations of a flare-up in the tunnel. As former Vale manager John Rudge said: "If Dave says it's Wednesday, then it's Wednesday!".

Colchester U (Signed from Windsor & Eton on 25/8/88) FL 19+1 FLC 2 FAC 3+2 Others 3 (Freed in June 1988)
West Bromwich A (Free from Edmonton Oilers on 13/10/89)
Walsall (Free on 17/7/90) FL 4+1 FLC 2 (Free to Kidderminster Harriers on 1/10/90)
Barnet (£10,000 on 29/2/92) FL 58+1/3 FLC 5 FAC 3 Others 5
Birmingham C (£150,000 on 20/12/93) FL 45+1 FLC 1 FAC 5 Others 8
Dunfermline Ath (Free on 18/7/97) SL 21/1 SLC 3 SC 2
Port Vale (Free on 20/3/98) FL 34+2/1 FAC 1

BARNETT Jason Vincent
Born: Shrewsbury, 21 April 1976
Height: 5'9" Weight: 11.6
A popular right back whose season at Lincoln in 1998-99 was badly affected by injuries, a groin problem keeping him out of the summer campaign and, when he was eventually fit again, he played only five matches before suffering ligament damage, following a late challenge from a Manchester City player. He fought back again and was a virtual ever present after mid December, but finished fighting against a knee injury. Was out of contract in the summer, having turned down initial offers from City.
Wolverhampton W (From trainee on 4/7/94)
Lincoln C (£5,000 on 26/10/95) FL 122+8/3 FLC 5 FAC 7 Others 8

BARR William (Billy) Joseph
Born: Halifax, 21 January 1969
Height: 5'11" Weight: 10.8
The club captain, Billy's season at Carlisle was again disrupted by injury although he still featured in half the team's league programme in 1998-99. Most of his matches were at right back, where his tackling and other defensive qualities were used to best advantage and, although at times he looked less confident in an attacking role, he can take some pride in United's defensive record during the campaign.
Halifax T (From trainee on 6/7/87) FL 178+18/13 FLC 8+1/2 FAC 11+1/2 Others 14+3
Crewe Alex (Free on 17/6/94) FL 73+12/6 FLC 2 FAC 4 Others 8+1
Carlisle U (Free on 18/7/97) FL 60+2/3 FLC 6 FAC 1 Others 3

BARRAS Anthony (Tony)
Born: Billingham, 29 March 1971
Height: 6'0" Weight: 13.0
After missing the start of last season because of injury, the commanding centre half once again became the kingpin in York's defence before failure to agree terms for a new contract saw him initially arrive on loan at Reading, prior to signing a two-year contract within days. Although competing with several other defenders for a regular place in the side, Tony helped his cause by scoring a vital goal in a 1-1 draw at Luton. A tall and composed defender, he was used mostly as a substitute towards the end of the campaign.
Hartlepool U (From trainee on 6/7/89) FL 9+3 FLC 2 FAC 1 Others 1
Stockport Co (Free on 23/7/90) FL 94+5/5 FLC 2 FAC 7 Others 19+1
Rotherham U (Loaned on 25/2/94) FL 5/1
York C (Signed on 18/7/94) FL 167+4/11 FLC 16/2 FAC 10/1 Others 8+1/1
Reading (£20,000 on 19/3/99) FL 4+2/1

BARRETT Adam Nicholas
Born: Dagenham, 29 November 1979
Height: 5'10" Weight: 12.0
Formerly a trainee with Leyton Orient, Adam decided to take up a football scholarship in the USA in the summer of 1998 but, on being homesick, he became a late-season signing as extra cover in the heart of Plymouth's defence last January, making his only appearance as a 75th-minute substitute against Scunthorpe. A quick and strong left-sided central defender, who likes to work the ball, and has a great attitude, he looks likely to be one for the future.
Plymouth Arg (Free from USA football scholarship on 13/1/99) FL 0+1

BARRETT Earl Delisser
Born: Rochdale, 28 April 1967
Height: 5'10" Weight: 11.7
Club Honours: Div 2 '91; FLC '94; CS '95
International Honours: E: 3; B-4; U21-4
This vastly experienced Sheffield Wednesday defender found himself out in the cold at Hillsbrough last season. Just a few substitute appearances early on and then nothing at all appeared to indicate that Danny Wilson did not see him as a vital member of his squad. At his best a hard-tackling full back who can stand in reliably in the centre of defence when required, Earl is still blessed with a fair turn of speed and able to read a game well. Released during the summer, when fully fit, he is still capable of a man-to-man marking assignment with the best of them.
Manchester C (From trainee on 26/4/85) FL 2+1 FLC 1
Chester C (Loaned on 1/3/86) FL 12
Oldham Ath (£35,000 on 24/11/87) FL 181+2/7 FLC 20/1 FAC 14/1 Others 4
Aston Villa (£1,700,000 on 25/2/92) F/PL 118+1/1 FLC 15/1 FAC 9 Others 7
Everton (£1,700,000 on 30/1/95) PL 73+1 FLC 4 FAC 2 Others 3
Sheffield U (Loaned on 16/1/98) FL 5
Sheffield Wed (Free on 25/2/98) PL 10+5 FLC 0+1

BARRETT Paul David
Born: Newcastle, 13 April 1978
Height: 5'11" Weight: 11.5
International Honours: E: Yth
Paul joined Wrexham on a three-year contract just before the transfer deadline at the end of last March, having been a trainee with his home town club and progressing through the Centre of Excellence before turning pro. Although finding it difficult to break through into the first-team set up, his impressive form in the Pontins League prompted Wrexham's Brian Flynn to make a move for him. The Wrexham manager described Paul, whose father was on the books of Arsenal, as "A very mobile player, comfortable on both the right and left-hand side of midfield, a neat and tidy passer, and aggressive as well". Signed as an investment for the future and as part of the team's rebuilding plans, he certainly looked impressive when included towards the end of the campaign at the Racecourse.
Newcastle U (From trainee on 20/6/96)
Wrexham (Free on 24/3/99) FL 8+2

BARRETT Scott
Born: Ilkeston, 2 April 1963
Height: 6'0" Weight: 14.4
Club Honours: GMVC '92; FAT '92
Out of favour at Cambridge United in 1998-99, following the arrival of Arjan van Heusden from Port Vale during the 1998 close season, Scott moved to Leyton Orient on a free in January and immediately took over the goalkeeping duties from an out-of-form Chris MacKenzie. Playing in the final 23 matches of the campaign, and showing himself to be a commanding custodian who leads from the back, he also proved to be an excellent shot stopper who was good at taking crosses cleanly. Saved two penalties in the second leg of the play offs against Rotherham which were instrumental in taking Orient to Wembley. With his contract up for grabs in the summer, it remains to be seen whether the impressive 'keeper stays at Brisbane Road.
Wolverhampton W (Signed from Ilkeston T on 27/9/84) FL 30 FLC 1 FAC 1 Others 3
Stoke C (£10,000 on 24/7/87) FL 51 FLC 2 FAC 3 Others 4
Colchester U (Loaned on 10/1/90) FL 13
Stockport Co (Loaned on 22/3/90) FL 10 Others 2
Gillingham (Free on 14/8/92) FL 51 FLC 7 FAC 4 Others 4
Cambridge U (Free on 2/8/95) FL 119 FLC 6 FAC 7 Others 3
Leyton Orient (Free on 25/1/99) FL 20 Others 3

BARRICK Dean
Born: Hemsworth, 30 September 1969
Height: 5'9" Weight: 12.0
Club Honours: Div 3 '96
A free transfer signing in the summer of 1998 from Preston, Dean was an automatic choice at left-wing back for Bury in the opening three months of last season. During that time, the team climbed as high as third position in Division One, and the newcomer claimed his first goal for the Shakers in a 3-0 home win against Swindon. Soon after, he was publicly named as being responsible for the only goal conceded in a 1-0 away defeat at Wolves, and with his Gigg Lane career seeming to nose dive after this he lost his place in the team to firstly Chris Billy, then Paul Williams. Transfer listed in December, he was subsequently allowed to join Ayr United on an extended loan deal.
Sheffield Wed (From trainee on 7/5/88) FL 11/2
Rotherham U (£50,000 on 14/2/91) FL 96+3/7 FLC 6 FAC 8 Others 5/1
Cambridge U (£50,000 on 11/8/93) FL 90+1/3 FLC 7/1 FAC 7/1 Others 6
Preston NE (Signed on 11/9/95) FL 98+11/1 FLC 7+1/1 FAC 5 Others 6
Bury (Free on 3/7/98) FL 16+4/1 FLC 5
Ayr U (Loaned on 19/2/99) SL 6

BARRON Michael James
Born: Chester le Street, 22 December 1974
Height: 5'11" Weight: 11.9
A Hartlepool central defender who rarely has a bad game and, who despite his relative inexperience, was handed the club captaincy at the start of 1998-99. An automatic choice since being signed, and a player who likes to be involved, having twice made an extremely speedy recovery from injury, he again attracted the interest of other clubs but demonstrated his commitment to Pool by signing a new two-year contract. Honoured by being chosen the supporters' "Player of the Year" for the last two seasons.
Middlesbrough (From trainee on 2/2/93) P/FL 2+1 FLC 1 Others 3+3
Hartlepool U (Loaned on 6/9/96) FL 16
Hartlepool U (Free on 8/7/97) FL 70+1/1 FLC 3 FAC 2 Others 5

BARRY Gareth
Born: Hastings, 23 February 1981
Height: 6'0" Weight: 12.6
International Honours: E: U21-3; Yth
After breaking into the Aston Villa first team at the end of 1997-98, Gareth continued to build in confidence and went from strength to strength during last season. With Villa's deal to bring David Unsworth to the club having fallen through, he was then given the opportunity to replace Steve Staunton on the left-hand side of the defence, an opportutnity he grabbed with both hands. Featuring in most of Villa's games, he tended to remain injury free before tweaking an achilles tendon in a collision with the advertising boards in the match against Derby. This subsequently forced him to miss his first opportunity to play in Europe. During the final weeks, a change of playing formation saw him dropped to the subs' bench and, at home to Nottingham Forest, he was brought on to play in a midfield role. However, as unperturbed as ever, he made the most of it to score his first senior goal for the club, clearly showing signs of versatility. The club were so impressed with his progress that, on his 18th birthday, they signed him up on a five-year contract, merely confirming him to be a youngster with a bright future ahead of him. One of his major strengths is that he is very comfortable on the ball, is rarely panicked into making mistakes, and is always looking to create something. Was promoted to the England U21 squad and featured regularly.
Aston Villa (From trainee on 27/2/98) PL 28+6/2 FAC 2 Others 3

Gareth Barry

BART-WILLIAMS Christopher (Chris) Gerald
Born: Freetown, Sierra Leone, 16 June 1974
Height: 5'11" Weight: 11.6
Club Honours: Div 1 '98
International Honours: E: B-1; U21-16; Yth
After helping Nottingham Forest back to the Premiership in 1997-98, Chris again made his mark in the top division, operating mainly on the left-hand side but able to play in central midfield and up front if requested. Sidelined at the start of last season, he made his opening appearance in a 2-0 defeat at Newcastle in September and played in the next 18 games, scoring Forest's opener in a 2-2 draw against Aston Villa at the City Ground. He then gave way to the subs' bench and made few appearances until coming back strongly to score the winner in a surprise 2-1 victory at Blackburn. Under new management in 1999-2000, his stamina and commitment will be needed if the club are to climb out of the First Division.
Leyton Orient (From trainee on 18/7/91) FL 34+2/2 FLC 4 Others 2
Sheffield Wed (£275,000 on 21/11/91) F/PL 95+29/16 FLC 14+2/4 FAC 9+3/2 Others 1+3/2
Nottingham F (£2,500,000 on 1/7/95) F/PL 99+7/8 FLC 10 FAC 10 Others 7+1

BARTON Warren Dean
Born: Stoke Newington, 19 March 1969
Height: 6'0" Weight: 12.0
International Honours: E: 3; B-3
Warren is an important member of the Newcastle defensive squad, where his all-round abilities, flexibility, and honest professionalism equip him for a number of roles. Sturdy in the tackle, he enjoys raiding down the wing to cross dangerous balls into the opposition box, but his high level of fitness ensures he recovers in time to attend to his defensive duties. His career on Tyneside has been one of ups and downs with last season proving no exception. Primarily a right back, although he can also play the anchor role in midfield, it seemed that the presence of first choice Steve Watson, and the recent arrivals of Andy Griffin and Laurent Charvet, would deny him any first-team opportunities; indeed he spent the first three months on the bench, making only occasional substitute appearances. He displayed his character and his commitment to the club by patiently waiting his chance, working hard in training and, when given a run in the first team from mid-November on the "wrong" side at left back to cover injuries and suspensions, he turned in some of his best performances in his time at United, leading to a new three-and-a-half year contract in January. He was outstanding in the FA Cup-tie with Palace, when his passes led to both the goals and he left the field to a standing ovation from a previously sceptical St James' Park crowd. And continuing to be selected for most games, including the FA Cup semi final, he again gave an outstanding display, even finding time for some hitherto unsuspected trickery on the ball.
Maidstone U (£10,000 from Leytonstone on 28/7/89) FL 41+1 FLC 0+2 FAC 3/1 Others 7

Wimbledon (£300,000 on 7/6/90) F/PL 178+2/10 FLC 16/1 FAC 11 Others 2
Newcastle U (£4,500,000 on 5/6/95) PL 78+18/4 FLC 9/1 FAC 12+2 Others 9+2

BARTRAM Vincent (Vince) Lee
Born: Birmingham, 7 August 1968
Height: 6'2" Weight: 13.4
Having been on loan towards the end of the 1997-98 season from Arsenal, he joined Gillingham on a permanent basis during the summer on a free transfer. In the home game with Oldham last November, he injured his ankle during the pre-match practice and had to be substituted by Jim Stannard. Fortunately, the injury was not serious and he only missed two league games. Went through a bad spell in March, but manager Tony Pulis stuck by him, and his agility in the last few games was one of the reasons why the Gills reached the play offs.
Wolverhampton W (From juniors on 17/8/85) FL 5 FLC 2 FAC 3
Blackpool (Loaned on 27/10/89) FL 9 Others 2
Bournemouth (£65,000 on 24/7/91) FL 132 FLC 10 FAC 14 Others 6
Arsenal (£400,000 on 10/8/94) PL 11 FLC 0+1
Huddersfield T (Loaned on 17/10/97) FL 12
Gillingham (Free on 20/3/98) FL 53 FLC 2 Others 7

BASFORD Luke William
Born: Croydon, 6 January 1980
Height: 5'6" Weight: 8.10
A confident, attacking left-full back, Luke took the limited opportunities at Bristol Rovers to play first-team football in 1998-99, always looking comfortable in possession. Proving a capable deputy for Trevor Challis, he made five league starts but failed to be on a winning side in any of those matches, although he could always be relied upon to give a wholehearted performance. A nose and throat operation kept him sidelined for two months, and he had to wait to regain his place in March.
Bristol Rov (From trainee on 9/7/98) FL 11+5 Others 3

BASHAM Michael (Mike)
Born: Barking, 27 September 1973
Height: 6'2" Weight: 13.9
Club Honours: AMC '94
International Honours: E: Yth; Sch
The former England youth international exhibited signs of his outstanding pedigree on a regular basis in 1998-99, and he developed into an integral part of Barnet's rejuvenated backline. Initially, he was hindered by a recurring groin injury which restricted his number of first-team outings, but in the latter stages of the season he forged a great understanding with both Greg Heald and Mark Arber in the centre of the defence, which enabled the Bees to record four clean sheets in a row. His distribution, particularly over a long distance, was exceptional and he rarely ever sent a pass astray. "Bash" is also extremely proficient at reading the game and anticipating opponent's attacking moves, and following a series of commanding displays in the heart of defence, he signed a new contract, which was a suitable reward for his endeavours.
West Ham U (From trainee on 3/7/92)

Colchester U (Loaned on 18/11/93) FL 1
Swansea C (Free on 24/3/94) FL 27+2/1 FAC 6 Others 8+2
Peterborough U (Free on 18/12/95) FL 17+2/1 FLC 1 FAC 0+1
Barnet (Free on 5/8/97) FL 51+1/2 FLC 1 Others 3

BASHAM Steven (Steve) Brian
Born: Southampton, 2 December 1977
Height: 5'11" Weight: 12.0
Once again finding it difficult to hold down a senior squad place at Southampton, although making just five appearances from the bench for Saints he least managed to score his first Premiership goal, in a 2-0 win at Blackburn, before being loaned to Preston in February. Having been pursued by North End for several months, the young striker was an instant hit, scoring twice on his full debut, at home to Wycombe, and netting ten in all during his three-month stay at the club. Strong, quick, and possessing powerful heading ability, he was always keen to contribute to defending and recovering the ball, which made him extremely popular with the fans. Unavailable for the play offs, Steve refused Preston's initial approaches for the move to become permanent while needing time to consider Southampton's new terms during the summer.
Southampton (From trainee on 24/5/96) PL 1+18/1 FLC 0+1
Wrexham (Loaned on 6/2/98) FL 4+1
Preston NE (Loaned on 5/2/99) FL 15+2/10

BASS David
Born: Frimley, 29 November 1974
Height: 5'11" Weight: 12.7
Unable to get his place back at Rotherham, following a hamstring operation, David joined Carlisle on transfer deadline day last March and gave some battling performances in midfield in the last desperate weeks of the campaign. In one or two matches, notably that against Torquay, his passing and vision gave the sort of dimension that was too often lacking in the midfield during much of the term, but, sadly, he too was unable to sustain this higher level of performance. Nevertheless, he played his part in the club's rather narrowly achieved battle to keep its league status.
Reading (From trainee on 14/7/93) FL 7+4
Rotherham U (Free on 7/7/97) FL 13+5 FLC 1 FAC 0+1
Carlisle U (Free on 25/3/99) FL 8+1

BASS Jonathan (Jon) David
Born: Weston super Mare, 1 January 1976
Height: 6'0" Weight: 12.2
International Honours: E: Sch
The Birmingham defender suffered a double hernia prior to the start of 1998-99 and, on coming back, he struggled to make any sort of headway with Gary Rowett firmly entrenched in the right-back position. However, when Rowett moved temporarily to centre back in February and March, Jon was called up, playing with great vigour and intelligence and never letting the side down. Unlucky to be left out when the latter returned after the signing of David Holdsworth just before the transfer deadline, he came back at Bristol City as the side pushed for a play-off place. Steady and cool under pressure, he is also a hard worker.

Birmingham C (From juniors on 27/6/94) FL 55+4 FLC 5+1 FAC 4
Carlisle U (Loaned on 11/10/96) FL 3

BASTOW Darren John
Born: Torquay, 22 December 1981
Height: 5'11" Weight: 12.0
Darren was definitely the Plymouth find of last season. A young midfielder who has plenty of time on the ball, he showed maturity with his distribution, and proved to be a strong tackler with a good eye for goal. His promotion from the youth ranks saw him coming off the bench after 83 minutes to make his first-team debut in a home league fixture against Brentford and, within two minutes, smashing in a right-footed shot from the edge of the box to make it a 3-0 scoreline. Signing professional forms in January, his subsequent displays in Argyle's midfield meant that he came to the notice of the Premiership scouts and is unlikely to play Third Division football for long. Thus, it was no surprise that he won the trophy for "Young Player of the Year" at Home Park.
Plymouth Arg (From trainee on 13/1/99) FL 21+8/2 FAC 3 Others 1

BATES James (Jamie) Alan
Born: Croydon, 24 February 1968
Height: 6'2" Weight: 14.0
Club Honours: Div 3 '92, '99
A tall and commanding centre back, Jamie was a regular in Brentford's three-man central defensive partnership in 1998-99 until February, when he was dropped and lost the captaincy. After three more games, and seeing that he had no future at Griffin Park, the third highest appearance maker for the Bees became a crucial free signing for Wycombe just before the transfer deadline as a replacement for the injured Jason Cousins. Interestingly, he returned to Wycombe some 12 years after making his one previous appearance for the club, in the Isthmian League on loan as a young Bee. Playing in nine of the last ten games of the season, he steadied a sometimes rocky defence with some brilliant displays in the centre of the defence, his partnership with Paul McCarthy being particularly effective. In the mould of a stopper centre half, he is dominant in the air and able to head the ball a long way, but is also surprisingly comfortable on the ball and always passes constructively out of defence. Won a Third Division championship medal on Bees winning the title.
Brentford (From trainee on 1/6/87) FL 399+20/18 FLC 37+3/3 FAC 20+1/2 Others 44/1
Wycombe W (Free on 25/3/99) FL 9

BATTERSBY Anthony (Tony)
Born: Doncaster, 30 August 1975
Height: 6'0" Weight: 12.7
A striker who made his debut for Lincoln as a substitute in the opening match of 1998-99 at Bournemouth, while on loan from Bury, Tony did well enough for City to pay a club record fee for him just a week later. He was a regular in the team until being dropped at the start of March and, although he won his place back, he missed the end of the season through injury. Having led the Imps' scoring

charts for most of the campaign, he was overtaken in early May by Lee Thorpe.
Sheffield U (From trainee on 5/7/93) FL 3+7/1 FLC 1+1 Others 2+1/1
Southend U (Loaned on 23/3/95) FL 6+2/1
Notts Co (£200,000 on 8/1/96) FL 20+19/8 FLC 1 FAC 0+3 Others 4
Bury (£125,000 on 3/3/97) FL 37+11/8 FLC 3+1/1 FAC 2
Lincoln C (£75,000 on 8/8/98) FL 35+4/7 FLC 2/1 FAC 2/1 Others 2/1

BATTY David
Born: Leeds, 2 December 1968
Height: 5'8" Weight: 12.0
Club Honours: Div 2 '90, Div 1 '92; CS '92
International Honours: E: 40; B-5; U21-7
Widely recognised for the fierce tackling and combative approach he brings to the game, which has made him such an important player, the fiery midfielder's workrate is invariably very high and he constantly makes himself available to any colleague with the ball. Whilst in possession he rarely wastes a pass, although he usually prefers to play a short-ball game. He appeared in all of England's games in the 1998 World Cup, being unfortunate to be the one who missed a vital penalty in the shoot out against Argentina. Following three dismissals in 1997-98 he started the 1998-99 season with a six-match suspension, so took the opportunity to undergo an operation he needed for an achilles tendon problem on his left ankle. After making his first start of the campaign in the away tie at Partizan Belgrade in the European Cup Winners Cup, in which he conceded the critical penalty which eliminated Newcastle, he remained a regular in the side, adding grit and determination to the midfield until he returned to his home club of Leeds in December. Amid a rapturous welcome, he made his second debut against Coventry at Elland Road and, not only picked up a booking, but also a nasty rib injury which kept him sidelined for 15 games. On his return to action, although not 100 per-cent match fit, he immediately settled into a holding role, this benefiting both Lee Bowyer and David Hopkin. The expectation of Leeds' fans is that in 1999-2000 the "real" David Batty will be the difference between winning and challenging for the games' major honours. Made five international appearances for England in 1998-99.
Leeds U (From trainee on 3/8/87) F/PL 201+10/4 FLC 17 FAC 12 Others 17
Blackburn Rov (£2,750,000 on 26/10/93) PL 53+1/1 FLC 6 FAC 5 Others 6
Newcastle U (£3,750,000 on 2/3/96) PL 81+2/3 FLC 6 FAC 9/1 Others 16
Leeds U (£4,400,000 on 9/12/98) PL 10

BAYES Ashley John
Born: Lincoln, 19 April 1972
Height: 6'1" Weight: 13.5
International Honours: E: Yth
1998-99 was another good season for the Exeter number one, who continued to confirm his placing as the club's first-choice 'keeper. This inspired confidence and Ashley's continued improvement was evident for all to see, his form making sure that City had one of the best defensive

records in the Third Division. Having torn an ankle ligament in the warm up against Rotherham, he stayed on the field to keep a clean sheet before missing the next four games and breaking his ever-present sequence.
Brentford (From trainee on 5/7/90) FL 4 FLC 5 FAC 2 Others 1
Torquay U (Free on 13/8/93) FL 97 FLC 7 FAC 9 Others 6
Exeter C (Free on 31/7/96) FL 127 FLC 6 FAC 8 Others 4

BAYLISS David (Dave) Anthony
Born: Liverpool, 8 June 1976
Height: 5'11" Weight: 12.4
Dave started last season at centre half, but then switched to right back until an injury cost him his place in the Rochdale squad in October. With Keith Hill, Mark Monington and Alan Johnson at the heart of defence, he was unable to regain a place in the side and looked to be on the way out until a succession of injuries and suspensions gave him another chance in February. His change of fortune saw him playing a starring role in victories over high flying Brentford and Scunthorpe, even netting a rare goal to win the game at Scunthorpe. Although small for a centre back, he always relishes a battle with a big centre forward.
Rochdale (From trainee on 10/6/95) FL 93+14/3 FLC 6 FAC 2+3 Others 7+1

BAZELEY Darren Shaun
Born: Northampton, 5 October 1972
Height: 5'10" Weight: 11.7
Club Honours: Div 2 '98
International Honours: E: U21-1
A versatile, pacy player who spent most of last season at right back for Watford, though he can also play as a winger or striker, he was a consistent outlet for clearances, while his own attacking inclinations made him a potent source of accurate right-wing crosses. His own goal return was perhaps a little disappointing, despite including a memorable solo effort at Bury. Out of contract during the summer, Darren has now made more than 250 first-team appearances for his only club.
Watford (From trainee on 6/5/91) FL 187+53/21 FLC 13+5/2 FAC 12+1/3 Others 9+1/1

BEADLE Peter Clifford
Born: Lambeth, 13 May 1972
Height: 6'1" Weight: 13.7
Transferred to Port Vale from Bristol Rovers during the 1998 close season, he took time to settle in but then scored some cracking goals, especially against Wolves and Crystal Palace, that helped lift the club off the foot of the table. Although a recurring ankle often interrupted his progress, he was joint leading scorer with six goals when a change of manager led to a change of opinion and a move to Notts County in February in a bid to help them avoid relegation. A big, strong centre forward, Peter scored three times in 14 appearances for the Magpies after his move, and when fully fit it is anticipated that he will be a strong force in the penalty area, hopefully scoring lots of goals. Is a capable leader of the line and good target man.

Gillingham (From trainee on 5/5/90) FL 42+25/14 FLC 2+4/2 FAC 1+1 Others 1
Tottenham H (£300,000 on 4/6/92)
Bournemouth (Loaned on 25/3/93) FL 9/2
Southend U (Loaned on 4/3/94) FL 8/1
Watford (Signed on 12/9/94) FL 12+11/1 FLC 1
Bristol Rov (£50,000 on 17/11/95) FL 98+11/39 FLC 2+1 FAC 5/2 Others 7+1/1
Port Vale (£300,000 on 6/8/98) FL 18+5/6 FLC 2 FAC 1
Notts Co (£250,000 on 18/2/99) FL 13+1/3

BEAGRIE Peter Sydney
Born: Middlesbrough, 28 November 1965
Height: 5'8" Weight: 12.0
International Honours: E: B-2; U21-2
After a barren spell without a goal dating back to 5 November 1996, mainly due to spending a long time out injured, the clever midfielder opened his Bradford account with a penalty in the opening game of last season at home to Stockport. He certainly made up for lost time, scoring more goals during the campaign than any other, and playing the best football of his illustrious career. A revelation, usually celebrating goals with his famous somersault, he played 39 consecutive cup and league games before picking up a calf injury. Has signed a new contract that will keep him at City until June 2000.
Middlesbrough (From juniors on 10/9/83) FL 24+9/2 FLC 1 Others 1+1
Sheffield U (£35,000 on 16/8/86) FL 81+3/11 FLC 5 FAC 5 Others 4
Stoke C (£210,000 on 29/6/88) FL 54/7 FLC 5 FAC 3/1
Everton (£750,000 on 2/11/89) F/PL 88+26/11 FLC 7+2/3 FAC 7+2 Others 5+1/1
Sunderland (Loaned on 26/9/91) FL 5/1
Manchester C (£1,100,000 on 24/3/94) F/PL 46+6/3 FLC 8/1 FAC 4+1/1
Bradford C (£50,000 on 2/7/97) FL 74+3/12 FLC 7/3 FAC 3
Everton (Loaned on 26/3/98) PL 4+2

Peter Beagrie

BEALL Matthew (Billy) John
Born: Enfield, 4 December 1977
Height: 5'7" Weight: 10.12

Billy's transfer from Cambridge to Leyton Orient was a long drawn-out deal, which took until the end of last October to sort out before finally going to a tribunal. Having left United during the summer, as soon as Billy started playing you could see why Tommy Taylor, Orient's manager, was eager to sign him and why the U's were so reluctant to let him go. A tigerish midfielder, and recognised as an excellent box-to-box player who, despite his size, is not frightened to get a foot in. Is also a valuable attacking force, scoring the winner at Hull, and a good passer of the ball.
Cambridge U (From trainee on 28/3/96) FL 73+8/7 FLC 2 FAC 6/2 Others 1+1
Leyton Orient (Signed on 26/10/98) FL 21+2/2 FAC 5 Others 3

BEARD Mark
Born: Rochampton, 8 October 1974
Height: 5'10" Weight: 11.3
Signed from Sheffield United during the summer of 1998, Mark was one of the few successes of a dismal Southend season, making the right-wing-back position his own with a good run of committed displays. Although his combative style resulted in more bookings than were necessary, he could never be accused of not giving of his best and could be one of the players that United build their new season around.
Millwall (From trainee on 18/3/93) FL 32+13/2 FLC 3+1 FAC 4/1
Sheffield U (£117,000 on 18/8/95) FL 22+16 FLC 2+1 FAC 2+2
Southend U (Loaned on 24/10/97) FL 6+2 Others 1
Southend U (Free on 6/7/98) FL 36+1 FLC 1 FAC 1 Others 1

BEARDSLEY Peter Andrew
Born: Newcastle, 18 January 1961
Height: 5'8" Weight: 11.7
Club Honours: Div 1 '88, '90; Div 2 '99; FAC '89; CS '88, '89
International Honours: E: 59; B-2
Starting last season with Fulham, Peter played a significant role in their early successes but, when Geoff Horsfield and Barry Hayles arrived, he gave way and signed for struggling Hartlepool at the end of December. He made an immediate impact at his new club, scoring on his debut against Peterborough with a blistering volley after just 18 minutes. Despite not being the player he had once been he did show occasional touches of brilliance, playing a central midfield role and feeding the ball around the park to create chances. Although extremely well paid for his services, Hartlepool's gamble paid off with increased crowds, while off the field he was a fine ambassador for the club. Significantly, it was his second goal for Pool, which secured a fine 1-0 win over Leyton Orient, that virtually secured the team's safety away from the bottom of Division Three.
Carlisle U (Free from Wallsend BC on 9/8/79) FL 93+11/22 FLC 6+1 FAC 15/7 Others 2 (£275,000 to Vancouver Whitecaps on 1/4/82)
Manchester U (£300,000 on 9/9/82) FLC 1 (Free to Vancouver Whitecaps on 1/3/83)
Newcastle U (£150,000 on 23/9/83) FL 146+1/61 FLC 10 FAC 6 Others 1
Liverpool (£1,900,000 on 24/7/87) FL 120+11/46 FLC 13+1/1 FAC 22+3/11 Others 5/1

Everton (£1,000,000 on 5/8/91) F/PL 81/25 FLC 8/5 FAC 4/1 Others 2/1
Newcastle U (£1,400,000 on 16/7/93) PL 126+3/47 FLC 11/4 FAC 11/3 Others 11/4
Bolton W (£450,000 on 20/8/97) PL 14+3/2 FLC 3 FAC 0+1
Manchester C (Loaned on 17/2/98) FL 5+1
Fulham (Free on 26/3/98) FL 19+2/4 FLC 4+1/1 Others 1/1
Hartlepool U (Free on 31/12/98) FL 22/2 Others 2

BEASANT David (Dave) John
Born: Willesden, 20 March 1959
Height: 6'4" Weight: 14.3
Club Honours: Div 4 '83, Div 2 '89; Div 1 '98; FAC '88; FMC '90
International Honours: E: 2; B-7
The veteran goalkeeper rolled back the years in 1998-99 when establishing himself as Nottingham Forest's number one 'keeper ahead of Mark Crossley. In producing a string of fine performances for a side that was looking relegation material long before the end of the campaign, he was an ever present until shipping 11 goals in two successive home games, against Manchester United and Chelsea. Released during the summer on reaching the age of 40, he captained the side on a couple of occasions when Steve Chettle was injured.
Wimbledon (£1,000 from Edgware T on 7/8/79) FL 340 FLC 21 FAC 27 Others 3
Newcastle U (£800,000 on 13/6/88) FL 20 FLC 2 FAC 2 Others 1
Chelsea (£725,000 on 14/1/89) F/PL 133 FLC 11 FAC 5 Others 8
Grimsby T (Loaned on 24/10/92) FL 6
Wolverhampton W (Loaned on 12/1/93) FL 4 FAC 1
Southampton (£300,000 on 4/11/93) PL 86+2 FLC 8 FAC 9
Nottingham F (Free on 22/8/97) P/FL 67 FLC 5 FAC 2

BEATTIE James Scott
Born: Lancaster, 27 February 1978
Height: 6'1" Weight: 12.0
International Honours: E: U21-4
1998-99 turned out to be an excellent season for the young Southampton striker. An England U21 international, he was signed during the summer of 1998 from Blackburn when Kevin Davies moved in the opposite direction for £7.5m. Expecting a year of consolidation with occasional first-team outings, he was thrown into the thick of the relegation battle and won instant acclaim with the Saints' fans for his non-stop effort and passion. His magnificent winner against Leicester, when he hit a side-footed volley over the 'keeper, Kasey Keller, further enhanced his standing. Very strong in the air and having great physical presence in and around the opponents' box, he scored a total of five Premiership goals, all of them vital. Looking set for a full international cap in the future, James was voted Southampton's "Player of the Year".
Blackburn Rov (From trainee on 7/3/95) PL 1+3 FLC 2 FAC 0+1
Southampton (£1,000,000 on 17/7/98) PL 22+13/5 FLC 1+1/1 FAC 2

BEAUCHAMP Joseph (Joey) Daniel
Born: Oxford, 13 March 1971
Height: 5'10" Weight: 12.11

1998-99 was not the best of seasons for Joey at Oxford, after his best-ever show the year before, and he will have been disappointed to have scored just four goals. To add to his frustrations, he was also red carded twice – the first in his career – and almost moved to other clubs on a few occasions; Southampton, Nottingham Forest, Manchester City and Fulham all reported to have been interested in signing a player who, on his day, can take apart the best defences from his wide role, using a mixture of pace and skill.

Oxford U (From trainee on 16/5/89) FL 117+7/20 FLC 6+1/2 FAC 8/3 Others 5+1
Swansea C (Loaned on 30/10/91) FL 5/2 Others 1
West Ham U (£1,000,000 on 22/6/94)
Swindon T (£850,000 on 18/8/94) FL 39+6/3 FLC 7+2/1 FAC 2 Others 4
Oxford U (£75,000 on 4/10/95) FL 136+22/31 FLC 16/6 FAC 5+3/1 Others 0+2

BEAUMONT Christopher (Chris) Paul
Born: Sheffield, 5 December 1965
Height: 5'11" Weight: 11.12
Chris enjoyed his best season yet for Chesterfield in 1998-99, although he did not start as a first teamer. Injury to Paul Holland gave him a chance in central midfield, and he put in many marvellously consistent, hard-working displays, his astute passing and strong running enabling the Spireites to sustain a play-off challenge. After Holland's return, he retained a first-team spot in left midfield and was rewarded for his diligence and attitude in February by being given another year on his contract. He played out the last three months of the season with a cracked fibia.

Rochdale (Free from Denaby U on 21/7/88) FL 31+3/7 FLC 0+1/1 FAC 2/1 Others 2
Stockport Co (£8,000 on 21/7/89) FL 238+20/39 FLC 14+3/3 FAC 15/2 Others 34+2/7
Chesterfield (£30,000 on 22/7/96) FL 96+15/4 FLC 8+2 FAC 6+2/1 Others 3

BEAVERS Paul Mark
Born: Blackpool, 2 October 1978
Height: 6'3" Weight: 13.5
Yet to play for Sunderland's first team, and in order to keep match fit, Paul had spells on loan at Shrewsbury (December) and Oldham (March) in 1998-99. After playing for Town at home against Wycombe in the Auto Windscreens Shield, he made his league debut at Mansfield, and appeared once more before returning home, having had little chance to impress in a struggling side. At Oldham, however, the young striker immediately made an impact with his strong running and presence, scoring twice – one of them winning the vital penultimate game of the campaign against Stoke – and almost certainly securing Latics' Second Division safety.

Sunderland (From trainee on 14/4/97)
Shrewsbury T (Loaned on 7/12/98) FL 2 Others 1
Oldham Ath (Loaned on 25/3/99) FL 7/2

BECK Mikkel
Born: Aarhus, Denmark, 12 May 1973
Height: 6'2" Weight: 12.9
International Honours: Denmark: 15
Having spent almost as much time on the bench for Middlesbrough in 1998-99 than

starting, and having scored just five goals, he jumped at the opportunity of joining Derby in transfer deadline week – Jim Smith, the County manager, persuading him to sign a four-year contract for a nominal fee under the Bosman ruling. Preferring to play as a left-sided striker, and noted for making intelligent runs into space either side of a central striker, he had a rather frustrating start to his Derby career and there was notable relief when, in his fourth game for the club, he netted the winner at Leicester. However, he impressed the fans with some very hard-working performances which bode well for the coming season, when he will hope to revive his international career – a major reason for his move to Pride Park.

Middlesbrough (Free from Fortuna Cologne, via Kolding and B1909, on 13/9/96) F/PL 66+25/24 FLC 14+2/5 FAC 5+3/2
Derby Co (£500,000 on 26/3/99) PL 6+1/1

BECKETT Luke John
Born: Sheffield, 25 November 1976
Height: 5'11" Weight: 11.6
Undoubtedly one of Kevin Ratcliffe's best signings for Chester, Luke arrived from Barnsley at the start of last season and was an instant hit with the fans with two goals in the Worthington Cup-tie at Port Vale. Unfortunately, he was restricted to only 29 games with City due to injuries, but still managed to score 13 goals, some of them in spectacular fashion. Soon became a favourite with the fans because of his tremendous workrate and eye for goal, and there were no doubts among them that if he'd had a full season in the team he would have been amongst the division's leading goalscorers.

Barnsley (From trainee on 20/6/95)
Chester C (Free on 11/6/98) FL 24+4/11 FLC 1/2

David Beckham

BECKHAM David Robert Joseph
Born: Leytonstone, 2 May 1975
Height: 6'0" Weight: 11.12

Club Honours: FAYC '92; PL '96, '97, '99; FAC '96, '99; CS '96, '97; EC '99
International Honours: E: 23; U21-9; Yth
An excellent Manchester United midfielder, with a sublime range of passing and shooting skills, David returned to England a marked man, following his altercation with Argentina's Deigo Simeone in the World Cup finals during the summer of 1998. Seen by certain English fans, notably of rival Premiership clubs, as the main reason for the nation's loss against the South Americans, it was feared that he might have to move abroad to escape the fierce hostility shown towards him. However, demonstrating that he had the necessary character to rise above it, he was an ever present throughout the course of the campaign. Although his goal count was slightly down on the previous tally, the quality of his goals remained of the very highest order and, having opened his account in the Premiership against Leicester at Old Trafford last August, his equalising goal against Barcelona in the Champions' League at Old Trafford in September was right out of the top drawer. With further strikes against Brondby, Wimbledon, and Middlesbrough, he was an important cog as United progressed on the trophy hunt on three fronts, his performance against Inter Milan in the Champions' League quarter final at Old Trafford was simply world class. On the eve of that match, Inter's Simeone confessed that he had intentionally fallen to the ground when David kicked him during their bust up in the World Cup during the summer. Simeone said, "Let's just say the ref fell into the trap. You could say that my falling transformed a yellow card into a red card but, in fact, the most appropriate punishment was a yellow one." When David's father, Ted, asked him what he would do if Simeone came up to him, he answered, "What can I do. I'll shake his hand." After the match, he not only shook the Argentinian's hand, but the pair swopped shirts. Now that's character! Scoring his first goal in three months against Everton in the Premiership in March, he then hit a 25-yard screamer against Arsenal in the FA Cup semi-final replay, which helped United to another cup final appearance at Wembley. An automatic choice in Kevin Keegan's first England squad for the European qualifier against Poland, David remains a highly-influential player for both club and country. As a key member of the treble-winning side, he was selected by his fellow professionals for the PFA award-winning Premiership team.

Manchester U (From trainee on 29/1/93) PL 128+16/30 FLC 5+2 FAC 16+2/5 Others 35+1/6
Preston NE (Loaned on 28/2/95) FL 4+1/2

BEDEAU Anthony (Tony) Charles Osmond
Born: Hammersmith, 24 March 1979
Height: 5'10" Weight: 11.0
A steadily improving young Torquay striker whose best performances were probably away from Plainmoor, where his pace and close control were used effectively on the break, Tony combined well with Eifion

Williams during the latter part of the campaign, and the two should form a dangerous partnership this coming term. Added impressively to his scoring account with nine goals, only one of them coming in a game that was lost.

Torquay U (From trainee on 28/7/97) FL 46+36/14 FLC 3+1/1 FAC 2+3 Others 0+6

Tony Bedeau

BEECH Christopher (Chris)
Born: Congleton, 5 November 1975
Height: 5'10" Weight: 11.12
International Honours: E: Yth; Sch
Signed from Cardiff during the summer of 1998, Chris had a very good start to the first two months of last season, putting in some fine displays at left back for Rotherham before suffering a knee injury which kept him out for a long time. Battled on to win his place back in March and April, but then was a victim of the squad system of which he was a very reliable member.

Manchester C (From trainee on 12/11/92)
Cardiff C (Free on 7/8/97) FL 46/1 FLC 2 FAC 6
Rotherham U (Free on 30/6/98) FL 24 FLC 2

BEECH Christopher (Chris) Stephen
Born: Blackpool, 16 September 1974
Height: 5'11" Weight: 11.12
Unable to agree terms, he began 1998-99 with Hartlepool on a week-to-week contract, but on the field this attacking midfielder was at the top of his form, carrying on from were he had finished off the previous season. He played to his strengths, scoring several memorable goals, and with nine from the first 16 games he was well up with the Division Three leading scorers. Unfortunately, as the weeks passed his dispute was not settled, and matters came to a head when a proposed move to Sheffield United fell through. Previously a very popular player, he upset the supporters by walking out and was in limbo for several weeks until joining Huddersfield on loan at the end of November, before a permanent move

followed in February. He continued to show impressive form with his new club, and stepped off the bench to gain a regular place with some all-out attacking displays. A good header of the ball, and an intelligent passer, he scored a wonderful headed goal in the rain-swept Boxing Day clash with Grimsby, and soon repaid the fee with three goals in four games, two of them against Derby in the FA Cup. Unfortunately, his campaign was ended by an ankle injury with a few games remaining.

Blackpool (From trainee on 9/7/93) FL 53+29/4 FLC 4+4 FAC 1 Others 3+3/2
Hartlepool U (Free on 18/7/96) FL 92+2/23 FLC 5/1 FAC 3/1 Others 3/1
Huddersfield T (£65,000 on 27/11/98) FL 13+4/2 FAC 2/2

BEESLEY Paul
Born: Liverpool, 21 July 1965
Height: 6'1" Weight: 12.6
Signed from Manchester City early in 1998-99, Paul, an experienced defender, found a new lease of life in the autumn of his career with Port Vale, proving solid and dependable, and making the majority of his appearances in central defence, either in a back four or three, before struggling a bit when moved to left back for a spell. In October he hit a purple patch of three goals in six games, including one after just 35 seconds against Bristol City. Although 12 bookings led to a few suspensions and an appearance before the FA, he gave everything and did particularly well towards the campaign's close, before being released during the summer.

Wigan Ath (Free from Marine on 22/9/84) FL 153+2/3 FLC 13 FAC 6 Others 11
Leyton Orient (£175,000 on 20/10/89) FL 32/1 FAC 1 Others 2/1
Sheffield U (£300,000 on 10/7/90) F/PL 162+6/7 FLC 12+1 FAC 9+2/1 Others 3/1
Leeds U (£250,000 on 2/8/95) PL 19+3 FLC 5+1 FAC 5 Others 2+2
Manchester C (£500,000 on 7/2/97) FL 10+3
Port Vale (Loaned on 24/12/97) FL 5
West Bromwich A (Loaned on 12/3/98) FL 8
Port Vale (Signed on 28/8/98) FL 33+2/3 FAC 1

Paul Beesley

BEETON Alan Matthew
Born: Watford, 4 October 1978
Height: 5'11" Weight: 11.12
This young left-footed defender enjoyed a run of 11 games for Wycombe early last season, but then lost his place as left-wing back to new signing, Chris Vinnicombe. This seemed a little harsh at the time for a very competitive and athletic player with no mean speed, who looks particularly comfortable going down the wing. In fact, during Wanderers' dreadful start to 1998-99, he was one of perhaps only two or three players who always gave their all. Made some substitute appearances towards the end of the campaign and will be hoping that Lawrie Sanchez makes more use of him in 1999-2000.

Wycombe W (From trainee on 1/7/97) FL 26+10 FLC 2 FAC 1+2

BEHARALL David
Born: Jarrow, 13 April 1979
Height: 6'0" Weight: 11.12
A graduate of the Newcastle School of Excellence, David led the club's juniors to the Northern Intermediate League title in 1997-98, and established himself in the reserves during the early part of 1998-99, captaining the side on occasion, clearly being a young man who relishes responsibility. A tall and slim centre back, who is comfortable on the ball and, who displays a first-class attitude, he worked hard to improve his all-round game, particularly his passing, being rewarded with a place on the bench for the home game with Wimbledon in November, and then his debut at home to Everton in April. He was unlucky to encounter a Goodison side fighting for Premiership survival and United lost 3-1 after conceding a first-minute goal. However, David settled in and became increasingly assured as the game progressed to earn himself three further appearances and justify his growing reputation as a fine prospect for the future.

Newcastle U (From trainee on 4/7/97) PL 4

BELL Michael (Mickey)
Born: Newcastle, 15 November 1971
Height: 5'9" Weight: 11.4
A talented Bristol City full back, Mickey was cruelly struck down by a broken leg at a crucial stage of the season last February. His partnership with Brian Tinnion on the left was often the team's most effective method of attack and, as in the promotion season, his dead-ball strikes brought the team many goals. Was just approaching his best form as a vital member of the squad, and benefiting by playing behind Brian Tinnion, when suffering the injury during the West Bromwich Albion game at the Hawthorns.

Northampton T (From trainee on 1/7/90) FL 133+20/10 FLC 7+1 FAC 5/1 Others 9+2/1
Wycombe W (£45,000 on 21/10/94) FL 117+1/5 FLC 5 FAC 9/2 Others 3+1
Bristol C (£150,000 on 2/7/97) FL 77/15 FLC 7 FAC 3 Others 2

BELLAMY Craig Douglas
Born: Cardiff, 13 July 1979
Height: 5'9" Weight: 10.12
International Honours: W: 7 U21-8; Yth; Sch

Craig enjoyed a fantastic season for Norwich in 1998-99 and, but for a terrible knee injury sustained at Wolverhampton in mid December, would surely have scored even more goals. Playing almost exclusively up front alongside Iwan Roberts, he won many new admirers with his clinical finishing and clever footwork on the ball, particularly amongst certain Premiership clubs who continue to monitor his progress. At international level, he added to his collection of Welsh caps, most notably by scoring Wales' winning goal in Denmark during their Euro 2000 qualifying match.

Norwich C (From trainee on 20/1/97) FL 68+11/30 FLC 6/2 FAC 1

Craig Bellamy

BENALI Francis (Franny) Vincent
Born: Southampton, 30 December 1968
Height: 5'10" Weight: 11.0
International Honours: E: Sch

Always a great competitor, the Southampton left back or central defender came back strongly towards the end of last season after missing three months with a broken arm suffered at Leicester in December. Typically, he played on for half an hour, despite the pain, the break only being revealed by X Rays later! Having seemingly lost his place to new signing, Patrick Colleter, Franny won his place back, giving his usual inspiring performance in the run in to the end of the campaign. It is fair to say that he improves each season with experience, and his disciplinary record is also much better. Has now played more than 200 games for Saints in 12 years at his only club.

Southampton (From apprentice on 5/1/87) F/PL 244+32/1 FLC 21+7 FAC 20 Others 3+1

BENJAMIN Trevor Junior
Born: Kettering, 8 February 1979
Height: 6'2" Weight: 13.2

This powerfully-built young Cambridge

striker made a big impact in 1998-99. A terrifying sight for defences as he builds up steam on one of his left-wing runs, he hit the headlines during United's Worthington Cup run, and his buccaneering style helped see off Premiership Sheffield Wednesday. Although a dip in form followed during the winter, he ended the campaign back to his marauding best. Certainly, a number of Third Division full backs and goalkeepers will be pleased to see the back of "Bruno", who now has the chance to play in a higher league in 1999-2000.

Cambridge U (From trainee on 21/2/97) FL 54+25/15 FLC 5+3/4 FAC 4+1/2 Others 3+2

Trevor Benjamin

BENNETT Frank (Frankie)
Born: Birmingham, 3 January 1969
Height: 5'7" Weight: 12.1

A stocky, pacy wide player, Frankie recovered from potential career-threatening surgery on both his knees in June 1998 to regain his fitness. Returning to league action with Bristol Rovers, when making a 62nd-minute substitute appearance on 24 April in a vital 2-1 victory at Blackpool, he became the 33rd different player to be used by Rovers during the season as he strived to be rewarded with another contract. Starting for the first time in 1998-99, in the final match of the season at Macclesfield, he scored in a remarkable 4-3 victory that saw Rovers come from 2-0 down to take maximum points.

Southampton (£7,500 from Halesowen T on 24/2/93) PL 5+14/1 FLC 1+2 FAC 0+1
Shrewsbury T (Loaned on 25/10/96) FL 2+2/3
Bristol Rov (£15,000 on 22/11/96) FL 15+19/4 FLC 1+1 FAC 0+2 Others 3/2

BENNETT Gary Ernest
Born: Manchester, 4 December 1961
Height: 6'1" Weight: 13.0
Club Honours: Div 3 '88

Released by Scarborough during the 1998 close season, Gary, a vastly experienced player, joined Darlington as player/coach, but missed the first quarter of 1998-99 through injury. Operating in both midfield

and central defence, and using his wide knowledge of the game to assist younger players around him, he scored his first goal for Darlington in the live Sky TV clash at home to his first club, Manchester City, and contributed four more in the league.

Manchester C (Free from Ashton U on 8/9/79)
Cardiff C (Free on 16/9/81) FL 85+2/11 FLC 6/1 FAC 3
Sunderland (£65,000 on 26/7/84) FL 362+7/23 FLC 34+1/1 FAC 17+1 Others 21/1
Carlisle U (Free on 16/11/95) FL 26/5 Others 5/1
Scarborough (Free on 2/8/96) FL 86+2/18 FLC 6/3 FAC 4 Others 3
Darlington (Free on 8/7/98) FL 26+3/4 FAC 3/1 Others 1

BENNETT Gary Michael
Born: Liverpool, 20 September 1962
Height: 5'11" Weight: 12.0
Club Honours: AMC '85; WC '95

Due to a knee injury which resulted in an operation, Gary was restricted to just seven appearances in the Chester team during 1998-99. The popular forward scored the only goal of the game at Southend in August to give City victory, and then played virtually no part in the rest of the season. A deadly finisher at his best, and also creative.

Wigan Ath (Free from Kirby T on 9/10/84) FL 10+10/3 FAC 1 Others 3+1/1
Chester C (Free on 22/8/85) FL 109+17/36 FLC 6+4/1 FAC 8+1/5 Others 10/5
Southend U (Signed on 11/11/88) FL 36+6/6 FLC 4/4 FAC 1 Others 2+1
Chester C (£20,000 on 1/3/90) FL 71+9/15 FLC 8/2 FAC 5/1 Others 4+1/1
Wrexham (Free on 12/8/92) FL 120+1/77 FLC 17/9 FAC 7/3 Others 9/9
Tranmere Rov (£300,000 on 13/7/95) FL 26+3/9 FLC 4
Preston NE (£200,000 on 27/3/96) FL 15+9/4 Others 1/1
Wrexham (£100,000 on 28/2/97) FL 15/5 FAC 0+1
Chester C (£50,000 on 25/7/97) FL 42+6/12 FLC 3+1 FAC 2

BENNETT Ian Michael
Born: Worksop, 10 October 1971
Height: 6'0" Weight: 12.10
Club Honours: Div 2 '95; AMC '95

Having kept eight clean sheets in Birmingham's opening 14 games of 1998-99, Ian pulled a hamstring at Norwich on 26 September, an injury which let Gary Poole in for the remainder of the campaign. Known for his exploits as a shot-stopping 'keeper, and one who had dramatically improved his ability to deal well with crosses from the flanks, it was a bitter pill to swallow, especially as he had earlier been rated as one of the best goalies outside the Premiership. Nevertheless, he will undoubtedly be back.

Newcastle U (Free from Queens Park R juniors on 20/3/89)
Peterborough U (Free on 22/3/91) FL 72 FLC 10 FAC 3 Others 4
Birmingham C (£325,000 on 17/12/93) FL 187 FLC 25 FAC 13 Others 11

BENNETT Michael (Micky) Richard
Born: Camberwell, 27 July 1969
Height: 5'11" Weight: 11.11

Released by Leyton Orient in the summer of 1998, Micky joined up with Brighton in

time for the start of 1998-99. Initially played a holding role in midfield before injuries necessitated him playing at centre half and right back, as a born-again Christian he was the victim of a racial attack when a home fan ran on the pitch during the away game at Swansea in February. Likes to get involved, but his early performances flattered to deceive and he never quite reached those levels again before being released by Micky Adams at the end of the season.

Charlton Ath (From apprentice on 27/4/87) FL 24+11/2 FLC 4 FAC 1 Others 6+1
Wimbledon (£250,000 on 9/1/90) FL 12+6/2 FLC 1+1 FAC 0+1 Others 1+1
Brentford (£60,000 on 14/7/92) FL 40+6/4 FLC 4+1 FAC 1 Others 6+1
Charlton Ath (Free on 24/3/94) FL 19+5/1 FAC 1
Millwall (Free on 16/5/95) FL 1+1
Cardiff C (Free on 14/8/96) FL 5+9/1 FLC 2 FAC 1+1 Others 0+1 (Free to Cambridge C in December 1996)
Leyton Orient (Free on 8/12/97) FL 1+1 Others 1
Brighton & Hove A (Free on 3/8/98) FL 37+1 FLC 2 FAC 1 Others 1

BENNETT Thomas (Tom) McNeill
Born: Falkirk, 12 December 1969
Height: 5'11" Weight: 11.8
An energetic and enthusiastic midfielder, Tom bounced back from a career-threatening knee injury in March 1999. Ever popular with the Stockport faithful, he spent the last few months of the season re-establishing himself in Gary Megson's first team and will be looking forward to the 1999-2000 season as a regular in the County midfield. Before the injury, he was touted as a possible Scotland "B" international, another target he will aiming to achieve.

Aston Villa (From apprentice on 16/12/87)
Wolverhampton W (Free on 5/7/88) FL 103+12/2 FLC 7 FAC 5+2 Others 3+1
Stockport Co (£75,000 on 23/6/95) FL 97+4/5 FLC 20/2 FAC 9 Others 6+1

BENT Junior Antony
Born: Huddersfield, 1 March 1970
Height: 5'6" Weight: 10.9
A speedy Blackpool winger who uses his pace to get behind the full back, Junior was used only sporadically last season, depending on whatever system was being used. The scorer of the club's first league goal, at home to Oldham, he followed that up with another at Scunthorpe in the Worthington Cup before his striking rate dried up as he spent more and more time coming off the bench to get at defences late in the game. Is a great crowd favourite.

Huddersfield T (From trainee on 9/12/87) FL 25+11/6 FLC 1 FAC 3+1/1 Others 4
Burnley (Loaned on 30/11/89) FL 7+2/3
Bristol C (£30,000 on 22/3/90) FL 142+41/20 FLC 10+3/1 FAC 12+3/2 Others 7+3
Stoke C (Loaned on 26/3/92) FL 1
Shrewsbury T (Loaned on 24/10/96) FL 6
Blackpool (Signed on 29/8/97) FL 46+29/4 FLC 2+1/1 FAC 2+1 Others 4

BENT Marcus Nathan
Born: Hammersmith, 19 May 1978
Height: 6'2" Weight: 12.4
International Honours: E: U21-2
Marcus never found the form of the previous season at Crystal Palace in 1998-99 and, despite scoring six goals in the reserves, the striker was unable to replicate those performances in the first team before joining Port Vale in January. As John Rudge's final signing for Vale, and seemingly able to beat defenders with some ease, he looked to be getting back on course. Unfortunately, however, it all went wrong when he caught sight of goal, and during the run-in he made only spasmodic appearances.

Brentford (From trainee on 21/7/95) FL 56+14/8 FLC 7/1 FAC 8/3 Others 5+1/1
Crystal Palace (£150,000 + on 8/1/98) P/FL 13+15/5 FLC 0+2 FAC 0+1
Port Vale (£375,000 on 15/1/99) FL 10+5

BERESFORD David
Born: Middleton, 11 November 1976
Height: 5'5" Weight: 11.4
International Honours: E: Yth; Sch
The tricky Huddersfield winger finally put 14 months of injury worries behind him in 1998-99 and was able to concentrate on gaining a regular first-team slot. He began the campaign with two subs' appearances in the Worthington Cup against Everton, causing the Premiership outfit all kinds of problems with his lightning pace and accurate crossing, before making his first two starts against Queens Park Rangers and Sunderland, and putting on dazzling displays. Always willing to get forward to support the strikers, goals followed at Norwich and West Bromwich, and the "Man of the Match" award in the return game against Norwich at the McAlpine merely highlighted his astute performances on the right-hand side of midfield.

Oldham Ath (From trainee on 22/7/94) P/FL 32+32/2 FLC 3+3 FAC 0+1 Others 3
Swansea C (Loaned on 11/8/95) FL 4+2
Huddersfield T (£350,000 on 27/3/97) FL 24+9/3 FLC 1+2 FAC 1+1

BERESFORD John
Born: Sheffield, 4 September 1966
Height: 5'7" Weight: 12.0
Club Honours: Div 1 '93
International Honours: E: B-2; Yth; Sch
A left-sided defender or midfield player who signed for Southampton in February 1998 and gave some sound displays, it was thought that his presence would be of great benefit to the team as they strove to improve on 1997-98's 12th place. However, he was just seven minutes into last season when he was taken off against Liverpool with badly damaged cruciate knee ligaments, only reappearing as a substitute in three of the last four games of the campaign. Defensively sound and having the skill and pace of a winger, it is to be hoped that this experienced player will fully recover for the coming season.

Manchester C (From apprentice on 16/9/83)
Barnsley (Free on 4/8/86) FL 79+9/5 FLC 5+2/2 FAC 5/1
Portsmouth (£300,000 on 23/3/89) FL 102+5/8 FLC 12/2 FAC 11 Others 2
Newcastle U (£650,000 on 2/7/92) F/PL 176+3/3 FLC 17 FAC 17+1/1 Others 17+1/4
Southampton (£1,500,000 on 6/2/98) PL 11+3

BERESFORD Marlon
Born: Lincoln, 2 June 1969
Height: 6'1" Weight: 13.6
Middlesbrough's faithful stand-in shot-stopper has yet to finish on the losing side in the Premiership, despite conceding seven goals in just four outings in 1998-99. After opening his account with three straight clean sheets the previous term he furthered the Boro's unbeaten sequence whenever he was named as cover for Mark Schwarzer. During his custodianship he claimed two "Man of the Match" awards and saved a penalty in the Worthington Cup match against Everton along the way. Sadly, that game turned out to be his only reverse thus far whilst on first-team duty. Is renowned for the accuracy of his clearances and ball distribution, whether from a throw or a kick, and has launched many counter attacks from his own goal line, in giving confidence to the defenders playing in front of him.

Sheffield Wed (From trainee on 23/9/87)
Bury (Loaned on 25/8/89) FL 1
Northampton T (Loaned on 27/9/90) FL 13 Others 2
Crewe Alex (Loaned on 28/2/91) FL 3
Northampton T (Loaned on 15/8/91) FL 15
Burnley (£95,000 on 28/8/92) FL 240 FLC 18 FAC 20 Others 16
Middlesbrough (£500,000 on 10/3/98) P/FL 7 FLC 3

BERG Henning
Born: Eidsvoll, Norway, 1 September 1969
Height: 6'0" Weight: 12.7
Club Honours: PL '95, '99
International Honours: Norway: 62
A solid Manchester United central defender whose timing and judgement is always impeccable, Henning had a frustrating start to last season, when he struggled with persistent injury problems. After playing as a substitute against Arsenal in the Charity Shield opener in August, he made only seven full starts up to the end of December. Whether it was the Yuletide cheer, or the unstinting work of United physio' David Fevre that worked the oracle, remains unsure, but his season really burst into life following the festivities. Starting with a solid performance in the FA Cup third round against Middlesbrough at Old Trafford, he certainly looked the part alongside Jaap Stam. His defensive qualities really came to the fore, however, in the Champions' Cup quarter final against Inter Milan at Old Trafford, when an outstanding goal-line clearance denied Inter the chance of a precious away goal. Two weeks later, he was a star performer in the San Siro, keeping Ronaldo and company at bay with a series of exquisite tackles. With so many top-class defenders vying for that exclusive position alongside Stam, Henning proved he had all the necessary qualities to make it his very own. Barring further injuries, he could well become a permanent fixture in the first team for many more seasons to come.

Blackburn Rov (£400,000 from Lillestrom on 26/1/93) PL154+5/4 FLC 16 FAC 10 Others 9
Manchester U (£5,000,000 on 12/8/97) PL 33+10/1 FLC 3 FAC 7 Others 8+4/1

BERGER Patrik

Born: Prague, Czechoslovakia, 10 November 1973
Height: 6'1" Weight: 12.6
International Honours: Czechoslovakia: 30

After some close season doubts that he would return to his native Czechoslovakia, Patrik remained at Liverpool to enjoy one of his finest seasons. In the opening two games of 1998-99, there were doubts that he was going to be used once again as the player to be withdrawn if a substitute was to be introduced into a game, but a scintillating display against Newcastle in a 4-1 victory at St James' Park destroyed that theory. As the campaign progressed, so did his contributions. His deep, penetrating runs and ability to find the back of the net meant that he won several "Man of the Match" awards throughout a difficult time for the club. However, while his direct approach and powerful shooting excites the crowd, his defensive play can let him down on occasion but, no doubt, that can be tightened up. Continued to feature for his country.

Liverpool (£3,250,000 from Borussia Dortmund, via Slavia Prague, on 15/8/96) PL 49+28/16 FLC 6+1/2 FAC 3+2 Others 13+1/4

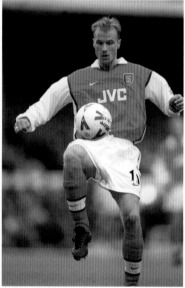

Dennis Bergkamp

BERGKAMP Dennis

Born: Amsterdam, Holland, 18 May 1969
Height: 6'0" Weight: 12.5
Club Honours: PL '98; CS '98
International Honours: Holland: 68

Is a genuine world-class striker with the ability to destroy any team on his day. Also capable of scoring spectacular goals from any angle, and from dead-ball situations, his early season form at Arsenal in 1998-99, however, suffered badly from the demands of the World Cup finals during the previous summer. A subsequent back injury also caused him to miss a number of matches during the first half of the campaign. But once he returned to full fitness he struck up a good understanding with his main strike partner, Nicolas Anelka, and his precision passing created a number of goals for other team mates. This was particularly evident when he laid on four in the 5-0 win over Leicester in February. He was also particularly instrumental in the 4-0 victory at West Ham two weeks earlier. Has the overall class crucial to win closely-fought games against top opposition.

Arsenal (£7,500,000 from Inter Milan, via Ajax, on 3/7/95) PL 117+2/51 FLC 14/8 FAC 16/7 Others 6/2

BERGSSON Gudni

Born: Reykjavik, Iceland, 21 July 1965
Height: 6'1" Weight: 12.3
Club Honours: Div 1 '97
International Honours: Iceland: 77

Although one of the most consistent performers in the First Division, 1998-99 proved to be a somewhat frustrating one for Gudni. As reliable as ever during the first half of the campaign, he provided his trademark solid displays for Bolton until a recurring groin problem put him out of action in November. It would be four months until he made his comeback away to Oxford, appearing as a substitute in a much-changed team to the one he left in November, and then had to settle for a place on the bench for much of the remainder of the season. Is still considered to be an invaluable and highly-experienced member of the Trotters' squad, whilst still appearing with some regularity in the Icelandic national team.

Tottenham H (£100,000 from Valur on 15/12/88) F/PL 51+20/2 FLC 4+2 FAC 2+2 Others 5+1
Bolton W (£115,000 on 21/3/95) P/FL 121+6/9 FLC 15+1 FAC 4 Others 3+2

BERKLEY Austin James

Born: Dartford, 28 January 1973
Height: 5'10" Weight: 11.6

1998-99 was an excellent season for the left-sided Shrewsbury midfield player as he continued his good work of 1997-98 and added a bite to his game, which saw him more involved in tackling and defending. Very tricky with the ball at his feet when running at defences, Austin packed a wicked shot with a much stronger appetite for goals, and doubled his career total in just one campaign.

Gillingham (From trainee on 13/5/91) FL 0+3 Others 0+3
Swindon T (Free on 16/5/92) FL 0+1 FLC 0+1 Others 3+1/1
Shrewsbury T (Free on 29/7/95) FL 125+14/12 FLC 4+2 FAC 6+1 Others 11/1

BERKOVIC Eyal

Born: Haifa, Israel, 2 April 1972
Height: 5'7" Weight: 10.2
International Honours: Israel: 51

Once again the Israeli midfield playmaker had an excellent season in West Ham's colours, and certainly put the John Hartson training incident well behind him. Combining good skills on the ball with intelligent movement off it, he was generally involved in all of the Hammers' attacking moves in 1998-99, and was a major reason for their success in finishing fifth in the Premiership. There was no doubt that when he played well the team played well, and he was outstanding in games at Derby and Tottenham – victories that went a long way towards the side's high league placing. Having settled down well in London – living with his family in Golders Green, a predominantly Jewish area – he continued to be a regular for Israel on the international front. Stop Press: Moved to Glasgow Celtic for £5.5 million on 9 July.

Southampton (Leased from Maccabi Tel Aviv on 11/10/96) PL 26+2/4 FLC 5+1/2 FAC 1
West Ham U (£1,700,000 on 30/7/97) PL 62+3/10 FLC 6 FAC 7+1/2

BERNAL Andrew (Andy)

Born: Canberra, Australia, 16 May 1966
Height: 5'10" Weight: 12.5
International Honours: Australia: 14

Unable to find a regular place in Reading's back four until last November, Andy adjusted to the demands of playing either at wing back or centre back quite quickly, his combative style continuing to make him a favourite with the fans. Two sendings off during the season, however, brought his total to eight in five seasons but, despite being at the veteran stage, he is still a vital part of the Royals' set up.

Ipswich T (Free from Sporting Gijon on 24/9/87) FL 4+5 Others 0+2
Reading (£30,000 from Sydney Olympic on 26/7/94) FL 160+4/2 FLC 14+1 FAC 10 Others 3

BERNTSEN Robin

Born: Tromso, Norway, 16 July 1970
Height: 5'11" Weight: 11.9

A midfield player who joined Port Vale on loan from the Norwegian club, Tromso, last November, Robin made his debut against Sunderland, lasting an hour. He then expressed a wish to play in the back four, which manager John Rudge promptly disagreed with. The player was unhappy at this juncture, caught the next plane back to Norway, and was not seen at Vale Park again.

Port Vale (Loaned from Tromso, via VIF and Tromsdalen, on 13/11/98) FL 1

BERRY Trevor John

Born: Haslemere, 1 August 1974
Height: 5'7" Weight: 11.2
Club Honours: AMC '96
International Honours: E: Yth

Sidelined for the start of last season at Rotherham, having to undergo a hernia operation, after getting back to full fitness at the turn of the year he had a relapse. The highlight of the campaign for this speedy winger was a spectacular goal in the FA Cup replay win against Rochdale. Fully fit he is a major asset to the team and will be hoping for better fortunes in 1999-2000.

Aston Villa (£50,000 from Bournemouth juniors on 3/4/92)
Rotherham U (£20,000 on 8/9/95) FL 103+23/16 FLC 3+1 FAC 7+3/3 Others 9/1

BERTHE Mohamed
Born: Guyana, 12 September 1972
Height: 6'2" Weight: 15.2
Signed by West Ham from the Austrian club, Graz Ajaccio, in March 1998, Mohamed joined Bournemouth in the 1998 close season, having failed to make an appearance for the Hammers. A powerful midfielder who can also play at centre back, can shoot with either foot and is a good crosser of the ball, things did not work out for him at Dean Court and, after making 17 starts and four substitute appearances, he joined Hearts in March before the Scottish club subsequently released him at the end of the campaign.
West Ham U (Free from Graz Ajaccio on 26/3/98)
Bournemouth (Free on 10/7/98) FL 12+3/2 FLC 4 FAC 1 Others 0+1

BERTI Nicola
Born: Parma, Italy, 14 April 1967
Height: 6'1" Weight: 12.2
International Honours: Italy: 39
A very experienced Italian central midfielder who arrived at Tottenham from Inter Milan in January 1998, initially on a six-month loan period, he quickly showed his worth when proving instrumental to the club's Premiership survival in 1997-98, prior to signing a permanent contract. A very effective box-to-box player, with an excellent range of passing skills, and strong in the tackle, he never quite attained the form he had shown during the previous term and, following the arrival of a new manager, George Graham, he was placed on the transfer list in October. Having played just four early games, and feeling that he had no future at White Hart Lane, he moved to Alaves on 7 January 1999.
Tottenham H (Loaned from Inter Milan, via Parma and Fiorentina, on 9/1/98) PL 21/3 FAC 2

BESWETHERICK Jonathan (Jon) Barry
Born: Liverpool, 15 January 1978
Height: 5'11" Weight: 11.4
Jon is another young Plymouth player who developed well throughout 1998-99. A tall left back who has a good turn of pace, he grew in confidence with a run in the first team and became a far more attacking player when providing some excellent crosses for the forward line. Made his first starting appearance at Shrewsbury in the league last October.
Plymouth Arg (From trainee on 27/7/96) FL 18+6 FAC 4 Others 1

BETSY Kevin Eddie Lewis
Born: Seychelles, 20 March 1978
Height: 6'1" Weight: 11.12
International Honours: E: SP-1
A very promising young player signed by Fulham from Woking early last season, Kevin played as a wing back and then as a striker in the reserves, where he was the top scorer with 17 goals. He had already played as a substitute in cup matches at Anfield and Old Trafford, before making his full league debut against Millwall in April and scoring in a 4-1 win.

Fulham (£80,000 + from Woking on 16/9/98) FL 1+6/1 FLC 0+1 FAC 0+1 Others 1

BETTS Simon Richard
Born: Middlesbrough, 3 March 1973
Height: 5'7" Weight: 11.4
Although once again never completely sure of his place in the Colchester team at any time, Simon played in over half the league games again last season, split between each full-back position. Following Steve Wignall's resignation, he marked his recall to the team under Steve Whitton's caretaker managership with the opening goal at Stoke – a 20-yard volley – then welcomed new manager, Mick Wadsworth, to Layer Road with a 35-yard special in the first minute against York. Having lost his place to Fabrice Richard later in the campaign, he was released in the summer.
Ipswich T (From trainee on 2/7/91)
Wrexham (Free on 13/8/92)
Scarborough (Free on 3/11/92)
Colchester U (Free on 11/12/92) FL 182+9/11 FLC 9 FAC 8+2 Others 14/2

BIGNOT Marcus
Born: Birmingham, 22 August 1974
Height: 5'10" Weight: 11.2
International Honours: E: SP-1
A speedy Crewe full back, having secured his place in the 1997-98 he lost it midway during last January when removed after 70 minutes of a 4-1 defeat at Bradford. Replaced by David Wright, the former England semi-professional star, who competes for every ball with great enthusiasm, is determined to regain the right-back slot during the coming term. Has yet to score for Alex.
Crewe Alex (£150,000+ from Kidderminster Hrs on 1/9/97) FL 68 FLC 5 FAC 2

BILIC Slaven
Born: Split, Croatia, 11 September 1968
Height: 6'2" Weight: 13.8
International Honours: Croatia: 43
After playing a starring role for Croatia during their unexpected third-place finish in the World Cup finals, Everton supporters finally hoped to see the best of this classy, ball-playing centre half. Unfortunately, that dream remained unfilled, as a niggling hip injury picked up in France continued to dog Slaven throughout 1998-99 and saw him make just five appearances before bowing to the inevitable and undergoing surgery. Despite speculation linking him with a return to West Ham, Evertonians remain sure that they will eventually see his true ability displayed in royal blue in 1999-2000.
West Ham U (£1,300,000 from Karlsruhe, via Hajduk Split, on 4/2/96) PL 48/2 FLC 5/1 FAC 1
Everton (£4,500,000 on 16/7/97) PL 26+2 FLC 3 FAC 1

BILLY Christopher (Chris) Anthony
Born: Huddersfield, 2 January 1973
Height: 5'11" Weight: 11.8
A Plymouth midfielder and right-sided wing back who had been tracked by Sam Allardyce for some time before becoming his first 1998 close-season signing for Notts County, Chris never really settled at

Meadow Lane and was allowed to rejoin his former manager, Neil Warnock, at Bury last September, thus beginning his third stretch under the latter. Able to perform in a variety of positions (he wore nine different shirt numbers), he virtually became an automatic choice on his arrival, turning out mainly in midfield or at right back, despite struggling to find his form at times. Has excellent skills and pace, loves to run at defenders, and can always be relied upon to give 100 per-cent effort.
Huddersfield T (From trainee on 1/7/91) FL 76+18/4 FLC 8+2 FAC 5 Others 15+2/2
Plymouth Arg (Signed on 10/8/95) FL 107+11/8 FLC 5 FAC 8/1 Others 5+1
Notts Co (Free on 2/7/98) FL 3+3 FLC 2
Bury (Free on 17/9/98) FL 35+2 FAC 1

BIMSON Stuart James
Born: Liverpool, 29 September 1969
Height: 5'11" Weight: 11.12
Lincoln left back who was brought in from the wilderness of reserve-team football and produced some excellent performances in 1998-99. His near perfect in-swinging corners brought him two goals direct from flag kicks and caused chaos in opponents defences on numerous other occasions and, although he struggled against a knee injury at the end of April, he managed to complete the season. Was given a two-year extension to his contract during the summer.
Bury (£12,500 from Macclesfield T on 6/2/95) FL 36 FLC 5 Others 3
Lincoln C (Free on 29/11/96) FL 50+8/3 FAC 3+1 Others 4+1/1

BIRCHAM Marc Stephen John
Born: Wembley, 11 May 1978
Height: 5'10" Weight: 12.4
International Honours: Canada: 1
A product of the Millwall youth system, Marc made his debut against Preston in January 1997 as a full back, a position he largely continued to fill in senior games, in spite of playing predominantly in midfield as a junior. A forceful, competitive player with bags of enthusiasm, he earned himself a new contract towards the end of 1997-98 and, although not having regular first-team football last season, whenever he played he acquitted himself well, and was part of the squad for the Auto Windscreens Shield final. His continued good form, also saw him gain full Canadian honours, scoring his first goal against Northern Ireland.
Millwall (From trainee on 22/5/96) FL 29+9 FLC 0+1 FAC 1+1 Others 3+1

BIRD Anthony (Tony)
Born: Cardiff, 1 September 1974
Height: 5'10" Weight: 12.8
International Honours: W: U21-8; Yth
A three-match suspension at the start of last season saw Swansea's top goalscorer of the previous campaign revert to a substitute role for most of 1998-99, making more than 20 league appearances from the bench. With the Steve Watkin and Julian Alsop partnership establishing themselves in the Swan's first-team line-up, plus a much reduced reserve-team programme, Tony found it difficult retaining his sharpness in front of goal when called into action.

Cardiff C (From trainee on 4/8/93) FL 44+31/13 FLC 8/2 FAC 4+1/1 Others 12+4/3 (Free to Barry T in January 1996)
Swansea C (£40,000 on 8/8/97) FL 43+27/17 FLC 2+1 FAC 2+1 Others 3+2/3

BISHOP Charles (Charlie) Darren
Born: Nottingham, 16 February 1968
Height: 6'0" Weight: 13.7
Club Honours: Div 3 '97
A solid central defender for Northampton, Charlie missed most of 1997-98 through injury. Looking for a bright start, he began the 1998-99 season as one of the three central defenders, but after a disastrous game against Blackpool in September both player and club decided to part company. Following that decision, he signed for non-league Ilkeston Town a few weeks later and joined his family business.
Watford (Free from Stoke C juniors on 17/4/86)
Bury (Free on 10/8/87) FL 104+10/6 FLC 5 FAC 4/1 Others 12+1
Barnsley (£50,000 on 24/7/91) FL 124+6/1 FLC 11+1 FAC 9 Others 5
Preston NE (Loaned on 12/1/96) FL 4
Burnley (Loaned on 28/3/96) FL 9
Wigan Ath (£20,000 on 28/6/96) FL 27+1 FLC 1 Others 2
Northampton T (£20,000 on 12/12/97) FL 11 FLC 2 FAC 1 Others 1

BISHOP Ian William
Born: Liverpool, 29 May 1965
Height: 5'9" Weight: 10.12
International Honours: E: B-1
After six appearances at the end of 1997-98, Ian spent the summer sharpening his game, but then injured his knee ligaments in a pre-season friendly. This kept him out of Manchester City's first-team squad until the end of October, although he appeared in four reserve games. Playing his first Second Division game at home against Colchester, as a second half substitute, he then played the next five games, although being substituted in four of them. Although trying to regain full fitness, his skill was still there but he found it hard to adapt in the more basic physical game. However, that changed over the Christmas period, where his old flair and midfield passing began to show, and he contributed to two good results. Despite spending the next eight games on the bench, playing twice, following the Chesterfield away game he was given a consistent spell in the side, looking sharper and more involved, his contribution being excellent in the unbeaten run of results.
Everton (From apprentice on 24/5/83) FL 0+1
Crewe Alex (Loaned on 22/3/84) FL 4
Carlisle U (£15,000 on 11/10/84) FL 131+1/14 FLC 8/1 FAC 5/1 Others 4
Bournemouth (£35,000 on 14/7/88) FL 44/2 FLC 4 FAC 5 Others 1
Manchester C (£465,000 on 2/8/89) FL 18+1/2 FLC 4/1 Others 1
West Ham U (£500,000 on 28/12/89) F/PL 240+14/11 FLC 21+1/1 FAC 22+1/3 Others 4+1/1
Manchester C (Free on 26/3/98) FL 25+6 FAC 1+1 Others 0+1

BJORNEBYE Stig-Inge
Born: Elverum, Norway, 11 December 1969
Height: 5'10" Weight: 11.9
Club Honours: FLC '95
International Honours: Norway: 71

The Norwegian international enjoyed his eighth season for Liverpool in 1998-99, whether appearing on the left of the defence or in midfield. Strong and reliable, and an excellent tackler, he is known for his deep, surging runs which often end in goals. Not always a regular this time round, sometimes giving way to the returning Steve Staunton, he can always be relied on when on the field, especially with his corners and potent crosses which, as ever, were whipped in with some power and often deceived goalkeepers and defenders. With this player you always know what you are going to get.
Liverpool (£600,000 from Rosenborg, via Kongsvinger, on 18/12/92) PL 132+7/2 FLC 16 FAC 11+2 Others 16/2

BLACK Kingsley Terence
Born: Luton, 22 June 1968
Height: 5'9" Weight: 11.2
Club Honours: FLC '88; FMC '92; AMC '98
International Honours: E: Sch. NI: 30; B-3; U21-1
Once again Kingsley had to vie with David Smith for a place on Grimsby's right flank. The Mariners' increasing injury problems as the 1998-99 season progressed, saw him, however, pressed into a new role in the centre of midfield, supporting a lone striker, a role to which he adopted with consummate ease. His skill either in this position or on the right flank was such that he was able to rekindle his international career, having been recalled to the Northern Ireland "B" squad against Wales.
Luton T (From juniors on 7/7/86) FL 123+4/26 FLC 16+2/1 FAC 5+1/2 Others 3+2/1
Nottingham F (£1,500,000 on 2/9/91) F/PL 80+18/14 FLC 19+1/5 FAC 4 Others 4+2/1
Sheffield U (Loaned on 2/3/95) FL 8+3/2
Millwall (Loaned on 29/9/95) FL 1+2/1 FLC 0+1
Grimsby T (£25,000 on 16/7/96) FL 72+33/6 FLC 11 FAC 5+1 Others 2+5/1

BLACK Michael James
Born: Chigwell, 6 October 1976
Height: 5'8" Weight: 11.8
Club Honours: FAYC '94
International Honours: E: Sch
A strong, skilful winger with good natural pace, Michael came through the youth ranks at Arsenal. During the last two seasons, however, he has spent more time recovering from a series of injuries than playing. His set backs include a dislocated shoulder, hernia, and cartilage problems, all necessitating surgery. 1997-98 saw him have a successful loan spell at Millwall before suffering a further injury. Although the injuries could easily have affected him psychologically, he has shown great determination in getting back to fitness. Having made his first-team debut when he came off the bench in the Champions League away leg at Panathinaikos in 1998-99, he continued his progress by playing regularly in the reserves, before being released during the summer.
Arsenal (From trainee on 1/7/95) Others 0+1
Millwall (Loaned on 3/10/97) FL 13/2 Others 1

BLACKMORE Clayton Graham
Born: Neath, 23 September 1964
Height: 5'8" Weight: 11.12
Club Honours: FAC '90; ECWC '91; ESC '91; PL '93; Div 1 '95
International Honours: W: 39; U21-3; Yth; Sch
A great servant to Middlesbrough since being snapped up as one of manager Bryan Robson's first signings on his appointment to Boro, Clayton soon fitted into Bryan's way of doing things by helping the club to win promotion at the first attempt, his cheerful outlook and ready humour endearing him to his team mates in the dressing room, and especially to the developing young aspirants coming through the system. With his appearances getting fewer each term, although he played in over 60 Boro first-team games and scored some memorable goals, he left late last season, having made one appearance in the Worthington Cup, to join former Boro favourites, John Hendrie and Craig Hignett at Barnsley. Sad to see him leave, his many Teesside fans will always harbour pleasant memories of a very skilful and aggressive midfielder who never shirked a tackle and sprayed passes around the park with unerring accuracy. Signed by the Tykes because of a crippling injury list that saw few left-sided players being fit for selection, he filled in at left-wing back despite being short of match fitness due to non selection at the Riverside, before being freed during the summer.
Manchester U (From apprentice on 28/9/82) F/PL 150+36/19 FLC 23+2/3 FAC 15+6/1 Others 19/4
Middlesbrough (Free on 11/7/94) P/FL 45+8/4 FLC 4+2 FAC 4+1 Others 1
Bristol C (Loaned on 1/11/96) FL 5/1
Barnsley (Free on 26/2/99) FL 4+3 FAC 1

BLACKWELL Dean Robert
Born: Camden, 5 December 1969
Height: 6'1" Weight: 12.7
International Honours: E: U21-6
Having come through the youth set up at Wimbledon to make his debut in 1989, Dean has served the club well for many years, and had a first-class season in 1998-99, his partnership with Chris Perry being as good as any in the Premiership. Is a strong, commanding and popular figure in the Dons' defence, and produced some of the best form of his career to date. The timing of his tackles were again excellent and he was very difficult to pass. With statistics showing him to be one of the fairest defenders in the league, this ex-England U21 international gave his all in a worrying season and is now well on the way to 250 appearances for his only team.
Wimbledon (From trainee on 7/7/88) F/PL 159+23/1 FLC 15 FAC 22+1 Others 1
Plymouth Arg (Loaned on 15/3/90) FL 5+2

BLAKE Nathan Alexander
Born: Cardiff, 27 January 1972
Height: 5'11" Weight: 13.2
Club Honours: WC '92, '93; Div 3 '93, Div 1 '97
International Honours: W: 11; B-1; U21-5; Yth

Following on from his successful stint in the Premiership, great things were expected of Nathan at Bolton in 1998-99, and he duly obliged when part of a three-pronged strike force comprising Dean Holdsworth and Arnar Gunnlaugsson – scoring seven times in five games. Continuing in this vein until he had, by his own high standards, a barren patch during October, it still came as a great surprise to the fans to hear that he was transferring to Blackburn at the end of that month. However, although starting well with a goal at Old Trafford and a vital second-half brace at Nottingham Forest, the New Year saw his appearances restricted by a combination of a virus, an old neck injury, and achilles tendon trouble. Having sorted his differences out with Bobby Gould and returning to international duty with Wales during the season, he is yet another Rovers' forward player who will be looking for better luck in 1999-2000.

Cardiff C (Free from Chelsea juniors on 20/8/90) FL 113+18/35 FLC 6+2 FAC 10/4 Others 13+2/1
Sheffield U (£300,000 on 17/2/94) P/FL 55+14/34 FLC 3+1/1 FAC 1 Others 1
Bolton W (£1,500,000 on 23/12/95) F/PL 102+5/38 FLC 10+1/8 FAC 6/2
Blackburn Rov (£4,250,000 on 30/10/98) PL 9+2/3 FAC 1+2

Nathan Blake

BLAKE Noel Lloyd George
Born: Jamaica, 12 January 1962
Height: 6'1" Weight: 14.2
As Exeter's assistant manager, Noel played in only a handful of games last season. This was due, in part, to the continuing defensive improvement of the side which coped admirably without him. However, his vast experience – including his playing at the top level – was undeniably helpful to a predominantly youthful side in the centre of defence.

Aston Villa (Signed from Sutton Coldfield T on 1/8/79) FL 4
Shrewsbury T (Loaned on 1/3/82) FL 6
Birmingham C (£55,000 on 15/9/82) FL 76/5 FLC 12 FAC 8
Portsmouth (£150,000 on 24/4/84) FL 144/10 FLC 14/1 FAC 10/2 Others 5/1

Leeds U (Free on 4/7/88) FL 51/4 FLC 4+1 FAC 2 Others 4
Stoke C (£175,000 on 9/2/90) FL 74+1/3 FLC 6 FAC 3+1 Others 4+1
Bradford C (Loaned on 27/2/92) FL 6
Bradford C (on 20/7/92) FL 38+1/3 FLC 2+1 FAC 5/1 Others 4
Dundee U (Free on 10/12/93) SL 52+2/2 SLC 2 SC 5 Others 3
Exeter C (Free on 18/8/95) FL 130+5/9 FLC 6 FAC 6 Others 3

BLAKE Robert (Robbie) James
Born: Middlesbrough, 4 March 1976
Height: 5'9" Weight: 12.6
Robbie missed Bradford's first three games of last season through suspension, then had to wait another five matches before he got his chance due to an injury to Izzy Rankin. In outstanding form after he formed a striking partnership with Lee Mills, he also showed his versatility by playing on both flanks when used as a wide man. This was also his best ever season for scoring goals, his close control of the ball and his ability to ghost past defenders being outstanding.

Darlington (From trainee on 1/7/94) FL 54+14/21 FLC 4+2/1 FAC 3+1 Others 3+1/1
Bradford C (£300,000 on 27/3/97) FL 61+17/23 FLC 3+2/1 FAC 3

BLATHERWICK Steven (Steve) Scott
Born: Nottingham, 20 September 1973
Height: 6'1" Weight: 14.6
Chesterfield snapped up this solid central defender from Burnley last December after a loan spell. Denied much chance to impress by the fine form of Mark Williams and Ian Breckin, "Blathers" played as an emergency striker at times, but is naturally a stopper. It is reassuring to know that, if Mark Williams exercises his right to a "Bosman" in the summer, the Spireites have an accomplished replacement already at the club. Steve is a powerful header of the ball and scored against Stoke in April with a bullet from around 12 yards.

Nottingham F (Free from Notts Co juniors on 2/8/92) FL 10 FLC 2 FAC 1 Others 2
Wycombe W (Loaned on 18/2/94) FL 2 Others 1
Hereford U (Loaned on 11/9/95) FL 10/1 Others 2
Reading (Loaned on 27/3/97) FL 6+1
Burnley (£150,000 on 18/7/97) FL 16+8 FLC 5 FAC 1+1 Others 3
Chesterfield (Loaned on 18/9/98) FL 2
Chesterfield (£50,000 on 1/12/98) FL 7+5/1 Others 2

BLOMQVIST Lars Jesper
Born: Tavelsjo, Sweden, 5 February 1974
Height: 5'9" Weight: 11.6
Club Honours: EC '99; FAC '99; PL '99
International Honours: Sweden: 8
The Swedish "Player of the Year" for 1993, the flying left-winger, with excellent ball control, and good crossing skills to match, arrived at Manchester United in the summer of 1998 as back-up cover for Ryan Giggs. Although many Reds' fans questioned his commitment when he said that he would have preferred to stay at Parma than move to Old Trafford, he quickly showed them what he could do. His seering runs down the left flank soon put them in mind of another famous Jesper who wore the red shirt in the '80s – Jesper Olsen. Alex Ferguson was

certainly impressed. He said, "If we'd had Jesper last March, we would have won the title." After a blank August, he made his Premiership debut against Charlton at Old Trafford at the beginning of September and never looked back. Although he scored only one goal during the campaign, against Everton at Goodison in October, he created many more for Andy Cole, Dwight Yorke, Paul Scholes and company in Giggs's absence. With only fleeting appearances in the side during December, he was recalled in January when Giggs suffered more injury problems. Although he was injured himself in training on the eve of United's second-leg European tie against Inter Milan, he made a good recovery and, despite unfounded rumours that he was unsettled at the club in March, he remained an important member of the squad, seemingly assured of a long-term future at Old Trafford.

Manchester U (£4,400,000 from Parma, via Gothenburg and AC Milan, on 31/7/98) PL 20+5/1 FLC 0+1 FAC 3+2 Others 6+1

BLOOMER Matthew Brian
Born: Grimsby, 3 November 1978
Height: 6'0" Weight: 13.0
A Grimsby Town central defender, this junior professional is the third generation of a well-known local footballing family to appear for the Mariners. And, as a highly promising member of the reserve squad, he made a brief senior appearance in 1998-99 as substitute in the Nationwide League home game with Crystal Palace. Will be looking for more opportunities this coming term.

Grimsby T (From juniors on 3/7/97) FL 0+4 Others 0+1

BLUNT Jason John
Born: Penzance, 16 August 1977
Height: 5'9" Weight: 10.10
International Honours: E: Yth
Having failed to make a first-team appearance at Leeds in 1997-98, Jason signed for Blackpool during the 1998 close season and made his debut for the Seasiders in the opening game of the new campaign. Surprisingly, the young midfielder was then consigned to the reserves until coming back to score a cracking goal in the first round FA Cup-tie at Wigan. Back in the reserves, he was released by mutual consent in March, hoping to emigrate to Australia.

Leeds U (From trainee on 1/1/95) PL 2+2 FLC 0+1
Blackpool (Free on 2/7/98) FL 1+1 FAC 1/1 Others 1

BOA MORTE Luis Pereira
Born: Lisbon, Portugal, 4 August 1977
Height: 5'10" Weight: 11.5
Club Honours: PL '98; CS '98
A very pacy Portuguese U21 international winger, cum striker, with Arsenal whose best position is on the right flank. Although he failed to command a regular first-team place in 1998-99, he made a major contribution in a difficult third round FA Cup-tie at Preston, scoring the first goal and setting up two others in a 4-2 victory after the Gunners had come back from two down.

He also scored in the Champions' League away leg at Panathinaikos. Is at present very much a squad player whose difficulty is in competing for places with Nicolas Anelka, Dennis Bergkamp and Marc Overmars. Is a striker noted for shooting on sight of goal.

Arsenal (£1,750,000 + from Sporting Lisbon on 25/6/97) PL 6+17 FLC 3/2 FAC 2+3/1 Others 2+3/1

BOATENG George
Born: Nkawkaw, Ghana, 5 September 1975
Height: 5'9" Weight: 11.7
Coventry's enormously popular all-action midfielder did not have a happy first half of last season, and failed to reproduce the dazzling form of 1997-98, being rested in November in favour of the Belgian, Philippe Clement. After Christmas, however, playing in a wider right-wing position he blossomed once more with some tigerish tackling, good control and goals. He had an excellent game and scored twice in the 4-1 win at Villa Park, netting with a brave diving header against Liverpool, and was on the spot to score the vital winner against Southampton. Although his over exuberance resulted in a large number of yellow cards, two of which saw him have an early bath in the FA Cup win at Leicester, in April he publicly expressed his preference for a central midfield role after another lacklustre appearance on the wing. Rumoured to be the subject of a transfer bid from Villa near the end of the campaign, he finished on a high note, creating both goals in the win over Wimbledon when playing in a free midfield role.

Coventry C (£250,000 from Feyenoord, via Excelsior, on 19/12/97) PL 43+4/5 FLC 3/1 FAC 8/1

George Boateng

BODLEY Michael (Mick) John
Born: Hayes, 14 September 1967
Height: 6'1" Weight: 13.2
Club Honours: GMVC '91
Although starting the first 15 games for Peterborough last season, the central defender struggled with injuries after that and was eventually allowed to leave for non-

league St Albans City in March. A whole-hearted player who preferred the pass to the "boot", the fans were sad to see him leave.

Chelsea (From apprentice on 17/9/85) FL 6/1 FLC 1 Others 1
Northampton T (£50,000 on 12/1/89) FL 20 Others 2
Barnet (£15,000 on 1/10/89) FL 69/3 FLC 2 FAC 10 Others 9
Southend U (Free on 15/7/93) FL 66+1/2 FLC 3 FAC 2 Others 7
Gillingham (Loaned on 23/11/94) FL 6+1 Others 1
Birmingham C (Loaned on 23/1/95) FL 3
Peterborough U (£75,000 on 27/7/96) FL 86/1 FLC 9 FAC 8 Others 6

BOERTIEN Paul
Born: Haltwhistle, 20 January 1979
Height: 5'10" Weight: 11.2
The latest starlet to emerge from Carlisle's youth ranks in 1998-99, injury having sidelined him for over a year until he returned to the side last February at Swansea, he scored his debut league goal in the match and kept his place in midfield until Derby signed him just before the transfer deadline. An all-round performer, preferably on the left-hand side, his early promise with County's reserves, where he showed good attacking ability, led to a first-team call up as the season drew to an end, and he came off the bench at Chelsea for the last eight minutes. Should have a bright future in the game if nurtured properly.

Carlisle U (From trainee on 13/5/97) FL 16+1/1 FLC 0+2 FAC 1 Others 1
Derby Co (£250,000 on 25/3/99) PL 0+1

BOGIE Ian
Born: Newcastle, 6 December 1967
Height: 5'8" Weight: 12.0
International Honours: E: Sch
The playmaking Port Vale midfielder was a regular in the side right up until last March's transfer deadline day when he was ousted from his role by new signing, Dave Brammer. Despite having the ability to put his foot on the ball and pull the strings behind the team's attacking moves, this became harder as they battled against relegation. Scored two goals during the season, both away from home, at Wolves and a late season winner at Norwich.

Newcastle U (From apprentice on 18/12/85) FL 7+7 FLC 0+1 FAC 1+2 Others 3/1
Preston NE (Signed on 9/2/89) FL 67+12/12 FLC 3+1 FAC 3 Others 4+1
Millwall (£145,000 on 16/8/91) FL 44+7/1 FLC 1 FAC 2 Others 3
Leyton Orient (Signed on 14/10/93) FL 62+3/5 FLC 2 FAC 2 Others 8+1
Port Vale (£50,000 on 23/3/95) FL 125+20/9 FLC 9/1 FAC 8+2/2 Others 8

BOHINEN Lars
Born: Vadso, Norway, 8 September 1969
Height: 6'0" Weight: 12.10
International Honours: Norway: 49
In his second season at Derby, the Norwegian international midfield player did not manage to be the automatic first-team choice he may have expected to have been due to the competition for places. Playing in a withdrawn role, usually on the right-hand side of the field, very adept at reading the

play in front of him, and known as a very astute passer of the ball, he was disappointed at not converting some good opportunities into goals – a problem shared by others at Pride Park in 1998-99. Suffered a couple of calf strains which kept him out of action for short periods throughout the season.

Nottingham F (£450,000 from Young Boys of Berne, via Valergengen and Viking, on 5/11/93) F/PL 59+5/7 FLC 7+1/2 FAC 2/1 Others 1
Blackburn Rov (£700,000 on 14/10/95) PL 40+18/7 FLC 3+2/1 FAC 2+1/1
Derby Co (£1,450,000 on 27/3/98) PL 38+3/1 FAC 3

BOLAND William (Willie) John
Born: Ennis, Ireland, 6 August 1975
Height: 5'9" Weight: 11.2
International Honours: Ei: B-1; U21-11; Yth; Sch
An Irish-born midfielder, Willie, a product of the Coventry youth scheme and a skilful midfielder who rarely wastes the ball, played only one game for the club last season, in the Worthington Cup. Although his chances were limited by the glut of midfield players at Highfield Road, he turned down an offer of a move to Dundee United in mid term, preferring to see the campaign out with City in the knowledge that his contract would be expiring in the summer and that he would be receiving an offer of re-engagement.

Coventry C (From juniors on 4/11/92) PL 43+20 FLC 6+1 FAC 0+1

BOLDER Adam Peter
Born: Hull, 25 October 1980
Height: 5'8" Weight: 11.0
A combative midfielder who made his senior Hull debut when coming on for the final half hour of the vital 4-0 win against Hartlepool last January, Adam was beginning to prove a lucky charm as he had been a non-playing sub in the FA Cup win at Luton a month earlier. Along with fellow trainees, Michael Blythe and Paul Wilson, he was due to be rewarded with a pro contract at the end of the season. His younger brother, Chris, is currently a trainee at the club.

Hull C (Trainee) FL 0+1

BOLI Roger Zokou
Born: Adjame, Ivory Coast, 29 June 1965
Height: 5'8" Weight: 11.0
Transferred from Walsall to Dundee United during the 1998 close season, Roger joined Bournemouth last October from the Terrors, having scored just once in five appearances. Although a lot was expected from the striker, due to a series of injuries he was restricted to just five starts and five substitute appearances. Quick and dangerous, and willing to shoot from anywhere, barring further injuries he will be hoping to make a bigger contribution to the Cherries' 1999-2000 campaign.

Walsall (Free from Lens on 8/8/97) FL 41/12 FLC 6/2 FAC 4/4 Others 6/6
Dundee U (£150,000 on 20/7/98) SL 3 SLC 2/1
Bournemouth (£50,000 on 21/10/98) FL 5+1 FLC 0+1 FAC 0+2 Others 0+1

BOLLAND Paul Graham
Born: Bradford, 23 December 1979
Height: 5'11" Weight: 11.0
Although appearing in four matches for Bradford City at the beginning of 1998-99 as cover for Stuart McCall, he then moved back to the reserve team before joining Notts County on loan in January. His strength and maturity in midfield certainly impressed manager Sam Allardyce and the move was made permanent in April. Still only 19, Paul has much potential for the future, and is expected to become a strong and even more talented midfield player. He was also required to play at the back, where he worked hard and impressed there.
Bradford C (From trainee on 20/3/98) FL 4+8 FLC 2
Notts Co (£75,000 on 14/1/99) FL 12+1

BONALAIR Thierry
Born: Paris, France, 14 June 1966
Height: 5'9" Weight: 10.8
Club Honours: Div 1 '98
Following Nottingham Forest's successful promotion back to the Premiership in 1997-98, Thierry was rewarded with a new one-year contract, having shown good ability before going down with an achilles injury. Starting 1998-99 in possession of a first-team place, the former French U21 international proved to be a versatile player, on either flank, operating at wing back, in midfield, and as a sweeper on occasion. In what proved to be a difficult season, with the club struggling for their Premiership lives most of the time, he always did of his best and could not be faulted. Scored in a 3-2 defeat at Sheffield Wednesday.
Nottingham F (Free from Neuchatel Xamax, via Nantes, Auxere and Lille, on 17/7/97) P/FL 48+11/3 FLC 4 FAC 1

Thierry Bonalair

BONNER Mark
Born: Ormskirk, 7 June 1974
Height: 5'10" Weight: 11.0
Released by Blackpool during the 1998 close season, Mark joined Cardiff and soon proved himself to be a gutsy midfield player. Neat, tidy, thoughtful, and efficient, he showed gritty determination when he lost his place through injury and was allowed out on loan to Hull City in January, making a dramatic debut with the winner against Rotherham, before damage to his ankle in a freak training accident saw him return to Ninian Park. At that stage there were real doubts about his Cardiff future, but he battled back and finished the season as first choice in the centre of midfield as the Bluebirds were promoted. In showing the qualities manager Frank Burrows was looking for, he is sure to figure in City's plans for 1999-2000.
Blackpool (From trainee on 18/6/92) FL 156+22/14 FLC 15+3 FAC 11 Others 10+3/1
Cardiff C (Free on 17/7/98) FL 21+4/1 FLC 2 Others 1
Hull C (Loaned on 8/1/99) FL 1/1

BONNOT Alexandre (Alex)
Born: Boissy, France, 31 July 1973
Height: 5'8" Weight: 11.4
A defensive midfielder signed on a free transfer from the French club, SCO Angers, last November, Alex made his first-team debut for Watford as a substitute at Portsmouth in January, and his full debut at home to Crewe at the end of the campaign, when he impressed with his firm tackling and accurate passing. Out of contract during the summer, off the field his engaging manner and taste for English life made him many new friends.
Watford (Free from SCO Angers on 10/11/98) FL 1+3

BOOTH Andrew (Andy) David
Born: Huddersfield, 6 December 1973
Height: 6'0" Weight: 13.0
International Honours: E: U21-3
Andy had to wait for 13 matches last season before notching his first goal for Sheffield Wednesday and, although putting in plenty of effort and working hard for the team, he found goals difficult to come by. An injury suffered in January did not help his cause either. Strong in the air, he requires good service from the wings and, ideally, a pacy striker to play alongside him. The Wednesday manager, Danny Wilson, stood by him throughout the campaign in order to boost his confidence, and he remained an integral part of a Wednesday outfit that continued to secure its place in the Premiership.
Huddersfield T (From trainee on 1/7/92) FL 109+14/54 FLC 6+1/3 FAC 8/3 Others 12+1/4
Sheffield Wed (£2,700,000 on 8/7/96) PL 87+5/23 FLC 4 FAC 7+1/3

BOOTY Martyn James
Born: Kirby Muxloe, 30 May 1971
Height: 5'8" Weight: 11.2
Although he began last season as Reading's regular choice at right back, his form dipped to the point where he was reduced to substitute then left out of the squad

altogether, before being loaned, then sold to Southend, where he quickly returned to first-team action. A neat defender and good passer of the ball, who never realised his potential at Reading, he immediately displayed his quality and positional sense from left back and, despite his campaign being brought to a premature end by a dubious suspension, will look to being a regular for the Blues during the coming term.
Coventry C (From trainee on 30/5/89) FL 4+1 FLC 2 FAC 2
Crewe Alex (Free on 7/10/93) FL 95+1/5 FLC 6 FAC 8/1 Others 13
Reading (£75,000 on 18/1/96) FL 62+2/1 FLC 10+1 FAC 7/1
Southend U (Free on 7/1/99) FL 18+2

BORBOKIS Vassilios (Vass)
Born: Serres, Greece, 10 February 1969
Height: 5'11" Weight: 12.0
International Honours: Greece: 1
As in the previous campaign, Vass scored in Sheffield United's opening two games, both trademark shots from outside the area. His excellent play as a right-wing back created many openings for the forwards and, high in the goal assists table, he was called into the Greek international squad. Injured against Cardiff in the FA Cup, and then denied permission to return to Greece, he went anyway. Fined and placed on the transfer list, he never played for United again, and signed for Derby in February, a deal which saw two players plus a cash adjustment given in exchange. The Greek international who specialises in playing in a right-wing back role, can also switch to the left-hand side of defence, as he was asked to do on his debut for the club. Possessing an explosive shot and showing a willingness to move forward, after only three full games he suffered a fractured jaw which ruled him out of action for the rest of the campaign. His versatility will be a useful factor in the coming season.
Sheffield U (£900,000 from AEK Athens, via Apollon, on 9/7/97) FL 55/4 FLC 9/3 FAC 9/1 Others 1/1
Derby Co (£600,000 + on 12/3/99) PL 3+1

BORROWS Brian
Born: Liverpool, 20 December 1960
Height: 5'10" Weight: 11.12
International Honours: E: B-1
This former Everton, Bolton and Coventry defender once again excelled at Swindon as a central defender and skipper, this time in 1998-99. Missing very few games, what he lacked in pace he made up for in experience, and as well as defending, his surging runs often caused the opposition all sorts of problems. Retiring from football at the end of the campaign, Brian can look back with pride at playing over 700 senior games after starting out as an associated schoolboy at Everton in October 1975.
Everton (From juniors on 23/4/80) FL 27 FLC 2
Bolton W (£10,000 on 24/3/83) FL 95 FLC 7 FAC 4 Others 4
Coventry C (£80,000 on 6/6/85) F/PL 396+13/11 FLC 42/1 FAC 26/1 Others 10+1
Bristol C (Loaned on 17/9/93) FL 6
Swindon T (Free on 5/9/97) FL 80 FLC 2 FAC 1

BORTOLAZZI Mario
Born: Verona, Italy, 10 January 1965
Height: 5'9" Weight: 11.4
An experienced midfielder who appeared in well over 300 games in Italy's Serie "A" and "B" Divisions before joining West Bromwich for the start of 1998-99, Mario proved to be an excellent passer of the ball and an expert with free kicks. However, after having a very useful first half to the season, he faded somewhat after Christmas when the grounds got heavier and suffered with niggling knee and ankle injuries which interrupted his football. Was released by Albion in May 1999.
West Bromwich A (Free from Genoa, via Fiorentina, AC Milan, Parma and Atalanta, on 11/8/98) FL 25+10/2 FAC 1

BOS Gijsbert
Born: Spakenburg, Holland, 22 February 1973
Height: 6'4" Weight: 13.7
A tall and skilful central striker with aerial ability, Gijsbert made just one start for Rotherham in 1998-99 and played so poorly that he wasn't considered again before eventually having his contract terminated and returning to his native Holland.
Lincoln C (£10,000 from Ijsselmeervogels on 19/3/96) FL 28+6/6 FLC 6/3 FAC 1/1 Others 1
Rotherham U (£20,000 on 4/8/97) FL 7+11/4 FLC 1+1

BOSNICH Mark John
Born: Sydney, Australia, 13 January 1972
Height: 6'2" Weight: 14.2
Club Honours: FLC '94, '96
International Honours: Australia: 15
Mark commenced last season in Aston Villa's goal, being a key figure in a defence that was an integral part of Aston Villa's early success and playing in the opening ten games, conceding just four goals during their unbeaten run. He then sustained a shoulder injury in a collision with Coventry's George Boateng and, when the problem persisted keyhole surgery was eventually required, which ruled him out until mid February. Having come back to make a couple of appearances on the subs' bench, before regaining his place at Derby in early March, after a spell of seven games "Bossie" was ruled out of the home fixture against Nottingham Forest due to a foot injury, which only served to raise controversy within the media as to his future. In the final year of his contract, and with speculation continuing to abound as to where he would be playing next season, he was voted Oceana's "Goalkeeper of the Century" in a poll organised by the International Federation of Football History and Statistics. Stop Press: Was installed as Peter Schmeichel's successor at Manchester United under the Bosman ruling – returning to the club he left eight years earlier – when signing a four-year contract on 2 June in a deal worth around £7 million.
Manchester U (Free from Sydney Croatia on 5/6/89) FL 3
Aston Villa (Free on 28/2/92) F/PL 179 FLC 20+1 FAC 17 Others 11

BOULD Stephen (Steve) Andrew
Born: Stoke, 16 November 1962
Height: 6'4" Weight: 14.2
Club Honours: Div 1 '89, '91; PL '98; ECWC '94; FAC '98; CS '98
International Honours: E: 2; B-1
Despite his advancing years, Steve remains a solid and thoroughly reliable central defender at Arsenal. Although no longer ever present in the Premiership's longest-serving back-line, he can always be relied upon to do a professional job when called up, providing the perfect partner to either Tony Adams or Martin Keown. This was recognised by the Gunners' manager, Arsene Wenger, who gave him an extension of his contract. Good in the air, hard tackling, and an excellent man marker, he is particularly dangerous at set-pieces with his familiar near-post flick-ons. Deputising as captain when Tony Adams was injured in 1998-99, he showed that he was a natural leader and had an exceptional game against Liverpool, his skill and timing eliminating the threat of Michael Owen. Although prone to injuries, he is one of the most difficult-to-pass central defenders in the Premiership when fully fit. Stop Press: Joined Sunderland on 2 July for a fee believed to be around £500,000.
Stoke C (From apprentice on 15/11/80) FL 179+4/6 FLC 13/1 FAC 10 Others 5
Torquay U (Loaned on 19/10/82) FL 9 FAC 2
Arsenal (£390,000 on 13/6/88) F/PL 271+16/5 FLC 33/1 FAC 27+2 Others 18+6/2

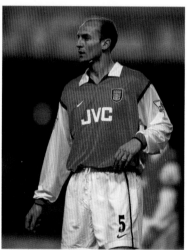
Steve Bould

BOUND Matthew Terence
Born: Melksham, 9 November 1972
Height: 6'2" Weight: 14.6
The left-sided central defender forged an excellent partnership with Jason Smith at the heart of the Swansea defence in 1998-99, displaying a consistency which was a major part in the club's defensive strategy. Dangerous in free-kick situations around the opposition penalty area, Matthew was well capable of regularly getting himself on the goalscoring chart, as his goals against Cardiff and Shrewsbury proved.

Southampton (From trainee on 3/5/91) F/PL 2+3
Hull C (Loaned on 27/8/93) FL 7/1
Stockport Co (£100,000 on 27/10/94) FL 44/5 FLC 1 FAC 3/1 Others 3/1
Lincoln C (Loaned on 11/9/95) FL 3+1 Others 1
Swansea C (£55,000 on 21/11/97) FL 73/2 FLC 2 FAC 5 Others 5/2

BOWEN Jason Peter
Born: Merthyr Tydfi, 24 August 1972
Height: 5'7" Weight: 11.0
Club Honours: AMC '94
International Honours: W: 2; B-1; U21-5; Yth; Sch
Although playing in two early season games for Reading in 1998-99, Jason was substituted in both, then told he could leave the club as soon as he was able to find another one willing to take him. After a spell in the reserves, the tricky winger eventually moved to Cardiff, where he helped the Welsh club gain promotion from Division Three. Capable of hitting the heights, he impressed at City where his two-footed ability saw him play as a main striker alongside Kevin Nugent.
Swansea C (From trainee on 1/7/90) FL 93+31/26 FLC 6+1/2 FAC 9+2/1 Others 15+3/8
Birmingham C (£350,000 on 24/7/95) FL 35+13/7 FLC 4+6/2 FAC 1+4 Others 2/2
Southampton (Loaned on 2/9/97) PL 1+2
Reading (£200,000 on 24/12/97) FL 12+3/1 FLC 1+1 FAC 5
Cardiff C (Free on 12/1/99) FL 10+7/2 FAC 0+1

BOWEN Mark Rosslyn
Born: Neath, 7 December 1963
Height: 5'8" Weight: 11.11
Club Honours: EUFAC '84
International Honours: W: 41; U21-3; Yth; Sch
Missed most of last season with a groin injury, not appearing in the Charlton first team until April when he came in as a substitute at West Ham, one of his former clubs. Is a vastly experienced defender who, although favouring his right foot, can play in either full-back berth or in midfield, reads the game well, and is very calm under pressure. Mark also distributes the ball well and likes to get forward and join the attack, although he has yet to score for the club in open play. Was released during the summer.
Tottenham H (From apprentice on 1/12/81) FL 14+3/2 FAC 3 Others 0+1
Norwich C (£97,000 on 23/7/87) F/PL 315+5/24 FLC 34/1 FAC 28/1 Others 17/1
West Ham U (Free on 10/7/96) PL 15+2/1 FLC 3 (Free to Shimizu SP on 17/3/97)
Charlton Ath (Free on 16/9/97) P/FL 36+6 FAC 3 Others 3

BOWLING Ian
Born: Sheffield, 27 July 1965
Height: 6'3" Weight: 14.8
Now in his fifth season as Mansfield's regular custodian, this left footer missed the first game of 1998-99 through suspension, following a sending off in the last game of the previous term. He played through part of the campaign with an injury as no replacement could be signed due to a transfer embargo. Eventually, following an operation in mid-January, he came back as good as ever a month later to put in some

sterling performances and win the supporters' "Player of the Year" award. On the day he received the award he broke his right arm trying to prevent what turned out to be Exeter's winner at Field Mill.

Lincoln C (£2,000 from Gainsborough Trinity on 23/10/88) FL 59 FLC 3 FAC 2 Others 4
Hartlepool U (Loaned on 17/8/89) FL 1
Bradford C (Loaned on 25/3/93) FL 7
Bradford C (£27,500 on 28/7/93) FL 29 FLC 2 FAC 2+1 Others 1
Mansfield T (Free on 11/8/95) FL 160 FLC 8 FAC 8 Others 6

BOWMAN Robert (Rob)
Born: Durham City, 21 November 1975
Height: 6'1" Weight: 12.10
Club Honours: FAYC '93
International Honours: E: Yth

Rob's first full match of the 1998-99 campaign did not come until last October but, thereafter, he featured at right back in the majority of Carlisle's games. A full back who often looks most comfortable going forward, he was frequently up in support of the front men and was offered terms for the new season.

Leeds U (From trainee on 20/11/92) PL 4+3 FLC 0+1 Others 1
Rotherham U (Free on 21/2/97) FL 13
Carlisle U (Free on 14/8/97) FL 30+1/2 FAC 1 Others 2

BOWRY Robert (Bobby) John
Born: Hampstead, 19 May 1971
Height: 5'9" Weight: 10.8
Club Honours: Div 1 '94

A neat, skilful Millwall midfielder with the ability to make telling passes, as well as getting back and defending well, it took him a while to win over the fans at the Den, but he now has their respect. Had mixed fortunes last season with injury and suspension but when he played he gave some excellent performances, some of them being in the Auto Windshield Trophy, which helped the club to reach Wembley.

Queens Park R (Signed on 8/8/90)
Crystal Palace (Free from Carshalton on 4/4/92) F/PL 36+14/1 FLC 10 FAC 1
Millwall (£220,000 on 5/7/95) FL 122+12/5 FLC 9 FAC 6 Others 4

BOWYER Lee David
Born: London, 3 January 1977
Height: 5'9" Weight: 10.6
International Honours: E: U21-11; Yth

Prior to the start of 1998-99, the verdict on Lee was that this was to be his third and most important season at Elland Road. And what a season he had, translating all the promise he had shown into giving consistently top-drawer performances. At the same time, he blossomed into a real all-action midfielder, looking a cross between the two Davids, Batty and Platt. He also weighed in with his fair share of goals, eight by the end of March. Unfortunately, the downside of his tigerish play brought about a high number of bookings, but offset against that he proved to have a wonderful "engine" and could run all day, with an eye for a shooting chance. During the campaign, press reports suggested he would deservedly be chosen for the full England squad, if the

FA hierarchy could forgive him for turning down a belated invitation to play in the Toulon U21 tournament the previous summer. That they did to a certain extent, when he starred in the 5-0 victory over Poland U21, and scored a superb solo goal to show just what he could do. One of the final nominations for the PFA "Young Player of the Year", no one deserved it more.

Charlton Ath (From trainee on 13/4/94) FL 46/8 FLC 6+1/5 FAC 3/1 Others 2
Leeds U (£2,600,000 on 5/7/96) PL 88+4/16 FLC 4+1/1 FAC 11/2 Others 4

Lee Bowyer

BOXALL Daniel (Danny) James
Born: Croydon, 24 August 1977
Height: 5'8" Weight: 11.6
Club Honours: Div 3 '99
International Honours: Ei: U21-2

This attacking Brentford right back arrived at Griffin Park in the 1998 close season from Crystal Palace and soon settled into the number two shirt, his good close skills being very impressive. Sometimes chose the wrong passing selection, but this will improve with experience. As a regular in the Eire U21 side, he gained further caps against Croatia, Malta and Yugoslavia, and was delighted to win a Third Division championship medal as the Bees turned things around immediately.

Crystal Palace (From trainee on 19/4/95) F/PL 5+3 FLC 1+1
Oldham Ath (Loaned on 21/11/97) FL 5 Others 1
Oldham Ath (Loaned on 27/2/98) FL 12
Brentford (Free on 9/7/98) FL 37+1/1 FLC 4 FAC 2 Others 2

BOYCE Emmerson Orlando
Born: Aylesbury, 24 September 1979
Height: 5'11" Weight: 11.10

Another member of Luton's youth team to turn pro after coming through the club's trainee ranks, Emmerson is at home as a right back or as a central defender. Cool and capable in possession, commanding in the air, and possessing great pace, he is yet another player who impressed in both youth and reserve outings in 1998-99 before making the first team. Given his senior

debut in the early January 3-0 Auto Windscreens Shield defeat by Walsall, the youngster came back to be given a further opportunity towards the end of the season, at home to Lincoln. Although out of contract during the summer, at the time of going to press the club had made him an offer of re-engagement.

Luton T (From trainee on 2/4/98) FL 1 Others 1

BRABIN Gary
Born: Liverpool, 9 December 1970
Height: 5'11" Weight: 14.8
International Honours: E: SP-4

The powerhouse midfielder became an instant cult hero at Hull last January following his move from Blackpool and a period on loan at Lincoln, having agreed to a two-year contract despite interest from two other clubs and City being bottom of the Football League. A former nightclub bouncer, Gary takes no prisoners, but there is much more to his game. A colleague of new signings, Jon Whitney, Jason Perry and Colin Alcide at Lincoln, his midfield promptings were backed up by a succession of priceless goals.

Stockport Co (From trainee on 14/12/89) FL 1+1 Others 1+1
Doncaster Rov (£45,000 from Runcorn on 26/7/94) FL 58+1/11 FLC 2 FAC 2 Others 4
Bury (£125,000 on 29/3/96) FL 5
Blackpool (£200,000 on 30/7/96) FL 50+13/5 FLC 7+1 FAC 2 Others 2+2
Lincoln C (Loaned on 11/12/98) FL 3+1 Others 1
Hull C (Free on 8/1/99) FL 21/4

BRACE Deryn Paul John
Born: Haverfordwest, 15 March 1975
Height: 5'8" Weight: 10.12
Club Honours: WC '95
International Honours: W: U21-8; Yth

As now seems the norm, injuries continued to hinder the progress of this combative Wrexham performer who, as previously, always gave 110 per cent in 1998-99. Held a regular full-back slot in the side during the early part of the campaign, but suffered a bad ankle injury which required an operation in late November. Having fought his way back into the first-team set up by the latter part of the season, Deryn, who has a "never-say-die" spirit which the Racecourse faithful appreciate, can adjust to either full-back position and pushes forward whenever he can.

Norwich C (From trainee on 6/7/93)
Wrexham (Free on 28/4/94) FL 76+6/2 FLC 6 FAC 5 Others 6

BRACEWELL Paul William
Born: Heswall, 19 July 1962
Height: 5'9" Weight: 12.5
Club Honours: CS '84, '85; ECWC '85; Div 1 '85, '93, '96; Div 2 '99
International Honours: E: 3; U21-13 (UEFAC '84)

Paul's 1998-99 season looked like being ended by an injury in early February, but his excellent distribution and linking the defence with the attack had already helped to put Fulham into first position in the Second Division, which they retained for the rest of the campaign. After four players

were injured in a bruising encounter at Burnley, he came back in the last week and when Kevin Keegan left to take the England job full time, Paul, who had been the Cottagers' player/coach, was appointed as manager.

Stoke C (From apprentice on 6/2/80) FL 123+6/5 FLC 6 FAC 6/1
Sunderland (£250,000 on 1/7/83) FL 38/4 FLC 4 FAC 2
Everton (£425,000 on 25/5/84) FL 95/7 FLC 11/2 FAC 19+2 Others 17+2/1
Sunderland (£250,000 on 23/8/89) FL 112+1/2 FLC 9 FAC 10 Others 6
Newcastle U (£250,000 on 16/6/92) F/PL 64+9/3 FLC 3+1/1 FAC 6+2 Others 2
Sunderland (£100,000 on 23/5/95) P/FL 76+1 FLC 8 FAC 3
Fulham (£75,000 on 10/10/97) FL 61+1/1 FLC 4 FAC 8 Others 2

Paul Bracewell

BRADBURY Lee Michael
Born: Isle of Wight, 3 July 1975
Height: 6'2" Weight: 13.10
International Honours: E: U21-3
Having started 1998-99 in good form with a well-taken goal in the opening fixture at home to Blackpool, the bustling Manchester City striker played 17 league and cup games, scoring four goals, before joining up with his former manager, Terry Venables, at Crystal Palace at the end of October. Became a father at Christmas and celebrated with a brilliant headed goal in the FA Cup at Newcastle but, despite working hard for the team, he could only register four goals. Then, with only half of his fee paid, and Palace in serious financial difficulties, he moved to Birmingham on loan until the end of the campaign before another appearance for Palace would have meant the balance having to be paid.

Portsmouth (Free from Cowes on 14/8/95) FL 41+13/15 FLC 1+2 FAC 4/2
Exeter C (Loaned on 1/12/95) FL 14/5
Manchester C (£3,000,000 + on 1/8/97) FL 34+6/10 FLC 6/1
Crystal Palace (£1,500,000 on 29/10/98) FL 19+3/4 FAC 1/1
Birmingham C (Loaned on 25/3/99) FL 6+1 Others 1+1

BRADLEY Shayne
Born: Gloucester, 8 December 1979
Height: 5'11" Weight: 13.2
International Honours: E: Sch
A professional signing for Southampton in January 1998 after coming through the trainee ranks, the former England schoolboy international came off the bench three times for Saints in 1998-99, his debut coming in a 1-0 defeat at Everton in December. Despite doing well with the reserve side, scoring six goals, in order to further his experience he was loaned to Swindon in transfer deadline week and played seven times before returning to the Dell. Yet to score in senior football, the striker shows good movement on and off the ball, and has the ability to get into good positions.

Southampton (From trainee on 16/1/98) PL 0+3
Swindon T (Loaned on 25/3/99) FL 6+1

BRADSHAW Carl
Born: Sheffield, 2 October 1968
Height: 5'11" Weight: 11.11
Club Honours: AMC '99
International Honours: E: Yth
Club captain at Wigan, Carl proved his versatility in 1998-99 when playing in a number of positions. Starting the season as the main choice left back, his sureness in the tackle and no lack of confidence saw him also occupy the other full-back berth, as well as a holding position in midfield. Showing wholehearted commitment, he performed well with fairness, and was delighted to lift the Auto Windscreens Shield at Wembley. As the club's regular penalty taker, his only goal came from open play in the 3-2 victory at Oldham.

Sheffield Wed (From apprentice on 23/8/86) FL 16+16/4 FLC 2+2 FAC 6+1/3 Others 1
Barnsley (Loaned on 23/8/86) FL 6/1
Manchester C (£50,000 on 30/9/88) FL 1+4 FAC 0+1 Others 0+1
Sheffield U (£50,000 on 7/9/89) F/PL 122+25/8 FLC 10+1/2 FAC 12+1/3 Others 4
Norwich C (£500,000 on 28/7/94) P/FL 55+10/2 FLC 6+1/1 FAC 2
Wigan Ath (Free on 6/10/97) FL 66+1/7 FLC 3 FAC 3 Others 6

BRADSHAW Mark
Born: Ashton under Lyne, 7 September 1969
Height: 5'10" Weight: 12.0
International Honours: E: SP-1
A Halifax signing from Macclesfield in 1995, once again Mark made the left-back position his own in 1998-99, always looking to attack, and during Town's lean spell in February and March he scored three goals. A consistent defender, who previously represented England at semi-professional level, he can also push up into midfield if required. Out of contract during the summer, at the time of going to press the club had offered him terms of re-engagement.

Blackpool (From trainee on 9/12/87) FL 34+8/1 FLC 3/1 FAC 5+1 Others 1+2 (Free to Stafford R during 1991 close season)
York C (Loaned on 16/4/91) FL 0+1
Halifax T (Free from Macclesfield T on 18/5/95) FL 41/4 FLC 3 FAC 1 Others 1/1

BRADY Garry
Born: Glasgow, 7 September 1976
Height: 5'10" Weight: 11.0
International Honours: S: Yth
Following a contract dispute with his club, Tottenham, Garry arrived at Newcastle in the summer of 1998 for a fee determined by tribunal. A Scottish youth international, he is a midfielder who likes to play in the central area and get forward to support the attack at every opportunity. Had a lengthy wait to show his abilities, making his first appearance as a substitute striker, at Goodison in late November. Another gap of six weeks ensued before he began to figure more often in the first-team squad, and he is clearly a player whom Ruud Gullit hopes will develop and grow as he gains experience alongside the foreign stars in the United squad.

Tottenham H (From trainee on 9/9/93) PL 0+9 FAC 1+1
Newcastle U (£650,000 on 15/7/98) PL 3+6 FAC 2+1

BRAMBLE Titus Malachi
Born: Ipswich, 31 July 1981
Height: 6'1" Weight: 13.10
Titus broke into the Ipswich first team just before last Christmas after producing some good performances in the reserve and academy sides, making his debut in the televised game at Sheffield United. He made quite an impression on everybody with his apparent lack of nerves and general coolness, coupled with undoubted talent in the middle of Town's defence. His second appearance was also in front of cameras – at the Stadium of Light – and again he did not look out of place. Sidelined for much of the second half of the season with a foot injury, he picked up the "Academy Player of the Year" award complete with plaster cast.

Ipswich T (From trainee on 24/8/98) FL 2+2 FAC 0+1

BRAMMER David (Dave)
Born: Bromborough, 28 February 1975
Height: 5'10" Weight: 12.0
It was assumed by many critics that Dave would be able to step up in class, having continued his impressive form of the previous campaign as a strong-running midfielder at Wrexham in 1998-99. A fine passer of the ball, and not afraid to join the attack to unload powerful shots, he eventually became a deadline day arrival in the Port Vale midfield. As a battling player who never gave up, he helped to plug a hole that had been there all season and did much to aid the team's ultimately successful battle against relegation. Ironically, he is now playing for his father's home-town team and has quickly settled into First Division football for the first time in his career.

Wrexham (From trainee on 2/7/93) FL 118+19/12 FLC 6+2 FAC 8+2/1 Others 13+2/1
Port Vale (£350,000 + on 24/3/99) FL 9

BRANAGAN Keith Graham
Born: Fulham, 10 July 1966
Height: 6'0" Weight: 13.2
Club Honours: Div 1 '97
International Honours: Ei: 1; B-1

Last season proved to be a very frustrating one for the Bolton goalkeeper, especially when you consider the confidence with which he had played in the previous season's Premiership campaign. Having missed the start of 1998-99 with ligament damage, he did not make his first appearance for the club until the 2-1 home defeat by Watford in October and, while he managed to play in four consecutive games, his ligament problem re-occurred and surgery was needed, keeping him out for the remainder of the season. Previously a vital player in the team, Keith will now have a fight on his hands to regain his place, such was the form of Steve Banks and Jussi Jaaskelainen.

Cambridge U (From juniors on 4/8/83) FL 110 FLC 12 FAC 6 Others 6
Millwall (£100,000 on 25/3/88) FL 46 FLC 1 FAC 5 Others 1
Brentford (Loaned on 24/11/89) FL 2 Others 1
Gillingham (Loaned on 1/10/91) FL 1
Bolton W (Free on 3/7/92) P/FL 203 FLC 30 FAC 10 Others 6

BRANCA Marco
Born: Grosseto, Italy, 6 January 1965
Height: 6'0" Weight: 11.7
The former Inter Milan "Hot Shot" struggled throughout last season with a mystery injury that eventually sidelined him and rendered him unable to continue playing at the demanding level of fitness required of Premiership players. The club took many specialist opinions before declaring the termination of his engagement, and he was freed to return home. Great things had been predicted for him after Middlesbrough's triumphant return to the top, especially when bearing in mind his prolific goalscoring exploits during his first year. Sadly, with his appearances being limited to just one off the bench, and with no goals to his credit this time around, the very popular striker slipped into Premiership oblivion.

Middlesbrough (£1,000,000 from Inter Milan, via Grosseto, Cagliari, Udinese, Sampdoria and Parma, on 17/2/98) P/FL 11+1/9 FLC 2/1

BRANCH Graham
Born: Liverpool, 12 February 1972
Height: 6'2" Weight: 12.2
Arriving at Stockport on a free transfer under the Bosman ruling in July 1998, County boss, Gary Megson, felt he was a Premiership standard player who had been under-achieving at Tranmere, and he hoped his no-nonsense style of management would bring out the best in a player gifted with immense natural skill. A tricky right winger or an awkward central striker, who is keen to get the defender on the back foot in either position and run directly at goal, having impressed in his first few games (he scored three goals, including one in the televised clash with Barnsley) before his form and confidence dipped, he was placed on the transfer list and moved to Burnley in December. Going straight into his new side on the left wing, and making an immediate impression with his speed and directness, scoring at Bristol Rovers, Andy Cooke's absence in March saw him moved to a central striking position, before dropping to

the bench when Stan Ternent abandoned the two-winger formation.

Tranmere Rov (Free from Heswall on 2/7/91) FL 55+47/10 FLC 4+8/1 FAC 2+1 Others 2+1
Bury (Loaned on 20/11/92) FL 3+1/1 Others 1
Wigan Ath (Loaned on 24/12/97) FL 2+1
Stockport Co (Free on 31/7/98) FL 10+4/3 FLC 1
Burnley (Free on 31/12/98) FL 14+6/1

BRANCH Paul Michael
Born: Liverpool, 18 October 1978
Height: 5'10" Weight: 11.7
International Honours: E: U21-2; Yth; Sch
A lightning-fast young Everton striker, Michael endured a frustrating season in 1998-99 after struggling to overcome a hamstring injury. Loaned out to Manchester City at the end of October, he played well in four league games and, as much as City manager Joe Royle wanted him on a more permanent basis, it was not to be. Returning to Goodison, and handed a surprise first appearance of the campaign in the Anfield derby match, it was unfair to expect too much from him on such an intense occasion. And, substituted after an hour never to figure again in 1998-99, he was made available for transfer during the summer.

Everton (From trainee on 24/10/95) PL 16+25/3 FLC 0+1 FAC 1+2
Manchester C (Loaned on 29/10/98) FL 4

BRANNAN Gerard (Ged) Daniel
Born: Prescot, 15 January 1972
Height: 6'0" Weight: 12.3
Out of favour at Manchester City in 1998-99, Ged started on loan at Norwich as a sub five games into the new campaign before going on to make 11 starts. An experienced midfielder, he certainly bolstered the Canaries' squad at a time when injuries deprived Bruce Rioch of Neil Adams, Shaun Carey, and Mike Milligan from his resources in that area of the pitch. Although asked to perform in the unfamiliar role on the right-hand side, he did very well for the team, particularly in terms of his passing skills, and scored City's goal in the 2-1 defeat at Sheffield United. Back at Maine Road, he was transferred to the Scottish League side, Motherwell, on 28 October.

Tranmere Rov (From trainee on 3/7/90) FL 227+11/20 FLC 26+1/4 FAC 10+1 Others 26+1/1
Manchester C (£750,000 on 12/3/97) FL 38+5/4 FLC 2 FAC 1
Norwich C (Loaned on 21/8/98) FL 10+1/1 FLC 1

BRANSTON Guy Peter Bromley
Born: Leicester, 9 January 1979
Height: 6'0" Weight: 13.12
Yet to make an appearance for Leicester, this strong young centre back was loaned out to Colchester (August) and Plymouth (November) to further his football education in 1998-99. Initially suspended following United's play-off game at Barnet in 1997-98, in which he was sent off, he then struggled with injury, making just one appearance, at Oldham as a sub, before returning to Filbert Street. He next spent a three-month loan period with Argyle, slotting in comfortably alongside the Argyle skipper, Mick Heathcote, and, more often

than not, being a threat at set pieces. Scored two goals in his eight-match spell.

Leicester C (From trainee on 3/7/97)
Colchester U (Loaned on 9/2/98) FL 12/1 Others 1
Colchester U (Loaned on 7/8/98) FL 0+1
Plymouth Arg (Loaned on 20/11/98) FL 7/2 Others 1

BRASS Christopher (Chris) Paul
Born: Easington, 24 July 1975
Height: 5'10" Weight: 12.6
Last season was generally a disappointing one for Burnley's former "Player of the Year", and he began the campaign at right back but was soon moved to a midfield role in which he never looked comfortable. And, for a time, he was not even an automatic first-team choice. An injury to Brian Reid in March finally let him back in his best position, at centre back, where his determination and interception skills were soon seen at their best. Also very effective as a pure man marker, as Bournemouth's Mark Stein would testify.

Burnley (From trainee on 8/7/93) FL 116+11/1 FLC 7+1 FAC 6+1 Others 8+1
Torquay U (Loaned on 14/10/94) FL 7 FAC 2 Others 1

BRAYSON Paul
Born: Newcastle, 16 September 1977
Height: 5'4" Weight: 10.10
International Honours: E: Yth
Although he played in 31 first-team matches for Reading last season, the small and compact striker rarely completed a full game, either being withdrawn or appearing as a late substitute. This clearly affected his confidence and he failed to score at senior level, though he regularly found the net for the reserves. Probably needs to be more aggressive to succeed in the rigours of Division Two football, but he is a natural goalscorer who will progress with experience.

Newcastle U (From trainee on 1/8/95) FLC 1+1
Swansea C (Loaned on 30/1/97) FL 11/5
Reading (£100,000 on 26/3/98) FL 15+19/1 FLC 0+1 FAC 1 Others 1

BRAZIER Matthew Ronald
Born: Leytonstone, 2 July 1976
Height: 5'8" Weight: 11.6
Loaned to Cardiff early on last season, Matthew proved a huge success during a 11-game stay and would have remained longer had it not been for a back injury. A skilful wide player who scored two cracking goals while at Ninian Park, with Rufus Brevett occupying the left-wing-back role to such good effect that he was named in the Divison Two PFA team, he had to be content with only four first-team starts with Fulham. Although unlucky with injuries as well, he did not let the side down when given a rare chance.

Queens Park R (From trainee on 1/7/94) P/FL 36+13/2 FLC 3+2/1 FAC 3
Fulham (£65,000 on 20/3/98) FL 4+5/1 FAC 2+1 Others 1
Cardiff C (Loaned on 28/8/98) FL 11/2

BREACKER Timothy (Tim) Sean
Born: Bicester, 2 July 1965
Height: 6'0" Weight: 13.0

Club Honours: FLC '88
International Honours: E: U21-2

Initially signed on loan last October from West Ham United, he was used by Queens Park Rangers as cover to injuries to the regular defenders. However, he made just two appearances before getting injured himself against Huddersfield and going back to Upton Park. In February, Tim returned to Rangers on a permanent basis, having been signed on a free transfer, playing on the right-hand side of defence and equally comfortable as a centre or wing back.

Luton T (From apprentice on 15/5/83) FL 204+6/3 FLC 22+2 FAC 21 Others 7
West Ham U (£600,000 on 12/10/90) F/PL 229+11/8 FLC 20+1 FAC 27+1 Others 7
Queens Park R (Loaned on 2/10/98) FL 2
Queens Park R (Free on 10/2/99) FL 16/1

BREBNER Grant Iain
Born: Edinburgh, 6 December 1977
Height: 5'10" Weight: 12.0
Club Honours: FAYC '95
International Honours: S: U21-17

One of the undoubted Reading successes of last season, Grant will always have the distinction of scoring the first-ever league goal at the Madejski Stadium, a close-range volley in the 3-0 victory over Luton. An enterprising, skilful midfielder who ended the campaign as joint-leading goalscorer with ten goals, and who also captained the Scottish U21 team, he is one of the best players who have appeared for the Royals in recent years.

Cambridge U (Loaned on 9/1/98) FL 6/1
Hibernian (Loaned on 26/2/98) SL 9/1
Reading (£300,000 on 15/6/98) FL 36+3/9 FLC 3/1 FAC 1

Grant Brebner

BRECKIN Ian
Born: Rotherham, 24 February 1975
Height: 6'0" Weight: 12.9
Club Honours: AMC '96

Ian developed into a fine, perceptive Chesterfield defender in 1998-99, operating equally well in the centre of a back four, or as one of three centre halves, as tactics demand. His reading of the game and anticipation has come on so much over one season that terrace wags nicknamed him "Breckinbauer". To the unsuspecting, he looks as though he might benefit from a diet of Guinness and steak but, as soon as the whistle blows, he neither gives nor expects any quarter against the most physical opponents.

Rotherham U (From trainee on 1/11/93) FL 130+2/6 FLC 6 FAC 5 Others 11
Chesterfield (£100,000 on 25/7/97) FL 84+3/3 FLC 7 FAC 4/1 Others 2

BREEN Gary Patrick
Born: Hendon, 12 December 1973
Height: 6'2" Weight: 12.0
International Honours: Ei: 20; U21-9

A skilful, right-footed central defender who likes to bring the ball out of defence and who is also very good in the air, Gary started last season at Coventry as the first-choice centre half alongside Jean-Guy Wallemme. Although he lost his place to Paul Williams after injury forced him out in November, he was, however, able to regain his place in the Republic of Ireland team, for whom he always played well. Returned to the City side as a right back, following Roland Nilsson's serious injury and was more comfortable in that role than previously, before playing the last three games of the season at centre half. In his absence, the side missed his presence at the near post on corners, but off-the-field problems such as missing the team bus to Southend did not help his case, and he indicated that he would like to move on during the summer.

Maidstone U (Free from Charlton Ath juniors on 6/3/92) FL 19
Gillingham (Free on 2/7/92) FL 45+6 FLC 4 FAC 5 Others 1
Peterborough U (£70,000 on 5/8/94) FL 68+1/1 FLC 6 FAC 6 Others 6/1
Birmingham C (£400,000 on 9/2/96) FL 37+3/2 FLC 4 FAC 1
Coventry C (£2,400,000 on 1/2/97) PL 59+5/1 FLC 5+1 FAC 6

BRENNAN James (Jim) Gerald
Born: Toronto, Canada, 8 May 1977
Height: 5'9" Weight: 12.5

A Canadian international who, in the opinion of the Bristol City coach, Benny Lennartsson, has shown the biggest improvement of all the players during his time at the club. In 1998-99 at right back he was switched to his more natural role of left back. Has great pace, the ability to get forward to support the front players and, in addition to his dangerous crosses, he possesses a strong shot. Was a strong candidate for City's "Player of the Season".

Bristol C (Free from Sora Lazio on 25/10/94) FL 40+3/1 FLC 2 FAC 1

BRESLAN Geoffrey (Geoff) Francis
Born: Torbay, 4 June 1980
Height: 5'8" Weight: 11.0

Although Geoff is still a trainee, he again did exceptionally well for Exeter last term. After progressing through the City ranks, the midfielder's eye-catching displays had the scouts visiting St James' Park, and he chipped in with a share of the goals, including the only goal of the game at play-off hunting Mansfield in April. Playing on the wide left, he is also a good crosser of the ball.

Exeter C (From trainee on 7/1/99) FL 24+11/4 FLC 2 FAC 1+2 Others 2

BREVETT Rufus Emanuel
Born: Derby, 24 September 1969
Height: 5'8" Weight: 11.6
Club Honours: Div 2 '99

A great crowd pleaser, Rufus' sorties down the left flank brought Fulham several vital goals in their successful quest for promotion in 1998-99, while his selection for the PFA award-winning side and Second Division championship medal was well earned. Very strong and quick into the tackle, with an excellent recovery rate, next season in Division One will give him more opportunity to show his defensive qualities. Missed just two games throughout the campaign, his first full one at the Cottage, and scored his first goal for the club in a 1-0 home win over Stoke.

Doncaster Rov (From trainee on 8/7/88) FL 106+3/3 FLC 5 FAC 4 Others 10+1
Queens Park R (£250,000 on 15/2/91) F/PL 141+11/1 FLC 9+1 FAC 8
Fulham (£375,000 on 28/1/98) FL 56/1 FLC 5 FAC 5 Others 2

BRIDGE Wayne Michael
Born: Southampton, 5 August 1980
Height: 5'10" Weight: 11.11
International Honours: E: U21-1; Yth

Signing pro forms in early 1998, this Southampton midfielder graduated from the youth team. Usually playing wide and possessing great pace, Wayne made 16 starts in 1998-99, his first season at senior level, plus another eight as a substitute and grew in confidence as a result. Making his first-team debut when coming off the bench at home to Liverpool in the opening match, and notching his first start at Charlton a few days later, his rapid progress earned him an England U21 cap in May.

Southampton (From trainee on 16/1/98) PL 15+8 FLC 1

BRIDGE-WILKINSON Marc
Born: Nuneaton, 16 March 1979
Height: 5'6 Weight: 11.0

A young reserve midfielder who made his Derby debut as a sub in the 2-1 win at Liverpool last November, he proved to be a forceful and positive player, hence the move up. Not afraid to shoot from distance, having a good scoring record for the reserves, he was loaned out to Carlisle in March to further his experience. Despite his obvious pedigree and ability on the ball, Derby's former "Young Player of the Year" never really imposed himself on the game in a way that might have been hoped and he returned to Pride Park in early April. It is thought that his versatility will be a useful factor in the coming campaign.

Derby Co (From trainee on 26/3/97) PL 0+1
Carlisle U (Loaned on 5/3/99) FL 4+3

BRIDGES Michael
Born: North Shields, 5 August 1978
Height: 6'1" Weight: 10.11
Club Honours: Div 1 '96, '99
International Honours: E: U21-2; Yth; Sch
Sunderland's quicksilver England U21 striker found his first-team opportunities limited last season, but still picked up a second First Division championship medal, weighing in with some typically outstanding goals, including braces against Oxford and Sheffield United, and a truly classy finish in the Worthington Cup at Everton. Tall, speedy, and tremendously skilful, Michael gained further Young England honours against France in February, but was unfairly asked to play up front on his own and was subbed at half time. Nevertheless, speculation constantly linked him to a host of top clubs and, at the time of writing, Sunderland have taken steps to alleviate fans' fears that he could leave by preparing a new six-year contract for him.
Sunderland (From trainee on 9/11/95) P/FL 31+48/16 FLC 8+3/5 FAC 2

BRIGHT Mark Abraham
Born: Stoke, 6 June 1962
Height: 6'1" Weight: 12.2
Club Honours: FMC '91
An experienced striker, Mark did not make his first start last season until the game at Everton near the end of the campaign, having made only a handful of substitute appearances for Charlton. He scored with his head shortly after coming on as a substitute against Newcastle at The Valley, helping the Addicks secure a 2-2 draw. Tall and dangerous in the air, he was at his most effective running on to crosses put in by the wingmen. Having announced his intention to retire during the summer, it is his intention to work in the media.
Port Vale (Free from Leek T on 15/10/81) FL 18+11/10 FLC 1+1 FAC 0+1/1 Others 2
Leicester C (£33,000 on 19/7/84) FL 26+16/6 FLC 3+1 FAC 1
Crystal Palace (£75,000 on 13/11/86) F/PL 224+3/92 FLC 22/11 FAC 13+1/2 Others 23/9
Sheffield Wed (£1,375,000 on 11/9/92) PL 112+21/48 FLC 20+1/11 FAC 13/7 (Free to Sion on 27/1/97)
Millwall (Loaned on 13/12/96) FL 3/1 Others 1
Charlton Ath (Free on 4/4/97) P/FL 18+10/10 FLC 0+3 FAC 2+2 Others 3

BRIGHTWELL David John
Born: Lutterworth, 7 January 1971
Height: 6'2" Weight: 13.5
Signed from Northampton during the 1998 close season, this experienced and powerful central defender was another recruit to Carlisle ranks for 1998-99. Ever present, apart from a handful of games missed through injury, his influence on the side grew as the term progressed, not just as a very solid centre half but in an attacking role at set pieces. His 25-yard equalising volley in the vital Plymouth game at the end of the campaign brought United back into contention and provided the platform for Jimmy Glass' astonishing finale.
Manchester C (From juniors on 11/4/88) F/PL 35+8/1 FLC 2+1 FAC 5+2/1
Chester C (Loaned on 22/3/91) FL 6

Lincoln C (Loaned on 11/8/95) FL 5 FLC 2
Stoke C (Loaned on 11/9/95) FL 0+1 Others 1
Bradford C (£30,000 on 22/12/95) FL 23+1 FAC 1 Others 2
Blackpool (Loaned on 12/12/96) FL 1+1
Northampton T (Free on 29/7/97) FL 34+1/1 FLC 2 FAC 5 Others 2+1
Carlisle U (Free on 10/7/98) FL 41/4 FLC 2 FAC 1 Others 1

BRIGHTWELL Ian Robert
Born: Lutterworth, 9 April 1968
Height: 5'10" Weight: 12.5
International Honours: E: U21-4; Yth
Released during the 1998 close season, the ex-Manchester City defender joined Coventry in June 1998, but was hampered by injuries for most of the campaign. When fit he was unable to put pressure on the consistent Roland Nilsson and played in only one game, the dismal Worthington Cup defeat at Luton. However, by the end of the season his injury problems had cleared up and he was a regular for the reserves in central defence, before being given a free transfer during the summer. Is the brother of Carlisle's David, and the son of two famous Olympic athletes.
Manchester C (From juniors on 7/5/86) F/PL 285+36/18 FLC 29+2 FAC 19+4/1 Others 4+3
Coventry C (Free on 2/7/98) FLC 1

BRIGHTWELL Stuart
Born: Easington, 31 January 1979
Height: 5'6" Weight: 10.11
International Honours: E: Sch; Yth
Diminutive right winger who trained with Hartlepool at the end of 1997-98, before signing a contract in the 1998 close season to get first-team football after ten years experience in the junior ranks at Manchester United. Although getting his chance early on it was only when he had lost some weight that he began to play his best football. However, always on the fringe of the senior squad despite a lengthy run in mid term, as the weeks progressed his chances became fewer. Was released on a free transfer during the summer.
Manchester U (From trainee on 8/2/96)
Hartlepool U (Free on 20/7/98) FL 8+9/1 FLC 0+1 FAC 1+1 Others 0+1/1

BRISCO Neil Anthony
Born: Wigan, 26 January 1978
Height: 6'0" Weight: 11.5
Released by Manchester City during the summer of 1998, Neil, a lively midfield player, joined Port Vale prior to the start of last season, initially on trial, before gaining a contract a month later. He made a surprise debut on live television against Liverpool in the FA Cup and held his place for the following league game at Birmingham before returning to the reserves. A tough tackler who never gives up, he has signed a new contract and looks to have a bright future in the game.
Manchester C (From trainee on 4/3/97)
Port Vale (Free on 7/8/98) FL 1 FAC 1

BRISCOE Lee Stephen
Born: Pontefract, 30 September 1975
Height: 5'11" Weight: 11.12
International Honours: E: U21-5

Although a promising left-sided midfielder or defender, Lee was again unable to obtain a regular place in the Sheffield Wednesday side last season. full of commitment and endeavour, he always gave his all when selected but somehow failed to find the consistency to impress the new boss, Danny Wilson. Typical of his luck was his superb last-minute winner against Arsenal at Hillsbrough. It was such a great goal, but it was completely overshadowed by the Paulo Di Canio incident with the referee. So his big moment came and went and he only played the odd game thereafter. A neat, athletic player with a good left foot, he deserves a consistent first-team place. Maybe 1999-2000 will be his season!
Sheffield Wed (From trainee on 22/5/94) PL 41+21/1 FLC 3+1 FAC 0+2
Manchester C (Loaned on 20/2/98) FL 5/1

Lee Briscoe

BRISSETT Jason Curtis
Born: Wanstead, 7 September 1974
Height: 5'10" Weight: 12.7
Signed free from Bournemouth in July 1998, his blistering pace and his ability to run at opponents made him a vital part of Walsall's attacking force in 1998-99. Though sent off three times during the season, both dismissals against Preston were extremely harsh, and he came back to play a vital role in the win against Oldham. Seen at his best when attacking down the left-hand side to get in crosses, he can also play up front to good effect.
Peterborough U (Free from Arsenal juniors on 14/6/93) FL 27+8 FLC 5+1/1 FAC 2+1/1 Others 3+1/1
Bournemouth (Free on 23/12/94) 96+28/8 FLC 5+2 FAC 4 Others 6+2/2
Walsall (Free on 31/7/98) FL 27+8/2 FLC 2 FAC 1 Others 3+2

BRODIE Stephen (Steve) Eric
Born: Sunderland, 14 January 1973
Height: 5'7" Weight: 10.6
The pacy Scarborough striker was a big favourite with the fans in 1998-99, missing just three games, and was always willing to run and chase every ball. He made much of

his own luck and scored some spectacular goals into he bargain, including a stunning 25-yard volley to earn a 1-0 win at Torquay. Asked to be put on the transfer list when the club dropped into the Conference.

Sunderland (From trainee on 1/7/91) FL 1+11
Doncaster Rov (Loaned on 31/8/95) FL 5/1
Scarborough (Free on 20/12/96) FL 109+2/27 FLC 4 FAC 3 Others 2+1

BROOKER Paul

Born: Hammersmith, 25 November 1976
Height: 5'8" Weight: 10.0

With a total of 35 minutes first-team action in two substitute appearances for Fulham in 1998-99, Paul obviously didn't figure in Kevin Keegan's plans, and had a trial with Portsmouth just before the end of the season. Is still the same exciting right-sided midfielder or striker, who was the fans' hero in Fulham's 1996-97 promotion campaign, but was unable to find the vital final pass or shot to go with his superb dribbling ability.

Fulham (From trainee on 1/7/95) FL 13+43/4 FLC 1+2/1 FAC 1+3/1 Others 3+3

BROOMES Marlon Charles

Born: Birmingham, 28 November 1977
Height: 6'0" Weight: 12.12
International Honours: E: U21-2; Yth; Sch

A freak pre-1998-99 season injury that caused his leg to be placed in plaster because of ligament damage was yet another set back in an injury-strewn career at Blackburn. It was not until November that he could join the first-team squad, but by the turn of the year he had taken over from Darren Peacock and was playing superbly. Although lacking height, he is superbly athletic and attacks the high ball with aggression. His close-range shot blocking was almost "Colin Hendry-like" and during January he was improving every game. Tragedy struck again when he was sucked into a dispute with Gianluca Vialli at Chelsea that earned both men a dismissal, although it was difficult to see what offence Marlon committed. Lightning was almost to strike twice when, felled by a blow from Dennis Bergkamp at Arsenal, he was booked for alleged diving. For a young player he is remarkably mature and is one of the defence's talkers.

Blackburn Rov (From trainee on 28/11/94) PL 10+7 FLC 1 FAC 4
Swindon T (Loaned on 22/1/97) FL 12/1

BROUGHTON Drewe Oliver

Born: Hitchin, 25 October 1978
Height: 6'3" Weight: 12.0

Starting last season with Norwich, the tall, rangy forward found it difficult to create an impact at the club after showing so much promise on breaking into the side in 1996-97, and was allowed to leave for Brentford at the end of October. Surprisingly, he made just one appearance for the Bees, being substituted and transferred to Peterborough inside three weeks. Possessing an excellent first touch for such a big man, he flitted in and out of his new team but still managed seven goals in 14 league starts.

Norwich C (From trainee on 6/5/97) FL 3+6/1

Wigan Ath (Loaned on 15/8/97) FL 1+3
Brentford (Signed on 30/10/98) FL 1
Peterborough U (Signed on 17/11/98) FL 14+11/7 Others 1+1/1

BROWN Aaron Wesley

Born: Bristol, 14 March 1980
Height: 5'10" Weight: 11.12
International Honours: E: Sch

A former England Schoolboy international who has progressed through the Bristol City Football Academy, Aaron made his first-team debut for the club in 1998-99, his highlight being an outstanding performance in midfield at West Bromwich Albion. Showing great promise when played in central midfield, with strong tackling and the ability to get forward in support of the front players, City has big hopes for him. All in all, he is an excellent prospect who is sure to do well in the coming campaign.

Bristol C (From trainee on 7/11/97) FL 14

BROWN Daniel (Danny)

Born: London, 12 September 1980
Height: 6'0" Weight: 12.0

A young Leyton Orient left-sided midfielder, and a first-year professional, Danny was rewarded for his good performances in the youth team and reserves with a call up to the senior side that played in the Auto Windscreens Shield game at Peterborough last season. Hungry for the ball, he competes well and likes to run at defenders. Is also a good passer. Stop Press: Signed for Barnet on 24 May.

Leyton Orient (From trainee on 5/5/98) Others 1

BROWN David Alistair

Born: Bolton, 2 October 1978
Height: 5'10" Weight: 12.6

A pre-season capture from Manchester United, David was high on manager Mark Hateley's shopping list, having impressed in a seven-game loan spell at the end of 1997-98. Despite his lack of experience, young "Brownie" was given the thankless task of shouldering the attacking responsibility of a struggling team, and made an impressively manful job of it. Doing very well to reach double figures, he should do even better with the likes of Colin Alcide alongside him up front.

Manchester U (From trainee on 27/10/95)
Hull C (Free on 26/3/98) FL 45+4/13 FLC 4/3 FAC 3 Others 2

BROWN Grant Ashley

Born: Sunderland, 19 November 1969
Height: 6'0" Weight: 11.12

This Lincoln central defender was in and out of the team for much of last season and finished the campaign as a regular on the subs' bench. His 21 league starts brought his career total with City to 324, giving him the fourth highest total in the club's history after ten seasons at Sincil Bank. Scored just one goal, in the 4-3 home defeat at the hands of Preston North End.

Leicester C (From trainee on 1/7/88) FL 14 FLC 2
Lincoln C (£60,000 on 20/8/89) FL 324+1/13 FLC 20/1 FAC 13 Others 18+1/2

BROWN Gregory (Greg) Jonathan

Born: Manchester, 31 July 1978
Height: 5'11" Weight: 12.6

On non-contract forms in 1997-98, Greg signed professional forms in the 1998 close season to play in the newly formed Macclesfield reserve team. Playing a solid part in a fairly invincible reserve defence and attracting a host of non-league scouts, in the second half of the campaign he was loaned out to Chorley and Morecambe, eventually being called back from the latter to fill a defensive position in the first team, when injuries and suspensions left a gap. Not afraid to go forward, he was the nearest Macclesfield player to scoring in his Second Division debut, at Walsall.

Chester C (From trainee on 20/6/96) FL 1+3 FAC 0+1 Others 0+1
Macclesfield T (Free on 19/12/97) FL 7

BROWN Jonathan (Jon)

Born: Barnsley, 8 September 1966
Height: 5'10" Weight: 11.6

As a Halifax ever dependable, Jon is a good passer of the ball, can play in a variety of positions and, although a regular in the midfield, he also excels as sweeper if required. Never short of a word or two, and the club joker, his continued absence on the score sheet did not get to him. Was released in the summer.

Exeter C (£1,500 from Denaby U on 1/7/90) FL 149+15/3 FLC 9 FAC 12+1/1 Others 17/1
Halifax T (Free on 12/7/95) FL 32+8 FLC 3 FAC 1 Others 0+1

Jon Brown

BROWN Kenneth (Kenny) James

Born: Upminster, 11 July 1967
Height: 5'9" Weight: 11.6

Having failed to make an appearance at Millwall last season, Kenny was signed on transfer deadline day until the end of the

season, his experience being vital to Gillingham's cause as they battled to reach the play offs. In the 4-1 victory at Oldham in late April, he was involved in a four-man move that resulted in one of Gills' goals of the season, when Paul Smith headed home his pin-point cross. A player who can play in any number of defensive positions, possibly being more effective as a right-wing back where he gets forward well, he is the son of the former West Ham and England centre half, Ken (senior).

Norwich C (From juniors on 10/7/85) FL 24+1 Others 3
Plymouth Arg (Free on 10/8/88) FL 126/4 FLC 9 FAC 6 Others 3
West Ham U (£175,000 on 2/8/91) F/PL 55+8/5 FLC 2+1 FAC 7+2/1 Others 2+2
Huddersfield T (Loaned on 7/9/95) FL 5
Reading (Loaned on 27/10/95) FL 12/1 FLC 3
Southend U (Loaned on 1/3/96) FL 6
Crystal Palace (Loaned on 28/3/96) FL 5+1/2 Others 3/1
Reading (Loaned on 9/9/96) FL 5
Birmingham C (£75,000 on 27/12/96) FL 11 FAC 1
Millwall (£40,000 + on 31/7/97) FL 45 FLC 4 FAC 1 Others 2
Gillingham (Free on 25/3/99) FL 2+2 Others 0+1

BROWN Michael (Mickey) Antony
Born: Birmingham, 8 February 1968
Height: 5'9" Weight: 11.12
Club Honours: Div 3 '94
Continuing his third spell with Shrewsbury in 1998-99, Mickey was asked to play in attack, midfield and as a wing back during the season. Combined effectively up front with marksman, Lee Steele, but was most at home on the right wing. Never gets the goals his contribution deserves but, when they come, they're usually spectacular. Out of contract during the summer, he is strong on the ball and brilliant in tight spots.

Shrewsbury T (From apprentice on 11/2/86) FL 174+16/9 FLC 17/2 FAC 10/1 Others 11
Bolton W (£100,000 on 15/8/91) FL 27+6/3 FLC 0+1 FAC 3 Others 2
Shrewsbury T (£25,000 on 23/12/92) FL 66+1/11 FLC 8/1 FAC 3 Others 2
Preston NE (£75,000 on 30/11/94) FL 11+5/1 FLC 0+1 Others 1
Rochdale (Loaned on 13/9/96) FL 5
Shrewsbury T (£20,000 on 12/12/96) FL 56+27/5 FLC 1+1 FAC 1 Others 4+1

BROWN Michael Robert
Born: Hartlepool, 25 January 1977
Height: 5'9" Weight: 11.8
International Honours: E: U21-4
After an indifferent 1997-98 season, Michael was only on the fringe of Manchester City's first team in 1998-99 and up until the end of November had played only one full game and made seven substitute appearances. Brought back into the senior team for the FA Cup replay at home against Darlington, he was a born-again player. His approach was consistent and he capped an excellent display when scoring a spectacular goal to win the game in extra time, after dribbling through the defence, passing three defenders, and placing the ball from an angle into the net. (One equal in quality to Georgiou Kinkladze's of past seasons). It was also his

first goal for the club. This was the start of an unbroken run that saw him become established in midfield, covering the field and foraging and chasing loose balls for 90 minutes. Following a chat with Joe Royle, City's manager, his attitude became more mature, he began to walk away from confrontations and showed much more composure. There was no doubting that his performances made a big impact towards the team's successes in the second half of the campaign, before he was surprisingly released in the summer.

Manchester C (From trainee on 13/9/94) F/PL 67+22/2 FLC 1+4 FAC 10+1/2 Others 4
Hartlepool U (Loaned on 27/3/97) F/PL 41+17 FLC 1+3 FAC 8/1

BROWN Steven (Steve) Byron
Born: Brighton, 13 May 1972
Height: 6'1" Weight: 13.10
Steve was brought into the Charlton side early last season in his favoured central defensive position after Richard Rufus was suspended. A tall, versatile, right-sided defender, who had played most of his previous games for the Addicks at right back, he featured in about half of the Premiership games and was a revelation, usually looking the best central defender on show. Excellent in the air, and a player who distributes the ball well and possesses an extremely hard shot, he is also a very capable emergency goalkeeper. This was seen to good advantage when he came on for the last quarter of an hour in a 4-2 win at Aston Villa, replacing the red-carded Andy Petterson, and immediately made a brilliant save from the resulting free kick.

Charlton Ath (From trainee on 3/7/90) P/FL 139+21/5 FLC 7+2 FAC 13/1 Others 3+2

BROWN Steven (Steve) Ferold
Born: Northampton, 6 July 1966
Height: 6'0" Weight: 11.8
A popular left-footed midfielder for Wycombe, who is both an effective tackler with his long legs, and a creative passer of the ball. He likes to run at defences and shoot, and the pick of his five goals were a long-range volley against Swindon in the Worthington Cup and a 25-yard shot at home to Lincoln. Disappointed with his disciplinary record, which brought about a number of suspensions and disrupted both his and the team's rhythm, when on top form, which he was mid season, he is one of the outstanding midfielders at this level.

Northampton T (From juniors on 11/8/83) FL 14+1/3 (Free to Irthlingborough T in December 1985)
Northampton T (Free on 21/7/89) FL 145+13/19 FLC 10/1 FAC 12/2 Others 10+1/1
Wycombe W (£60,000 on 9/2/94) FL 186+13/14 FLC 13+2/2 FAC 10+1 Others 7+2

BROWN Steven (Steve) Robert
Born: Southend, 6 December 1973
Height: 6'0" Weight: 12.7
Signed from Lincoln during the summer of 1998, and looking impressive up front in Macclesfield's first pre-season run out, Steve, an experienced, hard-running, bustling striker broke down in training with

shin splints and had to sit it out until the end of August before making his first-team debut. However, he failed to impress manager, Sammy McIlroy, after four games and was consigned to the reserves, where he was a prolific goalscorer. Had a three-month loan spell with Irish club, Waterford, from November through to February, and then signed on loan for Conference outfit, Dover, at the end of February.

Southend U (From trainee on 10/7/92) FL 10/2 FAC 0+1 Others 1
Scunthorpe U (Free on 5/7/93)
Colchester U (Free on 27/8/93) FL 56+6/17 FLC 2 FAC 5/1 Others 4/1
Gillingham (Signed on 22/3/95) FL 8+1/2
Lincoln C (£20,000 on 6/10/95) FL 47+25/8 FLC 0+3 FAC 3+1 Others 3+1/1
Macclesfield T (Free on 21/7/98) FL 1+1 FLC 1+1

BROWN Wayne Larry
Born: Southampton, 14 January 1977
Height: 6'1" Weight: 11.12
Now in his third season with the club, indifferent form in 1998-99 saw Wayne share the goalkeeper's jersey with Neil Cutler, finally making 23 appearances in the league. Is a good shot stopper who looks to have a future in the game, given a little more experience.

Bristol C (From trainee on 3/7/95) FL 1 (Free to Weston super Mare during 1996 close season)
Chester C (Free on 30/9/96) FL 38 FLC 3 FAC 2 Others 1

BROWN Wayne Lawrence
Born: Barking, 20 August 1977
Height: 6'0" Weight: 12.6
Despite the promise of the previous season, Wayne was unable to force his way into Ipswich's 1998-99 record-equalling defence and, indeed, found himself further back in the ranking with Titus Bramble given preference over him when opportunities arose. A central defender with good aerial strength, he made just the one substitute appearance in the televised game at Sheffield United.

Ipswich T (From trainee on 16/5/96) FL 1+1
Colchester U (Loaned on 16/10/97) FL 0+2

BROWN Wesley (Wes) Michael
Born: Manchester, 16 March 1979
Height: 6'1" Weight: 12.2
Club Honours: EC '99; PL '99
International Honours: E: 1; U21-7; Yth; Sch
A solid Manchester United full back, or central defender, who is good in the air, with pace and confidence to match, Wes sent out a message of hope to all those promising youngsters who are worried about the growing influx of cosmopolitan stars flocking to these shores: "If you're good enough, you'll still get there." Of course, Wes is not just good enough, he is something really special, as his progression from Lancashire League to Champions' League in two seasons so ably demonstrates. Brought into the side at the beginning of last October, as a substitute against Southampton at the Dell, he gave some sterling performances in the Premiership, the Worthington Cup (where he became the 22nd United youngster to be given a League

Cup outing) and the Champions' League. His quality really came to the fore, however, during United's vital European Cup-tie against Bayern at Old Trafford in December, when one tackle on the former World Cup winner, Luther Matthais, convinced everyone that here was a boy with a tremendous future. Although he only made three starts in December, he was back in contention after Christmas, giving an impressive display against Chelsea in the FA Cup, when Jaap Stam was serving a one-match suspension. Playing at the peak of his form, it came as no surprise when Kevin Keegan rewarded him with a full England cap for the friendly against Hungary in April. The following day, Alex Ferguson gave him a new five-year contract. For Wes, the only way is up! Played seven times for the England U21 side in 1998-99.

Manchester U (From trainee on 13/11/96) PL 12+4/2 FLC 0+1 FAC 2 Others 3+1

Wes Brown

BROWNE Anthony (Tony)
Born: Sheerness, 12 February 1977
Height: 5'10" Weight: 11.10
Having played for Gravesend & Northfleet following a YTS apprenticeship at West Ham, this left back impressed while on trial in the reserves at Brighton last October and was initially awarded a one-month contract which was later extended to the end of the season. Excelled in his debut at Barnet, his first Football League match, but lost his place as a result of suspension and illness and, despite a further appearance at home to Leyton Orient, he never broke back into the side before being disappointingly released at the end of the campaign.
Brighton & Hove A (Free from Gravesend & Northfleet on 22/10/98) FL 13 FAC 1 Others 1

BROWNE Stafford Ernet
Born: Haywards Heath, 4 January 1971
Height: 5'10" Weight: 12.8
A lively centre forward who signed for

Brighton from Hastings Town last July, after a trial period, he unfortunately suffered injuries which restricted his chances to impress, and found it difficult to adjust to the pace of the professional game. Was released in October and joined Welling United in November.
Brighton & Hove A (Free from Hastings T on 31/7/98) FL 2+1

BROWNING Marcus Trevor
Born: Bristol, 22 April 1971
Height: 6'0" Weight: 12.10
International Honours: W: 5
Having started last season for Huddersfield at Bury, little did this industrious midfielder know that after just nine minutes he would be thrust in goal to deputise for the sent-off 'keeper. Even in this position he performed admirably. Adaptable in a midfield or forward role, Marcus then joined Gillingham in November on loan, but his debut was cut short at Manchester City after 69 minutes when he suffered serious cruiciate knee ligament damage. The Gills' manager, Tony Pulis, kept a check on his fitness and in transfer deadline week, he signed him on a permanent basis but, unfortunately, his injury problems continued when he lasted just 16 minutes in the 2-0 victory at Wycombe in early April. A strong tackler, whose forward runs take him into dangerous positions, hopefully, he can come back renewed in 1999-2000.
Bristol Rov (From trainee on 1/7/89) FL 152+22/13 FLC 7+3 FAC 8/1 Others 13+5/3
Hereford U (Loaned on 18/9/92) FL 7/5
Huddersfield T (£500,000 on 17/2/97) FL 25+8 FLC 2+2
Gillingham (Loaned on 20/11/98) FL 1
Gillingham (£150,000 on 25/3/99) FL 0+3

BRUCE Paul Mark
Born: London, 18 February 1978
Height: 5'11" Weight: 12.0
Not selected for Queens Park Rangers in 1998-99, having promised much the previous season, Paul was loaned out to bolster the Cambridge team in the promotion run-in. An attack-minded left-sided player who can perform equally well in midfield or further forward, he failed to make an immediate impact, but his pin-point crosses and deadly free kicks promised much for the future.
Queens Park R (From trainee on 15/7/96) FL 1+4/1 FAC 0+3
Cambridge U (Loaned on 25/3/99) FL 2+2

BRUCE Stephen (Steve) Roger
Born: Corbridge, 31 December 1960
Height: 6'0" Weight: 13.0
Club Honours: Div 2 '86, PL '93, '94, '96; FLC '85, '92; FAC '90, '94; CS '93, '94; ECWC '91; ESC '91
International Honours: E: B-1; Yth
Signed from Birmingham during the 1998 close season, Steve made his debut as Sheffield United's player/manager on the opening day of 1998-99 at home to Swindon and thus became the first United manager to appear for the club in a league fixture. Performing his usual defensive role, although not as fast as in the past his

experience showed through. His final game of the season was the 4-0 home defeat by Sunderland, a hamstring problem preventing him playing again, although he hopes to be available for the coming term. Stop Press: Having left Sheffield United the previous week, Steve signed a three-year deal as manager of Huddersfield on 24 May.
Gillingham (From apprentice on 27/10/78) FL 203+2/29 FLC 15/6 FAC 14/1
Norwich C (£125,000 on 24/8/84) FL 141/14 FLC 20/5 FAC 9/1 Others 10
Manchester U (£800,000 on 18/12/87) F/PL 309/36 FLC 32+2/6 FAC 41/3 Others 32+2/7
Birmingham C (Free on 17/6/96) FL 70+2/2 FLC 6 FAC 6/1
Sheffield U (£200,000 on 22/7/98) FL 10 FLC 1

BRUMWELL Phillip (Phil)
Born: Darlington, 8 August 1975
Height: 5'8" Weight: 11.0
One of only three players remaining at Darlington from the Wembley play-off team of 1996, Phil proved an invaluable squad player in 1998-99, operating in almost every defensive and midfield position during the season. One of the few local members of the team, he can always be relied upon to give everything for his hometown club and is a strong-tackling, tenacious performer.
Sunderland (From trainee on 30/6/94)
Darlington (Free on 11/8/95) FL 97+41/1 FLC 5+2 FAC 6+4/2 Others 5+3

BRYAN Derek (Del) Kirk
Born: London, 11 November 1974
Height: 5'10" Weight: 11.5
Club Honours: Div 3 '99
Speedy right-sided Brentford forward and former non-leaguer, Del was out injured until last November, but came back strongly as a regular in the 14 strong squad to win himself a Third Division championship medal. Often thrown into a game late on to use his pace to create chances, he weighed in with four goals and continued to show much promise.
Brentford (£50,000 from Hampton on 28/8/97) FL 11+20/6 FAC 0+3 Others 1+1

BRYAN Marvin Lee
Born: Paddington, 2 August 1975
Height: 6'0" Weight: 12.2
This Blackpool full back was again seen at his best, in 1998-99, when getting down the right flank to cause problems to the opposing defence; just what you would expect of a former out-and-out wingman. Also difficult to pass at the back, due to speed of recovery, Marvin got his usual goal, a last-minute equaliser at Reading when all seemed lost.
Queens Park R (From trainee on 17/8/92)
Doncaster Rov (Loaned on 8/12/94) FL 5/1
Blackpool (£20,000 on 10/8/95) FL 158+6/4 FLC 10+2 FAC 6 Others 12

BRYANT Matthew (Matt)
Born: Bristol, 21 September 1970
Height: 6'1" Weight: 13.2
A back injury sustained last March, meant that Matt had to miss Gillingham's surge into the play offs, although he was struggling to gain a regular first-team place at the time. Probably the quickest defender

on the club's books, and excellent in the air at both ends of the pitch, he was used in the early part of the season in the unaccustomed position of full back.

Bristol C (From trainee on 1/7/89) FL 201+2/7 FLC 9+1 FAC 11 Others 9
Walsall (Loaned on 24/8/90) FL 13 FLC 4
Gillingham (£65,000 on 8/8/96) FL 79+18 FLC 9+1 FAC 3+1 Others 4

BRYSON James Ian Cook
Born: Kilmarnock, 26 November 1962
Height: 5'11" Weight: 12.12
Club Honours: Div 3 '96

After missing the first few games of 1998-99, Ian became Rochdale's most influential midfielder as they recovered from a dire start to the season. His contribution was especially vital in the FA Cup, with goals in both games against Scarborough, running half the length of the field to settle the replay with a last-minute winner. The injury jinx of the previous campaign hit again, though, and he was sidelined in February, only reappearing in the final weeks, before being released in the summer.

Kilmarnock (Signed from Hurlford on 22/10/81) SL 194+21/40 SLC 12+7/1 SC 14+2/3
Sheffield U (£40,000 on 24/8/88) F/PL 138+17/36 FLC 11+2/1 FAC 18+4/4 Others 7/3
Barnsley (£20,000 on 12/8/93) FL 16/3 FLC 2/1 Others 2
Preston NE (£42,500 on 29/11/93) FL 141+10/19 FLC 6+1/1 FAC 7+2/1 Others 12/1
Rochdale (Free on 21/7/97) FL 43+11/1 FLC 1 FAC 5/2 Others 2

BUBB Byron James
Born: Harrow, 17 December 1981
Height: 5'7" Weight: 10.5

Another product of the Millwall youth policy, turning professional in December 1998, after putting in some good performances in the reserves he made his first-team debut last season against Colchester and helped the Lions to a 2-0 victory after they fielded a reserve side prior to the Auto Windshields final. A fast and tricky winger who can also play in midfield, his pace is outstanding and he looks to be a great prospect for the future.

Millwall (From trainee on 30/12/98) FL 1+2

BUCKLE Paul John
Born: Hatfield, 16 December 1970
Height: 5'8" Weight: 11.10
Club Honours: Div 3 '92

Paul enjoyed another all-action season in Colchester's engine room, and was the only player in the club to feature in the squad for every game in 1998-99. A regular until losing his automatic place when Aaron Skelton briefly returned to fitness, he then fought his way back into the team and finished the campaign spectacularly with some dynamic performances. Scored the opening goals in two bottom-of-the-table six pointers against Notts County and Northampton. Out of contract during the summer, at the time of going to press it was known that the club had made him an offer of re-engagement.

Brentford (From trainee on 1/7/89) FL 42+15/1 FLC 5+1 FAC 3+1 Others 6+5

Torquay U (Free on 3/2/94) FL 57+2/9 FLC 8 FAC 3 Others 1
Exeter C (Free on 13/10/95) FL 22/2 FAC 1 Others 2
Northampton T (Free on 30/8/96)
Wycombe W (Free on 18/10/96)
Colchester U (Free on 28/11/96) FL 96+9/7 FLC 4 FAC 2 Others 10/3

BUCKLEY Adam Christian
Born: Nottingham, 2 August 1979
Height: 5'9" Weight: 11.2

Formerly a trainee at West Bromwich Albion, Adam followed his dad, Alan – once of Albion, but now the Grimsby manager – to Blundell Park and turned professional during the 1997 close season. Held back for obvious reasons, the young midfielder was finally given a taste of first-team football when coming off the bench at Swindon for seven minutes last April to make his Football League debut. Following this up with a ten-minute spell at Watford, he looks set to get more opportunities in 1999-2000.

Grimsby T (Signed from West Bromwich A juniors on 7/8/97) FL 0+2

BULL Garry William
Born: West Bromwich, 12 June 1966
Height: 5'10" Weight: 12.2
Club Honours: GMVC '91

Signed from York during the summer of 1998, Gary spent most of last season in Scunthorpe's reserve squad, where his good touch and goal-poaching abilities were still in evidence as a prolific scorer throughout the campaign. The striker could not take that form into the first team though, and found starting opportunities restricted, being brought on mainly as a substitute and failing to open his account for the club. Was released during the summer.

Southampton (Signed from Paget R on 15/10/86)
Cambridge U (Signed on 29/3/88) FL 13+6/4 FLC 0+1 Others 0+2
Barnet (£2,000 on 1/3/89) FL 83/37 FLC 4/4 FAC 11/3 Others 8/2
Nottingham F (Free on 21/7/93) F/PL 4+8/1 FLC 2 FAC 0+3

Birmingham C (Loaned on 12/9/94) FL 10/6 Others 2/1
Brighton & Hove A (Loaned on 17/8/95) FL 10/2 Others 1/2
Birmingham C (Free on 29/12/95) FL 3+3 FLC 0+1 FAC 0+2 Others 1/1
York C (Free on 4/3/96) FL 66+17/11 FLC 7+2/2 FAC 5+1
Scunthorpe U (Free on 24/7/98) FL 4+20 FLC 0+1 FAC 0+1 Others 0+2

BULL Ronald (Ronnie) Rodney
Born: Hackney, 26 December 1980
Height: 5'8" Weight: 10.12

Still a trainee, Ronnie gave some outstanding performances in the reserves at Millwall in 1998-99 and followed them up with an excellent first-team debut against Colchester. Extremely assured at left back, where he challenged hard, delivered a good ball, and did not know what it meant to give it up, he could be the next "Harry Cripps".

Millwall (From trainee on 12/5/99) FL 1

BULL Stephen (Steve) George
Born: Tipton, 28 March 1965
Height: 5'11" Weight: 12.11
Club Honours: Div 4 '88, Div 3 '89; AMC '88
International Honours: E: 13; B-5; U21-5

Steve remained at Wolves during the summer as other strikers departed, making an impressive start to 1998-99 and scoring in the third match at Oxford, which ended a long run without a goal. He followed that up with a hat trick against Barnet, his 18th for the club, yet his first at Molineux since 1991. By now, playing more as a target man, and forming a good partnership with Robbie Keane, he headed the winner against Bury before struggling with a knee injury again. In the first 15 games he only missed the Worthington Cup ties with Bournemouth but, as in 1997-98, the required surgery was delayed, leaving his career in doubt. His last appearance was on 3 October, though he again proved people wrong by making a brave comeback for the reserves in March, a game which attracted over 8,000 fans to

Steve Bull

Molineux. He then scored in four more games for the reserves before returning to the first team as a sub at Birmingham in April.

West Bromwich A (Free from Tipton T on 24/8/85) FL 2+2/2 FLC 2/1 Others 1+2
Wolverhampton W (£35,000 on 21/11/86) FL 461+13/249 FLC 32+1/18 FAC 18+2/7 Others 33+1/32

BULLIMORE Wayne Alan

Born: Sutton in Ashfield, 12 September 1970
Height: 5'9" Weight: 12.1
International Honours: E: Yth

An experienced player who was a regular in the Scarborough midfield in 1998-99 until losing his place towards the end of the campaign, having earlier been released by Peterborough during the summer. He certainly impressed in the pre-season friendlies, especially when giving a "Man of the Match" performance against Manchester City, but scored only one goal in the real competitions before being released when the club found itself relegated to the Conference.

Manchester U (From trainee on 16/9/88)
Barnsley (Free on 9/3/91) FL 27+8/1 FLC 2+1 FAC 1+1
Stockport Co (Free on 11/10/93)
Scunthorpe U (Free on 19/11/93) FL 62+5/11 FLC 2+2/1 FAC 7/1 Others 5/1
Bradford C (£40,000 on 15/12/95) FL 1+1
Doncaster Rov (Loaned on 20/9/96) FL 4
Peterborough U (Free on 26/3/97) FL 10+11/1 FLC 0+3 FAC 0+1 Others 1
Scarborough (Free on 5/8/98) FL 33+2/1 FLC 1 FAC 2 Others 1

BULLOCK Anthony (Tony) Brian

Born: Warrington, 18 February 1972
Height: 6'1" Weight: 12.13

Making a belated debut in the Football League with Barnsley, having been signed on transfer deadline day in 1996-97 from Leek Town, the goalkeeper came into the side because of Dave Watson's injury and Lars Leese's loss of form. An excellent shot stopper who commanded his area well and proved a good organiser, he made the position his own in keeping clean sheets against several of the sides at the top of the First Division.

Barnsley (£20,000 from Leek T on 27/3/97) FL 32 FLC 2 FAC 5

Tony Bullock

BULLOCK Darren John

Born: Worcester, 12 February 1969
Height: 5'9" Weight: 12.10

This physical midfielder was a permanent fixture under Steve McMahon at Swindon in 1998-99, but his replacement, Jimmy Quinn, had other ideas and wanted more creativity in the centre of the field. Although he showed his trademark aggression, a flurry of suspensions saw him fall out of favour and transferred to Bury in February. Brought in as a direct replacement for Burnley-bound Lenny Johnrose, he made an immediate impression, lasting just 12 minutes into his debut, against Norwich, when (harshly) sent off the field of play. Following that, he continued to impress with his enthusiasm and determination, and scored a superb first goal for the club, against Sunderland, which was duly voted "Goal of the Season" by the supporters.

Huddersfield T (£55,000 from Nuneaton Borough on 19/11/93) FL 127+1/16 FLC 11/1 FAC 8/2 Others 9/1
Swindon T (£400,000 on 24/2/97) FL 55+11/2 FLC 2 FAC 1
Bury (£150,000 + on 15/2/99) FL 12/1

BULLOCK Lee

Born: Stockton, 22 May 1981
Height: 5'9" Weight: 11.7

A promising young York midfielder, and still a trainee, he was due to sign a full professional contract during the close season after impressing in the reserves and intermediates. His one senior appearance came at Wrexham in the second round of the FA Cup, and he helped the youth team reach the fifth round of the FA Youth Cup. He was also voted the most promising youngster for 1998-99 at Bootham Crescent.

York C (Trainee) FAC 1

BULLOCK Martin John

Born: Derby, 5 March 1975
Height: 5'5" Weight: 10.7
International Honours: 10.7

1998-99 must be summed up as a disappointing season for the diminutive Barnsley winger. He showed in the previous term that he was capable of beating experienced international defenders and it was hoped that he would carry this form into the First Division. However, his performances were fitful and he found himself on the substitutes' bench for long periods before publicly announcing his intentions to leave the club under the Bosman ruling in the summer, which did not endear him to the fans.

Barnsley (£15,000 from Eastwood T on 4/9/93) F/PL 92+71/3 FLC 9+3 FAC 4+11/3 Others 1

BULMAN Dannie

Born: Ashford, 24 January 1979
Height: 5'10" Weight: 12.3

A 1998 summer signing from Combined Counties League side, Ashford Town, after being a trialist in four reserve games the previous season, Danny joined Wycombe as a future prospect. However, after the team's terrible start to the season, he was soon pitched in at the deep end, enjoying a dramatic debut in first-class football when,

with Wycombe trailing 1-0 at home to Bristol Rovers on Bank Holiday Monday, he came on as a last-minute substitute. He immediately chased down a back pass to the visitor's 'keeper, who only succeeded in thumping the ball against the back of his thigh and into the net for the equalising goal, just 26 seconds after he had entered the field of play, and surely one of the fastest debut goals of all time. In his six starts and nine substitute appearances he was used as a striker, and his tireless workrate and nuisance value to opposing defences quickly endeared him to the supporters. Although he had an uncanny knack of finding himself in good positions, he was rested from the first team at the end of November and made no more appearances, an injury not helping. It was a huge step up from football seven levels below but he should be back in contention for a first-team place soon.

Wycombe W (£5,000 + from Ashford T on 17/6/98) FL 5+6/1 FLC 1+1 FAC 0+2

BURGESS Daryl

Born: Birmingham, 24 January 1971
Height: 5'11" Weight: 12.4

Able to occupy the right-back, centre-half and sweeper positions, Daryl failed to establish himself at West Bromwich during the first half of last season, being made to fight for a place with four other similar defenders! However, he stuck to his task and towards the end of the campaign returned to the side. He even took over the captain's armband when producing some sterling displays, none better than the one at Molineux when Albion dented Wolves' play-off hopes in April with a 1-1 draw.

West Bromwich A (From trainee on 1/7/89) FL 293+10/9 FLC 16+3/3 FAC 8 Others 14

BURNETT Wayne

Born: Lambeth, 4 September 1971
Height: 5'11" Weight: 12.6
Club Honours: AMC '98
International Honours: E: Yth

A 1998 close season hernia, followed by a possibly premature and abortive return to the game, meant that this skilful Grimsby midfielder was sidelined for most of 1998-99 and it was not until Easter that he returned to the side. There is no doubt that his midfield skills were sadly missed and that his absence accounted greatly for Town's sparse goals-for tally during the campaign. Despite picking up a further groin injury on the final day, Wayne is hoping to be fully restored in time for the coming term.

Leyton Orient (From trainee on 13/11/89) FL 34+6 FLC 3+1/1 FAC 3+1 Others 4
Blackburn Rov (£90,000 on 19/8/92)
Plymouth Arg (Signed on 9/8/93) FL 61+9/3 FLC 3 FAC 8 Others 4+1
Bolton W (£100,000 on 12/10/95) F/PL 0+2
Huddersfield T (Signed on 6/9/96) FL 44+6 FLC 6+1/1 FAC 1+1
Grimsby T (£100,000 on 9/1/98) FL 35+6/3 FLC 2+1 Others 8/3

BURNS Alexander (Alex)

Born: Bellshill, 4 August 1973
Height: 5'8" Weight: 10.6

A small, quick Scottish midfielder with excellent balance, Alex joined Southend from SC Heracles during the summer of 1998 and soon became a crowd favourite, his jinking skills and strong shot bringing him some early-season goals in 1998-99. Unfortunately, injury and the poor form of the team saw him lose his place, and he finally left the club to return to Scotland to be with his family.

Motherwell (Signed from Shotts Bon Accord on 6/8/91) SL 39+37/8 SLC 5+1/1 SC 6+1/2 Others 2+1/2 (Free to SC Heracles during 1997 close season)
Southend U (Free on 3/7/98) FL 26+5/5 FLC 3 FAC 1 Others 1

BURNS John Christopher
Born: Dublin, 4 December 1977
Height: 5'10" Weight: 11.0
Signed from Belvedere back in 1994, the young Irishman had to wait patiently in the wings at Nottingham Forest for his first taste of first-team football which finally came in 1998-99. A battling, tough-tackling midfielder, once termed as the new "Roy Keane", John made his debut when coming off the bench for the return leg of the Worthington Cup tie against Leyton Orient. Although a regular in the reserves, that was to be his only opportunity during a long and hard campaign which saw the club ultimately relegated to the First Division. He is sure to be offered further chances during the coming term.

Nottingham F (From Belvedere YC on 4/12/94) FLC 0+1

BURNS Liam
Born: Belfast, 30 October 1978
Height: 6'0" Weight: 12.12
International Honours: NI: U21-6; Yth
A Port Vale defender who was only called upon on a handful of occasions in 1998-99, a nightmare appearance as a substitute when he was not the first to get given the runaround by West Bromwich's Lee Hughes, led to a five-month spell out of the first-team picture. Although the new manager, Brian Horton, gave Liam his first start, against Huddersfield, he was then substituted after just 37 minutes at Wolves and spent the remainder of the campaign in the reserves. Nevertheless, Liam was a regular for the Northern Ireland U21s.

Port Vale (From trainee on 2/7/97) FL 2+3

BURROWS David
Born: Dudley, 25 October 1968
Height: 5'9" Weight: 11.8
Club Honours: CS '89; Div 1 '90; FAC '92
International Honours: E: B-3; U21-7
A left-sided Coventry defender who had a very solid season in 1998-99, despite injuring a hamstring at the end of September and not being back in first-team action until early January, his tough tackling, good positional play, and strength in the air came to the fore in the second half of the campaign. While he does not get up in support of his attack as often as he used to at Anfield, when he does overlap his crossing is excellent. Although picking up a number

of yellow cards, David missed only one game through suspension.

West Bromwich A (From apprentice on 8/11/86) FL 37+9/1 FLC 3+1 FAC 2 Others 1
Liverpool (£550,000 on 20/10/88) F/PL 135+11/3 FLC 16 FAC 16+1 Others 14
West Ham U (Signed on 17/9/93) PL 29/1 FLC 3/1 FAC 3
Everton (Signed on 6/9/94) PL 19 FLC 2 FAC 2
Coventry C (£1,100,000 on 2/3/95) PL 95+1 FLC 8 FAC 9

BURTON Deon John
Born: Ashford, 25 October 1976
Height: 5'9" Weight: 11.9
International Honours: Jamaica: 18
A popular, pacy striker at Derby who, after representing Jamaica in France 98, found himself out of the reckoning for a first-team place during the first half of 1998-99. To gee him up, Jim Smith sent him out on loan to First Division Barnsley for a month, which seemed to have the desired effect as, upon his return, he netted twice in the FA Cup at Plymouth and was involved constantly in subsequent league and cup games. Another double against Everton was the highlight of his season and, at last, he showed a level of consistency only hinted at previously. Continuing to be a first-choice striker for his country, he missed the last handful of games with a hamstring injury.

Portsmouth (From trainee on 15/2/94) FL 42+20/10 FLC 3+2/2 FAC 0+2/1
Cardiff C (Loaned on 24/12/96) FL 5/2 Others 1
Derby Co (£1,000,000 + on 9/8/97) PL 26+24/12 FLC 2 FAC 7/3
Barnsley (Loaned on 14/12/98) FL 3

BURTON-GODWIN Osagyefo (Sagi) Lenin Ernesto
Born: Birmingham, 25 November 1977
Height: 6'2" Weight: 13.6
After making his first-team debut in 1997-98, the well-built young Crystal Palace right back came into the side last season as a deputy for the injured Jamie Smith, having scored in three successive reserve games and netted his first senior goal in a 3-2 home win over Wolves. Good in the air, he eventually gave way to the returning Smith before coming back into contention towards the end of a campaign that had been fraught with financial problems for Palace. Stop Press: Signed for Colchester on 28 May.

Crystal Palace (From trainee on 26/1/96) P/FL 19+6/1 FLC 1 FAC 0+1

BUSHELL Stephen (Steve) Paul
Born: Manchester, 28 December 1972
Height: 5'9" Weight: 11.6
Signed from York during the 1998 close season, the busy, hard-working midfielder made quite an impact at Blackpool in 1998-99 with his tackling and strong running. Having opened his account with a goal in the club's first home league game, he got great pleasure from scoring against his old side, despite the Seasiders losing at Bloomfield Road. Unfortunately, he suffered a broken foot in mid March and was forced to sit out the rest of the campaign.

York C (From trainee on 25/2/91) FL 156+18/10 FLC 8+1/2 FAC 5 Others 11+2/1
Blackpool (Free on 2/7/98) FL 31/3 FLC 4 FAC 1

BUTLER Philip Anthony (Tony)
Born: Stockport, 28 September 1972
Height: 6'2" Weight: 12.0
A strong central defender, who would have been free to leave Blackpool at the end of 1998-99 under the Bosman ruling, Tony joined Port Vale on transfer deadline day last March and made his debut in a defeat at Bristol City. Unfortunately, after settling down, as the team conceded one goal in their next three games which was a far cry from how things had been going, he picked up a hamstring injury that forced him to miss the remainder of the campaign. Not many forwards get the better of Tony, especially in the air.

Gillingham (From trainee on 13/5/91) FL 142+6/5 FLC 12 FAC 12+1 Others 5+1/1
Blackpool (£225,000 on 30/7/96) FL 98+1 FLC 7 FAC 4 Others 4/1
Port Vale (£115,000 on 25/3/99) FL 4

BUTLER Martin Neil
Born: Wordsley, 15 September 1974
Height: 5'11" Weight: 11.9
This lively striker started last season at Cambridge in the same way as he finished the old – by scoring goals. With the record books now showing his name regularly, he ended 1998-99 having scored his first hat trick, against Mansfield, and as the club's leading goalscorer for the second consecutive term. Strong and fast, he was rewarded by his fellow professionals with a place in the PFA Division Three team and, as the workaholic of United's front line, if he continues to score at the present rate, he could soon be the club's leading goalscorer ever.

Walsall (From trainee on 24/5/93) FL 43+31/8 FLC 2+1 FAC 2+5/2 Others 2+2/2
Cambridge U (£22,500 on 8/8/97) FL 74+3/27 FLC 7/3 FAC 4+2/3 Others 3+1/1

BUTLER Paul John
Born: Manchester, 2 November 1972
Height: 6'2" Weight: 13.0
Club Honours: Div 2 '97; Div 1 '99
Having joined Sunderland from Bury in the summer of 1998, and picking up a deserved First Division championship medal in his first season with the club, this powerful, no-nonsense centre back did not taste defeat in a league game until December. At that stage of the campaign, he had missed only one game, the home defeat by Barnsley in November emphasising how crucial his suspension-induced absence was. Dominant in the air, Paul formed a solid partnership with a rejuvenated Andy Melville and his impressive form earned him a place in the PFA First Division select, prompting Eire boss, Mick McCarthy, to select him for a "B" international against the National League in February. Thus, when the inevitable first cap arrives, his old club, Bury, will be entitled to a further £200,000.

Rochdale (From trainee on 5/7/91) FL 151+7/10 FLC 8+1 FAC 6+2 Others 12+1
Bury (£100,000 on 22/7/96) FL 83+1/4 FLC 8 FAC 2 Others 3/1
Sunderland (£600,000 + on 15/7/98) FL 44/2 FLC 6+1 FAC 2

BUTLER Peter James
Born: Halifax, 27 August 1966
Height: 5'9" Weight: 11.1
Released by West Bromwich Albion, Peter joined his hometown club, Halifax, in the summer of 1998 as player/coach. An experienced midfielder who has played at the highest level, he got red carded in his first match against Wrexham in the League Cup, but soon won over the majority of the fans with his battling qualities.
Huddersfield T (From apprentice on 21/8/84) FL 0+5
Cambridge U (Loaned on 24/1/86) FL 14/1 Others 1
Bury (Free on 8/7/86) FL 9+2 FLC 2/1 FAC 1
Cambridge U (Free on 10/12/86) FL 55/9 FLC 4 FAC 2 Others 2
Southend U (£75,000 on 12/2/88) FL 135+7/9 FLC 12/1 FAC 2 Others 11/2
Huddersfield T (Loaned on 24/3/92) FL 7
West Ham U (£125,000 on 12/8/92) F/PL 70/3 FLC 4 FAC 3 Others 1
Notts Co (£350,000 on 4/10/94) FL 20 FLC 2 FAC 2 Others 3
Grimsby T (Loaned on 30/1/96) FL 3
West Bromwich A (£175,000 on 28/3/96) FL 52+8 FLC 2+1 FAC 1+2
Halifax T (Free on 1/8/98) FL 33/1 FLC 2 FAC 1 Others 1

BUTLER Stephen (Steve)
Born: Birmingham, 27 January 1962
Height: 6'2" Weight: 12.12
Club Honours: GMVC '89
International Honours: E: SP-3
After finding himself out in the cold, once Gillingham had signed Carl Asaba from Reading late last August, Steve moved to Peterborough as the player/coach at the end of October and opened his goalscoring account with the winner at Torquay. The veteran striker continued to play into February, scoring two more goals, before being allowed to move on loan to non-league Stevenage in March.**Brentford** (Free from Windsor & Eton on 19/12/84) FL 18+3/3 Others 2
Maidstone U (Free on 1/8/86) FL 76/41 FLC 4/3 FAC 18/7 Others 10/4
Watford (£150,000 on 28/3/91) FL 40+22/9 FLC 4+3 FAC 1 Others 2+1
Bournemouth (Loaned on 18/12/92) FL 1
Cambridge U (£75,000 on 23/12/92) FL 107+2/51 FLC 4+1 FAC 6/5 Others 3
Gillingham (£100,000 on 15/12/95) FL 77+31/20 FLC 7+1/1 FAC 5/1 Others 1
Peterborough U (Free on 29/10/98) FL 13+1/2 FAC 1 Others 1/1

BUTT Nicholas (Nicky)
Born: Manchester, 21 January 1975
Height: 5'10" Weight: 11.3
Club Honours: FAYC '92; CS '96, '97; PL '96, '97, '99; FAC '96; EC '99
International Honours: E: 8; U21-7; Yth (UEFA Yth '93); Sch
A gritty midfielder with neat skills and a hardened edge, Nicky had a promising start to last season, playing in Manchester United's opening five games before being forced out for an operation on four wisdom teeth. He had just recovered from that ordeal, when he was sent off twice in five days, against Barcelona in the Champions' League, and Arsenal in the Premiership.

Although he was given a one-match ban by UEFA for his hand-ball offence against Barca, it was suddenly increased to two, which meant he missed the important ties against Bayern and Brondby. After playing in only two games during October, he scored his first Premiership goal of the season against Leeds in November, then netted his second against Middlesbrough at Old Trafford in December. But just when it seemed like he was beginning to show the sort of form that had put him on the verge of a World Cup place in the summer, he sustained a hip injury before United's vital FA Cup-tie against Chelsea in March. Having made a remarkable recovery, however, he was a steadying influence in a side vying for honours on three fronts, whilst also becoming a vital member of Kevin Keegan's new England team. Won European Cup and Premier League championship medals for his endeavours.
Manchester U (From trainee on 29/1/93) PL 119+27/13 FLC 5 FAC 16+2/1 Others 29+6/1

BUTTERFIELD Daniel (Danny) Paul
Born: Boston, 21 November 1979
Height: 5'10" Weight: 11.10
Club Honours: AMC '98
International Honours: E: Yth
Another graduate of John Cockerill's fruitful Grimsby youth scheme, this highly skilled young right-wing back is forecast to follow Gary Croft and John Oster to the highest level. A solid defender, and fast and tenacious when going forward, it was, however, a frustrating season for Danny as the consistent form and fitness of John McDermott and Tony Gallimore limited his chances at senior level. When called to the squad he continued to show why he is so highly thought of, and a late-season injury to McDermott gave him an opportunity for an extended run. Following some sterling performances and a couple of "Man of the Match" awards it was no great surprise when he picked up the club's "Young Player of the Year" trophy.
Grimsby T (From trainee on 7/8/97) FL 13+6 FLC 2+1 FAC 0+1 Others 1+1/1

BUTTERS Guy
Born: Hillingdon, 30 October 1969
Height: 6'3" Weight: 14.2
International Honours: E: U21-3
Forcing his way back to full fitness after breaking his leg in March 1998, the Gillingham manager, Tony Pulis, selected him in early December and after a few tentative appearances he regained his composure and strength to reclaim his place at the heart of the defence. One of the unsung performers at the club, Guy is a good tackler, is sound in the air, and a good man to have around at set plays.
Tottenham H (From trainee on 5/8/88) FL 34+1/1 FLC 2+1 FAC 1
Southend U (Loaned on 13/1/90) FL 16/3 Others 2
Portsmouth (£375,000 on 28/9/90) FL 148+6/6 FLC 15+1/1 FAC 7 Others 7+2
Oxford U (Loaned on 4/11/94) FL 3/1 Others 1
Gillingham (£225,000 on 18/10/96) FL 84/10 FLC 2 FAC 5 Others 7

BYFIELD Darren
Born: Birmingham, 29 September 1976
Height: 5'11" Weight: 11.11
1998-99 was a somewhat disappointing season for Darren, an up-and-coming youngster at Aston Villa with the potential to become a future star of the game. After breaking in to the first-team squad in 1997-98, the pacy forward was expected to push hard for further senior opportunities, but was only featured in four of Villa's games, and two of those were on the subs' bench. Loaned to Preston in November, he scored on his debut, against Burnley, but picked up a knee injury and returned to Villa Park early, after refusing a place on the bench against Wrexham at the end of December. In the final weeks of the campaign, having played in the reserves alongside Paul Merson, he increased his workrate and began to apply more effort in training in an attempt to raise his fitness level and prove to the manager that he is worth a regular place in the side this coming term.
Aston Villa (From trainee on 14/2/94) PL 1+6 FLC 1 FAC 0+1 Others 1
Preston NE (Loaned on 6/11/98) FL 3+2/1 Others 1

BYRNE Christopher (Chris) Thomas
Born: Manchester, 9 February 1975
Height: 5'9" Weight: 10.4
International Honours: E: SP-1
Having established himself as a regular first-team member in his first year at Stockport, Chris was an integral part of Gary Megson's plans for the 1998-99 campaign. Skilful and pacy with the ball at his feet, and with the knack of arriving in the box at the right time to score goals, Chris was showing great form at the start of the season. Therefore, it came as a massive blow to the club when he suffered serious damage to his cruciate ligament in a game against Huddersfield in late September. Ruled out for the rest of the term, the club is hoping that an off-field problem will not hamper his efforts to play for County in 1999-2000.
Sunderland (Signed from Macclesfield T on 11/6/97) FL 4+4 FLC 1+1
Stockport Co (£200,000 on 21/11/97) FL 32+5/9 FLC 2/1 FAC 1+1

BYRNE Desmond (Dessie)
Born: Dublin, 10 April 1981
Height: 5'7" Weight: 10.8
International Honours: Ei: Yth
A teenager who played a key role for the Republic of Ireland U16 squad which won the European championship in 1998, Dessie started out as a centre half with Cherry Orchard in Dublin but made the breakthrough into Stockport's first team, while still a trainee, as a left back against Bradford in January 1999. Another impressive display against Norwich City suggested he had a great future in the game, but, unfortunately, he was involved in a serious altercation in a nightclub and, sacked by County, was forced to return home to Ireland.
Stockport Co (Trainee) FL 2

C

CABALLERO Fabian
Born: Argentina, 31 October 1978
Height: 5'10" Weight: 13.0
An Argentinian trialist on loan at Arsenal until the end of last season. He is an aggressive striker who is good in the air and particularly quick when getting into his stride. His forte is in and around the penalty box and, given a sight of goal, will always attempt to score. His knowledge of the English style of play improved greatly once he began full-time training with the first-team squad and he made his debut when coming off the bench in the 5-0 home Worthington Cup defeat at the hands of London rivals, Chelsea. Also came on as a substitute against Middlesbrough (Premiership) and at Preston (FA Cup), where he will probably be remembered for all of the wrong reasons, when appearing to catch a defender with his arm to allow Manu Petit to slot in, unchallenged on the edge of the six-yard box to score the third goal in the 4-2 third-round win.
Arsenal (Loaned from Serro Portino on 29/10/98) PL 0+1 FLC 0+1 FAC 0+1

CADAMARTERI Daniel (Danny) Leon
Born: Bradford, 12 October 1979
Height: 5'7" Weight: 11.12
Club Honours: FAYC '98
International Honours: E: U21-1; Yth
A powerful young Everton forward with an explosive burst of pace, Danny continued in 1998-99 to build on the rich promise he displayed in his first Premiership campaign. Employed more regularly as an influential substitute than as a member of the Blues' starting line-up, he stepped off the bench at Middlesbrough to inspire a 2-2 draw from a 2-0 deficit. He also committed his international future to England by coming on, typically, as a substitute in an U21 European championship qualifier against the Czech Republic – despite rival claims from several other countries. Still learning his craft, the youngster looks sure to enjoy a bright future in the game.
Everton (From trainee on 15/10/96) PL 26+31/8 FLC 4+3/1 FAC 4+1

CADETTE Nathan Daniel
Born: Cardiff, 6 January 1980
Height: 5'10" Weight: 11.1
International Honours: W: Yth
Nicknamed "Shaper", the Cardiff-born trainee earned a senior contract during the summer of 1998, before going on loan to Telford United during last season for extra experience. Made four cup appearances, in the FAW Premier Cup, and came off the bench in both the Worthington Cup and FA Cup, but remained some way off a league call-up. Enthusastic and willing, Nathan constantly encourages his team mates, and is a midfielder with a good attitude.
Cardiff C (From Trainee on 1/6/98) FL 0+4 FAC 0+1 Others 0+1

CAHILL Timothy (Tim)
Born: Sydney, Australia, 6 December 1979
Height: 5'10" Weight: 10.11
One of a number of promising youngsters to have made good progress at Millwall in 1998-99, the young Aussie had a remarkable first full season in league football, culminating in a Wembley appearance against Wigan in the Auto Windscreens Shield. Tim actually scored the goal which enabled the Lions to take a narrow lead to the Bescot Stadium for the second leg of the area final, a game which he had to miss through suspension. Although carrying a good shot, his seven goals included a number of headers, proof that he can get up remarkably well for a lad of only average height. Also supports the attack well from midfield and is a good defender, being strong in the challenge.
Millwall (Signed from Sydney U on 31/7/97) FL 35+2/6 FLC 0+1 Others 5/1

CAIG Antony (Tony)
Born: Whitehaven, 11 April 1974
Height: 6'1" Weight: 13.4
Club Honours: Div 3 '95; AMC '97
One of Carlisle's most consistent performers in recent years, "Caigy's" shot-stopping skills again provided a reassuring presence at the back of the United defence in 1998-99. Despite the club's poor league form, the Cumbrians had conceded only just over one goal per game when he surprisingly joined Blackpool during transfer deadline week, his last match being at Darlington which ended a run of over 160 consecutive first-team appearances stretching back almost three years. There was much surprise at him being allowed to leave at such a critical stage of the campaign, but, out of contract in the summer, the club decided to get a fee for him. Required by the Seasiders to replace the transferred Steve Banks, he made his debut the following Saturday, at Chesterfield, and impressed during the remaining nine games.
Carlisle U (From trainee on 10/7/92) FL 223 FLC 16 FAC 13 Others 29
Blackpool (£40,000 on 25/3/99) FL 10

CALDERWOOD Colin
Born: Glasgow, 20 January 1965
Height: 6'0" Weight: 12.12
Club Honours: Div 4 '86; FLC '99
International Honours: S: 33; Sch
A vastly experienced central defender whose versatility stretches to midfield was dogged by injury and a drop in form which saw him sidelined at Spurs for much of 1998-99. As competition for places hotted up at White Hart Lane, Colin became disappointed at the prospect of only occasional appearances, resulting in him losing his international spot in Scotland's defence. Good in the air, and with a high level of personal fitness, he was delighted to get a switch to Aston Villa as cover for the injured Ugo Ehiogu, despite being reluctant to leave a club for which he had worked hard and been a loyal servant of. Having made his last appearance on the subs' bench in January in the Worthington Cup semi final against Wimbledon, he moved during transfer deadline week in the hope of finding his form once more in a bid to win back his much coveted international place. Playing in the last eight games, he immediately struck up a good understanding with Gareth Southgate in the centre of Villa's defence as the side began to concede less goals than previously. Is recognised by manager John Gregory for his no-nonsense defending.
Mansfield T (Signed on 19/3/82) FL 97+3/1 FLC 4 FAC 6/1 Others 7
Swindon T (£30,000 on 1/7/85) FL 328+2/20 FLC 35 FAC 17/1 Others 32
Tottenham H (£1,250,000 on 22/7/93) PL 152+11/7 FLC 19+1 FAC 15+1/1
Aston Villa (£225,000 on 24/3/99) PL 8

CALVO-GARCIA Alexander (Alex)
Born: Ordizia, Spain, 1 January 1972
Height: 5'10" Weight: 11.12
A regular in the Scunthorpe midfield in 1998-99, Alex remained a crowd favourite who loved to get forward, and chipped in with his fair share of goals. Very skilful on the ball, and with an excellent work-rate, he has made a superb transition into English football, being a key member of the promotion-chasing squad. Scored his tenth goal of the season, the only goal of the game, to give United a 1-0 promotion play-off win over Leyton Orient at Wembley.
Scunthorpe U (Free from Eibar on 4/10/96) FL 88+12/16 FLC 6/3 FAC 9/1 Others 7/2

Alex Calvo-Garcia

CAMPAGNA Samuel (Sam) Patrick Philip
Born: Worcester, 9 November 1980
Height: 6'1" Weight: 11.7
After impressing all and sundry at Swindon in 1998-99, the youth-team captain made his first-team debut when coming off the bench at Premiership-bound Bradford City in November before being used as a sub at home to Barnsley in the final fixture of the campaign. A centre back who has shown good ability in the air, and is more than

comfortable on the ground, Sam was expected to sign a two-year professional contract in the past summer.
Swindon T (Trainee) FL 0+2

CAMPBELL Andrew (Andy) Paul
Born: Stockton, 18 April 1979
Height: 5'11" Weight: 11.7
International Honours: E: Yth
At the tender age of just 16 years, Andy made his Premiership debut for Middlesbrough when coming off the bench against Sheffield Wednesday in 1996-97, and then celebrated his 20th birthday with two fine goals during his loan transfer to Sheffield United (against Grimsby in the Nationwide First Division) in 1998-99, sparking off a tug of war for his manager to resolve with Steve Bruce, who wanted to make the transfer permanent. United had taken the speedy young striker on loan in January and February and, although injury restricted him to five appearances, he went back to Bramall Lane in March, on loan until the end of the season, and continued to impress with his strong, direct running up front, both down the middle and on the flanks. "Robbo" rates the striker very highly and should demonstrate his esteem by thwarting the Blade's second attempt to buy his protege, who has been groomed from trainee to Premier League status with a great future being predicted for him.
Middlesbrough (From trainee on 4/7/96) F/PL 7+13 FLC 4+3/1 FAC 2/1
Sheffield U (Loaned on 10/12/98) FL 5/1
Sheffield U (Loaned on 25/3/99) FL 6/2

CAMPBELL Jamie
Born: Birmingham, 21 October 1972
Height: 6'1" Weight: 12.11
The ever-present Cambridge left back from 1997-98 continued his reliable form into 1998-99, missing just one game through suspension. Possessing a sweet left foot, which made him dangerous going forward and at set plays, he was not often on the score sheet, but those he put away always seem to be memorable. Out of contract during the summer, at the time of going to press the club had offered him terms of re-engagement.
Luton T (From trainee on 1/7/91) FL 10+26/1 FLC 1+1 FAC 1+3 Others 1+2
Mansfield T (Loaned on 25/11/94) FL 3/1 FAC 2
Cambridge U (Loaned on 10/3/95) FL 12
Barnet (Free on 11/7/95) FL 50+17/5 FLC 3+3/1 FAC 4+2/1 Others 1
Cambridge U (Free on 8/8/97) FL 91/6 FLC 7 FAC 6/1 Others 4

CAMPBELL Kevin Joseph
Born: Lambeth, 4 February 1970
Height: 6'1" Weight: 13.8
Club Honours: FAYC '88; FLC '93; FAC '93; ECWC '94; Div 1 '98
International Honours: E: B-1; U21-4
After an unhappy spell in Turkey with Trabzonspor, having left Nottingham Forest during the summer of 1998, Kevin exploded back onto the Premiership scene in an astonishing loan spell with Everton, which began last March in transfer deadline week. Shamefully discriminated against by the

Trabzonspor President, Mehhmet Ali Yilmaz, he angrily quit the Turks and soon found himself the object of hero worship at Goodison Park. His nine goals in eight games – including a hat trick against West Ham – saw him end the campaign as Everton's top scorer and their saviour. Quick, strong, and good in the air, he was an unlikely inheritor of Duncan Ferguson's number nine jersey and, as 1998-99 came to a halt, the club immediately began moves to make his loan deal permanent.
Arsenal (From trainee on 11/2/88) F/PL 124+42/46 FLC 14+10/6 FAC 13+6/2 Others 15+4/5
Leyton Orient (Loaned on 16/1/89) FL 16/9
Leicester C (Loaned on 8/11/89) FL 11/5 Others 1/1
Nottingham F (£3,000,000 on 1/7/95) F/PL 79+1/32 FLC 12 FAC 11/3 Others 3 (£2,500,000 to Trabzonspor on 7/8/98)
Everton (Loaned on 25/3/99) PL 8/9

CAMPBELL Neil Andrew
Born: Middlesbrough, 26 January 1977
Height: 6'2" Weight: 13.7
Having started the opening four games at Scarborough in 1998-99, the talented young striker became unsettled and, following a spell on loan at non-league Telford United, he moved to Southend in January after turning down Colchester. Built like an old-fashioned centre forward, he struggled to find his form and touch, although one of his two strikes in the victory at Leyton Orient in April was excellent. Neil was one of Alvin Martin's final signings as the United manager.
York C (From trainee on 21/6/95) FL 6+6/1 FLC 1 FAC 0+2 Others 2
Scarborough (Free on 5/9/97) FL 23+22/7 FLC 2 FAC 0+2 Others 3/1
Southend U (Free on 22/1/99) FL 9+3/2

CAMPBELL Paul Andrew
Born: Middlesbrough, 29 January 1980
Height: 6'1" Weight: 11.0
After breaking into the Darlington first team at the end of 1997-98, Paul had to wait until last December before appearing again. Then he did not make the side again until mid April, but played in the last seven games of the season, scoring once at Carlisle. A tall, graceful midfielder, and accurate passer of the ball, he promises much as he gains in strength and confidence.
Darlington (From trainee on 8/7/98) FL 10+5/2 Others 1

CAMPBELL Stuart Pearson
Born: Corby, 9 December 1977
Height: 5'10" Weight: 10.8
Club Honours: FLC '97
International Honours: S: U21-13
A right-sided Leicester midfielder, Stuart once again made the majority of his appearances, this time in 1998-99, from the substitutes' bench, where he sat to earn a medal at Wembley. Has not quite managed to secure a regular first-team berth as yet, but continued to gain valuable experience with both club and the Scottish U21 team. His clear target for the coming term will be to force his way into the starting line-up more frequently, in order to begin to fulfil

the obvious promise that is present in his game.
Leicester C (From trainee on 4/7/96) PL 11+22 FLC 2+3 FAC 3

CAMPBELL Sulzeer (Sol) Jeremiah
Born: Newham, 18 September 1974
Height: 6'2" Weight: 14.1
Club Honours: FLC '99
International Honours: E: 27; B-1; U21-11; Yth (UEFA Yth '93)
1998-99 was another terrific season for this accomplished central defender, whose value to both Tottenham and England increased with every performance. At the heart of Spurs' defence, showing a high level of commitment and competitive attitude which was second to none, Sol faced some of the best attackers both at Premiership and world level, and emerged as one of the most complete central defenders to be found. His strength and pace, complimented by a maturity which saw him embrace his responsibilities as club captain, were just two of his most notable attributes. But, his superior aerial ability, remains his outstanding trademark, along with his tremendous recovery powers. The campaign saw another side of his game with eight league and cup goals. Among the most memorable came the two at home to Manchester United in December, when deep into injury time, he salvaged a much-deserved point, Spurs finishing the game all square at 2-2. Snatching a result from games that Tottenham looked certain to lose was also memorably demonstrated in September when, again, deep into injury time, he scored the equaliser in the 3-3 draw with Leeds. In April, he was recognised by his fellow professionals when being voted into the Premiership "Team of the Season" at the annual PFA awards, and with interest in this highly-rated defender growing both at home and abroad and expected to further increase as the side come under the spotlight in Europe in 1999-2000, it is little surprise that George Graham is anxious for him to sign an extension to the remaining two years left on his current contract, an anxiety shared by the Tottenham faithful.
Tottenham H (From trainee on 23/9/92) PL 196+9/8 FLC 25/4 FAC 21+2/1

CANHAM Scott Walter
Born: Newham, 5 November 1974
Height: 5'9" Weight: 11.7
Signed on a free transfer last August from Brentford, Scott played only a couple of times in Leyton Orient's senior team, used mainly as a right-wing back, but when called upon he never let the team down. Excellent with dead-ball kicks, he made his full league debut in January, at home to Darlington, and set up two goals with his excellent crosses. Will be looking to earn a regular first-team place this coming term.
West Ham U (From trainee on 2/7/93)
Torquay U (Loaned on 3/11/95) FL 3
Brentford (Loaned on 19/1/96) FL 14
Brentford (£25,000 + on 29/8/96) FL 24+11/1 FLC 4+2 FAC 1+1 Others 1+2
Leyton Orient (Free on 10/8/98) FL 2+6 Others 1

CAPLETON Melvyn (Mel) David
Born: Hackney, 24 October 1973
Height: 5'11" Weight: 12.0
Signed on non-contract forms as goalkeeping cover for Chris MacKenzie in August, having been at non-league Grays Athletic, Mel only played one game for Leyton Orient, in the Worthington Cup-tie at Nottingham Forest, and he managed to keep a clean sheet. Joined his old club, Southend, in October, again on non-contract terms, and performed very well after replacing Martyn Margetson two thirds of the way through the season, making many spectacular saves and giving the defence confidence in proving himself to be both agile and commanding. The possessor of a mighty kick, he hopes to open the new campaign in United's goal.
Southend U (From trainee on 1/7/92)
Blackpool (Free on 1/8/93) FL 9+2 FLC 1 (Free to Grays Ath on 18/10/95)
Leyton Orient (Free on 14/9/98) FLC 1
Southend U (Free on 23/10/98) FL 14

CARBON Matthew (Matt) Phillip
Born: Nottingham, 8 June 1975
Height: 6'2" Weight: 13.6
International Honours: E: U21-4
A strong, positive West Bromwich centre back who put in some solid displays at the heart of the Baggies' defence in 1998-99. It was difficult at times for the former Derby player, when injuries and suspension meant that his central defensive partner was often changed, but Matt battled on well and was never found wanting, despite Albion's failure to prevent goals being scored against them!
Lincoln C (From trainee on 13/4/93) FL 66+3/10 FLC 4/1 FAC 3 Others 4+3
Derby Co (£385,000 on 8/3/96) P/FL 11+9 FLC 1 FAC 0+1
West Bromwich A (£800,000 on 26/1/98) FL 54+1/3 FLC 2 FAC 1

CARBONARI Horacio Angel
Born: Argentina, 2 May 1973
Height: 6'3" Weight: 13.4
Signed in the 1998 close season from Rosario Central, for what was a record transfer fee for Derby, he proved to be a powerful defender who could play anywhere at the back and proved equally adept when performing as a sweeper or as a man-to-man marker. He also displayed a willingness to get forward and support the attack at any set pieces, as well as possessing a tremendous shooting ability at free kicks. Sustained a knee injury early on in 1998-99, but was an automatic first choice upon his return, where his ability in the air was more noticeable. Scored winning goals against Southampton and Nottingham Forest, though his exuberant celebrations in the latter were deemed not quite appropriate for the occasion.
Derby Co (£2,700,000 from Athletico Rosario Central on 1/7/98) PL 28+1/5 FAC 4

CARBONE Benito
Born: Begnara, Italy, 14 August 1971
Height: 5'6" Weight: 10.8
This small, but highly-skilled playmaker had a truly excellent season for Sheffield Wednesday in 1998-99, often being the Owls' only inspirational player. As you would expect, he chipped in with his usual supply of goals, but was mainly a creator of chances for others. In establishing his importance to the side under Danny Wilson, who has helped restore the Italian's confidence, he also seemed to flourish following the Paolo di Canio incident, perhaps realising that Wednesday needed his flair more than ever. A good player to build a future side around, he gives his all, and can be expected to shine this coming term with the Hillsborough faithful right behind him. Won the supporters' "Player of the Season" award.
Sheffield Wed (£3,000,000 from Inter Milan, via Torino, Reggina, Casert, Ascoli and Napoli, on 18/10/96) PL 83+6/23 FLC 3 FAC 7/1

Benito Carbone

CARDEN Paul
Born: Liverpool, 29 March 1979
Height: 5'8" Weight: 11.10
After a couple of substitute appearances in Rochdale's pre-season games, this energetic youngster looked to have been forgotten, but was brought into the side at the end of last November and immediately carved out a place for himself, solving Dale's problems on the right of midfield and then filling in successfully at right-wing back. Against Swansea, he had the strange experience of being "sent off" and subsequently suspended a week after the game, when the clearing up of a case of mistaken identity involving team-mate Mark Williams led to the latter's second yellow card being cancelled and given to Paul, who had already had one caution during the game itself!
Blackpool (From trainee on 7/7/97) FL 0+1 FAC 0+1 Others 1
Rochdale (Free on 3/3/98) FL 27+5 FAC 3 Others 3

CAREY Brian Patrick
Born: Cork, 31 May 1968
Height: 6'3" Weight: 14.4
International Honours: Ei: 3; U21-1
Continuing to impress at the heart of Wrexham's defence in 1998-99, organising the back four superbly, his height was a great advantage in either penalty area. In the running to be recognised as one of the Racecourse club's best-ever acquisitions, Brian was always prominent in the contest for "Player of the Season", despite having two spells out with injury while undergoing two ops – a cartilage in September, and an ankle that required surgery in December. Thankfully, he has a rapid rate of recovery and was back to fitness in next to no time, controlling his back four. Scored an important winning goal against Gillingham near the end of April when relegation began to loom.
Manchester U (£100,000 from Cork C on 2/9/89)
Wrexham (Loaned on 17/1/91) FL 3
Wrexham (Loaned on 24/12/91) FL 13/1 FAC 3 Others 3
Leicester C (£250,000 on 16/7/93) F/PL 51+7/1 FLC 3 FAC 0+1 Others 4
Wrexham (£100,000 on 19/7/96) FL 117/3 FLC 6 FAC 15 Others 7

CAREY Louis Anthony
Born: Bristol, 22 January 1977
Height: 5'10" Weight: 11.10
International Honours: S: U21-1
A local-born defender who, during a difficult campaign for Bristol City in 1998-99, appeared in central defence and at full back. Louis never quite reached the peak of the previous season when playing alongside Shaun Taylor, but always gave 100 per-cent effort to the cause. Was undoubtedly affected by the uncertain start, when the team found it difficult to cope with the demands made by the higher standard of football. However, well thought of at Ashton Gate, his best days are still to come!
Bristol C (From trainee on 3/7/95) FL 139+5 FLC 7+1 FAC 9 Others 3+2

CAREY Shaun Peter
Born: Kettering, 13 May 1976
Height: 5'9" Weight: 10.10
International Honours: Ei: U21-2
The 1998-99 campaign proved to be a bitter-sweet one for Norwich's former Republic of Ireland U21 international midfielder. Having won Bruce Rioch's approval during the pre-season build-up, Shaun started the first three games of the season, winning praise for his excellent workrate and passing skills. However, a snapped achilles tendon sustained in the game at Stockport, ruled him out of first-team contention for over seven months, before he returned against Huddersfield in late March. A tenacious and dogged character, he did remarkably well to fight back from such a debilitating injury.
Norwich C (From trainee on 1/7/94) FL 32+15 FLC 3+2 FAC 1+1

CARLISLE Clarke James
Born: Preston, 14 October 1979
Height: 6'1" Weight: 12.7
A young Blackpool central defender who

became a regular member of the side last season, Clarke continued to show the promise that had Premier League scouts running the rule over him. He also continued to score, diving in to head the first goal in a memorable 3-1 victory at Stoke. Good in the air, he has no mean ability on the ground either.

Blackpool (From trainee on 13/8/97) FL 42+8/3 FLC 2+1 Others 2

Clarke Carlisle

CARLISLE Wayne Thomas
Born: Lisburn, 9 September 1979
Height: 6'0" Weight: 11.6
International Honours: NI: Yth
On Steve Coppell replacing Terry Venables as manager at Crystal Palace last season, this young Northern Ireland youth international was one of the first of the newcomers to be selected for the first-team, making a solid defensive debut at Selhurst against Birmingham in January. Most certainly a player for the future, the youngster went back to the reserves while looking for further opportunities from the bench.
Crystal Palace (From trainee on 18/9/96) FL 2+4

CARPENTER Richard
Born: Sheerness, 30 September 1972
Height: 6'0" Weight: 13.0
Signed from Fulham during the 1998 close season, Richard played a crucial role in Cardiff's promotion campaign in 1998-99. Having been promoted from the Third Division three times, with Gillingham, Fulham and now the Bluebirds, he is a strong, tough-tackling midfield player. Lost his place during the promotion run-in, when Frank Burrows was worried his midfield was becoming too predictable, although not

scoring the goals he would have liked – finishing with only one – he made more than 50 first-team appearances, and will aim to bounce back from that late season blip in 1999-2000.
Gillingham (From trainee on 13/5/91) FL 107+15/4 FLC 2+1 FAC 9+1 Others 7/1
Fulham (£15,000 on 26/9/96) FL 49+9/7 FLC 4/1 FAC 2/1 Others 2
Cardiff C (£35,000 on 29/7/98) FL 41+1/1 FLC 2 FAC 4

CARR Darren John
Born: Bristol, 4 September 1968
Height: 6'2" Weight: 13.7
Signed from Chesterfield the day before the start of last season, Darren had the misfortune to score the only goal of the game on his debut for Gillingham, against Walsall. Unfortunately, it turned out to be the winning goal for the Midlands side! A regular in the team up until Guy Butters regained his first-team place, he is strong in the tackle, and not many forwards get the better of him in aerial duels. Turned down a transfer deadline move to Lincoln.
Bristol Rov (From trainee on 20/8/86) FL 26+4 FLC 2+2 FAC 3 Others 2
Newport Co (£3,000 on 30/10/87) FL 9
Sheffield U (£8,000 on 10/3/88) FL 12+1/1 FLC 1 FAC 3+1 Others 1
Crewe Alex (£35,000 on 18/9/90) FL 96+8/5 FLC 8 FAC 12/2 Others 10
Chesterfield (£30,000 on 21/7/93) FL 84+2/4 FLC 9 FAC 6+3 Others 8
Gillingham (£75,000 on 7/8/98) FL 22+8/2 FLC 2 FAC 1 Others 3+1

CARR Graeme
Born: Chester le Street, 28 October 1978
Height: 5'9" Weight: 11.0
A player who came through the ranks to sign professional forms last September, the young defender, cum midfielder, made good progress during the campaign after making his debut as a sub in a 0-0 draw at Plymouth. His first full appearance came in front of a 14,000 crowd at Hull City, and he cleared a goalbound shot off the line to earn the side a point in a 1-1 draw. Looks to have a good future in the game, despite the club plummeting into the Conference.
Scarborough (From trainee on 3/9/97) FL 5+5

CARR Stephen
Born: Dublin, 29 August 1976
Height: 5'9" Weight: 12.2
Club Honours: FLC '99
International Honours: Ei: 3; U21-12; Yth; Sch
A tenacious Spurs' wing back who incredibly missed only one game of the 1998-99 Premiership campaign, and that through a suspension, Stephen continued to grow into his role as a sturdy midfielder with good pace, and impressed his new manager, George Graham, known for high expectations from his defenders. Consistent throughout the season, as his confidence continued to grow so did his appetite to get forward down the flanks and turn provider. Enjoying the occasional shot on target, he was also rewarded with his first senior goal, in the Worthington Cup second round first leg at Brentford. At international level, as

the understudy to Denis Irwin in the Republic of Ireland squad, he got his deserved senior debut for his country in April, when coming in as a replacement for the injured Irwin. For someone so consistent it is difficult to single out any one performance as his best, but his contribution in the goalless draw away to Arsenal would be an achievement any player would be pleased to recall, along with his part in the 1-0 victory over Leicester in the Worthington Cup final at Wembley in March.
Tottenham H (From trainee on 1/9/93) PL 99+3 FLC 14/1 FAC 11

Stephen Carr

CARR-LAWTON Colin
Born: South Shields, 5 September 1978
Height: 5'11" Weight: 11.7
In or on the fringe of Burnley's first team during the club's injury-plagued opening three months of last season, Colin looked too lightweight to pose a serious threat to the first-choice strikers and was eventually loaned out to a Greek club, along with Carl Smith.
Burnley (From trainee on 21/1/97) FL 2+3 FLC 0+2 Others 1+1

CARRAGHER James (Jamie) Lee
Born: Bootle, 28 January 1978
Height: 6'1" Weight: 13.0
Club Honours: FAYC '96
International Honours: E: 1; B-2; U21-19; Yth
Jamie grew up a lot in the centre of Liverpool's defence in 1998-99, despite it not being his most natural position, and having to play there due to a combination of injuries and a dearth of defensive talent. Always a fierce tackler, he was tried in a central defensive role and initially looked out of position. But Roy Evans and Gerard Houllier kept faith with him in that role and, to his credit, he coped extremely well, learning his trade and gaining England U21 honours, as well as a call up to the full England squad. Won his second "Man of the Match" award in the defeat against Charlton

at the Valley for his outstanding defensive display and, if he continues to make solid progress, the young Liverpudlian could well earn a full England cap.

Liverpool (From trainee on 9/10/96) PL 52+4/2 FLC 4+1 FAC 2 Others 7

CARRAGHER Matthew (Matty)
Born: Liverpool, 14 January 1976
Height: 5'9" Weight: 11.4
Club Honours: Div 3 '97

This hard-working Port Vale right back was just beginning to establish himself in the team in 1998-99 when he picked up a cruciate injury at Bolton in November that ended his campaign early. A battling player who always give his all, and has a promising future in the game, he will be raring to go again this time around.

Wigan Ath (From trainee on 25/11/93) FL 102+17 FLC 6+1/1 FAC 10+1/2 Others 7+1
Port Vale (Free on 3/7/97) FL 34+2 FLC 2

CARROLL David (Dave) Francis
Born: Paisley, 20 September 1966
Height: 6'0" Weight: 12.0
Club Honours: FAT '91, '93; GMVC '93
International Honours: E: Sch

As an ever present in the Wycombe midfield for the last ten years, it came as a shock when Dave was dropped after the first ten games of 1998-99, apparently for lack of effort. Having to be content with a substitutes' role until his recall in December, after a spell out with injury he showed magnificent form in the final weeks of the season, scoring four further goals, including a brace against Oldham, and laying on numerous others. A very honest player, there are few more skilful at this level, he has now passed the 500 appearance mark for Wycombe, and is only six goals short of his century. His total of seven goals in 30 starts was impressive for a midfielder in a struggling team.

Wycombe W (£6,000 from Ruislip Manor in 1988 close season) FL 232+10/37 FLC 18+1 FAC 24/5 Others 14/3

CARROLL Roy Eric
Born: Enniskillen, 30 September 1977
Height: 6'2" Weight: 12.9
Club Honours: AMC '99
International Honours: NI: 2; U21-8; Yth

A virtual ever present in the Wigan Athletic goal in 1998-99, once again displaying a presence and maturity way beyond his years, his excellent performances were rewarded at international level, with Northern Ireland U21 caps against Germany and Moldova. Continuing to blossom, and maintaining a high level of consistency between the posts, speculation abounded with stories of a move to a top Premiership club. Very agile for a big man, his performances saw him win an Auto Windscreens winners medal and named runner up in the "Player of the Year" awards. He also made a full appearance against the Republic.

Hull C (From trainee on 7/9/95) FL 46 FLC 2 FAC 1 Others 1
Wigan Ath (£350,000 on 16/4/97) FL 72 FLC 5 FAC 5 Others 11

CARRUTHERS Martin George
Born: Nottingham, 7 August 1972
Height: 5'11" Weight: 11.9

Injured early last season, and unable to win his place back in the Peterborough side, he was loaned to York in January but was unable to find the net in six outings. Having returned to London Road, the experienced, skilful front runner was signed on transfer deadline day by Darlington to partner Marco Gabbiadini up front. In showing himself to be good in the air and willing to run all day, the pair immediately struck up an understanding which produced nine goals between them in the last ten games, with Martin getting two and Marco seven.

Aston Villa (From trainee on 4/7/90) F/PL 2+2 FAC 0+1 Others 0+1
Hull C (Loaned on 31/10/92) FL 13/6 Others 3
Stoke C (£100,000 on 5/7/93) FL 60+31/13 FLC 7+3/1 FAC 3+1 Others 10+4/6
Peterborough U (Signed on 18/11/96) FL 63+4/21 FLC 5+1/2 FAC 6/4 Others 6
York C (Loaned on 29/1/99) FL 3+3
Darlington (Signed on 25/3/99) FL 11/2

CARRUTHERS Matthew
Born: Dover, 22 July 1976
Height: 6'0" Weight: 12.4

In coming to Mansfield on trial just before last Christmas from Dover Athletic, the young striker, who was still in the army, made only four appearances from the subs' bench before returning to the Nationwide Conference. A raw talent, who played in a central position and looked strong and quick, he will be looking for further opportunities to play a higher level of football in the future.

Mansfield T (Free from Dover Ath on 18/2/99) FL 0+5

CARSLEY Lee Kevin
Born: Birmingham, 28 February 1974
Height: 5'10" Weight: 11.11
International Honours: Ei: 11; U21-1

A tough-tackling central midfielder who is at his best operating in a protective role just in front of the central defenders, Lee started 1998-99 as an automatic selection for Derby. His eighth season at the club also saw him as a regular for the Republic of Ireland squad, though a rare knee injury sustained in October meant that he missed the Euro 2000 qualifier against Yugoslavia as well as three league matches. Although the subject of various transfer rumours during the first half of the campaign, it was still something of a surprise when he decided to join Blackburn in transfer deadline week. Coming straight into the Rovers' side for the last eight matches, despite performing well, it was a shock to find himself in a team that was relegated from the Premiership when the final whistle went.

Derby Co (From trainee on 6/7/92) PL 122+16/5 FLC 10+3 FAC 12 Others 3
Blackburn Rov (£3,375,000 on 23/3/99) PL 7+1

CARSON Daniel (Danny)
Born: Liverpool, 2 February 1981
Height: 5'6" Weight: 10.7

A product of Chester's youth policy, and still

a trainee, Danny made his league debut for the club when coming on as substitute in the game at Brentford last November, before being given his full debut at Shrewsbury later in the season. The youngster looked comfortable in a central midfield role and will no doubt be knocking on the door for a regular place in 1999-2000.

Chester C (Trainee) FL 1+1

CARSS Anthony John
Born: Alnwick, 31 March 1976
Height: 5'10" Weight: 12.0

Signed during the 1998 close season, the former Cardiff utility player suffered a woeful start to his Chesterfield career. As the first of a rake of left-sided players to come to the club in 1998-99, he would have been in first-team contention but for a broken leg suffered when appearing as an over-age player in a Youth Alliance game. He recovered to make it as far as the bench in April, and turned in fine performances for the reserves before finally making his first-team debut as a substitute against Notts County.

Blackburn Rov (Free from Bradford C juniors on 29/8/94)
Darlington (Free on 11/8/95) FL 33+24/2 FLC 5/1 FAC 2+1 Others 4
Cardiff C (Free on 28/7/97) FL 36+6/1 FLC 2 FAC 5+1 Others 1
Chesterfield (Free on 7/9/98) FL 2+2

CARTER Alfonso (Alfie) Jermaine
Born: Birmingham, 23 August 1980
Height: 5'10" Weight: 10.6

In graduating from the Walsall YTS ranks to sign professional last April, Alfie enjoyed an outstanding season in the reserve team that just missed out on the Pontins League Division Three championship, his fine crossing of the ball from the left echoing David Beckham. Having made his first-team debut in the final home game against Fulham, replacing Darren Wrack for the last 12 minutes, the young midfielder will be expected to be in the running for places this coming term.

Walsall (From trainee on 30/4/99) FL 0+1

CARTER James (Jimmy) William Charles
Born: Hammersmith, 9 November 1965
Height: 5'10" Weight: 11.1
Club Honours: Div 2 '88

The second coming of Jimmy at Millwall arrived when he turned up in June 1998 on a free from Portsmouth after an absence of some seven years, during which time he earned big money moves to both Liverpool and Arsenal. A fast and tricky winger who became an asset to the team, he had a great start to 1998-99, playing the first 16 games before a back injury sidelined him for the rest of the season, which was a severe blow to both club and player. His biggest disappointment, however, was in not being available to play at Wembley in the Auto Windscreens Shield final before he was released in the summer.

Crystal Palace (From apprentice on 15/11/83)
Queens Park R (Free on 30/9/85)
Millwall (£15,000 on 12/3/87) FL 99+11/10 FLC 6+1 FAC 6+1/2 Others 5+1

Liverpool (£800,000 on 10/1/91) FL 2+3 FAC 2 Others 0+1
Arsenal (£500,000 on 8/10/91) F/PL 18+7/2 FLC 1 FAC 2+1
Oxford U (Loaned on 23/3/94) FL 5
Oxford U (Loaned on 23/12/94) FL 3+1
Portsmouth (Free on 6/7/95) FL 60+12/5 FLC 5+1/1 FAC 0+2
Millwall (Free on 2/7/98) FL 16 FLC 2 FAC 0+1

CARTER Michael David
Born: Darlington, 13 November 1980
Height: 5'11" Weight: 12.3
A young striker who, after scoring prolifically for the youth and reserve teams, was given a chance in the Darlington first team and scored on his debut against Scarborough last November. However, this was his only start, although he came on as a substitute at Manchester City in the FA Cup. Still a trainee, he is one to watch for the future.
Darlington (Trainee) FL 1/1 FAC 0+1

CARTER Timothy (Tim) Douglas
Born: Bristol, 5 October 1967
Height: 6'2" Weight: 13.2
International Honours: E: Yth
Released by Millwall during the 1998 close season, the experienced goalkeeper joined Football League newcomers, Halifax, but was desperately unlucky with injuries throughout his first season at the club. After making his debut as a second-half substitute at Scunthorpe in October, his next appearance, at Carlisle, saw him suffer another injury which he never really recovered from. Freed during the summer, to his credit, Tim played in some matches with broken fingers.
Bristol Rov (From apprentice on 8/10/85) FL 47 FLC 2 FAC 2 Others 2
Newport Co (Loaned on 14/12/87) FL 1
Sunderland (£50,000 on 24/12/87) FL 37 FLC 9 Others 4
Carlisle U (Loaned on 18/3/88) FL 4
Bristol C (Loaned on 15/9/88) FL 3
Birmingham C (Loaned on 21/11/91) FL 2 FLC 1
Hartlepool U (Free on 1/8/92) FL 18 FLC 4 FAC 1 Others 2
Millwall (Free on 6/1/94) FL 4 FLC 0+1
Blackpool (Free on 4/8/95)
Oxford U (Free on 18/8/95) FL 12 FLC 4 Others 1
Millwall (Free on 6/12/95) FL 62 FLC 5 FAC 3 Others 1
Halifax T (Free on 13/7/98) FL 9+1 Others 1

CARTWRIGHT Lee
Born: Rawtenstall, 19 September 1972
Height: 5'8" Weight: 11.0
Club Honours: Div 3 '96
1998-99 was a memorable season for many reasons for Preston's senior pro', who made 14 substitute appearances in both the league and other competitions. Having finally started a match in the FA Cup First Round, after which he was a regular until injured in February, the absence of his pace and the ability to beat his marker adversely affected the promotion push. However, in the interim, he reached 250 league and 300 career games for the club, the first player at Preston to do either since the 1980s. A speedy and direct winger, he also contributed a few goals to the club's promotion effort.
Preston NE (From trainee on 30/7/91) FL 212+47/20 FLC 10+2/2 FAC 15+2/1 Others 17+4/1

CARTWRIGHT Mark Neville
Born: Chester, 13 January 1973
Height: 6'2" Weight: 13.6
The sale of Andy Marriott to Sunderland gave Mark the opportunity to establish himself as Wrexham's first team custodian in 1998-99. An ever present up to the end of February, he blew "hot and cold" on many occasions, often distinguishing himself with some superb stops, but also getting caught out and epitomising the old saying that goalkeepers have to be crazy! Although his concentration was a little awry on occasions, there is no reason why he cannot go on to improve, given the right encouragement. Lost his place in March after Brian Flynn brought in Tommy Wright on loan from Manchester City to give him a rest from first-team duties.
Stockport Co (Free from York C juniors on 17/8/91. Released during 1992 close season)
Wrexham (Signed from USA soccer scholarship on 5/3/94) FL 37 FLC 2 FAC 6 Others 6

CASEY Ryan Peter
Born: Coventry, 3 January 1979
Height: 6'1" Weight: 11.2
Club Honours: Ei: Yth
Despite scoring the first league goal of his career against Cambridge in Swansea's first away game of last season, Ryan has yet to convince the supporters he is worthy of a regular slot in the first-team line-up. On his day, capable of not only beating defenders with skill, he also has the pace that enables him to get to the byline and provide crosses for his strikers. Was included in the Irish youth squad for the World U21 Youth championships in Nigeria last April.
Swansea C (From trainee on 7/5/97) FL 10+16/1 FLC 1+1 Others 1

CASIRAGHI Pierluigi
Born: Monza, Italy, 4 March 1969
Height: 5'11" Weight: 12.3
Club Honours: ESC '98
International Honours: Italy: 44
In their latest instalment to transform themselves from the Blues into the Azzurri, Chelsea broke their transfer record during the 1998 close season and lured "Gigi" to the Bridge to join Gianfranco Zola and former Serie "A" team-mates Roberto Di Matteo (Lazio) and Gianluca Vialli (Juventus). Having become a national hero when he scored the winning goal in the World Cup qualifier play off against Russia which sent Italy to France, he was inexplicably omitted from the 22-man squad by Cesare Maldini, along with the other hero of the qualifying campaign – Franco Zola. A self-confessed Mark Hughes fan, he replaced the Welsh legend, who moved on to Southampton, and led the line in the same muscular fashion – quite happy to receive the ball and lay it off to supporting colleagues. Initially, he suffered some bad luck, but his first goal in English football, in his tenth match, was worth waiting for. At Anfield – the Blues' hoodoo ground – he collected a long ball, dribbled past David James and squeezed it home from a narrow angle to give Chelsea the lead, his third goal at the ground following two for Italy in Euro 96. After breaking his goalscoring "duck", his misfortune in front of goal continued – against FC Copenhagen his superb header rebounded off the crossbar for Brian Laudrup to head back in for the winning goal. His ill luck was compounded in the tenth Premiership match of the campaign when he sustained a serious knee injury at Upton Park, following a collision with two West Ham players, which prevented him playing for the rest of the season. It is an indication of the Italian's popularity that his team mates paraded his shirt during the following home game to rapturous applause. After such a fleeting glimpse of their record signing, the Chelsea faithful are hopeful that this top-class centre forward will return fully recovered and receive his share of good fortune which is long overdue.
Chelsea (£5,400,000 from Lazio, via Juventus, on 15/7/98) PL 10/1 Others 3+2

Pierluigi Casiraghi

CASKEY Darren Mark
Born: Basildon, 21 August 1974
Height: 5'8" Weight: 11.9
International Honours: E: Yth (UEFAYC '93); Sch
Reading fans at last began to see the best of Darren, one of the most consistent performers during a difficult season in 1998-99. He made more first-team appearances than any other player, weighed in with some vital goals from midfield, and continued to dominate not just with crunching tackles but also long, raking passes which could open up opposing defences.
Tottenham H (From trainee on 6/3/92) PL 20+12/4 FLC 3+1/1 FAC 6+1
Watford (Loaned on 27/10/95) FL 6/1
Reading (£700,000 on 28/2/96) FL 102+13/9 FLC 5+2/2 FAC 3+1/1 Others 1

CASPER Christopher (Chris) Martin
Born: Burnley, 28 April 1975
Height: 6'0" Weight: 11.11
Club Honours: FAYC '92
International Honours: E: U21-1; Yth
(EUFAC '93)
The tall central defender arrived on loan from Manchester United last September and so impressed during his spell with Reading that the club made the move a permanent one. Although he accumulated ten bookings and one sending off during the season, those figures belie the player's undoubted ability to make important and well-timed interceptions in and around the penalty area. Contracted to the Royals until 2002, Chris is the son of Frank, the former Burnley striker.
Manchester U (From trainee on 3/2/93) PL 0+2 FLC 3 FAC 1 Others 0+1
Bournemouth (Loaned on 11/1/96) FL 16/1
Swindon T (Loaned on 5/9/97) FL 8+1/1
Reading (£300,000 on 16/9/98) FL 32 FLC 1 FAC 1 Others 1

CASTLE Stephen (Steve) Charles
Born: Barking, 17 May 1966
Height: 5'11" Weight: 12.10
A tireless, hard-working Peterborough midfielder, who always puts the team first, Steve assisted the club on the coaching side last season but still found time to make nearly 30 appearances. A great favourite of the fans, unfortunately, injuries stopped him from being a regular. With a proven record of scoring vital goals, he netted four during the campaign, all of them being in drawn games or those that were won by the odd goal.
Leyton Orient (From apprentice on 18/5/84) FL 232+11/55 FLC 15+1/5 FAC 23+1/6 Others 18+2
Plymouth Arg (£195,000 on 30/6/92) FL 98+3/35 FLC 5/1 FAC 8/2 Others 6/1
Birmingham C (£225,000 on 21/7/95) FL 16+7/1 FLC 11 FAC 1 Others 3/1
Gillingham (Loaned on 15/2/96) FL 5+1/1
Leyton Orient (Loaned on 3/2/97) FL 4/1
Peterborough U (Free on 14/5/97) FL 60+3/7 FLC 5+1 FAC 3+1/2 Others 3+1

CASTLEDINE Stewart Mark
Born: Wandsworth, 22 January 1973
Height: 6'1" Weight: 12.13
Had a terrible run of injuries at Wimbledon during the 1998-99 season and made just one first-team appearance – a very difficult game at Highbury against a rampant Arsenal team who eventually won 5-1. An aggressive midfielder with tremendous workrate, and a player who never gives the opposition a rest, one thing that you can be sure of is that the female Dons' fans will be hoping to see more of him next season.
Wimbledon (From trainee on 2/7/91) F/PL 18+10/4 FLC 4/3 FAC 2+3
Wycombe W (Loaned on 25/8/95) FL 7/3

CHALK Martyn Peter Glyn
Born: Swindon, 30 August 1969
Height: 5'6" Weight: 10.0
A tricky little Wrexham winger who can cause the opposing defence many problems when in the mood, delivering important crosses for his strikers, Martyn was once again an important member of the squad in 1998-99, despite receiving an ankle injury in

August which kept him out of action until October. Could do with adding a little more consistency to his play, but is very popular with the supporters and was given a two-year contract for his efforts.
Derby Co (£10,000 from Louth U on 23/1/90) FL 4+3/1 FAC 3/1 Others 0+1
Stockport Co (£40,000 on 30/6/94) FL 29+14/6 FLC 7+1/2 FAC 2+3 Others 2+2
Wrexham (Signed on 19/2/96) FL 87+29/6 FLC 3+1 FAC 11+3 Others 6

CHALLINOR David (Dave) Paul
Born: Chester, 2 October 1975
Height: 6'1" Weight: 12.6
International Honours: E: Yth; Sch
Best known as the possessor of the longest throw in the Football League, Dave's projectiles can indeed be potent missiles, and set up many goalscoring opportunities for his team mates. Standing out for his distributional skills, he has an excellent all-round game, is never less than dependable, while his favourite position is being tucked in just behind the midfield, from where he contributed two league goals last season. Something of a closet intellectual, he turned down a university place to pursue a football career.
Tranmere Rov (Signed from Brombrough Pool on 18/7/94) FL 61+10/3 FLC 3+1 FAC 4

CHALLIS Trevor Michael
Born: Paddington, 23 October 1975
Height: 5'9" Weight: 11.4
International Honours: E: U21-1; Yth
Signed from Queens Park Rangers during the 1998 close season, and immediately looking comfortable in possession, the former England U21 full back quickly made an impression at Bristol Rovers with his distribution and ability to get forward to support the strikers. It was no surprise when he was appointed captain in December, the extra responsibility given to him by the manager, Ian Holloway, acknowledging him as Rovers' most consistent performer. Despite being sent off at Gillingham and Northampton in his first half-dozen league appearances, Trevor's wholehearted tackling won him many admirers with Rovers' supporters and he picked up the "Player of the Season" award.
Queens Park R (From trainee on 1/7/94) F/PL 12+1 FAC 2
Bristol Rov (Free on 15/7/98) FL 38 FLC 2 FAC 6 Others 1

CHAMBERLAIN Alec Francis Roy
Born: March, 20 June 1964
Height: 6'2" Weight: 13.9
Club Honours: Div 1 '96; Div 2 '98
Alec has now clocked up more than 500 league appearances for five different clubs, and over 600 senior appearances in all. A player who sets remarkable standards of consistency, this experienced Watford goalie always remains calm and fully focused on the game, and enjoys the full confidence of his defence. An ever present in the league for the second consecutive season, the highlight of a successful term was probably the remarkable save that frustrated Stockport's Brett Angell.
Ipswich T (Free from Ramsey T on 27/7/81)
Colchester U (Free on 3/8/82) FL 188 FLC 11 FAC 10 Others 12
Everton (£80,000 on 28/7/87)
Tranmere Rov (Loaned on 1/11/87) FL 15
Luton T (£150,000 on 27/7/88) FL 138 FLC 7 FAC 7 Others 7
Sunderland (Free on 8/7/93) FL 89+1 FLC 9 FAC 8 Others 1
Watford (£40,000 on 10/7/96) FL 96 FLC 5 FAC 6 Others 3

CHAPMAN Benjamin (Ben)
Born: Scunthorpe, 2 March 1979
Height: 5'7" Weight: 11.0
Having made his Grimsby first-team debut in 1997-98, Ben went back to the reserves, where he impressed as a hard-tackling left-sided defender when putting together many determined and uncompromising displays in 1998-99. Despite the feeling that he was being overlooked, the youngster was finally given another all too brief taste of senior football when coming off the bench in the final minute of the last game of the season to make his Football League debut. Hopefully, he can add to that in 1999-2000.
Grimsby T (From trainee on 11/7/97) FL 0+1 Others 0+1

CHAPPLE Philip (Phil) Richard
Born: Norwich, 26 November 1966
Height: 6'2" Weight: 13.1
Club Honours: Div 3 '91
Signed from Charlton during the 1998 close season, the Peterborough manager, Barry Fry, said of Phil: "In bringing him to London Road, the club has captured the best central defender in the Third Division". Unfortunately, carrying an injury, he made just one appearance, at Leyton Orient, and the fans are still waiting to see how good he is. If they are lucky they will find him to be a strong tackler, good in the air, and a player who gives nothing less than 100 per-cent effort. He can also get vital goals from free kicks and corners.
Norwich C (From apprentice on 10/7/85)
Cambridge U (Signed on 29/3/88) FL 183+4/19 FLC 11/2 FAC 23/1 Others 17
Charlton Ath (£100,000 on 13/8/93) FL 128+14/15 FLC 11 FAC 9 Others 5
Peterborough U (Free on 2/7/98) FL 1 Others 1

CHARLERY Kenneth (Kenny) Leroy
Born: Stepney, 28 November 1964
Height: 6'1" Weight: 13.12
International Honours: St Lucia: 3
It was a truly remarkable campaign for Kenny, and it was no surprise that he scooped the award for Barnet's "Most Improved Player". As you can imagine, it is not normally an accolade associated with a 34-year old, but he proved to be a revelation during a difficult season and won over a previously sceptical Underhill crowd in emphatic style. In October, he was allocated the captain's armband and, responding admirably to his new role, he managed to net 16 goals, including two braces (at Southend and at Cambridge). To cap a magnificent nine months, he was then selected to play for St Lucia in the Copa Caribe Cup and proceeded to score two

goals on his international debut, against Martinique. Both he and Warren Hackett made history when they took to the field, being the first players to have ever gained full international recognition whilst on the club's books. His main strengths are shielding the ball in attack, and using his experience to capitalise on opponents' defensive errors.

Maidstone U (£35,000 from Fisher on 1/3/89) FL 41+18/11 FLC 1+3/1 FAC 0+3 Others 5+4
Peterborough U (£20,000 on 28/3/91) FL 45+6/19 FLC 10/5 FAC 3/1 Others 11/7
Watford (£350,000 on 16/10/92) FL 45+3/13 FLC 3 FAC 1 Others 0+1
Peterborough U (£150,000 on 16/12/93) FL 70/24 FLC 2 FAC 2+1/3 Others 2/1
Birmingham C (£350,000 on 4/7/95) FL 8+9/4 FLC 3+1/2 Others 2+1
Southend U (Loaned on 12/1/96) FL 2+1
Peterborough U (Signed on 9/2/96) FL 55+1/12 FLC 4/1 FAC 6/6 Others 6/1
Stockport Co (£85,000 on 25/3/97) FL 8+2
Barnet (£80,000 on 7/8/97) FL 58+16/22 FLC 5+1 FAC 2 Others 2+1

CHARLES Gary Andrew
Born: Newham, 13 April 1970
Height: 5'9" Weight: 11.8
Club Honours: FMC '92; FLC '96
International Honours: E: 2; U21-4

Having signed a new long-term contract in the summer of 1998, Gary made a promising start to Aston Villa's 1998-99 campaign, looking fitter and sharper than he had been for years, and was a key figure when playing in an attacking right-wing-back role. Encouraged to get forward as much as possible to supply crosses for the forwards, his form was so good that John Gregory suggested that the England manager, Glenn Hoddle – take a look at him. He also managed to get on the scoresheet a couple of times – against Middlesbrough and Stromgodset. However, following the arrival of Steve Watson from Newcastle in October, he lost his Villa place and was eventually sold to the Portuguese side, Benfica, for £1.5 million in January, after spending four years at Villa Park.

Nottingham F (From trainee on 7/11/87) F/PL 54+2/1 FLC 9 FAC 8+2/1 Others 4+2
Leicester C (Loaned on 16/3/89) FL 5+3
Derby Co (£750,000 on 29/7/93) FL 61/3 FLC 5+1 FAC 1 Others 9
Aston Villa (Signed on 6/1/95) PL 72+7/3 FLC 9+1 FAC 5+2 Others 6+3/1

CHARLTON Simon Thomas
Born: Huddersfield, 25 October 1971
Height: 5'8" Weight: 11.10
International Honours: E: Yth

A valuable member of the Birmingham defence in 1998-99, his tigerish tackling and fine passing bolstering the left flank, Simon shrugged off a groin injury which kept him out of action for three months, to come back strongly. Although crossing and adventurous running made him a key attacking component, his ability to hoist long throws into dangerous areas gave City further options. Is a player who really enjoys the game.

Huddersfield T (From trainee on 1/7/89) FL 121+3/1 FLC 9/1 FAC 10 Others 14

Southampton (£250,000 on 8/6/93) PL 104+10/2 FLC 9+4/1 FAC 8+1
Birmingham C (£250,000 on 5/12/97) FL 50+2 FLC 3 FAC 1

CHARNOCK Philip (Phil) Anthony
Born: Southport, 14 February 1975
Height: 5'11" Weight: 11.2

Having just completed his third year at Crewe since arriving from Liverpool, Phil has already signed a new contract. A hard-working central midfielder, who misses very few games, just two in 1998-99, he also added two goals to his overall total during the campaign – one in a 4-4 home draw against Bolton and the other effectively securing three points in a 2-1 win at Swindon. He is also a good passer who strikes the ball well, and is always looking to set up attacks. Can also play at full back if needed.

Liverpool (From trainee on 16/3/93) FLC 1 Others 0+1
Blackpool (Loaned on 9/2/96) FL 0+4
Crewe Alex (Signed on 30/9/96) FL 97+12/6 FLC 7 FAC 4 Others 6

CHARVET Laurent Jean
Born: Beziers, France, 8 May 1973
Height: 5'10" Weight: 12.3
Club Honours: ECWC '98

Having joined Newcastle during the 1998 close season, when Chelsea decided against a permanent move following his loan period with them, Laurent proved a dependable member of the United defence in 1998-99. Although probably best in his preferred position of right back, injuries led to him being pressed into service at centre back for large parts of the season, and he performed that role with great credit. His aggression and strength suits him well for the position, as he is deceptively quick, is rarely beaten for pace and, although not particularly tall, he is difficult to beat in the air. He made a good start for his new club, being "Man of the Match" on his debut in the opening game of the season. Despite Ruud Gullit's known liking for rotating his squad, he was a regular selection, missing only four games until a knee-ligament injury ruled him out of the FA Cup semi final and all subsequent Premiership games, before returning to play in the FA Cup Final. Also enjoys supplementing the attack whenever he can, although not a frequent scorer, and his only counter of the campaign came when he contributed an important goal at Middlesbrough that helped earn a point.

Chelsea (Loaned from Cannes on 22/1/98) PL 7+4/2 FLC 0+1 Others 0+1
Newcastle U (£750,000 on 23/7/98) PL 30+1/1 FLC 4 FAC 5 Others 2

CHENERY Benjamin (Ben) Roger
Born: Ipswich, 28 January 1977
Height: 6'0" Weight: 12.5

A right back in his second season at Cambridge in 1998-99, he was virtually ever present, having fought back from a horrific head injury in 1997-98. Comfortable on the ball, good positionally, and known as "Mr Reliable", he came on in leaps and bounds last season after comfortably seeing off Sheffield Wednesday's lively foreign

wingers in the Worthington Cup-tie at Hillsborough.

Luton T (From trainee on 3/3/95) FL 2 FAC 1
Cambridge U (Free on 3/7/97) FL 80/2 FLC 7 FAC 6 Others 3

CHERRY Steven (Steve) Reginald
Born: Nottingham, 5 August 1960
Height: 6'1" Weight: 13.0
Club Honours: AIC '95
International Honours: E: Yth

Released by Rotherham and joining non-league Rushden & Diamonds in March 1997, the experienced goalkeeper came back into the Football League with Notts County in March 1998 from Stalybridge before moving to Mansfield under the Bosman ruling during the 1998 close season. A player with well over 500 league games under his belt, due to the suspension of Ian Bowling Steve was called into action for the opening match of 1998-99, the 3-0 defeat at Brentford being his only first-team game, and he left for Oldham in transfer deadline week on a short-term, non-contract basis.

Derby Co (From apprentice on 22/3/78) FL 77 FLC 5 FAC 8
Port Vale (Loaned on 26/11/80) FL 4 FAC 4
Walsall (£25,000 on 10/8/84) FL 71 FLC 10 FAC 7 Others 6
Plymouth Arg (£17,000 on 23/10/86) FL 73 FLC 4 FAC 5 Others 1
Chesterfield (Loaned on 1/12/88) FL 10 Others 3
Notts Co (£70,000 on 16/2/89) FL 266 FLC 17 FAC 14 Others 31
Watford (Free on 14/7/95) FL 4
Plymouth Arg (Signed on 19/2/96) FL 16 Others 3
Rotherham U (Free on 15/7/96) FL 20 FLC 2 Others 1 (Free to Rushden & Diamonds on 7/3/97)
Notts Co (Free from Stalybridge Celtic on 26/3/98)
Mansfield T (Free on 30/7/98) FL 1
Oldham Ath (Free on 25/3/99)

Steve Chettle

CHETTLE Stephen (Steve)
Born: Nottingham, 27 September 1968
Height: 6'1" Weight: 13.3
Club Honours: FMC '89, '92; FLC '89, '90; Div 1 '98
International Honours: E: U21-12

A model of consistency, Steve took over the captaincy at Nottingham Forest following Colin Cooper's move to Middlesbrough early last season. Having established himself as a defensive lynch pin at the City Ground over the last 11 years, the former England U21 international recorded his 500th appearance for the club when coming off the bench at West Ham in February, in what was his testimonial year. A player who rarely grabs the limelight, and one who missed few games for Forest in difficult circumstances, he again looked comfortable in possession, especially when looking to make the right pass. Scored two penalties in drawn matches at home to Blackburn and Southampton.

Nottingham F (From apprentice on 28/8/86) F/PL 388+16/10 FLC 45+3/1 FAC 36+1 Others 21+2/2

CHRISTIE Iyseden
Born: Coventry, 14 November 1976
Height: 6'0" Weight: 12.6
Missed only a handful of matches for Mansfield in 1998-99, coming off the subs' bench in over 20 of them as the management favoured the Lee Peacock/Tony Lormor partnership up front. However, he still managed a useful number of goals, despite Town's play-off ambitions disappearing. And while his temperament is sometimes questionable, it is more down to his enthusiasm getting the better of him than anything malicious. Is a striker who always looks to test the 'keeper.

Coventry C (From trainee on 22/5/95) PL 0+1 FLC 0+1
Bournemouth (Loaned on 18/11/96) FL 3+1
Mansfield T (Loaned on 7/2/97) FL 8
Mansfield T (Free on 16/6/97) FL 44+37/18 FLC 4/5 FAC 0+4 Others 2+1

CHRISTIE Malcolm Neil
Born: Peterborough, 11 April 1979
Height: 5'6" Weight: 11.4
Spotted by Derby playing in non-league football, the young striker was signed from Nuneaton Borough last November for an initial fee which, depending upon appearances, could rise by a further £100,000. Top scorer at the time of his transfer, his potential was soon displayed when he came on as a substitute at Sheffield Wednesday and, through on goal, was pulled down by the 'keeper, resulting in a red card for the latter. He also impressed in the reserves, and with the right training will surely continue to develop in the coming seasons.

Derby Co (£50,000 + from Nuneaton Borough on 2/11/98) PL 0+2

CLAPHAM James (Jamie) Richard
Born: Lincoln, 7 December 1975
Height: 5'9" Weight: 10.11
Jamie played in every game for Ipswich last season, although not an ever present, having been dropped for the trip to Watford before coming on as a substitute. Had a mixed start to the campaign, during which he struggled to find the level of form that he had attained previously, compounded by the fact that Bobby Petta was also having form problems. With the manager settling on a

formation of three big defenders at the back, he was asked to undertake the left-sided, attacking wing-back role and, at times, was solely responsible for all the thrust and width down that flank, whilst not neglecting his defensive responsibilities. Had a tremendous finish to 1998-99, being voted as "Player of the Year" by the supporters, who also voted his effort against Port Vale as the "Goal of the Season" at Portman Road. It was his first goal and, as debut goals go it was a cracker latching onto the ball on the left, he cut in and fired a right-foot screamer into the top right-hand corner of the net.

Tottenham H (From trainee on 1/7/94) PL 0+1
Leyton Orient (Loaned on 29/1/97) FL 6
Bristol Rov (Loaned on 27/3/97) FL 4+1
Ipswich T (£300,000 on 9/1/98) FL 67+1/3 FLC 3+1 FAC 2 Others 3

CLARE Daryl Adam
Born: Jersey, 1 August 1978
Height: 5'9" Weight: 11.12
Club Honours: AMC '98
International Honours: Ei: U21-4
1998-99 was a frustrating season for this Grimsby striker who, although impressing at international level for Eire, scoring goals against an Irish FA XI for the "B" side, and Croatia in an U21 Euro 2000 match, failed to make his mark at Blundell Park. This, despite the Mariners' constant injury problems up front and lack of fire power. The general view amongst Town's fans was that this youngster should have been given far more opportunities, especially as he displays an abundance of skill and speed around the box.

Grimsby T (From trainee on 9/12/95) FL 15+30/3 FLC 0+3/1 FAC 1+4 Others 4+2

Daryl Clare

CLARIDGE Stephen (Steve) Edward
Born: Portsmouth, 10 April 1966
Height: 5'11" Weight: 12.10
Club Honours: Div 3 '91, Div 2 '95; AMC '95; FLC '97
Signed from Wolves at the start of 1998-99, his nine league goals helping to keep

Portsmouth in the First Division for another season, Steve's bustling, never-say-die attitude on the pitch gave him an autonomous relationship with the hometown supporters as he battled, often on his own up front, through a difficult campaign on the south coast. Given more support, he would have netted more goals for Pompey, but his on-the-ball skills, dribbling, and general footballing ability gave him the "menace" tag, whoever the opposition. His untidy pitch appearance belies his skill to hold the ball up well, and nicknamed "Gypsy" by his fellow players, this footballing veteran should complete his 400th league game this coming term.

Bournemouth (Signed from Fareham on 30/11/84) FL 3+4/1 Others 1 (£10,000 to Weymouth in October 1985)
Crystal Palace (Signed on 11/10/88)
Aldershot (£14,000 on 13/10/88) FL 58+4/19 FLC 2+1 FAC 6/1 Others 5/2
Cambridge U (£75,000 on 8/2/90) FL 56+23/28 FLC 2+4/2 FAC 1 Others 6+3/1
Luton T (£160,000 on 17/7/92) FL 15+1/2 FLC 2/3 Others 2/1
Cambridge U (£195,000 on 20/11/92) FL 53/18 FLC 4/3 FAC 4 Others 3
Birmingham C (£350,000 on 7/1/94) FL 86+2/35 FLC 14+1/2 FAC 7 Others 9+1/5
Leicester C (£1,200,000 on 1/3/96) P/FL 53+10/17 FLC 8/2 FAC 4/1 Others 3+1/1
Portsmouth (Loaned on 23/1/98) FL 10/2
Wolverhampton W (£400,000 on 26/3/98) FL 4+1 FAC 1
Portsmouth (£200,000 on 10/8/98) FL 39/9 FLC 2+1 FAC 2/1

CLARK Ian David
Born: Stockton, 23 October 1974
Height: 5'11" Weight: 11.7
1998-99 was a mixed season for this Hartlepool left-sided utility player. For most of it he was played at left back and as a defender who was able to overlap effectively while doubling as a wing forward. However, despite being determined to succeed, he was not as regular a goalscorer as he would have liked, but as the possessor of a powerful shot he was always dangerous when getting into a forward position.

Doncaster Rov (Free from Stockton on 11/8/95) FL 23+22/3 FLC 1+2 FAC 1+1 Others 4/1
Hartlepool U (Free on 24/10/97) FL 55+8/9 FLC 2 FAC 2+1 Others 4

CLARK Lee Robert
Born: Wallsend, 27 October 1972
Height: 5'8" Weight: 11.7
Club Honours: Div 1 '93, '99
International Honours: E: U21-11; Yth; Sch
The Sunderland schemer suffered terrible luck on the opening day of last season, breaking his leg against Queens Park Rangers – an injury which kept him on the sidelines until November, when he returned in the Worthington Cup-tie at Everton as a substitute and scored from the spot in the penalty shoot-out victory. Possessing vision and good passing ability, Lee added a second First Division championship medal to the one he won with Newcastle in 1992, and is one of the few players who is revered by both clubs' fans. Was also picked by his fellow professionals, for the second year

Lee Clark

running, as a member of their award winning First Division select. Stop Press: Having been at the centre of an embarrasment to the club, Lee moved to Fulham for £3 million on 8 July.

Newcastle U (From trainee on 9/12/89) F/PL 153+42/23 FLC 17 FAC 14+2/3 Others 7+5/1
Sunderland (£2,750,000 on 25/6/97) FL 72+1/16 FLC 4+1 FAC 4 Others 3

CLARK Martin Alan
Born: Accrington, 12 September 1970
Height: 5'9" Weight: 10.12
Unfortunately, Martin was yet another Rotherham player who failed to make an impact in 1998-99, his one and only appearance coming in late February. A player who can play at full back or as a sweeper, he was released at the end of the season.

Rotherham U (Free from Southport on 25/6/97) FL 29 FLC 2 FAC 3

CLARK Peter James
Born: Romford, 10 December 1979
Height: 6'1" Weight: 12.7
The former Arsenal trainee had a promising first season in the Football League with his new club, having joined Carlisle in time for the start of 1998-99. A left-sided player who featured both in defence and midfield, he played with enthusiasm and commitment using his undoubted pace to good effect. And, while he still has a lot to learn, playing in a more successful side should help to develop his undoubted ability. Thus he can view the new campaign with some degree of anticipation.

Carlisle U (Signed from Arsenal juniors on 6/8/98) FL 35+1 FAC 1 Others 2

CLARK Simon
Born: Boston, 12 March 1967
Height: 6'1" Weight: 12.12
Simon was again a first-team regular for Leyton Orient, this time in 1998-99, and again proved to be an excellent central defender and a threat in the opponents' area at set pieces. Although not scoring as many goals as in the previous season, he still contributed with vital strikes, whilst being part of one of the best defences in the Third Division at the other end of the pitch. Big and strong, he thrives on aerial battles.

Peterborough U (Free from Stevenage Borough on 25/3/94) FL 102+5/3 FLC 5 FAC 12 Others 7+1/1
Leyton Orient (£20,000 on 16/6/97) FL 79/9 FLC 5 FAC 7 Others 4

CLARK William (Billy) Raymond
Born: Christchurch, 19 May 1967
Height: 6'0" Weight: 12.4
Billy's appearances were restricted at Exeter last season, mainly due to a long-standing toe injury. However, his commanding presence, whether in defence or midfield, and his awareness and ability at set pieces was crucial to City. Being granted a free transfer at the end of the term was merely indicative of the ability of the crop of young defenders coming through the ranks at the club.

Bournemouth (From apprentice on 25/9/84) FL 4
Bristol Rov (Signed on 16/10/87) FL 235+13/14 FLC 11+1 FAC 8+1 Others 19+2/1
Exeter C (Free on 30/11/97) FL 39+2/3 FLC 2 FAC 4+1/1 Others 3/1

CLARKE Adrian James
Born: Cambridge, 28 September 1974
Height: 5'10" Weight: 11.0
Club Honours: FAYC '94
International Honours: E: Yth; Sch
Adrian seemed to suffer more than most as Southend's slide continued during the 1998-99 season, his confidence almost totally evaporating. An exciting wide player when on form, he began the campaign as a regular but lost his place and only contributed to the side occasionally afterwards. His close control and pace are an attribute that any team would welcome, so it's hoped that the arrival of Alan Little as manager will see a return of the player of old, despite him being out of contract during the summer.

Arsenal (From trainee on 6/7/93) PL 4+3 FAC 1+1
Rotherham U (Loaned on 2/12/96) FL 1+1 Others 1
Southend U (Free on 27/3/97) FL 63+13/8 FLC 7/1 FAC 3 Others 1

CLARKE Andrew (Andy) Weston
Born: Islington, 22 July 1967
Height: 5'10" Weight: 11.7
Club Honours: GMVC '91
International Honours: E: SP-2
Not in line for first-team representation at Wimbledon, Andy was loaned to Port Vale last August in order to help arrest the club's poor start, making his debut at Swindon, but could only manage six appearances, four of them from the bench, and never really looked the part before returning to Selhurst Park. His next stop on loan was at Northampton in January, playing just four times prior to going home. A fast and energetic striker who at his best could leave defenders in his wake, and probably at his most dangerous out wide, the supporters remembered him for beating the whole Lincoln defence prior to having his shot well saved by the 'keeper. Released by the Dons on 23 April, he signed for Peterborough on 4 May.

Wimbledon (£250,000 from Barnet on 21/2/91) F/PL 74+96/17 FLC 13+12/4 FAC 9+8/2
Port Vale (Loaned on 28/8/98) FL 2+4
Northampton T (Loaned on 15/1/99) FL 2+2

CLARKE Clive Richard
Born: Dublin, 14 January 1980
Height: 6'1" Weight: 12.3
International Honours: Ei: Yth
Having come through Stoke's ranks as a trainee, and showing good promise to be taken on as a professional in January 1997, the young Republic of Ireland U18 international left back was given his opportunity in 1998-99, and played the last two games of the season. A player who looks to break through this coming term, he performed particularly well and, indeed, may have won his chance earlier but for injury.

Stoke C (From trainee on 25/1/97) FL 2

CLARKE Darrell James
Born: Mansfield, 16 December 1977
Height: 5'10" Weight: 11.6
Still developing, this talented 21-year-old Mansfield midfielder was in and out of the side throughout last season due to injury and

loss of form. A local lad who graduated from the YTS scheme, which helps make him popular with the Field Mill faithful, if he can steer clear of injury to retain a regular place he should develop into a fine player.

Mansfield T (From trainee on 3/7/96) FL 68+22/11 FLC 3/1 FAC 3+1/1 Others 0+2

CLARKE Timothy (Tim) Joseph
Born: Stourbridge, 16 May 1965
Height: 6'3" Weight: 15.2
Club Honours: AMC '96

A big, commanding goalkeeper, Tim started last season as Scunthorpe's first choice and held down that place until Christmas. Then, a slight dip in form saw him lose out to Tommy Evans during the second half of the campaign, though his experience proved useful in helping the reserves to promotion. Returned to the side for the two play-off matches against Swansea, before being left out for the final at Wembley.

Coventry C (£25,000 from Halesowen T on 22/10/90)
Huddersfield T (£15,000 on 22/7/91) FL 70 FLC 7 FAC 6 Others 8 (Free to Halesowen on 19/8/93)
Rochdale (Loaned on 12/2/93) FL 2
Shrewsbury T (Free from Altrincham on 21/10/93) FL 30+1 FLC 3 Others 1 (Free to Witton A during 1996 close season)
York C (Free on 7/9/96) FL 17 FLC 1 FAC 4 Others 1
Scunthorpe U (Signed on 21/2/97) FL 78 FLC 5 FAC 6 Others 5

CLARKSON Ian Stewart
Born: Solihull, 4 December 1970
Height: 5'11" Weight: 12.0
Club Honours: AMC '91

A busy Northampton right-wing back, and a strong defender who likes to get forward, Ian's 1998-99 season ended in August when he received a broken leg in the 0-0 draw with Lincoln at Sixfields. His recovery was long and his presence missed in the Cobblers' side, especially as he could also play midfield and sweeper, if needed. Was released during the summer.

Birmingham C (From trainee on 15/12/88) FL 125+11 FLC 12 FAC 5+1 Others 17+1
Stoke C (£40,000 on 13/9/93) FL 72+3 FLC 6 FAC 5 Others 8+2
Northampton T (Free on 2/8/96) FL 90+2/1 FLC 7+1 FAC 6 Others 10/1

CLARKSON Philip (Phil) Ian
Born: Garstang, 13 November 1968
Height: 5'10" Weight: 12.5

Blackpool's midfield dynamo hardly missed a game last season and, although his goal tally was down on the previous term, he still managed to hit the target in four out of five consecutive early matches before having a lean spell. Good in the air, despite his lack of real height, he is a valuable utility player who can be used either up front or in midfield with confidence.

Crewe Alex (£22,500 from Fleetwood T on 15/10/91) FL 76+22/27 FLC 6+2/1 FAC 3+2/2 Others 7+4/1
Scunthorpe U (Loaned on 30/10/95) FL 4/1
Scunthorpe U (Free on 13/2/96) FL 45+3/18 FLC 2/1 FAC 3/2 Others 1
Blackpool (£80,000 on 6/2/97) FL 103+3/27 FLC 7 FAC 3/2 Others 4/1

CLAYTON Gary
Born: Sheffield, 2 February 1963
Height: 5'10" Weight: 12.8
International Honours: E: SP-1

Unfortunately, this vastly experienced Torquay midfielder was forced to quit the game last March, after what initially appeared to be a run-of-the-mill knee injury turned out to be far more serious than originally suspected. A player who was much admired by the Plainmoor faithful, his leadership and eye for a telling pass will be greatly missed.

Doncaster Rov (Signed from Burton A on 23/8/86) FL 34+1/5 FLC 2 FAC 3 Others 2
Cambridge U (£10,000 on 2/7/87) FL 166+13/17 FLC 17+1/3 FAC 9 Others 7/2
Peterborough U (Loaned on 25/1/91) FL 4
Huddersfield T (£20,000 on 18/2/94) FL 15+4/1 FAC 0+1 Others 4/2
Plymouth Arg (Signed on 10/8/95) FL 32+6/2 FLC 2 FAC 2 Others 1
Torquay U (Free on 21/8/97) FL 56/2 FLC 4 FAC 4/1 Others 4

CLEAVER Christopher (Chris) William
Born: Hitchin, 24 March 1979
Height: 5'10" Weight: 11.3

A young Peterborough striker, Chris failed to make his mark last season, coming off the bench just three times and failing to get among the goals. Still a youngster, and one who will run all day for the cause, he was loaned out to non-league Grantham in January in an effort to sharpen him up. Hopefully, he will warrant more opportunities in 1999-2000.

Peterborough U (From trainee on 22/3/97) FL 10+19/3 FLC 0+2 FAC 0+2 Others 1+2

CLEGG Michael Jaime
Born: Ashton under Lyne, 3 July 1977
Height: 5'8" Weight: 11.8
Club Honours: FAYC '95
International Honours: E: U21-2

A very able Manchester United full back who is good in the tackle and excellent on the overlap, Michael found that the challenge for first-team places was particularly frantic at Old Trafford in 1998-99, with so many youngsters vying for a chance in the side. Despite making only fleeting appearances, he was particularly impressive during United's short-lived Worthington Cup run against Bury, Nottingham Forest and Spurs, and is sure to feature again before too long.

Manchester U (From trainee on 1/7/95) PL 4+3 FLC 4 FAC 3+1 Others 0+1

CLELAND Alexander (Alex)
Born: Glasgow, 10 December 1970
Height: 5'8" Weight: 11.6
Club Honours: SPL '95, '96, '97; SC '94, '96
International Honours: S: B-2; U21-11; Sch

Regarded as the best uncapped full back in Scotland when Everton took advantage of his freedom of contract to snap him up from Glasgow Rangers in July 1998, Alex made a bright impression in the Premiership before a torn calf muscle ended his campaign prematurely last Janaury. However, until then the tidy and versatile defender had been a regular in Toffees' first team, figuring in a

variety of positions – right and left-wing back, right midfield, and was playing in central defence more than competently when he sustained his season-ending injury. He also came close to opening his English goals account in style with a "David Beckham" type strike from the halfway line against Leeds in September, which whistled inches wide of the target.

Dundee U (From juniors on 18/6/87) SL 131+20/8 SLC 10+1 SC 7+2 Others 8+1/1
Glasgow R (Signed on 26/1/95) SL 90+6/4 SLC 8+2 SC 13+1 Others 13+1
Everton (Free on 3/7/98) FL 16+2 FLC 2+1 FAC 1

CLEMENCE Stephen Neal
Born: Liverpool, 31 March 1978
Height: 5'11" Weight: 11.7
Club Honours: FLC '99
International Honours: E: U21-1; Yth; Sch

The son of the former Liverpool and England goalkeeper, Ray, this athletic midfielder, who enjoys playing a central role, missed much of last season after picking up an injury in September. Alas, though Stephen made it as far as the substitutes' bench on a number of occasions thereafter, lack of match fitness meant that starting places in the line up were rare, and Tottenham were deprived of his pace and intelligent passing, along with his ability to create from midfield, be it as a provider or when running at the opponents' defence. As a player of such promise, he will surely feature in the first team in 1999-2000, especially with George Graham at the helm, and he is sure to be given every opportunity to impress at White Hart Lane. Represented England at U21 level at the beginning of the campaign.

Tottenham H (From trainee on 3/4/95) PL 21+14 FLC 4+1 FAC 2+1/1

CLEMENT Neil
Born: Reading, 3 October 1978
Height: 6'0" Weight: 12.3
International Honours: E: Yth; Sch

Neil arrived on loan from Chelsea last November, having already made two subs' appearances in the Worthington Cup, and had a run of 12 games at Reading, either at left back or on the left-hand side of midfield, and scored a superb goal, a scudding 30 yarder against Lincoln. However, a dip in form and an excessive transfer fee demand by the London club meant that no permanent deal was arranged. Unable to get further games at Chelsea, he joined Preston during transfer deadline week and made a memorable debut at Colchester, when sent off for two bookable offences. A classy young defender of whom much is expected, he is the son of Dave, the former Queens Park Rangers and England full back.

Chelsea (From trainee on 8/10/95) PL 1 FLC 0+2
Reading (Loaned on 19/11/98) FL 11/1 Others 1
Preston NE (Loaned on 25/3/99) FL 4

CLEMENT Philippe
Born: Antwerp, Belgium, 22 March 1974
Height: 6'1" Weight: 12.7
International Honours: Belgium: 9

Signed from Belgian side, Racing Genk, in

the summer of 1998, after starring for the little-known club the previous season, the hard-working Coventry defensive midfielder whose main asset is his physical strength, was selected for the Belgian World Cup squad and played in two matches. His baptism to the English game was fierce, fracturing a cheek bone in a pre-season game, and unable to start a first-team game until November when he set up a goal for Darren Huckerby in the win at Blackburn. He then pulled a hamstring in the home match with Leicester and finally injured his back at Leeds. His early form was good, adding steel to the City midfield, however, the absence through injury put him down the pecking order and, recalled for the FA Cup-tie at Everton, like many of his team mates that day he gave a lacklustre performance. Subsequent appearances were from the bench, before returning to Belgium on 29 June when joining Club Brugge for £750,000.

Coventry C (£625,000 from Racing Genk on 17/7/98) PL 6+6 FLC 1+1 FAC 1+1

CLITHEROE Lee John
Born: Chorley, 18 November 1978
Height: 5'10" Weight: 10.4
Having come through at Oldham in 1997-98, there were high hopes at the club that this attacking right winger, who is both quick and skilful, and an excellent crosser of the ball, would consolidate in 1998-99. Unfortunately, though, injuries and selection meant that he only played once prior to the Walsall home league fixture in December, a game that turned into a disaster for him. Up against his old team-mate, Neil Pointon, the two went for a 50/50 ball, and Lee ended up going to hospital with a broken leg, his season over.

Oldham Ath (From trainee on 1/7/97) FL 2+3

CLODE Mark James
Born: Plymouth, 24 February 1973
Height: 5'10" Weight: 10.10
Club Honours: AMC '94
Mark had to wait until the beginning of January before he was given his first outing in the Swansea team last season, against Gillingham in an Auto Windscreens Shield match. Having recovered from a broken ankle, ligament damage, and a shin injury, the full back also had to contend with the impressive form displayed by Michael Howard in defence and in March he was given a free transfer.

Plymouth Arg (From trainee on 30/3/91)
Swansea C (Free on 23/7/93) FL 109+10/3 FLC 7+2 FAC 6 Others 10+2

COATES Jonathan Simon
Born: Swansea, 27 June 1975
Height: 5'8" Weight: 10.4
International Honours: W: B-1; U21-5; Yth
Jonathan struggled at the start of last season in an unaccustomed central midfield role at Swansea but, after recovering from ankle ligament damage sustained in a Welsh Premier Cup-tie at Wrexham, he was back in contention around the Christmas period, displaying all his usual close-ball skills. Evidence of his ability to play at a higher

level was given during the Swans' FA Cup run, when he was not overshadowed by players from a higher division. This form saw him being rewarded with a place in the Welsh "B" side, and a seat on the substitutes' bench against Switzerland for the full Welsh international side in March.

Swansea C (From trainee on 8/7/93) FL 117+27/11 FLC 6+1/1 FAC 7 Others 10+2

COBIAN Juan Manuel
Born: Buenos Aires, Argentina, 11 September 1975
Height: 5'9" Weight: 11.10
Signed for a nominal sum from Boca Juniors during the 1998 close season, this young Argentinian right-sided full back appeared at ease in the Sheffield Wednesday side straight away. He started eight out of the first ten games in 1998-99, looking very capable both defending and, when called upon, attacking down the right flank. Then he was inexplicably dropped from the team and made only one further appearance as a substitute, before being released during the summer and expecting to have trials with Barnsley prior to the start of the new season.

Sheffield Wed (Signed from Boca Juniors on 13/8/98) PL 7+2 FLC 1

COID Daniel (Bradley) John
Born: Liverpool, 3 October 1981
Height: 5'11" Weight: 11.7
Known as Bradley despite being christened Daniel, the young first-year trainee impressed all at Blackpool last season, so much so that he was given his first-team debut when coming off the bench to participate in the final game of 1998-99, a 2-1 home win over Colchester. A left-sided midfielder who shows many of the attributes valued by the modern player, he is expected to progress smartly at Bloomfield Road.

Blackpool (Trainee) FL 0+1

COLDICOTT Stacy
Born: Redditch, 29 April 1974
Height: 5'8" Weight: 11.8
Signed from West Bromwich Albion during the 1998 close season, Stacy was yet another player to move from the Hawthorns to Grimsby as a result of Alan Buckley's penchant to surround himself with former Baggies. A solid and strong-tackling midfielder who can also play as an overlapping full back if required, he established himself firmly in the number six shirt, when his commitment to the cause went down well with the fans.

West Bromwich A (From trainee on 4/3/92) FL 64+40/3 FLC 8+1 FAC 2+2/1 Others 7+3
Cardiff C (Loaned on 30/8/96) FL 6
Grimsby T (£125,000 on 6/8/98) FL 35+2/3 FLC 2 FAC 1

COLE Andrew (Andy) Alexander
Born: Nottingham, 15 October 1971
Height: 5'11" Weight: 11.12
Club Honours: Div 1 '93; PL '96, '97, '99; FAC '96, '99; CS '97; EC '99
International Honours: E: 5; B-1; U21-8; Yth, Sch
A quick and elusive Manchester United striker with lightning speed and good skills

to match, Andy started last season as a possible transfer target of Aston Villa manager, John Gregory, following Dwight Yorke's move to Old Trafford in September. Although the speculation mounted when Alex Ferguson left him out of the side for a month, he made a goalscoring return, hitting four in three games against Southampton, Wimbledon and Brondby in October. After that 6-2 victory over the Danes in Copenhagen, Andy hailed his double act with Dwight Yorke as one of the best he had played in. "The partnership is superb," he said. "It reminds me of the successful one I had with Peter Beardsley when I was at Newcastle United." It certainly had European defences worried, with Holland's World Cup defender, Michael Reiziger, quoting: "They are two of the best strikers in the world." After hitting four goals in his next seven games, he launched a scathing attack on Glenn Hoddle in November for persistently leaving him out of the England squad. However, when Hoddle resigned in January he was recalled to the side by temporary boss, Howard Wilkinson, for the friendly against France, and was also named in Kevin Keegan's first squad for the European qualifier against Poland in March. With the goals coming in regular abundance, including a brace apiece against West Ham, Leicester and Nottingham Forest, one of his most vital strikes came in the European Cup semi-final clash against Juventus, which earned United a place in the final. Widely accepted as one of the best strikers in Europe and ending the campaign with European Cup, FA Cup and Premiership winners medals, transfer speculation is now a thing of the past.

Arsenal (From trainee on 18/10/89) FL 0+1 Others 0+1
Fulham (Loaned on 5/9/91) FL 13/3 Others 2/1
Bristol C (£500,000 on 12/3/92) FL 41/20 FLC 3/4 FAC 1 Others 4/1
Newcastle U (£1,750,000 on 12/3/93) F/PL 69+1/55 FLC 7/8 FAC 4/1 Others 3/4
Manchester U (£6,000,000 on 12/1/95) PL 116+21/62 FLC 2 FAC 18+2/9 Others 21+4/11

COLE Joseph (Joe) John
Born: London, 8 November 1981
Height: 5'9" Weight: 11.0
Club Honours: FAYC '99
International Honours: E: Yth
After much media hype, and a professional for only a matter of days, the talented West Ham midfielder, cum forward, finally made his first-team bow last January when coming off the bench in the home FA Cup-tie against Swansea. Taking it all in his stride, with a shimmy here and a dummy there, he showed enough in the 25 minutes he was on the pitch to suggest that he will be a future star. His manager, Harry Redknapp, went on to use him wisely, giving him a senior start at Wimbledon, followed by another at Liverpool, and bringing him off the bench in three of the remaining five games of the season to set him up for 1999-2000. Having represented England in the European Youth championships, and played a big part in helping the Hammers win the FA Youth Cup, Joe is well on course to both follow

Joe Cole

and surpass many of the homegrown talents produced at Upton Park over the years.
West Ham U (From trainee on 11/12/98) PL 2+6 FAC 0+1

COLEMAN Christopher (Chris)
Born: Swansea, 10 June 1970
Height: 6'2" Weight: 14.6
Club Honours: WC '89, '91; Div 1 '94; Div 2 '99
International Honours: W: 24; U21-3; Yth; Sch
A tower of strength in a Fulham defence which conceded only 32 league goals in 1998-99, the club captain showed all the qualities of an international defender, rarely wasting a ball and always appearing to have plenty of time. Chris was selected for the award-winning PFA Second Division side for the second successive year and, alongside Kit Symons, was also a regular in the Welsh team. Won a Second Division championship medal as the club returned to the First Division after two years.
Swansea C (From from Manchester C juniors on 1/9/87) FL 159+1/2 FLC 8 FAC 13/1 Others 15
Crystal Palace (£275,000 on 19/7/91) F/PL 143+11/13 FLC 24+2/2 FAC 8/1 Others 2
Blackburn Rov (£2,800,000 on 16/12/95) PL 27+1 FLC 2 FAC 2
Fulham (£2,100,000 on 1/12/97) FL 71/5 FLC 5/1 FAC 8 Others 3

COLEMAN Simon
Born: Worksop, 13 June 1968
Height: 6'0" Weight: 11.8
In a Southend team that suffered from a distinct lack of confidence throughout 1998-99, Simon formed a partnership with Rob Newman that at times was excellent. A fully committed player, he unfortunately played in a defence whose errors were invariably quickly punished by opposition goals but, along with Newman, he was often the rock which held the back line together.
Mansfield T (From juniors on 29/7/85) FL 96/7 FLC 9 FAC 7 Others 7/1
Middlesbrough (£600,000 on 26/9/89) FL 51+4/2 FAC 5 Others 10/1
Derby Co (£300,000 on 15/8/91) FL 62+8/2 FLC 5+1 FAC 5 Others 12
Sheffield Wed (£250,000 on 20/1/94) PL 11+5/1 FLC 3 FAC 2
Bolton W (£350,000 on 5/10/94) P/FL 34/5 FLC 4 FAC 2
Wolverhampton W (Loaned on 2/9/97) FL 3+1
Southend U (Free on 20/2/98) FL 55+1/4 FLC 4 FAC 1 Others 1

Patrick Colleter

COLLETER Patrick
Born: Brest, France, 6 November 1965
Height: 5'10" Weight: 10.10
A French "B" international left back signed from Brest last December, Patrick immediately showed great skill and pace combined with excellent crossing ability at Southampton. He also liked to come inside and have a go at goal, such as the one he scored from 30 yards against Charlton at home in January. Strong and determined defensively, making 18 consecutive starts until injured against Blackburn at the Dell, he proved to be a valuable asset in the relegation battle.
Southampton (£300,000 from Brest on 23/12/98) PL 16/1 FAC 2

COLLETT Andrew (Andy) Alfred
Born: Stockton, 28 October 1973
Height: 6'0" Weight: 12.10
Andy was Bristol Rovers' deputy 'keeper to Lee Jones in 1998-99 and added just three league games to his century of appearances for the Pirates, when replacing the latter for a brief period of suspension in early September. He then kept a clean sheet against Chesterfield at the Memorial Stadium. Following a brief trial with Leyton Orient in December, in March he joined Rushden & Diamonds on loan until the end of the season in an attempt to relaunch his career, before being released during the summer.
Middlesbrough (From trainee on 6/3/92) PL 2 Others 3
Bristol Rov (£10,000 on 18/10/94) FL 107 FLC 4 FAC 7 Others 8

COLLINS James Ian
Born: Liverpool, 28 May 1978
Height: 5'8" Weight: 10.0
A product of Crewe's youth team, having made a few subs' appearances in 1997-98 and performing well in the summer friendlies, he made his full league debut at Gresty Road against Barnsley early last season, and then opened his scoring account in a 2-1 home win over Bradford. Highly thought of by the club, the talented midfielder made just six starts and a subs' appearance during the campaign, but will be looking to go better in 1999-2000.
Crewe Alex (From trainee on 4/7/96) FL 5+2/1 FLC 1+1

COLLINS John Angus Paul
Born: Galashiels, 31 January 1968
Height: 5'7" Weight: 10.10
Club Honours: SC '95
International Honours: S: 53; U21-8; Yth
Signed from AS Monaco during the 1998 close season, the experienced Scottish international midfielder recovered from the shock of seeing a penalty kick saved on his Everton home debut to enjoy a solid start to his Premiership career. Ironically, Aston Villa's Mark Bosnich saved the effort, after watching the Scot score an identically struck effort against Brazil during the World Cup finals! A hard-working, left-sided midfielder with a venomous shot, he opened his goals account in England with two excellent strikes against Middlesbrough and Sunderland in the Worthington Cup, before a niggling injury hindered him more and more as the season progressed and

eventually forced him to undergo surgery. That ended his campaign on 28 December. Unfortunately, for a player who prides himself on his physical condition, it was the first serious injury of his career.

Hibernian (From Hutchison Vale BC on 9/8/84) SL 155+8/16 SLC 7+3/1 SC 17/3 Others 4/1
Glasgow C (Signed on 13/7/90) SL 211+6/47 SLC 22/3 SC 21/3 Others 13/1 (Free to AS Monaco on 2/7/96)
Everton (£2,500,000 on 7/8/98) PL 19+1/1 FLC 2+2/1

John Collins

COLLINS Lee
Born: Bellshill, 3 February 1974
Height: 5'8" Weight: 11.6
The 1998-99 season will be one to forget for Lee. The battling Swindon midfielder missed almost the entire season due to a shoulder injury that required surgery, but to his and the physio's credit he managed to bounce back against Tranmere in March. An excellent, tough-tackling midfielder who stays with his opponent, despite having toned his aggression down considerably, after a two-game spell at full back in which he failed to shine, he was placed on the transfer list. With no takers at the time of going to press, the Scot will be looking for a way back in 1999-2000.

Albion Rov (Signed from Pollock on 25/11/93) SL 43+2/1 SLC 2 SC 2 Others 2
Swindon T (£15,000 on 15/11/95) FL 29+10/1 FAC 3 Others 1

COLLINS Lee David
Born: Birmingham, 10 September 1997
Height: 6'1" Weight: 12.6
Lee was well known to Brian Little from his stay at Villa Park, and was tracked for some time before being released on a free transfer last February. A tall, commanding central defender who went straight into the Stoke side for his league debut, he is one very much for the future. Was unfortunate to break his nose after a short while at the club.

Aston Villa (From trainee on 5/7/96)
Stoke C (Free on 19/2/99) FL 4

COLLINS Samuel (Sam) Jason
Born: Pontefract, 5 June 1977
Height: 6'3" Weight: 14.0
Having made his first-team debut for Huddersfield during the previous campaign, Sam returned to training earlier than anyone else in an effort to maintain his place in 1998-99. This dedication paid off and he soon established a solid defensive partnership with first Andy Morrison, and then Kevin Gray. A willingness to win every header and to get in crunching tackles kept him in the side for the opening 17 matches until jadedness caught up with him. Minor injuries followed in February, before a recall came in the early FA Cup rounds and allowed him to make good use of his long throws, which undoubtedly worried the majority of defences. Missing another 13 games, he came back at the tail-end of the season and looks to establish himself as a permanent first choice this coming term.

Huddersfield T (From trainee on 6/7/94) FL 34+3 FLC 6+1 FAC 3

COLLINS Simon Jonathan
Born: Pontefract, 16 December 1973
Height: 5'11" Weight: 13.0
An extremely versatile Plymouth player, and an excellent squad member, Simon was one of the most consistent members of the team in 1998-99, appearing in 40 league matches. The campaign saw him deployed mainly as a central defender, arguably his best position, where he continued to prove himself to be strong, competent in the air, and a very good distributor of the ball, which is why he is equally comfortable in midfield. Apart from a ten-match spell of missing games, he played his way through the campaign, despite struggling with several niggling injuries. Is now out of contract.

Huddersfield T (From trainee on 1/7/92) FL 31+21/3 FLC 6+3/2 FAC 1+4 Others 1+3
Plymouth Arg (£60,000 on 6/3/97) FL 81+3/5 FLC 2 FAC 1 Others 1

COLLINS Wayne Anthony
Born: Manchester, 4 March 1969
Height: 6'0" Weight: 12.0
Club Honours: Div 2 '97
Wayne had more than his fair share of injuries in the last campaign and, when he was fit, sometimes found it difficult to regain his place with Fulham playing so well. Although central midfield is his normal position he filled in on the right and, when he could not break back into the first team, showed his versatility by playing in the Combination side on the right of the back three. The scorer of two vital winning goals, against Colchester and Bristol Rovers, he also collected a Second Division championship medal after Fulham finished top of the league.

Crewe Alex (£10,000 from Winsford U on 29/7/93) FL 102+15/14 FLC 5/1 FAC 8+1 Others 14+1/2
Sheffield Wed (£600,000 on 1/8/96) PL 16+15/6 FLC 2 FAC 1
Fulham (£400,000 + on 23/1/98) FL 28+6/3 FLC 4 FAC 3+1 Others 4

COLLYMORE Stanley (Stan) Victor
Born: Cannock, 22 January 1971
Height: 6'3" Weight: 13.10
International Honours: E: 3
Having reported back for summer training a week earlier than the rest of the Aston Villa squad, to ensure that he was in tip-top condition for the start of 1998-99, an injury during a pre-season friendly resulted in him missing the first two games. Returned for just one match before a thigh strain saw him miss the next four, Stan came back via the subs' bench at home to Derby at the end of September, and went on to score a hat trick at Stromgodset in the first round of the UEFA Cup. Following that, he only appeared sporadically, with a hamstring strain, a stomach bug, and suspension all playing their part, before spending most of his time on the subs' bench and openly expressing his frustration about being left out of the starting line-up. Then, in mid January, a statement was issued that Stan would be seeking counselling for stress and depression and, although he came back into the side, following the home defeat against Chelsea on 21 March the club announced that he was to receive full-time counselling from then on and would be out of action for the rest of the campaign. As a striker with both pace and power, who can run at defenders and force mistakes, and a natural talent, it was a time in his life that is best forgotten.

Wolverhampton W (From trainee on 13/7/89)
Crystal Palace (£100,000 from Stafford R on 4/1/91) FL 4+16/1 FLC 2+3/1
Southend U (£100,000 on 20/11/92) FL 30/15 FAC 3/3
Nottingham F (£2,000,000 on 5/7/93) F/PL 64+1/41 FLC 9/2 FAC 2/1 Others 2/1
Liverpool (£8,500,000 on 3/7/95) PL 55+6/26 FLC 2+2 FAC 9/7 Others 5+2/2
Aston Villa (£7,000,000 on 16/5/97) PL 34+11/7 FLC 1 FAC 5/3 Others 9+1/5

CONLON Barry John
Born: Drogheda, 1 October 1978
Height: 6'3" Weight: 13.7
International Honours: Ei: U21-4
A young Irishman brought in from Manchester City by the Southend manager, Alvin Martin, last September, Barry had the worst possible start, playing in a team performing badly, and he made only a dozen appearances before being dropped. He did return, however, and looked much more the part, showing his excellent first-time control, passing, and battling qualities, and will undoubtedly prove to be a class player in the Third Division in 1999-2000. Continued to play for the Republic of Ireland's U21 side.

Manchester C (Free from Queens Park R juniors on 14/8/97) FL 1+6 FLC 0+1
Plymouth Arg (Loaned on 26/2/98) FL 13/2
Southend U (£95,000 on 4/9/98) FL 28+6/7 FAC 1 Others 1

CONNELLY Gordon Paul John
Born: Glasgow, 1 November 1976
Height: 5'11" Weight: 12.4
Signed in the summer of 1998 from Airdrie, Gordon proved to be a fast and clever right winger who made an immediate impact at

York in 1998-99, and had an excellent first half of the season. Unfortunately, after netting four goals, including outstanding efforts against Luton and Manchester City, the Scot lost his form and place in the side during the closing weeks.
Airdrieonians (From Milngarvie W on 11/8/95) SL 16+17/1 SC 0+1 Others 3+2/1
York C (Free on 10/8/98) FL 28/4 FLC 2 FAC 3 Others 1

CONNELLY Sean Patrick
Born: Sheffield, 26 June 1970
Height: 5'10" Weight: 11.10
Described by Stockport manager Gary Megson as one of the best right backs in the First Division, Sean has earned the tag of "Mr Consistency" at Edgeley Park. He reads the game particularly well and is superb in his timing of the tackle, while in the air he is surprisingly competent considering his height. A regular in the County side up until last January, injury and then suspension forced him on to the sidelines for the remainder of the campaign.
Stockport Co (Free from Hallam on 12/8/91) FL 239+7/3 FLC 25/1 FAC 14+1 Others 15+1

CONNOLLY David James
Born: Willesden, 6 June 1977
Height: 5'8" Weight: 11.4
International Honours: Ei: 18
The diminutive, pacy Republic of Ireland striker arrived at Wolves from Feyenoord in August 1998 after long negotiations, but even then it was on a loan basis for the season. Began with five successive games as a sub, as he strove to recover match fitness, and finally started one at Bournemouth before making 15 appearances (including six as a sub) without scoring, although continuing to work hard. Ironically, it all came good in the first match following Mark McGhee's departure in November, David hitting four at Bristol City! He quickly added his first Molineux goal and during the autumn played his 14th match for Eire, coming on as a sub in Yugoslavia. He then only made two starts for Wolves in December and none in January or February as he fell out of favour. Yet in the latter month he got his seventh goal for Eire, having replaced Robbie Keane against Paraguay. Scored for Wolves in March at Barnsley, having come on for the same player, the latter's subsequent absence put him back in the team, but he did not impress in a four-game run and was dropped at Birmingham. At his best, David is able to turn defenders while using good close control to his best advantage.
Watford (From trainee on 15/11/94) FL 19+7/10 FLC 1 FAC 3+3/4 Others 1/1 (Free to Feyenoord during 1997 close season)
Wolverhampton W (Loaned on 21/8/98) FL 18+14/6 FLC 2 FAC 0+1

CONNOLLY Karl Andrew
Born: Prescot, 9 February 1970
Height: 5'10" Weight: 11.2
Club Honours: WC '95
Predominantly left footed, Karl is generally regarded as the "jewel" in the Wrexham side, and the most gifted player at the club.

Again not one of his best seasons, during an in-and-out type of term for him in 1998-99, often seeming to be not firing on all cylinders. However, his skilful and penetrating play is a delight to watch when on song, and whilst still the leading goalscorer at the Racecourse it is still a bone of contention that he is far more effective when operating on the left flank! Has a penchant for scoring important cup goals, and last season was no different with a return of seven, including a hat trick in the home third round FA Cup-tie with Scunthorpe.
Wrexham (Free from Napoli, in local Sunday League, on 8/5/91) FL 302+15/79 FLC 20/4 FAC 33/15 Others 31+1/6

Karl Connolly

CONNOR Daniel Brian
Born: Dublin, 31 January 1981
Height: 6'2" Weight: 12.9
International Honours: Ei: Yth
Having come through the ranks at Peterborough to sign professional forms in April 1998, the young Irish youth international goalkeeper was not expected to make an appearance last season, especially as he had not long recovered from cruciate ligament damage. However, with Mark Tyler and Bart Griemink both injured he was rushed into service at Brighton in January, and could not be faulted for the only goal of the game. Showing a good pair of hands and commanding the six-yard box well for a youngster, he then played in a 5-2 home win over Barnet, before unluckily suffering a broken leg in an end-of-term academy game.
Peterborough U (From trainee on 29/4/98) FL 2

CONNOR Paul
Born: Bishop Auckland, 12 January 1979
Height: 6'1" Weight: 11.5
Still unable to force his way into the

Middlesbrough first team in 1998-99, and even at times the reserves, Paul went out on loan to Stoke in transfer deadline week in an effort to further his football education, having done similarly at Hartlepool a year earlier. Tall and quick, he soon started scoring with the City reserve side before being given his chance against Burnley and Oldham, prior to scoring twice in the last game of the campaign, at home to promoted Walsall – the first being a superb diving header. However, back at the Riverside, he was released during the summer.
Middlesbrough (From trainee on 4/7/96)
Hartlepool U (Loaned on 6/2/98) FL 4+1
Stoke C (Loaned on 25/3/99) FL 2+1/2

CONROY Michael (Mick) Kevin
Born: Glasgow, 31 December 1965
Height: 6'0" Weight: 13.3
Club Honours: Div 4 '92
An experienced striker, Mick did not figure in many games for Blackpool last season, and spent two spells on loan at Chester as manager Kevin Ratcliffe tried to add more firepower to·his attack. The first time round, in December, his experience paid dividends as City lost only two games during his ten games, Mick netting three goals, but although he returned for a further temporary stay in March he was limited to just five appearances as a sub. The highlight of his time at Blackpool in 1998-99, came when he scored a cracking long-range goal in a 1-0 home win over Scunthorpe in the Worthington Cup.
Clydebank (Free from Coventry C juniors on 15/5/84) SL 92+22/38 SLC 4+1 SC 5+2
St Mirren (Signed on 12/12/87) SL 9+1/1 SC 0+1
Reading (£50,000 on 28/9/88) FL 65+15/7 FLC 3+2 FAC 8+2/1 Others 2+2
Burnley (£35,000 on 16/7/91) FL 76+1/30 FLC 4/1 FAC 9+1/4 Others 7+1/4
Preston NE (£85,000 on 20/8/93) FL 50+7/22 FLC 2+1 FAC 7/2 Others 2+3
Fulham (£75,000 on 9/8/95) FL 88+6/32 FLC 11/6 FAC 5+1/3 Others 4/1
Blackpool (£50,000 on 26/3/98) FL 12+2 FLC 2/1 Others 0+1
Chester C (Loaned on 12/12/98) FL 10+3
Chester C (Loaned on 25/3/99) FL 1+4

COOK Andrew (Andy) Charles
Born: Romsey, 10 August 1969
Height: 5'9" Weight: 12.0
Signed from Portsmouth in January 1998 to bring much needed balance on the left-hand side of the Millwall defence, in only his second appearance for the Lions Andy suffered a hamstring injury which effectively ended his 1997-98 season. Then, having battled his way back to fitness after working hard during the summer, and keen to establish himself in the side, it was not to be as a recurrence of the injury kept him out of action for most of 1998-99, except for playing the odd reserve game. Equally at home at left back or pushing forward in a wing-back or wide midfield role, he had his first full game against Colchester when Millwall fielded a reserve side prior to Wembley.
Southampton (From apprentice on 6/7/87) FL 11+5/1 FLC 4 FAC 1 Others 1
Exeter C (£50,000 on 13/9/91) FL 70/1 FLC 2 FAC 7/1 Others 6/1

Swansea C (£125,000 on 23/7/93) FL 54+8 FLC 2 FAC 3 Others 9+1/2
Portsmouth (£35,000 on 20/12/96) FL 7+2
Millwall (£50,000 on 8/1/98) FL 4+1

COOK James (Jamie) Steven
Born: Oxford, 2 August 1979
Height: 5'10" Weight: 11.6
A wide player who is more at home on the left, Jamie had hoped to make an Oxford first-team berth his own after impressing the year before, but remained on the fringes, scoring just once to help earn a vital point with Huddersfield. Hard working and full of running, he played in 22 games but, with half of those as a substitute, he would have been disappointed. However, he is still young and looks set to feature more prominently this season.
Oxford U (From trainee on 1/7/97) FL 18+21/3 FLC 0+1 FAC 2+1

COOK Paul Anthony
Born: Liverpool, 22 June 1967
Height: 5'11" Weight: 11.0
Having started last season as Stockport's midfield playmaker, his vision and range of passing being crucial to the creative side of the club's game, he was injured in December for a month and, on coming back and being sent off in the FA Cup fourth round at Sheffield Wednesday, he was loaned out to Burnley in March. Providing the coolness and clear vision that the Clarets had previously lacked in that department, he made his debut in an unlucky defeat at home to Preston, being voted "Man of the Match", and remained a key figure during the unbeaten run as the campaign reached the closing stages. After scoring his first goal for the club in the final game, against Northampton, he would be a very popular permanent signing if terms could be agreed.
Wigan Ath (Signed from Marine on 20/7/84) FL 77+6/14 FLC 4 FAC 6+1 Others 5+1/1
Norwich C (£73,000 on 23/5/88) FL 3+3 Others 1+1
Wolverhampton W (£250,000 on 1/11/89) FL 191+2/19 FLC 7/1 FAC 5+2 Others 6+1/1
Coventry C (£600,000 on 18/8/94) PL 35+2/3 FLC 3 FAC 3
Tranmere Rov (£250,000 on 29/2/96) FL 54+6/4 FLC 8 FAC 1
Stockport Co (£250,000 on 24/10/97) FL 48+1/3 FLC 1+1 FAC 2
Burnley (Loaned on 12/3/99) FL 12/1

COOKE Andrew (Andy) Roy
Born: Shrewsbury, 20 January 1974
Height: 6'0" Weight: 12.8
A disrupted and, on the whole, disappointing season for the Burnley striker, despite rumours of a bigger-club interest in him still surfacing from time to time. Very much the supporting player to Andy Payton during 1998-99, he too often looked lethargic and was unable to recapture his scoring touch of the previous campaign. Sidelined in March following the removal of his appendix, he returned to a more settled side looking keener and more like his old self.
Burnley (Signed from Newtown on 1/5/95) FL 91+33/42 FLC 4+2/3 FAC 3+3/1 Others 9+2/2

COOKE Terence (Terry) John
Born: Birmingham, 5 August 1976
Height: 5'7" Weight: 11.4
Club Honours: FAYC '95
International Honours: E: U21-4; Yth
Signed on loan from Manchester United for three months last January, Terry made his Manchester City debut at home to Fulham as a traditional right winger, showing immediate promise to fill the main deficiency in the team's game. Following that, his contribution consistently improved to the extent that he made it known that he would like to come to Maine Road permanently. His wing play was fast and direct, and climaxed with accurate crosses which stood out in the Second Division. He can also score on occasion. At Reading, he struck two quality goals, both free kicks from outside the area, each one curled and beating the whole defence to finish in the bottom corner. Having made a tremendous contribution to the club's push for automatic promotion, he signed a three-year contract in April and looks certain to become the "darling" of the Maine Road crowd. Earlier in the season, having recovered from a long-term injury that kept him out of action throughout 1997-98, Terry was loaned out to Wrexham in order to get match fit.
Manchester U (From trainee on 1/7/94) PL 1+3 FLC 1+2/1 Others 0+1
Sunderland (Loaned on 29/1/96) FL 6
Birmingham C (Loaned on 29/11/96) FL 1+3
Wrexham (Loaned on 30/10/98) FL 10 Others 1
Manchester C (£1,000,000 on 13/1/99) FL 21/7 Others 3

COOKSEY Scott Andrew
Born: Birmingham, 24 June 1972
Height: 6'3" Weight: 13.10
International Honours: E: SP-1
A goalkeeper signed mid last season from Conference club, Hednesford, Scott found his opportunities at Shrewsbury limited to an Auto Windscreens game and deputising for injuries. Having earlier appeared in league football with Peterborough, before winning a semi-pro cap for England, he will have to bide his time, especially if Paul Edwards is still in brilliant form.
Derby Co (From trainee on 25/7/90)
Shrewsbury T (Free on 7/2/91)
Peterborough U (£25,000 from Bromsgrove Rov on 30/12/93) FL 15 FLC 2 FAC 2 Others 1 (Free to Hednesford on 1/6/95)
Shrewsbury T (£20,000 on 22/10/98) FL 2 Others 1

COOPER Colin Terence
Born: Sedgefield, 28 February 1967
Height: 5'10" Weight: 11.9
Club Honours: Div 1 '98
International Honours: E: 2; U21-8
Signed form Nottingham Forest early in 1998-99, and currently enjoying his second term at Middlesbrough, "Coops" was thrilled by the prospect of teaming up again with former favourite, Gary Pallister, when "Robbo" brought the duo back to strengthen his push for Premiership consolidation. Always in the thick of the action, he delivered many sterling performances and has never looked back since relinquishing the captain's arm band at Forest. Strong and fearless in the tackle, skilfully adept at clearing his lines, and the scourge of many Premiership predators in his domain, he is now completely re-established as the (defensive) law enforcement officer at the Cellnet.
Middlesbrough (From juniors on 17/7/84) FL 183+5/6 FLC 18 FAC 13 Others 19+1/2
Millwall (£300,000 on 25/7/91) FL 77/6 FLC 6 FAC 2 Others 2
Nottingham F (£1,700,000 on 21/6/93) F/PL 179+1/20 FLC 14/2 FAC 12/1 Others 7
Middlesbrough (£2,500,000 on 22/8/98) PL 31+1/1 FLC 1 FAC 1

COOPER Kevin Lee
Born: Derby, 8 February 1975
Height: 5'7" Weight: 10.7
The tricky Stockport winger struggled to find the kind of form he had enjoyed in 1997-98 last season, mainly because he played most of the campaign with a knee injury. County's boss, Gary Megson, praised his attitude and commitment to the team and Kevin's efforts were rewarded when he returned from having an operation on the problem area in February, again reproducing the creative skills and accurate crossing that is integral to the team's style of play.
Derby Co (From trainee on 2/7/93) FL 0+2 FLC 0+2 Others 0+1
Stockport Co (£150,000 on 24/3/97) FL 68+20/12 FLC 4+2/1 FAC 2 Others 1

COOTE Adrian
Born: Great Yarmouth, 13 September 1978
Height: 6'2" Weight: 12.0
International Honours: NI: 2; B-1; U21-9
1998-99 proved to be a frustrating season for this Northern Ireland U21 international, as the form of Iwan Roberts and Craig Bellamy prevented him from playing the number of senior matches for Norwich he would have liked. However, he continued to score goals at a prolific rate in the reserves, finishing as top scorer for the third campaign in a row. A powerful and brave front runner, he has time on his side and is likely to receive his chance at first-team level again in the season ahead. Made his debut for the full international side, playing against Canada and the Republic, and represented the "B" team against Wales.
Norwich C (From trainee on 3/7/97) FL 13+16/2 FLC 0+1

CORAZZIN Giancarlo (Carlo) Michele
Born: Canada, 25 December 1971
Height: 5'10" Weight: 12.7
International Honours: Canada: 27
This talented striker, with a thunderbolt shot, signed from Plymouth during the summer of 1998 and marked his Northampton debut (versus Stoke) with a stunning free kick from 25 yards, giving the 'keeper no chance. In a season where goals were at a premium, Carlo was the only regular goalscorer and regular penalty taker, but sadly missed the final run in when a leg injury kept him out of the side and forced him to collect his "Player of the Year" trophy on crutches. Can hold the ball up well, and is a goal supplier as well as a scorer, and is a great favourite with the Town crowd.

Cambridge U (£20,000 from Vancouver 86ers on 10/12/93) FL 104+1/39 FLC 4/2 FAC 5 Others 3/2
Plymouth Arg (£150,000 on 28/3/96) FL 61+13/23 FLC 1+1 FAC 0+2/1 Others 2+1
Northampton T (Free on 2/7/98) FL 36+3/16 FLC 4+1 FAC 2 Others 1/1

CORDEN Simon Wayne
Born: Leek, 1 November 1975
Height: 5'9" Weight: 11.3
The Port Vale left winger again failed to grasp his big chance to claim a regular first-team berth, this time in 1998-99. Although he has plenty of skill, and is an excellent crosser of the ball, good games in the reserves never managed to transfer themselves to the senior team and he only managed five starts. He did appear as a regular substitute, but would probably have benefited from a loan spell in the lower divisions where he would have been able to pick up more match practice. Has now completed seven years at the club with few starts.
Port Vale (From trainee on 20/9/94) FL 30+34/1 FLC 4 FAC 2+1/1

CORICA Stephen (Steve) Christopher
Born: Cairns, Australia, 24 March 1973
Height: 5'8" Weight: 10.10
International Honours: Australia: 9
Injury had restricted the Wolves' midfielder to just three-minutes play in 1997-98, and after lining up for the opening match of 1998-99 he suffered a hamstring problem and did not start again for the first team until 15 September. From early October, Steve played ten in a row, and in the 2-0 win over Grimsby he was a good link between the midfield and forwards. Having lost his place in January, he started two games at the end of March, and in the latter, against Crewe, he ran well with the ball as he strove for his first competitive Molineux goal. From then on, he played at least a part in most games and was looking livelier, starting and finishing a move that brought him a welcome winning goal at Birmingham. Is excellent off the ball, where his ability to drag defenders out of position makes chances for others.
Leicester C (£325,000 from Marconi on 11/8/95) FL 16/2 FAC 2
Wolverhampton W (£700,000 on 16/2/96) FL 70+15/4 FLC 3+1 FAC 2

CORNFORTH John Michael
Born: Whitley Bay, 7 October 1967
Height: 6'1" Weight: 13.12
Club Honours: Div 3 '88; AMC '94
International Honours: W: 2
A playmaker in Wycombe's midfield, John had another unsettled season of small runs of games followed by periods of injury or as substitute in 1998-99. In total, he started 13 games and appeared as substitute on five occasions, and his one goal was a penalty in the 2-1 defeat at Preston. He thoroughly enjoyed his midfield duel with Paul Gascoigne in the two Worthington Cup games with Middlesbrough and, with two good feet and excellent passing ability, he can still contribute much at this level if he can regain his former mobility and fitness. Was released during the summer.

Sunderland (From apprentice on 11/10/85) FL 21+11/2 FLC 0+1 Others 1+3
Doncaster Rov (Loaned on 6/11/86) FL 6+1/3 Others 2
Shrewsbury T (Loaned on 23/11/89) FL 3 Others 2
Lincoln C (Loaned on 11/1/90) FL 9/1
Swansea C (£50,000 on 2/8/91) FL 147+2/16 FLC 14 FAC 11/1 Others 19/1
Birmingham C (£350,000 on 26/3/96) FL 8
Wycombe W (£50,000 on 5/12/96) FL 35+12/6 FLC 6 FAC 2/2 Others 0+2
Peterborough U (Loaned on 13/2/98) FL 3+1

CORNWALL Lucas (Luke) Clarence
Born: Lambeth, 23 July 1980
Height: 5'11" Weight: 11.0
A first-year Fulham professional, in normal circumstances last season it would have been Luke's breakthrough to a regular place in the first team but, with Barry Hayles and Geoff Horsfield in such great form, he had no chance. Even his end-of-season loan spell at Queens Park Rangers was notable only for a hat trick against Fulham in a 5-1 Combination win. But his pace and scoring ability will surely mean a fine career, even if not at Fulham. Having made his senior debut for the Cottagers, when coming off the bench at Notts County in mid September, he scored his first senior goal in a 3-3 draw at home to York.
Fulham (From trainee on 6/7/98) FL 1+3/1 FLC 1

CORT Carl Edward Richard
Born: Southwark, 1 November 1977
Height: 6'4" Weight: 12.7
International Honours: E: U21-5
Another product of Wimbledon's excellent youth scheme, Carl will make a good choice to partner Jason Euell in the attack more often this coming term. Although showing good, close ball control, and at 6'4" tall an intimidating sight for any defender, his appearances were limited last season due to the calibre of strikers at the club. Despite that, he continued to play for the England U21 side, and furthered his development, holding the ball up well and growing in confidence. Some idea of his potential can be gauged by the fact that he scored three Premiership goals, two of them away from home against top four sides. A great prospect, hopefully, he will play a major part in the club's future.
Wimbledon (From trainee on 7/6/96) PL 22+17/7 FLC 3+2/2 FAC 4+4/1
Lincoln C (Loaned on 3/2/97) FL 5+1/1

COSTA Ricardo
Born: Portugal, 10 January 1973
Height: 5'8" Weight: 11.9
A skilful, diminutive ball player who arrived at Darlington on loan from Portuguese side, Boavista, at the turn of 1999, although restricted to just four substitute appearances before returning to his native country he was a great favourite with the fans, and scored once with a header in the 5-1 rout over Mansfield. Needless to say, Ricardo would be welcomed back any time.
Darlington (Loaned from Boavista on 11/1/99) FL 0+3/1 Others 0+1

Tony Cottee

COTTEE Anthony (Tony) Richard
Born: West Ham, 11 July 1965
Height: 5'9" Weight: 12.6
International Honours: E: 7; U21-8; Yth
A pint-sized livewire striker, Tony enjoyed the kind of season, in 1998-99, that he could only have dreamed about as he neared veteran status. Scored goals regularly throughout the campaign, including all three in the two-legged Worthington Cup semi-final victory over Sunderland that took the Foxes to Wembley. Sadly, there was no fairy tale ending for Tony beneath the twin towers, where that elusive winners medal was snatched from his grasp once again. He bounced back a fortnight later, ironically against Tottenham, to record his 200th career league goal. Strangely, both his first (for West Ham) and his 100th (for Everton) were also scored against Spurs. He led City's goalscoring charts throughout the campaign, yet hardly ever seemd to find the net from outside the six-yard box, proving that his true striking instincts were as sharp as ever. Missed the month of November due to a thigh strain, but came back as hungry and eager as ever.
West Ham U (From apprentice on 1/9/82) FL 203+9/92 FLC 19/14 FAC 24/11 Others 1/1
Everton (£2,300,000 on 2/8/88) F/PL 161+23/72 FLC 19+4/11 FAC 15+6/4 Others 11+2/12
West Ham U (Signed on 7/9/94) PL 63+4/23 FLC 8/4 FAC 5/1 (Signed by Selangor on 3/3/97)
Leicester C (£500,000 on 14/8/97) PL 36+14/14 FLC 6/5 FAC 1+2/2 Others 0+1
Birmingham C (Loaned on 14/11/97) FL 4+1/1

COUSINS Jason Michael
Born: Hayes, 14 October 1970
Height: 5'11" Weight: 12.4
Club Honours: GMVC '93; FAT '93
1998-99 was a storming season from the Wycombe team captain, who seemingly improves with every year. In spite of the poor form of the team, Jason always led by example in the centre of defence, giving total commitment and effort. He simply hates losing and, as the sort of player every manager needs in a team, it was no surprise when he comfortably won the supporters' "Player of the Year" award. A particularly good timer of the last-ditch tackle, when he always seems to win the ball cleanly, and is dominant in the air, his second goal of the campaign, in the 2-0 win at Bristol Rovers in March, proved to be the end of his action as he turned his ankle when bravely heading the ball in. Was the first player to be offered, and sign, a new contract by Lawrie Sanchez towards the end of the season.
Brentford (From trainee on 13/7/89) FL 20+1 Others 2+2
Wycombe W (Free on 1/7/91) FL 201+7/5 FLC 16/1 FAC 22 Others 15

COUZENS Andrew (Andy)
Born: Shipley, 4 June 1975
Height: 5'10" Weight: 11.11
Club Honours: FAYC '93
International Honours: E: U21-3
Having arrived at Carlisle with a considerable reputation as a former England U21 cap, in his two years at Brunton Park this undoubted promise was rarely fulfilled. A skilled passer of the ball, he enjoyed a more settled spell in the side following the arrival of Nigel Pearson as manager in 1998-99, and showed some class touches, notably in the winning goal he set up at Southend for Steve Finney. However, he lost his place soon afterwards before going to Blackpool on loan in early March, a move that was firmed up in transfer deadline week after he had proved most competitive. Was also used in a full-back capacity.
Leeds U (From trainee on 5/3/93) PL 17+11/1 FLC 4+1/1 Others 0+2
Carlisle U (£100,000 on 21/7/97) FL 28+14/2 FLC 3+1/1 Others 1+3
Blackpool (Free on 5/3/99) FL 6

COWAN Thomas (Tom)
Born: Bellshill, 28 August 1969
Height: 5'9" Weight: 11.10
Prior to returning to action at Huddersfield last December, having been out injured for 18 months due to cruciate damage to his right knee, this tough-tackling Scot had become a father, an author, a radio presenter, and an after-dinner speaker. Returning to his usual left-back berth as though he had never been away, playing heroically in the 4-0 demolition of Crystal Palace, the Kilner Bank faithful were in raptures following his trade-mark after-the-match celebrations. His wholehearted displays quickly gained him a regular place, testing the opposition with his strong heading and long-throw abilities, before he suffered a broken jaw in the FA Cup encounter at Wrexham and was

sidelined for a further six matches. With his contract surprisingly not renewed, he joined Burnley in March, an initial loan spell quickly being made a permanent move, as he made an immediate impression in the problem left-back position. Not the most subtle of defenders, he more than made up for that with his commitment to the cause, and his spectacular over-head kick against Macclesfield that saw him score one of the goals of the season and did no harm at all to his crowd-favourite status. Was out of contract during the summer.
Clydebank (From Netherdale BC on 11/7/88) SL 16/2 SC 2
Glasgow R (Signed on 9/2/89) SL 8+4 SC 0+1 Others 2
Sheffield U (£350,000 on 1/8/91) F/PL 45 FLC 5 FAC 2 Others 1
Stoke C (Loaned on 1/10/93) FL 14 FLC 1 Others 3
Huddersfield T (£150,000 on 24/3/94) FL 137/7 FLC 13/1 FAC 9/1 Others 6
Burnley (£20,000 on 12/3/99) FL 12/1

COWE Steven (Steve) Mark
Born: Gloucester, 29 September 1974
Height: 5'7" Weight: 10.10
As in 1997-98, Steve was another of Swindon's forwards who failed to make their mark in 1998-99, being occasionally used as sub, showing plenty of hustle and bustle, but was impeded by his height and small frame. A player with undoubted quality and skill, in a bid to give him more competitive football, he enjoyed much more success with a loan spell at non-league Hereford after arriving there in mid February.
Aston Villa (From trainee on 7/7/93)
Swindon T (£100,000 on 22/3/96) FL 42+29/9 FLC 3+2 FAC 1+2

COX Ian Gary
Born: Croydon, 25 March 1971
Height: 6'0" Weight: 12.2
The Bournemouth skipper had another impressive season in 1998-99, at the heart of a very mean Cherries' defence. A former midfielder, he excelled at centre back and only missed one game throughout the campaign, being good in the air and comfortable carrying the ball forward from defence. He also scored six league and cup goals.
Crystal Palace (£35,000 from Carshalton on 8/3/94) F/PL 2+13 FLC 1+2/1
Bournemouth (Free on 28/3/96) FL 144/16 FLC 9 FAC 7 Others 10/1

COX James (Jimmy) Darryl
Born: Gloucester, 11 April 1980
Height: 5'6 Weight: 10.7
A first-year professional at Luton in 1998-99, having come through the junior ranks, Jimmy made his first-team debut when playing in midfield against Ipswich in the Worthington Cup clash, and went on to make a further nine appearances before being surprisingly released during the summer. With pace and dribbling skills, and at his best when playing off the front men, it was felt by some good judges that he had a future at the club, but it was not to be.
Luton T (From trainee on 7/5/98) FL 3+5 FLC 1+1

COX Neil James
Born: Scunthorpe, 8 October 1971
Height: 6'0" Weight: 13.7
Club Honours: FLC '94; Div 1 '95
International Honours: E: U21-6
Neil had his best season yet for Bolton in 1998-99, producing some wonderful displays for the club and proving himself a bargain at the £1.2 million which secured his services from Middlesbrough in 1997. A rock in the right-back position, his wholehearted displays making him one of the fans' favourites and rightly so, his no-nonsense style of play worked wonders. He even found his goalscoring touch, the pick of which were two similar pile-driving efforts from 25 yards in the three games against Norwich and West Bromwich Albion at the beginning of the year.
Scunthorpe U (From trainee on 20/3/90) FL 17/1 FAC 4 Others 4+1
Aston Villa (£400,000 on 12/2/91) F/PL 26+16/3 FLC 5+2 FAC 4+2/1 Others 2
Middlesbrough (£1,000,000 on 19/7/94) P/FL 103+3/3 FLC 14+1 FAC 5/1 Others 2
Bolton W (£1,200,000 on 27/5/97) P/FL 62+3/5 FLC 5 FAC 1+1 Others 3

COYNE Christopher (Chris)
Born: Brisbane, Australia, 20 December 1978
Height: 6'1" Weight: 13.10
Signed from the Australian club, Perth SC, early in 1996, but yet to appear for West Ham, the young strong-tackling centre back was loaned out to Brentford (August) and Southend (March) to further his experience of the game. Made eight starts at Brentford in place of the injured Danny Cullip, making his Football League debut in the 2-0 home win over Brighton, and performed reasonably well before going back to reserve-team football at Upton Park. At Southend, however, he came off the bench just once, but was then recalled by the Hammers to provide cover following an injury to Rio Ferdinand, which saw him come off the bench in the home 5-1 defeat at the hands of Leeds.
West Ham U (£150,000 from Perth SC on 13/1/96) PL 0+1
Brentford (Loaned on 21/8/98) FL 7 FLC 1
Southend U (Loaned on 25/3/99) FL 0+1

COYNE Daniel (Danny)
Born: Prestatyn, 27 August 1973
Height: 5'11" Weight: 13.0
International Honours: W: 1; B-1; U21-9; Yth; Sch
After undergoing a summer's hard work in the 1998 close season to ensure his complete recovery from a series of injuries, Danny found himself second choice to Steve Simonsen in Tranmere's goal until the latter's move to Everton. However, his return between the sticks was short lived, due to a recurrence of a persistent groin injury which necessitated an operation to remove a piece of bone in October. Back in the first team by Christmas, he showed that his handling skills and positional sense were undiminished. Unfortunately, his groin injury came back to haunt him again in

March, and his appearance against Birmingham proved to be his last for the team. A fine off-the-field ambassador for the club, he became a free agent under the Bosman ruling at the end of the campaign, and looks likely to move on. Represented the Welsh "B" side that played against Northern Ireland.
Tranmere Rov (From trainee on 8/5/92) FL 110+1 FLC 13 FAC 2 Others 2

CRADDOCK Jody Darryl
Born: Bromsgrove, 25 July 1975
Height: 6'1" Weight: 12.4
Having established himself as a regular first teamer in 1997-98, Jody found himself one of the victims of Sunderland's failure to achieve promotion in that campaign and lost his centre-back berth in the side last season to new boy, Paul Butler. Nevertheless, when called upon, the ball-playing defender proved extremely reliable and turned in excellent displays in two vital promotion battles in March, against Bolton and West Bromwich dealing comfortably with the threats posed by quality strikers such as Dean Holdsworth and Lee Hughes. Still only in his mid 20s, his pace and heading ability make him a valuable squad member who could still establish himself in the club in the Premiership.
Cambridge U (Free from Christchurch on 13/8/93) FL 142+3/4 FLC 3/1 FAC 6 Others 5
Sunderland (£300,000 + on 4/8/97) FL 34+4 FLC 6+2 FAC 2 Others 3

CRAMB Colin
Born: Lanark, 23 June 1974
Height: 6'0" Weight: 12.6
Club Honours: B&Q '93
Colin had an unhappy season at Bristol City in 1998-99, being left out for most of the time before being loaned out to Walsall in February. Given his debut in the defeat at Notts County, he then made a considerable impact with two goals, including a penalty, in the league game at Millwall, and another two, which again included a spot kick, in the home game against Bristol Rovers. His powerful running and coolness from the penalty spot left Walsall regretting that City recalled him after a month and would not agree to the original option of the loan being extended to the end of the campaign. A popular player, who many fans felt should have been given more games and the chance to link play between midfield and attack, Colin was subject to a transfer deadline bid by Bristol Rovers that failed to materialise.
Hamilton Ac (From juniors on 1/6/93) SL 29+19/10 SC 0+1 Others 1+3
Southampton (£75,000 on 8/6/93) PL 0+1
Falkirk (Signed on 30/8/94) SL 6+2/1 SLC 0+1
Hearts (Signed on 1/3/95) SL 3+3/1
Doncaster Rov (£25,000 on 15/12/95) FL 60+2/25 FLC 2/1 FAC 1/1 Others 1/1
Bristol C (£250,000 on 10/7/97) FL 38+15/9 FLC 3+1 FAC 1/1 Others 1+1
Walsall (Loaned on 27/2/99) FL 4/4 Others 2

CRAVEN Dean
Born: Shrewsbury, 17 February 1979
Height: 5'7" Weight: 10.10
In his first full season at Shrewsbury in

1998-99, the local youngster showed bags of enthusiasm. Still only 20, the diminutive "Tarzan" has good control and likes to run at defences and, while not quite a regular, being mainly used as substitute, his time will come.
West Bromwich A (From trainee on 1/7/97)
Shrewsbury T (Free on 26/3/98) FL 7+4 FLC 2

CRAWFORD James (Jimmy)
Born: Chicago, USA, 1 May 1973
Height: 5'11" Weight: 11.6
Club Honours: S Div 1 '93; SLC '94
International Honours: Ei: U21-2
Jimmy held a regular place in the team at Reading between last September and January, but a series of niggling injuries and consequent loss of form meant that he was confined to reserve-team football after the turn of the year. Earlier, he had shown himself to be a steady, neat right-sided player with an eye for the penetrating crossfield pass.
Newcastle U (£75,000 from Bohemians on 23/3/95) PL 0+2 FLC 0+1
Rotherham U (Loaned on 27/9/96) FL 11
Dundee U (Loaned on 20/2/98) SL 0+1
Reading (£50,000 on 26/3/98) FL 14+3 FLC 1 FAC 1 Others 1

CREANEY Gerard (Gerry) Thomas
Born: Coatbridge, 13 April 1970
Height: 5'11" Weight: 13.6
International Honours: S: B-1; U21-11
Freed by Manchester City, Gerry moved up to Scotland last October and joined St Mirren, making 12 appearances while scoring three goals. Then, with a view to get back into the Football League, he signed a week-to-week contract at Notts County in February, with the chance of a permanent move a possibility. Although scoring in his first home game, a 2-1 win against Walsall, he played mainly in midfield, and captained the side on a few occasions. A player who never stops talking and organising the players around him, and a scorer of valuable goals, despite appearing in 16 of County's last 18 games, he was not retained for 1999-2000.
Glasgow C (From juniors on 15/5/87) SL 85+28/36 SLC 9+1/7 SC 9/8 Others 6+3/3
Portsmouth (£500,000 on 25/1/94) FL 60/32 FLC 7/3 FAC 2/1
Manchester C (£2,000,000 on 8/9/95) P/FL 8+13/4 FAC 0+4/1
Oldham Ath (Loaned on 28/3/96) FL 8+1/2
Ipswich T (Loaned on 25/10/96) FL 6/1
Burnley (Loaned on 19/9/97) FL 9+1/8 FLC 1
Chesterfield (Loaned on 2/1/98) FL 3+1
St Mirren (Free on 13/10/98) SL 11+1/3
Notts Co (Free on 18/2/99) FL 13+3/3

CRESSWELL Richard Paul Wesley
Born: Bridlington, 20 September 1977
Height: 6'0" Weight: 11.8
International Honours: E: U21-4
Big, strong, and good at dealing with high balls, also having skills on the ground, Richard had an outstanding season at York in 1998-99, in fulfilling all early promise. Capped at England U21 level, becoming the first City player to represent the home country, the young striker netted 19 goals in 42 games prior to being snapped up by

Sheffield Wednesday during transfer deadline week. After making his first start at Wednesday in a 2-1 win at Hillsborough against Coventry, he participated in six of the last seven games of the campaign from the bench, scoring his debut goal for his new club in the home 1-0 win over Liverpool. With both pace and confidence, and a liking to be involved in build-up play as well as finishing, he is seen by the fans as the kind of goalscorer who has been missing at the club over the past few years.
York C (From trainee on 15/11/95) FL 72+23/21 FLC 3+3 FAC 4+2/3 Others 4
Mansfield T (Loaned on 27/3/97) FL 5/1
Sheffield Wed (£950,000 + on 25/3/99) PL 1+6/1

CRICHTON Paul Andrew
Born: Pontefract, 3 October 1968
Height: 6'1" Weight: 12.2
The much-travelled goalkeeper made his Burnley debut in last season's opening game against Bristol Rovers, but was then promptly recalled by West Bromwich. He returned to Turf Moor, this time on a permanent basis, in November, making his second "debut" in a 5-0 defeat at Bournemouth. In several heavy defeats, Paul was more often the last line of a very poor defence rather than being the villain himself and, in general, he performed capably enough, although happier as a shot stopper than dealing with awkward crosses.
Nottingham F (From juniors on 23/5/86)
Notts Co (Loaned on 19/9/86) FL 5
Darlington (Loaned on 30/1/87) FL 5
Peterborough U (Loaned on 27/3/87) FL 4
Darlington (Loaned on 28/9/87) FL 3 FLC 1 Others 1
Swindon T (Loaned on 24/12/87) FL 4
Rotherham U (Loaned on 9/3/88) FL 6
Torquay U (Loaned on 25/8/88) FL 13 FLC 2
Peterborough U (Signed on 3/11/88) FL 47 FAC 5 Others 3
Doncaster Rov (Free on 25/8/90) FL 77 FLC 5 FAC 3 Others 5
Grimsby T (Free on 9/7/93) FL 133 FLC 7 FAC 8 Others 2
West Bromwich A (£250,000 on 9/9/96) FL 32 FLC 1 FAC 1
Burnley (Loaned on 7/8/98) FL 1
Burnley (£100,000 on 19/11/98) FL 28 Others 1

CRITTENDEN Nicholas (Nick) John
Born: Ascot, 11 November 1978
Height: 5'8" Weight: 11.0
With so many star names at Chelsea vying for a first-team slot, Nick was never considered for selection at the Bridge in 1998-99, instead, having to play with the reserves. Probably at his best in a right-wing-back role, although fairly flexible throughout the midfield, he was loaned to Plymouth in October, but only made two appearances, one from the bench, before going home. Still a promising youngster, who is at his best when driving down the flank, 1999-2000 will be an important season for him.
Chelsea (From trainee on 9/7/97) PL 0+2 FLC 1
Plymouth Arg (Loaned on 19/10/98) FL 1+1

CROFT Gary
Born: Burton on Trent, 17 February 1974
Height: 5'9" Weight: 11.8
International Honours: E: U21-4

During the 1998-99 pre-season, Gary lost the battle for Blackburn's number three shirt to Callum Davidson and was resigned to back up appearances until he got the chance to play right back in Brian Kidd's first game in charge, against Charlton. He coped surprisingly well for a left-footed player, and was selected again in the role in March against Everton. This time, unfortunately, he had to leave the field after dislocating his shoulder when making a splendid tackle. At his best when left to cover a wide area, he returned from injury in April, but clearly came back sooner than advisable.

Grimsby T (From trainee on 7/7/92) FL 139+10/3 FLC 7 FAC 8+2/1 Others 3
Blackburn Rov (£1,700,000 on 29/3/96) PL 33+7/1 FLC 6 FAC 4+2

CROOKS Lee Robert
Born: Wakefield, 14 January 1978
Height: 6'0" Weight: 12.1
International Honours: E: Yth
Lee made a late start for recognition in 1998-99, with only two substitute appearances for Manchester City in the first 16 games. However, in mid October at Wigan on a waterlogged pitch, having been selected at right back, he had an outstanding game, being very confident and cool under pressure. The press certainly made noises for all to take notice. Following that, he made the position his own, missing only four games to the end of the season. His main asset is to go forward and dispatch accurate and telling crosses from the right-hand side into the opposing goal area. Scored his first goal for the club in the 1-1 draw at Chesterfield with a powerful low drive from 30 yards and played for the Football League U21 side against the Italian League U21s. Once he can settle into his acquitted role further honours should come his way.

Manchester C (From trainee on 14/1/95) FL 43+11/1 FLC 0+1 FAC 5 Others 3

CROSBY Andrew (Andy) Keith
Born: Rotherham, 3 March 1973
Height: 6'2" Weight: 13.7
Andy was Chester's first signing under the Bosman ruling when he joined the club from Darlington during the 1998 close season. And, made captain by Kevin Ratcliffe, he scored his first goal for City against Hull City in a 2-2 draw. A good, steady centre back, he assumed the role of penalty taker during the campaign, scoring twice from the spot with tremendous shots.

Doncaster Rov (Free from Leeds U juniors on 4/7/91) FL 41+10 FLC 1+1 FAC 2 Others 4+1/1
Darlington (Free on 10/12/93) FL 179+2/3 FLC 10 FAC 11/1 Others 9
Chester C (Free on 8/7/98) FL 41/4 FLC 3 FAC 1 Others 1

CROSS Jonathan (Jon) Neil
Born: Wallasey, 2 March 1975
Height: 5'10" Weight: 11.7
After being released by Wrexham, Jon was recommended to Chester and signed during the 1998 close season. Although being able to play almost anywhere, he made 39 appearances for City in the left-back spot, joining in the attack to great effect with his speed and searching crosses. Was one of six players at the club who were out of contract during the summer but offered terms of re-engagement.

Wrexham (From trainee on 15/11/92) FL 92+27/12 FLC 4+3/1 FAC 4+1/1 Others 9+6/1
Hereford U (Loaned on 2/12/96) FL 5/1 Others 1
Chester C (Free on 4/8/98) FL 33+2/1 FLC 4 FAC 1 Others 1

CROSSLEY Mark Geoffrey
Born: Barnsley, 16 June 1969
Height: 6'0" Weight: 16.0
International Honours: E: U21-3. W: 2; B-1
Having been sidelined for most of 1997-98 with a back injury, and being loaned out to Millwall for match fitness, Mark was again in the wings at Nottingham Forest in 1998-99 as the club looked forward to being back in the Premiership. Unable to dislodge Dave Beasant, the Welsh international goalkeeper kept his cool, remained patient, and finally got back into the side in February after the latter had been on the receiving end of 11 goals in successive home defeats at the hands of Manchester United (8-1) and Chelsea (3-1). Playing his first Premiership game for almost two years he came back into the side at Charlton to save a penalty in the 0-0 draw. Big and strong, and a goalie who excels in one-on-one situations with the forwards, he won his second Welsh cap during the season, against Switzerland. Also kicks long and hard from his hands.

Nottingham F (From trainee on 2/7/87) F/PL 282+1 FLC 35+1 FAC 32 Others 18
Millwall (Loaned on 20/2/98) FL 13

CROUDSON Steven (Steve) David
Born: Grimsby, 14 September 1979
Height: 6'0" Weight: 12.4
Having come through the trainee ranks at Grimsby to sign professional forms during the 1998 close season, and performing well in the youth side, the rookie 'keeper was suddenly thrust in to first-team reckoning following the acrimonious departure of Aidan Davison and an injury to Andy Love. Making his debut in the penultimate game of 1998-99, at home to a Wolves' side desperately seeking to clinch the fourth play-off place, Steve made a string of fine saves to win the "Man of the Match" award and a place in the last match of the campaign, at Watford.

Grimsby T (From trainee on 6/7/98) FL 2

CROWE Dean Anthony
Born: Stockport, 6 June 1979
Height: 5'5" Weight: 11.3
Dean started last season in tremendous goalscoring form with four goals in Stoke's first three league games. However, he was clearly not Brian Little's first choice and the City fans did vent their frustrations at times that they were not seeing enough of the lad who, all too often came off the bench to test a tiring opposition defence. There is still much to come from "Deano".

Stoke C (From trainee on 5/9/96) FL 29+25/12 FLC 2+1 Others 1/1

CROWE Glen Michael
Born: Dublin, 25 December 1977
Height: 5'10" Weight: 13.1
International Honours: Ei: U21-2; Yth
Unable to find his feet at Molyneux in 1998-99, Glen was loaned out to Exeter last August, where he made ten appearances without getting on the scoresheet, before being released in February and signing a short-term contract at Plymouth. A bustling centre forward who gives defences no peace at all, he is quick and strong, and showed the Argyle fans why he has appeared at a higher level. Scored his first goal for the club in the last home game of the season against Cambridge, before leaving in the summer.

Wolverhampton W (From trainee on 3/7/96) FL 6+4/1
Exeter C (Loaned on 21/2/97) FL 10/5
Cardiff C (Loaned on 24/10/97) FL 7+1/1 Others 1
Exeter C (Loaned on 6/8/98) FL 3+6 FLC 1
Plymouth Arg (Signed on 4/2/99) FL 3+8/1

CROWE Jason William
Born: Sidcup, 30 September 1978
Height: 5'9" Weight: 10.9
International Honours: E: Yth; Sch
An attacking wing back who came through from the youth team at Arsenal, Jason is good in the air for his size and uses both feet well. Although his best position is on the right-hand side of the back four, he has also played at centre back and in midfield for the reserves. Has good strength and speed which he uses to get forward at every opportunity. Added to his Gunners' first-team appearances in 1998-99, when coming off the bench in the Worthington Cup win at Derby, and spent a period on loan at Crystal Palace in November after Terry Venables, who was hit by a mixture of injuries and international call ups at Palace, gave him eight games, albeit all of them being the losing variety. Nonetheless, it was all good experience for a youngster who hopes to make his way in the game, preferably at Highbury.

Arsenal (From trainee on 13/5/96) FLC 0+2 FAC 0+1
Crystal Palace (Loaned on 10/11/98) FL 8

CRUYFF Jordi
Born: Amsterdam, Holland, 9 February 1974
Height: 6'0" Weight: 11.0
Club Honours: PL '97; CS '96, '97
International Honours: Holland: 9
A versatile Manchester United front-line player with excellent skills and a terrific shot in either foot, Jordi vowed to repay the huge debt he owed to Alex Ferguson for keeping faith in him during two injury-hit seasons. Mainly used as a substitute in 1998-99, his most prolific spell came during October, when he scored two goals against Southampton and Derby. Unable to hold a place down in such a star-studded line-up, his last appearance for United came in January against West Ham, before he went on loan to Celtic Virgo until the end of the campaign.

Manchester U (£1,400,000 from Barcelona, via Ajax, on 12/8/96) PL 14+12/5 FLC 4 FAC 0+1 Others 3+6

CUERVO Philippe
Born: Calais, France, 13 August 1969
Height: 5'11" Weight: 12.6
This skilful Frenchman was beset with bad luck last season and made only two appearances in Swindon's first team, having sustained an horrendous knee injury in a late tackle in a reserve game. Despite a number of operations, he is back on his feet but a long way off any football and, at the time of going to press, it is difficult to determine when he will be back. Greatly missed, he is a player who is effective in any number of positions, including the right-wing-back role, although he is probably at his best as a conventional midfielder deployed behind the front men. The fans are anxiously awaiting his return.
Swindon T (Free from St Etienne on 8/8/97) FL 16+13 FLC 2+1

CULLEN David Jonathan (Jon)
Born: Durham City, 10 January 1973
Height: 6'0" Weight: 12.0
A regular in the reserves in 1998-99, the tall Sheffield United central defender who signed the previous season from Hartlepool, failed to break through into the senior side, making just two appearances as a late substitute in the second half of the campaign. As a player who can also perform well in midfield and up front, where his direct, strong runs cause problems for defenders, he will be keen to become a regular member of the first-team squad this coming term.
Doncaster Rov (From trainee on 16/9/91) FL 8+1 FLC 2+1/1 FAC 0+1 Others 1 (Free to Spennymoor in September 1993)
Hartlepool U (Free from Morpeth on 27/3/97) FL 33+1/12 FLC 2 FAC 1 Others 2
Sheffield U (£250,000 on 26/1/98) FL 0+4

CULLIP Daniel (Danny)
Born: Bracknell, 17 September 1976
Height: 6'1" Weight: 12.7
Unfortunately, this Brentford centre back sustained a serious knee injury in the fourth game of last season (against West Bromwich Albion in the Worthington Cup) and was sidelined for the rest of the campaign. A player with a future in the game, it is hoped that he comes back as good as new.
Oxford U (From trainee on 6/7/95)
Fulham (Free on 5/7/96) FL 41+9/2 FLC 8 FAC 2 Others 1
Brentford (£75,000 on 17/2/98) FL 15 FLC 2

CULVERHOUSE Ian Brett
Born: Bishops Stortford, 22 September 1964
Height: 5'10" Weight: 11.2
Club Honours: UEFAC '84; Div 2 '86, '96
International Honours: E: Yth
Released by Swindon during the 1998 close season, after becoming a free agent under the Bosman ruling, the experienced sweeper signed for Brighton on a monthly contract last August following a brief spell with Kingstonian in the Football Conference. Initially released in October because the then boss, Brian Horton, wanted to play a flat-back-four system, he re-signed a week later and was immediately installed as captain in the absence through injury of Gary Hobson. Given a contract in November until the end of the season, which was later extended until June 2000 when, following Horton's departure, Jeff Wood became manager and appointed him as reserve-team coach.
Tottenham H (From apprentice on 24/9/82) FL 1+1
Norwich C (£50,000 on 8/10/85) F/PL 295+1/1 FLC 23 FAC 28 Others 22/1
Swindon T (£250,000 on 9/12/94) FL 95+2 FLC 9 FAC 10 Others 1 (Free to Kingstonian during 1998 close season)
Brighton & Hove A (Free on 18/8/98) FL 35 FLC 1 FAC 1 Others 1

CUMMINS Michael Thomas
Born: Dublin, 1 June 1978
Height: 6'0" Weight: 11.11
International Honours: Ei: U21-1; Yth
A pro at Middlesbrough since 1995, Michael is a strong-running midfielder who favours covering as much ground as possible, and gives his all over 90 minutes. He is also a strong tackler whose preference is simply to win the ball every time he engages the opposition. Only the wealth of young talent at "Robbo's" disposal kept him out of the first-team squad for so long, and his senior debut in the final game of last season, at West Ham, despite a 4-0 defeat for the club, was much welcomed. Having made his debut for the Republic of Ireland's U21 side, and very highly thought of, his day will surely come on a regular basis.
Middlesbrough (From trainee on 1/7/95) PL 1

CUNDY Jason Victor
Born: Wimbledon, 12 November 1969
Height: 6'1" Weight: 13.13
International Honours: E: U21-3
Jason's season at Ipswich in 1998-99, as it turned out, was over before it even began when he injured his ankle during a fitness exercise at home the day before he was due to report back for summer training. It took a long time to diagnose exactly what the problem was and, eventually, an operation was required. He finally regained his fitness by the end of March but, with the defence playing so well, a place on the substitutes' bench was the best he could hope for. Given a free transfer at the end of the season for "financial reasons", he became the first casualty of the club's failure to reach the Premiership. A powerfully built central defender who is excellent in the air with pace and good recovery powers on the ground, his last campaign at Portman Road, was a picture of the realities of football – from captain to cast-off in nine cruel months. Stop Press: Signed for Portsmouth on 28 June.
Chelsea (From trainee on 1/8/88) FL 40+1/1 FLC 6 FAC 6 Others 4
Tottenham H (£750,000 on 26/3/92) F/PL 23+3/1 FLC 2
Crystal Palace (Loaned on 14/12/95) FL 4
Bristol C (Loaned on 23/8/96) FL 6/1
Ipswich T (£200,000 on 29/10/96) FL 54+4/5 FLC 8 FAC 4 Others 2

CUNNINGHAM Kenneth (Kenny) Edward
Born: Dublin, 28 June 1971
Height: 6'0" Weight: 11.8
International Honours: Ei: 21; B-2; U21-4; Yth
A versatile and reliable attacking full back who is a valued member of the Wimbledon squad, Kenny again enjoyed getting down the right-hand flank regularly in 1998-99 to provide accurate crosses for the front men. Is also able to slot in at centre back, if needed, and has served the Republic of Ireland well in this position. With an excellent footballing brain, and a player who gives valuable verbal support to his fellow team mates, he was voted the "Irish Player of the Year" at the end of 1998. He is both hard working and comfortable on the ball.
Millwall (Signed from Tolka Rov on 18/9/89) FL 132+4/1 FLC 10 FAC 1 Others 5+1/1
Wimbledon (Signed on 9/11/94) PL 163+1 FLC 18+1 FAC 24

CURCIC Sasa
Born: Belgrade, Yugoslavia, 14 February 1972
Height: 5'9" Weight: 11.2
International Honours: Yugoslavia: 14
A highly popular Crystal Palace midfielder, despite being moody and said to be a difficult trainer, he scored on the opening day last season, at home to Bolton, and scored a further three goals when coming off the bench. Having played for Yugoslavia against Brazil in September, and thought to be one of the players that the club would be building on in 1998-99, he only appeared sporadically for Palace from then on and was devastated by the NATO bombings on his homeland. An attacking player with excellent vision, passing skills, and a talent for long-range shooting opportunities, at the time of going to press it is difficult to see where his future lies.
Bolton W (£1,500,000 from Partizan Belgrade, via OFK Belgrade, on 28/10/95) PL 28/4 FLC 3/1 FAC 2/2
Aston Villa (£4,000,000 on 23/8/96) PL 20+9 FLC 1+1 FAC 2/1 Others 0+1
Crystal Palace (£1,000,000 on 26/3/98) P/FL 10+13/5 FLC 2

CURETON Jamie
Born: Bristol, 28 August 1975
Height: 5'8" Weight: 10.7
International Honours: E: Yth
A local-born striker, Jamie recovered from a broken leg and started last season in a wide role on Bristol Rovers' left wing, before being moved up front in November following the transfer of Barry Hayles. Enjoying another good campaign in being the only ever present in the club, he scored four goals in the second half against Reading in a remarkable 6-0 win at the Madjeski Stadium, and added another second-half hat trick at Walsall on 20 March with his final equalising goal coming in injury time after a wayward clearance by the home goalkeeper hit him full in the face. Developed a potent goalscoring partnership with Jason Roberts, both scoring over 20 goals apiece, and took his tally to 29 on the last day of the season with another hat trick,

this time at Macclesfield, which ensured that he won the Second Division's "Golden Boot" award.

Norwich C (From trainee on 5/2/93) P/FL 13+16/6 FLC 0+1 FAC 0+2
Bournemouth (Loaned on 8/9/95) FL 0+5 Others 0+1
Bristol Rov (£250,000 on 20/9/96) FL 118+9/49 FLC 3+1/1 FAC 9/2 Others 4/1

CURLE Keith
Born: Bristol, 14 November 1963
Height: 6'1" Weight: 12.12
Club Honours: AMC '86; FMC '88
International Honours: E: 3; B-4

The Wolves captain had a pre-1998-99 season row about his contract but, thankfully, the issue was settled. He then took three penalties in the first five matches, scoring twice, while Simon Osborn scored in the scramble that followed the other one. An ever present in the league until the end of October, though some felt the central defender was not as assured as previous, he did not miss another match until the end of March, playing 24 times and showing his true form with fine tackling and distribution. After Bristol City had tried to get him to become their assistant manager early in December, Wolves soon appointed him reserve-team coach, so he could continue playing as well as improving his future development in football.

Bristol Rov (From apprentice on 20/11/81) FL 21+11/4 FLC 3 FAC 1
Torquay U (£5,000 on 4/11/83) FL 16/5 FAC 1/1 Others 1
Bristol C (£10,000 on 3/3/84) FL 113+8/1 FLC 7+1 FAC 5 Others 14+1
Reading (£150,000 on 23/10/87) FL 40 FLC 8 Others 5
Wimbledon (£500,000 on 21/10/88) FL 91+2/3 FLC 7 FAC 5 Others 6/1
Manchester C (£2,500,000 on 14/8/91) F/PL 171/11 FLC 18/2 FAC 14 Others 1
Wolverhampton W (£650,000 on 2/8/96) FL 104+1/7 FLC 5 FAC 9/1 Others 2

CURRAN Christopher (Chris)
Born: Birmingham, 17 September 1971
Height: 5'11" Weight: 12.4

Chris enjoyed a good, full season of action at Exeter in 1998-99 after recovering fully from the knee-ligament injury he endured the previous term. His neat link up play and vision enabled the team to keep things tighter at the back, especially away from home, where conceding goals had become a seasonal ritual. Is a hard-working central defender who is fully committed to the team and contests every ball.

Torquay U (From trainee on 13/7/90) FL 144+8/4 FLC 15 FAC 8 Others 10/1
Plymouth Arg (£40,000 on 22/12/95) FL 26+4 FLC 1+1 FAC 1 Others 4
Exeter C (£20,000 on 31/7/97) FL 39+4/4 FLC 4 FAC 3 Others 2

CURRAN Daniel (Danny) Lee
Born: Brentwood, 13 June 1981
Height: 5'8" Weight: 9.0

Danny is an exciting young Leyton Orient trainee forward who, after scoring a lot of goals in the youth team and reserves, was given his chance when coming off the bench against Peterborough in the Auto Wind-

screens Shield last season and played like he was a first-team regular. He also made brief appearances against Darlington in the league and Bristol Rovers in the FA Cup. Definitely a player to watch out for in the future, and one who is full of tricks with pace to match, he will be looking to earn a place in the senior squad this season.

Leyton Orient (Trainee) FL 0+1 FAC 0+1 Others 0+1

CURRIE Darren Paul
Born: Hampstead, 29 November 1974
Height: 5'11" Weight: 12.7

Signed from Plymouth during the summer of 1998, Darren made a whirlwind start to last season where he struck two magnificent goals for Barnet in successive games. Following the latter, which was scored against Wolves and consequently awarded the "Goal of the Season" title, he relinquished his goalscoring duties and adopted the role of provider. He quickly developed a marvellous rapport with the Underhill crowd, and his ability to deliver accurate crosses was clearly appreciated by the fans. Although his talent was usually utilised on the left flank he proved against Rotherham in September that he was equally adept at performing on the right wing and, although not bestowed with scintillating pace, the combination of great balance and sleight of feet made him a very difficult player to tackle when he was in possession. However, as the campaign progressed, his first-team outings away from home became increasingly limited as the Bees adopted a more defensive line-up on their travels. Often plagued with comparisons between himself and his legendary uncle Tony (Currie), if he can maintain a level of consistency then he has the skill to establish himself as a talent in his own right.

West Ham U (From trainee on 2/7/93)
Shrewsbury T (Loaned on 5/9/94) FL 10+2/2
Shrewsbury T (Loaned on 3/2/95) FL 5
Leyton Orient (Loaned on 16/11/95) FL 9+1
Shrewsbury T (£70,000 on 7/2/96) FL 46+20/8 FLC 2+1/1 FAC 3
Plymouth Arg (Free on 26/3/98) FL 5+2
Barnet (Free on 13/7/98) FL 33+5/4 FLC 2/1 FAC 1/1 Others 1

CURTIS John Charles
Born: Nuneaton, 3 September 1978
Height: 5'10" Weight: 11.9
Club Honours: FAYC '95
International Honours: E: B-1; U21-15; Yth; Sch

A solid Manchester United full back, with good tackling and recovery skills, John had very few opportunities to show United fans what he could do in 1998-99 after first coming to prominence during the 1997-98 campaign. Facing stiff opposition from the new kid on the block, Wes Brown, he only made eight appearances all season, the first as a substitute in the Premiership against Wimbledon in October, and his last against Everton in March. However, highly thought of at Old Trafford, he is certain to get more chances before too long, especially with the side being involved in so many competitions in 1999-2000. Despite a lack of senior

appearances, he was still an ever present for the England U21 side during the term.

Manchester U (From trainee on 3/10/95) PL 4+8 FLC 4

CURTIS Thomas (Tom) David
Born: Exeter, 1 March 1973
Height: 5'8" Weight: 11.7

Recovering well from a broken toe last September to put in some gutsy, harrying displays in the Chesterfield midfield in 1998-99, Tom developed cartilage trouble at Burnley in January, but put off an operation in order to aid the Spireites' play-off push. It speaks volumes for his selflessness that he would do this, and run the risk of appearing to under-perform as a result. Unfortunately, the injury got the better of him in April, and he was forced to sit out the rest of the season.

Derby Co (From juniors on 1/7/91)
Chesterfield (Free on 12/8/93) FL 218+4/12 FLC 17+1 FAC 18/1 Others 11+1

CUSACK Nicholas (Nicky) John
Born: Maltby, 24 December 1965
Height: 6'0" Weight: 12.8

Nicky was one of the automatic choices in midfield for Swansea throughout 1998-99, displaying consistent performances throughout with his all-round style of play, linking up well with his strikers, or as an extra defender when needed. During the Wrexham Welsh Premier Cup-tie he had to have six stitches in a head wound after coming on as a substitute. An excellent professional who rarely receives the credit he deserves, he took over the captaincy after the early-season injury to Keith Walker.

Leicester C (Signed from Alvechurch on 18/6/87) FL 5+11/1 FAC 0+1 Others 1+1
Peterborough U (£40,000 on 29/7/88) FL 44/10 FLC 4/1 FAC 4/1 Others 2
Motherwell (£100,000 on 2/8/89) SL 68+9/17 SLC 5/4 SC 3+1/2 Others 1+1/1
Darlington (£95,000 on 24/1/92) FL 21/6
Oxford U (£95,000 on 16/7/92) FL 48+13/10 FLC 3/2 FAC 4+2/1 Others 2+1
Wycombe W (Loaned on 24/3/94) FL 2+2/1
Fulham (Free on 4/11/94) FL 109+7/14 FLC 6+4/1 FAC 7+1/1 Others 5+2/3
Swansea C (Free on 30/10/97) FL 74+1/1 FLC 2/1 FAC 6 Others 4

CUTLER Neil Anthony
Born: Birmingham, 3 September 1976
Height: 6'1" Weight: 12.0
International Honours: E: Yth; Sch

Released by Crewe, this former England youth international goalkeeper joined Chester at the start of last season after a spell on loan with the club during 1997-98. Started 1998-99 as second choice, but took over the number-one spot in November and played 20 consecutive league games before losing his place to Wayne Brown. Still young enough to reach the top, he returned for the final three games of the campaign.

West Bromwich A (From trainee on 7/9/93)
Chester C (Loaned on 27/3/96) FL 1
Crewe Alex (Signed on 30/7/96)
Chester C (Loaned on 30/8/96) FL 5
Chester C (Free on 8/7/98) FL 23 FLC 1 FAC 1 Others 1

D

DABELSTEEN Thomas
Born: Copenhagen, Denmark, 6 March 1973
Height: 6'1" Weight: 11.12
Coming to England during the Scandinavian mid-season break, having been with the Danish side, Kolding, the striker joined Scarborough on non-contract forms last November. Having scored for the reserves on his debut, he also found the net in the third of five senior games, a 3-1 defeat at Peterborough, before linking up with the East-Anglian side at the end of the campaign.
Scarborough (Free from Kolding on 27/11/98) FL 5/1

Nicos Dabizas

DABIZAS Nikolaos (Nicos)
Born: Amyndaeo, Greece, 3 August 1973
Height: 6'1" Weight: 12.7
International Honours: Greece: 28
Nikos is a versatile Newcastle player who is a regular in the Greek national side and is best deployed at the heart of the defence, although his confidence and ability on the ball means he can also be used in midfield if desired. His spring enables him to be very good in the air, a quality which proved valuable in both penalty boxes last season. His importance to Newcastle is demonstrated by his appearance record. Thus, despite Ruud Gullit's known liking for rotating his squad, he was a regular throughout the campaign, his main absences being because twice he was shown two yellow cards, and therefore a red card, in a game, which led to suspensions. Scored three times in six games early in the season, all headers, and this probably persuaded the

manager to put him on as an auxiliary attacker when he came off the bench in the local derby at Middlesbrough in December. Within a couple of minutes, he had scored the equaliser with another header to win a point for his club. Played a key role in the FA Cup semi final, when he assumed responsibility for marshalling the defence to deny Spurs a goal following Steve Howey's unfortunate first-half departure through injury.
Newcastle U (£1,300,000 from Olympiakos on 13/3/98) PL 35+6/4 FLC 2 FAC 8 Others 2/1

DACOURT Olivier
Born: Paris, France, 25 September 1974
Height: 5'9" Weight: 11.6
A sharp and classy midfield playmaker, Olivier was one of Everton's players of last season, despite a disciplinary record which included 14 bookings, one red card and sparked four separate bans. Signed from Strasbourg immediately prior to 1998-99 kicking off, after impressing manager Walter Smith with the way he dominated Paul Ince in a UEFA Cup-tie the previous season, the Frenchman constantly excelled. An incisive tackler, with a good range of passing and the ability to score spectacular goals – as he proved at Anfield after only 39 seconds – cheeky team mates christened him "The Vieira of the North!" A close friend of the Arsenal star, his excellence inevitably led to talk of him being lured away from Goodison Park and, although he soured his relationship with the Everton supporters somewhat, he still remained one of the success stories of a sorry season at Goodison. Stop Press: Signed for Lens on 29 June, a £6.5 million fee securing his transfer.
Everton (£4,000,000 from Strasbourg on 7/8/98) PL 28+2/2 FLC 4/1 FAC 2

Olivier Dacourt

DAHLIN Martin
Born: Udevalla, Sweden, 16 April 1968
Height: 6'0" Weight: 13.2
International Honours: Sweden: 60

It was a great surprise when Martin returned in time for the start of Blackburn's 1998-99 Premiership campaign, his back problem alleviated by medical treatment in the USA during the summer, and he was by far the best of Rovers' strikers during the pre-season games, scoring against PSV Eindhoven and generally looking back to his sharpest. Surprisingly, he then found himself on the bench until the end of September before getting sent off in his second game and being loaned to Hamburg, with the Germans having an option to purchase. Unfortunately, the Swede again injured his back and seldom played. At his best very sharp around the box, with excellent touches and movement, he is contracted at Rovers until June 2000.
Blackburn Rov (£2,500,000 from Roma, via Malmo and Moenchengladbach, on 23/7/97) PL 13+13/4 FLC 2/2 FAC 0+1 Others 0+1

DAILLY Christian Eduard
Born: Dundee, 23 October 1973
Height: 6'0" Weight: 12.10
Club Honours: SC '94
International Honours: S: 13; B-1; U21-34; Yth; Sch

Signed from Derby one week into last season, ostensibly to replace the departed Colin Hendry, it was curious why he was given his Blackburn debut in midfield and later installed at right back. Distinctly ill at ease in that position, he struggled until replacing Darren Peacock in central defence in December. Although he gave glimpses of the ease on the ball and the composure that had made him a member of the Scottish squad, not the least of his problems was his alignment in the offside trap. Out of the side when he pulled a calf muscle at the end of December, it was strange that he never returned when fit again, and he really needs an injury-free time before judgement is made. At his best, a quality player very much in the mould of the top Europeans.
Dundee U (From juniors on 2/8/90) SL 110+33/18 SLC 9/1 SC 10+2 Others 8+1/1
Derby Co (£1,000,000 on 12/8/96) PL 62+5/4 FLC 6 FAC 4+1
Blackburn Rov (£5,300,000 on 22/8/98) PL 14+3 FLC 2 Others 2

DALEY Anthony (Tony) Mark
Born: Birmingham, 18 October 1967
Height: 5'8" Weight: 11.7
Club Honours: FLC '94
International Honours: E: 7; B-1; Yth
The former England winger came to Watford on a trial basis at the start of last season, having been released by Wolves following a serious cruciate ligament injury. He then promptly suffered a thigh injury that also needed surgery, but having proved his fitness was rewarded with a contract in January to the end of the campaign. A winger who likes to run on to passes played ahead of him, he remains very quick and his ball skills are much appreciated by the crowd. As an ex-Villa player, he must have been delighted to score his first Watford goal – a match-winner – at Birmingham, before being given a free transfer during the summer.

Aston Villa (From apprentice on 31/5/85) F/PL 189+44/31 FLC 22+2/4 FAC 15+1/2 Others 15+2/1
Wolverhampton W (£1,250,000 on 6/6/94) FL 16+5/3 FLC 4/1 FAC 0+2
Watford (Free on 7/8/98) FL 6+6/1 FLC 1+1

Paul Dalglish

DALGLISH Paul
Born: Glasgow, 18 February 1977
Height: 5'10" Weight: 10.0
International Honours: S: U21-3
It is always difficult for a man to follow a famous father in the same profession, and being the son of a legend like Kenny, who was also his club manager at Newcastle, Paul has had major challenges to face, particularly as he resembles his father both physically and in a number of aspects of his footballing style. Is a lively, mobile player, with burning pace and instinctive striking skills which he deploys with intelligence, and is seen to best advantage when playing off a target man. His level headedness helped him cope with a difficult season in 1998-99, a season which saw his father leave his job as Newcastle manager after only two games. Paul remained determined, having had a good pre-season in which he scored twice in the friendly at Bray, and he worked hard enough to earn himself a chance in the Newcastle first team on merit. After three substitute appearances, he was given his first start against Derby in October and had a run of eight games, scoring the winner at Tranmere in the Worthington Cup when he rounded the 'keeper in a style reminiscent of his father, and the point-saving equaliser against Wednesday in the Premiership. During this period he also made a scoring debut for Scotland U21s against Estonia. However, he then fell out of favour at Newcastle and, after a couple of further substitute appearances, he joined Norwich on transfer deadline day on loan until the end of the season.

Glasgow Celtic (From juniors on 20/7/95)
Liverpool (Free on 14/8/96)
Newcastle U (Free on 21/11/97) PL 6+5/1 FLC 2/1
Bury (Loaned on 21/11/97) FL 1+11 FAC 1
Norwich C (Loaned on 25/3/99) FL 3+2

DALTON Paul
Born: Middlesbrough, 25 April 1967
Height: 5'11" Weight: 13.0
Having missed Huddersfield's back end of 1997-98 through injury, the gifted winger could not wait to make an impact on the First Division last season. He soon thrilled the McAlpine crowd with a winning performance after coming off the bench, when scoring the winning goal from the spot against Mansfield in the Worthington Cup. Continued to impress with some skilful, attacking displays, scoring three cracking goals in ten games, before injury struck again when a foot-tendon injury put him firmly on the sidelines.

Manchester U (£35,000 from Brandon U on 3/5/88)
Hartlepool U (£20,000 on 4/3/89) FL 140+11/37 FLC 10/2 FAC 7/1 Others 9/3
Plymouth Arg (£275,000 on 11/6/92) FL 93+5/25 FLC 5/2 FAC 7/5 Others 6
Huddersfield T (Signed on 11/8/95) FL 79+19/25 FLC 9+3/2 FAC 5+1

DARBY Duane Anthony
Born: Birmingham, 17 October 1973
Height: 5'11" Weight: 12.6
Although leaving Hull City under the Bosman ruling, amidst a storm of controversy, when signing for Notts County during the 1998 close season, Duane was unable to get a first-team opportunity at his new club because he had snapped an achilles tendon in one of his first training sessions, and returned to City on loan during transfer deadline week. A determined striker who is very strong on his right side, he appeared in eight of Hull's final nine matches before going back to Meadow Lane, where he has yet to play.

Torquay U (From trainee on 3/7/92) FL 60+48/26 FLC 4+3/1 FAC 1+4 Others 5+3/2
Doncaster Rov (£60,000 on 19/7/95) FL 8+9/4 FLC 2 FAC 0+1 Others 1+1
Hull C (Signed on 27/3/96) FL 75+3/27 FLC 5/1 FAC 4/6 Others 4/2
Notts Co (Free on 2/7/98)
Hull C (Loaned on 25/3/99) FL 4+4

DARBY Julian Timothy
Born: Bolton, 3 October 1967
Height: 6'0" Weight: 11.4
Club Honours: AMC '89
International Honours: E: Sch
Preston's experienced midfielder had to bide his time for a first-team chance in 1998-99, not starting a match until December, following two earlier substitute appearances. The second of these saw him score his first goal for the club, against Ford United in the FA Cup first round, a feat he repeated at Hartlepool in the Auto Windscreens Shield. Gary Parkinson's injury saw Julian fill in at right back from January onwards, where he gave a good account of himself, using his height and strength in the tackle to good effect until the signing of Graham Alexander saw him return to the role of squad member. Was released in the summer.

Bolton W (From trainee on 22/7/86) FL 258+12/36 FLC 25/8 FAC 19/3 Others 31+1/5
Coventry C (£150,000 on 28/10/93) PL 52+3/5 FLC 3/1 FAC 2+2
West Bromwich A (£200,000 on 24/11/95) FL 32+7/1 FAC 1 Others 4
Preston NE (£150,000 on 13/6/97) FL 18+14/1 FLC 1+1 FAC 2+2/1 Others 2+2/1
Rotherham U (Loaned on 26/3/98) FL 3

DARCHEVILLE Jean-Claude
Born: French Guyana, 25 July 1975
Height: 5'8" Weight: 11.12
A newcomer to English football, the Frenchman became Dave Bassett's first 1998 summer signing in preparation for Nottingham Forest's return to the Premiership when he joined the club on an extended loan from the French First Division side, Stade Rennais. A powerfully-built striker, who could also operate on the right-hand side of midfield, he looked to follow the example of his countryman, Thierry Bonalair, in making his mark at the City Ground. Started well enough with two goals in his first five games, including a cracker in a 2-1 win at Southampton, but then lost his place shortly afterwards and never got back in again on a regular basis.

Nottingham F (Loaned from Stade Rennais on 20/7/98) PL 14+2/2 FLC 1+2

Jean-Claude Darcheville

DARLINGTON Jermaine Christopher
Born: Hackney, 11 April 1974
Height: 5'7" Weight: 10.10
Once of Charlton, Jermaine came back into the Football League with Queens Park Rangers when they signed him from Aylesbury United during transfer deadline week last March. An attacking left-wing back who made his first-team debut for Rangers in the 2-1 home win against West Bromwich in April, before making three more appearances, he is yet another of Gerry Francis' finds from the non-league area, and one who is expected to challenge the established wing backs for the number-three shirt in 1999-2000.

Charlton Ath (From trainee on 30/6/92) FL 1+1 (Free to Dover Ath on 23/9/93)
Queens Park R (£25,000 from Aylesbury U on 25/3/99) FL 4

David D'Auria

D'AURIA David Alan
Born: Swansea, 26 March 1970
Height: 5'10" Weight: 12.6
Club Honours: WC '94
International Honours: W: Yth
Having captained Scunthorpe to within a point of the play offs in 1997-98, David lived near Hull and, being a close friend of Gregor Rioch, it was not a surprise when Hull beat off Swansea, Cardiff and Scarborough for his signature during the 1998 close season. At his best in the centre of midfield, he soon took over the skipper's armband, as he became one of their most regular performers in a turbulent campaign. Subject to a £50,000 bid from Plymouth in November, the right-footed player is learning the tricks of the building trade in preparation for his eventual non-playing future.
Swansea C (From trainee on 2/8/88) FL 27+18/6 FLC 2+2 FAC 1 Others 4 (Free transfer to Merthyr Tydfil during 1991 close season)
Scarborough (Signed from Barry T on 22/8/94) FL 49+3/8 FLC 3+2/1 FAC 4+1 Others 2
Scunthorpe U (£40,000 on 6/12/95) FL 103+4/18 FLC 6 FAC 7/1 Others 4+1
Hull C (Free on 16/7/98) FL 42/4 FLC 4 FAC 2 Others 2/1

DAVENPORT Peter
Born: Birkenhead, 24 March 1961
Height: 5'11" Weight: 12.10
Club Honours: FMC '90; GMVC '97
International Honours: E: 1; B-1
Peter spent most of the 1998-99 season as team coach at Macclesfield but, because of limited resources and a small squad at the club, the former England striker was included among the five-named substitutes for three FA Cup games, making a five-minute appearance in the second round 4-1 victory over Cambridge, when replacing the tiring left winger. In March 1999 he was appointed as assistant manager, when the previous holder of the job was made up to Director of Football.

Airdrie (Free during 1993 close season) SL 35+3/9 SLC 3/1 SC 3+2
Nottingham F (Free from Camel Laird on 5/1/82) FL 114+4/54 FLC 10/1 FAC 7+1/1 Others 10+1/2
Manchester U (£750,000 on 12/3/86) FL 73+19/22 FLC 8+2/4 FAC 2+2
Middlesbrough (£750,000 on 30/11/88) FL 53+6/7 FLC 2 FAC 4 Others 7+1/1
Sunderland (£350,000 on 19/7/90) FL 72+27/15 FLC 5+2/1 FAC 9+1/2 Others 14+1
St Johnstone (Free on 16/8/94) SL 12+10/4 SLC 3 SC 0+1 Others 2/1
Stockport Co (Free on 23/3/95) FL 3+3/1 (Free to Southport on 24/8/95)
Macclesfield T (Free on 21/1/97) FL 2+3/1 FAC 0+1

DAVIDSON Callum Iain
Born: Stirling, 25 June 1976
Height: 5'10" Weight: 11.8
Club Honours: S Div 1 '97
International Honours: S: 7; U21-2
A success early last season, when his quick tackling, enthusiastic forward running, and fine positional covering marked him as a real prospect, and saw him drafted into the Scottish team, Callum scored his Blackburn debut goal against West Ham with a stunning right-footed shot from long range. A victim of foul play on international duty, he missed games because of recurring headaches and thereafter was seldom as incisive as he had been early on. However, fit and well, he will undoubtedly be back for Rovers in 1999-2000.
St Johnstone (From juniors on 8/6/94) SL 38+5/4 SLC 1 Others 3
Blackburn Rov (£1,750,000 on 12/2/98) PL 35/1 FLC 2+1 FAC 2 Others 1+1

DAVIDSON Ross James
Born: Chertsey, 13 November 1973
Height: 5'9" Weight: 12.4
Voted Chester's "Player of the Season" for 1998-99, Ross is a reliable right back who is equally at home when joining the attack. A skilful player, who likes to get forward and has a tremendous shot, when required he can also play at the centre of defence. Is also a strong tackler. Was one of six players at the club who were out of contract during the summer, but were offered terms of re-engagement.
Sheffield U (Signed from Walton & Hersham on 5/6/93) FL 2 Others 2
Chester C (Free on 26/1/96) FL 123/6 FLC 7 FAC 3+1 Others 4

DAVIES Gareth Melville
Born: Hereford, 11 December 1973
Height: 6'1" Weight: 11.12
International Honours: W: U21-8
The tall Welsh centre back made just one appearance at Reading in 1998-99, the opening game at Wrexham, before he was sidelined by the manager and forced to train on his own until the PFA were called in to settle the dispute. Freed in March, Gareth signed up for First Division Swindon, where he linked up once again with his former Royals' boss, Jimmy Quinn. After quickly stamping his presence in the centre of Town's defence, unfortunately, a hamstring injury forced him out of action for the last few games. Good on the ground, and able to play as a midfielder, not only is he a sound

tackler but he also enjoys the passing game.
Hereford U (From trainee on 10/4/92) FL 91+4/1 FLC 5+2 FAC 4 Others 5
Crystal Palace (£120,000 on 1/7/95) F/PL 22+5/2 FAC 2 Others 1
Cardiff C (Loaned on 21/2/97) FL 6/2
Reading (£100,000 on 12/12/97) FL 18+1 FLC 1 FAC 3
Swindon T (Free on 2/3/99) FL 6

DAVIES Jamie
Born: Swansea, 12 February 1980
Height: 6'0" Weight: 11.9
Two substitute appearances in the Welsh Premier Cup games against Barry Town were Jamie's only first-team starts during the first half of last season. At the end of January, however, John Hollins was impressed with the young striker's form sufficiently to offer him a further 12-months extension to his contract. A first-year professional, he made his league debut as a second-half substitute against Carlisle United at the Vetch in February.
Swansea C (From trainee on 16/7/98) FL 0+1

DAVIES Kevin Cyril
Born: Sheffield, 26 March 1977
Height: 6'0" Weight: 13.6
International Honours: E: U21-2; Yth
Signed from Southampton during the 1998 close season for a fee in excess of £7 million, Kevin's first appearance in 1998-99 was eagerly awaited by the Blackburn fans. Unfortunately, for both player and club, in rehabilitating from a long absence through injury the striker found it difficult to adjust to the pace of the game and recurring spells of tonsilitis sidelined him for further spells. A much-admired player, especially when he performed miracles for Chesterfield, he scored just twice, both goals coming against Charlton, but on a more positive note he showed that he had lost none of the strength and power that allows him to pass defenders. However, with Rovers fighting to stem the relegation tide it was hardly conducive for good football. At his best, he likes taking defenders on, mainly from wide positions, has plenty of power, and has skill to match. All at Ewood will be hoping that he can put last season behind him and produce the goods in the coming campaign. Added to his England U21 cap with an appearance against the Czech Republic.
Chesterfield (From trainee on 18/4/94) FL 113+16/22 FLC 7+2/1 FAC 10/6 Others 9+2/1
Southampton (£750,000 on 14/5/97) PL 20+5/9 FLC 3+1/3 FAC 1
Blackburn Rov (£7,250,000 on 2/6/98) PL 9+12/1 FLC 3 FAC 2/1 Others 1

DAVIES Lawrence
Born: Abergavenny, 3 September 1977
Height: 6'1" Weight: 11.8
International Honours: W: Yth
Unable to get a game at Bradford last season, Lawrence was loaned to Hartlepool in early September to put some much needed first-team football under his belt but, after just two starts and an appearance from the bench, he returned to Valley Parade. He eventually became Jeff Wood's first signing as manager of Brighton in February when joining the club for the rest of the season. A

striker, who despite hard running and good approach play, failed to find the net in his limited appearances, he scored a hat trick for the reserves against Barnet, but when this failed to earn him a place on the bench for the next senior game he asked the new manager, Micky Adams, to release him from his contract.

Leeds U (From trainee on 19/8/96)
Bradford C (Free on 11/7/97) FL 1+3
Darlington (Loaned on 1/12/97) FL 2 Others 1
Hartlepool U (Loaned on 11/9/98) FL 2+1
Brighton & Hove A (Free on 12/2/99) FL 2+6

DAVIES Simon
Born: Haverfordwest, 23 October 1979
Height: 5'10" Weight: 11.4
International Honours: W: B-1; U21-5; Yth

As one of the most sought after young players in the Football league, Simon blossomed at Peterborough last season, missing just three games, and appeared at Welsh U21 and "B" team levels to mark his promise. With vision, touch, pace, and two good feet, the brilliant young midfielder was recognised by his fellow professionals when selected for the award-winning PFA Third Division team, and was the supporters' "Player of the Year". Surprisingly, he only scored four times, all in the league, and all in games that were either won or drawn, but if there is a weakness in his make up it is in that department and he will undoubtedly look to put it right in 1999-2000.

Peterborough U (From trainee on 21/7/97) FL 47+2/4 FLC 2 FAC 1 Others 3

DAVIES Simon Ithel
Born: Winsford, 23 April 1974
Height: 6'0" Weight: 11.11
Club Honours: FAYC '92
International Honours: W: 1

The former Manchester United man was again unable to exert his influence on the left side of Luton's midfield, this time in 1998-99, suffering from a mixture of form loss and injuries, and played just two games before signing for Macclesfield in December. Big and strong, despite making a good start with Town while showing some skilful ball play, he lost form and was rested at the beginning of March. However, he played memorably at Manchester City, revelling in the derby atmosphere, and showed up well when beating four defenders before being denied by the 'keeper. Scored his first goal for the club, at Luton of all places, within six minutes of coming off the bench.

Manchester U (From trainee on 6/7/92) PL 4+7 FLC 4+2 Others 2+1/1
Exeter C (Loaned on 17/12/93) FL 5+1/1 FAC 1
Huddersfield T (Loaned on 29/10/96) FL 3
Luton T (£150,000 on 5/8/97) FL 10+12/1 FLC 3+1 FAC 0+1 Others 3
Macclesfield T (Signed on 17/12/98) FL 9+3/2 FAC 1

DAVIS Daniel (Danny) Jonathan Steven
Born: Brighton, 3 October 1980
Height: 5'9" Weight: 11.1

A Brighton & Hove Albion trainee, the 18-year-old midfielder was a regular in the youth team during two successful cup runs. Hailing from nearby Saltdean, he made his

full senior debut when coming on as a substitute during the disastrous 4-0 home defeat by Darlington in March, but had the misfortune to give away the penalty which led to the fourth goal. Micky Adams was due to reward him with a one-year professional contract during the summer.

Brighton & Hove A (Trainee) FL 0+1

DAVIS Kelvin Geoffrey
Born: Bedford, 29 September 1976
Height: 6'1" Weight: 14.0
International Honours: E: U21-3; Yth

A goalkeeper who began to establish himself in 1997-98 after ousting the American, Ian Feuer, from the number-one spot at Luton, Kelvin had a brilliant season in 1998-99, missing just three games and keeping 11 clean sheets. With shot-stopping ability high on his agenda, added experience has seen him begin to control the box more and to stand up to create a bigger target. Began the campaign well when pulling off a string of fine saves in a pre-season friendly against the Premier League champions, Arsenal, and ended it supremely when being both the players' and supporters' choice as Town's "Player of the Year".

Luton T (From trainee on 1/7/94) FL 92 FLC 7 FAC 2 Others 6
Torquay U (Loaned on 16/9/94) FL 2 FLC 1 Others 1
Hartlepool U (Loaned on 8/8/97) FL 2 FLC 1

DAVIS Neil
Born: Bloxwich, 15 August 1973
Height: 5'9" Weight: 11.10

Released by Aston Villa during the 1998 close season, Neil spent a month on trial at Walsall at the beginning of 1998-99, before signing for non-league Hednesford Town, having made a brief appearance in the opening game at Gillingham when he replaced Jason Brissett and skimmed the bar from a narrow angle. A striker, who is hard working, has good control, and links up well, he could well come again.

Aston Villa (£25,000 from Redditch on 4/5/91) PL 0+2 FAC 0+1
Wycombe W (Loaned on 25/10/96) FL 13 Others 1
Walsall (Free on 6/8/98) FL 0+1

DAVIS Sean
Born: Clapham, 20 September 1979
Height: 5'10" Weight: 12.0

Having made his first-team debut for Fulham in October 1996, this very promising young player was described by the club's Director of Youth, Alan Smith, as the best midfielder he had seen in Academy U19 matches last season. Despite the strength in depth of the senior squad, Sean took part in nine games and showed improvement with each outing, gaining the confidence to spray the ball around and have a shot when the opportunity arose.

Fulham (From trainee on 2/7/98) FL 1+6 FLC 1+1 FAC 1

DAVIS Solomon (Sol) Sebastian
Born: Cheltenham, 4 September 1979
Height: 5'8" Weight: 11.0

Having come through Swindon's junior ranks, the left-sided full back, cum wing

back, was offered his first pro contract in the summer of 1998 after a series of impressive performances in the reserves, and following a fine league debut as a substitute at home to Queens Park Rangers shortly after his 18th birthday in 1997-98. Able to get up and down the left flank all day long, despite his final ball sometimes letting him down, youth is on his side, and he is expected to develop into a good player. Had a good run of appearances in mid term at Town in 1998-99 before tailing off, and will be looking to build upon that this coming season.

Swindon T (From trainee on 29/5/98) FL 26+5 FAC 1

DAVIS Stephen (Steve) Mark
Born: Hexham, 30 October 1968
Height: 6'2" Weight: 14.7
Club Honours: Div 4 '92

A solid barrier in his central defensive role, and very dangerous with his ability in the air, both in defence and in the opponents' penalty box, Steve was a Luton player you could rely upon in 1998-99. As well as being sure footed in his ball skills, Town's captain showed his class by scoring one of the most memorable goals in recent times. Not very happy with the movement up front he carried the ball from the half-way line, took a return pass in his stride, bore down on the Hull goalkeeper, and rounded him to put the ball into an empty net. However, even that failed to stop the team going down to a FA Cup second round defeat, and he was soon taking the return journey to Burnley, one of his former clubs, on the last day of December, having scored ten goals in 29 games. As Burnley's favourite player of the decade, his transfer to Turf Moor was arguably manager Stan Ternent's most popular move, and he soon displayed his familiar defensive solidity, exciting forward runs, and was particularly dangerous at set pieces. His best scoring season to date, 13, he was rewarded with a place in the PFA Second Division select.

Southampton (From trainee on 6/7/87) FL 5+1
Burnley (Loaned on 21/11/89) FL 7+2
Notts Co (Loaned on 28/3/91) FL 0+2
Burnley (£60,000 on 17/8/91) FL 162/22 FLC 10/2 FAC 18/1 Others 13
Luton T (£750,000 on 13/7/95) FL 137+1/21 FLC 19/3 FAC 5/2 Others 10/1
Burnley (£800,000 on 21/12/98) FL 19/3

DAVIS Steven (Steve) Peter
Born: Birmingham, 26 July 1965
Height: 6'0" Weight: 12.12
International Honours: E: Yth

1998-99 was a wretched season for the experienced Oxford central defender, who lost almost all of it to an achilles injury. Indeed, after picking up the knock at Crystal Palace in the team's third league game he did not appear again until April, as a non-playing sub in the defeat at Port Vale. Good in the air, and a good tackler, he was missed.

Crewe Alex (Free from Stoke C juniors on 17/8/83) FL 140+5/1 FLC 10 FAC 3 Others 7+1
Burnley (£15,000 on 3/10/87) FL 147/11 FLC 7 FAC 9 Others 19/1
Barnsley (£180,000 on 26/7/91) FL 103+4/10 FLC 9 FAC 3
York C (Loaned on 12/9/97) FL 2/1
Oxford U (£75,000 on 16/2/98) FL 18/2

DAVISON Aidan John
Born: Sedgefield, 11 May 1968
Height: 6'1" Weight: 13.12
Club Honours: AMC '98
International Honours: NI: 3; B-1
A highly dependable Grimsby goalkeeper, whose consistency behind a solid back four produced one of the meanest defences in the First Division, and one that enabled the Mariners to hold down a respectable place, despite a dearth of goals. Once again called to the Northern Ireland squad but, regrettably, failing to make the bench, following a late-season thumb injury, Aidan's Blundell Park career ended acrimoniously in a dispute over terms for a new contract and was released during the summer.
Notts Co (Signed from Billingham Synthonia on 25/3/88) FL 1
Bury (£6,000 on 7/10/89)
Millwall (Free on 14/8/91) FL 34 FLC 3 FAC 3 Others 2
Bolton W (£25,000 on 26/7/93) P/FL 35+2 FAC 8 Others 4
Hull C (Loaned on 29/11/96) FL 9 Others 1
Bradford C (Free on 14/3/97) FL 10
Grimsby T (Free on 16/7/97) FL 77 FLC 10 FAC 7 Others 10

DAWS Nicholas (Nick) John
Born: Manchester, 15 March 1970
Height: 5'11" Weight: 13.2
Club Honours: Div 2 '97
Bury's only ever present in 1998-99, the ever reliable midfielder has now completed 165 consecutive league games for the Shakers, after managing once again to steer clear of injury and suspension. Now approaching seven years at Gigg Lane, Nick's non-stop running and well-timed tackles have made him a favourite with the fans and a succession of Bury managers. He also scored three goals in 1998-99, his third being a screamer against Sunderland at Gigg Lane.
Bury (£10,000 from Altrincham on 13/8/92) FL 269+13/11 FLC 21+3/3 FAC 13 Others 13+2/1

DAWSON Andrew Stephen
Born: York, 8 December 1979
Height: 6'0" Weight: 11.7
Having signed professional forms during the 1998 close season, this local-born lad made a sensational start to his York career in 1998-99, when coming on as a substitute in the closing minutes of the game against Manchester City in December and scoring the winner with his first touch of the ball. Equally at home in defence or midfield, he had an extended run in the senior side during the closing weeks of the campaign.
York C (From trainee on 2/7/98) FL 7+4/1

DAWSON Andrew (Andy)
Born: Northallerton, 20 October 1978
Height: 5'9" Weight: 10.2
A young player who came through Nottingham Forest's junior ranks to turn professional in October 1995, Andy finally made his long awaited first-team debut for Forest when called up to play in the home leg of the Worthington Cup tie against Leyton Orient. Loaned out to Scunthorpe

just before Christmas to further his football education, he became an immediate favourite when making some outstanding performances from left back. Eventually, with both Preston and Aberdeen rumoured to be interested in signing him, he moved to United on a permanent basis in March and scored his first goal for the club in the play-off game at home to Swansea, which helped the team to Wembley and promotion. Can also be used to good effect in midfield.
Nottingham F (From trainee on 31/10/95) FLC 1
Scunthorpe U (£70,000 on 18/12/98) FL 24 Others 4/1

DAY James (Jamie) Russell
Born: Bexley, 13 September 1979
Height: 5'7" Weight: 10.12
International Honours: E: Sch
A second-year professional at Arsenal, having come through the club's junior ranks and unable to see much of a future at Highbury, Jamie joined Bournemouth at the beginning of last March, making two substitute appearances during the remainder of the season. A left-sided defender, who can play either as an orthodox full back or in a wing-back role, he is another investment in the Cherries' future.
Arsenal (From trainee on 3/7/97)
Bournemouth (£20,000 on 3/3/99) FL 0+2

DEAN Michael James
Born: Weymouth, 9 March 1978
Height: 5'10" Weight: 11.12
Michael found it difficult to secure a Bournemouth first-team place during 1998-99, making only one start and eight substitute appearances. A central midfielder who has good vision and is a good passer of the ball, he will be hoping to further his career with more senior opportunities in 1999-2000.
Bournemouth (From trainee on 4/7/96) FL 18+16 FAC 1 Others 1

DEANE Brian Christopher
Born: Leeds, 7 February 1968
Height: 6'3" Weight: 12.7
International Honours: E: 3; B-3
Having carved his niche in soccer history by becoming the first-ever goalscorer in the Premier League on its inception in 1992, his Middlesbrough goals in 1998-99 were credited with greater importance by the manager and the supporters, not least his sixth goal for the club, which condemned Nottingham Forest to relegation from the higher echelons of world domestic soccer. Extremely powerful in the shot, especially the volley, he surprised and brought the best out of many of the Premiership's top 'keepers after arriving at the Cellnet from Benfica last October. Although having a reputation as a goalscorer, he struggled to find the back of the net for a while, but his overall match contributions and developing partnership with Hamilton Ricard ultimately proved his substantial worth to Boro's cause.
Doncaster Rov (From juniors on 14/12/85) FL 59+7/12 FLC 3 FAC 2+1/1 Others 2+2
Sheffield U (£30,000 on 19/7/88) F/PL 197/82 FLC 16/11 FAC 23+1/11 Others 2/2

Leeds U (£2,900,000 on 14/7/93) PL 131+7/32 FLC 8+3/2 FAC 13+3/4 Others 3
Sheffield U (£1,500,000 on 29/7/97) FL 24/11 FLC 4/2 FAC 1 (£1,000,000 to Benfica on 15/1/98)
Middlesbrough (£3,000,000 on 16/10/98) PL 24+2/6 FLC 0+1 FAC 1

Brian Deane

DEARDEN Kevin Charles
Born: Luton, 8 March 1970
Height: 5'11" Weight: 13.4
An excellent lower division goalkeeper, and great shot stopper, after spending five years as Brentford's first-choice custodian, Kevin was unfortunate to lose his place to Jason Pearcey at the start of 1998-99. Apart from two appearances, he returned to the side in December, following Pearcey's finger injury, and kept four clean sheets in nine games before undeservedly losing his position to new signing, Andy Woodman. Was then loaned to Barnet before having a similar spell at Huddersfield, where he failed to get a game.
Tottenham H (From trainee on 5/8/88) PL 0+1 FLC 1
Cambridge U (Loaned on 9/3/89) FL 15
Hartlepool U (Loaned on 31/8/89) FL 10
Swindon T (Loaned on 23/3/90) FL 1
Peterborough U (Loaned on 24/8/90) FL 7
Hull C (Loaned on 10/1/91) FL 3
Rochdale (Loaned on 16/8/91) FL 2
Birmingham C (Loaned on 19/3/92) FL 12
Brentford (Free on 30/9/93) FL 205 FLC 17 FAC 13 Others 19
Barnet (Loaned on 5/2/99) FL 1

DE FREITAS Fabian
Born: Surinam, 28 July 1972
Height: 6'0" Weight: 12.2
Having been away from English football, this strong, powerful striker joined West Bromwich at the beginning of 1998-99 after two years in Spanish football with Osasuna, scoring twice on his Baggies home debut when coming off the bench against Norwich. Afterwards, however, he struggled

with his form and indeed his fitness, and amazingly failed to turn up for the Easter Bank holiday home game with Crewe Alexandra, thinking it was an evening kick off instead of an afternoon start! Punished with a hefty fine by his manager, he later returned to the team and scored.

Bolton W (£400,000 from Volendam on 19/8/94) F/PL 24+16/7 FLC 2+4 FAC 1 Others 0+2/2 (Free to Osasuna on 6/9/96)

West Bromwich A (Free on 21/8/98) FL 22+15/7 FAC 0+1

DEGN Peter

Born: Aarhus, Denmark, 6 April 1977
Height: 5'10" Weight: 12.6

An attacking right-wing back with pace and athleticism, Peter was snapped up by Everton last February from the Danish club, Aarhus, for a nominal fee before he became a free agent. Spotted by the Toffees when on international duty for Denmark U21s, he was handed his first taste of Premiership football in daunting circumstances – against Manchester United at Old Trafford. He went on to make a handful of substitute appearances and looks set to enjoy a bright future in English football.

Everton (£200,000 from Aarhus on 23/2/99) PL 0+4

DE GOEY Eduard (Ed) Franciscus

Born: Gouda, Holland, 20 December 1966
Height: 6'6" Weight: 15.0
Club Honours: FLC '98; ECWC '98; ESC '98
International Honours: Holland: 31

Amidst the controversy of Luca Vialli's rotational policy in 1998-99, one position was clarified – the giant Dutch 'keeper took over from Dmitri Kharine for Premiership matches. The popular Ed played superbly during Chelsea's 21-match unbeaten league run, particularly in away matches at Blackburn, Liverpool, Manchester United, and Leeds, where he saved a Jimmy Floyd Hasselbaink penalty. He then kept five consecutive clean sheets – a period of 504 minutes – during December and January, and his agility and calm assurance were crucial factors in the Blues' rise to the top of the table. He developed a firm understanding with the revamped back four in front of him and this contributed to the club's most consistent and defensively-solid season for many years. Played in the first 33 Premiership matches before a fractured toe interrupted his sequence and allowed Kevin Hitchcock an opportunity between the sticks. After a tough baptism in the Premiership, Ed has worked hard on the training ground with goalkeeping coach, Eddie Niedzwiecki, and his fellow-'keepers, to acclimatise to the demands of English football, and has become one of the most reliable of contemporary custodians.

Chelsea (£2,250,000 from Feyenoord, via Sparta Rotterdam, on 10/7/97) PL 63 FLC 4 FAC 7 Others 18

DELANEY Mark Anthony

Born: Haverfordwest, 13 May 1976
Height: 6'1" Weight: 11.7

A strong, straight-running right-wing back who was plucked from the League of Wales

side, Carmarthen, Mark was Frank Burrows' first 1998 close season signing and Cardiff fans cried out: "Who wants a League of Wales player." However, he quickly won them over with some exciting displays and smashed a thrilling goal against Chester in the FA Cup, before being selected by his peers for the PFA award winning Third Division team. Sold to the Premiership's Aston Villa for an eventual £500,000 in March, the Bluebirds' fans complained bitterly because the club had let him go! At Villa Park, he figured mainly with the reserves, scoring two goals before making his first-team debut when coming off the bench for Steve Stone at home to Nottingham Forest. On 31 March, he received a shock call up for the Welsh squad to play Switzerland, but was not called upon.

Cardiff C (Free from Carmarthen on 3/7/98) FL 28 FLC 2 FAC 5/1

Aston Villa (£250,000 + on 10/3/99) PL 0+2

DELAP Rory John

Born: Sutton Coldfield, 6 July 1976
Height: 6'0" Weight: 12.10
Club Honours: AMC '97
International Honours: Ei: 3; B-1; U21-4

A right-sided Derby wing back with notable attacking flair and ball control, the Republic of Ireland international started off 1998-99 as a regular choice for Jim Smith until a poor display against Arsenal in the Worthington Cup saw him rested from first-team duty. This was followed by a mysterious illness linked to the intake of energy drinks and, upon being restored to the side, a medial ligament injury led to him missing a number of games before it was aggravated in a comeback with the reserve team. Will be hoping for better luck in the coming season, and looks to a longer run in the team. Possesses a notable long throw.

Carlisle U (From trainee on 18/7/94) FL 40+25/7 FLC 4+1 FAC 0+3 Others 12+2

Derby Co (£500,000 + on 6/2/98) PL 31+5 FLC 3/1 FAC 0+1

DELLAS Trianos

Born: Thessaloniki, Greece, 31 January 1976
Height: 6'4" Weight: 15.0

The tall Greek's season at Sheffield United in 1998-99 was hampered by hamstring problems and his appearances were intermittent, despite him showing impressive passing ability from midfield. Not easily flustered, with good balance, and possessing a fine shot which he used to score from a good 35 yards out against Portsmouth, he was used as a front man on occasions, with particular success against Tranmere, where he scored twice in the 3-2 win – United coming back from 2-0 down.

Sheffield U (£300,000 from Aris Salonika on 26/8/97) FL 14+12/3 FLC 2 FAC 0+2 Others 0+1

DEL RIO Walter Jose

Born: Buenos Aires, Argentina, 16 June 1976
Height: 5'11" Weight: 12.4

Signed by Terry Venables from Boca Juniors on a year's loan last September, the

Argentinian made his Crystal Palace debut in a 4-0 defeat at Barnsley almost immediately, but then he faded from the scene after two more appearances, having failed to come to terms with the English game. An attacking midfielder, he is unlikely to be around this coming season.

Crystal Palace (Loaned from Boca Juniors on 7/9/98) FL 1+1 FLC 0+1

DERRY Shaun Peter

Born: Nottingham, 6 December 1977
Height: 5'10" Weight: 10.13
Club Honours: Div 3 '98

An operation on his kneecap kept Shaun out of action at Sheffield United until last November, but then he turned in a series of impressive performances on the right-hand side of defence and in midfield. Still only 21, he always seems calm and unhurried, is a good tackler, shows good distribution, has a good long throw, and should play a key role for United in 1999-2000. Was put on stand-by to play for the Football League against the Italian League in November.

Notts Co (From trainee on 13/4/96) FL 76+3/4 FLC 4+1 FAC 6+1/1 Others 3

Sheffield U (£700,000 on 26/1/98) FL 31+7 FAC 4

DESAILLY Marcel

Born: Accra, Ghana, 7 September 1968
Height: 6'1" Weight: 13.5
Club Honours: ESC '98
International Honours: France: 54

Using their tried and tested Italian connections, Chelsea clinched the signing of possibly the world's greatest central defender from AC Milan shortly before the 1998 World Cup. That claim was no exaggeration as Marcel played outstandingly for the victorious French team, being voted into every critic's World XI and picking up a World Cup winner's medal to go with the Champions' League medals won with Marseille and Milan in an illustrious career. His golden touch continued when, in only his third match for the Blues, he won a European Super Cup winners' medal to round off an incredible summer. By his own admission, he returned from the World Cup only 70 per-cent fit, owing to ankle, knee and rib injuries, which was fortunate for Premiership strikers because even at this level of fitness his performances were awesome. His first goal for Chelsea was vital, with the team trailing to a Bjarne Goldbaek goal against FC Copenhagen at Stamford Bridge, Marcel struck three minutes from time. Picking the ball up on the left corner of the penalty area, he stepped inside a challenge and curled a sweet right-footed shot into the opposite corner – as cool as you like as if on the training pitch! This maintained Chelsea's 40-year unbeaten home record in European football, and pulled around a tie which seemed to be slipping away from them. One of the key factors in his decision to move to Chelsea was the physical element of English football – he loves tackling, being aptly nicknamed "The Rock", and when a forward is tackled by Marcel they stay tackled!

Allied to this power, aggression, and determination, he also has good distribution and coolness in possession, which allows him to play in midfield when required. His partnership with fellow World Cup winner, Frank Leboeuf, was instrumental in Chelsea's defensive solidarity and their dogged pursuit of more silverware.

Chelsea (£4,600,000 from AC Milan, via Nantes and Marseilles, on 14/7/98) PL 30+1 FAC 6 Others 8/1

Marcel Desailly

DE SOUZA Miquel Juan
Born: Newham, 11 February 1970
Height: 5'11" Weight: 13.8

In an effort to sharpen him up for last season, the Peterborough manager, Barry Fry, loaned Miquel out to Southend where he started three of the opening six games. A strong front man, with good aerial capabilities, on suffering from a lack of striking support, he returned to London Road and made three starts before having a second spell on loan, this time at Rochdale at the end of October. At Spotland, Miquel looked just what was needed when he laid on the winning goal for Robbie Painter at Barnet on his debut but, unfortunately, the partnership never blossomed after that. On arriving back home, Posh exchanged him for Rushden & Diamonds' Richie Hanlon on 9 December and, in more comfortable surrounds, he immediately won the Conference "Player of the Month" award.

Charlton Ath (Signed from Clapton on 4/7/89)
Bristol C (Free on 1/8/90)
Birmingham C (£25,000 from Dagenham & Redbridge, via Yeovil T, Dorchester T and Bashley, on 1/2/94) FL 5+10 FLC 2 Others 1
Bury (Loaned on 25/11/94) FL 2+1
Wycombe W (£80,000 on 27/1/95) FL 73+10/29 FLC 8/2 FAC 6/2 Others 3
Peterborough U (£50,000 on 26/3/97) FL 20+16/5 FLC 1+1 Others 1/1
Southend U (Loaned on 11/8/98) FL 2 FLC 1+1
Rochdale (Loaned on 29/10/98) FL 5

DEVENNEY Michael Paul
Born: Bolton, 8 February 1980
Height: 5'8" Weight: 10.5

A young Burnley defender, who was not a regular member of the first-team squad in 1998-99, Michael made his Clarets' debut as a substitute in the Auto Windscreens Shield game against Preston. The subsequent influx of new blood at Turf Moor may have delayed his next chance, but the first-year professional has the time to wait.

Burnley (From trainee on 6/7/98) Others 0+1

DEVINE Sean Thomas
Born: Lewisham, 6 September 1972
Height: 6'0" Weight: 13.6
Club Honours: FAYC '91
International Honours: Ei: B-1

Sean endured a disappointing 1998-99 in a Barnet shirt, and a mixture of ill fortune and lack of confidence saw him score just one goal before losing his place in the side to young Marlon King. Desperate for first-team football, he was loaned to Wycombe in March to replace the outgoing Keith Scott, and scored within minutes of coming on as a sub at Reading, striking with a left-footed pin-point shot from 25 yards. His next goal was a 20-yard strike with his right foot at Bristol Rovers and, in linking up very well with Andy Baird, the two laid on each others goals in the memorable win at Manchester City. He ended the campaign with eight priceless goals from the last 12 games to become the club's top scorer, and he even laid on the goal in the final game at Lincoln which kept them up. There is every chance that Wycombe would have been relegated without those goals, and his signing was made permanent before the season's end, the fee being a record for the club. He really is the complete predator striker, with two good feet, excellent control, dangerous anywhere within shooting distance, and having a good football brain. Needless to say he was a huge hit with the supporters, managing to finish third in the "Player of the Year" award in spite of being just six weeks at Adams Park.

Millwall (From trainee on 4/5/91) (Free to Bromley in August 1992)
Barnet (£10,000 from Famagusta on 5/10/95) FL 112+14/47 FLC 9/3 FAC 5/5 Others 6
Wycombe W (£220,000 + on 18/3/99) FL 11+1/8

DEVLIN Paul John
Born: Birmingham, 14 April 1972
Height: 5'9" Weight: 11.5
Club Honours: AIC '95

Starting last season as a squad member, most of his appearances were from the Sheffield United bench until he moved on loan to Notts County in October, before being recalled after Petr Katchouro's injury and Dean Saunders' departure and given an extended run in the side. Taking his opportunity well he turned in some impressive performances on the right wing with some fast, tricky play and searching crosses that set up several goals, as well as scoring himself.

Notts Co (£40,000 from Stafford R on 22/2/92) FL 132+9/25 FLC 11+1/1 FAC 8/1 Others 17+2/4

Birmingham C (Signed on 29/2/96) FL 61+15/28 FLC 8+1/4 FAC 3+1/2
Sheffield U (£200,000 + on 13/3/98) FL 27+16/6 FLC 0+3 FAC 4/1 Others 2
Notts Co (Loaned on 23/10/98) FL 5

DE VOS Jason Richard
Born: Canada, 2 January 1974
Height: 6'4" Weight: 13.7
International Honours: Canada

Darlington's only current international since the war set off in great form at the start of last season and had a host of bigger clubs watching him. Surprisingly, however, the tall Canadian chose to move to Scotland, and signed for Dundee United for a club record fee of £500,000 in October. His aerial power was sadly missed after his departure, particularly at set pieces, where his bullet-type header against Sheffield United took the Worthington Cup-tie into extra time last August.

Darlington (Free from Montreal Impact on 29/11/96) FL 43+1/5 FLC 3/1 FAC 4 Others 1

DEWHURST Robert (Rob) Matthew
Born: Keighley, 10 September 1971
Height: 6'3" Weight: 14.0

1998-99 was another season of desperately bad luck with injuries for the big Hull City defender, who continued to be one of the most popular Tigers. A double hernia operation in the summer meant he missed the start of the campaign and it wasn't until November that he was recalled. Made a sensational impact with a giant-killing FA Cup winner at Luton, and looked to be getting back to his formidable best when struck down by a thigh injury in the following game at Torquay. With manager, Warren Joyce, successfully rebuilding his defence, he was unable to break back into the side, but still played an important role with his encouragement from the sidelines before being released in the summer.

Blackburn Rov (From trainee on 15/10/90) FL 13 FLC 2 Others 1
Darlington (Loaned on 20/12/91) FL 11/1 Others 1
Huddersfield T (Loaned on 2/10/92) FL 7
Hull C (Free on 5/11/93) FL 132+6/13 FLC 8 FAC 8/1 Others 7

DE ZEEUW Adrianus (Arjan) Johannes
Born: Castricum, Holland, 16 April 1970
Height: 6'1" Weight: 13.11

It looked like Arjan would be leaving Barnsley after the club's relegation from the Premier League but a change of manager brought a change of heart and he signed a one-year deal. Strong and powerful in the air, and good in the tackle, he had everything a centre back should have, despite seeming to struggle a little due to the constant changing of the defence. Always a threat at set pieces, as his two goals against West Bromwich showed on the opening day of the campaign, he also scored the only goal of the game in the 1-0 win at Stockport. Out of contract during the summer, at the time of going to press it was unclear as to whether the Dutchman had accepted the club's offer of re-engagement.

Barnsley (£250,000 from Telstar, via Vitesse 22, on 3/11/95) F/PL 138/7 FLC 12 FAC 14

DIAWARA Kaba
Born: Toulon, France, 16 December 1975
Height: 5'11" Weight: 11.8

A former French U21 international striker who joined Arsenal from Bordeaux last January, he settled in quickly and adapted well to the English style of play. Burly and strong, Kaba consequently thrived in physical games, and looked to be a good finisher both on the ground and in the air. Is quick for a big man, and can perform equally well as a front striker or out on the wing if required. Yet to play for the full 90 minutes, either when coming off the bench or unable to complete a game, his first-team debut saw him play the last 16 minutes of Arsenal's 1-0 home Premiership win over a rampant Chelsea. Interestingly, he made his first start for the Gunners in the sensational FA Cup fifth round game at Highbury against Sheffield United, but was not on the pitch when Marc Overmars scored the "so-called unsporting" second goal in a 2-1 win, having been substituted 11 minutes earlier.
Arsenal (£2,500,000 from Bordeaux, via FC Girardins, on 29/1/99) PL 2+10 FAC 1+2

DIAZ Isidro (Izzy)
Born: Valencia, Spain, 15 May 1972
Height: 5'7" Weight: 9.6
Club Honours: Div 3 '97

A tricky winger, and one of the "three amigos" at Wigan when Rochdale boss, Graham Barrow, was the manager there, Izzy signed up for his old boss just after the start of last season, having spent a couple of weeks at Tranmere on trial, and gave the Dale their first win of the campaign when he netted from almost the goal line at Carlisle. After a couple of months as a regular in the side, he gradually faded from the picture and his contract was cancelled in December to allow him to return home to Spain.
Wigan Ath (Free from Balaguer on 25/7/95) FL 57+19/16 FAC 4+1/2 Others 3
Wolverhampton W (Free on 8/8/97) FL 1
Wigan Ath (Free on 18/12/97) FL 1+1
Rochdale (Free on 14/8/98) FL 12+2/2 FLC 1 FAC 1+2

DI CANIO Paolo
Born: Rome, Italy, 9 July 1968
Height: 5'9" Weight: 11.9

This hugely talented, but temperamental star player left Sheffield Wednesday under a cloud, following the well-documented refereeing incident at Hillsborough against Arsenal last September. Subsequently suspended for 12 matches, and fined by the FA, Wednesday allowed him to go home to Italy in order to escape the media but, supposed to return for the Boxing Day match against Leicester, he failed to arrive stating that he was suffering from stress. Despite prolonged efforts by Wednesday officials to persuade him to return being to no avail, following a successful bid from West Ham for his services he arrived at Upton Park at the end of January. Paolo soon set the Hammers alight with his special brand of skill and was a joy to watch as he bamboozled one defence after another. As well as making goals for others he scored a handful himself, including a brilliant

individual effort against Newcastle when he glided through United's defence, rounded the 'keeper, and scored.
Glasgow C (Signed from AC Milan, via AC Milan, Lazio, Ternana, Juventus and Napoli, on 3/7/96) SL 25+1/12 SLC 2 SC 6/3 Others 2+1
Sheffield Wed (£3,000,000 on 8/8/97) PL 39+2/15 FLC 4/2 FAC 3
West Ham U (£1,700,000 on 28/1/99) PL 12+1/4

DICHIO Daniele (Danny) Salvatore Ernest
Born: Hammersmith, 19 October 1974
Height: 6'3" Weight: 12.3
Club Honours: Div 1 '99
International Honours: E: U21-1; Sch

Although Danny made more substitute appearances than starts last season, he played an extremely important role in Sunderland's promotion to the Premiership, collecting a deserved First Division championship medal. When called upon to deputise for Niall Quinn or Kevin Phillips, the big striker led the line well, chipping in with 12 goals, including a late winner against Bury in October when coming off the bench, and a typically brave strike versus Portsmouth, when suffering a bad concussion for his efforts after heading home. Strong in the air, he was voted the Nationwide "Player of the Month" for August and will no doubt be pushing for a regular first-team place this coming term.
Queens Park R (From trainee on 17/5/93) P/FL 56+19/20 FLC 6/2 FAC 3+3 (Free to Sampdoria during 1997 close season)
Barnet (Loaned on 24/3/94) FL 9/2
Sunderland (£750,000 from Lecce on 28/1/98) FL 18+31/10 FLC 4+1/2 FAC 1+1 Others 1+2

Paul Dickov

DICKOV Paul
Born: Livingston, 1 November 1972
Height: 5'6" Weight: 11.9
Club Honours: ECWC '94
International Honours: S: U21-4; Yth; Sch
Signed a new two-year contract for Manchester City at the beginning of last

season, before playing in the first 11 league and cup games and scoring four goals, despite being substituted seven times during this period. Following that he was in and out of the team due to inconsistent form and a couple of injuries. A popular player with the fans, based on his 100 per-cent non-stop working and chasing loose balls, Paul shields himself well from big defenders who have a habit of leaning on him to stifle his small frame. Although his close control and sharp dashes make him an exciting player, because of his stature and treatment from the opposition he has the tendency to keep complaining to the referee, which often gets him booked. Manager Joe Royle then has to have quiet words with him to keep him on track. Scored a brilliant hat trick within 14 minutes at Maine Road against Lincoln, followed by one more in the following game.
Arsenal (From trainee on 28/12/90) PL 6+15/3 FLC 2+2/3
Luton T (Loaned on 8/10/93) FL 8+7/1
Brighton & Hove A (Loaned on 23/3/94) FL 8/5
Manchester C (£1,000,000 on 23/8/96) FL 68+26/24 FLC 5+2/2 FAC 4+3/1 Others 3/2

DICKS Julian Andrew
Born: Bristol, 8 August 1968
Height: 5'10" Weight: 13.0
International Honours: E: B-2; U21-4

Having been out of the game for ten months, the tough-tackling West Ham left back made a remarkable comeback in the Worthington Cup-tie against Northampton, eight games into 1998-99. Showing tremendous character in battling his way back from such a serious injury, he is still a fiery and intimidating defender despite losing some of his pace. Had excellent games against Everton and Leicester, and rescued West Ham in the FA Cup when scoring a late equaliser against Swansea.
Birmingham C (From apprentice on 12/4/86) FL 83+6/1 FLC 5+1 FAC 5 Others 2
West Ham U (£300,000 on 25/3/88) FL 159/29 FLC 19/5 FAC 14/2 Others 11/4
Liverpool (£1,500,000 on 17/9/93) PL 24/3 FLC 3 FAC 1
West Ham U (£1,000,000 on 20/10/94) PL 103/21 FLC 11/3 FAC 9/1

DIGBY Fraser Charles
Born: Sheffield, 23 April 1967
Height: 6'1" Weight: 13.10
Club Honours: Div 2 '96
International Honours: E: U21-5; Yth; Sch

A surprise signing for Crystal Palace at the start of 1998-99, having left Swindon under the Bosman ruling, the goalkeeper was snapped up to replace the recently departed Carlo Nash as Kevin Miller's understudy. However, following a shaky start to the season by the latter, Fraser came in for his debut, at home to Oxford, and kept a clean sheet in a 2-0 win. Agile, and a shot stopper, who sets up attacks with good early throws, he then held his own in Palace's goal until Christmas, when suffering a long-term injury and losing out to Miller.
Manchester U (From apprentice on 25/4/85)
Swindon T (£32,000 on 25/9/86) F/PL 417 FLC 33 FAC 21 Others 33+1
Crystal Palace (Free on 8/8/98) P/FL 18 FLC 3

DI LELLA Gustavo Martin
Born: Buenos Aires, Argentine, 6 October 1973
Height: 5'8" Weight: 10.7
A stylish midfielder who played well at times for Hartlepool during 1998-99, Gustavo disappointingly failed to make the anticipated breakthrough to establish a regular first-team place. A real battler, his competitive attitude was much appreciated by some supporters but, as the possessor of a fiery temperament, he was twice sent off during the campaign. After being out of the senior picture for some time he was encouraged to have been recalled by the new manager, Chris Turner, in the closing weeks of the season.
Darlington (Free from Blyth Spartans on 2/12/97) FL 0+5 (Free to Blyth Spartans on 3/2/98)
Hartlepool U (Free on 20/3/98) FL 19+9/4 FLC 1 FAC 2 Others 1

DILLON Paul William
Born: Limerick, 22 October 1978
Height: 5'9" Weight: 10.11
International Honours: Ei: U21-1; Yth
Having shaken off a pre-season heel injury, Paul was a regular on the left side of Rotherham's defence in 1998-99, giving some excellent performances with his never-say-die attitude, before having to miss a chunk of the campaign after undergoing an operation in December. With speed and tackling ability, he still has age on his side, and is likely to become a key factor in United's immediate future.
Rotherham U (From trainee on 7/3/97) FL 50+5/2 FLC 2 FAC 4 Others 3

DI MATTEO Roberto (Robbie)
Born: Switzerland, 29 May 1970
Height: 5'10" Weight: 12.5
Club Honours: FAC '97; FLC '98; ECWC '98; ESC '99
International Honours: Italy: 34
Probably best known for goalscoring exploits, particularly in Wembley Cup finals against Middlesbrough, Robbie was asked to play a deeper, more unglamorous role in 1998-99 – covering, tackling back, and launching counter attacks with raking crossfield passes. He adapted superbly, allowing fellow midfielders, Dan Petrescu and Gus Poyet, to get forward and notch vital goals, while he made sure the "the back door was locked". Although he did not open his goalscoring account until January, to use a cockney street trader's cliché: "Every one's a winner!", a fierce left-footed drive from the edge of the box, deep into injury time, against Coventry, maintained Chelsea's lead at the top of the Premiership. In February, a dramatic 85th-minute header gave the Blues an FA Cup victory at Hillsborough and set up the titanic quarter-final clash with Manchester United. His third of the season was the only goal at the Valley on Easter Saturday, which put Chelsea right back in the championship race. His long-range passing was as good as ever, two inch-perfect 30-yard passes creating the Blues' goals in the televised match against Leicester City. This superb

midfield player, who is eagerly coveted by a host of Serie "A" clubs, has pledged his future to Chelsea, his outstanding displays since his arrival three years ago having been a key factor in the club's renaissance from sleeping giants to the forefront of European football.
Chelsea (£4,900,000 from Lazio, via FC Aarac, FC Zurich and Schaffhausen, on 17/7/96) PL 87+7/13 FLC 8+1/3 FAC 12+2/3 Others 17/3

DINNING Tony
Born: Wallsend, 12 April 1975
Height: 6'0" Weight: 12.11
A hard-working, strong-tackling defensive player whose versatility has become vital to Stockport's small squad, Tony was called upon to fill a number of roles in 1998-99, from right back to centre half and midfield. He was also the side's regular penalty taker, scoring five times from the spot. Perhaps his ability and willingness to swop positions meant he did not spend as much time as he would have liked in his preferred central defensive role, but he remains an important player for County.
Newcastle U (From trainee on 1/10/93)
Stockport Co (Free on 23/6/94) FL 110+31/13 FLC 9+5/1 FAC 3+7 Others 6+1/2

DIXON Lee Michael
Born: Manchester, 17 March 1964
Height: 5'9" Weight: 11.8
Club Honours: Div 1 '89, '91; PL '98; FAC '93, '98; ECWC '94; CS '98
International Honours: E: 22; B-4
As a long-serving member of the ageless Arsenal back line, Lee was almost ever present in 1998-99, and his consistently good form throughout the season resulted in his recall to the England team for the international against France in March. Having impressed, he then had the misfortune to come out of a heavy challenge suffering from concussion and had to leave the field. Fortunately for the Gunners, he recovered quickly. A natural attacking, right-sided wing back with good speed to get forward to deliver telling crosses to his front men, he is equally solid in a defence which is harder to break down than any other in the Premiership. Out of contract during the summer, at the time of going to press the club had offered him terms of re-engagement.
Burnley (From juniors on 21/7/82) FL 4 FLC 1
Chester C (Free on 16/2/84) FL 56+1/1 FLC 2 FAC 1 Others 3
Bury (Free on 15/7/85) FL 45/5 FLC 4 FAC 8/1 Others 1
Stoke C (£40,000 on 18/7/86) FL 71/5 FLC 6 FAC 7 Others 4
Arsenal (£400,000 on 29/1/88) PL 382+6/20 FLC 45 FAC 41/1 Others 37

D'JAFFO Laurent
Born: Aquitane, France, 5 November 1970
Height: 6'0" Weight: 13.5
French striker who joined Bury on a free transfer from Ayr United in July 1998 after impressing in the Shakers' early pre-season games. Laurent was the club's first-choice striker virtually throughout 1998-99 and missed only a handful of games, largely due

to a troublesome achilles injury sustained in early January which saw his leg put in plaster and meant that he was sidelined for more than a month. An exciting player who wears his heart on his sleeve, he finished the season as the side's top scorer with nine league and cup goals.
Ayr U (Signed from Red Star Paris on 13/10/97) SL 21+3/10 SC 2+1
Bury (Free on 28/7/98) FL 35+2/8 FLC 4+1/1 FAC 1

Laurent D'Jaffo

DOBBIN James (Jim)
Born: Dunfermline, 17 September 1963
Height: 5'10" Weight: 11.0
International Honours: S: Yth
Originally released by Grimsby at the end of 1997-98, the experienced midfielder was later offered terms, mainly to add experience to a young reserve squad. However, the Mariners mounting injury problems saw him come off the bench on a few occasions. He also spent a month on loan helping out former Mariner, Paul Futcher, at Southport during the Pontins League mid-winter break, before being freed during the summer.
Glasgow C (Free from Whitburn BC on 9/10/80) SL 1+1 SLC 4/1
Motherwell (Loaned on 1/2/84) SL 1+1
Doncaster Rov (£25,000 on 19/3/84) FL 56+8/13 FLC 5/1 FAC 2 Others 3
Barnsley (£35,000 on 19/9/86) FL 116+13/12 FLC 3+1 FAC 11 Others 4/1
Grimsby T (£55,000 on 15/7/91) FL 154+10/21 FLC 13/3 FAC 7+1/1 Others 5/1
Rotherham U (Free on 2/8/96) FL 17+2 FLC 0+1 FAC 1 Others 1
Doncaster Rov (Free on 22/8/97) FL 28+3 FAC 1 Others 1
Scarborough (Free on 20/3/98) FL 1
Grimsby T (Free on 26/3/98) FL 1+5 FLC 0+1

DOBIE Robert **Scott**
Born: Workington, 10 October 1978
Height: 6'1" Weight: 12.8
This big, raw-boned Carlisle forward gave some influential performances in the second

half of last season, following a loan spell at Clydebank in early November which seemed to have refreshed him. With his height and natural aggression, he showed signs of becoming an effective target man for the club, his aerial power bringing him several goals, including a brace against Shrewsbury, while his long-range lob in the Exeter match was one of the most opportunist goals of the campaign. He can look forward to 1999-2000 with some confidence.

Carlisle U (From trainee on 10/5/97) FL 35+23/8 FLC 1+5 FAC 0+1 Others 3+1
Clydebank (Loaned on 3/11/98) SL 6

DOBSON Anthony (Tony) John
Born: Coventry, 5 February 1969
Height: 6'1" Weight: 13.2
Club Honours: FAYC '87
International Honours: E: U21-4
Not in line for first-team consideration at West Bromwich at the start of 1998-99, Tony was loaned to Gillingham with a view to a permanent signing early in September due to an injury crisis at Priestfield. Making his debut at Chesterfield before appearing in a 3-2 home defeat by Northampton, he must have done something right in that game because he was snatched from under the Gills' noses when signed by Town just two days later. A classy and stylish defender who can play in most defensive positions, having both flair and pace, he quickly settled in with the Cobblers until an injury after just seven games saw him end up on the operating table and out of action for most of the campaign. Pencilled in to make his comeback in April, he made some reserve appearances around the start of that month and returned to the senior side for the final few games of the relegation dog fight that was ultimately unsuccessful.

Coventry C (From apprentice on 7/7/86) FL 51+3/1 FLC 5+3 Others 0+1
Blackburn Rov (£300,000 on 17/1/91) F/PL 36+5 FLC 5 FAC 2 Others 1
Portsmouth (£150,000 on 22/9/93) FL 48+5/2 FLC 6 FAC 1+2 Others 4/1
Oxford U (Loaned on 15/12/94) FL 5
Peterborough U (Loaned on 29/1/96) FL 4
West Bromwich A (Free on 8/8/97) FL 6+5 FLC 0+2 FAC 2
Gillingham (Loaned on 4/9/98) FL 2
Northampton T (£25,000 on 11/9/98) FL 8+3 FLC 0+1

DODD Jason Robert
Born: Bath, 2 November 1970
Height: 5'10" Weight: 12.3
International Honours: E: U21-8
Southampton club captain who has now been with the Saints for ten years, having originally been at Bath City. Recognised as a right back, and versatile enough to perform just as well in the centre of defence or midfield, he was badly hit by injury in 1998-99 and missed many games, while in others he needed injections to see him through. Nonetheless, he always gave 100 per-cent and could always be relied upon whatever the predicament. Reads the game well and packs a powerful shot, scoring his customary goal, from the penalty spot, in the home win against Newcastle.

Southampton (£50,000 from Bath C on 15/3/89) PL 242+17/8 FLC 30+1 FAC 24/1 Others 5

DOHERTY Gary Michael Thomas
Born: Carndonagh, 31 January 1980
Height: 6'2" Weight: 13.1
International Honours: Ei: Yth
Despite preferring a central defensive role, where his solid performances would no doubt help tighten up Luton's defence, it is as a striker that he is recognised, his added height making him an ideal target man. Although he struggled to make an early appearance for Town in 1998-99, coming off the bench five times before making a start, he netted back-to-back goals, against Lincoln and Manchester City, in that period to open his goals account for the Hatters. Scoring six in total, a further three of them again in successive games, he definitely looks to be one for the future.

Luton T (From trainee on 2/7/97) FL 6+24/6 FLC 0+1 FAC 1+2 Others 0+1

DOHERTY Lee Joseph
Born: Camden Town, 6 February 1980
Height: 6'2" Weight: 11.8
Formerly a trainee at Arsenal, Lee crossed over London to Charlton last October. A tall, strong central defender, he played for Athletic's reserve and U19 sides before being signed by Jeff Wood when Brighton took over his contract in March, and made his debut in the 0-0 draw at Hartlepool. Made a couple of further appearances before falling out of favour, and was released by Micky Adams at the end of the season.

Charlton Ath (Signed from Arsenal juniors on 29/10/98)
Brighton & Hove A (Free on 19/3/99) FL 3

DOHERTY Thomas (Tommy) Edward
Born: Bristol, 17 March 1979
Height: 5'8" Weight: 9.13
The highlight of this young Bristol City midfielder's season in 1998-99, was his recognition by the Republic of Ireland. Another who suffered from injury problems which disrupted the campaign, the club missed his tigerish approach in midfield and his ability to play the ball around consistently well. While only glimpses were seen of his best form, the one outstanding memory was of his winning battle with Swindon's Darren Bullock, in the Christmas holiday game at Ashton Gate.

Bristol C (From trainee on 8/7/97) FL 37+16/3 FLC 3/1 FAC 1+1

DOIG Christopher (Chris) Ross
Born: Dumfries, 13 February 1981
Height: 6'2" Weight: 12.6
The tall Scottish-born central defender made his first-team debut for Nottingham Forest last Boxing Day, when coming off the bench at Old Trafford of all places after 69 minutes with Manchester United already 3-0 to the good. He then made his initial start for Forest a couple of weeks later at Coventry and did not look out of place despite the side losing 4-0. Another product of the youth team, he had to be driven to Manchester by his father as he was back home with his parents when the call-up came. Good in the

air and, as you would expect of a youngster who has come up through the Forest academy, he looks to play the ball out of defence.

Nottingham F (From trainee on 7/3/98) PL 1+1

DOLAN Joseph (Joe)
Born: Harrow, 27 May 1980
Height: 6'3" Weight: 12.12
International Honours: NI: Yth
Released by Chelsea in April 1998, Joe made a dream start to his senior career with Millwall in 1998-99, winning the "Man of the Match" award on his debut in the Auto Windscreens area semi-final success against Gillingham, when he found himself up against the formidable strike force of Robert Taylor and Carl Asaba. Following that, he went on to establish himself as a regular in the side and was not overawed when facing some of the top forwards in the Second Division. Scored his first league goal at Chesterfield in March with a strong header, but missed the area final first leg whilst away on international duty with the Northern Ireland U18 side. However, he returned to play a full part in the second leg. Is a tall, strong central defender who is very hard in the challenge, good in the air and difficult to knock off ball, and if you add these attributes to his pace and passing ability he has every chance of becoming a player of real quality.

Millwall (Free from Chelsea juniors on 15/4/98) FL 9/1 Others 3

DOMI Didier
Born: Sarcelles, France, 2 May 1978
Height: 5'10" Weight: 11.4
Didier is a classy French U21 international who is equally at home in an orthodox left-back position or the modern wing-back role. His slight figure belies his strength in the tackle, and his alertness and highly developed positional sense, sharp for one who as yet is relatively inexperienced, enables him to anticipate situations and stifle them before they develop into real danger for his side. He displays surprisingly good aerial ability for his height, and uses his sound distribution skills to adroitly turn defence into attack. Calm and composed when defending, his good pace and solid technique enable him to overlap down the wing to provide a telling service for his strikers. Coming through the same French development process as Arsenal's Nicolas Anelka, he joined Newcastle at the end of 1998 from Paris St Germain and went straight into the first team, regardless of not having played for some time. He looked so at home that he remained first choice, despite the club's wealth of full-back talent, until injury caused him to miss three weeks during April, including the FA Cup semi final. He looks a real star of the future.

Newcastle U (£3,250,000 + from Paris St Germain on 5/1/99) PL 14 FAC 4

DOMINGUEZ Jose Manuel Martins
Born: Lisbon, Portugal, 16 February 1974
Height: 5'3" Weight: 10.0
Club Honours: Div 2 '95; FLC '99
International Honours: Portugal: 3

An excellent dribbler out on the left flank, Jose proved at Tottenham in 1998-99 that he could also hold his own in midfield, having the energy and determination to turn a game by his introduction. This factor of his game being best demonstrated at home to Southampton and Aston Villa in the Premiership, when, brought off the subs' bench, he injected new life and pace into games that Spurs seemed to be losing their grip of. In an amazing mid-season turn-around, when Jose had reportedly been told by his new boss, George Graham, that his services were no longer required, the little Portuguese international pledged his love of the club and his determination to win Graham over, which he rightly did. Graham went on to tell him that, following a run of fine form and his contribution to Tottenham's improved performances, that he could stay at the club as cover for David Ginola. A great crowd favourite who rises to every opportunity he gets, the fans will be hoping that he remains a member of the squad for 1999-2000.
Birmingham C (£180,000 from Benfica on 9/3/94) FL 0/3 FLC 1+2 FAC 2+1 Others 2+2/1 (£1,800,000 to Sporting Lisbon on 1/8/95)
Tottenham H (£1,600,000 on 12/8/97) PL 10+21/4 FLC 2+3/1 FAC 1

DONALDSON O'Neill McKay
Born: Birmingham, 24 November 1969
Height: 6'0" Weight: 12.4
A pacy striker signed from Stoke last September, O'Neill's Torquay career was blighted by injuries, the final blow being a broken right leg sustained against Hartlepool just after making an encouraging return. A bubbly and enthusiastic character, who had only just come back from an injury suffered in his second game at Stoke – an injury that ultimately saw him leave the club – hopefully he will put it behind him. Scored in the 4-0 home wins over Halifax.
Shrewsbury T (Free from Hinckley T on 13/11/91) FL 15+13/4 Others 1
Doncaster Rov (Free on 10/8/94) FL 7+2/2 FLC 2 Others 0+1
Mansfield T (Loaned on 23/12/94) FL 4/6 FAC 1/1
Sheffield Wed (£50,000 on 9/1/95) PL 4+10/3
Oxford U (Loaned on 30/1/98) FL 6/2
Stoke C (Free on 13/3/98) FL 2
Torquay U (Free on 7/9/98) FL 7+5/1

DONIS Georgios
Born: Greece, 22 October 1969
Height: 6'0" Weight: 12.6
International Honours: Greece: 22
The Greek International signed for Sheffield United during transfer deadline week last March at least until the end of the season. Several clubs were reported to be interested in his services when he left AEK Athens as a free agent after a court ruled in his favour over a financial dispute with the Greek club, and he quickly showed his pace down the wing, along with his ability to take on and beat defenders to cross the ball. Stop Press: Became Steve Bruce's first signing for Huddersfield on 4 June.
Blackburn Rov (Free from Panathanaikos on 5/7/96) PL 11+11/2 FLC 3 FAC 0+1 (Free to AEK Athens on 20/9/97)
Sheffield U (Free on 25/3/99) FL 5+2/1

DONOVAN Kevin
Born: Halifax, 17 December 1971
Height: 5'8" Weight: 11.2
Club Honours: AMC '98
Kevin was yet another Grimsby player for whom 1998-99 was a frustrating season. A long-term recuperation from a back injury, including a brief and premature return in September, meant it was December before he properly regained his place in midfield, and it was almost Easter before he showed traces of the skill, pace and confidence in running through opposing defences that made him such a vital part of the previous campaign's promotion winning side. Hopefully the Millenium season will see him restored to full form and fitness.
Huddersfield T (From trainee on 11/10/89) FL 11+9/1 FLC 1+1 FAC 1/2 Others 4
Halifax T (Loaned on 13/2/92) FL 6
West Bromwich A (£70,000 on 1/10/92) FL 139+29/19 FLC 9+2/6 FAC 7+1/3 Others 15+1/4
Grimsby T (£300,000 on 29/7/97) FL 73+1/16 FLC 6+1/1 FAC 7/1 Others 9/3

DOOLAN John
Born: Liverpool, 7 May 1974
Height: 6'1" Weight: 13.0
Perhaps one of the most underrated players in the Barnet side, and a hugely influential figure in the line up, John commenced 1998-99 on the substitutes' bench before being allocated the number eight shirt, which he wore for the majority of the season. The strongest attributes in his style of play is his committed nature in the tackle, and also his ability to unleash pin-point, accurate passes over long distances. Enjoying numerous productive games, most notably against Hull City and Rotherham at home, and also at Southend and Leyton Orient, he rarely received the applause that his industrious presence deserved, and many casual observers failed to recognise the importance that both he and Stevie Searle played in the outcome of a game. Having strived to improve his level of physical fitness, and also his accuracy in front of goal, his final performance at Leyton Orient indicated that he is evolving into a gifted midfielder with a robust edge to his game.
Everton (From trainee on 1/6/92)
Mansfield T (Free on 2/9/94) FL 128+3/10 FLC 8/1 FAC 7/2 Others 4+1/1
Barnet (£60,000 on 13/1/98) FL 57+2/2 FLC 1+1 FAC 1 Others 1

DORIGO Anthony (Tony) Robert
Born: Australia, 31 December 1965
Height: 5'9" Weight: 10.10
Club Honours: Div 2 '89, Div 1 '92; FMC '90; CS '92
International Honours: E: 15; B-7; U21-11
An experienced left back whom Derby gave a trial to last October, and who eventually signed on a free transfer from Torino, Tony immediately brought a new dimension to County's attacking moves with his pacy runs down the left wing and excellent crossing skills, winning a "Man of the Match" award against Arsenal in December. One of several players at the club who can take any penalty kicks awarded, he has an explosive shot from distance, one such effort helping to dispatch Huddersfield from the FA Cup.

Unfortunate to suffer a couple of hamstring injuries towards the end of the season, which limited his appearances, by then he had also showed himself to be defensively sound, especially when covering well behind the centre backs.
Aston Villa (From apprentice on 19/7/83) FL 106+5/1 FLC 14+1 FAC 7 Others 2
Chelsea (£475,000 on 3/7/87) FL 146/11 FLC 14 FAC 4 Others 16/1
Leeds U (£1,300,000 on 6/6/91) F/PL 168+3/5 FLC 12+1 FAC 16 Others 9/1 (Free to Torino during 1997 close season)
Derby Co (Free on 23/10/98) PL 17+1/1 FLC 1 FAC 3/2

DORNER Mario
Born: Baden, Austria, 21 March 1970
Height: 5'10" Weight: 13.0
This hard-running Austrian forward, who had ended as second-top scorer for Darlington the previous season, was limited to only 13 starts with another 15 appearances as a substitute, because of injury problems in 1998-99. Consequently, he was only able to register four goals, two of which were match winners, while another was a crucial equaliser against Burnley in the FA Cup. Is very strong, holds the ball up well, and has some delightful touches.
Motherwell (Free from VFB Modling on 1/7/97) SL 2 SLC 0+2
Darlington (Free on 17/10/97) FL 34+15/13 FLC 2 FAC 4+2/2 Others 1

DOUGLAS Andrew Stephen
Born: Barrow, 27 May 1980
Height: 5'10" Weight: 11.2
A promising forward from Carlisle's youth ranks, and a first-year professional, Andy received a surprise call up in the FA Cup-tie against Hartlepool in 1998-99 and earned a star man rating on the day. Making his league debut seven days later, when he came off the bench against Rotherham, his progress will be watched with interest by United fans.
Carlisle U (From trainee on 27/7/98) FL 0+1 FAC 1

DOUGLAS Stuart Anthony
Born: Enfield, 9 April 1978
Height: 5'9" Weight: 11.5
Very much a regular for Luton in 1998-99, Stuart finally put the subs' tag he was carrying around behind him, making just one appearance all season from the bench, while missing only six available games. Persistent, pacy, and aggressive up front, and constantly chasing lost causes, the striker notched 11 goals to share the club's highest scorer accolade with Phil Gray. Despite never netting more than one goal in a game, only two of them were in matches that Town lost, and another reward for his efforts comes in the shape of free kicks awarded, which set up good goalscoring opportunities from free kicks.
Luton T (From trainee on 2/5/96) FL 52+24/11 FLC 9+2/3 FAC 2+1 Others 0+1

DOWIE Iain
Born: Hatfield, 9 January 1965
Height: 6'1" Weight: 13.11
International Honours: NI: 56; U23-1; U21-1

Appointed as reserve-team boss in the summer, following the departure of John Hollins to Swansea, Iain remained a Queens Park Rangers' player and continued to appear for Northern Ireland, where he added to his goalscoring record and gained his 50th full international cap against Turkey in September. He took over as a caretaker/manager between Ray Harford's resignation and Gerry Francis' arrival and became part of the new management team when appointed player/coach. He then gained a place in the first team following an injury to, and subsequent transfer of Mike Sheron. A player in the mould of the old-fashioned centre forward, who can be relied on for knock downs from centres, he used his experience to coach the reserve side during his relatively successful season.

Luton T (£30,000 from Hendon on 14/12/88) FL 53+13/16 FLC 3+1 FAC 1+2 Others 5/4
Fulham (Loaned on 13/9/89) FL 5/1
West Ham U (£480,000 on 22/3/91) FL 12/4
Southampton (£500,000 on 3/9/91) F/PL 115+7/30 FLC 8+3/1 FAC 6/1 Others 4
Crystal Palace (£400,000 on 13/1/95) P/FL 19/6 FAC 6/4
West Ham U (£500,000 on 8/9/95) PL 58+10/8 FLC 10+1/2 FAC 3+1/1
Queens Park R (Signed on 30/1/98) FL 16+14/2 FLC 0+1 FAC 0+1

DOWNER Simon
Born: Romford, 19 October 1981
Height: 5'11" Weight: 12.0

Another Leyton Orient trainee who, like Danny Brown, was rewarded with a game against Peterborough in the Auto Windscreens Shield last season, Simon also made a brief appearance as a substitute in the final league match, against Barnet. Very quick and strong, and a good passer, the young central defender also showed maturity when he played in a summer friendly against West Ham and had to mark John Hartson. At the same time he showed good aerial power, despite not being the biggest.

Leyton Orient (Trainee) FL 0+1 Others 1

DOZZELL Jason Alvin Winans
Born: Ipswich, 9 December 1967
Height: 6'1" Weight: 13.8
Club Honours: Div 2 '92
International Honours: E: U21-9; Yth

An experienced forward or midfielder with lots of top-level experience, having left Northampton during the summer, Jason began last season without a club and trained at Colchester to maintain his fitness. After impressing in the reserves, he accepted a month-to-month contract and soon won a regular first-team place. Played as a target man for most of the second half of the campaign, he scored four goals – remarkably, all headers – most notably the winner against Bournemouth which took United to safety. Despite being out of contract during the summer, the club made him an offer of re-engagement for the coming season.

Ipswich T (From apprentice on 20/12/84) F/PL 312+20/52 FLC 29+1/3 FAC 22/12 Others 22/4
Tottenham H (£1,900,000 on 1/8/93) PL 68+16/13 FLC 8+2 FAC 4+1/1

Ipswich T (Free on 2/10/97) FL 8/1 FLC 2/1
Northampton T (Free on 19/12/97) FL 18+3/4 FAC 1 Others 3
Colchester U (Free on 14/10/98) FL 23+6/4 FAC 1 Others 0+1

DRAPER Mark Andrew
Born: Long Eaton, 11 November 1970
Height: 5'10" Weight: 12.4
Club Honours: FLC '96
International Honours: E: U21-3

Having signed a new long-term contract during the summer of 1998, 1998-99 was a frustrating season for Mark as he struggled to gain a first-team place at Aston Villa, with most of his appearances coming from the subs' bench. During November and December, the classy midfielder missed a spell of five games following an operation on his ankle and, although he returned for the next five fixtures, he only managed to start one of them. This was mainly due to a reoccurrence of the ankle problem. While a second operation was not required it ruled him out for a further five games, but after regaining his place in the starting line-up at the end of February he began to produce a string of impressive appearances, especially when being able to get forward more. This was highlighted by the fact that he scored two goals in three games; his goal against Southampton being a fine display of individual effort and came after he picked the ball up just inside the Saints' half, beat a number of players and slotted it past the 'keeper. An on-song Mark Draper is a key link between midfield and the forwards.

Notts Co (From trainee on 12/12/88) FL 206+16/40 FLC 14+1/2 FAC 10/2 Others 21+2/5
Leicester C (£1,250,000 on 22/7/94) PL 39/5 FLC 2 FAC 2
Aston Villa (£3,250,000 on 5/7/95) PL 108+11/7 FLC 11+1/2 FAC 10/2 Others 12+1

DREYER John Brian
Born: Alnwick, 11 June 1963
Height: 6'1" Weight: 13.2

John started last season as Bradford's regular centre back alongside Darren Moore, but after 18 games he sustained a bad toe injury and was out injured for ten weeks. He then found it hard to get back into the side, due to the form of Andy O'Brien, Ashley Westwood and Moore. A good hard-working professional, he can play equally well at left back, centre back or in midfield. At the start of 1998-99 John was on a monthly contract but later signed up until the end of the campaign, and was due to decide during the summer whether to take up the club's offer of re-engagement.

Oxford U (Signed from Wallingford on 8/1/85) FL 57+3/2 FLC 10+1 FAC 2 Others 3
Torquay U (Loaned on 13/12/85) FL 5
Fulham (Loaned on 27/3/88) FL 12/2
Luton T (£140,000 on 27/6/88) FL 212+2/13 FLC 13+1/1 FAC 14 Others 8/1
Stoke C (Free on 15/7/94) FL32+17/3 FLC 5 FAC 1 Others 4+1/1
Bolton W (Loaned on 23/3/95) FL 1+1 Others 1+1
Bradford C (£25,000 on 6/11/96) FL 61+5/1 FLC 7+2 FAC 3/3

DRURY Adam James
Born: Cambridge, 29 August 1978
Height: 5'10" Weight: 11.8

A young Peterborough defender, who had given advance notice of his promise in 1997-98 before suffering a dislocated shoulder, Adam held down the left-back position in 1998-99 with some ease, apart from the odd minor injury and, at the same time, looked to be a star of the future. With his pace and positional ability always seemingly giving him plenty of time on the ball, he was the subject of a £500,000 bid on transfer deadline day. And, while "Posh" turned it down, they may be hard pressed to hold on to him for much longer. Has both confidence and much enthusiasm for the game.

Peterborough U (From trainee on 3/7/96) FL 68+9/1 FLC 4 FAC 2 Others 6

DRYDEN Richard Andrew
Born: Stroud, 14 June 1969
Height: 6'0" Weight: 13.12
Club Honours: Div 4 '90

Southampton central defender who was a surprise buy from Bristol City in 1996 when Graeme Souness was manager. Played the first three games of last season, but appeared only one more time in the first team (in the away win at Blackburn) when a knee injury, which required surgery, kept him out for three months and robbed him of further opportunities. Having great strength at either end of the park, and dangerous at set pieces, Richard always performs with great composure when called upon.

Bristol Rov (From trainee on 14/7/87) FL 12+1 FLC 2+1 FAC 0+2 Others 2
Exeter C (Loaned on 22/9/88) FL 6
Exeter C (Signed on 8/3/89) FL 86/13 FLC 7/2 FAC 2 Others 4
Notts Co (£250,000 on 9/8/91) FL 30+1/1 FLC 1+1 FAC 2+1 Others 2
Plymouth Arg (Loaned on 18/11/92) FL 5 Others 1
Birmingham C (£165,000 on 19/3/93) FL 48 FLC 5 FAC 1
Bristol C (£140,000 on 16/12/94) FL 32+5/2 FLC 4 FAC 1+1 Others 2
Southampton (£150,000 on 6/8/96) PL 43+3/1 FLC 7/3

DRYSDALE Leon Anthony
Born: Walsall, 3 February 1981
Height: 5'9" Weight: 11.13

The young trainee made an impressive league debut for Shrewsbury in the home defeat against Rotherham last season. A right-sided wing back, Leon looked very useful going forward, with accurate passing from defence belying his years, and appeared to be an excellent prospect.

Shrewsbury T (Trainee) FL 2

DUBERRY Michael Wayne
Born: Enfield, 14 October 1975
Height: 6'1" Weight: 13.6
Club Honours: FLC '98; ECWC '98; ESC '99
International Honours: E: U21-5

When Chelsea acquired Marcel Desailly to resume his World Cup-winning defensive partnership with Frank Leboeuf in 1998-99, many pundits felt that Michael would be forced to leave the Blues, but the young central defender responded magnificently to prove the doubters wrong. Replacing the

injured Desailly, who was carrying calf and knee strains, "Doobs" turned in a string of good performances, which recalled his arrival on the scene three years earlier. Indeed, he was so successful that the versatile Desailly was switched to midfield on his return to action. Sadly, the injury hoodoo re-occurred to interrupt his career yet again – a torn hamstring at Highbury in January limiting his second half of the season to two Premiership starts and a handful of substitute outings. A product of the highly successful Chelsea youth policy, he is totally committed to the side and his stated long-term ambition is to captain the Blues in the future.

Chelsea (From trainee on 7/6/93) PL 77+9/1 FLC 8 FAC 12/2 Others 9
Bournemouth (Loaned on 29/9/95) FL 7 Others 1

DUBLIN Dion
Born: Leicester, 22 April 1969
Height: 6'1" Weight: 12.4
Club Honours: Div 3 '91
International Honours: E: 4

As a vital element of Coventry's opening game of last season, scoring the second goal in a 2-1 home win over Chelsea, it would have been unthinkable for the City fans to contemplate that this larger-than-life striker would be playing for their midland rivals, Aston Villa, a few weeks later. However, after starting the first 12 games, and scoring four goals, he moved to Villa in early November and successfully commenced his career there by scoring seven goals in his first three games – two against Spurs, a hat trick at Southampton, and two in a 4-2 defeat at the hand of Liverpool. Initially, there were signs that a formidable strike partnership would be struck up with Stan Collymore, but as that petered out a very successful link up with Julian Joachim was formed. Although playing in most games, after missing Fulham and Newcastle matches at the end of January it was felt that he might require a hernia operation but, in the event, it was postponed until the summer. His strengths lie in him having an eye for goal, commanding the air waves, and possessing the ability to be comfortable, whether it be at centre forward or at centre half. Still very much in the mind of the international selectors, he played for England against the Czech Republic in November, and looks forward to picking up where he left off at Villa Park this coming term.

Norwich C (From Oakham U on 24/3/88)
Cambridge U (Free on 2/8/88) FL 133+23/52 FLC 8+2/5 FAC 21/11 Others 14+1/5
Manchester U (£1,000,000 on 7/8/92) PL 4+8/2 FLC 1+1/1 FAC 1+1 Others 0+1
Coventry C (£2,000,000 on 9/9/94) PL 144+1/61 FLC 11+2/4 FAC 13/7
Aston Villa (£5,750,000 on 6/11/98) PL 24/11

DUBLIN Keith Barry
Born: High Wycombe, 29 January 1966
Height: 6'0" Weight: 12.10
International Honours: E: Yth

After what was his best season in the blue shirt of Southend in 1997-98, Keith's appearances in 1998-99 were restricted by Simon Coleman, Rob Newman, David Morley, and Leo Roget, who were all chosen at centre half in front of him. Although always showing his strong defensive qualities when called upon, he could not force his way into the team on a permanent basis, and spent part of the season on loan, first to Colchester United (November) and then at Canvey (March), before being released in the summer.

Chelsea (From apprentice on 28/1/84) FL 50+1 FLC 6 FAC 5 Others 5+1
Brighton & Hove A (£3,500 on 14/8/87) FL 132/5 FLC 5 FAC 7/1 Others 7
Watford (£275,000 on 17/7/90) FL 165+3/2 FLC 12 FAC 4 Others 6
Southend U (Signed on 21/7/94) FL 175+4/9 FLC 10+1 FAC 5 Others 3
Colchester U (Loaned on 9/11/98) FL 2

DUDLEY Craig Bryan
Born: Newark, 12 September 1979
Height: 5'10" Weight: 11.2
Club Honours: Div 3 '98
International Honours: E: Yth

A product of the Notts County youth system, where he scored at a phenomenal rate, Craig did not figure much last season and left for Hull on loan in November to gain some league experience. Hurriedly drafted in on the day that Warren Joyce became City's caretaker manager, making his debut only hours later, against Brighton, before returning to Meadow Lane in mid February, he made a big impression at Boothferry, especially with the vital last-gasp winner against Carlisle. Transferred to Oldham during the transfer deadline week, he looks forward to making his debut for the Latics in 1999-2000. Has good pace, on and off the ball.

Notts Co (From trainee on 2/4/97) FL 11+20/3 FLC 1+2/1 FAC 1+2
Shrewsbury T (Loaned on 8/1/98) FL 3+1
Hull C (Loaned on 10/11/98) FL 4+3/2
Oldham Ath (Free on 25/3/99)

DUERDEN Ian Christopher
Born: Burnley, 27 March 1978
Height: 5'9" Weight: 12.6

Having made his sole appearance in the Football League for Burnley in 1997-98, the young striker was released during the following summer and joined Halifax on non-contract forms, hoping to gain a contract. Started the first game of last season as Town played their first competitive league match, at Peterborough, after a five-year absence but, following two months of reserve football, Ian signed for Doncaster Rovers where he made a big impression.

Burnley (From trainee on 11/7/96) FL 1
Halifax T (Free on 7/8/98) FL 1+1 FLC 0+1

DUFF Damien Anthony
Born: Ballyboden, Ireland, 2 March 1979
Height: 5'10" Weight: 9.7
International Honours: Ei: 9; B-1; Yth; Sch

Started 1998-99 with a pre-season operation for a hernia, Damien did not really regain his place at Blackburn until Jason Wilcox was absent for the same reason. Although a player capable of creating a breach in the opposition ranks with his quick darts and left-wing crosses, he seldom played to anything like his true potential and was utilised by Brian Kidd, essentially as a substitute, before opening his scoring account in April with a long-range volley against Liverpool. A regular in the Republic of Ireland's full side, he missed a month of football near the end of the campaign when representing the U20 select in Nigeria.

Blackburn Rov (Signed from Lourdes Celtic on 5/3/96) PL 36+19/5 FLC 5+1 FAC 6+2/1 Others 1

DUFFIELD Peter
Born: Middlesbrough, 4 February 1969
Height: 5'6" Weight: 10.4

After a long period in Scottish football, Peter returned to the Football League when he was loaned from Falkirk last January to partner Marco Gabbiadini up front at

Damien Duff

Darlington. His intelligent holding up of the ball worked well and in their four games together the pair scored seven goals between them, with Peter getting two. However, after only ten starts he was relegated to the substitutes' bench following the arrival of Martin Carruthers on transfer deadline day.

Middlesbrough (From apprentice on 4/11/86)
Sheffield U (Free on 20/8/87) FL 34+24/16 FLC 3+5/2 FAC 6+2/1 Others 3+2/3
Halifax T (Loaned on 7/3/88) FL 12/6 Others 1
Rotherham U (Loaned on 7/3/91) FL 17/5
Blackpool (Loaned on 23/7/92) FL 3+2/1 FLC 0+1
Stockport Co (Loaned on 19/3/93) FL 6+1/4 Others 2+1
Crewe Alex (Loaned on 15/1/93) FL 0+2 FAC 0+1
Hamilton Ac (Signed on 24/9/93) SL 69+3/38 SLC 2/1 SC 2 Others 3/3
Airdrie (Signed on 21/7/95) SL 19+5/7 SLC 2+2/2 SC 3/3 Others 1
Raith Rov (Signed on 2/3/96) SL 37+14/11 SLC 2+1/3 SC 2 Others 1+1
Morton (Signed on 8/11/97) SL 27+1/9 SLC 1 SC 1
Falkirk (Signed on 27/8/98) SL 9+6/2
Darlington (Signed on 15/1/99) FL 10+4/2

DUGUID Karl Anthony
Born: Hitchin, 21 March 1978
Height: 5'11" Weight: 11.7
1998-99 will be remembered as the season when Karl established himself as a regular in Colchester's starting line-up. After three seasons as a super sub, "Doogie" seemed to have become physically stronger, while retaining his impressive pace, and enjoyed a run in the team as a central striker, paired up front with Jason Dozzell, where his mobility complemented his partner's experience. Finished the campaign on four goals, including valuable equalisers in the away games at Reading, Gillingham and Northampton late in the season.
Colchester U (From trainee on 16/7/96) FL 46+44/11 FLC 0+3 FAC 3+3 Others 1+5

DUNCAN Andrew (Andy)
Born: Hexham, 20 October 1977
Height: 5'11" Weight: 13.0
International Honours: E: Sch
Following his move from Manchester United in early 1998, Andy has become a regular member of the Cambridge first team. Missing only one game, through suspension, in 1998-99 and forming a key partnership with Marc Joseph, he eventually took over the senior role in the heart of the defence when partnering youngster, Martin McNeill. He also captained the side in the absence of Paul Wanless, and displaying strength on the ground and in the air, along with an ability to read the game, he was a much improved player.
Manchester U (From trainee on 10/7/96)
Cambridge U (£20,000 on 9/1/98) FL 63+1/1 FLC 5 FAC 2 Others 3

DUNDEE Sean William
Born: Durban, South Africa, 7 December 1972
Height: 6'1" Weight: 12.8
Signed from Karlsruhe during the 1998 close season, the South African was limited to a substitute appearance against Fulham in the Worthington Cup in 1998-99, and cannot hope for much of a first-team future at Liverpool with the wealth of striking talent which abounds within the club. During the

summer, he had a great game as a sub against Crewe, but picked up an annoying injury which prevented him from making more of an impact. He is, in truth, a player bought more to provide the regular strike force with some competition, rather than being a potent striker in his own right, and during the campaign he was the subject of some transfer speculation when the French club, Auxerre, put in an offer. However, Sean had already committed himself to the Reds, despite being fourth in the pecking order of strikers.
Liverpool (£2,000,000 from Karlsruhe, via Bay View, D'Alberton Callis, Suttgarter and Ditzingen, on 5/6/98) PL 0+3 FLC 0+1 Others 0+1

DUNGEY James Andrew
Born: Plymouth, 7 February 1978
Height: 5'10" Weight: 12.0
International Honours: E: Yth; Sch
Released by Exeter during the 1998 close season, the former England youth 'keeper spent most of 1998-99 playing for local league side, Bodmin Town. However, in signing non-contract forms for Plymouth as cover for Jon Sheffield, he was called upon in the last weeks of the campaign due to an injury to Sheffield, having earlier deputised for him in the FA Cup game at Wycombe. Although James is quite small for a 'keeper he makes up for this with incredible agility and, in his eight appearances during the campaign, he showed he is still capable of performing at a good level.
Plymouth Arg (From trainee on 3/10/95) FL 9+1 Others 4
Exeter C (Free on 10/12/97) FL 1 (Free to Bodmin during 1998 close season)
Plymouth Arg (Free on 7/8/98) FL 7 FAC 1 Others 1

DUNN David John Ian
Born: Blackburn, 27 December 1979
Height: 5'10" Weight: 12.3
International Honours: E: U21-1; Yth
A member of the Blackburn side that reached the final of the FA Youth Cup in 1998, David was not expected to feature with the first team in 1998-99, but injuries necessitated his promotion. He displayed great temperament when slotting home the winning penalty in the Worthington Cup shoot-out victory at Newcastle, and scored his maiden goal in the win at Aston Villa. A tough tackler and hard worker, he has the marking ability to cope with the midfield scramble and gets forward strongly, making use of the wing when the opportunity presents itself. Made his England U21 debut with an appearance against the Czech Republic.
Blackburn Rov (From trainee on 30/9/97) PL 10+5/1 FLC 1+1 FAC 2+1

DUNNE Joseph (Joe) John
Born: Dublin, 25 May 1973
Height: 5'9" Weight: 11.6
International Honours: Ei: U21-1; Yth; Sch
A very combative and competitive Colchester defender, Joe played most of last season in his regular position of right back, before being switched to left back late on to accommodate the arrival of Fabrice Richard. Highly placed in the players' "Player of the Year" voting, he unfortunately broke his arm

in the home game against Walsall, bringing his season to a premature end and denying United his regular late-season spectacular goal. Was somewhat surprisingly released during the summer.
Gillingham (From trainee on 9/8/90) FL 108+7/1 FLC 7 FAC 5+1 Others 4+2
Colchester U (Free on 27/3/96) FL 79+22/3 FLC 3+1/1 FAC 5+1 Others 7+1

DUNNE Richard Patrick
Born: Dublin, 21 September 1979
Height: 6'1" Weight: 14.0
Club Honours: FAYC '98
International Honours: Ei: B-1; U21-1; Yth; Sch
A big and powerful centre half, Richard's delight at helping the Republic of Ireland to a shock European Youth championship success during the summer of 1998 was tempered by a foot injury he picked up in Cyprus. He eventually recovered to claim his first-team place in an unfamiliar right-wing back role at Everton in 1998-99, and applied himself diligently. Deceptively quick, his immense physical presence still suggests that central defence is his most natural position. Selected to represent the Republic of Ireland at the World Youth championships in Nigeria, he was prevented from travelling by a hamstring injury which effectively curtailed his season in March. Also made his first appearance for the Republic's U21 side.
Everton (From trainee on 8/10/96) PL 23+3 FLC 2 FAC 4

DUNWELL Michael
Born: Middlesbrough, 6 January 1980
Height: 5'11" Weight: 12.2
A first-year professional with a reputation for goalscoring, having been Hartlepool juniors' leading scorer in 1997-98, he had little luck in 1998-99, his best performance being a hat trick for the reserves in a game which was later declared void. However, with Pool's safety at the bottom of Division Three assured, he was given his debut, touching the ball just once, when coming on as substitute and playing in the last minute of the last game of the season at Southend.
Hartlepool U (From trainee on 3/7/98) FL 0+1

DURKAN Kieran John
Born: Chester, 1 December 1973
Height: 5'11" Weight: 12.10
Club Honours: WC '95
International Honours: Ei: U21-3
With stiff competition from the other wingers at Macclesfield in 1998-99, Kieran had to sit out first-team duties in mid season because of inconsistent performances. However, he got his place back at the start of March due to squad injuries, and his play was instrumental in the team's upward change of form, three successive victories being the end product. A provider for several goals with sorties down either wing and pin-point crosses to the strikers, he also scored two goals at Burnley in the narrow 4-3 defeat, the first coming from 15 yards out when he lobbed the 'keeper from the right after a superb run down the flank.
Wrexham (From trainee on 16/7/92) FL 43+7/3 FLC 3+1 FAC 4+2/2 Others 15/1

Stockport Co (£95,000 on 16/2/96) FL 52+12/4 FLC 10+1 FAC 4/3 Others 4+2
Macclesfield T (£15,000 on 25/3/98) FL 25+5/3 FLC 1+2 FAC 0+2 Others 0+1

DURNIN John Paul
Born: Bootle, 18 August 1965
Height: 5'10" Weight: 11.10
Another consistent player for Portsmouth in 1998-99, now in his seventh season for the Hampshire club, John is able to play either in midfield or in attack where, given the support, he is a very capable and strong performer. At 34, his strike rate was still valuable as he repeated his end of 1997-98 flurry of goals to help keep the club in the First Division, including a spectacular "Goal of the Season", a looping volley in a 2-2 draw at the Hawthorns in April. Though occasionally hot-tempered, he forms an effective partnership with whoever he plays alongside, whether it be at right back, midfield, or in the number ten jersey. A charismatic Liverpudlian whom Pompey fans have nicknamed "Johnny Lager", his battling, 90-minute efforts should help carry the side through another campaign, whilst reaching his 200th league game for the club.
Liverpool (Free from Waterloo Dock on 29/3/86) FLC 1+1
West Bromwich A (Loaned on 20/10/88) FL 5/2
Oxford U (£225,000 on 10/2/89) FL 140+21/44 FLC 7/1 FAC 7/1 Others 4+1/1
Portsmouth (£200,000 on 15/7/93) FL 116+63/31 FLC 13+2/2 FAC 5+2 Others 4+2

DUXBURY Lee Edward
Born: Keighley, 7 October 1969
Height: 5'10" Weight: 11.13
1998-99 was another great season for the Oldham captain, and he climaxed it when winning the supporters' "Player of the Year" award and leading the Latics to Second Division safety. The midfield general also scored seven times in 48 appearances – including three in a row at one stage – three of them critical to the cause. Leading by example, when the going got tough, Lee got going, his strong-tackling displays pulling the side through at times. Inspirational in breaking down attacks, and able to play from box to box, once again he also showed excellent passing skills from the centre of midfield. Where would Athletic be without him!
Bradford C (From trainee on 4/7/88) FL 204+5/25 FLC 18+1/3 FAC 11 Others 13
Rochdale (Loaned on 18/1/90) FL 9+1 FAC 1
Huddersfield T (£250,000 on 23/12/94) FL 29/2 FLC 1 Others 3
Bradford C (£135,000 on 15/11/95) FL 63/7 FLC 2 FAC 5 Others 3
Oldham Ath (£350,000 on 7/3/97) FL 89+2/11 FLC 4 FAC 8/1 Others 2

DYCHE Sean Mark
Born: Kettering, 28 June 1971
Height: 6'0" Weight: 13.10
1998-99 was a disappointing season for the Bristol City central defender, whose return from injury was expected to compensate for the continuing absence of Shaun Taylor. In the event, the club captain made a shaky start before being dropped, never able to show the form he had exhibited at Chesterfield, and was allowed to go to Luton on loan in January. Well known for his tough-tackling and motivational skills, he remained at Town virtually throughout the remainder of the campaign, firing in the winner at home to Gillingham, and gradually recovering his form despite missing six games due to injury. Stop Press: Completed a £150,000 move to Millwall on 5 July.
Nottingham F (From trainee on 20/5/89)
Chesterfield (Free on 1/2/90) FL 219+12/8 FLC 9 FAC 13/1 Others 16
Bristol C (£350,000 on 11/7/97) FL 14+3 FLC 2+1
Luton T (Loaned on 4/1/99) FL 14/1 Others 1

DYER Alexander (Alex) Constantine
Born: Forest Gate, 14 November 1965
Height: 6'0" Weight: 12.0
Alex again showed himself to be "Mr Versatile" at Notts County in 1998-99, appearing all over the park whenever a specialised job was required. Played as a centre back, full back, midfielder, and even a target man in emergencies. An intelligent player, who is always confident on the ball, he has yet to find the net for County. Is cool, calm, and collected, especially when under pressure. Prefers the left-hand side.
Blackpool (Free from Watford juniors on 20/10/83) FL 101+7/19 FLC 8+1/1 FAC 4+1 Others 7/1
Hull C (£37,000 on 13/2/87) FL 59+1/14 FLC 2 FAC 4/1
Crystal Palace (£250,000 on 11/11/88) FL 16+1/2 FLC 3+1 FAC 1+1 Others 3+1/3
Charlton Ath (£100,000 on 30/11/90) FL 60+18/13 FLC 2+1 FAC 1/1 Others 3+1
Oxford U (Free on 26/7/93) FL 62+14/6 FLC 4/1 FAC 5/1 Others 5
Lincoln C (Free on 21/8/95) FL 1 FLC 1
Barnet (Free on 1/9/95) FL 30+5/2 Others 1 (Freed on 9/5/96)
Huddersfield T (Signed from FA Maia on 13/8/97) FL 8+4/1 FLC 3/1
Notts Co (Free on 2/3/98) FL 29+10 FLC 0+2 FAC 3+1

DYER Bruce Antonio
Born: Ilford, 13 April 1975
Height: 6'0" Weight: 11.3
International Honours: E: U21-11
Started 1998-99 in the Crystal Palace first team, scoring two goals, before a transfer to Fulham collapsed, only for Barnsley to sign him the following week, last October. In making a steady start at Oakwell, he had just begun to show his potential when he was sidelined for a number of games due to a stomach injury. A strong-running striker who is capable of beating defenders with skill and pace, he returned to action after taking some time to regain full fitness, and once again began to terrorise defences with his powerful play. Selected by his fellow professionals for the award-winning PFA First Division side, he also netted some spectacular goals.
Watford (From trainee on 19/4/93) FL 29+2/6 FLC 4/2 FAC 1 Others 2/1
Crystal Palace (£1,100,000 on 10/3/94) F/PL 95+40/37 FLC 9+5/1 FAC 7+3/6 Others 3+2
Barnsley (£700,000 on 23/10/98) FL 28/7 FAC 2/1

DYER Keiron Courtney
Born: Ipswich, 29 December 1978
Height: 5'7" Weight: 9.7
International Honours: E: B-2; U21-10; Yth

Keiron continued his development as one of the country's most promising youngsters last season, culminating in a call up to the full England squad and a nomination for the second successive year in the PFA First Division select. With a love of running with the ball, and attacking opposing defences, he had more of a free role in Ipswich's midfield, which enabled him to display his skills to the full, scoring five goals, including his first at Portman Road – against Portsmouth – and the only goal in the away win at Stockport when he ran on to a defence-splitting ball from Jon Hunt and calmly chipped the oncoming goalkeeper. Fractured his left leg early in the match with Watford in March, but played on and scored the opening goal of the game before leaving the field on a stretcher. Coming back for the last five fixtures, only really regaining full-match fitness in the final game of the league campaign, he scored a double in the home leg of the play-off semi final against Bolton – a right-foot shot and an astute header – but it was not enough to save his side from a third successive play-off exit. He has also become something of a character locally since starting a weekly column in the Green 'Un – the local Saturday sports paper. Made four appearances for the England U21 side in 1998-99.
Ipswich T (From trainee on 3/1/97) FL 79+12/9 FLC 11/1 FAC 5 Others 5+1/2

DYER Wayne
Born: Birmingham, 24 November 1977
Height: 6'1" Weight: 11.7
Having been at Birmingham without a game, Wayne signed for Walsall last August after spending some time with non-league Moor Green, and went on to make an 18th-minute substitution for Dean Keates in the league game at Wycombe, and a 14th-minute appearance from the bench for the same player in the Worthington Cup second leg at Queens Park Rangers before signing for Hereford United in mid November. Is more of a front man, where he can use his height to good effect.
Birmingham C (From trainee on 5/7/96. Freed on 8/4/97)
Walsall (Free from Moor Green on 20/8/98) FL 0+1 FLC 0+1

DYSON Jonathan (Jon) Paul
Born: Mirfield, 18 December 1971
Height: 6'1" Weight: 12.12
Having to watch Huddersfield rise to the top of the First Division, the former "Player of the Year" came to be known as "Mr Patience", as regular action was seen only from the subs' bench. But, always one to depend on, he finally started at Swindon prior to going down with an ankle injury two games later. Then, on coming back, he lost out again when being sent off at the McAlpine against Tranmere. Versatile and consistent, and able to play anywhere in the back four or in midfield, Jon was recalled for the FA Cup matches against Derby, before injury and illness sidelined him until the latter end of the campaign. Enjoyed his first goal for 14 months, at Crystal Palace, before being carried off with concussion.
Huddersfield T (From juniors on 29/12/90) FL 135+20/4 FLC 14+2 FAC 9 Others 7+4

Match Winning Tackle?

OR

Career Ending Injury?

are you covered?

SPECIALIST SPORTS INSURANCE
WINDSOR
Security in a Competitive World

There is a stark reality to Professional Sport.

For example, every year over fifty Professional Footballers

have to retire through injury.

Don't risk it. Don't believe that it will never happen to you.

It might.

Make that call ~ 0171 407 7144

EADEN Nicholas (Nicky) Jeremy
Born: Sheffield, 12 December 1972
Height: 5'9" Weight: 12.8
Again a regular on the right-hand side of the Barnsley defence in 1998-99, he was far more comfortable when going forward, although this suffered when his fellow wing-back, Darren Barnard, was injured and so much of the attacking play came down the right. An excellent crosser when going forward, it was noticeable that when Nicky played well so did the Tykes. Skippered the team on a number of occasions.
Barnsley (From juniors on 4/6/91) F/PL 243+8/9 FLC 16+1/1 FAC 19 Others 2

EADIE Darren Malcolm
Born: Chippenham, 10 June 1975
Height: 5'8" Weight: 11.6
International Honours: E: U21-7; Yth
1998-99 will not go down as one of Darren's finest. Two knee operations interrupted his progress for both club and country, and the speedy Norwich winger will be looking for much better things in the season ahead. A former England U21 international, he signed a new extended contract at the outset of the campaign and in the games he played once again looked the class act everyone knew him to be. He has tremendous acceleration, the ability to go past opponents on either side, and a powerful left-foot shot which has brought him close on 40 first-team goals.
Norwich C (From trainee on 5/2/93) P/FL 141+14/34 FLC 23+1/2 FAC 7+1/1 Others 1+1

Robbie Earle

EARLE Robert (Robbie) Gerald
Born: Newcastle under Lyme, 27 January 1965
Height: 5'9" Weight: 10.10
International Honours: Jamaica: 9
One of the most popular players ever to have played for Wimbledon, and an excellent ambassador for the club, last season saw Robbie continuing to show that he had not lost his goalscoring touch with some vital strikes that included one which proved that, even at the age of 34, he is as agile as ever – when scoring with a spectacular over-head kick against Spurs in the FA Cup. A commanding figure in the Wimbledon midfield, and an inspiration to the rest of the team, he competed for Jamaica in the World Cup of 1998, and had the honour of scoring Jamaica's first ever World Cup final goal. Began 1998-99 well when heading in an Alan Kimble free kick from fully 20 yards to open the Dons' scoring account for the new campaign in a 3-1 home win over Spurs. An attacking midfielder who has great energy, and who times his runs into the box with great precision to score or to pass to players better positioned. How would the Dons do without him!
Port Vale (From juniors on 5/7/82) FL 284+10/77 FLC 21+2/4 FAC 20+1/4 Others 18+1/5
Wimbledon (£775,000 on 19/7/91) F/PL 257+2/56 FLC 26/6 FAC 34/8 Others 1/1

EARNSHAW Robert
Born: Zambia, 6 April 1981
Height: 5'8" Weight: 10.10
International Honours: W: U21-3; Yth
Opened last season with a stunning goal on his debut start, at Hartlepool in the opening Third Division match, an overhead kick which set Cardiff fans celebrating and saw one jump off a barrier and knock himself out on a goalpost as he landed. Pacy and sharp, the young striker spent loan spells with Fulham and Middlesbrough without being called up, merely being in the shop window. Although born in Zambia, Robert moved to Wales as a youngster and has opted to play for his adopted country. Indeed, he has already played for the U18s and marks every goal he scores with a somersault.
Cardiff C (Trainee) FL 1+9/1 FLC 0+1 FAC 0+1 Others 0+1

EASTON Clint Jude
Born: Barking, 1 October 1977
Height: 5'11' Weight: 10.8
Club Honours: Div 2 '98
International Honours: E: Yth
A left-sided midfield player who is an elegant passer of the ball and reads the game well, Clint must have hoped for a consistent run in Watford's first team last season, but had to be content with sporadic appearances, not least because he was hampered by groin problems which needed surgery in the summer.
Watford (From trainee on 5/7/96) FL 32+4/1 FLC 2+1 FAC 3+1 Others 3

EASTWOOD Phillip (Phil) John
Born: Blackburn, 6 April 1978
Height: 5'10" Weight: 12.2
Still not a regular in Burnley's side, Phil, formerly a striker, was more often employed in a deeper role for his occasional Second Division outings in 1998-99. A capable performer behind the front two, he scored his first league goal in the 4-1 defeat at Preston, but continued to rely on injuries for first-team chances, before being released in the summer.
Burnley (From trainee on 5/7/96) FL 7+9/1 FAC 1 Others 1

EBDON Marcus
Born: Pontypool, 17 October 1970
Height: 5'10" Weight: 12.4
International Honours: W: U21-2; Yth
Marcus established himself as a regular at Chesterfield during 1998-99, combining the defensive and attacking aspects of midfield play to great effect. His tackling and positional play improved as the season wore on, and he hardly wasted a pass, finding time in the pandemonium of Second Division midfield play to look up and pick out his forwards before stroking another perfectly-weighted ball into their path. Is an exciting player to watch!
Everton (From trainee on 16/8/89)
Peterborough U (Free on 15/7/91) FL 136+11/15 FLC 14+2 FAC 12+3/1 Others 11+1
Chesterfield (£100,000 on 21/3/97) FL 79+6/4 FLC 3+1 FAC 4 Others 2

Marcus Ebdon

ECKHARDT Jeffrey (Jeff) Edward
Born: Sheffield, 7 October 1965
Height: 6'0" Weight: 11.7
Able to play at the back, in midfield, or up front, this consistent and gutsy player proved a point at Cardiff in 1998-99. Having lost his place and, with his contract at an end, things looked bleak. City were even prepared to sell him to Hull City. But Jeff stuck it out, won his place back in the team and earned a new contract when convincing manager Frank Burrows that he can still do

a job in the Second Division. Whatever happens, he will never be criticised for a lack of effort.

Sheffield U (From juniors on 23/8/84) FL 73+1/2 FLC 7 FAC 2 Others 5
Fulham (£50,000 on 20/11/87) FL 245+4/25 FLC 13 FAC 5+1 Others 15/3
Stockport Co (£50,000 on 21/7/94) FL 56+6/7 FLC 6+2/1 FAC 5/4 Others 2
Cardiff C (£30,000 on 22/8/96) FL 84+7/13 FLC 1+2/1 FAC 7+1/1 Others 5/1

EDGE Roland
Born: Gillingham, 25 November 1978
Height: 5'9" Weight: 11.6
A local-born player, and a second-year professional, Roland made his first-team debut for Gillingham when he came on as a substitute in the cauldron of Preston's Deepdale ground after 58 minutes for Adrian Pennock last September. Able to fill in anywhere along the back and midfield, being neat and tidy with good control, he was a regular member of Gillingham's Combination side in 1998-99.
Gillingham (From trainee on 10/7/97) FL 1+7 FAC 1 Others 2

EDGHILL Richard Arlon
Born: Oldham, 23 September 1974
Height: 5'9" Weight: 11.5
International Honours: E: B-1; U21-3
At the beginning of the 1998-99 season, Richard was the longest-serving professional at Manchester City being only 23 years old, and was awarded a new four-year contract. Played in the first 16 league and cup games, mainly at right back, showing consistent form. His fast acceleration going forward or on the overlap is a big asset of his game, and he will shoot on sight of the target. However, he is still waiting for his first goal for the club after over 100 appearances. Although he received a mysterious foot injury at Wycombe in November, which kept him out of the team for the next two games, other than that he was an ever present, except for suspension.
Manchester C (From trainee on 15/7/92) P/FL 123 FLC 14 FAC 4 Others 3

EDINBURGH Justin Charles
Born: Brentwood, 18 December 1969
Height: 5'10" Weight: 12.0
Club Honours: FAC '91; FLC '99
The experienced Spurs' left back was rediscovered by George Graham just when it had looked as though the introduction of Paolo Tramezzani had put paid to Justin's first-team hopes at White Hart Lane in 1998-99. As it was, the gritty defender found himself to be a regular and playing some of his finest football for three years. Still quick off the mark, and with a tremendous appetite for the 50-50 ball, he looked inspired back in his old role, and was rewarded with another trip to Wembley in March for the Worthington Cup final. His commitment and passion in that game was dramatically and controversially thwarted after a clash with Leicester's Robbie Savage, Justin describing the sending off as the worst moment of his career. Fortunately for the Spurs' man, his side grabbed victory

in the closing moments to put the icing on a memorable season for him. Still able to offer a great deal at Premiership level this term.
Southend U (From trainee on 5/8/88) FL 36+1 FLC 2+1 FAC 2 Others 4+1/1
Tottenham H (£150,000 on 30/7/90) PL 183+22/1 FLC 24+4 FAC 26+1 Others 3

[EDINHO] Amaral Neto Edon Do
Born: Brazil, 21 February 1967
Height: 5'9" Weight: 12.9
The previous campaign's joint-leading goalscorer for Bradford, Edinho played in the first game of last season, but failed to make the starting line-up again, moving to the Scottish League side, Dunfermline, in mid November on a three-month loan. Returning to Valley Parade in February, the bustling forward moved on a free transfer to Portugese Division Two leaders, Portomenusu, on 23 March 1999. As you would expect from a Brazilian, flamboyance and skill are important features of his make up.
Bradford C (£250,000 from VSC Guimaraes on 6/2/97) FL 50+9/15 FLC 2+1/1 FAC 1
Dunfermline Ath (Loaned on 13/11/98) SL 5+5/1

EDMONDSON Darren Stephen
Born: Coniston, 4 November 1971
Height: 6'0" Weight: 12.11
Club Honours: Div 3 '95; AMC '97
Injured at the start of 1998-99, on recovering the Huddersfield defender was loaned to Plymouth in mid September to fill the troubled right-wing-back role. Although he arrived at Home Park with a view to a permanent transfer, he made just four appearances before suffering further injury and leaving for the McAlpine. Eventually, a return to action saw him back in the frame for a defensive call-up after producing some consistent displays with the reserves. A good passer of the ball, he came on as a sub at Queens Park Rangers in the FA Cup, and followed it up in the two encounters with Derby, when playing a solid defensive role but, although continuing to be involved, it was mainly from the subs' bench.
Carlisle U (From trainee on 17/7/90) FL 205+9/8 FLC 15/1 FAC 15/3 Others 22/3
Huddersfield T (£200,000 + on 3/3/97) FL 26+6 FLC 2 FAC 2+2
Plymouth Arg (Loaned on 11/9/98) FL 4

EDWARDS Andrew (Andy) David
Born: Epping, 17 September 1971
Height: 6'3" Weight: 12.10
A commanding Peterborough central defender who was promoted to captain in Steve Castle's absence last season, Andy likes the ball to feet, rather than thumping it clear, and is a great help to all the younger, inexperienced players around him. Virtually ever present, apart from a handful of games, he again got himself on the scoresheet with two goals, while continuing to show himself to be a danger at set pieces. With his ability in the air, and his speed of recovery in the tackle, where would Posh be without him.
Southend U (From trainee on 14/12/89) FL 141+6/5 FLC 5 FAC 4 Others 9/2
Birmingham C (£400,000 on 6/7/95) FL 37+3/1 FLC 12/1 FAC 2 Others 5/1

Peterborough U (Signed on 29/11/96) FL 112/4 FLC 6 FAC 8 Others 11/1

EDWARDS Christian (Chris) Nicholas Howells
Born: Caerphilly, 23 November 1975
Height: 6'2" Weight: 12.8
International Honours: W: 1; B-2; U21-7
Despite signing for Nottingham Forest inside the March, 1998 transfer deadline, Christian failed to make an appearance for the club in 1997-98, coming off the bench to make his first-team debut last November in a 2-0 defeat at Tottenham before being loaned out to Bristol City in mid December. Unfortunately, for City, the big central defender was recalled to Forest after just three games, the team conceding only two goals and looking to have found a defensive stability which up to that time had been missing. A commanding presence, who shines in aerial battles and can be used with the utmost confidence in set pieces further forward, he made his first start at Charlton, and played through the rest of a campaign that ended with relegation from the Premiership. Represented the Welsh "B" side that played against Northern Ireland.
Swansea C (From trainee on 20/7/94) FL 113+2/4 FLC 5 FAC 4 Others 9+1
Nottingham F (£175,000 + on 26/3/98) PL 7+5
Bristol C (Loaned on 11/12/98) FL 3

EDWARDS Jake
Born: Prestwich, 11 May 1976
Height: 6'2" Weight: 13.0
Although born in the north west of England, Jake was brought up in America and only returned to this country two years ago to take up trials with Tranmere Rovers and Wrexham. He then returned to the States to complete his degree at college, but the Robins had been impressed with him during his period at the Racecourse and he was invited back in the summer of 1998. Continuing to develop, earning a contract until the end of the season, he was brought into the first team to try and pep up the attack, and was on target on his senior debut in the Auto Windscreens Shield tie at Macclesfield, and in his first full league start at Luton. Along with fellow post graduate Andy Morrell, and Oxford "professor" Steve Rishworth, he is one of the "bright" boys to have made their league debuts in 1998-99.
Wrexham (Free from James Maddison University on 13/8/98) FL 4+5/1 Others 1+4/2

EDWARDS Michael
Born: Hessle, 25 April 1980
Height: 6'1" Weight: 12.0
An incredibly mature performer for his age, Michael brought calm and authority to the heart of the Hull defence in 1998-99 as they clawed their way to league survival in the second half of the season. It was no coincidence that the former youth team captain re-established his place in the first team at the same time, but he has clearly benefited from the greater experience of such as Justin Whittle and Jon Whitney, and shows every prospect of going on to play at a much higher grade. Uses his height and strength well, prefers his right foot, but is

not afraid to use his left when needed. His high standard of performance was recognised by supporters and management alike as he deservedly won both of the club's "Young Player of the Season" awards.

Hull C (From trainee on 16/7/98) FL 48+3 FLC 2+1 FAC 3 Others 3

EDWARDS Neil Ryan
Born: Aberdare, 5 December 1970
Height: 5'9" Weight: 11.10
International Honours: W: U21-1; Yth; Sch
"Taffy" was the automatic first choice between the posts for Rochdale in 1998-99, and his tremendous shot-stopping feats came to be taken for granted by the fans. Well known, as being too small for a goalkeeper, the Dale skipper's string of outstanding performances led to his supporters pushing for recognition by the Welsh team. During the season he signed a new long-term contract that will keep him at Spotland until 2002.

Leeds U (From trainee on 10/3/89) Others 1
Stockport Co (£5,000 on 3/9/91) FL 163+1 FLC 11 FAC 11 Others 31
Rochdale (£25,000 on 3/11/97) FL 72 FLC 2 FAC 4+1 Others 4

EDWARDS Paul
Born: Liverpool, 22 February 1965
Height: 5'11" Weight: 11.5
Club Honours: Div 3 '94
The goalkeeper had another excellent season, when completing his seventh year at Shrewsbury in 1998-99, probably his best so far. His strength as a shot stopper was complimented with considerable improvement in the air and in his kicking. Many important saves meant that the points were often down to "Eagle", a highly regarded club man.

Crewe Alex (Free from Leek T on 24/2/89) FL 29 FLC 4 FAC 3 Others 4
Shrewsbury T (Free on 6/8/92) FL 246 FLC 15 FAC 16+1 Others 16

Neil Edwards

Paul Edwards

EDWARDS Robert (Rob)
Born: Manchester, 23 February 1970
Height: 5'9" Weight: 12.4
Always dependable and committed, the Huddersfield left-sided midfielder started last season again deputising at left back, a position he made his own after giving some consistent performances. His solid contributions were rewarded with a cracking goal against Queens Park Rangers at the McAlpine, which was followed by a two-year extension to his contract. November saw the determined tackler make his 100th league appearance against Norwich, followed by some "Man of the Match" performances, and another cracking free-kick goal, this time against Ipswich at home. He also enjoyed returning to his former club, Crewe, when captaining Town. Missing just one game due to suspension, Rob was very comfortable on the ball and liked pushing forward, whether it was from full back or his natural midfield position, which he occupied towards the end of 1998-99.

Crewe Alex (From trainee on 11/7/88) FL 110+45/44 FLC 8/5 FAC 13+5/5 Others 9+8/4
Huddersfield T (£150,000 on 8/3/96) FL 108+21/13 FLC 10+1/1 FAC 7+1/1

EDWARDS Robert (Rob) William
Born: Kendal, 1 July 1973
Height: 6'0" Weight: 12.2
International Honours: W: 4; B-2; U21-17; Yth
Much was expected of Rob at Bristol City in 1998-99, the Welsh international being one of the few players at the club with previous First Division experience. However, due to injury problems, he was never able to play the midfield anchor role, to which he is well suited, on a consistent basis. As a ball winner with good passing skills, in the games he did play he provided an important role in the side and was sorely missed when absent. Out of contract during the summer, his future at Ashton Gate was uncertain at the time of going to press.

Carlisle U (From trainee on 10/4/90) FL 48/5 FLC 4 FAC 1 Others 2+1
Bristol C (£135,000 on 27/3/91) FL 188+28/5 FLC 16+3/1 FAC 13+2 Others 12+1/2

EDWORTHY Marc
Born: Barnstaple, 24 December 1972
Height: 5'8" Weight: 11.10
Coventry signed the utility defender in

August 1998 from Crystal Palace, where he had been the "Player of the Season" in their relegation campaign. His strongest positions are right back or in central defence, but his first-team chance came when David Burrows was injured early in the season at Charlton. Marc's slip unfortunately resulted in Charlton's equaliser. However, he recovered from that error to put in some sterling performances on the left, his speed being evident as well as his good passing ability. He then lost his place when Burrows recovered fitness in early January , but was recalled for the 3-0 FA Cup win at Leicester where he did a good job on the dangerous Steve Guppy. Finally, in May, with injuries stretching the squad, he was chosen at right back and played extremely well before making way for the return of Roland Nilsson. With Nilsson leaving for Sweden during the summer, Marc is the logical replacement.

Plymouth Arg (From trainee on 30/3/91) FL 52+17/1 FLC 5+2 FAC 5+2 Others 2+2
Crystal Palace (£350,000 on 9/6/95) F/PL 120+6 FLC 8+1/1 FAC 8 Others 6
Coventry C (£850,000 + on 28/8/98) PL 16+6 FAC 1

EHIOGU Ugochuku (Ugo)

Born: Hackney, 3 November 1972
Height: 6'2" Weight: 14.10
Club Honours: FLC '96
International Honours: E: 1; B-1; U21-15
Not only was 1998-99 an excellent season for Aston Villa but it was also a great one for this imposing central defender, until he was involved in a collision with Alan Shearer at Newcastle which left him with a fractured left-eye socket. It was initially thought that the injury would rule him out for the rest of the campaign. But almost three months and three operations later, Ugo made a surprising, although welcome return to the team via the subs' bench, at home to Nottingham Forest on 24 April, and received a standing ovation when coming on after 71 minutes. There was no doubting that his presence had been sorely missed during his prolonged absence and contributed greatly to Villa dropping away from the top of the Premiership. Both solid and pacy, and great in the air, he can confidently be relied upon as a man marker as well as putting himself about at the other end of the pitch at set pieces. Despite the horrific injury, it was still a fantastic season for him and he continues to wait patiently for the call up to the England squad, which surely must come sooner rather than later.

West Bromwich A (From trainee on 13/7/89) FL 0+2
Aston Villa (£40,000 on 12/7/91) F/PL 191+13/11 FLC 16+1/1 FAC 16+2/1 Others 16/1

EKOKU Efangwu (Efan) Goziem

Born: Manchester, 8 June 1967
Height: 6'2" Weight: 12.0
International Honours: Nigeria: 5
A big, strong Wimbledon forward who is equally capable with the ball in the air or at his feet. After missing most of 1997-98 through injury, the "Chief" was looking back to his very best at the start of last

season when he was red hot, scoring twice in the 3-1 win over Spurs on the opening day. It was therefore a real blow to everyone involved with the club when he requested a move just a few games into the season, and with only 11 league starts he still remains an important part of the Dons' squad. Interestingly, all of his Premiership goals came in games that were either won or drawn, including the winner at home to Arsenal, the eventual league runners-up. A striker who combines well with his team mates, he has very quick feet, while his pace will always put him in for goalscoring opportunities.

Bournemouth (£100,000 from Sutton U on 11/5/90) FL 43+19/21 FLC 0+2 FAC 5+2/2 Others 3+1/2
Norwich C (£500,000 on 26/3/93) PL 26+11/15 FLC 3/1 FAC 1+1 Others 3/1
Wimbledon (£900,000 on 14/10/94) PL 102+21/37 FLC 11+2/4 FAC 16+1/3

ELLINGTON Lee Simon

Born: Bradford, 3 July 1980
Height: 5'10" Weight: 11.0
Having signed a professional contract in the summer, and starting the first three games of the season, 1998-99 turned out to be a frustrating campaign for the young Hull striker as he became one of the victims of a Tigers' mass re-building programme. Much of his football being restricted to the junior team, where he determinedly continued to learn his craft.

Hull C (From trainee on 16/7/98) FL 7+8/2 FLC 1+2 FAC 0+3 Others 0+3

ELLINGTON Nathan Levi Fontaine

Born: Bradford, 2 July 1981
Height: 5'10" Weight: 12.10
Bristol Rovers signed the exciting 17-year-old striker from non-league Walton & Hersham in February, despite interest shown by Arsenal and West Ham. Nathan immediately made an impression with his pace and close control, and was given his league debut when used as a substitute, on 23 February against Gillingham at the Memorial Stadium. Nicknamed the "Duke", and scoring a cracking goal in the 2-0 victory over York after coming on in his third match as substitute, it is expected that he will be a real asset in the future and provide worthy competition for a regular place in the Rovers' starting line-up.

Bristol Rov (£150,000 from Walton & Hersham on 18/2/99) FL 1+9/1

ELLIOTT Anthony (Tony) Robert

Born: Nuneaton, 30 November 1969
Height: 6'0" Weight: 13.7
Club Honours: WC '90
International Honours: E: Yth; Sch
The hugely popular Scarborough goalie pulled off some brilliant saves during his time at the club, but was unfortunate to suffer a serious back injury midway through last season, after making 24 consecutive appearances, which ultimately led to him having to retire from the game prematurely. Off the field an excellent ambassador for Boro, he will be sorely missed.

Birmingham C (From apprentice on 3/12/86) FLC 1
Hereford U (Free on 22/12/88) FL 75 FLC 5 FAC 6 Others 9
Huddersfield T (Free on 29/7/92) FL 15 FLC 2 FAC 3 Others 3
Carlisle U (Free on 28/6/93) FL 21+1 FAC 1 Others 5
Cardiff C (Free on 4/7/96) FL 38+1 FLC 2 FAC 2 Others 1
Scarborough (Free on 12/2/98) FL 35 FLC 2 FAC 2 Others 2

ELLIOTT Matthew (Matt) Stephen

Born: Wandsworth, 1 November 1968
Height: 6'3" Weight: 14.10
International Honours: S: 7
A right-footed Leicester central defender, who is commanding in the air, Matt regularly took over the captain's armband whenever Steve Walsh was injured in 1998-99. Was a member of the Scotland squad for France '98, but did not see any action, though he has since become a regular choice at the heart of his adoptive country's defence. Picking up a broken nose on the opening day at Old Trafford, his goals were scarcer last season, but still vitally important, netting a late equaliser against Wimbledon and the strike that set the Foxes on the way to a crucial Easter victory at White Hart Lane. Always solid and formidable at the back, having also added spot-kick responsibility to his duties, he was also employed as an emergency striker at various points during the campaign, especially when City's lack of squad depth was sometimes exposed by injuries.

Charlton Ath (£5,000 from Epsom & Ewell on 9/5/88) FLC 1
Torquay U (£10,000 on 23/3/89) FL 123+1/15 FLC 9/2 FAC 9/2 Others 16/1
Scunthorpe U (£50,000 on 26/3/92) FL 61/8 FLC 6 FAC 2 Others 8
Oxford U (£150,000 on 5/11/93) FL 148/21 FLC 16/1 FAC 11/2 Others 6
Leicester C (£1,600,000 on 18/1/97) PL 90/14 FLC 9 FAC 6 Others 2

ELLIOTT Robert (Robbie) James

Born: Newcastle, 25 December 1973
Height: 5'10" Weight: 11.6
International Honours: E: U21-2; Yth
1998-99 was a big season for Robbie, having missed the vast majority of the previous campaign with a broken leg. That particular injury kept him out of action until he made his first appearance in the Worthington Cup game at Norwich, where he promptly scored. However, he found it difficult to maintain a decent run in the team after this, due to the left-back competition from Mike Whitlow and Jimmy Phillips, although a number of assured performances meant that his tally for the season was well into double figures. A versatile player who can play at left back or on the left wing, Robbie will be looking to return to his Newcastle form and make the left-back position his own when the new season begins.

Newcastle U (From trainee on 3/4/91) F/PL 71+8/9 FLC 5 FAC 7+3 Others 5+1
Bolton W (£2,500,000 + on 2/7/97) P/FL 18+8 FLC 1/1 Others 3

ELLIOTT Steven William
Born: Swadlincote, 29 October 1978
Height: 6'1" Weight: 14.0
International Honours: E: U21-3

The former youth-team captain and "Young Player of the Year" at Derby continued making good progress in 1998-99, and the first half of the season saw him with the first-team squad on an almost constant basis. An effective central defender, he had an outstanding game at Anfield, having been unexpectedly drafted into the side at the last minute. The second half of the campaign, however, saw him playing more regularly for the reserves due to the competition for senior places and tactical changes, and his season ended on a disappointing note with a sprained ankle in April.

Derby Co (From trainee on 26/3/97) PL 10+4 FLC 3+1 FAC 1+2

ELLIOTT Stuart Thomas
Born: Willesden, 27 August 1977
Height: 5'9" Weight: 12.0

A hard-working left-sided midfielder who, despite looking to be surplus to requirements at Newcastle, had turned down a £100,000 move to Wrexham prior to being loaned out to Gillingham (October), Hartlepool (January), and then Wrexham (March). Having showed some neat touches with the Gills, he eventually arrived at Hartlepool and, determined to do well, had some success alongside Peter Beardsley before returning to St James' Park. Signing for Wrexham, his third loan period of the season, during transfer deadline week, he came into the side against Wigan in the northern final second-leg tie of the Auto Windscreens game and produced a combative display, coupled with good passing ability. He then went on to prove a useful addition to the Racecourse staff, being rather similar to his predecessor, Dave Brammer.

Newcastle U (From trainee on 28/8/95)
Hull C (Loaned on 28/2/97) FL 3
Swindon T (Loaned on 20/2/98) FL 1+1
Gillingham (Loaned on 23/10/98) FL 4+1
Hartlepool U (Loaned on 29/1/99) FL 5
Wrexham (Loaned on 22/3/99) FL 8+1 Others 1

ELLIS Anthony (Tony) Joseph
Born: Salford, 20 October 1964
Height: 5'11" Weight: 11.0

Starting just three games for Bury in 1998-99, he seldom looked like being involved in manager Neil Warnock's plans, and had been on the transfer list for two months before he teamed up again with Gary Megson, this time at Stockport in early February. Had an immediate impact on a side struggling to find the net, scoring in vital wins over Crewe, Swindon, and Bolton, and playing a major role in County's best run of the season – six wins, four draws and two defeats from 12 games. His ability to hold the ball up and bring other players into the attack resulted in a more threatening looking side, and his experience bodes well for all the young forwards at Edgeley Park.

Oldham Ath (Free from Horwich RMI on 22/8/86) FL 5+3 FLC 1 Others 1
Preston NE (£23,000 on 16/10/87) FL 80+6/27 FLC 3 FAC 5 Others 11+1/5
Stoke C (£250,000 on 20/12/89) FL 66+11/19 FLC 5+1/1 FAC 1+4 Others 3+2
Preston NE (£140,000 on 14/8/92) FL 70+2/48 FLC 4/2 FAC 6/3 Others 6/3
Blackpool (£165,000 on 25/7/94) FL 140+6/55 FLC 10+1/6 FAC 7/1 Others 8/3
Bury (£75,000 on 12/12/97) FL 24+14/8 FLC 2+2
Stockport Co (£25,000 on 3/2/99) FL 16/6

Tony Ellis

ELLISON Anthony Lee
Born: Bishop Auckland, 13 January 1973
Height: 5'11" Weight: 12.3
Club Honours: Div 4 '91

After gaining a year's contract following his return to Darlington at the end of the 1997-98 season, Lee failed to re-establish himself as a regular in the first team in 1998-99 and made only three starts and 19 substitute appearances. A striker with a good eye for a goal, he was unable to add to his 23 for the Quakers and was released again during the summer.

Darlington (From trainee on 8/11/90) FL 54+18/17 FLC 2+1 FAC 4+2/2 Others 3+1/1
Hartlepool U (Loaned on 25/3/93) FL 3+1/1
Leicester C (Free on 12/8/94)
Crewe Alex (Free on 23/8/95) FL 3+1/2 FLC 1 Others 0+1 (Free to Halifax during 1996 close season)
Hereford U (Free on 11/10/96) FL 0+1 (Freed on 23/10/96)
Darlington (Signed from Bishop Auckland on 26/3/98) FL 7+21/3 Others 0+2

EMBERSON Carl Wayne
Born: Epsom, 13 July 1973
Height: 6'2" Weight: 14.7
Club Honours: FAYC '91

Carl left Colchester briefly in the 1998 close season after failing to agree terms, but fortunately signed up in time for pre-season and began 1998-99 as first-choice 'keeper once again. In the first half of the campaign, he made at least one top-class save in every match as the U's struggled to adjust to life at a higher level, until he was rather unluckily sent off at Fulham on Boxing Day. The

resulting suspension brought his unbroken run of appearances to an end, but he quickly regained his place with the change of managers, and stayed in the team until a broken finger in training ruled him out of the last six games. Was runner up in most of the "Player of the Year" awards and has now kept 49 clean sheets in his United career, which places him third behind Mike Walker (141) and Percy Ames (80).

Millwall (From trainee on 4/5/91) Others 1
Colchester U (Loaned on 17/12/92) FL 13
Colchester U (£25,000 on 6/7/94) FL 178+1 FLC 9 FAC 8 Others 16

EMBLEN Neil Robert
Born: Bromley, 19 June 1971
Height: 6'1" Weight: 13.11

Very much a utility player, Neil began last season in a central defensive role at Wolves, but any hopes of a more settled campaign were thwarted by an injury after two games, He did not start another match until 22 September, this time in a more advanced midfield role, and often tended to be the scapegoat when other players returned from injury. However, in December he got his first goal for the club since March 1996 after coming on as a sub to bundle in an equaliser against Bolton. After showing his flexibility by playing as a forward against Ipswich at Christmas, and doing well, in January he had the first suspension of his career, missing one game after receiving five bookings. Nevertheless, he gradually asserted himself in the team more, his determination and strong runs always stirring the crowd, and he scored with a neat headed goal at Barnsley. From then on, he was more effective in defence, playing in the last 11 matches.

Millwall (£175,000 from Sittingbourne on 8/11/93) FL 12 Others 1
Wolverhampton W (£600,000 on 14/7/94) FL 80+8/9 FLC 2+2/1 FAC 7+2 Others 2+1
Crystal Palace (£2,000,000 on 21/8/97) PL 8+5 FAC 1+1/2
Wolverhampton W (£900,000 on 26/3/98) FL 36+4/2 FLC 2+1 FAC 2

EMBLEN Paul David
Born: Bromley, 3 April 1976
Height: 5'11" Weight: 12.5

An end of August 1998 loan signing from Charlton, Paul, the brother of Neil at Wolves, immediately looked at home in his central midfield role at Wycombe, and signed permanently after a month at Adams Park. He was first choice until December when he fell out of favour with Neil Smillie, but was recalled in March under the new manager, Lawrie Sanchez, and played a crucial part in the club staying up. A fierce tackler with two good feet, he has incredible stamina and can spend the 90 minutes running everywhere on the pitch. This was exemplified in the penultimate game of the season, at home to Wigan, when his non-stop performance probably did most to secure the win. He also scored the winning goal in that match and, even more crucially, scored the only goal at Lincoln on the final day, a perfectly placed looping header seven minutes from time, which kept the club in Division Two.

Charlton Ath (£7,500 + from Tonbridge on 16/5/97) FL 0+4
Brighton & Hove A (Loaned on 4/11/97) FL 15/4
Wycombe W (£60,000 on 28/8/98) FL 28+7/2 FLC 2 FAC 2+1 Others 1

[EMERSON] THOME August
Born: Porto Alegre, Brazil, 30 March 1972
Height: 6'1" Weight: 13.4
What a great season 1998-99 was for Sheffield Wednesday's Brazilian-born stopper, his first complete one in England. Built along traditional English lines for his position, and possessing lots of skill on the ball, as well as good tackling capabilities, he formed a great partnership with the evergreen Des Walker, thus helping to make the Wednesday defence better than for many a year. A real "thinking" defender, "Emo" continued to impress the Wednesday crowd with his enthusiastic displays and penchant to enjoy his football. In the current football scene, there is no doubt, especially at Hillsborough, that he is one of the better "foreigners" to have hit these shores and Owls' fans would like to see him tied to the club in a long-term capacity.
Sheffield Wed (Free from Benfica on 23/3/98) PL 44/1 FLC 2 FAC 3/1

ERANIO Stefano
Born: Genoa, Italy, 29 December 1966
Height: 5'11" Weight: 12.2
International Honours: Italy: 20
The former Italian international right-sided Derby wing back, cum midfielder, had a frustrating 1998-99 season after a loss of form at the start of the campaign, followed by a succession of niggling injuries. This was after he had forced his way back into first-team contention. Prefers the greater involvement of the midfield role, where he displays an excellent understanding with fellow Italian, Francesco Baiano, while his excellent ball control and positional awareness can combine to play some delightful passes into space for the strikers to run onto. A great favourite of the home supporters, he scored just one goal, a penalty in the 3-0 FA Cup victory at Plymouth.
Derby Co (Free from AC Milan, via Genoa, on 15/7/97) PL 41+7/5 FLC 3 FAC 5/1

ETHERINGTON Craig
Born: Brentwood, 16 September 1979
Height: 6'0" Weight: 11.10
Yet to make his debut for West Ham, having been a professional since the 1997 close season, Craig joined Halifax for a loan spell last February. Although the young central midfielder's talent was there for all to see during his month's stay, an injury meant that he had to return to Upton Park earlier rather than later. However, he is an exciting prospect who should make a name for himself in the game.
West Ham U (From trainee on 9/7/97)
Halifax T (Loaned on 4/2/99) FL 4 Others 1

ETHERINGTON Matthew
Born: Truro, 14 August 1981
Height: 5'10" Weight: 11.2
International Honours: E: Yth
The jewel in the Peterborough side in 1998-99, having played three games in the previous campaign and signed professional forms during the summer of 1998, Matthew was supposedly the focus of a number of bids in the region of £2 million over the last 12 months. A fast, attacking, left-sided midfielder, who has quick feet, excellent control, and a powerful shot on him, his rapidly improving form saw him picked to play for England at U18 and U20 levels, and selected by his fellow professionals for the award-winning PFA Third Division side. The youngest ever to win this honour, despite being on the frail side he is rapidly filling out, and the fans cannot wait to see him in action this coming term.
Peterborough U (From trainee on 15/8/98) FL 24+8/3 FLC 0+1 FAC 0+1 Others 2

EUELL Jason Joseph
Born: Lambeth, 6 February 1977
Height: 6'0" Weight: 12.7
International Honours: E: U21-6
Voted by Wimbledon supporters as the most improved player in 1998-99, Jason has proved to be a talented and adaptable team member. At his most impressive in the first half of the season, when he put in some starring performances, he scored a brace of goals against Sheffield Wednesday and Coventry, where his all-round performances earned him rave reviews. Most definitely one for the future, his ten goals were also an excellent tally, especially considering the number of games he played in midfield. While there was no doubt that he was very effective playing in this area, passing with precision, making well-timed runs into danger areas, turning defenders inside out

with his quick feet and ball control, he is just as effective further forward. Having turned down offers to play for both Barbados and Jamaica, it is an England cap that he cherishes. Continued to be chosen at U21 level for England, picking up four more caps during the term.
Wimbledon (From trainee on 1/6/95) PL 53+15/18 FLC 9+2/3 FAC 6+5/1

EUSTACE Scott Douglas
Born: Leicester, 13 June 1975
Height: 6'0" Weight: 14.2
Released by Mansfield during the 1998 close season, Scott signed for Chesterfield in time for the start of 1998-99, but failed to make a first-team start, coming off the bench in a 3-0 Worthington Cup defeat at Leicester, before arriving at Cambridge early in the New Year. Reading the game well, the centre back deputised soundly for Marc Joseph in the middle of a solid defence, but needed a sustained performance to earn a contract for 1999-2000. Is currently on non-contract forms at the Abbey.
Leicester C (From trainee on 9/7/93) FL 0+1
Mansfield T (Free on 9/6/95) FL 90+8/6 FLC 3 FAC 5/1 Others 3+1
Chesterfield (Free on 7/8/98) FLC 0+1
Cambridge U (Free on 8/1/99) FL 15+1

EVANS Michael (Micky) James
Born: Plymouth, 1 January 1973
Height: 6'1" Weight: 13.4
International Honours: Ei: 1
Once again Micky's season was marred by injuries and he spent more time on the physio's couch than he did on the pitch at West Bromwich in 1998-99, being presented with the fictitious BUPA "Player of the

Jason Euell

Year" award by the club's physio, Nick Worth. A battler through and through, he did, however, have the pleasure of scoring Albion's goal in their 1-1 draw at Molineux against rivals and play-off chasing Wolves. Not only a strong, hard-running, pacy forward, he can be used with confidence on the wide right if required.

Plymouth Arg (From trainee on 30/3/91) FL 130+33/38 FLC 8+1 FAC 10+2/3 Others 10/2
Southampton (£500,000 on 4/3/97) PL 14+8/4 FLC 2+1/1
West Bromwich A (£750,000 on 27/10/97) FL 19+11/3 FLC 2/1 FAC 1+1

EVANS Nicholas (Nicky) Andrew
Born: Carmarthen, 12 May 1980
Height: 5'8" Weight: 12.5

A hard-working midfielder, and one of seven YTS players to be signed by Hartlepool as first-year professionals during the 1998 close season, less than a month into 1998-99 he was the first of this intake to win a place in the senior squad, making his debut when coming on as substitute in what was Hartlepool's first-ever televised game, a Friday night match at Halifax. It was a tough baptism, but, surprisingly, this was to be his only first-team appearance and he was forced to bide his time in the reserves. However, he has now been offered a short-term contract to prove his worth to the new manager, Chris Turner.

Hartlepool U (From trainee on 3/7/98) FL 0+1

EVANS Paul Simon
Born: Oswestry, 1 September 1974
Height: 5'8" Weight: 11.6
Club Honours: Div 3 '94, '99
International Honours: W: U21-4; Yth

A rarity, Paul was so grateful to Shrewsbury, who taught him his trade, that on being transferred to Brentford last March he chose to be "sold" rather than await a summer "Bosman". A strong tackler with a lethal shot, as Town's club captain and penalty taker, his had been the first name on the team sheet. Having scored nine goals for Town, including a Worthington Cup hat trick, the all-action midfielder was appointed captain on his arrival at Griffin Park and scored three times, a fine shot against Plymouth and a 40 yarder at Chester, and a 25-yard rocket against Swansea. Winning a championship medal first time round, he was also selected by his fellow professionals for the PFA award-winning Third Division side.

Shrewsbury T (From trainee on 2/7/93) FL 178+20/26 FLC 12+2/4 FAC 12+1/2 Others 12/4
Brentford (£110,000 on 3/3/99) FL 14/3

EVANS Stephen (Steve) James
Born: Caerphilly, 25 September 1980
Height: 6'1" Weight: 11.6
International Honours: W: Yth

Having come through Crystal Palace's junior ranks as a trainee before turning professional last October, Steve was given his first-team debut when coming off the bench in a 1-1 home draw against Birmingham in February. A tall left-sided winger with a Welsh international youth cap to his name, he impressed enough to be given further opportunities as a sub before the campaign ended. Is a young man you should be hearing more from.

Crystal Palace (From trainee on 31/10/98) FL 0+4

EVANS Thomas (Tommy) Raymond
Born: Doncaster, 31 December 1976
Height: 6'0" Weight: 13.2

Unlucky to be pipped by Tim Clarke as Scunthorpe's first choice at the start of last season, the goalie had to wait patiently until Boxing Day for his chance. Following that, he never looked back, with a string of clean sheets and performances that got better every game. Superb in one-on-one situations, and an excellent shot stopper, he could well play at a higher level.

Sheffield U (From trainee on 3/7/95)
Crystal Palace (Free on 14/6/96)
Scunthorpe U (Free on 22/8/97) FL 29 FLC 1 FAC 1 Others 2

EVANS Duncan Wayne
Born: Abermule, 25 August 1971
Height: 5'10" Weight: 12.5

Last season the consistency of Chris Marsh and Neil Pointon limited Wayne's first-team opportunities at Walsall, but he deputised at various times for both, and was his usual wholehearted self in the 13 games in which he was called upon. Released during the summer, he is still a strong tackler who can operate on either side at the back, and was a good man to have at the club.

Walsall (Free from Welshpool on 13/8/93) FL 173+10/1 FLC 14+1/1 FAC 15+1 Others 12+3

EVERS Sean Anthony
Born: Hitchin, 10 October 1977
Height: 5'9" Weight: 9.11

A busy, bustling midfielder who moves the ball quickly from defence to attack, and is not afraid to shoot, Sean had hoped that in turning down the Republic of Ireland's offer of an U21 cap would lead to a call up for England at the same level, but it was not to be. After starting 1998-99 in good form at Luton, missing just one of the opening 38 games, and playing for the Nationwide U21 side in Terni – and scoring – against their Italian counterparts, he left the Hatters to sign for Reading in transfer deadline week. However, due to a series of injuries, he was unable to make his debut until coming on as a second-half sub in the final game of the campaign, at Oldham, and hopes to be one of the first names on the team sheet in 1999-2000.

Luton T (From trainee on 16/5/96) FL 43+9/6 FLC 9/1 FAC 2 Others 6
Reading (£500,000 on 25/3/99) FL 0+1

EYJOLFSSON Sigurdur (Siggi)
Born: Iceland, 1 December 1973
Height: 6'2" Weight: 12.0

Signed by Walsall from IF Akranes (Iceland) last January, he made his debut when going on as a substitute for Jason Brissett in the 1-0 win at Northampton in February, scored his first goal in the last minute of the Auto Windscreens southern final against Millwall, and seconds later almost pulled the tie out of the fire with another fine effort which was saved by the goalkeeper. Despite scoring the vital third goal in the unforgettable promotion-winning game against Oldham the tall forward has yet to make a full appearance. Although a great favourite with Bescot fans he returned home on 11 May.

Walsall (Free from IF Akranes on 27/1/99) FL 0+10/1 Others 0+1/1

EYRE John Robert
Born: Hull, 9 October 1974
Height: 6'0" Weight: 12.7

1998-99 was John's best season at Scunthorpe, with him given a new role wide on the right. Very direct with superb skills he tormented opposition defences by running at them, and also had his best campaign in terms of scoring goals, many spectacular strikes being from long distance. Suffered from a recurrent hamstring injury at one stage, which forced him to be rested for selected games in the run-in, but he was always a first choice when fit. Scored his first Football League hat trick, against Brighton, in March, before being sent off in the home play-off game against Swansea and missing out on a Wembley appearance through suspension. Stop Press: Joined Hull City on 7 June under the Bosman ruling.

Oldham Ath (From trainee on 16/7/93) P/FL 4+6/1 FLC 0+2
Scunthorpe U (Loaned on 15/12/94) FL 9/8
Scunthorpe U (£40,000 on 4/7/95) FL 151+13/43 FLC 9/2 FAC 12/3 Others 8+1/3

EYRE Richard Paul
Born: Poynton, 15 September 1976
Height: 5'11" Weight: 11.6

A promising Port Vale right winger who waited patiently for his first-team chance, having risen through the junior ranks, he made his full debut at Queens Park Rangers in 1998-99 but, despite doing quite well, he had to wait another five months for his next appearance, by which time Brian Horton had taken over as manager. A pacy player, with bags of enthusiasm, he occupied a wing-back role in some games in the run-in towards the end of the season.

Port Vale (From trainee on 29/6/95) FL 8+4

EYRES David
Born: Liverpool, 26 February 1964
Height: 5'11" Weight: 11.8

Now at the veteran stage, David continued to give good service on Preston's left flank in 1998-99, despite missing a total of 16 matches through two bad injuries. He made his 50th appearance for North End in October, and scored against his former club, Burnley, in the next match. Earlier in the season, he demonstrated his awareness when volleying a poor clearance back past the Reading 'keeper from near the halfway line, one of several goals scored during the campaign. And, as well as being an attacking force, he also provided admirable defensive back up, as befits a former wing back.

Blackpool (£10,000 from Rhyl on 15/8/89) FL 147+11/38 FLC 11+1/1 FAC 11/2 Others 13+2/4
Burnley (£90,000 on 29/7/93) FL 171+4/37 FLC 17/7 FAC 14/8 Others 9/3
Preston NE (£80,000 on 29/10/97) FL 59+3/12 FLC 2 FAC 5/2 Others 5/3

we've
isolated
the

childhood
leukaemia

family **cancer**

survival
rate

major
new

of
cancer *drug* **testicular**
cancer
registered **cured**

eac*h* **year**

but

others like Harry still
need your *help*

people now
successfully

You can help The Cancer Research Campaign in many ways – to find out more please contact us.

research cures cancer
research needs money

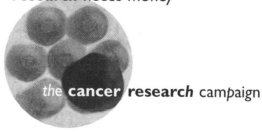

the **cancer research** campaign

10 Cambridge Terrace, London, NW1 4JL 020 7224 1333 www.crc.org.uk

FACEY Delroy Michael
Born: Huddersfield, 22 April 1980
Height: 5'11" Weight: 13.10
Every club up and down the country had a young talent waiting to burst onto the scene in 1998-99 and Huddersfield were no different. In Town's case it was Delroy. A fast-developing teenager who had already impressed in pre-season, Delroy came off the bench on the opening day at Bury and, in the following weeks, showed enough to be recognised by the England selectors at U18 level. He rejoined first-team action in November, having been laid up with a minor injury, and scored his first goal, at Barnsley, before repeating the act in the 4-0 demolition of Crystal Palace. Always a handful in the air, with pace and power on the ground, he was often released from the subs' bench late in a game to damage a tiring opposition defence. If he continues to improve at the same rate, it's only a matter of time!
Huddersfield T (From trainee on 13/5/97) FL 7+19/3 FAC 0+2

FAIRCLOUGH Courtney (Chris) Huw
Born: Nottingham, 12 April 1964
Height: 5'11" Weight: 11.7
Club Honours: Div 2 '90, Div 1 '92, '97; CS '92
International Honours: E: B-1; U21-7
A highly experienced central defender who developed across the River Trent at Nottingham Forest, while his younger brother joined Notts County, Chris is a talented defender who found it difficult at first to adjust to the Division Two heavyweights after leaving Bolton during the 1998 close season. Having made just 19 starts for County, he was loaned to York in mid March and produced some outstanding performances for them. Returning at the end of the season vowing to fight for his place in his hometown, his skill and organising ability was a big factor in York pulling clear of the relegation zone.
Nottingham F (From apprentice on 12/10/81) FL 102+5/1 FLC 9+1/1 FAC 6 Others 9+2
Tottenham H (£387,000 on 3/7/87) FL 60/5 FLC 7 FAC 3
Leeds U (£500,000 on 23/3/89) FL 187+6/21 FLC 17+2/2 FAC 14+1 Others 14
Bolton W (£500,000 on 4/7/95) F/PL 89+1/8 FLC 11 FAC 5
Notts Co (Free on 30/7/98) FL 16/1 FLC 2 FAC 1
York C (Loaned on 17/3/99) FL 11

FARLEY Adam John
Born: Liverpool, 12 January 1980
Height: 6'1" Weight: 10.11
Club Honours: FAYC '98
Another product of Everton's impressive youth set-up, Adam is a tall, powerful central defender. An FA Youth Cup winner at the end of the previous season, he made just one appearance in the Premiership during 1998-99, as a substitute at Derby, and will be

hoping for plenty more opportunities in 1999-2000.
Everton (From trainee on 16/2/98) PL 0+1

FARRELL Andrew (Andy) James
Born: Colchester, 7 October 1965
Height: 5'11" Weight: 12.3
Club Honours: Div 4 '92
Rochdale's veteran utility man again figured in central defence and in midfield roles in 1998-99, playing his 500th league game just after the start of the season. Losing his place briefly, when Dale adopted a new system, Andy was soon pressed back into service again as one of the three-centre backs when injuries and suspensions hit the regular trio, and he performed with his customary steadiness. He also appeared at full back towards the end of the campaign, before being released in the summer.
Colchester U (From apprentice on 21/9/83) FL 98+7/5 FLC 9 FAC 8 Others 6
Burnley (£13,000 on 7/8/87) FL 237+20/19 FLC 17+4/1 FAC 19+2 Others 27+3/3
Wigan Ath (£20,000 on 22/9/94) FL 51+3/1 FLC 3 FAC 4+1 Others 5/1
Rochdale (Free on 3/7/96) FL 113+5/6 FLC 6 FAC 5+1 Others 5

FARRELL David (Dave) William
Born: Birmingham, 11 November 1971
Height: 5'10" Weight: 11.9
Asked to play a little deeper for Peterborough last season, Dave still managed to give opposing defenders the run-around on occasions, his mazy, pacy, left-sided runs often taking him into the danger areas, where he looked to score more than he ultimately did. After starting the opening match, at home to Halifax, he then spent quite some time on the bench before coming back with a goal in a 2-0 home win over Rochdale, and notching three more, including the winner at London Road against Mansfield, before the campaign came to an end. With good feet and excellent crossing ability, he is yet another Posh player the scouts are looking at with interest.
Aston Villa (£45,000 from Redditch U on 6/1/92) F/PL 5+1 FLC 2
Scunthorpe U (Loaned on 25/1/93) FL 4+1/1 Others 2
Wycombe W (£100,000 on 14/9/95) FL 44+16/6 FLC 6 FAC 3+2 Others 2
Peterborough U (Free on 21/7/97) FL 68+11/10 FLC 4+1/1 FAC 4 Others 5/1

FARRELL Sean Paul
Born: Watford, 28 February 1969
Height: 6'0" Weight: 13.7
Club Honours: Div 3 '98
Having established an excellent strike partnership with Gary Jones at Notts County in 1997-98, Sean started off well enough last season, scoring two goals on the opening day against Oldham, before being hampered by a string of unlucky injuries which led him to spend the vast majority of the campaign on the sidelines. When fit, he is dangerous in any penalty area, with his height and strength being of great advantage, and is a hard-working, selfless target man who always puts the team first.
Luton T (From apprentice on 5/3/87) FL 14+11/1 FAC 2+1/1 Others 1+2/2

Colchester U (Loaned on 1/3/88) FL 4+5/1
Northampton T (Loaned on 13/9/91) FL 4/1
Fulham (£100,000 on 19/12/91) FL 93+1/31 FLC 5+1/3 FAC 2/3 Others 8/1
Peterborough U (£120,000 on 5/8/94) FL 49+17/20 FLC 4+2/1 FAC 4+1/3 Others 3+1/1
Notts Co (£80,000 on 14/10/96) FL 49+11/19 FLC 2 FAC 6/1 Others 1

FARRELLY Gareth
Born: Dublin, 28 August 1975
Height: 6'0" Weight: 13.0
International Honours: Ei: 5; B-1; U21-11; Yth; Sch
Despite being the man whose spectacular goal kept Everton in the Premiership on the final day of 1997-98, Gareth figured for just 13 minutes of an intensely frustrating 1998-99 campaign. That fleeting appearance came as a substitute against Leeds, although a knee injury which required exploratory surgery later on did not help his claims. The left-sided midfielder with full international experience, the young Irishman simply didn't figure in Walter Smith's plans and was made available for transfer during the summer.
Aston Villa (From trainee on 21/1/92) PL 2+6 FLC 0+1
Rotherham U (Loaned on 21/3/95) FL 9+1/2
Everton (£700,000 + on 9/7/97) PL 18+9/1 FLC 1/1 FAC 1

FAULCONBRIDGE Craig Michael
Born: Nuneaton, 20 April 1978
Height: 6'1" Weight: 13.0
The rangy Coventry forward was given his first taste of senior English football with a loan move to Third Division strugglers, Hull City, last December until the end of the season. Quick and mobile for a tall lad, Craig struggled to adapt to the rough and tumble of the basement grade, and it was notable that his most impressive performance was arguably in the FA Cup-tie at Aston Villa.
Coventry C (From trainee on 5/7/96)
Dunfermline Ath (Loaned on 27/3/98) SL 1+12/1 SLC 0+1
Hull C (Loaned on 18/12/98) FL 4+6 FAC 1 Others 1+1

FEAR Peter Stanley
Born: Sutton, 10 September 1973
Height: 5'10" Weight: 11.7
International Honours: E: U21-3
A local lad, Peter's appearances – two from the bench and one start – for Wimbledon in 1998-99 were few and far between due to injury and strong competition for places in the midfield and defensive areas. Despite being popular with Dons' fans, and providing good support for the younger players coming through the ranks, he was released during the summer. As a player who tackles and cuts down an opponent's space well, and who can also create chances for others, he should have no difficulty in finding another team.
Wimbledon (From trainee on 2/7/92) PL 51+22/4 FLC 9+2/1 FAC 4

FENN Neale Michael Charles
Born: Edmonton, 18 January 1977
Height: 5'10" Weight: 12.6
International Honours: Ei: B-1; U21-7; Yth
Unable to grasp anything at Spurs in 1998-99, Neale was loaned to Swindon

(November) and Lincoln (December) in an effort to keep him match fit. Although finding life difficult in the First Division with Swindon, playing four games, he fared better at Lincoln, and made a promising debut in the Auto Windscreens Shield against Mansfield. Subsequently used only as an occasional substitute during the extended term, despite making appearances for the Republic of Ireland "B" team, he earned the praise of the Lincoln coaching staff who described him as the most skilful striker on the club's books. A player who is recognised for his ability to twist and turn around the box, being especially difficult to mark when he has his back to the defenders, while possessing vision and skill in abundance, the Premiership seems to be passing him by.

Tottenham H (From trainee on 1/7/95) PL 0+8 FAC 2/1
Leyton Orient (Loaned on 30/1/98) FL 3
Norwich C (Loaned on 26/3/98) FL 6+1/1
Swindon T (Loaned on 13/11/98) P/FL 4
Lincoln C (Loaned on 31/12/98) FL 0+4 Others 1

FENTON Graham Anthony
Born: Wallsend, 22 May 1974
Height: 5'10" Weight: 12.10
Club Honours: FLC '94, '96
International Honours: E: U21-1

As a Leicester right-sided striker, and occasional midfielder, Graham started last season by damaging ankle ligaments in the opening reserve fixture, and then struggled to force his way into regular contention, though he did have a run as replacement for the injured Tony Cottee during November. Sadly, his opportunity coincided with a general dip in team form, and thereafter his chances were confined to the occasional run out as substitute, his only goal of the campaign coming in the Worthington Cup victory at Chesterfield that set the Foxes on the road to Wembley.

Aston Villa (From trainee on 13/2/92) PL 16+16/3 FLC 2+5
West Bromwich A (Loaned on 10/1/94) FL 7/3
Blackburn Rov (£1,500,000 on 7/11/95) PL 9+18/7 FLC 0+2 FAC 0+1
Leicester C (£1,100,000 on 8/8/97) PL 12+20/3 FLC 2+1/1 FAC 0+1 Others 0+2

FENTON Nicholas (Nicky) Leonard
Born: Preston, 23 November 1979
Height: 5'10" Weight: 10.4
International Honours: E: Yth

Made his Manchester City first-team debut in the Worthington Cup against Notts County last season and gave a mature performance. This was followed with a further 15 league and cup games. Showing confident skill, and working for Gerard Wiekens very well in the centre, his style was nicely composed and he did not make rash moves in playing the ball out of defence. Has acquired noticeable skill with the long ball, which showed up particularly in the home game with Walsall when he crossed for Shaun Goater to head in. Although the second half of the season saw Nicky left out of the squad primarily as not to rush him, he is certainly a player for the future, and was selected for the England U18 side that met Israel.

Manchester C (From trainee on 26/11/96) FL 15 FLC 3 Others 1

FERDINAND Leslie (Les)
Born: Acton, 8 December 1966
Height: 5'11" Weight: 13.5
Club Honours: FLC '99
International Honours: E: 17; B-1

Strong in the air, and a powerful striker of the ball, Les had an indifferent season at Tottenham in 1998-99, which was also hampered by injury. When at his best, he commanded the attack, was always first to the ball from the kick out, and used his knowledge of the game to spread the play wide and then position himself on the box ready for the return ball. With only a disappointing five goals tally throughout the campaign, he looked to be losing confidence in his abilities, which often resulted in him taking the ball an extra yard in a bid to be clearer on goal, as opposed to unleashing one of his trademark drives that had brought such great success for him at Newcastle. Still able to finish clinically though, he showed his goalscoring prowess in the 1-0 early season away victory over Everton, and again in the 4-1 return leg at home in December. With speculation of a close season move being reported, he returned from injury in the final game to stake his claim for a place in 1999-2000 with an exquisite opener in the title decider against Manchester United. Looking sharp and pacy going forward, whilst strong and committed when tracking back, an in-form Les is undoubtedly an asset from which Tottenham could still benefit, but he still has more to prove to his new boss, George Graham.

Queens Park R (£15,000 from Hayes on 12/3/87) F/PL 152+11/80 FLC 11+2/7 FAC 6+1/3 Others 1
Brentford (Loaned on 24/3/88) FL 3
Newcastle U (£6,000,000 on 7/6/95) PL 67+1/41 FLC 6/3 FAC 4+1/2 Others 5/4
Tottenham H (£6,000,000 on 5/8/97) PL 41+4/10 FLC 3+2 FAC 8+1

FERDINAND Rio Gavin
Born: Peckham, 7 November 1978
Height: 6'2" Weight: 12.1
International Honours: E: 8; U21-4; Yth

In 1998-99, the young West Ham central defender continued his progress to show a maturity beyond his years, being outstanding throughout the campaign while becoming a regular in the England squad. "Man of the Match" on any number of occasions, and a big favourite at Upton Park, he is not a "clear-at-all-costs" type but a player who brings the ball out of defence well, and has excellent distribution to match. He seems a resilient type as well. Despite picking up a groin problem after just three games which, at the time, was thought might have to be cured by surgery, and then injuring ankle ligaments in the 0-0 draw at Aston Villa towards the end of the season, on both occasions he was back three games later. A superb natural talent, his manager, Harry Redknapp, enthuses over his ability, and many good judges in the game feel that if he continues to improve at the rate he has thus far, he will be head and shoulders above the competition. Also, in this day and age of red cards, Rio is a very fair-minded defender, and is rarely seen making rash tackles. Is the cousin of Tottenham's Les Ferdinand.

West Ham U (From trainee on 27/11/95) PL 77+5/2 FLC 6+1 FAC 8
Bournemouth (Loaned on 8/11/96) FL 10 Others 1

FERGUSON Darren
Born: Glasgow, 9 February 1972
Height: 5'10" Weight: 11.10
Club Honours: PL '93
International Honours: S: U21-5; Yth

The son of Manchester United's manager, Alex, and a neat passing Wolves' midfielder, he was not involved in the first nine games of 1998-99 before coming on as a sub at Bournemouth and promptly equalising. He began matches on 17 and 20 October but, unfortunately, Wolves lost them both, and in the autumn he had a trial with the Italian club, Cosenza. However, their supporters were unhappy about the departure of the coach, rioting on the day Darren arrived, and he quickly returned to the midlands before going on loan to Sparta Rotterdam early in 1999.

Manchester U (From trainee on 11/7/90) F/PL 20+7 FLC 2+1
Wolverhampton W (£250,000 on 13/1/94) FL 94+23/4 FLC 13+2/3 FAC 9+2/3 Others 6

Duncan Ferguson

FERGUSON Duncan
Born: Stirling, 27 December 1971
Height: 6'4" Weight: 14.6
Club Honours: SL '94; SLC '94; FAC '95
International Honours: S: 7; B; U21-7; Yth; Sch

Duncan is a tall, quick, physically strong and fearless centre forward of the old school who had become an idol of the Goodison crowd, so much so that unrest following his signing for Newcastle led to the resignation of Everton chairman, Peter Johnson. His formidable power in the air makes him a excellent target man, and he is essentially a team player who is excellent at holding up the

ball and using his mobility, while his deceptively good first touch with his left foot creates space and scoring opportunities for colleagues. He scored twice on his debut against Wimbledon, and much was anticipated of his partnership with Alan Shearer. Unfortunately, the "Toon Army" is still waiting to see this pairing establish itself as Alan was injured at the time of Duncan's arrival and then, just as he was returning to full fitness, having played twice alongside Duncan, the latter suffered a recurrence of a long-standing groin problem when he tore a muscle against Liverpool in December, that necessitated an operation which sidelined him for over three months. Although not fully match fit, he returned to a great ovation as a late substitute in the FA Cup semi final, where his presence helped turn the game in Newcastle's favour, and it was his pass for Gary Speed which Sol Campbell handled to concede a vital penalty. Unable to play again until May, on the eve of the FA Cup Final, in which he appeared as a second-half sub, it was determined that he needed an adducton muscle operation during the summer. Having retired from international football during 1997-98, since his signing for Newcastle the Scottish manager, Craig Brow, has intimated that the door remains ajar with a return to the national side not ruled out. However, Duncan has, as yet, to respond.

Dundee U (Signed from Carse Thistle on 1/2/90) SL 75+2/27 SLC 2+1/2 SC 6/4
Glasgow R (£4,000,000 on 20/7/93) SL 8+6/2 SLC 2+2/3 SC 0+3 Others 1
Everton (£4,400,000 on 4/10/94) PL 110+6/38 FLC 8/1 FAC 8+1/4
Newcastle U (£7,000,000 + on 25/11/98) PL 7/2 FAC 0+2

FERNANDES Tamer Hasan
Born: Paddington, 7 December 1974
Height: 6'3" Weight: 13.7
International Honours: E: Yth

A patient deputy to first-choice goalkeeper Carl Emberson at Colchester in 1998-99, Tamer's big chance finally arrived in the New Year when he was selected for three games around the time of Emberson's suspension. Returned to the team for the closing stages of the season, and was delighted to finally be in a winning team, against Notts County in mid April. Indeed, he was seen to be praying to Allah as Warren Aspinall scored the late, winning penalty – before being released during the summer.

Brentford (From trainee on 12/7/93) FL 10+2 FAC 2 Others 2+1
Colchester U (Signed on 29/1/98) FL 8

FERRARESI Fabio
Born: Fano, Italy, 24 May 1979
Height: 5'9" Weight: 11.2

A young Italian who was signed from Cesena early on in 1998-99, Fabio soon became a regular in Aston Villa's reserve side, featuring as an attack-minded central midfielder, and sat on the first-team bench a number of times to give him experience of the big occasion. Only once used, he came on in the away leg of the first round UEFA Cup match against Stromgodset, and will be looking for further opportunities this coming term.

Aston Villa (Free from Cesena on 19/8/98) Others 0+1

FERRER Albert Llopes
Born: Barcelona, Spain, 6 June 1970
Height: 5'7" Weight: 10.6
Club Honours: ESC '98
International Honours: Spain: 35

To bolster their defensive strength, Chelsea swooped on Spain's Chantilly training camp to sign this experienced, tough-tackling right back on the eve of the 1998 World Cup. A native Catalan, who had been with his local club, Barcelona, for 15 years, Albert had been highly successful, winning five Spanish Liga titles, the Spanish Cup, plus European Cup-Winners' Cups. Incredibly, he became the third Olympic gold medallist on Chelsea's books in 1998-99, along with Celestine Babayaro and Dmitri Kharine. He was an automatic choice for Spain under Javier Clemente, and Chelsea beat off a host of European rivals to lure him away from the Nou Camp after he became a casualty of Louis van Gaal's Dutch "revolution". Having settled into English football immediately, his third match for Chelsea brought victory in the European Super Cup over his old nemesis from Spain, Real Madrid. A fast, reliable full back who is very confident on the ball going forward, he is a key member of Chelsea's revamped back four which provided the club's best defensive record for many years. He also proved himself to be one of the top right backs in the Premiership, subduing almost every winger he faced and, his acquisition was one of the transfer coups of the season.

Chelsea (£2,200,000 from Barcelona on 15/8/98) PL 30 FLC 0+1 FAC 2 Others 8

FERRI Jean-Michel
Born: Lyon, France, 7 February 1969
Height: 6'1" Weight: 13.4
International Honours: France: 5

Signed from Istanbulspor last December, the Frenchman had to bide his time at Anfield before making his debut for Liverpool in a 2-1 defeat at Chelsea. Stamford Bridge is not an easy place these days for an initiation and, in coming on for Paul Ince after 48 minutes, that was certainly the case. However, reserve football showed him to be a classy defender, cum midfielder, and he should get further opportunities in the coming campaign as Gerard Houllier examines his side further.

Liverpool (£1,500,000 + from Istanbulspor, via FC Nantes, on 4/12/98) PL 0+2

FESTA Gianluca
Born: Cagliari, Italy, 15 March 1969
Height: 6'0" Weight: 13.6

A brilliant, adventure-seeking, tough-tackling, no-nonsense Middlesbrough stopper in the mould of so many classic defenders in the English way, the only difference is that Gianluca believes he can get back to cover his lines from the forages he makes deep into hostile territory. Despite the defence being left floundering with a man short at the back occasionally, his performances in 1998-99 won him many new admirers, a few "Man of the Match" awards, a handful of goals, and a

fistful of yellow cards from unsympathetic referees. Nevertheless, he is still a firm favourite with the fans.

Middlesbrough (£2,700,000 from Inter Milan, via Cagliari, on 18/1/97) P/FL 76/5 FLC 13/1 FAC 7/1

FETTIS Alan William
Born: Belfast, 1 February 1971
Height: 6'1" Weight: 12.10
International Honours: NI: 25; B-3; Yth; Sch

Although only playing two first-team games for Blackburn in 1998-99, when both Tim Flowers and John Filan were injured, he did not concede a goal and contributed two good saves from free kicks in the game against Charlton. Disappointingly, the lack of senior football cost him his place with Northern Ireland, and towards the end of the season he struggled with a chipped bone in his hand. At his best, Alan is an excellent shot stopper who is both brave and agile.

Hull C (£50,000 from Ards on 14/8/91) FL 131+4/2 FLC 7+1 FAC 5 Others 7
West Bromwich A (Loaned on 20/11/95) FL 3
Nottingham F (£250,000 on 13/1/96) PL 4 FLC 1 FAC 0+1
Blackburn Rov (£300,000 on 12/9/97) PL 9+1 FAC 1

FICKLING Ashley Spencer
Born: Sheffield, 15 November 1972
Height: 5'10" Weight: 11.6
International Honours: E: Sch

Signed from Grimsby, when Ashley joined Scunthorpe in the summer of 1998 many thought he was to be a squad player, but he was a regular over the first three quarters of the season, playing at right back or as one of three central defenders. A solid if unspectacular defender, he scored an own goal on his debut against Shrewsbury, and could count himself unlucky to be omitted for the closing two months of the campaign. Out of contract during the summer, it was reported that the Iron had offered him terms of re-engagement.

Sheffield U (From juniors on 26/7/91) FLC 2+1 Others 3
Darlington (Loaned on 26/11/92) FL 14 Others 1
Darlington (Loaned on 12/8/93) FL 1 FLC 1
Grimsby T (Free on 23/3/95) FL 26+13/2 FLC 2+1 FAC 2+1
Darlington (Loaned on 26/3/98) FL 8
Scunthorpe U (Free on 24/7/98) FL 28+1 FLC 2 FAC 2 Others 2

FILAN John Richard
Born: Sydney, Australia, 8 February 1970
Height: 5'11" Weight: 13.2
International Honours: Australia: 1

Commencing 1998-99 in Blackburn's first team because Tim Flowers was suspended, the Australian goalie was unlucky to have to stand down immediately. In November he had to deputise for the latter, who was injured, and the new manager, Brian Kidd, stood by him even when Flowers was fit. By that time John had been little short of brilliant with an epic showing against Leeds, when the team was down to ten men, and another incredible display at Highbury. Superbly agile on the line, he saved two penalties, and was decisive when leaving his goal to punch.

Not short of confidence, he also managed to pick up three yellow cards.

Cambridge U (£40,000 from Budapest St George on 12/3/93) FL 68 FLC 6 FAC 3 Others 3
Coventry C (£300,000 on 2/3/95) PL 15+1 FLC 2
Blackburn Rov (£700,000 on 10/7/97) PL 33 FLC 2 FAC 4

FINNAN Stephen (Steve) John
Born: Limerick, 20 April 1976
Height: 5'10" Weight: 11.6
Club Honours: Div 3 '98; Div 2 '99
International Honours: Ei: B-1; U21-8

A very talented winger who was always popular with the Notts County fans, being both speedy and tricky down the flanks, Steve could also play well as a right-wing back. However, the chance of football in a higher division eventually led him to leave Meadow Lane for Fulham last November, and he started with his new club in the right-wing-back slot where his runs and crosses brought several goals. With Kevin Keegan wanting to try him out in central midfield, the opportunity arose with the loan signing of Jamie Smith from Crystal Palace, and he backed up his manager's judgement with several excellent performances in the latter matches. Winning a Second Division championship medal as the Fulham revival continued, it is not often that a player wins championship medals in successive seasons with different clubs, but he did. Also selected by his peers for the PFA award-winning divisional side.

Birmingham C (£100,000 from Welling U on 12/6/95) FL 9+6/1 FLC 2+2 Others 2+1
Notts Co (Loaned on 5/3/96) FL 14+3/2 Others 3/1
Notts Co (£300,000 on 31/10/96) FL 71+9/5 FLC 4 FAC 7/1 Others 1
Fulham (£600,000 on 13/11/98) FL 21+1/2 FAC 4 Others 1

FINNEY Stephen (Steve) Kenneth
Born: Hexham, 31 October 1973
Height: 5'10" Weight: 12.8
Club Honours: Div 2 '96

Released by Swindon, this skilful forward returned to his native Cumbria in the 1998 close season but took a while to get into his stride at Carlisle in 1998-99. His best performances came in the New Year, when he took over the number nine shirt and netted several times in this spell. His goal at Darlington in March was the 4000th league goal in United's history, but it also proved to be his swansong – signing for Leyton Orient just two days later. Joining the O's as cover for Steve Watts and Amara Simba, having scored against Orient earlier in the season, he impressed Tommy Taylor with his running and ability on the ball, and was unfortunate not to play more. Was released during the summer.

Preston NE (From trainee on 2/5/92) FL 1+5/1 FAC 0+1 Others 1+1
Manchester C (Free on 12/2/93)
Swindon T (Free on 15/6/95) FL 47+26/18 FLC 6+1/1 FAC 2+5/2 Others 2+1/1
Cambridge U (Loaned on 10/10/97) FL 4+3/2
Carlisle U (Free on 3/7/98) FL 22+11/6 FLC 1+1 FAC 1 Others 2
Leyton Orient (Free on 25/3/99) FL 2+3

FINNIGAN John Francis
Born: Wakefield, 29 March 1976
Height: 5'8" Weight: 10.11

A central midfield player who was one of Lincoln's successes in what proved to be a disappointing season for the club in 1998-99, John had spent the last few weeks of 1997-98 on loan at Sincil Bank before the move became permanent in the 1998 close season. He proved effective both as a ball winner and a creator of chances, and netted his first goal for the club to earn a valuable point at Burnley in December. However, injury forced him out of several games in the second half of the campaign, and his influence was badly missed.

Nottingham F (From trainee on 10/5/93)
Lincoln C (£50,000 on 26/3/98) FL 42+1/1 FLC 2 FAC 3/1 Others 1

FISH Mark Anthony
Born: Capetown, South Africa, 14 March 1974
Height: 6'3" Weight: 13.2
International Honours: South Africa: 46

A tower of strength at the heart of the Bolton defence in 1998-99, Mark had an excellent season, starting the campaign full of confidence, having appeared in all three of South Africa's games in the 1998 World Cup. Although his skill and experience marshalled the Trotters' rearguard superbly in the early stages of the term, unpleasant club versus country wrangles did not help his cause, and he frequently had to make energy sapping trips around the globe to play in the African Nations Cup. Despite this, he always returned as swiftly as possible to fight for the Bolton cause. Although he did not score as many goals as he would have liked (his overhead kick at Swindon being particularly memorable), you can bet that he will feature on the scoresheet at some stage during the coming season, due to his trademark pacy, probing runs up field whenever the chance arises.

Bolton W (£2,500,000 from Lazio, via Orlando Pirates, on 16/9/97) P/FL 58/3 FLC 6 FAC 2 Others 3

FISHER Neil John
Born: St Helens, 7 November 1970
Height: 5'10" Weight: 11.0

After being released on a free transfer at the end of 1997-98, Neil found himself back at Chester on a non-contract basis on transfer deadline day last March, having been at Bangor City in the interim. Still a skilful midfield player, after making seven appearances for City he will no doubt be looking to return to league football on a more permanent basis.

Bolton W (From trainee on 12/7/89) FL 17+7/1 FLC 4 FAC 1
Chester C (Free on 5/6/95) FL 91+17/4 FLC 8 FAC 6 Others 3 (Released during 1998 close season)
Chester C (Free from Bangor C on 25/3/99) FL 7+1

FITZGERALD Scott Brian
Born: Westminster, 13 August 1969
Height: 6'0" Weight: 12.12
International Honours: Ei: B-1; U21-4

After suffering injury problems throughout the 1997-98 campaign, Scott started last season well, and was a regular in the Millwall defence for 30 continuous matches before

injury and suspension sidelined him. Then, after the appearance of Joe Dolan, he found it hard to get back into the first team, and must have been bitterly disappointed not to appear at Wembley in the Auto Windscreens Shield. A good reader of the game, this central defender is effective in the air, very difficult to get round, and is strong in the challenge. Hopefully, he will be back to his best in 1999-2000.

Wimbledon (From trainee on 13/7/89) F/PL 95+11/1 FLC 13 FAC 5 Others 1
Sheffield U (Loaned on 23/11/95) FL 6
Millwall (Loaned on 11/10/96) FL 7
Millwall (£50,000 + on 28/7/97) FL 48+2/1 FLC 3 FAC 1 Others 4

FITZHENRY Neil
Born: Wigan, 24 September 1978
Height: 6'0" Weight: 12.3

A former young player of the year at Wigan, Neil's 1998-99 season was dogged by injuries, which included surgery on his lateral ligament. An old-style centre back, hard tackling and enthusiastic, his only start in an Athletic shirt came in the home match against Preston. Sadly, a recurrence of the knee problem saw him last only 12 minutes, thus forcing him to miss the rest of the campaign.

Wigan Ath (From trainee on 4/7/97) FL 2+2 Others 1

FITZPATRICK Trevor Joseph James
Born: Frimley, 19 February 1980
Height: 6'1" Weight: 12.10
International Honours: Ei: Yth

Trevor forced his way into first-team reckoning early in 1998-99, showing a knack for being in the right place at the right time in front of goal. Rewarded for his efforts when winning Republic of Ireland U19 honours, good coaching will polish the goalscorers skill he obviously possesses. A product of the Southend youth system, and a first-year professional, he is one to watch for in 1999-2000.

Southend U (From trainee on 6/7/98) FL 8+18/5 FLC 1+2 FAC 0+1

FJORTOFT Jan-Aage
Born: Aalesund, Norway, 10 January 1967
Height: 6'3" Weight: 14.2
International Honours: Norway: 72

A striker with good control and an eye for a goal, Jan-Aage was not happy when it became obvious that he was not going to be a regular first choice at Barnsley in 1998-99, and he spent some time on the transfer list early in the campaign. However, back in the side he soon showed he had lost none of his natural goalscoring instinct when given a run, netting six times before losing his place when the manager brought in Bruce Dyer. Was transferred to Eintracht Frankfurt (Germany) on 26 November 1998 for £450,000.

Swindon T (£500,000 from Rapid Vienna, via Hamar and Lillestrom, on 29/7/93) P/FL 62+10/28 FLC 9/9 FAC 3+1/2 Others 1+1
Middlesbrough (£1,300,000 on 31/3/95) P/FL 37+4/10 FLC 7/2 FAC 0+2/1
Sheffield U (£700,000 on 31/1/97) FL 30+4/19 FLC 2+1/1 FAC 1+1/2 Others 3/1
Barnsley (£800,000 on 16/1/98) P/FL 21+13/9 FLC 5+1/4

FLACK Steven (Steve) Richard
Born: Cambridge, 29 May 1971
Height: 6'2" Weight: 13.2
Last season, Steve was the first-choice striker for Exeter, while his partners up front were chopped and changed throughout the campaign. His strength, aerial ability and goals were the subject of several substantial six-figure transfer bids, some of which were from higher division clubs. It was a measure of how highly the club rates him that all of the bids were dismissed.
Cardiff C (£10,000 from Cambridge C on 13/11/95) FL 6+5/1
Exeter C (£10,000 on 13/9/96) FL 95+17/29 FLC 3+1 FAC 7/3 Others 4+1/2

FLAHAVAN Aaron Adam
Born: Southampton, 15 December 1975
Height: 6'1" Weight: 11.12
In what should have been a promising 1998-99 for Aaron, in taking over as first-choice Portsmouth goalkeeper from the record-breaking Alan Knight, an injury curtailed his season twice, spookily against the same opposition. A leaky defensive line in front of him brought less clean sheets than the eight in 26 he managed during 1997-98, and he collapsed suddenly alone in the goalmouth during a 5-2 win over Swindon, after suffering a mystery illness, before recovering to play the rest of the game. His confidence in the area was shaken in mid season, allowing Knight to return, and an on-loan 'keeper brought in. Then cruelly, in his return match at Swindon, he was badly hurt in a mid-air save, resulting in broken ribs, jawbone and teeth, thus placing him out of action for the rest of the campaign. Confidence and fitness restored, his capabilities of reflex saves and command of the penalty area should hopefully see him back as Pompey's regular number one, a position he has patiently waited for, having learned so much from the legendary Knight.
Portsmouth (From trainee on 15/2/94) FL 63 FLC 8

FLASH Richard Garfield
Born: Birmingham, 8 April 1976
Height: 5'9" Weight: 11.10
Signed in the 1998 close season from Watford, he looked a very good acquisition for Plymouth in the pre-season games. A quick and agile wing back with a very good right foot, sadly his campaign ended prematurely at Cardiff last September, when an injury was found to be damaged knee ligaments which required surgery. Made his comeback for the reserves in March and, hopefully, will have a full term to look forward to in 1999-2000.
Manchester U (From trainee on 1/7/94)
Wolverhampton W (Free on 22/9/95)
Watford (Free on 25/7/96) FL 0+1
Lincoln C (Loaned on 2/10/97) FL 2+3
Plymouth Arg (Free on 4/8/98) FL 4+1 FLC 1

FLECK Robert William
Born: Glasgow, 11 August 1965
Height: 5'8" Weight: 11.9
Club Honours: SPD '87; SLC '87, '88
International Honours: S: 4; U21-6; Yth
A former Scottish international, Robert scored in Reading's first ever league match

at the Madejski Stadium – a 3-0 win over Luton – but a serious back problem meant that he had to retire from soccer and return home to Norwich. Managing only a handful of games for the Royals in 1998-99, he remained in football by coaching Gorleston, a team in the Eastern Counties League.
Glasgow R (Free from Possil YM on 14/7/83) SL 61+24/29 SLC 3+5/2 SC 1+1 Others 3+4/3
Partick Th (Loaned in November 1983) SL 1+1/1
Norwich C (£580,000 on 17/12/87) FL 130+13/40 FLC 13/11 FAC 16+2/11 Others 7/4
Chelsea (£2,100,000 on 13/8/92) PL 35+5/3 FLC 7/1 FAC 1
Bolton W (Loaned on 17/12/93) FL 6+1/1 Others 1
Bristol C (Loaned on 12/1/95) FL 10/1
Norwich C (£650,000 on 29/8/95) FL 93+11/16 FLC 9+2/2 FAC 3
Reading (£60,000 on 26/3/98) FL 5+4/1 FLC 1

FLEMING Craig
Born: Halifax, 6 October 1971
Height: 6'0" Weight: 12.10
A tremendously consistent central defender whose partnership with Matt Jackson has provided a solid base for Norwich's rearguard, Craig enjoyed an outstanding season in 1998-99. Strong in the tackle, being particularly adept at getting ahead of his opponent to win the ball cleanly, he is also useful in the air, and a natural competitor. Having scored only twice in his career prior to the 1998-99 campaign, he doubled his tally with headed goals at Bury, and at home to Port Vale.
Halifax T (From trainee on 21/3/90) FL 56+1 FLC 4 FAC 3 Others 3+2
Oldham Ath (£80,000 on 15/8/91) F/PL 158+6/1 FLC 12+1 FAC 11 Others 4
Norwich C (£600,000 on 30/6/97) FL 55+4/4 FLC 6 FAC 1+1

Curtis Fleming

FLEMING Curtis
Born: Manchester, 8 October 1968
Height: 5'11" Weight: 12.8
Club Honours: Div 1 '95

International Honours: Ei: 10; U23-2; U21-5; Yth
Long-serving Curtis is one of Middlesbrough's most consistent performers, well capable of filling either of the full-back berths, and yet still able, with his turn of speed, to overlap as a flying wing back to supply quality crosses, or to take advantage of those supplied to him to score his customary seasonal goal. His effort in the 89th minute of the nail-biting game against Blackburn Rovers in 1998-99 was good enough to secure three priceless points for Boro at the Cellnet. Although injuries plagued his season, no doubt this talented Eire international will already be looking towards next term's battlegrounds to prove his durability.
Middlesbrough (£50,000 from St Patricks on 16/8/91) F/PL 184+17/3 FLC 18+2/1 FAC 13+1 Others 7+1

FLEMING Terence (Terry) Maurice
Born: Marston Green, 5 January 1973
Height: 5'9" Weight: 10.9
A hard-working player who captained Lincoln during the 1998-99 campaign, he mostly appeared in central midfield, but was also used on the right flank and as an emergency full back. Terry was one of Lincoln's most consistent players throughout the season, but suffered by switching positions on a regular basis. He also had disciplinary problems, collecting a total of 11 yellow cards.
Coventry C (From trainee on 2/7/91) F/PL 8+5 FLC 0+1
Northampton T (Free on 3/8/93) FL 26+5/1 FLC 2 FAC 0+1 Others 0+1
Preston NE (Free on 18/7/94) FL 25+7/2 FLC 4 FAC 0+1 Others 3+2
Lincoln C (Signed on 7/12/95) FL 134+8/3 FLC 9+1/1 FAC 8/2 Others 3

FLETCHER Carl Neil
Born: Camberley, 7 April 1980
Height: 5'10" Weight: 11.7
A product of Bournemouth's youth policy who signed professional forms during the 1998 close season, after turning out for the first team in 1997-98 while still a trainee, he followed that up with another substitute appearance during 1998-99, when coming on against Chesterfield in a striking role. He is, however, predominantly a midfielder, and another for the Cherries' emerging prospects who will be pushing for a regular senior spot during the new term.
Bournemouth (From trainee on 3/7/98) FL 0+2

FLETCHER Steven (Steve) Mark
Born: Hartlepool, 26 July 1972
Height: 6'2" Weight: 14.9
Steve has now notched up over 250 appearances for Bournemouth and finished 1998-99 with ten goals, despite having missed ten games of the season through injury. A tall striker who is good in the air and adept at holding the ball up until his fellow players join him in attack, he struck up a good partnership with fellow striker, Mark Stein, which he will be keen to renew in the coming campaign.

Hartlepool U (From trainee on 23/8/90) FL 19+13/4 FLC 0+2/1 FAC 1+2 Others 2+2/1
Bournemouth (£30,000 on 28/7/92) FL 213+17/43 FLC 19/3 FAC 11/1 Others 12/2

FLITCROFT David (Dave) John
Born: Bolton, 14 January 1974
Height: 5'11" Weight: 13.5
As the brother of Blackburn's Gary, Dave is a skilful midfielder in his own right, and was used down the flanks by Chester in 1998-99 with great effect. Not afraid to battle for the ball, and a good all-round team player who likes to shoot from a distance, he made his 200th league appearance for City, against Halifax in April. Out of contract during the summer, he can also deliver excellent crosses from the wide right.
Preston NE (From trainee on 2/5/92) FL 4+4/2 FLC 0+1 Others 0+1
Lincoln C (Loaned on 17/9/93) FL 2 FLC 0+1
Chester C (Free on 9/12/93) FL 146+21/18 FLC 10+1 FAC 7 Others 8/1

FLITCROFT Garry William
Born: Bolton, 6 November 1972
Height: 6'0" Weight: 12.2
International Honours: E: U21-10; Yth; Sch
Gary was enjoying the best football of his spell at Blackburn, in 1998-99, making the midfield role his own with a series of energetic, ball-hunting performances that might have earned him England selection. However, in the middle of October he had to have surgery on his knee, and his recovery was much slower than anticipated. Ironically, he had just developed an ability to score goals that he had never shown previously, timing his runs from deep into the penalty area and finishing with power. Two goals in the game against West Ham, and a magnificent equaliser in Lyon, were just a hint of a talent that was emerging.
Manchester C (From trainee on 2/7/91) PL 109+6/13 FLC 11+1 FAC 14/2
Bury (Loaned on 5/3/92) FL 12
Blackburn Rov (£3,200,000 on 26/3/96) PL 66+6/5 FLC 3+1/1 FAC 3+1 Others 2/1

FLO Havard
Born: Norway, 4 April 1970
Height: 6'1" Weight: 13.6
International Honours: Norway: 16
The brother of Chelsea's Tore Andre, this tall Norwegian striker was signed by Wolves from Werder Bremen last January after protracted negotiations, having made an impact in the World Cup when scoring against Scotland. It snowed on his debut as he made a quiet start, but the next week he showed his qualities in the air, scoring against Arsenal in the FA Cup, and later hitting the post with a shot. Despite making a 16th appearance for Norway, he did not score in his first seven league games in England and, with Steve Froggatt long gone, he needed somebody to provide the service to him. He finally broke the duck against Bristol City, and later that afternoon he scored again with a fine half volley.
Wolverhampton W (£700,000 from Werder Bremen, via Stryn and Sogndal, on 12/1/99) FL 18+1/5 FAC 1/1

FLO Tore-Andre
Born: Strin, Norway, 15 June 1973
Height: 6'4" Weight: 13.8
Club Honours: FLC '98; ECWC '98; ESC '98
International Honours: Norway: 35
A magnificent, world-class centre forward who had an outstanding World Cup for Norway, during which he terrorised the Brazilian defence for the second time in 12 months, he scored a superb individual goal which clinched victory and put Norway into the second stage at the expense of Scotland and Morocco. A cult hero with the Chelsea faithful, he suffered the frustration of starting last season on the subs' bench as a high-profile "victim" of the club's controversial rotation policy. In the fifth Premiership match of the season, with the Blues trailing 3-2 at their bogey ground of Ewood Park with just ten minutes left, Tore came off the bench to score two brilliant goals within three minutes to secure Chelsea's first league victory at Blackburn for 22 years. But it was back to the bench for Tore until Pierluigi Casiraghi's serious knee injury at West Ham in November forced Gianluca Vialli's hand, and saw him forge a partnership with Gianfranco Zola, which often proved devastating. He scored consistently up to the turn of the year as the Blues reached English football's summit for the first time for nine years, his goals included an injury-time header which inflicted Aston Villa's second Premiership defeat, a classic diving header against Tottenham, and a smartly-taken Boxing Day volley at Southampton. Sadly, for Chelsea and Tore, disaster struck when everything seemed set fair, an ankle cartilage injury sustained in a third round FA Cup-tie at Oldham sidelining him for eight matches. There was no doubting that his absence, along with Gus Poyet's, severely undermined Chelsea's bid for the Premiership title. Fortunately, he returned earlier than expected and continued in his rich goalscoring form – goals at Valerenga and Wimbledon, plus two brilliantly-taken efforts in a televised match at Villa Park demonstrating just how much he had been missed. Although superb in the air, he likes to "drop off" opposing defenders, collect the ball in midfield and use his mazy dribbling skills to create opportunities for himself and his fellow strikers. His close control and trickery remind older supporters of an earlier Chelsea hero – Peter Osgood, and from Blues' fans there can be no greater tribute.
Chelsea (£300,000 from Brann Bergen, via Sogndal and Tromso, on 4/8/97) PL 34+30/21 FLC 5+2/3 FAC 3+1 Others 7+7/4

FLOWERS Timothy (Tim) David
Born: Kenilworth, 3 February 1967
Height: 6'2" Weight: 14.0
Club Honours: PL '95
International Honours: E: 10; U21-3; Yth
1998-99 was a season to forget for Tim. Commencing late at Blackburn because of suspension, the goalie was never at ease and conceded four goals from free kicks from the edge of the area. He also displayed the other side of his game at Lyon, where he contributed a couple of excellent saves.

After a torn bicep had cost him his place and two months of football, on not displacing John Filan he immediately submitted to a transfer request as he saw his England squad place disappear. At his best, he is an excellent shot stopper who inspires others.
Wolverhampton W (From apprentice on 28/8/84) FL 63 FLC 5 FAC 2 Others 2
Southampton (£70,000 on 13/6/86) F/PL 192 FLC 26 FAC 16 Others 8
Swindon T (Loaned on 23/3/87) FL 2
Swindon T (Loaned on 13/11/87) FL 5
Blackburn Rov (£2,400,000 on 4/11/93) PL 175+2 FLC 14 FAC 13+1 Others 12

FLYNN Michael (Mike) Anthony
Born: Oldham, 23 February 1969
Height: 6'0" Weight: 11.0
The Stockport captain was undoubtedly the team's player of the 1998-99 season his gritty displays reputedly attracting the attention of Birmingham, Huddersfield, and Spurs. However, the fans were able to breathe again when the popular centre half finally agreed to sign a four-and-a-half-year extension to his contract in March 1999. Superb in the air, and wholly committed in the challenge, his marshalling of the defence was one of the main reasons for County's survival in Division One.
Oldham Ath (From apprentice on 7/2/87) FL 37+3/1 FLC 1+1/1 FAC 1 Others 2
Norwich C (£100,000 on 22/12/88)
Preston NE (£125,000 on 4/12/89) FL 134+2/7 FLC 6 FAC 6+1/1 Others 13
Stockport Co (£125,000 on 25/3/93) FL 270+1/13 FLC 26/2 FAC 16/1 Others 19

FLYNN Sean Michael
Born: Birmingham, 13 March 1968
Height: 5'8" Weight: 11.8
A hard-working, right-sided or central midfielder who once again had a useful season for West Bromwich, this time in 1998-99, he again put together some determined performances. A dedicated professional, unfortunately, Sean blotted his copybook when he was sent off for the first time in his career in the home game with Ipswich. Skippered Albion during the course of the campaign, and led by example – shouting, gesticulating, and urging his team mates on to the bitter end.
Coventry C (£20,000 from Halesowen T on 3/12/91) F/PL 90+7/9 FLC 5/1 FAC 3
Derby Co (£250,000 on 11/8/95) F/PL 39+20/3 FLC 3 FAC 3
Stoke C (Loaned on 27/3/97) FL 5
West Bromwich A (£260,000 on 8/8/97) FL 63+10/4 FLC 6 FAC 0+2

FOE Marc-Vivien
Born: Nkolo, Cameroon, 1 May 1975
Height: 6'3" Weight: 13.6
International Honours: Cameroon: 31
In becoming West Ham's record signing, when joining the club from RC Lens last January, the Cameroon international central midfielder quickly got into the action, making his debut at Wimbledon a few days later. It did not take long to show himself to be a big, powerful player who gave the side a presence in the middle of the park, especially when breaking up attacks with precision tackling and moving the ball on. Superb at Chelsea, in a shock 1-0 win, he was

unlucky to have a goal ruled out because of an infringement, but it was his all-round ability that the Hammers brought him to Upton Park for, not his goals. Playing in 13 of the final 16 games, his height was used to good effect either in shoring up a defence under pressure or up front at set pieces.

West Ham U (£4,200,000 from RC Lens, via Canon Younde, on 28/1/99) PL 13

FOLAN Anthony (Tony) Stephen
Born: Lewisham, 18 September 1978
Height: 5'11" Weight: 11.8
Club Honours: Div 3 '99
International Honours: Ei: U21-5

An extremely skilful and tricky two-footed Brentford winger who has the potential to go to the very top, Tony arrived at the club last September from Crystal Palace and, after a spell on the bench, became a regular when making a name for himself by scoring spectacular goals. A mazy run, beating four defenders before shooting in at Peterborough was then eclipsed by an incredible 45 yarder from the right wing against Cambridge. Lost his place to the more experienced Andy Scott late in the campaign, but had enough appearances under his belt to qualify for a Third Division championship medal and is certain to figure strongly in 1999-2000. Came on as a sub for the Eire U21 side versus Malta.

Crystal Palace (From trainee on 22/9/95) PL 0+1
Brentford (£100,000 on 22/9/98) FL 19+10/4 FLC 0+1 FAC 3/2 Others 2

FOLEY Dominic Joseph
Born: Cork, 7 July 1976
Height: 6'1" Weight: 12.8
International Honours: Ei: U21-8

Although the Wolves' striker was not involved early in the 1998-99 season, despite the departures of some of his rivals for a place, it began for him on 29 September when he came on as a sub against Queens Park Rangers and scored with a neat downward header. Not involved in the next two fixtures, he then came on as a sub again before making only his third ever start for Wolves, scoring again as they beat Grimsby. He retained his place but was disappointing and, having been involved in five out of seven games, he faded before going on loan to Notts County in December. Following his spell at Meadow Lane, Dominic went on loan to Ethnikos in Greece, scoring a hat trick on his debut, but returned in March as Wolves were not receiving his wages. Despite the circumstances, he was then unable to play until he was given international clearance, before being released during the summer. Shows composure on the ball, and has a powerful shot. Stop Press: Joined Watford on 8 July.

Wolverhampton W (£35,000 from St James' Gate on 31/8/95) FL 4+16/3 FLC 0+3 FAC 0+1 Others 0+2
Watford (Loaned on 24/2/98) FL 2+6/1
Notts Co (Loaned on 7/12/98) FL 2 Others 1

FORAN Mark James
Born: Aldershot, 30 October 1973
Height: 6'4" Weight: 14.3

As in 1997-98, Mark had very few opportunities at Crewe last season, but always gave of his best when they arose, especially when standing in for Dave Walton and Steve Macauley in the centre of the defence. Very competitive, and tall, and commanding, he wins aerial battles at both ends of the pitch, but was only required for six starts in mid term, as others performed solidly during a difficult campaign.

Millwall (From trainee on 3/11/90)
Sheffield U (£25,000 on 28/8/93) FL 10+1/1 FLC 1 Others 0+1
Rotherham U (Loaned on 26/8/94) FL 3
Wycombe W (Loaned on 11/8/95) FL 5 FLC 2
Peterborough U (£40,000 on 8/2/96) FL 22+3/1 FAC 1 Others 2
Lincoln C (Loaned on 22/1/97) FL 1+1
Oldham Ath (Loaned on 3/3/97) FL 0+1
Crewe Alex (£25,000 + on 12/12/97) FL 14+4/1 FAC 1

FORBES Adrian Emmanuel
Born: Ealing, 23 January 1979
Height: 5'8" Weight: 11.10
International Honours: E: Yth

Norwich's flying winger found it hard to sustain the impact he created in his first full season in 1997-98, making only limited appearances in 1998-99, Bruce Rioch's first season in charge at Carrow Road. However, still only 20 years old, Adrian's future in the game remains bright, his tremendous pace and direct style capable of unnerving the best of defenders. And, although his final ball can sometimes be awry, his unpredictability can also be a great asset. 1999-2000 will be a big season for this homespun right winger as he tries to re-assert himself in the first-team picture.

Norwich C (From trainee on 21/1/97) FL 38+20/4 FLC 0+2 FAC 1+1

FORBES Steven (Steve) Dudley
Born: Stoke Newington, 24 December 1975
Height: 6'2" Weight: 13.2

A strong-running midfielder, Steve missed the early part of last season with an injury from a summer friendly, but forced his way into the Colchester team for a run of games in September, during which he scored the late winner at York after coming on as substitute, and the equaliser against Wycombe at Layer Road. Having lost his place to Jason Dozzell, sadly his last two full appearances were in the FA Cup disasters against Bedlington and Gillingham, before he spent the last few months of 1998-99 on loan at Peterborough, where he started just one game.

Millwall (£45,000 from Sittingbourne on 11/7/94) FL 0+5 FLC 0+1 FAC 0+1
Colchester U (Signed on 14/3/97) FL 34+17/4 FLC 1+2 FAC 3/1 Others 4+1
Peterborough U (Loaned on 3/3/99) FL 1+2

FORD Jonathan (Jon) Steven
Born: Birmingham, 12 April 1968
Height: 6'1" Weight: 13.12
Club Honours: AMC '94

With a central defensive injury crisis afflicting Barnet at the beginning of last season, Jon was the most experienced player in a make-shift back four, and his solid, uncompromising style of play, coupled to a

good organisational mind, enabled the Bees to overcome their injury troubles and record two good results in their opening couple of games. However, after defeats at Wolves and Plymouth, he was dropped from the side before returning to help record a clean sheet at Shrewsbury, and adding some much-needed stability to the defence. Unfortunately, in the next match, at home to Peterborough, he was sent off following a clash with United's Jimmy Quinn, and his suspension consequently enabled Mark Arber to establish himself in the side at his expense. His most accomplished display was in the home victory against Torquay in November, when he netted his only goal of the campaign, but sensing his first-team chances were limited he left to join Kidderminster Harriers in February.

Swansea C (£5,000 from Cradley T on 19/8/91) FL 145+15/7 FLC 12+1 FAC 8+5/2 Others 15+5
Bradford C (£21,000 on 26/7/95) FL 18+1 FLC 4 FAC 2 Others 1
Gillingham (£15,000 on 16/8/96) FL 2+2 FLC 3 FAC 0+1 Others 1
Barnet (£25,000 on 21/2/97) FL 47/2 FLC 6 FAC 2 Others 1

FORD Liam Anthony
Born: Dewsbury, 8 September 1979
Height: 5'6" Weight: 9'10"

Having signed professional forms for Plymouth during the 1998 close season, after coming through the club's youth system, the young left-sided midfielder made his first-team debut as an 81st-minute substitute for veteran Steve McCall at Shrewsbury last October. A talented and cultured youngster who likes to take the ball upfield and join the forwards, although he needs building up, is likely to get more first team exposure in 1999-2000.

Plymouth Arg (From trainee on 9/7/98) FL 0+1

FORD Mark Stuart
Born: Pontefract, 10 October 1975
Height: 5'8" Weight: 10.8
Club Honours: FAYC '93
International Honours: E: U21-2; Yth

A broken ankle sustained in the first match of last season kept Mark on the Burnley sidelines for three months, and he never seemed to fully regain favour, although his subsequent performances probably exceeded his form of the previous campaign. Never to be faulted in terms of enthusiasm, he remained at his best, playing just in front of the defence, but was also quite capable of sparking attacking moves. Was released during the summer.

Leeds U (From trainee on 5/3/93) PL 27+2/1 FLC 7 FAC 5 Others 0+1
Burnley (£250,000 on 18/7/97) FL 43+5/1 FLC 2 FAC 1+1 Others 5+1

FORD Michael (Mike) Paul
Born: Bristol, 9 February 1966
Height: 6'0" Weight: 12.6
Club Honours: WC '88

As Frank Burrows' most crucial signing, Mike rejoined Cardiff during the summer of 1998, after ten seasons with Oxford, and was soon named captain. His ability to lead, organise, and inspire, was crucial, and he was the key figure in City's promotion campaign.

An attacking full back who is equally good in the centre of the defence, when he was playing City did well, and when he was out injured they struggled. That says it all.

Leicester C (From apprentice on 11/2/84)
Cardiff C (Free from Devizes T on 19/9/84) FL 144+1/13 FLC 6 FAC 9 Others 7
Oxford U (£150,000 on 10/6/88) FL 273+16/18 FLC 27+1/2 FAC 12+1/1 Others 8/1
Cardiff C (Free on 29/7/98) FL 25 FAC 5

FORD Robert (Bobby) John
Born: Bristol, 22 September 1974
Height: 5'9" Weight: 11.0

The start of Bobby's first full season at Sheffield United in 1998-99 was hindered by injury but, when he did make the side, his battling and harrying qualities in midfield were to the fore. Preferring his midfield role, he did, on occasions, play as a right-wing back, with the extra defensive responsibilities. Whatever the position, he quietly gave his 100 per cent, although both he and his fans were hoping for a few more goals.

Oxford U (From trainee on 6/10/92) FL 104+12/7 FLC 14+2/1 FAC 10/2 Others 7/1
Sheffield U (£400,000 on 28/11/97) FL 47+6/1 FLC 2/1 FAC 9+4 Others 2

Bobby Ford

FORD Tony
Born: Grimsby, 14 May 1959
Height: 5'10" Weight: 13.0
Club Honours: Div 3 '80; FLGC '82
International Honours: E: B-2

As Mansfield's oldest ever player, Tony completed his 900th Football League appearance against Plymouth at Home Park last January, which is a record for an outfield player. This record was testament to his professionalism and fitness as he fast approached his 40th birthday. Bringing sound positional sense to bear, he spent most of 1998-99 in midfield, where he competed with Lee Williams. Is also Town's assistant manager.

Grimsby T (From apprentice on 1/5/77) FL 321+34/54 FLC 31+3/4 FAC 15+4/2 Others 2
Sunderland (Loaned on 27/3/86) FL 8+1/1
Stoke C (£35,000 on 8/7/86) FL 112/13 FLC 8 FAC 9 Others 6/1
West Bromwich A (£145,000 on 24/3/89) FL 114/14 FLC 7 FAC 4/1 Others 2+1
Grimsby T (£50,000 on 21/11/91) FL 59+9/3 FLC 1 FAC 3
Bradford C (Loaned on 16/9/93) FL 5 FLC 2
Scunthorpe U (Free on 2/8/94) FL 73+3/9 FLC 4/1 FAC 7/1 Others 4 (Free to Barrow on 22/8/96)
Mansfield T (Free on 25/10/96) FL 97+6/7 FLC 4/1 FAC 4/1 Others 5

Tony Ford

FORINTON Howard Lee
Born: Boston, 18 September 1975
Height: 5'11" Weight: 11.4

Despite being allowed to go on loan to Plymouth last December, scoring his first league goals, three in eight appearances, Birmingham refused to let him move on a more permanent basis and he returned to St Andrews. A stocky striker, whose control and touch was greatly improved in 1998-99, Howard was the club's leading scorer in the Pontins League, having made his first start for the Blues in the 6-0 Worthington Cup win over Macclesfield in September. Scored the 86th-minute winner against Queens Park Rangers on 20 April in a must-win game that all but secured a play-off place.

Birmingham C (Signed from Yeovil T on 14/7/97) FL 0+4/1 FLC 1+1
Plymouth Arg (Loaned on 18/12/98) FL 8+1/3

FORREST Craig Lorne
Born: Vancouver, Canada, 20 September 1967
Height: 6'5" Weight: 14.4
Club Honours: Div 2 '92
International Honours: Canada: 46

Due to the excellent form of Shaka Hislop, Craig spent virtually the whole of last season on the West Ham substitutes' bench. However, keeping in good shape, his loyalty was rewarded with the captaincy of the Canadian national side that played against Northern Ireland in April, before being called up for the Hammers' final game of the season, at home to Middlesbrough. Good on crosses, and quick off his line to clear balls played in behind the defence, he did well to keep a clean sheet in a 4-0 win, a result that saw the club finish fifth in the Premiership. Stands up until the last moment, thus making it difficult for forwards.

Ipswich T (From apprentice on 31/8/85) F/PL 263 FLC 16 FAC 11 Others 14

Colchester U (Loaned on 1/3/88) FL 11
Chelsea (Loaned on 26/3/97) PL 2+1
West Ham U (£500,000 on 23/7/97) PL 14+1 FLC 3 FAC 4

FORREST Martyn William
Born: Bury, 2 January 1979
Height: 5'10" Weight: 12.2

The young striker who is a second-year professional at Bury – where his father John, a goalkeeper, played 430 league games in the 1970s. Marked his 20th birthday by being named as a substitute in Bury's FA Cup third round game against Stockport. He celebrated the occasion by making his club debut as a second-half substitute and impressing as he took up a right-wing role. Also made his league debut in February, again as a substitute, against Ipswich. Small in stature, but stocky, Martyn is highly rated by all Gigg Lane.

Bury (From trainee on 16/7/97) FL 0+1 FAC 0+1

FORRESTER Jamie Mark
Born: Bradford, 1 November 1974
Height: 5'6" Weight: 11.0
Club Honours: FAYC '93
International Honours: E: Yth (UEFAYC '93); Sch

Jamie had by far his best season in league football in 1998-99, reaching 17 goals for Scunthorpe by the turn of the year and leading the Third Division scoring charts for most of the campaign. A small striker, with plenty of pace and skill, he has developed a killer instinct for poaching goals in the penalty area and, as an ever present for United, he won a place in the PFA Division three select team. Left United two days after their Wembly play-off triumph to join Utrecht FC in Holland on a three-year contract.

Leeds U (£60,000 from Auxerre on 20/10/92) PL 7+2 FAC 1+1/2
Southend U (Loaned on 1/9/94) FL 3+2
Grimsby T (Loaned on 10/3/95) FL 7+2/1
Grimsby T (Signed on 17/10/95) FL 27+14/6 FLC 0+2 FAC 3+1/3
Scunthorpe U (Signed on 21/3/97) FL 99+2/32 FLC 6/2 FAC 7/4 Others 7

FORRESTER Mark
Born: Middlesbrough, 15 April 1981
Height: 5'9" Weight: 10.3

Mark, a young second-year Torquay trainee midfielder, made a number of substitute appearances after coming off the bench at Cambridge, followed by a full debut at Peterborough, and showed an encouraging mobility and awareness which bodes well for the future. Was due to sign on full terms for the coming campaign in the summer.

Torquay U (Trainee) FL 1+4

FORSSELL Mikail
Born: Steinfurt, Germany, 15 March 1981
Height: 6'1" Weight: 12.8

Chelsea beat off a host of European giants such as Ajax, Bayern Munich, Inter Milan, and Sampdoria, plus British rivals, Liverpool and Rangers, to clinch the signing of Mikael from HJK Helsinki in December 1998. The 17-year-old goalscoring prodigy had already played against Benefica, PSV Eindhoven and Kaiserslautern in the Champions' League for

the Finnish champions, before committing himself to a five-year contract with the Blues. The loss of front-line goalscorers Pierluigi Casiraghi, Gus Poyet, and Tore Andre Flo, with lengthy injuries forced Blues' boss, Gianluca Vialli, into rushing the youngster into first-team action before he would have wished. He first appeared as a substitute for 16 minutes against Arsenal at Highbury in January, but made a tremendous impact on his full debut four days later at Stamford Bridge. Oxford had become particularly stubborn opposition in an FA Cup fourth round replay, but Mikael turned the match in Chelsea's favour with two stunning right-foot drives within eight second-half minutes, to grab the headlines on the following morning's sports pages. His first league goal, two weeks later, in his second Premiership start, was also one to remember – at the City Ground he walked the ball around the ex-England 'keeper, Dave Beasant, and rolled it home with all the aplomb of a veteran. This incredible beginning to his English career promises a bright future ahead, and it will be fascinating to compare his progress with other teenage sensations Michael Owen and Joe Cole.

Chelsea (Free from HJK Helsinki on 18/12/98) PL 4+6/1 FAC 1+2/2

FORSTER Nicholas (Nicky) Michael
Born: Caterham, 8 September 1973
Height: 5'10" Weight: 11.5
International Honours: E: U21-4

Nicky went on Birmingham's transfer list at his own request last season after struggling to hold down a regular place. Often used from the bench, his pace causing problems for tiring defences, he continued to give his all to the cause, and scored two vital goals in a 4-2 home win against Bristol City, when making a rare start in a bid to halt a faltering spell by City. With good feet, and the ability to turn half chances into goals, injuries have been his bugbear, but sooner or later goals will start coming his way again.

Gillingham (Signed from Horley T on 22/5/92) FL 54+13/24 FLC 3+2 FAC 6/2
Brentford (£100,000 on 17/6/94) FL 108+1/39 FLC 11/3 FAC 8/1 Others 7+1/4
Birmingham C (£700,000 on 31/1/97) FL 24+44/11 FLC 2+2/1 FAC 3+1

FORSYTH Michael (Mike) Eric
Born: Liverpool, 20 March 1966
Height: 5'11" Weight: 12.2
Club Honours: Div 2 '87
International Honours: E: B-1; U21-1; Yth

A reliable left-footed central defender, Mike spent most of 1998-99 at Wycombe recovering from a knee injury from the previous campaign. Despite setbacks with other injuries during his rehabilitation, he finally made his first appearance in the end-of-season match at Manchester City, where he replaced the suspended Jamie Bates. His superb performance in the epic 2-1 win was the more remarkable, given his lack of first-team football, and he went on to play three more games. Unfortunately, manager Lawrie Sanchez was unable to renew his contract, given his age and budget considerations, and

the supporters were sorry to see the departure of a truly professional and likeable player.

West Bromwich A (From apprentice on 16/11/83) FL 28+1 FLC 1 FAC 2 Others 1
Derby Co (£25,000 on 28/3/86) FL 323+2/8 FLC 36/1 FAC 15+1 Others 29/1
Notts Co (£200,000 on 23/2/95) FL 7
Hereford U (Loaned on 27/9/96) FL 12
Wycombe W (£50,000 on 6/12/96) FL 51+1/2 FLC 2 FAC 2 Others 2

FORSYTH Richard Michael
Born: Dudley, 3 October 1970
Height: 5'11" Weight: 13.0
International Honours: E: SP-3

Last season was an injury troubled time at Stoke for Richard, with groin and hamstring injuries to contend with. Indeed, his first appearance was not until November, although, typically, he scored on that day against Luton. As the team's fortunes faded, the left-sided midfielder's form dipped, and he looked less than pleased when substituted early in the televised game at home to Manchester City. Was released during the summer.

Birmingham C (£50,000 from Kidderminster Hrs on 13/7/95) FL 12+14/2 FLC 7+2 FAC 2 Others 3+1
Stoke C (£200,000 on 25/7/96) FL 90+5/17 FLC 7/1 FAC 4 Others 1+1

FORTUNE-WEST Leopold (Leo) Paul Osborne
Born: Stratford, 9 April 1971
Height: 6'3" Weight: 13.10

Much was expected of Leo when he signed for Lincoln in the summer of 1998 from Gillingham, but he failed to find his form and was dropped to the subs' bench after scoring just one goal in his first nine appearances. He was left out of the squad altogether after the home defeat by Fulham, and quickly moved out on loan to Rotherham, scoring four goals in five appearances, before being transferred to Brentford. Surprisingly, he was virtually only used as a late substitute until a move to Rotherham in February put him out of his misery. A big, strong striker, Leo netted an all-headed hat trick in just eight minutes in April to endear himself to the supporters.

Gillingham (£5,000 from Stevenage Borough on 12/7/95) FL 48+19/18 FLC 3+1/2 FAC 3+1/2
Leyton Orient (Loaned on 27/3/97) FL 1+4
Lincoln C (Free on 6/7/98) FL 7+2/1 FLC 2
Rotherham U (Loaned on 8/10/98) FL 5/4
Brentford (£60,000 on 17/11/98) FL 2+9 FAC 0+1 Others 2+1/1
Rotherham U (£35,000 on 26/2/99) FL 15/8 Others 2

FOSTER Craig Andrew
Born: Australia, 15 April 1969
Height: 5'11" Weight: 12.4
International Honours: Australia: 19

Yet another of Terry Venables' former players who signed for Crystal Palace during last season, Craig came from Portsmouth in October, and later became the club's PFA spokesman during the financial troubles over the non-payment of wages. He also captained the side. A busy midfield general, the Australian international scored his first goal against his old club at Selhurst four weeks after a difficult debut had culminated in a 3-0 defeat at Ipswich, and was a virtual regular

throughout the most difficult of campaigns, especially off the field.

Portsmouth (£320,000 from Marconi on 19/9/97) FL 13+3/2 FAC 2/2
Crystal Palace (Free on 2/10/98) FL 30+2/2 FAC 1

Craig Foster

FOSTER John Colin
Born: Manchester, 19 September 1973
Height: 5'11" Weight: 13.2
International Honours: E: Sch

Out of contract at Carlisle, John went to Bury on trial in the 1998 close season and impressed manager Neil Warnock sufficiently to earn a three-month contract, which was later extended until the end of the season. A right back who is also able to turn out at centre half or in midfield, he found competition for places tough at Gigg Lane though, and started just six games for the Shakers – mostly isolated appearances when deputising in midfield. Put on the transfer list early in 1999, he was given a free transfer in May 1999.

Manchester C (From trainee on 15/7/92) P/FL 17+2 FLC 2+1 FAC 2+1
Carlisle U (Free on 26/3/98) FL 7
Bury (Free on 31/7/98) FL 6+1

FOSTER Stephen (Steve)
Born: Mansfield, 3 December 1974
Height: 6'1" Weight: 12.0

The central defender once again proved to be one of Bristol Rovers' most consistent and reliable players in, at times, a young inexperienced defence in 1998-99, taking over briefly as captain in the absence of Andy Tillson. During the course of the season, he had six different partners with him in central defence. A good man-to-man marker, Steve also provided an imposing presence in opponents' penalty areas for set pieces, and was rewarded with his first-ever league goal in the important 4-1 win at Stoke City on 10 April. Only Jamie Cureton made more appearances for Rovers, in what proved to be a difficult campaign.

Mansfield T (From trainee on 15/7/93) FL 2+3 FLC 2 (Free to Telford on 22/1/94)
Bristol Rov (£150,000 from Woking on 23/5/97) FL 73+4/1 FLC 3 FAC 9 Others 5

FOSTER Stephen (Steve) John
Born: Warrington, 18 September 1980
Height: 5'11" Weight: 11.0
Having come through Crewe's youth ranks to sign professional forms at the start of 1998-99, much was expected of the young central defender who had played at the back and impressed in the summer friendlies. Made his first-team debut when coming off the bench for the last 18 minutes in a 1-0 defeat at Bury, and was a sub in the Worthington Cup a few weeks later at Bristol City, but those were his sum appearances for the season. With good strength and aerial ability, 1999-2000 could be his season.
Crewe Alex (From trainee on 19/9/98) FL 0+1 FLC 0+1

FOTIADIS Panos Andrew
Born: Hitchin, 6 September 1977
Height: 5'11" Weight: 11.7
International Honours: E: Sch
The young all-action Luton striker with pace and aggression was looking to break through as a first-team regular in 1998-99 but, in the event, his campaign stuttered along with ankle ligament damage being the main problem. Of his 25 appearances, 15 were from the bench, and while scoring three times, all in winning games, Andrew will be looking to put the campaign behind him in an effort to call upon the ability the club know he does possess. It will be interesting to see how he goes in 1999-2000.
Luton T (Free from juniors on 26/7/96) FL 22+31/6 FLC 1+4/1 FAC 1 Others 2+2

FOWLER Jason Kenneth
Born: Bristol, 20 August 1974
Height: 6'3" Weight: 11.12
An attacking midfielder, Jason provided one of Cardiff's highlights of last season with his chipped goal during the 4-1 win against Brentford at home. A player of great ability, he signed a new contract last season and was a key component of City's promotion effort. With great touch, passing skills, and an ability to produce the unexpected, he was always a threat to the opposition, and it was no surprise that he was selected by his fellow professionals to grace the award-winning PFA Third Division side.
Bristol C (From trainee on 8/7/93) FL 16+9 FLC 1+2 Others 1+1
Cardiff C (Signed on 19/6/96) FL 107+5/13 FLC 5/1 FAC 10+1/4 Others 3/1

FOWLER Robert (Robbie) Bernard
Born: Liverpool, 9 April 1975
Height: 5'11" Weight: 11.10
Club Honours: FLC '95
International Honours: E: 9; B-1; U21-8; Yth (UEFAYC '93)
Having returned from injury, and having regained his prowess as a goalscorer par excellence at Liverpool in 1998-99, Robbie proceeded to shoot himself in the foot with some extraordinary examples of well-documented behaviour, in which he appeared

to have allowed his personal views to get in the way of his footballing talent. Returning as a strike partner to Michael Owen against Charlton, he scored twice in a 3-3 draw to announce his presence once again amongst football's goalscoring elite, before going on to play twice more for England. A superb hat trick against Southampton in the 7-1 victory earned him the "Man of the Match" award, but thereafter his season declined into one in which he unnecessarily incurred the wrath of the Football Association's hierarchy. A player with consummate ability, especially when in sight of goal, he looks to return to the path which took him to glory in the first instance.
Liverpool (From trainee on 23/4/92) P/FL 179+6/106 FLC 27/21 FAC 18+1/10 Others 18+2/10

Robbie Fowler

FOX Ruel Adrian
Born: Ipswich, 14 January 1968
Height: 5'6" Weight: 10.10
Club Honours: FLC '99
International Honours: E: B-2
Despite Ruel being a formidable winger with great dribbling skills and tremendous pace, he found competition for midfield places hot up at Spurs in 1998-99, as Darren Anderton returned to fitness, and David Ginola became the club's number one asset. Starting the season well, with a goal in the opening game at Wimbledon, and going on to score a further three in the remainder of the campaign, his commitment was never in doubt as he strived hard to win back his place, even with the introduction of both Steffen Freund and Tim Sherwood. While speculation may be high as to whether he will survive the reported summer clear out at Tottenham, there should be no doubt that he still has a tremendous amount to offer at Premiership level.

Norwich C (From apprentice on 20/1/86) F/PL 148+24/22 FLC 13+3/3 FAC 11+4 Others 12+4
Newcastle U (£2,250,000 on 2/2/94) PL 56+2/12 FLC 3/1 FAC 5 Others 4/1
Tottenham H (£4,200,000 on 6/10/95) PL 94+9/13 FLC 7+3/1 FAC 10/1

FOYLE Martin John
Born: Salisbury, 2 May 1963
Height: 5'10" Weight: 12.0
Club Honours: AMC '93
An evergreen striker who finished last season as Port Vale's leading scorer, it was a fitting reward for a player who always gives his all despite being in the autumn of his career. It probably wasn't intended for him to be as regular as it turned out, but injuries elsewhere dictated and he ran all day for the cause. Able to hold the ball up well, and dangerous in the air, he became only the second player in Vale's history to top over 100 goals for the club. Out of contract during the summer, Martin was a worthy winner of the supporters' "Player of the Year" award.
Southampton (From apprentice on 13/8/80) FL 6+6/1 FLC 0+2/2
Aldershot (£10,000 on 3/8/84) FL 98/35 FLC 10/5 FAC 8/5 Others 6
Oxford U (£140,000 on 26/3/87) FL 120+6/36 FLC 16/4 FAC 5/3 Others 3+1/1
Port Vale (£375,000 on 25/6/91) FL 213+61/76 FLC 18+4/7 FAC 13+4/9 Others 13+3/9

FRAIL Stephen (Steve)
Born: Glasgow, 10 August 1969
Height: 5'11" Weight: 12.3
Club Honours: S Div 1 '92; B & Q '91
Happiest at either right back or wing back, the Scot endured a wretched season at Tranmere in 1998-99, and spent the majority of his time in the treatment room rather than on the field. A serious and recurrent knee injury ensured that his campaign was in effect over by mid October, but both Steve and the Rovers' management must be hoping that he will be fulfilling his considerable potential when fully match-fit. Solid and versatile, he can also be creative, and is not afraid to marshal his colleagues.
Dundee U (Free from Possilpark YM on 10/8/85) SL 91+8/1 SLC 2 SC 7 Others 3
Hearts (Signed on 31/3/94) SL 45+9/4 SLC 5+1 SC 4+1 Others 1
Tranmere Rov (£90,000 on 30/1/98) FL 9+2 FLC 1

FRAIN John William
Born: Birmingham, 8 October 1968
Height: 5'9" Weight: 11.9
Club Honours: AMC '91
An inspirational club skipper and left back for Northampton, John is one of the club's free-kick specialists, and no Town supporter will ever forget his Wembley winner in the 1997 play-off final versus Swansea. John also appeared in 1998-99 as a left-sided midfield player, and as a sweeper, but is at his best when making surging runs down the left wing, and many of his telling crosses result in goals.
Birmingham C (From apprentice on 10/10/86) FL 265+9/23 FLC 28/1 FAC 12 Others 22/2
Northampton T (Free on 24/1/97) FL 98+1/1 FLC 6 FAC 7 Others 13/2

FRAMPTON Andrew (Andy) James Kerr
Born: Wimbledon, 3 September 1979
Height: 5'11" Weight: 10.10
Another of the Crystal Palace youngsters given a chance by Steve Coppell after the mass clear out of players during transfer deadline week last March, Andy made his first-team debut at right back in a 1-0 win at Norwich and showed much promise. An attacking full back who can play on either flank, but predominately left footed, he turned professional in May 1998, having come through the trainee ranks.
Crystal Palace (From trainee on 8/5/98) FL 4+2

FRANCIS Damien Jerome
Born: London, 27 February 1979
Height: 6'1" Weight: 11.2
Confident and strong on the ball, and full of ambition and enthusiasm, Damien performed well both in defence and in midfield with Wimbledon's reserves last season, having previously been noted as a bustling striker who held the ball up well while waiting for others to arrive. Despite all of the promise, the club obviously wanted to protect him and, on that basis, he was given just two first-team games – playing in both Worthington Cup-ties against Birmingham. Rated highly by the management, he is another youngster who is expected to have a bright future ahead of him.
Wimbledon (From trainee on 6/3/97) PL 0+2 FLC 2

FRANCIS Kevin Michael
Born: Birmingham, 6 December 1967
Height: 6'7" Weight: 16.10
Club Honours: Div 2 '95; AMC '95
Big "Kev" was another Oxford player to suffer long-term injury in 1998-99. Having picked up a knee injury in the summer which resulted in three operations, he returned to action in the FA Cup fourth round tie and was unlucky – witnessed by millions on television – to concede an injury-time penalty to rescue Chelsea, who were, at the time, serious Premiership title challengers. He then struggled to get into the goalscoring groove he had shown the year before, and scored just once, a consolation in a defeat by Norwich, before ending the campaign being carried off with an achilles injury that will keep him sidelined until at least this coming Christmas. Often ungainly on the ground, his aerial strength can better most defenders.
Derby Co (Free from Mile Oak Rov on 2/2/89) FL 0+10 FLC 1+2 FAC 1+2/1 Others 0+1
Stockport Co (£45,000 on 21/2/91) FL 147+5/88 FLC 12/5 FAC 25/18
Birmingham C (£800,000 on 20/1/95) FL 32+41/13 FLC 6+5/5 FAC 3+3/2 Others 4/1
Oxford U (£100,000 + on 17/2/98) FL 27+6/8 FAC 0+2

FRANCIS Stephen (Steve) Stuart
Born: Billericay, 29 May 1964
Height: 6'0" Weight: 14.0
Club Honours: FMC '86, '88
International Honours: E: Yth
With senior opportunities limited at Huddersfield in 1998-99, it was inevitable that Steve would seek pastures new, having started the season understudying the new number one, Nico Vaesen. Eventually, due to

the latter being suspended, the 34-year-old goalie gained three first-team opportunities, the first of these being at Grimsby, only his second run out under the new manager, Peter Jackson. After bowing out with the Terriers at the McAlpine, in games against Crystal Palace and West Bromwich in December, where he again showed his ability as a classy shot stopper, he joined Northampton on a free transfer. Brought to the club as an experienced back up for Billy Turley, he made his debut at Reading, one of his old clubs, and kept a clean sheet in a 1-0 win. Released during the summer, he was the 35th player used during the campaign – a club record.
Chelsea (From apprentice on 28/4/82) FL 71 FLC 6 FAC 10 Others 1
Reading (£20,000 on 27/2/87) FL 216 FLC 15 FAC 15 Others 13
Huddersfield T (£150,000 on 1/8/93) FL 186 FLC 20 FAC 9 Others 12
Northampton T (Free on 27/1/99) FL 3

Per Frandsen

FRANDSEN Per
Born: Copenhagen, Denmark, 6 February 1970
Height: 6'1" Weight: 12.6
Club Honours: Div 1 '97
International Honours: Denmark: 18
A powerhouse midfield general who is a vital player in the Bolton set-up, Per started last season having made two appearances for Denmark in the World Cup, and looked as fresh as ever with his bustling, effective displays. Always guaranteed to get a good goal return he did not disappoint, and scored a few of his trademark thunderbolts from outside the box, notching important goals in the victories against Birmingham, Huddersfield, and Portsmouth. His central

midfield pairing with Claus Jensen seemed to improve with each game during the latter stages of the campaign, and can be expected to come to fruition this time round. Was selected by his fellow professionals for the PFA award-winning First Division side.
Bolton W (£1,250,000 from F.C. Copenhagen, via Lille, on 7/8/96) F/PL 122+1/15 FLC 12+1/2 FAC 4+1 Others 3/1

FRASER Stuart James
Born: Cheltenham, 1 August 1978
Height: 6'0" Weight: 12.0
Starting out with his hometown club, Cheltenham Town, Stuart was soon spotted by Stoke scouts and moved to the Victoria Ground as a professional in the 1996 close season. Impressing those around him, the reserve goalie earned his chance and made his debut in the closing stages of the final game of the season against promoted Walsall, after Carl Muggleton had been injured. Agile and brave, he is sure to be given further opportunities this coming term.
Stoke C (Signed from Cheltenham T on 8/7/96) FL 0+1

FRASER Stuart Thomas
Born: Edinburgh, 9 January 1980
Height: 5'9" Weight: 11.4
Another Luton youngster who made his first-team debut in 1997-98, the left back continued his improvement last season to finish on a high, when starting the last four games. Despite being recognised as a left-sided player, he showed that he was more than comfortable on the right at Notts County when performing a wing-back role. With Luton playing with wing backs much of the time, he gets forward to cross but, at the same time, he is also a firm tackler.
Luton T (From trainee on 2/4/98) FL 6+3 Others 1

FREEDMAN Douglas (Dougie) Alan
Born: Glasgow, 21 January 1974
Height: 5'9" Weight: 11.2
International Honours: S: B-1; U21-8; Sch
Signed from Wolves in August 1998, the striker renewed his acquaintance with Dave Bassett, then manager at Nottingham Forest, who had brought him to the City Ground to score Premiership goals. Despite not having a regular partner all season he did well, scoring twice in the first leg of the Worthington Cup-tie at Leyton Orient before breaking his league duck at Liverpool. He then scored in four matches that ended in draws, against Cambridge, Derby, Aston Villa, and Blackburn, before he came back with a run of goals at the end of the campaign, including three in successive matches, and the opener in a 2-1 win at Blackburn. An intelligent ball-playing striker, who turns defenders well, Dougie will be looking for more of the same in 1999-2000, in his quest to take Forest back to the Premiership and put the pain of relegation behind them.
Queens Park R (From trainee on 15/5/92)
Barnet (Free on 26/7/94) FL 47/27 FLC 6/5 FAC 2 Others 2
Crystal Palace (£800,000 on 8/9/95) F/PL 72+18/31 FLC 3+2/1 FAC 2+1 Others 3+2/2

Wolverhampton W (£800,000 on 17/10/97) FL 25+4/10 FAC 5+1/2
Nottingham F (£950,000 on 12/8/98) PL 20+11/9 FLC 4/3 FAC 1

FREEMAN Darren Barry Andduet
Born: Brighton, 22 August 1973
Height: 5'11" Weight: 13.0
Club Honours: Div 3 '99

A right-sided Brentford striker, instantly recognisable by his long blond hair, Darren came to Griffin Park from Fulham during the 1998 close season. Often in the right place at the right time to convert chances, he became a regular in the side until February, only missing matches due to injury or suspension. Then, despite his great pace, he was suddenly out of contention for a place for the rest of the campaign, apart from one subs' appearance. However, his previous appearances were enough for him to win a Third Division championship medal.

Gillingham (Free from Horsham on 31/1/95) FL 4+8 FAC 0+1 Others 2/1
Fulham (£15,000 + on 4/7/96) FL 32+14/9 FLC 2 Others 3/1
Brentford (Free on 7/7/98) FL 16+6/6 FLC 4/1 FAC 3/2 Others 1

FREESTONE Christopher (Chris) Mark
Born: Nottingham, 4 September 1971
Height: 5'11" Weight: 11.7
Club Honours: AMC '97

An out-and-out striker, Chris started 1998-99 well enough with Northampton, scoring two excellent goals against West Ham in the Worthington Cup, but the goals dried up as the side struggled to find form, and he became a big money signing for Hartlepool shortly before the transfer deadline in March. Seen as the final piece of the jigsaw, as the new manager, Chris Turner, attempted to build a Pool squad capable of holding on to their Nationwide League status, in the closing weeks of the season he formed an experienced striking partnership with the club's other new signing, Gary Jones. To his credit, of the two he had the most success as a goalscorer.

Middlesbrough (£10,000 from Arnold T on 2/12/94) P/FL 2+7/1 FLC 1+1/1 FAC 0+2
Carlisle U (Loaned on 3/3/97) FL 3+2/2 Others 2
Northampton T (£75,000 on 8/12/97) FL 40+17/13 FLC 4/3 FAC 1+2 Others 6+1/3
Hartlepool U (£75,000 on 25/3/99) FL 9+1/3

FREESTONE Roger
Born: Newport, 19 August 1968
Height: 6'3" Weight: 14.6
Club Honours: Div 2 '89; AMC '94
International Honours: W: U21-1; Yth; Sch

For the first time in his career, a ruptured disc forced Roger to miss a number of league matches through injury. Following his 500th league and cup appearance for Swansea last Christmas, he was set to break the Swans' 368 league appearance record held by the legendary Johnny King. A shot stopper with good, safe hands, he is still recognised as one of the top goalkeepers outside the First Division.

Newport Co (From trainee on 2/4/86) FL 13 Others 1
Chelsea (£95,000 on 10/3/87) FL 42 FLC 2 FAC 3 Others 6

Swansea C (Loaned on 29/9/89) FL 14 Others 1
Hereford U (Loaned on 9/3/90) FL 8
Swansea C (£45,000 on 5/9/91) FL 349+1/3 FLC 20 FAC 24 Others 37

FRENCH Jonathan (Jon) Charles
Born: Bristol, 25 September 1976
Height: 5'10" Weight: 10.10

Following a trial with Hull in February 1998, Jon left his native Bristol for Hull in the summer, having been associated with Rovers since the age of nine. Usually filling the right-wing-back berth, he was in or around Mark Hateley's squad for much of the first half of the season, but with a change of manager, and an ankle injury in January, he was largely restricted to the sidelines in 1999.

Bristol Rov (From trainee on 15/7/95) FL 8+9/1 FLC 0+1 FAC 0+3 Others 2+1/1
Hull C (Free on 28/7/98) FL 9+6 FLC 2+1 FAC 1 Others 0+1

Steffen Freund

FREUND Steffen
Born: Brandenburg, Germany, 19 January 1970
Height: 5'11" Weight: 11.6
Club Honours: FLC '99
International Honours: Germany: 21

Signed from Borussia Dortmund last December, the natural midfielder was quick to impress the White Hart Lane crowds with his gritty determination in bringing a much-needed physical presence to the heart of the Tottenham midfield. Making his debut at Sheffield Wednesday in early January, Steffen took up a role as midfield anchor man, feeding the wings and running at opponents through the centre of midfield. Courageous in the challenge, particularly for the 50-50 ball, he used his experience and self confidence to steady the team in an area which had been a weakness until his arrival. Quickly adjusting to the Premiership, pace being one of his natural attributes, meant that he could anticipate the play well and move intelligently off the ball, and create space around him. Among his notable perform-

ances was the Worthington Cup final where he gave little away in the centre, and provided tremendous service to Darren Anderton and David Ginola on the flanks. Steffan's European experience will be extremely valuable in the UEFA Cup in 1999-2000.

Tottenham H (£750,000 from Borussia Dortmund, via Motor Sud, Stahl Brandenburg and Schalke 04, on 29/12/98) PL 17 FLC 3 FAC 6

FRIEDEL Bradley (Brad) Howard
Born: Lakewood, USA, 18 May 1971
Height: 6'3" Weight: 14.7
International Honours: USA: 59

An American import, Brad was preferred earlier last season to David James in Liverpool's goal. Having acquitted himself well in those opening games, he then had problems of his own in the 3-3 home draw with Charlton in September. In the following match, he conceded two more goals against Manchester United, and paid the price. Roy Evans and Gerard Houllier introduced James into the number-one spot, and he was forced to play out the majority of the rest of the season in the reserves, or in other minor competitions, until a recall against Blackburn in late April. Made a great save in the 2-2 end of season draw against Manchester United, but whether he will be able to force his way back into the first team on a regular basis in 1999-2000 is debatable.

Liverpool (£1,000,000 from Columbus Crew on 23/12/97) PL 23 FLC 2 Others 1+1

FROGGATT Stephen (Steve) Junior
Born: Lincoln, 9 March 1973
Height: 5'10" Weight: 11.11
International Honours: E: U21-2

Having signed from Wolves at the end of last September, the former Aston Villa left winger made his Coventry debut at home to Villa, and quickly made an impression with his speed, skill, and crossing ability. Primarily bought for his crosses to the head of Dion Dublin, the two only played together three times before Dion was sold to Villa. His goal against Everton in November was a superbly-hit shot from outside the area, which deservedly won BBC's "Goal of the Month" award. Further goals came in the FA Cup games with Macclesfield and Leicester and, with some steadier shooting and a bit of luck, he would have scored more. His return to Villa Park in February saw him set up two goals in the 4-1 victory, before he picked up a hamstring injury at Easter that disrupted the run in to the end of the campaign.

Aston Villa (From trainee on 26/1/91) F/PL 30+5/2 FLC 1+1 FAC 5+2/1
Wolverhampton W (£1,000,000 on 11/7/94) FL 99+7/7 FLC 10+1/2 FAC 3 Others 2
Coventry C (£1,900,000 on 1/10/98) PL 23/1 FAC 3/2

FRY Christopher (Chris) David
Born: Cardiff, 23 October 1969
Height: 5'10" Weight: 10.7
International Honours: W: Yth

Stamina, passing, and a penchant for getting forward to join the attack were just some of the qualities seen in Chris last season at

Exeter. Although a favourite with the fans for his first-class attitude, the midfielder was given a free transfer at the end of 1998-99, but should have no trouble in finding another club. Missed six weeks after suffering an ankle tendon injury against Hartlepool in February.

Cardiff C (From trainee on 3/8/88) FL 22+33/1 FLC 1+2 FAC 0+2 Others 0+2
Hereford U (Free on 2/8/91) FL 76+14/10 FLC 6+2 FAC 8+2/1 Others 6+1
Colchester U (Signed on 24/10/93) FL 102+28/16 FLC 3+3/1 FAC 3+1 Others 12+2/1
Exeter C (Free on 29/7/97) FL 43+17/3 FLC 0+4 FAC 3+1 Others 2

FUGLESTAD Erik
Born: Randaberg, Norway, 13 August 1974
Height: 5'10" Weight: 11.4
This former Norwegian U21 international gave some excellent displays of attacking left-back play, although the early part of his 1998-99 season was disrupted by a series of niggling thigh injuries. Erik has developed the defensive aspects of his position, having always enjoyed the attacking elements, and has the ability to deliver a tremendous range of crosses from the left flank. It is that skill, allied to his extra strength and defensive resolve, that make him an important member of the Canaries' squad.

Norwich C (Free from Viking Stavanger on 8/11/97) FL 45+3/2 FLC 1 FAC 2

FULLARTON James (Jamie)
Born: Glasgow, 20 July 1974
Height: 5'10" Weight: 10.6
International Honours: S: U21-17
Starting last season for Crystal Palace in the Inter-Toto Cup, Jamie received a nasty knee injury which unfortunately kept him out of action until January. However, after coming back to form the fiery midfielder was loaned to Bolton in transfer deadline week, to provide some much needed back up for the existing midfield with the end of the season looming. Made just one start for the club, in the 0-0 draw at Oxford, and spent the rest of his time on the bench, despite having joined Wanderers with a reputation as a tough-tackling, no-nonsense type in the David Batty/Paul Ince mode.

St Mirren (Free from Motherwell BC on 13/6/91) SL 93+9/3 SLC 2 SC 4 Others 4+1 (Transferred to Bastia during 1996 close season)
Crystal Palace (Free on 7/8/97) P/FL 26+6/1 FLC 2 FAC 3
Bolton W (Loaned on 25/3/99) FL 1

[FUMACA] ANTUNES Jose Rodriguez Alves
Born: Bahia, Brazil, 15 July 1976
Height: 6'0" Weight: 11.8
The first Brazilian to grace a Colchester team, having arrived at the club on trial last March, Fumaca made his debut in the Sky Pay-per-View game against Manchester City, and had the City defence chasing shadows in what was a football master-class. A typical South American midfielder, cum forward, he was already firmly established as a Layer Road hero before suffering a serious head injury in a challenge with City's Andy Morrison, following which he was carried off

unconscious to hospital. Sadly for all at the club, they never saw him again as he had signed for Barnsley before the next match – short lived but extremely sweet!

Colchester U (Free from Catuense on 17/3/99) FL 1
Barnsley (Free on 25/3/99)

FURLONG Paul Anthony
Born: Wood Green, 1 October 1968
Height: 6'0" Weight: 13.8
Club Honours: FAT '88
International Honours: E: SP-5
After opening his account, while scoring Birmingham's first goal last season in a 2-0 win at Port Vale, the big striker pulled a hamstring and missed the next 15 games. He came back strongly to score in a 3-1 home victory against Crewe, his second match back, but was dogged by injuries throughout the campaign, and made only sporadic appearances in the last quarter. His best spell came at the turn of the year, when ten goals in ten games helped the Blues' play-off charge to gather pace. As City fans had come to expect, Paul held the ball up superbly, strength and power being his major asset, and marked his 100th appearance for the club with his 42nd goal – from the spot at Crystal Palace on 6 February.

Coventry C (£130,000 from Enfield on 31/7/91) FL 27+10/4 FLC 4/1 FAC 1+1 Others 1
Watford (£250,000 on 24/7/92) FL 79/37 FLC 7/4 FAC 2 Others 4
Chelsea (£2,300,000 on 26/5/94) PL 44+20/13 FLC 3+1 FAC 5+4/1 Others 7/3
Birmingham C (£1,500,000 on 17/7/96) FL 85+12/38 FLC 9/3 FAC 5/3 Others 2

Paul Furlong

GABBIADINI Marco
Born: Nottingham, 20 January 1968
Height: 5'10" Weight: 13.4
Club Honours: Div 3 '88
International Honours: E: B-1; FL-1; U21-2
Signed from York immediately prior to the start of 1998-99, Marco was undoubtedly the most exciting player to wear Darlington's colours for many seasons, and ended the campaign as top scorer in the Third Division with 24 league goals, the first time a Quaker has ever achieved this honour. It is 35 years since a Darlington player has scored as many goals in a season, Jimmy Lawton getting 25 in the league in 1964-65. His great strength in holding off challenges, and his ability to turn defenders, treated the long suffering Feethams' fans to displays they had not witnessed from a striker since those distant days, and they must pray for more of the same in 1999-2000.
York C (From apprentice on 5/9/85) FL 42+18/14 FLC 4+3/1 Others 4/3
Sunderland (£80,000 on 23/9/87) FL 155+2/74 FLC 14/9 FAC 5 Others 9/4
Crystal Palace (£1,800,000 on 1/10/91) FL 15/5 FLC 6/1 FAC 1 Others 3/1
Derby Co (£1,000,000 on 31/1/92) F/PL 163+25/50 FLC 13/7 FAC 8+1/3 Others 16+1/8 (Free to Panionios during 1997 close season)
Birmingham C (Loaned on 14/10/96) FL 0+2
Oxford U (Loaned on 31/1/97) FL 5/1
Stoke C (Free on 24/12/97) FL 2+6 FAC 1/1
York C (Free on 20/2/98) FL 5+2/1
Darlington (Free on 8/7/98) FL 40/24 FLC 2 FAC 3 Others 1+1/1

GABBIDON Daniel (Danny) Leon
Born: Cwmbran, 8 August 1979
Height: 5'10" Weight: 11.2
International Honours: W: U21-6; Yth
A 1998 close season signing from the trainee ranks, the young West Bromwich full back was blooded by manager Denis Smith at a difficult stage of last season – at home to promotion-chasing Ipswich, a week after Albion had crashed 4-0 in the local derby at Birmingham. Danny did well and was not overawed, even in front of a 41,000 crowd at the Stadium of Light in his second senior outing for the club. And, although he missed the tail end of the campaign with an ankle injury, he is most certainly one for the future, says his boss, having already represented Wales at two different levels.
West Bromwich A (From trainee on 3/7/98) FL 2

GADSBY Matthew John
Born: Sutton Coldfield, 6 September 1979
Height: 6'1" Weight: 11.12
Having made his debut in the closing game of 1997-98, this tall, home-grown Walsall defender played his first full game at Reading last September, and proved himself reliable whenever called upon, not least in the vital win at Lincoln in late April. A youngster with good passing skills, and with an eye for the goal, he is equally adept in a midfield role.
Walsall (From trainee on 12/2/98) FL 3+4 Others 0+2

GAGE Kevin William
Born: Chiswick, 21 April 1964
Height: 5'10" Weight: 12.11
Club Honours: Div 4 '83
International Honours: E: Yth
Although the veteran defender started the first three games of the 1998-99 campaign for Hull, he was soon troubled by the calf injury that dogged his first term at Boothferry Park. As the injury showed little sign of clearing up, the club's new owners sought a mutually agreed settlement to his contract that was terminated in January, leaving Kevin to concentrate his efforts on his pub/restaurant business in the Peak District.
Wimbledon (From apprentice on 4/1/82) FL 135+33/15 FLC 7+2/1 FAC 8+3/1 Others 0+1
Aston Villa (£100,000 on 17/7/87) FL 113+2/8 FLC 13/3 FAC 9/1 Others 8
Sheffield U (£150,000 on 15/11/91) F/PL 107+5/7 FLC 6 FAC 10+2 Others 1
Preston NE (Free on 28/3/96) FL 20+3 FAC 1
Hull C (Free on 26/9/97) FL 10+3 FLC 1 FAC 1+1 Others 1

GAIN Peter Thomas
Born: Hammersmith, 11 November 1976
Height: 6'1" Weight: 11.0
Unable to get a game at Spurs, this tall, left-sided midfield player joined Lincoln under the extended loan system at the end of December, and impressed enough for the club to sign him on a permanent basis three months later. His only first-team start was in the Auto Windscreens Shield at Hartlepool, but he made four brief appearances as a substitute in league matches. Is regarded as a talented player with a promising future.
Tottenham H (From trainee on 1/7/95)
Lincoln C (Loaned on 31/12/98) FL 0+1 Others 0+1
Lincoln C (Signed on 26/3/99) FL 0+3

GALE Shaun Michael
Born: Reading, 8 October 1969
Height: 6'1" Weight: 11.10
The hard-working Shaun continued to show improvement in his play within the Exeter defence in 1998-99. Although he did not get on the score sheet, he liked to get into the final third of the pitch whenever possible, and contributed to a number of goals. Is a recognised corner-kick taker, and an accurate passer, whether long or short.
Portsmouth (From trainee on 12/7/88) FL 2+1 Others 0+1
Barnet (Free on 13/7/94) FL 109+5/5 FLC 10 FAC 6 Others 3
Exeter C (£10,000 on 23/6/97) FL 63+7/4 FLC 4 FAC 3 Others 2+1

GALLACHER Kevin William
Born: Clydebank, 23 November 1966
Height: 5'8" Weight: 11.6
International Honours: S: 43; B-2; U21-7; Yth
The waspish Scot started last season wondering whether he had a future at Blackburn following Kevin Davies' arrival, particularly as a close-season hernia operation delayed his start. Returning in the third game, he opened the side's scoring, and a goal in the next game confirmed his position. However, on international duty he broke his arm, which kept him out of the game until November. Two goals in two games over the Christmas period cemented him as top scorer with the team, but he then sustained a calf strain which did not yield to treatment, and had a reaction with his hamstring when he returned to training. Expected to sit out the rest of the campaign, it was a surprise when he made an appearance at Southampton where his mobility and lateral action made everyone realise what the club had been lacking. Played four times for Scotland during the season.
Dundee U (Signed from Duntocher BC on 2/9/83) SL 118+13/27 SLC 13/5 SC 20+3/5 Others 15+6/3
Coventry C (£900,000 on 29/1/90) F/PL 99+1/28 FLC 11/7 FAC 4 Others 2
Blackburn Rov (£1,500,000 on 22/3/93) PL 129+10/46 FLC 8+1/2 FAC 13/4 Others 1+1

GALLEN Kevin Andrew
Born: Chiswick, 21 September 1975
Height: 5'11" Weight: 12.10
International Honours: E: U21-4; Yth (EUFAC '93); Sch
Kevin has progressed through Queens Park Rangers' junior ranks, with 1998-99 being his fifth season as a first-team player. Now fully recovered from a serious knee injury suffered two years ago, and a regular in the side, he is popular with the fans as he is a striker who always gives 100 per-cent effort in his games, and chases many lost causes. Had to make a number of adjustments, having had a number of different striking partners throughout the campaign, and due to these changes as well as suffering a little from a lack of confidence in front of goal his tally dropped significantly to just eight.
Queens Park R (From trainee on 22/9/92) P/FL 119+21/32 FLC 8+2/2 FAC 5+2/2

GALLIMORE Anthony (Tony) Mark
Born: Crewe, 21 February 1972
Height: 5'11" Weight: 12.6
Club Honours: Div 3 '95; AMC '98
1998-99 was undoubtedly "Gally's" best season since joining Grimsby. His solid defending, and forward runs down the left flank played a key part in the Mariners' tightness at the back, which, in view of the difficulties the forwards had in finding the net, contributed greatly to the team being able to maintain a respectable First Division place.
Stoke C (From trainee on 11/7/90) FL 6+5
Carlisle U (Loaned on 3/10/91) FL 8
Carlisle U (Loaned on 26/2/92) FL 8
Carlisle U (£15,000 on 25/3/93) FL 124/9 FLC 8/1 FAC 8 Others 24/1
Grimsby T (£125,000 on 28/3/96) FL 123+7/4 FLC 12 FAC 8 Others 10

GALLOWAY Michael (Mick) Anthony
Born: Nottingham, 13 October 1974
Height: 5'11" Weight: 12.4
Unable to hold down a regular place in Gillingham's side during 1998-99, his best game was probably at his old club, Notts County, on the final day of the campaign,

when he ran the show from his position on the left-side of midfield. On top of his game, Mick is good going forward, and an accurate passer, but last season his form fluctuated to such an extent that he made just 25 starts.

Notts Co (From trainee on 15/6/93) FL 17+4 FLC 2 FAC 0+1 Others 4
Gillingham (£10,000 + on 27/3/97) FL 57+16/5 FLC 3 FAC 1+2 Others 5

Mick Galloway

GANNON James (Jim) Paul

Born: Southwark, 7 September 1968
Height: 6'2" Weight: 13.0

As Stockport's longest-serving player, Jim enjoyed another highly successful season at Edgeley Park in 1998-99, his versatility and experience being invaluable. Employed in a central defensive position, and midfield role, as well as having a stint at right back, his polished performances kept the normal first-choice full back, Sean Connelly, out of the side. On the verge of quitting the game to return to his native Ireland in the summer of 1998, Stockport fans were grateful for his change of mind.

Sheffield U (Signed from Dundalk on 27/4/89)
Halifax T (Loaned on 22/2/90) FL 2
Stockport Co (£40,000 on 7/3/90) FL 330+24/52 FLC 32+3/3 FAC 18+1/1 Others 37+2/8
Notts Co (Loaned on 14/1/94) FL 2

GARCIA Anthony (Tony)

Born: Pierre Patte, France, 18 March 1972
Height: 6'0" Weight: 12.2

After unsuccessfully trialling at Sheffield United early in 1998-99, Tony arrived at Notts County in September on a month-to-month basis. Having at one time worked with Arsene Wenger at Marseilles, that pedigree was reflected in his exceptional talent. A midfield playmaker or a deep-lying striker who has the ability to turn a game with a touch of genius, Tony had difficulty settling in England and was released on 26 April to return to his native France. Scored twice, both in home 1-1 draws, against Bristol Rovers and Wrexham.

Notts Co (Signed from Lille OSC on 21/9/98) FL 10+9/2 FAC 3+2 Others 1

GARDE Remi

Born: L'Arbresle, France, 3 April 1966
Height: 5'9" Weight: 11.7
Club Honours: PL '98
International Honours: France: 6

Remained an important and versatile squad member at Arsenal in 1998-99, his best position being in midfield. Although he suffered from a bout of glandular fever last season and announced that he was going to retire, on his return to good health, however, he had second thoughts and signed a new one-year contract. A strong tackler and good passer of the ball, Remi was voted "Man of the Match" by a number of newspapers after the winning game against Chelsea at Highbury. And when he led the Gunners out against Derby in the Worthington Cup, he became the first non-British player ever to captain Arsenal, before being released during the summer.

Arsenal (Free from Strasbourg, via Lyon, on 14/8/96) PL 19+12 FLC 2 FAC 3+2 Others 3+2

GARDNER Anthony

Born: Birmingham, 10 September 1980
Height: 6'5" Weight: 13.8

Tall central defender with such a bright future predicted for him that Port Vale signed him on a professional contract a year before his apprenticeship was up. Very skilful on the ball for such a big man, although he made an impressive debut against Sheffield United in 1998-99, it wasn't until Brian Horton took over that he had a regular run in the side. Often getting out of trouble, thanks to his pace, he suffered a hamstring injury in March, at home to Grimsby, before returning for the final two games of the campaign and scoring his first goal, against Queens Park Rangers. Also won the "Young Player of the Year" award.

Port Vale (From trainee on 31/7/98) FL 14+1/1

GARDNER James (Jimmy)

Born: Dunfermline, 27 September 1967
Height: 5'11" Weight: 11.8

Deployed on either flank at times during 1998-99, Jimmy was an integral part of the Exeter team from the turn of the year. Extremely versatile, able to play out wide on either flank, and good at shipping in crosses to the front men, he assisted in a number of goals, although he did not get on the score sheet himself. Was surprisingly given a free transfer at the end of the season.

Queens Park R (Free from Ayresome North AFC on 1/4/87) SL 1+2
Motherwell (Signed on 1/7/88) SL 8+8 SC 0+1
St Mirren (Signed on 7/9/93) SL 31+10/1 SLC 1 SC 0+2 Others 2
Scarborough (Free on 25/8/95) FL 5+1/1
Cardiff C (Free on 28/9/95) FL 51+12/5 FLC 0+1 FAC 3 Others 4+1
Exeter C (Free on 29/7/97) FL 42+8/1 FLC 2+1 FAC 4+1/1 Others 2

GARDNER Ricardo Wayne

Born: Jamaica, 25 September 1978
Height: 5'9" Weight: 11.0
International Honours: Jamaica: 24

Ricardo signed for Bolton in August 1998 from Harbour View, in Kingston, Jamaica, having made over 20 appearances for Jamaica and shown his ability in last year's World Cup, which brought him to the attention of a number of European teams. It took some time to sort out a work permit for him, and he made his debut as a substitute in the Worthington Cup victory over Hartlepool. Despite being of slight appearance, the Jamaican is a tenacious competitor who is capable of playing with sublime skill, as the Reebok faithful have already seen. Although he did not keep his place on the left wing throughout last season, such was the form of Scott Sellars, an injury enforced absence to the latter meant that he had a good run in the team toward the end of the campaign, and will be hoping to cement his place in the starting line-up come the start of the new season.

Bolton W (£1,000,000 from Harbour View on 17/8/98) FL 19+11/2 FLC 2+1/1 FAC 0+1 Others 3

GARNER Darren John

Born: Plymouth, 10 December 1971
Height: 5'9" Weight: 12.7
Club Honours: AMC '96

An all-action midfield workaholic, Darren missed just one of the first 40 league matches for Rotherham in 1998-99, before serving a one-match ban, and then picking up an injury to miss out on some of the late games. He had hit six goals before the turn of the year but, although they dried up afterwards, it did not prevent him from being the team's "engine room".

Plymouth Arg (From trainee on 15/3/89) FL 22+5/1 FLC 2+1 FAC 1 (Free to Dorchester T on 19/8/94)
Rotherham U (£20,000 on 26/6/95) FL 138+3/10 FLC 8 FAC 10/5 Others 7/1

GARNETT Shaun Maurice

Born: Wallasey, 22 November 1969
Height: 6'2" Weight: 13.4
Club Honours: AMC '90

Shaun is like good wine in that he matures with age. 1998-99 was another great season for him at Oldham, as he held the back line together, despite the club fighting against relegation for most of the campaign. Although his fierce tackling earned him more than a fair share of bookings, you know what you are going to get from this man. Scored two vital goals – at Boundary Park against Luton, and at Wrexham – as the Latics strove to remain in the Second Division and, with his aerial ability as good as ever, he was influential at both ends of the park.

Tranmere Rov (From trainee on 15/6/88) FL 110+2/5 FLC 13/1 FAC 4 Others 15+2
Chester C (Loaned on 1/10/92) FL 9
Preston NE (Loaned on 11/12/92) FL 10/2 Others 1
Wigan Ath (Loaned on 26/2/93) FL 13/1
Swansea C (£200,000 on 11/3/96) FL 15 FLC 2
Oldham Ath (£150,000 on 19/9/96) FL 90+4/6 FLC 2 FAC 7 Others 2

GARRATT Martin Blake George

Born: York, 22 February 1980
Height: 5'8" Weight: 10.7

An ex-youth player who had an outstanding first season as a professional for York in

1998-99, Martin made over 40 senior appearances, impressing at both left back and on the left side of midfield. Proving to be a talented ball player, he attracted the attention of a number of clubs, spending a couple of days on trial at Leeds. Netted a fine goal in a draw against Stoke.

York C (From trainee on 2/7/98) FL 33+5/1 FLC 1+1 FAC 3 Others 0+1

GARRAULT Regis
Born: Rennes, France, 28 March 1968
Height: 5'9" Weight: 11.0

Signed on non-contract forms last November, Regis substituted for Walter Otta in the last 20 minutes of the FA Cup defeat at Preston, and his pace down the left wing briefly raised Walsall's hopes. He then played just over half of the Auto Windscreens Shield game at Bristol Rovers before being replaced by Clive Platt and moving on.

Walsall (Free from Chateauroux on 27/11/98) FAC 0+1 Others 1

GARVEY Stephen (Steve) Hugh
Born: Stalybridge, 22 November 1973
Height: 5'9" Weight: 11.1

After joining Blackpool from Crewe during the 1998 close season, having suffered a series of injuries in 1997-98, Steve failed to figure much for the Seasiders in 1998-99, only coming off the bench for his debut 17 games into the campaign. A player who can be used to attack full backs on either flank, he made his first start on Boxing Day, and scored from fully 30 yards after latching on to a weak clearance from the goalie in the home league fixture against Wigan.

Crewe Alex (From trainee on 25/10/91) FL 68+40/8 FLC 6+7/2 FAC 3+4/2 Others 8+3/1
Chesterfield (Loaned on 17/10/97) FL 2+1
Blackpool (Free on 16/7/98) FL 6+9/1

GASCOIGNE Paul John
Born: Gateshead, 27 May 1967
Height: 5'10" Weight: 11.12
Club Honours: FAYC '85; FAC '91. SPL '96, '97; SLC '97; SC '96
International Honours: E: 57; B-4; U21-13; Yth

Take away the famous name and Middlesbrough's number eight enjoyed a fairly typical English football season in the quest to help win things for his club and its supporters in 1998-99. In the local community, and outside of football, he is the epitome of professionalism, doing so much for deprived youngsters in the area and giving back tenfold all that the game has given him. Stepping onto a football pitch though is quite a different matter for him, and he is at once accountable to every person in the stadium, (especially the referee) and many outside of it. Fortunately, his abundant skills, and astute midfield magic are above reproach and, despite being pilloried in most match reports, he works extremely hard. He also suffers with enormous dignity the agonies of being too slow nowadays to catch younger tearaways, and too fast of mind for slower-thinking colleagues. His incredibly focussed football

brain never fails to demonstrate how important it is for someone in the midfield to read and anticipate the unfolding action, and nobody does it better than "Gazz". To peel back the thinly tainted veneer that cynics have daubed him with is to reveal the heart and mind of the incurable football fanatic, his appearances on a football pitch never failing to excite or solicit comment, however unfavourable. Sadly, his style, charisma, unbelievable talent, and "ordinariness", never do. His real "kicks" come as ever from just playing football, and it shows every time he emerges from the tunnel.

Newcastle U (From apprentice on 13/5/85) FL 83+9/21 FLC 8/1 FAC 4/3 Others 2+1
Tottenham H (£2,000,000 on 18/7/88) FL /19 FLC 14+1/8 FAC 6/6 (£5,500,000 to Lazio on 1/5/92)
Glasgow R (£4,300,000 on 10/7/95) SL 64+10/30 SLC 7/4 SC 7+1/3 Others 16/2
Middlesbrough (£3,450,000 on 27/3/98) P/FL 32+1/3 FLC 2+1 FAC 1

GAUGHAN Steven (Steve) Edward
Born: Doncaster, 14 April 1970
Height: 6'0" Weight: 12.6

Back on his old stamping ground after his sojourn with Chesterfield, Steve never really re-established himself in Darlington's first team for any sustained spell in 1998-99, and made only 18 starts with a further ten appearances as a substitute during the season. His powerful running in midfield produced two goals on forward surges but, at the end of the campaign, although still under contract, he was told he was free to look for another club. Stop Press: Signed a two-year contract for Halifax on 8 July.

Doncaster Rov (Free from Hatfield Main Colliery on 21/1/88) FL 42+25/3 FLC 2+2 FAC 4+1 Others 5+1
Sunderland (Free on 1/7/90)
Darlington (£10,000 on 21/1/92) FL 159+12/15 FLC 8 FAC 6/1 Others 10+1
Chesterfield (£30,000 on 16/8/96) FL 16+4 FLC 1+1/1 FAC 0+1 Others 1
Darlington (Signed on 21/11/97) FL 35+12/3 FLC 2 FAC 5 Others 2

GAVIN Jason Joseph
Born: Dublin, 14 March 1980
Height: 6'1" Weight: 12.7

A prodigious young talent who has crammed stacks of international experience at U21 level for the Republic of Ireland into his developing career, Jason emerged with great credit from his debut in the crackling atmosphere of St James Park when blooded in the north-east derby against Newcastle United last season. A strong tackler when playing alongside Gary Pallister and Dean Gordon, and certainly not overawed, he will take some shifting once he makes the grade to the senior squad. And a great future at the highest level is well within his capabilities.

Middlesbrough (From trainee on 26/3/97) PL 2

GAYLE Brian Wilbert
Born: Kingston, 6 March 1965
Height: 6'1" Weight: 13.12

In his second season at Shrewsbury, Brian's ability to organise, along with his experience, was vital in the centre of the defence. Supposed to be carrying an injury,

it was never evident in the commanding role he fulfilled, while helping to bring on the youngsters around him. Always in the thick of the action, and a menace to opposition defenders at corners, it came as a surprise when he was released during the summer.

Wimbledon (From apprentice on 31/10/84) FL 76+7/3 FLC 7/1 FAC 8/1 Others 2
Manchester C (£325,000 on 6/7/88) FL 55/3 FLC 8 FAC 2 Others 1
Ipswich T (£330,000 on 19/1/90) FL 58/4 FLC 3 FAC 0+1
Sheffield U (£750,000 on 17/9/91) F/PL 115+2/9 FLC 9 FAC 11/1 Others 1/1
Exeter C (Free on 14/8/96) FL 10 FLC 1
Rotherham U (Free on 10/10/96) FL 19+1 FAC 1 Others 1
Bristol Rov (Free on 27/3/97) FL 23 FLC 2
Shrewsbury T (Free on 9/12/97) FL 66/1 FLC 2 FAC 1

GAYLE John
Born: Bromsgrove, 30 July 1964
Height: 6'2" Weight: 15.4
Club Honours: AMC '91

A regular in the Scunthorpe side last season, John's strength and power up front distracted defenders, and led to the club's other two strikers scoring over 40 goals between them. Struggled for goals himself, and missed six weeks at the start of the year with a knee injury, but the team always faltered when he was missing. Unfortunately, he still found himself targeted by referees, being sent off twice in three weeks, earlier in the season, and serving four separate bans during the campaign.

Wimbledon (£30,000 from Burton A on 1/3/89) FL 17+3/2 FLC 3
Birmingham C (£175,000 on 21/11/90) FL 39+5/10 FAC 2 Others 8+1/4
Walsall (Loaned on 20/8/93) FL 4/1
Coventry C (£100,000 on 13/9/93) PL 3 FLC 1+2
Burnley (£70,000 on 17/8/94) FL 7+7/3 FLC 1+1/1 FAC 1+1/1
Stoke C (£70,000 on 23/1/95) FL 14+12/4 FLC 2 FAC 0+1 Others 3+1
Gillingham (Loaned on 14/3/96) FL 9/3
Northampton T (£25,000 on 10/2/97) FL 35+13/7 FLC 1+1/2 FAC 4 Others 9+1/4
Scunthorpe U (Free on 27/7/98) FL 36+1/4 FLC 2 FAC 1 Others 4

GAYLE Marcus Anthony
Born: Hammersmith, 27 September 1970
Height: 6'1" Weight: 12.9
Club Honours: Div 3 '92
International Honours: E: Yth. Jamaica: 9

An excellent all-round Wimbledon striker, who is equally effective in a left-sided midfield position, the Jamaican international is a confident and experienced player, and his aerial power is not only evident when attacking but also when defending from corners and free kicks. A strong but fair-minded player, with the ball at his feet Marcus is one of the most skilful players in the Premiership, and when points were few and far between he scored vital match winners, including one on the night of Joe Kinnear's heart attack at Sheffield Wednesday, which turned out to be the last three pointer of the season. He also struck doubles at West Ham and at home to Middlesbrough, and ended the campaign as the club's top scorer, one ahead of Jason Euell.

Brentford (From trainee on 6/7/89) FL 118+38/22 FLC 6+3 FAC 6+2/2 Others 14+6/2
Wimbledon (£250,000 on 24/3/94) PL 139+29/27 FLC 17+1/6 FAC 16+3/3

GEMMILL Scot
Born: Paisley, 2 January 1971
Height: 5'11" Weight: 11.6
Club Honours: FMC '92; Div 1 '98
International Honours: S: 15; B-2; U21-4
Having refused to sign a new contract, following his return from the World Cup, where he was in the Scottish squad, Nottingham Forest put him on a weekly agreement for 1998-99. Although playing in the majority of Forest's Premiership games, he found it difficult to raise his game with the club continuously fighting against relegation, and joined Everton in transfer deadline week with just five minutes to spare. Instrumental in helping the Toffees escape the drop, he proved an inspired purchase, as he showed himself to be a neat and tidy central midfielder with the ability to link defence and attack. He also displayed his eye for goal, with an outstanding volley at Newcastle. As the son of former Scottish international, Archie, who once turned down a move to Everton, Evertonians were delighted that Scot decided to complete his move to Goodison.
Nottingham F (From trainee on 5/1/90) F/PL 228+17/21 FLC 29+2/3 FAC 19+2/1 Others 13+1/4
Everton (£250,000 on 25/3/99) PL 7/1

GEORGE Liam Brendan
Born: Luton, 2 February 1979
Height: 5'9" Weight: 11.3
International Honours: Ei: Yth
Having made his first-team debut for Luton in 1997-98, Liam was hoping to build on that experience and began last season well, appearing in the opening seven matches before breaking his foot – an injury that was to hold him back for a large chunk of the campaign. A young Republic of Ireland youth international striker, who was a prolific scorer at junior levels, and one who twists and turns defenders well, he came back for a few games but really needed a good rest in the summer to get back to match fitness.
Luton T (From trainee on 20/1/97) FL 7+6 FLC 0+4 Others 0+1

GEORGIADIS George
Born: Havala, Greece, 8 March 1972
Height: 5'9" Weight: 10.10
International Honours: Greece: 2
Well named for a player who, in the summer of 1998, joined Newcastle (Ron Atkinson in TV commentary referred to him as Geordiadis), George is lively and energetic with an eye for goal, demonstrated by his impressive tally of 21 strikes from midfield for Panathinaikos the previous season. Quick and neat on the ball, he was seen to best advantage playing wide in midfield where he was able to get behind the opposing defences. Signed by former manager, Kenny Dalglish, Ruud Gullit kept him waiting for an opportunity to display his talents, and it was November before he

made his debut – in the goalless draw at Old Trafford, where he had an excellent game on the right of midfield. Thereafter, he became a useful member of the squad, making a number of appearances, although he was disappointed by the lack of a regular spot in the side, a fact which has also cost him his place in the Greek national team. He did play an important part in helping his club to reach Wembley, as he came on as substitute against Everton in the FA Cup quarter final, and scored a crucial goal to put United 2-1 ahead, shortly after Everton had equalised, from where they went on to win 4-1. Stop Press: Moved to PAOK Salonika for £1 million on 1 July.
Newcastle U (£420,000 from Panathinaikos, via Doxa Drama, on 5/8/98) PL 7+3 FLC 1 FAC 0+2/1

GERMAIN Steven (Steve)
Born: Cannes, France, 22 June 1981
Height: 5'10" Weight: 12.6
A young French forward brought in on loan for the last few weeks of 1998-99, in an effort to boost the Colchester attack, Steve made only a handful of brief substitute appearances, having little chance to shine, before being given a full debut in the last game of the season at Blackpool. He showed some good touches and a willingness to work for the team, and it would have been nice to see more of him before he returned to Cannes.
Colchester U (Loaned from Cannes on 25/3/99) FL 1+5

GERRARD Paul William
Born: Heywood, 22 January 1973
Height: 6'2" Weight: 14.4
International Honours: E: U21-18
A tall goalkeeper with excellent shot-stopping reflexes, Paul made only one appearance for Everton during 1998-99. That display, in a Worthington Cup victory at Middlesbrough, was competent enough, but he found it impossible to dislodge Thomas Myhre from the first-choice slot at Goodison. He even lost his place on the substitutes' bench when Steve Simonsen was signed from Tranmere, and conceded that his future probably lay away from Goodison. Loaned out to Oxford in mid December, he spent three months at the Manor Ground, making 16 appearances, but the financial crisis at the First Division club meant that they could not make the move permanent. Still only 26, his best footballing days lie ahead of him.
Oldham Ath (From trainee on 2/11/91) P/FL 118+1 FLC 7 FAC 7 Others 2+1
Everton (£1,000,000 + on 1/7/96) PL 8+1 FLC 3
Oxford U (Loaned on 18/12/98) FL 16

GERRARD Steven George
Born: Huyton, 30 May 1980
Height: 6'2" Weight: 12.4
International Honours: E: Yth
Steve made his Liverpool first-team debut in the centre of midfield at Tottenham last December, tackling strongly, and delivering penetrating through balls to the front men, having played excellently in the reserves. Awarded the "Man of the Match" award in

the UEFA Cup game against Celta Vigo at Anfield, he was later invited to train with Kevin Keegan's England team in March. He also had a scare during the same month when diagnosed with a stress fracture at the base of his back, but was given the all-clear after several tests. This youngster looks to be another Anfield talent who might just go all the way.
Liverpool (From trainee on 26/2/98) PL 4+8 Others 1

GIBB Alistair (Ally) Stuart
Born: Salisbury, 17 February 1976
Height: 5'9" Weight: 11.7
A right winger, converted to wing back, Ally took over the Northampton right-wing back spot from Ian Clarkson when the latter broke his leg, and held it for most of last season. Relying on his speed to outstrip many a defender, one of his best games was against Premiership side, West Ham. Is a good crosser of the ball, and corner-kick taker.
Norwich C (From trainee on 1/7/94)
Northampton T (Loaned on 22/9/95) FL 9/1
Northampton T (£30,000 on 5/2/96) FL 45+63/3 FLC 8+3 FAC 4+3 Others 4+3

GIBBENS Kevin
Born: Southampton, 4 November 1979
Height: 5'10" Weight: 12.13
A product of the Southampton youth set up, this young midfielder made his debut in 1997-98, and followed it up with a run in the first team last September. Unfortunately, he suffered a groin injury, which required surgery, and did not start playing again (in the reserves) until March. Was unlucky not to open his scoring account in the 1-1 draw against Spurs, the 'keeper making a crucial block with his knees from a downward header in the dying seconds of the game.
Southampton (From trainee on 16/1/98) PL 4+2 FLC 2

GIBBS Nigel James
Born: St Albans, 20 November 1965
Height: 5'7" Weight: 11.11
Club Honours: FAYC '82; Div 2 '98
International Honours: E: U21-5; Yth
By chalking up his 15th season of senior appearances, Watford's stalwart full back set a club record. He also moved to third in the club's all-time list for first-team games – only Luther Blissett and Gary Porter having played more. Nigel lost his senior place after breaking a big toe against Bolton in October, but remained an uncomplaining and essential member of the squad.
Watford (From apprentice on 23/11/83) FL 371+13/5 FLC 22/2 FAC 39+1 Others 17

GIBBS Paul Derek
Born: Gorleston, 26 October 1972
Height: 5'10" Weight: 11.10
Out of contract at Torquay during the summer of 1998, Paul moved to Plymouth where he was quickly recognised as the most talented footballer on the club's books. Unfortunately, he had a frustrating 1998-99 season with niggling injuries and this bad luck followed him throughout the year when he broke his leg badly on the last day of the

campaign. In between the injuries, he produced some excellent displays as an attacking left-wing back, the performances ultimately earning him the accolade of being chosen by his fellow professionals for the PFA Third Division team.

Colchester U (Signed from Diss T on 6/3/95) FL 39+14/3 FAC 1+1 Others 8+1
Torquay U (Free on 26/7/97) FL 40+1/7 FLC 4/1 FAC 3/1 Others 3/1
Plymouth Arg (Free on 7/7/98) FL 27/3 FLC 2

GIBSON Neil David
Born: Rhyl, 11 October 1979
Height: 5'11" Weight: 10.10
International Honours: W: U21-3

Formerly a trainee, Neil made his league debut for Tranmere against Norwich at Prenton Park last November, having been a consistent performer in the reserve side all season. Another impressive graduate from Rovers' youth policy, he was later unfortunate to pick up a knee-ligament injury which precluded him taking any further part in the campaign. A midfielder who relishes pushing forward to support the attack, he must be hoping that 1999-2000 brings him the opportunity to mount a sustained bid for a regular first-team place. Made three appearances for the Welsh U21 side in 1998-99.

Tranmere Rov (From trainee on 27/11/97) FL 0+1

GIBSON Paul Richard
Born: Sheffield, 1 November 1976
Height: 6'3" Weight: 13.0
Club Honours: FAYC '95

Unable to get much joy at Old Trafford, as one of Manchester United's youngsters Paul was loaned out to Hull City last November, and looked set for a fair stay at Boothferry as City's new manager, Warren Joyce, had earlier been coaching United's U16s for a number of years. Unfortunately, after just three appearances the talented young goalie broke a finger in two places in the pre-match warm-up against Carlisle, and only played with the help of painkillers before going back to United. Released in March, having failed to dislodge his illustrious contemporaries, he joined Notts County and was given two months and a first-team chance, a 1-0 defeat at home to Gillingham in the final game of 1998-99, to earn a more permanent contract. Is an impressive shot stopper who will certainly improve with experience.

Manchester U (From trainee on 1/7/95)
Mansfield T (Loaned on 20/10/97) FL 13
Hull C (Loaned on 6/11/98) FL 4
Notts Co (Free on 25/3/99) FL 1

GIBSON Robin John
Born: Crewe, 15 November 1979
Height: 5'6" Weight: 10.7

Formerly a member of the Cheshire schoolboy team, and the Crewe Alexandra School of Excellence, Robin signed schoolboy forms for the Gresty Road club, but upon leaving school was declined a YTS place as he was considered too small!! A number of clubs showed interest before he decided to join Wrexham in July 1996, progressing enough to earn professional

terms in July 1998. A tricky, hard-working little player who likes to be involved, and is a fine crosser of the ball, he can also get up well to compete with taller opponents. Made his first-team debut last January in the Auto Windscreens Shield encounter with Hull City, and was starting to make an impression with the squad until sustaining knee-ligament damage in the home-leg northern final of the above competition at the end of March. Was the club's "Young Player of the Season".

Wrexham (From trainee on 3/7/98) FL 3+4/1 FAC 0+1 Others 2+3

GIGGS Ryan Joseph
Born: Cardiff, 29 November 1973
Height: 5'11" Weight: 10.9
Club Honours: ESC '91; FAYC '92; FLC '92; PL '93, '94, '96, '97, '99; CS '93, '94, '96, '97; FAC '94, '96, '99; EC '99
International Honours: W: 24; U21-1; Yth. E: Sch

A highly skilled Manchester United left winger, who packs a tremendous left-footed shot, Ryan made an excellent start to last season, netting important goals against Lodz and Barcelona in the Champions' League, until a badly bruised left foot kept him out of action for two games. After making a goalscoring return with his first Premiership strike of the season, against Wimbledon, he then hit a brace against Brondby in Copenhagen, before suffering a longer lay off with a broken left foot, which kept him out until the end of November. A first-team regular throughout December and January, he netted important goals against Nottingham Forest and Coventry in the Premiership, and Middlesbrough in the FA Cup. Although he broke his nose playing against Inter Milan in the Champions' League quarter final at Old Trafford in March, he returned to play an inspiring role against Chelsea in the FA Cup sixth round replay and, with the season reaching its exciting climax, he hit the all-important equaliser against Juventus in the European Cup semi final at Old Trafford, before scoring after a wonderous 60-yard run against Arsenal in the FA Cup semi final replay, which took United to Wembley. Whilst Alex Ferguson enthused, "It was a goal of genius," Ryan described it as probably the best he has scored for the club. Although Jesper Blomqvist will undoubtedly be staking his claim for Ryan's place when the new season begins, there is still no finer sight in English football than "Giggsy" skipping down the wing on one of his sparkling sorties and, despite suffering his fair share of injuries, he is still one of the club's most inspirational players and was a worthy recipient of the European Cup, FA Cup and Premier League winners medals. Continued to represent Wales, playing against Italy (twice) and Denmark.

Manchester U (From trainee on 1/12/90) F/PL 237+23/53 FLC 17+4/6 FAC 34+3/7 Others 36+2/10

GILCHRIST Philip (Phil) Alexander
Born: Stockton on Tees, 25 August 1973
Height: 5'11" Weight: 13.12

Phil deservedly won the Oxford "Player of the Year" award for a series of fine displays in the centre-half berth in 1998-99, missing just a handful of games, most of which came following a dislocated shoulder around the turn of the year. He scored three goals, the first of them coming in an FA Cup tie at Chelsea that gave United the lead, the other two being vital – a point earner at Tranmere and the important first goal in the final game of the season when the club needed a high-scoring win to stay up. Well known for his long throw, he has great pace, tackles well, and is sound in the air.

Nottingham F (From trainee on 5/12/90)
Middlesbrough (Free on 10/1/92)
Hartlepool U (Free on 27/11/92) FL 77+5 FLC 4+1 FAC 4 Others 5
Oxford U (£100,000 on 17/2/95) FL 172+4/10 FLC 16 FAC 9/1 Others 3

Phil Gilchrist

GILKES Michael Earl Glenis McDonald
Born: Hackney, 20 July 1965
Height: 5'8" Weight: 10.10
Club Honours: FMC '88; Div 3 '86, Div 2 '94

The Wolves left-sided player was restricted to three outings as a sub during the first 14 matches in 1998-99, before having a run in the side at left back, lasting six games. Later, he came on as a sub and helped the team fight back from 2-0 down to draw with Norwich in December, before having another spell in January. Eventually omitted, he soon got another chance in February and kept his place, still having the ability to beat a man and put a good cross in on occasions. Was released during the summer.

Reading (Free from Leicester C juniors on 10/7/84) FL 348+45/43 FLC 25+7/6 FAC 31+2/1 Others 26+2/2
Chelsea (Loaned on 28/1/92) FL 0+1 Others 0+1
Southampton (Loaned on 4/3/92) FL 4+2
Wolverhampton W (£155,000 on 27/3/97) FL 33+5/1 FLC 0+1 FAC 2

GILL James Oliver
Born: Plymouth, 11 October 1980
Height: 5'5" Weight: 8.7

Still a trainee, as the midfield dynamo of the Plymouth youth team, and a firm favourite of youth-team manager Kevin Summerfield, James made his first-team debut in the Auto

Windscreens Shield match at Brentford in 1998-99. Coming off the bench to replace Martin Barlow in the Argyle midfield, in order to gain some useful first-team experience, he definitely looks to be a kid with a chance of making it.

Plymouth Arg (Trainee) Others 0+1

GILL Jeremy (Jerry) Morley

Born: Clevedon, 8 September 1970
Height: 5'7" Weight: 11.0
International Honours: E: SP-1

Playing in Birmingham's first three matches last season, before giving way to Gary Rowett and having to accept a squad place, Jerry continued to prove a strong competitor who is no slouch, whether it be at right back or in midfield. A good passer, who gets on with the job with the minimum of fuss, the former England semi-pro international also captained the reserves.

Birmingham C (£30,000 from Yeovil T on 14/7/97) FL 6 FLC 1

GILL Matthew James

Born: Norwich, 8 November 1980
Height: 5'11" Weight: 12.10

Yet another of the excellent youth-team players coming out of the Peterborough Academy, and one who had been given a run out in the last two games of 1997-98, Matthew looked to consolidate in 1998-99, and started well before an error at London Road saw Carlisle win 1-0 and knock his confidence somewhat. However, the frail looking, but hard-working midfielder came back strongly in the final third of the campaign to show that he was prepared to run all day for the cause.

Peterborough U (From trainee on 2/3/98) FL 24+4 FLC 2 Others 0+1

GILLESPIE Keith Robert

Born: Bangor, 18 February 1975
Height: 5'10" Weight: 11.3
Club Honours: FAYC '92
International Honours: NI: 26; U21-1; Yth; Sch

A talented right winger who· is fast and tricky on the ball and able to put in telling crosses from both static and running positions. Having agreed to move from Newcastle to Middlesbrough during the 1998 close season, much to Kenny Dalglish's relief this was called off for medical reasons as Keith was still troubled by an injury to his left ankle. Happily, suggestions that the injury would bring an end to his career proved unfounded, and he had an excellent first game of the season when coming off the bench to help in the destruction of Southampton. Despite remaining a regular for Northern Ireland, he found it difficult to find a starting place in Ruud Gullit's team, being used primarily as a sub, and was eventually transferred to Blackburn in December to become Brian Kidd's first signing at Ewood Park. It was an attractive move for Keith as Brian had been his coach during their days at Manchester United together. Unfortunately, he continued to be troubled with ankle and hamstring problems, resulting in him

missing as many games that he played, while his best contributions seemed to be when tracking back when the team was reduced to ten men. His great speed allowed him to do that, but with Rovers consigned to the First Division it is imperative that both he and the club can get back to the kind of form that the footballing public knows they are capable of if they are to come back to the Premiership at the first attempt.

Manchester U (From trainee on 3/2/93) PL 3+6/1 FLC 3 FAC 1+1/1
Wigan Ath (Loaned on 3/9/93) FL 8/4 Others 2
Newcastle U (£1,000,000 on 12/1/95) PL 94+19/11 FLC 7+1/1 FAC 9+1/2 Others 11+5
Blackburn Rov (£2,250,000 on 18/12/98) PL 13+3/1 FAC 4/1

GINOLA David

Born: Gassin, France, 25 January 1967
Height: 6'0" Weight: 11.10
Club Honours: FLC '99
International Honours: France:17

This wonderfully talented Spurs' winger had his best season in English football to date in 1998-99, which was underlined with his capturing of both the Football Writers and PFA "Player of the Year" awards, along with selection for the PFA award-winning Premiership side, replicating the achievement of a few very special players. Unlike Clive Allen, who also achieved those honours while at Spurs, David was rewarded not for the quantity of goals scored but for the way in which he took his goals, his spectacular first touch, but mostly his breathtaking skill and pace when out on the flanks, attacking opponents' goals. Creating more goals than he scored, he will undoubtedly be remembered for his stunning 25-yard drive in the FA Cup fifth round replay victory over Leeds, and his exquisite individual effort in the 1-0 defeat of Barnsley in the quarter finals of the same competition. Adored by the White Hart Lane crowd, and grudgingly respected by away crowds alike, the Frenchman came back from the disappointment of not being selected to represent his country in the World Cup, to prove to even his fiercest of critics that he is one of the greatest players in his position in the world. Although appearing enigmatic, he shook off his label of lacking commitment to establish himself as the most exciting player in the Premiership and, most importantly, to prove his value to George Graham, who many had expected would make David his first casualty in the bid to build a title-challenging side. Rewarded when receiving a new three-year deal at the club, which rightly puts him in the ranks of the Premiership's highest earners, he promises more of the same to the Tottenham faithful this season, and relishes the opportunity to have his brilliance measured against the best in Europe.

Newcastle U (£2,500,000 from Paris St Germain, via Toulon, Racing Paris and Brest, on 6/7/95) PL 54+4/6 FLC 6 FAC 4 Others 7+1/1
Tottenham H (£2,000,000 on 18/7/97) PL 64/9 FLC 11/3 FAC 9/4

GIOACCHINI Stefano

Born: Rome, Italy, 25 November 1976
Height: 6'0" Weight: 11.12

The Italian striker was taken on loan from the Italian Serie "A" last January until the end of the season, having been a member of Venezia's promotion-winning team in 1997-98, but found himself on the fringe of the Coventry side in 1998-99. With a Manchester-born wife, he wanted to try and make a name for himself in the English game, and impressed in reserve games before making three brief substitute appearances. There is a strong possibility that he will earn himself a contract at Highfield Road.

Coventry C (Loaned from Venezia on 11/1/99) PL 0+3

GITTENS Jonathan (Jon) Antoni

Born: Birmingham, 22 January 1964
Height: 6'0" Weight: 12.10

Jon added his huge amount of experience to the Exeter defence last season after signing from neighbours, Torquay, during the previous summer, his strength and positional sense contributing greatly to the side. Rewarded with a new one-year contract for 1999-2000, he is an excellent man marker, is strong in the air, and difficult to pass on the ground.

Southampton (£10,000 from Paget R on 16/10/85) FL 18 FLC 4 FAC 1
Swindon T (£40,000 on 22/7/87) FL 124+2/6 FLC 15+1 FAC 9 Others 13+1/1
Southampton (£400,000 on 28/3/91) FL 16+3 FLC 4 Others 1
Middlesbrough (Loaned on 19/2/92) FL 9+3/1
Middlesbrough (£200,000 on 27/7/92) PL 13 FLC 0+1 FAC 1
Portsmouth (Free on 9/8/93) FL 81+2/2 FLC 10 FAC 3 Others 3/1
Torquay U (Free on 5/8/96) FL 78/9 FLC 6 FAC 4 Others 5/2
Exeter C (Free on 29/7/98) FL 44/2 FLC 2 FAC 3/1 Others 2

GIVEN Seamus (Shay) John

Born: Lifford, 20 April 1976
Height: 6'0" Weight: 13.4
Club Honours: Div 1 '96
International Honours: Ei: 23; U21-5; Yth

The Republic of Ireland's first-choice goal-keeper, Shay is also the dependable last line of Newcastle's defence, being blessed with very quick feet and a safe pair of hands. Although considered by many to be small for his position, his anticipation and agility mean he is rarely exposed on crosses. Held his position in the team throughout most of last season when fit, and was outstanding with a "Man of the Match" performance in the 2-0 home win over Forest. A shoulder injury incurred against Wimbledon resulted in him being substituted at half time and sidelined briefly, but he returned after two matches, only to be sent off in the FA Cup-tie against Palace for handling outside his area, which earned him a one-match suspension. An excellent save from Mickel Beck to earn Newcastle a win at Derby typified his ability to pull off "impossible saves" and gain his side valuable points. He repeated this with a critical flying save from Darren Anderton in the opening minutes of

the FA Cup semi final, when the loss of a goal so early might well have proved fatal to Newcastle's aspirations. Unfortunately, his own hopes were hit when his form dipped subsequently, and he lost his place to Steve Harper prior to the final at Wembley.

Blackburn Rov (Free from Glasgow Celtic juniors on 8/8/94) PL 2 FLC 0+1
Swindon T (Loaned on 4/8/95) FL 5
Sunderland (Loaned on 19/1/96) FL 17
Newcastle U (£1,500,000 on 14/7/97) PL 55 FLC 2 FAC 10 Others 8

Shay Given

GLASGOW Byron Fitzgerald
Born: Clapham, 18 February 1979
Height: 5'7" Weight: 10.12
A graduate of Reading's youth development scheme, Byron forced his way into a midfield slot in the first team and remained there for most of last season. Despite his lack of height and weight, he was one of the team's more reliable performers, and capped a promising campaign with his first goal for the club in a 1-1 draw at Notts County. Showed great maturity in ignoring considerable provocation in Royals' 1-0 victory at Manchester City. Stop Press: Reported by the national papers on 8 July to have been sacked by Reading after testing positive for drugs.

Reading (From trainee on 24/8/96) FL 31+8/1 FLC 2 FAC 1+1 Others 1

GLASS James (Jimmy) Robert
Born: Epsom, 1 August 1973
Height: 6'1" Weight: 13.4
Released by Bournemouth during the 1998 close season, Jimmy became the second-choice goalkeeper at Swindon Town in 1998-99, managing just four games during the season and letting in ten goals in two of them. He ended this disappointing spell with a month's loan at Carlisle in April after special dispensation was granted by the FA – United having sold Tony Craig to Blackpool in transfer deadline week, then saw his on-loan replacement Richard Knight being forced to return to Derby. Despite playing just three matches, his sensational injury-time goal, when he came up for a corner, kept Carlisle in the Football League, relegated Scarborough, and catapulted him to the Pantheon of United's all-time heroes.

Is a good, agile shot stopper who is reliable on crosses and organises the defence well.

Crystal Palace (From trainee on 4/7/91)
Portsmouth (Loaned on 10/2/95) FL 3
Bournemouth (Free on 8/3/96) FL 94 FLC 4 FAC 4 Others 7
Swindon T (Free on 24/6/98) FL 3 FLC 1
Carlisle U (Loaned on 22/4/99) FL 3/1

GLASS Stephen
Born: Dundee, 23 May 1976
Height: 5'9" Weight: 11.0
Club Honours: SLC '96
International Honours: S: 1; B-2; U21-11; Sch
Signed from Aberdeen during the 1998 close season, Stephen is a nimble Newcastle winger who supplements a high workrate with the ability to control the ball at speed, mazy dribbling to beat his man on either side, and pin-point crossing from any angle. He made his debut for United as a substitute against Liverpool in the third game of last season and was chosen as "Man of the Match", his subsequent performances earning him a regular place by bringing an important balance to the side and beginning to provide the service sought by Alan Shearer. New to the Premiership and of slight build, he was not out of place amongst Newcastle's stars and, although still searching for the necessary level of consistency, his all-round game was blossoming as the campaign progressed, one of his most notable performances coming in the home game with Villa in January, when his passes led to the two home goals. Against Coventry in mid February, he suffered a bad knee injury which failed to respond to treatment, and he eventually underwent an operation in mid April, which was expected to end his season. However, with the FA Cup final looming he made an earlier than expected return when coming on as a sub in the last two Premiership games of the season, and in the final itself. Earlier chosen as a substitute for Scotland against Estonia, though he did not play, he made his full debut, from the bench, against the Faroe Islands in October at his former home ground of Pittodrie in Aberdeen.

Aberdeen (Free from Crombie Sports on 25/10/94) SL 93+13/7 SLC 10/2 SC 7+2 Others 3/2
Newcastle U (£650,000 on 22/7/98) PL 18+4/3 FLC 2 FAC 2+2 Others 2

GLEDHILL Lee
Born: Bury, 7 November 1980
Height: 5'10" Weight: 11.2
A promising young Barnet defender, Lee made his senior debut as a substitute in the home defeat against Southend last season, having captained the club's youth team to their highest-ever league position in the South East Counties table. Despite still being a trainee, he was able to slot into a number of positions on the pitch, including his favoured role of right back, while his strongest attributes were his enthusiasm and tenacity in the tackle. In successfully progressing through the ranks, he was looking forward to receiving a professional contract in the summer, and will be hoping to build upon his progression within the club's set-up to establish himself in the senior squad during 1999-2000.

Barnet (Trainee) FL 0+1

GLOVER Edward Lee
Born: Kettering, 24 April 1970
Height: 5'11" Weight: 12.1
Club Honours: FLC '89; FMC '92
International Honours: S: U21-3; Yth
Lee kept up his scoring feats of the previous season with a ratio of one goal every two matches for Rotherham in 1998-99, as he displayed his ability to hold the ball and turn cleverly. However, a hamstring injury picked up in the FA Cup game against Bristol Rovers at the beginning of January ruled him out for the rest of the term, and it was some time before a replacement was found for his scoring skills.

Nottingham F (From apprentice on 2/5/87) F/PL 61+15/9 FLC 6+5/2 FAC 8+2/1 Others 4+1/1
Leicester C (Loaned on 14/9/89) FL 3+2/1
Barnsley (Loaned on 18/1/90) FL 8 FAC 4
Luton T (Loaned on 2/9/91) FL 1
Port Vale (£200,000 on 2/8/94) FL 38+14/7 FLC 5+1/4 FAC 0+2 Others 3+2/2
Rotherham U (£150,000 on 15/8/96) FL 70+8/28 FLC 5 FAC 9+1/3 Others 1+1
Huddersfield T (Loaned on 3/3/97) FL 11

GOATER Leonard Shaun
Born: Hamilton, Bermuda, 25 February 1970
Height: 6'1" Weight: 12.0
Club Honours: AMC '96
International Honours: Bermuda: 9
Settled in well at Manchester City in 1997-98, scoring three goals in the last seven games, despite having targeted himself to score 25 goals and falling short due to a run of 12 games in mid season where he only scored one goal. This, after scoring ten goals in the first 16 outings. A striker who starts his approach from midfield, laying off balls wide to wingers, and moving forward for the crosses, his football thinking is good but, on occasion, he is too easily knocked off the ball. The fans would like to see him be more aggresive and not back off when he loses the ball. Adopting this attitude after the middle of January, it resulted in more frequent goals, his highlight being three at Burnley in mid March. Is good at laying the ball off, especially in the air, for fellow forwards.

Manchester U (From juniors on 8/5/89)
Rotherham U (Free on 25/10/89) FL 169+40/70 FLC 13+4/4 FAC 12+3/7 Others 15+5/5
Notts Co (Loaned on 12/11/93) FL 1
Bristol C (£175,000 on 17/7/96) FL 67+8/40 FLC 7/2 FAC 5 Others 5+1/1
Manchester C (£400,000 on 26/3/98) FL 48+2/20 FLC 3/2 FAC 4/1 Others 3/1

GOLDBAEK Bjarne
Born: Nykobing Falster, Denmark, 6 October 1968
Height: 5'10" Weight: 12.4
International Honours: Denmark: 16
In an amazing 20-day period in 1998-99, the Danish international midfielder went from a proverbial thorn in Chelsea's side to playing a part in the Blues' 5-0 mauling of Arsenal at Highbury! As an FC Copenhagen player, Bjarne played impressively at the Bridge in the European Cup Winners' Cup, second round first leg, putting the Danes ahead in the tie with a precious away goal. After Brian Laudrup's header clinched the tie for Chelsea in Copenhagen, Bjarne moved in

the opposite direction to Brian, inherited his number seven shirt, and made two of Chelsea's five goals at Highbury in an excellent debut. A hard-working, right-sided midfield player, he proved to be an astute acquisition by the club as long-term injuries and suspensions wrought havoc to their midfield. He came off the bench at Hillsborough to lay on Roberto di Matteo's late winner with a superb cross in the FA Cup fifth round, and eight days later scored his first goals in the Premiership with a brace in a match-winning performance at Nottingham Forest. A sweetly-struck volley against Liverpool the following Saturday clinched the points, and his fourth goal in four Premiership matches was a fierce right-footed drive against Aston Villa to round off a purple patch, both for Bjarne and the Blues, as they regained their impetus in the Premiership race. He also struck a 30-yard thunderbolt at Tottenham in the penultimate game of the campaign, that brought the scores level at 2-2. In these days of multi-million pound transfer dealings, Bjarne's signing fee was the bargain of the season, as the Dane played a significant part in Chelsea's success – who'd have thought it would be the unheralded Bjarne rather than his famous compatriot, Brian Laudrup.

Chelsea (£350,000 from FC Copenhagen, via Naestved, FC Schalke, Kaiserslautern, Tennis Borussia and FC Koln, on 10/11/98) PL 13+10/5 FLC 2 FAC 2+4

GOMEZ Fernando Colomer
Born: Spain, 11 September 1965
Height: 5'10" Weight: 13.0
International Honours: Spain: 1

Signed from Valencia for free at the start of 1998-99, despite being a past full Spanish international, there was still, however, a considerable financial outlay for the club. Acquired for his much-needed guile, against Stockport the midfielder chested the ball down and crashed it in from 30 yards with his left foot. Yet he was not always an automatic choice, making less impact as the winter weather began to set in, and getting one or two knocks as well. Not selected from 10 November to January, when he began three consecutive games, although he got in a well-taken strike at Tranmere he was not seen after 16 January. Simon Osborn had missed two of the three games but appeared in the latter, and Colin Lee felt their styles were too similar for them to play together again and he was released during the summer.

Wolverhampton W (Free from Valencia on 14/8/98) FL 17+2/2 FLC 2 FAC 1

GOODEN Ty Michael
Born: Canvey Island, 23 October 1972
Height: 5'8" Weight: 12.6
Club Honours: Div 2 '96

Proving a real asset, either as a left-sided wing back or attacking midfielder at Swindon in 1998-99, his performances again caught the eye of a number of clubs as he continued to torment First Division defences with his speed and strength. Once of Arsenal as an apprentice, he crosses the ball superbly from the flanks, delivers fine in-swinging corners, and packs a powerful shot. Scoring just one goal, in the 1-1 draw at Birmingham, the art of finding the net more often is something he looks to address.

Swindon T (Free from Wycombe W on 17/9/93) FL 110+26/9 FLC 6+1/1 FAC 6+1 Others 3+1

GOODHIND Warren Ernest
Born: Johannesburg, South Africa, 16 August 1977
Height: 5'11" Weight: 11.6

It was a fairytale start to 1998-99 for Warren, the first ever product from Barnet's youth system to establish himself in the senior side, when given the honour of wearing the captain's armband for the Worthington Cup-tie at Wolves in August, and creating history as the youngest ever skipper in the club's history. In the pre-season friendlies, he was utilised in the role of right back, then in the formative stages of the season he was fielded in the centre of the defence. Later, in the away match at Cambridge, he operated on the left side of defence, while in the home clash against Scunthorpe he was instructed to play on the right side of midfield. Obviously, this underlines his tremendous versatility, and this, coupled with a flawless technique, conjures up an image of a player who John Still quite rightly values in the £1 million bracket. However, only four days after netting his solitary goal of the campaign, against Scunthorpe, he suffered a gut-wrenching blow that ended his season. He was only on the pitch at Hednesford in the FA Cup first round tie for ten minutes before sustaining a broken leg, which ruled him out of action for seven months. His attitude towards his recovery has been nothing short of inspirational, and the club does not harbour any doubts that he will return to reclaim his mantle as their most valued asset.

Barnet (From trainee on 3/7/96) FL 38+15/2 FLC 5+1 FAC 1 Others 3/1

GOODING Michael (Mick) Charles
Born: Newcastle, 12 April 1959
Height: 5'8" Weight: 11.10
Club Honours: Div 3 '81, Div 2 '94

Brought up from Plymouth during the 1998 close season for the post of assistant manager, Mick was called into action for Southend more often than he expected in 1998-99. With the club lurching from one crisis to another, his hard work and strong tackling in midfield was required in an attempt to instil some confidence in a team which ultimately only avoided demotion from the league by a few places. A real 100 per center, he is unbelievably fit for a man of 40 years of age, and puts some of the younger players to shame.

Rotherham U (Signed from Bishop Auckland on 18/7/79) FL 90+12/10 FLC 9/3 FAC 3
Chesterfield (Signed on 24/12/82) FL 12
Rotherham U (Signed on 9/9/83) FL 149+7/33 FLC 18/3 FAC 13/4 Others 7
Peterborough U (£18,000 on 13/8/87) FL 47/21 FLC 8/2 FAC 1/2 Others 4/2
Wolverhampton W (£85,000 on 20/9/88) FL 43+1/4 FLC 4 Others 5+1/1

Reading (£65,000 on 26/12/89) FL 303+11/26 FLC 19 FAC 18+1/2 Others 16/2 (Free to Plymouth Arg as coach on 26/3/98)
Southend U (Free on 9/7/98) FL 19+4 FLC 2 Others 1

GOODLAD Mark
Born: Barnsley, 9 September 1979
Height: 6'0" Weight: 13.2

Unable to see much of a future for himself at Nottingham Forest, the young 'keeper was loaned out to Third Division Scarborough last February to get in some match practice and, having impressed against Newcastle in a reserve match, he was given a baptism of fire on his Football League debut as Boro crashed to a 5-1 home defeat against Cambridge. He did reasonably well, despite the scoreline, but it was much of the same again when involved in a 3-1 defeat at Shrewsbury, before he helped the side to a 2-1 home win over Swansea prior to returning to the City Ground.

Nottingham F (From trainee on 2/10/96)
Scarborough (Loaned on 5/2/99) FL 3

GOODMAN Donald (Don) Ralph
Born: Leeds, 9 May 1966
Height: 5'10" Weight: 13.2
Club Honours: Div 3 '85

Able to play as an out-and-out forward, or wide on the flank, he signed for Barnsley on a three-month loan from Hiroshima Antlers last December, having been released by Wolves at the end of the previous campaign. As usual he gave his best when called upon, but was unable to break into the goalscoring charts, and suffered throughout with a hamstring injury which limited his appearances. At his best a brave, battling forward with aerial strength, he left to return to Japan in mid March before signing for Motherwell on transfer deadline day.

Bradford C (Free from Collingham on 10/7/84) FL 65+5/14 FLC 5+1/2 FAC 2+3/4 Others 4+1/2
West Bromwich A (£50,000 on 27/3/87) FL 140+18/60 FLC 11/1 FAC 7/1 Others 5/1
Sunderland (£900,000 on 6/12/91) FL 112+4/40 FLC 9/1 FAC 3/1 Others 4
Wolverhampton W (£1,100,000 on 6/12/94) FL 115+10/33 FLC 8+1/4 FAC 16+1/2 Others 3 (Free to Hiroshima Antlers during 1998 close season)
Barnsley (Loaned on 25/12/98) FL 5+3 FAC 2

GOODMAN Jonathan (Jon)
Born: Walthamstow, 2 June 1971
Height: 6'0" Weight: 12.3
International Honours: Ei: 4

Jon made only one first-team appearance for Wimbledon in 1998-99 – from the subs' bench at Charlton – due to severe knee injury problems for the second consecutive season. A powerful forward with pace and an eye for goal, he will be pushing hard for a spot next season, if injuries allow.

Millwall (£50,000 from Bromley on 20/8/90) FL 97+12/35 FLC 5+4/2 FAC 5+1 Others 3
Wimbledon (Signed on 9/11/94) PL 28+32/11 FLC 1+1 FAC 3+4/3

GOODRIDGE Gregory (Greg) Ronald St Clair
Born: Barbados, 10 July 1971
Height: 5'6" Weight: 10.0
International Honours: Barbados: 5

A match winner on his day, Greg was the

victim of Benny Lennartsson's controversial team selections at Bristol City in 1998-99, often sitting in the stand when the fans were crying out for his much-needed pace and width, especially at home. After failing to gain a place in the side, he returned to Barbados to represent his own national side, before coming back to Ashton Gate. Still a crowd favourite, his electric pace delights at times, and if only he could add consistency to his all-round play he would be a regular in most sides outside of the Premier.

Torquay U (Free from Lambada on 24/3/94) FL 32+6/4 FLC 4/1 FAC 2+1 Others 3+1/1
Queens Park R (£350,000 on 9/8/95) PL 0+7/1 FLC 0+1 FAC 0+1
Bristol C (£50,000 on 19/8/96) FL 62+27/14 FLC 7+1/1 FAC 5+2/1 Others 0+4

GORAM Andrew (Andy) Lewis

Born: Bury, 13 April 1964
Height: 5'11" Weight: 12.6
Club Honours: SPD '92, '93, '95, '96, '97; SLC '93, '97; SC '92, '93, '96
International Honours: S: 43; U21-1

Released by Glasgow Rangers during the 1998 close season, and following negative newspaper articles, the enigmatic Scottish international 'keeper moved to Notts County last September as a temporary stand in whilst Darren Ward was on international duty. So popular with Rangers fans was he that two bus loads of his own supporters' club travelled down from Glasgow for his solitary performance, a 1-0 home defeat at the hands of Wigan. Four days later, he moved up the road to Sheffield United as a stand in for Alan Kelly and Simon Tracey, who were both injured. As expected, he turned out to be a reliable performer, conceding 12 goals in nine league and cup appearances, and was in goal for the club's first clean sheet of the season, at Oxford, in October. The 55th goalie to play for United in the Football League, Andy moved back north of the border with Motherwell on 12 January. Is the son of Lewis, who played in goal for Bury between 1950 and 1956.

Oldham Ath (Free from West Bromwich A juniors on 22/8/81) FL 195 FLC 10 FAC 7 Others 3
Hibernian (£325,000 on 9/10/87) SL 138/1 SLC 7 SC 13 Others 4
Glasgow R (£1,000,000 on 27/6/91) SL 184 SLC 19 SC 26 Others 3
Notts Co (Free on 3/9/98) FL 1
Sheffield U (Free on 7/9/98) FL 7 FLC 2

GORDON Dean Dwight

Born: Croydon, 10 February 1973
Height: 6'0" Weight: 13.4
Club Honours: Div 1 '94
International Honours: E: U21-13

Transferred from Crystal Palace to Middlesbrough during the 1998 close season, the "flying wingback", as he is affectionately known, sums up perfectly Dean's contribution to Boro's team performance in 1998-99, and indeed to the beautiful game. He is a member of the select band of ever presents that every club yearns for, and his goals, rare yellow cards and "Man of the Match" awards bear testimony to his total professionalism. His signing

raised a few Teesside eyebrows when he arrived at the Cellnet, but any fears were quelled after his debut (against Leeds) on the opening day of the season. Aggressive and enthusiastic, he is a tenacious and hungry ball winner, possessing a powerful shot, and has the ability to supply pin-point crosses to colleagues waiting expectantly in the strike zone.

Crystal Palace (From trainee on 4/7/91) F/PL 181+20/20 FLC 16+5/2 FAC 14+1/1 Others 5+1
Middlesbrough (£900,000 on 17/7/98) PL 38/3 FLC 2 FAC 1

GORDON Kenyatta Gavin

Born: Manchester, 24 June 1979
Height: 6'1" Weight: 12.0

Gavin's first full season at Lincoln saw him win a regular place in the second half of 1998-99, partnering either Tony Battersby or Lee Thorpe up front. He made good progress, and his ability to win the ball in the air, combined with his powerful running, caused problems for opposing defences. Scored five league goals during the season, his last as a teenager, but with better luck he could have at least doubled his total.

Hull C (From trainee on 3/7/96) FL 22+16/9 FLC 1+4/1 Others 1+1
Lincoln C (£30,000 on 7/11/97) FL 30+10/8 FAC 4 Others 3+1

GOUGH Richard Charles

Born: Stockholm, Sweden, 5 April 1962
Height: 6'0" Weight: 12.0
Club Honours: SPD '83, '89, '90, '91, '92, '93, '94, '95, '96, '97; SLC '89, '91, '93, '94, '97; SC '92, '93, '96
International Honours: S: 61; U21-5

An experienced central defender who makes defending look easy, Richard came back to British football with Nottingham Forest on a short-term contract early last March, having left Glasgow Rangers for the American side, San Jose, in May 1998. Obviously fit, he made quite an impression with the Forest fans, and even his old club, Spurs, rated him so highly that they tried to re-sign him on transfer deadline day. Made his Premiership debut at home to Newcastle, looking elegant and good on the ball, his positional play allowing him time and space, and was unlucky to give a penalty away. Despite the club being doomed to the First Division, the Scot tried his hardest to no avail, and it is difficult to see where he goes from here after being released in the summer.

Dundee U (Free from Wits University on 21/3/80) SL 161+8/24 SLC 33+3/9 SC 19/2 Others 30+1/3
Tottenham H (£750,000 on 17/8/86) FL 49/2 FLC 10 FAC 6
Glasgow R (£1,500,000 on 2/10/87) SL 318/26 SLC 35/3 SC 37/2 Others 34/4 (Free to San Jose on 21/5/98)
Nottingham F (Free on 5/3/99) PL 7

GOWER Mark

Born: Edmonton, 5 October 1978
Height: 5'11" Weight: 11.12
Club Honours: FLC '99
International Honours: E: Yth; Sch

Graduating from the FA National School of Excellence, this promising young midfielder joined Tottenham as a trainee in 1995, and

signed professional terms in April 1997 before making his first-team debut in the Worthington Cup second round first leg at Brentford last September, when he came off the bench. Instantly relaxed and confident with good pace, Mark went on to make a further subs' appearance and looks a good prospect for the future.

Tottenham H (From trainee on 1/4/97) FLC 0+2

GRAHAM Gareth Lee

Born: Belfast, 6 December 1978
Height: 5'7" Weight: 10.2
International Honours: NI: U21-2

This ginger-headed youngster from Northern Ireland came through the Crystal Palace ranks as a trainee before turning professional in March 1997. A useful midfield prospect, he had hoped to break into the first team in 1997-98, but a broken leg held him back, and it was not until some impressive reserve displays saw him coming into senior reckoning towards the end of last season. Given his debut when coming off the bench for the last 13 minutes at Watford in April, Gareth looks to hold down a regular squad place this coming term.

Crystal Palace (From trainee on 19/3/97) FL 0+1

GRAHAM Richard Ean

Born: Dewsbury, 28 November 1974
Height: 6'2" Weight: 12.10
International Honours: Ei: U21-2

Recognised at Oldham as one of the most honest of players, when he crashed to the ground in sheer agony during the home match against Fulham last September, the fans knew there was something adrift, especially when it took him a while to recover. Although he appeared in six of the next seven matches, it was clear that his knee was giving him a lot of pain, and he was rested for ten games before playing against Brentford in the two FA Cup matches in December. Following that, told by the doctors that he would be out for the rest of the season, he was operated on in January and, despite the initial medical fears that he might not play again, Richard is back in training. A footballing central defender who is good in the air, but prefers the ball to feet where he can make attacking runs, he is also a danger from set pieces.

Oldham Ath (From trainee on 16/7/93) P/FL 125+8/12 FLC 11 FAC 11/1 Others 3

GRAHAM Richard Stephen

Born: Newry, 5 August 1979
Height: 5'8" Weight: 10.6
International Honours: NI: U21-2; Yth

Richard is another of the successes from Queens Park Rangers' youth programme. The younger brother of Mark, who is also at Rangers, he is a player who can perform equally well either on the wing or in central midfield. Made his first-team debut as a substitute in the victory at Wolverhampton Wanderers last September, and was included in the Northern Ireland U21 squad for the match against Germany in March.

Queens Park R (From trainee on 8/8/96) FL 0+2

GRAINGER Martin Robert
Born: Enfield, 23 August 1972
Height: 5'11" Weight: 12.0
Uncompromising in the tackle, and fully committed, Martin also provided Birmingham with superb dead-ball service and crosses from the left in 1998-99. Rated as the club's most improved player by manager Trevor Francis, he finally won the fans over when used mainly on the left of midfield, a role he dislikes. More than capable in defence if required, he also causes the opposition problems with throw ins and powerfully taken free kicks.
Colchester U (From trainee on 28/7/92) FL 37+9/7 FLC 3 FAC 3+2 Others 3/1
Brentford (£60,000 on 21/10/93) FL 100+1/12 FLC 6/1 FAC 9/1 Others 8/2
Birmingham C (£400,000 on 25/3/96) FL 86+18/9 FLC 6+2 FAC 5+1 Others 2

GRANT Anthony (Tony) James
Born: Liverpool, 14 November 1974
Height: 5'10" Weight: 10.2
Club Honours: CS '95
International Honours: E: U21-1
An elegant, cultured midfielder with the ability to deliver damaging and incisive passes through any defence, Tony appeared in danger of failing to live up to his undoubted potential in a disappointing 1998-99 season at Everton. He appeared fleetingly, and rarely showed the kind of sublime passing skills he undoubtedly possesses, before being made available for transfer in the summer. Deceptively sharp in the tackle, among other attributes, he would enhance all but the best first-team squads.
Everton (From trainee on 8/7/93) PL 43+16/2 FLC 5+1 FAC 4+4 Others 2+2/1
Swindon T (Loaned on 18/1/96) FL 3/1

GRANT Gareth Michael
Born: Leeds, 6 September 1980
Height: 5'9" Weight: 10.4
Having attended trials at Lilleshall in August for the England U18's squad, Gareth was involved in Bradford's first eight games last season but, with an abundance of strikers at the club, he was loaned to Halifax Town in February to get some first-team experience. Although regularly used on the subs' bench, when called upon his pace and trickery caused all sorts of problems to opposing defences. Back at Valley Parade, as a regular goalscorer in the reserves and leading goalscorer in the juniors, he is thought to have a big future in the game.
Bradford C (From trainee on 28/4/98) FL 2+6 FLC 1+1
Halifax T (Loaned on 12/2/99) FL 0+3 Others 0+1

GRANT Kim Tyrone
Born: Ghana, 25 September 1972
Height: 5'10" Weight: 11.6
International Honours: Ghana: 7
Made only a couple of subs' appearances for Millwall in 1998-99 before going to Notts County on loan in December, and scoring within seconds on his debut, against Northampton. Although popular with the County fans for his hard work and ability to turn, which provided many chances for himself and his team mates, he failed to hit the net again before injury forced him to return to the Den. On recovery, and with injuries and suspensions affecting other strikers, Kim finally got a chance or two, scoring a cracking goal in a 3-0 home win against Wrexham, and then striking both in a 2-0 home win over Colchester. A pacy striker with good shooting ability with either foot, it looked at one stage that he would be in line for a place in the Auto Windscreens Shield final at Wembley, but it was not to be as Richard Sadlier returned early from the U20 championships in Nigeria.
Charlton Ath (From trainee on 6/3/91) FL 74+49/18 FLC 3+9/1 FAC 8+5/5 Others 5+2/1
Luton T (£250,000 on 15/3/96) FL 18+17/5 FLC 4/2 FAC 0+2 Others 2+1/1
Millwall (Signed on 29/8/97) FL 35+20/11 FLC 3/1 FAC 0+1 Others 2+1/1
Notts Co (Loaned on 24/12/98) FL 6/1

GRANT Peter
Born: Glasgow, 30 August 1965
Height: 5'9" Weight: 11.9
Club Honours: SPL '86, '88; SC '89
International Honours: S: 2; B-2; U21-10; Yth; Sch
A model professional, Peter's vast experience gained during his 18 years with Glasgow Celtic proved more than useful for Norwich's Bruce Rioch to call upon in 1998-99, and to play alongside his usual youthful line-up. He worked tremendously hard, chasing and harrying the opposition when they had the ball, whilst always being available for a pass when City were in possession. A tremendous example to every young player, his contribution to the club's cause should not be underestimated.
Glasgow C (From juniors on 27/7/82) SL 338+27/16 SLC 40+3/3 SC 34+4/1 Others 27/1
Norwich C (£200,000 on 22/8/97) FL 64+4/3 FLC 4+1 FAC 2

GRANT Stephen Hubert
Born: Birr, 14 April 1977
Height: 6'1" Weight: 12.0
International Honours: Ei: U21-4; Sch
Although the arrival of Ian Moore and Tony Ellis at Stockport resulted in limited opportunities for the Republic of Ireland U21 international to break into the first team in 1998-99, he was often impressive in the reserve team as a strong-running striker always willing to shoot on sight of goal. At senior level, he was often used as a substitute, but failed to make an impression on manager Gary Megson's starting line-up, and was released during the summer.
Sunderland (Free from Athlone T on 10/8/95) (Free to Shamrock Rov on 17/10/96)
Stockport Co (£30,000 on 3/9/97) FL 10+19/4 FAC 0+1

GRANVILLE Daniel (Danny) Patrick
Born: Islington, 19 January 1975
Height: 5'11" Weight: 12.5
Club Honours: FLC '98, ECWC '98
International Honours: E: U21-4
When Danny joined Leeds from Chelsea in June 1998, George Graham saw the youngster as the answer to a long quest for a high-class left back. Unfortunately, Ian Harte's much improved fitness and form, and a thigh strain he picked up pre season, meant he was not an automatic selection for the first team. In fact, his first touch of the ball for his new club was to score in the penalty shoot out in the UEFA Cup victory against Martimo. Then, making his first full start, in the 1-1 home draw at Nottingham Forest, he lasted only 31 minutes before picking up his second yellow card of the match and collecting a sending off. Although remaining in the first team squad he was unable to break into the side, but at such a young age there is plenty of time to give his career a lift off.
Cambridge U (From trainee on 19/5/93) FL 89+10/7 FLC 3+2 FAC 2+2 Others 4+2
Chelsea (£300,000 + on 21/3/97) PL 12+6 FLC 3 Others 4+1/1
Leeds U (£1,600,000 on 8/7/98) PL 7+2 FLC 1 FAC 3 Others 0+1

GRAY Andrew (Andy) David
Born: Harrogate, 15 November 1977
Height: 6'1" Weight: 13.0
International Honours: S: Yth
Transferred to Nottingham Forest from Leeds last September, the son of the former Leeds' star, Frankie, was looking to relaunch his career after a frustrating spell at Elland Road. He started quite well at the City Ground but, in a side struggling to come to terms with life in the Premiership, he faltered and lost his place before having spells on loan at Preston (February) and Oldham (March). A right-footed left winger, with skill and excellent crossing ability, as you might expect from the nephew of the legendary Eddie Gray, he joined North End as cover for injuries to the wide men. However, unable to create an impression, he switched to Oldham at the end of his loan period, where he had much of the same. Hopefully, Andy will get the opportunity to rebuild his career at Forest in 1999-2000.
Leeds U (From trainee on 1/7/95) PL 13+9 FLC 3+1 FAC 0+2
Bury (Loaned on 11/12/97) FL 4+2/1
Nottingham F (£175,000 on 2/9/98) PL 3+5 FLC 2+1 FAC 0+1
Preston NE (Loaned on 23/2/99) FL 5
Oldham Ath (Loaned on 25/3/99) FL 4

GRAY David
Born: Rossendale, 18 January 1980
Height: 6'2" Weight: 13.2
After being an unused substitute for Rochdale in the final match of 1997-98, he made his first-team debut in the 1998-99 pre-season games, before making his first senior appearance when coming on at Plymouth on the opening day. An energetic and powerful front runner, he later made two more substitute appearances, before going on loan to non-league Chorley at the end of December after Dale had signed several more experienced strikers. Was released during the summer.
Rochdale (From trainee on 3/7/98) FL 0+3

GRAY Ian James
Born: Manchester, 25 February 1975
Height: 6'2" Weight: 13.0
Having arrived at Edgeley Park in the

summer of 1997, just before Gary Megson took over as manager, as understudy to Carlo Nash in 1998-99 Ian performed brilliantly in the reserve team and continued to develop into a more than promising goalkeeper. Unlucky not to get a chance in the first team until the final three games of the campaign, when he came in and was unfortunate to have nine goals put past him. Has another year to run on his current contract and could well make his mark in 1999-2000. Is agile and keen, with good handling ability.

Oldham Ath (From trainee on 16/7/93)
Rochdale (Loaned on 18/11/94) FL 12 Others 3
Rochdale (£20,000 on 17/7/95) FL 66 FLC 4 FAC 5 Others 4
Stockport Co (£200,000 + on 30/7/97) FL 6 FLC 2

GRAY Kevin John
Born: Sheffield, 7 January 1972
Height: 6'0" Weight: 14.0
Having firmly put the off-field issues of 1997-98 behind him, the no-nonsense Huddersfield defender gave some solid displays after coming off the subs' bench last season. Always committed to the cause, never shirking a tackle or aerial challenge, and having regained his first-team place, he was a colossus in the FA Cup against Queens Park Rangers, and equally magnificent against Derby and Everton in the Worthington Cup. After opening his goal-scoring account against Wolves, a powerful header cancelling out his "own" goal in the same game, he suffered an injured knee against Swindon on Easter Monday which effectively brought his campaign to an end.
Mansfield T (From trainee on 1/7/90) FL 129+12/3 FLC 8/1 FAC 6+1 Others 12+2/2
Huddersfield T (Signed on 18/7/94) FL 141+10/3 FLC 9+1 FAC 11 Others 3

GRAY Martin David
Born: Stockton on Tees, 17 August 1971
Height: 5'9" Weight: 11.4
An energetic Oxford midfielder who gives committed performances in every game, Martin missed just seven games last season, several of them being imposed following suspensions. However, you cannot change his displays, and if you were to take away his all-action style he would not be such an effective player. A good motivator of others who, sadly, could not weigh in with a goal this time around, he covers every part of the pitch, competes for every ball, and wins more than his fair share.
Sunderland (From trainee on 1/2/90) FL 46+18/1 FLC 6+2 FAC 0+3 Others 3+1
Aldershot (Loaned on 9/1/91) FL 3+2 Others 1
Fulham (Loaned on 20/10/95) FL 6 Others 1
Oxford U (£100,000 on 28/3/96) FL 115+6/4 FLC 9 FAC 4

GRAY Michael
Born: Sunderland, 3 August 1974
Height: 5'7" Weight: 10.10
Club Honours: Div 1 '96, '99
International Honours: E: 3
The Sunderland left back ended 1997-98 by missing the final penalty at Wembley in the play-off shoot-out, but ended 1998-99 by winning his first full England cap against

Hungary in Budapest – an achievement that epitomised his grit and determination, qualities that shine through in his play. As a former winger, he can be a potent attacker when moving forward, possessing pace and the ability to beat a man, while his crossing strengths provide numerous chances for the team's forwards. His partnership down the left flank with Allan Johnston was one of the vital components in Sunderland's First Division championship win and he picked up his second title medal, as well as being selected for the PFA Division One award-winning team for the second time.
Sunderland (From trainee on 1/7/92) P/FL 206+20/14 FLC 16+3 FAC 9+1/1 Others 2

GRAY Philip (Phil)
Born: Belfast, 2 October 1968
Height: 5'10" Weight: 12.5
International Honours: NI: 21; U23-1; Yth; Sch
Having suffered from injuries at Luton in 1997-98, Phil was hoping for a trouble-free ride last season after spending the summer recovering from his back and knee problems. Returned to enjoy his longest uninterrupted run in the team, playing in 31 of the opening 33 games and scoring in three successive matches, at Fulham, York, and at home to Oldham, he ended the campaign with 13 goals. An aggressive and sometimes unorthodox striker, whilst also inventive and intuitive, the experienced Northern Ireland international was eventually slowed down by ankle and toe injuries before coming back for the final game, at Millwall.
Tottenham H (From apprentice on 21/8/86) FL 4+5 FAC 0+1
Barnsley (Loaned on 17/1/90) FL 3 FAC 1
Fulham (Loaned on 8/11/90) FL 3 Others 2/1
Luton T (£275,000 on 16/8/91) FL 54+5/22 FLC 4/3 FAC 2/1 Others 2
Sunderland (£800,000 on 19/7/93) FL 108+7/34 FLC 9/4 FAC 8/3 Others 2 (Free to Nancy during 1996 close season)
Luton T (£400,000 from Fortuna Sittard on 19/9/97) FL 46+6/10 FLC 7/3 FAC 2/2 Others 0+1

GRAY Stuart
Born: Hallogate, 18 December 1973
Height: 5'11" Weight: 11.2
International Honours: S: U21-7
Reading's Scottish left back missed a large chunk in the middle of last season because of a run of injuries, but recovered around February time to regain a regular spot, either at left back or on the left-hand side of midfield. A steady, rather than spectacular defender, who is somewhat handicapped by a lack of pace, he possesses a good shot and scored a couple of well-taken goals late in the campaign.
Glasgow C (Free from Giffnock North AFC on 7/7/92) SL 19+9/1 SC 1 Others 2+1
Reading (£100,000 on 27/3/98) FL 32+2/2 FLC 4

GRAYSON Simon Nicholas
Born: Ripon, 16 December 1969
Height: 6'0" Weight: 13.7
Club Honours: FLC '97
Last season was a very quiet one for the Aston Villa defender, and one in which he had to contend with a place on the subs' bench far more times than he actually

played. In fact, Simon only featured in the starting line-up on seven occasions, but sustained his match fitness by playing in a number of reserve matches. It is possibly not surprising to hear that he remained fairly injury free in 1998-99, apart from the knee problem he picked up in a behind-closed-doors friendly at the beginning of March. Extremely versatile, although more comfortable in a right-sided wing-back role, he can also be relied upon as a man marker, while his aerial ability is important at both ends of the pitch.
Leeds U (From trainee on 13/6/88) FL 2 Others 1+1
Leicester C (£50,000 on 13/3/92) F/PL 175+13/4 FLC 16+2/2 FAC 9 Others 13+1
Aston Villa (£1,350,000 on 1/7/97) PL 32+16 FLC 1+1 FAC 4+1/2 Others 6+3

GRAZIOLI Giuliano Stefano Luigi
Born: Marylebone, 23 March 1975
Height: 5'11" Weight: 12.11
Loaned out to non-league Stevenage Borough in 1997-98, the Peterborough striker came to the nation's notice when scoring against the eventual FA Cup finalists, Newcastle. Back at London Road for 1998-99, after spending a couple of league games on the bench he came into the side at Barnet and scored five times in a 9-1 victory, but was surprisingly unable to hold down a regular place. As a player who picks up the pieces in the box, and capitalises on defenders' mistakes, Giuliano still finished the campaign as the club's leading goalscorer with 15 from 22 starts. Out of contract during the summer, it was reported that United had offered him terms of re-engagement.
Peterborough U (Free from Wembley on 19/10/95) FL 23+18/16 FLC 1+2 FAC 0+3/1 Others 0+2

GREAVES Mark Andrew
Born: Hull, 22 January 1975
Height: 6'1" Weight: 13.0
Starting last season on the transfer list, Mark's form suffered further with a "Di Canio" style sending off at Chester in August. It was November before a two-match ban was handed out, but with that out of the way, and Warren Joyce installed as manager, "Greavesie" became the revelation of the Tigers' New Year. Displaying the best form of his career, especially as one of the three centre halves, he also starred at right-wing back, and was rewarded with a two-year contract in March.
Hull C (Free from Brigg T on 17/6/96) FL 58+22/4 FLC 4 FAC 5 Others 1+1

GREEN Francis James
Born: Nottingham, 25 April 1980
Height: 5'9" Weight: 11.6
Having made his debut for Peterborough late in 1997-98, and scoring at Torquay, the young striker was expected to be given an early chance last season but, in the event, eventually came in for a few games from March onwards. However, he obviously likes playing against Torquay, his only goal of 1998-99 coming against them as in the previous campaign. A success of the U19

Academy team, when picked for the seniors he never let them down, and continued to show much promise and workrate.
Peterborough U (£25,000 + from Ilkeston T on 2/3/98) FL 5+6/2

GREEN Richard Edward
Born: Wolverhampton, 22 November 1967
Height: 6'1" Weight: 13.7
Having moved initially on loan from Gillingham last August to make his Walsall debut in the Worthington Cup first leg against Queens Park Rangers, Richard was signed on a more permanent basis a month later, and held his place until early in the New Year when he failed to regain it after Ian Roper had deputised for him when he was out with injury. Though he scored just once last season (in the win over Millwall in November), his flick-ons in opponents' penalty areas added an extra dimension to the play of this powerful central defender.
Shrewsbury T (From trainee on 19/7/86) FL 120+5/5 FLC 11/1 FAC 5 Others 5/1
Swindon T (Free on 25/10/90)
Gillingham (Free on 6/3/92) FL 206+10/16 FLC 12+1 FAC 16+1/1 Others 6+1
Walsall (Signed on 10/8/98) FL 22+8/1 FLC 2 FAC 2 Others 1

GREEN Robert Paul
Born: Chertsey, 19 January 1980
Height: 6'2" Weight: 12.2
International Honours: E: Yth
Graduating through the junior side to reach professional status at Norwich during the 1997 close season, but very much in the wings behind the impressive Andy Marshall, Robert finally got the break he was looking for when standing in for the latter to make his first-team debut in last season's 0-0 home draw against Ipswich. That was followed up with another start, a 2-2 home draw against Tranmere, and he looks set to put pressure on the latter in 1999-2000. An England youth international at U16, U17, and U18 levels, he has overcome a serious back injury to become a real prospect, being commanding, agile, and a goalie who stands up well in one-on-one situations.
Norwich C (From juniors on 3/7/97) FL 2

GREEN Ryan Michael
Born: Cardiff, 20 October 1980
Height: 5'8" Weight: 10.10
International Honours: W: 2; U21-7; Yth
At the end of 1997-98 Ryan had played twice for Wales at the age of 17, yet he had not even been close to a Wolves' debut. Although his international career continued at U21 level in 1998-99, the young right back had still not made the Wolves' team. Eventually, he got his chance when Kevin Muscat was suspended in November, and showed remarkable confidence against Sheffield United, repeatedly taking players on and looking very skilful until he went off injured in the second half. He then had a few fitness worries, but after playing for Wales U21s in March, and putting his problems behind him, he signed a contract for his club in April.
Wolverhampton W (From trainee on 25/10/97) FL 1

GREEN Scott Paul
Born: Walsall, 15 January 1970
Height: 5'10" Weight: 12.5
Club Honours: Div 1 '97; AMC '99
A highly versatile and valuable Wigan squad member, Scott held down the right-back berth for most of last season. With the club adopting a three-man central defensive formation for long periods, it gave him licence to push forward into what once was more familiar territory. A popular player among the fans, possessing a good engine and no lack of confidence on the ball, somewhat surprisingly he failed to score a goal during the campaign. Was delighted to be part of the side that won the Auto Windscreens Shield at Wembley.
Derby Co (From trainee on 20/7/88)
Bolton W (£50,000 on 17/3/90) P/FL 166+54/25 FLC 19+4/1 FAC 20+3/4 Others 16+4/1
Wigan Ath (£300,000 on 30/6/97) FL 69+6/1 FLC 6 FAC 6 Others 6+1

GREENACRE Christopher (Chris) Mark
Born: Halifax, 23 December 1977
Height: 5'11" Weight: 12.8
Placed on Manchester City's transfer list in August 1998, being one of many players the club looked at with a view to reduce the staff, he made his one and only appearance at Millwall in a tough game where, though brought into the team to resolve the lack of goals, he could not settle and was substituted after 52 minutes. Loaned out to Scarborough in mid December, he stayed for the maximum three months. This gave him first-team football, which he enjoyed, being a regular for most of the period and scoring the odd goal. Returned to the reserves at the end of March, scoring a hat trick against Coventry reserves, before being loaned out to Northampton, where he failed to get a senior opportunity. Is always looking to latch on to half chances, his busy play in the penalty area making him difficult to mark.
Manchester C (From trainee on 1/7/95) FL 3+5/1 FAC 0+1
Cardiff C (Loaned on 22/8/97) FL 11/2
Blackpool (Loaned on 5/3/98) FL 2+2
Scarborough (Loaned on 10/12/98) FL 10+2/2 Others 1

GREENALL Colin Anthony
Born: Billinge, 30 December 1963
Height: 5'11" Weight: 12.12
Club Honours: Div 3 '97; AMC '99
International Honours: E: Yth
Came out of retirement to enjoy his best ever campaign as a player. After starting 1998-99 as Wigan's reserve-team coach, injuries saw him return for a league match at Notts County in September. A virtual ever present thereafter, his leadership and organisational skills in a three-man central defence formed the back bone of the side that reached the play-off final. Crowned a memorable season, in which he played his 750th first-team game, with his first ever appearance at Wembley, when winning the "Man of the Match" award in the 1-0 Auto Windscreens Shield victory over Millwall. Dependable as ever, his vast experience was invaluable in a sweeper role, collecting both

the supporters' and players' "Player of the Year" awards for the second time in three seasons.
Blackpool (From apprentice on 17/1/81) FL 179+4/9 FLC 12/2 FAC 9 Others 2
Gillingham (£40,000 on 10/9/86) FL 62/4 FLC 3/1 FAC 6/1 Others 9/2
Oxford U (£285,000 on 15/2/88) FL 67/2 FLC 4 FAC 1 Others 2
Bury (Loaned on 4/1/90) FL 3 Other 1
Bury (£125,000 on 16/7/90) FL 66+2/5 FLC 3 FAC 1 Others 8/1
Preston NE (£50,000 on 27/3/92) FL 29/1
Chester C (Free on 13/8/93) FL 42/1 FLC 2 FAC 4/1 Others 4
Lincoln C (Free on 27/7/94) FL 43/3 FLC 6 FAC 3/1 Others 2
Wigan Ath (£45,000 on 19/9/95) FL 162/14 FLC 5+1/1 FAC 10/1 Others 15+1

GREENE David Michael
Born: Luton, 26 October 1973
Height: 6'3" Weight: 14.4
International Honours: Ei: U21-14
A tall centre half whose presence was vital in the Colchester rearguard during 1998-99, David deservedly claimed a clean sweep of all the "Player of the Year" awards at the end of an outstanding season. He was a pillar of strength throughout the year, and his appearance record was only blemished by suspension following a controversial sending off, along with former United forward, Carl Asaba, at Gillingham. Finished the campaign as second-top scorer with eight goals, many of them towering headers, but also scored the only Colchester goal direct from a free kick, to beat promotion-chasing Walsall at Layer Road. Once the record holder for the Republic of Ireland U21 appearances, he has now been overtaken by Alan Mahon of Tranmere.
Luton T (From juniors on 3/9/91) FL 18+1 FLC 2 FAC 1 Others 0+1
Colchester U (Loaned on 23/11/95) FL 14/1 Others 2
Brentford (Loaned on 1/3/96) FL 11
Colchester U (£30,000 on 21/6/96) FL 124/14 FLC 8 FAC 6 Others 10/2

GREENING Jonathan
Born: Scarborough, 2 January 1979
Height: 5'11" Weight: 11.7
Club Honours: EC '99
International Honours: E: U21-3; Yth
A highly talented young Manchester United forward, with pace, and an eye for goal, Jonathan made an impressive start to his United career, playing alongside Eric Cantona in the Munich Memorial game last August. Arguably the pick of the bunch during the Worthington Cup campaign, he made his Premiership debut as a substitute against Nottingham Forest in December and, following several first-team outings from the bench in the latter stages of the season, he appears to have a bright future ahead of him at Old Trafford. A non-playing sub for United in the European Cup final, good feet and good passing skills also allow him to play in midfield if required. Made his debut for the England U21 side in 1998-99, appearing three times in all.

York C (From trainee on 23/12/96) FL 5+20/2 FLC 0+1 Others 1
Manchester U (£500,000 + on 25/3/98) PL 0+3 FLC 3 FAC 0+1

GREGAN Sean Matthew
Born: Guisborough, 29 March 1974
Height: 6'2" Weight: 14.7
Preston's combative midfielder and captain had another tumultuous season in 1998-99, always playing with strength and aggression, whether attacking or defending, but suffered three suspensions in the process. His experience as a former centre half makes him a useful aerial force at both ends of the field, despite only scoring three times himself. Nevertheless, he remains one of North End's most important players, especially after tempering his desire to play long raking passes at every opportunity. Amongst his personal achievements during the campaign, he reached 100 games for the club, 200 in the Football League, and 250 career games. Selected by his fellow professionals for the PFA award-winning Second Division side, he was rewarded with a new two-and-half year contract in February.
Darlington (From trainee on 20/1/91) FL 129+7/4 FLC 8 FAC 7 Others 10+1/1
Preston NE (£350,000 on 29/11/96) FL 94+3/6 FLC 5 FAC 7/1 Others 7

GREGG Matthew (Matt) Stephen
Born: Cheltenham, 30 November 1978
Height: 5'11" Weight: 12.0
The young goalkeeper gave early notice of his potential in 1998-99, with some fine performances at Torquay and, following his Plainmoor Worthington Cup appearance against Crystal Palace, Palace's manager, Terry Venables, soon paid a substantial fee to secure his services. Unable to get a game at Selhurst with Fraser Digby in such good form, he had a spell on loan to Swansea in February, keeping two clean sheets in five league appearances, before returning to Palace when Digby was injured. Still to make his debut for the Eagles.
Torquay U (From trainee on 4/7/97) FL 32 FLC 5 FAC 1 Others 1
Crystal Palace (£400,000 on 24/10/98)
Swansea C (Loaned on 12/2/99) FL 5

GREGORY David Spencer
Born: Sudbury, 23 January 1970
Height: 5'10" Weight: 12.8
A true utility player, "Greggers" (senior) competed a marvellous season in 1998-99, in which he played as a full back, centre half, in midfield, and up front, not to mention finishing as Colchester's leading goalscorer for the second time in succession! His 14 goals included no less than nine penalties, all dispatched with a calm precision, no matter that several of them came very late, in both games against Wycombe, and also at Bristol Rovers, to win vital points for United. His other goals were all spectacular too, with the finish to a sweeping attack at Notts County and a splendid curling shot at Burnley, particularly memorable. Was very unlucky not to collect at least one of the end-of-season awards.

Ipswich T (From trainee on 31/3/87) F/PL 16+16/2 FLC 3+2 FAC 1 Others 3+2/4
Hereford U (Loaned on 9/1/95) FL 2 Others 1
Peterborough U (Free on 4/7/95) FL 0+3 FLC 1 FAC 1 Others 2
Colchester U (Free on 8/12/95) FL 124+12/17 FLC 5+1/2 FAC 6/2 Others 12/2

GREGORY Neil Richard
Born: Ndola, Zambia, 7 October 1972
Height: 5'11" Weight: 11.10
David's younger brother had a rather mixed season at Colchester in 1998-99, when he found goals a lot harder to come by than in Division Three the previous term. He started the campaign on the bench but, called in to replace the injured Tony Lock, he kept his place and picked up three goals by mid September. However, the goals then dried up and his next strike, against Bournemouth, was wiped out as the match was controversially abandoned at half time with a rampant United 3-1 up. Following that, he had to wait until the end of February for his only other first-team goal, before losing his place to the teenage sensation, Lomana Tresor Lua Lua.
Ipswich T (From trainee on 21/2/92) P/FL 18+27/9 FLC 2+3 FAC 0+1 Others 4+3/2
Chesterfield (Loaned on 3/2/94) FL 2+1/1
Scunthorpe U (Loaned on 6/3/95) FL 10/7
Torquay U (Loaned on 22/11/96) FL 5
Peterborough U (Loaned on 27/11/97) FL 2+1/1 Others 1
Colchester U (£50,000 on 2/1/98) FL 41+12/11 FLC 2 Others 4/2

GRIEMINK Bart
Born: Holland, 29 March 1972
Height: 6'4" Weight: 15.4
Although playing second fiddle to Mark Tyler at Peterborough for the past couple of seasons, and missing the whole of 1997-98, the Dutch goalkeeper had to overcome injuries of his own when standing in for the latter during 1998-99. However, when called upon he did well, despite the odd clanger, and showed good agility for such a large man. Is very popular with the fans.
Birmingham C (Free from WK Emmen on 9/11/95) FL 20 FLC 3 FAC 1 Others 1+1
Peterborough U (£25,000 on 11/10/96) FL 44 FLC 1 FAC 4 Others 4

GRIFFIN Andrew (Andy)
Born: Billinge, 7 March 1979
Height: 5'9" Weight: 10.10
International Honours: E: U21-1; Yth
Although naturally right footed, Andy is a talented young Newcastle full back who is equally at home on either flank, and one who looks to have a fine future ahead of him. Solid defensively, with a good turn of pace, he enjoys the wing-back role which gives him scope to press forward and supplement the attack. After sitting out the first few games of last season he came into the side for the away leg of the European Cup Winners Cup-tie at Partizan Belgrade, where he was one of United's best players, and then held his place, including a visit to Old Trafford where he successfully shackled David Beckham, until suffering a bad groin injury against Wednesday in November which necessitated surgery. He returned to

fitness after a couple of months, but was limited to only occasional appearances, and was unable to re-establish himself as regular first choice until the latter stages of the season. Although he was severely tested by David Ginola in the Premiership game at Tottenham, Ruud Gullit had enough confidence in him to select him for the FA Cup semi final, and he responded with a "Man of the Match" performance of such quality that the Spurs' winger was substituted in the second half. This released Andy to adopt a more attacking role, demonstrating his impressive stamina by making a number of late surges into the opposition danger area deep into the second half of extra time, his fine form earning him selection for the England U21 team for the friendly against Hungary at the end of April. Unfortunately, he twisted his ankle to end his Premiership campaign prematurely, although he did return for the FA Cup Final.
Stoke C (From trainee on 5/9/96) FL 52+5/2 FLC 4+1 FAC 2
Newcastle U (£1,500,000 + on 30/1/98) PL 18 FLC 1 FAC 3 Others 1

GRIFFIN Antony Richard
Born: Bournemouth, 22 March 1979
Height: 5'11" Weight: 11.2
As a product of Bournemouth's successful youth policy, 1998-99 saw him establish himself in the Cherries' first-team squad, making one start and five substitute appearances. Able to play either at left back or in midfield, looking comfortable in both positions, he also has a lot of pace. Looks an exciting prospect.
Bournemouth (From trainee on 7/7/97) FL 1+5

GRIFFIN Charles (Charlie) John
Born: Bath, 25 June 1979
Height: 6'0" Weight: 12.7
Just like his manger, Jimmy Quinn, Charlie started his career in non-league football, being signed by Swindon from Chippenham Town in January 1999 where he was top scorer in the Screwfix League with 30 goals. At 20 years of age, and a real prospect for the future, the coaching staff believe that he has shown plenty of promise after making his Football league debut from the bench at Sunderland of all places. He was given three more subs' appearances, looking quite sharp, before starting the final game of the season, at home to Barnsley, and scoring with a right-footed drive into the top corner from 20 yards. There is plenty more to come from this young man.
Swindon T (£10,000 from Chippenham T on 29/1/99) FL 1+4/1

GRIFFITHS Carl Brian
Born: Welshpool, 16 July 1971
Height: 5'11" Weight: 11.10
International Honours: W: B-1; U21-2; Yth
Although not as prolific as in the previous campaign, Carl still managed to add eight goals to Leyton Orient's promotion push before being allowed to join Wrexham on loan last January. A self-confessed Robins' fan, and originally with the club as a boy, he scored four goals in five games and

appeared to be the goalscoring answer to Wrexham's problems but, for some unexplained reason, the two clubs could not agree a fee, leaving Port Vale free to sign him during transfer deadline week. Unfortunately injured on his debut at Bristol City, being forced out of the fray after an hour, he did not return until the penultimate game of the campaign, against Queens Park Rangers. Leading the line well, and heading the side's second goal, a goal that ultimately clinched relegation safety, he showed himself to be good with both feet, alive to half chances, and able to hold the ball up well for others.

Shrewsbury T (From trainee on 26/9/88) FL 110+33/54 FLC 7+4/3 FAC 6/2 Others 7+3/3
Manchester C (£500,000 on 29/10/93) PL 11+7/4 FLC 0+1 FAC 2
Portsmouth (£200,000 on 17/8/95) FL 2+12/2 FLC 0+1
Peterborough U (£225,000 on 28/3/96) FL 6+10/2 FLC 0+2/1 FAC 1+1/1 Others 0+1
Leyton Orient (Loaned on 31/10/96) FL 5/3
Leyton Orient (£100,000 on 7/3/97) FL 60+5/29 FLC 7+1/3 FAC 5/2 Others 2
Wrexham (Loaned on 13/1/99) FL 4/3 Others 1/1
Port Vale (£100,000 on 25/3/99) FL 3/1

GRIFFITHS Gareth John

Born: Winsford, 10 April 1970
Height: 6'4" Weight: 14.0

A tall central defender recruited by Wigan on a free transfer from Port Vale in the 1998 close season, having been out of contract, Gareth started the campaign as a first-team regular until suffering a recurrence of a knee injury in an FA Cup-tie against Blackpool. Robust and hard to pass, and tremendously strong in the air, he proved to be an invaluable squad member when called upon on his return from injury. He also showed much composure during the long run in at the end of the campaign.

Port Vale (Signed from Rhyl on 8/2/93) FL 90+4/4 FLC 8 FAC 7/1 Others 7
Shrewsbury T (Loaned on 31/10/97) FL 6
Wigan Ath (Free on 2/7/98) FL 20 FLC 4/1 FAC 1 Others 1

GRIFFITHS Peter

Born: St Hellier, 13 August 1980
Height: 5'9" Weight: 11.6

The young unassuming winger brought to Macclesfield from Ashton United in pre-season to make up the newly-formed reserve team in 1998-99, he made his first-team debut as substitute in the Worthington Cup-tie at Birmingham, and immediately impressed as the only player with total commitment in a poor team. Following that, Peter was rewarded with a regular squad place until the side was strengthened with more experienced players in mid season. A fast winger who can dummy his way out of a tackle, and can provide pin-point crosses, he scored his first league goal at Colchester with a mazy 40-yard run, finished off by a fizzing shot that caught a looping deflection off a defender before dipping over the stranded 'keeper. Is definitely one for the future.

Macclesfield T (Free from Ashton U on 16/7/98) FL 4/1 FLC 0+1 FAC 0+1 Others 1

GRIMANDI Gilles

Born: Gap, France, 11 November 1970
Height: 6'0" Weight: 12.7
Club Honours: PL '98; FAC '98; CS '98

As in 1997-98, Gilles proved to be an essential squad player at Arsenal in 1998-99, and one who could play equally well at wing back, in the centre of defence, or in midfield. Having the advantage of being strong with either foot, he is good in the air, quick on the ground, and is an excellent reader of the game, an ability which enables him to break up attacks by the opposition. Also has great enthusiasm, and in terms of character is one of the best at joining in with the banter within the squad.

Arsenal (£1,500,000 from Monaco, via FC Gap, on 25/6/97) PL 19+11/1 FLC 6 FAC 4+3 Others 1+2

GRITTON Martin

Born: Glasgow, 1 June 1978
Height: 6'1" Weight: 12.7

Having impressed in trials during the 1998 close season, after playing for Porthleven, the tall, imposing centre forward signed on non-contract forms for Plymouth prior to the start of 1998-99. Given his first-team debut as a sub on the opening day against Rochdale, he made a further appearance from the bench as he combined football with his studies as an undergraduate at Portsmouth University.

Plymouth Arg (Free from Porthleven on 7/8/98) FL 0+2

GROBBELAAR Bruce David

Born: Durban, South Africa, 6 October 1957
Height: 6'1" Weight: 14.2
Club Honours: Div 1 '82, '83, '84, '86, '88, '90; FLC '82, '83, '84, '90; FAC '86, '89, '92; CS '82, '88, '89; EC '84
International Honours: Zimbabwe: 20

Signed by Bury on a non-contract basis last September, he became the oldest-ever player to turn out for the club – aged 40 years and 337 days – when he kept goal in a 1-0 defeat at Birmingham. With Dean Kiely called up for the Republic of Ireland, the Shakers had only an untried youngster, Pat Kenny, to call upon, and turned to Bruce, who was playing in the Ryman's League for Chesham, to appear in a one off. Following that, and following a goalkeeping crisis at Lincoln, the former Liverpool man turned up at Sincil Bank and kept a clean sheet against Colchester, but looked distinctly out of touch when conceding four goals at Wycombe the following Saturday, having just arrived back from a midweek trip to Zimbabwe. That proved to be it as far as City were concerned and he was released shortly afterwards.

Crewe Alex (On trial from Vancouver Whitecaps on 18/12/79) FL 24/1
Liverpool (£250,000 from Vancouver Whitecaps on 12/3/81) F/PL 440 FLC 70 FAC 62 Others 56
Stoke C (Loaned on 17/3/93) FL 4
Southampton (Free on 11/8/94) PL 32 FLC 3 FAC 5
Plymouth Arg (Free on 12/8/96) FL 36 FLC 2 FAC 3
Oxford U (Free on 17/9/97)
Sheffield Wed (Free on 23/9/97)

Oldham Ath (Free on 18/12/97) FL 4 (Free to Chesham during 1998 close season)
Bury (Free on 4/9/98) FL 1
Lincoln C (Free on 11/12/98) FL 2

GRONDIN David

Born: Paris, France, 8 May 1980
Height: 5'9" Weight: 11.11

A promising young left-sided defender who joined Arsenal from French club, St Etienne, during the summer of 1998, after an impressive youth career which saw him gaining honours with the French U17 and U18 squads. After making his first-team debut in the Worthington Cup victory at Derby, he played with great assurance in the Champions League in Panathinaikos, and was particularly impressive in the 0-0 draw at home to Liverpool. Is a promising young player who is likely to become the eventual replacement for Nigel Winterburn.

Arsenal (£500,000 from St Etienne on 23/7/98) PL 1 FLC 2 Others 1

GROVES Paul

Born: Derby, 28 February 1966
Height: 5'11" Weight: 11.5
Club Honours: AMC '98

What more is there left to say about this classy Grimsby midfielder! Now in his second spell at Blundell Park, Paul has played in every game during his six seasons at the club since coming off the bench during the opening game of the 1992-93 season against Charlton Athletic. A great choice as club captain, he added to his midfield skills and creative ball play in 1998-99 by becoming Town's leading scorer, his goals making a vital contribution to an otherwise meagre tally. Ended the campaign as the club's "Player of the Year".

Leicester C (£12,000 from Burton A on 18/4/88) FL 7+9/1 FLC 1/1 FAC 0+1 Others 0+1
Lincoln C (Loaned on 20/8/89) FL 8/1 FLC 2
Blackpool (£60,000 on 25/1/90) FL 106+1/21 FLC 6/1 FAC 9/4 Others 13/3
Grimsby T (£150,000 on 12/8/92) FL 183+1/38 FLC 10+1/2 FAC 12/2 Others 4/1
West Bromwich A (£600,000 on 8/7/96) FL 27+2/4 FLC 2/1 FAC 1
Grimsby T (£250,000 on 21/7/97) FL 92/21 FLC 11/3 FAC 7/1 Others 10/2

Paul Groves

GUDJOHNSEN Eidur Smari
Born: Rejkjavik, Iceland, 15 September 1978
Height: 6'1" Weight: 13.0
International Honours: Iceland: 1
Bolton's Colin Todd took what was, at the time, something of a risk when he signed Eidur in August 1998. Having started his career with Valur in Iceland he moved to PSV Eindhoven in 1995, where he played in the same team as a young Ronaldo, and three goals in six starts for them drew comparisions which rated him as highly as the gifted Brazilian, before a career-threatening broken ankle put the brakes on a promising career. His confidence shattered, he went back to Iceland where he eventually returned to first-team action with KR Reykjavic. When he first joined Bolton he was overweight and severely out of shape, and it was a number of months before Todd considered him fit enough for the rigours of the First Division, his first appearance coming as a substitute in the home victory over Birmingham in September. Following that, he had to wait until April for his first start for the club, away to Oxford. This followed two previous substitute appearances, in which he scored vital equalising goals against Swindon and Barnsley, and he carried on scoring until the end of the season, his contribution in the home win against promotion rivals, Ipswich, being particularly memorable. A strong, skilful forward, Eidur looks an amazing acquisition for a free transfer, and his performances towards the end of the campaign showed just why he was rated as highly as Ronaldo at PSV. If Bolton can manage to keep hold of him, the "Iceman" will definitely score goals in the future, no matter what league he is playing in.
Bolton W (Free from KR Reykjavic, via Valur and PSV Eindhoven, on 6/8/98) FL 8+6/5 FLC 0+1 Others 3

GUDMUNDSSON Johann Birnir
Born: Reykjavik, Iceland, 7 December 1977
Height: 5'9" Weight: 13.0
International Honours: Iceland:
Signed from Keflavic in March 1998, he came to Watford too late to participate in the 1997-98 league programme, but marked his debut against Port Vale in 1998-99 with two goals. A right winger or midfield player who is a full international for his native Iceland, Johann demonstrated neat skills, but was unable to command a regular first-team place.
Watford (Signed from Keflavik on 26/3/98) FL 6+7/2

GUINAN Stephen (Steve) Anthony
Born: Birmingham, 24 December 1975
Height: 6'1" Weight: 13.7
With Nottingham Forest back in the Premiership, Steve was afforded no opportunities at the City Ground in 1998-99, and was loaned out to first Halifax (October) and then Plymouth (March). Scoring on his debut for Town, his three-month spell with

the club brought him two goals in 12 appearances, his touch on the ball being his major quality. Following some more reserve football at Forest, Steve moved on to Plymouth as an excellent loan signing near the end of the campaign. Brought in to ensure the goals that were hoped would take Plymouth into the play offs, he certainly played his part, scoring seven from 11 starts, including an excellent hat trick against Scunthorpe. Argyle fans will be hoping that Plymouth can find the money to tempt the centre forward to sign on a more permanent basis.
Nottingham F (From trainee on 7/1/93) F/PL 2+4 FLC 1/1
Darlington (Loaned on 14/12/95) FL 3/1
Burnley (Loaned on 27/3/97) FL 0+6
Crewe Alex (Loaned on 19/3/98) FL 3
Halifax T (Loaned on 16/10/98) FL 12/2
Plymouth Arg (Loaned on 24/3/99) FL 11/7

GUIVARC'H Stephane
Born: Concarneau, France, 6 September 1970
Height: 6'0" Weight: 12.4
International Honours: France: 13
A strong, bustling striker who joined Newcastle just before the 1998 World Cup, where he gained a winners medal with France, he arrived on Tyneside with a big goalscoring reputation, having topped the goal charts in France for the previous two seasons, and been top scorer in the 1997-98 UEFA Cup with seven goals, although failing to find the net in the World Cup. Despite being injured in a pre-season friendly against Bray, twisting his left ankle, which caused him to miss the first two games of the season, he scored on his Premiership debut against Liverpool, but failed to find a permanent place in the team. Then, having made only two full and two substitute appearances, he moved on to Scotland with Rangers early in November, but struggled to make a major impact there too.
Newcastle U (£3,500,000 from Auxerre, via Brest and Guingamp, on 13/7/98) PL 2+2/1

GUNNLAUGSSON Arnar Bergmann
Born: Akranes, Iceland, 6 March 1973
Height: 6'0" Weight: 11.10
International Honours: Iceland: 28
It was said in last year's Factfile that it was only a matter of time before Arnar registered his first league goal for Bolton. How prophetic that statement turned out to be! The Reebok faithful were expecting some good performances from him after the promise he showed at the end of 1997-98, although no one could have expected the start this Icelandic international made last season. After missing the first couple of games, he was put into the side, initially to play off the front two of Nathan Blake and Dean Holdsworth, and carried this off in some style, scoring 11 goals in 18 games. This immediately made him a favourite of the fans, and also attracted the attentions of some Premier League teams. However, a dip in form during November, and tabloid rumours of him disliking life in the First Division, prompted some uneasy rumblings

from certain sections of the crowd, and he lost his place in the team during the festive period. This uneasy exchange continued between player and supporters until Martin O'Neill took him to Leicester in February. Made his first start in a thrashing at Highbury, which was quite an introduction, but impressed with his shooting in the home clash with West Ham, despite being out of luck. Scoring from the penalty spot for his country in a victory over Luxembourg, the left-footed midfielder, cum striker, is an important member of Iceland's challenge for a place in Euro 2000.
Bolton W (£100,000 from IA Akranes, via Feyenoord, Nuremberg and Sochaux, on 7/8/97) P/FL 24+18/13 FLC 6+3/2 FAC 1+1
Leicester C (£2,000,000 on 5/2/99) PL 5+4

GUPPY Stephen (Steve) Andrew
Born: Winchester, 29 March 1969
Height: 5'11" Weight: 11.12
Club Honours: FAT '91, '93; GMVC '93
International Honours: E: B-1; U21-1; SP-1
A left-sided Leicester midfielder, Steve can operate equally effectively as either a wing back or as an out-and-out left winger. Continued to deliver more Premiership crosses than any other player in 1998-99, and added the ability to crop up with the odd spectacular strike. Scored three carbon-copy goals with his much maligned right foot, against Nottingham Forest, Birmingham, and in the televised game at Chelsea, by cutting inside and curling the ball home from outside the penalty box. The most spectacular of all, though, was his fierce drive at Wimbledon, where he collected a miscued clearance from Neil Sullivan and rifled it into the top corner from fully 25 yards. His consistent level of performance regularly saw him touted as a possible England contender, particularly in light of the national side's paucity of naturally left-sided players, but so far to no avail.
Wycombe W (Signed in 1989-90) FL 41/8 FLC 4 FAC 8/2 Others 10
Newcastle U (£150,000 on 2/8/94) FLC 0+1
Port Vale (£225,000 on 25/11/94) FL 102+3/12 FLC 7 FAC 8 Others 7+1/1
Leicester C (£950,000 on 28/2/97) PL 87+1/6 FLC 9 FAC 4/1 Others 2

GURNEY Andrew (Andy) Robert
Born: Bristol, 25 January 1974
Height: 5'10" Weight: 11.6
A talented right-wing back, Andy failed to find the goalscoring touch at Torquay last season, but always gave 100 per-cent commitment, and most of the fans were sorry to see him leave to join Reading in January. Is an exciting player when he moves upfield though, and likes to shoot at the opposing goal at every opportunity. After making his Royals' debut in the disastrous 6-0 home defeat against Bristol Rovers, he was unable to hold down a regular place in the starting line-up, and played in only one of the last 12 matches.
Bristol Rov (From trainee on 10/7/92) FL 100+8/9 FLC 7/1 FAC 5 Others 15
Torquay U (Free on 10/7/97) FL 64/10 FLC 6 FAC 5/1 Others 3
Reading (£100,000 on 15/1/99) FL 5+3

Professional Footballers Association
20 Oxford Court
Bishopsgate
Manchester
M2 3WQ

Tel: 0161 236 0575
Fax: 0161 228 7229

* * * * *

PFA Financial Management
91 Broad Street
Birmingham
B15 1AU

Tel: 0121 644 5277
Fax: 0121 644 5288

* * * * *

PFA Enterprises Ltd
Suite 9, 4th Floor
52 Haymarket
London
SW1Y 4RP

Tel: 0171 839 8663
Fax: 0171 839 2097
email: gnelson@thepfa.co.uk

H

HAALAND Alf-Inge (Alfie) Rasdal
Born: Stavanger, Norway, 23 November 1972
Height: 5'10" Weight: 12.12
International Honours: Norway: 32
After the disappointment of not being selected for the Norwegian World Cup squad, Alfie had to endure something of a stop-start season at Leeds in 1998-99, with suspension and niggling injuries restricting his playing appearances. Although primarily a midfielder, his adaptability meant that he was used as a right back and in a defensive role, while his usual combative style and constant willingness to give no less than 100 per cent caused him to pick up 11 yellow cards by March and, following his suspension, he picked up a groin injury in training which saw him miss a number of games. This apart, he is still a valuable squad member at Elland Road.
Nottingham F (Signed from Bryne on 25/1/94) F/PL 66+9/7 FLC 2+5 FAC 5+1 Others 2+3
Leeds U (£1,600,000 on 17/7/97) PL 50+11/8 FLC 3 FAC 5+1 Others 2+1

HACKETT Warren James
Born: Plaistow, 16 December 1971
Height: 6'0" Weight: 12.5
Club Honours: FAYC '90
International Honours: St Lucia: 6
After doing so well for Mansfield in 1997-98, and winning international honours for St Lucia, his performances at Field Mill were inconsistent last season and he moved to Barnet on transfer deadline day. Immediately adding stability to the Bees' back-line, he made his debut in the victory at Brighton when he came on as a substitute, and comfortably slotted into the role of left back. His uncomplicated style at the back illustrated that he was both a solid and reliable performer, although the fans are eager to see what extra defensive option he can bring to the team once acclimatised. After being at the club for just a month, he was awarded the joint title of being their first internationally capped player, along with Kenny Charlery, and has established himself as one of the most highly-regarded full backs in the Caribbean. Also able to operate on the left-hand side of a central defensive trio, he appears to be an astute signing with plenty to offer in the 1999-2000 campaign.
Leyton Orient (Free from Tottenham H juniors on 3/7/90) FL 74+2/3 FLC 4 FAC 8/2 Others 7
Doncaster Rov (Free on 26/7/94) FL 46/2 FLC 4 FAC 1 Others 4
Mansfield T (£50,000 on 20/10/95) FL 114+3/5 FLC 4 FAC 7 Others 2
Barnet (Free on 25/3/99) FL 3+4

HADLAND Phillip (Phil) Jonathan
Born: Warrington, 20 October 1980
Height: 5'11" Weight: 11.0
Having graduated through Reading's youth and reserve teams, as a winger, who can play on either flank, Phil made his single appearance for the first team in last season's Worthington Cup-tie at home to Barnsley, whilst still a trainee. Despite only keeping the bench warm on a couple of other occasions, he has been offered a one-year professional contract and will aim for a more regular first-team berth during the coming term.
Reading (Trainee) FLC 1

HADLEY Shaun Leon
Born: Birmingham, 6 February 1980
Height: 5'9" Weight: 10.8
Having completed his YTS period at Torquay, this pacy young striker started last season on a month-to-month contract, and came off the bench in home games against Carlisle and Peterborough, before being released by the club in the middle of the campaign.
Torquay U (From trainee on 30/6/98) FL 0+2

HAILS Julian
Born: Lincoln, 20 November 1967
Height: 5'10" Weight: 11.1
Julian suffered a frustrating season for Southend in 1998-99, having to watch the majority of it from the sidelines. An injury sustained in October was supposed to be cleared up by Christmas, but he played no further part in the campaign, his raiding wing-back play being greatly missed. As a past "Player of the Year", he will be hoping that his commitment and passing skills will gain him a permanent place in the United team for the new season.
Fulham (Signed from Hemel Hempstead on 29/8/90) FL 99+10/12 FLC 5+1 FAC 2 Others 9/1
Southend U (Free on 2/12/94) FL 143+17/7 FLC 9+2 FAC 3+1 Others 3

HALL Gareth David
Born: Croydon, 12 March 1969
Height: 5'8" Weight: 12.0
Club Honours: Div 2 '89; Div 1 '96; FMC 90
International Honours: E: Sch. W: 9; U21-1
Signed from Sunderland under the Bosman ruling at the end of 1997-98, the 29-year-old defender arrived at Swindon with a wealth of experience. Although known as a full back, he is versatile enough to play anywhere across the back line or in midfield, and had an outstanding season at the heart of Town's defence in 1998-99 where his touch and intelligence proved invaluable. He also scored in the 2-2 home draw with West Bromwich Albion. A player with Premiership experience, having learned the basics at Chelsea, he shows 100 per-cent commitment and is a strong tackler.
Chelsea (From apprentice on 25/4/86) F/PL 120+18/4 FLC 12+1 FAC 6 Others 10+4/1
Sunderland (£300,000 on 20/12/95) P/FL 41+7 FLC 3 FAC 2
Brentford (Loaned on 3/10/97) FL 6
Swindon T (Free on 22/5/98) FL 39+2/1 FLC 2 FAC 2

HALL Marcus Thomas
Born: Coventry, 24 March 1976
Height: 6'1" Weight: 12.2
International Honours: E: B-1; U21-8
The left-sided Coventry defender, cum midfielder, had a miserable season with injury in 1998-99. After playing as a substitute in the opening game he did not make the first team because of a groin injury until the end of October, when he played at Luton, and in the home game with Arsenal. In the latter game he damaged cruciate ligaments and was sidelined until April, before reappearing in the senior team as a substitute at Leicester. Is an elegant and skilful player, who is always looking to make his passes count.
Coventry C (From trainee on 1/7/94) PL 58+15/1 FLC 10+1/1 FAC 7+2

Marcus Hall

HALL Paul Anthony
Born: Manchester, 3 July 1972
Height: 5'9" Weight: 11.0
International Honours: Jamaica: 24
After turning out for Jamaica in the 1998 World Cup, Coventry signed the right-sided attacker from Portsmouth in a surprise transfer move in August and he made his debut as a substitute in the opening-day win over Chelsea. A regular on the bench until November, before getting a place in the starting line-up at Anfield, and at home to Newcastle, as well as two Worthington Cup-ties, he scored one goal, the winner in the home tie with Southend. Generally appearing unable to bridge the gap between the Nationwide and the Premiership, he went on loan to Bury in the New Year, but returned to make some impressive reserve-team appearances, where his pace and ability to attack the full back was seen to good effect. Was placed on the transfer list at the end of the season.
Torquay U (From trainee on 9/7/90) FL 77+16/1 FLC 7 FAC 4+1/2 Others 5+1/1
Portsmouth (£70,000 on 25/3/93) FL 148+40/37 FLC 10+3/1 FAC 7+1/2 Others 6+2/2
Coventry C (£300,000 on 10/8/98) PL 2+7 FLC 2/1
Bury (Loaned on 18/2/99) FL 7

HALL Richard Anthony
Born: Ipswich, 14 March 1972
Height: 6'2" Weight: 13.11
International Honours: E: U21-11; Yth

Having made just one appearance in 1998-99, coming off the bench in the FA Cup replay at Swansea, the talented West Ham central defender was finally forced to quit the game in March following a long and courageous battle for fitness. For three seasons he had to suffer a recurring foot injury and after the comeback game a bad reaction in his foot proved the final straw. It was a sad end to a career that was never allowed to fully flower.

Scunthorpe U (From trainee on 20/3/90) FL 22/3 FLC 2 FAC 3 Others 4
Southampton (£200,000 on 13/2/91) F/PL 119+7/12 FLC 11+1/1 FAC 15/3 Others 3
West Ham U (£1,400,000 on 19/7/96) PL 7 FAC 0+1

HALL Wayne

Born: Rotherham, 25 October 1968
Height: 5'9" Weight: 10.6

A former left winger who settled in at left back down the years, but can still be used to good effect further up the flank, Wayne has now had over ten years service and 350 plus games with York. Although injuries caused him problems, which restricted his appearances in 1998-99, he was pleased to net his first goal for five seasons in a 3-3 Boxing Day draw against Burnley.

York C (Free from Hatfield Main Colliery on 15/3/89) FL 314+17/9 FLC 23+1 FAC 11+1/1 Others 21/1

HALLE Gunnar

Born: Oslo, Norway, 11 August 1965
Height: 5'11" Weight: 11.2
Club Honours: Div 2 '91
International Honours: Norway: 62

Although probably nearing the twilight of his career, Gunnar is basically a manager's dream, being able to play anywhere in midfield and defence, and very much the model professional. Capped more than 60 times for Norway, he played in the 1998 World Cup, surprisingly at the expense of Leeds' team-mate, Alfie Haaland. In 1998-99, he weighed in with his usual dependable performances, scoring in the draws at Nottingham Forest and Tottenham Hotspur with close range headers. In fact, despite being the eldest member of the squad, he was offered and signed a new two-year deal during the campaign, David O'Leary, his manager, merely proving what an excellent player he really is. Stop Press: Joined Bradford for £200,000 on 11 June.

Oldham Ath (£280,000 from Lillestrom on 15/2/91) F/PL 185+3/17 FLC 16/2 FAC 8/2 Others 4
Leeds U (£400,000 on 13/12/96) PL 65+5/4 FLC 3+1 FAC 8+1 Others 2

HALLWORTH Jonathan (Jon) Geoffrey

Born: Stockport, 26 October 1965
Height: 6'2" Weight: 14.10
Club Honours: Div 2 '91

By his own standards, Jon was a year behind schedule at Cardiff, having joined the Bluebirds believing they would earn promotion. The experienced 'keeper was easily City's first choice in 1998-99 until he broke two ribs at Leyton Orient on 10 April, and was forced to miss the last five matches. Delighted to see his understudy, Seamus

Kelly, do so well, and with Second Division football promised for this coming term the big goalie will be looking to get his huge goal kicks ready for the occasion. Not surprisingly, was selected by his fellow professionals for the PFA award-winning Third Division side.

Ipswich T (From apprentice on 26/5/83) FL 45 FLC 4 FAC 1 Others 6
Bristol Rov (Loaned on 1/1/85) FL 2 Others 1
Oldham Ath (£75,000 on 3/2/89) F/PL 171+3 FLC 20 FAC 20 Others 3
Cardiff C (Free on 6/8/97) FL 84 FLC 4 FAC 10 Others 1

HAMANN Dietmar

Born: Waldsasson, Germany, 27 August 1973
Height: 6'3" Weight: 12.2
International Honours: Germany: 16

Signing for Newcastle on a five-year contract after the 1998 World Cup, where he played in all five of Germany's games and was one of his country's main successes, "Didi" is a tall, slim midfielder of real quality, who likes to control the tempo of the game. Highly mobile, but tireless, strong in the tackle, with a deft touch on the ball, allied to powerful and accurate long-range shooting, he became a key player in the Newcastle engine room in 1998-99. After exciting the "Toon Army" with his pre-season play, particularly a stunning strike in the friendly against Juventus, he suffered ligament damage to his right knee against Liverpool in the third game of the campaign and was out for two months, even returning to Munich for treatment. Although recalled to the German squad immediately on recovery, he found establishing himself in the Newcastle team more difficult, and a dismissal at Liverpool was particularly disappointing for him and the club. However, he became a regular in midfield after the turn of the year, and his quality emerged as he gained in confidence and adjusted to the pace of the Premiership. His burgeoning partnership with Gary Speed was highly influential in United's progress as the season rolled on, and increasingly he looked to be developing into the playmaker which Newcastle have lacked for some time now. His 50-yard crossfield pass from which Louis Saha scored the winner in the FA Cup replay at Blackburn was a highlight of the season. His elder brother, Matthias, was previously a striker with Bayern Munich.

Newcastle U (£4,500,000 from Bayern Munich, via Wacker Munchen, on 5/8/98) PL 22+1/4 FLC 1 FAC 7/1

HAMILTON Derrick (Des) Vivian

Born: Bradford, 15 August 1976
Height: 5'11" Weight: 13.0
International Honours: E: U21-1

Unable to hold down a place at Newcastle under Ruud Gullit in 1998-99, Des was loaned out to Sheffield United (October) and Huddersfield (February). At Bramall Lane, playing at wing back or in midfield, he gave six impressive performances and was unlucky not to score on a number of occasions. However, with Steve Bruce unable to sign him on a more permanent

basis, due to United's lack of funds, he went back to St James' Park before arriving at the McAlpine for the remainder of the season. Strong on the ball, and linking well with the forwards, Huddersfield did not lose any of the opening nine fixtures that Des appeared in, and he even helped himself to a last-minute equaliser at Wolves, before a troublesome groin injury prematurely ended his time at Town with a few games remaining.

Bradford C (From trainee on 1/6/94) FL 67+21/5 FLC 6/1 FAC 6 Others 4+1/2
Newcastle U (£1,500,000 + on 27/3/97) PL 7+5 FLC 1+1/1 FAC 1 Others 1
Sheffield U (Loaned on 16/10/98) FL 6
Huddersfield T (Loaned on 15/2/99) FL 10/1

HAMILTON Ian Richard

Born: Stevenage, 14 December 1967
Height: 5'9" Weight: 11.3

He began his first full season at Sheffield United in 1998-99 as a regular member of the side, missing games only because of his two sendings off, working tirelessly in midfield, and always looking to deliver the probing pass. Often in a position to score, particularly from a distance, his goal tally could easily have been greater, but he missed seven games due to a hamstring injury at the turn of the year, and was again sidelined by a groin injury in April.

Southampton (From apprentice on 24/12/85)
Cambridge U (Signed on 29/3/88) FL 23+1/1 FLC 1 FAC 2 Others 2
Scunthorpe U (Signed on 23/12/88) FL 139+6/18 FLC 6 FAC 6/1 Others 14+1/3
West Bromwich A (£160,000 on 19/6/92) FL 229+11/23 FLC 13+2/1 FAC 10+1/1 Others 14+2/3
Sheffield U (Signed on 26/3/98) FL 35+3/3 FLC 4/1 FAC 2 Others 2

HAMMOND Nicholas (Nicky) David

Born: Hornchurch, 7 September 1967
Height: 6'0" Weight: 11.13

Nicky had to compete with two other goalkeepers for a first-team place at Reading in 1998-99, and unfortunately lost out to the extent that he managed only two appearances, in consecutive games in September. For the rest of the time he was restricted to reserve matches, but made a significant contribution to the development of the club's young 'keepers with his coaching sessions at the Reading Centre of Excellence.

Arsenal (From apprentice on 12/7/85)
Bristol Rov (Loaned on 23/8/86) FL 3
Swindon T (Free on 1/7/87) F/PL 65+2 FLC 11 FAC 10 Others 6
Plymouth Arg (£40,000 on 14/8/95) FL 4 FLC 2 Others 1
Reading (£40,000 on 13/2/96) FL 25 FLC 3 FAC 5

HANDYSIDE Peter David

Born: Dumfries, 31 July 1974
Height: 6'1" Weight: 13.8
Club Honours: AMC '98
International Honours: S: U21-7

Following the return, after 18 months, of Richard Smith to full fitness, Peter, along with the latter, formed a central defensive partnership for Grimsby in 1998-99 that was amongst the most formidable in the First Division. It was a factor which almost

certainly kept the Mariners clear of the relegation battle. His increasing confidence in going forward, and distribution from defence, must surely bring him back into Scotland international reckoning.

Grimsby T (From trainee on 21/11/92) FL 164+7/3 FLC 15+1 FAC 11 Others 13+1

HANLON Richard (Richie) Kenneth
Born: Wembley, 26 May 1978
Height: 6'1" Weight: 13.7
Came back into the Football League when joining Peterborough from Rushden & Diamonds last December, Miquel de Souza travelling in the opposite direction, but made only four subs' appearances before being loaned to Welling United in transfer deadline week. A former Chelsea trainee who can be used either up front or in midfield, he scored in a 1-1 home draw against Hull City prior to departing.

Southend U (Free from Chelsea juniors on 10/7/96) FL 1+1 (Free to Welling U during 1997 close season)
Peterborough U (Signed from Rushden & Diamonds on 9/12/98) FL 0+4/1 Others 1

HANMER Gareth Craig
Born: Shrewsbury, 12 October 1973
Height: 5'6" Weight: 10.3
1998-99 was another brilliant season for this Shrewsbury wing back, who continued to go forward on the left, putting over a stream of telling crosses and reaching passes he should have had no right to. A slightly-built player, who covers ground quickly to turn defenders and attackers, he tackles back well when covering the length of the pitch. Rarely troubled with injury, Gareth was an ever present in league and cup games and was never once substituted, thus giving him a continuous run of 91 games for Town without being replaced during a match.

West Bromwich A (£20,000 from Newtown on 18/6/96)
Shrewsbury T (£10,000 on 25/7/97) FL 85/1 FLC 3 FAC 3 Others 2

HANN Matthew
Born: Cambridge, 6 September 1980
Height: 5'9" Weight: 11.0
Introduced in the Auto Windscreens game at Bournemouth, after impressing in Peterborough's youth side, and still a trainee, he made his Football League debut when coming off the bench in a 2-2 draw at Halifax last January, showing fair promise in United's midfield before being injured two games later. Small and speedy, he can also play up front where he has a knack of picking up loose balls.

Peterborough U (From trainee on 6/1/99) FL 0+4 Others 1

HANSEN Bo
Born: Denmark, 16 June 1972
Height: 5'11" Weight: 11.10
International Honours: Denmark: 3
Bo signed for Bolton from Danish club, Brondby, last February, having scored 12 goals in 18 games for the team prior to his transfer, and figuring in all of their European Champions' League games. A striker of his experience was much needed at the time,

following the shock sales of Nathan Blake and Arnar Gunnlaugsson, but surprisingly, Bo did not make too many first-team appearances after his transfer, his outings being limited to a handful of starts and substitutions. When on the pitch he played with endeavour and spirit, looking to be a more than capable centre forward, and will surely be a valuable squad member, if not a more important factor in the Wanderers' fortunes this coming season.

Bolton W (£1,000,000 from Brondby on 12/2/99) FL 1+7 Others 0+3

HANSON David (Dave) Paul
Born: Huddersfield, 19 November 1968
Height: 6'0" Weight: 13.7
Signed by Halifax in January 1998 to bolster their chances of winning promotion to the Football League, on mission accomplished Dave formed a formidable partnership up front with Geoff Horsfield during the early part of last season. However, following Horsfield's departure to Fulham, and his subsequent hamstring injury, he never really regained his best form and, after returning to the side around the New Year, he was in and out of the team. Big and strong, he is a forward who is well suited to holding the ball up for others to feed off.

Bury (Free from Farsley Celtic on 19/7/93) FL 1 FLC 2 (Free to Halifax T on 18/8/94)
Leyton Orient (£50,000 from Hednesford T on 4/10/95) FL 26+22/5 FLC 1+1 FAC 1+1 Others 2+2
Chesterfield (Loaned on 10/3/97) FL 3/1
Halifax T (Free on 23/1/98) FL 19+12/2 FLC 4/2 Others 2/1

HAPGOOD Leon Duane
Born: Torbay, 7 August 1979
Height: 5'6" Weight: 10.0
A combative, hard-working Torquay midfielder who could always be relied upon to put heart and soul into his game, his first-team chances were limited in 1998-99 as Wes Saunders struggled to find a settled midfield. Having appeared two seasons earlier whilst still a first-year trainee, with added weight and experience he will look to hold down a regular place in 1999-2000.

Torquay U (From trainee on 21/5/98) FL 26+14/3 FLC 1+2 FAC 3+1 Others 0+2

HARDY Philip (Phil)
Born: Ellesmere Port, 9 April 1973
Height: 5'8" Weight: 11.8
Club Honours: WC '95
International Honours: Ei: U21-9
Phil continued to be the "hardy perennial" in 1998-99, and seems to have been around the Racecourse for years (which he has!), although still only 27-years old. The early season saw him competing with Deryn Brace for the left-back slot, before he went on to become a regular in that position. Selected for Ireland "B" against Northern Ireland, he was injured in training before the game, while misfortune also followed him after selection for the senior side against the Czech Republic in March, when he had to withdraw with an abscess. Now beginning to threaten those with the most appearances for Wrexham, he is a reliable defender who

rarely gives his opponents much room, while at the other end of the park the fans await his first ever goal!

Wrexham (From trainee on 24/11/90) FL 295+3 FLC 17 FAC 31 Others 37

HAREWOOD Marlon Anderson
Born: Hampstead, 25 August 1979
Height: 6'1" Weight: 11.0
A talented young Nottingham Forest striker who is right out of the Emile Heskey mould, Marlon was given his first Premiership start at home to West Ham last September, having made his Football League debut in 1997-98, followed by a string of impressive reserve performances and five subs' appearances at the beginning of 1998-99. Sharpened up by a spell on loan with the Finnish side, FC Haka, during the summer, he scored his first two senior goals in the Worthington Cup, while his first in the Premiership came in a 1-1 draw at Middlesbrough. Loaned to Ipswich at the end of January, with Jamie Scowcroft out injured, he certainly added to the attack, happy to be a team member rather than to promote himself, and before going back to the City Ground had scored at Bury. Involved in ten of Forest's final 11 games, he will benefit in a side not out of its depth this coming term.

Nottingham F (From trainee on 9/9/96) P/FL 12+12/1 FLC 2+2/2 FAC 0+1
Ipswich T (Loaned on 28/1/99) FL 5+1/1

HARGREAVES Christian (Chris)
Born: Cleethorpes, 12 May 1972
Height: 5'11" Weight: 12.2
Chris was a 1998 close season signing for Plymouth from the Conference side, Hereford United. A tricky midfielder who looked most comfortable in an orthodox left-wing position, his superb control allowed him to run at defenders and whip in excellent crosses for the forwards to attack. Although niggling injuries halted the fluency of his 1998-99 campaign, undoubtedly he will be looking to build on the good form he showed. Scored twice in the league, at home to Mansfield and at Chester.

Grimsby T (From trainee on 6/12/89) FL 15+36/5 FLC 2+2/1 FAC 1+2/1 Others 2+4
Scarborough (Loaned on 4/3/93) FL 2+1
Hull C (Signed on 26/7/93) FL 34+15 FLC 1 FAC 2+1/1 Others 3+1
West Bromwich A (Free on 13/7/95) FL 0+1 Others 0+1
Hereford U (Free on 19/2/96) FL 57+4/5 FLC 3+1 FAC 1 Others 2
Plymouth Arg (Free on 20/7/98) FL 30+2/2 FLC 2 FAC 4

HARKES John Andrew
Born: New Jersey, USA, 8 March 1967
Height: 5'10" Weight: 11.10
Club Honours: FLC '91
International Honours: USA: 70
From Washington DCU, John was another player who came to Nottingham Forest from American soccer in 1998-99, when arriving on loan last January. Previously in the Premiership with Sheffield Wednesday and West Ham, the former American captain

was looking to set up another successful spell in English football, but was unfortunate to arrive at Nottingham to play in a side bereft of ideas and facing almost certain relegation. Amazingly, his debut, a 1-0 win at Everton, coincided with the club's first league win in 20 games, and was only their third league victory of the season. His next appearance, however, brought home reality as Forest were smashed 8-1 on their own turf by Manchester United. A versatile player who can play effectively in midfield, or at right back, and has an explosive shot, John's time was up at Forest when the game at West Ham resulted in a 2-1 defeat, an injured calf, and an end to his campaign.

Sheffield Wed (£70,000 from North Carolina University on 3/10/90) F/PL 59+22/7 FLC 17/3 FAC 12+1/1 Others 7
Derby Co (Signed on 17/8/93) FL 67+7/2 FLC 5 Others 6/1 (£500,000 to USSF on 27/10/95)
West Ham U (Loaned on 28/10/95) PL 6+5 FAC 1+1
Nottingham F (Loaned from Washington DCU on 29/1/99) PL 3

HARKIN Maurice (Mo) Presley
Born: Derry, 16 August 1979
Height: 5'9" Weight: 11.11
International Honours: NI: Yth

This should have been the season when Mo went on to truly establish himself as the midfield playmaker for Wycombe Wanderers. However, after one start and two substitute appearances in 1998-99, this young and gifted two-footed player was struck by an ankle injury, forcing him to miss his Northern Ireland U21 debut. First estimates were for a Christmas return, but the recovery took longer than expected and eventually he was found to have a stress fracture of the ankle which needed an operation. By the end of the campaign he was well on the way to recovery and, after a period of rehabilitation at Lilleshall, he should be fighting for a place in 1999-2000.

Wycombe W (From trainee on 14/2/97) FL 14+27/2 FLC 1+2/1 FAC 1+2 Others 2/1

HARKNESS Steven (Steve)
Born: Carlisle, 27 August 1971
Height: 5'10" Weight: 11.2
International Honours: E: Yth

After a very good season at Liverpool in 1997-98, Steve was left on the bench during the early part of 1998-99. He then appeared in the centre of midfield against West Ham in September, before being left languishing on the subs' bench until the Arsenal match at Highbury in January, when he appeared on the left-hand side of midfield. His versatility was a double-edged sword, and he was often relegated to the bench. He further compounded his ill-luck with his wholehearted commitment to the Liverpool cause, when picking up injuries with his fierce tackling. Left Anfield on 9 March following a £750,000 bid from the Portuguese giants, Benfica, being accepted.

Carlisle U (From trainee on 23/3/89) FL 12+1
Liverpool (£75,000 on 17/7/89) F/PL 90+12/2 FLC 11+4/1 FAC 5+1 Others 13+3
Huddersfield T (Loaned on 24/9/93) FL 5 Others 1
Southend U (Loaned on 3/2/95) FL 6

HARLE Michael (Micky) James
Born: Lewisham, 31 October 1972
Height: 6'0" Weight: 13.8

Although eager to continue his fine level of consistency on the left side of Barnet's defence in 1998-99, a series of niggling injuries hindered his appearances, and a combination of tendonitis in his left foot and knee meant that he did not start in the opening five games. He returned to his familiar number three shirt in late August for the home match against Brentford, and kept his place in the side until October before suffering a severe foot injury, which kept him out for another five games. Then, having come back to play exceptionally well, he picked up a foot injury which was later diagnosed as a neuroma, and became increasingly more painful. Following the defeat at Mansfield in November, he underwent an operation and gradually progressed back to being on the fringes of the first team, before leaving the club on transfer deadline day to join Welling United in his native county of Kent. Micky was a reliable defender with a cultured left foot, who linked up well with Darren Currie on the flank to forge an attractive attacking option.

Gillingham (Trainee) FL 1+1
Millwall (£100,000 from Sittingbourne on 8/11/93) FL 12+9/1 FLC 1+1 FAC 1 Others 1
Bury (Loaned on 8/12/95) FL 0+1
Barnet (Free on 16/7/97) FL 53+1/2 FLC 4+1 FAC 2 Others 2

HARLEY Jonathan (Jon)
Born: Maidstone, 26 September 1979
Height: 5'9" Weight: 10.3
International Honours: E: Yth

A life-long Chelsea fan who broke into the first team at the back end of the previous campaign, but who only managed a minute's run in senior football during 1998-99, Jon replaced his boss, Gianluca Vialli, after the Italian's hat trick in the Worthington Cup third round tie against Aston Villa in October. Is a confident left-sided midfield player who uses the ball intelligently, packs a good shot, and is highly regarded at Chelsea. He is certainly one for the future.

Chelsea (From trainee on 20/3/97) PL 0+3 FLC 0+1

HARPER Kevin Patrick
Born: Oldham, 15 January 1976
Height: 5'6" Weight: 10.10
International Honours: S: B-1; U21-7; Sch

After six years spent at Hibernian in the Scottish Premier League , the former Scottish U21 international striker moved to Derby last September. A naturally right-footed player, who can play as a winger, up front, or in midfield, his versatility was much employed throughout the season but, in the main, from the substitutes' bench. Scored on his debut at Anfield, and his first two goals for the club both came from headers – not bad for a player of his height. Remained injury free throughout 1998-99, which enabled him to play in a variety of roles and when he was required, becoming a favourite with the fans and

proving to be a real bargain at the price. Is one for the future.

Hibernian (From Hutchison Vale BC on 3/8/92) SL 73+23/15 SLC 4+5 SC 9+1/3
Derby Co (£300,000 + on 11/9/98) PL 6+21/1 FLC 0+3 FAC 0+3/1

HARPER Lee Charles Phillip
Born: Chelsea, 30 October 1971
Height: 6'1" Weight: 13.11

Now in his third season at Queens Park Rangers, Lee started 1998-99 as the first-choice goalkeeper, but lost his place after arrival of Ludek Miklosko from West Ham United in October. An assured shot stopper, who stands up well, his appearances were then restricted to act as cover when the latter was injured.

Arsenal (£150,000 from Sittingbourne on 16/6/94) PL 1
Queens Park R (£125,000 + on 11/7/97) FL 51 FLC 6 FAC 1

HARPER Stephen (Steve) Alan
Born: Easington, 14 March 1975
Height: 6'2" Weight: 13.0

Steve is a reliable and agile Newcastle goalkeeper, and a good shot stopper with a safe pair of hands. During the 1998 close season he was pursued determinedly by Huddersfield after a successful loan period there in 1997-98, but remaining at St James' Park as third choice behind Shay Given and Lionel Perez, he was determined to establish himself as at least a squad member. After impressing the management in training, and playing in six consecutive reserve games in which he conceded but a single goal, he forced his way up to the number-two spot, and made his first-team debut when substituting for an injured Given after half time in the home game against Wimbledon at the end of November. Retained for the local derby at Middlesbrough, where he had an excellent game, and his performance was vital in helping to secure a draw, he confirmed his quality with another "Man-of-the-Match" performance in the following game at Blackburn, saving a penalty to help earn a useful point, before dropping back to the bench on Given's return to fitness. He was brought on as a substitute again when the latter was sent off in the FA Cup-tie against Palace, and he also played in the side when Given served his subsequent suspension. Well liked by the Newcastle crowd, United are fortunate to have such a high quality reserve 'keeper and in pushing Given hard, he successfully displaced him from the side for the visit to Wednesday in April and started the final three Premiership games, where his fine form earned him the FA Cup Final jersey in only his ninth appearance for the club. Is also a qualified referee.

Newcastle U (Free from Seaham Red Star on 5/7/93) PL 7+1 FAC 1+1
Bradford C (Loaned on 18/9/95) FL 1
Hartlepool U (Loaned on 29/8/97) FL 15
Huddersfield T (Loaned on 18/12/97) FL 24 FAC 2

HARPER Steven (Steve) James
Born: Newcastle under Lyme, 3 February 1969
Height: 5'10" Weight: 11.12
Club Honours: Div 4 '92

Was rarely missing from the Mansfield left-wing-back role in 1998-99, a role in which he has made his own since his switch to that position in 1996. Continued to frustrate the fans with some wayward crosses after working himself into good positions, he still played his part with some useful goals. In the latter part of the season he showed up in a much more withdrawn role, before being released in the summer.

Port Vale (From trainee on 29/6/87) FL 16+12/2 FLC 1+2 Others 1+1
Preston NE (Signed on 23/3/89) FL 57+20/10 FLC 1+1 FAC 1+2 Others 6+1/1
Burnley (Free on 23/7/91) FL 64+5/8 FLC 1+2 FAC 10/3 Others 8
Doncaster Rov (Free on 7/8/93) FL 56+9/11 FLC 2+1/1 FAC 3 Others 4
Mansfield T (£20,000 on 8/9/95) FL 157+3/18 FLC 6 FAC 8/1 Others 7

HARRIES Paul Graham
Born: Sydney, Australia, 19 November 1977
Height: 6'0" Weight: 13.7

Released by Portsmouth during the 1998 close season, he moved to Crystal Palace last September following a trial period when he scored three goals. However, unable to get a first-team opportunity at Selhurst, Paul was loaned to Third Division Torquay at the end of February. He certainly impressed everyone with his workrate, particularly at Plymouth and Cardiff, but, sadly, had few chances to show what he could do in front of goal, before being freed during the summer.

Portsmouth (Free from NSW Soccer Academy on 8/9/97) FL 0+1
Crystal Palace (Free on 7/9/98)
Torquay U (Loaned on 26/2/99) FL 5

HARRIS Andrew (Andy) David Douglas
Born: Springs, South Africa, 26 February 1977
Height: 5'10" Weight: 11.11

Andy was another Southend defender whose season was ruined by injury in 1998-99. An early problem, followed by another almost immediately after he regained full fitness meant that the United crowd saw very little of the strong tackling and teamwork they were used to from him. Released during the summer, having been tipped for great things only a year earlier, it should not be too difficult for him to find another club.

Liverpool (From trainee on 23/3/94)
Southend U (Free on 10/7/96) FL 70+2 FLC 5 FAC 3

HARRIS Jason Andre Sebastian
Born: Sutton, 24 November 1976
Height: 6'1" Weight: 11.7

Jason's loan move from Leyton Orient to Preston became permanent last September, after the pacy, young left-sided forward had impressed with his strength and aerial ability. Gained his first start at Maine Road, but was more often used from the bench with good effect, setting a new club record for substitute appearances in a season. Unluckily sent off at Northampton, he faded from the first-team scene for a while in April, after contributing several goals, almost all of which saw North End snatch late points.

Crystal Palace (From trainee on 3/7/95) FL 0+2 FLC 0+2
Bristol Rov (Loaned on 22/11/96) FL 5+1/2 Others 1/1
Lincoln C (Loaned on 11/8/97) FL 0+1
Leyton Orient (£20,000 on 23/9/97) FL 22+15/7 FLC 1 FAC 2 Others 1+1
Preston NE (Signed on 28/8/98) FL 9+25/6 FAC 2+1/1 Others 2+2

HARRIS Neil
Born: Orsett, 12 July 1977
Height: 5'11" Weight: 12.9

Signed from non-league Cambridge City (not Chelmsford as reported in last year's Factfile) just prior to the transfer deadline in March 1998, the striker followed up his two starts in 1997-98 to become the club's leading scorer in 1998-99 and a thorn in many a defender's side. Has very quick feet, is pacy, can hold the ball up well, has great shooting ability, and scored some cracking goals, none better than the one against Northampton when he cut in to the box and rifled the ball into the top corner. Having established himself as a great favourite with the crowd, it was no surprise when the supporters voted for Neil as the "Player of the Year".

Millwall (£30,000 from Cambridge C on 26/3/98) FL 39+3/15 FAC 0+1 Others 6/3

Neil Harris

HARRIS Richard
Born: Croydon, 23 October 1980
Height: 5'11" Weight: 10.9

Richard was yet another promising youngster given some first-team action at Crystal Palace last season, coming off the bench for the final 15 minutes of a 2-2 home draw against Huddersfield in the penultimate fixture, and having the crowd buzzing with his tremendous long throws. He also nearly scored with a far-post header. Not a bad start for a 19-year-old defender who came through the ranks as a trainee to sign pro in December 1997, he will be looking to consolidate in 1999-2000.

Crystal Palace (From trainee on 22/12/97) FL 0+1

HARRISON Craig
Born: Gateshead, 10 November 1977
Height: 6'0" Weight: 11.13

Now a fully fledged Middlesbrough squad member, although still of tender age, Craig can be relied on to give his all when called up for first-team duty. His powerful and fearless tackling, supported by well-timed and precision clearances with either foot, and launching lethal counter attacks, endorse the view of the coaches who appointed him on merit. He also remains a firm favourite of the fans who made him their first choice for the "Young Player of the Year" award. In a bid to further his experience, he was loaned out to Preston last January to provide cover for both of North End's injured left backs, and gave an impressive performance on his debut against Luton the following day, when setting up the equalising goal. His excellent composure and touch formed a great impression on the locals, before he returned to the Riverside seven games later.

Middlesbrough (From trainee on 4/7/96) P/FL 19+5 FLC 4+2 FAC 2
Preston NE (Loaned on 15/1/99) FL 6 Others 1

HARRISON Gerald (Gerry) Randall
Born: Lambeth, 15 April 1972
Height: 5'10" Weight: 12.12
International Honours: E: Sch

Out of contract at Burnley in the 1998 close season, Gerry arrived at Sunderland on a Bosman transfer but was unable to establish himself on Wearside, making just one appearance in the Worthington Cup against York in August before spending loan spells at Luton (December) and Hull City (March) following a bout of hepatitis. At his best in central defence, his solid, no-nonsense performances were often the barrier the Town's opposition broke up against, while his strong, powerful runs upfield always caused defenders problems. Reported to be set for a £100,000 permanent move to the Hatters, news that was quickly followed by Luton's dramatic fall into receivership, alerted Hull boss, Warren Joyce, and saw the player move to Boothferry Park, bringing a touch of class to Hull's defence. He would certainly be a popular addition to City's defence if still available.

Watford (From trainee on 18/12/89) FL 6+3 Others 1
Bristol C (Free on 23/7/91) FL 25+13/1 FLC 2+2 FAC 1 Others 4+1
Cardiff C (Loaned on 24/1/92) FL 10/1
Hereford U (Loaned on 19/11/93) FL 6 FAC 1 Others 1
Huddersfield T (Free on 24/3/94)
Burnley (Free on 5/8/94) FL 116+8/3 FLC 5+1 FAC 6+2 Others 7+1
Sunderland (Free on 29/7/98) FLC 1
Luton T (Loaned on 24/12/98) FL 14 Others 1
Hull C (Loaned on 25/3/99) FL 8

HARRISON Lee David
Born: Billericay, 12 September 1971
Height: 6'2" Weight: 12.7

Barnet's first choice custodian cemented his reputation as being one of the finest shot stoppers outside of the Premiership in 1998-99 by scooping the club's "Player of the Year" trophy for the second consecutive

year. Despite the Bees conceding 71 goals during the campaign, he was rarely at fault for any of them, and to highlight his importance it is interesting to note that in the three matches he missed Barnet conceded 15 goals. The lowest point of his campaign was his dismissal in the match at home to Shrewsbury in January, but that was the only blip in an otherwise impeccable term in which he amassed a total of 13 clean sheets, including two terrific displays against Darlington and a great performance at home against Cambridge in March. In fact, during the entire month of March he did not concede a goal, which epitomised his influence in the rejuvenation of the Bees' defence. His greatest attribute is his ability to conjure up reflex saves and deny opposing forwards from close range, and this is coupled with a good range of distribution.

Charlton Ath (From trainee on 3/7/90)
Fulham (Loaned on 18/11/91) Others 1
Gillingham (Loaned on 24/3/92) FL 2
Fulham (Free on 18/12/92) FL 11+1 FAC 1 Others 6
Barnet (Free on 15/7/96) FL 110 FLC 6 FAC 2 Others 5

HARSLEY Paul
Born: Scunthorpe, 29 May 1978
Height: 5'9" Weight: 11.5
A busy, skilful player who passes the ball well, Paul started off last season in the Scunthorpe midfield, but was then unlucky to be left out for two months. Won his place back in November, and was an ever present after that, either in midfield or in an effective right-sided wing-back role, which helped shore up the defence. Scored his only goal of the season, at Wrexham in the FA Cup third round, a spectacular 30-yard shot which won him a "Goal of the Week" competition.

Grimsby T (From trainee on 16/7/96)
Scunthorpe U (Free on 7/7/97) FL 43+6/1 FLC 2 FAC 2+1/1 Others 3

HART Gary John
Born: Harlow, 21 September 1976
Height: 5'9" Weight: 12.8
Was signed from Stanstead during the summer of 1998 for £1,000 plus a set of shirts, following some impressive performances whilst on trial for Brighton's reserve team at the end of 1997-98. A hard-working, natural goalscorer who possesses plenty of pace, he formed a successful partnership with Richard Barker and finished joint-top scorer with him on 12 goals, scooping all the "Player of the Season" awards in the process. Having had his one-year contract extended to the summer of 2001 by then manager, Brian Horton, the chairman, Dick Knight, publicly stated that he would not consider any offers under £500,000 for him.

Brighton & Hove A (£1,000 from Stansted on 18/6/98) FL 42+2/12 FLC 1+1 FAC 1 Others 1

HARTE Ian Patrick
Born: Drogheda, 31 August 1977
Height: 5'10" Weight: 11.8
International Honours: Ei: 19; U21-3

When left back David Robertson suffered his cartilage injury in February of the previous season, Ian came in and kept his place for the remainder of 1997-98. He then went away to work on maintaining his fitness during the summer, in the knowledge that the then manager, George Graham, had signed Danny Granville from Chelsea. Ian returned leaner and fitter, and a much much better player. In fact, he was virtually ever present at left back in 1998-99. Predominantly left sided, "Hartey" has tremendous power with either foot, is capable of switching play with an exquisite 60-yard pass, and as a defender will end his career with a healthy tally of goals. Not only is he deadly from long-range free kicks with his left foot, as Southampton and Nottingham Forest discovered, but he is equally adept at cutting inside from the left and scoring with his right, as Derby County found out at Elland Road. Still only 21 years of age, he should have a big future at Elland Road. Played for the Republic of Ireland in the game against Paraguay.

Leeds U (From trainee on 15/12/95) PL 58+7/6 FLC 3+2/1 FAC 7+2/2 Others 3

Ian Harte

HARTFIELD Charles (Charlie) Joseph
Born: Lambeth, 4 September 1971
Height: 6'0" Weight: 13.8
International Honours: E: Yth
Charlie, a left-sided Swansea midfield player, was given a trial by Lincoln last August and signed on loan the following month with a view to a permanent transfer. He scored at Wrexham, but the following week damaged stomach muscles in the warm up before the clash with Notts County at Meadow Lane, and had to withdraw from the team before the kick off. The injury caused him to return early to the Vetch, but although he had another brief trial with Lincoln in March he was unable to prove his fitness, and the move fell through for a second time.

Arsenal (From trainee on 20/9/89)

Sheffield U (Free on 6/8/91) F/PL 45+11/1 FLC 2+1 FAC 4+1 Others 1
Fulham (Loaned on 5/2/97) FL 1+1
Swansea C (Free on 28/11/97) FL 22/2 Others 1
Lincoln C (Loaned on 17/9/98) FL 3/1

HARTSON John
Born: Swansea, 5 April 1975
Height: 6'1" Weight: 14.6
International Honours: W: 18; U21-9; Yth
Struggling to find his form at West Ham last season, a well publicised training ground incident with Eyal Berkovic not really helping his cause, John briefly showed glimpses of his old form when scoring goals at Derby and at home to Coventry for the Hammers before signing for Wimbledon – who smashed their club record by nearly £5 million – in January, and then making his debut for his new club against his old one in a 0-0 draw. Much was made of Joe Kinnear's decision to sign the Welsh international centre forward, but despite criticism, the Dons' supporters were right behind the newcomer, knowing him to be strong, direct, and a real danger to any opposition in aerial confrontations. However, missing matches through suspension did not help initially, but when getting into his stride towards the end of what had been a difficult season for the Dons, he finally got off the mark with back-to-back goals against Newcastle and Coventry, which helped secure the club's Premiership safety.

Luton T (From trainee on 19/12/92) FL 32+22/11 FLC 0+1 FAC 3+3/2 Others 2
Arsenal (£2,500,000 on 13/1/95) PL 43+10/14 FLC 2+4/1 FAC 2+1/1 Others 8+1/1
West Ham U (£3,200,000 + on 14/2/97) PL 59+1/24 FLC 6/6 FAC 7/3
Wimbledon (£7,000,000 on 15/1/99) PL 12+2/2

HASLAM Steven Robert
Born: Sheffield, 6 September 1979
Height: 5'11" Weight: 10.10
International Honours: E: Yth; Sch
Locally born, the former England schoolboy international star came through the trainee ranks before turning professional for Sheffield Wednesday in September 1996. Having since represented the England U18 and U20 sides, and thought to have an excellent future in the game by the Owls' management, the stylish midfielder made his Premiership debut in the penultimate game of last season – a 1-0 home win against Liverpool – and followed that up with another start at Charlton. Is definitely a youngster with a future.

Sheffield Wed (From trainee on 12/9/96) PL 2

HASSELBAINK Jerrel (Jimmy Floyd)
Born: Surinam, 27 March 1972
Height: 6'2" Weight: 13.4
International Honours: Holland: 5
When you consider the fees being paid for top quality strikers these days, the £2,000,000 Leeds paid for Jimmy must rank as one of the best pieces of transfer business in the club's history. In only his second season, in 1998-99, he improved as a striker, particularly with his workrate and contri-

bution to team effort, Harry Kewell and Alan Smith both greatly benefiting from him. As the club's 1998 "Player of the Year" he was once again top scorer, and hit nine in nine games in November and December. Becoming even more deadly as the campaign progressed, with his long-range free kicks carrying both power and precision, his performance of the season came in the 2-1 victory at Aston Villa when, but for a post, he would have had a first-half hat trick, following a superb curling 20-yard free kick and an excellent solo strike. Many a Premiership defender suffered JFH's pace and power last season. Most definitely one of the game's top strikers, he was due to sit down with the club in the close season to discuss a new and improved contract, even though he has two years left to run on his present deal. Everyone connected to Leeds United hope things can be resolved successfully.

Leeds U (£2,000,000 from Boavista, via Campomairense, on 18/7/97) PL 66+3/34 FLC 5/2 FAC 9/5 Others 4/1

HASSELL Robert (Bobby) John Francis
Born: Derby, 4 June 1980
Height: 5'9" Weight: 12.6
Although he spent part of last season on the treatment table there was some surprise that his young Mansfield centre back, cum midfielder, was not called upon more often, having come through the youth team to turn professional during the summer. However, during his rare appearances in the first team he showed why so much is expected from him in the future.

Mansfield T (From trainee on 3/7/98) FL 9+3

HATELEY Mark Wayne
Born: Derby, 7 November 1961
Height: 6'3" Weight: 13.0
Club Honours: SPD '91, '92, '93, '94, '95; SC '92, '93; SLC '90, '92, '93
International Honours: E: 32; U21-10; Yth
Seven days after new owners – led by former Scunthorpe chairman, Tom Belton – took over at Hull City last November, Mark's nightmare finally came to a close. With still more than a year left on his player/manager contract, the former England international was invited to leave with the club stranded at the foot of the Football League. While the manager part of the post ended in disappointment, his playing influence led to utter frustration as he was only able to grace the black and amber shirt on 27 occasions. By his own high standards, the goals had also dried up, but at least he had the satisfaction of knowing his only Tigers' goal in open play proved to be priceless – a winner at fellow strugglers, Scarborough. It is to be hoped the bitter lessons he learned during his time in east Yorkshire will prove to be to his long-term benefit.

Coventry C (From apprentice on 1/12/78) FL 86+6/25 FLC 8/3 FAC 10+1/6
Portsmouth (£220,000 on 6/6/83) (£1,000,000 to AC Milan on 28/6/84) FL 38/22 FLC 4/2 FAC 2/1
Glasgow R (Signed from AS Monaco on 19/7/90) SL 158+7/85 SLC 15+3/11 SC 16/10 Others 17/7

Queens Park R (£1,500,000 on 3/11/95) P/FL 18+9/3 FLC 0+1 FAC 3+2/2
Leeds U (Loaned on 19/8/96) PL 5+1
Glasgow R (£300,000 on 14/3/97) SL 4
Hull C (Free on 8/8/97) FL 12+9/3 FLC 4+2

HAWES Steven (Steve) Robert
Born: High Wycombe, 17 July 1978
Height: 5'8" Weight: 11.10
Having trained with Hull for much of 1998, after being released by Sheffield United, "Hawsey" rejected the overtures of Oldham and Brentford to sign a two-year deal with the Tigers in the summer. A neat, tidy and hyperactive midfielder, Steve was a regular up to the turn of the year, but missed out as the team was re-organised in the fight for league survival.

Sheffield U (From trainee on 2/3/96) FL 1+3
Doncaster Rov (Loaned on 18/9/97) FL 7+1
Doncaster Rov (Free on 20/2/98) FL 1+2
Hull C (Free on 16/7/98) FL 18+1 FLC 4 FAC 1+1 Others 0+1

HAWORTH Simon Owen
Born: Cardiff, 30 March 1977
Height: 6'2" Weight: 13.8
Club Honours: AMC '99
International Honours: W: 5; B-1; U21-10; Yth
Having made just one appearance for Coventry in 1998-99, in a 5-1 defeat at Newcastle, this tall, strong and skilful centre forward became Wigan's record signing in October. Unfortunately, his season was hampered by hamstring problems, which saw him miss out on the majority of Athletic's games early on in the campaign, before he came back strongly in the last quarter to play at Wembley as part of the side that won the Auto Windscreens Shield. Of his 20 league games played, he averaged a goal every two games, his excellent first touch, strong aerial power, and ability to shield the ball to bring colleagues into the play, saw him net 14 goals in total. His strike rate saw him selected by Wales to captain their U21 side against Italy, while his most memorable goal came against his fellow countrymen, Wrexham, in the return leg of the area final of the Auto Windscreens Shield.

Cardiff C (From trainee on 7/8/95) FL 27+10/9 FLC 4 FAC 0+1 Others 4/1
Coventry C (£500,000 on 4/6/97) PL 5+6 FLC 2/1 FAC 0+1
Wigan Ath (£600,000 on 2/10/98) FL 19+1/10 FAC 1/1 Others 5/3

HAY Christopher (Chris) Drummond
Born: Glasgow, 28 August 1974
Height: 5'11" Weight: 12.5
Another Scot on Swindon's books, the striker was looking to build on his goalscoring at the club in 1997-98, but after just three starts in 1998-99 injury kept him out of the reckoning, and it was another ten games before he was available for selection. Back in the side again, following a dry spell he kick started his career, playing in 17 of the remaining 18 fixtures, and scoring a brace in the Portsmouth home game. Looks for a better term in 1999-2000.

Glasgow C (Free from Giffnock North AFC on 27/5/93) SL 9+16/4 SC 0+3 Others 0+2/1
Swindon T (£330,000 on 6/8/97) FL 46+17/20 FLC 2+1 FAC 2

HAYDON Nicholas (Nicky)
Born: Barking, 18 August 1978
Height: 5'10" Weight: 11.6
Another homegrown product at Colchester, Nicky came in to the team early on last season to replace injury-hit Richard Wilkins, and made an immediate impact with a goal in the win at Wrexham. However, in making only limited appearances throughout the first half of the campaign, playing in both full-back positions and in midfield, he went on loan to Kettering Town in the spring before being released in the summer.

Colchester U (From trainee on 10/8/95) FL 16+15/2 FLC 2 FAC 1+2 Others 1

HAYFIELD Matthew (Matt) Anthony
Born: Bristol, 8 August 1975
Height: 5'11" Weight: 12.2
Given a free transfer by Bristol Rovers during the 1998 close season, Matt joined Shrewsbury on a short-term contract, making just one full start and coming off the bench in another game before being released. Given little opportunity to shine, the young midfielder then signed for non-league Yeovil.

Bristol Rov (From trainee on 13/7/94) FL 24+17 FAC 4+1 Others 3+3
Shrewsbury T (Free on 17/8/98) FL 1+1

HAYLES Barrington (Barry) Edward
Born: Lambeth, 17 May 1972
Height: 5'9" Weight: 13.0
Club Honours: Div 2 '99
International Honours: E: SP-1
A firm crowd favourite, Barry played in Bristol Rovers' opening 20 games, scoring doubles against Wigan, Lincoln, and Walsall, and it was no surprise when his remarkable 18-month spell at the Memorial Stadium came to an end last November when he transferred his allegiance to Kevin Keegan's Fulham for a fee in excess of £2 million. Although coming to his new club with a huge price tag, Barry took a while to win over the Fulham faithful and, after two starts, during the second of which he opened his scoring account, he began several games on the subs' bench. To those who had seen him in action for Stevenage Borough only a couple of years before he was always going to come through, and the FA Cup-tie at Old Trafford was probably the turning point. Having had a brilliant game, his confidence rose, and he scored five times in the next 14 games, 12 of which were won. His pace and close control, together with the ability to get to the goal line and send over accurate crosses, also provided goals for his fellow strikers. Won a Second Division championship medal as Fulham galloped home with 14 points to spare.

Bristol Rov (£250,000 from Stevenage Borough on 4/6/97) FL 62/32 FLC 4/1 FAC 5/2 Others 3+2/2
Fulham (£2,100,000 on 17/11/98) FL 26+4/8 FAC 4/1

HAYTER James Edward
Born: Sandown, IoW, 9 April 1979
Height: 5'9" Weight: 11.2
James really made his mark in the Bournemouth first-team squad during the last third of 1998-99, making 16 starts and four substitute appearances from February until the end of the campaign. He also scored his first senior goal in his first appearance of the season, in the 4-0 victory over Stoke. A quick, exciting forward who played in a striking role or on either wing, he is an excellent prospect and looks to have secured a senior position for 1999-2000.
Bournemouth (From trainee on 7/7/97) FL 16+11/2 Others 0+1

HAYWARD Steven (Steve) Lee
Born: Pelsall, 8 September 1971
Height: 5'11" Weight: 12.5
Club Honours: AMC '97; Div 2 '99
International Honours: E: Yth
In his second season at Fulham, Steve exceeded all expectations, his free kicks and corners bringing several goals, but it was his accurate long passes which had the older Fulham fans comparing that part of his game with the great Johnny Haynes. Steve began 1998-99 on the bench but, once he was given his chance, played so well that he made it impossible for Kevin Keegan to leave him out of the starting line-up. Although five Fulham players made the PFA award-winning Second Division side, he was very unlucky not to be selected. But, despite that, he was well worth his Second Division championship medal as the Cottagers led the rest home by 14 points. Not a prolific scorer, but few will forget his superb drive to clinch Fulham's FA Cup win at Villa Park.
Derby Co (From juniors on 17/9/88) FL 15+11/1 FLC 0+2 FAC 1 Others 3+4
Carlisle U (£100,000 on 13/3/95) FL 88+2/14 FLC 6/1 FAC 4 Others 15/1
Fulham (£175,000 on 23/6/97) FL 74+3/7 FLC 8+1/2 FAC 7+2/2 Others 3

HAZAN Alon
Born: Ashdod, Israel, 14 September 1967
Height: 6'0" Weight: 13.4
International Honours: Israel: 64
The Israeli utility player was perhaps at his best for Watford in 1998-99 in a holding role in midfield, where his passing could be harnessed to maximum effect. Always seeming to have time on ball – the hallmark of a good player – he suffered hamstring problems in October, but otherwise he was a regular member of the first-team squad, who was often used to telling effect as a substitute.
Watford (£200,000 from Ironi Ashdod on 13/1/98) FL 15+18/2 FLC 1+1 Others 0+3

HEALD Gregory (Greg) James
Born: Enfield, 26 September 1971
Height: 6'1" Weight: 12.8
International Honours: E: Sch
Arguably the finest defender in the Third Division, his six-month absence during the first half of the 1998-99 campaign, due to a back injury sustained in summer training, proved to be hugely influential in Barnet's

fortunes. Back in late December, he was selected to sit on the bench in the home victory over Leyton Orient, and did not actually appear in the starting line-up until late January, where he occupied the number five shirt in the clash against Shrewsbury. Once he had returned to full fitness, he re-emerged as the defensive colossus that the Bees' fans had previously held in such high regard, his vast array of attributes including sublime aerial strength, which made him both a solid defender and a formidable weapon at set-piece plays. His positional sense is acute, and this is coupled with an uncompromising style in the tackle. After his return to the side, the Bees recorded seven clean sheets, and Greg scored on two occasions (at Hull and Rotherham).
Peterborough U (£35,000 from Enfield on 8/7/94) FL 101+4/6 FLC 8 FAC 8+1 Others 11/2
Barnet (Signed on 8/8/97) FL 62/5 FLC 4/1 FAC 1 Others 2/1

HEALD Paul Andrew
Born: Wath on Dearne, 20 September 1968
Height: 6'2" Weight: 14.0
Due to the excellent form and fitness of Wimbledon's number-one choice 'keeper, Neil Sullivan, Paul was restricted to playing just two games in the 1998-99 season, appearing in both legs of the Worthington Cup against Portsmouth, which the Dons won 5-3 on aggregate. An extremely popular member of the team who always finds time to sign autographs and have a joke with the younger Dons' fans, there was much speculation surrounding his future. Certainly, if Neil Sullivan does leave the club, as per press speculation, Paul may be called into action more this coming season. Safe and reliable, and a good shot stopper who stands up well, his quick reactions often allow him to make last-ditch saves.
Sheffield U (From trainee on 30/6/87)
Leyton Orient (Signed on 2/12/88) FL 176 FLC 13 FAC 9 Others 21
Coventry C (Loaned on 10/3/92) PL 2
Swindon T (Loaned on 24/3/94) PL 1+1
Wimbledon (£125,000 on 25/7/95) PL 20 FLC 7

HEALY Brian
Born: Glasgow, 27 December 1968
Height: 6'1" Weight: 12.7
International Honours: E: SP-1
A December 1998 signing from Conference club, Morecambe, although coming into league football at a relatively late age the midfielder made a big impression at Torquay with his passing and awareness. Also possessing a fine shot in either foot, Brian scored at Blackpool, in a 3-2 defeat, and netted a penalty in a 1-1 draw against Barnet at Plainmoor. Will benefit from a first full-time campaign, and big things are expected from this talented playmaker in 1999-2000.
Torquay U (£25,000 from Morecambe on 16/12/98) FL 16+3/2 Others 2

HEANEY Neil Andrew
Born: Middlesbrough, 3 November 1971
Height: 5'9" Weight: 11.6
Club Honours: FAYC '88
International Honours: E: U21-6; Yth

Although still retained by Manchester City, Neil spent most of last season in the reserve team, playing his only first-team game against Mansfield in the Auto Windscreens Shield, where nobody made their mark in a 2-0 home defeat. Linked to a number of clubs, but with nothing firmed up, he was loaned to Bristol City in mid March. There, he found his chances limited, with both Greg Goodridge and Scott Murray able to fill the wide role, and failed to make a big impression. A left winger with skill to match his pace, and the ability to deliver crosses into dangerous areas, he will have to see how 1999-2000 pans out for him at Maine Road.
Arsenal (From trainee on 14/11/89) F/PL 4+3 FLC 0+1
Hartlepool U (Loaned on 3/1/91) FL 2+1
Cambridge U (Loaned on 9/1/92) FL 9+4/2 FAC 1
Southampton (£300,000 on 22/3/94) PL 42+19/5 FLC 4+2 FAC 6/2
Manchester C (£500,000 on 25/11/96) FL 13+5/1 FAC 2/1 Others 1
Charlton Ath (Loaned on 26/3/98) FL 4+2 Others 3
Bristol C (Loaned on 12/3/99) FL 2+1

HEARY Thomas Mark
Born: Dublin, 14 February 1979
Height: 5'10" Weight: 11.12
International Honours: Ei: Yth; Sch
Due to suspensions late last season, the developing Huddersfield full back gained a recall against Barnsley at the McAlpine, his previous involvement in team affairs in 1998-99 being that of a non-playing sub on five occasions. Confident at right back or in midfield, and continuing to impress with good touch and vision, he was rewarded with an extension to his contract. A member of the Irish squad in the World Youth championships in Nigeria, he had earlier gained honours for the Republic's U20 side who beat Germany in the final of the UEFA championships in Cyprus.
Huddersfield T (From trainee on 17/2/96) FL 7+4 FLC 0+1 FAC 1

HEATH Robert
Born: Stoke, 31 August 1978
Height: 5'8" Weight: 10.0
One of the few locals in the current Stoke squad, Robert did not quite make the breakthrough into the side in 1998-99 that many had anticipated. Used as a full back on occasions, he failed to settle into a wing-back role and looks at his best in midfield. However, time is still on his side and further opportunities will come.
Stoke C (From trainee on 15/7/96) FL 11+5 Others 2

HEATHCOTE Michael (Mick)
Born: Kelloe, 10 September 1965
Height: 6'2" Weight: 12.5
Missing very few games in 1998-99, despite reaching the twilight of his career, the Plymouth captain is still extremely dependable. A strong and commanding central defender, his role in developing the youngsters was even more valuable and, as a good organiser, he was once again rewarded with the Argyle "Player of the Year" award. Excellent at set pieces, he

scored four goals, two of them in back-to-back matches, at home to Barnet and at Scunthorpe.

Sunderland (£15,000 from Spennymoor on 19/8/87) FL 6+3 Others 0+1
Halifax T (Loaned on 17/12/87) FL 7/1 FAC 1
York C (Loaned on 4/1/90) FL 3 Others 1
Shrewsbury T (£55,000 on 12/7/90) FL 43+1/6 FLC 6 FAC 5 Others 4
Cambridge U (£150,000 on 12/9/91) FL123+5/13 FLC 7/1 FAC 5+2/2 Others 7/2
Plymouth Arg (£100,000 on 27/7/95) FL 164+1/12 FLC 8/1 FAC 11/2 Others 8

HEBEL Dirk Josef

Born: Cologne, Germany, 24 November 1972
Height: 5'10" Weight: 12.1
Club Honours: Div 3'99

Unable to get an opportunity at Tranmere, having been signed from Bursaspor early in 1997-98, the German moved to Brentford at the end of last August, making his Football League debut in a 2-1 home win over Rochdale just three days later. A neat and tidy midfielder with good passing ability, he was a regular in the 14-man squad for three months until a foot injury put him out of action for eight weeks. Unfortunately, when fit, he was unable to get back into the team following the arrival of new signings, and was later released on 10 May, but not before taking a Third Division championship medal with him following the Bees' title win.

Tranmere Rov (Free from Bursaspor on 4/9/97)
Brentford (Free on 27/8/98) FL 6+9 FAC 2+1 Others 1

HECKINBOTTOM Paul

Born: Barnsley, 17 July 1977
Height: 5'11" Weight: 12.0

A left-sided defender who recognised that he needed a move from Sunderland if he was to make the grade, Paul joined Hartlepool on loan last September, and soon made his mark by scoring on his debut with a close-range shot against Peterborough after his header had been blocked. Although performing competently, he then struggled with a hamstring injury, and was allowed to return to Wearside, prior to having trials with Sheffield United, Bolton, and Stockport, before joining Darlington in a permanent deal just before the transfer deadline. Quickly getting down to business, he made the left-back spot his own with committed and hard-running displays, something he will be looking to repeat in 1999-2000.

Sunderland (Free from Manchester U juniors on 14/7/95)
Scarborough (Loaned on 17/10/97) FL 28+1 Others 1
Hartlepool U (Loaned on 25/9/98) FL 5/1
Darlington (Free on 25/3/99) FL 10

HEDMAN Magnus Carl

Born: Stockholm, Sweden, 19 March 1973
Height: 6'4" Weight: 13.10
International Honours: Sweden: 14

After 14 years as Coventry's number one, Steve Ogrizovic lost his mantle to Sweden's top 'keeper who, in his first full season (1998-99) in the English game, performed very well, his reflexes and shot stopping being exemplary, although a few doubts persisted about his command of the penalty area on crosses. Although a migraine problem kept him out of the two Christmas games, and he suffered an abdominal strain in the home game with Middlesbrough, Magnus carried on in controversial circumstances. His good form started on the opening day when he pulled off several world-class saves to deny Chelsea, and Pierluigi Casiraghi in particular, and he went on to perform heroics at Filbert Street in the FA Cup, including a late point-blank save when the score was 1-0, and at Highbury when he kept the score down to a respectable figure.

Coventry C (£500,000 from AIK Stockholm on 24/7/97) PL 50 FLC 3 FAC 6

HEGGEM Vegard

Born: Trondheim, Norway, 13 July 1975
Height: 5'10" Weight: 11.12
International Honours: Denmark: 11

Signed during the 1998 close season, the former Rosenborg right back was seen as yet another Norwegian import when he first donned a Liverpool shirt in 1998-99, but his move to Anfield effectively spelt the end of Rob Jones' career at Pool. However, he has since proved that he is a player of some quality with his displays throughout the season, showing skill and the ability to score goals, which adds yet another dimension to a team full of goalscoring ability. Having scored on his debut for Norway in a 3-3 draw against France, Vegard was unfortunately ruled out of the World Cup through injury. He can play on the right of the defence, or on the right-side of midfield, a position which truly utilises his ability to make deep, penetrating runs, and sometimes score vital goals. Playing in front of Rigobert Song, Liverpool look strong down the right.

Liverpool (£3,500,000 from Rosenborg, via Orkdal, on 27/7/98) PL 27+2/2 FLC 1 FAC 1 Others 4+1

Vegard Heggem

HEGGS Carl Sydney

Born: Leicester, 11 October 1970
Height: 6'1" Weight: 12.10

A ball-playing, talented striker, Carl started last season in the Northampton first team but struggled to find the net on a regular basis. In and out of the side, spending a lot of time on the bench, he soon made it clear that if he did not get regular senior football he would leave at the end of the season when his contract came up for renewal. Following that, he was sold to local non-league Rushden and Diamonds in October, along with Ray Warburton.

West Bromwich A (£25,000 from Leicester U on 22/8/91) FL 13+27/3 FLC 2 FAC 0+1 Others 6+3/1
Bristol Rov (Loaned on 27/1/95) FL 2+3/1
Swansea C (£60,000 on 27/7/95) FL 33+13/7 FLC 2 FAC 2 Others 4+1/1
Northampton T (£40,000 on 31/7/97) FL 29+17/5 FLC 3+2/2 FAC 4+1/1 Others 3+1/4

HEINOLA Antti Juhani

Born: Helsinki, Finland, 20 March 1973
Height: 5'10" Weight: 12.3
International Honours: Finland: 7

Antti was a regular member of the Queens Park Rangers' side in 1998-99, playing as an attacking right-wing back, before he suffered badly with injuries in the second half of the season. A fractured cheekbone incurred against Bury was followed by another serious head injury in his re-appearance against Bristol City. Called into the Finnish squad for their tournament in Cyprus at the beginning of 1999, but did not make an appearance.

Queens Park R (£150,000 from Heracles, via HJK Helsinki and Emmen, on 15/1/98) FL 23+10 FLC 3 FAC 1

HENCHOZ Stephane

Born: Billens, Switzerland, 7 September 1974
Height: 6'1" Weight: 12.10
International Honours: Switzerland: 37

One of the few Blackburn players to really prosper in 1998-99, Stephane compensated for the loss of Colin Hendry by becoming a real tower of strength in defence. Always cool, dominant in the air, and a calculating tackler, he occasionally appeared gauche but seldom made errors, while the lack of acceleration that caused him trouble in his first season appears to have been overcome. Despite an attempt to put aside negative publicity, regarding comments attributed to him about the area, his contract expires in the summer of 2000, and he is known to miss some of the facilities of mainland Europe. Brought to the club by Roy Hodgson, he was one of the players most affected by the club's decision to dismiss the manager.

Blackburn Rov (£3,000,000 from Hamburg, via Bulle and Neuchatel Xamax, on 14/7/97) PL 70 FLC 3+1 FAC 6 Others 2

HENDERSON Kevin Malcolm

Born: Ashington, 8 June 1974
Height: 6'3" Weight: 13.2

Still to be named in a starting line-up, taking into account his few appearances as a sub in

1998-99 Kevin looked the brightest of Burnley's second-string strikers. Always eager to impress, he has speed, crossing ability, and the finishing touch, which he proved with his first league goal against Lincoln. A muscle problem kept him out of contention in the later stages of the campaign, prior to him being released in the summer.
Burnley (Signed from Morpeth T on 17/12/97) FL 0+14/1 FLC 0+2 Others 0+4/1

HENDON Ian Michael
Born: Ilford, 5 December 1971
Height: 6'0" Weight: 12.10
Club Honours: FAYC '90; CS '91; Div 3 '98
International Honours: E: U21-7; Yth
1998-99 was a season of complete contrasts for Ian, who went from a highly popular club captain to desert the Notts County cause shortly before the transfer deadline in March – moving to a team almost doomed, Northampton Town. A quick and powerful right-sided full back, wing back or centre back who is comfortable on the ball, and possesses good pace, there was no questioning his commitment, when booked within ten minutes of his debut versus Preston. Manager Ian Atkins was hoping that he could inspire Town like he had County, but, ultimately, it was just too late, and he will be playing Third Division football in 1999-2000.
Tottenham H (From trainee on 20/12/89) FL 0+4 FLC 1 Others 0+2
Portsmouth (Loaned on 16/1/92) FL 1+3
Leyton Orient (Loaned on 26/3/92) FL 5+1
Barnsley (Loaned on 17/3/93) FL 6
Leyton Orient (£50,000 on 9/8/93) FL 130+1/5 FLC 6 FAC 7 Others 12/1
Birmingham C (Loaned on 23/3/95) FL 4
Notts Co (£50,000 on 24/2/97) FL 82/6 FLC 5/1 FAC 8+1
Northampton T (£30,000 on 25/3/99) FL 7

HENDRIE John Grattan
Born: Lennoxtown, 24 October 1963
Height: 5'8" Weight: 12.3
Club Honours: Div 3 '85, Div 2 '90, Div 1 '95
International Honours: S: Yth
Although in the veteran stage, but still capable of producing the odd flash leading to spectacular goals, John became the Barnsley player/manager on 6 July 1998 after Danny Wilson left for Sheffield Wednesday. Although his appearances were restricted, he did score the winning goal early in the season against Oxford, and made a couple of starts in the FA Cup run when injuries took their toll on the squad, before being released on 19 April 1999. Is the cousin of Aston Villa's rising star, Lee Hendrie.
Coventry C (From apprentice on 18/5/81) FL 15+6/2 FLC 2
Hereford U (Loaned on 10/1/84) FL 6
Bradford C (Free on 2/7/84) FL 173/46 FLC 17/3 FAC 11/6 Others 11/4
Newcastle U (£500,000 on 17/6/88) FL 34/4 FLC 2/1 FAC 4 Others 3
Leeds U (£600,000 on 20/6/89) FL 22+5/5 FLC 1 FAC 1 Others 2
Middlesbrough (£550,000 on 5/7/90) F/PL 181+11/44 FLC 22+2/6 FAC 10+2/2 Others 6/3
Barnsley (£250,000 on 11/10/96) F/PL 49+16/7 FLC 0+3 FAC 8/3

HENDRIE Lee Andrew
Born: Birmingham, 18 May 1977
Height: 5'10" Weight: 10.3
International Honours: E: 1; B-1; U21-7; Yth
Consistently featuring in Aston Villa's line-up in 1998-99, and showing much improved form, Lee was catapulted from England U21 status to that of full international when coming off the bench to make his debut against the Czech Republic in November. Unfortunately, after missing very few games, the young midfielder sustained an ankle injury at Liverpool in mid April that put him out of action for the rest of the season. Prior to that, however, he had proved to be a key member of John Gregory's title-chasing side, his attacking strengths, all-round hard work, and commitment to the cause, coming to the fore, despite a lack of goals. From a footballing family – his dad, Paul, played for Birmingham, and his cousin John is currently at Barnsley – he will only get better, and will be looking to build on his full England cap in 1999-2000. Sharing the Midland Football Writers "Young Midland Footballer of the Year" with Wolves' Robbie Keane, Lee continued to turn out for the England U21 side during the campaign.
Aston Villa (From trainee on 18/5/94) PL 46+10/6 FAC 5+4 Others 5+1

HENRY Nicholas (Nicky) Ian
Born: Liverpool, 21 February 1969
Height: 5'6" Weight: 10.12
Club Honours: Div 2 '91
Finally regaining fitness after a back operation, Nicky made his first appearance for Sheffield United last season as a sub against Tranmere in November and promptly sustained a broken hand. The energetic midfielder, unable to gain a permanent place, and spending much of his time on the bench, moved to Walsall in March, where his keen tackling and use of the ball showed up well in his debut game at the beginning of April. Playing with great commitment, he wore the number four shirt with distinction in the last few vital games of the campaign as promotion was clinched. Stop Press: Signed for Tranmere on 25 June under the Bosman ruling.
Oldham Ath (From trainee on 6/7/87) F/PL 264+9/19 FLC 30+4/3 FAC 21 Others 5
Sheffield U (£500,000 on 28/2/97) FL 13+3 FAC 2+1 Others 2
Walsall (Free on 25/3/99) FL 8

HENSHAW Terrence (Terry) Robert
Born: Nottingham, 29 February 1980
Height: 5'10" Weight: 11.0
Having made his first-team debut for Notts County while still a trainee, in 1997-98, he turned pro during the 1998 close season and was expecting to build on his earlier successes in 1998-99. Although a very promising young centre back, who followed a long line of graduates from the County youth squad, and continued to show midfield skills in reserve football, he was surprisingly released during the summer. Tall, and capable in the air, he could still come back to the league at a later stage.
Notts Co (From trainee on 20/7/98) FLC 0+1 Others 1+1

HERBERT Craig Justin
Born: Coventry, 9 November 1975
Height: 5'11" Weight: 11.6
In his second year at Shrewsbury in 1998-99, the central defender was unfortunate in as much that although rarely putting a foot wrong, he was usually fourth choice in a three-man central defence. Strong in the air and on the ground, and definitely improving his all-round performance, Craig always looked to take his chances when they came, and could become a regular when the opportunity next arises.
West Bromwich A (Free from Torquay U juniors on 18/3/94) FL 8 FLC 2 Others 1/1
Shrewsbury T (Free on 23/7/97) FL 29+3 FLC 3 FAC 2/1 Others 1

HERRERA Roberto (Robbie)
Born: Torquay, 12 June 1970
Height: 5'7" Weight: 10.6
Signed from Fulham early last August, the left-wing back returned to his roots, having been born in Torquay, and had a consistently good first season. His attacking pace and defensive positional play meant that this was an area of the team which manager Wes Saunders left well alone during a period of rebuilding.
Queens Park R (From trainee on 1/3/88) FL 4+2 FLC 1+2 Others 1+1
Torquay U (Loaned on 17/3/92) FL 11
Torquay U (Loaned on 24/10/92) FL 5
Fulham (Signed on 29/10/93) FL 143+2/1 FLC 15 FAC 13 Others 7+1
Torquay U (£30,000 on 4/8/98) FL 39+1 FLC 2 FAC 2 Others 2

Robbie Herrera

HESKEY Emile William Ivanhoe
Born: Leicester, 11 January 1978
Height: 6'2" Weight: 13.12
Club Honours: FLC '97
International Honours: E: 2; B-1; U21-14; Yth
A two-footed striker with power and pace, and an obvious threat to any defence, Emile

appeared to be on the brink of full international honours when a toe injury prevented his selection for England's prestige friendly with France. Although not as prolific as in previous seasons, he won the BBC "Goal of the Month" accolade for September with a classy solo effort against Arsenal, and also managed to turn Ramon Vega inside out before smashing home an unstoppable effort in the emotionally charged victory at home to Tottenham, on the night when the campaign to keep Martin O'Neill at Filbert Street reached a climax. Suffered with a back problem from Christmas onwards, which reduced his effectiveness right up to the Worthington Cup final, and continued to keep him out of the full England squad. A change in treatment saw him return to full speed to set up Tony Cottee's 200th league strike at White Hart Lane, leaving the pacy Sol Campbell in his wake, and further impressive games against Villa and West Ham saw him called up by Kevin Keegan for England's trip to Hungary. Finally, as a sub for Sunderland's Kevin Phillips, the big striker was called up for the last eight minutes in a 1-1 draw. Also played three times for the national U21 side.
Leicester C (From trainee on 3/10/95) PL 120+11/33 FLC 17+2/5 FAC 7 Others 5

HESSENTHALER Andrew (Andy)
Born: Dartford, 17 August 1965
Height: 5'7" Weight: 11.5
International Honours: E: SP-1
Gillingham's inspirational midfield worker and captain. By his own standards, he had a poor start to the 1998-99 campaign, but his form from January onwards was exceptional and he finished up as runner up in the fans "Player of the Year" poll. He was always breaking from his midfield role to try his luck at goal, and he finished up with eight to his credit, his highest total in a season for six years!
Watford (£65,000 from Redbridge Forest on 12/9/91) FL 195/11 FLC 13/1 FAC 5/2 Others 4
Gillingham (£235,000 on 7/8/96) FL 116+3/9 FLC 11 FAC 6/1 Others 6/2

HESSEY Sean Peter
Born: Whiston, 19 September 1978
Height: 5'10" Weight: 12.6
Huddersfield's young central defender had a tough baptism to the start of last season, playing only 45 minutes against Portsmouth at the McAlpine, and not only conceding a penalty when played out of position at right back, but suffering bruised ribs into the bargain. Sean soon recovered though, and continued to impress with the reserves in their promotion push, before joining the first-team regulars in giving a sound and solid display at Crewe. The 20-year old then kept his place in the side, following some astute displays, looking to be strong in the air and a good passer. Unfortunately, injuries and illness plagued him after another encounter with Portsmouth, and apart from the odd game, that was it before he was released during the summer.

Leeds U (Free from Liverpool juniors on 15/9/97)
Wigan Ath (Free on 24/12/97)
Huddersfield T (Free on 12/3/98) FL 7+4 FAC 1

HEWITT James (Jamie) Robert
Born: Chesterfield, 17 May 1968
Height: 5'10" Weight: 11.9
Chesterfield's long-serving right back received a well-deserved testimonial against Sheffield Wednesday in May, following another season of consistency, with his coolness under pressure and his clear reading of the game reflecting his experience. And, in a rare midfield outing against Fulham in April, Jamie got forward to score the goal that kept the Cottagers' championship champagne on ice. Out of contract during the summer, at the time of going to press it was known that the club had made him an offer of re-engagement.
Chesterfield (From trainee on 22/4/86) FL 240+9/14 FLC 10/1 FAC 8+1 Others 11+2
Doncaster Rov (Free on 1/8/92) FL 32+1 FLC 3+1/1 FAC 1 Others 3
Chesterfield (Signed on 8/10/93) FL 209+7/12 FLC 14 FAC 14/1 Others 11/1

HEWLETT Matthew (Matt) Paul
Born: Bristol, 25 February 1976
Height: 6'2" Weight: 11.3
International Honours: E: Yth
Expected to make a big impression at Bristol City in 1998-99, injuries saw him miss a large part of the season, but he still needs to score more goals if he is to fulfil his potential. A player who can make good runs from midfield, Matt was loaned to Burnley in November, but showed little of his ability in just three appearances before returning to Ashton Gate. It was thought that he found it difficult to adapt to the needs of a struggling side at a lower level, but, nevertheless, 1999-2000 could be make-or-break time for him.
Bristol C (From trainee on 12/8/93) FL 106+14/9 FLC 10+2 FAC 4+1/2 Others 5+1
Burnley (Loaned on 27/11/98) FL 2 Others 1

HEYWOOD Matthew (Matty) Stephen
Born: Chatham, 26 August 1979
Height: 6'2" Weight: 14.0
Having only signed professional in July 1998, Matty was a beneficiary of early season injuries (not to mention Stan Ternent's abrupt jettisoning of half the defence), and made his debut in September against Wigan. A centre back of the old-fashioned, no-nonsense variety, he took his chance well to form an effective partnership with the more skilful Brian Reid, but the signing of Steve Davis ensured that, for the moment at least, his first-team days were limited.
Burnley (From trainee on 6/7/98) FL 11+2 FAC 1 Others 1

HIBBURT James Anthony
Born: Ashford, 30 October 1979
Height: 6'0" Weight: 12.8
International Honours: E: Sch
The captain of the Crystal Palace youth team, and a former England schoolboy international, James came on as a substitute in the Inter-Toto Cup in Turkey, and

followed that up with a Football League debut at Norwich last April after scoring twice at Carrow Road in a reserve match. A central defender who is at his best in aerial confrontations, he is a player who is obviously part of Palace's future.
Crystal Palace (From trainee on 2/11/96) FL 0+2

HICKS Graham
Born: Oldham, 17 February 1981
Height: 5'11" Weight: 13.0
A product of Rochdale's School of Excellence and the son of the coach, Keith – who played for Oldham, Hereford and Dale as a centre half – Graham gained a regular place in the club's reserve side last season before signing pro forms in January, having been a trainee. A defender like his father, he was named as a substitute for a couple of games towards the end of the season before being selected for his Football League debut by the caretaker boss, David Hamilton, in the final match, at Brighton, playing at right back. Is also a top class cricketer.
Rochdale (From trainee on 21/1/99) FL 1

HICKS Mark
Born: Belfast, 24 July 1981
Height: 5'8" Weight: 10.4
Signed from junior league football during the 1998 close season, Mark came on as substitute during the Colchester game, when Millwall fielded a reserve side, and made an immediate impact. This hard-working, right-sided player, who is equally at home in defence or attack, looks like having a good career in front of him, especially if he continues to progress along the right lines.
Millwall (Signed from juniors on 29/7/98) FL 0+1

HICKS Stuart Jason
Born: Peterborough, 30 May 1967
Height: 6'1" Weight: 13.0
Still a firm favourite with the Leyton Orient fans in 1998-99, Stuart is a big, strong, dominant central defender, who has a great will to win and a no-nonsense approach to the game. Sent off towards the end of the season, causing him to miss the first leg of the play offs, he came back into action after 115 minutes of the return leg to help the club reach the final. Yet to score for Orient, he will be looking to add goals to his armoury in the coming term.
Peterborough U (From apprentice on 10/8/84)
Colchester U (Free from Wisbech on 24/3/88) FL 57+7 FLC 2 FAC 5/1 Others 5
Scunthorpe U (Free on 19/8/90) FL 67/1 FLC 4 FAC 4/1 Others 8
Doncaster Rov (Free on 10/8/92) FL 36 FLC 2 FAC 1 Others 2
Huddersfield T (Signed on 27/8/93) FL 20+2/1 FLC 3 FAC 3 Others 1
Preston NE (Signed on 24/3/94) FL 11+1 FLC 2 Others 1/1
Scarborough (Signed on 22/2/95) FL 81+4/2 FLC 5 FAC 4 Others 3
Leyton Orient (Free on 5/8/97) FL 64 FLC 7 FAC 5 Others 1+1

HIDEN Martin
Born: Stainz, Austria, 11 March 1973
Height: 6'0" Weight: 11.9
International Honours: Austria: 7

139

Like many of his team mates imported from the continent, Martin was virtually unknown in England when signed by George Graham for Leeds. Nevertheless, he settled in very well, and showed his tremendous versatility by playing all along the back line. However, although he began last season in the right-back slot vacated by an injury to Gary Kelly, and was playing consistently well, he unfortunately suffered a cruciate ligament injury in the 3-2 defeat at Old Trafford in November, which caused him to miss the rest of the campaign. Martin's strengths are his ability to read the game, and the timing of his tackles, either as a sweeper, centre back, or full back, and his injury was a big loss to the club.

Leeds U (£1,300,000 from Rapid Vienna on 25/2/98) PL 25 FLC 1 FAC 1 Others 4

HIGNETT Craig John

Born: Prescot, 12 January 1970
Height: 5'9" Weight: 11.10
Club Honours: Div 1 '95

Out of contract at Middlesbrough during the 1998 close season, Craig spent a few months at Aberdeen before arriving at Barnsley last November, and proving to be a bargain as he cropped up at the right place and at the right time regularly to poach goals. Showing that he could drift past defenders, and was very good at linking up with the forwards, he was always a cool finisher in front of goal, and will be one of the Tykes main hopes for the coming season. Is also recognised for his powerful dead-ball kicking.

Crewe Alex (Free from Liverpool juniors on 11/5/88) FL 108+13/42 FLC 9+1/4 FAC 11+1/8 Others 6+1/3
Middlesbrough (£500,000 on 27/11/92) F/PL 126+30/33 FLC 19+3/12 FAC 9+2/3 Others 5+1
Aberdeen (Free during 1998 close season) SL 13/2 SLC 2
Barnsley (£800,000 on 26/11/98) FL 24/9 FAC 5/5

Craig Hignett

HILEY Scott Patrick

Born: Plymouth, 27 September 1968
Height: 5'9" Weight: 11.5
Club Honours: Div 4 '90

Signed on a free transfer from Manchester City in the summer of 1998 as full-back cover, Scott, in fact, played many times in the full-back positions when Jason Dodd was used in the centre of defence and midfield. A strong runner, and a consistent performer, he made no less than eight goal-line clearances during 1998-99 as Saints were consistently under pressure, especially away from home. Unlucky on occasions to be left out after playing well, he also showed up with good crossing skills.

Exeter C (From trainee on 4/8/86) FL 205+5/12 FLC 17 FAC 14 Others 16+2
Birmingham C (£100,000 on 12/3/94) FL 49 FLC 7 FAC 1 Others 2
Manchester C (£250,000 on 23/2/96) P/FL 4+5
Southampton (Free on 4/8/98) PL 27+2 FAC 1

HILL Clinton (Clint) Scott

Born: Knowsley, 19 October 1978
Height: 6'0" Weight: 11.6

Clint amply demonstrated his rugged, uncompromising and enthusiastic style of play by picking up four bookings in Tranmere's first four games of 1998-99, leading to a one-match ban. Obviously a no-nonsense tackler and, to his manager's chagrin, he was hauled before the FA for the second successive season after collecting his 11th booking, before being sent off for the sixth time in his career during the game at Barnsley. Awkward, and sometimes over-committed rather than vicious, he is a strong and dominating youngster who will have a bright future in the game if he can improve his disciplinary record. Scored four valuable league goals from midfield.

Tranmere Rov (From trainee on 9/7/97) FL 46+1/4 FLC 5 FAC 2+1/1

HILL Colin Frederick

Born: Uxbridge, 12 November 1963
Height: 6'0" Weight: 12.11
Club Honours: FLC '97
International Honours: NI: 27

A Northampton central defender with class and experience, 1998-99 was not one of Colin's best seasons. Sent off in the opening game of the season after seven minutes, following one of the best one-handed saves seen at Sixfields, he was in and out of the first team, although still being selected for the Northern Ireland squad. Despite being in the latter stages of his playing career, he still has the speed and stamina for league football. Was released during the summer.

Arsenal (From apprentice on 7/8/81) FL 46/1 FLC 4 FAC 1 (Free to Maritimo during 1986 close season)
Colchester U (Free on 30/10/87) FL 64+5 FLC 2 FAC 7/2 Others 3+1
Sheffield U (£85,000 on 1/8/89) FL 77+5/1 FLC 5 FAC 10+2 Others 3
Leicester C (£200,000 on 26/3/92) F/PL 140+5 FLC 10+2/1 FAC 8 Others 9+1 (Free to Trelleborg during 1997 close season)
Northampton T (Free on 7/11/97) FL 49+5 FLC 5 FAC 5 Others 6+1

HILL Daniel (Danny) Ronald

Born: Enfield, 1 October 1974
Height: 5'9" Weight: 11.10
International Honours: E: U21-4; Yth

Signed in the summer of 1998 on a free from Tottenham, Danny could not make a midfield place his own at Oxford in 1998-99 and, although a regular early on, on the bench, he started just one game at Crystal Palace, and made another nine appearances before moving on to help Cardiff in their promotion push in November. Although many felt that the rough and tumble of the Third Division would not suit him, despite lacking consistency he looked a gifted midfielder who, at times, seemed to float over the ground. Scored his first-ever senior goals, both at Ninian Park, against Shrewsbury and Torquay.

Tottenham H (From trainee on 9/9/92) PL 4+6 FLC 0+2
Birmingham C (Loaned on 24/11/95) FL 5 FLC 2
Watford (Loaned on 15/2/96) FL 1
Cardiff C (Loaned on 19/2/98) FL 7
Oxford U (Free on 30/7/98) FL 1+8 FLC 0+1
Cardiff C (Free on 12/11/98) FL 14+12/2 FAC 1+2 Others 1

HILL Keith John

Born: Bolton, 17 May 1969
Height: 6'0" Weight: 12.6

Keith was again an automatic choice at the back for Rochdale in 1998-99, either in the conventional flat back four used at the start of the season, or as one of three central defenders later on. With Dale relying heavily on their defence – six of their first eight victories were by one goal to nil – his power in the air was an integral part of the team. However, his luck in escaping injury ran out in February, and he missed most of the remaining games with a hamstring problem, his eventual return coinciding with an excellent defensive performance by the side in the draw away to leaders, Cambridge.

Blackburn Rov (From juniors on 9/5/87) F/PL 89+7/4 FLC 6/1 FAC 5+1 Others 3+2
Plymouth Arg (Signed on 23/9/92) FL 117+6/2 FLC 9 FAC 10 Others 9
Rochdale (Free on 3/7/96) FL 112+1/6 FLC 6 FAC 7 Others 2

HILL Kevin

Born: Exeter, 6 March 1976
Height: 5'8" Weight: 10.3

The hard-working Torquay midfielder was often overlooked by manager Wes Saunders in 1998-99, as he struggled to find his best combination. Nevertheless, his ability to take up dangerous attacking positions, and steal in unnoticed to score a vital goal is a talent which few midfielders possess. Three of his five scored came in drawn matches.

Torquay U (Free from Torrington on 8/7/97) FL 53+19/12 FLC 6 FAC 5 Others 3+1

HILL Matthew Clayton

Born: Bristol, 26 March 1981
Height: 5'7" Weight: 12.6

This highly rated young Bristol City player who graduated from the Academy to first-team football last season, impressed many people with his ability to read the game, to

go with his pace and tackling ability. A great prospect, the coaching staff claim him to be one of the best young defenders in the country, and one who could go right to the top. Matthew is one of the many young players at Ashton Gate on whom the club are hoping to build lasting success.
Bristol C (From trainee on 22/2/99) FL 0+3

HILLIER David
Born: Blackheath, 19 December 1969
Height: 5'10" Weight: 12.5
Club Honours: FAYC '88; Div 1 '91
International Honours: E: U21-1
David showed his effective midfield and defensive skills in a versatile start to last season for Portsmouth, playing in defence, midfield, and then for a December spell as a centre half. Possibly under-achieving as a goalscorer, his one goal, against Plymouth in the Worthington Cup, was disappointing, and when the playing staff had to be trimmed for financial reasons he was sold to Bristol Rovers in February. Thus, in becoming one of three former Pompey players to assist Rovers in their attempt to avoid relegation, the former Arsenal man brought much needed presence to a young team, and was always prepared to have a strike at goal when opportunities allowed.
Arsenal (From trainee on 11/2/88) F/PL 82+22/2 FLC 13+2 FAC 13+2 Others 5+4
Portsmouth (£250,000 on 2/11/96) FL 62+5/4 FLC 3/2 FAC 4/1
Bristol Rov (£15,000 on 24/2/99) FL 13

HILLS John David
Born: Blackpool, 21 April 1978
Height: 5'9" Weight: 11.2
A young Blackpool left back who can perform with equal reliability in midfield, John has a liking to get forward at every possibility, and is a free-kick specialist from almost anywhere around the box. Unfortunately, for both him and the club, two repeat six-week injury lay offs decimated his season in 1998-99 but, when available, his enthusiastic play made him a crowd favourite. Not only good when going forward, at the back his last-ditch tackling ability often rescues the side.
Blackpool (From trainee on 27/10/95)
Everton (£90,000 on 4/11/95) PL 1+2
Swansea C (Loaned on 30/1/97) FL 11
Swansea C (Loaned on 22/8/97) FL 7
Blackpool (£75,000 on 16/1/98) FL 46+1/2 FLC 2 FAC 1 Others 3

HIMSWORTH Gary Paul
Born: Pickering, 19 December 1969
Height: 5'8" Weight: 10.6
The utility player was again a useful squad member for York, but failure to maintain a regular first-team place at the club in 1998-99 saw him return to Darlington in early March, almost exactly three years after leaving for Bootham Crescent. He immediately took up where he left off in midfield with busy, hard-running performances, and only missed one game from joining and ending the campaign. Probably at his best on the left-hand side, being both quick and skilful, he can do a good job for you wherever he plays.

York C (From trainee on 27/1/88) FL 74+14/8 FLC 5 Others 5+2
Scarborough (Free on 5/12/90) FL 83+9/6 FLC 7+2/1 FAC 1+1 Others 6+1
Darlington (Free on 16/7/93) FL 86+8/8 FLC 5+1 FAC 6 Others 7/4
York C (£25,000 on 16/2/96) FL 60+9/3 FLC 4 FAC 6+2/1 Others 3/1
Darlington (Signed on 5/3/99) FL 14/1

HINCHCLIFFE Andrew (Andy) George
Born: Manchester, 5 February 1969
Height: 5'10" Weight: 13.7
Club Honours: FAC '95; CS '95
International Honours: E: 7; U21-1; Yth
Sheffield Wednesday's Andy had a consistently brilliant season in 1998-99, and appeared unlucky not to be an England regular despite being a constant member of the squad. Strong on the left side defensively, he continued to supply wicked crosses, and once again showed how well suited he is to the modern wing-back position. He also chipped in with the regular goal or two. There is no doubt that, injury free, he is a class act, and the supporters appreciated his wholehearted, enthusiastic approach to the game. There was no doubting that his classy contributions helped keep the defence watertight compared to recent campaigns.
Manchester C (From apprentice on 13/2/86) FL 107+5/8 FLC 11/1 FAC 12/1 Others 4/1
Everton (£800,000 on 17/7/90) F/PL 170+12/6 FLC 21+2/1 FAC 12+2/1 Others 8
Sheffield Wed (£2,850,000 on 30/1/98) PL 47/4 FLC 2 FAC 2

HINDS Richard Paul
Born: Sheffield, 22 August 1980
Height: 6'2" Weight: 11.0
A first-year professional, this tall 18-year-old Yorkshireman made his league debut for Tranmere towards the end of last season at Grimsby. A surprise inclusion, his preferred position being at centre back, he started the game at right back and finished it at right-wing back! Having turned in some impressive performances for the Pontins League side, where he was calm and assured in front of goal, and made any number of vital clearances, Richard gave the Rovers' management some food for thought, although they are already backing him for great things in the new season.
Tranmere Rov (From juniors on 20/7/98) FL 1+1

HINSHELWOOD Daniel (Danny) Martin
Born: Bromley, 12 December 1975
Height: 5'9" Weight: 11.4
International Honours: E: Yth
A tenacious full back – and son of Brighton's Director of Youth Football, Martin – Danny signed for the club last August after being released by Portsmouth, but was subsequently freed by the Albion in the New Year before joining Bognor Regis Town. Made limited appearances for the first team, and was substituted early on in one of those against Leyton Orient after suffering concussion.
Nottingham F (From trainee on 14/12/92)
Portsmouth (Free on 28/2/96) FL 5
Torquay U (Loaned on 3/3/97) FL 7+2
Brighton & Hove A (Free on 28/8/98) FL 3+1

HIRST David Eric
Born: Cudworth, 7 December 1967
Height: 5'11" Weight: 13.10
Club Honours: FLC '91
International Honours: E: 3; B-3; U21-7; Yth
A player who has sustained more than his fair share of injuries, the former England international striker suffered a freak fall on a Southampton training run during the 1998 close season, resulting in a badly damaged knee which threatened an end to his career. However, having missed most of 1998-99, he fought back and re-appeared from the bench at Aston Villa and Derby in April. Hopefully, he will fully recover to add to Saints' striking force this coming term, his strength and all-round abilities having been greatly missed. At his best a striker who can run with the ball and finish resoundingly, and brave in the air, how the team could have done with some of that during the campaign.
Barnsley (From apprentice on 8/11/85) FL 26+2/9 FLC 1
Sheffield Wed (£200,000 on 11/8/86) F/PL 261+33/106 FLC 26+9/11 FAC 12+7/6 Others 8/5
Southampton (£2,000,000 on 17/10/97) PL 28+2/9 FLC 1 FAC 1

Shaka Hislop

HISLOP Neil Shaka
Born: Hackney, 22 February 1969
Height: 6'4" Weight: 14.4
Club Honours: Div 2 '94
International Honours: E: U21-1. Trinidad: 1
Signed on a free transfer from Newcastle during the summer of 1998, the big goalie quickly became a favourite at West Ham in 1998-99, while missing just one game and keeping 17 clean sheets, including the opening three matches. Excellent throughout the campaign, he not only made crucial saves, but his all-round game, which saw him improve on crosses, and his command of the box, inspired confidence in the Hammers' defence. This was typified by his "Man of the Match" display against Derby at

Upton Park during April, when he produced three brilliant saves from Dean Sturridge and Daryl Powell in the first quarter of an hour before the team ran out 5-1 winners. He ended the season as the "Hammer of the Year" and a Trinidad international, after deciding to play for the country of his birth against Jamaica.

Reading (Signed from Howard University on 9/9/92) FL 104 FLC 10 FAC 3 Others 9
Newcastle U (£1,575,000 on 10/8/95) PL 53 FLC 8 FAC 6 Others 4
West Ham U (Free on 8/7/98) PL 37 FLC 2 FAC 2

HITCHCOCK Kevin Joseph
Born: Canning Town, 5 October 1962
Height: 6'1" Weight: 13.4
Club Honours: AMC '87; FAC '97; FLC '98; ECWC '98

On Easter Saturday 1999 at the Valley, an "old friend" re-appeared between the sticks of Chelsea for the second half against Charlton. The popular Kevin, the Blues' longest-serving player, replaced the flu-stricken Ed de Goey to a warm reception, and kept a clean sheet as the side clinched a narrow victory in their quest for the Premiership title. Almost the "forgotten man" at the Bridge, it was his first Premiership outing for over two years, following a dislocated shoulder sustained against Manchester United in February 1997. Amazingly, he was called upon twice more before the season's end, when a fractured toe ended Ed de Goey's 100 per cent Premiership record – keeping another clean sheet at Hillsborough in the goalless draw against Sheffield Wednesday, and appearing at Tottenham in the London derby. During his long career at Chelsea, Kevin has competed with five international 'keepers for the number-one jersey, but when called upon has never let the Blues down, and there is no more popular player at Stamford Bridge with fans and team mates alike.

Nottingham F (£15,000 from Barking on 4/8/83)
Mansfield T (£14,000 on 1/2/84) FL 182 FLC 12 FAC 10 Others 20
Chelsea (£250,000 on 25/3/88) F/PL 92+4 FLC 12 FAC 14 Others 13
Northampton T (Loaned on 28/12/90) FL 17 Others 1

HITCHEN Steven (Steve) James
Born: Salford, 28 November 1976
Height: 5'8" Weight: 11.8

Steve must be the most improved player at Macclesfield after their first season in Division Two. He did not get to break into the first team until squad injuries allowed him last September, but this versatile full back, who can play on either side, became first choice for the team sheet from then on. A small player, yet a tenacious one, who overlaps well with the wingers on a break, he returns quickly to defend after good distribution of the ball, and can take corners accurately, usually pin-pointing his man. Swept the board at the "Player of the Season" awards.

Blackburn Rov (From trainee on 4/7/95)
Macclesfield T (Free on 14/7/97) FL 36+1 FLC 1+1 FAC 4

HJELDE Jon Olav
Born: Levanger, Norway, 30 April 1972
Height: 6'1" Weight: 13.7
Club Honours: Div 1 '98

Having made a highly promising start in English football with Nottingham Forest in 1997-98, the big Norwegian central defender started at Arsenal on the opening day of the Premiership programme last season and, following an injury which saw him substituted, he missed the next six games. Still looking to be selected for his national side, it was hardly of benefit that he was continuously being sidelined with injuries throughout a tough campaign in which Forest were regularly being tipped for relegation. Very strong in the air, after scoring in a 2-1 defeat at West Ham he was forced out of competitive football in order to have a hernia operation before coming back with four games to go.

Nottingham F (£600,000 from Rosenborg on 8/8/97) P/FL 39+6/2 FLC 4/2 FAC 2

HOBSON Gary
Born: Hull, 12 November 1972
Height: 6'1" Weight: 13.3

Brighton's club captain, who suffered an injury-ravaged season in 1998-99 with a persistent hamstring problem, was originally told by Jeff Wood that he would be allowed to leave, but was later reinstated to the team by caretaker boss, Martin Hinshelwood, in the 2-1 win at Plymouth, which immediately followed Wood's departure. The new manager, Micky Adams, has made it clear that he would like him to stay and see out the rest of his contract. A central defender or left back, who always gives 100 per-cent commitment, and is comfortable in possession, he played in the last six games of the campaign.

Hull C (From trainee on 17/7/91) FL 135+7 FLC 13+1 FAC 2+2/1 Others 6
Brighton & Hove A (£60,000 on 27/3/96) FL 86+6/1 FLC 5 FAC 3 Others 2

HOCKING Matthew (Matt) James
Born: Boston, 30 January 1978
Height: 5'11" Weight: 11.12

The cultured right-footed centre back, or wing back, continued to be a regular during Mark Hateley's reign at Hull in 1998-99, developing a partnership with new signing, Neil Whitworth. Unfortunately, Matt became one of the victims of the major Tigers' re-structure, and became a peripheral figure under Warren Joyce, ending the campaign on loan at York City. Stop Press: Signed for York on 26 May.

Sheffield U (From trainee on 16/5/96)
Hull C (£25,000 on 19/9/97) FL 55+2/2 FLC 6 FAC 4 Others 4
York C (Loaned on 25/3/99) FL 4+2

HOCKTON Daniel (Danny) John
Born: Barking, 7 February 1979
Height: 5'11" Weight: 11.11

Yet another who has progressed through the youth ranks at Millwall, Danny found himself thrust into the starting line-up at the beginning of 1997-98, and responded with valuable goals. Last season, however, he was forced to spend most of his time on the

subs' bench due to the stiff competition from the other strikers at the club. When he played, though, he gave his all, and scored one of the goals in the Auto Windscreens Shield win at Brighton. A pacy striker who can shoot with either foot, he is also good in the air and holds the ball up well.

Millwall (From trainee on 8/3/97) FL 11+25/4 FLC 2+1/2 FAC 0+1 Others 0+4/1

HODGE John
Born: Skelmersdale, 1 April 1969
Height: 5'7" Weight: 11.12
Club Honours: AMC '94

Out of contract at Walsall during the 1998 close season, John, a skilful winger who can go past his full back with ease and cross accurately, started 1998-99 as a regular in the Gillingham line-up. From November onwards, however, he found himself out in the cold and on the bench, but he was still capable of changing the course of a game, none more so than the cross in the last minute of the home fixture against Fulham, when he set up the winner for Robert Taylor. It was therefore no surprise that his 27 league appearances as a playing substitute was a club record!

Exeter C (Signed from Falmouth T on 12/9/91) FL 57+8/10 FLC 3/1 FAC 2 Others 8+2/1
Swansea C (Signed on 14/7/93) FL 87+25/10 FLC 6+2/3 FAC 6 Others 13+4
Walsall (Free on 23/9/96) FL 67+9/12 FLC 5 FAC 7+1/2 Others 5+2
Gillingham (Free on 10/7/98) FL 7+27/1 FLC 2 FAC 0+1 Others 2+4

HODGES Glyn Peter
Born: Streatham, 30 April 1963
Height: 6'0" Weight: 12.10
Club Honours: Div 4 '83
International Honours: W: 18; B-1; U21-5; Yth

Offered a one-year contract at the beginning of 1998-99, the former Welsh international midfielder surprisingly played in Nottingham Forest's opening three matches before going back to the reserves and coming off the senior subs' bench on a couple of occasions. Very experienced, he moved to Scarborough on non-contract terms at the end of January, but lasted just 25 minutes of a 5-1 defeat at Scunthorpe.

Wimbledon (From apprentice on 3/2/81) FL 200+3/49 FLC 14+2/3 FAC 13+2/2 Others 0+1
Newcastle U (£200,000 on 15/7/87) FL 7
Watford (£300,000 on 1/10/87) FL 82+4/15 FLC 5/2 FAC 8/1 Others 2+1/1
Crystal Palace (£410,000 on 16/7/90) FL 5+2 FLC 2+2/1
Sheffield U (£450,000 on 17/1/91) F/PL 116+31/19 FLC 4+3 FAC 13+3/3 Others 1
Derby Co (Free on 15/2/96) FL 1+8 (Freed during 1996 close season)
Hull C (Free from Sin Tao, Hong Kong on 22/8/97) FL 13+5/4 FLC 1 FAC 1 Others 2
Nottingham F (Free on 20/2/98) PL 3+2
Scarborough (Free on 26/1/99) FL 1

HODGES Lee Leslie
Born: Plaistow, 2 March 1978
Height: 5'5" Weight: 10.2

Once again Lee found it difficult to break into West Ham's senior side, this time in 1998-99. Small of stature, but tough, and a midfielder who likes being in the action

zone, he only made just one appearance for the Hammers, when coming off the bench at Blackburn in a 3-0 defeat, before going out on loan to Ipswich (November), where he came off the bench on four occasions, and Southend (March). Brought in at United for the end of season run-in, Lee demonstrated his fantastic skill and vision at that level, winning a succession of "Man of the Match" awards as the club battled to save its league status. At the same time, he showed guts and determination, and once he controls the urge to win a match on his own he will become star material.

West Ham U (From trainee on 2/3/95) PL 0+3 FAC 0+3
Exeter C (Loaned on 13/9/96) FL 16+1
Leyton Orient (Loaned on 28/2/97) FL 3
Plymouth Arg (Loaned on 6/11/97) FL 9 Others 1
Ipswich T (Loaned on 20/11/98) FL 0+4
Southend U (Loaned on 25/3/99) FL 10/1

HODGES Lee Leslie
Born: Epping, 4 September 1973
Height: 6'0" Weight: 12.1
International Honours: E: Yth
Lee returned to senior action in Reading's game against York last January, as a 58th-minute substitute. It was his first involvement in first-team action for 11 months after a serious knee injury, but further injury problems meant that it was also his last appearance of the season at this level. Although he managed a fit in a few reserve matches later on, he will hope for better luck in 1999-2000.
Tottenham H (From trainee on 29/2/92) PL 0+4
Plymouth Arg (Loaned on 26/2/93) FL 6+1/2
Wycombe W (Loaned on 31/12/93) FL 2+2 FAC 1 Others 1
Barnet (Free on 31/5/94) FL 94+11/26 FLC 6+1 FAC 6+1/4 Others 3+1
Reading (£100,000 on 29/7/97) FL 20+5/6 FLC 5+1 FAC 4+1

HODGSON Douglas (Doug) John
Born: Frankston, Australia, 27 February 1969
Height: 6'2" Weight: 13.10
A hard-tackling, no-nonsense central defender, Doug was signed by Northampton last October from Oldham as a replacement for Ray Warburton. Having given some outstanding displays in defence, both his tackling and heading being first class, after ten games and a goal, he picked up an injury to his neck which later turned out to be more serious than first thought. Told that he had to give up the game, as future damage to the neck could lead to paralysis, he was offered an administration job by the club.
Sheffield U (£30,000 from Heidelberg Alex on 22/7/94) FL 24+6/1 FLC 3+1 FAC 2+1 Others 1
Plymouth Arg (Loaned on 10/8/95) FL 3+2
Burnley (Loaned on 17/10/96) FL 1
Oldham Ath (Signed on 28/2/97) FL 33+8/4 FLC 0+2 FAC 3
Northampton T (£20,000 on 9/10/98) FL 7+1/1 FLC 1 FAC 1

HOLDSWORTH David Gary
Born: Walthamstow, 8 November 1968
Height: 6'1" Weight: 12.10
International Honours: E: U21-1; Yth
A bad knee injury last September against Huddersfield caused the Sheffield United

captain to miss a run of 23 games, his calm authority and anticipation in defence being much missed, and during his absence the team managed only one clean sheet. Scored on his return, and also two games later in the dramatic FC Cup victory against Notts County, before playing in both matches against Bolton, when he found himself up against his twin brother, Dean, who scored twice. Having regained full fitness, the club's directors decided to accept Birmingham's offer for David, although he had signed a four-year contract earlier in the season, and he left Bramall Lane just before the March deadline. In what was a record fee for a Blues' defender, he slipped impressively into the back four, immediately becoming a hit with the fans due to his firm tackling and excellent distribution. Scored with a header on his St Andrew's debut, against Watford.
Watford (From apprentice on 8/11/86) FL 249+9/10 FLC 20/2 FAC 14+1/1 Others 8+2
Sheffield U (£450,000 on 8/10/96) FL 93/4 FLC 7 FAC 13/3 Others 5
Birmingham C (£1,200,000 on 22/3/99) FL 8/1 Others 2

Dean Holdsworth

HOLDSWORTH Dean Christopher
Born: Walthamstow, 8 November 1968
Height: 5'11" Weight: 11.13
Club Honours: Div 3 '92
International Honours: E: B-1
Dean enjoyed a much more successful season in 1998-99, as opposed to his first with Bolton in the Premiership two years ago, and rediscovered his golden touch. Whilst still trying to shake off the tag of being Bolton's record signing, he produced some hard-working performances to win over the hearts of the Bolton fans, and developed a prolific partnership with Bob Taylor after Arnar Gunnlaugsson's transfer to Leicester, the two player's styles complimenting each other perfectly. Injury kept him out of the final few league games

and, although the competition for striking places was fierce at Bolton, his new-found lease of life will set him in good stead for the start of the new season. The brother of Birmingham's David, and well known for his work as a male model, Dean is a natural goalscorer whose trademark is his ability to arrive in the box just at the right moment.
Watford (From apprentice on 12/11/86) FL 2+14/3 Others 0+4
Carlisle U (Loaned on 11/2/88) FL 4/1
Port Vale (Loaned on 18/3/88) FL 6/2
Swansea C (Loaned on 25/8/88) FL 4+1/1
Brentford (Loaned on 13/10/88) FL 2+5/1
Brentford (£125,000 on 29/9/89) FL 106+4/53 FLC 7+1/6 FAC 6/7 Others 12+2/9
Wimbledon (£720,000 on 20/7/92) PL 148+21/58 FLC 16+3/11 FAC 13+7/7
Bolton W (£3,500,000 on 3/10/97) P/FL 39+13/15 FLC 3+1 FAC 1

HOLLAND Christopher (Chris) James
Born: Whalley, 11 September 1975
Height: 5'9" Weight: 11.5
International Honours: E: U21-10; Yth
Chris struggled to keep a regular place at Birmingham in 1998-99 due to Martyn O'Connor's excellent form in central midfield, making his first start against Wimbledon in the Worthington Cup at the end of October. Although going on to play in the 3-1 win over West Bromwich at the Hawthorns he lost his place in December, and was very much a fringe player from then on. Despite playing with vibrancy and great energy in the reserves, the call hardly ever came, and he will undoubtedly be looking for better in 1999-2000. A good passer of the ball, in recent seasons he has added more bite to his game.
Preston NE (Trainee) FL 0+1 Others 1
Newcastle U (£100,000 on 20/1/94) PL 2+1 FLC 0+1
Birmingham C (£600,000 on 5/9/96) FL 37+19 FLC 4+4 FAC 3 Others 1+1

HOLLAND Matthew (Matt) Rhys
Born: Bury, 11 April 1974
Height: 5'9" Weight: 11.12
Since joining Ipswich from Bournemouth in 1997, Matt has not missed a first-team match, notching over 100 appearances, but there were, however, some close calls regarding his fitness last season. Playing in central midfield, covering every blade of grass between the penalty areas, snatching vital goals, and making vital interceptions, he captained the side when Tony Mowbray was sidelined, and is the type of player who always gives maximum effort every game. His performance in the last game of the season – versus Bolton in the play offs – typified the man. He opened the scoring when he ran through from midfield and slotted the ball past the 'keeper, popped up from nowhere to prevent Bolton equalising, and then fired home from outside the area to seal the win. To underline his commitment to the club, Matt topped the table of personal appearances by the players during the campaign.
West Ham U (From trainee on 3/7/92)
Bournemouth (Signed on 27/1/95) FL 97+7/18 FLC 6 FAC 3 Others 3
Ipswich T (£800,000 on 31/7/97) FL 92/15 FLC 11/4 FAC 6 Others 4/2

HOLLAND Paul
Born: Lincoln, 8 July 1973
Height: 5'11" Weight: 12.10
International Honours: E: U21-4; Yth; Sch
Strong, energetic, and determined, Paul operated up and down the middle of the park for Chesterfield in 1998-99, and was also pulled back to a sweeper role when a five-man defence was called for. Although missing the run-up to Christmas with a knee injury, an exploratory operation revealed no damage, and he returned to first-team action for important games against the division's high flyers in February and March. He then suffered the season's most unusual injury, a cut ear, after some dressing-room high-jinks. Enough said . . .
Mansfield T (From juniors on 4/7/91) FL 149/25 FLC 11 FAC 7/3 Others 9/1
Sheffield U (£250,000 on 20/6/95) FL 11+7/1 FLC 2/1
Chesterfield (Signed on 5/1/96) FL 104+6/11 FLC 9/2 FAC 11 Others 1

HOLLIGAN Gavin Victor
Born: Lambeth, 13 June 1980
Height: 5'10" Weight: 12.0
The young striker was playing his football for Kingstonian when first spotted by West Ham towards the end of last year but, with the non-league side still involved in the FA Cup it was agreed by all parties concerned that Gavin could move to Upton Park once the Kings were out of the competition. Bought as one for the future he was soon scoring freely for the Hammers youth team, bagging two hat tricks in quick succession, before becoming a shock substitute at Anfield in February prior to him being officially registered with the club. Coming off the bench for the final ten minutes, within a matter of seconds he was foiled by the Liverpool goalie, David James, in a one-on-one situation, before he was back to reality when scoring three against Millwall reserves. Looks a very good prospect indeed.
West Ham U (£100,000 from Kingstonian on 5/3/99) PL 0+1

HOLLOWAY Christopher (Chris) David
Born: Swansea, 5 February 1980
Height: 5'10" Weight: 11.7
International Honours: W: U21-2
In his first full season as a professional, Chris made great in-roads into claiming a regular first-team place at Exeter for himself in 1998-99. Having broken into the Welsh U21 squad, his deft touch and accurate passing from midfield will no doubt ensure that he plays a big part in City's team this coming term.
Exeter C (From trainee on 9/7/98) FL 31+9/1 FLC 0+1 FAC 1 Others 1

HOLLOWAY Darren
Born: Bishop Auckland, 3 October 1977
Height: 5'10" Weight: 12.2
International Honours: E: U21-1
Sunderland defender Darren ended last season by returning to the first-team frame after a campaign ruined by a persistent back injury. The previous term, the attacking full back had established himself as the club's

regular number two, and as a member of the England U21 squad, but fitness problems, coupled with the good form of Chris Makin, kept him on the sidelines until February, when he returned for the historic first pay-per-view TV game, at Oxford. Showed his versatility by making several substitute appearances in midfield as Sunderland clinched the First Division title and, fully fit, will be eager to make up for lost time in the Premiership this term.
Sunderland (From trainee on 12/10/95) FL 33+5 FAC 2 Others 3
Carlisle U (Loaned on 29/8/97) FL 5

HOLLOWAY Ian Scott
Born: Kingswood, 12 March 1963
Height: 5'8" Weight: 10.10
Club Honours: Div 3 '90
The Bristol Rovers' player/manager continued to enjoy his ball-winning midfield role when adding to and almost reaching his 400th league appearance for his beloved home town club in 1998-99. Comfortable on the ball, Ian's presence on the pitch was certainly essential in assisting the Rover's inexperienced youngsters, and on his day he remains one of the most competitive players and best passers of the ball in the Second Division. He also remains an inspiration and a wonderful example to his team mates, and has no intention of hanging up his boots just yet.
Bristol Rov (From apprentice on 18/3/81) FL 104+7/14 FLC 10/1 FAC 8/2 Others 5
Wimbledon (£35,000 on 18/7/85) FL 19/2 FLC 3 FAC 1
Brentford (£25,000 on 12/3/86) FL 27+3/2 FLC 2 FAC 3 Others 0+1
Torquay U (Loaned on 30/1/87) FL 5
Bristol Rov (£10,000 on 21/8/87) FL 179/26 FLC 5 FAC 10/1 Others 20/3
Queens Park R (£230,000 on 12/8/91) F/PL 130+17/4 FLC 12+1 FAC 7+1/1 Others 1+1
Bristol Rov (Free on 22/7/96) FL 96+11/1 FLC 6 FAC 8/1 Others 2

HOLLUND Martin
Born: Stord, Norway, 11 August 1975
Height: 6'0" Weight: 12.9
1998-99 was a season of twists and turns for Hartlepool's Norwegian-born goalkeeper. He began the season in great style with some fine performances, most notably that at Bolton in a Worthington Cup-tie. Unfortunately, as the weeks progressed, his form dipped and he went through a terrible spell, losing his confidence, his first team place, and looking set for a quiet departure. However, against the odds he was recalled to the first team, steadily proving himself a more than adequate goalkeeper and, with a stronger defence in front of him, kept ten clean sheets in the last 18 games – a vast improvement on what had gone on before.
Hartlepool U (Free from SK Brann Bergen on 21/11/97) FL 69 FLC 2 FAC 2 Others 5

HOLMES Matthew (Matty) Jason
Born: Luton, 1 August 1969
Height: 5'7" Weight: 11.0
Another unlucky and frustrating time for Matty, this time in 1998-99, his campaign being plagued by injury. In truth, he has never really recovered from the dreadful

tackle that broke his left leg in Charlton's FA Cup-tie at Molineux in November 1997. Although attempting a comeback in mid term, making one appearance when coming on as a substitute in the FA Cup-tie at Blackburn in January, he later needed more surgery and played no further part in the season. Likes to play wide on the left, and is a good crosser of the ball.
Bournemouth (From trainee on 22/8/88) FL 105+9/8 FLC 7 FAC 8+2 Others 5
Cardiff C (Loaned on 23/3/89) FL 0+1
West Ham U (£40,000 on 19/8/92) F/PL 63+13/4 FLC 4 FAC 6 Others 3/1
Blackburn Rov (£1,200,000 on 15/8/95) PL 8+1/1 Others 2+1
Charlton Ath (£250,000 on 24/7/97) FL 10+6/1 FAC 1+2

HOLMES Paul
Born: Stocksbridge, 18 February 1968
Height: 5'10" Weight: 11.3
Paul had a mixed season for West Bromwich in 1998-99. Injured early on, his play at times was steady rather than brilliant but, for a defender with good technique, his crossing let him down too often. A player with Premier League experience, he contested the right-back position with Andy McDermott, and was perhaps unlucky to be dropped in favour of the young Australian in early March, his ability on the overlap always likely to give the team another option. Likes to get forward and have a shot on goal.
Doncaster Rov (From apprentice on 24/2/86) FL 42+5/1 FAC 3+1/1 Others 1
Torquay U (£6,000 on 12/8/88) FL 127+11/4 FLC 9 FAC 9+2 Others 13+3
Birmingham C (£40,000 on 5/6/92) FL 12 FAC 1
Everton (£100,000 on 19/3/93) PL 21 FLC 4 FAC 1 Others 0+2
West Bromwich A (£80,000 on 12/1/96) FL 102+1/1 FLC 5 FAC 4 Others 3

HOLMES Richard
Born: Grantham, 7 November 1980
Height: 5'10" Weight: 10.7
An excellent young Notts County trainee who was on the verge of signing pro forms for the club, Richard came off the bench for his debut in the home game against York last March, prior to the unexpected transfer of Ian Hendon providing further opportunities. The talented right back was quick to grasp his chance and rapidly developed in the first team environment, showing himself to be a good tackler with pace and ability to provide dangerous crosses.
Notts Co (From trainee on 23/3/99) FL 3+5

HOLMES Steven (Steve) Peter
Born: Middlesbrough, 13 January 1971
Height: 6'2" Weight: 13.0
This Lincoln central defender's outstanding form during 1998-99 saw him voted as the club's "Player of the Season" by the supporters. Although he started badly, being dropped after the opening day defeat at Bournemouth, he got back into the team by the end of September and never really looked back. He was the club's third-top scorer with six goals, despite playing at the back, and was appointed captain towards the end of the season in the absence of Terry Fleming.

Lincoln C (From trainee on 17/7/89)
Preston NE (£10,000 from Guisborough T, via Gainsborough Trinity, on 14/3/94) FL 13/1 FAC 3 Others 1
Hartlepool U (Loaned on 10/3/95) FL 5/2
Lincoln C (Loaned on 20/10/95) FL 12/1 Others 2
Lincoln C (£30,000 on 15/3/96) FL 121+1/15 FLC 6/2 FAC 7/1 Others 3/1

HOLSGROVE Lee
Born: Wendover, 13 December 1979
Height: 6'2" Weight: 12.5
Signed from Millwall in March 1998 after impressing in the Wycombe youth and reserve teams as both central defender and midfielder, and on a three-month loan spell at Ryman premier side, Aldershot Town, Lee made his senior debut for Wanderers in the penultimate game of last season, the important 2-1 home victory over Wigan. As a late substitute, he immediately looked at home at senior level, producing several excellent passes with his left foot, and not looking at all nervous in a very pressurised situation. Is the son of John Holsgrove, the experienced Wolves and Sheffield Wednesday centre half of the 60s and 70s.
Millwall (From juniors on 5/7/96)
Wycombe W (£7,500 on 24/3/98) FL 0+1

HOLSTER Marco
Born: Weesp, Holland, 4 December 1971
Height: 5'7" Weight: 10.11
Signed in the 1998 close season from the Dutch side, Heracles, it took Marco quite some time to adjust to English football at Ipswich in 1998-99. A left-footed central midfielder, he made his debut in the opening game at Grimsby – his only full appearance of the campaign – and was on the bench intermittently from then on, being unable to dislodge Matt Holland or Kieron Dyer from the first team. Regardless of that, he looks to be a useful man to have around.
Ipswich T (Free from SC Heracles, via AZ 67 Alkmaar, on 20/7/98) FL 1+9 FLC 0+1 FAC 0+1

HOLT Andrew (Andy)
Born: Stockport, 21 April 1978
Height: 6'1" Weight: 12.7
Last season was a tremendous one for the Oldham youngster, missing just three games throughout, while coming on in leaps and bounds. A fast, strong, predominately left-sided full back, who can also play with ease in central defence, being fearless in the tackle and good in the air, when in possession his terrific pace frightened the lives out of Second Division defenders in 1998-99. It was hardly surprising that – despite Athletic trying to resist relegation for much of the campaign – Andy was not only one of the great successes, but had the scouts flocking to Boundary Park to see what all the fuss was about. He also possesses one of the longest throws in football.
Oldham Ath (From trainee on 23/7/96) FL 46+12/5 FLC 2 FAC 4+1 Others 1

HOLT Michael Andrew
Born: Burnley, 28 July 1977
Height: 5'10" Weight: 11.12
Signed initially on loan from Preston last

November, following a loan spell at Macclesfield, to try and solve Rochdale's shortage of goals, Michael scored the equaliser at Chester on his second appearance, as a substitute. After the arrival of the giant, Andy Morris, the diminutive goal poacher really came into his own, with six goals in nine games, including a brace (of headers!) in the live televised game against Hull. Although the goals dried up for a while, his eager running continued to threaten opposing defences and he ended the campaign as joint-top scorer.
Preston NE (Free from Blackburn Rov juniors on 16/8/96) FL 12+24/5 FLC 2+2/1 FAC 1+3 Others 0+1
Macclesfield T (Loaned on 25/9/98) FL 3+1/1
Rochdale (Signed on 16/11/98) FL 17+7/7 Others 3/1

HOOPER Dean Raymond
Born: Harefield, 13 April 1971
Height: 5'11" Weight: 11.6
International Honours: E: SP-1
Signed from non-league Kingstonian immediately prior to the start of last season, having earlier had a loan spell at Peterborough when with Swindon, the fiery right-sided wing back came back into the league on the opening day and impressed. Booked on numerous occasions, although often not warranted, he is probably the only player to be cautioned for getting his face in the way of a fist! A no-nonsense, hard-tackling player who likes to push forward, Dean scored his first-ever league goals, against Barnet and Torquay.
Swindon T (£15,000 from Hayes on 3/3/95) FL 0+4 FLC 0+2 Others 2 (Free to Hayes on 4/10/96)
Peterborough U (Loaned on 15/12/95) FL 4
Peterborough U (Signed from Kingstonian on 6/8/98) FL 36+2/2 FLC 2 FAC 0+1 Others 1

HOPE Christopher (Chris) Jonathan
Born: Sheffield, 14 November 1972
Height: 6'1" Weight: 12.7
The Scunthorpe skipper deservedly won a place in the PFA Third Division team of the year after another outstanding season in 1998-99. Virtually unbeatable in the air, and good on the ground, United turned down £150,000 from Reading for him in the summer of 1998, and he soon signed a long-term contract at Glanford Park. Chipped in with a number of vital goals, and was not even cautioned throughout the campaign as he set a new club record of over 150 successive Football League appearances.
Nottingham F (Free from Darlington juniors on 23/8/90)
Scunthorpe U (£50,000 on 5/7/93) FL 235+8/16 FLC 11+1 FAC 17/1 Others 17/2

HOPE Richard Paul
Born: Middlesbrough, 28 June 1978
Height: 6'2" Weight: 12.6
The son of former Darlington goalkeeper, John, Richard was surprisingly transferred to Northampton last October after figuring in most of the games since the start of 1998-99. Equally at home in the centre of defence or at left back, this strong-tackling defender looked to be established in the side after being a regular the previous season. With Town in the midst of an injury crisis, he

went straight into the team alongside Ian Sampson, Lee Howey and Colin Hill, and performed well, having earlier had a trial at the club that came to nothing. Is also good in the air.
Blackburn Rov (From trainee on 9/8/95)
Darlington (Free on 17/1/97) FL 62+1/1 FLC 3 FAC 1 Others 0+1
Northampton T (Signed on 18/12/98) FL 17+2 Others 1

HOPKIN David
Born: Greenock, 21 August 1970
Height: 5'9" Weight: 11.0
International Honours: S: 5; B-1
What a difference a season makes. Following his arrival at Leeds in the summer of 1997, David, for a variety of reasons, including injury, illness, and family bereavements, failed to live up to expectations; this culminated in him being left out of the Scotland World Cup squad. However, 1998-99 saw "Hoppy" emerge as a key figure, "gelling" with Lee Bowyer to form a fine midfield partnership, which then became a trio following the arrival of David Batty. Although not prolific, he began to find the net again. Indeed, his first goal of the campaign, against Coventry in the 2-0 victory in December, was his first for 15 months. But, on numerous occasions, he took control of the centre of the park and looked every bit an international player, his excellent form seeing him being recalled to the Scotland set up. A player with a very sharp football brain, David should play a big part in the emergence of Leeds United.
Morton (Signed from Port Glasgow BC on 7/7/89) SL 33+15/4 SLC 2/2 SC 2/1
Chelsea (£300,000 on 25/9/92) PL 21+19/1 FLC 0+1 FAC 3+2
Crystal Palace (£850,000 on 29/7/95) FL 79+4/21 FLC 6/6 FAC 3 Others 4/2
Leeds U (£3,250,000 on 23/7/97) PL 54+5/5 FLC 6 FAC 6 Others 4

HOPPER Tony
Born: Carlisle, 31 May 1976
Height: 5'11" Weight: 12.8
Club Honours: AMC '97
One of the few members of the squad who actually hails from Carlisle, Tony's first-team appearances before last Christmas were relatively few, but from mid January onwards he featured in the majority of matches, and earned plaudits for his workrate and never-say-die attitude. He is another player who is perhaps at his best in a defensive ball-winning role, although he still has time on his side to develop his attacking qualities.
Carlisle U (From trainee on 18/7/94) FL 50+23/1 FLC 0+1 FAC 3+1/1 Others 6+2

HORLAVILLE Christophe
Born: Rouen, France, 1 March 1969
Height: 5'9" Weight: 12.1
A French striker who wanted to try his luck in England, Christophe joined Port Vale on loan from Le Havre last November, but struggled to adjust to the pace of the game and managed just the one start, at Oxford. Never afraid to have a shot, he also made a handful of substitute appearances, including one in the FA Cup on national TV against

145

Liverpool, before returning home to join FC Metz in January.

Port Vale (Loaned from Le Havre, via En Avant Guingamp, on 13/11/98) FL 1+1 FAC 0+1

HORLOCK Kevin

Born: Bexley, 1 November 1972
Height: 6'0" Weight: 12.0
Club Honours: Div 2 '96
International Honours: NI: 17; B-2

Kevin had another satisfying season for Manchester City in 1998-99, adopting a role of forward or midfielder, as opposed to the previous campaign where he was more a full back. Although covering the field for 90 minutes, sometimes his pace was against him in the Second Division. Despite that, he scored three goals in two consecutive games, his performance in the 3-0 win at Oldham Athletic being outstanding, but also he picked up a booking in each game. Unfortunately, while not an aggressive player, he picked up more than his share of yellow and red cards, something which he will try to remedy. As an established member of the Northern Ireland team, he appeared in midfield in four out of the five Euro 2000 qualifying games played, missing the away tie in Moldova through injury.

West Ham U (From trainee on 1/7/91)
Swindon T (Free on 27/8/92) F/PL 151+12/22 FLC 15+2/1 FAC 12/3 Others 5+2
Manchester C (£1,250,000 on 31/1/97) FL 79+1/18 FLC 5/1 FAC 3 Others 3/1

HORNE Barry

Born: St Asaph, 18 May 1962
Height: 5'9" Weight: 12.2
Club Honours: WC '86; FAC '95; CS '95
International Honours: W: 59

After an influential debut season for Huddersfield in 1997-98, the club quickly snapped up the former Welsh international on a one-year contract. An inspirational figure, Barry was soon captaining the side and, with his leadership coinciding with some outstanding performances, the team soon went to the top of the First Division. Although Town's form eventually dipped, it had nothing to do with the captain. Playing an anchor role in midfield, he showed great positional play, getting forward at all opportunities, and was rewarded with a sensational 30-yard strike at Bristol City. Always in the thick of the action, he showed his character in the Worthington Cup encounters with Everton, and was magnificent in the top-of-the-table clash against Sunderland. Unfortunately, in his 50th league appearance for Town, in the local derby against Bradford, he suffered medial ligament damage, an injury that ended his campaign prematurely. Was out of contract during the summer.

Wrexham (Free from Rhyl on 26/6/84) FL 136/17 FLC 10/1 FAC 7/2 Others 15/3
Portsmouth (£60,000 on 17/7/87) FL 66+4/7 FLC 3 FAC 6
Southampton (£700,000 on 22/3/89) FL 111+1/6 FLC 15+2/3 FAC 15/3 Others 7/1
Everton (£675,000 on 1/7/92) PL 118+5/3 FLC 12+1 FAC 11+1 Others 3
Birmingham C (£250,000 on 10/6/96) FL 33 FLC 3 FAC 3
Huddersfield T (Free on 13/10/97) FL 49+1/1 FLC 4 FAC 2

HORSFIELD Geoffrey (Geoff) Malcolm

Born: Barnsley, 1 November 1973
Height: 5'10" Weight: 11.0
Club Honours: Div 2 '99

Starting last season with Football League newcomers, Halifax, where he left off during the previous campaign, his potential was such that Kevin Keegan's Fulham snapped him up in October. Looking a typical old-time centre forward, his ratio of goals to games played confirming it, he scored with headers, close-range and long-distance efforts among his 17 goals for Fulham, but there was so much more to his game than that. Extremely strong, he held up the ball well, bringing other players into the game, and worked so hard that he immediately became the idol of the crowd. "Horsfield for England" was a frequently heard chant when Kevin Keegan became caretaker/manager of the national side. Was recognised by his peers with selection to the PFA award-winning Second Division side.

Scarborough (From juniors on 10/7/92) FL 12/1 FAC 1 Others 0+2 (Free to Halifax T on 31/3/94)
Halifax T (Free from Witton A on 8/5/97) FL 10/7 FLC 4/1
Fulham (£325,000 on 12/10/98) FL 26+2/15 FAC 5+1/2

Geoff Horsfield

HOTTE Mark Stephen

Born: Bradford, 27 September 1978
Height: 5'11" Weight: 11.1

A young Oldham midfielder who can also play in the defence, Mark is very much in the David Batty mould, being a gritty youngster who fights for every ball, and never gives anything away. Still at the learning stage, he only made one subs' appearance last season, in what was a difficult campaign, but his good form at reserve level did not go unnoticed with the offer of a new three-year contract coming his way. His main asset is his speed – in going into the tackle or when coming away with the ball.

Oldham Ath (From trainee on 1/7/97) FL 0+2

HOUGHTON Raymond (Ray) James

Born: Glasgow, 9 January 1962
Height: 5'7" Weight: 10.10
Club Honours: FLC '86, '94; Div 1 '88, '90; CS '88; FAC '89, '92
International Honours: Ei: 73

The Republic of Ireland international was given a free transfer by Reading at the end of last season, having never held down a regular place in midfield. Although the veteran's legs just would not take him through 90 minutes of Division Two hurly-burly football, having only ever scored one goal for the Royals, he was a great encourager of the younger players, and much respected for his long and distinguished career in the game.

West Ham U (From juniors on 5/7/79) FL 0+1
Fulham (Free on 7/7/82) FL 129/16 FLC 12/2 FAC 4/3
Oxford U (£147,000 on 13/9/85) FL 83/10 FLC 13/3 FAC 3 Others 6/1
Liverpool (£825,000 on 19/10/87) FL 147+6/28 FLC 14/3 FAC 26+1/4 Others 8/3
Aston Villa (£900,000 on 28/7/92) PL 83+12/6 FLC 11+2/2 FAC 7/2 Others 4+2/1
Crystal Palace (£300,000 on 23/3/95) P/FL 69+3/7 FLC 6 FAC 4 Others 4/1
Reading (Free on 21/7/97) FL 33+10/1 FLC 7+2 FAC 2+2

HOUGHTON Scott Aaron

Born: Hitchin, 22 October 1971
Height: 5'7" Weight: 12.4
Club Honours: FAYC '90
International Honours: E: Yth; Sch

After making yet another injury-hit start to a season at Peterborough, Scott was allowed to go on loan to Southend last November, with the move being made permanent two days before Christmas. Able to play on either flank, he came into his own at Roots Hall following a switch from winger to wing back, and his ability to get forward, along with his tenacious tackling, gave him a whole new role in the side. Pacy, and skilful, he is capable of scoring goals wherever he lines up.

Tottenham H (From trainee on 24/8/90) FL 0+10/2 FLC 0+2 Others 0+2
Ipswich T (Loaned on 26/3/91) FL 7+1/1
Gillingham (Loaned on 17/12/92) FL 3
Charlton Ath (Loaned on 26/2/93) FL 6
Luton T (Free on 10/8/93) FL 7+9/1 FLC 2+1 FAC 0+1 Others 2
Walsall (£20,000 on 2/9/94) FL 76+2/14 FLC 0+1/1 FAC 10/3 Others 4
Peterborough U (£60,000 + on 12/7/96) FL 57+13/13 FLC 6+2 FAC 7/1 Others 1+1/1
Southend U (Signed on 20/11/98) FL 26+1/3 Others 1

HOULT Russell

Born: Ashby de la Zouch, 22 November 1972
Height: 6'3" Weight: 14.9

A tall and commanding Derby goalkeeper who, having vied with Mart Poom in 1997-98 to be the first-team choice, made the most of the latter's illness at the start of last season to keep his place for the majority of 1998-99. Looked more confident than ever before, following the introduction of an individual training programme for him, and made some outstanding saves to sustain County's early season challenge at the top of

Russell Hoult

the table. Sustained a neck injury in November at Nottingham Forest, which kept him out for a couple of months, but as the campaign wore on he developed a fine understanding with the defenders in front of him, and improved communication led to one of the better defensive records of the Premiership. Lost his place at the culmination of the season, due to suspension after being sent off against Forest in April, but will be hoping to have done enough to start 1999-2000 as first choice.

Leicester C (From trainee on 28/3/91) FL 10 FLC 3 Others 1
Lincoln C (Loaned on 27/8/91) FL 2 FLC 1
Bolton W (Loaned on 3/11/93) FL 3+1 Others 1
Lincoln C (Loaned on 12/8/94) FL 15 Others 1
Derby Co (£300,000 on 17/2/95) F/PL 111+2 FLC 5 FAC 7

HOUSHAM Steven (Steve) James
Born: Gainsborough, 24 February 1976
Height: 5'10" Weight: 12.7
Injuries continued to plague this hardworking, committed Scunthorpe player who missed the opening two months of last season with a groin problem. Used as a wing back when available, injuries restricted him to mainly a substitutes' role, and his bad luck continued when a clash of heads with a team mate saw him suffer a broken nose against Brentford in April.

Scunthorpe U (From trainee on 23/12/93) FL 84+22/4 FLC 3+1 FAC 6+2/1 Others 6+4/2

HOWARD Jonathan (Jon)
Born: Sheffield, 7 October 1971
Height: 5'11" Weight: 12.6
Jon developed his forward play to pleasing effect for Chesterfield in 1998-99, goals coming from flashes of genius, and from his ability to be in the right place at the right time for simple tap-ins. Quick off the mark, persistent and perceptive, he was the subject of an unsuccessful bid from Bury shortly before he signed a new two-and-a-half-year contract in January. However, March saw him lose a little form for the first time in four seasons, as he struggled with a groin

problem, and missed key matches towards the end of the term, as the team's play-off hopes withered.

Rotherham U (From trainee on 10/7/90) FL 25+11/5 FLC 0+1 FAC 4/2 Others 3+1 (Free to Buxton on 11/11/94)
Chesterfield (Free on 9/12/94) FL 107+42/27 FLC 9/1 FAC 11+1/2 Others 7+3/2

HOWARD Michael Anthony
Born: Birkenhead, 2 December 1978
Height: 5'9" Weight: 11.13
After being rewarded with a contract following his trial period towards the end of 1997-98, Michael started last season as Swansea's first-choice left back, displaying good defensive qualities, and giving good attacking options to his team mates. As the campaign progressed he made the position his own, with not many opponents getting the better of him. Signed an extension to his contract at the Vetch Field, tying him to the Swans until June 2001.

Tranmere Rov (From trainee on 9/7/97)
Swansea C (Free on 6/2/98) FL 40+2/1 FLC 2 FAC 5 Others 3

HOWARD Steven (Steve) John
Born: Durham, 10 May 1976
Height: 6'2" Weight: 14.6
At the beginning of 1998-99 this big, old-fashioned type of centre forward was having a frustrating time at Hartlepool, with his confidence suffering badly as he failed to score goals regularly. Always a fierce competitor, over a matter of weeks his form improved dramatically, and he became the crowd favourite. Although Pool rejected offers for him from both Scunthorpe and Northampton, it eventually made economic sense when he accepted a move to Northampton in February. A target man who is good in the air and holds the ball up for others, and is not afraid to get stuck in, he missed part of Town's campaign through suspensions picked up earlier, but, as a real crowd

pleaser, there are high hopes for him at Sixfields in 1999-2000.

Hartlepool U (Free from Tow Law on 8/8/95) FL 117+25/26 FLC 7+1/1 FAC 5/2 Others 7/3
Northampton T (£120,000 on 22/2/99) FL 12

HOWARTH Neil
Born: Farnworth, 15 November 1971
Height: 6'2" Weight: 13.6
Club Honours: GMVC '95, '97; FAT '96
International Honours: E: SP-1
Following an import of new squad players for Macclesfield's first sortie into Division Two in 1998-99, Neil was not only unable to get a regular start in his preferred central defending role, but neither could he get in at full back, the position he played most at during 1997-98, having to be content with a bench place for much of the season, and only getting a start when injury or suspension left the squad short. However, he did get one unusual start when the manager, remembering a screamer of a goal from earlier days, experimented by putting him in the striker role at Wigan during a Macclesfield goal drought. He finally got despondent, not having a settled place, and transferred to Conference highflyers, Cheltenham, for £7,000 at the end of February.

Burnley (From trainee on 2/7/90) FL 0+1
Macclesfield T (Free on 3/9/93) FL 49+11/3 FLC 3 FAC 2+2 Others 2

HOWE Edward (Eddie) John Frank
Born: Amersham, 29 November 1977
Height: 5'10" Weight: 11.10
International Honours: E: U21-2
Had an excellent season at centre back for Bournemouth in 1998-99, missing just one game, while producing many outstanding performances along the way, and scoring five league and cup goals. Rightly recognised as the club's "Player of the Year", Eddie is a commanding centre back who is good in the air, a fierce tackler and, at just 21 years of age, is surely one of the lower divisions' brightest prospects.

Bournemouth (From trainee on 4/7/96) FL 87+16/3 FLC 6+1/1 FAC 7/2 Others 6+2

HOWE Stephen **Robert (Bobby)**
Born: Annitsford, 6 November 1973
Height: 5'7" Weight: 10.4
International Honours: E: Yth
Stephen, who likes to be known as Bobby, is an attacking midfielder who signed for Swindon in January 1998 from Nottingham Forest, where his first-team opportunities had dried up. After a slow start in 1998-99, he eventually recaptured the form that made him so popular at Forest to make the number seven jersey his own, scoring three goals in the process. An excellent passer of the ball, and ideally suited to a striking role or tucking in just behind the front men, he is rapidly becoming a crowd pleaser at Town, where he is expected to become one of the key figures in the club's battle to better themselves.

Nottingham F (From trainee on 5/12/90) P/FL 6+8/2 FLC 2 Others 1+1
Ipswich T (Loaned on 17/1/97) FL 2+1 FLC 1
Swindon T (£30,000 on 16/1/98) FL 29+4/3 FAC 2

147

HOWELLS David
Born: Guildford, 15 December 1967
Height: 5'11" Weight: 12.4
Club Honours: FAC '91
International Honours: E: Yth
A very experienced midfielder who was snapped up by Southampton on a free transfer from Spurs during the summer of 1998, David was in and out of the side in 1998-99, appearing in nine of the opening 12 games prior to undergoing a knee operation. The highlight of that period came when he scored the vital equaliser at Arsenal (Tottenham's arch rivals), a goal that would eventually deny the Gunners the Premiership title. Later on in the campaign, when looking for match fitness, he was loaned to Bristol City in transfer deadline week and marked his first game for the club with a tremendous goal in a 2-0 home win over Port Vale. Despite having to battle on to full recovery, right from the start it was apparent that he was bringing Premiership quality to Ashton Gate, having the ability to put his foot on the ball to direct operations, and the City fans would certainly like to see his kind in the side in 1999-2000.
Tottenham H (From apprentice on 28/1/85) F/PL 238+39/22 FLC 26+5/4 FAC 18+4/1 Others 7
Southampton (Free on 2/7/98) PL 8+1/1 FLC 1 FAC 1
Bristol C (Loaned on 25/3/99) FL 8/1

HOWEY Lee Matthew
Born: Sunderland, 1 April 1969
Height: 6'3" Weight: 14.6
Club Honours: Div 1 '96
Began last season partnering Steve Blatherwick in the centre of Burnley's defence but, along with Blatherwick and two others, was told by Stan Ternent after a home defeat by York that his services were no longer required. He subsequently joined Northampton, first on loan and later permanently, where he initially reverted to striker, managing six goals from set pieces, including one against his old club in the final game of the season, which kept Burnley uncomfortably close behind Burnley near the foot of the Second Division table. His aerial power is second to none, and he is a commanding figure in the back line.
Ipswich T (From trainee on 2/10/86) (Free to Blyth Spartans in March 1988)
Sunderland (Free from Bishop Auckland on 25/3/93) P/FL 39+30/8 FLC 1+4/2 FAC 2+4/1 Others 0+1
Burnley (£200,000 on 11/8/97) FL 24+2 FLC 5/1 FAC 2 Others 0+1
Northampton T (£50,000 on 6/11/98) FL 25/6 Others 1

HOWEY Stephen (Steve) Norman
Born: Sunderland, 26 October 1971
Height: 6'2" Weight: 11.12
Club Honours: Div 1 '93
International Honours: E: 4
Long serving Steve is an authoritative Newcastle centre back of real quality. Tall and commanding in the air, he is equally at home when the ball is on the ground, using either his pace and anticipation to head off danger before it develops, or his strength in the tackle to dispossess threatening opponents. Comfortable on the ball, he prefers to carry it forward out of defence to launch new attacks, or to use it accurately, long or short, to a colleague, rather than resorting to route-one tactics. A long-standing calf problem was again disruptive early in 1998-99, and it was eventually diagnosed that his general level of strength and fitness needed to be increased, to which end he spent three weeks at the FA's rehabilitation centre at Lilleshall to give himself the necessary foundation on which to build. He returned in November against Wimbledon, proudly captaining the team in the absence of Robert Lee and Alan Shearer, and turned in an excellent performance, both personally and in the way he marshalled the defence, leading manager Ruud Gullit to declare that Steve's return was like making a £5m signing! And, indeed, Steve signed a new four-year contract in February. His performances led some to suggest a return to international duty was imminent, but a further injury disrupted his season in March. Although returning for the FA Cup semi final, and being in fine form, he suffered yet another serious blow during the first half, rupturing his right achilles tendon, an injury which is likely to put him out for up to eight months.
Newcastle U (From trainee on 11/12/89) F/PL 160+22/6 FLC 14+2/1 FAC 20+2 Others 10+2

HOWIE Scott
Born: Glasgow, 4 January 1972
Height: 6'2" Weight: 13.7
Club Honours: S Div 2 '93
International Honours: S: U21-5
The tall, well-built Reading goalkeeper forced his way into the side for the fifth game of last season, and remained a permanent fixture in the team, despite competition from Nicky Hammond and Peter van der Kwaak. Although he proved himself to be an excellent shot stopper, with lightning reflexes, and great bravery, he will need to work on tightening up other parts of his footballing make-up, something which should come with added experience of the English game.
Clydebank (Signed from Ferguslie U on 7/1/92) SL 55 SLC 3 SC 4 Others 1
Norwich C (£300,000 on 12/8/93) PL 1+1
Motherwell (£300,000 on 13/10/94) SL 69 SLC 4 SC 5 Others 1
Reading (£30,000 on 26/3/98) FL 49 FLC 2 FAC 1 Others 1

HOYLAND Jamie William
Born: Sheffield, 23 January 1966
Height: 6'0" Weight: 13.2
International Honours: E: Yth
Out of contract at Burnley during the 1998 close season, Jamie teamed up with Scarborough prior to 1998-99 getting underway, as the player/coach and team captain. Despite the team being relegated to the Conference, in doubling up as a solid defender or in midfield, he won a host of "Man of the Match" awards, missed just two matches, and was named the "Boro Player of the Year". Is the son of Tommy, who played for Sheffield United and Bradford City between 1949 and 1962.

Manchester C (From apprentice on 12/11/83) FL 2 FLC 0+1/1
Bury (Free on 11/7/86) FL 169+3/35 FLC 14+1/5 FAC 6 Others 12/2
Sheffield U (£250,000 on 4/7/90) F/PL 72+17/6 FLC 5+3/1 FAC 8+2/1 Others 5/1
Bristol C (Loaned on 4/3/94) FL 6
Burnley (£130,000 on 14/10/94) FL 77+10/4 FLC 5 FAC 7 Others 5+1
Carlisle U (Loaned on 20/11/97) FL 5
Scarborough (Free on 6/8/98) FL 44/3 FLC 2 FAC 2 Others 1

HREIDARSSON Hermann
Born: Iceland, 11 July 1974
Height: 6'1" Weight: 13.1
Club Honours: Div 3 '99
International Honours: Iceland: 17
Signed from Ron Noades' old club, Crystal Palace, this tall, classy left-footed centre back joined Brentford for a club record fee last September, and soon showed an ability clearly well above that of division Three. Especially good at bringing the ball forward out of defence before passing it forward, he weighed in with some useful goals. Also added to his international caps for Iceland during the campaign, and was selected by his fellow professionals for the award-winning PFA divisional side before going on to win a Third Division championship medal when the Bees were promoted.
Crystal Palace (Signed from IBV on 9/8/97) P/FL 32+5/2 FLC 5/1 FAC 4
Brentford (£850,000 on 24/9/98) FL 33/4 FAC 2/1 Others 3/1

HRISTOV Georgi
Born: Bitola, Macedonia, 30 January 1976
Height: 5'11" Weight: 12.2
International Honours: Macedonia: 23
Having suffered serious knee-ligament damage in only the second league fixture of last season, he did not reappear until April and was obviously short of match fitness. A major hope for Barnsley to get promotion at the first attempt, his loss was a severe blow, and all at Oakwell will be hoping that he stays fit for the forthcoming season. On his game, Georgi can often prove outstanding, his ability on the ground and in the air bringing spectacular goals.
Barnsley (£1,500,000 from Partizan Belgrade on 23/7/97) P/FL 13+13/4 FLC 1+2/1 FAC 1+1

HUCK William Roger Fernend
Born: Paris, France, 17 March 1979
Height: 5'10" Weight: 11.13
Unable to further his career at Highbury, William was signed from Arsenal last March, having previously been at Monaco. Predominantly a left winger, who is quick and an excellent crosser of the ball, he managed six starts and one substitute appearance for Bournemouth, despite suffering a niggling injury. This season should see him firmly established in the Cherries' senior side, and he looks an excellent prospect for the future.
Arsenal (Signed from Monaco on 6/11/98)
Bournemouth (£50,000 on 25/3/99) FL 6+2

HUCKERBY Darren Carl
Born: Nottingham, 23 April 1976
Height: 5'10" Weight: 11.12
International Honours: E: B-1; U21-4

Although 1998-99 was a frustrating season for Coventry's young England striker, he started where he left off by ripping open the Chelsea defence with his pace, to score in the opening day win. For the next few games he looked to be carrying an injury, and a knee problem forced him to miss five games. While the sale of his striking buddy, Dion Dublin, was a blow, he immediately set up an excellent partnership with Noel Whelan, which resulted in three goals in four games for him, including the runner up in the BBC "Goal of the Month", against Everton, a long cross from Steve Froggatt being met with a superb piece of control and a devastating finish. He really hit the headlines in January though, with seven goals in three games, including back-to-back hat tricks against Macclesfield and Nottingham Forest, with his speed and control, allied to deadly finishing, being seen at its best. His third goal against Forest stands out as one of the finest on the ground for many years. In a run from the half-way line he beat four or five men before rounding the 'keeper to score to win another BBC "Goal of the Month" award. Sadly, the remainder of the campaign was an anti-climax, and Darren found goals hard to come by despite constantly unnerving defences with his deadly bursts of speed.

Lincoln C (From trainee on 14/7/93) FL 20+8/5 FLC 2 Others 1/2
Newcastle U (£400,000 on 10/11/95) PL 0+1 FAC 0+1
Millwall (Loaned on 6/9/96) FL 6/3
Coventry C (£1,000,000 on 23/11/96) PL 84+9/28 FLC 2+1 FAC 12/6

HUDSON Daniel (Danny) Robert
Born: Doncaster, 25 June 1979
Height: 5'9" Weight: 10.3
A highly promising young Rotherham midfielder with the ability to run at defenders, Danny had to work hard to try and establish himself as an automatic choice in the first team in 1998-99. The highlight of his season was undoubtedly his hat trick at Peterborough, where the Millers turned a 2-0 half-time deficit into a 4-2 win. Definitely has the ability to carve out a regular place in 1999-2000.
Rotherham U (From trainee on 25/6/97) FL 25+11/5 FLC 0+2 FAC 3+2/2 Others 2+1

HUGHES Aaron William
Born: Magherafelt, 8 November 1979
Height: 6'0" Weight: 11.2
International Honours: NI: 8; B-2; Yth
In an era of bought-in foreign players, Aaron is something of a rarity at Newcastle – an established talent developed through the youth team! Tall, slim, and comfortable on the ball, he is able to play at both centre back and full back, on either flank, although preferring the right, and he displays a cool head on young shoulders. Having signed a new four-year contract in the summer of 1998, he is already established in the Northern Ireland squad, where he played regularly at full back until missing the Euro 2000 qualifier at home to Moldova in November with a calf injury. Despite that, he found it difficult to secure a regular place

in his club side, and his early-season appearances were restricted to games for the reserves and the U19 youth team. He patiently applied himself with determination, being given his chance in the first team in November, and retained his place through to January, before finding himself back on the bench again until the latter stages of the campaign. Nonetheless, he has become one of the top young talents in the British game and looks set for a fine future. He came on in the first half of the FA Cup semi final as a substitute for the injured Steve Howey, and played with a calm assurance which belied his tender years, to help deny Spurs a goal and assist his side in reaching Wembley.
Newcastle U (From trainee on 11/3/97) PL 16+2 FLC 2 FAC 1+2 Others 0+2

HUGHES Andrew (Andy) John
Born: Manchester, 2 January 1978
Height: 5'11" Weight: 12.1
Club Honours: Div 3 '98
Andy had a disappointing 1998-99 at Notts County after a bright start, before recovering to produce some of his familiar all-action form towards the end of the campaign. A box-to-box, hard-running midfielder who is good on the ball, he continued to contribute valuable goals, scoring in the 1-1 home draw against Macclesfield in the penultimate game, which endeared him to the fans. Much is hoped of him for this coming season, especially if he can regain fitness and form after some injury problems which obviously held him back in mid term.
Oldham Ath (From trainee on 20/1/96) FL 18+15/1 FLC 1+1 FAC 3+1 Others 1+2
Notts Co (£150,000 on 29/1/98) FL 33+12/5 FLC 1 FAC 3 Others 1

HUGHES Bryan
Born: Liverpool, 19 June 1976
Height: 5'10" Weight: 11.2
Club Honours: WC '95
A highly talented midfielder who provided an elusive attacking threat when coming off the flank at Birmingham in 1998-99, Bryan was unfortunately hampered by an achilles tendon injury early in the campaign, and at Christmas suffered a personal tragedy when his partner lost the child they were expecting. After being given compassionate leave, he returned to the side and produced some brilliant performances. Scored a goal-of-the-season candidate against Portsmouth on 6 March, when dribbling past three players from the half-way line before finishing strongly.
Wrexham (From trainee on 7/7/94) FL 71+23/12 FLC 2 FAC 13+3/7 Others 14+1/3
Birmingham C (£750,000 + on 12/3/97) FL 64+15/8 FLC 5+1/1 FAC 3+1/2 Others 1

HUGHES Ceri Morgan
Born: Pontypridd, 26 February 1971
Height: 5'10" Weight: 12.7
International Honours: W: 8; B-2; Yth
Out at the start of last season due to an operation in the summer on his knee, having given some promising performances in the reserves the tenacious midfielder finally broke back into the Wimbledon first team

during the second half of the campaign. Although often on the bench, he ended the season in fine form and will no doubt be hoping to continue this into 1999-2000. An enthusiastic player who is full of potential, and shows no signs of shying away from the Premiership's big occasions, Ceri is always comfortable on the ball, looks to take on defenders down either flank, and will be hoping to get back into the Welsh international side this coming term.
Luton T (From trainee on 1/7/89) FL 157+18/17 FLC 13/1 FAC 11/2 Others 6
Wimbledon (£400,000 + on 4/7/97) PL 21+10/1 FLC 2+1 FAC 2+3

HUGHES Daniel Paul
Born: Bangor, 13 February 1980
Height: 5'10" Weight: 13.0
Despite being released by Wolves last March, this young midfielder was rated sufficiently highly by Chris Turner that he wasted little time in signing him for Hartlepool after his appointment there as manager. Previously unproven at league level, he justified the faith of his former coach, winning a first-team place, and not looking out of place in several appearances as Pool battled to avoid demotion to the Nationwide Conference. Is a ball winner who gets up and down the field, and has good distribution to go with natural stamina.
Wolverhampton W (From trainee on 13/7/98)
Hartlepool U (Signed on 2/3/99) FL 6+2

HUGHES David Robert
Born: St Albans, 30 December 1972
Height: 5'10" Weight: 11.8
International Honours: W: U21-1. E: Sch
A midfielder with undoubted potential, having been signed by Southampton from Weymouth in 1991, unfortunately his career has continually been interrupted by injury. The catalogue of misfortune, includes broken ankles, back problems, cracked ribs, hamstring problems, and a knee injury which needed an operation in August 1998. This ruled him out until last February, when he come on as a late sub in the 2-1 home win against Newcastle. Following that, he started six matches and came off the bench twice more. A fully-fit David, a former U21 international, would surely challenge for a regular first-team place, and it is hoped that he can now keep clear of any further problems.
Southampton (From Weymouth on 2/7/91) PL 21+33/3 FLC 3+1 FAC 1+5/1

HUGHES Garry
Born: Birmingham, 19 November 1979
Height: 6'0" Weight: 12.2
A young Northampton central defender who came through the ranks to make his debut in the F A Cup defeat by non-league Yeovil, as a substitute, Garry played in many of the pre-season friendlies, having been given a professional contract during the summer. He is the first player to come through the youth and reserve team since the club moved to Sixfields.
Northampton T (From trainee on 7/7/98) FAC 0+1

HUGHES Ian

Born: Bangor, 2 August 1974
Height: 5'10" Weight: 12.8
Club Honours: Div 2 '97
International Honours: W: U21-12; Yth

Able to be used anywhere in defence or midfield with complete confidence, Ian ended last season as Blackpool's captain following Tony Butler's departure. Very competitive, as well as being composed and comfortable on the ball, he scored his first ever goal for the Seasiders when gaining the club a point at Colchester. Is the son of a former Bury player.

Bury (From trainee on 19/11/91) FL 137+23/1 FLC 13+3 FAC 6+2 Others 14+4/1
Blackpool (£200,000 on 12/12/97) FL 51+3/1 FLC 4 Others 4

HUGHES Lee

Born: Birmingham, 22 May 1976
Height: 5'10" Weight: 11.6
International Honours: E: SP-2

The country's leading scorer in 1998-99 with 32 goals, Lee was in terrific form for West Bromwich during the first half of the season and, although his goals dried up from January onwards (not helped by a shoulder injury and a short suspension), he was always a threat to opposing defenders. As keen as mustard, with the knack of being in the right place at the right time, he is now valued at around £6 million, and scored three hat tricks during the campaign – the first Albion player since Derek Kevan in 1961-62 to score over 30 league goals. Was voted Albion's "Player of the Year" by the supporters, and selected by his fellow professionals for their award-winning PFA First Division team.

West Bromwich A (£250,000 + from Kidderminster Hrs on 19/5/97) FL 60+19/45 FLC 2+2/1 FAC 3

Lee Hughes

Mark Hughes

HUGHES Leslie Mark

Born: Wrexham, 1 November 1963
Height: 5'11" Weight: 13.0
Club Honours: FAC '85, '90, '94, '97; ECWC '91, '98; ESC '91; FLC '92, '98; PL '93, '94; CS '93, '94
International Honours: W: 72; U21-5; Yth; Sch

A vastly experienced and accomplished striker who was awarded an MBE in 1998 for his services to football, Mark decided to accept Southampton's offer for his services during the 1998 close season as the competition for the striking positions at Chelsea had increased, feeling he could still command a regular Premiership place. In the event, he actually made more appearances for his new club in midfield than he did as a striker, where his strength on the ball and ability to resist challenges were a great asset as the team fought to avoid relegation. This deeper role, and lack of the sort of service he had been used to, resulted in him only managing to score one goal throughout the campaign. Although his frustration was added to by picking up 14 cautions, his overall contribution was undoubted. Renowned for his ability to hold the ball and release at the right moment, he possesses a tremendous volley. Is still a regular in the Welsh team.

Manchester U (From apprentice on 5/11/80) FL 85+4/37 FLC 5+1/4 FAC 10/4 Others 14+2/2 (£2,500,000 to Barcelona on 1/7/86)
Manchester U (£1,500,000 on 20/7/88) F/PL 251+5/82 FLC 32/12 FAC 34+1/13 Others 27+1/8
Chelsea (£1,500,000 on 6/7/95) PL 88+7/25 FLC 7+3/3 FAC 13+1/9 Others 1+3/2
Southampton (£650,000 on 15/7/98) PL 32/1 FLC 2 FAC 1+1

HUGHES Michael Eamonn

Born: Larne, 2 August 1971
Height: 5'7" Weight: 10.13
International Honours: NI: 47; U23-2; U21-1; Yth; Sch

At £1.6 million, Michael could be the best buy Wimbledon have ever made. An influential and talented winger who can play on either flank, he produced some excellent performances during the first half of last season which coincided with the Dons' best run of form. A real delight to watch, especially when running at defenders, he is confident on the ball and has a powerful shot, although surprisingly scoring just twice in the league – one against Charlton with a long-range effort on Boxing Day, and a superb strike against Leeds in a 1-1 draw, giving Nigel Martyn no chance, not to mention the penalty which knocked the holders Chelsea out of the Worthington Cup. Having had an operation on a groin injury in April, he will be hoping to be fit for the start of the coming campaign.

Manchester C (From trainee on 17/8/88) FL 25+1/1 FLC 5 FAC 1 Others 1 (£450,000 to RS Strasbourg in 1992 close season)
West Ham U (Loaned on 29/11/94) PL 15+2/2 FAC 2
West Ham U (Loaned on 2/10/95) PL 28 FLC 2 FAC 3/1
West Ham U (Free on 12/8/96) PL 33+5/3 FLC 5 FAC 2
Wimbledon (£1,600,000 on 25/9/97) PL 57+2/6 FLC 4/1 FAC 6/2

HUGHES John Paul

Born: Hammersmith, 19 April 1976
Height: 6'0" Weight: 12.6
International Honours: E: Sch

With no opportunities coming his way at Chelsea during 1998-99, Paul was loaned to Stockport (December) and Norwich (March) before returning to Stamford Bridge at the end of the season. He certainly impressed all at Stockport, including the manager Gary Megson, who wanted to extend the loan period. But, following seven games he picked up an injury and, following his recovery, Norwich moved in smartly to take him to Carrow Road for the remaining six weeks of the term. A creative influence in the centre of the park with a good range of passing skills to go with the vision to see openings early, unfortunately, he missed a few games through injury, but the class was there for all to see. By nature an attacking midfielder, and one who likes to be the focal point within the build up of the team's offensive moves, he scored his only goal of the campaign in his final match for City, a 2-1 home win over Swindon.

Chelsea (From trainee on 11/7/94) PL 13+8/2 FAC 2 Others 1
Stockport Co (Loaned on 17/12/98) FL 7
Norwich C (Loaned on 24/3/99) FL 2+2/1

HUGHES Richard

Born: Glasgow, 25 June 1979
Height: 5'9" Weight: 9.12
International Honours: S: U21-4; Yth

Being of Scottish birth, Richard was a surprise Arsenal signing from Atalanta in August 1997 but, unable to make a breakthrough at Highbury, he moved to Bournemouth prior to the start of 1998-99, and made his debut in the first game of the season, against Lincoln. Immediately establishing himself in the first team, and becoming an integral part of the Cherries' midfield, he showed that he could play

either on the left or in central midfield. Despite not being blessed with the greatest of pace he is, nevertheless, an excellent dribbler of the ball with a good left foot shot. He also proved to be versatile, playing at centre back against West Bromwich in an FA Cup third round game and giving a faultless performance. Came to the fore at junior international level in 1998-99, making four appearances for the Scottish U21 side.

Arsenal (Free from Atalanta on 11/8/97)
Bournemouth (£20,000 on 5/8/98) FL 43+1/2 FLC 5 FAC 4 Others 3

HUGHES Stephen (Steve) John
Born: Reading, 18 September 1976
Height: 6'0" Weight: 12.12
Club Honours: FAYC '94; PL '98; CS '98
International Honours: E: U21-8; Yth; Sch
Despite being a member of the England U21 squad, Stephen has yet to become a regular first-team choice for Arsenal. A talented central and left-sided midfield player, he is an extremely valuable squad member, and a natural replacement whenever either Manu Petit or Patrick Viera are indisposed. Although the majority of his appearances last season were from the substitutes' bench, he made some particularly impressive contributions. Scored a valuable last-minute goal from long range at Leicester to earn the Gunners a draw, and had a mature, controlled game in the Worthington Cup victory at Derby, while also scoring in the Champions' League game at Dynamo Kiev. Has the ability to succeed at the highest level, but will have to be patient if he remains at Highbury.

Arsenal (From trainee on 15/7/95) PL 21+26/4 FLC 5+3/1 FAC 7+5/1 Others 2+3/1

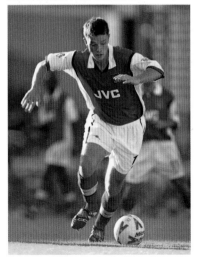
Steve Hughes

HULBERT Robin James
Born: Plymouth, 14 March 1980
Height: 5'9" Weight: 10.5
International Honours: E: Yth; Sch
As an England U18 player, Robin has excelled at youth level and now seems to

have settled in to the senior game without any trouble, his pace and quick feet resulting in him being utilised by Swindon as a right-wing back and in midfield. Although not a possession winner, when he has the ball to feet he can create chances further forward, and in 1998-99 he followed up his promise of the previous campaign with some useful performances. With several big clubs running the rule over him, he is expected to make further progress during the coming term.

Swindon T (From trainee on 25/9/97) FL 7+10 FLC 0+1 FAC 2

HULME Kevin
Born: Farnworth, 2 December 1967
Height: 5'10" Weight: 13.2
As Halifax's club captain, Kevin was always an inspiration to the rest of the team in 1998-99. His quality tackling and competitiveness, wherever he played, always there to see. Twice forced to appear in goal, remarkably keeping a clean sheet on both occasions, Kevin signed an extension to his contract last January. Predominantly a central midfielder, as you can see he can play just about anywhere.

Bury (£5,000 from Radcliffe Borough on 16/3/89) FL 82+28/21 FLC 4+3/2 FAC 4+1/1 Others 4+8/2
Chester C (Loaned on 26/10/89) FL 4
Doncaster Rov (£42,500 on 14/7/93) FL 33+1/8 FLC 2/1 FAC 1 Others 2
Bury (£42,500 on 11/8/94) FL 24+5 FLC 2 FAC 2 Others 2
Lincoln C (Signed on 28/9/95) FL 4+1 FAC 1 Others 1+1 (Free to Macclesfield T on 15/12/95)
Halifax T (Free on 22/11/96) FL 30/4 FLC 4 Others 2

HUMES Anthony (Tony)
Born: Blyth, 19 March 1966
Height: 5'11" Weight: 12.0
Along with fellow defender, Brian Carey, Tony is among Brian Flynn's finest investments at Wrexham. Unfortunately, like the previous campaign, he struggled with injury, having to undergo an appendix operation in early December, which curtailed any further activity with the first team. A manager's dream, he is the type of player who will give you 100 per-cent effort and more, his battling qualities always being to the fore, especially when appearing in midfield.

Ipswich T (From apprentice on 26/5/83) FL 107+13/10 FLC 6 FAC 4/1 Others 10/1
Wrexham (£40,000 on 27/3/92) FL 191+8/8 FLC 8 FAC 19/1 Others 13

HUMPHREYS Richard (Richie) John
Born: Sheffield, 30 November 1977
Height: 5'11" Weight: 14.6
International Honours: E: U21-3
1998-99 was yet another frustrating season for this young Sheffield Wednesday striker, cum midfield player, as he failed to command a regular place in the team. Nevertheless, he at least had the pleasure of scoring his first goals for the club in nearly two years, but, despite that, his potential remains partially untapped. Although not blessed with startling pace, the stockily-built youngster has a fair amount of skill and a doggedness to worry even Premiership

defences, but needs a regular run to prove his value. Having been played in a holding role in midfield earlier in his career appears to have done him no favours, and a boost to his confidence is required. There is no doubt that he is highly thought of at Hillsbrough, by both fans and management, and a few goals in 1999-2000 could do the trick.

Sheffield Wed (From trainee on 8/2/96) PL 27+33/4 FLC 1+2 FAC 5+4/4

HUNT Andrew (Andy)
Born: Thurrock, 9 June 1970
Height: 6'0" Weight: 12.0
Signed on a free transfer from West Bromwich Albion under the Bosman ruling during the 1998 close season, Andy was immediately given a first-team place at Charlton alongside play-off hero, Clive Mendonca, in the Addicks' attack. Despite working extremely hard, holding the ball up well, and winning his fair share of aerial battles, he failed to find the net on a regular basis. Scored twice in the 2-2 draw with Tottenham at White Hart Lane in November, doubling his previous goals tally, but only managed three more goals all season, which was obviously a disappointing return for a main striker.

Newcastle U (£150,000 from Kettering T on 29/1/91) FL 34+9/11 FLC 3/1 FAC 2/2 Others 3
West Bromwich A (£100,000 on 25/3/93) FL 201+11/76 FLC 12/4 FAC 7/2 Others 8+1/3
Charlton Ath (Free on 2/7/98) PL 32+2/7 FLC 2 FAC 1

HUNT James Malcolm
Born: Derby, 17 December 1976
Height: 5'8" Weight: 10.3
This dynamic Northampton midfield player held his own in the first team last season with some sterling displays, showing pace, aggressiveness, and the ability to take on his man, as well as being a good passer of the ball. Linking well with Roy Hunter, no Town supporter will ever forget his last-minute headed equaliser versus Preston at Sixfields in October.

Notts Co (From trainee on 15/7/94) FL 15+4/1 FAC 0+1 Others 2+2/1
Northampton T (Free on 7/8/97) FL 38+18/2 FLC 2+2 FAC 2+3 Others 6+1

HUNT Jonathan (Jon) Richard
Born: Camden, 2 November 1971
Height: 5'10" Weight: 11.12
Club Honours: Div 2 '95; AMC '95
A talented attacking midfielder who is best employed in a left-sided role, Jon was only on the fringes of the first-team action at Derby in 1998-99, being loaned to Sheffield United (August) and Ipswich (October) prior to arriving at United on a permanent basis in mid March. Started the campaign, games wise, at United, making five appearances and scoring in a 3-1 home win over Crewe, before returning to Pride Park and thence to Ipswich. Impressing to some degree at Portman Road, but not enough to stay, he was eventually given nine appearances from the bench by the County manager, Jim Smith, scoring a dramatic last-minute winner at Middlesbrough in December, before signing for Sheffield

United, along with Rob Kozluk, as part of the players plus cash deal that took Vass Borbokis to Derby. Playing in eight of the final 11 games he soon showed his ability to pass the ball well from midfield – one of the main reasons for Steve Bruce signing him – and became the main taker of corners and free kicks.

Barnet (From juniors in 1989-90) FL 12+21 FLC 1 FAC 0+1 Others 6+2
Southend U (Free on 20/7/93) FL 41+8/6 FLC 1+3 FAC 1 Others 6+1
Birmingham C (£50,000 on 16/9/94) FL 67+10/18 FLC 10+5/2 FAC 3+1/1 Others 8/4
Derby Co (£500,000 on 23/5/97) PL 7+18/2 FLC 2+2 FAC 0+3
Sheffield U (Loaned on 20/8/98) FL 4+1/1
Ipswich T (Loaned on 20/10/98) FL 2+4
Sheffield U (Signed on 12/3/99) FL 8/1

HUNTER Barry Victor
Born: Coleraine, 18 November 1968
Height: 6'3" Weight: 13.2
International Honours: NI: 13; B-2; Yth

Yet another Reading player who had to recover from a long-term knee injury, Barry went on loan to Southend to regain match fitness last February, then returned home to play in the last two league matches of the season. He also won back his place in central defence in the Northern Ireland side which met Canada in April. A stylish central defender, who hopes to sign a new contract in the summer, he has good touch, good awareness, and is excellent in the air – something he showed during his time at Southend, when he chipped in with two goals. Hopefully, he can look forward to an injury-free 1999-2000.

Newcastle U (Signed from Coleraine on 2/11/87. Freed during 1988 close season)
Wrexham (£50,000 from Crusaders on 20/8/93) FL 88+3/4 FLC 6 FAC 7+1/1 Others 15/1
Reading (£400,000 on 12/7/96) FL 28+2/2 FLC 1 FAC 1
Southend U (Loaned on 12/2/99) FL 5/2

HUNTER Roy Ian
Born: Middlesbrough, 29 October 1973
Height: 5'10" Weight: 12.8

A Northampton midfield dynamo, Roy missed the latter part of 1997-98 through injury, but made his comeback in late August 1998, only to pick up a leg injury in September and be forced to miss two months of this season. Still a great favourite with the crowd, he was last season's "Player of the Year", his high workrate, commitment, and tenaciousness being his trademark. Has been the target for several clubs.

West Bromwich A (From trainee on 4/3/92) FL 3+6/1 Others 4+1
Northampton T (Free on 2/8/95) FL 95+21/10 FLC 8 FAC 9/2 Others 11/1

HURST Paul Michael
Born: Sheffield, 25 September 1974
Height: 5'4" Weight: 9.4
Club Honours: AMC '96

After starting last season on the sidelines, having turned down the offer of a new contract, Paul battled his way back into the Rotherham team and subsequently signed a new deal. Very much a crowd favourite for his never-say-die spirit, he is equally at home on the left side of the back line, or in

midfield. Made more first-team appearances than in any previous campaign since joining United from school.

Rotherham U (From trainee on 12/8/93) FL 118+31/6 FLC 4 FAC 12/2 Others 12+1

HUTCHINGS Carl Emil
Born: Hammersmith, 24 September 1974
Height: 5'11" Weight: 11.0

Signed from Brentford during the 1998 close season, Carl began 1998-99 with several promising performances for Bristol City, before being troubled by a groin injury which saw him lose his place in the team. Up until that time, he had given the fans hope that he might just be the box-to-box midfield player that the club had been looking for. Although strong in the air, and with an eye for goal, he will have to wait until the coming term to prove that he can make the jump from the Second Division to meet the higher demands of the First.

Brentford (From trainee on 12/7/93) FL 144+18/7 FLC 9+1 FAC 11+1 Others 11+3
Bristol C (£130,000 on 6/7/98) FL 16+5/2 FLC 2+1/1 FAC 0+1

HUTCHISON Donald (Don)
Born: Gateshead, 9 May 1971
Height: 6'1" Weight: 11.8
International Honours: S: 2 B-1

A central midfielder with all of the qualities required to make a success of the role, Don enjoyed his best Premiership season at Everton in 1998-99. Voted "Player of the Season" by the club's supporters, he was also recognised within the game, his manager, Walter Smith, naming him first-team captain on several occasions, and Craig Brown rewarding him with a long awaited call up to the Scotland squad. He then celebrated his full international debut with a winning goal against the European Champions, Germany, on German soil! A committed tackler, an astute passer of the ball, and with a good eye for goal, the only asset missing from his make up is burning pace, something he makes up for with the intelligence of his play. He proved a revelation when he was switched – in an emergency – to a striking role at Goodison, and it was in that role he won his first Scotland cap as a substitute against the Czech Republic. However, it is in central midfield where he is most comfortable, and he looks set to go from strength to strength this season.

Hartlepool U (From trainee on 20/3/90) FL 19+5/2 FLC 1 FAC 2 Others 1
Liverpool (£175,000 on 27/11/90) F/PL 33+12/7 FLC 7+1/2 FAC 1+2 Others 3+1/1
West Ham U (£1,500,000 on 30/8/94) PL 30+5/11 FLC 3/2 FAC 0+1
Sheffield U (£1,200,000 on 11/1/96) FL 70+8/5 FLC 3+2 FAC 5/1 Others 2+1
Everton (£1,000,000 + on 27/2/98) PL 40+4/4 FLC 3+1/1 FAC 4

HUTT Stephen Graham
Born: Middlesbrough, 19 February 1979
Height: 6'3" Weight: 12.0

Stephen, a talented young midfielder, was again unable to make the breakthrough to win a regular place in the Hartlepool first team, this time in 1998-99. Having picked

up a series of niggling injuries early on, there was a general agreement that he needed to put on some weight if he was to become more effective, and he had a particularly good game against Preston in the Auto Windscreens Shield match. However, in March, he was loaned out to Unibond League team, Bishop Auckland, before being released on a free transfer during the summer.

Hartlepool U (From trainee on 8/7/97) FL 6+3 FAC 0+1 Others 1+1

HYDE Graham
Born: Doncaster, 10 November 1970
Height: 5'8" Weight: 11.11

Started last season at Sheffield Wednesday, but having struggled with niggling injuries for the past few campaigns he did not figure strongly in new manager Danny Wilson's plans, and made just one appearance from the bench before being allowed to move to Birmingham on a free transfer in February. A tenacious midfielder, Graham added bite to City's promotion bid, his busy, battling style helping to protect the back four and knit play together. Is a player who will always give the manager 100 per-cent effort, and has no little skill to go with his endeavours.

Sheffield Wed (From trainee on 17/5/88) F/PL 126+46/11 FLC 17+3/2 FAC 13+5/2 Others 4/1
Birmingham C (Free on 5/2/99) FL 13

HYDE Micah Anthony
Born: Newham, 10 November 1974
Height: 5'9" Weight: 11.5
Club Honours: Div 2 '98

A combative player, Micah remained first choice in Watford's central midfield, along with partner Richard Johnson in 1998-99. He again proved to be a consistent player, rarely being injured, and has now made over 200 senior appearances. The one disappointment during the season was his lack of goals, which seemed to stem from a lack of confidence – surely misplaced – with his shooting. However, he finally got off the mark against Bolton in April, it being his first goal for over a year, and was scored two days after the birth of his first son.

Cambridge U (From trainee on 19/5/93) FL 89+18/13 FLC 3 FAC 7+2 Others 4+1
Watford (£225,000 on 21/7/97) FL 83+1/6 FLC 6/1 FAC 6 Others 3

Micah Hyde

IFEJIAGWA Emeka
Born: Nigeria, 30 October 1977
Height: 6'3" Weight: 14.0
International Honours: Nigeria: 2
Signed by Charlton from the Nigerian club, Hdoji United, at the beginning of 1998-99, having previously won two international caps for the country of his birth, "Iffy" was loaned to Brighton last October in order to gain first-team experience, and had a tremendous debut when scoring the only goal of the game with a looping header, as Albion won at Barnet. A giant at the heart of the defence, he only made one further appearance, in the 3-2 home win against Hartlepool, before work permit problems caused his loan spell to be cut short in January. Currently believed to be somewhere in France!
Charlton Ath (£20,000 from Hdoji U on 12/8/98)
Brighton & Hove A (Loaned on 23/10/98) FL 2/1

IFILL Paul
Born: Brighton, 20 October 1979
Height: 6'0" Weight: 12.10
Yet another of the Millwall youngsters who burst onto the scene last season and, with less than a dozen senior appearances behind him, Paul fulfilled the ambition of every player to play at Wembley. A central striker who adapted to the role wide on the right, he gave many a defender a torrid time with his pace and trickery, which also got him into good goalscoring positions, and he scored his first league goal against Preston when finishing with the coolness of a seasoned campaigner.
Millwall (From trainee on 2/6/98) FL 12+3/1 Others 2+1

IGOE Samuel (Sammy) Gary
Born: Spelthorne, 30 September 1975
Height: 5'6" Weight: 10.0
Pint-sized in stature, but triple that for ability and determination, Sammy promised a good 1998-99 season at Portsmouth with his entertaining style of attacking play, good first touch, and general awareness around him. Despite scoring two goals in one match against Swindon early on, his flashes of brilliance and loss of form became a paradox, and the teams' slide down the table coincided with a poor second half of the campaign. So effective on his day, something which has attracted Premier clubs to Fratton Park, Sammy will he hoping to perform more consistently, and score more goals, if he is to play at a higher level.
Portsmouth (From trainee on 15/2/94) FL 86+48/10 FLC 6+4 FAC 2+3

ILIC Sasa
Born: Melbourne, Australia, 18 July 1972
Height: 6'4" Weight: 14.0
International Honours: Macedonia: 3. Yugoslavia

A tall, commanding goalkeeper, who is surprisingly agile for his size, Sasa started last season as the first-choice Charlton 'keeper, not conceding a goal in the first three matches, and putting in some brilliant performances. Then, injured at Chelsea in October, leaving the field with concussion and missing the next two games, he returned to the side only to lose form and eventually be dropped in January. Although coming back in March, when Simon Royce was injured, he followed suit himself at West Ham on Easter Monday, once again suffering concussion and a knee injury, and did not play again during the campaign. Once of Macedonia, he now represents Yugoslavia.
Charlton Ath (Free from St Leonards Stamcroft on 5/10/97) P/FL 37 FLC 2 FAC 1 Others 3

Sasa Ilic

IMPEY Andrew (Andy) Rodney
Born: Hammersmith, 13 September 1971
Height: 5'8" Weight: 11.2
International Honours: E: U21-1
Having started last season in such fine form, playing in a new right-sided wing-back role, and showing outstanding form at Nottingham Forest and Newcastle, a shock transfer saw him leave West Ham bound for Leicester in November, amidst controversial circumstances which were well documented at the time. Made a highly promising start in the 1-1 draw at Coventry, but then suffered a thigh strain at Newcastle, an injury which plagued him throughout the campaign. For quite a while he did not seem to be the same player, only occasionally giving glimpses of the pace and ability that everyone knew him to possess. However, gradually showing signs of settling in, especially against Aston Villa at Easter, Andy began to pose a threat to the opposition as 1998-99 drew to a close and obviously looks to extend that into the new term.
Queens Park R (£35,000 from Yeading on 14/6/90) F/PL 177+10/13 FLC 15+1/3 FAC 7+3/1 Others 0+2/1
West Ham U (£1,300,000 on 26/9/97) PL 25+2 FLC 4 FAC 3
Leicester C (£1,600,000 on 25/11/98) PL 17+1 FAC 1

INCE Paul Emerson Carlyle
Born: Ilford, 21 October 1967
Height: 5'11" Weight: 12.2

Club Honours: CS '93, '94; FAC '90, '94; ECW '91; ESC '91; FLC '92; PL '93, '94
International Honours: E: 45; B-1; U21-2; Yth
Into his second campaign with Liverpool in 1998-99, having returned to English football from Inter Milan, it was not one of his or the club's better campaigns. In short, by the Reds' high standards the fans could sense that the team would not be among the top three, and so it proved. As the cousin of Nigel Benn, Britain's former world boxing champion, he was as tigerish as ever, but was unable to make his tackles count as in previous years. And, at the age of 32, it is probably fair to say that he will not improve, but it is also reasonable to assume that any team he turns out for, and that includes the England side, will always find him playing his socks off. At his best, a midfield dynamo who breaks up attacks and gets forward to link up with the front men, his best moment during the season would have to be the home game against Manchester United, one of his former clubs. With Liverpool 2-0 down, and ready to hand over three valuable Premiership points in the tense race for the title, Jamie Redknapp pulled one back with a penalty, before Paul stormed through to equalise with a minute left on the clock. Having taken much stick from the United supporters, there was no doubting his delight.
West Ham U (From apprentice on 18/7/85) FL 66+6/7 FLC 9/3 FAC 8+2/1 Others 4/1
Manchester U (£1,000,000 on 14/9/89) F/PL 203+3/24 FLC 23+1/2 FAC 26+1/1 Others 24/1 (£8,000,000 to Inter Milan on 13/7/95)
Liverpool (£4,200,000 on 22/7/97) PL 65/14 FLC 6/1 FAC 3/1 Others 7/1

INGLEDOW Jamie Graeme
Born: Barnsley, 23 August 1980
Height: 5'6" Weight: 9.7
Another of Rotherham's highly promising youngsters, Jamie surprised a lot of people by starting off last season – his first as a senior pro – as the first-team right-wing back, although he had previously played as a midfielder. Settled in confidently to defy his inexperience, and should be another success from United's youth production line.
Rotherham U (From trainee on 1/7/98) FL 15+6/2 FLC 2 FAC 5 Others 1

INGLETHORPE Alexander (Alex) Matthew
Born: Epsom, 14 November 1971
Height: 5'11" Weight: 11.6
Alex's season at Leyton Orient in 1998-99 was spoilt by injury. Now the club's longest serving player, just when he seemed to get his chance in the team he would pick up another injury, although he still managed to score some vital goals. An attacking midfielder, who has often played up front, and has both pace and skill in abundance, he will be looking to have an injury-free run in the team in 1999-2000.
Watford (From juniors on 1/7/90) FL 2+10/2 FLC 1+2 Others 1+1/1
Barnet (Loaned on 23/3/95) FL 5+1/3
Leyton Orient (Signed on 19/5/95) FL 93+14/30 FLC 5/3 FAC 3+3 Others 3+3/1

INGRAM Stuart Denevan (Denny)
Born: Sunderland, 27 June 1976
Height: 5'10" Weight: 12.1
An adaptable defender or midfielder, and well used to the trials and tribulations of being a Hartlepool player, having been a first teamer for over five years, he was again used, this time in 1998-99, in a variety of positions as circumstances demanded. And again he struggled to get the supporters on his side. Shortly before the transfer deadline, with a move to Hull City looking likely, he persevered and turned in some exemplary performances in a Pool defence that was much improved in the latter weeks of the season.
Hartlepool U (From trainee on 5/7/94) FL 186+6/10 FLC 12+1 FAC 7 Others 8

INGRAM Rae
Born: Manchester, 6 December 1974
Height: 5'11" Weight: 12.8
Rae, one of 14 professionals released by Manchester City in the 1998 close season, was happy to join Macclesfield after his previous successful loan spell there, starting last season as the regular left back, being good on the overlap, and an excellent crosser of the ball. However, he suffered a knee injury during mid September and was out for two weeks and, when fit, he found it difficult to get a regular starting place until an injury in the squad allowed him back in November. He then courageously played through a month in mid term suffering with glandular fever, which turned into the awful debilitating illness, ME. This was a carefully guarded secret within the club until Rae could no longer stand the pain and stress, and it was publicly announced in late April. He is hoping with a careful diet and plenty of rest, to resume playing in the not too distant future.
Manchester C (From trainee on 9/7/93) P/FL 18+5 FLC 1 FAC 4
Macclesfield T (Free on 19/3/98) FL 28+6 FLC 2 FAC 2+1 Others 1

INMAN Niall Edward
Born: Wakefield, 6 February 1978
Height: 5'8" Weight: 11.6
International Honours: Ei: U21-8; Yth
1998-99 was yet another season when this Republic of Ireland U21 international failed to break into the Peterborough senior side on a permanent basis, making just one start and three subs' appearances. A left-sided wide player, with pace, tricks, and good crossing skills, Niall came off the bench three times to get at defenders late in games, and scored in his only start, a 4-2 home defeat at the hands of Rotherham. Still has time on his side.
Peterborough U (From trainee on 3/7/96) FL 6+5/2 FLC 1+1 FAC 0+1

INNES Mark
Born: Glasgow, 27 September 1978
Height: 5'10" Weight: 12.1
Very much a star in the making, Mark burst onto the scene at Oldham in 1998-99 to have a storming last two months, especially valued by a club fighting against relegation right down to the final match. Written up last year as a youngster of some quality, who could also play down the left-hand side, either in a defensive or attacking role, and a good tackler and passer of the ball, the agile midfielder improved two fold thanks to playing alongside John Sheridan. Impressing all who saw him, watch him go in 1999-2000.
Oldham Ath (From trainee on 10/10/95) FL 10+7/1 Others 1

IORFA Dominic
Born: Lagos, Nigeria, 1 October 1968
Height: 6'1" Weight: 12.2
International Honours: Nigeria: 4
Having played for Southend, before leaving at the start of 1996 and going on to appear for a number of sides outside the Football League, Dominic rejoined the club last December on non-contract terms in an attempt to solve United's goalscoring problems. A strong-running forward, with four Nigerian caps to his credit, he came off the bench twice, against Shrewsbury and Carlisle, in January before moving back to non-league football.
Queens Park R (£145,000 from Royal Antwerp on 23/3/90) FL 1+7 FLC 1 (Signed for Galatasaray on 1/12/91)
Peterborough U (Free on 24/10/92) FL 27+33/9 FLC 2+1 FAC 2+2 Others 1/1
Southend U (£15,000 on 3/8/94) FL 5+5/1 FLC 2 Others 0+3
Falkirk (Free on 31/1/96) SL 3+1/1 (Free to Hong Kong during 1996 close season)
Southend U (Free from Billericay on 18/12/98) FL 0+2

IPOUA Gui (Guy)
Born: Douala, Cameroon, 14 January 1976
Height: 6'1" Weight: 12.0
A powerful forward, fluent in four languages, Guy arrived from Spain prior to the start of 1998-99, after making an impression at Bristol Rovers, and being given a one-year contract. The younger brother of Cameroon international, Samuel Ipoua, who played in the 1998 World Cup finals in France, he had previously enjoyed brief spells with Nancy, Turin, Athletico Madrid, Seville, and Alicante, before moving to England. Having scored after coming on as a substitute in the first home match of the season against Reading, following the sale of Barry Hayles he failed to establish himself as Rovers' target man and found it difficult to find the net, scoring just three in 15 full league appearances, before leaving during the summer.
Bristol Rov (Free from Seville on 7/8/98) FL 15+9/3 FLC 1+1 FAC 3+1 Others 1

IROHA Benedict (Ben)
Born: Aloa, Nigeria, 29 November 1969
Height: 5'8" Weight: 11.10
International Honours: Nigeria: 33
Ben, a Nigerian World Cup player, joined Watford on a free transfer from Elche last December and, on making his debut at home to Bristol City, he almost scored an own goal with his first touch. A versatile left-sided player with an excellent long throw, who was used mainly at left back, he showed that he could also play up front, his skill on the ball and eagerness to get forward being impressive. In January he was honoured with a dance of welcome performed by fellow members of the Igbo tribe before the match against WBA. Unfortunately, it brought no luck on the pitch, as Watford went on to lose 2-0. Less exotically, he missed the last three months of the campaign with painful bunions.
Watford (Signed from Elche on 3/12/98) FL 8+2 FAC 1

IRONS Kenneth (Kenny)
Born: Liverpool, 4 November 1970
Height: 5'10" Weight: 12.2
The nearest that Tranmere had to an ever present in 1998-99, Kenny enjoyed his best season so far for the club, every appearance being solid and impressive. As Rovers' captain, and easily their top scorer with 18 goals, he was commanding in his favourite midfield position, often taking responsibility in all areas of the field and never less than influential. His presence was vital to the success of the team, and he provided fire, inspiration, and creativity, in his pivotal role, being named "Man of the Match" on 12 occasions. In the peak form of his career, being Rovers' driving force and the hub of the side's best and most profitable moves, he could never be accused of being speedy, but few read the game better, or provide a better example of a dedicated professional. Stop Press: Was transferred to Huddersfield for £500,000 on 14 June.
Tranmere Rov (From trainee on 9/11/89) FL 313+39/54 FLC 24+7/7 FAC 14+2/3 Others 28+3/3

Kenny Irons

IRVINE Stuart Christopher
Born: Hartlepool, 1 March 1979
Height: 5'9" Weight: 11.10
Young striker who began the 1998-99

season in Hartlepool's first team after being in great goalscoring form during the summer build up. He played several games, despite his magic touch having deserted him, but as the leading goalscorer for the reserves, many thought it would only be a matter of time before he would eventually establish himself at first-team level. Being Hartlepool born he will have been pleased to score in the match against arch-rivals, Darlington, but this was an isolated achievement and, at the end of the season, he was given a free transfer.

Hartlepool U (From trainee on 8/7/97) FL 13+18/2 FLC 1+1 FAC 0+2 Others 0+3

IRWIN Joseph **Denis**
Born: Cork, 31 October 1965
Height: 5'8" Weight: 11.0
Club Honours: CS '93, '96, '97; ECWC '91; ESC '91; FLC '92; PL '93, '94, '96, '97, '99; FAC '94, '96; EC '99
International Honours: Ei: 51; B-1; U23-1; U21-3; Yth; Sch
A highly experienced Manchester United defender, who is a model of consistency, and a specialist goalscorer from set-plays, Denis was a regular first teamer throughout the early stages of last season, playing in ten of United's opening 11 games before a knee injury ruled him out for most of October. Despite that set back, he returned to play a major role in United's quest for the treble, netting important penalties against Liverpool in the Premiership in September, Middlesbrough in the FA Cup in January, and Liverpool again in May. Unfortunately, he was also red carded in that latter match against Liverpool, which ruled him out of the FA Cup final. With so many youngsters vying for his place in the side, one would have expected him to be a worried man, but he actually relished the challenge. Although it cut deep into his pride when it appeared he was being kept at the back of the queue for a new contract, he was given a one-year extension in January and, despite a host of glittering honours under his wing during nine highly-successful years at Old Trafford, he was delighted to add European Cup and Premier League winners medals to the pile come the end of the club's best-ever season. Was one of five United players selected by his fellow professionals for the PFA award-winning Premiership side. Also played three times for the Republic of Ireland.

Leeds U (From apprentice on 3/11/83) FL 72/1 FLC 5 FAC 3 Others 2
Oldham Ath (Free on 22/5/86) FL 166+1/4 FLC 19/3 FAC 13 Others 5
Manchester U (£625,000 on 20/6/90) F/PL 301+9/19 FLC 28+3 FAC 41+1/7 Others 51/2

IVERSON Steffen
Born: Oslo, Norway, 10 November 1976
Height: 6'1" Weight: 11.10
Club Honours: FLC '99
This extremely agile and tenacious Spurs' striker opened his account in 1998-99 with a goal in his first appearance of the season, at home to Leeds in September. Having been out for most of the previous campaign,

Steffen looked lean and ambitious, even if not fully match fit. After scoring both goals in the 2-0 home win over Newcastle in October he appeared to be back to his best, effortlessly unleashing powerful shots at goal, and gracefully controlling the ball with his first touch. When Wimbledon and Tottenham seemed to be playing each other every week as FA Cup and Worthington Cup fixtures piled up, it was Steffen who took the club back to Wembley after a nine-year absence, scoring the only goal, an exquisite 25-yard chip in the 1-0 Worthington Cup semi-final victory at Selhurst Park. During a season which underlined his value to the club, he is sure to be a part of George Graham's long-term plans at Tottenham.

Tottenham H (£2,700,000 from Rosenborg, via Nationalkam, on 7/12/96) PL 46+10/15 FLC 6/2 FAC 5+2/2

IZZET Mustafa (Muzzy) Kemmel
Born: Mile End, 31 October 1974
Height: 5'10" Weight: 10.12
Club Honours: FLC '97
The right-footed Leicester midfielder showed outstanding form during the first half of last season, being touted as a possible England international, but the call eluded him. Whilst forming a highly influential midfield partnership with Neil Lennon, and occasionally operating as an emergency striker during times of injury crisis, Muzzy retained the knack of scoring spectacular goals, none more so than his acrobatic volley from outside the box to clinch a home victory over Tottenham on a highly emotional Monday night, when the crowd

were demonstrating for Martin O'Neill to remain at Filbert Street. No less brilliant was his controlled but instinctive volley over Nigel Martyn to turn the Worthington Cup-tie against Leeds a few weeks later, before a hamstring injury curtailed his appearances towards the end of the campaign.

Chelsea (From trainee on 19/5/93)
Leicester C (£650,000 + on 28/3/96) P/FL 109+2/13 FLC 13/2 FAC 7 Others 5

Muzzy Izzet

Steffen Iverson

PFA Enterprises Ltd
2 Oxford Court
Bishopsgate
Manchester
M2 3WQ

Tel: 0161 228 2733
Fax: 0161 236 4496
email: gberry@thepfa.co.uk

* * * * *

Football in the Community
11 Oxford Court
Bishopsgate
Manchester
M2 3WQ

Tel: 0161 236 0583
Fax: 0161 236 4459

* * * * *

F.F.E. & V.T.S. Ltd
2 Oxford Court
Bishopsgate
Manchester
M2 3WQ

Tel: 0161 236 0637
Fax: 0161 228 7229

JAASKELAINEN Juusi
Born: Vaasa, Finland, 19 April 1975
Height: 6'3" Weight: 12.10
International Honours: Finland: 1

Having signed for Bolton from VPS Vaasa in November 1997, the goalkeeper was unexpectedly thrown into first-team action at the start of last season, following Keith Branagan's ligament problem, and played for the majority of the campaign. Proving himself to be a promising young 'keeper, in giving some assured displays, Jussi produced some fine performances for Wanderers, especially in the nine-match spell in the early part of this year when he kept six clean sheets. The rigours of his first full season seemed to catch up with him in the latter stages, and his form deserted him, prompting Colin Todd to buy extra cover in the form of Steve Banks. An excellent shot stopper, the Finnish international should relish the challenge.
Bolton W (£100,000 + from VPS Vassa, via MPS, on 14/11/97) FL 34 FLC 5 FAC 1

JACK Rodney Alphonso
Born: Kingstown, St Vincent, 28 September 1972
Height: 5'7" Weight: 10.9
International Honours: St Vincent

A record signing from Torquay a week into 1998-99, Rodney quickly became a firm favourite with the Crewe fans after scoring twice in a 2-0 Worthington Cup home win over Oldham on his first-team debut. Although he went without a goal for considerable periods he was always likely to strike spectacularly and, in a difficult season, two in a 2-2 draw at Barnsley, another brace in a 3-1 win at Bolton, and the first in a 2-1 victory at Swindon were his most vital. Speedy and skilful, and capped for St Vincent – his place of birth – he can be used to good effect either through the middle or out wide, where his pace takes him into dangerous positions.
Torquay U (Free from Lambada, St Vincent on 10/10/95) FL 82+5/24 FLC 6/1 FAC 6 Others 6/3
Crewe Alex (£650,000 on 14/8/98) FL 37+2/9 FLC 2/2 FAC 1

JACKSON Darren
Born: Edinburgh, 25 July 1966
Height: 5'10" Weight: 11.0
Club Honours: SPL '98
International Honours: S: 28; B-1

The Scottish international striker came on a three-month loan to Coventry last November, having lost form and confidence at Glasgow Celtic only months after playing for his country in the 1998 World Cup. At a time when City had fears that Dion Dublin could not be adequately replaced, Darren gave Gordon Strachan another option. In the event, Noel Whelan and Darren Huckerby rose to the occasion and the Scot spent most

of his time with the club on the bench. Although he was only called upon three times, he left the club with his confidence restored and, after an abortive trial in China, he transferred to Hearts, where he won a first-team place.
Meadowbank Thistle (From Broxburn Amateurs on 24/5/85) SL 45+3/22 SLC 2/1 SC 2+1/1
Newcastle U (£70,000 on 13/10/86) FL 53+16/7 FLC 5/1 FAC 5/1 Others 2
Dundee U (Signed on 16/12/88) SL 79+8/30 SLC 6/3 SC 11+1/3 Others 4/1
Hibernian (Signed on 14/7/92) SL 160+12/50 SLC 12+1/3 SC 16/3 Others 2/1
Glasgow Celtic (Signed on 14/7/97) SL 13+16/3 SLC 3/1 SC 0+3/1 Others 5+6/2
Coventry C (Loaned on 20/11/98) PL 0+3

JACKSON Elliot
Born: Swindon, 27 August 1977
Height: 6'2" Weight: 15.2

Elliot did not get too many chances to impress at Oxford in 1998-99, but many thought that he kept goal well when pitched into the club's FA Cup-ties. He had a rare league appearance on the sale of Phil Whitehead, but after an indifferent game against Bradford he was replaced by the loan 'keeper, Paul Gerrard, who was cup-tied. This gave the youngster some action, and he impressed in the three games he got, two of them against Chelsea, before ending the campaign on loan at Stevenage and given a free in the summer clear out.
Oxford U (From trainee on 2/7/96) FL 7 FLC 3 FAC 3

Justin Jackson

JACKSON Justin Jonathan
Born: Nottingham, 10 December 1974
Height: 6'0" Weight: 11.6
Club Honours: Div 3 '98

Although Sam Allardyce gave Justin an opportunity to prove himself as a striker when Notts County were desperate for goals in 1998-99, he was eventually allowed to go

to Rotherham on loan in January, and then permanently to Halifax (February) after not scoring for the Magpies at all last season in 15 appearances. Having arrived at Rotherham to plug a striker's injury crisis, he played just two matches, scoring on his debut in a 4-2 win at Halifax, before moving to the Shay less than two weeks later. Settling in well with his new club, he scored three goals in the last five games, which included a stunner in the 1-0 home win over Brighton. With pace his major asset, allied to tireless running, there was no doubt that at this level he can get at defences.
Notts Co (£30,000 from Woking on 26/9/97) FL 7+18/1 FAC 3+2 Others 1
Rotherham U (Loaned on 21/1/99) FL 2/1
Halifax T (£30,000 on 11/2/99) FL 16/3

JACKSON Mark Graham
Born: Barnsley, 30 September 1977
Height: 6'0" Weight: 11.12
International Honours: E: Yth

Unable to get a game in the very successful young Leeds' side that finished fourth in the Premiership, Mark was loaned out to Huddersfield last October in a move to give him match practice. Arriving at Town as defensive cover, and making five starts before going back to Elland Road, he showed both his class and his battling qualities, never afraid to launch himself into the tackle, while passing the ball well out of defence. A useful youngster to have on your staff, he can perform equally well in the centre of the defence or in midfield.
Leeds U (From trainee on 1/7/95) PL 11+8 FAC 4
Huddersfield T (Loaned on 29/10/98) FL 5

JACKSON Matthew (Matt) Alan
Born: Leeds, 19 October 1971
Height: 6'1" Weight: 12.12
Club Honours: FAC '95
International Honours: E: U21-10; Sch

Norwich City's captain once again, in 1998-99, proved himself to be a central defender with the ability to remain calm even in the tensest of occasions. A consistent performer, Matt is excellent in the air, competing with the biggest of strikers and winning his fair share. He also reads the game very well, making interceptions look so easy, and snuffing out opposition attacks before they have really begun. A red card shown to him in last November's home match against Wolves was later rescinded when video evidence cleared him of stamping on full-back Lee Nayor.
Luton T (From juniors on 4/7/90) FL 7+2 FLC 2 Others 0+1
Preston NE (Loaned on 27/3/91) FL 3+1 Others 1
Everton (£600,000 on 18/10/91) F/PL 132+6/4 FLC 9 FAC 14/2 Others 4
Charlton Ath (Loaned on 26/3/96) FL 8 Others 2
Queens Park R (Loaned on 20/8/96) FL 7
Birmingham C (Loaned on 31/10/96) FL 10
Norwich C (£450,000 on 24/12/96) FL 94+3/6 FLC 3 FAC 3

JACKSON Michael James
Born: Runcorn, 4 December 1973
Height: 6'0" Weight: 13.8
Club Honours: Div 2 '97
International Honours: E: Yth

Outstanding in the centre of Preston's defence for all of last season, where his coolness, powerful heading, and superbly timed tackles were a real asset to the promotion push, Michael could easily play at a higher level. Finally finding his goalscoring range, he became a potent threat, scoring all of his goals from free kicks or corners. Now a senior pro' at the club, he reached 250 senior and 200 league games during the season, being unavailable for few matches (through suspension), when his organisational skills were definitely missed by his defensive colleagues.

Crewe Alex (From trainee on 29/7/92) FL 5 FLC 1 FAC 1 Others 2
Bury (Free on 13/8/93) FL 123+2/9 FLC 9/1 FAC 3 Others 12
Preston NE (£125,000 on 26/3/97) FL 90+1/10 FLC 6 FAC 6 Others 8

JACKSON Richard
Born: Whitby, 18 April 1980
Height: 5'8" Weight: 10.12
An exciting young right back who came up through the ranks at Scarborough to claim a regular first-team place in 1998-99, his consistent and promising displays soon brought him to the notice of Derby's Jim Smith, who offered him a contract after impressing in trials at Pride Park. Tipped as a player to watch for, he immediately earned himself a place on the County bench for several of the latter games, and came close to getting a call up.

Scarborough (From trainee on 27/3/98) FL 21+1 FLC 2
Derby Co (£30,000 + on 25/3/99)

JACOBS Wayne Graham
Born: Sheffield, 3 February 1969
Height: 5'9" Weight: 11.2
Although Bradford's longest serving player, Wayne was out of the starting line-up for the first six games of 1998-99, but injuries to Lee Todd and John Dreyer gave him his chance. A regular from then on, apart from figuring at left back, he also played on the left-hand side of midfield and was just as consistent. Loves to go on runs down the wing to get his crosses in, and is usually involved in the taking of free kicks and corners, the team benefiting from his strong and accurate left foot.

Sheffield Wed (From apprentice on 3/1/87) FL 5+1 FLC 3 Others 1
Hull C (£27,000 on 25/3/88) FL 127+2/4 FLC 7 FAC 8 Others 6
Rotherham U (Free on 5/8/93) FL 40+2/2 FLC 4 FAC 1 Others 2
Bradford C (Free on 5/8/94) FL 181+4/9 FLC 14 FAC 10/2 Others 5

JACOBSEN Anders
Born: Norway, 18 April 1969
Height: 6'3" Weight: 13.7
International Honours: Norway: 4
The big, strong and experienced Norwegian centre back joined Sheffield United last December for a small fee from IK Start, where he had been captain, making his debut as a late substitute against Notts County in the FA Cup. His first start was against Norwich and, although he took time

to adjust, he showed himself to be a solid and reliable defender who had a good turn of speed when necessary. Out of contract during the summer, he quickly improved with experience of the English game.

Sheffield U (Signed from IK Start on 24/12/98) FL 8+4 FAC 0+1

JAGIELKA Stephen (Steve)
Born: Manchester, 10 March 1978
Height: 5'8" Weight: 11.5
A striker in his second season at Shrewsbury in 1998-99, Steve followed much the same pattern as his first, alternating between the starting line-up and the bench. Very fast and tireless, and a prolific scorer in the reserves, he just failed to realise that potential in the first team, having to wait until April for his first goal of the season.

Stoke C (From trainee on 15/7/96)
Shrewsbury T (Free on 30/7/97) FL 17+30/2 FLC 2+2 FAC 1 Others 0+1

JAMES David Benjamin
Born: Welwyn Garden City, 1 August 1970
Height: 6'5" Weight: 14.5
Club Honours: FAYC '89; FLC '95
International Honours: E: 1; B-1; U21-10; Yth
1998-99 was yet another season in which Liverpool supporters saw both sides of David's enigmatic character. On his day, a 'keeper of the highest quality, and a magnificent shot-stopper, his vital stops at crucial moments in some games saved several points. However, on the other hand, his rushes of blood occasionally let points slip away, often against teams of lower ability. Despite that, some supporters feel that he is harshly blamed for the shortcomings of a poor back four, but still needs to develop greater self belief to go with his natural talent. Stop Press: Signed for Aston Villa on 17 June, a fee of £1.7 million securing him as a replacement for Mark Bosnich.

Watford (From trainee on 1/7/88) FL 89 FLC 6 FAC 2 Others 1
Liverpool (£1,000,000 on 6/7/92) PL 213+1 FLC 22 FAC 19 Others 22

JAMES Lutel Malik
Born: Manchester, 2 June 1972
Height: 5'9" Weight: 11.0
International Honours: St Kitts & Nevis: 3
Having previously been discarded by Scarborough and playing non-league football with Hyde United in recent seasons, the pint-sized striker was given a second chance in the Football League by Bury boss, Neil Warnock, when he was handed a professional contract last October. After just one reserve game for the Shakers, he found himself making his debut for Bury in the Worthington Cup – against Manchester United at Old Trafford – before starting ten games for Bury, terrifying many defenders with his pace, and scoring two goals for the club, his first coming in a game at Sheffield United in November. In April he gained international recognition for the first time, playing three games for St Kitts & Nevis.

Scarborough (Free from Yorkshire Amateurs on 22/2/93) FL 0+6 (Free to Guiseley during 1993 close season)
Bury (Free from Hyde U on 26/10/98) FL 10+7/2 FLC 0+1

JANSEN Matthew (Matt) Brooke
Born: Carlisle, 20 October 1977
Height: 5'11" Weight: 10.13
Club Honours: AMC '97
International Honours: E: U21-5; Yth
A classy England U21 international striker, Matt scored Crystal Palace's opening goal of last season, and added six more before Blackburn secured his services in January, in a transfer induced by Palace's financial difficulties. Quickly introduced to Premiership football by Brian Kidd, a superb volley on his Rovers' debut opened his scoring account, and his quick darts, feints, and mazy dribbling brought him much attention. Like a lot of goalscorers he is obsessive about opportunities, and his two goals against Wimbledon were classic poached goals, following up broken play. However, within a fortnight he had to undergo cartilage surgery but, rehabilitating well, he will undoubtedly be a threat this coming campaign. Once his play becomes more polished, a great future could be in store for him.

Carlisle U (From trainee on 18/1/96) FL 26+16/10 FLC 4+1/3 FAC 1+3 Others 3+3
Crystal Palace (£1,000,000 + on 12/2/98) P/FL 23+3/10 FLC 4 FAC 0+1
Blackburn Rov (£4,100,000 on 19/1/99) PL 10+1/3

JANSSON Jan
Born: Kalmar, Sweden, 26 January 1968
Height: 5'10" Weight: 12.4
International Honours: Sweden: 7
A skilful Port Vale midfielder whose season in 1998-99 hardly began due to a succession of niggling injuries, he started the campaign in the team before the first injury struck after just four games and he was not seen again until just before Christmas, when helping the team to a crucial victory over Bury. He also played in what proved to be John Rudge's final game, against Swindon, before the new boss, Brian Horton, freed him a month later in February, and after a trial at Walsall he returned to his native Sweden with Norrkoping.

Port Vale (£200,000 from Norrkoping on 4/11/96) FL 37+14/6 FLC 2+1 FAC 1

JARMAN Lee
Born: Cardiff, 16 December 1977
Height: 6'3" Weight: 13.3
International Honours: W: U21-9; Yth
Rated by his former manager, Kenny Hibbitt, as the "best footballer at Ninian Park", Cardiff-born "Jamma" undoubtedly has real ability with his right foot, but new manager, Frank Burrows, spent hours working on his heading ability, aggression, and defensive duties. If he sticks with it and continues to learn under Burrows, Lee has the ability to make the grade despite a disappointing 1998-99. The talented right back is a player who could well break through in the Second Division this coming

term. Having represented Wales at under 21 level, the talented right back could well break through this coming term.

Cardiff C (From trainee on 23/8/95) FL 78+15/1 FLC 3+1 FAC 3+3/1 Others 5+2

JARRETT Jason Lee Mee
Born: Bury, 14 September 1979
Height: 6'0" Weight: 12.4
As a first-year Blackpool professional, having come through the club's junior ranks, Jason made his first-team debut when coming off the bench in the losing FA Cup-tie at Wigan last season. Recognised as one for the future, the young midfielder made only the odd senior appearance from then on but, in starring for the reserve team, had the aplomb to notch two penalties at Rotherham.

Blackpool (From trainee on 3/7/98) FL 2 FAC 0+1 Others 1

JASZCZUN Antony (Tommy) John
Born: Kettering, 16 September 1977
Height: 5'10" Weight: 10.10
Having come through the Aston Villa junior ranks to turn professional in the 1996 close season, Tommy then had to wait patiently in the wings before receiving a first-team opportunity, which he did in 1998-99. After sitting on the subs' bench for a number of games, he eventually got the call at Stamford Bridge in October when coming on for the final 16 minutes of the 4-1 Worthington Cup defeat at the hands of Chelsea. Predominantly a defender, he played in the left-wing-back position, showing himself to be a fair crosser of the ball and good in recovery. Looking to be one for the future, he is quoted as saying: "My strengths are hard work, being able to get up and down the pitch, and passing the ball".

Aston Villa (From trainee on 5/7/96) FLC 0+1

JEAN Earl Jude
Born: St Lucia, 9 October 1971
Height: 5'8" Weight: 11.4
International Honours: St Lucia: 4
Earl left Plymouth near the end of the 1998-99 campaign, having had plenty of offers from abroad to continue his career. Although the West Indian started the season as Argyle's first-choice striker, he found goals hard to come by after scoring three times in the opening six matches, and he appeared to lose confidence. However, surprisingly good in the air for a small forward, his approach play allowed others into the game.

Ipswich T (Free from Uniao de Coimbra Felgueiras on 6/12/96) FL 0+1
Rotherham U (Free on 23/1/97) FL 7+11/6
Plymouth Arg (Free on 7/8/97) FL 37+28/7 FLC 3/1 FAC 6/1 Others 1+1

JEANNE Leon Charles
Born: Cardiff, 17 January 1980
Height: 5'8" Weight: 10.10
International Honours: W: U21-3; Yth
Leon is another of the young players that have made it to the Queens Park Rangers first team from the successful Academy scheme. The young forward made his debut

last February as a substitute against Watford, and his performance was such that he won a place in the starting line-up for the next match before being named "Man of the Match" in the following two fixtures. Playing for the Welsh U21 side in their match against Portugal in November, he became yet another player to suffer a serious injury which kept him out of football for a month. Was named the "First Division Player of the Month" for March.

Queens Park R (From trainee on 18/11/97) FL 7+3

JEFFERS Francis
Born: Liverpool, 25 January 1981
Height: 5'10" Weight: 10.7
Club Honours: FAYC '98
International Honours: E: Yth; Sch
A young striker with a predatory eye for goal, who had made just one subs' appearance for Everton in 1997-98, Francis enjoyed an outstanding fuller introduction to the English Premiership in 1998-99. Not blessed with burning acceleration, and still filling out physically, the youngster more than made up for those deficiencies with the intelligence of his runs up front, and the quality of his finishing. Given a full Premiership debut in a televised match at Derby County in February, he saw a debut strike snatched off his toes by team-mate Nick Barmby. However, he made up for that with a goal on his home debut seven days later and never looked back, ending the season as second top scorer with seven goals, and being rewarded for his endeavours with a call up to the full England squad for a trip to Hungary in April. The quality of one performance, at home to Charlton, had the BBC analyst, Alan Hansen, comparing the young striker to Dennis Bergkamp! There seems to be no doubt that he is clearly set for a big future in the game.

Everton (From trainee on 20/2/98) PL 11+5/6 FAC 2/1

JEMSON Nigel Bradley
Born: Hutton, 10 August 1969
Height: 5'11" Weight: 12.10
Club Honours: FLC '90; AMC '96
International Honours: E: U21-1
A proven goalscorer throughout his career, Nigel's spell so far at Bury has been both frustrating and unproductive – with just one penalty to show in his first two seasons at Gigg Lane. He seldom looked like working his way into Neil Warnock's plans during 1998-99, but did get an extended run of four games in January. Having spent much of the campaign on the transfer list, he turned down offers to join both Halifax Town and Hull City on loan, and so found himself playing Pontins League football once again.

Preston NE (From trainee on 6/7/87) FL 28+4/8 FAC 2/1 Others 5+1/5
Nottingham F (£150,000 on 24/3/88) FL 45+2/13 FLC 9/4 FAC 3+1/3 Others 1
Bolton W (Loaned on 23/12/88) FL 4+1
Preston NE (Loaned on 15/3/89) FL 6+3/2 Others 2/1
Sheffield Wed (£800,000 on 17/9/91) F/PL 26+25/9 FLC 3+4 FAC 3+3/1 Others 2+2/1

Grimsby T (Loaned on 10/9/93) FL 6/2 Others 1
Notts Co (£300,000 on 8/9/94) FL 7+7/1 FLC 2+2/1 Others 1
Watford (Loaned on 12/1/95) FL 3+1
Rotherham U (Loaned on 15/2/96) FL 16/5 Others 3/4
Oxford U (£60,000 on 23/7/96) FL 68/27 FLC 12/6 FAC 2
Bury (£100,000 on 5/2/98) FL 17+12/1 FLC 0+2 FAC 0+1

JENKINS Jamie
Born: Pontypool, 1 January 1979
Height: 5'8" Weight: 10.7
Having turned professional for Bournemouth in the 1997 close season, Jamie finally made his league debut for the Cherries when coming on as a substitute against Stoke, his only appearance of the campaign. A product of the club's youth policy, who plays in midfield, he is full of running and has good pace. Was surprisingly released during the summer.

Bournemouth (From trainee on 7/7/97) FL 0+1

JENKINS Lee David
Born: Pontypool, 28 June 1979
Height: 5'9" Weight: 11.0
International Honours: W: U21-1; Yth; Sch
Lee showed signs last season that he was recovering the form of two years ago when he made his senior debut for Swansea at the age of 17. A versatile youngster who can play at wing back or in midfield, he was a regular inclusion in the first team in 1998-99, and was selected for the Welsh U21 squad to play Italy last season at Wrexham.

Swansea C (From trainee on 20/12/96) FL 41+14/2 FLC 0+1 FAC 1+1 Others 4

JENKINS Stephen (Steve) Matthew
Born: Bristol, 2 January 1980
Height: 6'1" Weight: 13.0
Yet to be given an opportunity for Southampton after coming through the junior ranks, the left-sided defender was loaned to Brentford on transfer deadline day, making his debut as a late substitute at Hartlepool in place of Andy Scott. A promising youngster, he seems sure to build on the experience.

Southampton (From trainee on 16/1/98)
Brentford (Loaned on 25/3/99) FL 0+1

JENKINS Stephen (Steve) Robert
Born: Merthyr, 16 July 1972
Height: 5'11" Weight: 12.3
Club Honours: AMC '94
International Honours: W: 12; U21-2; Yth
The Welsh international enjoyed his best season with Huddersfield in 1998-99, giving solid and lively performances throughout, and even sendings off against Port Vale and Bradford failed to blight his contributions. A hard-working right back who pushes forward with purpose and crosses well, he clocked up his 100th appearance for the club at Tranmere, wearing the captain's arm band, and promptly led the Terriers to the top of the First Division. Rewarded with a superb volleyed goal against Stockport at the McAlpine, a further reward was his continued involvement with the Welsh national side. Unbelievably, he was called

into the Welsh squad on three separate occasions and made captain of the "B" team, only to miss them all due to injury problems.

Swansea C (From trainee on 1/7/90) FL 155+10/1 FLC 12+1 FAC 10+1 Others 26
Huddersfield T (£275,000 on 3/11/95) FL 128+1/3 FLC 13 FAC 11

JENKINSON Leigh
Born: Thorne, 9 July 1969
Height: 6'0" Weight: 12.2
International Honours: W: B-1

A tricky left winger recruited by Wigan from St Johnstone in the 1998 close season. After starting the campaign as a first-team regular, and playing in the opening four matches of 1998-99, he found opportunities limited following a change to the wing-back formation. And, after failing to settle, Leigh returned north of the border to join Scottish Premier League outfit, Hearts, at the end of December.

Hull C (From trainee on 15/6/87) FL 95+35/13 FLC 7+2 FAC 6+1 Others 9+2/1
Rotherham U (Loaned on 13/9/90) FL 5+2
Coventry C (£300,000 on 12/3/93) PL 22+10/1 FLC 0+1 FAC 3
Birmingham C (Loaned on 1/11/93) FL 2+1
St Johnstone (Signed on 8/12/95) SL 56+11/11 SLC 1 SC 6 Others 2
Wigan Ath (Free on 31/7/98) FL 3+4 FLC 3 FAC 0+1 Others 0+1

JENSEN Claus William
Born: Nykobing, Demark, 29 April 1977
Height: 5'11" Weight: 12.6

Claus joined Bolton in July 1998 from Danish club, Lyngby, having scored 11 goals and finished as their top scorer – an impressive return for a midfielder, and one which surely prompted Colin Todd to reach for the cheque book. Claus started last season in the centre of midfield with Per Frandsen, and continued in that vein for the rest of the campaign, missing only two league games in the process. A supremely gifted player with great technical ability, his pairing with Frandsen looking a formidable one, his one shortfall last season was that he did not score as many goals as he would have liked. However, if he carries on playing with the style and confidence which he showed in 1998-99 then he will surely rectify that record during the new season. A Danish U21 international, he will certainly be a name to watch in the future.

Bolton W (£1,600,000 from Lyngby, via Naestued, on 14/7/98) FL 44/2 FLC 6/2 FAC 1 Others 3

JEPSON Ronald (Ronnie) Francis
Born: Stoke, 12 May 1963
Height: 6'1" Weight: 13.7
Club Honours: Div 2 '97

A veteran striker who had often been bad news for Burnley – he scored against them for four former clubs – he finally arrived at Turf Moor in the 1998 close season on a free from Oldham. After impressing, usually in a prompting role behind the main strikers in the early games, a calf injury ruled him out for four months, but on his return he proved a valuable sub, often breathing new life into a jaded side. He certainly contributed a few

points to the side, despite not finding the net himself until scoring the winner in the safety-clinching home win against Fulham. Out of contract during the summer, at the time of going to press the club were known to have made an offer of re-engagement.

Port Vale (Free from Nantwich T on 23/3/89) FL 12+10 FLC 1+1 FAC 1+1
Peterborough U (Loaned on 25/1/90) FL 18/5
Preston NE (£80,000 on 12/2/91) FL 36+2/8 FLC 2 Others 3/4
Exeter C (£60,000 on 29/7/92) FL 51+3/21 FLC 6/2 FAC 3/1 Others 4/1
Huddersfield T (£80,000 on 7/12/93) FL 95+12/36 FLC 6+1/2 FAC 4/3 Others 6/1
Bury (£40,000 on 27/7/96) FL 31+16/9 FLC 7/1 FAC 0+3 Others 1+1/2
Oldham Ath (£30,000 on 16/1/98) FL 9/4
Burnley (Free on 29/7/98) FL 3+12/1 FLC 2

JERMYN Mark Stephen
Born: West Germany, 16 April 1981
Height: 6'0" Weight: 11.6

A second year Torquay YTS central defender, Mark made just one substitute appearance against Halifax, when coming on for the last 18 minutes at Plainmoor last March, but his pace and strength in the tackle saw him rewarded with a full pro contract during the summer. Looks to be an excellent prospect.

Torquay U (Trainee) FL 0+1

JEVONS Philip
Born: Liverpool, 1 August 1979
Height: 5'11" Weight: 11.10
Club Honours: FAYC '98

As top scorer in Everton's reserve team in 1998-99, Philip was rewarded and enjoyed his only Premiership outing when coming off the bench after 18 minutes to perform on the right of midfield. A tall, rangy front runner with superb finishing skills, the youngster saw his first-team chances limited last season by the progress of Francis Jeffers, but will be hoping for more opportunities in 1999-2000.

Everton (From trainee on 10/11/97) PL 0+1

JIHAI Sun
Born: China, 30 September 1977
Height: 5'10" Weight: 10.7
International Honours: China: 10

Along with Fan Zhiyi, he became the first Chinese international to play in the Football League after signing for Crystal Palace from Dalian Wanda last September. Terry Venables, the then Palace manager, had spotted the pair playing for China in the World Cup qualifiers when he was in charge of the Australian national side. A strong-tackling defender, who preferred being at left back from where he could get forward, he made his first-team debut in the Worthington Cup match at Bury, having waited a month for his work permit. Unfortunately, he missed a fair amount of games before Christmas due to suspensions and international call-ups, but was a virtual ever present towards the end of the campaign as the club fought for financial survival.

Crystal Palace (£500,000 from Dalian Wanda on 10/9/98) FL 22+1 FLC 1 FAC 1

JOACHIM Julian Kevin
Born: Boston, 20 September 1974
Height: 5'6" Weight: 12.2
International Honours: E: U21-9; Yth (UEFAC '93)

Following the departure of Dwight Yorke early on last season, and the problems surrounding Stan Collymore, Julian gained himself a regular place at Aston Villa and celebrated with goals. With the exception of just nine games, the high-scoring forward featured in all of Villa's starting line-ups, and came off the bench eight times to finish the campaign as the club's leading goalscorer. Having waited patiently for his chance, his main strength was undoubtedly his lightning pace, and his ability to take advantage of it when running at defenders and causing them all kinds of problems. Although he often had to adjust to a different strike partnership throughout the campaign, ending it with Dion Dublin, he gave many brilliant displays and put himself in line for an England call up. As Villa supporters' "Player of the Season", watch out for him and Dublin this time round.

Leicester C (From trainee on 15/9/92) F/PL 77+22/25 FLC 7+2/3 FAC 4+1/1 Others 4+2/2
Aston Villa (£1,500,000 on 24/2/96) PL 52+36/27 FLC 2 FAC 4+1/1 Others 5+1/1

Julian Joachim

JOBLING Kevin Andrew
Born: Sunderland, 1 January 1968
Height: 5'9" Weight: 12.0
Club Honours: AMC '98
Signed from Grimsby in the summer of 1998 after 11 seasons at the club, following an indifferent start at Shrewsbury Kevin settled into the midfield well and became captain in March when Paul Evans left for Brentford. Quickly became Town's long-throw man, which led to more than one goal, and while not too prolific in front of goal himself he proved to have a good shot when he used it.
Leicester C (From apprentice on 9/1/86) FL 4+5 FAC 0+1 Others 3/2
Grimsby T (Signed on 19/2/88) FL 251+34/10 FLC 13+4/1 FAC 10+3/2 Others 7+7
Scunthorpe U (Loaned on 10/1/94) Others 1
Shrewsbury T (Free on 29/7/98) FL 41/1 FLC 2/1 Others 1

JOHANSEN Michael Bro
Born: Glostrup, Denmark, 22 July 1972
Height: 5'6" Weight: 10.5
Club Honours: Div 1 '97
Probably Bolton's most cheerful player (if not the league's), who always plays the game with a wide smile on his face, he made the right-wing position his own last season, after his sporadic appearances in the previous Premiership season. His mazy runs caused all sorts of problems for opposing left backs and it is fair to say that Michael enjoyed his best time since joining the club. Playing with such enthusiasm and confidence, he also achieved an impressive goals tally of nine in all competitions, the highlights being his two fine goals in the 4-0 win over local rivals, Bury, especially the supreme individual effort in which Michael beat almost half of the Shakers' team before slotting the ball into the net. Also, one would find it difficult to forget his goal in the 1-0 defeat of Ipswich in the first leg of the First Division play-off semi final, which proved vital in getting Wanderers to Wembley.
Bolton W (£1,250,000 from FC Copenhagen, via KB Copenhagen and B1903, on 14/8/96) F/PL 68+24/13 FLC 8+3/1 FAC 2+1 Others 3/1

JOHNROSE Leonard (Lenny)
Born: Preston, 29 November 1969
Height: 5'10" Weight: 12.6
Club Honours: Div 2 '97
An important and immediate choice in Bury's first team for the past six seasons, Lenny had clearly become unhappy at Gigg Lane by the time that he left the club to join Burnley in February. His form had dipped dramatically with rumours rife for weeks that former boss, Stan Ternent, was once again about to swoop on Gigg Lane and carry away the midfield battler. His early season form had been as consistent as ever, and he had also managed to conjure up four goals – including two in the home Worthington Cup-tie against Crystal Palace. Joining an already sizeable contingent of ex-Bury players at Turf Moor, despite being sent off in his second game he became a

regular in Clarets' midfield, basically working hard and trying to push forward at every opportunity. Scored his first goal in a 3-1 win against Colchester.
Blackburn Rov (From trainee on 16/6/88) FL 20+22/11 FLC 2+1/1 FAC 0+3 Others 2
Preston NE (Loaned on 21/1/92) FL 1+2/1
Hartlepool U (£50,000 on 28/2/92) FL 59+7/11 FLC 5+1/4 FAC 5/1 Others 5
Bury (Signed on 7/12/93) FL 181+7/20 FLC 16+2/2 FAC 9/1 Others 9/1
Burnley (£225,000 on 12/2/99) FL 9+3/1

JOHNSEN Jean Ronny
Born: Norway, 10 June 1969
Height: 6'2" Weight: 13.2
Club Honours: PL '97, '99; CS '97; FAC '99; EC '99
International Honours: Norway: 41
A classy midfielder, or central defender, the Norwegian international made an excellent start to 1998-99, playing in Manchester United's opening six games before sustaining an ankle injury after scoring against Coventry at Old Trafford in September. Returning to action at the start of December, he netted two goals in the Reds' 3-0 demolition of Nottingham Forest on Boxing Day, until more injuries ruled him out until February. Making his third comeback of the season against Derby in the Premiership at the start of that month, he played a major role in United's quest for the treble, and was delighted to be the proud possessor of European Cup, FA Cup, and Premier League winners medals come the end of the club's most successful season ever. An outstanding performer alongside Jaap Stam, and a wonderfully gifted player when on the top of his form, he is now hopeful that his injury problems are well and truly behind him.
Manchester U (£1,200,000 from Besiktas, via Lyn and Lillestrom, on 26/7/96) PL 63+12/5 FLC 2 FAC 8+2/1 Others 22+2/1

JOHNSON Alan Keith
Born: Wigan, 19 February 1971
Height: 6'0" Weight: 12.0
After missing the whole of the previous season through injury, the hard man got himself fit in time for the opening of Rochdale's 1998-99 campaign, before being hit by a string of further niggling injuries. When on song, Alan, his old partner Keith Hill, and new signing Mark Monington, provided a formidable central defensive barrier to opposing forwards, but, unfortunately, a knee injury necessitated another long spell of rehabilitation at Lilleshall at the turn of the year, and he was released during the summer.
Wigan Ath (From trainee on 1/4/89) FL 163+17/13 FLC 7+2/2 FAC 14+2/1 Others 14+3/3
Lincoln C (Signed on 15/2/94) FL 57+6 FLC 2 FAC 3 Others 3+1/1
Preston NE (Loaned on 1/9/95) FL 2
Rochdale (Free on 16/8/96) FL 59+3/4 FLC 4 FAC 3/1 Others 1

JOHNSON Andrew (Andy)
Born: Bedford, 10 February 1981
Height: 5'9" Weight: 9.7
International Honours: E: Yth
A first-year professional, Andy became the

fourth youngest ever Birmingham debutant when coming on for the last 22 minutes at Bradford last August, and followed that up with more appearances from the bench throughout the campaign. The young forward's quickness and physique likened him to Michael Owen, and he went on to win U18 caps, playing in all England's games in the World Youth championships in Nigeria. He also caught the eye of Sunderland after starring in a reserve match against them.
Birmingham C (From juniors on 11/3/98) FL 0+4 FLC 0+2

JOHNSON Andrew (Andy) James
Born: Bristol, 2 May 1974
Height: 6'0" Weight: 13.0
Club Honours: Div 1 '98
International Honours: E: Yth. W: 4
The tenacious midfielder who always gives 100 per-cent effort, started last season in the Nottingham Forest line-up, having been a member of the side that were promoted to the Premiership in 1997-98. Involved in the first 11 games, and scoring in the 5-1 Worthington Cup win over Leyton Orient, he suffered a cracked rib before being asked by the club to undergo a hernia operation while recuperating. Came back as good as new, re-appearing in the Aston Villa game at the City Ground at the end of November, and played virtually right through as Forest ultimately were relegated. Also able to play in defence, and as a forward if required, he is very quick, an excellent passer, and links well with the front men. An England youth international, he made his full international debut for Wales, qualifying through his grandmother.
Norwich C (From trainee on 4/3/92) F/PL 56+10/13 FLC 6+1/2 FAC 2
Nottingham F (£2,200,000 on 4/7/97) P/FL 49+13/4 FLC 4+1/1 FAC 1

JOHNSON Damien Michael
Born: Lisburn, 18 November 1978
Height: 5'9" Weight: 11.2
International Honours: NI: 1; U21-8; Yth
His previous season's debut for Blackburn had been disappointing, but Damien proved in the pre-season that he was equipped to challenge for a role wide on the right in 1998-99. Indeed, no player shone brighter, and he must have been disappointed that he had to wait until the UEFA Cup-tie in Lyons for his baptism. When Sebastian Perez was subsequently hospitalised, the Irish youngster compensated with several displays where he employed quick feet and strong running. Has a tendency to cut inside, and is less effective in the final third of the field, but he is not afraid to track back and tackles with relish. Despite his size, he gets up well to head the ball, and the goal he scored against Arsenal was a great example of intelligent positioning at the far post, followed by an unstoppable header. Made his Northern Ireland debut against the Republic, and was also capped five times at U21 level.
Blackburn Rov (From trainee on 2/2/96) PL 14+7/1 FLC 4 Others 0+1
Nottingham F (Loaned on 29/1/98) FL 5+1

Damien Johnson

JOHNSON David Anthony
Born: Kingston, Jamaica, 15 August 1976
Height: 5'6" Weight: 12.3
Club Honours: FAYC '95; Div 2 '97
International Honours: E: B-1; Sch.
Jamaica: 2

Started last season at Ipswich where he left off the previous one – scoring goals. His form, and that of strike partner Jamie Scowcroft, kept Alex Mathie on the bench, and he maintained a regular supply of goals until a problem with his knee meant that he required an operation. Because Scowcroft was injured he came back too soon, taking time to get his match fitness back, and the goals dried up while he struggled to regain his pace, one of his main assets. However, he continued to work at his overall game and, although still tending to have a pot at goal if possible, does look to bring team mates into the play as shown by the number of "assists" he contributed during the campaign. Played in a couple of friendlies for Jamaica during 1998-99 – "testing the water" before committing himself to an international country.
Manchester U (From trainee on 1/7/94)
Bury (Free on 5/7/95) FL 72+25/17 FLC 8+3/4 FAC 1+1 Others 3+2/1
Ipswich T (£800,000 on 14/11/97) FL 71+2/33 FLC 4/1 FAC 6/2 Others 4

JOHNSON Ian Grant
Born: Dundee, 24 March 1972
Height: 5'11" Weight: 11.13
International Honours: S: U21-6
Having impressed in 1997-98, his first season at Huddersfield, Grant continued in the same vein in 1998-99, when giving some gritty performances in midfield. Showing great stamina, covering all areas between defence and midfield, and making unselfish forward runs coupled to tough tackling, he added a new dimension to his game with a few goals, kicking his seasonal tally off with a classy strike at the McAlpine against Mansfield in the Worthington Cup. Only suspensions ended his continuous run of appearances, but he was soon back to cap some battling displays with home goals against Bury, Bristol City, and Bolton, before injury ended his campaign in early April.
Dundee U (Free from Broughty Ferry on 7/9/90) SL 72+13/7 SLC 5/2 SC 4 Others 4+1/2
Huddersfield T (£90,000 on 14/11/97) FL 64+1/5 FLC 4/1 FAC 7

JOHNSON Marvin Anthony
Born: Wembley, 29 October 1968
Height: 6'0" Weight: 13.6
Despite being a Luton Town old stager, having been a professional at his only club for 13 years, and having his previous season ruined by injury, Marvin came back strongly to miss just six games in 1998-99. Appointed team captain on a permanent basis was just reward for all of his endeavours, which included 100 per-cent commitment and a never-say-die attitude in the central defensive position, meaning that few forwards got the better of him. Very popular at Kenilworth Road, he is strong in the air, hard to pass, and has good feet.
Luton T (From apprentice on 12/11/86) FL 288+14/6 FLC 26+2/2 FAC 12+1/1 Others 12

JOHNSON Michael Owen
Born: Nottingham, 4 July 1973
Height: 5'11" Weight: 11.12
Club Honours: AIC '95

Described as one of the best centre backs in the First Division by his manager, Trevor Francis, despite his lack of height, he has the ability to get up with the best of them. That, coupled to blistering pace and outstanding positional play, which improved beyond all recognition in 1998-99, saw him named as Birmingham's vice captain to Martyn O'Connor after Gary Ablett was injured. Also scored vital goals, including the winner at Tranmere in March, which catapulted the Blues into serious promotion contention. Has two good feet, always looks to pass the ball rather than clear his lines, and can be used as a man marker with some confidence.
Notts Co (From trainee on 9/7/91) FL 102+5 FLC 9 FAC 4 Others 15+1
Birmingham C (£225,000 on 1/9/95) FL 124+27/7 FLC 10+6/2 FAC 3+3 Others 6

JOHNSON Richard Mark
Born: Newcastle, Australia, 27 April 1974
Height: 5'11" Weight: 12.0
Club Honours: Div 2 '98

Richard missed the first month of last season with a thigh strain, but was a regular for Watford thereafter, anchoring the midfield with Micah Hyde. Hard working, and always involved, he now has the talent and confidence to impose himself on matches, while his most eye-catching asset remains his long-range shooting ability, perhaps best illustrated by a fine brace at Bristol City. He also scored a first-minute goal against Tottenham in the FA Cup third round, and was controversially sent off against Tranmere. Still only 25, he has made over 200 first-team appearances for Watford, his only club, and could soon be a candidate for the Australian national squad.
Watford (From trainee on 11/5/92) FL 184+20/17 FLC 12+1/1 FAC 12+1/1 Others 5+1

JOHNSON Ross Yorke
Born: Brighton, 2 January 1976
Height: 6'0" Weight: 12.12

A locally-born central defender who is currently Brighton's longest serving player, he scored his first league goals in the 2-2 away draw at Swansea last February, but has had a stop-start season due to recurring back spasms, which have restricted his appearances. Renowned for his long throw-ins, Ross is a cultured defender who is immensely popular with fans, and it was therefore surprising when Micky Adams announced at the end of the season that he would be available for transfer, despite having a year left on his contract.
Brighton & Hove A (From trainee on 22/7/94) FL 109+14/2 FLC 3+1 FAC 3 Others 4+1

JOHNSON Seth Art Maurice
Born: Birmingham, 12 March 1979
Height: 5'10" Weight: 11.0
International Honours: E: U21-6; Yth

Another Crewe youngster who has made it through the ranks, Seth got off to a flier in 1997-98, and built on it last season, rarely missing a game. Chased by a posse of scouts from the higher divisions, and recognised by

his selection for the England U21 side, he plays mainly in midfield, but can fill the full-back position if required, and is extremely versatile for a youngster. Scored five goals, including the winner at home to Bristol City, and was a runaway winner of the supporters' "Player of the Year" award. Stop Press: On 21 May, the £3 million rated Seth signed for the Premiership's Derby County, whose manager, Jim Smith, said: "he was delighted that his new charge had been so loyal to Alex during their successful fight to avoid relegation, it was something that showed him having great character".
Crewe Alex (From trainee on 12/7/96) FL 89+4/6 FLC 5 FAC 2/1 Others 0+3

JOHNSTON Allan
Born: Glasgow, 14 December 1973
Height: 5'9" Weight: 10.10
Club Honours: Div 1 '99
International Honours: S: 6; B-2; U21-3
"Magic" enjoyed a marvellous season at Sunderland in 1998-99, winning a First Division championship medal, four full Scotland caps, and earning selection to the PFA First Division award-winning side. The tricky winger, who excels at crossing, and can turn full backs inside out on either flank, also contributed in the goalscoring stakes – scoring twice in the vital promotion battle against Bolton in March, and netting one of the goals of the season at the Stadium of Light, a right-foot volley, against Huddersfield in April. Having made his debut for Scotland versus Estonia in a European championship qualifier, Allan has since established himself in Craig Brown's squad, playing a starring role in the victory over Germany in Bremen last April.
Hearts (Free from Tynecastle BC on 23/6/90) SL 46+38/12 SLC 3+2/2 SC 4+1 (Signed for Rennes during 1996 close season)
Sunderland (£550,000 on 27/3/97) FL 82+4/19 FLC 8+1/1 FAC 3 Others 3

JOHNSTON Raymond (Ray)
Born: Bristol, 5 May 1981
Height: 6'0" Weight: 12.5
International Honours: E: Sch
A former England schoolboy international goalkeeper, Ray has continued to maintain his promise in Bristol Rovers' youth team as a trainee, and was deemed good enough to be given a senior opportunity in the final game of last season at Macclesfield. Just three days after his 18th birthday, the youngster took the field and, despite conceding a third-minute goal and having to face a penalty in the first half, grew in confidence to pull off several excellent saves that ultimately secured three points for Rovers on their first-ever visit to Moss Rose. Having accepted a pro contract, he will be looking to challenge for the number-one spot on a regular basis in 1999-2000.
Bristol Rov (Trainee) FL 1

JONES Barry
Born: Prescot, 30 June 1970
Height: 5'11" Weight: 11.12
Club Honours: WC '95
Very steady and reliable, the central defender was a virtual ever present for York in 1998-99, captaining the side and netting vital goals in successive away wins at Oldham and Wycombe in mid term. Voted "Clubman of the Year" by the supporters, Barry can also operate at right back, where he once showed consistent form for Wrexham.
Liverpool (Signed from Prescot Cables on 19/1/89) Others 0+1
Wrexham (Free from 10/7/92) FL 184+11/5 FLC 14+1/1 FAC 11+2 Others 21+1
York C (£40,000 on 17/12/97) FL 67+1/4 FLC 2 FAC 3 Others 1

JONES Gary
Born: Huddersfield, 6 April 1969
Height: 6'1" Weight: 12.9
Club Honours: Div 3 '98
After scoring 29 league goals and winning the "Golden Boot" award at Notts County in 1997-98, Sam Allardyce kept with Gary for 36 games last season. However, failing to rediscover the form that helped lead County to the Third Division championship in the previous campaign, after scoring only eight times the player was then allowed to leave to try and find his prolific scoring touch at Hartlepool in March. As United's record signing, a lot was expected of him, and although playing some good stuff as Pool battled for their safety, he would have been disappointed not to have scored more goals. However, just like Chris Turner's other major signings, he is on contract until the 2001 close season and is seen as a class signing who can play a major role in re-establishing the club's respectability.
Doncaster Rov (Free from Rossington Main Colliery on 26/1/89) FL 10+10/2 FLC 1 (Free to Grantham on 1/11/89)
Southend U (£25,000 from Boston U, via Kettering T, on 3/6/93) FL 47+23/16 FLC 3/1 FAC 2 Others 6+1/2
Lincoln C (Loaned on 17/9/93) FL 0+4/2 Others 0+1
Notts Co (£140,000 on 1/3/96) FL 103+14/38 FLC 5+1/1 FAC 9+1/7 Others 2+1
Scunthorpe U (Loaned on 21/2/97) FL 9+2/5
Hartlepool U (Signed on 10/3/99) FL 12/1

JONES Gary Roy
Born: Birkenhead, 3 June 1977
Height: 5'10" Weight: 12.0
Midfielder Gary was in and out of the Rochdale side in the early part of last season, eventually losing the right-flank position to Paul Carden. Regularly used as a substitute thereafter, he converted a crucial penalty soon after coming on in the Auto Windscreens Shield win at Halifax. Was also tried briefly at right back.
Swansea C (Signed from Caernarfon T on 11/7/97) FL 3+5 FLC 0+1
Rochdale (Free on 15/1/98) FL 28+9/2 FLC 1 FAC 1+2 Others 1+1/1

JONES Gary Steven
Born: Chester, 10 May 1975
Height: 6'3" Weight: 14.0
Able to play either at centre half or centre forward, Gary was in grave danger of becoming the forgotten man of Tranmere in 1998-99 until he hit goals in consecutive games against Birmingham and Oxford. Unfortunately, he was out with a foot injury

in November and December, but this all-rounder never contributes less than 100 per-cent effort wherever he is asked to perform. Big and tall, although not particularly quick, he will always be awkward for opponents to handle and, despite a limited number of appearances, bagged five league goals. Quiet and dependable, rather than vociferous or flamboyant, he performed well in a number of positions, being a grafter as well as a true team man.
Tranmere Rov (From trainee on 5/7/93) FL 90+57/25 FLC 12+4/3 FAC 5+2/2 Others 1+1

JONES Graeme Anthony
Born: Gateshead, 13 March 1970
Height: 6'0" Weight: 12.12
Club Honours: Div 3 '97; AMC '99
A bustling Wigan centre forward, Graeme had yet another season, this time in 1998-99, that was hampered by injuries. Strong in the air, he damaged his cruciate ligaments in the match against Blackpool in September, which forced him to miss the majority of the campaign. On his return, he found it hard to regain his place, and was used mainly as a substitute as the club made the play offs. A popular player and squad member, he turned down a move to Hull City in transfer deadline week.
Doncaster Rov (£10,000 from Bridlington T on 2/8/93) FL 80+12/26 FLC 4+1/1 FAC 2+1/1 Others 5/1
Wigan Ath (£150,000 on 8/7/96) FL 75+18/43 FLC 4+1/1 FAC 4/1 Others 6+2/6

JONES Jason Andrew
Born: Wrexham, 10 May 1979
Height: 6'2" Weight: 12.7
International Honours: W: Yth
Following two games for the Swansea first team in the Welsh Premier Cup against Caernarfon Town last season, the goalkeeper was given his league opportunity following a back injury to Roger Freestone at the end of January. During his third league game, however, Jason was involved in an accidental collision with Swans' defender, Steve Jones, resulting in concussion, with the club being forced to bring in Matt Gregg from Crystal Palace on loan. At the end of March he was named as substitute for the Welsh U21 team against Switzerland.
Swansea C (Free from Liverpool juniors on 29/12/97) FL 4

JONES Jonathan (Jon) Berwyn
Born: Wrexham, 27 October 1978
Height: 5'10" Weight: 11.5
A product of Chester's youth team who, due to the number of forwards at the club, found his chances of first-team football limited to just eight league appearances during last season, he joined League of Wales club Barry Town on loan in March. Is able to get into good positions on the flanks or through the middle due to his terrific pace.
Chester C (From trainee on 27/3/97) FL 7+25/2 FLC 0+1 FAC 0+2 Others 1+2

JONES Keith Aubrey
Born: Dulwich, 14 October 1965
Height: 5'8" Weight: 11.2
International Honours: E: Yth; Sch

A hard-working, competitive midfield player who was a valuable squad member for Charlton during last season, Keith was often called upon to carry out a man-marking job, having one of his best performances, against Middlesbrough at the Valley, when playing Paul Gascoigne out of the game. He likes to get forward whenever possible, and scored the winning goal against Liverpool at home, thus giving the Addicks three valuable points. Keith works hard, never hides, and can always be relied upon to do a good job when brought into the side.

Chelsea (From apprentice on 16/8/83) FL 43+9/7 FLC 9+2/3 FAC 1 Others 4+1
Brentford (£40,000 on 3/9/87) FL 167+2/13 FLC 15/2 FAC 13/4 Others 16/1
Southend U (£175,000 on 21/10/91) FL 88+2/11 FLC 4 FAC 5 Others 9/1
Charlton Ath (£150,000 on 16/9/94) P/FL 126+15/5 FLC 6+1 FAC 4+2/1 Others 3

JONES Lee

Born: Pontypridd, 9 August 1970
Height: 6'3" Weight: 14.4
Club Honours: AMC '94

Having established himself as Bristol Rovers' first-choice goalkeeper, the tall and commanding Lee was very unfortunate to have been sent off in the final minute of a tense goalless draw at Gillingham on 22 August. He made up for this with some fine performances, none more so than an Auto Windscreens Shield tie at Walsall in December when he made three saves in an exciting penalty shoot-out. He even volunteered to take a spot kick himself, but it was saved by his opposite number, James Walker. Called up as cover for the Welsh "B" squad for an international against Northern Ireland on 9 February, a groin and ankle injury halted his fine run of 30 consecutive matches in March.

Swansea C (£7,500 from AFC Porth on 24/3/94) FL 6 Others 1
Bristol Rov (Signed on 7/3/98) FL 40 FLC 2 FAC 6 Others 3

JONES Philip Lee

Born: Wrexham, 29 May 1973
Height: 5'9" Weight: 10.8
International Honours: W: 2; B-1; U21-14; Yth

Little went right for the ex-Liverpool player at the start of last season, and he seemed not to figure in John Aldridge's plans, but when he showed signs of a possible return to his previous free-scoring best, the manager was quick to restore him to the Tranmere first team. Although Lee's campaign was disrupted by a series of niggling injuries, he remained enthusiastic, imaginative, and committed to the team cause. Pacy, and a good reader of the game, playing just in front of the midfield rather than as an out-and-out forward, he scored one league goal, and two in the Worthington Cup.

Wrexham (From trainee on 5/7/91) FL 24+15/10 FLC 2 FAC 1+2/1 Others 4+1/2
Liverpool (£300,000 on 12/3/92) PL 0+3 FLC 0+1
Crewe Alex (Loaned on 3/9/93) FL 4+4/1

Wrexham (Loaned on 26/1/96) FL 20/8
Wrexham (Loaned on 31/1/97) FL 2+4
Tranmere Rov (£100,000 on 27/3/97) FL 55+17/16 FLC 6+3/2 FAC 0+1

JONES Mark Andrew

Born: Walsall, 7 September 1979
Height: 5'9" Weight: 11.7
International Honours: E: Sch

The young Wolves' striker was well down the order in 1998-99 until, prompted by the summer departures, he came on as a sub after 80 minutes against Barnet, while his first league action followed on at Bristol in November. After having an outing for Swindon reserves in February, as he was lacking match fitness, by April he had come off the bench four times for Wolves, and was top scorer for the reserves with 12 before signing a further one-year contract.

Wolverhampton W (From trainee on 25/9/96) FL 0+2 FLC 0+2

JONES Matthew Graham

Born: Llanelli, 1 September 1980
Height: 5'11" Weight: 11.5
Club Honours: FAYC '97
International Honours: W: B-1; U21-6; Yth

By the time this 18-year-old midfielder made his first-team debut for Leeds in the FA Cup victory at Portsmouth last season, he already had a string of Welsh youth and U21 caps to his name. He then made his full debut in the 2-1 victory at Aston Villa, before being given further substitute appearances, never letting anyone down, and always making a good impression. Although the most recent youngster to make United's first team, Matthew has long been tipped as one of the most exciting talents to come out of the extraordinary bunch which won the FA Youth Cup in 1997.

Leeds U (From trainee on 3/9/97) PL 3+5 FAC 0+1

JONES Matthew Neil

Born: Shrewsbury, 11 October 1980
Height: 6'0" Weight: 12.0

A second-year trainee, and very much one for the future at Shrewsbury, having impressed throughout last season he was given a senior debut at Torquay in the final game of the campaign when coming off the bench after 60 minutes. Along with Glyn Thompson, who also made the most of his first appearance at first-team level in the same match, the young midfielder gave due notice that he would be very much in the reckoning before too long.

Shrewsbury T (Trainee) FL 0+1

JONES Nathan Jason

Born: Rhondda, 28 May 1973
Height: 5'7" Weight: 10.12

Although beginning last season at Southend in contention for a place, Nathan was unable to get into the starting line-up on more than six occasions, while virtually being a regular on the bench. A skilful left-sided midfielder, who works hard for the team, but really needed more starts if he was to further his career, he was loaned to Scarborough and

played in eight of the final ten matches of a campaign which saw them relegated to the Conference.

Luton T (£10,000 from Merthyr on 30/6/95. Freed on 20/12/95)
Southend U (Free from Nomincia on 5/8/97) FL 39+17 FLC 5+1 FAC 2+1/1 Others 0+2
Scarborough (Loaned on 25/3/99) FL 8+1

JONES Paul Steven

Born: Chirk, 18 April 1967
Height: 6'3" Weight: 14.8
International Honours: W: 11

As Southampton's "Player of the Season" in 1997-98, the Welsh international 'keeper had mixed fortunes at the Dell last season. Had a nervous start against Liverpool in August, and had five put past him in the next game at Charlton before recovering to get back to his best form. Then, suffering a freak back injury in the warm up before an international game in March, it was thought then that he would not play again in 1998-99. However, showing much keenness and powers of recovery, he returned to play his part in the great end of season run, keeping clean sheets at Wimbledon, and in the last game at home to Everton, results which saw the Saints remain in the Premiership by the "skin of their teeth". A good shot stopper who fills the goal well and made vital saves, some of the most important being in the 1-1 draw at Arsenal in October, he ended the campaign bringing vital confidence to the defence.

Wolverhampton W (£40,000 from Kidderminster Harriers on 23/7/91) FL 33 FLC 2 FAC 5 Others 4
Stockport Co (£60,000 on 25/7/96) FL 46 FLC 11 FAC 4 Others 4
Southampton (£900,000 on 28/7/97) PL 69 FLC 6 FAC 3

JONES Scott

Born: Sheffield, 1 May 1975
Height: 5'10" Weight: 12.8

Scott suffered an achilles tendon injury on the opening day of last season and did not return to the Barnsley line-up until October. He then showed his versatility by playing either at centre back, at left-wing back, or as a defensive full back. Strong in the tackle, and very good in the air for a man of his size, he also became a good dead-ball specialist, netting on a couple of occasions from free kicks. Valued highly by the club, he signed an extended three-year contract in February.

Barnsley (From trainee on 1/2/94) F/PL 56+7/4 FLC 2 FAC 4+3/2
Mansfield T (Loaned on 7/8/97) FL 6 FLC 2

JONES Stephen (Steve) Gary

Born: Cambridge, 17 March 1970
Height: 6'1" Weight: 12.12

Big, strong, and quick, Steve started only a handful of times for Charlton last season, but was used as a substitute in almost half of the Premiership matches. The striker only found the net on one occasion, against Liverpool at Anfield, when he scored with a spectacular goal after coming on as a substitute to earn the Addicks a 3-3 draw. Unable to obtain an automatic place in the

starting line-up, despite the lack of goals from the regular attack, it must be considered a disappointing campaign for him. When he did get a run in the side in December, he pulled a hamstring at Southampton in early January, subsequently being unable to regain his place on being fit again, before coming back for the final two games and being involved in three of the four goals that saw Aston Villa off in the penultimate match of the campaign.

West Ham U (£22,000 from Billericay T on 16/11/92) PL 8+8/4 FAC 2+2/1 Others 1+1
Bournemouth (£150,000 on 21/10/94) FL 71+3/26 FLC 4/3 FAC 3/1 Others 3
West Ham U (Signed on 16/5/96) PL 5+3 FLC 0+1 FAC 2
Charlton Ath (£400,000 on 14/2/97) P/FL 27+23/8 FLC 3+1 FAC 1 Others 1+2
Bournemouth (Loaned on 24/12/97) FL 5/4 Others 1/1

Steve Jones (Swansea City)

JONES Stephen (Steve) Robert
Born: Bristol, 25 December 1970
Height: 5'10" Weight: 12.2

A fearless defender who, returning to first-team duty in 1998-99 after missing all of the previous season recovering from a broken leg, re-established his first-team place, only to be sidelined again with a broken jaw sustained in a collision with his own goalkeeper. Not to be put off, Steve was back in the side before the end of April as the Swans made a challenge for one of the play-off places. Prior to his broken jaw, he had steadily rebuilt his fitness, and scored a glorious 25-yard goal against Brighton at the Vetch Field, which will rank as one of the goals of the season. Besides being a strong tackler, he always makes himself available for overlapping situations.

Swansea C (£25,000 from Cheltenham T on 14/11/95) FL 93+2/3 FLC 2 FAC 7 Others 7

JONES Vincent (Vinny) Peter
Born: Watford, 5 January 1965
Height: 6'0" Weight: 11.12
Club Honours: FAC '88 DIV 2 '90
International Honours: W: 9

Following the departure of John Hollins in the summer of 1998, Vinny was appointed as Queens Park Rangers' assistant manager by Ray Harford. However he started only one game before the departure of Harford and being passed over for the caretaker role. After Gerry Francis' arrival he was again not appointed to a coaching role and, although he still had over three years of his contract remaining, he did not appear for the club again. Having made a successful film debut in *Lock, Stock and Two Smoking Barrels*, he announced his retirement from football in March after negotiating a settlement with the club for the remaining period of his contract.

Wimbledon (£10,000 from Wealdstone on 20/11/86) FL 77/9 FLC 6+2 FAC 11+2/1 Others 3
Leeds U (£650,000 on 20/6/89) FL 44+2/5 FLC 2 FAC 1 Others 4
Sheffield U (£700,000 on 13/9/90) FL 35/2 FLC 4 FAC 1 Others 1
Chelsea (£575,000 on 30/8/91) F/PL 42/4 FLC 1 FAC 4/1 Others 5/2
Wimbledon (£700,000 on 10/9/92) F/PL 171+6/12 FLC 21+1/2 FAC 21+1/1
Queens Park R (£500,000 on 26/3/98) FL 8+1/1

JONK Wim
Born: Volendam, Holland, 12 December 1966
Height: 6'0" Weight: 12.2
International Honours: Holland: 48

A Dutch international with close on 50 international appearances behind him, and having competed for Holland in the World Cup, Wim moved from PSV Eindhoven to Sheffield Wednesday in time for the start of 1998-99. Although being an ever present, and impressing as a skilful midfielder who was extremely comfortable on the ball, always looking for the right pass, he was not always appreciated by the fans for his laid-back style. However, his calming presence was certainly helpful for the younger members of the team, a feature of his play that was backed up by Match Magazine who rated him the top midfielder at the club. Scored his first goal in English football against the Premier League's champions elect, Manchester United, in a surprise 3-1 win at Hillsborough, but only added one more. Having lost his place in the Dutch national side, it will be interesting to see what 1999-2000 holds for him.

Sheffield Wed (£2,500,000 from PSV Eindhoven, via FC Volendam, Ajax and Inter Milan, on 12/8/98) PL 38/2 FLC 2 FAC 3

Wim Jonk

JORDAN Andrew Joseph
Born: Manchester, 14 December 1979
Height: 6'1" Weight: 13.1

As the son of the former Scottish international and Bristol City manager, Joe, the young central defender made his debut for City in the final game of last season, against Norwich. A product of the club's youth policy, and highly rated by the coaching staff, his progress during the campaign was hampered by illness and injury, which prevented him making a claim for a first-team squad place earlier on. Andrew displays many of the qualities of his famous father, being very strong in the air, and in the tackle, while always looking to play the ball from the back when the opportunity arises. Has the ability to develop into a specialist dead-ball kicker, and has already scored goals from free kicks around the box in youth and reserve team football.

Bristol C (From trainee on 5/12/97) FL 1

JORDAN Scott Douglas
Born: Newcastle, 19 July 1975
Height: 5'10" Weight: 11.8

The talented and constructive midfielder had perhaps his best-ever season for York in 1998-99, winning his place back in the side in October, and scoring in a victory at Blackpool. He also hit one of the goals in the FA Cup win over Enfield and, in the closing weeks became a free-kick expert, scoring

three times from 25 yards, including one that earned a vital point at Northampton.
York C (From trainee on 21/10/92) FL 91+36/10 FLC 4+1/1 FAC 5+2/2 Others 6+4

Scott Jordan

JOSEPH Marc Ellis
Born: Leicester, 10 November 1976
Height: 6'0" Weight: 12.10
A cool, quick Cambridge United centre back who made good progress in 1998-99, when forming an excellent partnership with Andy Duncan. As an ever present for the first three months, before missing a few games in mid season prior to regaining his place, Marc showed himself to be good in the air and on the ground until a thigh injury finally curtailed him in early March. Can also be used in a sweeper capacity.
Cambridge U (From trainee on 23/5/95) FL 80+10 FLC 7 FAC 0+2 Others 4+1

JOSEPH Matthew (Matt) Nathan Adolphus
Born: Bethnal Green, 30 September 1972
Height: 5'8" Weight: 10.7
International Honours: E: Yth
An excellent attacking Leyton Orient right-wing back who, despite his size can also play sweeper or centre half, he is also a player who can read the game well, and uses his pace to make vital last-ditch tackles. His attack-minded play saw him appear in the centre-forward position during the Shrewsbury game last April, and outjump the opposing defence to head the ball across the goal for Amara Simba to score in a 6-1 win. Absent for the opening seven games in 1998-99, once in the side Matt missed few opportunities to play.
Arsenal (From trainee on 17/11/90)
Gillingham (Free on 7/12/92) (Free to Ilves during 1993 close season)
Cambridge U (Signed on 19/11/93) FL 157+2/6 FLC 6+1 FAC 7 Others 5
Leyton Orient (£10,000 on 22/1/98) FL 48/1 FLC 2 FAC 4+1 Others 1

JOSEPH Roger Anthony
Born: Paddington, 24 December 1965
Height: 5'11" Weight: 11.10
International Honours: E: B-2
Roger was used mainly as a squad player by Leyton Orient in 1998-99, but when called upon he let nobody down, using all his top-flight experience with Wimbledon to good effect. Unfortunate not to play more games, the form of the central defenders in the queue in front of him preventing it, he remained in contention throughout the campaign. Although not having the great pace of yesteryear, his ability to strike long balls in behind defenders, remains undiminished.
Brentford (Free from Southall on 4/10/85) FL 103+1/2 FLC 7 FAC 1 Others 8
Wimbledon (£150,000 on 25/8/88) F/PL 155+7 FLC 17+2 FAC 11+1 Others 6
Millwall (Loaned on 2/3/95) FL 5
Leyton Orient (Free on 22/11/96) FL 15 Others 1
West Bromwich A (Free on 28/2/97) FL 0+2
Leyton Orient (Free on 7/8/97) FL 26+23 FLC 3+2 FAC 0+2 Others 4

JOYCE Warren Garton
Born: Oldham, 20 January 1965
Height: 5'9" Weight: 12.0
Missing the first two months of last season at Hull with a rib and back injury was an inauspicious start to the most remarkable campaign in Warren's long career. In September, he was promoted as assistant to manager Mark Hateley following Billy Kirkwood's departure to St Johnstone. With Hateley's dismissal in November, new chairman, Tom Belton, immediately installed the former Burnley midfielder as caretaker boss and, although the Tigers were some six points adrift at the bottom of the Football League, Mr Belton was so impressed with the rookie boss that he was given the permanent post, despite the applications of a host of experienced managers. One of his first tasks was to appoint John McGovern – Warren was his first professional signing at Bolton in 1982 – as his assistant. They set about totally restructuring the Tigers' squad, and their transformed team produced an amazing string of results in the New Year to ensure the club's league survival. Not only has it created a new managerial partnership that promises to be a major force in the years to come, but Warren continued to exert his on-field influence with his non-stop midfield displays, despite nagging rib and back injuries. To use his own words, he "worked his socks off" to deservedly become a leading figure in Hull City's long and proud history. Is the son of the former Burnley star, Walter. His remarkable achievements, both on and off the field, were rewarded with the "Clubman of the Season" award, having signed a three-year contract before the final home game.
Bolton W (From juniors on 23/6/82) FL 180+4/17 FLC 14+1/1 FAC 11/1 Others 11/2
Preston NE (£35,000 on 16/10/87) FL 170+7/34 FLC 8/2 FAC 6/1 Others 19/7
Plymouth Arg (£160,000 on 19/5/92) FL 28+2/3 FLC 6/1 FAC 2 Others 2

Burnley (£140,000 on 7/7/93) FL 65+5/9 FLC 8/1 FAC 4/1 Others 8/1
Hull C (Loaned on 20/1/95) FL 9/3
Hull C (£30,000 on 10/7/96) FL 118+1/11 FLC 6+1/1 FAC 6/1 Others 5/1

Mark Jules

JULES Mark Anthony
Born: Bradford, 5 September 1971
Height: 5'8" Weight: 11.1
Mark went on Chesterfield's transfer list last November after the arrival of Shane Nicholson had pushed him out of the left-back position. Ironically, he hardly missed a match for a long time after this, injuries to Nicholson, Chris Perkins, and Tom Curtis, leading to him fulfilling a number of defensive and midfield duties with his usual understated effectiveness. Released during the summer, and with an eye on his future, he began a PFA-sponsored BSc in sports fitness.
Bradford C (From trainee on 3/7/90) FLC 0+1
Scarborough (Free on 14/8/91) FL 57+20/16 FLC 6+2/2 FAC 1+1 Others 6/4
Chesterfield (£40,000 on 21/5/93) FL 155+31/4 FLC 12+3/2 FAC 13+2 Others 10+1

JUPP Duncan Alan
Born: Haslemere, 25 January 1975
Height: 6'0" Weight: 12.12
International Honours: S: U21-10
A capable Wimbledon right back who only made a handful of appearances in the 1998-99 season due mainly to the fine form of the regular right back, Kenny Cunningham, he continued to perform to a high standard for the reserves. Still only 24 years of age, and a former Scottish U21 international, Duncan will hope to be given more opportunities to prove himself in the first team in the future. Composed in possession, and a player who likes to attack the full back, he is both solid and versatile.
Fulham (From trainee on 12/7/93) FL 101+4/2 FLC 10+2 FAC 9+1/1 Others 9+1/1
Wimbledon (£125,000 + on 27/6/96) PL 12+3 FLC 4 FAC 3+2

KAAMARK Pontus Sven
Born: Vasteras, Sweden, 5 April 1969
Height: 5'11" Weight: 12.7
Club Honours: FLC '97
International Honours: Sweden: 43
A right-footed Leicester defender who can operate either as wing back or as a central defender, Pontus had few opportunities of first-team action last season following the arrival of both Frank Sinclair and Gerry Taggart, but continued to look a cultured operator whenever called on. Came close to opening his scoring account against both Manchester United and Tottenham, but failed to find the necessary composure when the opportunity arose to deliver "typical defender's efforts." Although having to miss an international cap in October, due to a bout of tendonitis, he was a vital member of the Sweden team that continued to sweep all before them at the head of England's qualifying group for Euro 2000. Is looking to spend more time with his young daughter back in Gothenburg in future, which may result in either a commuting arrangement or a return to his homeland at the end of his contract during the summer.
Leicester C (£840,000 from IFK Gothenberg on 2/11/95) P/FL 60+5 FLC 5+1 FAC 4 Others 2

KACHLOUL Hassan
Born: Agadir, Morocco, 19 February 1973
Height: 6'1" Weight: 11.12
International Honours: Morocco: 4
A Moroccan international, following a successful trial at the Dell last October, Hassan joined Southampton from the French club, St Etienne. As a skilful and hard-working playmaker, who has good vision and passes the ball well, and can play on the left or the right-hand side, he soon became a great favourite of the fans, who appreciated his commitment to the cause. They also delighted in his vital goals, especially those in the 1-1 draw at Nottingham Forest, and the 1-0 home win over West Ham. Once in the side he was rarely out of it, and having opened his goals account against Wimbledon at the Dell, he closed it with one in the penultimate game, a 2-0 win over the same team. Signed until the summer, it will be interesting to see whether he lines up for 1999-2000.
Southampton (£250,000 from St Etienne, via Nimes, Dunkerque and Metz, on 20/10/98) PL 18+4/5 FAC 2

KANDOL Tresor Osmar
Born: Zaire, 30 August 1981
Height: 6'2" Weight: 11.7
Born in Zaire, but coming through Luton's trainee ranks to turn professional last September, the young striker started 1998-99 in Town's youth team and celebrated with a goal in a game against Leyton Orient. Having signed a two-year contract, he ended the campaign in the first-team squad, after making his senior debut as a sub in the Auto Windscreens Shield 3-0 home defeat at the hands of Walsall in early January, as well as being the management's choice as "Best Young Player". Excellent in the air, if he can stay clear of injuries this impressive young player could well become a regular.
Luton T (From trainee on 26/9/98) FL 2+2 Others 0+1

KANU Nwankwo
Born: Owerri, Nigeria, 1 August 1976
Height: 6'4" Weight: 13.3
International Honours: Nigeria: 9
A Nigerian international bought from Inter Milan last February, his first appearance in an Arsenal shirt will be remembered for the wrong reasons, because he set up the "illegal" goal against Sheffield United in the fifth round FA Cup-tie. Represented his country in the 1998 World Cup finals in Paris, but was then sidelined with a series of leg and knee injuries. Two years earlier, he had undergone heart surgery which raised serious doubts about his future in the game. A relaxed, yet determined young man, he has bravely overcome those set backs to become a valuable member of the Arsenal squad. Skilful and creative, both through midfield and in a strikers' role, he holds the ball up well and opens up tactical options. Following his first-team introduction, he was involved in a number of match-changing situations, especially when coming off the bench to score the crucial only goal against Derby that took Arsenal into the FA Cup semi finals. Has quickly become a cult figure with the Highbury fans, and looks a good investment for the future, provided his fitness prevails.
Arsenal (£4,500,000 from Inter Milan, via Fed Works, Iwuanyanwu National and Ajax, on 4/2/99) PL 5+7/6 FAC 0+5/1

KATCHOURO Petr
Born: Minsk, Belarus, 2 August 1972
Height: 5'11" Weight: 12.6
International Honours: Belarus: 23
Kept out of action until last October by a pre-season cartilage injury, Petr made an instant impact up front for Sheffield United, scoring six goals in eight games. Playing much better than the previous season, his running off the ball created space for others as well as for himself, and earned him a substitute appearance for Belarus against Wales. Unfortunately, a damaged kidney, sustained against Sunderland in November, put him out of action until the end of March. Out of contract during the summer, at the

Nwankwo Kanu

time of going to press it was known that the club had made him an offer of re-engagement.

Sheffield U (£650,000 from Dinamo Minsk on 19/7/96) FL 42+30/18 FLC 5+3/1 FAC 2+6 Others 3/1

KAVANAGH Graham Anthony
Born: Dublin, 2 December 1973
Height: 5'10" Weight: 12.11
International Honours: Ei: 3; B-1; U21-9; Yth; Sch

At times last season, "Kav" looked as though he was poised at last to make a huge step up in standards by adding consistency to the undoubted gifts of vision and shooting. As Stoke's leading scorer for most of the campaign after Brian Little gave him his chance up front, he let himself down with disciplinary issues that saw him sent off twice and booked too often. Was called into the Republic of Ireland Euro 2000 squad on occasions, and selected by his fellow professionals for the PFA award-winning Second Division side.

Middlesbrough (Signed from Home Farm on 16/8/91) F/PL 22+13/3 FLC 1 FAC 3+1/1 Others 7
Darlington (Loaned on 25/2/94) FL 5
Stoke C (£250,000 + on 13/9/96) FL 112+6/20 FLC 8+1/6 FAC 3 Others 2/1

KAVANAGH Jason Colin
Born: Meriden, 23 November 1971
Height: 5'9" Weight: 12.7
International Honours: E: Yth; Sch

Wycombe's first-choice right-wing back until Matt Lawrence joined last October, Jason then spent his time on the substitutes' bench, either side of an ankle ligament injury, before being recalled in February by the new manager, Lawrie Sanchez. However, after a brief run he decided that his future lay away from Adams Park and was allowed to join Stoke on a free transfer, before his contract expired at the end of the season. With pace and stamina to work the right flank, he quickly established himself in the side, and played a key role in turning City's fortunes around.

Derby Co (From trainee on 9/12/88) FL 74+25/1 FLC 3+2 FAC 7 Others 8+8
Wycombe W (£25,000 on 1/11/96) FL 84+6/1 FLC 6 FAC 3+1 Others 4
Stoke C (Free on 8/3/99) FL 8

KAY John
Born: Great Lumley, 29 January 1964
Height: 5'9" Weight: 11.6
Club Honours: Div 3 '88

John, a tough, no-nonsense Scarborough full back, who never knows when he is beaten, did not enjoy the best of seasons in 1998-99, especially with the campaign ending in relegation to the Conference for the club, and a free transfer for him. Although the former Boro captain's experience often shone through when playing alongside the younger members of the side, he was sent off twice and missed the final 12 fixtures through injury. And, at 35 years of age, he will be pondering his next move during the summer.

Arsenal (From apprentice on 7/8/81) FL 13+1
Wimbledon (£25,000 on 20/7/84) FL 63/2 FLC 3 FAC 3 Others 1

Middlesbrough (Loaned on 8/1/85) FL 8
Sunderland (£22,500 on 22/7/87) FL 196+3 FLC 19 FAC 12 Others 6
Shrewsbury T (Loaned on 28/3/96) FL 7 Others 1
Preston NE (Free on 23/8/96) FL 7 FLC 3
Scarborough (Free on 27/9/96) FL 97+1 FLC 2 FAC 4/1 Others 3

KEANE Robert (Robbie) David
Born: Dublin, 8 July 1980
Height: 5'9" Weight: 11.10
International Honours: Ei: 9; B-1

Having helped Eire win the European Youth championship in Cyprus in the summer of 1998, despite already being established in their senior team, he scored for Wolves on the opening day and was to play more as an out-and-out striker last season, showing wonderful improvisation with a goal against Barnet. After winning a fourth full inter-national cap against Croatia, and getting eight goals in Wolves' first 12 matches, he scored two for Eire as they beat Malta 5-0 but picked up a knee injury whilst away. Robbie then missed seven games entirely, and was reduced to being a sub for the next two, though he did help Wolves recover from 1-0 down to defeat Birmingham 3-1 in the latter. He was back on the goal trail in December, and showed sharp reflexes to head in at Bolton in the FA Cup in January. With Wolves entertaining holders, Arsenal, in the next round, there was much speculation about the young Irishman joining them, or another leading club. But despite having a busy afternoon, he did not make a major impact. Then, on 13 February, he grabbed his 16th goal of the campaign for Wolves, and later that month made his sixth full appearance for Eire. Sadly, by March, injections and illness were taking their toll. The treatment was in preparation for his trip to Nigeria for an U20 World tournament, the club being very unhappy to lose him at a vital stage of their season. When he was replaced at Barnsley, it was his sixth game without a goal, and his last before the trip. Ironically, he made little impact in Nigeria, and Eire did not progress much either.

Wolverhampton W (From trainee on 26/7/97) FL 64+7/22 FLC 7+1/3 FAC 3+2/2

KEANE Roy Maurice
Born: Cork, 10 August 1971
Height: 5'10" Weight: 12.10
Club Honours: FMC '92; CS '93, '96, '97; PL '94, '96, '97, '99; FAC '94, '96, '99
International Honours: Ei: 42; U21-4; Yth; Sch

An inspirational Manchester United mid-fielder with excellent skills and a hardened edge, Roy certainly made up for lost time in 1998-99, after missing most of the previous season with a serious knee injury. Absent from the Worthington Cup only, his leader-ship qualities were very much in evidence as United forged for major honours on three fronts and, missing only seven games all season, he netted some vital goals in both the Premiership and European campaigns. His equaliser in the European Cup against Bayern Munich at Old Trafford helped to secure United's place in the quarter final, when even Carol Vorderman would have found it difficult to work out the permu-

tations of qualification had United lost the tie. Continuing to marshal his troops towards a hopeful treble, he was on top form for the FA Cup semi final against Arsenal, where he had a goal disallowed in the first tie, and was red carded in the replay. And, despite scoring United's first goal against Juventus in the European Cup semi final in Turin, a yellow card offence ruled him out of the final. Although protracted wranglings over a new contract led to rumours that he might be forced to leave the club at the turn of the year, surely a player of his calibre is worth a king's ransom to the Reds. Despite missing out on a European Cup winners medal, he now has four Premier League and three FA Cup winners medals in the trophy room, so it was not all bad news. Again represented the Republic of Ireland, playing four times.

Nottingham F (£10,000 from Cobh Ramblers on 12/6/90) F/PL 114/22 FLC 17/6 FAC 18/3 Others 5/2
Manchester U (£3,750,000 on 22/7/93) PL 149+7/19 FLC 9+2 FAC 29+1/1 Others 32/7

Roy Keane

KEARTON Jason Brett
Born: Ipswich, Australia, 9 July 1969
Height: 6'1" Weight: 11.10
Club Honours: FAC '95

A very popular member of the Crewe staff, the Australian goalkeeper has proved to be one of the best custodians ever to play for the club, and in nearly three years has missed just seven league and cup games. Ever present last season, keeping nine clean sheets in a backs-to-the-wall campaign, he was often the difference between winning and losing. Very consistent, comes out well for crosses, and good in one-on-one situations, Jason is an excellent shot stopper who instils confidence in his defenders.

Everton (Free from Brisbane Lions on 31/10/88) PL 3+3 FLC 1 FAC 1
Stoke C (Loaned on 13/8/91) FL 16 Others 1
Blackpool (Loaned on 9/1/92) FL 14
Notts Co (Loaned on 19/1/95) FL 10 Others 2
Crewe Alex (Free on 16/10/96) FL 119 FLC 6 FAC 6 Others 6

KEATES Dean Scott
Born: Walsall, 30 June 1978
Height: 5'6" Weight: 10.10
In his second full season at Walsall, this midfield dynamo missed the occasional game in 1998-99, but always came back with renewed enthusiasm to snatch some useful goals, such as the match winner at Reading in February. A little player with a big heart, Dean could go a long way in the game with added weight.
Walsall (From trainee on 14/8/96) FL 71+7/3 FLC 7+1 FAC 6 Others 11/2

KEEN Kevin Ian
Born: Amersham, 25 February 1967
Height: 5'7" Weight: 10.10
International Honours: E: Yth; Sch
Kevin was yet another player who fairly blossomed under Brian Little's 5-3-2 style in 1998-99, carving swathes through Second Division defences in the early part of a season that saw him an early candidate for Stoke's "Player of the Year" award. Occasionally called on to play at right-wing back, whilst he always gave his all he did lose some of his early edge. But, as the side's form returned in the spring, the hard-working midfielder was soon firing on all cylinders once again, before being released in the summer.
West Ham U (From apprentice on 8/3/84) FL 187+32/21 FLC 21+1/5 FAC 15+7/1 Others 14+2/3
Wolverhampton W (£600,000 on 7/7/93) FL 37+5/7 FLC 2+1 FAC 5/1 Others 4/1
Stoke C (£300,000 on 19/10/94) FL 127+27/9 FLC 10+2/1 FAC 5 Others 3+1

KEISTER John Edward Samuel
Born: Manchester, 11 November 1970
Height: 5'8" Weight: 11.0
International Honours: Sierra Leone: 3
Walsall's tough-tackling Sierra Leone international midfielder had the cruel luck to suffer a serious knee injury against Northampton in the second league game of last season, and spent the rest of 1998-99 bravely striving to rehabilitate himself. A very popular player at the Bescot, who gives his all to the cause, he is not only a destroyer but can also pass the ball into dangerous areas effectively. Out of contract during the summer, at the time of going to press the club had made him an offer of re-engagement.
Walsall (Free from Faweh FC on 18/9/93) FL 78+27/2 FLC 4 FAC 10+2 Others 2+2

KELLER Francois
Born: Colmar, France, 27 October 1973
Height: 5'10" Weight: 10.10
Signed from Strasbourg last December, and known to be a midfielder with an eye for goal, Francois played several Football Combination games for Fulham, but his only first-team start, which came at Torquay in the Auto Windscreens Shield, saw him in the back three where he looked far less comfortable. Having earlier made his debut for the Cottagers, when coming off the bench at home to Burnley not long after arriving at the club, it will be interesting to see where he plays in 1999-2000, having been released during the summer.
Fulham (£30,000 from Strasbourg on 9/12/98) FL 0+1 Others 1

KELLER Kasey C
Born: Washington, USA, 27 November 1969
Height: 6'2" Weight: 13.12
Club Honours: FLC '97
International Honours: USA: 39
The Leicester goalkeeper with a middle initial of C, which does not stand for anything, Kasey was very much the first choice for the Foxes in 1998-99, though an intermittent back problem contributed to the occasional dip in form as much as the uncertainty over his future. Having often expressed a wish to try his luck on the continent at some stage of his career, he continued to keep his options open as his contract expiry date loomed, and he ultimately decided to leave the club in the summer of 1998. Nevertheless, he still produced some of his best form when it mattered, and was blameless for the winner at Wembley where he had performed with customary confidence. Previously, a top-class effort to deny Niall Quinn in the closing moments of the semi final against Sunderland had done much to ensure Leicester's trip to the twin towers, whilst outstanding saves in both league fixtures against Spurs earned a double that was equally precious in Premiership terms. He also turned in a top-class performance in the goalless draw at Middlesbrough.
Millwall (Free from Portland University on 20/2/92) FL 176 FLC 14 FAC 8 Others 4
Leicester C (£900,000 on 17/8/96) PL 99 FLC 16 FAC 8 Others 2

KELLER Marc
Born: Colmar, France, 14 January 1968
Height: 5'11" Weight: 12.4
International Honours: France: 6
A former French international who signed for West Ham in the summer of 1998, after leaving Karlsruhe, although he can play on either wing he was used mainly on the left, and also did well when called upon to appear in a wing-back role. Scored a spectacular goal against Everton in December, when his cross floated into the net, but the contender for "Goal of the Season" came at Derby when he crashed a 20 yarder into the top corner in Hammers' 2-0 win. He also scored the equaliser, direct from a corner, in a 2-2 draw at Liverpool. As you would expect from someone of his calibre, he passes the ball well, always being comfortable in possession, and is a good early crosser.
West Ham U (Free from Karlsruhe, via Colmar, Mulhouse and Strasbourg, on 27/7/98) PL 17+4/5 FLC 1

KELLY Alan Thomas
Born: Preston, 11 August 1968
Height: 6'2" Weight: 14.3
International Honours: Ei: 22; U23-1; Yth
Again competing with Simon Tracey for the Sheffield United goalkeeping spot in 1998-99, Alan was first choice at the start of the season, before a cartilage injury at Darlington kept him out, apart from one game, until mid December when he reached his 200th league appearance for the club, against Huddersfield. In producing many fine performances, on more than one occasion he kept the team in the game. Missed further matches in March, due to a groin strain, but added to his Republic of Ireland caps against Paraguay, and was in the squad at other times.
Preston NE (From apprentice on 25/9/85) FL 142 FLC 1 FAC 8 Others 13
Sheffield U (£200,000 on 24/7/92) FL 213+3 FLC 15 FAC 22 Others 2

Jason Kearton

KELLY David Thomas
Born: Birmingham, 25 November 1965
Height: 5'11" Weight: 12.1
Club Honours: Div '93
International Honours: Ei: 26; B-3; U23-1; U21-3

Unfortunately, "Ned" suffered a recurrence of an old injury early on last season, and the rest of it proved to be a very up-and-down affair for him. His experience was missed by Tranmere, but when he did appear in the first team, he was his usual hard-working, resourceful, quick-thinking self to contribute five goals, and was gradually coming back to full fitness at the end of the campaign. Although David is a striker who often sacrifices his own welfare for the team cause, and is a valuable member of the squad, he makes no secret of his support for West Bromwich Albion!

Walsall (Signed from Alvechurch on 21/12/83) FL 115+32/63 FLC 11+1/4 FAC 12+2/3 Others 14+3/10
West Ham U (£600,000 on 1/8/88) FL 29+12/7 FLC 11+3/5 FAC 6 Others 2+1/2
Leicester C (£300,000 on 22/3/90) FL 63+3/22 FLC 6/2 FAC 1 Others 2/1
Newcastle U (£250,000 on 4/12/91) FL 70/35 FLC 4/2 FAC 5/1 Others 4/1
Wolverhampton W (£750,000 on 23/6/93) FL 76+7/26 FLC 5/2 FAC 11/6 Others 4/2
Sunderland (£1,000,000 on 19/9/95) P/FL 32+2/2 FLC 2+1 FAC 3
Tranmere Rov (£350,000 on 5/8/97) FL 44+12/15 FLC 7/5 FAC 3

Gary Kelly

KELLY Gary Alexander
Born: Preston, 3 August 1966
Height: 5'11" Weight: 13.6
Club Honours: FAYC '85
International Honours: Ei: B-1; U23-1; U21-8

In missing just one game throughout last season, a backs-to-the-wall campaign for Oldham as they fought against relegation almost from day one, where would they be without this superb shot-stopping goalie. Although he kept just ten clean sheets – especially vital in the last two fixtures of 1998-99 – his all-round ability saved many a match, and is probably the main reason that the Latics are still in the Second Division. As the son of Alan (senior), and brother to Alan (junior), currently at Sheffield United, both Republic of Ireland international 'keepers, the closest Gary has got to that is a "B" cap, and he would have surely joined them had it not been for a lack of inches. His enthusiasm and agility always gives confidence to the defence.

Newcastle U (From apprentice on 20/6/84) FL 53 FLC 4 FAC 3 Others 2
Blackpool (Loaned on 7/10/88) FL 5
Bury (£60,000 on 5/10/89) FL 236 FLC 14 FAC 13 Others 29
Oldham Ath (£10,000 on 27/8/96) FL 113 FLC 6 FAC 9 Others 2

KELLY Seamus
Born: Tullamore, Eire, 6 May 1974
Height: 6'1" Weight: 13.0

An impressive goalkeeper, Seamus moved to Cardiff just before 1998-99 got underway, having been spotted playing for University College, Dublin (League of Ireland). He then stepped into the City first team at a crucial stage – five games from the end of their promotion campaign after Jon Hallworth had suffered two broken ribs at Leyton Orient. Making his debut four days later, he looked nervous initially, but made some good saves and kept a clean sheet in a 1-0 win. Indeed, he conceded only one goal in his first four appearances as Cardiff clinched promotion before the final match of the season, at Mansfield, when three whistled past him. Having set such high standards, he returned on holiday to his hometown of Tullamore, where his dad runs a public house, and will probably be pinching himself . . .

Cardiff C (Free from UCD Dublin on 3/8/98) FL 5

KENNA Jeffrey (Jeff) Jude
Born: Dublin, 27 August 1970
Height: 5'11" Weight: 12.2
International Honours: Ei: 26; B-1; U21-8; Yth; Sch

A struggling start to last season resulted in Jeff losing his first-team place at Blackburn

Jeff Kenna

to Christian Dailly, but at the beginning of October he got back on the pitch as a substitute and retained his position until a pulled calf muscle at the end of February terminated his campaign. Ironically, he had been playing for some weeks with injury, and frequently turned out when he ought not to have played, his form being patchy with tricky wingers a problem. However, he covered resolutely, and competed well. Thrust into the role of penalty taker he had a disastrous time, missing a last-minute spot kick against Newcastle in the Worthington Cup, and repeating the feat even more expensively in the league game at Ewood. Represented the Republic of Ireland twice during 1998-99.

Southampton (From trainee on 25/4/89) F/PL 110+4/4 FLC 4 FAC 10+1 Others 3
Blackburn Rov (£1,500,000 on 15/3/95) PL 137+1/1 FLC 11 FAC 11 Others 7

KENNEDY John Neil
Born: Newmarket, 19 August 1978
Height: 5'8" Weight: 10.5

Given his chance in the Ipswich first team following Mauricio Taricco's transfer last December, and Micky Stockwell's subsequent injury, he made his first full appearance in the win at Barnsley. Playing in seven of the next ten games, this run enabled him to grow in confidence to develop his game from one where he concentrated solely on his defensive responsibilities to one where he was able to join in the attack regularly and provide the thrust down the right with some excellent crosses. Nicknamed "Spider" by his team mates because of his resemblance to the character of the same name in Coronation Street!

Ipswich T (From trainee on 2/6/97) FL 6+2 FAC 1

KENNEDY Mark
Born: Dublin, 15 May 1976
Height: 5'11" Weight: 11.9
International Honours: Ei: 22; U21-7; Yth; Sch

A left-sided Wimbledon winger possessing outstanding pace, Mark joined the Dons from Liverpool with promise but had just a handful of starts in the league in 1998-99. An excellent crosser of the ball, providing power and accuracy, he showed in the final game against Southampton just what a danger he could be when he runs at defenders. And, if he can consistently produce similar performances then he will surely feature more in the first team this coming term, which would please the fans, who feel this talented player has a lot to offer the club if given more of a chance. Stop Press: Having continued to represent the Republic of Ireland, he was transferred to Manchester City on 8 July for a £1 million plus fee.

Millwall (From trainee on 6/5/92) FL 37+6/9 FLC 6+1/2 FAC 3+1/1
Liverpool (£1,500,000 on 21/3/95) PL 5+11 FLC 0+2 FAC 0+1 Others 0+2
Queens Park R (Loaned on 27/1/98) FL 8/2
Wimbledon (£1,750,000 on 27/3/98) PL 11+10 FLC 4+1/1 FAC 2

KENNEDY Peter Henry James
Born: Lurgan, 10 September 1973
Height: 5'9" Weight: 11.11
Club Honours: Div 2 '98
International Honours: NI: 2; B-1

The left-sided Watford midfield player made a slow start to last season, but soon got to grips with the new challenges presented by Division One football. Peter, who is blessed with a fine left foot, proved once again what an excellent crosser of the ball he is, and was always a danger at set pieces. As the only outfield player to be an ever present, it was fitting that he should score the goal against Grimsby that clinched the Hornets' place in the play offs, and having made his full debut for the Northern Ireland team against Moldova in November he looks set to be a fixture in the squad.

Notts Co (£100,000 from Portadown on 28/8/96) FL 20+2 FLC 1 FAC 2+1/1 Others 0+1
Watford (£130,000 on 10/7/97) FL 80/17 FLC 6/1 FAC 6/2 Others 3

KENTON Darren Edward
Born: Wandsworth, 13 September 1978
Height: 5'10" Weight: 11.11

Darren made a promising start to 1998-99, scoring in Norwich's opening day 2-1 home win against Crewe at Carrow Road. A series of excellent performances during the first half of the season had him knocking on the door of the England U21 set-up, but injuries and a slight loss of form saw him out of the side in the latter weeks of the campaign. For one so young, he has a remarkably unhurried approach to his game and, despite being occasionally caught out of position, his recovery tackling is top class. With such a good temperament to go with his composure and maturity, he should develop into a quality full back who is able to play on either flank.

Norwich C (From trainee on 3/7/97) FL 29+4/1 FLC 5

KEOWN Martin Raymond
Born: Oxford, 24 July 1966
Height: 6'1" Weight: 12.4
Club Honours: PL '98; FAC '98; CS '98
International Honours: E: 23; B-1; U21-8; Yth

A central defender of the highest quality who was almost ever present in the now familiar Arsenal back-four in 1998-99, he has gone from strength to strength in recent seasons. With exceptional speed for a big man, his distribution skills match his tremendous strengths in tackling and in the air. And, as an extremely effective man marker when the occasion warrants, his partnerships with both Tony Adams and Steve Bould are arguably the finest in the Premier Division. Very dangerous at set pieces, he scored winning goals against Panathinaikos in the Champions' League, and Nottingham Forest in the Premiership. Was a member of the England squad at the 1998 World Cup, and although he did not start a match he was recalled for international duty during last season.

Arsenal (From apprentice on 2/2/84) FL 22 FAC 5
Brighton & Hove A (Loaned on 15/2/85) FL 21+2/1 FLC 2/1 Others 2/1

Aston Villa (£200,000 on 9/6/86) FL 109+3/3 FLC 12+1 FAC 6 Others 2
Everton (£750,000 on 7/8/89) F/PL 92+4 FLC 11 FAC 12+1 Others 6
Arsenal (£2,000,000 on 4/2/93) PL 181+18/3 FLC 16+2/1 FAC 19+2 Others 17+5/1

KERR David William
Born: Dumfries, 6 September 1974
Height: 5'11" Weight: 12.7

Played in over half of Mansfield's matches in 1998-99 in a midfield role, although he can also play in defence if requested, and showed some neat touches and good tackling ability. Came back well from a serious double fracture of the leg the season before last to play a useful part in the Stags' attempt to make the play offs. Out of contract during the summer, it was reported that the club had offered him terms of re-engagement.

Manchester C (From trainee on 10/9/91) PL 4+2
Mansfield T (Loaned on 22/9/95) FL 4+1 Others 1
Mansfield T (£20,000 on 31/7/96) FL 46+16/4 FLC 1+1 FAC 0+1 Others 3

KERRIGAN Steven (Steve) John
Born: Baillieston, 9 October 1972
Height: 6'1" Weight: 12.4
Club Honours: S Div 2 '97

Having joined Shrewsbury the previous season, Steve was again a very popular player with the crowd in 1998-99. Always in the thick of the action up front, and acting as target man in the long-term absence of the injured Devon White he formed an effective partnership with Lee Steele. Although a provider more than a scorer, he had a respectable haul, especially as he missed some games with injury.

Albion Rov (Free from Newmains Juveniles on 22/7/92) SL 46+7/14 SLC 2/1 SC 1 Others 1
Clydebank (Signed on 11/2/94) SL 17+13 SLC 1+1 Others 2+1/2
Stranraer (Signed on 4/11/95) SL 19+2/5 SC 1
Ayr U (Signed on 25/6/96) SL 26+7/17 SLC 2/2 SC 1 Others 2/2
Shrewsbury T (£25,000 on 21/1/98) FL 43+8/12 FLC 1 FAC 1

Steve Kerrigan

KERSLAKE David
Born: Stepney, 19 June 1966
Height: 5'9" Weight: 12.3
International Honours: E: U21-1; Yth; Sch
For such a gifted and experienced right back, 1998-99 was really a nightmare season for David at Swindon. After battling for the number two jersey with Mark Robinson, and picking up an abdominal injury that just would not go away, despite returning to make a few substitute appearances he looked a shadow of the player he was before being freed during the summer. Once of the Premiership, and at his best when getting forward to deliver quality crosses to the forwards after his pace had taken him clear of the defenders, he left the club just three short of 200 appearances in all competitions.
Queens Park R (From apprentice on 1/6/83) FL 38+20/6 FLC 6+2/4 FAC 2+2 Others 2+2
Swindon T (£110,000 on 24/11/89) FL 133+2/1 FLC 12 FAC 8 Others 10
Leeds U (£500,000 on 11/3/93) PL 8
Tottenham H (£450,000 on 24/9/93) PL 34+3 FLC 5 FAC 1+1
Swindon T (Loaned on 29/11/96) FL 8
Charlton Ath (Free on 8/8/97)
Ipswich T (Free on 22/8/97) FL 2+5 FLC 1+1
Wycombe W (Loaned on 12/12/97) FL 9+1 Others 1
Swindon T (Free on 10/3/98) FL 22+2

KETSBAIA Temuri
Born: Georgia, 18 March 1968
Height: 6'0" Weight: 13.0
International Honours: Georgia: 31
The shaven head of the effervescent, livewire Temuri has become a popular sight for Newcastle's Toon Army of supporters. Unpredictable to colleagues as well as opponents, he is a hard worker who will always give of his best, even when played out of position as he was for much of last season. Preferring to play just behind the front line, where he can make tell his ability to run at pace with the ball under close control, and exploit his explosive shooting, he has been most often used as one of the main strikers. In and out of the team during the earlier part of 1998-99, he secured a more regular place after the turn of the year when he hit a purple patch, contributing some important goals and laying assists. Probably his best game came in the FA Cup quarter final when, having run Everton ragged, he scored twice and then with a hat trick beckoning he unselfishly laid the ball off for Alan Shearer to score. A former regular in the Georgian national team, he was voted second to David Beckam as the world's most exciting player in a poll of Russian fans.
Newcastle U (Free from AEK Athens, via Dynamo Sukhumi, Dynamo Tbilsi and Anorthosis Famagusta, on 10/7/97) PL 30+27/8 FLC 1+1 FAC 8+4/4 Others 5+5/1

KEWELL Harold (Harry)
Born: Smithfield, Australia, 22 September 1978
Height: 6'0" Weight: 11.10
Club Honours: FAYC '97
Of all the youngsters at Leeds, Harry is the "jewel in the crown". After his emergence in 1997-98, which had the media drooling, Harry had a mediocre start to last season. In fact, his long-range deflected goal in the Worthington Cup was his first after 14 games. But from then on, "H" regained his form and proved that he was equally adept, whether as a central striker or on the left flank. Superb when running at defenders, he showed the balance and ability to mesmerise defenders in the same way in which Eddie Gray, now assistant manager at Elland Road, used to. As the goals began to come on a more regular basis, he was a main figure in the passing and movement style of David O'Leary's young side, also showing that he had a good attitude to match his football prowess. One of six nominations for the PFA "Young Footballer of the Year", he was placed third behind Nicolas Anelka and Michael Owen, and is a young player of immense talent.
Leeds U (Signed from the Australian Academy of Sport on 23/12/95) PL 64+6/11 FLC 4/3 FAC 9/3 Others 4

Harry Kewell

KEY Lance William
Born: Kettering, 13 May 1968
Height: 6'2" Weight: 14.6
In having the unenviable job of under-studying Rochdale's number one, Neil Edwards, in 1998-99, his one appearance of the season only lasted a few minutes – when the latter got stuck in traffic on his way to the cup tie against Scarborough. Having been handed the goalies' jersey, Edwards, named as a substitute, came on to replace him as soon as he arrived at the ground! Lance also spent some time on loan at Northwich Victoria.
Sheffield Wed (£10,000 from Histon on 14/4/90) FAC 0+1
Oldham Ath (Loaned on 12/10/93) PL 2
Oxford U (Loaned on 26/1/95) FL 6

Lincoln C (Loaned on 11/8/95) FL 5
Hartlepool U (Loaned on 15/12/95) FL 1
Rochdale (Loaned on 1/3/96) FL 14
Dundee U (Free on 26/7/96) SL 4
Sheffield U (Free on 14/3/97)
Rochdale (Free on 6/8/97) FL 19 FLC 2 FAC 1

KHARINE Dmitri Victorvitch
Born: Moscow, Russia, 16 August 1968
Height: 6'2" Weight: 13.9
International Honours: Russia: 38
The impressive Russian goalkeeper was replaced by Ed de Goey in 1998-99 as Blues' boss, Gianluca Vialli, abandoned his goalkeeping rotational policy of the previous season, and the giant Dutchman became automatic choice for all competitions. Dmitri started just four matches during the campaign – the first round European Cup Winners Cup-tie against Helsingborg and Worthington Cup-ties against Aston Villa, Arsenal, and Wimbledon. Following the last of these matches, in December, the Russian was usurped by Kevin Hitchcock for the goalkeeping spot on the bench, and spent the rest of the season playing for the reserves, before a surprise recall saw him pull off a series of superb saves to deny Derby a share of the spoils in the final match of the campaign. However, since sustaining a serious knee injury in September 1996, he has started a mere 14 first-team fixtures and, with the current defence playing so consistently, he was released during the summer, joining Celtic on 22 June.
Chelsea (£200,000 from CSKA Moscow on 22/12/92) PL 118 FLC 11 FAC 12 Others 5

KIDD Ryan Andrew
Born: Radcliffe, 6 October 1971
Height: 6'0" Weight: 12.10
Club Honours: Div 3 '96
Ryan's season at Preston in 1998-99 was once again disrupted by niggling injuries, despite an ankle operation during the summer. A knee injury in September put him out for three games, when his abilities on the left side of central defence, or at left back, were sorely missed. Returned to reach several personal milestones at the turn of the year, including 200 league and 250 senior games in both his career and for North End, before further ankle trouble required yet another operation, and put him out of action for ten weeks. Predominantly left footed, he scored his now traditional right-foot goal, against Chesterfield in August.
Port Vale (From trainee on 12/7/90) FL 1 FLC 0+2 Others 0+1
Preston NE (Free on 15/7/92) FL 195+14/9 FLC 13+1/1 FAC 14 Others 14+1/1

KIELY Dean Laurence
Born: Salford, 10 October 1970
Height: 6'1" Weight: 13.5
Club Honours: Div 2 '97
International Honours: E: Yth; Sch
1998-99 was another particularly consistent season for Bury's highly-rated goalkeeper. He would have completed his third straight ever-present season for the Shakers had a call-up for the Republic of Ireland squad in

September not necessitated him missing the away game at Birmingham. His C.V. included 19 clean sheets in league games during the season, despite playing in a team which was ultimately relegated, and the runner-up spot in Bury's "Player of the Season" poll. Stop Press: The club's relegation was expected to accelerate Dean's departure from Gigg Lane, as he was clearly too good for Division Two, and it was not unexpected when he signed for Charlton Athletic in a £1 million deal on 25 May.

Coventry C (From trainee on 30/10/87)
York C (Signed on 9/3/90) FL 210 FLC 9 FAC 4 Others 16
Bury (Signed on 15/8/96) FL 137 FLC 13 FAC 4 Others 3

KILBANE Kevin Daniel
Born: Preston, 1 February 1977
Height: 6'0" Weight: 12.10
International Honours: Ei: 5; U21-11

A strong-running left winger, and a firm favourite with the West Bromwich fans, Kevin put in some useful performances both at home and away in 1998-99, but perhaps lacked consistency. Nevertheless, he always gave 100 per-cent effort out on the park, scoring some excellent goals, including Albion's "Goal of the Season" against Bolton Wanderers at home, and the clincher in the tension-packed local derby win over Wolves at the Hawthorns. Continued to represent the Republic of Ireland at full and U21 level.

Preston NE (From trainee on 6/7/95) FL 39+8/3 FLC 4 FAC 1 Others 1+1
West Bromwich A (£1,000,000 on 13/6/97) FL 86+1/10 FLC 7 FAC 3/1

KILFORD Ian Anthony
Born: Bristol, 6 October 1973
Height: 5'10" Weight: 11.0
Club Honours: Div 3 '97; AMC '99

Central midfielder for Wigan with a lovely touch and an eye for an opening. Once again called upon to fill a variety of roles from right back to left wing, last season saw him complete over 150 Football League appearances. However, towards the end of the campaign, the club's longest-serving player found it difficult to hold down a regular first-team shirt but, as always, was a willing servant.

Nottingham F (From trainee on 3/4/91) FL 0+1
Wigan Ath (Loaned on 23/12/93) FL 2+1/2 FAC 0+1
Wigan Ath (Free on 13/7/94) FL 127+26/27 FLC 8+1 FAC 9+2/1 Others 9+2/2

KILTY Mark Thomas
Born: Sunderland, 24 June 1981
Height: 5'11" Weight: 12.5

Still a trainee, this promising young player, who has come through the junior and youth ranks at Darlington, made his debut as a substitute at Feethams on Easter Saturday 1999 against Rotherham, and impressed with his skills in midfield. Making one more appearance from the bench before the end of the season, he is expected to go a long way in the game.

Darlington (Trainee) FL 0+2

KIMBLE Alan Frank
Born: Dagenham, 6 August 1966
Height: 5'9" Weight: 12.4
Club Honours: Div 3 '91

An experienced left back who put in another consistent season for Wimbledon in 1998-99. Although a defender who always looks to get the ball upfield, and with pace and an accurate left foot, his forward runs are watched with much anticipation by Dons' fans. A player that can be relied upon to give 100 per-cent effort, Alan is much feared as a set-piece specialist, where he came close many times during the campaign. Since signing from Cambridge in 1993, he has proved to be one of Joe Kinnear's best bargains, and has been retained for 1999-2000.

Charlton Ath (From juniors on 8/8/84) FL 6
Exeter C (Loaned on 23/8/85) FL 1 FLC 1
Cambridge U (Free on 22/8/86) FL 295+4/24 FLC 23+1 FAC 29/1 Others 22
Wimbledon (£175,000 on 27/7/93) PL 144+9 FLC 15+3 FAC 22

KINDER Vladimir (Vlad)
Born: Bratislava, Czechoslovakia, 9 March 1969
Height: 5'9" Weight: 13.0
International Honours: Czechoslovakia: 1. Slovakia: 39

A strong-running, left-sided Middlesbrough defender, who loves to go forward and have a shot at goal, the Czechoslovakian international brought the house down with his opening goal against Coventry in Boro's recent surge from relegation fodder to European contenders in 1998-99. His appearances last season were almost all from off the bench and, although strictly limited, he still found the target on two occasions.

Middlesbrough (£1,000,000 from Slovan Bratislava on 18/1/97) F/PL 29+8/5 FLC 7+1 FAC 3+1

KING Ledley
Born: London, 12 October 1980
Height: 6'2" Weight: 13.6
International Honours: E: Yth

A talented young defender who joined Tottenham as a trainee in July 1997, and signed professional terms a year later, Ledley made it as far as the subs' bench in the FA Cup semi finals as Tottenham went out of the competition to Newcastle after extra time. He then went on to make his first-team debut at Liverpool in May, when coming on for the second half as a replacement for Stephen Clemence, with Spurs looking to plug the gaps, and seems certain to feature in the senior team again this coming season.

Tottenham H (From trainee on 22/7/98) PL 0+1

KING Marlon Francis
Born: Dulwich, 26 April 1980
Height: 6'1" Weight: 11.12

1998-99 was a truly phenomenal debut campaign for the teenage Barnet striker, who had only signed professional terms in early September. Having impressed John Still, his progression into the first team followed a series of outstanding displays for the reserve side, and he was rewarded for his goalscoring exploits with a substitute appearance against Rochdale at home in late October. After scoring his first goal for the senior team in the victory at Southend in December, and with Scott McGleish and Sean Devine out of favour, he was able to establish himself as a regular, and forged a productive partnership with Kenny Charlery in attack. Playing alongside the experienced Charlery proved to be immeasurably beneficial to him, and his knowledge of the game evolved as a result. His greatest attributes are his blistering pace, superb balance, and lethal accuracy in front of goal, but he is still very raw. Various scouts from the Premiership observed his displays during the latter stages of the campaign, and they would have witnessed some breathtaking strikes at Peterborough and at home against Cambridge and Scarborough.

Barnet (From trainee on 9/9/98) FL 17+5/6 FAC 0+1 Others 1

KING Philip (Phil) Geoffrey
Born: Bristol, 28 December 1967
Height: 5'10" Weight: 12.7
Club Honours: FLC '91
International Honours: E: B-1

Unable to figure in the first team at Swindon in 1998-99, as in the previous campaign, Phil moved to Brighton in mid March following an impressive performance in the reserves whilst on trial. An experienced, attacking left back who still retains his passing and crossing ability, despite lacking the pace of yesterday, he made just three starts before leaving Albion by mutual consent in April.

Exeter C (From apprentice on 7/1/85) FL 24+3 FLC 1 Others 1+2
Torquay U (£3,000 on 14/7/86) FL 24/3 FLC 2 FAC 1 Others 2
Swindon T (£155,000 on 6/2/87) FL 112+4/4 FLC 11 FAC 5 Others 13
Sheffield Wed (£400,000 on 30/11/89) F/PL 124+5/2 FLC 17 FAC 9 Others 4
Notts Co (Loaned on 22/10/93) FL 6 Others 2
Aston Villa (£250,000 on 1/8/94) PL 13+3 FLC 3 Others 4
West Bromwich A (Loaned on 30/10/95) FL 4 Others 1
Swindon T (Free on 26/3/97) FL 5
Blackpool (Loaned on 20/10/97) FL 6
Brighton & Hove A (Free on 19/3/99) FL 3

KING Stuart Samuel David
Born: Derry, 20 March 1981
Height: 5'10" Weight: 10.4
International Honours: NI: Yth

Signed as a full pro' after one year as a trainee at Preston, the young Northern Ireland youth international made his debut as a sub at Hartlepool in the Auto Windscreens Shield. The direct left winger played out on the right, showing some neat touches on a very heavy pitch, before volunteering to take the decisive penalty in the shoot-out, which unfortunately was saved. He is sure to come back stronger for the experience, and showed his powers of recovery by playing again the following night – his third game in three days!

Preston NE (From trainee on 18/5/98) Others 0+1

KINSELLA Mark Anthony
Born: Dublin, 12 August 1972
Height: 5'9" Weight: 11.8
Club Honours: GMVC '92; FAT '92
International Honours: Ei: 9; B-1; U21-8;
Yth

An immensely talented right-sided midfield player who is Charlton's club captain, and a regular in the Republic of Ireland international side, Mark is very comfortable on the ball, controls the midfield, and most of the team's attacking moves stem from him. Working well with Neil Redfearn and Graham Stuart in the centre of the midfield, he had another fine season in 1998-99, taking the step up to Premiership football in his stride. Although an ever present in the league, goals were rare, and he only found the net on three occasions, against Everton and Spurs at the Valley and at Old Trafford. Is capable of scoring spectacular goals from long range, and is the side's free-kick specialist. Voted "Player of the Year" by the fans for the second consecutive season.
Colchester U (Free from Home Farm on 18/8/89) FL 174+6/27 FLC 11/3 FAC 11/1 Others 9+1/5
Charlton Ath (£150,000 on 23/9/96) P/FL 121/15 FLC 3 FAC 5/1 Others 3

KITSON Paul
Born: Murton, 9 January 1971
Height: 5'11" Weight: 10.12
International Honours: E: U21-7

1998-99 was a frustrating season for the West Ham striker, who suffered groin surgery, broken toes, and a succession of strains. Whilst in the side his workrate was excellent, and he was always prepared to scrap for possession. A good man to be able to call upon, after scoring the winner against Chelsea in March he scored a great goal a week later against Newcastle, when he beat two defenders before drilling a low 12 yarder into the net. Hopefully, he can put this all behind him in 1999-2000, and get back to his best as a brave front-line player with two good feet, an ability to hold play up well to bring others into the game, added to pace and, of course, tremendous workrate.
Leicester C (From trainee on 15/12/88) FL 39+11/6 FLC 5/3 FAC 1+1/1 Others 5/1
Derby Co (£1,300,000 on 11/3/92) FL 105/36 FLC 7/3 FAC 5/1 Others 13+1/9
Newcastle U (£2,250,000 on 24/9/94) PL 26+10/10 FLC 3+2/1 FAC 6+1/3 Others 0+1
West Ham U (£2,300,000 on 10/2/97) PL 39+5/15 FLC 2 FAC 2/1

KIWOMYA Christopher (Chris) Mark
Born: Huddersfield, 2 December 1969
Height: 5'9" Weight: 11.2
Club Honours: Div 2 '92

Signed on a free transfer from Arsenal in August 1998, Chris made his Queens Park Rangers' debut as a substitute in the home game against Bury. However, his appearances were restricted by a foot injury suffered in September, which kept him out of contention until the New Year. On his return he made a few appearances, mostly again from the bench, before gaining a recall for the game against Swindon, and scoring his first two goals for Rangers. Released

during the summer, at his best he is an athletic striker with pace who can get in behind defences without breaking the off-side rule.
Ipswich T (From trainee on 31/3/87) F/PL 197+28/51 FLC 14+1/8 FAC 14/2 Others 5+1/3
Arsenal (£1,500,000 on 13/1/95) PL 5+9/3 Others 1+2 (Free to Selangar on 21/8/97)
Queens Park R (Free on 28/8/98) FL 12+4/6 FLC 0+1 FAC 0+1

KIZERIDIS Nicos
Born: Thessalonika, Greece, 20 April 1971
Height: 5'6" Weight: 11.7

Signed from Paniliakos in July 1998, the Greek midfielder could not settle in England after playing in pre-season with Portsmouth, and in six of the first eight games. There was no doubt that he excited the supporters with one-touch football and good ball play with delightful "shimmies", but hungry for first-team action and not mastering the English language, he returned home to Greece in October somewhat bewildered. Although capable of playing on the wing, his lightweight build resulted in him being easily challenged.
Portsmouth (£100,000 from Paniliakos on 10/7/98) FL 2+2 FLC 2

KNARVIK Thomas (Tommy)
Born: Bergen, Norway, 1 November 1979
Height: 5'8" Weight: 11.0
Club Honours: FAYC '97

This young Norwegian who joined Leeds on his 17th birthday, and went on to become the "Young Player of the Year" in 1997-98 is viewed as one of the brightest midfield prospects at Elland Road. Although his only appearance of 1998-99 was for eight minutes in the 5-1 FA Cup victory at Portsmouth, he was a regular in the reserves as a goalscoring midfielder and is definitely a young man with a big future.
Leeds U (Free from IL Skjerjard on 20/11/96) FAC 0+1

KNIGHT Alan Edward
Born: Balham, 3 July 1961
Height: 6'1" Weight: 13.11
Club Honours: Div 3 '83
International Honours: E: U21-2; Yth

Expected to be on hand for Portsmouth in 1998-99, in case of injury to Aaran Flahavan, this goalkeeping legend (the longest serving custodian in English football), notched another 20 league games, due to his younger rival's injuries and the

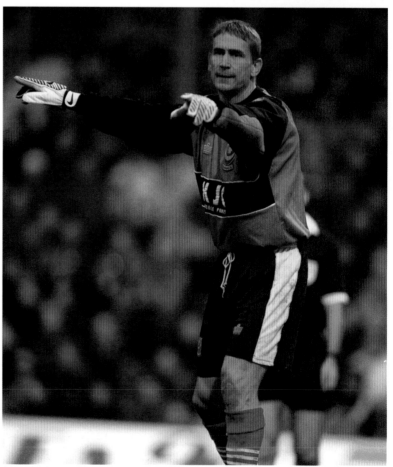

Alan Knight

on-loan 'keeper being recalled. Alan is still an excellent shot stopper and reflex 'keeper, even at the age of 39, and 21 years after his league debut. Having signed a three-year goalkeeping coach contract with Portsmouth to extend his one-club association to a remarkable 23 years, he is still registered as a goalkeeper for cover. At the start of 1999-2000, he will be only 82 league appearances short of the Pompey all-time record – Jimmy Dickinson's 764 – and has played in all four divisions for the club.

Portsmouth (From apprentice on 12/3/79) FL 682 FLC 51+1 FAC 43 Others 21

KNIGHT Richard
Born: Burton, 3 August 1979
Height: 6'1" Weight: 14.0
International Honours: E: Yth

Signed from non-league Burton Albion in June 1997, Richard waited patiently in the wings at Derby for his chance in 1998-99, but with Russell Hoult and Mart Poom showing excellent form he was confined to the reserves to learn his goalkeeping trade. His opportunity to play a higher grade of football came when he was loaned to Carlisle during transfer deadline week last March, after they had transferred their 'keeper to Blackpool without proper back up. It was not the easiest of situations in which to make his league debut, but after a slightly hesitant start he produced some fine performances in his six games for the club, before an injury crisis caused his return to Pride Park.

Derby Co (Signed from Burton A on 25/6/97)
Carlisle U (Loaned on 26/3/99) FL 6

Alan Knill

KNILL Alan Richard
Born: Slough, 8 October 1964
Height: 6'3" Weight: 13.0
Club Honours: WC '89
International Honours: W: 1; Yth

Rotherham's vastly experienced, tall central defender continued to give good service again at the heart of the defence in 1998-99, where he won many aerial battles, while proving invaluable in opposing penalty areas. He also showed great courage in

fending off problems caused by a back injury to play a vital role in the team's successful campaign, before being released in the summer.

Southampton (From apprentice on 14/10/82)
Halifax T (Free on 13/7/84) FL 118/6 FLC 6 FAC 6 Others 6
Swansea C (£15,000 on 14/8/87) FL 89/3 FLC 4 FAC 5 Others 7
Bury (£95,000 on 18/8/89) FL 141+3/8 FLC 7 FAC 8/1 Others 14+1/1
Cardiff C (Loaned on 24/9/93) FL 4
Scunthorpe U (Signed on 5/11/93) FL 131/8 FLC 5 FAC 10 Others 8
Rotherham U (Free on 7/7/97) FL 73+1/5 FLC 4 FAC 4/1 Others 4

KNOWLES Darren Thomas
Born: Sheffield, 8 October 1970
Height: 5'6" Weight: 11.6

For the second year running, Darren was Hartlepool's only ever present, and also voted the supporters' "Away Player of the Year". Proud to have 111 consecutive first-team appearances behind him at the end of 1998-99, it was a testament to the effective playing style of this popular right back, who always displays a fiercely competitive spirit. Yet, despite all that, he still managed to avoid the disciplinary problems that have dogged several of his team mates.

Sheffield U (From trainee on 1/7/89)
Stockport Co (£3,000 on 14/9/89) FL 51+12 FLC 2+4 Others 14+1
Scarborough (Free on 4/8/93) FL 139+5/2 FLC 11+1 FAC 9 Others 7
Hartlepool U (Free on 27/3/97) FL 99/1 FLC 4 FAC 3 Others 5

KONCHESKY Paul Martyn
Born: Barking, 15 May 1981
Height: 5'10" Weight: 10.12
International Honours: E: Yth

A first-year professional, Paul became the youngest ever Charlton player when he made his debut in 1997, and became their youngest Premiership player when he played at the Valley against Newcastle as a second-half substitute in 1998-99. Although his only start came against Wimbledon, also at the Valley, he aquitted himself well in both games, actually beginning the move which set up Martin Pringle for his last-minute equaliser in the Newcastle match. Very self assured, and composed, he uses the ball well when coming out of defence, and is a great prospect for the future.

Charlton Ath (From trainee on 25/5/98) P/FL 3+2 FLC 1

KONDE Oumar
Born: Binnengen, Switzerland, 19 August 1979
Height: 6'1" Weight: 12.6

Signed last November from FC Basle, the tall, young Swiss midfield player took some time to adjust to the English game at Blackburn. Selected as a substitute for two FA Cup-ties, he received his first taste of action when brought on at Newcastle, proving a tidy player who was able to keep himself mobile, although he failed to make his presence felt. His qualities on the ball were good, but he did not colour the game, and found it difficult to sustain his place,

even in the reserves. Stop Press: Left for SC Frieburg of Germany on 7 June.

Blackburn Rov (£500,000 from FC Basle on 13/11/98) FAC 0+1

KONJIC Muhamed
Born: Bosnia, 4 May 1970
Height: 6'4" Weight: 13.7
International Honours: Bosnia: 16

"Big Mo", as he is nicknamed by his colleagues, is the captain of Bosnia and the first Bosnian to play in the Premier League, having joined City last February from the French club, AS Monaco. In 1997-98 he played 19 league games and several Champions' League ties as Monaco reached the semi finals of the competition before losing to Juventus. As a tough, uncompromising defender, making his bow for the Sky Blues as a substitute in the league game at Tottenham, his first start came against Alan Shearer in a 4-1 defeat at Newcastle. Following that, it appeared that the man from Bosnia would take some time to adapt to the English game, but the fans remain optimistic that he will be ready to go this coming term.

Coventry C (£2,000,000 from AS Monaco, via Slobada Tuzla, Croatia Belisce, Croatia Zagreb and FC Zurich, on 5/2/99) PL 3+1

KOOGI Anders Bo
Born: Denmark, 8 September 1979
Height: 5'10" Weight: 11.1

This young Danish youth international finally made it to the Peterborough senior side, having come though the ranks as a trainee, when coming off the bench for the final two minutes of the last home game of 1998-99, a 3-0 win over Leyton Orient. A midfielder, who is expected to go further, Anders is a classy midfielder with vision, good passing ability, and a liking to get forward to join up with the attack. Watch out for him.

Peterborough U (From trainee on 21/7/97) FL 0+1

KOORDES Rogier
Born: Haarlem, Holland, 13 June 1972
Height: 6'1" Weight: 12.11

A left-sided midfield player who spent the majority of last season with Port Vale before being freed in February, the strong-running Dutchman started a dozen games but had his season continually interrupted by injury. His best games were probably in the victories at Crystal Palace and Barnsley, while his farewell appearance came in what was manager John Rudge's last game, against Swindon Town.

Port Vale (£75,000 from Telstar on 12/2/97) FL 29+9 FLC 0+1

KORSTEN Willem
Born: Boxtell, Holland, 21 January 1975
Height: 6'3" Weight: 12.10

The former Dutch U21 international, and a left-sided midfielder, cum striker, Willem joined Leeds on a three-month loan deal from Vitesse Arnhem last January. He quickly showed deft skill and excellent pace for someone so tall, and almost created a

scoring opportunity when coming on against Middlesbrough in January. Then, having settled into the squad very well, and scoring fine solo goals against Everton and Derby County, he was due to complete a permanent £1,500,000 transfer to Elland Road, but mysteriously turned the move down. Stop Press: Signed for Spurs during the summer, a transfer fee of £1.5 million doing the trick.
Leeds U (Loaned from Vitesse Arnhem, via NEC Nijmegen, on 11/1/99) PL 4+3/2 FAC 2+1

KOUMAS Jason
Born: Wrexham, 25 September 1979
Height: 5'10" Weight: 11.0
A confident midfielder, and one of the cornerstones of Tranmere's Pontins League team in 1998-99, Jason made his full first-team debut when he came on as a sub at Sunderland. His first goal came less than a fortnight later – an unstoppable thunderbolt against Huddersfield at Prenton Park. He is a quick-thinking, hard-running youngster, who is willing to look for the attacking option rather than making a negative pass, as well as being blessed with imagination and plenty of energy. In picking up two "Man of the Match" awards, and scoring four goals, he attracted a myriad of scouts from the top clubs, but seems content to consolidate his position with the Birkenhead outfit for now.
Tranmere Rov (From trainee on 27/11/97) FL 11+12/3 FLC 3+1/1

KOZLUK Robert (Rob)
Born: Mansfield, 5 August 1977
Height: 5'8" Weight: 11.7
International Honours: E: U21-2
A former "Young Derby Player of the Year", the right-wing back found it difficult to break into the County squad in 1998-99, making just ten appearances of sorts before finding his way to Sheffield United in mid March, along with Jon Hunt, as part of the players plus cash deal that took Vass Borbokis to Pride Park. At Bramall Lane, however, things improved, and he immediately slotted in on the right-hand side of defence as a wing back when making his debut at Tranmere. And, in making a most encouraging start with his pace being a great asset to the side, it was also his long throw that was used to good effect. The management have high hopes of this youngster.
Derby Co (From trainee on 10/2/96) PL 9+7 FLC 3 FAC 2+1
Sheffield U (Signed on 12/3/99) FL 10

KRIZAN Ales
Born: Slovenia, 25 July 1971
Height: 5'9" Weight: 12.12
International Honours: Slovenia: 25
Ales made only fleeting appearances for Barnsley under the management of John Hendrie in 1998-99, a Worthington Cup game early in the season, being followed by a chance in the league at home to Sheffield United in April. Tragically breaking his leg after only eight minutes, this composed left-sided defender will be hoping for a change of luck in the coming campaign.
Barnsley (£400,000 from Marbor Branik on 30/7/97) P/FL 13 FLC 4 FAC 1

KROMHEER Elroy Patrick
Born: Amsterdam, Holland, 15 January 1970
Height: 6'4" Weight: 13.12
A massive centre back who was signed by Reading from the Dutch side, FC Zwolle, following Royals' 1998 summer tour of Holland, Elroy failed to live up to expectations, despite having had earlier experience of British football with Motherwell. His place in the team was always at risk, after the club had signed Chris Casper last September, and he played out the latter part of the season in the reserve side. As you would expect, nothing much gets past him in aerial confrontations.
Motherwell (Signed from FC Volendam on 14/7/92) SL 11+1 SLC 1 SC 1 (Free to FC Volendam on 28/1/94)
Reading (£150,000 from FC Zwolle on 7/8/98) FL 11 FLC 1

KUBICKI Dariusz
Born: Warsaw, Poland, 6 June 1963
Height: 5'10" Weight: 11.12
Club Honours: Div 1 '96
International Honours: Poland: 47
Released by Wolves during the summer of 1998, the former Polish international had a short spell at right back for Carlisle in the opening weeks of last season, and proved yet again what a dependable performer he was, giving some useful displays in defence, before his connection with the club ended on him signing for Darlington in mid October. Studying at Sunderland University, he made just four appearances, all at left back, before he announced that he was returning home after eight years in this country, having completed his studies.
Aston Villa (£200,000 from Legia Warsaw, via Mielec and Zastra, on 28/8/91) F/PL 24+1 FLC 3 FAC 4+1 Others 1
Sunderland (£100,000 on 4/3/94) P/FL 135+1 FLC 7 FAC 7
Wolverhampton W (Free on 8/8/97) FL 12 FLC 4
Tranmere Rov (Loaned on 3/3/98) FL 12
Carlisle U (Free on 30/7/98) FL 7 FLC 2
Darlington (Free on 16/10/98) FL 2+1 Others 0+1

KUIPERS Michels
Born: Amsterdam, Holland, 26 June 1974
Height: 6'2" Weight: 14.10
An amateur with Amsterdam based SDW, Michels impressed in trials with Bristol Rovers in 1998-99 and, on being offered a two-year contract by the club, he bought himself out of the Dutch marines to pursue a full-time professional career in England. A tall, strong goalkeeper, with a superb attitude, the 24-year-old Dutchman made the breakthrough when making his league debut at Dean Court against Bournemouth. Will need further experience in the professional game, and will be pressing the current first-choice goalkeeper, Lee Jones, for the number-one jersey in 1999-2000.
Bristol Rov (Free from SDW Amsterdam on 20/1/99) FL 1

KULCSAR George
Born: Budapest, Hungary, 12 August 1967
Height: 6'2" Weight: 13.4
International Honours: Australia: 1

In his second season at Queens Park Rangers, George did not gain regular selection before the New Year, but in the second half of the campaign he was one of the many players tried in midfield. Normally playing in central midfield, he was used in a number of defensive positions in emergency situations, and scored his first goal for the club in the final game, a 6-0 home win over Crystal Palace. Is a strong ball winner who controls the area well and never stops running.
Bradford C (£100,000 from Royal Antwerp on 7/3/97) FL 23+3/1
Queens Park R (£250,000 on 17/12/97) FL 28+1/1 FLC 0+2

KVAL Frank Petter
Born: Bergen, Norway, 17 July 1974
Height: 6'0" Weight: 13.0
A Norwegian who remained second choice behind successive loan 'keepers at Burnley in 1998-99, after arriving at the club from Brann Bergen, before getting his break in the FA Cup-tie at the Riverside Stadium against Darlington. Unfortunately, after a capable, if occasionally eccentric performance, it all went wrong as the Clarets conceded three goals in the last ten minutes, and Frank failed to make the first-team line-up again, before being released during the summer.
Burnley (Signed from Brann Bergen on 6/10/98) FAC 1

KVARME Bjorn Tore
Born: Trondheim, Norway, 17 June 1972
Height: 6'1" Weight: 12.9
International Honours: Norway:1
Bjorn enjoyed a good early season for Liverpool in 1998-99, with his powerful, penetrating runs and fierce tackling skills, but the acquisition of Rigobert Song from Metz meant that his days were numbered at Anfield, often being relegated to the bench, and only brought on to offer the Reds options late in the game. A Norwegian international, who can also provide attacking choices when he gets forward, the club may well decide that he is too useful a player to let go, should injuries or suspensions rob them of key players.
Liverpool (Free from Rosenborg on 17/1/97) PL 39+6 FLC 2 FAC 2 Others 5

KYD Michael Robert
Born: Hackney, 21 May 1977
Height: 5'8" Weight: 12.10
Once again, this time in 1998-99, injury disrupted this young Cambridge striker's season – still only 23 years old but already in the top 20 United goalscorers. Limited to just ten full appearances as knee problems persisted, he managed to feature in a few games towards the end of the campaign, where he showed signs of recapturing his form of old. Fast and skilful, and often looking to be playing at too low a level, he needs an injury-free season to show what he is made of.
Cambridge U (From trainee on 18/5/95) FL 76+30/20 FLC 5+2/1 FAC 6+2/1 Others 3+2

LACEY Damien James
Born: Ogur, 3 August 1977
Height: 5'9" Weight: 11.3
Damien had his first game for Swansea last season against Gillingham in the Auto Windscreens Shield competition in January, followed by the match against Derby in the FA Cup tie, when replacing the injured Martin Thomas, and remaining in the first-team squad for the rest of the campaign. An extremely fit player, he is a good competitor, capable of playing well at full back or in midfield, with excellent passing qualities.
Swansea C (From trainee on 1/7/96) FL 32+12/1 FLC 2 FAC 1 Others 2

LAMBERT Christopher **James (Jamie)**
Born: Henley, 14 September 1973
Height: 5'7" Weight: 11.2
Booked and substituted in his only first-team match, in Reading's opening game of last season away to Wrexham, thereafter Jamie was sidelined by the manager, and forced to train on his own before spending a month on loan at Walsall in mid October, where he played on the left-hand side of midfield in four games, three of which were won. Reading eventually paid up his contract in March, and he played local football for Checkendon before going on trial at Walsall towards the end of 1998-99. Shows exciting dribbling skills, flair, and goals when at his best.
Reading (From juniors on 3/7/92) FL 77+48/16 FLC 8+3/2 FAC 9+2/1 Others 2+3/1
Walsall (Loaned on 16/10/98) FL 4+2

LAMBOURDE Bernard
Born: Guadaloupe, 11 May 1971
Height: 6'1" Weight: 12.4
Club Honours: FLC '98
A prerequisite for any club challenging for honours on two or three fronts is a utility player who is comfortable in a variety of positions. Chelsea are fortunate in having such a player in this man, and he filled in admirably at right back, central defence, and midfield when called upon. A calm, unflappable character, who is confident on the ball and has good positional sense, Bernard showed that he also has an eye for goal, and he lashed in his first for the Blues in Norway to put the European Cup Winners Cup beyond the reach of a gallant Valerenga.
Chelsea (£1,600,000 from Bordeaux, via Cannes, on 10/7/97) PL 17+7 FLC 5+1 FAC 2 Others 3+3/1

LAMPARD Frank James
Born: Romford, 21 June 1978
Height: 6'0" Weight: 12.6
International Honours: E: B-1; U21-13; Yth
As the only West Ham ever present, 1998-99 was a very impressive season for this young midfielder, who really seems to have come of age, and looks an outstanding bet for a top-class career. With football in his blood – his uncle, Harry Redknapp, currently manages the side, while his father, Frank (senior), played nearly 600 league games for the Hammers and is the club's assistant manager, and his cousin, Jamie Redknapp, is now with Liverpool – it is hardly surprising that he aspires to be one of the stars of the Premiership. Now established as England's U21 skipper, scoring against Poland and Luxembourg, and being called up for the full squad to play Hungary, he is surely in line to make the transition before too long. Has vision, allied to great passing skills, and can finish with the best of them, two 25-yard shots that notched up goals against Leicester and Middlesbrough merely proving the point. He was also the subject of transfer speculation, the club reportedly rejecting a £5 million offer from Spurs, followed by a statement from Harry Redknapp saying that Frank was going nowhere. Watch this space.
West Ham U (From trainee on 1/7/95) PL 68+16/10 FLC 8+1/5 FAC 8/1
Swansea C (Loaned on 6/10/95) FL 8+1/1 Others 1+1

LANCASHIRE Graham
Born: Blackpool, 19 October 1972
Height: 5'10" Weight: 11.12
Club Honours: Div 4 '92, Div 3 '97
Graham started 1998-99 in fine form with three goals in two pre-season Lancashire Cup games, and then scoring Rochdale's goal on the opening day of the season proper. Injured a couple of games later, he soon reappeared, scoring in each of his first two matches back. However, injury struck again, and he missed almost the entire campaign with a long-lasting thigh-muscle problem.
Burnley (From trainee on 1/7/91) FL 11+20/8 FLC 1+1 FAC 2+2/1 Others 2+4
Halifax T (Loaned on 20/11/92) FL 2 Others 1+1
Chester C (Loaned on 21/1/94) FL 10+1/7
Preston NE (£55,000 on 23/12/94) FL 11+12/2 Others 1+1
Wigan Ath (£35,000 on 12/1/96) FL 20+10/12 FLC 2+1/4
Rochdale (£40,000 on 2/10/97) FL 27+11/12 FLC 1+1 Others 1+1

LANCASTER Martyn Neil
Born: Wigan, 10 November 1980
Height: 6'0" Weight: 12.7
One of the highlights of Chester's season in 1998-99 was the progression of Martyn from the reserves to the first team. Still only 18, and probably City's hottest prospect, after making his league debut at Brentford in November he went on to make a further ten appearances at the heart of the defence, attracting the attention of many visiting scouts. As well as being strong in the tackle, he is a great athlete, is confident on the ball, and no doubt has a great future ahead of him.
Chester C (From trainee on 23/1/99) FL 8+3 FAC 0+1 Others 0+1

LANDON Richard John
Born: Worthing, 22 March 1970
Height: 6'3" Weight: 13.12
Despite being out of favour as the club's first-choice striker for most of the 1997-98 season, big Richard decided to see out his contract, thus remaining with Macclesfield for another year, and started the first game in Division Two against Fulham before falling from favour again. Having spent much of the campaign on loan at non-league Nuneaton and Atherstone, he received another chance in March, and regained form and favour with two goals in the first three games before being a provider for a further two in his next match. Was released during the summer.
Plymouth Arg (£30,000 from Bedworth U on 26/1/94) FL 21+9/12 FLC 0+1 FAC 0+1 Others 4
Stockport Co (£50,000 on 13/7/95) FL 7+6/4 FLC 0+1 FAC 0+1
Rotherham U (Loaned on 3/3/97) FL 7+1
Macclesfield T (Free on 11/7/97) FL 16+16/9 FLC 2 FAC 0+1 Others 0+1

LANGAN Kevin
Born: Jersey, 7 April 1978
Height: 6'0" Weight: 11.2
A product of Bristol City's youth policy, Kevin failed to make the hoped for breakthrough into regular first-team football in 1998-99. However, having impressed in the reserves, the steady and reliable full back was introduced by Benny Lennartsson in the vital home game against Bury but, on a night when the team failed to perform, he was substituted and left out for the following game. Is a strong tackler who could still become a regular at Ashton Gate.
Bristol C (From trainee on 4/7/96) FL 1+3 FAC 0+1 Others 1

LANGLEY Richard Barrington Michael
Born: Harlesden, 27 December 1979
Height: 5'10" Weight: 11.4
International Honours: E: Yth
Richard has made a rapid rise, progressing from the Queens Park Rangers' youth academy to becoming a first-team player. Having had just one reserve game last season before coming on as a substitute at Swindon, the next game saw him making his full debut and scoring a goal after just eight minutes. Unfortunately, the young midfielder suffered a serious leg injury against Ipswich at the beginning of December, which kept him out of action until late March.
Queens Park R (From trainee on 31/12/96) FL 7+1/1

LARUSSON Bjarnolfur (Bjarne)
Born: Iceland, 11 March 1976
Height: 5'11" Weight: 12.8
Signed from Hibernian, initially on loan, Bjarne made his Walsall debut in the 1-0 win at Luton near the end of last September, and joined on a more permanent basis on 16 October. The strong, hard-running forward scored twice, including the last-minute winner in the 4-3 win at Bristol Rovers at the end of October and, a few weeks later, starred against Rovers again, in the Auto Windscreens Shield, netting from the penalty spot in the 2-2 draw and also in the penalty shoot-out that took the Saddlers through. Was voted "Man of the Match" in the showpiece final home game against fellow promotion winners, Fulham.

Hibernian (Signed from IB Vestmanna on 17/10/97) SL 3+4/1
Walsall (Free on 25/9/98) FL 33+3/3 FAC 2 Others 6/1

LAUDRUP Brian

Born: Vienna, Austria, 22 February 1969
Height: 6'0" Weight: 13.2
Club Honours: SPD '95, '96, '97; SC '96; SLC '97; ESC '98
International Honours: Denmark: 82
Brian's performances for Denmark during the 1998 World Cup, particularly his dazzling display against reigning world champions, Brazil, had Chelsea fans drooling in anticipation of the world-class Dane taking his place in their star-studded line-up. Alas, Brian's stay was all too short because of his family's inability to settle in London, and he agreed to join European Cup Winners' Cup opponents, FC Copenhagen, after the 1-1 first leg at the Bridge, his father Finn having joined the Danish club as commercial manager. The second leg was precariously poised for Brian's last match in the famous blue shirt, but even Copenhagen's most famous son, Hans Christian Anderson, could not have written a more dramatic finale. Only victory guaranteed Chelsea's survival, and when Gigi Casiraghi's header came back off the crossbar who should nod home the rebound for the winning goal but Brian himself, thus ensuring his ex-club's progress at the expense of his new employers! It was his first and only goal for Chelsea in a career that had promised so much, but encompassed just ten starts. A slight back strain limited him to only two starts from the first seven matches, and he expressed his dissatisfaction with the club's rotation policy, although he was an automatic choice until his move. Chelsea's declared ambition was a four-pronged assault on the major trophies and, to be successful, a strong, talented squad was a necessity to overcome injuries, suspensions, and fixture pile-ups. The Dane's departure was exacerbated by the loss of Casiraghi just three days later, and the "Great Dane" left Blues' fans with just fleeting memories of cameo appearances.
Glasgow R (Signed from AC Milan, via Brondby, Uerdingen, Bayern Munich and Fiorentina, on 15/6/94) SL 114+2/33 SLC 4/3 SC 13/5 Others 16+1/3
Chelsea (Free on 17/6/98) PL 5+2 Others 3+1/1

LAUNDERS Brian Terence

Born: Dublin, 8 January 1976
Height: 5'10" Weight: 11.12
International Honours: Ei: U21-9; Yth
The former Crystal Palace midfielder was taken on loan by Derby's Jim Smith last September from Veendam in Holland until the end of 1998-99. Also able to play as a striker if required, he stayed in the reserves before making one substitute appearance at Leeds in March, prior to being loaned out until the end of the season to Second Division Colchester. Unfortunately, selected as an attacking midfielder he picked up a knee injury on his debut at Bournemouth, which finished his season and saw him become another member of United's "one game only club".

Crystal Palace (Signed from Cherry Orchard on 2/9/93) P/FL 1+3 FLC 0+2
Crewe Alex (Free on 8/8/96) FL 6+3 FLC 1+1 (Free to BV Veendam during 1997 close season)
Derby Co (Loaned on 11/9/98) PL 0+1
Colchester U (Loaned on 25/3/99) FL 1

LAURSEN Jacob

Born: Vejle, Denmark, 6 October 1971
Height: 5'11" Weight: 12.0
International Honours: Denmark: 26
Virtually an ever present in 1998-99, the Danish international defender had another very consistent season at the heart of the Derby defence. Rated as one of the best man markers in the league in a central position, though also able to play as a wing back when necessary, having appeared in one game at France 98, he subsequently found himself out in the cold for the Euro 2000 qualifiers after being asked to play out of position. Possibly his best performance was in the back-to-the-wall display at Arsenal in the FA Cup, County only losing out to a last-minute goal. Has delighted the fans by signing a new contract which will keep him at Pride Park till 2002 and, in the absence of Igor Stimac, is a capable deputy as club captain. His consistency resulted in him being named as "Player of the Year" by the fans, where he took more than 50 per cent of the vote.
Derby Co (£500,000 from Silkeborg on 17/7/96) PL 99+2/2 FLC 7 FAC 7

LAVIN Gerard

Born: Corby, 5 February 1974
Height: 5'10" Weight: 11.0
International Honours: S: U21-7
For fully 18 months, Gerard was sidelined by a knee injury he feared might mean the end of his career, but, then, just a year ago, he battled his way back to first-team football, hoping and praying that his knee would stand up to the stresses and strains. A virtual ever present in 1998-99, who scored his first Millwall goal in the Auto Windscreens Shield tie at Brighton, he is a pacy full back with the ability to get past fellow defenders to deliver good crosses. Surprisingly released in the summer, he is still hard in the tackle, while his reading of the game is an asset to any defence.
Watford (From trainee on 11/5/92) FL 121+5/3 FLC 11/1 FAC 6 Others 2+1
Millwall (£500,000 on 23/11/95) FL 67+7 FLC 2 FAC 3+1 Others 8/1

LAW Brian John

Born: Merthyr Tydfil, 1 January 1970
Height: 6'2" Weight: 13.6
International Honours: W: 1; U21-2; Yth; Sch
During the course of a difficult first season in 1997-98 at Millwall, Brian proved himself a consistent performer and was appointed skipper at the beginning of 1998-99, a position he kept until a knee injury sidelined him for the rest of the campaign. Released during the summer, he must hope that the coming term will bring different fortunes, as the last three years have seen nothing but injuries for this strong-tackling, well motivated central defender.

Queens Park R (From trainee on 15/8/87) FL 19+1 FLC 2+1 FAC 3 Others 1
Wolverhampton W (£134,000 on 23/12/94) FL 26+5/1 FLC 1+1 FAC 7
Millwall (Free on 31/7/97) FL 45/4 FLC 5 FAC 1 Others 2

LAWRENCE James (Jamie) Hubert

Born: Balham, 8 March 1970
Height: 5'11" Weight: 12.11
Club Honours: FLC '97
Having signed a new contract in the summer of 1998 to keep him at Bradford until 2001, Jamie started the first seven games in 1998-99 before being out for 11 matches with a medial knee-ligament injury. Began the campaign in midfield, but on coming back to the side, and due to injuries in the right-back position, he found himself playing as a wing back. Regularly moved back for tactical reasons, he always gave 100 per-cent effort in every game, wherever he played, a fact proven by his "Man of the Match" awards. Fast, skilful, and a good tackler, he is very much appreciated at Valley Parade.
Sunderland (Signed from Cowes on 15/10/93) FL 2+2 FLC 0+1
Doncaster Rov (£20,000 on 17/3/94) FL 16+9/3 FLC 2 FAC 1 Others 3
Leicester C (£125,000 on 6/1/95) P/FL 21+26/1 FLC 3+4/2 FAC 1+1
Bradford C (£50,000 on 17/6/97) FL 71+7/5 FLC 4+1 FAC 3/1

LAWRENCE Matthew (Matty) James

Born: Northampton, 19 June 1974
Height: 6'1" Weight: 12.12
International Honours: E: Sch
Having played 54 games, more than anyone else at Fulham in 1997-98, it came as a big surprise when the right back, cum midfielder, rejoined Wycombe last October. It was obvious that he had returned a much better player, and he immediately slotted into the right-wing back role, where he impressed with his tigerish defending and creative attacking play, and ability to whip useful in-swinging crosses into the box. Also had a spell as a central midfielder, where his strong tackling and thrusting runs came to the fore, before ending the season very strongly in what is probably his best position of right back. There are few better right backs in Division Two, especially one with a positive attitude towards the game that all managers look for in a player.
Wycombe W (£20,000 from Grays Ath on 19/1/96) FL 13+3/1 FLC 4 FAC 1 Others 0+1
Fulham (Free on 7/2/97) FL 57+2 FLC 4+1 FAC 2 Others 5
Wycombe W (£86,000 + on 2/10/98) FL 34/2 FAC 3 Others 2

LAWSON Ian James

Born: Huddersfield, 4 November 1977
Height: 5'11" Weight: 11.5
Having celebrated his 21st birthday by signing a new two-year contract for Huddersfield in 1998-99, Ian immediately signed up for the first of two loan spells with Second Division Blackpool, scoring three goals in five games in his first spell in November, but failing to find the net the second time round. Back at the McAlpine,

the pacy striker did not see too much first-team action – only an early December run out at home to West Bromwich – before coming off the subs' bench against Queens Park Rangers and promptly scoring his first goal of the season for Town. Three days later he repeated the act against Swindon. Excellent in the air, and showing much promise, he continues to be a part of the club's plans.

Huddersfield T (From trainee on 26/1/95) FL 13+29/5 FLC 1+4 FAC 1+1
Blackpool (Loaned on 6/11/98) FL 5/3
Blackpool (Loaned on 8/1/99) FL 4

LAZARIDIS Stanley (Stan)
Born: Perth, Australia, 16 August 1972
Height: 5'9" Weight: 11.12
International Honours: Australia: 21

Last season was a disappointing one for West Ham's Australian international left winger, who found it difficult to maintain defensive duties in a new wing-back role. At his best when going forward, and using his pace to attack defenders – either going down the flank on a direct route, or going on a mazy dribble – a groin strain sidelined him in September and, on coming back, he failed to hold down a regular place, making just 14 starts in all. If only he could add consistency to his other exciting talents.

West Ham U (£300,000 from West Adelaide on 8/9/95) PL 53+16/3 FLC 6+1 FAC 9+1

LEABURN Carl Winston
Born: Lewisham, 30 March 1969
Height: 6'3" Weight: 13.0

This powerful striker who is in the John Fashanu mould, enjoyed a long spell in the Wimbledon first team during the first half of last season. Although his only goal came in the Worthington Cup 4-1 home win over Portsmouth, his ability to hold the ball up well, and his flick ons and headers provided many opportunities for his fellow team mates. Joining from Charlton in January 1998 after progressing from their youth team, he is well respected within the football world. Is an excellent team player to be able to call upon.

Charlton Ath (From apprentice on 22/4/87) FL 276+46/53 FLC 19/5 FAC 19+2/4 Others 9+5/4
Northampton T (Loaned on 22/3/90) FL 9
Wimbledon (£300,000 on 9/1/98) PL 29+9/4 FLC 3+4/1 FAC 3

LEADBITTER Christopher (Chris) Jonathan
Born: Middlesbrough, 17 October 1967
Height: 5'9" Weight: 10.6
Club Honours: Div 3 '91

This vastly experienced Torquay player was probably the pick of the Gulls' midfield in 1998-99, a season during which they struggled in this department. A very strong tackler, and full of running for a player in the latter stages of his career, he was a big inspiration to the younger members of the side. With him being out of contract during the summer, at the time of going to press the club had already offered him new terms.

Grimsby T (From apprentice on 4/9/85)
Hereford U (Free on 21/8/86) FL 32+4/1 FLC 2 FAC 2 Others 3

Cambridge U (Free on 2/8/88) FL 144+32/18 FLC 12/3 FAC 16+2/3 Others 11+2/1
Bournemouth (£25,000 on 16/8/93) FL 45+9/3 FLC 6+1 FAC 5 Others 2
Plymouth Arg (Free on 27/7/95) FL 46+6/1 FLC 2 FAC 6/1 Others 5+1/1 (Free to Dorchester T during 1997 close season)
Torquay U (Free on 27/11/97) FL 58+5/2 FLC 1 FAC 1+2 Others 5+1

LEAH John David
Born: Shrewsbury, 3 August 1978
Height: 5'9" Weight: 12.0

Arriving at Darlington in the summer of 1998, on trial from League of Wales club, Newtown, the young midfielder was rewarded with a season's contract after impressing with his workrate and strong shooting. A player with a future, he made nine starts, including an appearance in the FA Cup (at Manchester City), and scored his first Football League goal with a fierce drive the Scunthorpe 'keeper could not hold.

Darlington (Signed from Newtown on 8/7/98) FL 7/1 FAC 1+1 Others 1

LEANING Andrew (Andy) John
Born: Goole, 18 May 1963
Height: 6'1" Weight: 14.7

Andy again proved to be an excellent club servant in 1998-99, taking his status as Chesterfield's reserve 'keeper with good grace, and performing with coolness and distinction when called upon. This was no more apparent than at Maine Road in September, where an excellent penalty save capped a resolute show that earned a point in a heated atmosphere. Out of contract during the summer, at the time of going to press the club had made an offer of re-engagement.

York C (Free from Rowntree Mackintosh on 1/7/85) FL 69 FLC 4 FAC 8 Others 5
Sheffield U (Free on 28/5/87) FL 21 FLC 2 FAC 2
Bristol C (£12,000 on 27/9/88) FL 75 FLC 5 FAC 7 Others 2
Lincoln C (Free on 24/3/94) FL 36 FLC 6 FAC 3 Others 6 (Freed during 1996 season)
Dundee U (Free on 19/7/96)
Chesterfield (Free on 1/10/96) FL 16 FLC 2 FAC 2 Others 1

LEBOEUF Frank
Born: Marseille, France, 22 January 1968
Height: 6'0" Weight: 12.6
Club Honours: FAC '97; FLC '98; ECWC '98
International Honours: France: 22

In the dark, pre-Ruud Gullit days it was inconceivable that a Chelsea player would appear in a World Cup final, but such has been Frank's phenomenal impact that he looked perfectly at home in this exalted company. A complete all-round, modern defender, who turns defence into attack with long, raking passes to the front men, he also wins the ball with crunching tackles, and has formed a formidable central defensive barrier with fellow-World Cup winner, Marcel Desailly – a crucial partnership in the team's quest for honours in 1998-99. He was also a central figure in one of the most controversial incidents of the season. In a scenario a million miles away from the World Cup final at Saint-Denis – the Manor Ground, Oxford, to be precise – he

demonstrated ice-cool nerves to slot home a 93rd-minute penalty in the FA Cup fourth round, to tie up the scores after the referee, Mike Reed, had adjudged Luca Vialli to have been fouled in the box. This maintained his 100 per-cent record from the spot since joining Chelsea – 15 in succession, and followed one of the goals of the season – against Coventry City at the Bridge – when he collected the ball on the halfway line, stormed forward, stepped inside a challenge, and lashed an unstoppable 20-yard drive past the 'keeper. As Chelsea's stand-in skipper – he had plenty of opportunities last season owing to Dennis Wise's disciplinary problems! – Frank has been a pivotal influence in Chelsea's cup successes over the past three seasons. Like the rest of the "Foreign Legion", he is a confirmed Anglophile and, as befits an articulate man, writes a column in a Broadsheet newspaper; has addressed the Oxford Union and Eton, and met the Prime Minister at 10 Downing Street. To the delight of all Blues' fans, the Frenchman signed a new three-year contract in March that will keep him at the club until 2002.

Chelsea (£2,500,000 from Strasbourg, via Hyeres, Meaux and Laval, on 12/7/96) PL 91/15 FLC 8/1 FAC 12/2 Others 17/2

Frank Leboeuf

LEE Alan Desmond
Born: Galway, 21 August 1978
Height: 6'2" Weight: 13.9
International Honours: Ei: U21-3

Unable to get a game at Aston Villa, this big, strong striker went on loan to Torquay last November, and had a highly impressive spell with the Gulls, scoring vital goals at Exeter, and a classic "Golden Goal" header which defeated Kevin Keegan's Fulham in the Auto Windscreens Shield. A player who holds the ball up well, he had another period on loan, this time at Port Vale, scoring goals against Bradford and Tranmere, and staying on until the end of the season. Was also capped at U21 level for the Republic of Ireland.

Aston Villa (From trainee on 21/8/95)
Torquay U (Loaned on 27/11/98) FL 6+1/2 Others 2/1
Port Vale (Loaned on 2/3/99) FL 7+4/2

LEE Christian (Chris) Earl
Born: Aylesbury, 8 October 1976
Height: 6'2" Weight: 11.7
A tall and speedy Northampton striker. With so many forwards on the books last season Chris found it hard to hold down a first-team place, although he was quite prolific in the reserves, failing to find the form that bagged him nine goals at the start of the 1996-97 season. However, with youth on his side, he still has time to establish himself.
Northampton T (Free from Doncaster Rov juniors on 13/7/95) FL 25+34/8 FLC 2/2 FAC 3+3 Others 6+2

LEE David John
Born: Bristol, 26 November 1969
Height: 6'3" Weight: 14.7
Club Honours: Div 2 '89; FLC '98
International Honours: E: U21-10; Yth
Released by Chelsea in December after a decade at Stamford Bridge, the experienced central defender joined his home town club, Bristol Rovers, who he had supported as a youngster. It provided him with an opportunity to play in his more favoured central midfield role, where his accurate distribution proved useful to a developing young team. David scored twice – a cracking goal against Burnley at the Memorial Stadium and another against Leyton Orient in the fourth round of the FA Cup, which ensured Rovers first appearance in the fifth round for over 20 years. Was released during the summer.
Chelsea (From trainee on 1/7/88) F/PL 119+32/11 FLC 13+7/1 FAC 10+4 Others 6+2/1
Reading (Loaned on 26/3/92) FL 5/5
Plymouth Arg (Loaned on 26/3/92) FL 9/1
Portsmouth (Loaned on 12/8/94) FL 4+1
Sheffield U (Loaned on 19/12/97) FL 5
Bristol Rov (Free on 23/12/98) FL 10+1/1 FAC 3/1

LEE David Mark
Born: Manchester, 5 November 1967
Height: 5'7" Weight: 11.0
Club Honours: Div 1 '97; AMC '99
David was still an invaluable member of the Wigan squad in 1998-99, and figured in over half of the games, both in the starting line-up and as a substitute. At his best, the right winger can use his acceleration to go past defenders to get accurate crosses into the box. Also good for a few goals, one of his seven strikes came with a spectacular lob from the edge of the penalty box in the away victory over Macclesfield.
Bury (From juniors on 8/8/86) FL 203+5/35 FLC 15/1 FAC 6 Others 19+1/4
Southampton (£350,000 on 30/1/92) F/PL 11+9 FAC 0+1 Others 1+1
Bolton W (£300,000 on 2/11/92) P/FL 124+31/17 FLC 19+1/2 FAC 13+2 Others 8+1/1
Wigan Ath (£250,000 on 16/7/97) FL 61+18/11 FLC 6/2 FAC 4+2/2 Others 5+4/1

LEE Graeme Barry
Born: Middlesbrough, 31 May 1978
Height: 6'2" Weight: 13.7
Unfortunately, 1998-99 was not the best of

seasons for Hartlepool's promising young central defender, despite being rated a £1 million prospect. Although early on he was reputedly attracting the attention of bigger clubs, playing well alongside Michael Barron, as the weeks progressed his form was affected by a troublesome ankle injury, and it was this that eventually brought his season to a premature end. At 21 years old, and still learning, he should benefit greatly from playing alongside the experienced central defender, Gary Strodder, in 1999-2000.
Hartlepool U (From trainee on 2/7/96) FL 84+7/6 FLC 3+2/1 FAC 4 Others 5+1/1

LEE Jason Benedict
Born: Forest Gate, 9 May 1971
Height: 6'3" Weight: 13.8
Club Honours: Div 2 '98
Signed from Watford, John Duncan's long pursuit of this tall front man ended last August when he joined Chesterfield for a club record fee. Jason's height and physical presence were obvious qualities. He also displayed a good first touch which, allied to his ability to hold the ball up, might have made him an important member of the side but for an early suspension and a succession of niggling injuries. Most of the fans have taken to him, and were delighted to see his first goal for the club against Blackpool in March.
Charlton Ath (From trainee on 2/6/89) FL 0+1 Others 0+2
Stockport Co (Loaned on 6/2/91) FL 2
Lincoln C (£35,000 on 1/3/91) FL 86+7/21 FLC 6 FAC 2+1/1 Others 4
Southend U (Signed on 6/8/93) FL 18+6/3 FLC 1 FAC 1 Others 5+3/3
Nottingham F (£200,000 on 4/3/94) F/PL 41+35/14 FLC 4+3/1 FAC 0+5 Others 4+2
Charlton Ath (Loaned on 5/2/97) FL 7+1/3
Grimsby T (Loaned on 27/3/97) FL 2+5/2 FAC 1
Watford (£200,000 on 16/6/97) FL 36+1/11 FLC 4 FAC 4 Others 1
Chesterfield (£250,000 on 28/8/98) FL 14+8/1 FAC 0+1 Others 0+2

LEE Martyn James
Born: Guildford, 10 September 1980
Height: 5'6" Weight: 9.0
Having signed pro terms for Wycombe last January, Martyn, a left-footed central midfielder, progressed from last year's youth team to earn two starts in the second half of the season, at Chesterfield and Notts County. Although diminutive, he impressed with his accurate left foot and nice touches on the ball and, on his debut, was confident enough to want to take all of the free kicks near the penalty area. Will almost certainly feature more strongly during the coming term.
Wycombe W (From trainee on 30/1/99) FL 2+1

LEE Robert (Rob) Martin
Born: West Ham, 1 February 1966
Height: 5'11" Weight: 11.13
Club Honours: Div 1 '93
International Honours: E: 21; B-1; U21-2
Rob, a powerful all-round Newcastle midfield player, is particularly adept at making box-to-box surges with the ball under close control, and has an engine

which enables him to do so throughout even the most demanding of games. His strength makes him difficult to shake off the ball, and he enjoys joining his strikers for shots on goal, whilst he rarely wastes a ball with his passing. Following his disappointment at missing out on Euro 96 he was delighted to be included in the England squad for the 1998 World Cup, and he made a substitute appearance against Colombia. Starting last season in good form in his preferred position of central midfield as a popular Newcastle club captain with a new three-year contract in his pocket, he was struck down by a troublesome virus in October, and then a few games after his comeback he suffered an achilles tendon injury against Leeds on Boxing Day, which sidelined him for two months. Then, on his return, he was unable to regain his starting place in the side. His appearances thereafter were largely restricted to substitutions, but whenever he played he always made his full contribution, such as in the home game with Arsenal when he drove the team forward to eventually gain a deserved point. During this period of absence from the team, Alan Shearer was appointed to replace him as club captain, although Rob still led the team out whenever Alan was absent. His non appearance in the regular starting line-up led to rumours that he was about to return to one of the London sides, but nothing materialised before transfer deadline day. Playing in the FA Cup semi final, where he had a fine game on the right, he helped young Andy Griffin to successfully subdue the menace of David Ginola, whilst also finding time to make an important contribution in midfield. Played in England's opening three games of 1998-99.
Charlton Ath (Free from Hornchurch on 12/7/83) FL 274+24/59 FLC 16+3/1 FAC 14/2 Others 10+2/3
Newcastle U (£700,00 on 22/9/92) F/PL 226+9/43 FLC 15/3 FAC 23/4 Others 19/4

LEESE Lars
Born: Cologne, Germany, 18 August 1969
Height: 6'4" Weight: 14.5
Having played a few games for Barnsley in 1997-98, while very much a stand-by goalkeeper, Lars got his chance last season following the injury to first-choice David Watson just eight games into 1998-99. However, as the team's form was in and out, he was one of the players to suffer, losing his place due to the excellence of the replacement, Tony Bullock, and never regaining it. Is a good shot stopper, and great on crosses, having a commanding presence in the box. Was released during the summer.
Barnsley (£250,000 from Bayern Leverkusen on 23/7/97) P/FL 16+1 FLC 4

LEGG Andrew (Andy)
Born: Neath, 28 July 1966
Height: 5'8" Weight: 10.7
Club Honours: WC '89, '91; AIC '95
International Honours: W: 5
Andy was yet another Reading player who was given his chance in early games last season but, on failing to impress the manager, being placed on the transfer list

and excluded from training with the other players. The left back, and long throw-in expert, spent a month on loan at Peterborough in mid October, where he was an immediate hit with the fans, before signing a two-and-a-half-year contract with Cardiff in December after leaving the Royals on a free transfer. Returning home to Wales, he was given a great reception when showing total commitment to the team and an ability to take on the opposition. Representing Wales against Denmark, he shows great workrate in midfield, and can also fill in at full back if needed.

Swansea C (Signed from Britton Ferry on 12/8/88) FL 155+8/29 FLC 9+1 FAC 16/4 Others 15+3/5
Notts Co (£275,000 on 23/7/93) FL 85+4/9 FLC 11 FAC 7+1 Others 13+2/6
Birmingham C (Signed on 29/2/96) FL 31+14/5 FLC 3+1 FAC 2+1
Ipswich T (Loaned on 3/11/97) FL 6/1 FLC 1
Reading (£75,000 on 20/2/98) FL 12 FLC 1
Peterborough U (Loaned on 15/10/98) FL 5
Cardiff C (Free on 16/12/98) FL 18+6/2 FAC 0+3

LEHMANN Dirk Johannes
Born: Aachen, Germany, 16 August 1971
Height: 6'0" Weight: 11.10
Signed from German Second Division side, Cottbus, immediately prior to the start of 1998-99, Dirk made his Fulham debut in a 4-2 pre-season victory at Ryman League Hendon, netting his first goal with a second-minute header. A regular in the first team until the arrival of Geoff Horsfield, he played an important role later in the campaign, in helping to keep all the strikers fresh, with several appearances from the bench. Also, his uncanny ability to hang in the air when he had seemed to jump too early, fooled most defenders, and created chances for his team mates. Although making a good start with three goals in his first three games, nine goals in 13+1 Combination games gives a better indication of his ability than his overall senior strike rate. Stop Press: Was surprisingly released during the summer and joined Hibernian on 8 July.

Fulham (£30,000 from Cottbus, via Molenbeek, on 7/8/98) FL 16+10/2 FLC 5/2 FAC 2+2/1 Others 1

LEITCH Donald Scott
Born: Motherwell, 6 October 1969
Height: 5'9" Weight: 12.2
This well-travelled Scottish midfield anchorman continued to be an instrumental figure at Swindon in 1998-99 with his tackling and ability to spread play from the centre of the park. Unfortunately, his appearances were somewhat limited due to a knee injury that dogged him for much of the season, and he will look to come back strongly this coming term. At his best operating just in front of the defence, when he is available the team plays better.

Dunfermline Ath (Free from Shettleston Juniors on 4/4/90) SL 72+17/16 SLC 6+1/3 SC 3 Others 1
Hearts (Signed on 6/8/93) SL 46+9/2 SLC 1+2/1 SC 3 Others 2
Swindon T (£15,000 on 29/3/96) FL 91+2/1 FLC 7/2 FAC 2

LENAGH Steven (Steve) Michael
Born: Durham, 21 March 1979
Height: 6'4" Weight: 13.9
As a central defender or midfielder, Steve's reserve displays show a composure and class that belies his youth. Having broken through into Chesterfield's first team over last Christmas in the unaccustomed position of forward, during an injury crisis, despite an obvious lack of familiarity with his role, he showed an excellent, committed attitude. Holding the ball up well, thinking about the game, and showing plenty of skill on the ball, he was rewarded for his efforts with his first league goal, in a 2-1 win at York in April.

Chesterfield (Free from Sheffield Wed juniors on 3/11/97) FL 6+7/1 Others 1+1

LENNON Neil Francis
Born: Lurgan, 25 June 1971
Height: 5'9" Weight: 13.2
Club Honours: FLC '97
International Honours: NI: 27; B-1; U23-1; U21-2; Yth
Neil, a fiery right-footed Leicester midfield dynamo, has now fully inherited the role of chief playmaker for the Foxes. As a consistent high class performer for both club and country in 1998-99, who added to his international goal tally against Moldova in Belfast, he also scored with a rare header to clinch Leicester's Worthington Cup quarter-final victory over Blackburn. His first league goal of the campaign was delayed until March but was worth waiting for, as an interchange of passes with fellow Irish international, Gerry Taggart, culminated in a finely judged curler from the corner of the box that went in off the far post. His deft but incisive passing around the box also set up several City goals, notably Tony Cottee's vital equaliser in the semi-final win over Sunderland, and only the gradual accumulation of yellow cards denied him an ever-present tag. Stop Press: Agreed a four-year contract during the summer.

Manchester C (From trainee on 26/8/89) FL 1
Crewe Alex (Free on 9/8/90) FL 142+5/15 FLC 8+1/1 FAC 16/1 Others 5
Leicester C (£750,000 on 23/2/96) P/FL 123+1/5 FLC 16/2 FAC 6 Others 5

LEONARD Mark Anthony
Born: St Helens, 27 September 1962
Height: 6'0" Weight: 13.3
The veteran front man opened the 1998-99 campaign in possession of the Rochdale number-nine shirt, but after only two league games he was relegated to the subs' bench as a niggling back injury took its toll. Despite sessions with specialists, and a trip to the rehabilitation centre at Lilleshall, Mark was eventually forced to end a career league spanning 17 seasons.

Everton (Signed from Witton A on 24/2/82)
Tranmere Rov (Loaned on 24/3/83) FL 6+1
Crewe Alex (Free on 1/6/83) FL 51+3/15 FLC 4/2 FAC 2 Others 3+1
Stockport Co (Signed on 13/2/85) FL 73+23 FLC 5/2 FAC 1 Others 2/3
Bradford C (£40,000 on 27/9/86) FL 120+37/29 FLC 13+5/6 FAC 6+3/1 Others 6+5/3
Rochdale (£40,000 on 27/3/92) FL 9/1

Preston NE (£40,000 on 13/8/92) FL 19+3/1 FLC 2
Chester C (Free on 13/8/93) FL 28+4/8 FLC 2 FAC 3/1 Others 3
Wigan Ath (Signed on 15/9/94) FL 60+4/12 FLC 2 FAC 6/2 Others 6/2
Rochdale (Free on 3/7/96) FL 74+6/6 FLC 5 FAC 2 Others 1

LEONHARDSEN Oyvind
Born: Kristiansund, Norway, 17 August 1970
Height: 5'10" Weight: 11.2
International Honours: Norway: 60
Another Norwegian international at Liverpool, Oyvind was restricted to just a handful of appearances in 1998-99, following a successful introduction to Anfield the previous term. A tireless individual who appears to be able to run all day, and shake off challenges in the tightest of Premiership midfields, he arrived from Wimbledon to bring that little bit extra to the club, but in a difficult season where the new manager, Gerard Houllier, was taking a good look around, he failed to be given many opportunities to shine. A player who gets forward, and whose strength allows him to hold the ball up well, he scored at Blackburn, and it is this part of his game that should be adding another attacking dimension to an already potent strike force.

Wimbledon (£660,000 from Rosenborg, via Clausenengen and Molde, on 8/11/94) PL 73+3/13 FLC 7+2/1 FAC 17/2
Liverpool (£3,500,000 on 3/6/97) PL 34+3/7 FLC 4+2 FAC 1 Others 3+2

LEONI Stephane
Born: Metz, France, 1 September 1976
Height: 5'11" Weight: 11.8
A former French U21 international full back, who was offered a two-year contract after impressing in a one-week trial last August, Stephane was thrown into first-team action just one week later as Bristol Rovers went into extra time against Leyton Orient in a Worthington Cup first-round tie at the Memorial Stadium. Having a good first touch, and able to play in midfield or in both full back positions, he scored an impressive winning goal, his only one of the season, in the FA Cup third round at Rotherham.

Bristol Rov (Free from Metz on 17/8/98) FL 25+5 FLC 0+1 FAC 4/1 Others 1

LE SAUX Graeme Pierre
Born: Jersey, 17 October 1968
Height: 5'10" Weight: 12.2
Club Honours: PL '95; FLC '98; ESC '98
International Honours: E: 35; B-2; U21-4
Controversy followed Graeme throughout 1998-99, beginning with clashes against Arsenal which saw Lee Dixon sent off for a nasty challenge on him, and then Graeme himself was dismissed, along with Blackburn's Sebastien Perez, after a contretemps at Ewood Park which cost him a three-match ban. His unfortunate season culminated in the unsavoury Robbie Fowler "incident" in March which brought him another suspension. That having been said, this feisty left back again demonstrated that he was still England's first choice for the

position, withstanding the challenges of Andy Hinchliffe and Philip Neville. At Chelsea he formed a particularly strong partnership with Celestine Babayaro on the left flank, and is a superb crosser of the ball who loves to get forward to link up with the attack. He showed this quality to perfection against Leeds in May at the Bridge, when he burst down the left wing and delivered an inch-perfect cross onto the head of Gustavo Poyet, who nodded home the only goal of the match to clinch Champions' League qualification.

Chelsea (Free from St Paul's, Jersey, on 9/12/87) F/PL 77+13/8 FLC 7+6/1 FAC 7+1 Others 8+1
Blackburn Rov (Signed on 25/3/93) PL 127+2/7 FLC 10 FAC 8 Others 6+1
Chelsea (£5,000,000 on 8/8/97) PL 56+1/1 FLC 4/1 FAC 7/1 Others 12

LESCOTT Aaron Anthony
Born: Birmingham, 2 December 1978
Height: 5'8" Weight: 10.9
International Honours: E: Sch
Having come through the ranks at Aston Villa, and a former England schoolboy international, Aaron is a right-sided midfielder, despite being left footed. A player who can also be used as a right-wing back due to his ability to attack the flank to find the forwards with good early crosses, he made his senior debut for Villa in 1998-99 when coming off the bench against Hull City in the third round FA Cup match. Now that he has made the breakthrough, after three seasons as a professional, it will be interesting to see whether he can make further advances.

Aston Villa (From trainee on 5/7/96) FAC 0+1

LESTER Jack William
Born: Sheffield, 8 October 1975
Height: 5'10" Weight: 11.8
Club Honours: AMC '98
International Honours: E: Sch
Yet another Grimsby player for whom 1998-99 was a frustrating season. A suspension followed by a lengthy spell of injury limited his strike opportunities and, without a doubt, his speed and ball skills in the box, along with his ability to cause consternation amongst the opposing defence was sadly missed. Returning to first-team duties over the Easter period, Jack showed he had not lost any of his enthusiasm, but had not yet regained full fitness. Most Mariners' supporters feel that as a marked man, several valid penalty claims went unrewarded during the campaign.

Grimsby T (From juniors on 8/7/94) FL 70+37/13 FLC 8+4/3 FAC 5+2/2 Others 4+4
Doncaster Rov (Loaned on 20/9/96) FL 5+6/1

LE TISSIER Matthew (Matt) Paul
Born: Guernsey, 14 October 1968
Height: 6'1" Weight: 13.8
International Honours: E: 8; B-6; Yth
Southampton's midfielder, cum striker, who again played a most important part in his club's fight against relegation, this time in 1998-99. Perhaps a bit down after not being selected for the England World Cup squad, he was left out of the starting line-up at the beginning of the campaign and, when he did

get in regularly – his runs in the team were interrupted by nagging injuries, which began to plague him. Still deadly accurate at set pieces and, although his personal goal total of seven was lower than usual, he continued to create many more for other members of the team. Surprisingly, in fact, three of last season's goals came from his head, and he virtually scored direct from a corner in the penultimate game, at Wimbledon, Hassan Kachoul ultimately claiming it. Regularly named in the national press's teams of the week, Matt cares deeply about the club, and is a huge favourite with the fans, who can be pretty certain of seeing him in the red and white stripes for some time to come.

Southampton (From apprentice on 17/10/86) F/PL 366+47/158 FLC 41+6/26 FAC 30+2/12 Others 11+1/9

Matt Le Tissier

LEVER Mark
Born: Beverley, 29 March 1970
Height: 6'3" Weight: 13.5
Club Honours: AMC '98
After a successful return to first-team action in 1997-98, when his solid performances at the centre of defence played a vital part in what was arguably one of Grimsby Town's most successful seasons, Mark was unfortunate in finding himself relegated to third choice, following the return to full fitness of Richard Smith. However, when given the opportunity, he turned in the dependable performances that Mariners' fans have come to expect of him.

Grimsby T (From trainee on 9/8/88) FL 308+18/8 FLC 22+1 FAC 15+3 Others 18

L'HELGOUALCH Cyrille
Born: St Nazaire, France, 25 September 1970
Height: 5'9" Weight: 13.0
After spending a couple of weeks on trial at Walsall, the Frenchman arrived at the Field Mill last December for one match, a victory

over Shrewsbury, which took Mansfield briefly to the top of the table. Preferring to play at the back, but equally at home in midfield, he left for France with several stitches in a leg wound after the Shrewsbury match but returned a couple of months later for the end of season run-in, scoring a spectacular goal against Rochdale on his comeback before departing.

Walsall (Free from Angers on 27/11/98)
Mansfield T (Free on 10/12/98) FL 3+1/1

LIBURD Richard John
Born: Nottingham, 26 September 1973
Height: 5'9" Weight: 11.1
Out of contract at Carlisle in the summer of 1998, the local boy came to Notts County on a free transfer, having first made his reputation at Middlesbrough. A tough-tackling full back who can play on either flank, he also operated as a wing back, and although taking time to achieve full match fitness from mid season onwards he established himself as a regular team member, being one of the first on the team sheet. With a liking to get further up the park, where he can join in the play, he scored in a 3-2 win at Stoke in March when firing in the second from the edge of the box.

Middlesbrough (£20,000 from Eastwood T on 25/3/93) FL 41/1 FLC 4 FAC 2 Others 5
Bradford C (£200,000 on 21/7/94) FL 75+3/3 FLC 6+2 FAC 2+2 Others 2
Carlisle U (Free on 26/2/98) FL 9
Notts Co (Free on 4/8/98) FL 27+8/1 FLC 1+1 FAC 3+3

LIDDELL Andrew Mark
Born: Leeds, 28 June 1973
Height: 5'7" Weight: 11.6
Club Honours: AMC '99
International Honours: S: U21-11
Started last season at Barnsley playing just behind the front two but, when this was not a success, opportunities became limited, and a thigh injury did not help. In order to play regular first-team football, he signed for Wigan in October, and proved to be a hard worker who never gave less than 100 per cent, while his ability to unlock defences resulted in many opportunities for his striking partners. Showed his quality netting ten league goals, including a brace in the final Football League game at Springfield Park against Chesterfield. An integral member of the side that won the Auto Windscreens Shield at Wembley, his bravery saw him continue to play through the pain barrier with a groin injury during the club's hectic run in to make the play offs.

Barnsley (From trainee on 6/7/91) F/PL 142+56/34 FLC 11+2/3 FAC 5+7/1 Others 2+1
Wigan Ath (£350,000 on 15/10/98) FL 28/10 Others 7

LIDDLE Craig George
Born: Chester le Street, 21 October 1971
Height: 5'11" Weight: 12.7
After impressing Darlington, when on loan from Middlesbrough at the end of the previous season, Craig was signed permanently in the summer of 1998, and continued to demonstrate what an excellent defender he was throughout the 1998-99 campaign, missing only two games. Hard

tackling and composed, his Premiership knowledge was obvious through his reading of the game and succession of dependable performances at the heart of the defence.
Aston Villa (From trainee on 4/7/90) (Free to Blyth Spartans in August 1991)
Middlesbrough (Free on 12/7/94) P/FL 20+5 FLC 3+2 FAC 2 Others 2
Darlington (Free on 20/2/98) FL 59/3 FLC 2 FAC 3 Others 2

LIGHTBOURNE Kyle Lavince
Born: Bermuda, 29 September 1968
Height: 6'2" Weight: 12.4
International Honours: Bermuda: 6
Kyle was another player who, after the horrendous start to his Stoke career through illness and injury the previous relegation campaign, had to work hard to win the supporters over in 1998-99. But, ultimately, he did, and his partnership up front with Peter Thorne was clearly City's best option. Indeed, he was really looking the business before a calf injury in November came at just the wrong time for both him and the side. Although a hard-working player, with pace and good ability in the air and on the ground, he continued to find it hard to please everyone.
Scarborough (Signed on 11/12/92) FL 11+8/3 FLC 1 Others 0+1
Walsall (Free on 17/9/93) FL 158+7/65 FLC 8/3 FAC 16+2/12 Others 7/5
Coventry C (£500,000 + on 18/7/97) PL 1+6 FLC 3
Fulham (Loaned on 13/1/98) FL 4/2 Others 1/1
Stoke C (£500,000 on 16/2/98) FL 37+12/9 FLC 1 FAC 1/1 Others 1

LIGHTFOOT Christopher (Chris) Ian
Born: Warrington, 1 April 1970
Height: 6'2" Weight: 13.6
An experienced and versatile Crewe player, who can operate in any of the defensive positions, or fit into a midfield role with ease, Chris was not available for the whole of last season, having four spells out of the side due to injury, etc. When playing, however, he could be relied upon to give wholehearted performances, none more so than when coming off the bench after 46 minutes at Gresty Road against Barnsley in August to score the second and third goals in a 3-1 win. The first, a towering header from a free kick, merely emphasised how effective he could be at both ends of the park, and the second saw him react the quickest to a loose ball from another set piece. Is both aggressive and strong in possession, with good passing technique. Was out of contract during the summer.
Chester C (From trainee on 11/7/88) FL 263+14/32 FLC 15+2/1 FAC 16+2/1 Others 14+2/5
Wigan Ath (£87,500 on 13/7/95) FL 11+3/1 FLC 2 FAC 2 Others 3
Crewe Alex (£50,000 on 22/3/96) FL 47+19/4 FLC 3+1 FAC 1+1/1 Others 3+2

LILLEY Derek Symon
Born: Paisley, 9 February 1974
Height: 5'11" Weight: 12.7
Club Honours: S Div 2 '95
International Honours: S: Yth
A strong and quick Scottish striker with Leeds, who once again had to settle for a place on the substitute's bench at the start of

last season, coming on at Middlesbrough on the opening day, at Everton in September – almost scoring with a last minute effort – and finally at home to Maritimo in the UEFA Cup. Then, after David O'Leary replaced George Graham at the helm, and finding himself out of the first-team picture, he joined Hearts on loan in December with a view to a permanent move, although that never materialised. Having returned, he joined Bury on loan in transfer deadline week as a direct replacement for a previous on-loan player, Paul Hall, who had been recalled by Coventry. Although he toiled hard and was rewarded when notching the winning goal in the Shakers' only away win of the season, at Oxford, he later suffered a hamstring injury at Grimsby which caused him to sit out the final two games. Is under contract at United until June 2000.
Greenock Morton (Free from Everton BC on 13/8/91) SL 157+23/56 SLC 5+1/4 SC 9+4/4 Others 6+4/5
Leeds U (£500,000 + on 27/3/97) PL 4+17/1 FLC 0+3 FAC 0+1 Others 0+1
Heart of Midlothian (Loaned on 30/12/98) SL 3+1/1 SC 1
Bury (Loaned on 25/3/99) FL 5/1

LING Martin
Born: West Ham, 15 July 1966
Height: 5'8" Weight: 10.8
Club Honours: Div 2 '96
Although unable to recapture his form of the previous season, Martin was still able to create a lot of chances from Leyton Orient's midfield in 1998-99, and always seemed to have so much time on the ball. Missed very few games throughout the campaign, just three in all, and scored several important goals, including a brilliant lob over the 'keeper at Brisbane Road against Cambridge, and one of the penalties that took the club to the play-off final at Wembley. Still one of the best passers of the ball in the Third Division, his skill on the ball often makes defenders seem statuesque.
Exeter C (From apprentice on 13/1/84) FL 109+8/14 FLC 8 FAC 4 Others 5
Swindon T (£25,000 on 14/7/86) FL 2 FLC 1+1
Southend U (£15,000 on 16/10/86) FL 126+12/31 FLC 8/2 FAC 7/1 Others 11+1/3
Mansfield T (Loaned on 24/1/91) FL 3
Swindon T (£15,000 on 28/3/91) F/PL 132+18/10 FLC 11+1/1 FAC 10+1/1 Others 12+1/1
Leyton Orient (Free on 23/7/96) FL 129+5/7 FLC 10 FAC 9 Others 5/1

LINIGHAN Andrew (Andy)
Born: Hartlepool, 18 June 1962
Height: 6'3" Weight: 13.10
Club Honours: Div 1 '91; FLC '93; FAC '93; ECWC '94
International Honours: E: B-4
A highly experienced, strong-tackling central defender, Andy, who was the oldest player at Crystal Palace in 1998-99, had two spells in the side before joining Queens Park Rangers on loan in the club's mass clear out during transfer deadline week. The brother of Brian and David, and the son of Brian senior, all professional footballers, he still relishes the challenge, and remains competitive, his height being valuable at both ends of the park. Continued to show his ability to hit long, accurate passes out of defence.

Hartlepool U (Free from Henry Smiths BC on 19/9/80) FL 110/4 FLC 7+1/1 FAC 8 Others 1/1
Leeds U (£20,000 on 15/5/84) FL 66/3 FLC 6/1 FAC 2 Others 2
Oldham Ath (£65,000 on 17/1/86) FL 87/6 FLC 8/2 FAC 3 Others 4
Norwich C (£350,000 on 4/3/88) FL 86/8 FLC 6 FAC 10 Others 4
Arsenal (£1,250,000 on 4/7/90) F/PL 101+17/5 FLC 13+1/1 FAC 12+2/1 Others 9+1/1
Crystal Palace (£150,000 on 27/1/97) F/PL 64+1/2 FLC 3+2 FAC 2+2 Others 3
Queens Park R (Loaned on 25/3/99) FL 4+3

LINIGHAN David
Born: Hartlepool, 9 January 1965
Height: 6'2" Weight: 13.0
Club Honours: Div 2 '92
Transferred to Dunfermline from Blackpool during the 1998 close season, David, a veteran with over 500 league appearances under his belt, was signed on transfer deadline day last March to bolster Mansfield's flagging defence. The stopper-type central defender's appearance in the side for the last 11 matches of the campaign certainly helped to plug a leaky defence, but the "Stags" still slipped to mid table. Still good in the air and on the ground, he remains difficult to pass. Out of contract during the summer, it was reported that Town had made him an offer of re-engagement.
Hartlepool U (From juniors on 3/3/82) FL 84+7/5 FLC 3+1/1 FAC 4 Others 2
Derby Co (£25,000 on 11/8/86)
Shrewsbury T (£30,000 on 4/12/86) FL 65/1 FLC 5 FAC Others 1
Ipswich T (£300,000 on 23/6/88) F/PL 275+2/12 FLC 21 FAC 18/1 Others 11
Blackpool (£80,000 on 17/11/95) FL 97+3/5 FLC 6/2 FAC 2/1 Others 8
Dunfermline Ath (Free during 1998 close season) SL 1 SLC 1
Mansfield T (Free on 25/3/99) FL 10

LINTON Desmond (Des) Martin
Born: Birmingham, 5 September 1971
Height: 6'1" Weight: 13.10
Having made just nine appearances for Peterborough in 1998-99 spread over two different spells, and not seeming to figure in Barry Fry's future plans, the strong-tackling right back was loaned to Swindon in March before being released at the end of the campaign. Despite performing steadily in seven games for Town, manager Jimmy Quinn was looking to strengthen other areas and was thus unable to secure anything more permanent for him. A player who always looks to use the ball rather than "lumping" it, and one who always appears to have time in possession, he should have no difficulty in finding another team.
Leicester C (From trainee on 9/1/90) FL 6+5 FLC 0+1 Others 1
Luton T (Signed on 22/10/91) FL 65+18/1 FLC 4+1 FAC 8 Others 7
Peterborough U (£25,000 on 26/3/97) FL 41+5 FLC 2 FAC 3+1 Others 2
Swindon T (Loaned on 19/3/99) FL 7+1

LISBIE Kevin Anthony
Born: Hackney, 17 October 1978
Height: 5'8" Weight: 10.12
International Honours: E: Yth
Kevin's expected breakthrough at Charlton

in 1998-99 failed to materialise, and he made just two subs' appearances before being loaned to Gillingham in early March. A quick, ball-playing striker, he soon showed his ability at Priestfield, with four goals in seven appearances, before ruptured medial knee ligaments sustained during the Gills' 3-0 defeat at Fulham curtailed his campaign. Able to also play wide on the right, where his pace enables him to get to the byline and deliver crosses into the box, his goalscoring prowess was shown nationwide on Sky, when he netted a late winner against Bournemouth.

Charlton Ath (From trainee on 24/5/96) P/FL 5+38/2 FLC 0+5 FAC 0+1
Gillingham (Loaned on 5/3/99) FL 4+3/4

LITTLE Colin Campbell
Born: Wythenshawe, 4 November 1972
Height: 5'10" Weight: 11.0
A nippy Crewe forward who seems to be able to raise his game in the important fixtures, he started last season with two goals at Oldham in a 3-2 Worthington Cup defeat, and then notched another ten in the league as the team fought desperately to avoid the drop into the Second Division. Having come back from a short-term injury, his brace in a 3-1 Gresty Road win against Portsmouth in the penultimate league game of 1998-99 was particularly welcome, especially as the result almost certainly saved Alex from relegation. Is at his best when running at defenders in the box.

Crewe Alex (£50,000 from Hyde U on 7/2/96) FL 66+40/24 FLC 6+1/2 FAC 4 Others 5/3

LITTLE Glen Matthew
Born: Wimbledon, 15 October 1975
Height: 6'3" Weight: 13.0
Tall, unconventional, and skilful, and occasionally used as a striker but more commonly employed on the right of midfield, Glen had another fine season in a struggling Burnley side in 1998-99. He was often the one creative element of the team, and contributed towards many a goal for Andy Payton, as well as occasionally finding the net himself. Injury, suspension and a hernia operation made for a stop-start campaign, and he was invariably missed when absent, Burnley having no other player as capable of getting past defenders to either cross accurately or to cut into the centre. The club's new influx of funds may make it easier to hold on to him, but there will be no shortage of admirers from the higher divisions.

Crystal Palace (From trainee on 1/7/94) (Free to Glentoran on 11/11/94)
Burnley (£100,000 on 29/11/96) FL 56+11/9 FLC 2+2 FAC 2+1 Others 3+1/1

LITTLEJOHN Adrian Sylvester
Born: Wolverhampton, 26 September 1970
Height: 5'9" Weight: 11.0
International Honours: E: Yth
Having started last season at Oldham, scoring in the Worthington Cup win at Boundary Park and notching two more later on, the striker moved to Bury in mid November. At his best when running at defenders, on either flank or through the

middle, and known by the Shakers' manager, Neil Warnock, from their days at Oldham together, he was brought in as a direct replacement for the Stockport-bound Rob Matthews. Despite his great pace, and an ability to get behind the opposition, it did not quite come off for him at Gigg Lane, and he only started five games after the turn of the year, spending most of his time on the subs' bench before being placed on the transfer list at the end of the campaign.

Walsall (Free from West Bromwich A juniors on 24/5/89) FL 26+18/1 FLC 2+1 FAC 1+1 Others 4+1
Sheffield U (Free on 6/8/91) F/PL 44+25/12 FLC 5+1 FAC 3+2/1 Others 2/1
Plymouth Arg (£100,000 on 22/9/95) FL 100+10/29 FLC 6 FAC 6+2/3 Others 6
Oldham Ath (Signed on 20/3/98) FL 16+5/5 FLC 2/1
Bury (£75,000 on 13/11/98) FL 11+9/1 FAC 1

LIVETT Simon Robert
Born: Plaistow, 8 January 1969
Height: 5'10" Weight: 12.9
After spells with West Ham, Leyton Orient, and Cambridge, Simon drifted into non-league football before being given a chance of resurrecting his league career with Southend during the 1998 close season. A hard-working midfielder, who also has the ability to pass well and deliver an excellent ball from set-pieces, he was treated rather poorly before being restored to the team for the final run-in by the new manager, Alan Little.

West Ham U (From trainee on 23/1/87) FL 1 FAC 0+1 Others 1
Leyton Orient (Free on 10/8/92) FL 16+8 FLC 2 FAC 2 Others 1/1
Cambridge U (Signed on 1/10/93) FL 12 FLC 1 FAC 3 Others 2 (Free to Dagenham & Redbridge during 1995 close season)
Southend U (Free from Grays Ath on 13/7/98) FL 19+4/1 FLC 1 FAC 1 Others 1

LIVINGSTONE Stephen (Steve) Carl
Born: Middlesbrough, 8 September 1968
Height: 6'1" Weight: 13.6
Club Honours: AMC '98
A strong, physical, and tireless Grimsby striker, with good timing in the air, and a sense of awareness in the box, in 1998-99 Steve was the subject of a projected move north of the border to St Johnstone which failed to materialise. However, during a season in which his opportunities up front were severely limited, being restricted by and large to his secondary role as an emergency central defender, he never once complained, filling in with all of his customary solid dependability.

Coventry C (From trainee on 16/7/86) FL 17+14/5 FLC 8+2/10 Others 0+1
Blackburn Rov (£450,000 on 17/1/91) F/PL 25+5/10 FLC 2 FAC 1/1
Chelsea (£350,000 on 23/3/93) PL 0+1
Port Vale (Loaned on 3/9/93) FL 4+1
Grimsby T (£140,000 on 29/10/93) FL 155+40/33 FLC 10+6/4 FAC 7+5/2 Others 4+3

LJUNGBERG Fredrik
Born: Sweden, 16 April 1977
Height: 5'9" Weight: 11.6
International Honours: Sweden: 8
A Swedish international, Fredrik joined

Arsenal from BK Halmstad in September 1998, shortly after he had scored the winning goal for his country against England in a European championship qualifier. Is a quick, skilful attacker, who can also play effectively in midfield. Came off the substitutes' bench to score against Manchester United at Highbury on his debut, before abdominal and ankle injuries kept him out of contention for some weeks during mid season. Following that, his first-team appearances were limited, despite him maintaining top form at international level, and scoring the winning goal against Poland in March. Is highly rated by the Swedish national coach, and has the skill and ability to become an Arsenal regular in the near future.

Arsenal (£3,000,000 from BK Halmstad on 17/9/98) PL 10+6/1 FLC 2 FAC 2+1

LLEWELLYN Christopher (Chris) Mark
Born: Swansea, 29 August 1979
Height: 5'11" Weight: 11.6
International Honours: W: 2; B-1; U21-7; Yth
Won his first full caps for Wales during their 1998 summer trips to Malta and North Africa, and maintained his international involvement with further U21 call ups in 1998-99. Able to play either as an orthodox striker, or on the left-hand side of midfield, his usual position for Norwich last season, he likes to run at defenders, using his pace and dribbling skills. And, although not a naturally wide player, he provided many telling crosses, especially for Iwan Roberts. Still only 19 years old, Chris has gained a wealth of first-team experience for one so young, and has the potential to develop into a very good player indeed.

Norwich C (From trainee on 21/1/97) FL 31+15/6 FLC 2+1 FAC 1+1

LOCK Anthony (Tony) Charles
Born: Harlow, 3 September 1976
Height: 5'11" Weight: 13.0
Tony had another impressive pre-season spell at Colchester, such that he displaced record signing, Neil Gregory, from the starting line-up for the opening game of 1998-99. Sadly, though, the striker picked up an injury during that game which kept him out for a few weeks, before he came back to regain a regular place for most of the first four months. Scored his only registered goal in a midweek draw at Walsall, but was cruelly denied a double strike the following Saturday, when the home game against Bournemouth was abandoned. Injury struck again soon afterwards, and he made only limited appearances thereafter, before being somewhat surprisingly released during the summer.

Colchester U (From trainee on 18/4/95) FL 29+35/9 FLC 0+2 FAC 1+3 Others 0+6

LOCKE Adam Spencer
Born: Croydon, 20 August 1970
Height: 5'11" Weight: 12.7
Although starring last season as Bristol City's right back after losing his place early on, he was re-instated by Benny

Lennartsson and gave some hard-working performances in midfield. With a liking to get forward, Adam gave the impression that in a balanced side he could get goals from midfield, something that was sadly missing at the club in 1998-99. The highlight of his season was a headed goal at Fratton Park on Easter Monday, which gave City a vital 1-0 win. Out of contract during the summer, at the time of going to press it was unclear as to whether he would be taking up the club's offer of re-engagement.

Crystal Palace (From trainee on 21/6/88)
Southend U (Free on 6/8/90) FL 56+17/4 FLC 5 FAC 2+1 Others 6+1
Colchester U (Loaned on 8/10/93) FL 4 Others 1
Colchester U (Free on 23/9/94) FL 64+15/8 FLC 5+1 FAC 5 Others 8+5
Bristol C (Free on 23/7/97) FL 61+4/4 FLC 6 FAC 3 Others 2/1

LOCKWOOD Matthew (Matt) Dominic
Born: Southend, 17 October 1976
Height: 5'9" Weight: 10.12
Signed on a free transfer last August from Bristol Rovers, this good, attacking left-wing back proved himself to be an excellent pin-point crosser of the ball at Leyton Orient, as well as being a constant threat at set plays, especially with his in-swinging corners. This was highlighted when he scored his first goal, at Southend, the ball going straight in from the corner. He also scored a 35 yarder against Torquay's Neville Southall, forcing the veteran 'keeper, along with the ball, over the line. Freed by Southend as a junior, Matt has moved on from those days to become a confident pro who can play all over the pitch, and one who is extremely comfortable in possession. Scored one of the penalties that took Orient to the play-off final at Wembley.

Queens Park R (Free from Southend U juniors on 2/5/95)
Bristol Rov (Free on 24/7/96) FL 58+5/1 FLC 2+1 FAC 6 Others 4+2
Leyton Orient (Free on 7/8/98) FL 36+1/3 FLC 2 FAC 4 Others 3

LOGAN Richard Anthony
Born: Barnsley, 24 May 1969
Height: 6'1" Weight: 13.3
Signed from Plymouth during the 1998 close season, Richard missed the start of 1998-99 with a badly broken nose, but soon won his place in the Scunthorpe midfield, where his workrate and tough tackling made him an important player. Switched to central defence after Christmas, he was a revelation, proving very strong in the air and solid on the ground, and chipping in with a number of goals from set pieces. The winner of the club's "Player of the Season" award, he also possesses a long throw which causes teams problems.

Huddersfield T (Free from Gainsborough Trinity on 15/11/93) FL 35+10/1 FLC 3 FAC 1 Others 9
Plymouth Arg (£20,000 on 26/10/95) FL 67+19/12 FLC 4/1 FAC 2+2 Others 8
Scunthorpe U (Free on 2/7/98) FL 38+3/6 FAC 3 Others 3

LOGAN Richard James
Born: Bury St Edmunds, 4 January 1982
Height: 6'0" Weight: 12.5

A local lad who has progressed from the YTS scheme through the Ipswich academy and reserve sides, where he scored regularly, to the fringes of the first team. Still a trainee, he made his senior debut at Wolverhampton just after Christmas, when coming on as a substitute in the last minute, and was given a longer run in the next game, at home to Grimsby, three days after signing professional, but has not featured in the side since. Is predominantly a right-footed striker who has a good turn of pace.

Ipswich T (From trainee on 6/1/99) FL 0+2

LOMAS James (Jamie) Duncan
Born: Chesterfield, 18 October 1977
Height: 5'11" Weight: 12.0
Looking to break through into Chesterfield's first team, this competent right-sided midfielder or defender began last season well, and made five appearances in a seven-game spell until being sidelined by a groin injury. He continued to put in consistent performances for the reserves, developing his tackling and reading of the game, and using his crossing ability to good effect. The club understandably opted for experienced heads as they chased a play-off place, and his chances of advancement were few and far between, but he is sure to come again.

Chesterfield (From trainee on 16/9/96) FL 7+6 FLC 1 Others 1+3

LOMAS Stephen (Steve) Martin
Born: Hanover, Germany, 18 January 1974
Height: 6'0" Weight: 12.8
International Honours: NI: 30; B-1; Yth; Sch
Badly missed early in 1998-99, when he was out of action for eight weeks after picking up an ankle injury at Coventry, the West Ham captain came back strongly to play in all but three of the remaining games, and lead the club into Europe, via fifth place in the Premiership. A good passer, with a lovely touch on the ball, he is a committed, competitive player who puts the side first, and is always in the thick of the action, even being called upon to play at right back for a few games, due to injuries. Despite being adept at making long, driving runs into the opposing penalty area, and having a good shot on him, he surprisingly gets few goals, there being only one last season – a 25 yarder in a 3-2 home win over Leicester – although he came close on a number of occasions. Almost a veteran at international level, Steve was proud to have captained Northern Ireland against Moldova, Germany and Canada.

Manchester C (From trainee on 22/1/91) P/FL 102+9/8 FLC 15/2 FAC 10+1/1
West Ham U (£1,600,000 on 26/3/97) PL 70/3 FLC 4 FAC 7/1

LOMAX Michael (Mike) John
Born: Manchester, 6 December 1979
Height: 5'11" Weight: 11.0
Released from Blackburn during the 1998 close season, having been a trainee at Ewood Park, Mike signed for Macclesfield, and was a key defender throughout 1998-99 in the newly formed Town reserves. Eventually making his first-team debut with a 12th-minute appearance from the bench in

the last Second Division game of the season, he showed himself to be a hard tackler with a good turn of speed.

Macclesfield T (Free from Blackburn Rov juniors on 16/7/98) FL 0+1

LOMBARDO Attilio
Born: Maria la Fossa, Italy, 6 January 1966
Height: 5'11" Weight: 12.6
International Honours: Italy: 18
Despite having a chance to join Chelsea during the 1998 close season, the bald Italian chose to stay at Crystal Palace, where he had become almost a cult figure. Started 1998-99 well, scoring three goals in the first five games, before being laid up after 22 consecutive matches, and eventually returning to Lazio in January for a reduced £500,000 fee, due to him being the highest paid player at Selhurst and the club desperate to reduce the wage bill. An elegant passer of the ball, both long and short, and having great control and vision, needless to say the classy midfielder was sorely missed.

Crystal Palace (£1,600,000 from Juventus, via Pergocrema, Cremonese and Sampdoria, on 9/8/97) P/FL 40+3/8 FLC 4/2

LONERGAN Darren
Born: Cork, 28 January 1974
Height: 6'0" Weight: 13.1
Darren was signed in the 1998 close season in order to make up the newly formed Macclesfield reserve team. The big central defender took an immediate command of the defence before getting his chance to show his mettle in the first team, with bench appearances in two of the four FA Cup games, but perhaps eight minutes in the first and 15 in the second, particularly when the team was already 5-0 down at Coventry, was not time enough. However, he had one moment of glory in his first appearance, scoring one of the penalties in the 9-8 shoot-out victory at non-league Slough in the FA Cup first round replay. His contract was cancelled in April 1999 after he had gone missing for some time.

Oldham Ath (Signed from Waterford on 2/9/94) FL 1+1
Bury (Free on 8/10/97)
Macclesfield T (Free on 6/8/98) FAC 0+2 Others 0+1

LONGWORTH Steven Paul
Born: Preston, 6 February 1980
Height: 5'9" Weight: 11.3
Following up his experiences of 1997-98, and having signed professional forms during the 1998 close season, the young Blackpool striker made his first start for the club in the losing Auto Windscreens game against Stoke last December. That, however, was to be his only first-team opportunity, and he had spells on loan at Lancaster City and Accrington Stanley before being released in the summer.

Blackpool (From trainee on 3/7/98) FL 0+2 FAC 0+1 Others 1

LORMOR Anthony (Tony)
Born: Ashington, 29 October 1970
Height: 6'0" Weight: 13.6

Signed from Preston, Mansfield finally got their man in the 1998 close season after a year-long chase, as a replacement for the previous campaign's leading scorer, Steve Whitehall. He was not an immediate hit with the fans, especially when he failed to score in his first ten matches, his cause not being helped by the fact that he was a former Spireite. However, when the goals eventually came he started to win over the terrace "boo boys" and always gave 100 per cent. A tall striker in the traditional mould, with the right kind of service he can lead the line well. Is persistent and pacy.

Newcastle U (From trainee on 25/2/88) FL 6+2/3
Lincoln C (£25,000 on 29/1/90) FL 90+10/30 FLC 1+2/3 FAC 4/2 Others 6
Peterborough U (Free on 4/7/94) FL 2+3 FAC 1 Others 1+1
Chesterfield (Free on 23/12/94) FL 97+16/35 FLC 8/4 FAC 5/3 Others 7+1/3
Preston NE (£130,000 + on 5/11/97) FL 9+3/3 FAC 3 Others 3
Notts Co (Loaned on 20/2/98) FL 2+5
Mansfield T (£20,000 on 16/7/98) FL 35+6/11 FLC 0+1 FAC 2/2 Others 2

LOUIS-JEAN Matthieu
Born: Mont St Aignan, France, 22 February 1976
Height: 5'9" Weight: 10.12
Matthieu became the third Frenchman to join Nottingham Forest in 1998-99 after Dave Bassett, the then Forest manager, had been impressed with him during a pre-season trial. Unable to agree a fee, Forest did the next best thing and borrowed the talented Le Havre defender until the end of the Premiership campaign. A quick and nimble full back who was good when going forward to get early balls into the danger areas, he showed that he was also a committed defender. Given his first-team debut when coming off the bench in the 5-1 Worthington Cup win at Leyton Orient, he made a few sporadic appearances until holding down a regular slot towards the end of the campaign.

Nottingham F (Loaned from Le Havre on 14/9/98) PL 15+1 FLC 2+1 FAC 1

LOVE Andrew (Andy) Mark
Born: Grimsby, 28 March 1979
Height: 6'1" Weight: 13.12
A tall and strongly built Grimsby goalkeeper, Andy again had limited league opportunities last season, but took his chance when an injury kept first-choice custodian, Aidan Davison, out for a spell towards the end of the campaign. Despite being called up during a period which coincided with a loss of form for Town, he once again showed himself to be a capable deputy.

Grimsby T (From trainee on 6/7/96) FL 12

LOVELL Stephen (Steve) William Henry
Born: Amersham, 6 December 1980
Height: 6'1" Weight: 12.7
Following some good performances for the Bournemouth reserve side in 1998-99, and still a trainee, Steve was promoted to the first team and made his league debut for the club when coming off the bench against Macclesfield at the beginning of April. He

then went on to make five further substitute appearances and one start during the remainder of the campaign. A tall striker who is another product of the Cherries' youth policy, he will be pushing hard for further senior appearances in 1999-2000.

Bournemouth (Trainee) FL 1+6

LOVELOCK Andrew (Andy) James
Born: Leamington, 20 December 1976
Height: 6'0" Weight: 12.8
International Honours: E: Sch
Started in league football with Coventry, coming through as a trainee to sign professional, before being released after suffering a serious knee injury that kept him out of soccer for two years. Then, having got himself match fit with non-league Southam in 1997-98, Andy trained with Crewe during the 1998 close season, and impressed enough to be offered a one-year contract. However, after making his first-team debut when coming off the bench at Oldham in the Worthington Cup last August, the tall midfielder failed to consolidate, and spent two spells on loan at Witton Albion prior to finishing the campaign at Altrincham.

Coventry C (From trainee on 20/12/93. Freed during 1996 close season)
Crewe Alex (Free from Southam U on 6/8/98) FLC 0+1

LOW Joshua (Josh) David
Born: Bristol, 15 February, 1979
Height: 6'1" Weight: 12.0
International Honours: W: U21-1; Yth
A fast, attacking winger, Josh continued to make the breakthrough and enjoyed making a number of first-team appearances for Bristol Rovers in 1998-99. His pace and ability to cross the ball into dangerous areas was always a threat and, although he lost his place following a suspension, he was rewarded for his progress as a young professional with a further two-year contract. He also made his Welsh U21 debut in Portugal on 18 November. Had a one-month loan spell with Conference club, Farnborough, before turning down an opportunity to join Rushden & Diamonds in February, in favour of a temporary move to Portsmouth, where he failed to put in an appearance. Stop Press: Signed for Leyton Orient on 27 May.

Bristol Rov (From trainee on 19/8/96) FL 11+11 FLC 0+2 FAC 2+2 Others 2

LOWE David Anthony
Born: Liverpool, 30 August 1965
Height: 5'10" Weight: 11.9
Club Honours: AMC '85; Div 2 '92, Div 3 '97
International Honours: E: U21-2; Yth
Wigan right-footed striker who is more of a creator of chances than a scorer. Hampered by injuries in 1998-99, this hard-working player was restricted to just five league starts, scoring his only goal in the home win over Fulham. Popular with the fans, the club's record scorer at least managed to complete a century of league appearances in his second spell, before being offered a combined playing and coaching role in the summer.

Wigan Ath (From apprentice on 1/6/83) FL 179+9/40 FLC 8 FAC 16+1/4 Others 18/9
Ipswich T (£80,000 on 26/6/87) FL 121+13/37 FLC 10/2 FAC 3 Others 10+2/6
Port Vale (Loaned on 19/3/92) FL 8+1/2
Leicester C (£250,000 on 13/7/92) F/PL 68+26/22 FLC 4+3/1 FAC 2+2 Others 3
Port Vale (Loaned on 18/2/94) FL 18+1/5
Wigan Ath (£125,000 on 28/3/96) FL 85+23/26 FLC 7 FAC 4+2/3 Others 5+1/1

LUA LUA Lomano Tresor
Born: Zaire, 28 December 1980
Height: 5'8" Weight: 12.2
Remember the name, it will be around for a very long time at the very top level! This Zaire-born, French national was picked up by Colchester's scouting system while playing college football in London, and was nurtured through the South-East Counties League side until making his senior debut as a second-half substitute at Chesterfield last January. Within minutes, he had scored his first league goal, and his performance lifted the side and supporters at a time of struggle in mid season. More substitute appearances followed, until a long-awaited full debut coincided with a first win for eight games, against second-placed Preston. Sadly sent off for retaliation at Burnley, this exciting natural talent will progress rapidly if the finer elements of team play can be allied to his immense skills. Scored a stunning hat trick in the space of the final three minutes to give United a 6-1 win over local rivals, Cambridge United, in the Avon Insurance Combination League in March.

Colchester U (Signed from Leyton College on 25/9/98) FL 6+7/1

LUCAS David Anthony
Born: Preston, 23 November 1977
Height: 6'2" Weight: 13.10
International Honours: E: Yth
David finally got his chance of a regular place at Preston last November, following an injury to Tepi Moilanen. Taking some time to re-acclimatise to first-team football after a year on the sidelines, his all-round game between the posts improved match by match. A superb shot stopper, and quick off his line, he gave an international class performance at Gillingham, making three top-class saves. Still has much to learn, particularly in commanding his box, but will surely add to his collection of junior international honours if he continues to improve as he did in 1998-99.

Preston NE (From trainee on 12/12/94) FL 40 FLC 1 FAC 4 Others 7
Darlington (Loaned on 14/12/95) FL 6
Darlington (Loaned on 3/10/96) FL 7
Scunthorpe U (Loaned on 23/12/96) FL 6 Others 2

LUCAS Richard
Born: Chapeltown, 22 September 1970
Height: 5'10" Weight: 12.6
Released by Hartlepool during the summer of 1998, Richard filled a variety of positions during 1998-99, his first season at Halifax. A left-sided player who operated at left back but was equally impressive playing in a more central position, his only goal to date was in the Auto Windscreens Shield second-

round tie against York City in January. Out of contract during the summer, at the time of going to press the club had offered him terms of re-engagement.

Sheffield U (From trainee on 1/7/89) FL 8+2 FAC 1 Others 0+1
Preston NE (£40,000 on 24/12/92) FL 47+3 FAC 4 Others 4+1
Lincoln C (Loaned on 14/10/94) FL 4 Others 2
Scarborough (Free on 5/7/95) FL 63+9 FLC 6 FAC 3+1 Others 2
Hartlepool U (Free on 27/3/97) FL 49/2 FLC 2 FAC 1 Others 1
Halifax T (Free on 7/8/98) FL 29+7 FLC 3 FAC 1 Others 2/1

LUCKETTI Christopher (Chris) James
Born: Littleborough, 28 September 1971
Height: 6'0" Weight: 13.6
Club Honours: Div 2 '97

As Bury's skipper, the central defender led by example once again, this time during 1998-99, having another highly consistent campaign despite the club's relegation. For the second successive season he picked up very few bookings – just five in 41 games – but crazily still faced a one-match suspension in the all-important penultimate league game at West Bromwich. A thigh strain picked up at Swindon in January accounted for the only other two games in which he was sidelined. Is both strong in the air and in possession on the ground. Stop Press: Signed for Huddersfield, who paid £1 million for his services on 11 June.

Rochdale (Trainee) FL 1
Stockport Co (Free on 23/8/90)
Halifax T (Free on 12/7/91) FL 73+5/2 FLC 2/1 FAC 2 Others 4
Bury (£50,000 on 1/10/93) FL 235/8 FLC 16 FAC 11/1 Others 15/1

LUDDEN Dominic James
Born: Basildon, 30 March 1974
Height: 5'8" Weight: 11.0
International Honours: E: Sch

A 1998 summer signing from Watford, after a year out with a back injury, Dominic quickly became a favourite at Preston in the left-back slot. Stunningly fast, he got forward well, and could be relied upon to deliver a string of telling crosses from the left flank, as well as being sound in defence. A hamstring injury in December meant he missed seven matches, including the Arsenal FA Cup-tie, but he returned for six games in February, before another hamstring injury saw him out again until April. The North End fans will be hoping to see more of his powerful, all-action play this coming season.

Leyton Orient (Signed from Billericay T on 6/7/92) FL 50+8/1 FLC 1 FAC 0+1 Others 6/1
Watford (£100,000 on 7/8/94) FL 28+5 FLC 3 FAC 2+1 Others 2
Preston NE (Free on 31/7/98) P/FL 26+6 FLC 1 FAC 2 Others 2

LUMSDON Christopher (Chris)
Born: Newcastle, 15 December 1979
Height: 5'7" Weight: 10.6

Chris, one of Sunderland's bright young hopes for the future, found it difficult to break into the first team last season due to the fine form of several more experienced players. Having made a substitute appearance in the Worthington Cup against Grimsby in October, he could perhaps count himself a little unlucky not to have appeared at least on the bench more often, as his form with the reserves was good. A midfielder, who can also play down either flank, his crossing and passing strengths have him marked down as a real prospect.

Sunderland (From trainee on 3/7/97) FL 1 FLC 0+1

LUNDEKVAM Claus
Born: Norway, 22 February 1973
Height: 6'3" Weight: 12.10
International Honours: Norway: 6

Norwegian international central defender brought to the Dell by Southampton from SK Brann in September 1996. A cultured and composed competitor who reads the game well and likes to bring the ball out of defence, Claus was a stalwart for the Saints last season, continuing his partnership for much of the time with Ken Monkou. The only real black spot of his campaign came when he was bizarrely sent off at Aston Villa in April for a second bookable offence, even though the team had been awarded a free kick for offside. Otherwise, he was consistently a class act.

Southampton (£400,000 from SK Brann on 3/9/96) PL 89+4 FLC 12+2 FAC 3

LUNDIN Pal Michael
Born: Osby, Sweden, 21 November 1964
Height: 6'5" Weight: 14.0

Pal, a free agent, joined Oxford last March from Osters IFV, a Swedish First Division club, after a trial period which saw him do well in a couple of reserve matches. A former team mate of Mark Watson at Osters, the former Swedish 'keeper (who had been on the bench for his country) was told he was not to be given a contract, before a change of mind saw him sign and playing in the last seven games, keeping three clean sheets. Tall with a very good clearance.

Oxford U (Free from Osters IFV on 2/3/99) FL 7

LUNT Kenneth (Kenny) Vincent
Born: Runcorn, 20 November 1979
Height: 5'10" Weight: 10.0
International Honours: E: Yth; Sch

Having come through the FA School at Lilleshall, playing at both schools and youth level for England, Crewe feel that they certainly have a player for the future in Kenny. Although his first-team opportunities were limited in 1998-99, following his breakthrough the previous season, mainly being from the bench until falling away in January, his second start saw him score the opening goal in a 2-1 home win over Bradford. A versatile midfielder, he is expected to fight his way back into contention before too long.

Crewe Alex (From trainee on 12/6/97) FL 35+24/3 FLC 2+3/1 FAC 0+1

LYDIATE Jason Lee
Born: Manchester, 29 October 1971
Height: 5'11" Weight: 12.3

Formerly with Blackpool, Jason moved over to Scarborough in time for the start of 1998-99, having been released by the Lancashire club. A strong, dominant defender, he impressed at the heart of the Boro defence before missing some key games through suspension, and then asking for a move so that he could be nearer his home in Manchester. With the request granted, he signed for Rochdale in February, initially on loan, and made his debut in the 3-0 win over Hull City that was televised live on Sky. Generally considered a central defender, Jason, in fact, slotted in more often than not as the defensive midfielder in Dale's line-up, playing in 14 of the final 19 matches, and scoring at Mansfield. Was released by the Boro during the summer, following their relegation from the league.

Manchester U (From trainee on 1/7/90)
Bolton W (Free on 19/3/92) FL 29+1 FLC 4 FAC 2 Others 1
Blackpool (£75,000 on 3/3/95) FL 81+5/2 FLC 7+2 FAC 6/1 Others 4+1
Scarborough (Signed on 6/8/98) FL 26+1/1 FLC 2 FAC 2 Others 1
Rochdale (Loaned on 12/2/99) FL 14/1

LYTTLE Desmond (Des)
Born: Wolverhampton, 24 September 1971
Height: 5'9" Weight: 12.13
Club Honours: Div 1 '98

Having been a regular for Nottingham Forest at right back, and occasionally in midfield, after signing from Swansea in 1993, Des was placed on the transfer list during the 1998 close season, and made few appearances in 1998-99 before going on loan to Port Vale in November. Made his debut as a wing back at Oxford, and did reasonably well during his stay, despite his upset on being substituted at Sunderland after 36 minutes when a change of formation was introduced. Had his loan extended for another month, but was recalled by Forest the day before the FA Cup third round as he was required to play against Portsmouth, and after appearing in the next two matches it was back to the reserves. Stop Press: Released during the summer, he signed for Watford on 8 July.

Leicester C (From trainee on 1/9/90)
Swansea C (£12,500 from Worcester C on 9/7/92) FL 46/1 FLC 2 FAC 5 Others 5
Nottingham F (£375,000 on 27/7/93) F/PL 177+8/3 FLC 19+1 FAC 16 Others 8
Port Vale (Loaned on 20/11/98) FL 7

LYTTLE Gerard Francis
Born: Belfast, 27 November 1977
Height: 5'8" Weight: 11.0
International Honours: NI: U21-6

Released by Glasgow Celtic during the 1998 close season, having failed to make an appearance for the Bhoys since signing pro forms in 1994, Gerard, who appeared promising in summer friendlies, made his first-team debut last August when coming off the bench for the final minute of the Worthington Cup-tie at London Road against Reading. A full back, cum midfielder, with a reputation of getting forward to deliver crosses to the front men, he was not heard from at senior level again.

Glasgow C (From juniors on 9/12/94)
Peterborough U (Free on 31/7/98) FLC 0+1

PFA Enterprises Ltd

Commercial Opportunities
with the Professional Footballers Association

The Professional Footballers Association has access to over 4,000 current and ex-players and has an enormously influential marque which provides the strongest possible accreditation, adding the status and appeal of the world's most popular sport to your own product, promotion or event.

PRODUCT ENDORSEMENTS

PERSONAL APPEARANCES

SPONSORSHIP OPPORTUNITIES

CORPORATE EVENTS

HOSPITALITY PACKAGES

BUSINESS PARTNERSHIPS

CARLING MASTERS LEAGUE FOOTBALL

PFA AWARDS DINNER

Official kit suppliers to the PFA   *Official car suppliers to the PFA*

**For more information on commercial opportunities with the
Professional Footballers Association, please contact:**

PFA Enterprises Ltd

Manchester
George Berry
Tel: 0161-228-2733
Fax: 0161-236-4496
Email: gberry@thepfa.co.uk

London
Garry Nelson
Tel: 0171-839-8663
Fax: 0171-839-2097
Email: gnelson@thepfa.co.uk

www.thepfa.co.uk

McALINDON Gareth Edward
Born: Hexham, 6 April 1977
Height: 5'10" Weight: 12.9
Club Honours: AMC '97

1998-99 was a disappointing campaign for "Macca" at Carlisle, and he was not retained at the end of the season. He made only three league starts, but came off the bench a further 13 times, though often too late in the game to make a substantive contribution. His commitment was never in doubt and, although he made the occasional telling pass, he was never able to register on the scoresheet.
Carlisle U (Free from Newcastle U juniors on 10/7/95) FL 22+37/5 FLC 4 FAC 1+1/1 Others 1+4/2

McALLISTER Brian
Born: Glasgow, 30 November 1970
Height: 5'11" Weight: 12.5
International Honours: S: 3

Having suffered an achilles heel injury in 1997-98, playing just ten times, a recurrence also ruled him out of a large amount of 1998-99, leaving him with only nine reserve starts and one Worthington Cup appearance for Wimbledon all season. A strong defender who has served the club handsomely, and known amongst Dons' fans as the "Scottish Womble", he can hold the ball well and is strong in the air, especially when dealing with the top strikers. Also possessing a good left foot, he is more than capable of hitting wonderful long passes behind the opposing full backs.
Wimbledon (From trainee on 1/3/89) F/PL 74+11 FLC 9+1 FAC 5+3 Others 1
Plymouth Arg (Loaned on 5/12/90) FL 7+1
Crewe Alex (Loaned on 8/3/96) FL 13/1 Others 2

McALLISTER Gary
Born: Motherwell, 25 December 1964
Height: 6'1" Weight: 11.12
Club Honours: S Div 1 '85; Div 1 '92; CS '92
International Honours: S: 57; B-2; U21-1

Having recovered from his cruciate ligament operation and returning to first-team duty last October, Gary took a short time to recover his timing and accuracy but, by the New Year, he was playing as well as he has ever done for Coventry. Although barracked by City fans in the defeat at West Ham at Christmas, that was more symptomatic of general frustration of the team. Within weeks he was being acclaimed by the same fans, scoring a superb goal direct from a free kick at Goodison in the FA Cup-tie, and a good goal at home to Middlesbrough. Sadly, the Scottish fans also barracked him on his return to the national side against the Czech Republic, and after the game he announced his international retirement after 57 caps. Three days later, when his mental state cannot have been perfect, he had the coolness to take and score a vital penalty at Hillsborough to set

the team on the way to an important win.
Motherwell (Signed from Fir Park BC on 5/9/81) SL 52+7/6 SLC 3+1 SC 7/2
Leicester C (£125,000 on 15/8/85) FL 199+2/47 FLC 14+1/3 FAC 5/2 Others 4
Leeds U (£1,000,000 on 2/7/90) F/PL 230+1/31 FLC 26/5 FAC 24/6 Others 14/4
Coventry C (£3,000,000 on 26/7/96) PL 81/9 FLC 9/3 FAC 7/1

McANESPIE Stephen (Steve)
Born: Kilmarnock, 1 February 1972
Height: 5'9" Weight: 10.7
Club Honours: S Div 1 '95; SLC '95; Div 1 '97
International Honours: S: Yth

A Fulham midfielder with a devastating free kick, Steve missed only three Football Combination fixtures last season, and would have been encouraged that two of his only three chances in the first team were in the final two matches of the campaign. Whereas he performed well in a central midfield role in the reserves, he played a lot of games as the middle man in the back three where he looked less assured. Is at his most positive when getting up the line to deliver crosses to the front men.
Aberdeen (From juniors on 12/5/88. Transferred to Vasterhauringe on 30/6/93)
Raith Rov (Signed on 25/1/94) SL 37+3 SLC 4 SC 3 Others 5
Bolton W (£900,000 on 30/9/95) F/PL 19+5 FLC 6
Fulham (£100,000 on 28/11/97) FL 3+4 FAC 1 Others 2+1
Bradford C (Loaned on 26/3/98) FL 7

McAREAVEY Paul
Born: Belfast, 3 December 1980
Height: 5'10" Weight: 11.0
International Honours: NI: Yth

Still a trainee, having made his Football League debut for Swindon in 1997-98 just

months after arriving at the club, and impressing, he continued to learn his trade with the junior and reserve sides in 1998-99 before being called upon in the penultimate game of the season. A tricky left-sided midfielder who loves the ball at his feet, and looking forward to signing a pro contract in the summer, he came off the bench for the final four minutes at Norwich – losing to a 90th-minute goal. Very highly thought of, he is expected to go well in 1999-2000.
Swindon T (Trainee) FL 0+2

McARTHUR Duncan Edward
Born: Brighton, 6 May 1981
Height: 5'9" Weight: 12.6

An 18-year-old YTS trainee, who is a left-footed, left sided midfielder, Duncan made his debut for Brighton in the 0-0 draw at Hartlepool last March. A combative player, whose physical presence disguises his age, he suffered disciplinary problems in the youth side, but following two impressive performances for the first team, he was awarded a one-year professional contract. This was subsequently revoked by manager Micky Adams after an alleged breach of club discipline.
Brighton & Hove A (Trainee) FL 3

McATEER Jason Wynn
Born: Birkenhead, 18 June 1971
Height: 5'10" Weight: 11.12
International Honours: Ei: 30; B-1

Although featuring on the right side of midfield in Liverpool's opening two games last season, it was clear that following the summer purchase of Vegard Heggem, Jason would be hard pushed to retain his place in the side. Although no one at Anfield ever questioned his enthusiasm and commitment

Gary McAllister

to the cause, with Rigobert Song already on his way to the club, the Blackburn manager, Brian Kidd, who was in the process of transferring Tim Sherwood to Spurs, moved quickly to get his man. Obviously a wrench to leave his home city, the Republic of Ireland international started in the centre of Rovers' midfield, but only had one game there before an injury to Jeff McKenna saw him move into his favoured role of right-wing back. His surging runs and power were certainly welcome, but he would not have found the tension of the relegation fight to his liking. However, being from a boxing family, his uncles Pat and Les were British middleweight champions, it is not surprising that he goes in where it hurts.

Bolton W (Signed from Marine on 22/1/92) P/FL 109+5/8 FLC 11/2 FAC 11/3 Others 8+1/2
Liverpool (£4,500,000 on 6/9/95) PL 84+16/3 FLC 12+1 FAC 11+1/3 Others 12+2
Blackburn Rov (£4,000,000 on 28/1/99) PL 13/1

McAULEY Sean

Born: Sheffield, 23 June 1972
Height: 5'11" Weight: 11.12
International Honours: S: U21-1; Yth

Started last season as Scunthorpe's left back, until indifferent performances saw him losing his place at Christmas, and eventually being loaned to Scarborough in transfer deadline week. A player with an excellent left foot, Sean made his debut as a sub in a 1-0 home win over Rochdale, and his first full appearance in front of 14,000 fans in a 1-1 draw at Hull City. He then made a further five starts before dropping out of the side.

Manchester U (From trainee on 1/7/90)
St Johnstone (Signed on 22/4/92) SL 59+3 SLC 3/1 SC 3 Others 1
Chesterfield (Loaned on 4/11/94) FL 1/1 FAC 1+1 Others 2
Hartlepool U (Free on 21/7/95) FL 84/1 FLC 6 FAC 3 Others 3
Scunthorpe U (Signed on 26/3/97) FL 55+6/1 FLC 5 FAC 5 Others 1
Scarborough (Loaned on 25/3/99) FL 6+1

MACAULEY Stephen (Steve) Roy

Born: Lytham, 4 March 1969
Height: 6'1" Weight: 12.0
Club Honours: FAYC '86

Having missed the whole of 1997-98 with a serious ankle injury, and having worked tremendously hard to regain his fitness, Steve was delighted to come off the bench for the last 15 minutes of Crewe's home game against Sunderland in early November, despite the team losing 4-1. It was good to be back and, apart from the odd spell out, he started the last five games as Alex fought to stave off relegation to the Second Division, actually scoring the winner at Ipswich to signal that he was well and truly back. A commanding central defender who is good at both ends of the park, being a powerful header of the ball, he can also be used up front if needed.

Manchester C (From trainee on 5/11/87. Released during 1988 close season)
Crewe Alex (£25,000 from Fleetwood T on 24/3/92) FL 173+12/21 FLC 12 FAC 12/1 Others 20/3

McAVOY Lawrence (Larry) David

Born: Lambeth, 9 July 1979
Height: 5'7" Weight: 11.0

A first-year professional at Cambridge, having come through the YTS ranks, Larry made an impressive debut for the senior side at Hull City last October and handled the pressure well. Ruled out for much of 1998-99 through injury, the young defender, who was described by the club as being an uncompromising, old-style right back, ended the campaign with some impressive performances in the reserves.

Cambridge U (From trainee on 14/5/98) FL 1

Steve McCall

McCALL Stephen (Steve) Harold

Born: Carlisle, 15 October 1960
Height: 5'11" Weight: 12.6
Club Honours: UEFAC '81
International Honours: E: B-1; U21-6; Yth

Out of contract at Torquay at the end of 1997-98, Steve returned to Plymouth, along with Kevin Hodges, for the start of 1998-99, the successful double act being tempted back to Argyle with Hodges as manager and Steve as player/assistant manager. Although he no longer has the legs, his reading of the game was second to none, and he was quite comfortably among the best passers in the division, while his skill on the ball created endless opportunities for his fellow midfielders and strikers. Obviously running the playing side of his career down, he made just 17 starts!

Ipswich T (From apprentice on 5/10/78) FL 249+8/7 FLC 29 FAC 23+1/1 Others 18+1/3
Sheffield Wed (£300,000 on 3/6/87) FL 21+8/2 FLC 2+3 FAC 1 Others 0+1
Carlisle U (Loaned on 8/2/90) FL 6
Plymouth Arg (£25,000 on 26/3/92) FL 97+3/5 FLC 5 FAC 6 Others 6
Torquay U (Free on 12/7/96) FL 43+8/2 FLC 3+1 Others 4/1
Plymouth Arg (Free on 7/8/98) FL 14+3 FLC 1+1 FAC 2+1

McCALL Andrew Stuart Murray

Born: Leeds, 10 June 1964
Height: 5'7" Weight: 12.0
Club Honours: Div 3 '85; SPL '92, '93, '94, '95, '96; SLC '92, '93; SC '92, '93, '96
International Honours: S: 40; U21-2

Having started with Bradford as an apprentice in 1980, and having gone on to play 40 times for Scotland, Stuart finally came home when returning to Valley Parade on being released by Glasgow Rangers during the 1998 close season. Given a three-year contract and appointed club captain, after missing four early games due to an ankle ligament injury, he quickly showed that he was a natural leader and an inspiration to the team. Although 34 years of age, he never stopped running, while his partnership with Gareth Whalley in the centre of midfield was outstanding. Won all of the "Player of the Year" awards.

Bradford C (From apprentice on 1/6/82) FL 235+3/37 FLC 16/3 FAC 12/3 Others 12+1/3
Everton (£850,000 on 1/6/88) FL 99+4/6 FLC 11/1 FAC 16+2/3 Others 8+1
Glasgow R (£1,200,000 on 15/8/91) SL 186+8/14 SLC 15/3 SC 25+2 Others 28/2
Bradford C (Free on 4/6/98) FL 43/3 FLC 3 FAC 2

McCAMMON Mark Jason

Born: Barnet, 7 August 1978
Height: 6'5" Weight: 14.5

A non-contract striker at Cambridge in 1998-99, Mark struggled to make the first team, playing at Southend and coming off the bench at home to Shrewsbury, both league games, before leaving the club by mutual consent and signing for Charlton on 17 March. Very tall, and decidedly pacy, he has yet to get a senior opportunity for Athletic, but was offered a new contract for the coming term.

Cambridge U (Free from Cambridge C on 31/12/96) FL 1+3 FAC 0+1 Others 1
Charlton Ath (Free on 17/3/99)

McCANN Gavin Peter

Born: Blackpool, 10 January 1978
Height: 5'11" Weight: 11.0

Gavin arrived at Sunderland from Everton last November to provide extra cover and competition for midfield places in the squad. A box-to-box player, he is a tremendous competitor who always contributes 100 per cent when called upon, and could well be seen by Peter Reid as the eventual successor to captain Kevin Ball in the midfield holding role. However, he can make good forward runs, epitomised by his winning goal at Lincoln in the FA Cup in January, and also gave Sunderland hope for the Worthington Cup semi final second leg with his 35-yard free kick which reduced the arrears at the Stadium of Light.

Everton (From trainee on 1/7/95) PL 5+6
Sunderland (£500,000 on 27/11/98) FL 5+6 FLC 1/1 FAC 1+1/1

McCARTHY Jonathan (Jon) David

Born: Middlesbrough, 18 August 1970
Height: 5'9" Weight: 11.5
International Honours: NI: 12; B-2

By his own admission, Jon had a poor first

season at Birmingham in 1997-98, but finally won the crowd over in 1998-99 when always giving nothing less than his best. However, his worrying lack of goals saw Bryan Hughes preferred on the wide right towards the end of the campaign as City went hunting for a promotion place. An unselfish player who always looks to get back to support the full back, the Northern Ireland international wingman has great pace and skill on the ball, which creates chances for others.

Hartlepool U (From juniors on 7/11/87) FL 0+1 (Free to Shepshed Charterhouse in March 1989)
York C (Free on 22/3/90) FL 198+1/31 FLC 8/1 FAC 11/3 Others 15/3
Port Vale (£450,000 on 1/8/95) FL 93+1/12 FLC 10/2 FAC 7/1 Others 8/2
Birmingham C (£1,850,000 on 11/9/97) FL 76+8/3 FLC 5 FAC 4 Others 2

McCARTHY Paul Jason
Born: Cork, 4 August 1971
Height: 5'10" Weight: 13.12
International Honours: Ei: U21-10; Yth; Sch
Strong central defender for Wycombe who recovered well from a hernia operation in the summer of 1998. Competition was strong in the centre of defence and, on being left out after the first six games, he was recalled last October for a long spell before an injury ruled him out until March. By that time he had become an automatic first choice, forming a formidable partnership with Jamie Bates, and shoring up what had become a leaky defence. He is a very powerful header of the ball, with a strong physical presence, and his good form was rewarded with a new two-year contract towards the end of the season.

Brighton & Hove A (From trainee on 26/4/89) FL 180+1/6 FLC 11/1 FAC 13 Others 12/1
Wycombe W (£100,000 on 5/7/96) FL 90+10/2 FLC 8+1/1 FAC 8 Others 3

McCARTHY Sean Casey
Born: Bridgend, 12 September 1967
Height: 6'1" Weight: 12.12
International Honours: W: B-1
Sean was yet another player returning to Plymouth in 1998-99 after a long absence. At the start of the season his signing was considered to be the missing link in the push for promotion, but, sadly, long-term injury deprived the side of his experience and expertise. His early appearances showed that he had lost none of his desire to battle, as he continued to chase lost causes and give defenders uncomfortable afternoons. An excellent target man who brings others into the game, a return to fitness will be a major boost for Argyle.

Swansea C (Signed from Bridgend T on 22/10/85) FL 76+15/25 FLC 4+1/3 FAC 5+2/4 Others 9+1/6
Plymouth Arg (£50,000 on 18/8/88) FL 67+3/19 FLC 7/5 FAC 3/1 Others 0+1/1
Bradford C (£250,000 on 4/7/90) FL 127+4/60 FLC 10+2/10 FAC 8/2 Others 8+1/7
Oldham Ath (£500,000 on 3/12/93) P/FL 117+23/43 FLC 10/1 FAC 6+1/1 Others 4/1
Bristol C (Loaned on 26/3/98) FL 7/1
Plymouth Arg (Signed on 7/8/98) FL 14+2/3 FLC 2/2 FAC 5

McCLARE Sean Patrick
Born: Rotherham, 12 January 1978
Height: 5'10" Weight: 11.12
International Honours: Ei: U21-2
Having risen through the junior ranks at Barnsley, Sean made an immediate impact when coming on as a substitute on his debut in 1997-98 and scoring after only ten minutes on the field. A hard-running box-to-box midfielder, he made a position in the first team his own until injury forced him to miss most of the latter part of the season. Showing an eye for goal, and now a Republic of Ireland U21 international, much will be expected of him in 1999-2000.

Barnsley (From trainee on 3/7/96) FL 23+7/3 FLC 4+1 FAC 5/1

McCLEN James (Jamie) David
Born: Newcastle, 13 May 1979
Height: 5'9" Weight: 10.12
It was a surprise when Jamie was handed his first-team debut for Newcastle against Tottenham at home late in 1998-99, but he acquitted himself well to justify his manager's faith in him, and to confirm his potential. He is a small, neat midfield player who works tirelessly for his side, and who likes to break forward at speed from the flanks, never afraid to have a shot at goal. As a product of the club's Centre of Excellence, having been with United from the age of ten, he made rapid progress last season which he started on the fringe of the reserves after playing a handful of games for them during the previous campaign. In and out of the reserve side until November, when he established himself as a regular, he continued his development in occasional training sessions with the senior squad to fully earn his call up.

Newcastle U (From trainee on 4/7/97) PL 1

McCONNELL Barry
Born: Exeter, 1 January 1977
Height: 5'10" Weight: 10.3
Although Barry made only a few appearances in the Exeter first team last season, the management have belief in his ability, which was shown with the offer of a new one-year contract for 1999-2000. A forward with close control, and a good striker of the ball, all that is needed is more consistency and a first-team place will surely be his.

Exeter C (From trainee on 4/8/95) FL 46+34/11 FLC 1+2 FAC 2+3 Others 0+1

McCORMICK Stephen (Steve)
Born: Dumbarton, 14 August 1969
Height: 6'4" Weight: 11.4
Club Honours: S Div 2 '96, S Div 1 '98
A gangly, left-sided forward with a good goalscoring record in Scottish football, Steve joined Leyton Orient on loan from Dundee last September, but found it difficult to adjust to the English game and returned to Dundee, before moving on to Airdrie after a month. Had one good run on his debut, when coming off the bench at Brisbane

Road against Mansfield, beating several players in a dribble from the half-way line but just could not find the finish.

Queens Park R (From Yoker Ath on 25/7/91) SL 108+14/37 SLC 5/1 SC 2+1 Others 4/1
Stirling A (Signed on 7/7/95) SL 67+5/33 SLC 4+1/3 SC 4/3 Others 8/3
Dundee U (Signed on 29/12/97) SL 6+9/5 SC 3+2/1
Leyton Orient (Loaned on 8/9/98) FL 1+3 FLC 2

McDERMOTT Andrew (Andy)
Born: Sydney, Australia, 24 March 1977
Height: 5'9" Weight: 11.3
Andy was in West Bromwich's reserves for the first six weeks of last season, then had an 11-match spell in the first team before losing his right-back slot to Paul Holmes. He then came back into contention in March, and played out the rest of the campaign very well, producing some excellent displays. A fine header of the ball, despite his height, although his distribution at times let him down, at his best his passing game is fine. Is also capable of playing in midfield.

Queens Park R (Signed from Australian Institute of Sport on 4/8/95) FL 6/2
West Bromwich A (£400,000 on 27/3/97) FL 39 FLC 2/1

McDERMOTT John
Born: Middlesbrough, 3 February 1969
Height: 5'7" Weight: 11.0
Club Honours: AMC '98
Now in his 13th season with Grimsby there is little new one can say about this consummate professional, who again firmly established himself as automatic choice at right back in 1998-99. Surprisingly fast for a defender, a strong tackler, a provider of excellent service for the front runners, and not averse to going forward with the ball, he worked well to establish a partnership with whichever left of midfield player he was teamed up with. As part of one of the most difficult to penetrate defences in the First Division, he played a vital part in the club maintaining a respectable place in the league.

Grimsby T (From trainee on 1/6/87) FL 396+15/7 FLC 29+1 FAC 27+1/2 Others 21

McDONALD Christopher (Chris)
Born: Edinburgh, 14 October 1975
Height: 6'1" Weight: 13.0
Club Honours: FAYC '94
International Honours: S: Sch
A popular left-sided central defender who, throughout his career, has been badly affected by injuries, he began 1998-99, his third season at Hartlepool, on a short-term contract, once again having to prove himself fit enough to justify a longer one. Although having a short first-team run, often wearing the number nine shirt, yet playing in a three-man central defence, with the playing staff needing to be reduced he was released on a free transfer at the end of September.

Arsenal (From trainee on 13/12/93)
Stoke C (Free on 31/8/95)
Hartlepool U (Free on 17/8/96) FL 18+2 FLC 3

McDONALD Martin Joseph
Born: Irvine, 4 December 1973
Height: 6'0" Weight: 11.12
International Honours: E: SP-1
A midfielder with a tremendous engine, and a tenacious tackler with an ability to run from box to box, Martin scored a brace of goals at Gillingham early last season, the second being a spectacular 22-yard drive that took a deflection to loop past the stranded 'keeper. However, on-field disciplinary problems led to a total of a seven match ban in November, which was followed by a two-week absence with a 'flu virus. Having "disappeared" after Christmas for four weeks, on his return he was immediately transferred to non-league neighbours, Altrincham, for an undisclosed fee rumoured to be around £10,000.
Stockport Co (Free from Bramhall on 5/8/92) (Free to Macclesfield T during 1993 close season)
Doncaster Rov (£20,000 from Southport on 1/8/96) FL 48/4 FLC 4 FAC 2
Macclesfield T (£20,000 on 10/12/97) FL 45/3 FLC 4 Others 1

McDOUGALD David Eugene **Junior**
Born: Big Spring, Texas, USA, 12 January 1975
Height: 5'11" Weight: 12.6
International Honours: E: Yth
Signed from Cambridge City during the 1998 close season, Junior returned to Millwall where he had once been on the books as a schoolboy and, although playing in many of the summer friendlies, he made just one first-team appearance, as a sub at Wigan, in the opening game of 1998-99. Following that, he joined Leyton Orient on non-contract forms in October, but was yet another player whose season was blighted by injury at Brisbane Road. However, when fit he was a real threat with his turn of pace, especially out wide. Also able to play as a forward, he will be looking to have an injury-free run this term.
Tottenham H (From trainee on 12/7/93)
Brighton & Hove A (Signed on 12/5/94) FL 71+7/14 FLC 7/2 FAC 4/3 Others 6/3
Chesterfield (Loaned on 28/3/96) FL 9/3
Rotherham U (£50,000 on 30/7/96) FL 14+4/2 FAC 1 Others 1 (Free to Toulon on 1/7/97)
Millwall (Free from Cambridge C on 3/7/98) FL 0+1
Leyton Orient (Free on 8/10/98) FL 3+5 FAC 1+1

McFARLANE Andrew (Andy) Antonie
Born: Wolverhampton, 30 November 1966
Height: 6'3" Weight: 13.8
Club Honours: AMC '94
Injuries ruined last season for Torquay's big striker and, at the time of writing, his future with the club was uncertain. Tall and awkward looking, on his few appearances he scored fine goals against Brentford at Plainmoor and Griffin Park. He also equalised at Halifax in a 1-1 draw.
Portsmouth (£20,000 from Cradley T on 20/11/90) FL 0+2
Swansea C (£20,000 on 6/8/92) FL 33+22/8 FLC 3/1 FAC 0+6 Others 3+4/3
Scunthorpe U (£15,000 on 4/8/95) FL 48+12/19 FLC 4/1 FAC 2+2/2 Others 3/2
Torquay U (£20,000 on 10/1/97) FL 42+14/11 FLC 3+1/1 Others 3+1/1

McGAVIN Steven (Steve) James
Born: North Walsham, 24 January 1969
Height: 5'9" Weight: 12.8
Club Honours: GMVC '92; FAT '92; Div 2 '95
An influential Wycombe midfield playmaker and striker, Steve appeared to have recovered from his fallen arch problem during the summer of 1998. Initially he began last season playing the substitutes' role, and had a good game starting at Middlesbrough in the Worthington Cup. The next match, however, saw the injury flare up again, and he remained sidelined until his comeback as a substitute in an Auto Windscreens Shield tie against Brentford. With a new manager in place, he then asked to be released from his contract at the end of January before it expired at the end of the season because of the need to be closer to his family in a time of two bereavements. The chairman reluctantly agreed, and he joined Southend on a short-term basis until the end of 1998-99. Performing in midfield, and up front on occasion, he showed signs of his skill in both positions, and also caused some defences problems but, with the side's morale low, he struggled to lift them.
Ipswich T (From trainee on 29/1/87) (Free to Thetford T in August 1987)
Colchester U (£10,000 from Sudbury T on 28/7/92) FL 55+3/17 FLC 2 FAC 6/2 Others 4
Birmingham C (£150,000 on 7/1/94) FL 16+7/2 FLC 1+1/1 FAC 3+1/2 Others 1+3
Wycombe W (£140,000 on 20/3/95) FL 103+17/14 FLC 5+2 FAC 6+1/3 Others 4+2
Southend U (Free on 2/2/99) FL 4+7

Pat McGibbon

McGIBBON Patrick (Pat) Colm
Born: Lurgan, 6 September 1973
Height: 6'2" Weight: 13.12
Club Honours: AMC '99
International Honours: NI: 6; B-5; U21-1; Sch
A Wigan central defender who is cool and assured under pressure and commanding in the air, Pat was a virtual ever present during the 1998-99 campaign, his aerial ability allowing him to net five goals, including a

dramatic last-second equaliser at Burnley. Once again his reliable performances were recognised at international level when called up by Northern Ireland. Was also a valuable member of the Wembley side that defeated Millwall 1-0 to win the Auto Windscreens Shield.
Manchester U (£100,000 from Portadown on 1/8/92) FLC 1
Swansea C (Loaned on 20/9/96) FL 1
Wigan Ath (£250,000 on 3/3/97) FL 77+4/6 FLC 5 FAC 5 Others 10

McGILL Derek
Born: Lanark, 14 October 1975
Height: 6'0" Weight: 12.8
Having moved from Raith Rovers to Queens Park last September, Derek arrived at Port Vale on trial in October on the recommendation of coach, Phil Bonnyman, who had seen him play in his native Scotland. A slightly-built striker, he played a few games for the reserves but found it difficult to break into the first team and made three appearances as a substitute, totalling just 23 minutes in all. For all that, he almost scored an equaliser at Stockport, but skewed his effort wide before being freed in November.
Hamilton Ac (From Dunfermline juniors on 25/6/93) SL 17+6/4 SC 1 Others 1 (Free to Glentoran during 1995 close season)
Falkirk (Free on 16/11/95)
Hamilton Ac (Free on 18/9/96) SL 8/4
Raith Rov (Free on 22/11/96) SL 14+11/4
Queens Park R (Free on 4/9/98)
Port Vale (Free on 2/10/98) FL 0+3

McGINLAY John
Born: Inverness, 8 April 1964
Height: 5'9" Weight: 11.6
Club Honours: Div 1 '97
International Honours: S: 13; B-2
Forced to have an achilles tendon operation in March 1998, the hard-running stiker was unable to get back into the Bradford side and signed for Oldham last October. Unfortunately, just six starts and four subs' appearances later, a re-occurrence of his knee injury ended a glorious career, but not before he had taken the Latics into the third round of the FA Cup. A great servant to football, with his wholehearted approach to the game, John always put the team first, even going in where it hurt at his own expense. Now in Boston, America coaching kids, he will be sorely missed by the fans.
Shrewsbury T (Signed from Elgin C on 22/2/89) FL 58+2/27 FLC 4 FAC 1/2 Others 3/2
Bury (£175,000 on 11/7/90) FL 16+9/9 FLC 1 FAC 1 Others 1+1
Millwall (£80,000 on 21/1/91) FL 27+7/10 FLC 2+1 FAC 2 Others 2/1
Bolton W (£125,000 on 30/9/92) P/FL 180+12/87 FLC 23+2/14 FAC 16+1/10 Others 11/7
Bradford C (£625,000 on 6/11/97) FL 12+5/3 FAC 0+1
Oldham Ath (Free on 23/10/98) FL 4+3/1 FAC 1+1/2 Others 1

McGINTY Brian
Born: East Kilbride, 10 December 1976
Height: 6'1" Weight: 12.6
Super "Bri's" silky skills might not be best suited to the battleground that is the Third

Division, but new boss Warren Joyce fully appreciated the former Ranger's contribution to the Hull City cause in 1998-99. Although restricted to the bench for much of the campaign, Joyce often referred to the midfielder's exemplary attitude and the part he played in the club's revival. Saved his best performance for the 4-0 win against fellow strugglers, Hartlepool, in January, with two cracking goals, before being released in the summer.

Glasgow R (From juniors on 1/7/93) SL 3 SLC 0+1
Hull C (Free on 28/11/97) FL 43+10/6 FLC 4/1 FAC 2+1/1 Others 3+1

McGLEISH Scott
Born: Barnet, 10 February 1974
Height: 5'9" Weight: 11.3
The 1998-99 campaign proved to be a roller-coaster season for the acrobatic striker, who is the undoubted darling of the Barnet faithful. Having commenced in dazzling form, and struck goals in consecutive games, including a strike against Wolves at Underhill, he then failed to find the net for seven matches, which paved the way for Sean Devine to reclaim his place. However, after Scott came on for Devine in the home match against Hull in September, and scored twice in a 4-1 victory, the tug of war for the number ten shirt between the pair took another twist when Italian side, Ancona, showed an interest in securing his services. The eventual trial in Italy proved to be unsuccessful, Scott returning to the starting line-up against Torquay in November to score an exceptional goal, which enabled

him to reclaim his place in the attack. He then endured a severe ankle injury in a reserve fixture in early February, and was ruled out of action for a month. Yet, once again he returned in style, when coming off the bench to score the second goal in the 3-0 home victory over Cambridge in March. He is incredibly effective in the air, despite his stature, and this, combined with an industrious workrate, paints a portrait of a striker who will regularly score goals in the basement division.

Charlton Ath (Free from Edgware T on 24/5/94) FL 0+6
Leyton Orient (Loaned on 10/3/95) FL 4+2/1 Others 1/1
Peterborough U (Free on 4/7/95) FL 3+10 FLC 0+1 FAC 0+1 Others 3+1/2
Colchester U (Loaned on 23/2/96) FL 10+5/6 Others 2
Cambridge U (Loaned on 2/9/96) FL 10/7 FLC 1
Leyton Orient (£50,000 on 22/11/96) FL 36/7 FLC 3/1 FAC 1 Others 1
Barnet (£70,000 on 1/10/97) FL 62+11/22 FLC 2/1 FAC 2 Others 2+2

McGLINCHEY Brian Kevin
Born: Derry, 26 October 1977
Height: 5'7" Weight: 10.2
International Honours: NI: B-1; U21-10
Signed from Manchester City during the 1998 close season, the Port Vale left back was used mainly as a reserve thanks to the consistency of Allen Tankard, and subsequently made only a handful of appearances in 1998-99. Despite being a pacy player, and a good crosser of the ball who managed to score at Oxford, he was released during the summer. However, with

youth on his side, and a permanent fixture for Northern Ireland at U21 level, he can only get better. He also represented the "B" team against Wales during the campaign.

Manchester C (From trainee on 4/12/95)
Port Vale (Free on 1/7/98) FL 10+5/1 FLC 0+1 FAC 1

McGORRY Brian Paul
Born: Liverpool, 16 April 1970
Height: 5'10" Weight: 12.8
Having gone out of the league with Hereford, this industrious, hard-working midfielder was Wes Saunders first signing as Torquay's manager during the 1998 close season. Had a good first part of the campaign when his passing was first class, but a series of niggling injuries spoilt the latter part and he was released during the summer. Scored his only goal for United in a 2-2 home draw against Carlisle.

Bournemouth (£30,000 from Weymouth on 13/8/91) FL 56+5/11 FLC 7 FAC 7+3/2 Others 5/1
Peterborough U (£60,000 on 10/2/94) FL 44+8/6 FLC 0+2 FAC 2 Others 2
Wycombe W (Free on 18/8/95) FL 0+4 FLC 1 Others 1/1
Cardiff C (Loaned on 22/3/96) FL 7
Hereford U (Signed on 26/3/97) FL 7/1
Torquay U (Free on 21/7/98) FL 31+3/1 FLC 2 FAC 2 Others 2

McGOVERN Brendan
Born: Camborne, 9 February 1980
Height: 5'10" Weight: 11.7
A first-year professional, the young Plymouth midfielder fully earned his promotion to the first team in the final week of the season, when he twice appeared as a substitute, replacing the assistant manager, Steve McCall, on both occasions. Although suffering a number of niggling injury problems throughout the campaign, the youngster came on in leaps and bounds, proving himself to be a big, strong, right-sided, attacking, battling player, as well as being a ball winner. In his manager's eyes, he is undoubtedly one for the future.

Plymouth Arg (From trainee on 9/7/98) FL 0+2

McGOWAN Gavin Gregory
Born: Blackheath, 16 January 1976
Height: 5'8" Weight: 11.10
Club Honours: FAYC '94
International Honours: E: Yth; Sch
After spending two loan spells at Luton in 1997, it was no great surprise when Arsenal freed him during the 1998 close season that he moved to Kenilworth Road on a more permanent basis. A strong full back who can play on either side but is more comfortable on the right, Gavin's only real downfall is his ability to collect cards. However, he is very quick, and will time his tackles better with experience. Also very skilful, he should become an asset to a side that harnesses bite to good football.

Arsenal (From trainee on 1/7/94) PL 3+3 FAC 1
Luton T (Loaned on 27/3/97) FL 2
Luton T (Loaned on 11/7/97) FL 6+2
Luton T (Free on 29/7/98) FL 27+4 FLC 7 FAC 2

Gavin McGowan

193

McGREAL John
Born: Liverpool, 2 June 1972
Height: 5'11" Weight: 12.8
One of the pivotal players of the Tranmere team in 1998-99, John is a cool-headed and assured central defender, now in his tenth season with the club. Solid at the back, and a good leader who is second to none in his reading of the game, he is rarely flustered even under constant pressure, and can be either an excellent anchor man or an adventurous carrier of the ball out of defence into attack. Possessing a touch of class, and confidently marshalling the players in front of him, unusually for him, he received two red cards early in the campaign, but fortunately remained free of serious injury. Still attracts the Premier League scouts to Prenton Park.
Tranmere Rov (From trainee on 3/7/90) FL 193+2/1 FLC 20+1 FAC 8 Others 7+2

McGREGOR Mark Dale Thomas
Born: Chester, 16 February 1977
Height: 5'11" Weight: 11.5
Mark continued to make progress at Wrexham in 1998-99, and is another youngster who seems to have been around the club for a long time due to his assured displays at the back. An adventurous right back who often comes though to try his luck at goal, his height enables him to play equally well at the heart of the defence when required, a position many observers believe is his best! Still only young, time is on his side if his ambitions to play in the higher echelons are to be realised.
Wrexham (From trainee on 4/7/95) FL 149+7/5 FLC 5 FAC 18+1 Others 10

McGREGOR Paul Anthony
Born: Liverpool, 17 December 1974
Height: 5'10" Weight: 11.6
Unable to get a game at Nottingham Forest in 1998-99, Paul had two loan spells interrupted by injury at Carlisle, but gave some impressive displays. Still highly thought of by many in the game, his three goals for the club, especially those against Barnet and Cambridge, provided some of the classiest moments seen at Brunton Park all season, and demonstrated a flair and touch not often seen in the Third Division. Unfortunately, United's attempts to secure a permanent deal were ultimately to no avail, and the right-sided striker signed for Preston in transfer deadline week, making his debut as a late sub just two days later. Fast and direct, he was used mainly from the bench, where his speed created problems for tiring defences, before he was surprisingly released during the summer.
Nottingham F (From trainee on 13/12/91) F/PL 7+23/3 FAC 0+3 Others 0+4/1
Carlisle U (Loaned on 25/9/98) FL 3/2
Carlisle U (Loaned on 20/11/98) FL 6+1/1 Others 1
Preston NE (Free on 24/3/99) FL 1+3

McGUCKIN Thomas Ian
Born: Middlesbrough, 24 April 1973
Height: 6'2" Weight: 14.2
Ian is a powerful central defender whose transfer from Hartlepool to Fulham in the 1997 close season did not turn out to be the

dream move he had envisaged. After an earlier permanent transfer back to Hartlepool had fallen through, and after having been out of first-team action for the best part of 18 months, a return move to his old club on loan last December looked to be an ideal opportunity for him to get his career back on track. Believing himself to be a better player, he did a good job under difficult circumstances, but, following the appointment of Chris Turner as the new Hartlepool manager, he was allowed to return to reserve football at Fulham.
Hartlepool U (From trainee on 20/6/91) FL 147+5/8 FLC 13+1/1 FAC 6 Others 6
Fulham (£75,000 on 16/6/97)
Hartlepool U (Loaned on 18/12/98) FL 8

McHUGH Frazer
Born: Nottingham, 14 July 1981
Height: 5'9" Weight: 12.5
Fraser was one of the leading lights in Swindon's youth team in 1998-99, and earned a two-year pro contract that was due to be signed in the summer. Playing in the centre of midfield, where his passing and ball control was a real asset to the attack, he made his Football league debut as a starter against Barnsley in the last game of the season and looked comfortable, having earlier come off the bench, two games into the campaign, during the 2-1 home Worthington Cup win over Wycombe. Is yet another of the highly promising youngsters who are important to Town's future.
Swindon T (Trainee) FL 1 FLC 0+1

McINDOE Michael
Born: Edinburgh, 2 December 1979
Height: 5'8" Weight: 11.0
After turning professional for Luton in April 1998, having graduated from the youth team, and being looked upon as a left-sided midfielder who was almost certain to be called up in 1998-99, Michael's impressive pre-season continued at non-league Hitchin Town, when he scored in a friendly game. Constructive and looking to make the right pass, he made his first-team debut in the first leg of the Worthington Cup, at home to Oxford, when coming off the bench for the last 12 minutes. Recognised by Town's management to be a player with a future, he made a further 27 appearances, which included him starting the final eight games of the campaign, and he probably cannot wait for 1999-2000 to get underway.
Luton T (From trainee on 2/4/98) FL 17+5 FLC 2+1 FAC 0+2 Others 1

McINNES Derek John
Born: Paisley, 5 July 1971
Height: 5'8" Weight: 12.0
Club Honours: S Div 2 '95; SPL '97
A hard-tackling Rangers midfield player, Derek came to Stockport for a three-month loan spell last November, after injury had robbed him of a place in Dick Advocaat's starting line-up at Ibrox. His intention was to get back to match fitness and return to Scotland, which he ultimately did, but that did not stop Stockport trying to secure him on a permanent basis following a series of

highly impressive displays. Within days of arriving at County, he became one of the most popular and influential of players at Edgeley Park, attracting the attention of a number of First Division clubs before returning north of the border.
Greenock M (From Gleniffer Thistle on 13/8/88) SL 196+25/19 SLC 7+1/1 SC 10+6 Others 10
Glasgow R (£250,000 on 13/11/95) SL 15+14/1 SLC 3+2/1 SC 0+1 Others 5+2/1
Stockport Co (Loaned on 6/11/98) FL 13 FAC 2

McINTOSH Martin Wyllie
Born: East Kilbride, 19 March 1971
Height: 6'2" Weight: 12.0
International Honours: S: B-2
In giving highly competent displays for Stockport in 1998-99, the reliable centre half underlined once again what a bargain Gary Megson got when he plucked him from Hamilton in 1997. Dominating in the air, and comfortable with the ball at his feet, attributes which have seen him capped by Scotland "B", he was a virtual ever present in the side, his partnership with Mike Flynn at the heart of the defence developing into one of the best in the division.
St Mirren (Free from Tottenham H juniors on 30/11/88) SL 2+2
Clydebank (Signed on 17/8/91) SL 59+6/10 SLC 2 SC 4+1/1 Others 3/1
Hamilton Ac (Signed on 1/2/94) SL 99/12 SLC 5 SC 5 Others 5/1
Stockport Co (£80,000 on 15/8/97) FL 79/5 FLC 3 FAC 4

McINTYRE James (Jim)
Born: Dumbarton, 24 May 1972
Height: 5'11" Weight: 12.2
Club Honours: SC '97
Despite a disappointing start at Reading in 1997-98, Jim proved himself to be a lively striker in 1998-99, and scored in the first-ever league match at the new Madejski Stadium, when sliding home the team's second goal in a 3-0 win against Luton. Thereafter the goals began to dry up, and he did not re-establish a regular place in the attack until December. His best performance coming when he scored twice in the 4-0 victory away to Stoke, Royals' highest win of the season.
Bristol C (Free from Duntochter BC on 10/10/91) FL 1 Others 0+1
Exeter C (Loaned on 11/2/93) FL 12+3/3 Others 4/1
Airdrie (Signed on 23/9/93) SL 32+22/10 SLC 3+3/1 SC 1+4 Others 2+2/2
Kilmarnock (Signed on 22/3/96) SL 42+3/9 SLC 2+1 SC 5+1/2 Others 2/1
Reading (£420,000 on 26/3/98) FL 28+10/6 FLC 1 Others 1

MACKAY Malcolm (Malky) George
Born: Bellshill, 19 February 1972
Height: 6'1" Weight: 11.7
Malky, as he is known, arrived at Norwich from Glasgow Celtic last September and quickly became a favourite with the City fans following a string of resolute displays at the heart of the defence. Almost a throwback to the days of the traditional, stopper-style centre half, he showed himself to be particularly strong in the air,

both defensively and as an attacking threat at set-play situations, when he was so unlucky with the amount of headers which were kept out by the woodwork. He also proved to be uncompromising in the tackle, and once into his stride is deceptively quick.

Queens Park R (From juniors on 8/12/89) SL 68+2/6 SLC 3/2 SC 2 Others 2
Glasgow Celtic (Signed on 6/8/93) SL 32+5/4 SLC 5+1 SC 4/1 Others 4+1
Norwich C (£350,000 on 18/9/98) FL 24+3/1 FLC 1+1 FAC 1

McKEEVER Mark Anthony
Born: Derry, 16 November 1978
Height: 5'9" Weight: 11.8
International Honours: NI: Yth. Ei: U21-4
Although signed by Sheffield Wednesday from Peterborough in April 1997, this smart youngster was brought along gently at Hillsborough and failed to make a first-team appearance in 1997-98. However, loaned out to Bristol Rovers last December, the tricky, pacy left winger played seven times in all for Rovers before going back and spending another spell on loan in March, this time at Reading. Scored at Stoke in his first match, and then netted the winner at Bournemouth to inflict the Cherries' first home defeat of the season. Although very impressive, especially with his dribbling skills and shooting ability, he was substituted a number of times late on in games. Selected for the Republic of Ireland squad while at the Madejski, he returned to Wednesday to make his senior debut at home to high-flying Chelsea. Looks to have a good chance of forging a successful career once he has filled out. Also played three times for the Republic at U21 level in 1998-99.

Peterborough U (Trainee) FL 2+1 FLC 1
Sheffield Wed (£500,000 + on 15/4/97) PL 1+2
Bristol Rov (Loaned on 10/12/98) FL 5+2
Reading (Loaned on 8/3/99) FL 6+1/2

MACKEN Jonathan Paul
Born: Manchester, 7 September 1977
Height: 5'10" Weight: 12.8
International Honours: E: Yth
A tremendously hard-working Preston forward, whose excellent positional sense and ability to hold the ball up was not always supported by his finishing in 1998-99, which netted few goals. He was often the forward replaced, especially early in the season, and was relegated to a regular place on the bench following the loan signing of Steve Basham, being used to pep up a tiring attack when coming on. With a very good footballing brain, and always giving 110 per cent to the cause, Jonathan seems particularly suited to playing just behind the front two, which he demonstrated late in the season when North End adopted a 4-3-3 formation on occasions.

Manchester U (From trainee on 10/7/96)
Preston NE (£250,000 on 31/7/97) FL 50+21/14 FLC 4+2/2 FAC 3+2 Others 4+3/1

McKENNA Paul Stephen
Born: Chorley, 20 October 1977
Height: 5'7" Weight: 11.12
Became a regular on the right of Preston's midfield early in 1998-99, and also featured wide on the left, although he preferred a more central role. Tigerish in the tackle, and quick to support both attack and defence, Paul's season was disrupted in the New Year, when knee and ankle injuries saw him in and out of the team for three months. Still relatively inexperienced, he will be looking for a long spell free of injury to firmly establish himself as a regular.

Preston NE (From trainee on 2/2/96) FL 39+7/1 FLC 1 FAC 1+1/1 Others 4

MacKENZIE Christopher (Chris) Neil
Born: Northampton, 14 May 1972
Height: 6'0" Weight: 12.6
Started last season as Leyton Orient's first-choice goalkeeper, playing in 35 of the opening 36 games, and showed himself, once again, to be an excellent shot stopper who was good at challenging for crosses. Had an outstanding game to keep the O's in the FA Cup at Kingstonian live on Sky TV, before losing his place in January to Scott Barrett, and going out on loan to Nuneaton Borough in March.

Hereford U (£15,000 from Corby on 20/7/94) FL 59+1/1 FLC 1 FAC 4 Others 8
Leyton Orient (Free on 17/10/97) FL 30 FLC 3 FAC 5 Others 2

McKENZIE Leon Mark
Born: Croydon, 17 May 1978
Height: 5'11" Weight: 11.2
Again unfortunate with injuries, Leon started last season on loan at Peterborough, scoring twice in his first game, a 3-1 win at Cardiff, and then at home to Exeter, before going back to Crystal Palace after four games when the injury jinx struck again. On recovery, he returned to London Road for a second loan spell and scored five goals in ten games. Then, after Posh's manager, Barry Fry, had failed to meet Palace's asking price to make the move permanent, the pacy, skilful, and busy young striker, with good heading ability, picked up his partnership with Clinton Morrison back at Selhurst, but was only able to find the net in a 2-1 defeat. From a boxing family – the son of Clinton, the former British light-welterweight champion, and nephew of Duke, a world champion at three different weights – he can be a star of the future if he can only stay clear of injury.

Crystal Palace (From trainee on 7/10/95) F/PL 18+34/3 FLC 4/1 FAC 1+4
Fulham (Loaned on 3/10/97) FL 1+2
Peterborough U (Loaned on 13/8/98) FL 4/3
Peterborough U (Loaned on 30/11/98) FL 10/5 Others 1/1

MacKENZIE Neil David
Born: Birmingham, 15 April 1976
Height: 6'2" Weight: 12.5
Successive Stoke managers have still to give Neil his chance of an extended run in the side. Tall with an excellent shot and good vision, the midfielder had his best game for

the club last term in the home fixture against Notts County but, whilst many saw opportunities opening up for him, Brian Little sent him to Cambridge on loan during transfer deadline week. Unfortunately, he suffered an ankle injury after a handful of games, having shown his class at set plays, and returned to the Victoria Ground.

Stoke C (Free from West Bromwich A juniors on 9/11/95) FL 15+25/1 FLC 1+1 FAC 0+1 Others 0+2
Cambridge U (Loaned on 24/3/99) FL 3+1/1

McKINLAY William (Billy)
Born: Glasgow, 22 April 1969
Height: 5'9" Weight: 11.6
International Honours: S: 30; B-1; U21-6; Yth; Sch
A pre-season hernia operation limited his early appearances for Blackburn in 1998-99, and the re-occurrence of the problem hospitalised him again in February. Then, an attempted comeback in April caused the problem to reappear and his absence was one of the main reasons why the club struggled so badly. His best game was against Leeds, when the team was reduced to ten men, and stout hearts and strong limbs were required, while his best position was when anchoring the midfield in front of the central defenders. With his tough tackling, and ability to keep mobile, was a valuable member of the side. Played twice for Scotland during the season.

Dundee U (Free from Hamilton Thistle on 24/6/85) SL 210+10/23 SLC 21/3 SC 23+3/4 Others 17/2
Blackburn Rov (£1,750,000 on 14/10/95) PL 76+14/3 FLC 4/1 FAC 7+1 Others 1

McKINNON Raymond (Ray)
Born: Dundee, 5 August 1970
Height: 5'8" Weight: 9.11
International Honours: S: U21-6; Sch
Released by Dundee United during the summer of 1998, Ray joined Luton on a one-year contract under the Bosman ruling in time for the start of 1998-99. Having been on top of Lennie Lawrence's wanted list, the Scottish midfielder quickly showed why with his calm and skilful play, and made his first-team debut in the opening game, playing well in a 1-0 win at Wycombe. Appearing in 39 of the 56 available games for Town, he would have played more often if not plagued by minor injuries throughout the campaign, a torn hamstring and sprained ankle holding him up. Is a player recognised for his ability to use both feet equally well.

Dundee U (From juniors on 12/8/86) SL 46+7/6 SLC 2 SC 5+1/1 Others 1
Nottingham F (£750,000 on 31/7/92) PL 5+1/1 FLC 1
Aberdeen (£300,000 on 8/2/94) SL 22+4 SLC 4+1 SC 3 Others 2
Dundee U (Signed on 3/11/95) SL 29+15/6 SLC 1+2 SC 6+3
Luton T (Free on 6/8/98) FL 29+1/2 FLC 4+1 FAC 2

McKINNON Robert
Born: Glasgow, 31 July 1966
Height: 5'10" Weight: 11.12
International Honours: S: 3; B-2
A strong-tackling left back, and a player

195

who was already a hero to Hartlepool fans from his first highly successful spell at the club, it was a great boost when caretaker manager, Brian Honour, signed him on loan from Hearts last February until the end of the season. He looked to be the perfect signing to fill what had been a troublesome position, but it was unfortunate that his relatively short stay coincided with a seven-match run without a win. Despite that, when Hearts had a change of mind to recall him for a return to their first team, the new Pool's manager, Chris Turner, was infuriated that the side had been left without adequate cover.

Newcastle U (Signed from Rutherglen Glencairn on 6/11/84) FL 1
Hartlepool U (Free on 5/8/86) FL 246+1/7 FLC 15 FAC 15 Others 15
Motherwell (Signed on 8/1/92) SL 93/5 SLC 4 SC 4 (Free to FC Twente on 9/8/96)
Heart of Midlothian (Free on 14/7/98) SL 12+1 SLC 1+1 Others 1
Hartlepool U (Loaned on 11/2/99) FL 7

McLAREN Andrew (Andy)
Born: Glasgow, 5 June 1973
Height: 5'10" Weight: 11.8
Club Honours: SC '94
International Honours: S: U21-4

Signed from Dundee last March to play as a wide-right midfielder at Reading, Andy showed glimpses of his ability to take players on and get forward, which had characterised his career in Scottish football, but failed to last the pace on a couple of occasions. However, there were glimpses of what might be in 1999-2000, and his last appearance of the season was highlighted by a superb headed goal in the 4-1 defeat at Wigan Athletic.

Dundee U (Free from Rangers BC on 20/6/89) SL 115+50/12 SLC 9+5/1 SC 12+5/3 Others 8+2/2
Reading (£100,000 on 25/3/99) FL 7/1

McLAREN Paul Andrew
Born: High Wycombe, 17 November 1976
Height: 6'0" Weight: 13.4

As a much improved Luton midfielder, Paul was expected to blossom in 1998-99, his ability to win the ball, and his strong running, allied to well-struck crosses, marking him out as a player with a future. Unfortunately, although appearing in four of the opening five games, scoring at Oxford in the second leg of the Worthington Cup, he was sidelined at Reading in the very next match when substituted after suffering what was thought to be medial ligament damage to his knee. Out of action for 15 games, he came back reasonably strongly before being replaced at Oldham after just ten minutes in early April when suffering from the same problem, his campaign over.

Luton T (From trainee on 5/1/94) FL 77+26/1 FLC 5+4/1 FAC 4 Others 8

McLEAN Ian James
Born: Leeds, 13 September 1978
Height: 5'10" Weight: 11.4

After coming through the ranks at Bradford to turn professional in January 1997, Ian failed to put in a first-team appearance, mainly due to a series of injuries keeping

him out of contention. However, signed by Oldham last October, he came straight into the side at left back and made five league starts before injury forced him out. Very much one for the future, part of his downfall is that he is a very strong tackler who does not hold back.

Bradford C (From trainee on 1/1/97)
Oldham Ath (Free on 13/10/98) FL 5

McLEARY Alan Terry
Born: Lambeth, 6 October 1964
Height: 5'11" Weight: 11.12
Club Honours: FLT '83; Div 2 '88
International Honours: E: B-2; U21-1; Yth

Appointed as Millwall's assistant manager in the 1998-99 season, Alan made a couple of first-team appearances through injury to other defenders, but still showed himself to be a vociferous player who got behind his team mates when the need required. A good motivator, along with "Rhino" Stevens, he helped Millwall into the Second Division's top ten with a bonus of a Wembley appearance, which must have been very rewarding in this, his first season of management.

Millwall (From apprentice on 12/10/81) FL 289+18/5 FLC 16+1 FAC 24+1/2 Others 22+1/2
Sheffield U (Loaned on 23/7/92) PL 3
Wimbledon (Loaned on 16/10/92) PL 4 FLC 2
Charlton Ath (Free on 27/5/93) FL 66/3 FLC 2 FAC 6 Others 3
Bristol C (Free on 31/7/95) FL 31+3 FLC 5
Millwall (Free on 21/2/97) FL 36 FLC 2 FAC 1

McLOUGHLIN Alan Francis
Born: Manchester, 20 April 1967
Height: 5'8" Weight: 10.10
International Honours: Ei: 38; B-3

In a team best described as mediocre last season, it was Alan's midfield skills that kept the Portsmouth side in some shape, making more starts than the rest of the side – 41 league matches. His return of ten league and cup goals was up to his seasonal average and 1999-2000, his eighth campaign with Pompey, should see his 300th league game and 50th goal for the south coast club. At 32, he reads the game well, has an ability to get forward into good attacking positions, and is still a valued member of the Republic of Ireland squad. Possessing good vision, off the field he takes the time to pass his knowledge on to younger players.

Manchester U (From apprentice on 25/4/85)
Swindon T (Free on 15/8/86) FL 101+5/19 FLC 11+3/5 FAC 4+2 Others 10/1
Torquay U (Loaned on 13/3/87) FL 21+3/4
Southampton (£1,000,000 on 13/12/90) FL 22+2/1 FLC 0+1 FAC 4 Others 1
Aston Villa (Loaned on 30/9/91) Others 1
Portsmouth (£400,000 on 17/2/92) FL 279+11/49 FLC 25/6 FAC 15+1/7 Others 9/1

McMAHON Samuel (Sam) Keiron
Born: Newark, 10 February 1976
Height: 5'10" Weight: 11.9

Unable to get a senior game at Leicester in 1998-99, this classy, right-footed midfield player was signed by Cambridge in March and, making his debut at Barnet, was "Man of the Match". Unfortunate not to be given

more opportunities to shine, he was released at the end of the season.

Leicester C (From trainee on 10/7/94) P/FL 1+4/1 FLC 0+2
Cambridge U (Free on 5/3/99) FL 1+2

McMANAMAN Steven (Steve)
Born: Bootle, 11 February 1972
Height: 6'0" Weight: 10.10
Club Honours: FAC '92; FLC '95
International Honours: E: 24; U21-7; Yth

After much transfer speculation, which inevitably upset the team's performance, Steve has sought new pastures in Spain. Liverpool will certainly miss his mazy dribbling skills, and his often spectacular goals – though he has still failed to find the net when wearing an England shirt. Some supporters would argue that for too long Liverpool built the side around him, and that his departure will force Gerard Houllier to examine new attacking options. Love him or loathe him, he will, indeed, be missed. He has been a good servant to Liverpool FC, and his ability to beat player after player and find the net at club level has been a welcome infusion of talent in a side often bereft of such skill during the 1990s. Played twice for England in 1998-99.

Liverpool (From trainee on 19/2/90) F/PL 258+14/46 FLC 32+1/10 FAC 28+1/5 Others 30/5

McMENAMIN Christopher (Chris)
Born: Donegal, 27 December 1973
Height: 5'10" Weight: 11.12

Despite starting last season in Peterborough's senior line-up, and making four further appearances, Chris' performances fell away and he moved to non-league Hitchin in transfer deadline week. However, the young right-wing back, who also looks at ease in midfield, has got what it takes to overcome this disappointment and could well be back.

Coventry C (Signed from Hitchin T on 20/9/96)
Peterborough U (Free on 8/8/97) FL 29+4 FLC 2 FAC 2 Others 3

McMILLAN Lyndon Andre (Andy)
Born: Bloemfontein, South Africa, 22 June 1968
Height: 5'11" Weight: 11.9

Now second in the all-time appearance list for York, the ever-popular right back was again a regular in the defence in 1998-99, and as reliable as ever. Cool and authoritative at the back, unfortunately, an injury caused him to miss the closing weeks of his testimonial year, just eight short of 500 games for the club.

York C (Signed on 17/10/87) FL 409+12/5 FLC 27 FAC 18 Others 26

McNAUGHTON Michael Ian
Born: Blackpool, 29 January 1980
Height: 6'3" Weight: 13.12

This teenage centre back progressed through the YTS ranks at Scarborough to become a regular in the reserves, before making his senior debut in a 0-0 draw at Plymouth, 12 games into 1998-99. Showing superb form in a struggling side, and scoring at

Mansfield, he made a first-team place his own, and capped an outstanding personal campaign when named as the supporters' "Away Player of the Season". He was one of the bonuses for a side that was ultimately relegated to the Conference.
Scarborough (From trainee on 6/7/98) FL 22+9/1 FAC 1 Others 1

McNEIL Martin James
Born: Rutherglen, 28 September 1980
Height: 6'1" Weight: 12.7
An 18-year-old trainee central defender at Cambridge, he was thrust into the first-team limelight when coming off the bench at home to Shrewsbury, before starting at Nottingham Forest in the Worthington Cup last October, and impressing. He then made six more starts, signed pro forms and, apart from another subs' appearance, virtually had his 1998-99 campaign ended early by injury, in that order. Cool, confident, and composed on the ground, and good in the air for his age, Martin looks to have a bright future ahead of him.
Cambridge U (From trainee on 15/12/98) FL 4+2 FLC 1 FAC 2

McNIVEN David Jonathan
Born: Leeds, 27 May 1978
Height: 5'11" Weight: 12.0
One of twins at Oldham, and the son of the former Leeds' man, David (senior), this David also hopes to be a star in his own right, but has a bit to do yet. With much expected of him, he had just two starts in 1998-99 and, while his running off the ball and ability to hold play up are first class, he needs to work on the scoring side of his game. Nevertheless, those in the know still believe in him.
Oldham Ath (From trainee on 25/10/95) FL 5+17/1 FLC 0+2

McNIVEN Scott Andrew
Born: Leeds, 27 May 1978
Height: 5'10" Weight: 12.1
International Honours: S: U21-1; Yth
As opposed to his twin, Scott had another excellent season for Oldham in 1998-99 and, improving all the time, would have been an ever present had it not been for injuries. Playing intelligently, and displaying good passing skills, along with strong running, it was no surprise that he got forward to score in successive home games – against Gillingham in the FA Cup and Wrexham in the league. Although comfortable in a number of positions, the club feel he is best suited to the right-wing-back role.
Oldham Ath (From trainee on 25/10/95) FL 84+13/2 FLC 6+1 FAC 9+1/1 Others 6

McPHAIL Stephen
Born: London, 9 December 1979
Height: 5'10" Weight: 12.0
Club Honours: FAYC '97
International Honours: Ei: U21-4; Yth
Another member of Leeds' successful youth system, this young Irish midfielder with the cultured left foot is tipped to go to the very top. His first game of last season

came in the UEFA Cup-tie at Roma, and after featuring in the next seven matches he picked up a niggling knee-ligament injury which took some time to heal and hampered his progress somewhat. When the injury cleared, Stephen was off to Nigeria with the Republic of Ireland side for the World Youth championships in April. A boy with bags of talent, he is a great passer of the ball, has superb control and vision, and should have a big future in the game. Also made his debut for the Republic's U21 side, appearing four times in all.
Leeds U (From trainee on 23/12/96) PL 11+10 FLC 1 Others 2

McPHERSON Keith Anthony
Born: Greenwich, 11 September 1963
Height: 5'10" Weight: 12.0
Club Honours: FAYC '81; Div 4 '87, Div 2 '94
Although holding down a regular place at the back from last September through to January, but unable to secure his position in the face of younger contenders, Keith left Reading bound for Brighton in March. The veteran central defender looked ill at ease during early performances in a sweeper system, but his form improved when Micky Adams arrived and declared his intention to play a more traditional formation. Thriving on the responsibility of being made captain towards the end of the season, he proved to be an excellent header of the ball who makes up for his advancing years by being a good reader of a game.
West Ham U (From apprentice on 12/9/81) FL 1
Cambridge U (Loaned on 30/9/85) FL 11/1
Northampton T (£15,000 on 23/1/86) FL 182/8 FLC 9/1 FAC 12 Others 13
Reading (Signed on 24/8/90) FL 264+7/8 FLC 21+1/1 FAC 12+1 Others 9+1
Brighton & Hove A (Free on 19/3/99) FL 10

McQUADE John
Born: Glasgow, 8 July 1970
Height: 5'8" Weight: 10.4
Club Honours: S Div 2 '92
A Scottish striker who joined Port Vale from Hamilton Academical in the summer of 1998 after a recommendation from new coach, Phil Bonnyman, John impressed in pre-season but was always on the fringe of the first team and managed just four appearances as a substitute. Also able to play in midfield, he was released in March 1999, returning to Scotland with Raith Rovers on trial.
Dumbarton (From juniors on 10/6/88) SL 142+23/50 SLC 6+1/1 SC 10/4 Others 2/1
Hamilton Ac (Signed on 31/8/93) SL 72+32/6 SLC 2+1 SC 2+1 Others 5+1
Port Vale (Free on 31/7/98) FL 0+3 FLC 0+1

McSHEFFREY Gary
Born: Coventry, 13 August 1982
Height: 5'7" Weight: 10.4
The Coventry-born striker set the FA Youth Cup and the youth leagues alight with his goalscoring feats in 1998-99, and was a major reason for the club's FA Youth Cup success, where he scored prolifically, including a hat trick in the semi final first leg at Newcastle. Became Coventry's

youngest ever debutant, and the Premier League's youngest ever player when he came on as a last-minute substitute at Villa Park, although he did not touch the ball. A great future is predicted for Gary.
Coventry C (Trainee) PL 0+1

McSPORRAN Jermaine
Born: Manchester, 1 January 1977
Height: 5'8" Weight: 10.10
Exciting right-footed striker signed by Wycombe last November from Ryman Division One side, Oxford City, from under the noses of several Premiership clubs, after he had failed to earn a contract at Arsenal in spite of scoring two goals as a trialist in a reserve game. He enjoyed an impressive game at Wigan when, in his third outing as a substitute, he stole the show with his extraordinary pace, and only two brilliant saves prevented him scoring. His first goal for the club was an Auto Windscreens "Golden" goal at Shrewsbury, which gave Wanderers their first away win of the campaign. In all, he made 12 starts and 16 substitute appearances and, although mainly used as a wide-right attacker, he was also very effective as a central striker running onto balls. Cool in the box, and with a very hard shot, he is as quick as they come and, in particular, his acceleration is phenomenal, catching out defenders who think they have more time to control the ball.
Wycombe W (Signed from Oxford C on 5/11/98) FL 11+15/4 Others 1+1/1

Jermaine McSporran

MADAR Mickael Raymond
Born: Paris, France, 8 May 1968
Height: 6'0" Weight: 13.2
International Honours: France: 3
The French striker made a significant impact in English football after being

lured to Everton from Deportivo La Coruna by Howard Kendall during 1997-98, but it soon transpired, however, that he was not new manager Walter Smith's cup of tea, and left Goodison after barely a year in royal blue. Not a typical continental striker, being good in the air, and leading the line with strength and intelligence, his willingness to work hard for the general good of the team was occasionally questioned, and he made only two league appearances – both uncompleted – before joining Paris St Germain at the end of December.

Everton (Free from Deportivo la Coruna, via Paris FC, Laval, Socheaux, Cannes and Monaco, on 31/12/97) PL 17+2/5 FLC 0+1

MADDISON Neil Stanley
Born: Darlington, 2 October 1969
Height: 5'10" Weight: 12.0

A dashing and versatile midfielder who was an integral part of Middlesbrough's promotion-winning team the previous season, he became a contender for the title of "Super Sub", since most of his appearances in 1998-99 saw him turn in some brilliant performances when coming off the bench. The surprise bargain buy from Southampton must qualify as one of "Robbo's" most astute signings, his ability to cover almost every playing position renders him especially valuable as cover for injuries and suspensions.

Southampton (From trainee on 14/4/88) F/PL 149+20/19 FLC 9+5 FAC 8+5 Others 1
Middlesbrough (£250,000 on 31/10/97) P/FL 26+17/4 FLC 5 FAC 4

MADDIX Daniel (Danny) Shawn
Born: Ashford, 11 October 1967
Height: 5'11" Weight: 12.2
International Honours: Jamaica: 1

Danny has been a stalwart of Queens Park Rangers' defence for the past ten years, and approaching 300 appearances for the club he was awarded a testimonial for the 1998-99 season. A solid and quick centre back, who has been a crowd favourite for a number of years, he gained another call up to the Jamaican squad but did not get an opportunity to prove himself at international level. During the home game against Oxford he suffered a bad injury when Ludek Mikosko's studs went into his hand, but he made a rapid comeback only two weeks later, being made captain in the absence of Karl Ready. Was released during the summer.

Tottenham H (From apprentice on 25/7/85)
Southend U (Loaned on 1/11/86) FL 2
Queens Park R (Free on 23/7/87) F/PL 241+34/12 FLC 23/3 FAC 21+2/2 Others 2+3

MAGILTON Jim
Born: Belfast, 6 May 1969
Height: 6'0" Weight: 14.2
International Honours: NI: 39; U23-2; U21-1; Yth; Sch

Never managing to convince the powers that be at Sheffield Wednesday in 1998-99, Jim made only a handful of appearances, subsequently losing his place in the Northern Ireland side, before going to Ipswich on loan in January. Making his debut at Sunderland, and immediately creating a good impression with his passing ability and his anchoring of the midfield to allow Kieron Dyer and Matt Holland more freedom to join the attack, his transfer became permanent on 23 March. A good dead-ball kicker, he soon got the job of taking corners and free kicks, and also proved that he was not afraid to have a shot from almost anywhere with either foot, opening his account at Huddersfield with a low shot from 15 yards after David Johnson's initial effort had rebounded off the 'keeper.

Liverpool (From apprentice on 14/5/86)
Oxford U (£100,000 on 3/10/90) FL 150/34 FLC 9/1 FAC 8/4 Others 6/3
Southampton (£600,000 on 11/2/94) PL 124+6/13 FLC 12+2/2 FAC 12/3
Sheffield Wed (£1,600,000 on 10/9/97) PL 14+13/1 FLC 2 FAC 1
Ipswich T (£682,500 on 15/1/99) FL 19/3 Others 2

MAHER Kevin Andrew
Born: Ilford, 17 October 1976
Height: 6'0" Weight: 12.5
International Honours: Ei: U21-4

Kevin suffered a poor season for Southend in 1998-99, when unable to find his form in a team that was struggling in all areas. A player possessing skill and tenacity, his ability was overridden by a lack of confidence, and he lost his place towards the end of the campaign. However, the arrival of a new manager at the club should

Danny Maddix

help restore him to the player he was in 1997-98, with his passing and vision coming to the fore.

Tottenham H (From trainee on 1/7/95)
Southend U (Free on 23/1/98) FL 52/5 FLC 4 FAC 1 Others 1/1

MAHON Alan Joseph
Born: Dublin, 4 April 1978
Height: 5'10" Weight: 11.5
International Honours: Ei; U21-8; Yth; Sch
Believed by many to be the most skilful player at Tranmere, Alan showed only occasional flashes of his best form in the previous season, when he was plagued by injury and loss of form. However, seemingly rejuvenated by the summer break, he tugged and tore at opposing defenders in 1998-99, and developed a probing and tricky style of play. Always an intelligent player, he found a rich seam of form and caused endless problems for his unfortunate markers, being at his happiest in a midfield berth from where he was often his team's main source of inspiration, and able to direct a supply of passes to his colleagues up front. He was also not frightened to take on an opponent, scoring six valuable goals, picking up eight "Man of the Match" awards, and continuing to mature as his confidence increased. A regular for the Republic of Ireland U21 side, he now holds the appearance record, one ahead of Colchester's David Greene.

Tranmere Rov (From trainee on 7/4/95) FL 51+33/9 FLC 2+6/1 FAC 0+1

MAHON Gavin Andrew
Born: Birmingham, 2 January 1977
Height: 6'0" Weight: 13.2
Club Honours: Div 3 '99
A skilful Brentford midfielder, Gavin returned to the league scene last November when signing from Hereford, and was a regular through to the end of the season. Very highly thought of by manager, Ron Noades, he was one of the very few players at Griffin Park who was never dropped or rested. Delighted to win a Third Division championship medal in his first season at the club, he sometimes got caught in possession, but will improve on that with experience.

Wolverhampton W (From trainee on 3/7/95)
Hereford U (Free on 12/7/96) FL 10+1/1 FLC 4
Brentford (£50,000 + on 17/11/98) FL 29/4 Others 3

MAKIN Christopher (Chris) Gregory
Born: Manchester, 8 May 1973
Height: 5'10" Weight: 11.2
Club Honours: Div 1 '99
International Honours: E: U21-5; Yth; Sch
The rock-solid Sunderland defender firmly established himself as the club's first-choice right back last term, picking up a deserved First Division championship medal. A naturally two-footed player, Chris is also comfortable on the opposite flank, and his tremendous tackling and willingness to get forward at every opportunity has made him one of the most popular players at the Stadium of Light. Indeed, the home supporters are eagerly awaiting the day

when one of his regularly attempted long-range efforts hits the back of the net.

Oldham Ath (From trainee on 2/11/91) F/PL 93+1/4 FLC 7 FAC 11 Others 1+1 (Transferred to Marseille during 1996 close season)
Wigan Ath (Loaned on 28/8/92) FL 14+1/2
Sunderland (£500,000 on 5/8/97) FL 60+3/1 FLC 10 FAC 3 Others 1+1

MALEY Mark
Born: Newcastle, 26 January 1981
Height: 5'9" Weight: 12.3
International Honours: E: Sch
A young Sunderland defender who made his first-team debut in the Worthington Cup against York City last August, the right back was one of the key players in the reserve's excellent form in the Pontins League, and could well become the next home-grown youngster to make the breakthrough into the first team at the Stadium of Light. Small of stature, but not lacking in determination, big things are expected of Mark.

Sunderland (From trainee on 30/1/98) FLC 1

MALKIN Christopher (Chris) Gregory
Born: Hoylake, 4 June 1967
Height: 6'3" Weight: 12.9
Club Honours: AMC '90
An experienced Blackpool striker who played more games last season than he had in the previous two campaigns, Chris put the injuries behind him as he began to get back to his best. Full of running and commitment up front, he was delighted to score against his old team, Tranmere, at Prenton in the Worthington Cup, before being forced to spend another spell on the sidelines. Surprisingly allowed to leave during the summer, his unselfish play also created chances for the other forwards.

Tranmere Rov (Free from Stork AFC on 27/7/87) FL 184+48/60 FLC 20+5/6 FAC 9+4/3 Others 26+7/7
Millwall (£400,000 on 13/7/95) FL 46+6/13 FLC 5/1 FAC 2/1
Blackpool (£275,000 on 14/10/96) FL 45+19/6 FLC 3+4/1 FAC 2+1 Others 0+3

MANN Neil
Born: Nottingham, 19 November 1972
Height: 5'10" Weight: 12.1
Despite missing much of the 1998-99 pre-season with a double hernia operation in May, and an eye injury in July, the midfielder's confidence blossomed in the opening months to produce by far the most consistent football of his career at Hull. Unfortunately, misfortune struck in the Humber derby at Scunthorpe in November when, in attempting a last-ditch goal-line clearance, he collided with a post and suffered career-threatening cruciate ligament damage. Overwhelmed by messages of support from the fans, Neil made a determined recovery and was given the added encouragement of a new two-year contract in March. Remarkably, the son of former Manchester City player, Arthur, returned as a substitute in the final game of the campaign at Swansea.

Grimsby T (Free from Notts Co juniors on 6/9/90)
Hull C (Free from Grantham T, via Spalding, on 30/7/93) FL 125+35/9 FLC 11+4 FAC 6+2/1 Others 8+2/1

MANNINGER Alexander (Alex)
Born: Salzburg, Austria, 4 June 1977
Height: 6'2" Weight: 13.3
Club Honours: FAC '98
The most capped player in the current Austrian U21 squad, Alex joined Arsenal two seasons ago and proved a more than capable deputy to David Seaman with a string of clean sheets in the Gunners' double winning season of 1997-98. A tremendous shot stopper who stands up well, he is equally strong in the air and on the ground, and shows great speed when coming off his line. Continued to develop well under the capable tuition of Bob Wilson in 1998-99 and, although his first-team appearances were limited, he performed consistently when called upon, keeping four consecutive clean sheets in the league during mid season. In late March, however, he sustained a serious wrist injury during a training session, which kept him out of action for the remainder of the campaign.

Arsenal (£500,000 from Graz, via Vorwaerts and Salzburg, on 17/6/97) PL 13 FLC 6 FAC 7

MANNION Sean
Born: Dublin, 3 March 1980
Height: 5'8" Weight: 11.5
Stockport central midfielder who was offered full professional terms during the summer of 1998, after arriving from the Dublin junior side, Stella Maris, in February. Having enjoyed an impressive season in 1998-99 with County's reserves, he was drafted in to Gary Megson's first-team plans during February after the small squad had suffered a series of injuries and suspension set backs. An unused substitute in the 2-0 win over Crewe at Gresty Road, Sean made his debut from the bench two games later in the defeat by West Bromwich. With Stockport three goals down he came on and showed composure and willingness to work hard for the team, qualities he will be hoping to demonstrate more often on the big stage during the 1999-2000 campaign.

Stockport Co (Free from Stella Maris on 11/2/98) FL 0+1

MANUEL William (Billy) Albert James
Born: Hackney, 28 June 1969
Height: 5'8" Weight: 12.7
Club Honours: Div 3 '92
Billy found that his first-team outings at Barnet were somewhat sporadic during 1998-99, making only three appearances in the starting line-up throughout the season. His solitary goal was a headed effort at Shrewsbury in late August when he came off the bench, and his experience proved to be a crucial factor in the outcome of the match. Fielded in the role of left back during the majority of his appearances, he appeared both comfortable and competent in that position, his infinite knowledge of the game compensating for his lack of pace. However, with the emphasis on introducing young players into the side, he proved to be an asset in the reserves and was an influential figure in helping the youth-team players acclimatise to the rigours of the Combination. With his

contract terminated in the middle of May, his final second-string appearance saw him strike twice in a 4-2 home defeat against West Ham to leave the fans with a fond parting memory of one of the true characters in the modern game.

Tottenham H (From trainee on 28/7/87)
Gillingham (Signed on 10/2/89) FL 74+13/5 FLC 2 FAC 3 Others 5
Brentford (£60,000 on 14/6/91) FL 83+11/1 FLC 7+1/1 FAC 4 Others 8+2
Peterborough U (Free on 16/9/94)
Cambridge U (Free on 28/10/94) FL 10 FAC 2
Peterborough U (Free on 28/2/95) FL 27/2 FLC 4/3 FAC 1+1 Others 2
Gillingham (Free on 26/1/96) FL 9+12 FAC 1 Others 1
Barnet (Free on 18/7/97) FL 13+16/1 FLC 2+2 FAC 1 Others 1+3

MARCELLE Clinton (Clint) Sherwin
Born: Trinidad, 9 November 1968
Height: 5'4" Weight: 10.0
International Honours: Trinidad & Tobago: 9
Despite having signed a new two-year deal at Barnsley for 1998-99, Clint found himself very much a peripheral player following the change of manager. Still showed the pace that made him a danger to defences, but only occasionally did he get the chance to show it, and failed to find the net. An automatic selection for the Trinidad & Tobago international team, he will be looking forward to better fortune in 1999-2000.
Barnsley (Free from Felgueiras on 8/8/96) F/PL 37+32/8 FLC 3+5 FAC 6+1/1

[MARCELO] Cipriano Dos Santos
Born: Niteroi, Brazil, 11 October 1969
Height: 6'0" Weight: 13.8
Marcelo's early season appearances for Sheffield United in 1998-99 were either from the bench or saw him being subbed, before the departures of Gareth Taylor and Dean Saunders finally gave him the opportunity of an extended run in the side. He responded well with 90 minutes of selfless running up front, week after week, his goals tally highlighting his sharp reactions, heading ability, and his knack of being in the right place at the right time. Finished as the club's top scorer.
Sheffield U (£400,000 from Dep Aleves on 6/10/97) FL 38+18/22 FLC 1+1 FAC 10+1/5 Others 1+1/1

MARCOLIN Dario
Born: Brescia, Italy, 28 October 1971
Height: 5'9" Weight: 11.8
Brought to Blackburn on loan from Lazio last October by Roy Hodgson, he suffered initially from being an unknown quantity for Brian Kidd, before returning to Italy around Christmas for a brief period. Consequently, he never became a regular and, while he displayed style and flair, he was not a dynamic presence. While Rovers indicated that they would not be exercising their option to sign him after the loan spell ended, the player will no doubt be delighted to take back the memory of a goal at Old Trafford when he returns to Italy.
Blackburn Rov (Loaned from Lazio on 30/10/98) PL 5+5/1 FLC 2 FAC 3

MARDON Paul Jonathan
Born: Bristol, 14 September 1969
Height: 6'0" Weight: 12.0
International Honours: W: 1; B-1
Paul did not have a happy time of it at West Bromwich in 1998-99, despite starting off reasonably well at right back. Injured in early September, and struggling for fitness and form, he spent a useful loan spell at Oldham in January with a view to getting him match fit. Made an immediate impact on the Boundary Park faithful, scoring the winner at Notts County on his debut, and netting two more, all headers, before going back to the Hawthorns. Needless to say, he was sorely missed. A player who is capable of performing well in a number of positions in midfield or defence, being sound in the air and on the ground, with his appetite back he was expected to regain a place in the side. Although giving it his all, he found himself losing out to the competition of Paul Raven, Daryl Burgess, Shaun Murphy, and Matthew Carbon, before coming back in the final match of the campaign. Represented the Welsh "B" team that played against Northern Ireland.
Bristol C (From trainee on 29/1/88) FL 29+13 FLC 3+3/1 Others 1
Doncaster Rov (Loaned on 13/9/90) FL 3
Birmingham C (£115,000 on 16/8/91) FL 54+10 FLC 11+1 FAC 1 Others 3
West Bromwich A (£400,000 on 18/11/93) FL 125+14/3 FLC 10 FAC 3 Others 2
Oldham Ath (Loaned on 8/1/99) FL 12/3

MARESCA Enzo
Born: Salerno, Italy, 10 February 1980
Height: 5'11" Weight: 12.0
An Italian U18 international skipper who joined West Bromwich on a free transfer from Cagliari early in 1998-99, signing a four-year contract, Enzo made a very encouraging start at the Hawthorns, scoring two goals into the bargain. Denis Smith, the Albion manager, believes that he will become an exceptionally fine player, having already added quality, aggression and skill to the club's midfield – and will contribute a lot more as his game develops. Now part of Zino Zoff's 40-man Italian squad preparing for the European championships, he was voted Albion's "Young Player of the Year" for 1998-99.
West Bromwich A (Free from Cagliari on 25/8/98) FL 9+13/2 FAC 1

MARGAS Javier
Born: Chile, 10 May 1969
Height: 6'1" Weight: 13.8
International Honours: Chile: 54
Big things were expected from the experienced Chilean international central defender when he joined West Ham in the summer of 1998. However, following a promising debut in the draw at Coventry, he had a torrid time in the Hammers' defence when they conceded four goals to both Wimbledon and Leeds, being caught out by the pace of Premiership football. Unfortunately, in the last named match, in December, he sustained a bad knee injury, and returned home to Chile for treatment, thus missing the rest of the season. His CV

shows him to be a tough, hard-tackling defender, with good aerial strength, and it will be interesting to see where he goes from here, especially in the light of press reports that quote him as saying he will not be returning to this country.
West Ham U (£2,000,000 from Catolica University on 3/8/98) PL 3

MARGETSON Martyn Walter
Born: Neath, 8 September 1971
Height: 6'0" Weight: 14.0
International Honours: W: B; U21-7; Yth; Sch
Signed from Manchester City after being surprisingly released prior to the start of 1998-99, Martyn performed well during the early season, behind a defence that, on occasions, gave him little cover. A very good shot stopper, his lack of confidence on crosses finally became his downfall, and he was replaced by Mel Capleton for the run-in. With good ability in dealing with back passes, and able to kick hard and long, he is sure to be in contention this coming term.
Manchester C (From trainee on 5/7/90) F/PL 51 FLC 2+2 FAC 3 Others 1
Bristol Rov (Loaned on 8/12/93) FL 2+1
Southend U (Free on 3/8/98) FL 32 FLC 4 FAC 1 Others 1

MARIC Silvio
Born: Zagreb, Croatia, 20 March 1975
Height: 5'10" Weight: 12.2
International Honours: Croatia: 16
Silvio is a highly-rated Croatian attacking midfielder with a reputation for goalscoring at international as well as club level. Technically gifted, and a skilled dribbler with a useful shot, a flexible player who prefers to play in a forward role just behind the main strikers, he can also take on the prime striking role, and looks set to become a key part of the Croatian team in the years ahead. Having won league and cup doubles with Croatia Zagreb in each of the last three years, scoring in last year's final, he was keen to broaden his skills with experience abroad, and he joined Newcastle last February to further that aim. Arriving at a time following the mid-season break in Croatia he lacked match fitness, and was used sparingly by Ruud Gullit, generally as a substitute or substituted player to allow him to adapt to the pace and style of the Premiership. Following his move to Tyneside, he was selected for the Croatian squad for the home game against Malta in March, but the match was postponed due to the Kosovo crisis.
Newcastle U (£3,650,000 from Croatia Zagreb on 26/2/99) PL 9+1 FAC 1+2

MARINKOV Alexandre (Alex)
Born: Grenoble, France, 2 December 1967
Height: 6'2" Weight: 12.10
Alex, a powerful and skilful centre back who joined Scarborough during the 1998 close season from the French Third Division club, Roanne L'Etape, on a one-year contract, started on the opening day of 1998-99 and showed outstanding form before swapping Boro's relegation battle for

chasing Scottish First Division honours with Hibernian in February, a £25,000 fee changing hands. Having become the club's penalty taker, with two under his belt against Brentford and Exeter, also scoring in a 3-2 win at Cambridge, and at home to Chester, his all-round abilities were badly missed.

Scarborough (Free from Roanne L'Etape on 6/8/98) FL 22/4 FLC 2 FAC 1

MARKER Nicholas (Nicky) Robert
Born: Budleigh Salterton, 3 May 1965
Height: 6'0" Weight: 12.11
The Sheffield United "Player of the Year" for 1997-98 was not in the starting line-up for the opening day of last season, and after one appearance in the Worthington Cup a move to Reading was imminent before an injury to David Holdsworth in September gave Nicky his chance. Captain for his first league start against Grimsby Town, scoring twice, he was almost ever present for four months, primarily in defence and, although perhaps lacking in pace, was always a reliable performer who was prepared to come forward. Relinquishing his place on Holdsworth's return, in February he moved to Plymouth Argyle on a one-month loan. Still has a year of his contract left, but does not appear to be at the forefront of Steve Bruce's plans.

Exeter C (From apprentice on 4/5/83) FL 196+6/3 FLC 11/1 FAC 8 Others 8/3
Plymouth Arg (£95,000 on 31/10/87) FL 201+1/13 FLC 15/3 FAC 9/1 Others 7/1
Blackburn Rov (£500,000 on 23/9/92) FL 41+13/1 FLC 3+1 FAC 4+1 Others 1+1
Sheffield U (£400,000 on 29/7/97) FL 60+1/5 FLC 7 FAC 9 Others 2
Plymouth Arg (Loaned on 26/2/99) FL 4

MARKSTEDT Peter
Born: Vasteras, Sweden, 11 January 1972
Height: 5'10" Weight: 13.10
Although making a promising start for Barnsley, having returned from a career-threatening neck injury sustained in 1997-98, Peter found first-team chances very limited last season. Each time he found himself in the squad he invariably became injured. Strong in the air, and composed on the deck, he will be hoping for an injury-free 1999-2000 because, at his best, he is an imposing central defender who can play the ball out from defence with some style.

Barnsley (£250,000 from Vasteras SK on 21/11/97) P/FL 8+1 FLC 0+1 FAC 1

MARRIOTT Andrew (Andy)
Born: Sutton in Ashfield, 11 October 1970
Height: 6'1" Weight: 12.6
Club Honours: Div 4 '92; FMC '92; WC '95
International Honours: E: U21-1; Yth; Sch. W: 5
The goalkeeper arrived at Sunderland from Wrexham early last season, primarily to act as cover for Thomas Sorensen, and made his first-team debut for the club at Grimsby in March. Deputising for the injured Dane, Andy played his part in a crucial 2-0 win, making two good saves when the game was still scoreless, and in having experience of the Premiership from his days at Nottingham Forest he will continue to be an

important squad member. His fine form with the reserves prompted the Welsh manager, Bobby Gould, to recall him to the full international squad in February.

Arsenal (From trainee on 22/10/88)
Nottingham F (£50,000 on 20/6/89) F/PL 11 FLC 1 Others 1
West Bromwich A (Loaned on 6/9/89) FL 3
Blackburn Rov (Loaned on 29/12/89) FL 2
Colchester U (Loaned on 21/3/90) FL 10
Burnley (Loaned on 29/8/91) FL 15 Others 2
Wrexham (£200,000 on 8/10/93) FL 213 FLC 10 FAC 22 Others 21
Sunderland (£200,000 + on 17/8/98) FL 1

MARSDEN Christopher (Chris)
Born: Sheffield, 3 January 1969
Height: 5'11" Weight: 10.12
Starting last season at Birmingham, and playing in the opening 25 games, his crisp passing and coolness under pressure was a big asset to the Blues' midfield. And, in orchestrating the play, the vice captain was invited to get forward more, obliging with five goals, one of them coming in the 1-1 draw at St Andrews against Swindon. Out of the side through injury from mid November, on getting back to fitness he signed for Southampton in February, and soon became an integral part of their midfield, having previously played under Saints' manager, Dave Jones, at Stockport. Proving himself to be a good all-round performer, even at Premiership level, he again showed a liking to push forward, scoring vital goals in the 3-3 draw against Blackburn, and the 2-1 victory against Leicester, both matches being at the Dell.

Sheffield U (From apprentice on 6/1/87) FL 13+3/1 FLC 1 Others 1
Huddersfield T (Signed on 15/7/88) FL 113+8/9 FLC 15+1 FAC 6+2 Others 10
Coventry C (Loaned on 2/11/93) PL 5+2
Wolverhampton W (£250,000 on 11/1/94) FL 8 FAC 3
Notts Co (£250,000 on 15/11/94) FL 10 FLC 1 Others 1/1
Stockport Co (£70,000 on 12/1/96) FL 63+2/3 FLC 13 FAC 4 Others 4/1
Birmingham C (£500,000 on 9/10/97) FL 51+1/3 FLC 5/3 FAC 2
Southampton (£800,000 on 2/2/99) PL 14/2

MARSH Christopher (Chris) Jonathan
Born: Sedgley, 14 January 1970
Height: 5'11" Weight: 13.2
Walsall's longest serving player had one of his best-ever seasons in 1998-99, operating on the right flank of the defence, and missing only four games. Also an excellent man-for-man marker, who earlier in his career was noted for his ability to hit the target when least likely, he overlapped splendidly, and scored the memorable second goal in the promotion clincher against Oldham.

Walsall (From trainee on 11/7/88) FL 311+34/23 FLC 19+2/1 FAC 31+1/3 Others 24+1/3

MARSH Simon Thomas Peter
Born: Ealing, 29 January 1977
Height: 5'11" Weight: 12.0
International Honours: E: U21-1
Simon was a virtual ever present for Oxford in 1998-99, prior to his enforced sale to Birmingham in December – a move

which gave United monetary breathing space and the Blues a player worth more than the giveaway fee. A more than competent and stylish left back, he weighed in with a couple of goals for the U's and, ironically, the game after his move he appeared for his new club at the Manor Ground, and went away after helping his new team mates to a 7-1 away win! He then impressed again in his next game, a home 0-0 draw against Sunderland, before being struck down with a back problem that required surgery. Is excellent at set pieces.

Oxford U (From trainee on 22/11/94) FL 49+7/3 FLC 6+2 FAC 2 Others 2
Birmingham C (£250,000 on 10/12/98) FL 6+1 FAC 1

MARSHALL Andrew (Andy) John
Born: Bury St Edmunds, 14 April 1975
Height: 6'2" Weight: 13.7
International Honours: E: U21-4
Now firmly established as Norwich's first-choice goalkeeper, Andy once again achieved a good level of consistency during the 1998-99 season, making some truly outstanding saves, including one phenomenal effort from Portsmouth's John Aloisi at Fratton Park, which had everyone raving. Very experienced for his relatively tender age, retaining his excellent reflexes and decisiveness in one-on-one situations, he has also worked hard on his distribution which, on occasions, has let him down. They say that goalkeepers improve with age, if so City fans will be relishing the prospect!

Norwich C (From trainee on 6/7/93) P/FL 109+1 FLC 9 FAC 3+1
Bournemouth (Loaned on 9/9/96) FL 11
Gillingham (Loaned on 21/11/96) FL 5 FLC 1 Others 1

MARSHALL Dwight Wayne
Born: Jamaica, WI, 3 October 1965
Height: 5'7" Weight: 11.8
Although appearing in Luton's opening five games of 1998-99, injury forced him on to the sidelines, and caused him to miss a call up for a Jamaican international squad training session, as well as keeping him out of action for the next six matches. With his contract terminated, he joined up with Plymouth until the end of the season, starting his return to the club slowly before finishing the campaign as the leading scorer with 12 goals, six of them coming in a seven match spell. A quick and agile forward who works hard in the front line, he is difficult to ignore as he can explode into action at any time, and is still a force to be reckoned with in the lower divisions. Despite suffering from hamstring and thigh problems, Argyle fans are hopeful he will sign an extension to his current deal in time for 1999-2000.

Plymouth Arg (£35,000 from Grays Athletic on 9/8/91) FL 93+6/27 FLC 8/1 FAC 7+2/4 Others 7+1/4
Middlesbrough (Loaned on 25/3/93) PL 0+3
Luton T (£150,000 on 15/7/94) FL 90+38/28 FLC 8+1/2 FAC 7+1/5 Others 6+3/3
Plymouth Arg (Free on 2/10/98) FL 25+3/12 FAC 1+2

MARSHALL Ian Paul
Born: Liverpool, 20 March 1966
Height: 6'1" Weight: 13.10
Club Honours: Div 2 '91
The Leicester left-footed striker injured a hamstring in pre-season and aggravated it in an early reserve outing, before making his return to first-team action until the end of last December. His lack of match fitness hampered his progress, but he did appear as a substitute at Wembley, where his header across goal almost set up a chance for Tony Cottee. Finally broke his duck with the winner at Anfield in the closing seconds, then repeated the dose in the following fixture to secure a home win over Coventry. Released during the summer, he always gives 100 per-cent effort for his team and is immensely popular on the terraces.
Everton (From apprentice on 23/3/84) FL 9+6/1 FLC 1+1/1 Others 7
Oldham Ath (£100,000 on 24/3/88) F/PL 165+5/36 FLC 17 FAC 14/3 Others 2+1/1
Ipswich T (£750,000 on 9/8/93) P/FL 79+5/32 FLC 4/3 FAC 9/3
Leicester C (£875,000 on 31/8/96) PL 47+15/18 FLC 1+1/1 FAC 6+1/3 Others 2/1

MARSHALL Lee Alan
Born: Nottingham, 1 August 1975
Height: 5'10" Weight: 10.8
A versatile and talented ball-player, Lee spent last season on the substitutes' bench for Scunthorpe, also figuring well in the reserves. Although he made a handful of starts at either right back or in midfield, he was at his best when used as a substitute, coming on to get the winner in the derby against Hull City in November.
Nottingham F (From trainee on 3/8/92)
Stockport Co (Free on 20/3/95) FL 1 (Free to Eastwood T on 24/8/96)
Scunthorpe U (£5,000 on 6/6/97) FL 17+23/2 FLC 0+2 FAC 2+2 Others 1

MARSHALL Lee Keith
Born: Islington, 21 January 1979
Height: 6'0" Weight: 11.11
International Honours: E: U21-1
What an incredible two seasons this former Enfield reserve player has enjoyed since he moved to Norwich in March 1997. Not only did he firmly establish his first-team credentials at Carrow Road in 1998-99, but he has also won international recognition, first for the Football League representative side in Italy, and then for the England U21 side against France at Pride Park. Lee is a very versatile performer, being able to play at full back, in the centre of defence or, as was the case most often last season, in the heart of the midfield. A tremendous worker, he displays a great deal of maturity and confidence for such a young man, and covers every inch of the pitch, working tirelessly when the opposition have the ball. And, when in possession, he has quick feet which enable him to make time and space for himself. His distribution is also good. A tremendous find for the Canaries, his progress will be closely monitored.
Norwich C (Signed from Enfield on 27/3/97) FL 40+8/3 FLC 5 FAC 1

MARSHALL Scott Roderick
Born: Edinburgh, 1 May 1973
Height: 6'1" Weight: 12.5
International Honours: S: U21-5; Yth
Signed by Southampton from Arsenal on a free transfer in July 1998, Scott comes from a footballing family, his father and brother having played for Hearts and Celtic, respectively. A footballing central defender who reads the game well while looking for the right pass, he was unable to command a regular first-team place, and moved to Celtic on loan in March, having made just two first-team appearances.
Arsenal (From trainee on 18/3/91) PL 19+5/1 FLC 1+1
Rotherham U (Loaned on 3/12/93) FL 10/1 Others 1
Sheffield U (Loaned on 25/8/94) FL 17
Southampton (Free on 3/8/98) PL 2

MARSHALL Shaun Andrew
Born: Fakenham, 3 October 1978
Height: 6'1" Weight: 12.12
Now in his fourth year as a professional, and a promising young goalkeeper, Shaun started 1998-99 as understudy to Arjan Van Heusden, but first-team action came in October after injury to the big Dutchman. His first game was at Cardiff, and he was the fans' "Man of the Match" in his first four appearances. Was given another chance at the end of the campaign, and handled the pressures of the promotion run in well.
Cambridge U (From trainee on 21/2/97) FL 22 FLC 1 FAC 2

MARTIN Andrew Peter
Born: Cardiff, 28 February 1980
Height: 6'0" Weight: 10.12
International Honours: W: U21-1; Yth
Andrew, one of Steve Coppell's colts, made his Crystal Palace first-team debut when starting in a 1-0 victory at Norwich last April. A left-sided striker who is good in the air and holds up play well, earlier, in December, he had been loaned out to non-league Merthyr in a bid to further his experience. Felt to have a promising career ahead of him, the Welsh youth international is sure to give it a go.
Crystal Palace (From trainee on 28/2/97) FL 2+1

MARTIN Jae Andrew
Born: Hampstead, 5 February 1976
Height: 5'11" Weight: 11.10
A pacy left-sided wide man, Jae was released by Lincoln during the summer of 1998 and moved down the road to Peterborough. Unfortunately, as in 1997-98, he was affected by a number of niggling injuries and failed to live up to his billing, making just four appearances from the bench last season before being released on loan to Grantham Town in transfer deadline week.
Southend U (From trainee on 7/5/93) FL 1+7 FLC 1+1 Others 0+1
Leyton Orient (Loaned on 9/9/94) FL 1+3 Others 1
Birmingham C (Free on 1/7/95) FL 1+6 Others 0+2
Lincoln C (Signed on 21/8/96) FL 29+12/5 FLC 5/1 FAC 1 Others 0+1
Peterborough U (Free on 2/7/98) FL 0+4

MARTIN John
Born: London, 15 July 1981
Height: 5'6" Weight: 9.12
John is a young Leyton Orient midfielder who started last season in the first team, having signed pro forms immediately prior to 1998-99 getting underway, playing a couple of games, before being rested in favour of a more experienced player. However, he is an exciting player who shows no nerves for one so young, and will be looking to gain a regular first-team place in 1999-2000.
Leyton Orient (From trainee on 6/8/98) FL 1+1 FLC 2 Others 1

MARTIN Lee Brendan
Born: Huddersfield, 9 September 1968
Height: 6'0" Weight: 13.0
International Honours: E: Sch
Having previously played in the Football League with Huddersfield and Blackpool, Lee, Halifax's first-choice goalkeeper, suffered a back injury last Christmas which kept him out of action for six weeks. He also suffered a cheek-bone injury during the Leyton Orient match in March, but again kept a number of clean sheets to earn the Shaymen some precious points. Was released during the summer.
Huddersfield T (From trainee on 1/7/87) FL 54 FAC 4 Others 5
Blackpool (Free on 31/7/92) FL 98 FLC 8 FAC 4 Others 7
Rochdale (Free on 8/11/96)
Halifax T (Free on 12/8/97) FL 37 FLC 4 FAC 1 Others 1

MARTINDALE Gary
Born: Liverpool, 24 June 1971
Height: 6'0" Weight: 12.1
Club Honours: Div 3 '98
Gary had a season he will not want to remember as he missed a large chunk of 1998-99 after undergoing a knee operation, leaving his first-team chances at Rotherham severely restricted. Just beginning to show his striking ability when he picked up his injury in October, it was typical of his cruel luck that when he returned on Easter Monday he sustained a broken jaw.
Bolton W (Signed from Burscough on 24/3/94)
Peterborough U (Signed on 4/7/95) FL 26+5/15 FLC 4/1 FAC 4 Others 4/2
Notts Co (£175,000 on 6/3/96) FL 34+32/13 FLC 3+1 FAC 3+1 Others 5+1/3
Mansfield T (Loaned on 7/2/97) FL 5/2
Rotherham U (Signed on 12/3/98) FL 13+5/4 FLC 0+2

MARTINEZ Roberto
Born: Balaguer Lerida, Spain, 13 July 1973
Height: 5'10" Weight: 12.2
Club Honours: Div 3 '97
The last of Wigan's "Three Amigos" still at the club, this cultured right-footed midfielder surprisingly made only ten league appearances during 1998-99. Skilful, with a clinical eye for finishing, Roberto is currently just one match short of 150 Football League games for Athletic.
Wigan Ath (Free from Balaguer on 25/7/95) FL 109+19/14 FLC 7/1 FAC 7+1/4 Others 5+2/1

MARTYN Antony **Nigel**
Born: St Austell, 11 August 1966
Height: 6'2" Weight: 14.7
Club Honours: Div 3 '90; FMC '91; Div 1 '94
International Honours: E: 9; B-6; U21-11
Recognised for many years as being one of the most consistent goalkeepers in England, Nigel has shown excellent form for Leeds since the day he signed for the club, and 1998-99 was no exception. The model of consistency, to list all of his superb saves would take too long, but his "Man of the Match" game in the 2-0 victory against Coventry City at Elland Road last December is one to stand out. Unfortunately, he had the misfortune to pick up a couple of injuries during the campaign. A rib injury suffered against Roma caused him to miss three games and, following a dive to make a brilliant full-length save in the 2-3 defeat at Manchester United, he missed a further game. "England's number one" is the chant often heard from the Leeds' followers, and Nigel picked up his ninth cap in a friendly against France. A vital part to the club's future success, everyone was delighted when he signed a two-year extension to his current contract, which already had 18 months to run. Was selected by his fellow professionals to take his place in the PFA award-winning Premiership side.
Bristol Rov (Free from St Blazey on 6/8/87) FL 101 FLC 6 FAC 6 Others 11
Crystal Palace (£1,000,000 on 21/11/89) F/PL 272 FLC 36 FAC 22 Others 19
Leeds U (£2,250,000 on 26/7/96) PL 108 FLC 8 FAC 13 Others 4

MASKELL Craig Dell
Born: Aldershot, 10 April 1968
Height: 5'10" Weight: 11.11
Craig started last season as a first-team regular at Leyton Orient, playing in the first eight games before losing his place in September. Despite taking a back seat, he remained a member of the squad, and when called upon he never let anybody down, but his lack of scoring obviously worked against him, although you couldn't fault his workrate and ability to hold the ball up during vital games. Was released during the summer.
Southampton (From apprentice on 15/4/86) FL 2+4/1
Huddersfield T (£20,000 on 31/5/88) FL 86+1/43 FLC 6/4 FAC 8/3 Others 7/4
Reading (£250,000 on 7/8/90) FL 60+12/26 FLC 2 FAC 5+1 Others 1
Swindon T (£225,000 on 9/7/92) F/PL 40+7/22 FLC 3+1/1 FAC 2+1 Others 4+1/4
Southampton (£250,000 on 7/2/94) PL 8+9/1 FAC 1+1
Bristol C (Loaned on 28/12/95) FL 5/1
Brighton & Hove A (£40,000 on 1/3/96) FL 68+1/20 FLC 4+1 FAC 3/1 Others 2/1 (Free to Happy Valley on 20/12/97)
Leyton Orient (Free on 26/3/98) FL 15+8/2 FLC 2 FAC 0+2 Others 1+2

MASON Gary Ronald
Born: Edinburgh, 15 October 1979
Height: 5'8" Weight: 10.6
International Honours: S: U21-1
An 18-year-old midfield player who came up through Manchester City's junior and reserve teams, he was thrust into the first home game against Blackpool last season. Made an immediate impact on both the game and the fans, akin to the style of Ian Bishop. His pace and game was continuous for 90 minutes, covering every part of the pitch, and he looked to be the fittest player at the club. His assist by a long ball out of defence to Paul Dickov, who in turn fed Lee Bradbury for the second goal, was as skilful as that of star players of yesteryear who controlled midfield. Having signed a four-year contract at the end of last August, and playing for Scotland U21s in Lithuania as a substitute for the last 20 minutes, he was extremely impressive for City on a heavy water-logged ground at Wigan. His 30-yard pass from the middle through to Shaun Goater, who scored the winning goal, was precision par excellence. Held back by the manager, Joe Royle, in the second half of the campaign so as not to burn him out, Gary is certainly a skilful midfield player for the future.
Manchester C (From trainee on 21/10/96) FL 18+1 FLC 3/1 FAC 2

MASON Paul David
Born: Liverpool, 3 September 1963
Height: 5'9" Weight: 12.1
Club Honours: SLC '90; SC '90
Able to play up front or in midfield with equal conviction, and noted for his shooting powers, Paul suffered a bad achilles tendon injury in December 1997, which brought his 1997-98 to an end. Out of contract during the summer of 1998, and a free agent under the Bosman ruling, he was told that he would be offered a new contract if he proved his fitness for 1998-99. However, after coming on as a substitute against Exeter in the Worthington Cup and scoring a cracking goal it appeared that he would stay at Portman Road, but the club had other ideas and he was on his way in October.
Aberdeen (£200,000 from FC Groningen on 1/8/88) SL 138+20/27 SLC 13+2/8 SC 11+1/1 Others 7/1
Ipswich T (£400,000 on 18/6/93) P/FL 103+10/25 FLC 10+1/5 FAC 4+3/3 Others 4/3

MATERAZZI Marco
Born: Perugia, Italy, 19 August 1973
Height: 6'4" Weight: 14.2
A tall, powerful Italian defender, Marco showed more ability on the ball than many forwards during his inaugural season in English football. Signed from Perugia during the 1998 close season, he delighted Evertonians with his classy skills on the ball and ability to spray passes out of defence. His first two goals in English football showed off that talent. One was a clever back heel in the Worthington Cup against Huddersfield, the other, a stunning 20-yard free kick that curled past Middlesbrough's defensive wall. Although he occasionally over did the ball play around his own penalty area, his biggest problem during the campaign was with referees, being dismissed three times and shown a yellow card on countless of other occasions. Stop Press: Transferred to Perugia for £3 million on 3 July.
Everton (£2,800,000 from Perugia on 31/7/98) PL 26+1/1 FLC 4/1 FAC 2

MATHIE Alexander (Alex)
Born: Bathgate, 20 December 1968
Height: 5'10" Weight: 11.7
International Honours: S: Yth
Alex struggled to get in the Ipswich side at the start of last season, and even though Jamie Scowcroft was injured, his situation was not helped by the club's lack of goals in their early matches – they failed to score in their first four games. Once Scowcroft was fit, and went straight into the side, his run of scoring meant that Alex was permanently on the bench, despite scoring against Crystal Palace when he came on in the last minute of the game and drove a low shot into the far corner from the edge of the box. The next week, on 16 October, he was on his way to Dundee United to seek the regular first-team place he deserved, but he will always be remembered at Ipswich for the first-half hat trick against the old enemy in 1997-98.
Glasgow C (From juniors on 15/5/87) SL 7+4 SC 1 Others 0+1
Morton (£100,000 on 1/8/91) SL 73+1/31 SLC 2/1 SC 5/3 Others 7/9
Port Vale (Loaned on 30/3/93) FL 0+3
Newcastle U (£285,000 on 30/7/93) PL 3+22/4 FLC 2+2
Ipswich T (£500,000 on 24/2/95) P/FL 90+19/38 FLC 10+3/8 FAC 2+2 Others 6/1

MATIAS Pedro Manuel Miguel
Born: Madrid, Spain, 11 October 1973
Height: 6'0" Weight: 12.0
Coming to Macclesfield for trials early last October, and wanting a chance to play football in England, the former Logrones, and Spanish U21 front man was introduced to manager Sammy McIlroy by the Spanish trio of Wigan players, following Town's match there. He immediately impressed both management and team in training, but negotiations were tedious and time consuming, and it was December before he finally signed a short-term contract. Despite not speaking any English, he fitted in well with the team, and made some mazy runs from midfield to turn the opposition easily and provide some all-important "assists" in the latter part of the season, before finally getting on to the scoresheet with his goal against Stoke.
Macclesfield T (Free from Logrones, via Real Madrid and Almeria, on 3/12/98) FL 21+1/2 FAC 1

MATTEO Dominic
Born: Dumfries, 28 April 1974
Height: 6'1" Weight: 11.12
International Honours: E: B-1; U21-4; Yth
Injuries apart, Dominic was reduced to something of a bit-part player at Liverpool in 1998-99. Overlooked for the start of the season, he made his first appearance as sub against West Ham, deputising for Steve Staunton, and following the purchase of Rigobert Song, and to some extent Vegard Heggem, competition for places were intensified. His best match of the campaign came in the 7-1 victory against Southampton, when he scored a goal and was outstanding in the central defensive role in a three-man defence. Against Coventry and Middlesbrough, he was moved to the

left of a three-man defence, and was sent off for a foul against Middlesbrough at Anfield. A player with the ability to break up an attack and bring the ball out of defence with some speed, he also played on the left-side of midfield against Derby at Anfield.

Liverpool (From trainee on 27/5/92) PL 80+15/1 FLC 9 FAC 5+1 Others 10+1
Sunderland (Loaned on 28/3/95) FL 1

MATTHEW Damian
Born: Islington, 23 September 1970
Height: 5'11" Weight: 10.10
Club Honours: Div 1 '94
International Honours: E: U21-9

A midfield player who possesses a good shot. After months of trying to sign Damien from Burnley, Cobblers' manager, Ian Atkins, finally got his man during the 1998 close season, yet the newcomer's Northampton career lasted just 53 minutes. On his debut he was taken off after seven minutes to be replaced by a defender, which followed another defender being sent off, and his second game ended for him at half time when he came off with a back injury. This led to an operation, and a long period of rehabilitation, before he started his comeback in the reserves in March.

Chelsea (From trainee on 13/6/89) F/PL 13+8 FLC 5 Others 1
Luton T (Loaned on 25/9/92) FL 3+2 Others 1
Crystal Palace (£150,000 on 11/2/94) F/PL 17+7/1 FLC 2+1 FAC 1
Bristol Rov (Loaned on 12/1/96) FL 8 Others 2/1
Burnley (£65,000 on 23/7/96) FL 50+9/7 FLC 6+1/1 FAC 2/1 Others 3
Northampton T (Free on 7/7/98) FL 1 FLC 1

MATTHEWS Lee Joseph
Born: Middlesbrough, 16 January 1979
Height: 6'3" Weight: 12.6
Club Honours: FAYC '97
International Honours: E: Yth

One of Leeds' good youngsters, and a member of their FA Youth Cup winners team, unable to get a break at Elland Road in 1998-99, Lee was loaned to Notts County at the end of September, but failed to make much of an impression and returned to United after five games and no goals. A young, tall striker with a good touch on the ball, he is very quick, and is still expected to make a name for himself.

Leeds U (From trainee on 15/2/96) PL 0+3 FLC 0+1
Notts Co (Loaned on 24/9/98) FL 4+1

MATTHEWS Robert (Rob) David
Born: Slough, 14 October 1970
Height: 6'0" Weight: 13.0
Club Honours: Div 2 '97
International Honours: E: Sch

With no right-footed players available in the midfield, Gary Megson swooped for Rob after he had scored in an impressive display for Bury against Stockport last October. He immediately gave County attacking options and trickery on the right flank, and also chipped in with some vital goals, including the winner against Sheffield United, which as good as secured the club's safety in Division One. Although substituted in almost every game he started for Stockport, his talent was nevertheless, highly valued.

Notts Co (Free from Loughborough University on 26/3/92) FL 23+2]0/11 FLC 0+2 FAC 3+2/2 Others 4+3
Luton T (£80,000 on 17/3/95) FL 6+5 FLC 0+1
York C (£90,000 on 8/9/95) FL 14+3/1 FAC 1 Others 3
Bury (£100,000 on 12/1/96) FL 54+20/11 FLC 4+5/3 FAC 1 Others 3
Stockport Co (£120,000 on 12/11/98) FL 19+4/2 FAC 1+1

MATTIS Dwayne Antony
Born: Huddersfield, 31 July 1981
Height: 6'1" Weight: 10.10
International Honours: Ei: Yth

Still a trainee, although expecting to sign pro forms in the summer, the young Republic of Ireland youth international midfielder made such an impression in the juniors and reserves at Huddersfield in 1998-99 that he was given two subs' appearances in the last two matches of the campaign, coming off the bench to make his debut at Crystal Palace before subbing at home to Crewe. Showed up well on both occasions, his passing qualities mixed with strong tackling, and he appears to have a good future in front of him.

Huddersfield T (Trainee) FL 0+2

MATTSSON Jesper Bo
Born: Sweden, 18 April 1968
Height: 6'1" Weight: 12.6
International Honours: Sweden: 1

Signed from the Swedish club, BK Halmstad, last December, this tall and dominant central defender was thrown straight into the Premiership fray at Leicester in a bid to shore up and stabilise the Nottingham Forest defence. Played in the next game, at home to Blackburn, but was then absent for a considerable period after sustaining rib and lung injuries. He re-appeared briefly when coming off the bench in the 8-1 home drubbing at the hands of Manchester United before playing three more times. With Forest in the First Division this coming term, the Swede should have a chance to regroup.

Nottingham F (£500,000 from BK Halmstad on 11/12/98) PL 5+1

MAUGE Ronald (Ronnie) Carlton
Born: Islington, 10 March 1969
Height: 5'10" Weight: 11.10

A forceful character both on and off the field, despite suspensions and a broken bone in his foot keeping his appearances down in 1998-99, Ronnie worked tirelessly in Plymouth's midfield with a high tackle count, his late runs into the penalty area giving him an extra string to his bow. Although given a free transfer at the end of the season, he will still go down in Argyle history for his winner at Wembley in the play-off final. Was called into the Trinidad and Tobago international squad in March.

Charlton Ath (From trainee on 22/7/87)
Fulham (Free on 21/9/88) FL 47+3/2 FLC 4 FAC 1 Others 2
Bury (£40,000 on 30/7/90) FL 92+16/10 FLC 8+2/2 FAC 8/2 Others 10+2
Manchester C (Loaned on 26/9/91) Others 0+1
Plymouth Arg (£40,000 on 22/7/95) FL 119+16/13 FLC 6 FAC 11/2 Others 5+1/1

MAVRAK Darko
Born: Mostar, Croatia, 19 January 1969
Height: 6'0" Weight: 12.11

Signed from Falkenburg, Sweden, at the end of last January, initially on non-contract forms, Darko made his debut in the 1-0 win at Reading a few days later. Operating up front, he calmly stabbed home the winner at Northampton in his fifth game, and got the opening goal at Blackpool at the beginning of April, when he again showed coolness in capitalising upon a defender's error.

Walsall (Free from Falkenburg on 27/1/99) FL 12+1/2 Others 3

MAY David
Born: Oldham, 24 June 1970
Height: 6'0" Weight: 13.5
Club Honours: CS '94, '96; PL '96, '97, '99; FAC '96, '99; EC '99

A very able Manchester United central defender, with good recovery skills and excellent heading ability to match, David had a frustrating start to last season when he suffered from a combination of thigh, knee and calf injuries. It certainly did not help his cause when Alex Ferguson shored up his defence with the acquisition of Jaap Stam and Henning Berg. After making his comeback in the Worthington Cup-ties against Bury and Nottingham Forest, opportunities remained few and far between. Although clearly frustrated at the lack of first-team opportunities, with Stam injured he was recalled right at the end of the campaign, and was a member of the side that clinched the Premiership championship with a 2-1 win over Spurs at Old Trafford. He was also delighted to win FA Cup and European Cup winners medals at the end of the club's most successful campaign in its lustrous history.

Blackburn Rov (From trainee on 16/6/88) F/PL 123/3 FLC 12+1/2 FAC 10/1 Others 5
Manchester U (£1,400,000 on 1/7/94) PL 65+14/6 FLC 7/1 FAC 6 Others 13+1/1

MAYBURY Alan
Born: Dublin, 8 August 1978
Height: 5'11" Weight: 11.7
Club Honours: FAYC '97
International Honours: Ei: 2; B-1; U21-6; Yth

Unable to get a kick of the ball at Leeds, the Republic of Ireland international arrived at Reading in March on loan, and was unfortunate to be sent off on his debut at home to Manchester City. He recovered from that set back to make a run of appearances, either at right-wing back or in midfield, but only played once on the winning side for Royals, in the 2-0 home victory over Millwall. Is a quality player who could still come good at Elland Road. Also represented the Republic at U21 level in 1998-99.

Leeds U (Free from St Kevin's BC on 17/8/95) PL 10+3 FLC 1 FAC 2
Reading (Loaned on 25/3/99) FL 8

MAYLETT Bradley
Born: Manchester, 24 December 1980
Height: 5'7" Weight: 10.2

Having signed professional forms for Burnley last February, after coming through

the trainee ranks, Bradley is undoubtedly the most promising player on the fringes of Clarets' first team. Still to make his full league debut, he was something of a secret weapon as a sub, a right winger with lightning speed, enthusiasm to spare, and a shot which will surely bring results in due course. Definitely one for the future.
Burnley (From trainee on 19/2/99) FL 0+17 Others 1

MAYO Kerry
Born: Haywards Heath, 21 September 1977
Height: 5'10" Weight: 13.4
Began last season in Brighton's midfield before suffering a knee injury. Returned to contention in late October and was in and out of the side for most of the remainder of the season before making the left-back position his own for the last six games. A tough-tackling player, who strikes the ball well when going forward, he scored two goals during the campaign, both in away defeats.
Brighton & Hove A (From trainee on 3/7/96) FL 86+7/7 FLC 4 FAC 1+2/1 Others 1+3

MEAKER Michael John
Born: Greenford, 18 August 1971
Height: 5'11" Weight: 12.0
International Honours: W: B-1; U21-2
After signing for Bristol Rovers during the summer, the tricky winger made a promising league debut against his former club, Reading, on the opening day of last season, but it was the best the supporters saw of him. Scoring that day in an emphatic 4-1 victory against the newly relegated Royals, at times he could be an exciting, attacking wide man, and at other times a frustrating player who tended to drift in and out of games. He added a second league goal in what turned out to be a consolation in a 3-1 defeat at Northampton Town, but was later sent off, before having a knee operation to cure a patella tendonitis problem which had been hampering his fitness for some time. Returned for the final match of the season, at Macclesfield.
Queens Park R (From trainee on 7/2/90) F/PL 21+13/1 FLC 2/1 FAC 3/1 Others 0+1
Plymouth Arg (Loaned on 20/11/91) FL 4 Others 1
Reading (£550,000 on 19/7/95) FL 46+21/2 FLC 3/1 FAC 0+3
Bristol Rov (Free on 7/8/98) FL 17+3/2 FLC 2 FAC 4+1

MEAN Scott James
Born: Crawley, 13 December 1973
Height: 5'11" Weight: 13.8
The slightly-built central midfielder once again had his season blighted by injury, having joined Port Vale on loan from West Ham to cover for injuries at the start of 1998-99, and being forced to limp out of his debut at home to West Bromwich after 74 minutes. That was his first start for three years and it turned out to be a cruciate ligament injury that ended his campaign there and then. Released during the summer, when fit enough to play, Scott is a stylish

player with good passing ability, who also enjoys making penetrating runs deep into the opposition territory.
Bournemouth (From trainee on 10/8/92) FL 52+22/8 FLC 7+1 FAC 2+1 Others 4
West Ham U (£100,000 on 18/7/96) PL 0+3
Port Vale (Loaned on 21/8/98) FL 1

MEECHAN Alexander (Alex) Thomas
Born: Plymouth, 29 January 1980
Height: 5'10" Weight: 10.10
Having made his debut for Swindon in 1997-98 while still a trainee, Alex signed pro forms for Bristol City during the 1998 close season, and came off the bench to make his first appearance in the last game of the campaign, at home to Norwich. Earlier, in the reserves, the young striker had shown a good turn of pace, and the ability to get into the box to score goals. Is another player who is highly regarded by the coaches at the club and who, if he maintains his progress, could make the breakthrough at a higher level.
Swindon T (Trainee) FL 0+1
Bristol C (Signed on 6/7/98) FL 0+1

MELLON Michael (Micky) Joseph
Born: Paisley, 18 March 1972
Height: 5'10" Weight: 12.11
A solid midfield support, Micky is an honest, hard-working player with an uncompromising style, and an eye for the early pass or darting, forward run to create chances for the front men. Also the possessor of a fiercesome shot himself, he moved from Tranmere to Burnley last January following Barry Kilby's appointment as chairman at Turf Moor. At his new club, he added a new dimension to what had been an over-defensive midfield unit, and continued to give the impression that he could always pop up with the odd goal.
Bristol C (From trainee on 6/12/89) FL 26+9/1 FLC 3 FAC 1+1 Others 5+3
West Bromwich A (£75,000 on 11/2/93) FL 38+7/6 FLC 3+2 FAC 0+1 Others 6/1
Blackpool (£50,000 on 23/11/94) FL 123+1/14 FLC 9/1 FAC 4 Others 7/2
Tranmere Rov (£285,000 on 31/10/97) FL 45+12/3 FLC 4 FAC 3+1
Burnley (£350,000 on 8/1/99) FL 20/2

MELTON Stephen
Born: Lincoln, 3 October 1978
Height: 5'11" Weight: 12.2
In a somewhat traumatic season for Nottingham Forest in 1998-99, although there were not many good things coming out of the City Ground, young Stephen was one of them. Having come through the club's trainee system to turn professional in October 1995, but patiently biding his time, with Forest already doomed to play in the First Division this coming campaign he was finally given a first-team debut in the last match of 1998-99, a 1-0 win at Leicester City. An industrious midfielder who looked to be good in the tackle, he also passed the ball skilfully, and could be one for the future.
Nottingham F (From trainee on 9/10/95) PL 1

MELVILLE Andrew (Andy) Roger
Born: Swansea, 29 November 1968
Height: 6'0" Weight: 13.10
Club Honours: WC '89; Div 1 '96
International Honours: W: 34; B-1; U21-2
The Welsh international centre back picked up his second First Division championship medal with Sunderland at the end of 1998-99, after a season in which even he must have been amazed at his change in fortunes. Having lost his first-team place the previous term, and been expected to depart Wearside, the towering defender spent the summer working hard on his fitness, returning to form to establish a solid rearguard in the team alongside new signing, Paul Butler. Andy's distribution from the back was again excellent, and he was a constant menace at set pieces, as was illustrated at West Bromwich in October when his headed goal began a fight back that turned a 2-0 deficit into a 3-2 win. Not surprisingly, his fine form was further recognised by Bobby Gould, who recalled him to the Welsh squad in February. Was somewhat surprisingly released during the summer.
Swansea C (From trainee on 25/7/86) FL 165+10/22 FLC 10 FAC 14+1/5 Others 13/2
Oxford U (£275,000 on 23/7/90) FL 135/13 FLC 12/1 FAC 6 Others 6/1
Sunderland (Signed on 9/8/93) P/FL 204/14 FLC 18+1 FAC 11 Others 2
Bradford C (Loaned on 13/2/98) FL 6/1

MENDES-RODRIGUEZ Alberto
Born: Nurnberg, Germany, 24 October 1974
Height: 5'11" Weight: 11.9
A quick, attacking midfield player with Arsenal, whose strength is in getting at defenders, he has excellent close skills and possesses a good shot with either foot. Scored the opening goal in the Gunners' 3-1 Champions' League victory at Panathinaikos with a powerful free kick in 1998-99 and, despite being only a squad player, he continued to learn the "English" game while waiting for his big chance.
Arsenal (£250,000 from FC Feucht on 21/7/97) PL 1+3 FLC 3+1/1 FAC 1 Others 1/1

MENDEZ Albert (Junior) Hillyard Andrew
Born: Balham, 15 September 1976
Height: 5'8" Weight: 11.0
A former Chelsea junior who went north to play senior football with St Mirren in April 1996, he joined Carlisle on loan from the Scottish club last November. Junior was the third on-loan striker to appear at Brunton Park during the first half of 1998-99, and he almost scored in the first minute of his debut against Rotherham. Generally looking to be an impressive performer in his spell at the club, showing enthusiasm and commitment, his goal against Hartlepool was a stylish piece of work.
Chelsea (From trainee on 1/7/95)
St Mirren (Free on 29/4/96) SL 70+17/17 SLC 4 SC 3/1
Carlisle U (Loaned on 18/11/98) FL 5+1/1

Clive Mendonca

MENDONCA Clive Paul
Born: Islington, 9 September 1968
Height: 5'10" Weight: 12.6
1998-99 was a frustrating time for Clive, who was troubled by various injuries throughout the season, including a persistent back problem. Very comfortable on the ball, although not the quickest of strikers the Charlton man has the ability to turn and gain a yard on defenders, and is deadly in front of goal. Although scoring a hat trick against Southampton at the Valley in the first home match of the campaign, he started only three games in 1999, but his tally of eight made him top scorer. One of his goals, a last-minute equaliser at Leicester, after he came on as substitute, earned the Addicks a valuable point.
Sheffield U (From apprentice on 10/9/86) FL 8+5/4 FLC 0+1 Others 1
Doncaster Rov (Loaned on 26/2/88) FL 2
Rotherham U (£35,000 on 25/3/88) FL 71+13/27 FLC 5+2/1 FAC 4+1/2 Others 4+2/1
Sheffield U (£110,000 on 1/8/91) FL 4+6/1 FLC 0+2 Others 0+1
Grimsby T (Loaned on 9/1/92) FL 10/3
Grimsby T (£85,000 on 13/8/92) FL 151+5/57 FLC 10+1/3 FAC 8/2 Others 2/1
Charlton Ath (£700,000 on 23/5/97) P/FL 59+6/31 FLC 5/1 FAC 2/1 Others 2/3

MERCER William (Billy)
Born: Liverpool, 22 May 1969
Height: 6'2" Weight: 13.5
Chesterfield's regular skipper and goalkeeper played for much of the early part of 1998-99 with a niggling thigh strain, although you would not have learned that from watching him. Billy bossed his area and handled the ball well all season, cleared with firmness and conviction, and got through ground and aerial work to a consistently high standard. The likeable

Liverpudlian is rated as one of the most reliable 'keepers in the Second Division.
Liverpool (From trainee on 21/8/87)
Rotherham U (Signed on 16/2/89) FL 104 FLC 12 FAC 12 Others 10
Sheffield U (Signed on 12/10/94) FL 4
Chesterfield (£93,000 on 5/9/95) FL 149 FLC 8 FAC 10 Others 7

Paul Merson

MERSON Paul Charles
Born: Harlesden, 20 March 1968
Height: 6'0" Weight: 13.2
Club Honours: Div 1 '89, '91; FLC '93; FAC '93; ECWC '94
International Honours: E: 21; B-4; U21-4; Yth
After seemingly resurrecting his career, and enjoying a World Cup squad place with England in France '98, Paul's return to Teeside took a turn for the worse as far as Middlesbrough were concerned when, having played in just three Premiership matches, and taking the "Man of the Match" award in two of them, he requested a move. Following that, he committed himself to Aston Villa for four years in mid September, scored on his debut at home to Wimbledon, and quickly proved to be an inspirational player among what was a young side. Predominantly playing in an attacking midfield role, behind the front two, he was just as comfortable in the out-and-out striker role, his versatility there for all to see. Selected for England against the Czech Republic and scoring, following the game it became apparent that he was carrying a back injury and, having come off at half time at Nottingham Forest, he was advised by a specialist that with damage to soft tissues rather than the disc only rest would cure the problem. After missing eight games, he came back with a bang in mid January,

coming off the bench to score at home against Everton, and proceeded to have his best spell at the club, before the arrival of Steve Stone in March saw a change to the playing formation, which resulted in him spending more time on the subs' bench than on the pitch. Hopefully, 1999-2000 will see a revitalised Paul Merson.
Arsenal (From apprentice on 1/12/85) F/PL 289+38/78 FLC 38+2/9 FAC 28+3/4 Others 27+2/7
Brentford (Loaned on 22/1/87) FL 6+1 Others 1+1
Middlesbrough (£4,500,000 + on 15/7/97) P/FL 48/12 FLC 7/3 FAC 3/1
Aston Villa (£6,750,000 on 10/9/98) PL 21+5/5 FAC 1

MIDDLETON Craig Dean
Born: Nuneaton, 10 September 1970
Height: 5'10" Weight: 11.12
Strong running, athletic, and a regular in Cardiff City's midfield, Craig is able to play in a number of positions, having appeared at full back, wing back, central defence, midfield, and just behind the front two. During 1998-99, he did an outstanding job for the Bluebirds and made more than 40 first-team appearances. Spent most of the season in midfield, and was the highest scoring player in that area, netting eight times.
Coventry C (From trainee on 30/5/89) F/PL 2+1 FLC 1
Cambridge U (Free on 20/7/93) FL 55+4/10 FLC 3 FAC 1 Others 1
Cardiff C (Free on 30/8/96) FL 88+21/8 FLC 2+1 FAC 13/3 Others 4+1

MIDGLEY Craig Steven
Born: Bradford, 24 May 1976
Height: 5'8" Weight: 11.7
On the small side, but a good all-round Hartlepool forward with a never-say-die attitude making him a constant menace to opposition defences, Craig was a regular goalscorer in the first half of 1998-99, and by mid season he had forged a successful strikeforce with big Steve Howard, which looked destined only to get better. Unfortunately, this was not to be, his campaign being brought to a premature end by a foot injury early in the New Year. And, although he continued to be involved at first-team level, he will be itching to get back in 1999-2000 in a stronger Pool squad.
Bradford C (From trainee on 4/7/95) FL 0+11/1 FAC 0+4 Others 1
Scarborough (Loaned on 7/12/95) FL 14+2/1
Scarborough (Loaned on 14/3/97) FL 6/2
Darlington (Loaned on 1/12/97) FL 1 Others 0+1/1
Hartlepool U (£10,000 on 13/3/98) FL 35+3/10 FLC 2 FAC 2/1 Others 3

MIGLIORANZI Stefan
Born: Pocos de Caldas, Brazil, 20 September 1977
Height: 6'0" Weight: 11.12
Born of Brazilian parents, but having an Italian passport through his paternal grandfather, Stefan moved to the United States aged 12 and played for St John's University in New York. Spotted by Everton scouts, but never kicking a ball on

Merseyside due to the weather, Portsmouth gave him a chance when bringing him over last March, and he showed some promising midfield skills in seven matches. Although he has yet to adapt to the English game, he shows signs of finding and creating space and, at 21, is an exciting prospect for Pompey supporters this season.

Portsmouth (Free from St John's University on 8/3/99) FL 4+3

MIKLOSKO Ludek (Ludo)
Born: Ostrava, Czechoslovakia, 9 December 1961
Height: 6'5" Weight: 14.0
International Honours: Czechoslovakia: 44

Ludo was initially signed on a month's loan from West Ham United last October, but this period was extended to the maximum three months allowable, before he became Gerry Francis' first transfer signing for a nominal fee on Christmas Day. The big goalkeeper chose Rangers on the recommendation of fellow Czech 'keeper, Jan Stejskal, who had played for the club in the early '90s. It was reported that he was so keen to leave the Hammers and sign for Rangers that he paid part of the transfer fee himself. Thus, it was no great surprise that he gained an immediate rapport with the fans. A tall and commanding 'keeper, he became the regular first choice after his arrival.

West Ham U (£300,000 from Banik Ostrava on 19/2/90) F/PL 315 FLC 25 FAC 25 Others 8
Queens Park R (£50,000 on 2/10/98) FL 31 FAC 1

MILBOURNE Ian
Born: Hexham, 21 January 1979
Height: 5'11" Weight: 11.2

Released by Newcastle during the 1998 close season, Ian was recruited by Scarborough immediately prior to the start of 1998-99. Skilful and pacy, the young striker quickly showed his ability to pass defenders, often with ease, and made his Football League debut in an opening day 2-1 home defeat at the hands of Southend. Unfortunately dogged by injuries, his appearances were restricted to being mainly from the bench, but he had a trial with Huddersfield in the final weeks of a campaign that ended with the side being relegated to the Conference, and seems determined to stay in the league.

Newcastle U (From trainee on 4/7/97)
Scarborough (Free on 5/8/98) FL 2+14 FLC 1+1 Others 0+1

MILLEN Keith Derek
Born: Croydon, 26 September 1966
Height: 6'2" Weight: 12.4
Club Honours: Div 3 '92; Div 2 '98

An experienced central defender who endured a frustrating season, having started 1998-99 as Watford's captain, he suffered a whole catalogue of injuries that prevented any first-team appearances after October. Firstly, it was a heel problem at the start of the campaign that set him back, then a hip injury and, finally, knee damage necessitating a cartilage operation. Despite being out of the game for long periods while at Vicarage Road, Keith will be looking forward with relish to the coming term.

Brentford (From apprentice on 7/8/84) FL 301+4/17 FLC 26/2 FAC 18/1 Others 30+1
Watford (Signed on 22/3/94) FL 163+2/6 FLC 10+1 FAC 14 Others 1

MILLER Alan John
Born: Epping, 29 March 1970
Height: 6'3" Weight: 14.6
Club Honours: FAYC '88; ECWC '94; Div 1 '95
International Honours: E: U21-4; Sch

Replaced between the posts at West Bromwich by Phil Whitehead after playing in 21 of Albion's opening 22 games in 1998-99, having again produced some excellent performances, a niggling back injury did not help matters, and this lingered on for quite some time. Well built and commanding, with good reflexes and safe hands, he ended the campaign in the reserves, and is now eager to regain his first-team place.

Arsenal (From trainee on 5/5/88) PL 6+2
Plymouth Arg (Loaned on 24/11/88) FL 13 FAC 2
West Bromwich A (Loaned on 15/8/91) FL 3
Birmingham C (Loaned on 19/12/91) FL 15 Others 1
Middlesbrough (£500,000 on 12/8/94) P/FL 57 FLC 3 FAC 2 Others 2
Grimsby T (Loaned on 28/1/97) FL 3
West Bromwich A (£400,000 on 28/2/97) FL 73 FLC 5 FAC 2

MILLER Charles (Charlie)
Born: Glasgow, 18 March 1976
Height: 5'9" Weight: 10.8
Club Honours: SPD '95, '96, '97; SLC '97
International Honours: S: U21-8

Signed on loan from Glasgow Rangers on transfer deadline day last March, Charlie joined Leicester and immediately impressed in several appearances for the reserves before making his Premiership debut from the bench on Easter Tuesday against Aston Villa at Hillsborough. Brought to the club with a view to a permanent move, the tenacious midfielder had few opportunities to show off his abilities at Premier level and, when finally making the starting line-up, at home to Newcastle, he was taken off with a dead leg after just 17 minutes. Injury problems at Rangers which curtailed much of his activity over the past couple of season, was one of the reasons the Scot travelled south to try his luck elsewhere, and the City manager, Martin O'Neill, would have debated hard and long whether to purchase him during the summer.

Glasgow R (From juniors on 2/7/92) SL 54+30/10 SLC 9+2/1 SC 5+1/2 Others 7+9/2
Leicester C (Loaned on 26/3/99) PL 1+3

MILLER Kevin
Born: Falmouth, 15 March 1969
Height: 6'1" Weight: 13.0
Club Honours: Div 4 '90

An excellent Crystal Palace goalkeeper who is a recognised shot stopper, is sound on crosses, and has a good rapport with his defence, to the surprise of many he started 1998-99 rather gingerly, being replaced by Fraser Digby after just three games. With the club experiencing financial difficulties, it was rumoured that Kevin would be joining Southampton, but in December he was in the side again and appeared to be getting back to his best. Is under contract until the end of 2000-01.

Exeter C (Free from Newquay on 9/3/89) FL 163 FLC 7 FAC 12 Others 18
Birmingham C (£250,000 on 14/5/93) FL 24 FLC 4 Others 2
Watford (£250,000 on 7/8/94) FL128 FLC 10 FAC 10 Others 3
Crystal Palace (£1,000,000 + on 21/7/97) P/FL 66 FLC 3 FAC 5

MILLER Paul Anthony
Born: Woking, 31 January 1968
Height: 6'0" Weight: 11.7

This versatile Lincoln player is equally at home in any of the midfield positions, but at his most effective making forward runs into the opposition penalty area. After struggling to win a first-team place in the early part of last season, he hit form after the chairman, John Reames, took over team affairs. Paul went on to become a key figure in the City team and, at the end of the campaign, was rewarded with a new two-year contract.

Wimbledon (From Yeovil T on 12/8/87) F/PL 65+15/10 FLC 3+3 FAC 3 Others 1
Newport Co (Loaned on 20/10/87) FL 6/2
Bristol C (Loaned on 11/1/90) FL 0+3 Others 2
Bristol Rov (£100,000 on 16/8/94) FL 100+5/22 FLC 7/1 FAC 5/4 Others 11/2
Lincoln C (Free on 8/8/97) FL 46+10/4 FLC 2 FAC 2 Others 2/1

MILLER Thomas (Tommy) William
Born: Easington, 8 January 1979
Height: 6'1" Weight: 11.12

The most successful of Hartlepool's recent youth-team products, this midfielder made great progress in 1998-99, not just winning a regular first-team place but also attracting the attention of bigger clubs, particularly Crystal Palace. A skilful player, good at bringing the ball forward, his game improved as he took on greater responsibilities, and he will have benefited greatly by playing alongside Peter Beardsley. Having had a memorable game against Preston in the Auto Windscreens Shield, scoring two goals and converting one of the deciding penalties, he has indicated his willingness to learn the game at Victoria Park by signing a new contract to the end of 2000-01.

Hartlepool U (From trainee on 8/7/97) FL 40+7/5 FLC 2 FAC 2/1 Others 3/2

MILLIGAN Jamie
Born: Blackpool, 3 January 1980
Height: 5'6" Weight: 9.12
Club Honours: FAYC '98
International Honours: E: Yth

Another product of Everton's highly successful youth academy, Jamie is a left-sided midfielder with a sweet left foot. After appearing several times in friendly internationals for Scotland, by virtue of his Scottish father, he appalled Walter Smith by opting for the lure of his native England to captain his country's U18s against Germany! The Toffees' manager, however, recoverd sufficiently to hand him several outings as a first-team substitute in 1998-99, and the youngster

looks set to enjoy a bright future in English football.

Everton (From trainee on 13/6/97) PL 0+3

MILLIGAN Michael (Mike) Joseph
Born: Manchester, 20 February 1967
Height: 5'8" Weight: 11.0
International Honours: Ei: 1; B-2; U23-1; U21-1

Early season injuries disrupted Mike's progress at Norwich in 1998-99, and he was placed on the transfer list in an attempt to revive his career. However, when called upon at either first or reserve-team level, this highly experienced midfielder never gave less than his best. A real enthusiast, who loves to be constantly involved in all the action, he is a tenacious tackler, uses the ball efficiently, and throughout his career has chipped in with some valuable goals.

Oldham Ath (From apprentice on 2/3/85) FL 161+1/17 FLC 19+1/1 FAC 12/1 Others 4
Everton (£1,000,000 on 24/8/90) FL 16+1/1 FLC 0+1 FAC 1 Others 4+1/1
Oldham Ath (£600,000 on 17/7/91) F/PL 117/6 FLC 11/1 FAC 9 Others 1/1
Norwich C (£800,000 on 27/6/94) P/FL 104+9/5 FLC 11+1 FAC 6

MILLS Daniel (Danny) John
Born: Norwich, 18 May 1977
Height: 5'11" Weight: 11.9
International Honours: E: U21-6; Yth

A strong and extremely fast right back or central defender, Danny was a regular member of the Charlton defence throughout last season, missing only two games. His commanding displays earning him a regular place in the England U21 side. Used as a right-wing back on occasions, with a penchant to get down the wing and get in telling crosses, he is not afraid to shoot, scoring one of Athletic's goals in the 4-2 defeat of West Ham at the Valley, and another from a free kick in the last minute to notch a 4-3 win at Villa Park. Good in the air, and a strong tackler, he is also the club's long-throw specialist. Stop Press: Was transferred to Leeds for £4 million on 15 June.

Norwich C (From trainee on 1/11/94) FL 46+20 FLC 3+2/1 FAC 2
Charlton Ath (£350,000 on 19/3/98) P/FL 45/3 FLC 3 FAC 1 Others 2

MILLS Daniel (Danny) Raymond
Born: Sidcup, 13 February 1975
Height: 6'0" Weight: 11.6

Signed during the summer of 1998 after being released by Barnet, Danny injured his knee in a pre-season friendly at Newcastle Town, which delayed his Brighton debut until late September. Able to play on either flank, and both pacy and tricky, he was transfer listed in November by Brian Horton after being sent off in a reserve game. Underwent groin surgery in the New Year, and was released at the end of the campaign.

Charlton Ath (From trainee on 1/7/93) Others 0+2
Barnet (Free on 29/9/95) FL 10+17 FLC 1 FAC 1+2 Others 0+1
Brighton & Hove A (Free on 3/7/98) FL 1+1

MILLS Rowan Lee
Born: Mexborough, 10 July 1970
Height: 6'1" Weight: 13.9

Signed from Port Vale at the beginning of last season, on a four-year contract, Lee became Bradford's first ever £1 million player. Starting late as a professional, after being turned down by both Sheffield clubs, Doncaster, Rotherham, and Barnsley, who said he would not make it, he proved them all wrong. Last season, having set himself the target of 20 goals, he easily beat that figure in his best ever campaign. It was not just his goalscoring that stood out, but also his brilliant defending when coming back for set pieces and corners. A non-stop worker in every game, and carrying a powerful shot in either foot from any distance or angle, he has become a real crowd pleaser at Valley Parade.

Wolverhampton W (Signed from Stocksbridge on 9/12/92) FL 12+13/2 FLC 1 FAC 3+1/1 Others 3/1
Derby Co (£400,000 on 24/2/95) FL 16/7
Port Vale (£200,000 on 1/8/95) FL 81+28/35 FLC 7+3/5 FAC 0+3 Others 6/4
Bradford C (£1,000,000 on 7/8/98) FL 44/23 FLC 4 FAC 2/1

MIMMS Robert (Bobby) Andrew
Born: York, 12 October 1963
Height: 6'3" Weight: 14.4
Club Honours: Div 1 '87; CS '87
International Honours: E: U21-3

Signed from Rotherham, the experienced 'keeper joined his hometown club, York, just after the start of the 1998-99 campaign.

Bobby Mimms

Still an excellent shot stopper, and agile for such a big man, he twice lost his senior place but returned in the closing weeks, giving some fine displays as City battled against relegation. Undertook some coaching duties in the second half of the season.
Halifax T (From apprentice on 5/8/81)
Rotherham U (£15,000 on 6/11/81) FL 83 FLC 7 FAC 3 Others 1
Everton (£150,000 on 30/5/85) FL 29 FLC 2 FAC 2 Others 4
Notts Co (Loaned on 13/3/86) FL 2 Others 1
Sunderland (Loaned on 11/12/86) FL 4
Blackburn Rov (Loaned on 23/1/87) FL 6
Manchester C (Loaned on 24/9/87) FL 3
Tottenham H (£325,000 on 25/2/88) FL 37 FLC 5 FAC 2
Aberdeen (Loaned on 16/2/90) SL 6 SC 2
Blackburn Rov (£250,000 on 22/12/90) F/PL 126+2 FLC 15 FAC 9 Others 4
Crystal Palace (Free on 30/8/96) FL 1
Preston NE (Free on 5/9/96) FL 27 FLC 2 FAC 2
Rotherham U (Free on 8/8/97) FL 43 FAC 4
York C (Signed on 14/8/98) FL 35 FLC 1 FAC 1 Others 1

MINTO Scott Christopher
Born: Heswall, 6 August 1971
Height: 5'9" Weight: 12.7
Club Honours: FAC '97
International Honours: E: U21-6; Yth
A left-sided player, who can play either as a wing-back or in a more defensive role, Scott joined West Ham from Benfica last January, having been with the Portuguese side since June 1997. Although he found the pace of the Premiership difficult at first, he soon settled, and was outstanding in a 1-0 win at his old club, Chelsea, a game which effectively finished off the Blues' championship hopes. Very fast, with good dribbling skills, and playing in 15 of the club's last 17 games, it was felt by the Upton Park faithful that, despite back-to-back defeats against Leeds and Everton at the end of the campaign, he was at last beginning to realise his undoubted talent.
Charlton Ath (From trainee on 2/2/89) FL 171+9/7 FLC 8/2 FAC 8+2 Others 7/1
Chelsea (£775,000 on 28/5/94) PL 53+1/4 FLC 3/1 FAC 9 Others 5+1 (Free to Benfica on 30/6/97)
West Ham U (£1,000,000 on 15/1/99) PL 14+1

MINTON Jeffrey (Jeff) Simon Thompson
Born: Hackney, 28 December 1973
Height: 5'6" Weight: 11.10
An enigmatic midfielder, and free-kick specialist, who is also Brighton's regular penalty taker, never having missed one for the Albion, it was once said that if Jeff played well then the side played well. Was among the leading scorers in 1998-99 until an ankle ligament injury in the televised match at Chester in January forced him to miss the next two months of the season. Reappeared after the transfer deadline had passed, and played until the end of the campaign without recapturing his early form. Named in the PFA Third Division team, he was offered a new contract by Micky Adams, but is more than likely to exercise the Bosman ruling to further his career elsewhere.
Tottenham H (From trainee on 11/1/92) FL 2/1 FLC 0+1
Brighton & Hove A (Free on 25/7/94) FL 167+7/31 FLC 12/1 FAC 7 Others 5

MIOTTO Simon Jonathan
Born: Australia, 5 September 1969
Height: 6'1" Weight: 13.3
An athletic goalkeeper signed by Hartlepool at the beginning of 1998-99, after missing out due to injury in a previous trial a year earlier, it had long been his ambition to become a professional footballer in England and, following a lengthy spell in the reserves, he got his chance when first-choice 'keeper, Martin Hollund, looked set to depart. A brave player, who was popular with supporters, he failed to make the position his own, and was soon back in the reserves before departing on 23 April, having received offers to play in Australia and Sweden.
Hartlepool U (Free from Riverside on 29/7/98) FL 5

MISKELLY David Thomas
Born: Newtonards, 3 September 1979
Height: 6'0" Weight: 12.9
International Honours: NI:
Having already represented his country at youth and U21 levels, Oldham feel they have a goalkeeper with a big, big future in front of him in David. With Gary Kelly unavailable, the youngster made his debut in a 1-1 draw at Reading last December and impressed. Strong in the air, and very agile, he commands the penalty area as if he owns it, and has excellent long kicking ability from both hands and feet. Watch out for him in 1999-2000.
Oldham Ath (From trainee on 1/7/97) FL 1

MITCHELL Graham Lee
Born: Shipley, 16 February 1968
Height: 6'1" Weight: 12.13

Jeff Minton

Starting slowly after joining Cardiff from Raith Rovers prior to the start of last season, Graham did not enjoy his stay in Scotland, but settled steadily with City and became their most consistent player in 1998-99. Always composed, and cool in possession, he made many crucial interceptions at the heart of the defence and was named the club's most improved player by supporters – at the age of 31. That was some tribute, and he earned it, having played exceptionally well after a rusty start with the Bluebirds.

Huddersfield T (From trainee on 16/6/86) FL 235+9/2 FLC 13+2/1 FAC 27/1 Others 24/1
Bournemouth (Loaned on 24/12/93) FL 4
Bradford C (Signed on 23/12/94) FL 64+1/1 FLC 8 FAC 2 Others 4
Raith Rov (Signed on 10/10/96) SL 22+1 SLC 0+1 SC 1 Others 0+1
Cardiff C (Free on 4/8/98) FL 46 FLC 2 FAC 5 Others 1

MOHAN Nicholas (Nicky)

Born: Middlesbrough, 6 October 1970
Height: 6'1" Weight: 14.0

Nicky started 1998-99 as Wycombe Wanderers' central defender, and was first choice until the turn of the year before becoming unsettled at the club after transfer speculation and a desire to move nearer to his family in Middlesbrough. He then arranged a move to Stoke on a free transfer and played his last game for Wycombe at the end of February. A strong physical presence, who is rarely beaten in the air, he had the height and strength that City were short of at the heart of their defence, and quickly showed his value to the fans. Known to the Stoke manager, Brian Little, from their days at Middlesbrough together, he made 15 starts out of a possible 16 and impressed.

Middlesbrough (From juniors on 18/11/87) F/PL 93+6/4 FLC 11 FAC 9+1 Others 11
Hull C (Loaned on 26/9/92) FL 5/1
Leicester C (£330,000 on 7/7/94) PL 23 FLC 2 FAC 1
Bradford C (£225,000 on 13/7/95) FL 83/4 FLC 8 FAC 5 Others 5
Wycombe W (Loaned on 14/8/97) FL 6
Wycombe W (£75,000 on 10/10/97) FL 52/2 FLC 3 FAC 4 Others 3
Stoke C (Free on 2/3/99) FL 15

MOILANEN Teuvo (Tepi) Johannes

Born: Oulu, Finland, 12 December 1973
Height: 6'5" Weight: 13.12
International Honours: Finland: 2

Ever present in Preston's goal in 1998-99 until injured at Northampton, the Finnish giant's fractured breastbone was slow to heal. Once fit again, however, David Lucas had staked his claim to a first-team spot, and Tepi had to settle for reserve football for the rest of the campaign. Obviously good on crosses because of his height, his groundwork showed great improvement before his injury, and he also made two tremendous saves in the penalty shoot-out against Grimsby in the Worthington Cup. Will be keenly contesting the starting spot with Lucas in the run-up to the coming season.

Preston NE (£120,000 from FF Jaro, via Ilves, on 12/12/95) FL 61 FLC 7 FAC 3 Others 1
Scarborough (Loaned on 12/12/96) FL 4
Darlington (Loaned on 17/1/97) FL 16

MOLENAAR Robert

Born: Zaandam, Holland, 27 February 1969
Height: 6'2" Weight: 14.4

A big, strong centre back, dubbed "The Terminator", Robert started last season in Leeds' first team and played consistently well. His reading of the game and cultured passing ability, typical of Dutch technique, combined with traditional defensive qualities, helped form a formidable partnership with Lucas Radebe, only one goal being conceded in the first six league games. Unfortunately, Robert suffered a serious cruciate injury at Highbury in December and, at the time of writing, was due to have his third operation after it snapped again. Not known when he will be able to return to action, it is a terrible blow to both player and club.

Leeds U (£1,000,000 from FC Volendam on 11/1/97) PL 47+4/5 FLC 4+1 FAC 5/1 Others 4

John Moncur

MONCUR John Frederick

Born: Stepney, 22 September 1966
Height: 5'7" Weight: 9.10

Although he did not play regularly in 1998-99, the West Ham midfielder could always be relied upon to do a good job. Has always possessed good passing skills, and last season saw him add more aggression to his play, which was evident in excellent displays against Liverpool and at Tottenham in April. At his best a player who could never get enough of the ball, and one who always made himself available by making space for himself.

Tottenham H (From apprentice on 22/8/84) FL 10+11/1 FLC 1+2
Doncaster Rov (Loaned on 25/9/86) FL 4
Cambridge U (Loaned on 27/3/87) FL 3+1
Portsmouth (Loaned on 22/3/89) FL 7
Brentford (Loaned on 19/10/89) FL 5/1 Others 1

Ipswich T (Loaned on 24/10/91) FL 5+1
Swindon T (£80,000 on 30/3/92) F/PL 53+5/5 FLC 4 FAC 1 Others 4/1
West Ham U (£900,000 on 24/6/94) PL 98+13/5 FLC 12/2 FAC 6+1/1

MONINGTON Mark David

Born: Bilsthorpe, 21 October 1970
Height: 6'1" Weight: 14.0
Club Honours: AMC '96

Rochdale's summer signing from Rotherham missed the first few games of 1998-99 though injury, but then quickly established himself alongside Keith Hill at the centre of the Dale's defence in place of the injured Alan Johnson. When Johnson was fit again, the club utilised all three of their experienced centre backs, and Mark starred in the centre-half role throughout the rest of the campaign with a succession of partners, despite three sendings off and three suspensions. His power in the air also brought him a useful return of goals at set pieces, including an extra-time "golden goal" winner at Halifax in the Auto Windscreens Shield. Was due to be out of contract during the summer, although the club have offered him terms of re-engagement.

Burnley (From juniors on 23/3/89) FL 65+19/5 FLC 5 FAC 4+1/1 Others 4+2
Rotherham U (Signed on 28/11/94) FL 75+4/3 FLC 3 FAC 1 Others 4
Rochdale (Free on 6/7/98) FL 37/3 FAC 4/1 Others 3/1

MONK Garry Alan

Born: Bedford, 6 March 1979
Height: 6'0" Weight: 13.0

Still a youngster, he appeared for Torquay in 1995-96 while on YTS forms before transferring his allegiance to Southampton at the end of that season. However, unable to break through at Premiership level, and with his former club in the midst of an injury crisis, the central defender went back to Plainmoor on loan last September and had an outstanding first game, at Halifax, when keeping the highly-rated Geoff Horsfield under wraps. Big, strong, and quick, he played six games before returning to the Dell and making his Premiership debut at Everton. Four more games followed, and he certainly looks to be one to watch out for.

Torquay U (Trainee) FL 4+1
Southampton (From trainee on 23/5/97) PL 4 FAC 0+1
Torquay U (Loaned on 25/9/98) FL 6

MONKHOUSE Andrew (Andy) William

Born: Leeds, 23 October 1980
Height: 6'1" Weight: 11.0

A highly skilful young player who will be one to watch in the future playing wide on the left, he marked his debut for Rotherham in 1998-99 as a substitute with a spectacular diving headed goal against Hartlepool in September. His only start was in the Auto Windscreens Shield, but he will surely get many opportunities, possibly this coming season.

Rotherham U (From trainee on 14/11/98) FL 0+5/1 FAC 0+1 Others 1

MONKOU Kenneth (Ken) John

Born: Surinam, 29 November 1964
Height: 6'3" Weight: 14.4
Club Honours: FMC '90
International Honours: Holland: U21

Despite missing half of last season's games due to niggling injuries, Ken had another outstanding campaign at the heart of Southampton's defence. Commanding in the air, strong on the ground, and a veteran of many successful relegation battles, he has been with Saints for seven years, having established a great partnership with Claus Lundekvam (when they are both available). Dangerous at corners, although his goals account shows just one to his credit in 1998-99, his presence often causes distraction in the opponent's penalty area, resulting in chances for others. Not only about defending, the man from Surinam is capable of hitting quality balls behind the opposing defence.

Chelsea (£100,000 from Feyenoord on 2/3/89) FL 92+2/2 FLC 12 FAC 3 Others 10
Southampton (£750,000 on 21/8/92) PL 190+8/10 FLC 18+1/2 FAC 16/1

MOODY Paul

Born: Portsmouth, 13 June 1967
Height: 6'3" Weight: 14.9

1998-99 was a dreadful season for "Moods" as he is popularly known at Fulham. After winning his place back, following a suspension carried over from the previous season, he sustained a broken leg in the home game against Stoke in early September. Having battled back to fitness, and having seven reserve outings, scoring twice, he was given a ten-minute spell in the penultimate game at Walsall. Then, with the final game at the Cottage against Preston scoreless at half time, Paul came off the bench to hit a 13-minute hat trick, including a penalty, and send the Fulham fans into raptures. On this form, he should have a big part to play in the coming season.

Southampton (£50,000 from Waterlooville on 15/7/91) F/PL 7+5 FLC 1 FAC 0+1
Reading (Loaned on 9/12/92) FL 5/1 Others 1
Oxford U (£60,000 on 19/2/94) FL 98+38/49 FLC 10+4/4 FAC 7+1/5 Others 3/3
Fulham (£200,000 on 4/7/97) FL 29+11/19 FLC 2+2 FAC 1+1 Others 2/1

MOONEY Thomas (Tommy) John

Born: Middlesbrough, 11 August 1971
Height: 5'10" Weight: 12.6
Club Honours: Div 2 '98

This valuable utility player has now made more than 300 league appearances for three different clubs. Able to play anywhere on the left side of the field, having played as part of a three-man defence in 1997-98, this time round he was mainly deployed as a striker, often coming on as substitute. Always a wholehearted performer, Watford's late push for a play-off place brought out the very best in him, and when injuries gave him a regular place in the starting line-up he responded with seven goals in six games to confirm his standing as the darling of the terraces. It was the first time for 48 years that a Watford player had scored in six consecutive league matches.

Aston Villa (From trainee on 23/11/89)
Scarborough (Free on 1/8/90) FL 96+11/30 FLC 11+2/8 FAC 3 Others 6/2
Southend U (£100,000 on 12/7/93) FL 9+5/5 FLC 1+1 Others 2+3
Watford (Signed on 17/3/94) FL 175+24/39 FLC 16/1 FAC 10+1/1 Others 4

Tommy Mooney

MOORE Alan

Born: Dublin, 25 November 1974
Height: 5'10" Weight: 11.4
Club Honours: Div 1 '95
International Honours: Ei: 8; U21-4; Yth; Sch

Alan's early promise at Middlesbrough has never really materialised, owing mainly to injuries and form lapses striking at the same time that other squad members peaked. His pace and skill are, and always have been, beyond reproach and, like his dedication, they leave nothing to be desired. He continued to win rave notices aplenty for his outstanding performances in the reserves who, courtesy of himself, enjoyed a super season in 1998-99, but in the Premiership he seems unable to rekindle the vital spark that makes the difference between winning and being an also ran. The real tragedy lies in the fact that in the past he has done it, running strongly, at rock-solid defences, jinking his way through to deliver telling passes, or unleashing powerful goal-bound missiles. Had a month on loan at Barnsley in October and November, his ball skills and ability to beat his man, making him an instant hit. However, although a permanent transfer was a real possibility, a change in the system to the team meant that as a natural left winger he was surplus to requirements, and he returned to the Riverside without delay.

Middlesbrough (From trainee on 5/12/91) F/PL 98+20/14 FLC 9+6/1 FAC 3+2/2 Others 3+1
Barnsley (Loaned on 30/10/98) FL 4+1

MOORE Craig Andrew

Born: Canterbury, Australia, 12 December 1975
Height: 6'1" Weight: 12.0
Club Honours: SPD '95, '96, '97; SLC '97
International Honours: Australia: 7

Craig turned out to be Terry Venables' best signing for Crystal Palace in 1998-99, after arriving from Glasgow Rangers in October. Another Australian international, the left-sided central defender made his debut in a 5-1 home win over Norwich, having replaced Dave Tuttle, and immediately impressed with his strength and tackling, allied to aerial ability. He also showed that he knew where the goal was, scoring three times in his first five games. Apart from missing a handful of matches, he was a regular, and it was a real blow when he was forced to return to Rangers at the end of March when the transfer fee was not forthcoming.

Glasgow R (Free from Australian Institute of Sport on 16/9/93) SL 68+6/5 SLC 8+1 SC 8+1 Others 13
Crystal Palace (£800,000 on 15/10/98) FL 23/3 FAC 1

MOORE Darren Mark

Born: Birmingham, 22 April 1974
Height: 6'2" Weight: 15.6

Bradford's "Bruno" is now playing the best football of his career. After the previous injury-hit campaign, he was the rock on which the whole defence was built on in 1998-99, despite him having three different centre-back partners. Showing great confidence in every game he played, his distribution came on in leaps and bounds, thus remedying an earlier weakness. Loves nothing better than to go on a run, and just charges through the opposition to have a shot or lay it off to one of his team mates. At the other end of the park, he does not mess about in the area, getting the ball away quickly, and is a tremendous tackler. Was selected by his fellow professionals for the award-winning PFA First Division side.

Torquay U (From trainee on 18/11/92) FL 102+1/8 FLC 6 FAC 7/2 Others 8/2
Doncaster Rov (£62,500 on 19/7/95) FL 76/7 FLC 4 FAC 1 Others 3/1
Bradford C (£310,000 + on 18/6/97) FL 62/3 FLC 5/1 FAC 2

MOORE Ian Ronald

Born: Birkenhead, 26 August 1976
Height: 5'11" Weight: 12.0
International Honours: E: U21-7; Yth

Strikers are ultimately judged on the number of goals they score and, although Ian enjoyed great form for much of last season, his goal tally of four was a disappointment. Signed from Nottingham Forest during the summer of 1998, he played with the burden of being Stockport's record signing by a long way. With pace in abundance, and creating a number of goals for strike partner, Brett Angell, he was employed out wide on the right as a winger towards the end of the campaign.

Tranmere Rov (From trainee on 6/7/94) FL 41+17/12 FLC 3+2/1 FAC 1+1 Others 0+1
Bradford C (Loaned on 13/9/96) FL 6
Nottingham F (£1,000,000 on 15/3/97) F/PL 3+12/1 FLC 0+2 FAC 1
West Ham U (Loaned on 26/9/97) PL 0+1
Stockport Co (£800,000 on 31/7/98) FL 32+6/3 FLC 2/1 FAC 2

MOORE Neil
Born: Liverpool, 21 September 1972
Height: 6'1" Weight: 12.9
After a promising first season at Turf Moor, Neil had a disappointing 1998-99 for Burnley. A knee injury ruled him out between September and January, and his comeback was relatively brief before suspension and then another injury effectively ended his season. Effective in central defence, he looked a fish out of water at right back where he was more often than not used during the campaign, before being released in the summer.
Everton (From trainee on 4/6/91) PL 4+1 FLC 0+1
Blackpool (Loaned on 9/9/94) FL 7 Others 1
Oldham Ath (Loaned on 16/2/95) FL 5
Carlisle U (Loaned on 25/8/95) FL 13 Others 2
Rotherham U (Loaned on 20/3/96) FL 10+1
Norwich C (Free on 8/1/97) FL 2
Burnley (Free on 29/8/97) FL 48+4/3 FLC 3+1 FAC 2/1 Others 4

MORALEE Jamie David
Born: Wandsworth, 2 December 1971
Height: 5'11" Weight: 11.0
Joining Brighton last August after a spell with Royal Antwerp of Belgium, Jamie was a regular choice at first, playing behind the front two of Richie Barker and Gary Hart, but was unable to score his first goal until 17 October in the 3-1 home defeat by Mansfield. Initially having a monthly contract, which was extended to the end of the season in December, he was relegated to the bench for much of the second half of the campaign, and became an Albion record-breaker when he was sent off just 90 seconds after coming on as a substitute at Scunthorpe. Stop Press: Although offered a new contract at the end of the season, he is believed to be joining Colchester United under the Bosman ruling.
Crystal Palace (From trainee on 3/7/90) FL 2+4
Millwall (Free on 3/9/92) FL 56+11/19 FLC 3+1/1 FAC 1 Others 3+1
Watford (£450,000 on 13/7/94) FL 40+9/7 FLC 6+1 FAC 5
Crewe Alex (Free on 8/8/96) FL 10+6 FLC 1+1 FAC 2 (Free to Royal Antwerp on 9/3/98)
Brighton & Hove A (Free on 10/8/98) FL 22+9/3 FLC 2 FAC 0+1 Others 1/1

MORGAN Alan Meredith
Born: Aberystwyth, 2 November 1973
Height: 5'10" Weight: 11.4
International Honours: W: U21-2; Yth; Sch
Alan endured a wretched, injury-wracked season at Tranmere in 1998-99, which prevented him from getting any sort of consistent first-team run, and just as he seemed to be getting himself back to full match fitness through the Pontins League team, he had the misfortune to tear a calf muscle which put him out of action until the coming term. A versatile performer who is as tricky as anyone on his day, he can play in virtually any outfield position, and must be hoping for better luck soon.
Tranmere Rov (From trainee on 8/5/92) FL 18+12/1 FLC 1+2 FAC 2

MORGAN Christopher (Chris) Paul
Born: Barnsley, 9 November 1977
Height: 5'10" Weight: 12.9
This local born defender was always fully committed to the cause of Barnsley in 1998-99. Good in the air, and exceptionally strong in the tackle, unfortunately he found himself to be a marked man with the referees, and looks to channel his natural aggression a little more carefully in the coming campaign. Is a great favourite with the crowd who, given a regular run in the side, could still go to the top.
Barnsley (From trainee on 3/7/96) P/FL 28+2 FLC 3 FAC 4

MORGAN Simon Charles
Born: Birmingham, 5 September 1966
Height: 5'10" Weight: 12.5
Club Honours: Div 2 '99
International Honours: E: U21-2
Nobody contributed more in 1998-99 to Fulham's first championship for 50 years than "Mr Fulham" himself. Playing in a back three between Kit Symons and Chris Coleman, "Morgs" was superb, and he also netted eight of the 23 goals the trio contributed to the Fulham cause. Strong in the tackle, being a motivator by deed, it is doubtful if he has ever played better in his nine years at the Cottage, and will relish the challenge of Division One football.
Leicester C (From apprentice on 15/11/84) FL 147+13/3 FLC 14/1 FAC 4+1 Others 3
Fulham (£100,000 on 12/10/90) FL 317+7/48 FLC 28/2 FAC 17/3 Others 17/4

MORGAN Stephen (Steve) Alphonso
Born: Oldham, 19 September 1968
Height: 5'11" Weight: 11.8
Club Honours: Div 3 '97
International Honours: E: Yth
Signed during the 1998 close season from Wigan by Burnley's new manager, Stan Ternent, Steve began 1998-99 as first-choice left back and, injury absence apart, remained there until the loan signing of Tom Cowan in March. While occasionally dangerous when pushing forward into midfield, he too often seemed a weak link in a defence that had its problems anyway, and was released during the summer.
Blackpool (From apprentice on 12/8/86) FL 135+9/10 FLC 13/2 FAC 16/1 Others 10+1/1
Plymouth Arg (£115,000 on 16/7/90) FL 120+1/6 FLC 7 FAC 6 Others 5
Coventry C (£110,000 on 14/7/93) PL 65+3/2 FLC 5/3 FAC 5
Bristol Rov (Loaned on 1/3/96) FL 5 Others 2
Wigan Ath (Free on 10/7/96) FL 31+5/2 FLC 2 FAC 1 Others 4
Bury (Loaned on 26/9/97) FL 5
Burnley (Free on 7/8/98) FL 17 FLC 2 FAC 1

MORLEY Benjamin (Ben)
Born: Hull, 22 December 1980
Height: 5'9" Weight: 10.1
Ben made national headlines last December when hitting a superb goal for Hull in the FA Cup at Luton to set up a money-spinning tie at Aston Villa, making his first-ever appearance as a forward at the age of 17. Usually seen at right-wing back, the former star of Hull schools Rugby League

side was rewarded with a two-and-a-half year pro contract months before the completion of his YTS. His progress is said to have already been monitored by a number of leading clubs.
Hull C (From trainee on 10/12/98) FL 6+14 FLC 1+1 FAC 2/1 Others 1+1

MORLEY David Thomas
Born: St Helens, 25 September 1977
Height: 6'2" Weight: 12.7
Having followed his team mate, Martyn Margetson, to Southend early last season, this tall and elegant centre half's skills were immediately in evidence after he signed from Manchester City. Strong in the air, and comfortable on the ground, David paid for the team's poor performances, being "banished" by manager Alvin Martin, before the latter's resignation saw his return to the side. Although not looking as polished as previous, he still showed some of the skills that will keep him in new manager Alan Little's thoughts for the coming campaign.
Manchester C (From trainee on 3/1/96) FL 1+2/1
Ayr U (Loaned on 14/3/98) SL 4
Southend U (Signed on 28/8/98) FL 26+1 FLC 2 FAC 0+1

MORRELL Andrew (Andy) Jonathan
Born: Doncaster, 28 September 1974
Height: 5'11" Weight: 12.0
A late starter in the game, Andy made his full football league debut for Wrexham at Millwall – in the same week he signed his first professional contract – the team suffering a 3-0 defeat last March. Initially, football was a part-time pursuit for Andy, who played at weekends for Newcastle Blue Star in the Northern League, while also graduating with a degree in sports studies at Newcastle University. After completing his course, he obtained employment as a fitness instructor in Leeds, but although getting on a bit in football terms, a chance meeting with Rob McCaffrey (a reporter with a satellite TV company) resulted in him making contact with a certain Joey Jones on Wrexham's coaching staff. Impressive displays with the reserves saw him develop a good understanding with another post graduate, Jake Edwards, with a reward of a contract until the end of 1999-2000. Is a player who shows keen awareness and movement off the ball, and chases lost causes, hoping to get on the end of things.
Wrexham (Free from Newcastle Blue Star on 18/12/98) FL 4+3 Others 0+1

MORRIS Andrew (Andy) Dean
Born: Sheffield, 17 November 1967
Height: 6'4" Weight: 15.12
Having made a welcome return to Chesterfield's first team as a substitute at Fulham last November, the long-serving centre forward joined Rochdale to give them some physical presence up front. Once he gained match fitness, after 18 months out of first-team action, he proved an awkward handful for opposition defenders, and in one spell scored four times in six games. Late in the season, he hit a crucial winner against Southend after Dale looked like they might

be dragged into the relegation dog-fight, and then netted a brilliant hat trick in the space of 25 minutes to beat Chester. Finished the campaign as the club's joint-top scorer.

Rotherham U (From juniors on 29/7/85) FL 0+7 FLC 0+1
Chesterfield (Signed on 12/1/88) FL 225+41/56 FLC 15+2/8 FAC 15+2/4 Others 18+4/3
Exeter C (Loaned on 4/3/92) FL 4+3/2
Rochdale (Free on 23/12/98) FL 25/7 Others 3/1

Jody Morris

MORRIS Jody Steven
Born: Hammersmith, 22 December 1978
Height: 5'5" Weight: 10.12
Club Honours: ECWC '98
International Honours: E: U21-6; Yth; Sch

Jody blossomed into a top-class Premiership midfield player during 1998-99, fulfilling his enormous potential, and looking comfortable alongside Chelsea's galaxy of international midfielders. Confident, and assured on the ball, he played a vital role for the Blues during the long absences of Gus Poyet and Dennis Wise, and his industry and workrate were appreciated by fans and team mates alike. Scored his first goal of the season in Chelsea's 25th Premiership match of the season, against Blackburn Rovers at the Bridge – incredibly, the first by an English-born Chelsea player! Earlier, concerned by his lack of first-team outings he contemplated a loan move to enhance his career, until reassured by Gianluca Vialli that he had a big part to play at the club. In hindsight, that proved to be a shrewd decision, and towards the end of the season he was deservedly awarded a new five-year contract. Played three times for the England U21 side during the campaign.

Chelsea (From trainee on 8/1/96) PL 29+14/2 FLC 5/2 FAC 5 Others 3+2

MORRIS Lee
Born: Blackpool, 30 April 1980
Height: 5'10" Weight: 11.2
International Honours: E: U21-1; Yth

Having had an impressive pre-1998-99 season, a stress fracture of the foot sustained whilst training with the England U18 squad, kept Lee out of the Sheffield United side until mid December. After eight sub appearances, he made his first start at Crewe at the end of January, followed by some impressive performances both on the left and up front, his speed, ball control, and quick thinking producing goals for others as well as for himself. His goal against West Bromwich was particularly memorable. Having played for the U18s in March, and signing a contract until 2002, former Blade, Keith Edwards, rates Lee as a natural striker – and he should know. Was selected for the England U21 side that played Bulgaria in the last fixture of the season.

Sheffield U (From trainee on 24/12/97) FL 14+11/6 FAC 2+5/2 Others 0+1

MORRIS Stewart Ian
Born: Newcastle, 21 September 1980
Height: 5'10" Weight: 11.10

A pacy young Scarborough trainee striker, and a prolific marksman for the club's youth team for a couple of seasons (23 goals in 1997-98), Stewart made his senior bow in the FA Cup at Rochdale last November when coming off the bench for the last six minutes and being booked. Despite the club being relegated to the Conference, he was due to sign pro forms in the summer.

Scarborough (Trainee) FAC 0+1

MORRISON Andrew (Andy) Charles
Born: Inverness, 30 July 1970
Height: 6'0" Weight: 14.8

Having come to Manchester City at the end of last October, initially on loan from Huddersfield Town, Andy made his debut at home against Colchester, his presence making such a difference in a 2-1 win. Big and solid, and a player who can compete with the strongest strikers in football, it was a very impressive debut, climaxing with him scoring the winning goal, a powerful header from a corner. In the following game, at Oldham, he scored again, this time a 30-yard rocket contributing to an impressive 3-0 win. This prompted Joe Royle to sign him permanently at a real bargain price and, with Gerard Wiekens, he went on to set up one of the best defensive duos in the Second Division. Because of his thick build and style of play, physical but not intimidating, he picked up a number of yellow cards, including one red card at Wimbledon in the FA Cup, which meant him missing vital games. That aside, he is an important player in central defence, his timing to reach high balls to head clear being so accurate.

Plymouth Arg (From trainee on 6/7/88) FL 105+8/6 FLC 10+1/1 FAC 6 Others 2+1
Blackburn Rov (£500,000 on 5/8/93) PL 1+4 FAC 1
Blackpool (£245,000 on 9/12/94) FL 47/3 FAC 2 Others 4
Huddersfield T (£500,000 on 4/7/96) FL 43+2/2 FLC 8 FAC 2
Manchester C (£80,000 on 29/10/98) FL 21+1/4 FAC 4 Others 1

Clint Morrison

MORRISON Clinton (Clint) Hubert
Born: Wandsworth, 14 May 1979
Height: 6'1" Weight: 11.2

Showing some of the qualities that drew obvious comparisons with Ian Wright, the young striker made the most of his chances at Crystal Palace in 1998-99. An exciting young player, as many of the big names left due to the club's financial plight, he moved on from being a regular on the bench to that of a regular in the starting line-up, and eventually becoming the club's leading scorer for the campaign. With good first touch to go with his speed off the mark, he holds play up well to bring other players in to danger areas, and is always looking to lose his marker when twisting and turning around the box.

Crystal Palace (From trainee on 29/3/97) P/FL 27+11/13 FLC 1+2/1 FAC 1

MORRISON David (Dave) Ellis
Born: Waltham Forest, 30 November 1974
Height: 5'11" Weight: 12.10

Dave returned to the Leyton Orient team in 1998-99 after his injury nightmare of the previous season. Still an excellent crosser of the ball, who added vital goals to his armoury this time round – scoring in a 1-1 draw at Swansea, the 90th-minute winner at home to Carlisle, another in a 4-3 win over Plymouth at Brisbane Road, and one of the penalties that took Orient to Wembley. Despite being used mainly as a winger, he also filled in at left back during the campaign, and had loan spells at Boreham Wood and St Albans in mid season. Out of contract during the summer, at the time of going to press the club had offered him terms of re-engagement.

Peterborough U (£30,000 from Chelmsford C on 12/5/94) FL 59+18/12 FLC 4+1/1 FAC 5+3 Others 6+2
Leyton Orient (£25,000 on 21/3/97) FL 16+17/3 FLC 1+3 FAC 1 Others 1+1

MORRISON John **Owen**
Born: Londonderry, 8 December 1981
Height: 5'8" Weight: 11.12
International Honours: NI: Yth; Sch
Although he signed professional forms a few weeks later this young trainee striker appeared almost from nowhere to make his first-team debut for Sheffield Wednesday at Hillsbrough against Leicester as a substitute, on Boxing Day 1998. Not very tall, but quite pacy, something the Owls were desperately short of at the time, he could be one for the future. When being called up for the Leicester game, Owen had yet to play for the reserves, being confined to the juniors, and there is no doubting that Danny Wilson sees him as a real talent and a star in the making.
Sheffield Wed (From trainee on 5/1/99) PL 0+1

MORRISSEY John **Joseph**
Born: Liverpool, 8 March 1965
Height: 5'8" Weight: 11.9
International Honours: E: Yth
As Tranmere's longest-serving player, and considered something of a veteran, John began most of his matches in 1998-99 on the bench, and could no longer consider himself a first-team regular for the Birkenhead club. Loves to operate on the wing, and always gave 100 per cent when called upon to try and add an extra dimension to Rovers' play, his skills still winning some valuable points. With his old-fashioned wide play, and willingness to take on and pass an opposing defender, there are still few more able to hold up the ball in a tight corner. Released on a free transfer at the end of last season, John, the son of the former Everton player of the 1960s (John senior), was due to don the number seven jersey for his well-deserved testimonial game against Everton in July 1999.
Everton (From apprentice on 10/3/83) FL 1 Others 0+1
Wolverhampton W (Free on 2/8/85) FL 5+5/1 FLC 1
Tranmere Rov (£8,000 on 2/10/85) FL 396+74/50 FLC 39+4/2 FAC 28+3/5 Others 39+3/6

MORROW Stephen (Steve) **Joseph**
Born: Bangor, 2 July 1970
Height: 6'0" Weight: 11.6
Club Honours: FAYC '88; FLC '93; ECEC '94
International Honours: NI: 37; B-1; U23-2; Yth; Sch
Steve was unable to gain Queens Park Rangers selection under the Ray Harford regime, and therefore started 1998-99 in the reserves. However, following the arrival of Gerry Francis, he moved from defence to midfield with great success, regaining the respect of the fans who had not really taken to him in his first season at the club. Due to injuries to the regular central defenders, he moved back to the defence, playing with renewed confidence despite missing several games after sustaining an injury against Watford in February. Although not a regular in the early part of the term, he retained his place in the Northern Ireland squad, and played in all of their Euro 2000 qualification matches.

Arsenal (From trainee on 5/5/88) F/PL 39+23/1 FLC 7+4/2 FAC 5+2 Others 1+4
Reading (Loaned on 16/1/91) FL 10
Watford (Loaned on 14/8/91) FL 7+1 Others 1
Reading (Loaned on 30/10/91) FL 3
Barnet (Loaned on 4/3/92) FL 1
Queens Park R (£1,000,000 on 27/3/97) FL 60/2 FLC 2 FAC 2

MORTIMER Paul **Henry**
Born: Kensington, 8 May 1968
Height: 5'11" Weight: 12.7
International Honours: E: U21-2
Another frustrating season for Paul, who was forced to miss the bulk of 1998-99 through injury. An extremely gifted left-sided midfield player, who when fit is undoubtedly the most skilful player at Charlton, he is comfortable on the ball, has good vision, and can pass with pin-point accuracy. He also has the ability to go past several players and score spectacular goals, which he did at Elland Road against Leeds, in what was probably the club's best goal of the campaign. Released during the summer, he can also play in defence if required, although he has rarely been used in this position in recent times.
Charlton Ath (Free from Farnborough T on 22/9/87) FL 108+5/17 FLC 4+1 FAC 8 Others 3+1
Aston Villa (£350,000 on 24/7/91) FL 10+2/1 FLC 2
Crystal Palace (£500,000 on 18/10/91) F/PL 18+4/2 FLC 1 FAC 1 Others 3
Brentford (Loaned on 22/1/93) FL 6 Others 2
Charlton Ath (£200,000 on 5/7/94) P/FL 67+19/15 FLC 4+1/1 FAC 3/1 Others 0+1

MOSES Adrian **Paul**
Born: Doncaster, 4 May 1975
Height: 5'10" Weight: 12.8
International Honours: E: U21-2
A solid Barnsley defender who never gives less than 100 per-cent effort, relegation from the Premiership in 1997-98 seemed to dent his confidence, and he took time to settle back into the demands of the First Division last season. Yet another player who was disrupted by the defensive line constantly being changed, at his brightest he is strong in the tackle, very quick, and can be used reliably as an effective man marker.
Barnsley (From juniors on 2/7/93) F/PL 114+11/3 FLC 9 FAC 15

MOSS Darren **Michael**
Born: Wrexham, 24 May 1981
Height: 5'10" Weight: 11.0
International Honours: W: Yth
Still a trainee, this 18-year-old product of Chester's youth policy made seven senior appearances last season, most of them in the right-back position. A creative ball player, and one to look out for in the future, the highlight of Darren's campaign was in being selected to represent Wales at U18 level in a youth tournament in Italy.
Chester C (Trainee) FL 5+2

MOSS Neil **Graham**
Born: New Milton, 10 May 1975
Height: 6'2" Weight: 13.10
Young Southampton goalkeeper who, in three-and-a-half years at the club, had only played three league games before last

season. Although deputising for Paul Jones in one game early on, a 3-0 defeat at Leeds, when Saints signed Michael Stensgaard from FC Copenhagen he was relegated to third choice, and was not expected to see further action for the time being. However, when Paul Jones suffered a back injury on international duty for Wales he was suddenly elevated to the first team, and played in all but the last two matches, while giving a very good account of himself, especially when keeping a clean sheet in the home draw with Arsenal.
Bournemouth (From trainee on 29/1/93) FL 21+1 FLC 1 FAC 3+1 Others 2
Southampton (£250,000 on 20/12/95) PL 10 FLC 2
Gillingham (Loaned on 8/8/97) FL 10 FLC 2

MOUNTFIELD Derek **Neal**
Born: Liverpool, 2 November 1962
Height: 6'1" Weight: 13.6
Club Honours: FAC '84; CS '84, '85; Div 1 '85, '87, Div 3 '95; ECWC '85
International Honours: E: B-1; U21-1
Released by Walsall during the 1998 close season, Derek signed for non-league Bromsgrove prior to coming back into the league with Scarborough as a non-contract player early last January. A veteran central defender, he started with six early games, and also helped out with the coaching at the club, before having a brief spell as the caretaker manager when Mick Wadsworth resigned to take over at Colchester. However, with Boro relegated to the Conference, he moved on during the summer.
Tranmere Rov (From apprentice on 4/11/80) FL 26/1 FLC 2 FAC 1
Everton (£30,000 on 2/6/82) FL 100+6/19 FLC 16/3 FAC 17/2 Others 14+1/1
Aston Villa (£450,000 on 6/6/88) FL 88+2/9 FLC 13/2 FAC 6/1 Others 11/5
Wolverhampton W (£150,000 on 7/11/91) FL 79+4/4 FLC 4/1 FAC 2 Others 2
Carlisle U (Free on 3/8/94) FL 30+1/3 FLC 4+1 FAC 4/1 Others 6/1
Northampton T (Free on 6/10/95) FL 4
Walsall (Free on 6/11/95) FL 96+1/2 FLC 8 FAC 9+1 Others 4 (Free to Bromsgrove during 1998 close season)
Scarborough (Free on 4/1/99) FL 5+1

MOWBRAY Anthony (Tony) **Mark**
Born: Saltburn, 22 November 1963
Height: 6'1" Weight: 13.2
International Honours: E: B-2
As Ipswich's club captain, Tony had a much better season in 1998-99, injury wise, although he did miss most of September. Again leading the side by example, he was a valuable member of the defence that equalled the club record of 26 clean sheets in a season. And, despite his advancing years, he was still a commanding figure in the centre of the Town defence, winning most of the aerial challenges when using his experience to anticipate how the play would develop, in making up for a lack of pace. Scored two goals, at Bury and Swindon, both resulting from corners, and came a close second to Jamie Clapham in the supporters' "Player of the Year" poll.
Middlesbrough (From apprentice on

27/11/81) FL 345+3/25 FLC 28+2/2 FAC 23/1 Others 23+1/1
Glasgow C (£1,000,000 on 8/11/91) SL 75+3/6 SLC 7 SC 5 Others 6
Ipswich T (£300,000 on 6/10/95) FL 90+2/4 FLC 7/1 FAC 8 Others 5/1

Carl Muggleton

MUGGLETON Carl David
Born: Leicester, 13 September 1968
Height: 6'2" Weight: 13.4
International Honours: E: U21-1
Carl opened last season in fine form, fully recovered from the finger injury that plagued him towards the end of the previous campaign, and played a key role in the early run that saw Stoke top the table almost exclusively until December. As the team's results turned the 'keeper lost a little confidence, and to bring competition for places Brian Little signed Gavin Ward, who went straight into the side. However, a groin injury to Ward saw Carl restored and back to his best form before the final whistle.
Leicester C (From apprentice on 17/9/86) FL 46 FAC 3 Others 5
Chesterfield (Loaned on 10/9/87) FL 17 Others 2
Blackpool (Loaned on 1/2/88) FL 2
Hartlepool U (Loaned on 28/10/88) FL 8 Others 2
Stockport Co (Loaned on 1/3/90) FL 4
Stoke C (Loaned on 13/8/93) FL 6 FLC 1 Others 2
Glasgow C (£150,000 on 11/1/94) SL 12 SC 1
Stoke C (£150,000 on 21/7/94) FL 137 FLC 14 FAC 3 Others 6
Rotherham U (Loaned on 1/11/95) FL 6 Others 1
Sheffield U (Loaned on 28/3/96) FL 0+1

MULLIN John Michael
Born: Bury, 11 August 1975
Height: 6'0" Weight: 11.10
The Sunderland striker has endured mixed fortunes in his four years at the club and last season was another combination of highs and lows. The tall, strong-running front man

was employed as an attacking midfielder, following Lee Clark's opening day injury, and took to his new position with aplomb, scoring in victories over Tranmere and Ipswich, after arriving in the box with perfect timing on both occasions. However, a groin injury sustained at Crewe in November consigned him to a lengthy spell on the treatment table, and effectively ended his first-team involvement for the campaign. And, with Peter Reid due to add to his squad in the summer, John was released.
Burnley (From trainee on 18/8/92) FL 7+11/2 FAC 2
Sunderland (£40,000 + on 12/8/95) P/FL 23+12/4 FLC 5+1 FAC 2+1
Preston NE (Loaned on 13/2/98) FL 4+3 Others 1
Burnley (Loaned on 26/3/98) FL 6

MULLINS Hayden Ian
Born: Reading, 27 March 1979
Height: 6'0" Weight: 11.12
International Honours: E: U21-3
Hayden was thought to be the most improved player at Crystal Palace in 1998-99, and justifiably won the club's "Player of the Year" award. Having given a good performance in the Inter Toto Cup in July 1998, he made his first-team debut on the opening day of the season at Selhurst Park against Bolton, before scoring his first senior goal in a 3-1 defeat at Birmingham, two games later. Although capable of playing in midfield, where his passing and good control stand out, his best position was found to be that of a sweeper, his coolness under pressure being excellent. His promise was eventually recognised at England U21 international level, and he made his debut when coming on for Frank Lampard in the 5-0 win over Poland.
Crystal Palace (From trainee on 28/2/97) FL 38+2/5 FLC 4 FAC 1

MULRYNE Phillip Patrick
Born: Belfast, 1 January 1978
Height: 5'8" Weight: 10.11
Club Honours: FAYC '95
International Honours: NI: 5; B-1; U21-3
Having already made full and U21 appearances for Northern Ireland in 1998-99, Phillip joined Norwich in transfer deadline week – a knock-down price for such a promising youngster. A highly talented midfielder whose senior opportunities at Old Trafford had been severely limited by the likes of Roy Keane, Nicky Butt, Paul Scholes and David Beckham, his range of passing was excellent, and he obviously possesses the vision to deliver those passes too. He also likes to dictate the pattern of play, and is always available to receive a pass. Something of a dead-ball specialist, he scored on his full debut for City, at Grimsby, last April.
Manchester U (From trainee on 17/3/95) PL 1 FLC 3 FAC 0+1
Norwich C (£500,000 on 25/3/99) FL 6+1/2

MURDOCK Colin James
Born: Ballymena, 2 July 1975
Height: 6'2" Weight: 13.0
International Honours: NI: B-3; Yth; Sch

Colin had a tremendous start to the 1998-99 season on the left side of Preston's central defence at Grimsby in the first round of the Worthington Cup, but was unable to claim a regular starting place, despite being called up by Northern Ireland's "B" squad. Particularly strong in the air, he came back well after being recalled following Ryan Kidd's injury problems, and found the consistency he had lacked earlier on, also scoring his first goal for 18 months into the bargain. He will be hoping to make further progress in the coming campaign, for both club and country.
Manchester U (From juniors on 21/7/92)
Preston NE (£100,000 on 23/5/97) FL 55+5/2 FLC 3 FAC 3+1 Others 6

MURPHY Daniel (Danny) Benjamin
Born: Chester, 18 March 1977
Height: 5'9" Weight: 10.8
International Honours: E: U21-2; Yth; Sch
An indefatigable midfield dynamo, Danny was restricted to just a few appearances for Liverpool in 1998-99, due to competition for places, and arrived at Crewe, his old team, on an extended loan in February. Starting the last 16 games of a tough campaign in which Alex were among the favourites for the drop into the Second Division, it was as if he had never been away, and he opened the scoring in a 3-1 home win over Oxford in his sixth match. A central midfielder who works hard and scores goals and, apart from his spell at Crewe, shone for the Reds' reserves, he looks forward to holding down a more regular place at Anfield in 1999-2000.
Crewe Alex (From trainee on 21/3/94) FL 110+24/27 FLC 7 FAC 7/4 Others 15+3/3
Liverpool (£1,500,000 + on 17/7/97) PL 6+11 FLC 1+1 FAC 0+1 Others 0+1
Crewe Alex (Loaned on 12/2/99) FL 16/1

MURPHY James (Jamie) Anthony
Born: Manchester, 25 February 1973
Height: 6'1" Weight: 13.10
Jamie had a stop-start season for Halifax in 1998-99 after forcing his way into the first team in October. Unfortunately, owing to a back injury he was forced to miss most of the second half of the campaign, and was put on the transfer list in March. A central defender who likes to get forward, he soon reappeared at right back in the absence of Andy Thackeray later that month.
Blackpool (From juniors on 23/8/90) FL 48+7/1 FLC 4/1 FAC 3 Others 2+3
Doncaster Rov (Free on 14/9/95) FL 47+7 FLC 2 FAC 1 Others 2
Halifax T (Free on 19/3/97) FL 21+2/1 FAC 1 Others 1

MURPHY John James
Born: Whiston, 18 October 1976
Height: 6'2" Weight: 14.0
The target of several bids on transfer deadline day last March, John is a tall central striker who is now in his fifth season at Chester, having initially come through the youth system. Although injuries have limited his games in previous terms, in 1998-99 he made 42 league appearances, scoring 12 goals, in what turned out to be his

best season for the club. Towards the end of the campaign, he formed a good partnership with Luke Beckett, which the club will be looking to continue into 1998-2000.
Chester C (From trainee on 6/7/95) FL 65+38/20 FLC 6+3/1 FAC 1+2 Others 3+1

MURPHY Matthew (Matt) Simon
Born: Northampton, 20 August 1971
Height: 6'0" Weight: 12.2
Matt had a good season, games wise, for Oxford in 1998-99, and was the second-top scorer after the departed Dean Windass, with eight goals. Three of those came in the first two games of the campaign when he was pushed up front, indeed most of his games were as a striker or just behind them in an attacking midfield role. Netted a brace at Crewe, but only scored twice at home, with another vital goal being a winner at Birmingham in a 1-0 success. Was released during the summer.
Oxford U (£20,000 from Corby T on 12/2/93) FL 85+75/21 FLC 4+8/4 FAC 5+3/2 Others 3+3/3
Scunthorpe U (Loaned on 12/12/97) FL 1+2 Others 1

MURPHY Shaun Peter
Born: Sydney, Australia, 5 November 1970
Height: 6'1" Weight: 12.0
Club Honours: AIC '95
Shaun did very well at West Bromwich for most of the 1998-99 season, especially when he lined up alongside Matt Carbon at the heart of the defence. Strong in the air, solid and determined in the tackle, he was resilient in his play, although at times he was tested to the limit by the more eager and nippy strikers he came up against. Nevertheless, he had a fine campaign, his best so far in Albion colours, before being surprisingly released in May.
Notts Co (Signed from Perth Italia on 4/9/92) FL 100+9/5 FLC 5+2 FAC 6/1 Others 12+1/1
West Bromwich A (£500,000 on 31/12/96) FL 60+11/7 FLC 3 FAC 4

MURPHY Stephen
Born: Dublin, 5 April 1978
Height: 5'11" Weight: 11.6
International Honours: Ei: Yth
Having joined Halifax in the summer of 1998 from Huddersfield, in his second match Stephen was unfortunately shown the red card in the away tie at Wrexham in the Worthington Cup. Although spending the majority of 1998-99 on the subs' bench, when called into first-team action the young left-sided defender acquitted himself quite well. Is a Republic of Ireland youth international.
Huddersfield T (Free from Belvedere YC on 16/5/95)
Halifax T (Free on 8/8/98) FL 10+2 FLC 2 FAC 0+1 Others 0+1

MURRAY Adam David
Born: Birmingham, 30 September 1981
Height: 5'8" Weight: 10.10
Despite being in his first year as a professional, having come through the trainee ranks, his inspired performances in both the Derby youth team and the reserves earned him a surprise call up to the first-team squad

in April, and then four promising substitute appearances, including games at West Ham, Arsenal, and Leicester. Playing on the right side of midfield, his combative nature and passing ability were among the late-season highlights at the club, and were instrumental in him being voted the "Young Player of the Season" at Pride Park. Is the son of ex-Port Vale player, Gary Porter, and is seen by County manager, Jim Smith, as having a big future in the game if he carries on making the same progress as in last season.
Derby Co (From trainee on 7/10/98) PL 0+4

MURRAY Paul
Born: Carlisle, 31 August 1976
Height: 5'9" Weight: 10.5
International Honours: E: B-1; U21-4; Yth
Paul is a left-footed Queens Park Rangers' midfield player who made a successful return to the side in 1998-99 after breaking his leg the previous season. His normal position is on the right-hand side of midfield, but he also operated in the right side of defence when necessary, due to injuries to other players. Not noted for his goalscoring, he did find the net on one occasion, at home to Norwich, but was not able to hold on to a regular place during the campaign, playing in only half of the available games. Cool and composed on the ball, hopefully he will recover the form that the fans know he is capable of in 1999-2000.
Carlisle U (From trainee on 14/6/94) FL 27+14/1 FLC 2 FAC 1 Others 6+1
Queens Park R (£300,000 on 8/3/96) P/FL 90+14/7 FLC 8/1 FAC 6

MURRAY Scott George
Born: Aberdeen, 26 May 1974
Height: 5'10" Weight: 11.0
In and out of the Bristol City side last season, featuring at right back, and wide on the right-hand side of midfield, Scott has great pace, which many felt could have been used more often, particularly in home games. Although often failing to produce a telling final ball, most of his best performances during the campaign, were when he was allowed to attack opponents down the right flank.
Aston Villa (£35,000 from Fraserburgh on 16/3/94) PL 4
Bristol C (£150,000 on 12/12/97) FL 37+18/3 FLC 2+2 FAC 1 Others 2

MURRAY Shaun
Born: Newcastle, 7 December 1970
Height: 5'8" Weight: 11.2
International Honours: E: Yth; Sch
One of a number of new players added to the Notts County championship squad, having signed from Bradford City during the 1998 close season, but doubtless the quickest to establish himself in the team and in the hearts of the fans in 1998-99. A highly talented, diminutive left-sided midfielder with excellent ball skills, Shaun played in central midfield and wide on the left as a playmaker, where he made good use of his passing and crossing capability. A regular, apart from injury, he also scored four goals, one of them being the winner in a 1-0 home victory over the Second Division champions elect, Fulham.
Tottenham H (From trainee on 10/12/87)

Portsmouth (£100,000 on 12/6/89) FL 21+13/1 FLC 2+1/1 FAC 1+3 Others 2+2
Scarborough (Signed on 1/11/93) FL 29/5 FAC 2 Others 2
Bradford C (£200,000 on 11/8/94) FL 105+25/8 FLC 7+2/1 FAC 4+2 Others 4/2
Notts Co (Free on 4/8/98) FL 32+3/3 FLC 2 FAC 6/1

Shaun Murray

MURTY Graeme Stuart
Born: Saltburn, 13 November 1974
Height: 5'10" Weight: 11.10
Transferred from York during the 1998 close season, Reading had to wait until February to see him in first-team action because of a long-term back injury. He then showed his class in a run of nine consecutive matches before his progress was once again halted, this time with a damaged ankle. In his brief spell of appearances he looked equally adept at defending and attacking, and should more than justify his transfer fee during the coming season.
York C (From trainee on 23/3/93) FL 106+11/7 FLC 10/2 FAC 5+1 Others 6+2
Reading (£700,000 on 10/7/98) FL 8+1

MUSCAT Kevin Vincent
Born: Crawley, 7 August 1973
Height: 5'11" Weight: 12.2
International Honours: Australia: 11
The Wolves' right back was expected to be under pressure to keep his place in 1998-99, but started the season well and, despite being booked in three successive matches in September, he missed only one game of the first 21. Eventually, a November suspension kept him out for two matches, and when he missed a couple of games in December he was forced to return at left back. Although uncomfortable there, he marked his first game in that role with a spectacular late

winner against high-riding Ipswich, before undergoing surgery on his hand in February, and being out for four matches. Returning at right back wearing a fibre-glass cast provided by the club physio, the competitive defender continued to set an example with his sheer effort, scoring his second penalty of the term against Crewe, and four days later notching another beauty from the edge of the area to break down Portsmouth. He was staying out of trouble too, apart from harshly getting his 11th booking of the season at Sheffield at Easter. A good tackler, he also likes to get forward.
Crystal Palace (£35,000 from South Melbourne on 16/8/96) FL 51+2/2 FLC 4/1 FAC 2 Others 2
Wolverhampton W (£200,000 on 22/10/97) FL 59+2/7 FLC 4 FAC 7

MUSSELWHITE Paul Stephen
Born: Portsmouth, 22 December 1968
Height: 6'2" Weight: 14.2
Club Honours: AMC '93
As the regular goalkeeper with Port Vale, Paul had a very good season in 1998-99 despite the battle against relegation. He began the campaign in the team, but a rocky spell in early November led to his axing for nine games, but when he returned he was better than ever, making a number of crucial saves, particularly during the run-in. He played on whilst injured at Norwich as Vale hung on for a crucial victory, and can feel well satisfied with his efforts.
Portsmouth (From apprentice on 1/12/86)
Scunthorpe U (Free on 21/3/88) FL 132 FLC 11 FAC 7 Others 13
Port Vale (£20,000 on 30/7/92) FL 282 FLC 14 FAC 20 Others 19

MUSTOE Neil John
Born: Gloucester, 5 November 1976
Height: 5'9" Weight: 12.10
Club Honours: FAYC '95
Signed from Wigan in July 1998, and an all-action left-sided midfielder who is tenacious in the tackle, he was initially hampered by a pre-season injury before establishing a place in Cambridge's midfield in 1998-99. He also scored three goals, one of which was a vital 90th-minute winner in a 3-2 home victory over Rotherham in December.
Manchester U (From trainee on 1/7/95)
Wigan Ath (Signed on 7/1/98) Others 0+1
Cambridge U (Free on 9/7/98) FL 28+6/3 FLC 3 FAC 0+1 Others 2

MUSTOE Robin (Robbie)
Born: Witney, 28 August 1968
Height: 5'11" Weight: 11.12
Club Honours: Div 1 '95
In any walk of life Middlesbrough's Robbie would automatically have assumed total control and responsibility for everything going on around him, and, would, most certainly, have beavered away to ensure that the "bacon" was well and truly brought home. On the football field he does exactly that, being the very essence of perpetual motion in midfield, adept at cancelling out the opposition playmakers, toiling incessantly to link his defenders to his strike force, and thinking nothing at all of taking over and playing either role whenever he feels that a colleague is not so well placed as himself. His

commitment was further endorsed in 1998-99 when he was on the subs' bench, having almost recovered from the effects of an injury best described as a raked stud thigh bone, and was asked to take the field in the 90th minute. Thirty seconds later the ref blew the final whistle, and when asked if he should be credited with an appearance he said: "yes, I certainly got a touch". Qualifying now, almost, for a well-earned testimonial, nobody, as they say, did it better or with more gusto.
Oxford U (From juniors on 2/7/86) FL 78+13/10 FLC 2 FAC 2 Others 3
Middlesbrough (£375,000 on 5/7/90) F/PL 265+11/22 FLC 40+1/7 FAC 21/2 Others 12+1/1

MYERS Andrew (Andy) John
Born: Hounslow, 3 November 1973
Height: 5'10" Weight: 13.11
Club Honours: FAC '97; ECWC '98
International Honours: E: U21-4; Yth
A versatile, left-sided Chelsea central defender or wing back who rose through the junior ranks, Andy found himself slipping down the pecking order at the Bridge in 1998-99, owing to the consistency shown by players such as Marcel Desailly, Frank Leboeuf, Michael Duberry, Bernard Lambourde, and Graeme le Saux. However, although unable to break into the first team until March, with two substitute appearances against Manchester United in the FA Cup sixth round and a Premiership start against West Ham, he showed that he could still be relied on to give good back up. Known as "Bruno", he is exceptionally fast, both in recovery and in getting forward, and is a tough man to get past. Stop Press: Was transferred to Bradford for £800,000 on 8 July.
Chelsea (From trainee on 25/7/91) F/PL 74+10/2 FLC 2+1 FAC 9+3 Others 4+3

MYHRE Thomas
Born: Sarpsborg, Norway, 16 October 1973
Height: 6'4" Weight: 13.12
International Honours: Norway: 5
A tall, commanding Everton goalkeeper with

outstanding reflexes, Thomas built on the promising impact he made at Goodison in 1997-98 to beat off the competition provided by the arrival of Steve Simonsen – signed for a British record transfer fee for a goalkeeper – and established himself as Norway's first choice in 1998-99. Despite the Toffees' disappointing season, at the mid-point of the campaign he actually topped the Premiership's clean sheet record, heading goalkeepers of the quality of David Seaman and Peter Schmeichel. However, there were a couple of shaky moments – most notably at West Ham (he was so disappointed he shaved his hair off afterwards as a punishment!) and Manchester United – but they ultimately failed to take the gloss off another very competent campaign. Was ever present in the Premiership, and saved his first penalty kick in English football, taken by England skipper, Alan Shearer, at St James' Park. Stop Press: Broke the fibula in his right leg in training with the Norwegian Euro 2000 squad during the summer.
Everton (£800,000 from Viking Stavanger on 28/11/97) PL 60 FLC 3 FAC 5

Thomas Myhre

Robbie Mustoe

Professional Footballers Association
Financial Management
Limited

The PFA has the job of looking after every aspect of a player's career: – his contract, advice on transfers, education and training, accident insurance, discipline and commercial matters. In line with these duties PFA Financial Management Limited was set up to provide the best possible financial and contractual advice to players during what is a very short-term career – an average of eight years.

Get in touch ... you deserve the best financial advice.

PFA Financial Management Limited
91 Broad Street
Birmingham
B15 1AU

Tel: 0121 644 5277
Fax: 0121 644 5288

NAISBETT Philip (Phil)
Born: Easington, 2 January 1979
Height: 5'11" Weight: 11.6
Having been freed by Sunderland during the 1998 close season, without making a senior appearance for the club, the young goalkeeper moved to non-league Gateshead before joining Scarborough on non-contract terms last January, as cover for the on-loan 'keeper, Nicky Weaver, following the long-term injury suffered by the regular number one, Tony Elliott. Making his first-team bow in the Auto Windscreens tie at Wigan, he made two further appearances before leaving in the summer.
Sunderland (From trainee on 14/4/97. Freed during 1998 close season)
Scarborough (Free from Gateshead on 29/1/99) FL 2 Others 1

NASH Carlo James
Born: Bolton, 13 September 1973
Height: 6'5" Weight: 14.1
1998-99 was a great first season at Stockport for the former male model. Having arrived under the Bosman ruling from Crystal Palace in the summer of 1998, he was an ever present in the side, bar the last three games, and grew in confidence as the season wore on. Relatively inexperienced when he arrived at County, his occasional mistakes were far outweighed by a number of match-saving performances, prompting Gary Megson to tip him as a goalkeeper destined for the top flight.
Crystal Palace (£35,000 from Clitheroe on 16/7/96) FL 21 FLC 1 Others 3
Stockport Co (Free on 7/6/98) FL 43 FLC 2 FAC 2

NAYLOR Anthony (Tony) Joseph
Born: Manchester, 29 March 1967
Height: 5'7" Weight: 10.8
The Port Vale striker had an injury ravaged season in 1998-99. After missing all of the pre-season friendlies he scored two in his first game, at Chester in the Worthington Cup, and remained in the team until suffering a knee injury against Norwich in October. He returned around Christmas for five games, scoring twice at West Bromwich, but the injury flared up again and he rarely appeared after that, and then only from the bench. The fact that his prowess as a nippy goalscorer was missing partly explained Vale's struggles on the pitch.
Crewe Alex (£20,000 from Droylsden on 22/3/90) FL 104+18/45 FLC 7+2/5 FAC 9/7 Others 12/9
Port Vale (£150,000 on 18/7/94) FL 141+34/51 FLC 11+1/6 FAC 10/1 Others 5+1/3

NAYLOR Glenn
Born: Goole, 11 August 1972
Height: 5'10" Weight: 11.10
There were only four games that this quick-footed front runner did not appear in throughout 1998-99, his third full campaign with Darlington, and his nine goals were just one short of his previous best of ten in 1997-98, taking his total for the club to 31 in all competitions. Was offered a new contract in the summer on the completion of his existing deal.
York C (From trainee on 5/3/90) FL 78+33/30 FLC 2+4 FAC 4+1/2 Others 3+4
Darlington (Loaned on 13/10/95) FL 3+1/1 Others 1+1
Darlington (Signed on 26/9/96) FL 100+21/27 FLC 3+1/1 FAC 9/2 Others 4

NAYLOR Lee Martyn
Born: Walsall, 19 March 1980
Height: 5'9" Weight: 11.8
International Honours: E: Yth
Although omitted from Wolves' opener in 1998-99, as the club's only out-and-out left back he was then in the team for 13 games running. Despite being often replaced, Lee hit the Sunderland bar with a 35-yard cracker before being given a rest for six games, and then playing in the next eight. Taking a goal chance against Birmingham coolly, and generally looking settled, except at Norwich after an opponent was sent off having challenged him, he was confident going forward and capable of getting in some good crosses. However, in 1999, he was reduced to the odd game as a sub, before signing a three-year extension to his contract in April.
Wolverhampton W (From trainee on 10/10/97) FL 31+8/1 FLC 5 FAC 4/1

NAYLOR Richard Alan
Born: Leeds, 28 February 1977
Height: 6'1" Weight: 13.7
1998-99 was a season of missed opportunities for Richard, who would have expected to be Ipswich's reserve striker once Alex Mathie had moved on. However, when David Johnson was sidelined by an operation the management turned to a loanee, Samassi Abou, rather than Richard, which must have been frustrating. But "Lady Luck" was on his side when, a week after Johnson entered hospital, Jamie Scowcroft broke his collarbone against Barnsley, and the first-team door was open. Taking the opportunity, Richard scored a last-minute winner in the televised game at Sheffield United, and then notched a double in the next match against Portsmouth, when he combined well with Abou to finish clinically. He kept his place in the side for the next four games, but the goals dried up, and when it became clear that Scowcroft's injury was taking longer to heal than originally thought another loan striker was brought in at his expense. Returning to the side to score the only goal at Bristol City, and striking the last goal against Sheffield United in the finale, the fans are waiting for him to blossom into a striker who deserves a regular senior place.
Ipswich T (From trainee on 10/7/95) FL 29+33/11 FLC 2+4/1 FAC 1+2 Others 0+2

NAYLOR Stuart William
Born: Wetherby, 6 December 1962
Height: 6'4" Weight: 12.10
International Honours: E: B-3; Yth
Unable to get a game at Bristol City last season, the veteran 'keeper moved to Mansfield on an extended loan in December, as cover for Ian Bowling who required an operation. After keeping a clean sheet on his debut, a 1-0 home win over Shrewsbury, he was injured in the second match, at Ninian Park, thus forcing Bowling back into action prematurely. Returning for four matches a month later – conceding ten goals in four games – to allow the latter to heal properly, he was freed by City and allowed to join Walsall in March. At his best a classy shot stopper, he was not used by the Saddlers and was freed during the summer.
Lincoln C (Free from Yorkshire Amateurs on 19/6/80) FL 49 FLC 4 FAC 2 Others 6
Peterborough U (Loaned on 23/2/83) FL 8
Crewe Alex (Loaned on 6/10/83) FL 38
Crewe Alex (Loaned on 23/8/94) FL 17 FLC 2 FAC 2 Others 3
West Bromwich A (£100,000 on 18/2/86) FL 354+1 FLC 22 FAC 13 Others 20
Bristol C (Free on 13/8/96) FL 37 FLC 4 FAC 4 Others 1
Mansfield T (Loaned on 11/12/98) FL 6
Walsall (Free on 8/3/99)

NDAH George Ehialimolisa
Born: Dulwich, 23 December 1974
Height: 6'1" Weight: 11.4
International Honours: E: Yth
By far and away Swindon's best and most exciting player in 1998-99, and a great favourite of the crowd, George started the season at centre forward partnering his old pal, Iffy Onuora, before dropping back to a left-sided midfield position. In this deeper role, he was able to use his electric pace much more effectively, while still showing an eye for goal, scoring 12 goals. His workrate allowed him to defend equally as well, and he showed himself to be a real all-rounder.
Crystal Palace (From trainee on 10/8/92) F/PL 33+45/8 FLC 7+6/2 FAC 3+1/1 Others 4+1
Bournemouth (Loaned on 13/10/95) FL 12/2 Others 1
Gillingham (Loaned on 29/8/97) FL 4
Swindon T (£500,000 on 21/11/97) FL 54+1/13 FLC 2/1 FAC 3

NDLOVU Peter
Born: Buluwayo, Zimbabwe, 25 February 1973
Height: 5'8" Weight: 10.2
International Honours: Zimbabwe: 19
Peter helped carry the load in attack at Birmingham in 1998-99 due to injuries, and continued to mesmerise defences with his electric pace, control, quick movement, and eye for the spectacular. Was distraught when sent off in the 1-1 home draw against Huddersfield in October for a second bookable offence – an alleged dive – despite the tackle on him deserving a penalty. However, after the referee watched the video, the card was scrubbed from the record books, although the expected home win went by the board. Very effective when coming from deep positions to leave defenders in his wake, the Zimbabwean international scored doubles against Macclesfield and close rivals, West Bromwich, while netting seven in an 11-game spell.

Coventry C (£10,000 from Highlanders on 16/8/91) F/PL 141+36/37 FLC 10/2 FAC 5+4/2 Others 0+1
Birmingham C (£1,600,000 on 15/7/97) FL 66+16/20 FLC 9/3 FAC 2+1/1 Others 1+1

NEIL Gary Derek Campbell
Born: Glasgow, 16 August 1978
Height: 6'0" Weight: 12.10
On a monthly contract at Leicester, and unable to make the senior side, this powerfully-built central defender had a spell on loan at Torquay, arriving at Plainmoor during transfer deadline week. Can also play in attack, but impressed at the back, and Wes Saunders was due to sign the young Glaswegian on a permanent contract in the summer after he was released by Leicester.
Leicester C (From trainee on 3/7/97)
Torquay U (Loaned on 25/3/99) FL 6+1

Stuart Nethercott

NEILL Lucas Edward
Born: Sydney, Australia, 9 March 1978
Height: 6'1" Weight: 12.0
Having exploded onto the scene during 1996-97, which culminated in him winning a full cap for Australia, and becoming the Millwall "Player of the Year", Lucas suffered a major setback when broken bones in both feet decimated his attempts to fulfil his potential. After a long fight to regain fitness, he got back into the first team in 1998-99, and the more he played the better he got. However, after making such strides to become an ever present, he was injured again, which put him out of the Wembley Auto Windscreens final. As a utility player who can play in defence as well as up front, he proved himself a formidable attacker, which was reflected in some big clubs wanting to sign him. He is also tricky with good pace, can shoot with either foot, and puts many defenders under pressure with his runs and crosses.
Millwall (Free from AIS on 13/11/95) FL 76+17/10 FLC 3+1 FAC 3 Others 7+1

NEILSON Alan Bruce
Born: Wegburg, Germany, 26 September 1972
Height: 5'11" Weight: 12.10
International Honours: W: 5; B-2; U21-7
1998-99 was a season that Alan will want to forget, especially in not playing enough games to qualify for a Second Division championship medal. It would have been difficult enough to break into the Fulham side with the brilliance of the back three, but he had the all-round game to have vied for another position if it had not been for a spate of injuries. It seemed that each time he got close to a recall, a troublesome calf injury flared up again to destroy his hopes, but with another two years left on his contract the Welsh international has the ability to do well in Division One if he can steer clear of injuries. The two FA Cup ties against his old club, Southampton, showed his class.
Newcastle U (From trainee on 11/2/91) F/PL 35+7/1 FLC 4 Others 4
Southampton (£500,000 on 1/6/95) PL 42+13 FLC 7 FAC 1+1
Fulham (£250,000 on 28/11/97) FL 20+1/1 FLC 0+1 FAC 4 Others 2

NETHERCOTT Stuart David
Born: Ilford, 21 March 1973
Height: 6'1" Weight: 13.8
International Honours: E: U21-8
A former England U21 international who grew up with the likes of Sol Campbell at Tottenham, his move to Millwall was initially on a loan basis and, in keeping with the club's fortunes on the injury front, he suffered a dislocated shoulder at Fulham in March 1998, leaving his 1997-98 campaign in tatters. However, having signed for the club on a permanent basis in the summer of 1998, when Scott Fitzgerald was injured early last season, Stuart was given his chance and was ever present bar a suspension. Made skipper, and a rock in defence with good motivating ability, he is a very good header of the ball, strong in the challenge and, without doubt, one of the best defenders in the Nationwide League. The pinnacle of his spell at the Den came when he led the side out at Wembley for the Auto Windscreens final against Wigan.
Tottenham H (From trainee on 17/8/91) PL 31+23 FAC 5+3/1
Maidstone U (Loaned on 5/9/91) FL 13/1 Others 1
Barnet (Loaned on 13/2/92) FL 3
Millwall (Signed on 22/1/98) FL 45+2/2 FAC 1 Others 7

NEVILLE Gary Alexander
Born: Bury, 18 February 1975
Height: 5'11" Weight: 12.8
Club Honours: FAYC '92; PL '96, '97, '99; FAC '96, '99; CS '96; EC '99
International Honours: E: 32; Yth (UEFAC '93)
A hard-tackling Manchester United full back, who is equally as effective in the centre of defence, Gary had a very busy

summer in 1998, playing for England in the World Cup finals, then co-launching his book: *For Club And Country*, with his brother Phil in early September. Playing regularly throughout the 1998-99 campaign, he missed only two Premiership games up to the start of December, before being forced out of the Boxing Day encounter against Nottingham Forest, following his red-card offence against Tottenham earlier that month. He then missed three games in a row with a groin strain in January. Returning in time for the important FA Cup-tie against Liverpool, he really came to the fore in the latter stages of the European Cup, where he showed true international form before scoring his first Premiership goal in nearly two years, against Everton in March. As one of United's most inspirational players as they mounted their continued quest for major honours, and an automatic choice in Kevin Keegan's first England squad for the vital European qualifier against Poland in March, it is safe to say that he has virtually made that right-back spot his very own. Was selected by his fellow professionals for the PFA award-winning Premiership side in advance of the club's best-ever season, which saw them get their hands on the European Cup, FA Cup, and last but not least, the Premiership title.
Manchester U (From trainee on 29/1/93) PL 145+4/2 FLC 4+1 FAC 21+2 Others 33+4

NEVILLE Philip (Phil) John
Born: Bury, 21 January 1977
Height: 5'11" Weight: 12.0
Club Honours: FAYC '95; PL '96, '97, '99; FAC '96, '99; CS '96, '97; EC '99
International Honours: E: 17; U21-7; Yth; Sch
A superb Manchester United right back, who is equally as adaptable as a central defender, Phil had a stop-start introduction to last season, after playing as a substitute in the Charity Shield opener against Arsenal at Wembley. Having then made his first full appearance of the campaign against Lodz in the Champions' Cup in August, he deputised for brother, Gary, and Denis Irwin in the next three games. Co-launching his book: *For Club And Country* with Gary in early September, he enjoyed an extended run in the side, and in November he netted his first ever goal in the Champions' League in United's 5-0 win over Brondby. After that run of nine successive games, however, he made only fleeting appearances in the side, though continuing to be a regular face on the sub's bench. Although given an extended run in February, rumours continued to abound about his long-term future at Old Trafford, but Alex Ferguson was quick to dispel such talk by giving him a massive vote of confidence, and he ended the season with European Cup, FA Cup, and Premier League winners medals, as did his brother. Made five international appearances for England in 1998-99.
Manchester U (From trainee on 1/6/94) PL 80+22/1 FLC 5+1 FAC 14+4 Others 14+7/1

NEVLAND Erik
Born: Stavanger, Norway, 10 November 1977
Height: 5'10" Weight: 11.12
International Honours: Norway: 3
A highly talented Manchester United striker, with an eye for a goal, Erik made only one appearance for United during the course of 1998-99, when he scored as a substitute against Bury in the Worthington Cup in October. With so many promising players vying for a regular place in the side, he decided to impress Alex Ferguson from afar, joining Gothenburg on loan for the Swedish season in January.
Manchester U (Signed from Viking Stavanger on 15/7/97) PL 0+1 FLC 0+2/1 FAC 2+1

NEWELL Michael (Mike) Colin
Born: Liverpool, 27 January 1965
Height: 6'2" Weight: 12.0
Club Honours: AMC '85; PL '95
International Honours: E: B-2; U21-4
Signed from Aberdeen on a free during transfer deadline week last March, Mike joined Crewe in an effort to help them get away from the First Division danger zone. As a forward with a wealth of experience, including a Premier League championship medal with Blackburn, he returned to the club where he first launched his career back in 1983, but in just one start and three appearances from the bench he hardly set the world on fire. At his best, a strong-running striker, who is good in the air, competes well, and holds the ball up for others to arrive, it will be interesting to see where he goes from here.
Crewe Alex (Free from Liverpool juniors on 28/9/83) FL 3
Wigan Ath (Free on 31/10/83) FL 64+8/25 FLC 6/1 FAC 8/6 Others 5+1/3
Luton T (£100,000 on 9/1/86) FL 62+1/18 FAC 5/1
Leicester C (£350,000 on 16/9/87) FL 81/21 FLC 9/5 FAC 2 Others 4
Everton (£850,000 on 27/7/89) FL 48+20/15 FLC 7+3/4 FAC 6+4 Others 6/2
Blackburn Rov (£1,100,000 on 15/11/91) F/PL 113+17/28 FLC 14+2/8 FAC 9+2/6 Others 9+1/6
Birmingham C (£775,000 on 26/7/96) FL 11+4/1 FLC 4/2 FAC 0+1
West Ham U (Loaned on 21/12/96) PL 6+1
Bradford C (Loaned on 17/3/97) FL 7
Aberdeen (£160,000 on 21/7/97) SL 27+12/5 SLC 4/4 SC 1+1
Crewe Alex (Free on 25/3/99) FL 1+3

NEWHOUSE Aidan Robert
Born: Wallasey, 23 May 1972
Height: 6'2" Weight: 13.10
International Honours: E: Yth
Despite starting last season as Swansea's first-choice striker, Aidan was injured during the first game against Exeter, leaving him sidelined until November. Showed signs against Millwall of his ability, especially in wide situations, but made just three more league appearances for the Swans before having his contract paid up just prior to the end of the campaign.
Chester C (From trainee on 1/7/89) FL 29+15/6 FLC 5+1 FAC 0+2 Others 2+3/1
Wimbledon (£100,000 on 22/2/90) F/PL 7+16/2 FLC 1+1 FAC 2 Others 0+1
Port Vale (Loaned on 21/1/94) FL 0+2 FAC 0+1
Portsmouth (Loaned on 2/12/94) FL 6/1

Torquay U (Loaned on 7/12/95) FL 4/2
Fulham (Free on 20/6/97) FL 7+1/1 FLC 3+1/3
Swansea C (£30,000 on 31/10/97) FL 8+6 FAC 2 Others 0+1

NEWMAN Richard (Ricky) Adrian
Born: Guildford, 5 August 1970
Height: 5'10" Weight: 12.6
Ricky had a season of mixed fortune in 1998-99, mainly because of injury. Although playing in the middle of the park in the holding role, he can get forward quickly to support the attack, has quick feet, and can shoot with either of them. When he did get his chance late on in the campaign he put in some excellent performances, which was the main factor in his being selected for the Wembley team that contested the Auto Windscreens Shield.
Crystal Palace (From juniors on 22/1/88) F/PL 43+5/3 FLC 5 FAC 5+2 Others 2
Maidstone U (Loaned on 28/2/92) FL 9+1/1
Millwall (£500,000 on 19/7/95) FL 130+6/5 FLC 11 FAC 5 Others 7

Rob Newman

NEWMAN Robert (Rob) Nigel
Born: Bradford on Avon, 13 December 1963
Height: 6'2" Weight: 13.4
Club Honours: AMC '86
Signed from Norwich during the 1998 close season, as a "Desperate Dan" type figure in the heart of the Southend defence, Rob soon became the fans' hero with his never-say-die attitude, immaculate distribution, and scoring prowess. In short, he displayed the type of application that all players should have, and if United had 11 Rob Newmans in their team they would not have found themselves in such a state!
Bristol C (From apprentice on 5/10/81) FL 382+12/52 FLC 29+1/2 FAC 27/2 Others 33/5

Shaun Newton

Norwich C (£600,000 on 15/7/91) F/PL 181+24/14 FLC 22+2/2 FAC 13/1 Others 7
Motherwell (Loaned on 12/12/97) SL 11 SC 3
Wigan Ath (Loaned on 26/3/98) FL 8
Southend U (Free on 28/7/98) FL 36/7 FLC 4/1 FAC 1 Others 1

NEWSOME Jonathan (Jon)
Born: Sheffield, 6 September 1970
Height: 6'2" Weight: 13.11
Club Honours: Div 1 '92; CS '92
Started last season on the injury list, and was never able to break up the Emerson – Des Walker central defensive pairing at Sheffield Wednesday, only managing a few appearances, mainly being relegated to the role of squad player. Now into his second spell at the club, the tall defender is an excellent tackler, and continues to work hard to bring all the other facets of his game up to the same standard. Loaned to Bolton last November, Jon made such a good impression that a permanent deal looked imminent at one time. However, he was too valuable a player for Wednesday not to be able to call upon, but needs regular football to do himself justice.
Sheffield Wed (From trainee on 1/7/89) FL 6+1 FLC 3
Leeds U (£150,000 on 11/6/91) F/PL 62+14/3 FLC 3 FAC 3+1 Others 5
Norwich C (£1,000,000 on 30/6/94) P/FL 61+1/7 FLC 9 FAC 5/1
Sheffield Wed (£1,600,000 on 16/3/96) PL 45+3/4 FLC 3 FAC 6+1
Bolton W (Loaned on 18/11/98) FL 6

NEWTON Christopher (Chris) John
Born: Leeds, 5 November 1979
Height: 6'0" Weight: 11.8

Locally born Chris came through the youth ranks at Halifax to make his full debut last Boxing Day against Darlington. An exciting prospect, whose wing play causes opponent full backs one or two problems, he was a regular in the reserve team, and will be looking to play first-team football on a consistent basis in 1999-2000.
Halifax T (From trainee on 17/7/98) FL 8+6/1 Others 0+1

NEWTON Edward (Eddie) John Ikem
Born: Hammersmith, 13 December 1971
Height: 5'11" Weight: 12.8
Club Honours: FAC '97; FLC '98; ECWC '98
International Honours: E: U21-2
This unfortunate Chelsea player endured his third successive injury-blighted season during 1998-99. After just one Premiership appearance, a broken ankle sustained in October kept him out of first-team action until February, when he re-appeared against Blackburn. Aptly nicknamed "Steady Eddie", the popular, locally-developed central midfielder was sorely missed throughout the campaign, where his crucial interceptions and intelligent distribution in the holding position make him the perfect foil to Chelsea's attacking midfielders. Released during the summer, it was a cruel twist of fortune for this dependable player who, before his broken leg three years ago, was considered to be a future England international. Stop Press: Was reported to have signed for Birmingham in early July.
Chelsea (From trainee on 17/5/90) F/PL 139+26/8 FLC 15+2/1 FAC 15+3/1 Others 11+2
Cardiff C (Loaned on 23/1/92) FL 18/4

NEWTON Shaun O'Neill
Born: Camberwell, 20 August 1975
Height: 5'8" Weight: 11.7
International Honours: E: U21-3
A right-sided winger who was a regular member of Charlton's first-team squad up until last February, although he did not play in the final run in. Shaun is at his best when getting the ball down to the byline and cutting back crosses to make full use of his lightning pace. Possesses a strong right-foot shot, but failed to score in the league last season, his only goal coming against Queens Park Rangers in the Worthington Cup. Would probably have played more games, but was sacrificed when Athletic adopted their 5-3-2 system, which they did in a good proportion of games during the season. Can also play in the right-wing back position.
Charlton Ath (From trainee on 1/7/93) P/FL 147+41/15 FLC 15+1/3 FAC 7+3 Others 7+1/2

NGONGE Felix Michel
Born: Zaire, 10 January 1967
Height: 6'0" Weight: 12.8
International Honours: Zaire: 4
Although a Zaire international striker, Michel joined Watford during the 1998 close season though most of his previous experience was gained in Belgium. Unusually for Graham Taylor, he was signed on the strength of video evidence, but he made an immediate impression when scoring on his debut, and was very impressive before a groin injury in October, which required an operation, set him back for a while. Returned to first-team action at the end of the campaign, and played a full part in the push for the play offs, his strength and exciting change of pace making him an effective foil for the rampant Tommy Mooney.
Watford (Free from Samsunspor, via KRC Harelbeks, on 17/7/98) FL 13+9/4 FLC 1/1 Others 3/1

NICHOLLS Kevin John Richard
Born: Newham, 2 January 1979
Height: 6'0" Weight: 11.0
International Honours: E: Yth
With Charlton in the Premiership, and unable to get a game, the fierce tackling midfielder signed for Brighton on a month's loan last February, scoring on his debut against Leyton Orient direct from a free kick. However, the loan period was cut short because of injury and suspension, after being booked in all four games he played for the Seagulls. Selected in the England squad for the World U20 championships in Nigeria, Kevin is good on the ball, and has good vision to match aggression. Stop Press: Was signed by Wigan in the summer for a fee of £250,000.
Charlton Ath (From trainee on 29/1/96) FL 4+8/1 FLC 2+2
Brighton & Hove A (Loaned on 26/2/99) FL 4/1

NICHOLLS Mark
Born: Hillingdon, 30 May 1977
Height: 5'10" Weight: 10.4
Club Honours: FLC '98
A young, quicksilver Chelsea striker who, although he did not begin a Premiership match during 1998-99, proved to be a valuable member of the Blues' squad. "Nicho", who was in an unenviable position, battling for a first-team place against world-class strikers such as Gianfranco Zola, Pierluigi Casiraghi, Tore-Andre Flo, Gianluca Vialli, and Brian Laudrup at various times during the season, plus the emerging Mikael Forssell, never let Chelsea down during his many substitute appearances, particularly during the January-February injury crisis when Vialli and Flo were the only front-rank strikers available. A product of the Chelsea youth policy, he would surely be an automatic choice at most Premiership clubs, and he still has time to make an impact at the highest level.
Chelsea (From trainee on 1/7/95) PL 11+25/3 FLC 4+2 FAC 1+3 Others 0+4

NICHOLS Jonathan Anthony
Born: Plymouth, 10 September 1980
Height: 6'0" Weight: 11.12
Still a trainee at Torquay, this second-year YTS full back, who can play on either flank, impressed when given his chance at Leyton Orient towards the end of 1998-99. More opportunities followed, and he looks to be on a full contract for the coming season. Was voted United's "Young Player of the Year".
Torquay U (Trainee) FL 5+1

NICHOLSON Shane Michael
Born: Newark, 3 June 1970
Height: 5'10" Weight: 12.2
Club Honours: GMVC '88
With his "bad boy" image now firmly behind him, this naturally left-footed defender added class to Chesterfield's backline in 1998-99, having trained with the club from the close season, and signing a contract upon being given the "all clear" by the Football Association in September. After impressing in the Spireites' autumn push towards the play-offs, he suffered an abdominal injury that kept him out until January, but happily returned to offer assurance at the back with well-timed tackles and perceptive distribution, and an accurate cross when going forward. Out of contract during the summer, at the time of going to press the club had made him an offer of re-engagement.
Lincoln C (From trainee on 19/7/88) FL 122+11/6 FLC 8+3 FAC 6/1 Others 7+1
Derby Co (£100,000 on 22/4/92) FL 73+1/1 FLC 4 FAC 4/1 Others 5
West Bromwich A (£150,000 on 9/2/96) FL 50+2 FLC 4 Others 4
Chesterfield (Free on 21/8/98) FL 23+1 Others 1

NIELSEN Allan
Born: Esbjerg, Denmark, 13 March 1971
Height: 5'8" Weight: 11.2
Club Honours: FLC '99
International Honours: Denmark: 29
A versatile, attacking midfielder who loves to get forward with the ball at his feet, Allan will look back at 1998-99, his most successful season at Spurs since joining. A real battler, he scored nine goals in the campaign, most notably his fine low drive in the 3-1 defeat of Liverpool in the Worthington Cup fourth round, and his headed winner late into injury time in the Worthington Cup final at Wembley in March. With the introduction of both Steffen Freund and Tim Sherwood, and suffering a spell of injury, the Dane battled hard for regular first-team action and, despite assurances that he featured in George Graham's long-term plans, a training ground dispute in May threw his future in doubt, before a written transfer request was submitted to the club. With a wealth of club and international experience under his belt, Tottenham fans will hope that any reported differences can be settled, and that Allan will still be at the Lane in 1999-2000.
Tottenham H (£1,650,000 from Brondby, via Esbjerg, Bayern Munich, Sion, Odense and FC Copenhagen, on 3/9/96) PL 73+9/12 FLC 10+1/3 FAC 3+2/3

NIESTROJ Robert Waldemar
Born: Poland, 2 December 1974
Height: 5'10" Weight: 11.3
The Polish-born German was the first signing made by Wolves' manager, Colin Lee, who described him as "one for the future". Arriving from Fortuna Dusseldorf last November, and playing in midfield, Robert came on as a sub at West Bromwich on 29 November, making his full debut against Ipswich a month later. A good passer of the ball, he retained his place for the next two matches, but, surprisingly, was not seen again until being used as a sub late in March.
Wolverhampton W (£300,000 + from Fortuna Dusseldorf on 13/11/98) FL 2+3 FAC 1

NIGHTINGALE Luke Raymond
Born: Portsmouth, 22 December 1980
Height: 5'10" Weight: 12.5
A former trainee at Fratton Park who broke into the first team last season, Luke made a dream debut after coming on as substitute – with Portsmouth 1-0 down – when scoring two goals to beat West Bromwich in November, aged just 17. He also scored other important goals against Leeds in the FA Cup, and at Queens Park Rangers. Top goalscorer in Pompey's youth team, and a regular scorer in the reserves, he is still learning, but has a promising career ahead of him. Alert, quick, strong, and skilful, with good ball distribution, he should blend in well during the forthcoming season, given the chance to pair up with elder colleagues. Is a very exciting prospect for the future.
Portsmouth (From trainee on 23/11/98) FL 6+13/3 FAC 1+1/1

NILSEN Roger
Born: Tromso, Norway, 8 August 1969
Height: 5'11" Weight: 12.6
International Honours: Norway: 31
After the first four games of last season, Roger sustained a calf injury which kept him out for Sheffield United's next seven matches. On his return, as a left-sided player at the back who enjoyed coming forward, he maintained his high standards, particularly in defence. Out of contract at the end of the season, he played his final game in early February, still having failed to score from open play in nearly 200 games for the Blades despite some near misses, and in March it was agreed he would move to Tottenham for the remainder of the campaign.
Sheffield U (£550,000 from Viking Stavanger on 2/11/93) P/FL 157+9 FLC 9+1 FAC 9+2 Others 2+1
Tottenham H (Free on 26/3/99) PL 3

NILSSON Nilsennart Roland
Born: Helsingborg, Sweden, 27 November 1963
Height: 5'11" Weight: 11.12
Club Honours: FLC '91
International Honours: Sweden: 99
Back in England with Coventry, and following up an excellent season in 1997-98 for him, Roland had an outstanding final campaign in the English game before sadly sustaining a nasty injury at Highbury in March. Having suffered fractured ribs and a punctured lung, he recovered to make an emotional final appearance, and has now returned to take up a player/coach role at Helsingborg in his native Sweden. A long-time Swedish international full back, his strengths included excellent positional play, fitness, and strong passing skills. He will certainly be missed by the Highfield Road faithful.
Sheffield Wed (£375,000 from IFK Gothenburg on 8/12/89) F/PL 151/2 FLC 16/1 FAC 15 Others 3+1 (Transferred to Helsingborg on 9/5/94)
Coventry C (£200,000 on 29/7/97) PL 60 FLC 3 FAC 6

NIXON Eric Walter
Born: Manchester, 4 October 1962
Height: 6'4" Weight: 14.6
Club Honours: AMC '90
A vastly experienced goalie, Eric began 1998-99 vying for the number-one jersey at Stockport with the new arrival, Carlo Nash, before a knee injury ruled him out of contention. With Nash and the reserve-team 'keeper, Ian Gray, he was pushed into the background until being recruited by Wigan in transfer deadline week to provide cover for Roy Carroll, who was on international duty. Tall and dominating, he had earlier spent a loan spell at the club in October. Having combined his duties with that of club goalkeeping coach at Stockport, he took up the same position at Springfield Park, thus linking up again with Ray Mathias, the Latics' manager.
Manchester C (£1,000 from Curzon Ashton on 10/12/83) FL 58 FLC 8 FAC 10 Others 8
Wolverhampton W (Loaned on 29/8/86) FL 16
Bradford C (Loaned on 28/11/86) FL 3
Southampton (Loaned on 23/12/86) FL 4
Carlisle U (Loaned on 23/1/87) FL 16

Tranmere Rov (£60,000 on 24/3/88) FL 341 FLC 34 FAC 19 Others 45+1
Reading (Loaned on 9/1/96) FLC 1
Blackpool (Loaned on 5/2/96) FL 20 Others 2
Bradford C (Loaned on 13/9/96) FL 12
Stockport Co (£100,000 on 28/8/97) FL 43 FLC 2 FAC 2
Wigan Ath (Loaned on 28/8/98) FL1
Wigan Ath (Free on 24/3/99) FL 2

NOEL-WILLIAMS Gifton Ruben Elisha
Born: Islington, 21 January 1980
Height: 6'1" Weight: 14.6
Club Honours: Div 2 '98
International Honours: E: Yth

1998-99 was a season of significant progress for the big centre forward, who is still only 19, but has already made 100 first-team appearances for Watford. The raw promise he had shown since making his debut as a 16-year old began to be translated into genuine striking talent, as evinced by his ten goals, his best-ever return, and enough to make him the Hornets' leading scorer. Gifton – generally abbreviated in Watford circles to GNW – was outstanding in the important victory at Bolton, and scored a terrific winning goal against Sunderland. Unfortunately, he cracked a thigh bone near the knee joint during that match, and had to miss the last three months of the campaign. On a disappointing note, he was selected for the Football League U21 squad against Italy in November, but injury restricted him to the bench.
Watford (From trainee on 13/2/97) FL 55+34/19 FLC 3+1/1 FAC 7/4

NOGAN Kurt
Born: Cardiff, 9 September 1970
Height: 5'11" Weight: 12.7
International Honours: W: U21-2

In his second full season at Preston, Kurt finally refound his goalscoring touch, netting on the opening day, and going on to grab the winner at Turf Moor, the fourth consecutive league match he has scored against his former club. Other highlights included two goals versus Arsenal in the televised FA Cup third round tie, and his 100th league goal, against his first club, Luton. He developed a particularly rewarding partnership with Steve Basham, and also played for Wales "B" in February, in what proved to be a tremendously successful season for both himself and the club.
Luton T (From trainee on 11/7/89) FL 17+16/3 FLC 1+3/1 Others 1+1
Peterborough U (Free on 30/9/92) Others 1
Brighton & Hove A (Free on 17/10/92) FL 97/49 FLC 10/7 FAC 5+1 Others 7/4
Burnley (£250,000 on 24/4/95) FL 87+5/33 FLC 8/5 FAC 3 Others 5/4
Preston NE (£150,000 + on 13/3/97) FL 58+13/23 FLC 3+1 FAC 3+1/3 Others 4+2/1

NOGAN Lee Martin
Born: Cardiff, 21 May 1969
Height: 5'9" Weight: 11.0
Club Honours: AMC '98
International Honours: W: 2; B-1; U21-1

1998-99 was a season in which this industrious and creative forward found himself in and out of the Grimsby side, as the manager, Alan Buckley, struggled to find the right strike force to remedy the paucity of goals that plagued the Mariners throughout the campaign. However, whenever called upon, the brother of Preston's Kurt never let the side down, and will be looking forward to getting back among the goals in 1999-2000. Out of contract during the summer, at the time of going to press Lee had yet to agree terms.
Oxford U (From trainee on 25/3/87) FL 57+7/10 FLC 4+1 FAC 2+1/1 Others 4+1/1
Brentford (Loaned on 25/3/87) FL 10+1/2
Southend U (Loaned on 17/9/87) FL 6/1 FLC 2 Others 1/1
Watford (£350,000 on 12/12/91) FL 97+8/26 FLC 5+2/3 FAC 2/1 Others 1+2
Southend U (Loaned on 17/3/94) FL 4+1
Reading (£250,000 on 12/1/95) FL 71+20/26 FLC 5+1/1 FAC 2 Others 3/2
Notts Co (Loaned on 14/2/97) FL 6
Grimsby T (£170,000 on 24/7/97) FL 63+11/10 FLC 9+1/2 FAC 4/2 Others 8/2

NOSWORTHY Nayron
Born: Brixton, 11 October 1980
Height: 6'0" Weight: 12.0

Although regarded by Gillingham as a midfield player, Nayron can also play at full back, in central defence, or even up front when required. Made his debut in the home clash with Fulham last November, while still a trainee, when he came on as a sub after 16 minutes and did not let the team down, in giving a mature performance. comfortable on the ball, and carrying a powerful right-foot shot, he turned professional at the end of last year.
Gillingham (From trainee on 30/12/98) FL 0+3 Others 0+1

NOTMAN Alexander (Alex)
Born: Edinburgh, 10 December 1979
Height: 5'7" Weight: 10.11
International Honours: S: U21-4

Yet another Manchester United youngster who has come through the ranks, this chunky little striker with a good appetite for goals first came to prominence at Old Trafford when he came off the bench to score twice against Eric Cantona's XI in the Munich Memorial match last August. Having made a promising first-team debut as a substitute in the Worthington Cup against Spurs in December, if the goals keep coming, he is now well placed in the pecking order for a regular place in the squad before too long. After being capped at U21 level for Scotland in 1998-99, making four appearances, he went on a three-month loan to Aberdeen in January.
Manchester U (From trainee on 17/12/96) FLC 0+1
Aberdeen (Loaned on 11/2/99) SL 0+2

NOWLAND Adam Christopher
Born: Preston, 6 July 1981
Height: 5'11" Weight: 11.6

Having made his first-team debut for Blackpool whilst still a 16-year-old junior in the final match of 1997-98, Adam continued to promise much in the junior side, and came off the bench to score a last-minute winner in the 1-0 league victory over Luton at Bloomfield Road last September. It came as no surprise when he was handed a professional contract in January, being no more than he deserved, and he followed that up with a run of games, which included the opening goal in the 2-1 win at Preston. Is certainly one to watch out for.
Blackpool (From trainee on 15/1/99) FL 13+25/3 FLC 0+1

NUGENT Kevin Patrick
Born: Edmonton, 10 April 1969
Height: 6'1" Weight: 13.3
International Honours: Ei: Yth

As Cardiff's "Player of the Year", winning the Supporters Club award, and being named as manager Frank Burrows' personal choice, Kevin enjoyed his best-ever season in 1998-99, leading the line with great skill, and scoring 18 goals in all. It was a tribute to him that he should return with such an impact following almost a year out through injury. If only he had more pace to add to his undoubted skill, he would have been playing in a far higher division last season, and it was a surprise for many when he missed out on being named in the PFA award-winning Third Division team.
Leyton Orient (From trainee on 8/7/87) FL 86+8/20 FLC 9+3/6 FAC 9/3 Others 9+1/1
Plymouth Arg (£200,000 on 23/3/92) FL 124+7/32 FLC 11/2 FAC 10/3 Others 5+3
Bristol C (Signed on 29/9/95) FL 48+22/14 FLC 2+2 FAC 3+2/1 Others 2+1
Cardiff C (£65,000 on 4/8/97) FL 42+3/15 FLC 2+1 FAC 7/4

NYAMAH Kofi
Born: Islington, 20 June 1975
Height: 5'9" Weight: 11.10

Released by Stoke during the summer of 1998, he joined Luton just after the start of last season and was expected to feature strongly as a left-sided wing back, excelling when taking on defenders, and known to be an excellent crosser. Inclined to get too far up the pitch at times, he scored in a reserve match at Swindon but, apart from two cup matches, he was never really in Lennie Lawrence's first-team plans, and his monthly contract was not renewed just before Christmas. From there he moved to non-league Kingstonian, before coming back into the league on non-contract forms with Cambridge United (March), but not making a senior appearance.
Cambridge U (From trainee on 19/5/93) FL 9+14/2 FLC 0+2 FAC 3+1/1 Others 4) Free to Kettering T during 1995 close season
Stoke C (£25,000 on 24/12/96) FL 9+8 FLC 1+1
Luton T (Free on 20/8/98) FLC 0+1 FAC 1

OAKES Andrew (Andy) Mark
Born: Northwich, 11 January 1977
Height: 6'4" Weight: 12.4
The cousin of Aston Villa's Michael Oakes jumped at the chance of kick starting his career at the other end of the Football League ladder when he quit his factory job to join Hull City from Winsford United last December. Although the least known of manager Warren Joyce's pre-Christmas captures, the giant 'keeper was very familiar to the Hull boss, as he had cleaned his boots whilst still a trainee at Burnley. With nothing appearing to worry him, Andy soon took to his new challenge, and seems set to maintain the high standard of recent Hull custodians such as Alan Fettis and Roy Carroll. Stop Press: Having won the club's "Away Player of the Season" award, he signed for Derby on 2 June, the £460,000 fee being the joint-third highest in City's history.
Hull C (Signed from Winsford U on 8/12/98) FL 19 Others 1

OAKES Michael Christian
Born: Northwich, 30 October 1973
Height: 6'2" Weight: 14.6
Club Honours: FLC '96
International Honours: E: U21-6
In 1998-99, Michael achieved his longest ever spell of football, using Mark Bosnich's injury-forced absence to promote himself as the regular Aston Villa goalkeeper. The extended run helped him feel more comfortable and more settled, and he strung together a series of fine performances which had the fans chanting his name. Having patiently learned his trade in reserve football, he took his opportunity with both hands, so to speak, and visibly grew in confidence before giving way to Bosnich towards the end of a season that saw Villa heading the Premiership for long periods. His biggest disappointment was when being sent off at Blackburn on Boxing Day for allegedly handling the ball outside the penalty area, although the referee has since admitted he was wrong and nullified the red card. The son of Alan, the former Manchester City star, Michael is keeping it in the family, being a brave shot stopper who comes out well for crosses and kicks long and hard.
Aston Villa (From juniors on 16/7/91) PL 49+2 FLC 3 FAC 2 Others 5
Scarborough (Loaned on 26/11/93) FL 1 Others 1

OAKES Scott John
Born: Leicester, 5 August 1972
Height: 5'11" Weight: 11.13
International Honours: E: U21-1
Scott made just one solitary substitute appearance for Sheffield Wednesday in 1998-99, and continued in his role of utility player, having been at Hillsbrough under three separate managers and never having a

decent run in the side. But his problem has appeared to be one of versatility, playing in defence, midfield, and as a striker, and failing to settle into a regular position. There is no doubting his level of skill, composure on the ball, and good shooting ability, but he needs regular football to do himself justice. Is the son of a member of the famous pop group, Showaddywaddy.
Leicester C (From trainee on 9/5/90) FL 1+2 Others 1
Luton T (Signed on 22/10/91) FL 136+37/27 FLC 3+3/1 FAC 12+2/5 Others 3+3/1
Sheffield Wed (£425,000 + on 1/8/96) PL 7+17/1 FLC 0+1 FAC 0+2

OAKES Stefan Trevor
Born: Leicester, 6 September 1978
Height: 5'11" Weight: 12.4
A right-footed midfielder, the talented younger brother of Scott Oakes of Sheffield Wednesday signed professional forms for Leicester in July 1997, having spent two years on the YTS scheme. After impressing with consistent displays for the reserves, and earning promotion to the bench during City's injury crisis in 1998-99, Stefan made his debut in the home defeat by a rampant Chelsea, replacing Graham Fenton during the second half. Will clearly be pushing for more regular inclusion this coming season.
Leicester C (From trainee on 3/7/97) PL 2+1

OAKLEY Matthew
Born: Peterborough, 17 August 1977
Height: 5'10" Weight: 12.1
International Honours: E: U21-4
Southampton midfielder who is strong in the tackle and at closing people down. Having struggled with a back problem early on last season, which had been caused by the long throw-ins for which he is well known, the former U21 international made 24 senior appearances, while scoring two goals. Able to play wide or in the middle, and an excellent link man, watch for further improvement as the side fights for its Premiership survival.
Southampton (From trainee on 1/7/95) PL 81+13/7 FLC 10+1 FAC 5+2/1

OATWAY Anthony (Charlie) Philip David Terry Frank Donald Stanley Gerry Gordon Stephen James
Born: Hammersmith, 28 November 1973
Height: 5'7" Weight: 10.10
Club Honours: Div 3 '99
Brentford's tigerish midfield ball-winner, who was named after Queens Park Rangers' players of the '70s, Charlie started 1998-99 as a regular sub, before dropping out of contention and being loaned to Lincoln in October. Returned to the 14-strong squad in December, and stayed there until the end of the campaign, being used to "dig in" and get the ball for the more skilful players to create. Having scored his first Brentford goal against West Bromwich Albion in the Worthington Cup in August, the season ended with him being the proud possessor of a Third Division championship medal as the Bees returned from whence they came in 1997-98.
Cardiff C (Free from Yeading on 4/8/94) FL 29+3 FLC 2/1 FAC 1+1 Others 3+1

Torquay U (Free on 28/12/95) FL 65+2/1 FLC 3 FAC 1
Brentford (£10,000 on 21/8/97) FL 37+20 FLC 1+2/1 FAC 4 Others 0+1
Lincoln C (Loaned on 21/10/98) FL 3

O'BRIEN Andrew (Andy) James
Born: Harrogate, 29 June 1979
Height: 6'3" Weight: 12.4
International Honours: E: U21-1; Yth; Ei: U21-1
Last season, Bradford's Andy gained his first International honours when playing for the England U21 side against France in the 2-1 win at Derby County. He had previously been voted "Man of the Match" in the Nationwide League U21s versus an Italian Seria "B" side in a 1-1 draw in November. Also played at right back and right of midfield, as he had to vie with Ashley Westwood and John Dreyer to see who partnered Darren Moore in the centre of City's defence. At only 20 years of age, he certainly has time on his side, and always gives it everything in every game. Has now decided to represent the Republic of Ireland because he feels he will have more chance of international honours with them, as England seem to have an abundance of young centre halves. Making his debut in an U21 friendly against Sweden, Andy qualified for the Republic because his father was born there. Is known as "Rash" because of his man-marking ability.
Bradford C (From trainee on 28/10/96) FL 60+19/2 FLC 3 FAC 5

O'BRIEN Liam Francis
Born: Dublin, 5 September 1964
Height: 6'1" Weight: 12.6
Club Honours: Div 1 '93
International Honours: Ei: 16; U23-1; Yth; Sch
The veteran midfielder was not fully match fit as last season kicked off, but soon forced his way back into the Tranmere first team, where his probing play added an extra dimension, and he was often the hub of their best moves. Liam's accomplished and solid style enabled him to organise the speed and shape of midfield, and he was never less than dependable and consistent. Although his fierce right-footed shot brought him two league goals, he was released on a free transer at the end of the campaign.
Manchester U (£60,000 from Shamrock Rov on 14/10/86) FL 16+15/2 FLC 1+2 FAC 0+2
Newcastle U (£250,000 on 15/11/88) F/PL 131+20/19 FLC 9/1 FAC 12+2/1 Others 9+2/1
Tranmere Rov (£300,000 on 21/1/94) FL 169+12/12 FLC 17+2/1 FAC 7+1/1 Others 5+1

O'CALLAGHAN George
Born: Cork, 5 September 1979
Height: 6'1" Weight: 10.10
The Republic of Ireland U18 international rose through the ranks in 1998-99 to become an accomplished midfield player with Port Vale, having turned professional at the start of the campaign. He made a promising debut in a victory over Wolves, but was then left out for a month until appearing in another victory, against Crewe. A slightly-built youngster, who has

a bright future, he played twice more over the Christmas period, although he has yet to make the breakthrough under the new manager, Brian Horton.

Port Vale (From trainee on 10/7/98) FL 4 FAC 0+1

O'CONNOR James Kevin
Born: Dublin, 1 September 1979
Height: 5'8" Weight: 11.6
Regulars at Stoke's reserves games had noted James' progress, and when he was eventually given his first-team opportunity in 1998-99 he took it with both hands, soon winning "Man of the Match" honours. A tough up and down midfield player, who loves to be involved in the play, he was also called into the Republic of Ireland U20 squad for the World Youth Cup championships.

Stoke C (From trainee on 5/9/96) FL 4 Others 0+1

O'CONNOR Jonathan (Jon)
Born: Darlington, 28 October 1976
Height: 5'11" Weight: 11.10
International Honours: E: U21-3; Yth
Having played in Sheffield United's pre-1998-99 season friendlies and been a regular in the reserves, the rangy defender made his first start for the Blades at Bristol City in December. Two further games soon followed, during which he equipped himself well, but was unable to make the breakthrough as a first-team regular. Equally at home at right back or in central defence, where his positional play is excellent, he will hope to achieve this in 1999-2000.

Everton (From trainee on 28/10/93) PL 3+2
Sheffield U (Signed on 10/2/98) FL 2+2 FAC 1

O'CONNOR Martyn John
Born: Walsall, 10 December 1967
Height: 5'9" Weight: 11.8
A wily campaigner who played consistently well in the centre of midfield for Birmingham last season, he was often seen breaking up opposition attacks and taking up intelligent positions to maintain the Blues' reputation for having a rigid midfield. As the team's penalty taker, Martyn slotted home the winner at Portsmouth in September, also scoring from the spot against Crystal Palace and Crewe, before missing six games in mid season due to injury. Not a spectacular player, as ever he was steady and reliable in everything he did.

Crystal Palace (£25,000 from Bromsgrove Rov on 26/6/92) FL 2 Others 1+1
Walsall (Loaned on 24/3/93) FL 10/1 Others 2/1
Walsall (£40,000 on 14/2/94) FL 94/21 FLC 6/2 FAC 10/2 Others 3/1
Peterborough U (£350,000 on 12/7/96) FL 18/3 FLC 4 FAC 2
Birmingham C (£500,000 + on 29/11/96) FL 91+3/9 FLC 7 FAC 4 Others 2

ODUNSI Saheed **Adeleke (Leke)**
Born: Lambeth, 5 December 1980
Height: 5'9" Weight: 11.8
Another product of Millwall's youth policy, although Leke made his senior debut as a

substitute in the Auto Windshields first-round tie against Cardiff in 1998-99, it took until late on in the season for him to make his first league start, against Colchester. Having played regularly in the reserves, where he proved to be a very good midfield player who was strong in the challenge and able to make killing passes, he will no doubt be looking for more appearances in the coming term.

Millwall (From trainee on 24/2/99) FL 2+1 Others 0+1

O'GORMAN David (Dave)
Born: Chester, 20 June 1972
Height: 6'0" Weight: 12.10
A very pacy, wide midfielder with an eye for goal, Dave started last season in Swansea's first-team squad, but after just five league appearances was told that he would not be retained. Following that, in February, the Swans paid up his contract, enabling him to join North Wales League of Wales side, Connah's Quay Nomads.

Wrexham (From trainee on 6/7/90) FL 8+9 FAC 1 Others 1 (Free to Northwich Vic during 1991 close season)
Swansea C (£20,000 from Barry T on 8/8/97) FL 13+26/5 FLC 3 Others 1

OGRIZOVIC Steven (Steve)
Born: Mansfield, 12 September 1957
Height: 6'4" Weight: 15.0
Club Honours: FAC '87
"Oggy" played only two first-team games for Coventry in 1998-99, both at Christmas, against Tottenham and West Ham, and did not let the side down. The big goalkeeper then spent the rest of the campaign on the bench, and playing reserve team football, before developing a severe neck problem which necessitated surgery in March. Hopes to be back playing in October, and the club have offered him a one-year extension to his contract, providing the operation is a success.

Chesterfield (Signed from ONRYC on 28/7/77) FL 16 FLC 2
Liverpool (£70,000 on 18/11/77) FL 4 Others 1
Shrewsbury T (£70,000 on 11/8/82) FL 84 FLC 7 FAC 5
Coventry C (£72,000 on 22/6/84) F/PL 504/1 FLC 49 FAC 34 Others 11

OKAFOR Samuel (Sam) Amaechi
Born: Xtiam, Nigeria, 17 March 1982
Height: 5'9" Weight: 12.0
A Colchester youth team and YTS midfield player who enjoyed a consistent season in the South-East Counties side in 1998-99, and impressed in several Combination games for the reserves, he was rewarded with a place on the bench for the final match of the campaign at Blackpool. One for the future, he replaced David Gregory at half time to make a first-team debut, and did not look out of place at all.

Colchester U (Trainee) FL 0+1

O'KANE John Andrew
Born: Nottingham, 15 November 1974
Height: 5'10" Weight: 12.2
Club Honours: FAYC '92; Div 2 '97

A neat and tidy defender, with the ability to operate in either the right or left-back positions, John suffered from yet another managerial change at Everton in the summer of 1998. Rarely figuring in Walter Smith's plans, he spent a fruitless spell on loan at Burnley last October, and at the end of the season was made available for transfer. His rare first-team opportunities during 1998-99 came in high pressure matches – an FA Cup quarter final at Newcastle, and a trip to Manchester United – and he did not let anyone down on either occasion. A technically adept performer, schooled at Manchester United, his career can still flourish.

Manchester U (From trainee on 29/1/93) PL 1+1 FLC 2+1 FAC 1 Others 1
Bury (Loaned on 25/10/96) FL 2+2/2
Bury (Loaned on 16/1/97) FL 9/1 Others 1
Bradford C (Loaned on 31/10/97) FL 7
Everton (£250,000 + on 30/1/98) PL 14 FAC 1+2
Burnley (Loaned on 31/10/98) FL 8

OLDFIELD David Charles
Born: Perth, Australia, 30 May 1968
Height: 5'11" Weight: 13.4
International Honours: E: U21-1
Released by Luton during the 1998 close season, it would have to be said that David was not an instant hit with the Stoke public, but if ever a player battled through to show the fans that he was worthy of their support it was him. A box-to-box player who was never accused of hiding, he also captained the side in Phil Robinson's absence.

Luton T (From apprentice on 16/5/86) FL 21+8/4 FLC 4+2/2 FAC 0+1 Others 2+1/2
Manchester C (£600,000 on 14/3/89) FL 18+8/6 FLC 2+1/2 Others 0+1/1
Leicester C (£150,000 on 12/1/90) F/PL 163+25/26 FLC 10+1/1 FAC 6/3 Others 11+3/2
Millwall (Loaned on 24/2/95) FL 16+1/6
Luton T (£150,000 on 21/7/95) FL 99+18/18 FLC 11/2 FAC 2 Others 7+2/4
Stoke C (Free on 2/7/98) FL 43+3/6 FLC 2 FAC 2 Others 1

O'LEARY Kristian Denis
Born: Port Talbot, 30 August 1977
Height: 6'0" Weight: 13.4
International Honours: W: Yth
With a knee injury forcing him to miss most of the first half of last season, his recall to the Swansea first team in the FA Cup game against Derby, to cover for the suspended Jason Smith, showed what a good prospect he was for the future. Appearing to be a lot fitter, Kristian was also prominent when playing in midfield, and always looked capable of scoring vital goals. Included as substitute for Wales U21 side that played Switzerland on March 30th, his consistent form made it difficult for the management to leave him out of the side, catching the eye in defence or midfield.

Swansea C (From trainee on 1/7/96) FL 52+9/3 FLC 1 FAC 3+1 Others 2+2

OLIVER Adam

Born: West Bromwich, 25 October 1980
Height: 5'9" Weight: 11.2
International Honours: E: Yth

A compact, hard-shooting, determined midfielder with a big future ahead of him, Adam made his first-team debut for West Bromwich when coming off the bench for the final four minutes of Albion's 2-1 Worthington Cup win over Brentford last August. Already named in the England U18 squad, he also made a subs' league appearance before the campaign closed.

West Bromwich A (From trainee on 15/8/98) FL 0+1 FLC 0+1

OLIVER Michael

Born: Middlesbrough, 2 August 1975
Height: 5'10" Weight: 12.4

This skilful and strong-running Darlington midfielder completed his third season with the club in 1998-99, appearing in 75 per-cent of the matches before being surprisingly released in the summer. Although his strong runs often took him through defences, his goalscoring touch eluded him, and he only managed one strike all season, against Shrewsbury at Feethams. Is a player who covers every inch of the pitch.

Middlesbrough (From trainee on 19/8/92) Others 0+1
Stockport Co (£15,000 on 7/7/94) FL 17+5/1 FLC 0+2 FAC 2 Others 1
Darlington (Free on 30/7/96) FL 100+14/12 FLC 6 FAC 7+1 Others 2+3

OMOYINMI Emmanuel (Manny)

Born: Nigeria, 28 December 1977
Height: 5'6" Weight: 10.7
International Honours: E: Sch

Despite producing outstanding performances when playing for West Ham reserves last season, Manny was only called upon for first-team duty on the odd occasion, making five appearances from the bench in the first half of 1998-99, before getting a start at Swansea in the FA Cup third-round game. Having great pace, and able to play down either flank, he was loaned to Leyton Orient in transfer deadline week to help the O's in their promotion quest, making his debut at Scunthorpe, and scoring with a header in the next game, a 2-1 win at Halifax. Two games later, he returned to Upton Park following an injury, but expects to be challenging for a place in 1999-2000.

West Ham U (From trainee on 17/5/95) PL 1+8/2 FLC 0+1 FAC 1+1
Bournemouth (Loaned on 30/9/96) FL 5+2
Dundee U (Loaned on 20/2/98) SL 1+3 SC 0+1
Leyton Orient (Loaned on 19/3/99) FL 3+1/1

O'NEILL John Joseph

Born: Glasgow, 1 January 1974
Height: 5'11" Weight: 12.0

1998-99 was another steady season for John who never quite managed to consolidate his first-team place at Bournemouth, making 22 starts and 13 substitute appearances, while scoring four league and cup goals. Able to play anywhere in a midfield or in a striking role, he is a player with good vision who is not afraid to run with the ball, and is versatile enough to fill in where needed.

Queens Park R (From school on 25/7/91) SL 70+21/30 SLC 2+1 SC 2 Others 0+1
Glasgow C (Signed on 16/5/94) SL 0+2
Bournemouth (Free on 29/3/96) FL 61+30/7 FLC 4+4 FAC 4+4/2 Others 5+4

O'NEILL Keith Padre Gerard

Born: Dublin, 16 February 1976
Height: 6'1" Weight: 12.7
International Honours: Ei: 12; U21-1; Yth; Sch

Having progressed through the Norwich youth ranks to blossom only briefly, Keith moved to Middlesbrough last March in a deal which should eventually land the Canaries £1 million. Before departing, he scored a fantastic 40-yard goal at Tranmere, and added to his tally of full caps for the Republic of Ireland, with an early season appearance against Croatia. Mainly regarded as a left winger, winning instant approval from the Boro fans on his arrival, he can also operate successfully as a central striker, having great pace and strength. Signed to give more bite and width to the strike force, he fitted the bill admirably, his electrifying pace and tenacious aggression ensuring that his selection in the Premiership line up became an accepted formality, while forming an excellent partnership with Hamilton Ricard up front.

Norwich C (From trainee on 1/7/94) P/FL 54+19/8 FLC 8+3/1 FAC 3
Middlesbrough (£700,000 + on 19/3/99) PL 4+2

O'NEILL Michael Andrew Martin

Born: Portadown, 5 July 1969
Height: 5'11" Weight: 11.10
Club Honours: AMC '99
International Honours: NI: 31; B-2; U23-1; U21-1; Yth; Sch

Unable to get any first-team action at Coventry in 1998-99, Michael became the new Wigan manager Ray Mathias' first signing when he arrived at Springfield Park in September. Still a quality performer, the midfielder enjoyed an excellent season which also saw him restored to Northern Ireland international duty. A classy dribbler with a crisp passing ability, he also chipped in with some important strikes as the club won the Auto Windscreens Shield, including the winner in the area final second-leg at Wrexham.

Newcastle U (Signed from Coleraine on 23/10/87) FL 36+12/15 FLC 2 FAC 3+2/1 Others 1
Dundee U (Signed on 15/8/89) SL 49+15/11 SLC 3+2/1 SC 2 Others 3+2/1
Hibernian (Signed on 20/8/93) SL 96+2/19 SLC 9/3 SC 6/2
Coventry C (£500.000 on 26/7/96) PL 3+2 FLC 1
Aberdeen (Loaned on 22/1/98) SL 4+1 SC 0+1
Reading (Loaned on 2/3/98) FL 9/1
Wigan Ath (Free on 18/9/98) FL 35+1 FLC 1 FAC 3 Others 7/3

ONUORA Ifem (Iffy)

Born: Glasgow, 28 July 1967
Height: 6'1" Weight: 13.10

Another of Swindon's rising stars, the bulky striker proved himself as lethal in the air as he was with the ball at his feet in 1998-99, and was a revelation, being in the top three goalscorers for Division One all year. Missing just three games for Town, he got himself off the mark in the 1-1 home draw against Sunderland three games into the new campaign, and hit the back of the net on a regular basis, scoring braces at home to Oxford and at Crewe and Barnsley. Big and strong, and effective when holding up play in the area, needless to say, he is a favourite with the Town faithful.

Huddersfield T (Signed from Bradford University on 28/7/89) FL 115+50/30 FLC 10+6/4 FAC 11+3/3 Others 13+3/3
Mansfield T (£30,000 on 20/7/94) FL 17+11/8 FAC 0+1 Others 1
Gillingham (£25,000 on 16/8/96) FL 53+9/23 FLC 6/1 FAC 4/2 Others 1
Swindon T (£120,000 on 13/3/98) FL 46+3/21 FLC 2 FAC 1+1

Udo Onwere

ONWERE Udo Alozie

Born: Hammersmith, 9 November 1971
Height: 6'0" Weight: 12.0

Udo began the 1998-99 campaign boasting the coveted title of being Barnet's leading scorer during the summer schedule, and he looked set to continue that form during the ensuing term. However, despite operating successfully in the latter stages, he failed to hold down a regular place in the starting line-up. A tremendous athlete, who is capable of covering large areas during a match, his neat distribution is often overlooked by supporters, while his most prominent attributes are his ability to win the ball in the middle of the park, and his lengthy throwing ability, which proved to be a useful set-piece weapon. Scored his first goal in the closing minutes of the 3-0 victory over Cambridge in March, and he continued the streak in front of goal in the next home match, against Halifax. However, his most proficient display for the Bees came in the 1-0 home win against Scarborough in April

when, after hitting the bar with a free kick, he carved open a glorious opportunity for Marlon King to net the winner. His season was ended prematurely when he suffered a severe groin injury in the middle of April, before being released in the summer.

Fulham (From trainee on 11/7/90) FL 66+19/7 FLC 4+2 FAC 1+1 Others 9

Lincoln C (Free on 12/8/94) FL 40+3/4 FLC 5 FAC 1 Others 4/1 (Free to Dover Ath in August 1996)

Blackpool (Free on 13/9/96) FL 5+4 FLC 1 FAC 1 Others 0+2

Barnet (Free on 5/8/97) FL 25+11/2 FLC 4+1 FAC 0+1 Others 1+1

OPARA Kelechi Chrysantus
Born: Oweri, Nigeria, 21 December 1981
Height: 6'0" Weight: 12.6

Another youth team regular in 1998-99, along with Sam Okafor, "KK" also made his first-team debut for Colchester in the latter stages of the closing League game at Blackpool. Although only given a few minutes on the pitch, he showed some good touches and nice positional play, and has set out his standards for the coming season's development.

Colchester U (Trainee) FL 0+1

O'REGAN Kieran Michael
Born: Cork, 9 November 1963
Height: 5'8" Weight: 10.12
International Honours: Ei: 4; U21-1; Yth

Kieran began 1998-99 as Halifax's player/manager, but his season was disrupted by injury, and his midfield ball-playing skills were sadly missed. Despite having been an integral part of the side that was promoted from the Conference, with the club's results being a major disappointment, he was dismissed, along with his assistant, Andy May, in April.

Brighton & Hove A (Signed from Tramore Ath on 9/4/83) FL 69+17/2 FLC 6+1 FAC 3 Others 2+1/1

Swindon T (Free on 12/8/87) FL 23+3/1 FLC 5+1 FAC 2+1 Others 3/1

Huddersfield T (Signed on 4/8/88) FL 187+12/25 FLC 15+1/1 FAC 16+1/3 Others 20+1/3

West Bromwich A (£25,000 on 8/7/93) FL 36+9/2 FLC 3+1 FAC 2 Others 3

Halifax T (Free on 17/8/95) FL 15+4/2 FLC 2+1 Others 1

ORLYGSSON Thorvaldur (Toddy)
Born: Iceland, 2 August 1966
Height: 5'11" Weight: 11.3
International Honours: Iceland: 41

Although he started the first 11 matches for Oldham in 1998-99, Toddy had another frustrating season, as he found himself in and out of the team. Recognised as a strong tackler, as well as a good passer of the ball, and effective on the wide right or in central midfield, he appeared to have lost his way at Boundary Park, and looked out of sorts for much of the time. And, with the manager expecting more from him, he was released during the summer.

Nottingham F (£175,000 from KA Akureyri on 9/12/89) F/PL 31+6/2 FLC 5+1/2 FAC 1 Others 0+1

Stoke C (Free on 5/8/93) FL 86+4/16 FLC 7/1 FAC 6/1 Others 7/1

Oldham Ath (£180,000 on 22/12/95) FL 65+11/1 FLC 7+1 FAC 3+1

ORMEROD Anthony
Born: Middlesbrough, 31 March 1979
Height: 5'10" Weight: 11.8
International Honours: E: Yth

A tricky young Middlesbrough winger who will long be remembered for his brilliant debut goal, against Bradford in 1997-98, having made just one subs' appearance for Boro last season before being loaned out to Carlisle in mid January in a bid to get match fit. Arriving at a club managed by his old team-mate, Nigel Pearson, he played in five games under difficult circumstances, and, while showing glimpses of his class, did not find the net. On a scoring note, his "forward flip" after hitting the target is a great favourite with Boro fans.

Middlesbrough (From trainee on 16/5/96) FL 8+10/3 FLC 2+2 FAC 2

Carlisle U (Loaned on 18/1/99) FL 5 Others 1+1

ORMEROD Brett Ryan
Born: Blackburn, 18 October 1976
Height: 5'11" Weight: 11.4

A hard-working young Blackpool striker, Brett built on earlier promises to become a regular member of the squad in 1998-99, his good form epitomised when coming off the bench to net the first in a 2-0 win at Bristol Rovers. Despite not scoring nearly as many goals as he would have liked, he was always working for the good of the team, and should, in time, develop into a very useful player.

Blackpool (£50,000 from Accrington Stanley on 21/3/97) FL 35+18/10 FLC 2 FAC 1+1/1 Others 3

ORMEROD Mark Ian
Born: Bournemouth, 5 February 1976
Height: 6'0" Weight: 12.11

A young Brighton goalkeeper who shared the position in 1998-99 with the more experienced Mark Walton, he is not spectacular, but is technically sound, particularly with positioning and organising his defence. After an impressive reserve-team performance in the 0-0 draw against an experienced Arsenal side, which contained Kanu, rumours abounded of interest from the Gunners which never materialised. Signed a new one-year contract at the end of the season.

Brighton & Hove A (From trainee on 21/7/94) FL 78 FLC 2 FAC 1 Others 3

OSBORN Simon Edward
Born: Croydon, 19 January 1972
Height: 5'9" Weight: 11.4

After curling in a neat goal at Barnet, the midfielder was hoping to establish himself with Wolves last season, having not really progressed as well as expected, and he played in the first 13 games before being injured against Bury and missing the next six. He came back amidst speculation that he would leave the club at the end of the campaign. Unfortunately, the crowd did not always appreciate the amount of

covering and chasing that he put in, which sometimes did not allow his creative skills to flourish. Scored a well-deserved goal at Sheffield on Easter Monday, equalising with a beautiful free-kick, and got a lot of tackles in, but eight bookings meant that he missed the visit to Birmingham, thus ending a 15-game run.

Crystal Palace (From trainee on 3/1/90) F/PL 47+8/5 FLC 11/1 FAC 2 Others 1+3

Reading (£90,000 on 17/8/94) FL 31+1/5 FLC 4 Others 3

Queens Park R (£1,100,000 on 7/7/95) PL 6+3/1 FLC 2

Wolverhampton W (£1,000,000 on 22/12/95) FL 113+4/11 FLC 5/2 FAC 9 Others 2

OSTENSTAD Egil
Born: Haugesun, Norway, 2 January 1972
Height: 6'0" Weight: 13.0
International Honours: Norway: 17

Norwegian international striker who signed for Southampton in 1996. Very strong in the air, and a powerful runner, perhaps his total of seven Premiership goals in 1998-99 was disappointing, even though he was the club's top scorer, but it reflected the problems the Saints had in creating chances. Despite having various striking partners during the campaign, as the manager revolved the squad in order to achieve the best combination and, more often than not, being left on his own up front, he was always looking to hurt defences. Is very popular with the Dell faithful.

Southampton (£800,000 from Viking Stavanger on 3/10/96) PL 77+16/28 FLC 9/3 FAC 3+1/2

OSTER John Morgan
Born: Boston, 8 December 1978
Height: 5'9" Weight: 10.8
International Honours: W: 3; B-1; U21-9; Yth

A gifted out-and-out winger with the ability to play on either the right or left, John endured a frustrating season at Everton in 1998-99. When on the top of his form he could be a devastating match winner, as evidenced by a solo goal in an FA Cup-tie against Coventry, but the youngster was never really given a long enough run in the side to show he could produce such performances regularly. Despite suffering the embarrassment of being sent off in an international for the second successive time – a Wales U21 match against Italy – he has no problems with his discipline. Was made available for transfer by the Blues at the end of a season which never really took off for him. Also represented the Welsh "B" team against Northern Ireland.

Grimsby T (From trainee on 11/7/96) FL 21+3/3 FAC 0+1/1

Everton (£1,500,000 on 21/7/97) PL 22+18/1 FLC 4+1/1 FAC 2+3/1

O'SULLIVAN Wayne St John
Born: Akrotiri, Cyprus, 25 February 1974
Height: 5'9" Weight: 11.2
Club Honours: Div 2 '96
International Honours: Ei: U21-2

A consistent, hard-working player who played a full part in Cardiff's promotion in 1998-99, Wayne can play at wing back on either side, or in midfield. Suffered a little after the departure of Mark Delaney to Aston Villa, as the player selected to replace him, with the fans constantly comparing the two. Whereas Delaney is a fast, straight-running player, and Wayne is a tricky, powerful-running figure, it was never a fair comparison, especially as the supporters rarely acknowledged his superiority over Delaney on the defensive side of his game. One of only two City players out of contract at the end of the campaign, he was offered new terms by the club.

Swindon T (From trainee on 1/5/93) FL 65+24/3 FLC 11/1 FAC 1+3 Others 3+2
Cardiff C (£75,000 on 22/8/97) FL 78+7/4 FLC 1+2 FAC 10/1 Others 2

OTTA Walter Nicolas
Born: Cordoba, Argentina, 20 December 1973
Height: 5'9" Weight: 11.2
A free agent, Walter signed from Deportes Temuco, Chile last November, and the following day went on as a substitute for Jamie Lambert in Walsall's 3-0 win over Millwall. Just three days later he got an injury-time winner against Lincoln, and then scored three more goals in the next few weeks while acting as a twin spearhead with Andy Rammell. He declined a longer contract, however, and left the Saddlers at the turn of the year.

Walsall (Free from Deportes Temuco on 6/11/98) FL 6+2/3 FAC 2 Others 1/1

OVENDALE Mark John
Born: Leicester, 22 November 1973
Height: 6'2" Weight: 13.2
An ever present for Bournemouth in 1998-99, making 58 league and cup appearances, Mark joined the club from League of Wales side, Barry Town, in the 1998 close season, and made a smooth transition to league football. He proved an enormous asset to the Cherries, in giving many outstanding performances as an integral part of a very solid defence. Is an excellent shot stopper who commands the penalty area, and makes gathering crosses and corners look easy.

Northampton T (Free from Wisbech on 15/8/94) FL 6 Others 2 (Free to Barry T during 1995 close season)
Bournemouth (£30,000 on 14/5/98) FL 46 FLC 5 FAC 4 Others 3

OVERMARS Marc
Born: Ernst, Holland, 29 March 1973
Height: 5'8" Weight: 11.4
Club Honours: PL '98; FAC '98; CS '99
International Honours: Holland: 51
On his day one of the most exciting left-sided wingers in the Premier League, and a regular for Holland, Marc was an automatic choice in the Arsenal line-up during 1998-99. Showing electrifying pace and wonderful dribbling skills, he could be relied upon to contribute his share of goals, frequently making runs from his own half, taking on opponents, and creating

confusion. A classic example of this was in the fourth round of the FA Cup at Wolves when he ran on to a pass from Tony Adams to attack and avoid four defenders before hitting a powerful shot into the net to help seal victory. His delivery of long crosses is first class, and during the season he continued to link well with his fellow Dutch international, Dennis Bergkamp, and Frenchman, Nicolas Anelka. Is a crucial figure in the future of the club.

Arsenal (£7,000,000 from Ajax on 10/7/97) PL 69/18 FLC 3/2 FAC 14+2/6 Others 7/2

OVERSON Vincent (Vince) David
Born: Kettering, 15 May 1962
Height: 6'2" Weight: 15.0
Club Honours: Div 3 '82, Div 2 '93; AMC '91, '92
Freed by Burnley during the 1998 close season, the tall centre back moved to Football League newcomers Halifax Town on non-contract terms in time for the start of last season. With the club obviously looking to call upon his great reservoir of experience as they looked to re-establish themselves in the league, unfortunately, after making just one appearance from the bench, he was plagued by injury problems and was released in September, joining non-league Padiham. A player who always brought 100 per-cent effort to his game, he left the league with close on 700 first-team appearances behind him.

Burnley (From apprentice on 16/11/79) FL 207+4/6 FLC 9/1 FAC 19 Others 10
Birmingham C (Free on 11/6/86) FL 179+3/3 FLC 11+1 FAC 8 Others 11/1
Stoke C (£55,000 on 29/8/91) FL 167+3/6 FLC 13/1 FAC 10 Others 23
Burnley (Free on 15/8/96) FL 6+2 FLC 1 Others 1
Shrewsbury T (Loaned on 18/9/97) FL 2
Halifax T (Free on 8/8/98) FLC 0+1

OWEN Gareth
Born: Chester, 21 October 1971
Height: 5'8" Weight: 12.0
Club Honours: WC '95
International Honours: W: B-1; U21-8
Awarded a testimonial in 1999-2000 for his loyalty to Wrexham, although now approaching 350 appearances and ten-years service with the Racecourse club, one gets the impression we have never really seen the best of Gareth. A fine long passer of the ball, and a strong forager, there is much to be admired about his play, despite a certain lack of consistency. Always more effective when pushing up to help his forwards with strong driving play, often unleashing a powerful shot, he scored some vital goals, similar to his glancing header against Bristol Rovers at the Racecourse in April which secured the points.

Wrexham (From trainee on 6/7/90) FL 245+44/31 FLC 9+1 FAC 22+6 Others 35+2/1

OWEN Michael James
Born: Chester, 14 December 1979
Height: 5'9" Weight: 11.2
Club Honours: FAYC '96
International Honours: E: 13; U21-1; Yth; Sch

1998-99 was yet another spectacular season for the boy genius. A brilliant hat trick against Newcastle at St James' Park in only the third game of the campaign augured well for the Reds and for Michael. However, while Liverpool's Premiership hopes disappeared into thin air, his career took off to gain new heights. At the start of the season there was much talk that this genius was tired, and that he had expended too much energy – both mental and physical – during England's World Cup campaign in France, but more goals and ceaseless running destroyed that particular myth. He continued to hit the back of the net with regularity in a manner which few other strikers in the league could match. But goalscoring apart, he runs relentlessly in the Liverpool cause, often chasing balls which appear to be going out of play, and chasing balls which other team mates have given up as lost. There is more than the merest hint of a Shankly player about him, and he continues to be chosen for his country. There is much more to come from this young man, and he is surely destined, injuries apart, to re-write the record books.

Liverpool (From juniors on 18/12/96) PL 65+3/37 FLC 6/5 FAC 2/2 Others 8+2/3

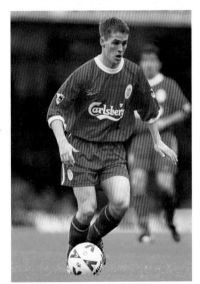

Michael Owen

OWERS Gary
Born: Newcastle, 3 October 1968
Height: 5'11" Weight: 12.7
Club Honours: Div 3 '88
Signed from Bristol City during the 1998 close season, Gary took time to settle at Notts County, but once he had moved his family to Nottingham he became one of the club's most consistent performers. Although usually occupying the central midfield holding position, where his vast experience was tested to the full in a difficult season, in the last few weeks he occupied the right-back slot due to the transfer of Ian Hendon, and injuries to

other players. Continuing to maintain his record of having scored in every season of his professional career, four being put away in 1998-99, he is a player you can rely upon, being two footed and sure in possession.

Sunderland (From apprentice on 8/10/86) FL 259+9/25 FLC 25+1/1 FAC 10+2 Others 11+1/1
Bristol C (£250,000 on 23/12/94) FL 121+5/9 FLC 9/1 FAC 9 Others 9/2
Notts Co (£15,000 on 30/7/98) FL 36+3/3 FLC 2 FAC 6/1

OWUSU Lloyd Magnus
Born: Slough, 12 December 1976
Height: 6'1" Weight: 14.0
Club Honours: Div 3 '99

Signed from non-league Slough during the summer of 1998, this strong and deceptively fast Brentford striker had an outstanding first league season, ending it as the Bees' top scorer. Scored hat tricks against Southend, home and away, and

Rotherham, and was especially effective at closing down opposing goalkeepers as they attempted to clear back passes. The winner of a Third Division championship medal at his first attempt, he developed cult status with the supporters, who loved his 100 per-cent effort, and chanted "Owusuuu" at every opportunity.

Brentford (£25,000 from Slough T on 29/7/98) FL 42+4/22 FLC 0+4/2 FAC 3/1 Others 2+1

Lloyd Owusu

P

PADOVANO Michele
Born: Turin, Italy, 28 August 1966
Height: 5'10" Weight: 10.10
International Honours: Italy: 1
Another talented Italian at Crystal Palace who suffered from the financial difficulties of last season, apart from coming off the bench twice Michele was restricted to the reserves, scoring four goals before going on loan to Metz (France) in November. Even there his luck was out, being injured in training before even getting a game. A striker who has super touches, and turns defenders well, and is contracted at Palace until the end of 1999-2000, it is difficult to see where he fits in at the club.
Crystal Palace (£1,700,000 from Juventus, via Asti, Cosenza, Pisa, Napoli, Genoa and Reggiana, on 18/11/97) P/FL 0+4/1 FLC 8+4/1

PAGE Robert John
Born: Llwynpia, 3 September 1974
Height: 6'0" Weight: 12.5
Club Honours: Div 2 '98
International Honours: W: 7; B-1; U21-6; Yth; Sch
A resolute central defender, Robert has now made over 150 appearances for Watford, his only club. Despite being club captain, he found himself in the reserves at the start of last season, but his setback only served to make him more determined. Injuries to Keith Millen and Dean Yates helped him regain both his first-team place and the captaincy, and he struck up an excellent understanding with Steve Palmer in the heart of the defence that gave the side's promotion aspirations a solid grounding. His consistent form, and extra maturity and assurance, earned him a recall to the Welsh squad, and he had the honour of captaining Wales "B" against Northern Ireland.
Watford (From trainee on 19/4/93) FL 137+7 FLC 9 FAC 10+1 Others 6/1

PAHARS Marians
Born: Latvia, 5 August 1976
Height: 5'9" Weight: 10.9
International Honours: Latvia: 18
The Latvian international striker was signed by Southampton just before last March's transfer deadline, having been refused a work permit twice. In fact, the club had wanted to sign him much earlier, but he was strangely deemed to be not good enough, and only on the third appeal was the permit allowed. coming on as a sub in the home match against Blackburn, he scored the vital equaliser, having had an earlier introduction to Premiership football when coming off the bench for 22 minutes at Coventry. Then, in the last match at home, against Everton, he scored both goals in a 2-0 win, the second a glorious diving header, to send the Saints' fans wild. Small and quick, Marians has been described as the Latvian Michael Owen, and great things are expected of him in the future.
Southampton (£800,000 from Skonto Riga on 25/3/99) PL 4+2/3

PAINTER Peter Robert (Robbie)
Born: Wigan, 26 January 1971
Height: 5'11" Weight: 12.2
When Graham Lancashire and Mark Leonard were injured early last season, Robbie was left as Rochdale's only recognised front man. Although he netted in three consecutive games in September, despite his non-stop running Dale's previous top scorer found goals hard to come by after that, and following the signings of Andy Morris and Michael Holt he was given a slightly deeper lying role, even being relegated to the bench for a few games. Out of contract during the summer, at the time of going to press the club had offered him terms of re-engagement.
Chester C (From trainee on 1/7/88) FL 58+26/8 FLC 2+2 FAC 7+1/3 Others 3+3
Maidstone U (£30,000 on 16/8/91) FL 27+3/5 FLC 2 FAC 1+1 Others 0+2
Burnley (£25,000 on 27/3/92) FL 16+10/2 FLC 2 FAC 1
Darlington (Signed on 16/9/93) FL 104+11/28 FLC 2+4/1 FAC 5+1/2 Others 9/3
Rochdale (Signed on 10/10/96) FL 101+11/30 FLC 3/1 FAC 7 Others 4+2

PALLISTER Gary Andrew
Born: Ramsgate, 30 June 1965
Height: 6'4" Weight: 14.13
Club Honours: FAC '90, '94, '96; CS '93, '94, '96, '97; ECWC '91; ESC '91; FLC '92; PL '93, '94, '96, '97
International Honours: E: 22; B-9
Signed from Manchester United during the 1998 close season, this vastly experienced centre back, who, just like the Prodigal Son, returned home to Middlesbrough in readiness for the start of last season, much to the delight of the fans. "Pally" is very much the local boy made good, and can do nothing wrong in the eyes of the faithful. Was a towering presence at the back, where he missed nothing in the air, and was "Robbo's" inspirational replacement for Nigel Pearson. Having formed a brilliant defensive partnership with hard-tackling Tony Mowbray in the heady days of the mid and late 1980s, when Bruce Rioch's youthful team was forging an existence for a liquidation threatened Boro, the rest as they say is history, and he returned from his duties with United to a vastly different set up from the one that he left. Gary will not mind being reminded of the super, even memorable goal he scored earlier in the season with a brilliant diving header. Sadly, it was at the wrong end as he strove valiantly to deny the opposition attack, and it helped Chelsea to a 2-0 victory over Boro.
Middlesbrough (Free from Billingham T on 7/11/84) FL 156/5 FLC 10 FAC 10/1 Others 13
Darlington (Loaned on 18/10/85) FL 7
Manchester U (£2,300,000 on 29/8/89) F/PL 314+3/12 FLC 36 FAC 38/1 Others 45+1/1
Middlesbrough (£2,500,000 on 24/7/98) PL 26 FAC 1

PALMER Carlton Lloyd
Born: Rowley Regis, 5 December 1965
Height: 6'2" Weight: 13.3
International Honours: E: 18; B-5; U21-4
Starting 1998-99 with Southampton, playing in all but two of the opening 24 games,

Carlton became Ron Atkinson's first signing for Nottingham Forest last January as the new manager desperately looked for the right formula that would turn around Forest's disappointing season. Mind you, things were tough at the Dell so swapping it for the City Ground probably did not seem to be a bad idea at the time. An experienced campaigner, who Atkinson knew from his days with him at West Bromwich and Sheffield Wednesday, and an awkward, gangly type with an all-action style, he was used both in midfield and as a centre back. Although his exciting, surging forward runs galvanised the crowd at times, and although starting with a win in his first game, at Everton, wins were few and far between, and in his next match he was a member of the Forest side that was annihilated 8-1 at home by Manchester United. With Forest back in the First Division in 1999-2000, Carlton will be among players who are looking to re-group.
West Bromwich A (From apprentice on 21/12/84) FL 114+7/4 FLC 7+1/1 FAC 4 Others 6
Sheffield Wed (£750,000 on 23/2/89) F/PL 204+1/14 FLC 31/1 FAC 18/2 Others 8+1/1
Leeds U (£2,600,000 on 30/6/94) PL 100+2/5 FLC 12 FAC 12/1 Others 4/1
Southampton (£1,000,000 on 26/9/97) PL 44+1/3 FLC 5 FAC 2
Nottingham F (£1,100,000 on 21/1/99) PL 13

PALMER Stephen (Steve) Leonard
Born: Brighton, 31 March 1968
Height: 6'1" Weight: 12.13
Club Honours: Div 2 '92, '98
International Honours: E: Sch
Having worn every Watford shirt the previous season, Steve confined himself to central defence in 1998-99, where his partnership with Robert Page proved a cornerstone of the team's promotion challenge, and made him a popular choice as the club's "Player of the Year". Has now clocked up more than 250 league appearances, and his fitness and wholehearted commitment remain exemplary. As an ex-Ipswich player, his goal against Norwich must have given him particular pleasure.
Ipswich T (Free from Cambridge University on 1/8/89) F/PL 87+24/2 FLC 3 FAC 8+3/1 Others 4+2
Watford (£135,000 on 28/9/95) FL 147+11/6 FLC 10+1 FAC 8+1 Others 7

PARKER Garry Stuart
Born: Oxford, 7 September 1965
Height: 5'11" Weight: 13.2
Club Honours: FLC '89, '90, '97; ESC '89
International Honours: E: B-1; U21-6; Yth
A right-footed Leicester midfielder, Garry started more often in the early rounds of the Worthington Cup than he did in the league last season, but still managed a vital contribution by netting the last-minute penalty to oust Leeds from the Worthington Cup, and keep the Foxes bound for Wembley. As the season wore on, however, he became more involved with coaching duties, and looks set to build on that role in the coming campaign.
Luton T (From apprentice on 5/5/83) FL 31+11/3 FLC 1+3/1 FAC 6+2

Hull C (£72,000 on 21/2/86) FL 82+2/8 FLC 5 FAC 4 Others 2/1
Nottingham F (£260,000 on 24/3/88) FL 99+4/17 FLC 22+1/4 FAC 16/5 Others 9/3
Aston Villa (£650,000 on 29/11/91) F/PL 91+4/13 FLC 12 FAC 10/1 Others 0+2
Leicester C (£300,000 on 10/2/95) P/FL 89+25/10 FLC 16+1/2 FAC 9+2/2 Others 4+1/2

PARKER Scott Matthew
Born: Lambeth, 13 October 1980
Height: 5'7" Weight: 10.7
International Honours: E: Yth; Sch

An extremely talented self-assured midfield player who made only four Premiership substitute appearances for Charlton during last season, his only start coming in the FA Cup at Blackburn, where he performed well. Scott has an excellent touch, reads the game well, likes to take players on, distributes the ball very well, being not afraid to try a long-range pass if appropriate, and packs a powerful shot. Able to play in central midfield, or wide on the right, it was a surprise that he did not make more appearances during the campaign.
Charlton Ath (From trainee on 22/10/97) P/FL 0+7 FLC 0+1 FAC 1+1

PARKIN Brian
Born: Birkenhead, 12 October 1965
Height: 6'3" Weight: 14.7
Club Honours: Div 3 '90

Released by Wycombe during the 1998 close season after failing to hold down a place in 1997-98, playing just once, this very experienced goalie signed Pontins' forms for Shrewsbury in 1998-99 before coming back into the League with Notts County as a non-contract player in October. An excellent shot stopper, Brian was a temporary signing to provide cover for Darren Ward, who was away on international duty, having been recommended by then assistant manager, Dennis Booth. Playing just once, a 3-2 home defeat at the hands of Lincoln, sadly, he failed to earn the chance of an offer of a permanent second-choice 'keeper role and moved on to Wimbledon before being released in the summer.
Oldham Ath (From juniors on 31/3/83) FL 6 FLC 2
Crewe Alex (Free on 30/11/84) FL 98 FLC 7 FAC 2 Others 6
Crystal Palace (Free on 1/7/88) FL 20 FLC 3 Others 2
Bristol Rov (Free on 11/11/89) FL 241 FLC 15 FAC 12 Others 23
Wycombe W (Free on 24/7/96) FL 25 FLC 4
Shrewsbury T (Free on 14/9/98)
Notts Co (Free on 2/10/98) FL 1
Wimbledon (Free on 26/3/99)

PARKIN Jonathan (Jon)
Born: Barnsley, 30 December 1981
Height: 6'4" Weight: 13.7

Having signed professional forms for Barnsley last January, he came on at Huddersfield in the 90th minute as the season drew to a close, to become the first player from the club's new academy to make his league debut. Equally at home in central defence or up front, Jon is a big, robust player, who all at Oakwell believe to have a big future in the game.
Barnsley (From trainee on 5/1/99) FL 0+2

PARKINSON Andrew (Andy) John
Born: Liverpool, 27 May 1979
Height: 5'8" Weight: 10.12

Andy's never-say-die attitude has made him a favourite among the Tranmere fans, and he became a regular first-team choice during 1998-99. His raw talent of the previous term matured into a more cultured sytle of play, and he never contributed less than 100 percent effort in any game. A pacy forward who is able to play on either the left or right, he relished taking on opposing defenders, became more thoughtful with experience, and contributed three goals in a very satisfactory season on which he can further build. Still only 20, he is likely to be given a pivotal role by cash-strapped Tranmere in the coming campaign.
Tranmere Rov (From Liverpool juniors on 12/4/97) FL 28+19/3 FLC 4+1/1 FAC 2+2/1

PARKINSON Gary Anthony
Born: Thornaby, 10 January 1968
Height: 5'11" Weight: 13.5

Preston's experienced right back played his 500th senior game at Wycombe, and 400th league game at Oldham last September, before sustaining a serious knee injury at Chesterfield in January, his 56th consecutive appearance since joining the club. Unfortunately, his attempted comeback at Reading lasted only 25 minutes before he suffered a recurrence which effectively ended his season, the resulting operation putting him out of action until well into 2000. Gary likes to get forward, delivering accurate crosses and corners from the flank, possesses a tremendous shot from free kicks around the box, and it was therefore somewhat surprising that he scored just twice, both penalties, after the previous year's return. It is hoped he is able to return to first-team action in 1999-2000.
Middlesbrough (Free from Everton juniors on 17/1/86) FL 194+8/5 FLC 20/1 FAC 17/1 Others 19
Southend U (Loaned on 10/10/92) FL 6
Bolton W (Free on 2/3/93) FL 1+2 Others 4
Burnley (Signed on 27/1/94) FL 134+1/4 FLC 12 FAC 10 Others 6/1
Preston NE (£50,000 on 30/5/97) FL 71+1/6 FLC 6 FAC 7/1 Others 6/1

PARKINSON Philip (Phil) John
Born: Chorley, 1 December 1967
Height: 6'0" Weight: 12.8
Club Honours: Div 2 '94

It seems unthinkable that Phil was almost allowed to join Wycombe Wanderers at the start of last season, because he was by far Reading's most consistent and resolute player in a long and difficult campaign in 1998-99. He captained the team, missed very few games, dominated in midfield, scored some vital goals, and all in all was a great favourite with the fans who elected him as their "Player of the Season" by a huge margin. He also found time to coach at the club's Centre of Excellence.
Southampton (From apprentice on 7/12/85)
Bury (£12,000 on 8/3/88) FL 133+12/5 FLC 6+1 FAC 4/1 Others 13/1
Reading (£37,500 on 10/7/92) FL 234+23/13 FLC 23+1/2 FAC 13/1 Others 5+2

PARKS Anthony (Tony)
Born: Hackney, 28 January 1963
Height: 5'10" Weight: 11.5
Club Honours: UEFAC '84; S Div 1 '94; B & Q '94

In pre season it looked likely that Tony would be Burnley's first-choice 'keeper in 1998-99, but the loan signings of first Paul Crichton and then Gavin Ward ensured that his only senior appearances were in the two early Worthington Cup games against Bury. Following that, the evergreen goalie signed for non-league Barrow in October before moving over to Scarborough when the Yorkshire club had a goalkeeping crisis in February. Despite giving some commanding performances in the final 15 games it was not enough to save Boro from the drop into the Conference, where they will be playing their football in 1999-2000.
Tottenham H (From apprentice on 22/9/80) FL 37 FLC 1 FAC 5 Others 5
Oxford U (Loaned on 1/10/86) FL 5
Gillingham (Loaned on 1/9/87) FL 2
Brentford (£60,000 on 24/8/88) FL 71 FLC 7 FAC 8 Others 5
Fulham (Free on 27/2/91) FL 2
West Ham U (Free on 15/8/91) FL 6 FAC 3
Stoke C (Free on 21/8/92) FL 2 FLC 1
Falkirk (Free on 14/10/92) SL 112 SLC 8 SC 4 Others 4
Blackpool (Free on 6/9/96)
Burnley (Free on 13/8/97) FLC 2 (Free to Barrow on 14/10/98)
Doncaster Rov (Loaned on 13/2/98) FL 6
Scarborough (Free on 26/2/99) FL 15

PARLOUR Raymond (Ray)
Born: Romford, 7 March 1973
Height: 5'10" Weight: 11.12
Club Honours: FLC '93; ECWC '94; PL '98; FAC '93, '98; CS '98
International Honours: E: 3; B-1; U21-12

Arguably the most improved player in the first-team squad at Arsenal in 1998-99, proving to be a strong tackler and good passer of the ball, his increased strength, fitness and pace also enabled him to score some good quality goals. Although a natural attacking right-sided midfielder, he showed that he could comfortably revert to the centre of midfield, or drop to the right-full-back position. Rarely had a bad game, a feature recognised by him being voted the Supporters' Club "Player of the Year". Such was his improvement last season that many critics believed he should have been selected for the England World Cup squad in France. However, as his good form continued, he received a belated call-up to the England squad for the match against Poland, and made his international debut when coming on as a substitute.
Arsenal (From trainee on 6/3/91) F/PL 170+35/17 FLC 17+3 FAC 26/2 Others 15+3

PARRISH Sean
Born: Wrexham, 14 March 1972
Height: 5'10" Weight: 11.8

An all-action midfield player, Sean came back to the Northampton first team at the beginning of last season after a long period out of the game with a broken leg. Also able to play in defence, he took time to recapture his form, but his bustling style of play brought him important goals during

the campaign, like the one he scored against Tottenham in the Worthington Cup that saw Town take the lead against the Premiership club.

Shrewsbury T (From trainee on 12/7/90) FL 1+2 FLC 1 Others 3 (Free to Telford during 1992 close season)
Doncaster Rov (£20,000 on 28/5/94) FL 64+2/8 FLC 3+1 FAC 2/1 Others 3
Northampton T (£35,000 + on 2/8/96) FL 82+2/10 FLC 8+1/1 FAC 2 Others 3/1

PARTRIDGE Scott Malcolm
Born: Leicester, 13 October 1974
Height: 5'9" Weight: 11.2
Club Honours: Div 3 '99

Had a wonderful season at Torquay in 1998-99, with 15 league and cup goals prior to joining Brentford for a six figure fee in February. Extremely fast and nippy, his close control and ability to bring others into play were a feature of his game, and the supporters were undoubtedly sorry to see him leave. However, Scott was due to leave in the summer on a free transfer under the Bosman ruling, so the sale represented good business for United. Brought in by Ron Noades to partner Lloyd Owusu, he scored three goals in his first four starts for the Bees, plus four games at the end of the campaign, and was delighted to win a Third Division championship winners medal for his pains.

Bradford C (From trainee on 10/7/92) FL 0+5 FLC 1+1
Bristol C (Free on 18/2/94) FL 24+33/7 FLC 2+3/1 FAC 1+3
Torquay U (Loaned on 13/10/95) FL 5/2
Plymouth Arg (Loaned on 22/1/96) FL 6+1/2
Scarborough (Loaned on 8/3/96) FL 5+2
Cardiff C (£50,000 on 14/2/97) FL 29+8/2 FLC 2 FAC 2 Others 1
Torquay U (Signed on 26/3/98) FL 33+1/13 FLC 2 FAC 2/1 Others 2/1
Brentford (£100,000 on 19/2/99) FL 12+2/7

PATERSON Jamie Ryan
Born: Dumfries, 26 April 1973
Height: 5'5" Weight: 10.6

Once again the Halifax fans' favourite, Jamie was troubled by an injury ravaged season in 1998-99. Despite his problems, he was the club's leading goalscorer, although he often played behind the front two. An exciting player on the ball, who has an ability to score from long range, he was voted the Conference "Player of the Season" during Town's championship-winning campaign of 1997-98.

Halifax T (From trainee on 5/7/91) FL 34+10/5 FLC 0+1 FAC 1 Others 3
Falkirk (Signed on 11/12/94) SL 1+3
Scunthorpe U (£18,000 on 12/10/95) FL 34+21/2 FAC 4+1/1 Others 3
Halifax T (Free on 30/7/97) FL 19+5/10 FLC 1+1/1 FAC 1

PATERSON Scott
Born: Aberdeen, 13 May 1972
Height: 5'11" Weight: 12.10

The former Liverpool player arrived from Bristol City during the 1998 close season, and made an early impression at Carlisle in 1998-99 with some assured defensive performances until losing his place through injury. He returned to the side, although

moved up into midfield. His performance at Brighton was outstanding in this role, and he also scored his only United goal in that encounter, but, remaining injury prone, he was released during the summer, having not featured on first-team duty since February.

Liverpool (£15,000 from Cove R on 19/3/92)
Bristol C (Free on 4/7/94) FL 40+10/1 FLC 6 FAC 2 Others 3
Cardiff C (Loaned on 7/11/97) FL 5
Carlisle U (Free on 23/7/98) FL 18+1/1 FLC 2 Others 0+1

PATTERSON Mark
Born: Leeds, 13 September 1968
Height: 5'10" Weight: 12.4

1998-99 was an excellent season for Mark in the wing-back position for Gillingham. Strong in the tackle, with good distribution, he liked to get forward at every opportunity, and scored his first goal for the club in the 2-1 home win over Oldham Athletic in November. Played on at the end of the season, despite requiring a hernia operation.

Carlisle U (From trainee on 30/8/86) FL 19+3 FLC 4 Others 1
Derby Co (£60,000 on 10/11/87) FL 41+10/3 FLC 5+2 FAC 4 Others 5+1/2
Plymouth Arg (£85,000 on 23/7/93) FL 131+3/3 FLC 3 FAC 8 Others 9
Gillingham (£45,000 on 30/10/97) FL 65/2 FLC 2 FAC 3 Others 4

PATTERSON Mark Andrew
Born: Darwen, 24 May 1965
Height: 5'8" Weight: 11.12
Club Honours: FMC '87

A battling midfield tiger, Mark made just nine starts in Bury's First Division team as he failed to settle at the club under the new boss, Neil Warnock. His longest run in the side came in February, when he played three consecutive games, but this was after he had been transfer listed, and just after he had completed a two-month loan spell with Blackpool. Despite still being under contract, a parting of player and club eventually became inevitable, and he was allowed to join Southend on a free transfer during transfer deadline week. Having spent a spell on loan at United in 1997-98 this was a welcome return, but this time round he found it more difficult to stamp his authority on the game and will look forward to a more positive 1999-2000 campaign.

Blackburn Rov (From apprentice on 1/5/83) FL 89+12/20 FLC 4/1 FAC 3+1 Others 2+4/1
Preston NE (£20,000 on 15/6/88) FL 54+1/19 FLC 4+1 FAC 4 Others 7/2
Bury (Signed on 1/2/90) FL 42/10 FLC 2 FAC 1 Others 4
Bolton W (£65,000 on 10/1/91) P/FL 158+11/11 FLC 16+4/2 FAC 17/1 Others 9
Sheffield U (£300,000 on 22/12/95) FL 72+2/4 FLC 9 FAC 3
Southend U (Loaned on 27/3/97) FL 4
Bury (£125,000 on 11/12/97) FL 27+4/2 FLC 4 FAC 1
Blackpool (Loaned on 11/12/98) FL 7
Southend U (Free on 25/3/99) FL 5

PAYNE Derek Richard
Born: Edgware, 26 April 1967
Height: 5'6" Weight: 10.8

Although available for selection at the start of 1998-99, Derek's disappearing act at the end of the previous campaign was

remembered by the Peterborough fans, and he was heckled continuously. Although he performed in his own hard-working way, and showed good distribution, the little midfielder found it difficult, making just nine appearances before being allowed to join non-league St Albans.

Barnet (£12,000 from Hayes on 1/12/88) FL 50+1/6 FLC 2 FAC 2 Others 3+1
Southend U (Free on 15/7/93) FL 32+3 FLC 2 FAC 1 Others 8/1
Watford (Signed on 21/7/94) FL 33+3/1 FLC 3 FAC 0+1 Others 2
Peterborough U (Free on 8/8/96) FL 79+3/4 FLC 7 FAC 9 Others 8

PAYNE Stephen (Steve) John
Born: Pontefract, 1 August 1975
Height: 5'11" Weight: 12.5
Club Honours: GMVC '95, '97; FAT '96
International Honours: E: SP-1

Steve has been the backbone of the Macclesfield defence throughout their two seasons in the Football League, and has worn the captain's armband for much of that time. The quiet unassuming centre back, who is good in the tackle, has an excellent turn of pace, and a liking for going forward for set pieces, scored his second goal in senior football from such a situation against Chesterfield in April, following a brilliant 25-yard volley. Unfortunately, he suffered a bout of 'flu after Christmas and, on returning, a loss of form saw him rested for a few games before he came back for the rest of the season.

Huddersfield T (From trainee on 12/7/93)
Macclesfield T (Free on 23/12/94) FL 71+6/2 FLC 6 FAC 5 Others 2

Andy Payton

PAYTON Andrew (Andy) Paul
Born: Whalley, 23 October 1967
Height: 5'9" Weight: 11.13

In a Burnley side constantly changed through injury, loss of form, suspension, and new signings, Andy seemed the one

constant factor in 1998-99, scoring the first goal of the season after two minutes, against Bristol Rovers on the opening day, and seldom looking back. Nicknamed the "Padiham Predator", he is just that, always on hand to pick up a loose ball if not scoring from solo efforts, such as his spectacular volley at Blackpool. Without his goals, the Clarets would have been in a really sorry state, and Second Division survival was down to his efforts as much as anyone.

Hull C (From apprentice on 29/7/85) FL 116+28/55 FLC 9+2/1 FAC 8 Others 3/1
Middlesbrough (£750,000 on 22/11/91) FL 8+11/3 FAC 1+3
Glasgow C (Signed on 14/8/92) SL 20+16/15 SLC 3+2/5 SC 1+1 Others 3
Barnsley (Signed on 25/11/93) FL 100+8/41 FLC 7/3 FAC 6+1/1
Huddersfield T (£350,000 on 4/7/96) FL 42+1/17 FLC 7/3 FAC 2
Burnley (Signed on 16/1/98) FL 58+1/29 FLC 1/1 FAC 1/2 Others 5/3

PEACOCK Darren

Born: Bristol, 3 February 1968
Height: 6'2" Weight: 12.12
Club Honours: WC '90

Signed from Newcastle during the 1998 close season, replacing Colin Hendry was never going to be easy, and Darren spent the early months of 1998-99 struggling at Blackburn. A fine competitive player, he found difficulty with changes of pace and spoiled many performances by an odd mistake. Injured at the end of November, he then lost his place to first Christian Dailly and then Marlon Broomes. When Broomes played splendidly it appeared his first team chances had slipped away, but an unlucky dismissal at Chelsea, which cost the latter a suspension, restored Darren to the team. Having settled at Ewood, he was a revelation, and in difficult circumstances with a disjointed side around him he became a major force, decisive, alert, and a hard man to play against. However, a miserable late display against Liverpool undid some of the good work, and he will be looking for a good start to the coming campaign.

Newport Co (From apprentice on 11/2/86) FL 24+4 FLC 2 FAC 1 Others 1+1
Hereford U (Free on 23/3/89) FL 56+3/4 FLC 6 FAC 6/1 Others 6
Queens Park R (£200,000 on 22/12/90) F/PL 123+3/6 FLC 12/1 FAC 3 Others 2
Newcastle U (£2,700,000 on 24/3/94) PL 131+2/2 FLC 13+1/2 FAC 11 Others 17+1
Blackburn Rov (Free on 2/7/98) PL 27+3/1 FLC 2 FAC 3 Others 2

PEACOCK Gavin Keith

Born: Eltham, 18 November 1967
Height: 5'8" Weight: 11.8
Club Honours: Div 1 '93
International Honours: E: Yth; Sch

As Queens Park Rangers' most experienced player, and an automatic choice for the central midfield position, Gavin missed few games last season. The first-choice penalty taker, he is most effective when making runs from midfield, and ended the campaign as the club's joint highest scorer. The son of Keith, the former Charlton player, he can also play up front if required,

and is always a danger to the opposition with his knack of playing one-twos that take him into scoring positions.

Queens Park R (From apprentice on 19/11/84) FL 7+10/1 FAC 0+1
Gillingham (£40,000 on 5/10/87) FL 69+1/11 FLC 4 FAC 2 Others 5/1
Bournemouth (£250,000 on 16/8/89) FL 56/8 FLC 6 FAC 2 Others 2
Newcastle U (£275,000 on 30/11/90) FL 102+3/35 FLC 6/5 FAC 6/2 Others 3/4
Chelsea (£1,250,000 on 12/8/93) PL 92+11/17 FLC 6/1 FAC 14+4/9 Others 7
Queens Park R (£1,000,000 on 22/11/96) FL 106+2/22 FLC 6/1 FAC 7/2

PEACOCK Lee Anthony

Born: Paisley, 9 October 1976
Height: 6'0" Weight: 12.8
Club Honours: AMC '97
International Honours: S: Yth

When starting his first full term in a Mansfield shirt last August, Lee looked a completely different player to the one signed for a record sum the previous season. Now fully fit, his goalscoring feats, strength, power, and enthusiasm helped the Stags into the play-off positions, his most notable achievement being the hat trick he scored against Barnet in November, in the first match to be played with the new fluorescent ball.

Carlisle U (From trainee on 10/3/95) FL 52+24/11 FLC 2+3 FAC 4+1/1 Others 6+4
Mansfield T (£90,000 on 17/10/97) FL 67+10/22 FLC 2 FAC 4 Others 4/2

PEACOCK Richard (Rich) John

Born: Sheffield, 29 October 1972
Height: 5'10" Weight: 11.5

With Hull City looking to restructure their squad, the right-sided midfield man moved to Lincoln last January as part of an exchange deal which saw Jason Perry and Jon Whitney travel in the opposite direction. City had chased Rich for two years, but after his arrival he struggled to make the starting line-up, and completed just three league appearances, plus a further seven as substitute. Hopefully, having been dogged by injury for the last year, this tricky player will come back as good as new in 1999-2000.

Hull C (Signed from Sheffield FC on 14/10/93) FL 144+30/21 FLC 12+3/2 FAC 7+1/1 Others 5+1
Lincoln C (Free on 21/1/99) FL 3+7

PEAKE Jason William

Born: Leicester, 29 September 1971
Height: 5'11" Weight: 12.10
International Honours: E: Yth; Sch

Released by Bury during the summer of 1998, Jason had somewhat of a stop-start return to Rochdale after two disappointing seasons away from Spotland. However, once he regained his form, along with a regular place in the side at the end of September, he quickly became the mainstay of Dale's midfield. He also rediscovered his shooting boots, and netted a number of spectacular goals, as well as keeping many an opposition goalkeeper on his toes with long-range efforts.

Leicester C (From trainee on 9/1/90) FL 4+4/1 Others 1+1
Hartlepool U (Loaned on 13/2/92) FL 5+1/1
Halifax T (Free on 26/8/92) FL 32+1/1 FAC 1 Others 2

Rochdale (Signed on 23/3/94) FL 91+4/6 FLC 3 FAC 5/2 Others 7/1
Brighton & Hove A (Signed on 30/7/96) FL 27+3/1 FLC 2 FAC 2 Others 1
Bury (Free on 8/10/97) FL 3+3
Rochdale (Free on 2/7/98) FL 36+2/5 FLC 2 FAC 4 Others 3

PEARCE Dennis Anthony

Born: Wolverhampton, 10 September 1974
Height: 5'10" Weight: 11.0
Club Honours: Div 3 '98

After pushing his way into regular league football at Notts County in 1997-98 Dennis had a difficult time in 1998-99, having first to recover from an early-season injury. A skilful left full back who loves to attack, he started well enough when scoring in a 1-1 draw at Burnley on his comeback, but then experienced difficulties in finding his old form. However, when his touch returns he will again be ranked amongst the best in his division.

Aston Villa (From trainee on 7/6/93)
Wolverhampton W (Free on 3/7/95) FL 7+2 FLC 1 FAC 1
Notts Co (Free on 21/7/97) FL 68+3/3 FLC 4 FAC 8+1 Others 2

PEARCE Alexander Gregory (Greg)

Born: Bolton, 26 May 1980
Height: 5'10" Weight: 11.7

A graduate of Chesterfield's blossoming youth system, the 1998-99 first-team career of this defender amounted to just seven minutes at Millwall in October. Although his patient wait for further opportunities went largely unrewarded, Greg continued to work hard as a regular reserve, showing a commendably good attitude throughout.

Chesterfield (From trainee on 24/3/98) FL 0+1 Others 0+1

PEARCE Ian Anthony

Born: Bury St Edmunds, 7 May 1974
Height: 6'3" Weight: 14.4
Club Honours: PL '95
International Honours: E: U21-3; Yth

1998-99 was another terrific season for the West Ham central defender. As one of the unsung heroes in the side, his consistent displays were one of the main reasons why the Hammers continued to do so well in the top half of the Premiership. An extremely versatile player, Ian can virtually perform to a high standard anywhere on the park, being a strong header of the ball, comfortable in possession, and whenever he joins the attack he can be deadly, scoring with headers in two successive home games, against Nottingham Forest and Blackburn. Thus it was a big blow to both club and player when he fractured his knee in the match at Tottenham in April, an injury that ruled him out for the remaining three fixtures. Expected to be fit in time for pre-season training, he was runner up in the "Hammer of the Year" award.

Chelsea (From juniors on 1/8/91) F/PL 0+4 Others 0+1
Blackburn Rov (£300,000 on 4/10/93) PL 43+19/2 FLC 4+4/1 FAC 1+2 Others 6+1
West Ham U (£1,600,000 + on 19/9/97) PL 63/3 FLC 5 FAC 7/1

PEARCE Stuart

Born: Hammersmith, 24 April 1962
Height: 5'10" Weight: 13.0
Club Honours: FLC '89, '90; FMC '89, '92
International Honours: E: 76; U21-1

Stuart remained a very popular member of the Newcastle squad in 1998-99, whether he was at centre back or at left back the supporters fully appreciating his wholehearted endeavour on the field, his consistent, no-nonsense approach to the game, and his thunderous left-footed shooting, particularly from set pieces. Although in the latter stages of his career, he is still formidable in the tackle, draws on his wealth of experience, and his ability to read the game compensates for his eroding pace. He survived an horrific road accident just prior to the season starting when his Rover car, with him in it, was crushed by a seven-ton lorry. But, as befits his reputation, he did not allow this to affect his performances, and he began the season ten days later in excellent form. He played in every game until he was sent off controversially at home against West Ham at the end of October, and having served his subsequent suspension he then found it very difficult to re-establish himself in the team, particularly after the signing of Didier Domi, and injury problems. Was appointed MBE in the New Year Honours list for services to football.
Coventry C (£25,000 from Wealdstone on 20/10/83) FL 52/4 FAC 2
Nottingham F (£200,000 on 3/6/85) F/PL 401/63 FLC 60/10 FAC 37/9 Others 24/6
Newcastle U (Free on 21/7/97) PL 37 FLC 2 FAC 7 Others 5+1/1

PEARCEY Jason Kevin

Born: Leamington, 23 July 1971
Height: 6'1" Weight: 13.12
Club Honours: Div 3 '99

Signed from Grimsby during the 1998 close season, this competent Brentford shot-stopping 'keeper started 1998-99 as his new club's first choice, keeping four clean sheets in his first four games before a shaky run where every shot he parried saw the rebound knocked in. After recovering his best form, before he broke a finger in November, he was replaced by Kevin Dearden, and then new signing, Andy Woodman, before spending the rest of the term in the reserves. However, his 17 league appearances qualified him for a Third Division championship medal when the Bees picked up the title at their first attempt.
Mansfield T (From trainee on 18/7/89) FL 77 FLC 5 FAC 2 Others 7
Grimsby T (£10,000 on 15/11/94) FL 49 FLC 3 FAC 1
Brentford (Free on 9/7/98) FL 17 FLC 3 FAC 2 Others 1

PEER Dean

Born: Stourbridge, 8 August 1969
Height: 6'2" Weight: 12.4
Club Honours: AMC '91

A midfielder and general utility man, Dean was not a regular member of the Northampton first team last season, but with so many injuries was called upon several times to fill a gap, always giving 100 per-cent effort and showing a very high workrate. Although missing over two months of the campaign through injury, he is an ideal man to have on the bench as he is equally at home in defensive situations. Was released during the summer.
Birmingham C (From trainee on 9/7/87) FL 106+14/8 FLC 14+1/3 FAC 2+1 Others 11+1/1
Mansfield T (Loaned on 18/12/92) FL 10 Others 1
Walsall (Free on 16/11/93) FL 41+4/8 FLC 2 FAC 4+2 Others 3
Northampton T (Free on 22/8/95) FL 91+28/5 FLC 6+2/1 FAC 6 Others 8+5

PEMBERTON Martin Calvin

Born: Bradford, 1 February 1976
Height: 5'11" Weight: 12.6

Released by Scunthorpe during the 1998 close season, this utility player was signed by Hartlepool on a short-term contract shortly afterwards. Unfortunately, his first-team appearances were limited to just five outings as a substitute in a defensive role, and had little time to impress before being put out of action with a dislocated shoulder and released at the end of September. He then joined Unibond League team, Harrogate Town, and was successful with them after being converted to play as a goalscoring forward.
Oldham Ath (From trainee on 22/7/94) FL 0+5 FLC 0+1 Others 0+1
Doncaster Rov (Free on 21/3/97) FL 33+2/3 FLC 0+1
Scunthorpe U (Free on 26/3/98) FL 3+3
Hartlepool U (Free on 3/7/98) FL 0+4 FLC 0+1

PENNANT Jermaine

Born: Nottingham, 15 January 1983
Height: 5'6" Weight: 10.0
International Honours: E: Yth; Sch

An England youth international, and still only 16, Jermaine made his debut for Notts County in early December to become the second youngest player to ever make a first-team appearance for the club. A talented youngster, he was quickly sold to Arsenal in January, where it is hoped he will continue to progress and become a star of the future. A brilliant right-sided midfielder, he made just two appearances at Meadow Lane, one in the FA Cup, and the other in the Auto Windscreens Shield, before leaving for Highbury where he was immediately inducted into the club's youth academy. Is an intelligent player with vision, speed, and dribbling skills, who like to attack defenders on route to goal. Also an excellent crosser, and all in all a tremendous prospect for the future.
Notts Co (Associated Schoolboy) FAC 0+1 Others 0+1
Arsenal (Trainee - £1,500,000 on 14/1/99)

PENNEY David Mark

Born: Wakefield, 17 August 1964
Height: 5'10" Weight: 12.0
Club Honours: WC '91

Ironically, David's only full Third Division appearance for Cardiff during 1998-99 was probably his best performance during his stay with the club. Despite Frank Burrows saying that the powerful, hard-working midfielder would continue as captain of the Bluebirds, within days he left to join Conference club, Doncaster Rovers, on 28 August 1998. Part of the problem was that David's family lived in the north of England, and Burrows insisted that all his players and families live within 45 minutes of Ninian Park.
Derby Co (£1,500 from Pontefract Collieries on 26/9/85) FL 6+13 FLC 2+3/1 FAC 1/1 Others 1+3/1
Oxford U (£175,000 on 23/6/89) FL 76+34/15 FLC 10+1 FAC 2+2/1 Others 3+1
Swansea C (Loaned on 28/3/91) FL 12/3
Swansea C (£20,000 on 24/3/94) FL 112+7/20 FLC 5+1/2 FAC 7/1 Others 14
Cardiff C (£20,000 on 24/7/97) FL 33+2/5 FLC 1+1 FAC 6

Adrian Pennock

PENNOCK Adrian Barry

Born: Ipswich, 27 March 1971
Height: 6'1" Weight: 13.5

Once again, this time in 1998-99, Adrian continued to impress for Gillingham, mainly in the sweeper position where he never looked troubled and played the simple ball. His motto being get in quickly or if in doubt kick it out! Also able to play in central midfield, or in central defence, it was noticeable that in the first two games he missed through suspension, Gills lost them both.
Norwich C (From trainee on 4/7/91) FL 1
Bournemouth (£30,000 on 14/8/92) FL 130+1/9 FLC 9 FAC 12/1 Others 8
Gillingham (£30,000 on 4/10/96) FL 85+1/2 FLC 2 FAC 3 Others 7/1

PENRICE Gary Kenneth

Born: Bristol, 23 March 1964
Height: 5'8" Weight: 11.7

An experienced midfielder, Gary started last season at Bristol Rovers under suspension, following his sending off against Brentford in the last league game of the previous campaign. Although his main role was to act as first-team coach, he could always be relied upon to add a little punch to Rovers' attack or midfield whenever he was called off the bench as a substitute. In scoring his 60th league goal on 4 April for the Pirates on his 250th league appearance, it was his first goal for almost 18 months, and proved to be a valuable point saver against Northampton.

Bristol Rov (Free from Mangotsfield on 6/11/84) FL 186+2/54 FLC 11/3 FAC 11/7 Others 13+2/2
Watford (£500,000 on 14/11/89) FL 41+2/18 FAC 4/1 Others 1/1
Aston Villa (£1,000,000 on 8/3/91) FL 14+6/1
Queens Park R (£625,000 on 29/10/91) F/PL 55+27/20 FLC 5+2/2 FAC 2+2/1 Others 1
Watford (£300,000 on 15/11/95) FL 26+13/2 FLC 2+1 FAC 1 Others 1+1
Bristol Rov (Free on 18/7/97) FL 48+18/6 FLC 2+1 FAC 7+3/2 Others 3

PEPPER Carl
Born: Darlington, 26 July 1980
Height: 5'11" Weight: 11.0
Having turned professional in the summer, Carl became yet another product of the Darlington youth team who broke through, making his debut at first-team level on the opening day of last season at right back, and continuing for the next five league and cup games. However, he then lost his place, making only one more start, but showed enough promise to be offered new terms at the end of the campaign.
Darlington (From trainee on 8/7/98) FL 5+1 FLC 2

PEPPER Colin Nigel
Born: Rotherham, 25 April 1968
Height: 5'10" Weight: 12.4
Last season, Nigel found himself the odd man out in Bradford's midfield after City had signed Stuart McCall and Gareth Whalley, and played just 11 games, when coming in for the injured Jamie Lawrence. A hard-tackling hustler, whose great strength is in closing the opposition's forwards down, he moved to Aberdeen last November for the sum of £300,000.
Rotherham U (From apprentice on 26/4/86) FL 35+10/1 FLC 1/1 FAC 1+1 Others 3+3
York C (Free on 18/7/90) FL 223+12/39 FLC 16+2/3 FAC 12/2 Others 15+1
Bradford C (£100,000 on 28/2/97) FL 47+5/11 FLC 4/1 FAC 1

PERCASSI Luca
Born: Milan, Italy, 25 August 1980
Height: 5'9" Weight: 11.0
The modern, forward-looking Chelsea have made a declared intent to scour Europe in a search for the best young talent to augment their own successful youth policy. The first young import to appear in the first team in 1998-99 was Luca, an Italian youth international right back, who played the last 13 minutes at Highbury in the 5-0 drubbing of Arsenal in November. Having joined Chelsea from Atalanta during the 1998 close season, along with Italian U16 captain, Samuele Dalla Bona, in deals which dismayed the Serie "A" club, the youngster is very highly regarded in his native Italy, and with Dalla Bona and the Finn, Mikael Forsell, represents the new wave of European talent who will lead the Blues into the new millennium. The fact that the club can compliment this continental talent with home-grown youngsters such as Jody Morris, John Terry, and Jon Harley, augurs well for the future.
Chelsea (Free from Atalanta on 5/8/98) FLC 0+1

PEREZ Sebastian
Born: St Chamond, France, 24 November 1973
Height: 5'10" Weight: 11.6
The move of the gifted Sebastian to Blackburn during the 1998 close season appeared doomed from the start. Slow international clearance, plus a pre-season injury limited his settling in, and although selected in consecutive years by French Football as the best right back in France he was played by Roy Hodgson wide on the right. With the service to him not being of the best he tended to drift inside looking for work, but still became a huge crowd favourite with his non-stop running and quick skills. After claiming his initial goal, against Chelsea, he was the victim of a travesty of another refereeing decision, as proved by television, when sent off after colliding with Graeme le Saux. Eight days later he was back in France for the UEFA tie in Lyon, where he contributed a superb headed goal, before coming off at half time because of problems caused by a floating bone in his knee. He remained in Marseilles for an operation, but when he returned he was unsettled with his infant daughter perpetually troubled by colds from the damp Lancashire weather. Understandably, the club agreed to release him, and he was loaned back to Bastia for the remainder of the campaign. Tantalisingly, he appeared to be not only a crowd favourite, but a player with a great future in the game. Stop Press: Having been on loan at Bastia, Marseilles paid £2.5 million for him on 30 May.
Blackburn Rov (£3,000,000 from Bastia, via St Etienne, on 22/7/98) PL 4+1/1 FAC 1 Others 2/1

PERKINS Christopher (Chris) Peter
Born: Nottingham, 9 January 1974
Height: 5'11" Weight: 11.0
Chris happily added a couple of rare goals to his sound, consistent play on the left-hand side of Chesterfield's defence and midfield in 1998-99. After losing his place to injury in January, he returned on his natural side, at right-back, replacing Jamie Hewitt for a few games, before moving to the left for the run-in to the end of the season. Out of contract during the summer, he is probably the fastest sprinter at the club, and is developing the ability to play well in a number of positions.
Mansfield T (From trainee on 19/11/92) FL 3+5 Others 0+1
Chesterfield (Free on 15/7/94) FL 136+11/3 FLC 9+1/1 FAC 13 Others 9+3/1

PERON Jean (Jeff) Francois
Born: France, 11 October 1965
Height: 5'9" Weight: 11.0
Having had French experience with Caen, RC Strasbourg, and Lens, Portsmouth snapped up this talented midfielder last September from Walsall, where he had been the "Player of the Season" in 1997-98. A no-nonsense, speedy ball chaser, whose intelligent passing and pace perked up Pompey's season, Jeff proved to be a goalmaker rather than scorer, his sole strike coming at Swindon being an excellent example of how well he carries the ball. As a player who has great vision, with possible new signings during the summer, the little Frenchman should fit in well to give the team a better campaign in 1999-2000.

Walsall (Free from Lens, via Caen and RC Strasbourg, on 22/8/97) FL 38/1 FLC 5 FAC 4 Others 5
Portsmouth (£125,000 on 3/9/98) FL 37+1/1 FLC 2 FAC 2

PERPETUINI David Peter
Born: Hitchin, 29 September 1979
Height: 5'8" Weight: 10.8
A young left-sided defender who could also be used in midfield, he impressed enough in the Watford reserve side in 1998-99 to warrant a first-team opportunity, and was duly rewarded with a debut at home to Bury in March. As a player who likes to get forward to get in crosses to the front men, he is combative, and has a good recovery rate.
Watford (From trainee on 3/7/97) FL 1

PERRETT Russell
Born: Barton on Sea, 18 June 1973
Height: 6'3" Weight: 13.2
Niggling injuries have kept this likeable centre half out of Portsmouth's regular line-up, having made the transformation from non-league football at Lymington straight into First Division life quite well. Strong in the air, with good ability on the ground, Russell enjoyed a 12-match run in the team in 1998-99 while Michail Vlachos was injured, and must now look to hold down a regular first-team place at First Division level. For too long he has only come into the reckoning when injuries and suspensions have hit the team and carrying knee injuries himself, an uninterrupted run in the side is long overdue.
Portsmouth (Signed from Lymington on 30/9/95) FL 66+6/2 FLC 5 FAC 4

PERRY Christopher (Chris) John
Born: Carshalton, 26 April 1973
Height: 5'8" Weight: 11.1
Chris finished yet another excellent season with Wimbledon, this time in 1998-99, and that he supported the Dons as a boy shone through in the commitment and passion that he showed on the pitch. Although relatively small for a central defender, he constantly wins aerial battles with forwards renowned for their heading ability, and reads the game as well as anyone in the top flight. Certainly, he would not be out of place on an international stage. The fans' favourite, this athletic player has the ability to time a tackle to perfection and has sparked interest from larger clubs due to his reputation to get to grips with the game. Stop Press: Wanted by George Graham, as he rebuilds the Tottenham defence, Chris was reported to have signed for the north-London club on 4 July for £4 million.
Wimbledon (From trainee on 2/7/91) PL 158+9/2 FLC 20 FAC 24/1

PERRY Jason
Born: Newport, 2 April 1970
Height: 6'0" Weight: 11.12
Club Honours: WC '92, '93; Div 3 '93
International Honours: W: 1; B-2; U21-3; Yth; Sch
Having moved from Bristol Rovers to Lincoln during the 1998 close season, Jason signed for Hull on the same last December day from Lincoln City as fellow Imp, Jon Whitney, the duo's commanding presence in the Tigers' defence soon earning the nickname of "The Kray Twins". With the

experience of his ten years at Cardiff, the former Welsh international did much to settle the club's leaky rearguard although, weeks after joining, an untimely calf injury sidelined him for three months. Showed enough to suggest that he will be a key figure in City's anticipated progress in 1999-2000.

Cardiff C (From trainee on 21/8/87) FL 278+3/5 FLC 22 FAC 14+1 Others 25+1
Bristol Rov (Free on 4/7/97) FL 24+1 FLC 2 FAC 2+1 Others 2
Lincoln C (Free on 14/7/98) FL 10+2 FLC 2 FAC 1
Hull C (Free on 18/12/98) FL 7+1 Others 2

PERRY Mark James
Born: Ealing, 19 October 1978
Height: 5'11" Weight: 12.10
International Honours: E: Yth; Sch
Mark is another of the successes of Queens Park Rangers' youth policy. After making his debut in 1997-98, the young midfielder made his first appearance of last season against Swindon in October, but was injured and was not able to complete the match. Although regaining match fitness, and making a comeback for the reserve side, he did not feature in the first team again before the end of the campaign. An excellent reader of the game, and comfortable on the ball, he can also play on the right-hand side of three at the back where he tackles and passes well. Hopefully, the youngster will be back as good as new in 1999-2000.

Queens Park R (From trainee on 26/10/95) FL 9+2/1 FLC 2

PESCHISOLIDO Paolo (Paul) Pasquale
Born: Scarborough, Canada, 25 May 1971
Height: 5'7" Weight: 10.12
Club Honours: Div 2 '99
International Honours: Canada: 29
From being Fulham's first £1 million player, and missing only one game in 1997-98, this fast, skilful striker had a very in-and-out season in 1998-99, despite winning a Second Division championship medal, being absent from the early games through suspension, before aggravating a groin injury which kept him out of action until October. His best spell of the campaign was from October through to December, when he looked really sharp and found the net eight times in 13 games, but after the purchase of Geoff Horsfield and Barry Hayles he was switched to a deeper role behind the front two, and when this did not work too well he spent much of his time coming off the bench in the later stages of the game. Undoubtedly, the highlight was his brilliant strike from near the touchline at Anfield, which brought Fulham back into the Worthington Cup-tie, and he hit a similar one against Chesterfield at the Cottage a month later. The Canadian international is married to Birmingham's managing director, Karen Brady.

Birmingham C (£25,000 from Toronto Blizzards on 11/11/92) FL 37+6/16 FLC 2/1 FAC 0+1 Others 1+1
Stoke C (£400,000 on 1/8/94) FL 59+7/19 FLC 6/3 FAC 3 Others 5+1/2
Birmingham C (£400,000 on 29/3/96) FL 7+2/1
West Bromwich A (£600,000 on 24/7/96) FL 36+9/18 FLC 4+1/3 FAC 1
Fulham (£1,100,000 on 24/10/97) FL 51+14/20 FLC 1+1/1 FAC 8/2 Others 2

PETERS Mark
Born: St Asaph, 6 July 1972
Height: 6'0" Weight: 11.3
This stalwart of the Mansfield defence played exceptionally well for most of last season, but was dropped, along with his centre-back partners following the 7-2 debacle at Cambridge in March. Returned to the side in April, following the suspension of Craig Allardyce, and kept his place for the last few games of the campaign. A hard, but fair tackler, he is lucky to still be playing after an horrific injury sustained in 1996 caused him to miss the whole of the following term. Was released during the summer.

Manchester C (From trainee on 5/7/90)
Norwich C (Free on 2/9/92)
Peterborough U (Free on 10/8/93) FL 17+2 FLC 2 Others 2
Mansfield T (Free on 30/9/94) FL 107+1/9 FLC 5/1 FAC 8 Others 7

PETHICK Robert (Robbie) John
Born: Tavistock, 8 September 1970
Height: 5'10" Weight: 11.12
An established tough-tackling full back who made the transformation from non-league football with Weymouth directly into First Division level with verve, Robbie lost his regular right-wing back place at Portsmouth early last term, and his powerful right foot and attacking play was sadly missed after he was allowed to leave for Bristol Rovers in February. As one of three ex-Pompey players who enjoyed the final third of the season at Rovers, he was always prepared to link up with the attack, showing good determination, and proved to be a popular signing.

Portsmouth (£30,000 from Weymouth on 1/10/93) FL 157+32/3 FLC 13+3 FAC 9 Others 3+1
Bristol Rov (£15,000 on 19/2/99) FL 9

PETIT Emmanuel (Manu)
Born: Dieppe, France, 22 September 1970
Height: 6'1" Weight: 12.7
Club Honours: PL '98; FAC '98; CS '98
International Honours: France: 29
Very much the driving force in the centre of the Arsenal midfield in 1998-99, so much so that whenever he was absent the Gunners often lacked a great deal of flair. His understanding with French international colleague, Patrick Vieira, made them the most formidable duo in the Premiership, and as a strong and exceptionally creative player he continued to show his ability to thread precision passes through defences for strikers to run on to. An excellent striker of the dead ball, his goal from a free kick in the FA Cup third round against Preston was of the highest class. Having won Premier League and FA Cup winners' medals in his first season in English football, unlike a number of other players who were also involved in the World Cup finals during the summer, he did not appear jaded. The low part of his season, however, was the number of games missed through suspension and injury. In frustration, he even talked of quitting English football before team mates convinced him to stay. Is a proven match winner who is crucial to the future success of the Gunners. Was one of three Arsenal men to be recognised by their fellow professionals with selection to the PFA award-winning Premiership side.

Arsenal (£3,500,000 from AS Monaco, via ES Argues, on 25/6/97) PL 58+1/6 FLC 3 FAC 10/2 Others 6

PETRESCU Daniel (Dan) Vasile
Born: Bucharest, Romania, 22 December 1967
Height: 5'9" Weight: 11.9
Club Honours: FAC '97; FLC '98; ECWC '98
International Honours: Romania: 80
Dan achieved two milestones during an impressive 1998 World Cup in France, his goal against ex-Chelsea mentor Glenn Hoddle's England making him the first Romanian to score in two World Cup finals, and his appearance against Croatia in the last 16 was his 25th cap as a Chelsea player – breaking Ray Wilkins' 19-year-old club record. At the beginning of last season he looked to be on his way out of Stamford Bridge, following the signing of Albert Ferrer, and the switch to a flat back-four. With Luca Vialli unable to guarantee him an automatic place in the starting line-up, clubs throughout Europe were alerted to his possible availability. But such was his affection for the club that he vowed to stay and fight for his place, and the Chelsea faithful who were aghast at rumours of his departure created banners pleading with him to stay. His natural attacking instincts and skill on the ball enabled him to slot into midfield, where his foraging down the right flank was an essential element in Chelsea's attacking strategy. As one of the stars of the 5-0 demolition of Arsenal, three days later he played superbly against Wimbledon – creating the Blues' second goal for Gustavo Poyet, and impudently scoring the third himself. His second Premiership goal of the season also inflicted defeat on an ex-Chelsea mentor – a clinical finish at St James' Park securing a 1-0 victory over Ruud Gullit's Newcastle to cement the side's position at the top of the league. Further valuable goals followed against Leicester and Everton, as Dan made a vital contribution to Chelsea's Champions' League qualification, and it was a great relief to everybody – fans and team mates alike – when he decided to stay at the Bridge. Just to show where his heart lay, he named his newly-born daughter, Chelsea!

Sheffield Wed (£1,250,000 from Genoa, via Steava and Foggia, on 6/8/94) PL 28+9/3 FLC 2 FAC 0+2
Chelsea (£2,300,000 on 18/11/95) PL 110+11/14 FLC 8/2 FAC 18/1 Others 11+3/2

PETRIC Gordon
Born: Belgrade, Yugoslavia, 30 July 1969
Height: 6'2" Weight: 13.9
Club Honours: SPD '96, '97; SLC '97; SC '94
International Honours: Yugoslavia: 4
Signed from Glasgow Rangers last November, the tall Yugoslav international defender came to Crystal Palace on the recommendation of his former Ibrox colleague, Craig Moore. Playing either in the centre of the defence or at left back, he looked to be an accomplished player, especially in the air, and apart from a fair spell out of the side he gave many solid performances following his debut at home to

Bristol City. Unfortunately, not long after scoring with a brilliant 35-yard shot at Sheffield United, his only goal of the season, he came under immense pressure due to his family living in the war zone, following the NATO attacks. Stop Press: Was released on 30 June to join AEK Athens.

Dundee U (Signed from Partizan Belgrade on 18/11/93) SL 60/3 SLC 3 SC 11 Others 2/1
Glasgow R (£1,500,000 on 1/8/95) SL 61+4/3 SLC 9 SC 8 Others 14+1/1
Crystal Palace (£300,000 on 6/11/98) FL 18/1

Bobby Petta

PETTA Robert (Bobby) Alfred Manuel
Born: Rotterdam, Holland, 6 August 1974
Height: 5'7" Weight: 11.3
1998-99 was a frustrating season for Bobby at Ipswich, the Dutchman never being able to emulate the consistency of form which he achieved in 1997-98, while his apparent reluctance to commit himself to the club by refusing to sign a new contract did not endear him to the supporters. However, he has a tremendous ability to take on defenders and beat them through speed or skill or a combination of both, but can equally disappear for long spells of the game. He scored just two goals during the campaign, against Birmingham and Huddersfield, but was an important part of the tactical changes introduced for the last two games at Portman Road when wins were vital, and Bobby demonstrated that he has the talent to play at the highest level when Town scored four times on each occasion.
Ipswich T (Free from Feyenoord on 12/6/96) FL 55+15/9 FLC 8+2 FAC 5+1 Others 3

PETTERSON Andrew (Andy) Keith
Born: Freemantle, Australia, 26 September 1969
Height: 6'2" Weight: 14.7
Andy started last season at Charlton as the second-choice 'keeper to Sasa Ilic, before coming off the bench at Chelsea when the latter was concussed. Losing his place in the side when Ilic was fit again, he was loaned to Portsmouth in November, and pulled off some magnificent saves to keep Pompey winning and drawing during the time he was on the south coast. Admired by the supporters, who did not want him to leave, his cover was required back at the Valley, and he arrived to find Simon Royce holding the number-one spot. A good shot stopper with a powerful kick, and not afraid to come off his line when necessary, he had the distinction of being a sub three times during the campaign, replacing Ilic again, at West

Ham, and Royce against Blackburn at the Valley. Although starting in six of the final seven matches, he left Athletic during the summer as a free agent.
Luton T (Signed on 30/12/88) FL 16+3 FLC 2 Others 2
Ipswich T (Loaned on 26/3/93) PL 1
Charlton Ath (£85,000 on 15/7/94) P/FL 68+4 FLC 6 FAC 1 Others 4
Bradford C (Loaned on 8/12/94) FL 3
Ipswich T (Loaned on 26/9/95) FL 1
Plymouth Arg (Loaned on 19/1/96) FL 6
Colchester U (Loaned on 8/3/96) FL 5
Portsmouth (Loaned on 13/11/98) FL 13

PETTY Benjamin (Ben) James
Born: Solihull, 22 March 1977
Height: 6'0" Weight: 12.5
Another signing for the future by Brian Little, Ben, who had captained Villa's reserve side, was quickly in the Stoke first-team squad, and made his league debut soon after arriving at the Britannia Stadium last November. At home anywhere across the defensive line, he looks a committed capture.
Aston Villa (From trainee on 10/5/95)
Stoke C (Free on 27/11/98) FL 9+2 FAC 1 Others 1

PHILLIPS David Owen
Born: Wegburg, Germany, 29 July 1963
Height: 5'10" Weight: 12.5
Club Honours: FAC '87
International Honours: W: 62; U21-4; Yth
Having been a regular at Huddersfield in 1997-98, David was struck down with a troublesome toe problem that put him out of action for the opening two months of 1998-99. However, back to full fitness, he quickly cemented his place in the side again, slotting into various positions in defence, and even into a midfield anchor role. With decisions made at Boothferry Park to release David, in order for him to eventually take on a coaching role, the experienced former Welsh international signed for Lincoln on transfer deadline day, and was used both on the right side of midfield and at left back during the run in to the end of the campaign. Even at 35, David still maintained his enthusiasm and passion for the game, and was given a contract to the end of 1999-2000.
Plymouth Arg (From apprentice on 3/8/81) FL 65+8/15 FLC 2+1 FAC 12+1 Others 4/1
Manchester C (£65,000 on 23/8/84) FL 81/13 FLC 8 FAC 5 Others 5/3
Coventry C (£150,000 on 5/6/86) FL 93+7/8 FLC 8 FAC 9/1 Others 5+1/2
Norwich C (£525,000 on 31/7/89) F/PL 152/18 FLC 12 FAC 14/1 Others 8/1
Nottingham F (Signed on 20/8/93) F/PL 116+10/5 FLC 16+1 FAC 10+2 Others 4
Huddersfield T (Free on 14/11/97) FL 44+8/3 FAC 7
Lincoln C (Free on 25/3/99) FL 9

PHILLIPS Gareth Russell
Born: Pontypridd, 19 August 1979
Height: 5'8" Weight: 9.8
International Honours: W: Yth; Sch
As a first-year Swansea professional who, despite making just the one substitute appearance during last season, was given an extension to his contract until June 2000. With plenty of workrate, the promising midfielder had a successful loan spell with

both Merthyr and League of Wales side, Carmarthen Town, during the campaign.
Swansea C (From trainee on 9/7/98) FL 0+8

PHILLIPS James (Jimmy) Neil
Born: Bolton, 8 February 1966
Height: 6'0" Weight: 12.7
Club Honours: Div 1 '97
Last season, Jimmy found it difficult to cement a place in the Bolton first team, due to the competition for the left-back berth from Mike Whitlow, Robbie Elliott and Hasney Aljofree, and although he made a handful of starts he had to be content with spending the majority of the campaign on the bench. One thing which you can be assured of with Jimmy is his never-say-die spirit and 100 per-cent commitment to the cause. Now in his second spell with the club, he enjoyed a well-deserved testimonial at the beginning of last season, attracting a full house to the Reebok to witness a 0-0 draw with Celtic. A skilful player who can make good use of his cultured left foot at set pieces, he links defence to attack well.
Bolton W (From apprentice on 1/8/83) FL 103+5/2 FLC 8 FAC 7 Others 14
Glasgow R (£95,000 on 27/3/87) SL 19+6 SLC 4 Others 4
Oxford U (£110,000 on 26/8/88) FL 79/8 FLC 3 FAC 4 Others 2/1
Middlesbrough (£250,000 on 15/3/90) F/PL 139/6 FLC 16 FAC 10 Others 5/2
Bolton W (£250,000 on 20/7/93) P/FL 195+3/2 FLC 26+2/1 FAC 10 Others 9/2

PHILLIPS Kevin
Born: Hitchin, 25 July 1973
Height: 5'7" Weight: 11.0
Club Honours: Div 1 '99
International Honours: E: 1; B-1
Sunderland fans are fast running out of superlatives to describe "Super Kev". A powerful, pocket-sized forward, who has a shoot on sight policy in front of goal, possesses electrifying pace, is adept at holding the ball up, and oozes self confidence, Kevin missed nearly four months of last season with a worrying persistent toe injury, yet returned to bag 25 goals, including four at Bury in April which clinched Sunderland's return to the Premiership. His partnership with Niall Quinn is already legendary on Wearside, and he celebrated another excellent campaign in which he won the Nationwide "Player of the Month" award for March and a First Division championship medal, before winning his first full England cap against Hungary in Budapest in April. Having scored a total of 60 goals in only two seasons at the club it should be fascinating to see him let loose on the Premiership.
Watford (£10,000 from Baldock on 19/12/94) FL 54+5/24 FLC 2/1 FAC 2 Others 0+2
Sunderland (£325,000 + on 17/7/97) FL 68+1/52 FLC 5/2 FAC 4 Others 3/2

PHILLIPS Lee
Born: Aberdare, 18 March 1979
Height: 6'1" Weight: 12.2
International Honours: W: Yth
It was a bitterly disappointing season at Cardiff for Lee during 1998-99, having few

chances – and only two in the league. He started against Peterborough in the second match of the campaign, but the Bluebirds lost 3-1 at home, and selected against Barnet away during February he limped off injured. The composed young right back was then named in the starting line-up against Second Division Wrexham in the FAW Premier Cup semi final, but was harshly sent off for two bookable offences. One of two players who were out of contract at the end of last season, both Lee and Wayne O'Sullivan were offered new terms.
Cardiff C (From trainee on 14/7/97) FL 11+2 FLC 2 Others 0+1

PHILLIPS Lee Paul
Born: Penzance, 16 September 1980
Height: 5'11" Weight: 12.0
Having made a fair start at Plymouth in 1997-98 the youngster turned professional during the summer of 1998, and despite limited opportunities in the first team in 1998-1999 he continued to show good progress. A young centre forward who possesses good pace and a well developed all-round game, Lee had the honour of scoring Plymouth's last goal of the season, a shot placed superbly in the corner of Carlisle's goal from the edge of the area.
Plymouth Arg (From trainee on 9/7/98) FL 11+16/1 FAC 3+2 Others 1+1

PHILLIPS Martin John
Born: Exeter, 13 March 1976
Height: 5'10" Weight: 11.10
Signed from Manchester City last August, Alan Ball, the Portsmouth manager, captured his signature for the third time, having played him at Exeter and Manchester City. Noted for his skill, and for being a tricky winger with an accurate cross, he came off the bench early in the season and scored in a 3-0 win over Queens Park Rangers. But, sadly, following that, the manager failed to give him a chance other than bringing him on to give the side width late on – two starts and 18 as a substitute – and he was loaned out to Bristol Rovers in February, making his debut for the Pirates at Lincoln. The subject of a possible exchange deal involving Rovers' Welsh U21 winger, Josh Low, he was unfortunate to be injured in his second appearance before returning to Fratton Park. With the ability to beat defenders, and display excellent ball skills, Portsmouth supporters will be hoping to see more of him in 1999-2000.
Exeter C (From trainee on 4/7/94) FL 36+16/5 FLC 1+2 FAC 2 Others 1+5
Manchester C (£500,000 on 25/11/95) P/FL 3+12 FLC 0+1
Scunthorpe U (Loaned on 5/1/98) FL 2+1 Others 1
Exeter C (Loaned on 19/3/98) FL 7+1
Portsmouth (£50,000 + on 27/8/98) FL 2+15/1 FLC 0+2 FAC 0+1
Bristol Rov (Loaned on 24/2/99) FL 2

PHILLIPS Steven (Steve) John
Born: Bath, 6 May 1978
Height: 6'1" Weight: 11.10
Steve forced his way into the Bristol City first team in 1998-99, after joining the club from non-league football in 1996. Although experiencing some difficulties, the

goalkeeper was not helped by the fact that there were constant changes in front of him, before being released on 20 May. Was involved in a controversial penalty decision, awarded in the last minute, which gave Sunderland a 1-0 victory at Ashton Gate.
Bristol C (Signed from Paulton Rov on 21/11/96) FL 15 FAC 1

PHILLIPS Wayne
Born: Bangor, 15 December 1970
Height: 5'10" Weight: 11.2
International Honours: W: B-2
Described by club captain, Mike Flynn, as the fittest player at Stockport, Wayne is a hard-working central or right-sided midfielder who covers a lot of ground. Playing a cautious game, he always delivers a sensible pass, and would undoubtedly have featured in the first team more often in 1998-99 but for an injury picked up in October, a hinderance which also affected his Welsh "B" international career. Stop Press: Transferred back to Wrexham for £50,000 on 8 July.
Wrexham (From trainee on 23/8/89) FL 184+23/16 FLC 17+1 FAC 12+2/1 Others 18+6/1
Stockport Co (£200,000 on 13/2/98) FL 14+8 FLC 1 FAC 1

PHILPOTT Lee
Born: Barnet, 21 February 1970
Height: 5'10" Weight: 5'10"
Club Honours: Div 3 '91
A left winger who signed for Lincoln in the summer of 1998 on a free transfer from Blackpool, Lee pulled a stomach muscle in pre-season training, and shortly after regaining his fitness he damaged a hamstring which kept him out until February. When given the ball he was often a revelation, with the ability to go round defenders almost at ease, and his form in his few appearances resulted in him being voted by the supporters as Lincoln's "Away Player of the Season".
Peterborough U (From trainee on 17/7/86) FL 1+3 FAC 0+1 Others 0+2
Cambridge U (Free on 31/5/89) FL 118+16/17 FLC 10/1 FAC 19/3 Others 15/2
Leicester C (£350,000 on 24/11/92) F/PL 57+18/3 FLC 2+1 FAC 6+2 Others 4+1
Blackpool (£75,000 on 22/3/96) FL 51+20/5 FLC 5/1 FAC 4 Others 0+2
Lincoln C (Free on 21/7/98) FL 15+9 FLC 0+1 FAC 1 Others 1+2

PICKERING Albert (Ally) Gary
Born: Manchester, 22 June 1967
Height: 5'10" Weight: 11.8
Right back had been a problem position for Burnley in 1998-99, only the inexperienced Chris Scott having looked at home there, before Ally's arrival from Stoke in December. With opportunities scarce at City due to a back injury, the club had allowed him a free transfer, and he immediately tightened things up at Turf Moor, looking calm and assured at the back, complimenting a good turn of speed going forward. Not a natural attacker, he nevertheless scored one of the Clarets' goals of the season, a solo run ending with a bending shot in the 4-1 win at Stoke, his former club. Was released during the summer.
Rotherham U (£18,500 from Buxton on 2/2/90) FL 87+1/2 FLC 6 FAC 9 Others 7

Coventry C (£80,000 on 27/10/93) PL 54+11 FLC 5+1 FAC 4/1
Stoke C (£280,000 on 15/8/96) FL 81+2/1 FLC 10 FAC 2
Burnley (Free on 17/12/98) FL 21/1

PILKINGTON Kevin William
Born: Hitchin, 8 March 1974
Height: 6'1" Weight: 13.0
Club Honours: FAYC '92
International Honours: E: Sch
The Port Vale reserve goalkeeper, who was signed from Manchester United during the 1998 close season following the departure of Arjan van Heusden, bided his time in the reserves until making his debut against Sunderland in November, and held his place for nine games. Unfortunately, he gave two penalties away during this spell, which included seven defeats, and although making some good saves he lost his place after the FA Cup defeat by Liverpool. Tall and commanding, he will be hoping to be more of a regular this time around.
Manchester U (From trainee on 6/7/92) PL 4+2 FLC 1 FAC 1
Rochdale (Loaned on 2/2/96) FL 6
Rotherham U (Loaned on 22/1/97) FL 17
Port Vale (Free on 1/7/98) FL 8 FAC 1

PINAMONTE Lorenzo
Born: Foggia, Italy, 9 May 1978
Height: 6'3" Weight: 13.4
An Italian-born striker who arrived at Bristol City on a free transfer from Foggia early last season, he made his only appearance in the final game of the campaign, and joined a list of players who have scored for the club on their debuts. A prolific scorer in the reserves, and making steady progress, he is big and strong, shows power in the air, and has the ability to strike the ball well, with his left foot. Ended 1998-99 leaving the fans feeling that there could be much more to come from him.
Bristol C (Free from Foggia on 18/9/98) FL 1/1

PINNOCK James Edward
Born: Dartford, 1 August 1978
Height: 5'9" Weight: 11.11
As a slightly-built forward, James struggled to gain a regular first-team place at Gillingham in 1998-99, due to the form of Carl Asaba and Robert Taylor, starting just once and coming off the bench on another seven occasions. Although a proven goalscorer at lower levels, where his movement in the box finds him getting on the end of half chances, he needs a run of senior games to see what he is made of.
Gillingham (From trainee on 2/7/97) FL 0+7 FLC 1+1 Others 0+3

[PIRI] MORI COSTA Francisco Javier
Born: Caneas de Onis, Spain, 10 November 1970
Height: 5'10" Weight: 11.8
Signed on loan until the end of the season from the Spanish club Merida last March, Piri was another left-sided midfielder to be tried by Barnsley. After making an impressive display in the reserves he was given a run out in the first team, but it was soon obvious that, despite him having a good touch with his left

foot, he needed to get some more games under his belt to find the pace of the game and to raise his fitness levels.

Barnsley (Loaned from Merida on 25/3/99) FL 2

PISTONE Alessandro
Born: Milan, Italy, 27 July 1975
Height: 5'11" Weight: 12.1

A stylish Italian U21 defender, who is at home in central defence or in his preferred position of left back. Pacy and cool on the ball, Alessandro enjoys raiding down the wings and delivering dangerous crosses for his strikers. He played in Newcastle's opening two games of the 1998-99 season, but lost his place following the arrival of new manager, Ruud Gullit, and thereafter made only a single substitute appearance. After returning home to Italy in January, on loan to Venezia, he struggled to establish himself as first choice there too.

Newcastle U (£4,300,000 from Inter Milan, via Vicenza, Solbiatese and Crevalcore, on 31/7/97) PL 30+4 FLC 1 FAC 5 Others 5

PLATT Clive Linton
Born: Wolverhampton, 27 October 1977
Height: 6'4" Weight: 13.0

Now in his fourth season at Walsall, Clive is a powerfully-built striker whom no defence can ignore, though the best has yet to be seen of him at Football League level. Good in the air, and strong on the ground, although his first touch will improve with experience, he played just ten times last season and scored against Colchester in October when deputising for Andy Rammell.

Walsall (From trainee on 25/7/96) FL 18+14/4 FLC 1+2/1 FAC 0+1 Others 1+6

PLATTS Mark Anthony
Born: Sheffield, 23 May 1979
Height: 5'8" Weight: 11.13
International Honours: E: Yth; Sch

Out of first-team reckoning at Sheffield Wednesday, having failed to make a senior appearance for three years, this highly-rated young left-sided midfielder initially signed for Torquay on non-contract terms last March, but is now a full professional. With loads of skill and pace, Mark showed glimpses of his undoubted talent in eight appearances, and there are better things to come.

Sheffield Wed (From trainee on 16/10/96) PL 0+2
Torquay U (Free on 9/3/99) FL 7+1

PLUMMER Christopher (Chris) Scott
Born: Isleworth, 12 October 1976
Height: 6'3" Weight: 12.9
International Honours: E: U21-5; Yth

A central defender who is poised and comfortable on the ball, Chris has been with Queens Park Rangers for six years, but has only made a few first-team appearances in that time. However, due to injuries to established players, he was given an extended run last season, before being unable to play in as many games as he should have after being injured himself in the game at Oxford United. His height makes him a danger to the opposition at set pieces and corners.

Queens Park R (From trainee on 1/7/94) F/PL 12+4 FLC 2

POINTON Neil Geoffrey
Born: Warsop, 28 November 1964
Height: 5'10" Weight: 12.10
Club Honours: Div 1 '87; CS '87

This vastly experienced defender moved to Walsall from Hearts during the summer of 1998, and in a magnificent first season missed only three games, taking over as skipper in the second half of the campaign. Firm in the tackle, and a great organiser, he had the bad luck to miss a penalty at Millwall in the Auto Windscreens southern final, after scoring in the shoot outs in earlier rounds at Bristol Rovers and Brentford. Possessing one of football's longest throw-ins, Neil can push forward to get in telling crosses with the best of them. With him being out of contract during the summer, at the time of going to press the club had offered him terms of re-engagement.

Scunthorpe U (From apprentice on 10/8/82) FL 159/2 FLC 9/1 FAC 13 Others 4
Everton (£75,000 on 8/11/85) FL 95+7/5 FLC 6+2 FAC 16+2 Others 9+3
Manchester C (£600,000 on 17/7/90) FL 74/2 FLC 8 FAC 4 Others 4
Oldham Ath (£600,000 on 10/7/92) F/PL 92+3/3 FLC 5 FAC 7+1/2
Hearts (£50,000 on 6/10/95) SL 64+3/3 SLC 7 SC 5 Others 2
Walsall (Free on 22/7/98) FL 43 FLC 2 FAC 2 Others 6

POLLITT Michael (Mike) Francis
Born: Farnworth, 29 February 1972
Height: 6'4" Weight: 14.0

Signed from Sunderland during the 1998 close season without making an appearance at the Stadium of Light, and spending a nomadic season on loan with several different clubs, Mike welcomed the opportunity to settle down at Rotherham in order to prove himself to be one of the best 'keepers in the Third Division. An ever present, he was confident with crosses, and pulled off some superb saves, including two penalty stops, which gave confidence to the rest of the defence.

Manchester U (From trainee on 1/7/90)
Bury (Free on 10/7/91)
Lincoln C (Free on 1/12/92) FL 57 FLC 5 FAC 2 Others 4
Darlington (Free on 11/8/94) FL 55 FLC 4 FAC 3 Others 5
Notts Co (£75,000 on 14/11/95) FL 10 Others 2
Oldham Ath (Loaned on 29/8/97) FL 16
Gillingham (Loaned on 12/12/97) FL 6
Brentford (Loaned on 22/1/98) FL 5
Sunderland (£75,000 on 23/2/98)
Rotherham U (Free on 14/7/98) FL 46 FLC 2 FAC 5 Others 3

POLLOCK Jamie
Born: Stockton, 16 February 1974
Height: 5'11" Weight: 14.0
Club Honours: Div 1 '95, '97
International Honours: E: U21-3; Yth

Having spent the summer of 1998 appraising his stature, he decided to follow a strict programme of exercise, resulting in him reducing his weight by one stone. As the 1998-99 season commenced one could see a new look Jamie, sharper on the ball, and more aggressive in midfield. Keen in the tackle, a feature of his play which resulted in three sending offs, he also missed eight games

during October and November, due to having a hernia operation. This took a lot out of him, and saw him recovering slowly in training before regaining fitness. Eventually, he came back into the first team as a substitute in the last minute of the FA Cup game with Halifax Town at Maine Road, and started the next few matches, but had to come off sometimes due to tiring. Once fully fit he took over the captaincy for a few games, and if he can keep himself in condition is sure to be a force this coming term.

Middlesbrough (From trainee on 18/12/91) F/PL 144+11/17 FLC 17+2/1 FAC 13+1/1 Others 4+1 (Free to Osasuna on 6/9/96)
Bolton W (£1,500,000 on 22/11/96) F/PL 43+3/5 FLC 4+1/1 FAC 4/2
Manchester C (£1,000,000 on 19/3/98) FL 32+2/2 FLC 4 FAC 3+1 Others 1+1

POLSTON John David
Born: Walthamstow, 10 June 1968
Height: 5'11" Weight: 11.12
International Honours: E: Yth

Signed from Norwich in the summer of 1998, John was yet another Reading player to suffer from a long-term injury in 1998-99, the central defender playing only four league matches, although finishing on the losing side just once. As soon as he became match fit he showed signs of his undoubted class, but lost his place after experiencing a calf injury in the game at Colchester in February. When Royals get him fully fit they will no doubt benefit from his no-frills defending, and great strength in the air and on the ground.

Tottenham H (From apprentice on 16/7/85) FL 17+7/1 FLC 3+1
Norwich C (£250,000 on 24/7/90) F/PL 200+15/8 FLC 20+1/2 FAC 17+1/1 Others 9/1
Reading (Free on 6/7/98) FL 4

POOLE Kevin
Born: Bromsgrove, 21 July 1963
Height: 5'10" Weight: 12.11
Club Honours: FLC '97

After replacing Ian Bennett in Birmingham's goal at the end of last September for the game at Portsmouth, and making his first appearance for the Blues in 1998-99, he made a game-turning save from John Aloisi early on to ensure a clean sheet and all three points in a 1-1 win. From then on, his sure reflexes and unflustered manner saw him maintain a regular place in the side, keeping nine clean sheets in a 15-match spell, and being rewarded with a two-year contract. Is sound on crosses and a recognised saver of penalties.

Aston Villa (From apprentice on 26/6/81) FL 28 FLC 2 FAC 1 Others 1
Northampton T (Loaned on 8/11/84) FL 3
Middlesbrough (Signed on 27/8/87) FL 34 FLC 4 FAC 2 Others 2
Hartlepool U (Loaned on 27/3/91) FL 12
Leicester C (£40,000 on 30/7/91) F/PL 163 FLC 10 FAC 8 Others 12
Birmingham C (Free on 4/8/97) FL 37 FLC 1 FAC 1 Others 2

POOM Mart
Born: Tallin, Estonia, 3 February 1972
Height: 6'4" Weight: 13.6
International Honours: Estonia: 65

The Estonian international goalkeeper, having ended 1997-98 as the first-choice 'keeper at Derby, would have hoped to continue in that

vein in 1998-99, but illness and a finger injury in the close season meant he had to spend the first three months of the new term on the substitutes' bench due to the inspired form of Russell Hoult. Injury to the latter returned him to the team, only for a broken finger sustained at Swansea to rule him out for a month. Took over in goal towards the end of the campaign, after suspension to Hoult, but his Estonian citizenship means he has to play in 75 per cent of all available games to qualify for a work permit, and this he did not do. With height and agility that allows him to deal especially well with balls crossed in, he kept nine clean sheets in 20 starts, and actually came on twice for Hoult, when keeping another blank.

Portsmouth (£200,000 from FC Wil on 4/8/94) FL 4 FLC 3 (Signed by Tallin SC on 9/5/96)
Derby Co (£500,000 on 26/3/97) PL 55+2 FLC 6 FAC 4

PORFIRIO Hugo Cardosa
Born: Lisbon, Portugal, 28 September 1973
Height: 5'5" Weight: 10.10
International Honours: Portugal: 3

No stranger to English football, having been at West Ham on loan in 1996-97, Hugo is yet another foreign-born player who was signed on loan by Nottingham Forest in 1998-99, arriving from Benefica in January. A very skilful and creative player, who could be used to good effect whether out wide or through the middle, the Premiership was hardly the ideal place for the little Portuguese international to perform, especially with a team staring relegation in the face for most of the campaign. Used initially from the bench, mainly because he was carrying a number of injuries, he came back strongly to fashion a goal from nowhere in a 2-0 home win over Sheffield Wednesday, with Forest already down.

West Ham U (Loaned from Sporting Lisbon on 27/9/96) PL 15+8/2 FLC 2/1 FAC 1+1/1
Nottingham F (Loaned from Benfica on 28/1/99) PL 3+6/1

PORTER Andrew (Andy) Michael
Born: Holmes Chapel, 17 September 1968
Height: 5'9" Weight: 12.0
Club Honours: AMC '93, '99

A hard-tackling Wigan midfield player recruited in the 1998 close season from Port Vale, while not an automatic choice in 1998-99, Andy gave everything when called into the team. Coming back strongly to become part of the side which reached the play offs, he scored just the one league goal, a stunning 20-yard drive on his Latics' start in the 2-2 draw at Preston. Winning an Auto Windscreens medal despite not being called upon at Wembley, he has now completed over 350 Football League games.

Port Vale (From trainee on 29/6/87) FL 313+44/22 FLC 22+1 FAC 20+4/3 Others 26+2/1
Wigan Ath (Free on 28/7/98) FL 6+10/1 FLC 0+2 FAC 1 Others 3+3

PORTER Gary Michael
Born: Sunderland, 6 March 1966
Height: 5'7" Weight: 11.0
Club Honours: FAYC '82
International Honours: E: U21-12; Yth

Very much a player's player, although not always appreciated by the fans at Walsall,

this very experienced midfielder began last season as the club skipper, playing 15 league games before moving to Scarborough in mid February. Although he showed touches of class in Boro's desperate struggle against relegation, he was released during the summer prior to the team beginning preparations for the Conference.

Watford (From apprentice on 6/3/84) FL 362+38/47 FLC 30+2/5 FAC 25+2/3 Others 12+1/2
Walsall (Free on 25/7/97) FL 39+5/1 FLC 4+2 FAC 3+1/2 Others 5+1
Scarborough (Free on 19/2/99) FL 11+2

POTTER Daniel (Danny) Raymond John
Born: Ipswich, 18 March 1979
Height: 6'0" Weight: 13.4

Originally signed on a short-term contract at the start of last season, having been freed by Colchester, Danny made his debut for Exeter at Shrewsbury after Ashley Bayes suffered an ankle injury, and showed the City fans what a competent and accomplished 'keeper he was. Once at Chelsea as a trainee, he seems certain to provide more than adequate competition for Bayes, and will be knocking hard for a regular place this coming term.

Colchester U (Free from Chelsea juniors on 3/10/97)
Exeter C (Free on 8/8/98) FL 5

POTTER Graham Stephen
Born: Solihull, 20 May 1975
Height: 6'1" Weight: 11.12
International Honours: E: U21-1; Yth

Able to play in any position down the left-hand side of the field, having excellent pace and crossing ability, Graham did not figure in manager Denis Smith's plans until halfway through last season but, on coming into the side, he did a positive job at left back when linking up with Kevin Kilbane and allowing Jason van Blerk to move into midfield. Broke a toe late on in the campaign.

Birmingham C (From trainee on 1/7/92) FL 23+2/2 FAC 1 Others 6
Wycombe W (Loaned on 17/9/93) FL 2+1 FLC 1 Others 1
Stoke C (£75,000 on 20/12/93) FL 41+4/1 FLC 3+1 FAC 4 Others 5
Southampton (£250,000 + on 23/7/96) FL 2+6 FLC 1+1
West Bromwich A (£300,000 + on 14/2/97) FL 25+8 FLC 0+1 FAC 1
Northampton T (Loaned on 24/10/97) FL 4 Others 1

POTTS Steven (Steve) John
Born: Hartford, USA, 7 May 1967
Height: 5'8" Weight: 10.11
International Honours: E: Yth

Once again, this time in 1998-99, the likeable West Ham defender played superbly when called upon. He reads the game well, makes up for his lack of height with his quickness and timely interceptions, and had an outstanding game against Liverpool at Upton Park when blunting the danger of Michael Owen and Robbie Fowler. West Ham are fortunate to have such a loyal player, who has now played over 450 games for the club. Despite sustaining a knee injury against Derby in April, which initially was thought to have

brought his campaign to a close, he bounced back four games later to appear in the final match, a 4-0 home win over Middlesbrough.

West Ham U (From apprentice on 11/5/84) F/PL 344+30/1 FLC 36+2 FAC 40+1 Others 14+1

Stephane Pounewatchy

POUNEWATCHY Stephane Zeusnagapa
Born: Paris, France, 10 February 1968
Height: 6'1" Weight: 15.2
Club Honours: AMC '97

A very experienced, strong and solid central defender who started last season as a free agent with Dundee in the new Scottish Premier League, having been released by Carlisle in the summer, before joining Port Vale at the end of August as cover for a crop of defensive injuries. With just two first-team games under his belt at Vale, he was brought to Layer Road by Mick Wadsworth in February, and immediately impressed with his composed defensive displays, bringing back some unhappy memories for the United faithful who remembered his "Man of the Match" display for Carlisle against the U's in the 1997 Auto Windscreens Shield final. This time the tale had a happier ending for United as Stephane's class helped the team to Division Two safety, and he was rewarded with his first Colchester goal, at Blackpool. Out of contract in the summer, hopefully, he will be persuaded to stay at Layer Road into the millennium.

Carlisle U (Free from Gueugnon on 6/8/96) FL 81/3 FLC 7 FAC 5 Others 9/2
Dundee U (Free on 1/7/98) SL 2+1 SLC 1
Port Vale (Free on 28/8/98) FL 2
Colchester U (Free on 17/2/99) FL 15/1

POUTON Alan
Born: Newcastle, 1 February 1977
Height: 6'0" Weight: 12.8

York's talented and strong-running midfielder had an outstanding start to last season, in which he played a big part in the club's rise to eighth in the Second Division. Unfortunately, a training ground injury in October sidelined him for four months, and

he struggled to find his best form after that, but netted a fine solo goal in a 1-1 draw at Wrexham in March.

Oxford U (Free from Newcastle U juniors on 7/11/95)

York C (Free on 8/12/95) FL 79+11/7 FLC 5+1 FAC 5/1 Others 2

Chris Powell

POWELL Christopher (Chris) George Robin
Born: Lambeth, 8 September 1969
Height: 5'10" Weight: 11.7

Signed from Derby during the 1998 close season, Chris was an ever present in the Charlton side in 1998-99, playing at left back or in a wing-back role. He also played one game against Wimbledon at the Valley on the left-hand side of midfield. Comfortable on the ball with good control, and a penchant to push forward down the left wing to put telling crosses into the opposition penalty area, he shows good awareness and distribution, being popular with the supporters. Yet to score his first goal for the club, although he has come close on a couple of occasions.

Crystal Palace (From trainee on 24/12/87) FL 2+1 FLC 0+1 Others 0+1

Aldershot (Loaned on 11/1/90) FL 11

Southend U (Free on 30/8/90) FL 246+2/3 FLC 13 FAC 8 Others 21

Derby Co (£750,000 on 31/1/96) F/PL 89+2/1 FLC 5 FAC 5/1

Charlton Ath (£825,000 on 1/7/98) PL 38 FLC 3 FAC 1

POWELL Darren David
Born: Hammersmith, 10 March 1976
Height: 6'3" Weight: 13.2
Club Honours: Div 3 '99

Another Brentford signing from non-league Hampton, the giant centre half's long legs made many crucial last-ditch tackles in 1998-99. Although sustaining a groin injury last November, which saw him miss 13 games, he came back strongly in the last third of 1998-99 playing alongside Hermann Hreidarsson, to cap a very impressive first league campaign. Was rewarded for his endeavours when picking up the club's

"Player of the Year" award to go with his Third Division championship medal.

Brentford (£15,000 from Hampton on 27/7/98) FL 33/2 FLC 3 Others 0+1

Darryl Powell

POWELL Darryl Anthony
Born: Lambeth, 15 November 1971
Height: 6'0" Weight: 12.10
International Honours: Jamaica: 8

An experienced central or left-sided Derby midfielder who, if required, can also play a left wing-back role, Darryl came back from a disappointing time in France 98 with Jamaica to claim a regular berth in the County midfield in 1998-99, where his strong tackling and adept distribution allowed the more flamboyant skills of others to flourish. Keeping free from injuries all season, and close to being an ever present in the first team, he failed to get his name on the scoresheet, but will be looking to do better in 1999-2000.

Portsmouth (From trainee on 22/12/88) FL 83+49/16 FLC 11+3/3 FAC 10 Others 9+5/4

Derby Co (£750,000 on 27/7/95) F/PL 106+20/6 FLC 6+1 FAC 6+1

POWELL Paul
Born: Wallingford, 30 June 1978
Height: 5'8" Weight: 11.6

Paul was one of the successes at Oxford in 1998-99. Having been a winger, cum midfielder at the start of the campaign, he made the left-back berth his own following the sale of Simon Marsh, and missed only two games after that. He often showed the form that gave him a chance in the England set up at U21 level, and scored three times, one of them in a 2-1 win over Port Vale. Should impress again this season to become one of the best attacking full backs in the Second Division. Has a good long throw.

Oxford U (From trainee on 2/7/96) FL 52+16/4 FLC 0+2 FAC 4 Others 0+2

POWER Graeme Richard
Born: Harrow, 7 March 1977
Height: 5'10" Weight: 10.10
International Honours: E: Yth

Released by Bristol Rovers during the 1998 close season, Graeme joined Exeter on a short-term contract, but his initial displays resulted in him being taken on for the whole of the campaign. A virtual ever present until hampered by a cracked rib endured at home to Darlington in March, he will be looking for another excellent term in 1999-2000. Able to play at full back or in the centre of the defence, his surging runs can often destabilise opposing defences.

Queens Park R (From trainee on 11/4/95)

Bristol Rov (Free on 15/7/96) FL 25+1 FAC 1 Others 1+2

Exeter C (Free on 6/8/98) FL 40 FLC 2 FAC 4 Others 2

POWER Lee Michael
Born: Lewisham, 30 June 1972
Height: 6'0" Weight: 11.10
International Honours: Ei: B-1; U21-13; Yth

Freed by Hibernian, Lee joined Plymouth during the 1998 close season and, although initially joining Halifax on loan, he made the move permanent last January. As a player who thrives on creating goals as much as scoring them, he should prove a great asset to the club for next season. Struggled with a back problem which hampered his first-team appearances, but should be raring to go in time for the new term.

Norwich C (From trainee on 6/7/90) F/PL 28+16/10 FLC 1 FAC 0+1 Others 0+2

Charlton Ath (Loaned on 4/12/92) FL 5

Sunderland (Loaned on 13/8/93) FL 1+2 FLC 2/1

Portsmouth (Loaned on 15/10/93) FL 1+1 Others 1

Bradford C (£200,000 on 8/3/94) FL 14+16/5 FLC 0+2 FAC 0+2/1 Others 1+1/1

Peterborough U (£80,000 on 26/7/95) FL 25+13/6 FLC 2+2 FAC 1+2 Others 1/1

Dundee U (Free on 14/12/96) SL 9+1/4 SC 3/2

Hibernian (Free on 20/3/97) SL 9+2/2 SLC 1

Plymouth Arg (Free on 4/8/98) FL 7+9 FLC 1+1 Others 0+1

Halifax T (Signed on 11/12/98) FL 14+4/4

Gus Poyett

POYET Gustavo (Gus) Augusto
Born: Montevideo, Uruguay, 15 November 1967
Height: 6'2" Weight: 13.0
Club Honours: ECWC '98; ESC '98
International Honours: Uruguay: 23

A fully-fit Gustavo opened last season with a bang, scoring in early Premiership matches against Coventry and Nottingham Forest. Sandwiched between these efforts was a real collector's item – the only goal of the European Super Cup final against Real Madrid in Monaco, which brought the Blues their first cup within 16 months. His fierce right-footed drive from the edge of the box ensuring that Chelsea became the fifth English winners, and the first since 1991. His hot streak continued with the 88th-minute winner, a near-post header from a corner against plucky Charlton, two against Arsenal in the 5-0 drubbing, a screamer from the edge of the box against Wimbledon, plus crucial goals against Leicester, Derby, Tottenham, and Southampton, which

stretched Chelsea's unbeaten Premiership run to 18 matches, and saw them top the league table for the first time in nine years. These exploits just underlined how seriously the classy Uruguayan had been missed by Chelsea the previous season, when a knee-ligament injury curtailed his involvement. Sadly, he took another knock on the same knee shortly after scoring at Southampton on Boxing Day, and was sidelined for 18 matches. To enhance the feeling of déjà vu, Gus returned to play in a European Cup-Winners' Cup semi final – just as he had 12 months earlier. Unfortunately, this time it went against the Blues as Real Mallorca squeezed through by a single goal. As a consolation, he grabbed the crucial match-winning goal against Leeds a few weeks later which confirmed Chelsea's qualification for the Champions' League at the expense of their Yorkshire rivals – his towering header putting the club amongst Europe's elite for the first time. It is fair to say that "Big Gus" was the most influential player in the Premiership during the first half of the season, as his awareness, passing ability, box-to-box workrate, and goalscoring opportunism, made him the cornerstone of Chelsea's sensational start to the campaign, and left all Blues' fans wondering what may have been if not for that unfortunate injury.

Chelsea (Free from Real Zaragoza, via Bella Vista, on 15/7/97) PL 32+10/15 FLC 3/2 Others 8+4/2

PREECE Andrew (Andy) Paul
Born: Evesham, 27 March 1967
Height: 6'1" Weight: 12.0

A summer capture from Blackpool on a free transfer, and a proven goalscorer, Andy struggled to find his form at Gigg Lane throughout last season. Despite starting 23 league and cup games in the Shakers' attack, and being involved as a substitute in the majority of other games, he scored just three goals, suffering something of a confidence crisis when supporters singled him out for criticism and barracking. He stuck manfully to the task though, and could always be counted upon to make his presence felt.

Northampton T (Free from Evesham on 31/8/88) FL 0+1 FLC 0+1 Others 0+1 (Free to Worcester C during 1989 close season)
Wrexham (Free on 22/3/90) FL 44+7/7 FLC 5+1/1 FAC 1/2 Others 5/1
Stockport Co (£10,000 on 18/12/91) FL 89+8/42 FLC 2+1 FAC 7/3 Others 12+2/9
Crystal Palace (£350,000 on 23/6/94) PL 17+3/4 FLC 4+2/1 FAC 2+3
Blackpool (£200,000 on 5/7/95) FL 114+12/35 FLC 8+2/1 FAC 2+3/2 Others 12/2
Bury (Free on 6/7/98) FL 19+20/3 FLC 4+1 FAC 0+1

PREECE David
Born: Sunderland, 26 August 1976
Height: 6'2" Weight: 12.3

As Darlington's only ever present in all 46 league games last season, this agile young goalkeeper showed more confidence in collecting high balls and commanding his area in his second full season with the Quakers, as well as continuing to show off his shot-stopping ability. Much of this improvement must go down to the appointment of former Sunderland star,

Jimmy Montgomery, as goalkeeping coach at the club, and saw 16 clean sheets in the league this time as opposed to only ten in 1997-98. Has something of a reputation for saving penalties.

Sunderland (From trainee on 30/6/94)
Darlington (Free on 28/7/97) FL 91 FLC 4 FAC 7 Others 2

PREECE David William
Born: Bridgnorth, 28 May, 1963
Height: 5'6" Weight: 11.6
Club Honours: FLC '88
International Honours: E: B-3

As Cambridge's player/coach, and one of the respected midfielders in the lower division, his first-team appearances were more limited last season, but his experience showed when he played. An excellent passer of the ball, who is able to dictate and control the tempo of the game, David also scored a couple of goals, his first ever for United.

Walsall (From apprentice on 22/7/80) FL 107+4/5 FLC 18/5 FAC 6/1 Others 1
Luton T (£150,000 on 6/12/84) FL 328+8/21 FLC 23/3 FAC 27/2 Others 8+1/1
Derby Co (Free on 11/8/95) FL 10+3/1 FLC 2
Birmingham C (Loaned on 24/11/95) FL 6 Others 1
Swindon T (Loaned on 21/3/96) FL 7/1
Cambridge U (Free on 6/9/96) FL 39+22/1 FLC 3+2 Others 1+1

PREECE Roger
Born: Much Wenlock, 9 June 1968
Height: 5'8" Weight: 10.11

Roger combined his coaching duties at Shrewsbury in 1998-99 with an important uncompromising midfield role. A strong and enthusiastic tackler who always gives his all, his season was interrupted once or twice with injury. Likes to have a go on goal when he can get forward.

Wrexham (Free from Coventry C juniors on 15/8/86) FL 89+21/12 FLC 2+1 FAC 5 Others 8+1/1
Chester C (Free to Southport on 14/8/90) FL 165+5/4 FLC 10 FAC 8/1 Others 11 (Freed on 18/10/96)
Shrewsbury T (Free from Telford on 4/7/97) FL 41+6/3 FLC 1 FAC 2

PRENDERGAST Rory
Born: Pontefract, 6 April 1978
Height: 5'8" Weight: 11.13

A young left-sided midfielder who arrived at York immediately prior to the start of 1998-99 getting underway, having earlier been on Barnsley's books after coming through the ranks as a trainee, Rory made his first-team debut as a sub in the home Worthington Cup-tie against Sunderland, two games into the campaign. After making five appearances in all, including a start at Wigan in the league, he was allowed to join Oldham in transfer deadline week on non-contract forms but, in failing to make an appearance, he was not retained. Has good ball-playing skills and crossing ability.

Barnsley (From trainee on 8/4/97)
York C (Free on 6/8/98) FL 1+2 FLC 0+1 FAC 0+1
Oldham Ath (Free on 25/3/99)

PRESSMAN Kevin Paul
Born: Fareham, 6 November 1967
Height: 6'1" Weight: 15.5
International Honours: E: B-3; U21-1; Yth; Sch

Despite playing in Sheffield Wednesday's

goal for the first 14 games of the season, and conceding an average of just one goal per game, Kevin found himself out of the side, being replaced by newly-signed Pavel Srnicek. His omission owing much to the team's poor form rather than his. On top of that, he must have been bitterly disappointed to lose his place in the England reckoning, albeit as fourth-choice 'keeper. Twice asked the club for a transfer, the second time round was after he played very well when Srnicek was suspended, and being dropped when the Czech was available again. Kevin's strengths remain his kicking ability and good shot-stopping technique, and it would appear to be only a matter of time that he reclaims his place at Wednesday.

Sheffield Wed (From apprentice on 7/11/85) F/PL 246+1 FLC 31 FAC 16 Others 4
Stoke C (Loaned on 10/3/92) FL 4 Others 2

PRICE Jason Jeffrey
Born: Pontypridd, 12 April 1977
Height: 6'2" Weight: 11.5
International Honours: W: U21-5

A regular inclusion in the Welsh U21 squad last season, showing his ability to play either at right-wing back, or in central defence, he was most effective for Swansea early on when operating in a wide midfield role where his electric pace was used to full effect. At the end of the campaign, in the game against Rochdale, Jason's pace off the mark saw him score two goals in what was his first full game for two months following a hamstring injury.

Swansea C (Free from Aberaman on 17/7/95) FL 57+7/7 FLC 4 FAC 3/1 Others 2+1

Ryan Price

PRICE Ryan
Born: Wolverhampton, 13 March 1970
Height: 6'5" Weight: 14.0
Club Honours: AMC '95; GMVC '97; FAT '96
International Honours: E: SP-5

A fearless giant of a 'keeper, who plays with £20,000 worth of titanium plates and screws in his face following an on-field accident two seasons ago, Ryan was ever present for

Macclesfield in 1997-98 with 19 clean sheets, but did not fare well in Division Two. However, having been rested for four matches following Town's heavy FA Cup third round defeat at Coventry, he maintained nine clean sheets last term, which was not bad considering that the team did not climb above 20th place. He also saved the defence from blushes on numerous occasions with split-second saves from point-blank shots.

Birmingham C (£40,000 from Stafford R on 9/8/94) Others 1
Macclesfield T (£15,000 on 3/11/95) FL 88 FLC 6 FAC 6 Others 2

Chris Priest

PRIEST Christopher (Chris)
Born: Leigh, 18 October 1973
Height: 5'9" Weight: 10.10
Making his 150th league appearance in Chester's midfield in the end of December game last season at home to Mansfield, Chris was once again the engine room of City's midfield. A strong tackler with a creative flair, who often produces goalscoring opportunities for his team mates, and chips in with vital goals himself, he is both consistent and reliable. Out of contract during the summer, at the time of going to press the club had offered him new terms.

Everton (From trainee on 1/6/92)
Chester C (Loaned on 9/9/94) FL 11/1 Others 2
Chester C (Free on 11/1/95) FL 151+5/25 FLC 6 FAC 6/1 Others 6

PRIESTLEY Philip (Phil) Alan
Born: Wigan, 30 March 1976
Height: 6'3" Weight: 13.5
Signed from non-league Atherton during the 1998 close season, Rochdale's young third-choice 'keeper was given the chance to perform at league level when Neil Edwards was injured before the visit of Plymouth, while reserve Lance Key was out on loan. Performing creditably in a 1-1 draw, he looks to have a fine future.

Rochdale (Free from Atherton LR on 23/9/98) FL 1

PRIMUS Linvoy Stephen
Born: Forest Gate, 14 September 1973
Height: 6'0" Weight: 14.0
Linvoy continued to show why his signing the previous season from Barnet had been such a shrewd investment by former Reading manager, Terry Bullivant. He was a steady, aggressive, yet composed defender, and it was no coincidence that his appearances in the team ran parallel to Royals' best spell of 1998-99 when they threatened to reach the play-off positions.

Charlton Ath (From trainee on 14/8/92) FL 4 FLC 0+1 Others 0+1
Barnet (Free on 18/7/94) FL 127/7 FLC 9+1 FAC 8/1 Others 4
Reading (£400,000 on 29/7/97) FL 67/1 FLC 9 FAC 2 Others 1

PRINGLE Martin Ulf
Born: Sweden, 18 November 1970
Height: 6'2" Weight: 12.3
International Honours: Sweden: 1
The tall, hard-working striker was signed by Charlton from Benfica last January, initially on loan, before the transfer was made permanent after he had given some impressive early performances. Made his debut against Southampton at the Dell as a substitute, and scored in his first full game against Newcastle at the Valley, where he got a last-minute equaliser. Two more goals followed in the next four games, but then they dried up. Covering a lot of ground, and having real pace, he also has a powerful shot with both feet, although favouring his right. With the correct service, Martin looks capable of producing the goods on a regular basis.

Charlton Ath (Signed from Benfica on 8/1/99) PL 15+3/3

PRIOR Spencer Justin
Born: Southend, 22 April 1971
Height: 6'3" Weight: 13.4
Club Honours: FLC '97
Signed from Leicester last August to replace the outgoing Christian Dailly, this tall, robust central defender was excellent in the air, strong in the tackle, and was an almost constant menace in a very impressive Derby rearguard in 1998-99. The only occasions on which he missed games were due to niggling medial ligament injuries, but recovery from these did not take long. Does not find the net too often, but scored the winning goal at Hillsbrough in January while helping to keep another clean sheet, and proved to be another bargain signing by the astute Jim Smith.

Southend U (From trainee on 22/5/89) FL 135/3 FLC 9 FAC 5 Others 7/1
Norwich C (£200,000 on 24/6/93) P/FL 67+7/1 FLC 10+1/1 FAC 0+2 Others 2
Leicester C (£600,000 on 17/8/96) PL 61+3 FLC 7 FAC 5 Others 2
Derby Co (£700,000 on 22/8/98) PL 33+1/1 FLC 2 FAC 4

PRITCHARD David Michael
Born: Wolverhampton, 27 May 1972
Height: 5'8" Weight: 11.5
International Honours: W: B-1
A ruptured tendon foot injury that had kept the combative full back out of the Bristol Rovers' team for seven months, David

returned to the first team in 1998-99 as a substitute in an Auto Windscreens Shield-tie at Walsall, which was eventually resolved with a penalty shoot-out. Interestingly, he was one of the eight players who missed their penalties, Walsall winning 5-4. He then made his first start on 23 January in a fourth round FA Cup victory over Leyton Orient, the first time Rovers had reached that far for 20 years. Out of contract at the end of the season, he turned down the opportunity to have a loan spell at Walsall just prior to transfer deadline, typically staying on to hold down his place in the final matches.

West Bromwich A (From trainee on 5/7/90) FL 1+4 (Free to Telford during 1992 close season)
Bristol Rov (£15,000 on 25/2/94) FL 135+2 FLC 7 FAC 12+1 Others 9+1

PROCTOR Michael Anthony
Born: Sunderland, 3 October 1980
Height: 5'11" Weight: 12.7
A young Sunderland striker who many people on Wearside are tipping to go on to great things, Michael is strong and pacy, and although making more appearances for the youths than the reserves last term, he was handed his first-team debut as a substitute against Premier League Everton in the Worthington Cup in November. Looking sharp and dangerous, if he continues to develop then a regular place may not be far away.

Sunderland (From trainee on 29/10/97) FLC 0+1

PROKAS Richard
Born: Penrith, 22 January 1976
Height: 5'9" Weight: 11.4
Club Honours: Div 3 '95; AMC '97
Richard can look back with some satisfaction on his performances at Carlisle in 1998-99, his favoured role as the midfield enforcer, and his determined style of play making him a popular figure among United supporters who appreciate his positive approach. Despite occasional forays up front, he failed to find the net, and will be looking to develop his role as an attacking midfielder in 1999-2000.

Carlisle U (From trainee on 18/7/94) FL 130+10/2 FLC 8+1 FAC 6 Others 17+3/1

PURSE Darren John
Born: Stepney, 14 February 1977
Height: 6'2" Weight: 12.8
International Honours: E: U21-2
Having been used occasionally from the bench by Birmingham in the early part of last season, apart from a start against Macclesfield, Darren was eventually given a run of ten games on coming in at Watford in October and starring as the "Man of the Match". A tough competitor in the centre of the defence, and strong in the air, he lost his place in the side when Trevor Francis decided to recall the experienced Gary Ablett. However, still relatively inexperienced, and still learning the game, his turn will undoubtedly come before too long.

Leyton Orient (From trainee on 22/2/94) FL 48+7/3 FLC 2 FAC 1 Others 7+1/2
Oxford U (£100,000 on 23/7/96) FL 52+7/5 FLC 10+1/2 FAC 2
Birmingham C (£800,000 on 17/2/98) FL 13+15 FLC 2+1 Others 0+1

QUAILEY Brian Sullivan
Born: Leicester, 21 March 1978
Height: 6'1" Weight: 13.11
A well-built striker who is strong and
mobile and, who in the main, acted as
reserve to Lee Hughes, Fabian de Freitas,
and Micky Evans at West Bromwich in
1998-99, he had a useful spell on loan at
Third Division Exeter in December before
returning to the Hawthorns and putting
pressure on the other three main front men.
At St James' Park, Brian stayed for the
maximum three months, his experience at a
higher level of football plain to see, and
contributed two goals.
West Bromwich A (Signed from Nuneaton
Borough on 22/9/97) FL 1+6 FLC 0+1
Exeter C (Loaned on 23/12/98) FL 8+4/2
Others 2/1

QUASHIE Nigel Francis
Born: Peckham, 20 July 1978
Height: 6'0" Weight: 12.4
International Honours: E: B-1; U21-4; Yth
Signed by Nottingham Forest from Queens
Park Rangers at the start of 1998-99, the
young Londoner took time to settle,
playing his first game for his new club at
home to Everton, but appeared on a
winning side just once – the 5-1
Worthington Cup victory at Leyton Orient
– before missing the rest of the campaign
with a broken foot. Despite the club's poor
form what he did show was that he had
quick feet, was brave enough to receive the
ball in difficult areas, and had a priceless
ability to get balls away quickly and
accurately, whether they were passed long
or short. The midfielder also has a strong
shot, and does not give possession away
without a struggle.
Queens Park R (From trainee on 1/8/95) PL
50+7/3 FLC 0+1 FAC 4/2
Nottingham F (£2,500,000 on 24/8/98) PL 12+4
FLC 2 FAC 0+1

QUAYLE Mark Leslie
Born: Liverpool, 2 October 1978
Height: 5'9" Weight: 10.6
Signed from Everton in the 1998 close
season, having failed to make a
breakthrough at Goodison, Mark impressed in reserve matches for Notts County,
but was allowed to go out on loan to non-
league Grantham Town where he also
impressed. Small, but quick, the young
forward figured in two starts plus six as a
substitute at County before the manager
decided to go with an alternative strike
force, and he was allowed to leave in the
summer after other new strikers with
greater experience were signed.
Everton (From trainee on 3/10/95)
Notts Co (Free on 23/6/98) FL 2+3 FAC 0+2
Others 0+1

QUINN Alan
Born: Dublin, 13 June 1979
Height: 5'9" Weight: 11.7
This young Irish midfielder was unable to
force his way into the Sheffield Wednesday
side last season, his only appearance coming
at Wimbledon early on. It could well be that
his lack of strength could hold him back, but
he is still growing and certainly has plenty of
commitment, and is still one for the future.
Sheffield Wed (Signed from Cherry Orchard on
6/12/97) PL 1+1

QUINN Barry Scott
Born: Dublin, 9 May 1979
Height: 6'0" Weight: 12.2
International Honours: Ei: U21-2; Yth
The young Irish midfield player came to the
fore during the 1998 World U18 championships which the Republic of Ireland won
under his captaincy, showing himself to be a
great prospect with silky ball skills, capable
of opening defences, and a coolness on the
ball that belies his tender years. He got his
first-team chance at Coventry early last
season at Old Trafford, making an impressive
debut, and in a run of five games he was not
overawed and gave a good account of
himself. Returning to reserve-team duty
he was a regular in the promotion-seeking
team, and in April he captained the
Republic's U20 side in the World
championships in Nigeria which reached the
quarter finals before losing on penalties to the
host nation. Barry was recalled to senior duty
when Gary McAllister was suspended, and
did not fail to impress. Also represented the
Republic at U21 level in 1998-99.
Coventry C (From trainee on 28/11/96) PL 6+1
FLC 1

Nigel Quashie

QUINN James (Jimmy) Martin
Born: Belfast, 18 November 1959
Height: 6'0" Weight: 13.10
Club Honours: Div 2 '94
International Honours: NI: 48; B-1

After starting 1998-99 as Barry Fry's right-hand man at Peterborough, while continuing to play and appearing in the first nine games, scoring five goals in the process – including two back-to-back doubles in wins against at home to Exeter and at Barnet – he was released on 5 November to become the manager at Swindon, thus following on from Steve McMahon. It was testimony to the striker's skill and guile in front of goal that Posh were never able to replace him, and despite him having tired legs he was still a model professional for the youngsters to follow.

Swindon T (£10,000 from Oswestry on 31/12/81) FL 34+15/10 FLC 1+1 FAC 5+3/6 Others 1/2
Blackburn Rov (£32,000 on 15/8/84) FL 58+13/17 FLC 6+1/2 FAC 4/3 Others 2/1
Swindon T (£50,000 on 19/12/86) FL 61+3/30 FLC 6/8 FAC 5 Others 10+1/5
Leicester C (£210,000 on 20/6/88) FL 13+18/6 FLC 2+1 FAC 0+1 Others 0+1
Bradford C (Signed on 17/3/89) FL 35/14 FLC 2/1 Others 1
West Ham U (£320,000 on 30/12/89) FL 34+13/19 FLC 4+2/2 Others 1
Bournemouth (£40,000 on 5/8/91) FL 43/19 FLC 4/2 FAC 5/2 Others 2/1
Reading (£55,000 on 27/7/92) FL 149+33/71 FLC 12+4/12 FAC 9/5 Others 6+3/6
Peterborough U (Free on 15/7/97) FL 47+2/25 FLC 6/1 FAC 3/3 Others 3+1/1

Jimmy Quinn (WBA)

QUINN Stephen James (Jimmy)
Born: Coventry, 15 December 1974
Height: 6'1" Weight: 12.10
International Honours: NI: 15; B-2; U21-1; Yth

An attacking midfield player, James also played as an out-and-out striker at West Bromwich in 1998-99, partnering Lee Hughes up front on several occasions. Good on the ball, he seemed to lose his confidence during the second half of the season, and was substituted on a number of occasions before losing his place in the side. But he is a gritty performer who will bounce back again, given the opportunity. Continued to play for Northern Ireland during the campaign.

Birmingham C (Trainee) FL 1+3
Blackpool (£25,000 on 5/7/93) FL 128+23/36 FLC 10+4/5 FAC 5+1/4 Others 7+4/2
Stockport Co (Loaned on 4/3/94) FL 0+1
West Bromwich A (£500,000 on 20/2/98) FL 51+5/8 FLC 2 FAC 1

Niall Quinn

QUINN Niall John
Born: Dublin, 6 October 1966
Height: 6'4" Weight: 15.10
Club Honours: FLC '87; Div 1 '99
International Honours: Ei: 69; B-1; U23-1; U21-6; Yth; Sch

Big Niall was many Sunderland fans' "Player of the Year" last term, as his goals helped to fire the Wearsiders to the First Division title, and earned him a richly-deserved championship medal. The giant Irish international striker was also selected for the PFA award-winning Division One side, which prompted Crystal Palace boss, Steve Coppell, to remark that he was one of the most difficult players to play against that he has ever seen. Certainly, his aerial strength was again phenomenal, but he was also extremely deft on the ground, and last term contained many highlights for him, including two goals in a vital 2-1 promotion victory over Ipswich in January, and a stint as emergency goalkeeper at Bradford in March when, having already scored to put Sunderland 1-0 up, he kept a clean sheet to secure three crucial points. Continuing to be a regular in the Eire side, and starring in their April win over England's Euro 2000 rivals, Sweden, he even had the honour of having a group of Sunderland fans release a single – *Niall Quinn's Disco Pants* – as a tribute to him.

Arsenal (From juniors on 30/11/83) FL 59+8/14 FLC 14+2/4 FAC 8+2/2 Others 0+1
Manchester C (£800,000 on 21/3/90) F/PL 183+20/66 FLC 20+2/7 FAC 13+3/4 Others 3/1
Sunderland (£1,300,000 on 17/8/96) F/PL 77+9/34 FLC 5+1/4 FAC 4/1 Others 2/2

QUINN Robert John
Born: Sidcup, 8 November 1976
Height: 5'11" Weight: 11.2
Club Honours: Div 3 '99
International Honours: Ei: U21-5

Signed from Crystal Palace during the summer of 1998, this competent defensive Brentford player made few mistakes. Commenced 1998-99 in midfield before moving to centre back, his best position, where he impressed with his strong tackling and good distribution. With the return to fitness of Darren Powell, and the change of tactics to a flat back four, Robert played some games in a defensive midfield slot or joined the action from the bench for the remainder of the campaign, and was good value for his Third Division championship medal at the end of a very successful season.

Crystal Palace (From trainee on 11/3/95) F/PL 18+5/1 FLC 2+1/1 Others 2+1
Brentford (£40,000 on 9/7/98) FL 34+9/2 FLC 4 FAC 3/1 Others 3/1

QUINN Wayne Richard
Born: Truro, 19 November 1976
Height: 5'10" Weight: 11.12
International Honours: E: B-1; U21-2; Yth

At the start of last season, Wayne was involved in an England get-together, and went on to play more games in 1998-99 than any other Blade, concentrating more on defence, where his spe/ed was more of an asset than previously. Continuing to show his crossing ability when coming forward, and always a threat with free kicks from just outside the area, he played mostly as a left-wing back, although occasionally in midfield.

Sheffield U (From trainee on 6/12/94) FL 69+3/3 FLC 8 FAC 9+1 Others 2

RABAT Didier
Born: Noumea, New Caledonia, 2 August 1966
Height: 6'1" Weight: 13.0
From New Caledonia, and a powerful and capable striker who was formerly with Paris St Germain and Toulon, he arrived at Notts County on trial as a potential free-transfer signing last December. Although he showed up rather well, especially in the air, in his one first-team match, the 1-0 home defeat by Hull City in the Auto Windscreens Shield, he was not retained and returned to France on 18 January.
Notts Co (Signed from Paris St Germain, via Toulon on 21/12/98) Others 1

RACHEL Adam
Born: Birmingham, 10 December 1976
Height: 5'11" Weight: 12.8
Following the long-term injury to Mark Bosnich, and prior to the signing of Peter Enckelman, Adam was the deputy 'keeper to Michael Oakes at Aston Villa in 1998-99, which resulted in him making 18 appearances on the subs' bench. Not overly tall for a goalie, he makes up for his lack of inches with agility and shot-stopping capabilities, which often see him reacting very quickly to dangerous goalmouth situations. He is also a reasonable kicker of the ball, from both feet and hands. Although his only first-team opportunity came when he was called off the bench at Blackburn after Michael Oakes had been dismissed for handling outside the area, and spent the next 33 minutes trying to keep Villa in the game before being beaten from close range by Tim Sherwood, there should be further call ups in 1999-2000, that is if he agrees to the club's offer of re-engagement.
Aston Villa (From trainee on 10/5/95) PL 0+1

RADEBE Lucas
Born: Johannesburg, South Africa, 12 April 1969
Height: 6'1" Weight: 11.8
International Honours: South Africa: 48
Captain of both club and country, Lucas is regarded almost unanimously as the "jewel in the crown" at Elland Road, and is the best defender to have pulled on a Leeds' shirt since Don Revie's days. His reading of the game is second to none, and his subsequent last-ditch tackles, along with his ability to smother opposition danger men as a top-class man marker distinguish him from the run of the mill Premiership defenders. Had another excellent season in 1998-99, leading by example. Although he picked up a knee-ligament injury at Derby, which caused him to miss the whole of November, he returned with performances of the highest order, and the young United central defender, Jonathan Woodgate, came on immensely while playing alongside him. The media courted many transfer rumours which prompted

David O'Leary to say that his skipper would leave "over his dead body", and thankfully Lucas signed a new four-year contract in December. Deservedly getting a contract which made him one of the highest paid players at the club, his undoubted commitment was highlighted when after African Nations Cup games he flew straight back to perform against Leicester and Liverpool on Monday nights, and produce consistent performances. With players like Lucas at the club, future success cannot be far away for United.
Leeds U (£250,000 from Kaizer Chiefs on 5/9/94) PL 102+11 FLC 7+3 FAC 12+2/1 Others 3

RADIGAN Neil Thomas
Born: Middlesbrough, 4 July 1980
Height: 5'8" Weight: 11.0
A first-year Scarborough professional, having progressed through the junior ranks to become a regular in the reserves, Neil made his senior bow last season when coming off the bench in the Worthington Cup home leg against Barnsley. Steady and consistent in midfield, and an accurate passer, he made virtually all of his appearances in the first half of the campaign, before being released in April when the team were up against it.
Scarborough (From trainee on 6/7/98) FL 4+5 FLC 0+2

RAE Alexander (Alex) Scott
Born: Glasgow, 30 September 1969
Height: 5'9" Weight: 11.12
Club Honours: Div 1 '99
International Honours: S: B-4; U21-8
Alex picked up a First Division championship medal with Sunderland last term, but will probably look back on the season with mixed emotions. The tough-tackling, attacking midfielder, who is equally effective in a central or wide position, is very popular at the Stadium of Light and, after missing the early weeks of the campaign through injury, returned with a bang, scoring twice as a substitute in the 7-0 demolition of Oxford. Sadly, the Scotsman was to be struck down by personal and stress-related problems, and when he re-appeared he suffered torn knee ligaments following a crude tackle at Blackburn in an FA Cup tie in January. Fully fit and raring to go, he will be an important part of next term's Premiership squad.
Falkirk (Free from Bishopbriggs on 15/6/87) SL 71+12/20 SLC 5/1 SC 2+1
Millwall (£100,000 on 20/8/90) FL 205+13/63 FLC 13+2/1 FAC 13/6 Others 10/1
Sunderland (£750,000 on 14/6/96) F/PL 49+18/7 FLC 5+1/2 FAC 3 Others 0+2

RAINFORD David John
Born: Stepney, 21 April 1979
Height: 6'0" Weight: 11.11
A homegrown Colchester product, who had scored many goals from midfield for the reserves and youth teams, David got his first-team debut late on in the win at York last September. Unfortunately, he never got the chance to build on that start, and went on loan to Scarborough at Christmas to get some first-team experience, before returning

to Layer Road later in the season. Strangely, Mick Wadsworth had already left Scarborough to take over as United's new manager, but the youngster did not manage to force his way into the squad and was released in the summer.
Colchester U (From trainee on 30/7/97) FL 0+1
Scarborough (Loaned on 31/12/98) FL 0+2 Others 1

RAMAGE Craig Darren
Born: Derby, 30 March 1970
Height: 5'9" Weight: 11.8
International Honours: E: U21-3
Craig, who had an horrific season at Bradford in 1998-99 when suffering a series of cartilage injuries, did not start a first-team game. A regular with the reserves, the tigerish midfielder made the odd senior appearance when coming off the bench, and will be looking to be fully fit in time for 1999-2000. Released during the summer, at his most capable of scoring the odd goal, he mixes up skilful passing with hard tackling.
Derby Co (From trainee on 20/7/88) FL 33+9/4 FLC 6+1/2 FAC 3+1/1 Others 0+3
Wigan Ath (Loaned on 16/2/89) FL 10/2 Others 0+1
Watford (£90,000 on 21/2/94) FL 99+5/27 FLC 8+1/2 FAC 7
Peterborough U (Loaned on 10/2/97) FL 7 Others 1
Bradford C (Free on 24/6/97) FL 24+11/1 FLC 0+2

RAMMELL Andrew (Andy) Victor
Born: Nuneaton, 10 February 1967
Height: 6'1" Weight: 13.12
A typical old-fashioned striker, Andy moved to Walsall from Southend during the summer of 1998, and made his debut on the opening day of last season in the club's 1-0 win at Gillingham. He then scored the decisive second goal at Wycombe a fortnight later, and in September netted in five successive games. His tireless running up front, and his power in the air made him a great crowd pleaser, while his tally of 20 goals was his best in ten seasons in the Football League. However, this tells only part of the story of his contribution to the Saddlers' promotion effort.
Manchester U (£40,000 from Atherstone U on 26/9/89)
Barnsley (£100,000 on 14/9/90) FL 149+36/44 FLC 11+3/1 FAC 12+1/4 Others 8/1
Southend U (Signed on 22/2/96) FL 50+19/13 FLC 3+3/1 FAC 2+1 Others 1
Walsall (Free on 15/7/98) FL 39/18 FLC 2/1 FAC 2 Others 5/1

RANKIN Isaiah (Izzy)
Born: London, 22 May 1978
Height: 5'10" Weight: 11.6
Signed from Arsenal during the 1998 close season, Izzy became Bradford's record signing, and came on as substitute for the Nationwide U21 side that played against the Italian Serie "B" select last November. Started last season as Lee Mills' strike partner, but when the manager changed the strike force he found himself out in the cold, being only used occasionally as a substitute. With great pace and an eye for goal, and still only 22 years old, the former Gunner has plenty of time to make a name for himself.

Arsenal (From trainee on 12/9/95) PL 0+1
Colchester U (Loaned on 25/9/97) FL 10+1/5 Others 1
Bradford C (£1,300,000 on 14/8/98) FL 15+12/4 FLC 2/1 FAC 0+1

Isiah Rankin

RANKINE Simon **Mark**
Born: Doncaster, 30 September 1969
Height: 5'9" Weight: 12.11
Missing just four league games for Preston in 1998-99, Mark regularly demonstrated his ability to disrupt the opposition midfield. Combative, and keen to get forward, he scored on the opening day, but managed few more during a season which saw him record the 450th senior appearance of his career. Having marked the occasion by scoring against Burnley, before suffering a bad facial injury, his consistent form was rewarded with a new two-year contract, and he will be hoping to remain a central figure in the first team for some time to come.
Doncaster Rov (From trainee on 4/7/88) FL 160+4/20 FLC 8+1/1 FAC 8/2 Others 14/2
Wolverhampton W (£70,000 on 31/1/92) FL 112+20/1 FLC 9+1 FAC 14+2 Others 7+2
Preston NE (£100,000 on 17/9/96) FL 95+5/4 FLC 8 FAC 7/1 Others 4

RAPLEY Kevin John
Born: Reading, 21 September 1977
Height: 5'9" Weight: 10.8
Club Honours: Div 3 '99
When the striker scored twice for Brentford, against Mansfield, on the opening day of 1998-99 it looked as though it would be his best season yet, but amazingly he was dropped for the next game. Although he continued to be part of the first-team squad his appearances were mainly from the bench, and he was loaned to Southend in October. At United, he immediately struck up a good relationship with the Roots Hall faithful, his darting near-post runs, quick turns, and striker's instincts were apparent straight away, and it was a shock when he decided to join Notts County on a permanent basis at the end of

his loan spell, instead of Southend. Having scored a goal on his debut at Luton to give County victory for the first time in two months, Kevin was perhaps a little unlucky, as one of several strikers brought in at around the same time, and ended up on the bench in later games. For the record, on Brentford winning promotion, and having played 12 times before leaving, he was happy to receive a Third Division championship medal for his efforts.
Brentford (From trainee on 8/7/96) FL 27+24/12 FLC 3+5/3 FAC 0+2 Others 1
Southend U (Loaned on 20/11/98) FL 9/4
Notts Co (£50,000 on 23/2/99) FL 10+6/2

RAVEN Paul Duncan
Born: Salisbury, 28 July 1970
Height: 6'1" Weight: 12.12
International Honours: E: Sch
A long-serving West Bromwich centre-back, Paul had a testimonial during last season – his last at the Hawthorns. Injuries ruined the campaign for the much-liked defender, who only made seven first-team appearances for Albion, plus 11 on loan to Rotherham, before being released in May. Loaned to United at the end of October to ease a crisis caused by many of the club's recognised defenders being out of action, he underlined his value by scoring three goals. Is strong in the air and on the ground.
Doncaster Rov (From juniors on 6/6/88) FL 52/4 FLC 2 FAC 5 Others 2
West Bromwich A (£100,000 on 23/3/89) FL 222+5/14 FLC 16/1 FAC 8/3 Others 15/1
Doncaster Rov (Loaned on 27/11/91) FL 7
Rotherham U (Loaned on 29/10/98) FL 11/3

RAWLINSON Mark David
Born: Bolton, 9 June 1975
Height: 5'10" Weight: 11.4
Mark had a somewhat disappointing 1998-99 season at Bournemouth in terms of first-team opoportunities, making only five starts and two substitute appearances. Predominantly a central midfielder, he is versatile enough to have played a couple of games at right back during the campaign, and is a good passer of the ball who is also not afraid to tackle.
Manchester U (From trainee on 5/7/93)
Bournemouth (Free on 1/7/95) FL 46+30/2 FLC 2+1 FAC 2+1 Others 3

RAYNOR Paul James
Born: Nottingham, 29 April 1966
Height: 6'0" Weight: 12.11
Club Honours: WC '89, '91
Paul spent the first part of last season at Leyton Orient on non-contract forms, being mainly used from the subs' bench as a utility player. Best known as an attacking right-sided midfielder, with excellent vision, and a good passer of the ball, he left to join Kettering in October when he was offered a permanent contract.
Nottingham F (From apprentice on 2/4/84) FL 3 FLC 1
Bristol Rov (Loaned on 28/3/85) FL 7+1
Huddersfield T (Free on 15/8/85) FL 38+12/9 FLC 3 FAC 2+1 Others 1
Swansea C (Free on 27/3/87) FL 170+21/27 FLC 11+1/3 FAC 8+1/1 Others 15+1/3
Wrexham (Loaned on 17/10/88) FL 6

Cambridge U (Free on 10/3/92) FL 46+3/2 FLC 5 FAC 1 Others 2+1/1
Preston NE (£36,000 on 23/7/93) FL 72+8/9 FLC 4+1 FAC 7/1 Others 10/2
Cambridge U (Signed on 12/9/95) FL 78+1/7 FLC 1+1 FAC 2 Others 1 (Free to Guang Deong during 1997 close season)
Leyton Orient (Free on 26/2/98) FL 6+9 FLC 1+1

READ Paul Colin
Born: Harlow, 25 September 1973
Height: 5'10" Weight: 12.11
International Honours: E: Sch
1998-99 was another frustrating season for this sharp Wycombe striker who, like last year, began brightly and scored two goals in his first two starts in August, including a left-footed bullet at Swindon in the Worthington Cup. With no success in the next six games, however, he endured a period in and out of the side, before scoring one further goal as a substitute at Plymouth in the FA Cup. His last appearance was in mid January, and after sustaining an injury he returned to fitness in April but played no further part in the club's relegation battle, prior to being released in the summer. Although finding it hard to establish himself at first-team level with Wanderers, there is no doubt that he has the instincts of a goalscorer.
Arsenal (From trainee on 11/10/91)
Leyton Orient (Loaned on 10/3/95) FL 11 Others 1
Southend U (Loaned on 6/10/95) FL 3+1/1 Others 1
Wycombe W (£130,000 on 17/1/97) FL 32+25/9 FLC 4/2 FAC 1+2/1 Others 1

READY Karl
Born: Neath, 14 August 1972
Height: 6'1" Weight: 13.3
International Honours: W: 5; B-2; U21-5; Sch
Welsh born Karl was appointed Queens Park Rangers' club captain by Ray Harford towards the end of the 1997-98 season, holding on to the captain's armband after the change in management. A solid player who can play anywhere across the back four, where he is good in the air and comfortable with the ball, he was an ever present in 1998-99 up to game number 37, when he was absent due to suspension. His most memorable moment of the campaign came against Bristol City in the first home game of the season. In order to try and retrieve something from a lost cause, he was moved up to the left-hand side of the forward line, and ended the match by scoring in injury time with a remarkable curling shot from the edge of the box.
Queens Park R (From trainee on 13/8/90) F/PL 155+15/8 FLC 8+2/1 FAC 8

REDFEARN Neil David
Born: Dewsbury, 20 June 1965
Height: 5'9" Weight: 13.0
Club Honours: Div 2 '91
A record signing for Charlton when he was secured from Barnsley during the 1998 close season, great things were expected of him, particularly in providing goals from midfield. Neil is a strong and determined player who tackles hard and likes to get into the opposition penalty area in order to get

shots on goal. Despite being a regular for most of 1998-99, he only managed three goals, including a penalty against West Ham at the Valley. Lost his place in the side when Graham Stuart was signed, but featured again towards the end of the campaign.

Bolton W (Free from Nottingham F juniors on 23/6/82) FL 35/1 FLC 2 FAC 4
Lincoln C (£8,250 on 23/3/84) FL 96+4/13 FLC 4 FAC 3/1 Others 7
Doncaster Rov (£17,500 on 22/8/86) FL 46/14 FLC 2 FAC 3/1 Others 2
Crystal Palace (£100,000 on 31/7/87) FL 57/10 FLC 6 FAC 1 Others 1
Watford (£150,000 on 21/11/88) FL 22+2/3 FLC 1 FAC 6/3 Others 5/1
Oldham Ath (£150,000 on 12/1/90) FL 56+6/16 FLC 3/1 FAC 7+1/3 Others 1
Barnsley (£150,000 on 5/9/91) F/PL 289+3/72 FLC 21/6 FAC 20/6 Others 5
Charlton Ath (£1,000,000 on 1/7/98) PL 29+1/3 FLC 2/1 FAC 1

REDKNAPP Jamie Frank
Born: Barton on Sea, 25 June 1973
Height: 6'0" Weight: 12.10
Club Honours: FLC '95
International Honours: E: 14; B-1; U21-19; Yth; Sch

For too long, Jamie sought to rid himself of the "Spice Boy" tag with which he had become associated, and in all fairness he has probably achieved that now. He had a fine season with Liverpool in 1998-99, in which he came to the peak of his career, proving once again that he is a fine footballer, possesses a fierce shot, is strong in the tackle, is a great passer of the ball, has vision, and is dedicated to the Reds' cause. Having had a magnificent game in the FA Cup against Manchester United with a compelling midfield performance, he continued to feature in successive England manager's plans, and it is likely that he will feature in Gerard Houllier's plans for several more seasons to come, unless foreign riches beckon him in the way that they did with Steve McManaman.

Bournemouth (From trainee on 27/6/90) FL 6+7 FLC 3 FAC 3 Others 2
Liverpool (£350,000 on 15/1/91) F/PL 187+24/27 FLC 25/5 FAC 17+1/2 Others 19+4/3

Jamie Redknapp

REDMILE Matthew Ian
Born: Nottingham, 12 November 1976
Height: 6'3" Weight: 14.10
Club Honours: Div 3 '98

This young giant of a Notts County centre half continued his steady development in 1998-99, and gradually forced his way into a regular first-team place, his best form coming in the first quarter of the season. Possesses great skill for such a big man and, under the watchful eye of manager, Sam Allardyce, is learning to eliminate mistakes and add the consistency which is required of him. Good in the air at both ends of the pitch, Matthew causes defenders all sorts of problems with his height at set pieces.

Notts Co (From trainee on 4/7/95) FL 94+4/6 FLC 6 FAC 12 Others 3

REDMOND Stephen (Steve)
Born: Liverpool, 2 November 1967
Height: 5'11" Weight: 11.7
Club Honours: FAYC '86
International Honours: E: U21-14; Yth

A seasoned professional, the central defender was a 1998 summer recruit for Bury on a free transfer from Oldham, and went straight into the Shakers' side, but struggled to recapture his form. Shortly after a dismissal at Bradford in October, Steve picked up a hamstring injury, and was missing for almost three months. However, he returned to the regular line-up from February onwards and was outstanding, reading the game well while always remaining in control. It was therefore a big blow for Bury when he chipped a bone in an ankle at Oxford in mid April, and missed the final three games of 1998-99. Out of contract during the summer, the club were known to have made him an offer of re-engagement.

Manchester C (From apprentice on 3/12/84) FL 231+4/7 FLC 24 FAC 17 Others 11
Oldham Ath (£300,000 on 10/7/92) P/FL 195+10/4 FLC 20 FAC 10+2 Others 1+1
Bury (Free on 3/7/98) FL 26 FLC 4

Steve Redmond

Adam Reed

REED Adam Maurice
Born: Bishop Auckland, 18 February 1975
Height: 6'1" Weight: 12.0

Returning to his first club, Darlington, during the 1998 close season, three years after leaving for Blackburn Rovers, having failed to break into the first team at Ewood Park, the experience has undoubtedly made him a better player, although his assured performances at right back and in the centre of defence were sadly limited by a couple of unfortunate injuries. With excellent aerial strength, and positional ability, he looks to make up for lost time in 1999-2000.

Darlington (From trainee on 16/7/93) FL 45+7/1 FLC 1+1 FAC 1 Others 3
Blackburn Rov (£200,000 on 9/8/95)
Darlington (Loaned on 21/2/97) FL 14
Rochdale (Loaned on 5/12/97) FL 10 Others 2/1
Darlington (Free on 17/7/98) FL 25+4/2 FAC 2 Others 0+1

REED Martin John
Born: Scarborough, 10 January 1978
Height: 6'0" Weight: 11.6

A strong-tackling, no-nonsense central defender who did well in his senior appearances for York in 1998-99, especially when giving a fine display in the vital away win at Lincoln late in the season. Is still highly thought of at Bootham Crescent.

York C (From trainee on 4/7/96) FL 31+5 FLC 2 FAC 3+1 Others 1

REES Jason Mark
Born: Aberdare, 22 December 1969
Height: 5'5" Weight: 10.2
International Honours: W: 1; U21-3; B-1; Yth; Sch

After playing for Exeter on loan during 1996-97, Jason signed up permanently from Cambridge during the 1998 close season. His competitiveness and awareness as a ball winner in the middle of the pitch were appreciated by the fans, and his ability was rewarded by the fact that he was virtually an ever present in the side.

Luton T (From trainee on 1/7/88) FL 59+23 FLC 3+2 FAC 2+1 Others 5+1/2
Mansfield T (Loaned on 23/12/93) FL 15/1 Others 1
Portsmouth (Free on 18/7/94) FL 30+13/3 FLC 2+1 FAC 0+1
Exeter C (Loaned on 31/1/97) FL 7
Cambridge U (Free on 8/8/97) FL 17+3 FLC 2 Others 1
Exeter C (Free on 29/7/98) FL 44/1 FLC 2 FAC 4 Others 1

REEVES Alan
Born: Birkenhead, 19 November 1967
Height: 6'0" Weight: 12.0
Having quit Wimbledon's "Crazy Gang" in search of first-team football with Swindon during the summer of 1998, the tall central defender, who is an excellent header of the ball, showed himself to be an asset in attack on set pieces, as well as adding experience at the back. Scoring in his second match, a 2-1 home Worthington Cup win over Wycombe, he then picked up an ankle injury part way through the campaign that kept him out of the side for three months, after which he never really won back his place.
Norwich C (Signed from Heswall on 20/9/88)
Gillingham (Loaned on 9/2/89) FL 18
Chester C (£10,000 on 18/8/89) FL 31+9/2 FLC 1+1 FAC 3 Others 3
Rochdale (Free on 2/7/91) FL 119+2/9 FLC 12/1 FAC 6 Others 5
Wimbledon (£300,000 on 6/9/94) PL 52+5/4 FLC 2+2 FAC 8
Swindon T (Free on 23/6/98) FL 23+1/2 FLC 2/1

REEVES David Edward
Born: Birkenhead, 19 November 1967
Height: 6'0" Weight: 12.6
Club Honours: Div 3 '95
Chesterfield's yo-yo king also finished 1998-99 as leading scorer, and might have doubled that tally at least, if it was not for the unselfish work that he put in for others, chasing after through balls to terrorise the right-hand side of opponents' defences. Dave formed a symbiotic partnership with Jon Howard for much of the season, linking well with Jason Lee just as a hernia flared up, and he was due to go under the surgeon's knife in the summer in order to return fully fit for the coming campaign.
Sheffield Wed (Free from Heswall on 6/8/86) FL 8+9/2 FLC 1+1/1 FAC 1+1 Others 0+1
Scunthorpe U (Loaned on 17/12/86) FL 3+1/2
Scunthorpe U (Loaned on 1/10/87) FL 6/4
Burnley (Loaned on 20/11/87) FL 16/8 Others 2/1
Bolton W (£80,000 on 17/8/89) FL 111+23/29 FLC 14+1/1 FAC 8+5/5 Others 9+2/7
Notts Co (£80,000 on 25/3/93) FL 9+4/2 FLC 1+1
Carlisle U (£121,000 on 1/10/93) FL 127/47 FLC 9/5 FAC 9/4 Others 23/7
Preston NE (Signed on 9/10/96) FL 45+2/12 FLC 3+1/3 FAC 2/3 Others 1
Chesterfield (Signed on 6/11/97) FL 63+3/15 FLC 3/1 FAC 2+1/1 Others 2

REID Brian Robertson
Born: Paisley, 15 June 1970
Height: 6'2" Weight: 11.12
International Honours: S: U21-4
Brian was a constant factor in Burnley's central defence for much of last season. Arriving from Morton in September, he partnered first Peter Swan, then Matty Heywood, and finally Steve Davis, looking

generally solid amid the chaos that sometimes surrounded him, and chipping in with a couple of vital goals. Injury finally cost him his place, and on recovery he was unable to displace Chris Brass before being released in the summer.
Greenock M (Free from Renfrew Waverley on 27/7/88) SL 57/1 SLC 2 SC 7 Others 2/1
Glasgow R (Signed on 25/3/91) SL 5
Greenock M (Signed on 11/3/96) SL 68/3 SLC 4 SC 3 Others 5
Burnley (Signed on 4/9/98) FL 30+1/3 FAC 1 Others 1

Paul Reid

REID Paul Robert
Born: Oldbury, 19 January 1968
Height: 5'9" Weight: 11.8
1998-99 was another good season for Paul, who unfortunately for Oldham fans has come to the end of his contract at the club and was set to become a free agent during the summer. Missed just a handful of games, due to more than his fair share of cautions, but the supporters appreciated his total commitment to Athletic's cause, especially with the club staring relegation in the face for most of the campaign. Still showing his hard-tackling, hard-running abilities from the left side of midfield, he will undoubtedly be missed. Both of his goals were penalties in winning games.
Leicester C (From apprentice on 9/1/86) FL 140+22/21 FLC 13/4 FAC 5+1 Others 6+2
Bradford C (Loaned on 19/3/92) FL 7
Bradford C (£25,000 on 27/7/92) FL 80+2/15 FLC 3/2 FAC 3 Others 5/1
Huddersfield T (£70,000 on 20/5/94) FL 70+7/6 FLC 9/1 FAC 5+1 Others 1
Oldham Ath (£100,000 on 27/3/97) FL 93/7 FLC 4/1 FAC 8 Others 1

REID Shaun
Born: Huyton, 13 October 1965
Height: 5'8" Weight: 12.2
After missing all of 1997-98 recovering from a career-threatening knee injury, Shaun

returned to the Chester midfield as a substitute at Exeter last September. His return to full fitness really was remarkable, and was a just reward for the determination that he showed throughout his 14-month lay off. Just like his brother, Sunderland manager, Peter, a tough-tackling midfielder and a firm favourite with the fans, he was appointed on to the youth coaching staff near the end of the season.
Rochdale (From apprentice on 20/9/83) FL 126+7/4 FLC 10/2 FAC 5/1 Others 12
Preston NE (Loaned on 12/12/85) FL 3
York C (£32,500 on 23/12/88) FL 104+2/7 FLC 7 FAC 4 Others 5/1
Rochdale (Free on 16/8/92) FL 106+1/10 FLC 8 FAC 5/1 Others 8+1/2
Bury (£25,000 on 5/7/95) FL 20+1 FLC 5 FAC 1 Others 2
Chester C (£30,000 on 25/11/96) FL 43+6/2 FLC 2 FAC 1 Others 3

Shaun Reid

REID Steven John
Born: Kingston, 10 March 1981
Height: 6'1" Weight: 12.4
International Honours: E: Yth
An England U16 international striker who made his league debut for Millwall at the age of 17, when coming on as a substitute in the final game of 1997-98, against Bournemouth, Steven was one of a significant number of local products who got their chance in 1998-99 due to injuries. Adapting himself very well, he went on to make an appearance at Wembley in the losing Auto Windscreens final against Wigan. A strong tackler for a winger, cum forward, and very good in the air, he loves running at defenders to put defences under pressure.
Millwall (From trainee on 18/5/98) FL 25+1 FLC 0+1 Others 6

REILLY Mark
Born: Bellshill, 30 March 1969
Height: 5'8" Weight: 10.7
Club Honours: SC '97
International Honours: S: B-1
A Scottish "B" international midfield player who arrived at Reading during the 1998 close season on a free transfer from Kilmarnock, he returned to the Scottish Premier League club for a small fee early in November. Never sure of a first-team place at the Madejski Stadium, Mark made only six starts during the campaign, being handicapped by a lack of pace and a couple of injuries.
Motherwell (From Wishaw Juniors on 23/8/85) SL 3+1
Kilmarnock (Signed on 5/7/91) SL 190+15/8 SLC 9+1 SC 19/1 Others 7+1/1
Reading (Free on 21/7/98) FL 4+2 FLC 2

REINELT Robert (Robbie) Squire
Born: Loughton, 11 March 1974
Height: 5'11" Weight: 12.0
Signed on a non-contract basis from Brighton last August, Robbie was used mainly as a substitute by Leyton Orient, but managed a couple of starts before joining non-league Stevenage permanently in October. An enthusiastic attacker who likes to chase the ball down, his one highlight was to score against Nottingham Forest in the Worthington Cup.
Aldershot (Trainee) FL 3+2
Gillingham (Free from Wivenhoe T on 19/3/93) FL 34+18/5 FLC 3/1 FAC 5+2/2 Others 5
Colchester U (Signed on 22/3/95) FL 22+26/10 FLC 4+1/2 FAC 1 Others 3/1
Brighton & Hove A (£15,000 on 13/2/97) FL 32+12/7 FLC 2 Others 1
Leyton Orient (Free on 10/8/98) FL 2+5 FLC 0+4/1

REMY Christophe Philippe
Born: Besancon, France, 6 August 1971
Height: 5'10" Weight: 12.6
1998-99 was a frustrating time for Christophe who was one of the most talented players in the Oxford squad. He started the season with a number of injuries, playing just twice up to December before having a run of games which culminated with his fine strike at Ipswich – his only goal for the club – when he got on the end of a fine through ball and slotted home. However, the right-sided wing back tailed off again towards the end and was released in the summer.
Oxford U (Signed from Auxerre on 25/7/97) FL 23+5/1 FLC 4 FAC 1+3

RENNIE David
Born: Edinburgh, 29 August 1964
Height: 6'0" Weight: 13.0
International Honours: S: Yth;
Disappointed to be told that he was due to be released by Peterborough at the end of 1998-99, following a long period out because of hernia problems, David still performed well despite having limited opportunities. At his best, a central defender who was good in the air, an excellent tackler, and whose long-passing abilities and skill at set pieces were a bonus, he could also get you a few goals.
Leicester C (From apprentice on 18/5/82) FL 21/1 FLC 2

Leeds U (£50,000 on 17/1/86) FL 95+6/5 FLC 7 FAC 7/1 Others 4/1
Bristol C (£175,000 on 31/7/89) FL 101+3/8 FLC 8 FAC 9 Others 5
Birmingham C (£120,000 on 20/2/92) FL 32+3/4 FLC 1 Others 1
Coventry C (£100,000 on 11/3/93) PL 80+2/3 FLC 6 FAC 3+1
Northampton T (Free on 5/8/96) FL 45+3/4 FLC 4 FAC 1 Others 5
Peterborough U (Free on 1/12/97) FL 27 Others 5

RENNISON Graham Lee
Born: Northallerton, 2 October 1978
Height: 6'0" Weight: 12.8
Having made his first-team debut for York while still a trainee in 1997-98, he signed professional forms during the summer of 1998 and, despite sitting on the bench a number of times, made just one substitute appearance in the FA Cup-tie at Wrexham in 1998-99. However, the young central defender is still highly regarded at Bootham Crescent, and expects to make good progress during the coming season.
York C (From trainee on 2/7/98) FL 1 FAC 0+1

RENNISON Shaun
Born: Northallerton, 23 November 1980
Height: 6'3" Weight: 11.12
Another of Scarborough's good youngsters, Shaun came through the ranks to turn professional last February, having already made his senior bow at Mansfield in December and scored against Scunthorpe in his next appearance. Recognised by the Boro youth-team coach as "the next Tony Adams", and obviously a central defender with a bright future in the game, he was a regular by the end of the campaign before being presented with the "Young Player of the Year" award.
Scarborough (From trainee on 9/2/99) FL 15/1 Others 1

RENSHAW Ian Francis
Born: Chelmsford, 14 April 1978
Height: 6'0" Weight: 11.6
Arriving at Scarborough at the end of last November as a non-contract player, Ian was given his only opportunity the following month when coming on in the 87th minute of the 3-1 defeat at Peterborough before leaving. Initially, in the town to visit his girlfriend, having taken leave of absence from his job at a London bank, and playing his football for Basildon United in the Essex League, he proved to be an attacking forward who could hold the ball up reasonably well.
Scarborough (Free from Basildon U on 27/11/98) FL 0+1

RIBEIRO Bruno
Born: Setubal, Portugal, 22 October 1975
Height: 5'8" Weight: 12.2
Having arrived at Elland Road in 1997-98 as an unknown quantity, Bruno quickly became a supporters' favourite for his gritty and skilful displays. However, an operation in the summer of 1998 took a while to heal, which meant he missed most of pre-season training, and he began 1998-99 on the bench. Recalled against Aston Villa in

September, he then picked up a thigh injury which caused him to be sidelined once more and, on returning in the UEFA Cup-tie at Roma, he hit a post and was sent off. Following that, he again found himself struggling for fitness, although he made scoring appearances against Wimbledon and Portsmouth to remind the fans of his undoubted skill. Despite being reported in the Press to be seeking a transfer, hopefully, he will remain at Elland Road and fare better in the coming season.
Leeds U (£500,000 from Vittoria Setubal on 18/7/97) PL 35+7/4 FLC 3+1/1 FAC 4/1 Others 1+1

Hamilton Ricard

RICARD Cuesta **Hamilton**
Born: Colombia, 12 January 1974
Height: 6'2" Weight: 14.5
International Honours: Colombia: 19
Middlesbrough never lost a Premiership game during which "Ham, the Man" scored a goal, the Colombian striker proving to be a lucky omen as well as a leading goalscorer. In 1998-99, he worked very hard to put the previous season's report, (could do better if he tried!) behind him, and certainly delivered the goods this time around. His strike rate was phenomenal, and the feeling at the Riverside is that he has not peaked yet, his boundless energy and developing relationship with Brian Deane, and more recently Keith O'Neill, augering well for the future. Big and strong, and difficult to dislodge, he gets better all the time.
Middlesbrough (£2,000,000 + from Deportivo on 13/3/98) P/FL 36+9/17 FLC 4/3 FAC 1

RICHARD Fabrice
Born: Santes, France, 16 August 1973
Height: 6'1" Weight: 12.4
A French defender signed by Colchester towards the transfer deadline last March to add defensive cover, he was an ever present in the team either at right back or his more natural position of centre half. Initially, he seemed rather exposed at full back, where the greater pace of the English game caused

some problems, but he looked much more comfortable when playing in the middle of defence, either in a flat back four or as a marker in a defensive three.

Colchester U (Signed from Cannes on 22/3/99) FL 10

Dean Richards

RICHARDS Dean Ivor
Born: Bradford, 9 June 1974
Height: 6'2" Weight: 13.5
International Honours: E: U21-4

The Wolves' central defender suddenly had a lot to prove after injuries and losses of form, and began last season competently, apart from the dreaded night that Wolves met Queens Park Rangers. When playing to his potential, Dean tackled splendidly, also having the skills to beat players too, but did not endear himself to the fans when he made comments, not for the first time, about leaving if Wolves did not gain promotion. He performed better in the New Year, looking good against Arsenal, and it seemed he might go to Newcastle before the transfer deadline. Although he scored an unlucky own goal at Barnsley his extra determination was typified by the fact he scored a powerful winning goal that day. As Wolves' most expensive signing ever, he could still leave for free because of the Bosman ruling.

Bradford C (From trainee on 10/7/92) FL 82+4/4 FLC 7/1 FAC 4/1 Others 3+2
Wolverhampton W (£1,850,000 on 25/3/95) FL 118+4/7 FLC 11 FAC 10/1 Others 2

RICHARDS Justin
Born: West Bromwich, 16 October 1980
Height: 5'10" Weight: 11.0

Having signed professional forms for West Bromwich last January, after coming through the trainee ranks, the young enterprising striker made his debut at senior level as a second-half substitute against Ipswich at the Hawthorns in March. Played very well in Albion's youth and reserve teams prior to that, and is looking ahead to a promising career with the club. Was named in the England U18 squad in 1999.

West Bromwich A (From trainee on 8/1/99) FL 0+1

RICHARDS Tony Spencer
Born: Newham, 17 September 1973
Height: 5'11" Weight: 13.1

Starting last season for Leyton Orient scoring in the opening two games, he then spent the next 12 matches on the sidelines before coming back to remain almost for the rest of 1998-99. Used both as a right winger and a centre forward during the campaign, he also managed to score more than his fair share of goals, his main highlight being a hat trick in the FA Cup-tie against Brighton. Bustling, aggressive, and hard running, Tony is always on the look out for a shot on goal.

West Ham U (From trainee on 14/8/92) Free to Hong Kong R during 1993 close season)
Cambridge U (Signed from Sudbury T on 10/8/95) FL 29+13/5 FLC 1 Others 3
Leyton Orient (£10,000 on 21/7/97) FL 38+8/9 FLC 2+2/1 FAC 2/3 Others 4

RICHARDSON Barry
Born: Wallsend, 5 August 1969
Height: 6'1" Weight: 12.1

Barry began 1998-99 in Lincoln's reserves, but won his place back in goal in mid September following an injury to John Vaughan. He then had a run of 15 consecutive appearances before being dropped after the 2-1 defeat at York City in early December, and his only subsequent game was in the Auto Windscreens Shield. Bearing that in mind, it was no surprise that he was placed on the transfer list at the end of the season.

Sunderland (From trainee on 20/5/88)
Scarborough (Free on 21/3/89) FL 30 FLC 1 Others 1
Stockport Co (Free on 6/8/91)
Northampton T (Free on 10/9/91) FL 96 FLC 4 FAC 5 Others 8
Preston NE (£20,000 on 25/7/94) FL 20 FLC 2 FAC 3 Others 2
Lincoln C (£20,000 on 20/10/95) FL 109 FLC 5 FAC 8 Others 2

RICHARDSON Ian George
Born: Barking, 22 October 1970
Height: 5'10" Weight: 11.1
Club Honours: Div 3 '98
International Honours: E: SP-1

Always one of the first names on the Notts County team sheet after joining the club from Birmingham City early in 1996, he was converted to a left-sided central defender, where he is now more usually at home. Suffered through injury last season, and for a time operated once again as a midfielder, scoring the club's opening goal of 1998-99, at Oldham, after controversially kicking the ball out of the 'keeper's hands as he attempted a clearance. Ever popular with the fans, and a scorer of set piece-goals, he scored back-to-back doubles, away to

Millwall and at home to York, in March, ending the campaign with seven strikes in total. Is also known for his exceptional leap.

Birmingham C (£60,000 from Dagenham & Redbridge on 23/8/95) FL 3+4 FLC 3+1 FAC 2 Others 1+2
Notts Co (£200,000 on 19/1/96) FL 79+8/10 FLC 4 FAC 7/1 Others 5

Jon Richardson

RICHARDSON Jonathan (Jon) Derek
Born: Nottingham, 29 August 1975
Height: 6'0" Weight: 12.6

Exeter's "Mr Reliable", Jon is now the player with the longest continuous service for the club. His consistency in the centre of City's defence made him a virtual ever present in the team in 1998-99, while his fondness for bringing the ball out to join the attack was rewarded with five league goals. Difficult to pass, he compliments his game with excellent tactical awareness.

Exeter C (From trainee on 7/7/94) FL 207+5/7 FLC 9/3 FAC 11/1 Others 9

RICHARDSON Kevin
Born: Newcastle, 4 December 1962
Height: 5'9" Weight: 12.0
Club Honours: FAC '84; CS '84; Div 1 '85, '89; ECWC '85; FLC '94
International Honours: E: 1

Signed from Southampton during the 1998 close season, Kevin immediately showed his experience and know how at Barnsley in 1998-99, and was made club captain. Always available to the player in possession, and invariably making good use of the ball, his organisational skills were evident on the pitch from day one. Despite suffering a knee injury in late September that kept him out of action for a couple of months, he came back strongly to lead with renewed vigour apart from another blip at the end of a long and hard campaign.

Everton (From apprentice on 8/12/80) FL 95+14/16 FLC 10+3/3 FAC 13/1 Others 7+2
Watford (£225,000 on 4/9/86) FL 39/2 FLC 3 FAC 7 Others 1
Arsenal (£200,000 on 26/8/87) FL 88+8/5 FLC 13+3/2 FAC 9/1 Others 3 (£750,000 to Real Sociedad on 1/7/90)
Aston Villa (£450,000 on 6/8/91) ßL 142+1/13 FLC 15/3 FAC 12 Others 10
Coventry C (£300,000 on 16/2/95) PL 75+3 FLC 8/1 FAC 7
Southampton (£150,000 on 10/9/97) PL 25+3 FLC 4 FAC 1
Barnsley (£300,000 on 17/7/98) FL 24+2 FLC 4 FAC 2+1

RICHARDSON Lee James
Born: Halifax, 12 March 1969
Height: 5'11" Weight: 11.0

Huddersfield's playmaker and skilful, ball-playing midfielder suffered early season ankle problems that kept him out of action for the opening six games of 1998-99. Then, back in the side for a handful of appearances, hamstring damage sustained at Tranmere put him out of action again. However, he finally got going in November to find his genuine form, and gave a brilliant performance on Boxing Day against Grimsby to win the "Man of the Match" award. Unfortunately, his season was blighted again, this time at Sheffield United, where an ankle injury forced him on to the sidelines until early April. As you would expect of him, he came back strongly, especially in the heart of midfield against soon-to-be-promoted, Sunderland, where his battling qualities stood out.
Halifax T (From trainee on 6/7/87) FL 43+13/2 FLC 4 FAC 4+2 Others 6
Watford (£175,000 on 9/2/89) FL 40+1/1 FLC 1+1 FAC 1
Blackburn Rov (£250,000 on 15/8/90) FL 50+12/3 FLC 1 Others 2+2
Aberdeen (£152,000 on 16/9/92) SL 59+5/6 SLC 2/1 SC 8/2 Others 3/1
Oldham Ath (£300,000 on 12/8/94) FL 82+6/21 FLC 6+2 FAC 9 Others 4
Stockport Co (Loaned on 15/8/97) FL 4+2
Huddersfield T (£65,000 on 24/10/97) FL 29+7/3 FAC 0+2

RICHARDSON Neil Thomas
Born: Sunderland, 3 March 1968
Height: 6'0" Weight: 13.9
Club Honours: AMC '96

Used as a squad player at Rotherham in the early months of last season, Neil found his opportunities limited to a handful of starts. As if that was not enough, just when he got back into the team for the two FA Cup games against Rochdale he suffered a broken foot in the replay in December and failed to regain his place. Still regarded as one of the best passers of a ball in the club, he was richly rewarded for his ten year's service with a testimonial before being freed in the summer.
Rotherham U (Signed from Brandon U on 18/8/89) FL 168+16/10 FLC 14+1/1 FAC 12+1/1 Others 11+2/1
Exeter C (Loaned on 8/11/96) FL 14 Others 2

RICHARDSON Nicholas (Nick) John
Born: Halifax, 11 April 1967
Height: 6'1" Weight: 12.6
Club Honours: Div 3 '93; WC '93

A stylish midfield player who missed only three games for Chester during 1998-99, Nick turned in some tremendous performances for City, being at the centre of most of their creative moves, and providing goalscoring opportunities for his team mates as well as chipping in with three strikes himself. Extremely versatile, he is comfortable at right back as well as in his more favoured midfield berth. Out of contract during the summer, at the time of going to press the club had offered him terms of re-engagement.
Halifax T (Free from Emley on 15/11/88) FL 89+12/17 FLC 6+4/2 FAC 2+1/1 Others 6/1
Cardiff C (£35,000 on 13/8/92) FL 106+5/13 FLC 4 FAC 6 Others 12+2/2
Wrexham (Loaned on 21/10/94) FL 4/2
Chester C (Loaned on 16/12/94) FL 6/1
Bury (£22,500 on 8/8/95) FL 3+2 FLC 1
Chester C (£40,000 on 7/9/95) FL 127+6/9 FLC 7 FAC 4/1 Others 4/1

RICKERS Paul Steven
Born: Leeds, 9 May 1975
Height: 5'10" Weight: 11.0

A virtual ever present for Oldham in 1998-99, missing just one game due to a car accident en-route to the ground, this skilful midfielder also chipped in with four very handy goals, none more important than the header in the 2-0 win over Reading on the last day of the season – the result keeping Latics in the Second Division. As always in the thick of things, his hard-working displays finding him up and down the pitch, tackling at one end and driving for goal at the other, Paul typifies the modern midfielder and looks to play a key role in any Athletic success.
Oldham Ath (From trainee on 16/7/93) FL 151+7/13 FLC 8 FAC 10+1 Others 2+1

RICKETTS Michael Barrington
Born: Birmingham, 4 December 1978
Height: 6'2" Weight: 11.12

Such was the competition for places up front for Walsall in 1998-99 that this tall striker started only two games, and for the first time in four seasons did not score a first-team goal. With a good football brain, good feet, and good aerial ability, he substituted in midfield on a number of occasions, and could still be one of the players of the future.
Walsall (From trainee on 13/9/96) FL 10+34/3 FLC 0+3 FAC 1+1 Others 3+1/1

RIDLER David (Dave) George
Born: Liverpool, 12 March 1976
Height: 6'1" Weight: 12.2

Now an established member of the Wrexham squad, Dave continued to improve at the heart of the defence in 1998-99, forming useful central defensive partnerships, primarily with Brian Carey, and also Dean Spink. An unhurried, controlled type of defender who likes to play his way out of trouble, he also scored his first Football League goal at Burnley in October, and continued in the goalscoring frame of mind with a strike at Lincoln City in the Auto Windscreens Shield. Can also fill in more than adequately at left back when required.
Wrexham (Free from Rockys on 3/7/96) FL 60+7/1 FLC 1 FAC 8 Others 7+1/1

RIEDLE Karl-Heinz
Born: Weiler, Germany, 16 September 1965
Height: 5'10" Weight: 11.6
International Honours: Germany: 42

Early in 1998-99, Karl-Heinz was favoured as the strike partner for Michael Owen at Liverpool. Taller, better in the air, and vastly more experienced, he seemed the ideal foil for the youthful Owen, and, indeed, in the opening game of the campaign against Southampton at the Dell, things went according to plan, with the German equalising and Owen hitting the winner. He even won the "Man of the Match" award, which he followed up by winning a second award against West Ham, when his goal two minutes from time gave Liverpool fresh hope. His vast experience and never-say-die spirit was useful to the Reds' cause, but as the season unfolded his style failed to gel with that of Owen's, and when Robbie Fowler returned to the fold he was forced onto the substitutes' bench. Always a good player to have in your squad, with his contract up for renewal in the summer it will be interesting to see what is in store for him in 1999-2000.
Liverpool (£1,600,000 from Borussia Dortmund, via Augsburg, Blau-Weiss 90, Werder Bremen and Lazio, on 4/8/97) PL 34+25/11 FLC 2+4 FAC 2 Others 3+4/2

RIGBY Anthony (Tony) Angelo
Born: Ormskirk, 10 August 1972
Height: 5'10" Weight: 12.12
Club Honours: Div 2 '97

After struggling for some time with a hernia problem, the skilful Bury midfield man thought he had overcome his troubles when he appeared in all the Shakers' pre-1998-99 season games, and was on the bench for the opening league and Worthington Cup games. However, on 17 August he entered hospital for an operation as the problem re-occurred, and on making a comeback in the reserves in October he again broke down. The following month he attempted another comeback in the reserve team, but was obviously severely lacking in fitness. This proved to be the case when he was picked to play in Bury's home clash against Ipswich in February and only lasted until half time. On 1 April, he was allowed to join Unibond League, Altrincham, on loan before being given a free transfer the following month.
Crewe Alex (From trainee on 16/5/90)
Bury (Free from Barrow, via Lancaster C and Runcorn & Burscough, on 6/1/93) FL 120+46/19 FLC 5+3/2 FAC 5+3/2 Others 13+3/2
Scarborough (Loaned on 14/2/97) FL 5/1

RIMMER Stephen (Steve) Anthony
Born: Liverpool, 23 May 1979
Height: 6'3" Weight: 13.4

Another promising young lad coming through Manchester city's reserve side in 1998-99, being a tall and strong centre back, Steve played in the Auto Windscreens Shield game against Mansfield Town and excelled himself well in spite of the defeat. Surprisingly, after being loaned out to non-league Doncaster Rovers for one month during January, he was made available for transfer at the end of February and was released during the summer.
Manchester C (From trainee on 29/5/96) Others 1

RIOCH Gregor (Greg) James
Born: Sutton Coldfield, 24 June 1975
Height: 5'11" Weight: 12.10
Greg's bubbly enthusiasm was never in danger of fading during a frustrating 1998-99, a thigh injury ruling him out of the early weeks of Hull City's season when a cartilage operation in November meant he was sidelined as the squad underwent a drastic overhaul. Never far away from the action, his FA Cup exploits for example, included a stunning goal at Salisbury, and a seven-second booking at Aston Villa. Having been seen as a left back or midfielder in the past, the son of Bruce Rioch also wholeheartedly filled in at centre half during the term. Was released during the summer.
Luton T (From trainee on 19/7/93)
Barnet (Loaned on 17/9/93) FL 3 FLC 2 Others 1
Peterborough U (Free on 11/8/95) FL 13+5 FLC 2 FAC 2+1 Others 2+1
Hull C (Free on 10/7/96) FL 86+5/6 FLC 7/3 FAC 5/1 Others 3

RIPLEY Stuart Edward
Born: Middlesbrough, 20 November 1967
Height: 5'11" Weight: 13.0
Club Honours: PL '95
International Honours: PL 172+15/13 FLC 18 FAC 14/3 Others 8+1
Signed by Southampton from Blackburn during the summer of 1998, having been an integral part of the championship winning team in 1995, and a member of the England squad, he came to the Dell with the reputation of being a strong-running wide player, who was noted for his excellent crossing ability and willingness to cover back quickly. Although he often showed good form, some troublesome injuries restricted his appearances, and his best run came during October and November when he played nine consecutive full games – being on the losing side only once. If he can get fully fit for 1999-2000, he will do a good job for the Saints, especially in giving them width down the right side.
Middlesbrough (From apprentice on 23/12/85) FL 210+39/26 FLC 21+2/3 FAC 17+1/1 Others 20+1/1
Bolton W (Loaned on 18/2/86) FL 5/1 Others 0+1
Blackburn Rov (£1,300,000 on 20/7/92) PL 172+15/13 FLC 18 FAC 14/3 Others 8+1
Southampton (£1,500,000 on 10/7/98) PL 16+6 FLC 1 FAC 0+1

RISHWORTH Stephen (Steve) Peter
Born: Chester, 8 June 1979
Height: 6'0" Weight: 12.0
Nicknamed "Professor" by his Wrexham team mates during his time at the Racecourse in 1998-99, Steve has temporarily hung up his boots in favour of a university education at Balliol College, Oxford, (a place which took in notables such as Asquith, Macmillan and Heath). As if that doesn't inspire him to greater things, he attended the same school as fellow "Robin", Ian Rush, at St Richard Gwyn Comprehensive in Flint, played alongside a certain Michael Owen for Flintshire Boys team, and represented Wales at U15 and 18 levels. Has now begun a four-year degree course in engineering science after earlier representing Manchester City youth team, before

playing for Wrexham. Having made his Wrexham debut as a sub at Gillingham last September, before enrolling at Oxford in October, the club decided to keep his registration as he has the potential to make it as a dashing winger. Others, such as Steve Heighway, Brian Hall, Steve Coppell, and Tony Galvin (not forgetting ex Robin and PFA Chairman, Barry Horne) have shown there is still a career in football after obtaining a degree.
Wrexham (From juniors on 11/8/98) FL 0+4

RITCHIE Andrew (Andy) Timothy
Born: Manchester, 28 November 1960
Height: 5'10" Weight: 12.9
Club Honours: Div 2 '91
International Honours: E: U21-1; Yth; Sch
As the Oldham team manager, Andy made just two appearances for the Latics during 1998-99, both coming from the bench, and after deciding to wind down his long and illustrious playing career he was granted a benefit year in 1999 as recognition for his services to the club, having scored over 100 goals for Athletic. At the peak of his game, a striker who had excellent skill and touch, coupled with the ability to pull away from defenders to create chances either for himself or others. How do you replace a legend!
Manchester U (From apprentice on 5/12/77) FL 26+7/13 FLC 3+2 FAC 3+1
Brighton & Hove A (£500,000 on 17/10/80) FL 82+7/23 FLC 3+1/1 FAC 9/2
Leeds U (£150,000 on 25/3/83) FL 127+9/40 FLC 11/3 FAC 9/1 Others 2+1
Oldham Ath (£50,000 on 14/8/87) F/PL 187+30/82 FLC 18+2/18 FAC 8+2/4 Others 3
Scarborough (Free on 3/8/95) FL 59+9/17 FLC 4+1/2 FAC 4/1 Others 1
Oldham Ath (Free on 21/2/97) FL 14+12/2 FLC 1/1 FAC 1+2

RIVERS Mark Alan
Born: Crewe, 26 November 1975
Height: 5'11" Weight: 11.2
A player who is always likely to score a few goals, Mark opened Crewe's account last season on the opening day in a 2-1 defeat at Norwich, and apart from illness was rarely absent from the line up as the club fought tooth and nail to avoid relegation from the First Division. Interestingly, other than the Norwich defeat, all of his following nine goals came in games that were either won or drawn, and included five in five outings earlier in the campaign. More effective in a wide role, his height also makes him a danger at corners and free kicks.
Crewe Alex (From trainee on 6/5/94) FL 116+22/29 FLC 8+1/4 FAC 9/3 Others 6+3/3

RIZA Omer Kerime
Born: Enfield, 9 November 1979
Height: 5'9" Weight: 11.2
A first-year professional striker with exceptional natural pace, Omer is another product of the successful Arsenal youth scheme. His speed gets him into good positions with the result that he has a good scoring rate with both the youth team and reserves. Despite needing to improve in the air, he is a player for the future. After making his first-team debut when coming off the bench at Derby in the Worthington

Cup, he joined the Dutch side, Ado Den Haag on loan in March to gain further experience, playing in an attacking midfield role. Out of contract during the summer, he looks likely to sign the club's new offer of re-engagement.
Arsenal (From trainee on 1/7/98) FLC 0+1

RIZZO Nicholas (Nicky) Anthony
Born: Sydney, Australia, 9 June 1979
Height: 5'10" Weight: 12.0
Another Aussie at Crystal Palace in 1998-99, Nicky joined the club in July 1998 from Liverpool, the fee being set by a tribunal, having been at Anfield for close on two years without a first-team game of any sort. After showing clear promise of skilful, hard-running on either flank in the reserves, his debut for Palace came when subbing at home to Port Vale in September, and four games after making a start against Bury in the Worthington Cup he scored in the 5-1 league win over Norwich. Highly popular with the fans, he missed the final months with a knee-ligament injury.
Liverpool (Signed from Sydney Olympic on 26/9/96)
Crystal Palace (£300,000 on 31/7/98) FL 13+6/1 FLC 1

ROACH Neville
Born: Reading, 29 September 1978
Height: 5'10" Weight: 11.1
Having worked his way up through the youth and reserve teams at Reading in previous season, the young striker made only a handful of appearances for the senior side in 1998-99 before being discarded by manager Tommy Burns. After being made to play in the unaccustomed role of wing back in the reserves, he went on trial to Bury, then resurrected his career when signed by Southend at the end of February. Both positive and strong, Neville showed flashes of his ability, and will be looking to an extended run in 1999-2000 to show the fans what he is made of.
Reading (From trainee on 10/5/97) FL 5+11/1 FLC 1+4/1 FAC 0+1 Others 0+1
Southend U (£30,000 on 26/2/99) FL 7+1/1

ROBERTS Andrew (Andy) James
Born: Dartford, 20 March 1974
Height: 5'10" Weight: 13.0
Club Honours: FAYC '91
International Honours: E: U21-5
Since his move from Crystal Palace in March 1998, Andy has shown himself to be a hard-working and committed player in Wimbledon's midfield. In 1998-99, he played a vital role in breaking up the oppositions' moves, and certainly filled the void left by the departure of Vinny Jones. On the scoresheet twice with well taken goals against Everton and Derby, the fans hope they will see him a lot more next season. Also able to play a sweeper role if required, and at his best in a right-sided position, his locker includes skill, awareness, and good passing technique.
Millwall (From trainee on 29/10/91) FL 132+6/5 FLC 12/2 FAC 7 Others 4/1
Crystal Palace (£2,520,000 on 29/7/95) F/PL 106+2/2 FLC 7+1 FAC 8 Others 6/1
Wimbledon (£1,200,000 + on 10/3/98) PL 35+5/3 FLC 3+1 FAC 2+1

ROBERTS Anthony (Tony) Mark
Born: Holyhead, 4 August 1969
Height: 6'0" Weight: 13.11
International Honours: W: 2; B-2; U21-2; Yth
Released by Queens Park Rangers during the 1998 close season, Tony joined Millwall because of injury to Nigel Spink but then sustained a serious hand injury himself which not only finished him for 1998-99, but looks like it could be even more serious. Freed in April, the tall, commanding goalkeeper, who stands up well, and is something of a shot stopper, will be looking for the green light that allows him to play on. Is well known for his kicking ability.
Queens Park R (From trainee on 24/7/87) F/PL 122 FLC 10 FAC 10+1 Others 2
Millwall (Free on 6/8/98) FL 8

ROBERTS Benjamin (Ben) James
Born: Bishop Auckland, 22 June 1975
Height: 6'1" Weight: 12.11
International Honours: E: U21-1
Unable to get a game at Middlesbrough in 1998-99, with Mark Schwartzer in great form, the young goalie was loaned out to Millwall in February and made his home debut in the Auto Windscreens clash with Gillingham. Despite an injury threatening to curtail his spell at the Den, he returned to face Walsall in the first leg of the area final and gave an excellent display, subsequently booking himself a place at Wembley. Back to his best, Ben was outstanding as a shot stopper who commanded his box with great gusto. Interestingly, he is probably the only 'keeper to concede a goal within the first and last minutes of a Wembley final – Boro versus Chelsea in the FA Cup, and Millwall versus Wigan in the Auto Windscreens Shield.
Middlesbrough (From trainee on 24/3/93) F/PL 15+1 FLC 2+1 FAC 6 Others 1
Hartlepool U (Loaned on 19/10/95) FL 4 Others 1
Wycombe W (Loaned on 8/12/95) FL 15
Bradford C (Loaned on 27/8/96) FL 2
Millwall (Loaned on 12/2/99) FL 11 Others 4

ROBERTS Christian (Chris) John
Born: Cardiff, 22 October 1979
Height: 5'10" Weight: 12.8
International Honours: W: U21-1; Yth
Cardiff-born striker who found life difficult during his first full season as a professional at Ninian Park in 1998-99. Did not start a match in the league, but was in the starting line-up during two Worthington Cup matches, finishing the season without a goal, although he did score a number for the reserves. However, Chris' pace and fierce shooting means he will aim to challenge for a first-team place during the coming term. Spent a month on loan with Conference club, Hereford United. Having spent a month on loan at Hereford United, he later broke into the Welsh U21 side, coming on as a sub.
Cardiff C (From trainee on 8/10/97) FL 5+10/3 FLC 2 FAC 0+2 Others 0+1

ROBERTS Darren Anthony
Born: Birmingham, 12 October 1969
Height: 6'0" Weight: 12.4

Although a great favourite with the Darlington crowd, and the club's leading scorer for the previous two campaigns, Darren never really set up a good understanding with his fellow striker, Marco Gabbiadini, and hit just six goals in 12 starts and 16 subs' appearances in 1998-99 before leaving for struggling Scarborough on an 18-month contract in early February. Full of non-stop running and effort, and skilful on the ball with a powerful shot, he was ever present for the rest of the campaign, scoring just twice, before netting Boro's last league goal prior to them dropping into the Conference.
Wolverhampton W (£20,000 from Burton A on 23/4/92) FL 12+9/5 FLC 0+1 Others 1+1
Hereford U (Loaned on 18/3/94) FL 5+1/5
Chesterfield (Free on 18/7/94) FL 10+15/1 FLC 3/1 FAC 1+1 Others 2+5/3
Darlington (Free on 30/7/96) FL 76+20/33 FLC 6+2/4 FAC 5/1 Others 3
Peterborough U (Loaned on 20/2/98) FL 2+1
Scarborough (Signed on 5/2/99) FL 18/3

ROBERTS Iwan Wyn
Born: Bangor, 26 June 1968
Height: 6'3" Weight: 14.2
International Honours: W: 7; B-1; Yth; Sch
Having, by his own admission, not enjoyed the best of first seasons at Norwich, Iwan reported for the 1998-99 campaign over a stone lighter and with a renewed appetite for the game. A centre forward in the traditional mould, who relishes the physical confrontation with his direct marker, he is exceptionally good in the air, possesses a great first touch for a big man, and his ability to link play by holding the ball up under pressure was at the heart of many of City's best moments during the campaign. As a proven goalscorer, he rediscovered his touch in front of goal, thriving on good service from the flanks to become a firm favourite with the Canary faithful, being named in several Welsh "B" squads and put on standby for the full international side.
Watford (From trainee on 4/7/88) FL 40+23/9 FLC 6+2/3 FAC 1+6 Others 5
Huddersfield T (£275,000 on 2/8/90) FL 141+1/50 FLC 13+1/6 FAC 12/4 Others 14/8
Leicester C (£100,000 on 25/11/93) ßL 92+8/41 FLC 5/1 FAC 5/2 Others 1
Wolverhampton W (£1,300,000 + on 15/7/96) FL 24+9/12 FLC 2 FAC 0+1 Others 2
Norwich C (£900,000 on 9/7/97) FL 69+7/24 FLC 5+2/5 FAC 1/1

ROBERTS Jason Andre Davis
Born: Park Royal, 25 January 1978
Height: 5'11" Weight: 12.7
International Honours: Grenada: 4
Captured from Wolves early last August, Jason, a powerful, well-built striker who was signed to replace Bristol Rovers' Peter Beadle, is the nephew of former West Bromwich Albion and England striker, Cyrille Regis. After opening his goalscoring account, he scored a remarkable hat trick, including his first goals for 14 matches, against Welling in the first round of the FA Cup, and his confidence grew. Particularly strong and accurate in his one on ones with opposing goalkeepers, he certainly enjoyed his first full season, and his contribution to the Rovers' team was remarkable. Following his 23rd goal in the penultimate match of the

campaign – against Manchester City – which secured the club's status in the Second Division, he missed the final game to win a further international cap for Grenada, a fitting reward for Rovers' "Young Player of the Season".
Wolverhampton W (£250,000 from Hayes on 12/9/97)
Torquay U (Loaned on 19/12/97) FL 13+1/6 Others 1
Bristol C (Loaned on 26/3/98) FL 1+2/1
Bristol Rov (£250,000 on 7/8/98) FL 32+5/16 FLC 2 FAC 5/7 Others 1

Jason Roberts

ROBERTS Neil Wyn
Born: Wrexham, 7 April 1978
Height: 5'10" Weight: 11.0
International Honours: W: B-1; U21-2; Yth
As is often the case, Neil suffered in his second season (1998-99) in the football league after showing impressive potential in his initial campaign for the Racecourse club, Wrexham. Still just 21 he has time on his side, and was not helped by having unsuitable attackers alongside him, in a team that found goals hard to come by. Deserving better support for his efforts, an unusual injury suffered in the second half of the campaign saw him out of action until the end of term. The problem started with a dead leg, which turned into a blood clot that calcified, the only cure for this condition being complete rest. Hopefully back to resume training in the summer in time for the new campaign, he has supported his hometown club since a boy. Appeared in two representative games last season, against Italy at U21 level, and Northern Ireland in a "B" international.
Wrexham (From trainee on 3/7/96) FL 40+16/11 FLC 1/1 FAC 6+1/2 Others 2+2/2

ROBERTS Stephen Wyn
Born: Wrexham, 24 February 1980
Height: 6'0" Weight: 12.7
International Honours: W: Yth
The younger brother of Neil, Stephen progressed through Wrexham's junior

ranks to turn professional in January 1998, and made his first-team debut in 1998-99 when coming off the bench in the Auto Windscreens Shield encounter at Hull City. Highly regarded by the coaching staff at the Racecourse, he is a central defender who seems to have time on the ball, looks for the right pass, and holds the line together, which augers well for the future.

Wrexham (From trainee on 16/1/98) Others 0+1

ROBERTS Stuart Ian
Born: Carmarthen, 22 July 1980
Height: 5'7" Weight: 9.8
International Honours: W: U21-3
The first-year Swansea professional made a name for himself at the start of last season after coming on as a substitute against Norwich in the first round of the Worthington Cup and supplying the cross for the Swans equaliser. A very quick, tricky ball player, with a lot of heart, Stuart became a regular inclusion in the first-team squad for the rest of the campaign, showing up well also in the FA Cup-ties against West Ham and Derby. At the age of 18, he was named as substitute for the Welsh "B" side that played against Northern Ireland at Wrexham, and celebrated by signing an extension to his contract with the Swans until June 2001. Scored his first league goals against Carlisle and Peterborough, followed by being capped at U21 level for Wales against Switzerland.

Swansea C (From trainee on 9/7/98) FL 15+17/3 FLC 0+2 FAC 3 Others 3+1

ROBERTSON Mark William
Born: Sydney, Australia, 6 April 1977
Height: 5'9" Weight: 11.4
A tenacious performer in midfield, and occasionally at full back last season, Mark had an extended run in Burnley's side prior to returning "home" to take part in a tournament in his native Australia. A hernia operation ruled him out subsequently, but he is an improving player and his best may be yet to come.

Burnley (Free from Marconi on 3/10/97) FL 27+13/1 FLC 0+1 Others 3+1

ROBINS Mark Gordon
Born: Ashton under Lyne, 22 December 1969
Height: 5'8" Weight: 11.11
Club Honours: FAC '90; ECWC '91; ESC '91; FLC '97
International Honours: E: U21-6
Signed on loan to the end of last season from the Greek side, Panionis, where he has been for the past 18 months, Mark was not 100 per-cent match fit when he arrived at Manchester City, but improved in the reserve games. Eventually, he came on as a substitute at Preston rather late, which did not give him time to influence the game, but he showed a marked improvement when coming off the bench at home against Lincoln City, showing up better against the other strikers. Unfortunately, despite having a good pedigree as a goal poacher, just what the team required

Stuart Roberts

bearing in mind the openings made but not executed, his loan period was cut short by a groin injury in training after just three substitute appearances. Was released during the summer.

Manchester U (From apprentice on 23/12/86) FL 19+29/11 FLC 0+7/2 FAC 4+4/3 Others 4+3/1
Norwich C (£800,000 on 14/8/92) PL 57+10/20 FLC 6+3/1 Others 1+1
Leicester C (£1,000,000 on 16/1/95) P/FL 40+16/12 FLC 5+4/5 FAC 4+2 Others 1+1
Reading (Loaned on 29/8/97) FL 5 (Signed by Deportivo Orense on 15/1/98)
Manchester C (Free from Panionis on 25/3/99) FL 0+2

ROBINSON Carl Phillip
Born: Llandrindod Wells, 13 October 1976
Height: 5'10" Weight: 12.10
International Honours: W: B-2; U21-6; Yth
The ball-winning Wolves' midfielder struggled in pre-season with doubts about his level of fitness, and after playing in the first two games of 1998-99 he did not appear again until October. Having had a good month for goals in November, coming on as a sub to score in two successive games, then hitting a couple of beauties against Birmingham, he had a 15-match run through to February, followed by selection for the Welsh "B" team. However, at club level he was not at his best, having to play on the right side rather than in his preferred central role. Five bookings caused a suspension in March, but even when things were going wrong Carl continued to try hard to score. After all if you don't buy a ticket. . . .

Wolverhampton W (From trainee on 3/7/95) FL 57+11/10 FLC 5 FAC 9/1
Shrewsbury T (Loaned on 28/3/96) FL 2+2 Others 1

ROBINSON Jamie
Born: Liverpool, 26 February 1972
Height: 6'1" Weight: 12.8
Club Honours: Div 3 '95
1998-99 was another good season for the no-nonsense Torquay central defender before a leg injury ended his campaign prematurely. Having formed a good

defensive partnership with the emerging Wayne Thomas, following Alex Watson's injury, he was surprisingly released during the summer. Scored his first-ever goal for the Gulls in his penultimate game, a 4-0 win over Halifax at Plainmoor. A menace at set pieces with flick ons, and able to play in midfield if the need be, Jamie should have no difficulty in finding another club.

Liverpool (From trainee on 4/6/90)
Barnsley (Free on 17/7/92) FL 8+1 Others 3
Carlisle U (Signed on 28/1/94) FL 46+11/4 FLC 1+2 FAC 3 Others 7+6/1
Torquay U (Free on 2/7/97) FL 75/1 FLC 6 FAC 5 Others 4

ROBINSON John Robert Campbell
Born: Bulawayo, Rhodesia, 29 August 1971
Height: 5'10" Weight: 11.7
International Honours: W: 16; U21-5
Now a regular in the Welsh international side, John had a good season for Charlton in 1998-99, despite picking up too many bookings for dissent, which resulted in two separate suspensions. A tricky winger who favours his right foot but is equally comfortable on the left, he can also play in a wing-back role, which he did on occasions. Likes to take players on, especially when getting to the byline or cutting inside, but only scored once, in the 5-0 defeat of Southampton at the Valley. Missed several games near the end of a long, hard campaign due to damaged ankle ligaments sustained on Easter Monday at West Ham, before returning for the last three matches and scoring in the 4-3 win at Aston Villa.

Brighton & Hove A (From trainee on 21/4/89) FL 57+5/6 FLC 5/1 FAC 2+1 Others 1+2/2
Charlton Ath (£75,000 on 15/9/92) P/FL 206+11/25 FLC 14+2/4 FAC 11+2/2 Others 5+1

ROBINSON Leslie (Les)
Born: Shirebrook, 1 March 1967
Height: 5'9" Weight: 12.4
Les gave another season of committed effort to Oxford's cause in 1998-99, missing just a couple of games. A full back, cum centre back, and occasional midfielder, the captain was again very consistent, passing the career

500 league game mark in the game against Norwich near the end of the campaign. Did not manage to score, but came close in the last game when his possible goal-bound header was helped in by Andy Thomson.

Mansfield T (Free from Nottingham F juniors on 6/10/84) FL 11+4 Others 1
Stockport Co (£10,000 on 27/11/86) FL 67/3 FLC 2 FAC 4 Others 4
Doncaster Rov (£20,000 on 24/3/88) FL 82/12 FLC 4 FAC 5 Others 5/1
Oxford U (£150,000 on 19/3/90) FL 333+5/3 FLC 33/8 FAC 17+1 Others 10

Les Robinson

ROBINSON Spencer **Liam**
Born: Bradford, 29 December 1965
Height: 5'7" Weight: 12.7

Liam, a very experienced and hard-working striker, suffered a succession of niggling injuries in 1998-99, which saw him failing to start a single match for Scarborough during the second half of the campaign. Very much the competitor, he had been unable to help stem the tide of bad results that saw the team relegated to the Conference on the final day, and was released during the summer.

Huddersfield T (Free from Nottingham F juniors on 5/1/84) FL 17+4/2
Tranmere Rov (Loaned on 18/12/85) FL 4/3
Bury (£60,000 on 8/7/86) FL 248+14/89 FLC 17+3/6 FAC 9/1 Others 24/4
Bristol C (£130,000 on 14/7/93) FL 31+10/4 FLC 2/1 FAC 5 Others 1
Burnley (£250,000 on 26/7/94) FL 43+20/9 FLC 5+1/2 FAC 5/1 Others 1+1
Scarborough (Free on 5/8/97) FL 45+20/7 FLC 2+1 FAC 2/1 Others 1+2

ROBINSON Mark James
Born: Rochdale, 21 November 1968
Height: 5'9" Weight: 12.4
Club Honours: Div 2 '96

As a regular and consistent performer since joining Swindon Town in the 1994 close season, Mark can play in central defence, but is at his best as an attacking full back. Although missing the end of the 1998-99 campaign due to a nasty ankle sprain, he was expected to be fully fit in time for 1999-

2000, where his enthusiasm and commitment will be much in demand. Very good defensively, he is also a player who enjoys getting forward to join up with the attack where he looks to cross quality balls into the middle. An excellent striker of the ball, his long passes from the back can sometimes be a revelation.

West Bromwich A (From apprentice on 10/1/87) FL 2 FLC 0+1
Barnsley (Free on 23/6/87) FL 117+20/6 FLC 7+2 FAC 7+1 Others 3+2/1
Newcastle U (£450,000 on 9/3/93) F/PL 14+11 FAC 1
Swindon T (£600,000 on 22/7/94) FL 180+5/3 FLC 17 FAC 11 Others 6+1

ROBINSON Marvin Leon St
Born: Crewe, 11 April 1980
Height: 6'0" Weight: 12.9

A young Derby striker, especially prolific and impressive in the reserves, who came into the first-team squad for the final few games of last season and played for ten minutes of the game at Arsenal (on live TV), where he looked very quick and made some intelligent runs to help take the pressure off the defence. Having come through the trainee ranks to turn pro during the summer of 1998, it will be very difficult for him to progress into the first team on a regular basis, but is one for the long-term future if he can keep learning.

Derby Co (From trainee on 8/7/98) PL 0+1

ROBINSON Matthew Richard
Born: Exeter, 23 December 1974
Height: 5'11" Weight: 11.8

Unable to hold a first-team place regularly at the Dell, Matthew made the rare move along the M27 to join Portsmouth last February, where he established himself as either a right-wing back or on the left, ably filling in when either position was free due to injury. Happy going forward, this hairless defender loves taking players on, and can beat his man with an educated left foot and great first touch. Starting the last 29 games, he scored his first-ever league goal at Fratton last season against Bury to win over the Pompey supporters, who foolishly doubted his ability due to him signing from arch-rivals, Southampton.

Southampton (From trainee on 1/7/93) PL 3+11 FAC 1+2
Portsmouth (£50,000 on 20/2/98) FL 42+2/1 FLC 0+1 FAC 2

ROBINSON Paul Peter
Born: Watford, 14 December 1978
Height: 5'9" Weight: 11.12
Club Honours: Div 2 '98
International Honours: E: U21-2

Having suffered an ankle-ligament injury in August, just when he had won a first-team place, the left back soon bounced back to play a significant part in Watford's promotion challenge. He also represented the Football League U21 squad against Italy in November and did well, despite playing out of position in central defence. Following that he was included in the England U21 squad to face Poland (along with his namesake from Leeds!), and crowned a success-

ful season by winning two caps. Watford born and bred, Paul is an irrepressible character both on and off the field, who occasionally lets his enthusiasm run away with him. Nevertheless, he has now made more than 50 League appearances.

Watford (From trainee on 13/2/97) FL 48+15/2 FLC 1+1 FAC 4+2 Others 5

ROBINSON Paul William
Born: Beverley, 15 October 1979
Height: 6'2" Weight: 13.4
Club Honours: FAYC '97

Another member of Leeds' successful youth side to make the breakthrough last season, following Nigel Martyn's rib injury in Roma, Paul made his full debut in the 0-0 draw with Chelsea in October, and was very impressive. Big and agile, he looks to be a very good shot stopper, making four more appearances, and looking sound in all of them. Very highly thought of, whilst on U21 duty in March he was called into the full England squad for training, and with him and Nigel Martyn in contention the club's goalkeeping spot should be in "safe hands" for the forseeable future.

Leeds U (From trainee on 13/5/97) PL 4+1 FLC 1

ROBINSON Philip Daniel
Born: Manchester, 28 September 1980
Height: 5'9" Weight: 11.0

A young Blackpool defender who was used on a number of occasions in the first half of last season, mainly from the bench, Phil impressed enough to sign professional forms in January. Still very inexperienced, the club have high hopes that he will follow in the path of the many stars developed at Bloomfield Road.

Blackpool (From trainee on 15/1/99) FL 2+3 FLC 0+1 FAC 1

ROBINSON Phillip (Phil) John
Born: Stafford, 6 January 1967
Height: 5'10" Weight: 11.7
Club Honours: Div 4 '88, Div 3 '89, '98; AMC '88, '91

Signed on a free from Notts County during the 1998 close season, Phil was named as Stoke's team captain on the eve of the campaign, and whilst many saw him as a midfielder he gave the side much as a central defender in a 5-3-2 formation. Occasionally used at full back, his pace did not allow him to work the touchline, and he returned to the heart of the defence, but in the second half of 1998-99, when Brian Little started to sign central defenders he slipped into a comfortable midfield role. Is a player who leads by example.

Aston Villa (From apprentice on 8/1/85) FL 2+1/1
Wolverhampton W (£5,000 on 3/7/87) FL 63+8/8 FLC 6 FAC 3/1 Others 8+2
Notts Co (£67,500 on 18/8/89) FL 65+1/5 FLC 6/1 FAC 1+1 Others 9+1
Birmingham C (Loaned on 18/3/91) FL 9 Others 2+1
Huddersfield T (£50,000 on 1/9/92) FL 74+1/5 FLC 4 FAC 8/1 Others 8
Northampton T (Loaned on 2/9/94) FL 14 FLC 1 FAC 1 Others 2
Chesterfield (£15,000 on 9/12/94) FL 60+1/17 FLC 1 FAC 2 Others 8/4
Notts Co (£80,000 on 16/8/96) FL 63+14/5 FLC 4 FAC 6+1/1 Others 1
Stoke C (Free on 23/6/98) FL 39+1/1 FLC 2 FAC 2

ROBINSON Stephen (Steve)
Born: Lisburn, 10 December 1974
Height: 5'9" Weight: 11.3
International Honours: NI: 3; B-4; U21-1;
Yth; Sch
An attacking midfielder who is equally comfortable in the middle or playing on either flank, Steve had an excellent season in 1998-99 for Bournemouth, ending up as the club's second top scorer with 17 goals. His consistently high performances also saw him gain further full international recognition with Northern Ireland, as well as helping the Cherries stay in contention with the promotion pack right until the end of the campaign. Recognised by his peers as being selected for the PFA award-winning Second Division side, during 1999-2000 he will no doubt be looking for further international opportunities.
Tottenham H (From trainee on 27/1/93) PL 1+1
Bournemouth (Free on 20/10/94) FL 187+13/43 FLC 10/1 FAC 12+1/4 Others 14/3

ROBINSON Steven (Steve) Eli
Born: Nottingham, 17 January 1975
Height: 5'9" Weight: 11.3
Refused a transfer request last September after becoming disheartened with being dropped following good displays, the popular Birmingham midfielder got back on track with a series of first-team starts which included the first goal, a cracking half volley in the 4-2 FA Cup defeat at Leicester in January. Has bags of energy, and continued to develop his distribution skills as the campaign went on.
Birmingham C (From trainee on 9/6/93) FL 48+23 FLC 6/1 FAC 1+1/1 Others 2
Peterborough U (Loaned on 15/3/96) FL 5

ROBSON Mark Andrew
Born: Newham, 22 May 1969
Height: 5'7" Weight: 10.2
Club Honours: Div 3 '98
After scoring the goal that won Notts County the Third Division championship in 1997-98, Mark spent much of last season on the sidelines, making just four appearances after some injury problems. The small and speedy winger is very popular with the County fans, and his ability to create opportunities with either foot was sorely missed in a season that lacked creativity and firepower. In an effort to get him some match practice he was loaned to Wycombe in October, and impressed with his attacking play in four games before returning to Meadow Lane, having arrived at Wanderers when their fortunes were reviving. Hopefully, he can get himself back on track in time for the coming season.
Exeter C (From apprentice on 17/12/86) FL 26/7 FAC 2 Others 2
Tottenham H (£50,000 on 17/7/87) FL 3+5 FLC 1
Reading (Loaned on 24/3/88) FL 5+2
Watford (Loaned on 5/10/89) FL 1
Plymouth Arg (Loaned on 22/12/89) FL 7
Exeter C (Loaned on 3/1/92) FL 7+1/1 Others 3/1
West Ham U (Free on 14/8/92) F/PL 42+5/8 FLC 2 FAC 2/1 Others 4+1
Charlton Ath (£125,000 on 17/11/93) FL 79+26/9 FLC 4+2 FAC 10/2 Others 2
Notts Co (Free on 23/6/97) FL 26+4/4 FLC 2+1 FAC 3 Others 1
Wycombe W (Loaned on 17/10/99) FL 1+3

ROCHE Stephen (Steve) Michael
Born: Dublin, 2 October 1978
Height: 6'0" Weight: 11.2
International Honours: Ei: Yth; Sch
Having lost his way somewhat in the 1997-98 season, and scheduled to be released during the summer, Millwall's new management elected to give Steve a new six-month contract for 1998-99, with the encouragement to resurrect his career. A very talented midfielder, with a sweet left foot, he had the ability to go on to do big things, but after just three first team and some reserve games the decision was made to release him.
Millwall (Free from Belvedere on 6/10/94) FL 7+4 FLC 1 Others 1

RODGER Simon Lee
Born: Shoreham, 3 October 1971
Height: 5'9" Weight: 11.9
Club Honours: Div 1 '94
As the longest-serving player at Crystal Palace, Simon probably thought he had seen everything there was to see in football until the problems that beset Selhurst Park last season. Once again he had a campaign that was disrupted by injuries, this time ligament damage as the main problem, but he managed to get a fair amount of starts in until finally sidelined. A tough-tackling, hard-working left-sided midfielder, who is known for his ability to take set pieces and score the occasional goal, there was just one in 1998-99, the first in a 1-1 home draw against Queens Park Rangers. Was out of contract during the summer.
Crystal Palace (£1,000 from Bognor Regis T on 2/7/90) F/PL 151+22/8 FLC 17+1 FAC 6+3 Others 5+2
Manchester C (Loaned on 28/10/96) FL 8/1
Stoke C (Loaned on 14/2/97) FL 5

RODRIGUEZ Daniel (Dani) Ferreira
Born: Madeira, Portugal, 3 March 1980
Height: 6'0" Weight: 11.8
Dani joined Bournemouth on loan from the Portuguese side, Farense, last October, making seven substitute appearances, having first come off the bench at Reading in the league. Although he proved to be a quick and very skilful striker, who showed great promise in his limited time at Dean Court, unfortunately the club experienced difficulties in signing him permanently and he was snapped up by south-coast neighbours, Southampton, in early March.
Bournemouth (Loaned from CS Farense on 1/10/98) FL 0+5 Others 0+2
Southampton (£170,000 on 3/3/99)

ROGAN Anthony (Anton) Gerard Patrick
Born: Belfast, 25 March 1966
Height: 6'0" Weight: 13.0
Club Honours: SPD '88; SC '88, '89
International Honours: NI: 18
Once again this tough-tackling Blackpool left back was faced by an injury crisis, this time in 1998-99, rarely being available for selection throughout the campaign and doubtless wondering whether his career was at an end. Obviously extremely resilient, Anton got back into the side for a handful of

the remaining matches before being released during the summer.
Glasgow C (Signed from Distillery on 9/5/86) SL 115+12/4 SLC 12+1 SC 18/1 Others 8
Sunderland (£350,000 on 4/10/91) FL 45+1/1 FLC 1 FAC 8 Others 4
Oxford U (Signed on 9/8/93) FL 56+2/3 FLC 4 FAC 4 Others 2
Millwall (Free on 11/8/95) FL 30+6/8 FLC 1 FAC 2 Others 1
Blackpool (Free on 18/7/97) FL 10+5 FLC 1

ROGERS Alan
Born: Liverpool, 3 January 1977
Height: 5'9" Weight: 12.6
Club Honours: Div 1 '98
International Honours: E: U21-3
Having been an ever present in his first season with Nottingham Forest, as a replacement for Stuart Pearce, he adapted well to the Premiership in 1998-99, despite the club's disastrous campaign which ended in relegation back to the First Division after just one year in the Premiership. A solid defender who likes to get forward, but also one who has an excellent recovery rate, he missed very few games, and showed his versatility when playing as a wing back and in central midfield. He also chipped in with some useful goals, especially one in a 3-1 win at Wimbledon. Having proved to be an excellent signing for Forest, his good form was recognised by selection to the England "B" side.
Tranmere Rov (From trainee on 1/7/95) FL 53+4/2 FLC 1 FAC 1
Nottingham F (£2,000,000 on 10/7/97) P/FL 80/5 FLC 8 FAC 1

ROGERS Paul Anthony
Born: Portsmouth, 21 March 1965
Height: 6'0" Weight: 12.0
Club Honours: Div 3 '97; AMC '99
International Honours: E: SP-6
A gritty and combative Wigan midfielder who missed only four league matches for the club throughout last season, and an unsung hero, his solid running for 90 minutes was again a feature of his game, his excellent performances being rewarded with the dramatic injury-time winner at Wembley in the final of the Auto Windscreens Shield. Finishing the campaign with a tally of three goals, the final games also saw him complete a century of league appearances for the club. Rejected a new contract offered by the club in favour of signing a two-year deal with Brighton and Hove Albion.
Sheffield U (£35,000 from Sutton U on 29/1/92) F/PL 120+5/10 FLC 8+1/1 FAC 4 Others 1
Notts Co (Signed on 29/12/95) FL 21+1/2 FAC 1 Others 6/1
Wigan Ath (Loaned on 13/12/96) FL 7+2/3
Wigan Ath (£50,000 on 7/3/97) FL 85+6/2 FLC 6 FAC 3 Others 8/1

ROGET Leo Thomas Earl
Born: Ilford, 1 August 1977
Height: 6'1" Weight: 12.2
Injury, suspension, and loss of form, all played a part in Leo's in-and-out season at Southend in 1998-99. A good, solid centre half, with very good timing in the tackle, he will have been disappointed in the way it

turned out, and will be looking for a regular place this coming term.
Southend U (From trainee on 5/7/95) FL 51+7/1 FLC 4 FAC 1

ROLLING Franck Jacques
Born: Colmar, France, 23 August 1968
Height: 6'1" Weight: 13.0
Club Honours: FLC '97
Freed by Bournemouth last September, the Frenchman moved on non-contract forms to Gillingham, a side struggling with injuries and suspensions, with a view to helping them out of a hole. Unfortunately, when making his first appearance for his new club, in a 1-0 defeat at Chesterfield, he lasted only 58 minutes before sustaining a nasty head injury and being removed from the pitch. Then, not required by the Gills, Franck went to Wycombe Wanderers on trial on 2 October before leaving for home later that month. A player who performs equally well at full back or in the centre of defence, being strong in the air and a passer with ball at feet, there is still some good football left in him if he remains injury free.
Ayr U (Signed from FC Pau on 8/8/94) SL 35/2 SLC 2 SC 1 Others 4
Leicester C (£100,000 on 4/9/95) P/FL 18 FLC 5 FAC 0+1
Bournemouth (Free on 8/8/97) FL 26+4/4 FLC 2/1 FAC 0+2 Others 3/3
Gillingham (Free on 4/9/98) FL 1

ROPER Ian Robert
Born: Nuneaton, 20 June 1977
Height: 6'3" Weight: 13.4
Deservedly chosen as Walsall's "Young Player of the Season" after making tremendous progress in 1998-99, during the early parts of the season he competed with Richard Green and Adrian Viveash for one of the central defensive positions, before making the number five shirt his own from January onwards. He also opened his scoring account with the FA Cup match winner against Gresley in November, and got another in the final home game against Fulham.
Walsall (From trainee on 15/5/95) FL 55+14/1 FLC 0+3 FAC 4+1/1 Others 11+1

ROSCOE Andrew (Andy) Ronald
Born: Liverpool, 4 June 1973
Height: 5'11" Weight: 12.0
Club Honours: AMC '96
A highly talented left-sided player, Andy has more Rotherham appearances to his credit than any other player on the books, topping 200 league and cup starts. Lost his first-team place during last January and February, but battled back to regain it for the run in to the end of the season before being freed in the summer. A dead-ball specialist, he scored some spectacular goals from free kicks.
Bolton W (Free from Liverpool juniors on 17/7/91) FL 2+1 Others 1+1
Rotherham U (£70,000 on 27/10/94) FL 184+18/18 FLC 10 FAC 10/2 Others 11/2

ROSE Andrew (Andy) Mark
Born: Ascot, 9 August 1978
Height: 5'9" Weight: 12.2

Andy remained very much on the fringe of the Oxford squad in 1998-99, and started just two games – one league, one cup, with a further three substitute appearances, and a few more sat on the bench. A defender or defensive midfielder, he will now have to show his promise elsewhere, having been given a free at the end of the season.
Oxford U (From trainee on 1/7/97) FL 1+4 FLC 1

ROSE Karl Barrie
Born: Barnsley, 12 October 1978
Height: 5'10" Weight: 11.4
Having come up through Barnsley's junior ranks, Karl made his debut for the Tykes last December, when injuries and suspensions hit the first team, and proved to be a hard-working striker who never gave less than 100 per-cent effort. Good in the air, and with no little skill on the ground, he also gave the opposition no time to think. Joined Mansfield on transfer deadline day to gain experience, but managed just 20 minutes in a Stags' shirt when he came on as substitute at Peterborough, before being forced back to his parent club with a cyst on his shin which finished his campaign.
Barnsley (From juniors on 7/11/95) FL 2+2 FAC 1+2
Mansfield T (Loaned on 25/3/99) FL 0+1

ROSE Matthew David
Born: Dartford, 24 September 1975
Height: 5'11" Weight: 11.1
Club Honours: FAYC '94
International Honours: E: U21-2
Matthew started 1998-99 as a right-sided defender, but was unable to command a regular spot in Queens Park Rangers' first team. After Gerry Francis was appointed manager, he regained his place in the side, initially in midfield, and his confidence returned. And, when needed, due to injuries, he performed very comfortably as a central defender, but despite several near misses and well saved shots he has yet to open his goalscoring account for the club. Is positionally sound and a good tackler.
Arsenal (From trainee on 19/7/94) PL 2+3
Queens Park R (£500,000 on 20/5/97) FL 40+5 FLC 3 FAC 1

ROSENTHAL Ronny
Born: Haifa, Israel, 11 October 1963
Height: 5'10" Weight: 12.13
Club Honours: Div 2 '98
International Honours: Israel: 60
The veteran Watford striker suffered a frustrating season through injury in 1998-99, as continuing knee problems necessitated a cartilage operation in September, which put him out of the game until December, whereupon he picked up a groin injury. Fit enough to play against his old club, Tottenham, in the FA Cup third round, he then succumbed to further knee injuries. At his best, confident on the ball, and willing to take the opposition on, he remained a regular and encouraging influence on the club bench.
Liverpool (Loaned from Standard Liege, via Maccabi Haifa and FC Bruges, on 22/3/90) FL 5+3/7

Liverpool (£1,000,000 on 29/6/90) F/PL 27+39/14 FLC 2+7/1 FAC 5+3 Others 2+4
Tottenham H (£250,000 on 26/1/94) PL 55+33/4 FLC 3/1 FAC 7+2/6
Watford (Free on 12/8/97) FL 25+5/8 FLC 5+1/1 FAC 2+1/2

ROUGIER Anthony (Tony) Leo
Born: Tobago, 17 July 1971
Height: 6'0" Weight: 14.1
International Honours: Trinidad & Tobago: 14
A striker, cum wide player, Tony joined Port Vale from Hibernian last January, having had to wait three weeks for a work permit before making an impressive debut at Birmingham. However, his next couple of games saw his form dip as he struggled to adapt to a new style of play, and he was subsequently dropped. Then, after scoring a remarkable goal for the reserves in April, he returned to the first team with a new lease of life and played his part in their climb to safety. Is an international with Trinidad and Tobago.
Raith Rov (Free from Trinity Prospect on 9/3/95) SL 47+10/2 SLC 3/3 SC 4+1/1 Others 4+1/1
Hibernian (Signed on 10/7/97) SL 34+11/4 SLC 4 Others 2
Port Vale (£175,000 on 4/1/99) FL 8+5

ROWBOTHAM Darren
Born: Cardiff, 22 October 1966
Height: 5'10" Weight: 12.13
Club Honours: Div 4 '90
International Honours: W: Yth
The player with the most appearances for Exeter, Darren is a big hit with the fans for his loyalty to the club, whom he first played for in 1987. Awareness, vision, and the knack for bringing other players into the game up front meant that he played a significant part in first-team action in 1998-99, despite a stomach muscle strain restricting his performances.
Plymouth Arg (From juniors on 7/11/84) FL 22+24/2 FLC 1 FAC 0+3/1 Others 1+1
Exeter C (Signed on 31/10/87) FL 110+8/47 FLC 11/6 FAC 8/5 Others 5/1
Torquay U (£25,000 on 13/9/91) FL 14/3 FAC 3/1 Others 2
Birmingham C (£20,000 on 2/1/92) FL 31+5/6 FLC 0+1 Others 3+1
Mansfield T (Loaned on 18/12/92) FL 4
Hereford U (Loaned on 25/3/93) FL 8/2
Crewe Alex (Free on 6/7/93) FL 59+2/21 FLC 3/1 FAC 4/3 Others 6+2/1
Shrewsbury T (Free on 28/7/95) FL 31+9/9 FLC 3+2/2 FAC 4/1 Others 1+3
Exeter C (Free on 24/10/96) FL 95+5/35 FLC 4 FAC 8/4 Others 2/1

ROWE Ezekiel (Zeke) Bartholomew
Born: Stoke Newington, 30 October 1973
Height: 5'11" Weight: 12.8
As in 1997-98, Zeke was used sporadically at Peterborough in 1998-99, only this time round all of his appearances in the league were from the subs' bench. A striker with pace, and once highly thought of at no less a club than Chelsea, he was unable to break into the side before being loaned to non-league Welling United early in March.
Chelsea (From trainee on 12/6/92)
Barnet (Loaned on 12/11/93) FL 9+1/2 FAC 2/1
Brighton & Hove A (Loaned on 28/3/96) FL 9/3
Peterborough U (Free on 4/7/96) FL 13+22/3 FLC 2 FAC 4+2 Others 0+3
Doncaster Rov (Loaned on 20/2/98) FL 6/2

ROWE Rodney Carl
Born: Huddersfield, 30 July 1975
Height: 5'8" Weight: 12.8
A striker with good close control, Rodney finished second top scorer with eight goals for York in 1998-99, netting twice in a 3-3 draw against Burnley, and hitting vital goals in crucial wins against Millwall and Macclesfield late in the season. Also able to play on the wide right, where his pace gets him past defenders and into dangerous shooting positions.
Huddersfield T (From trainee on 12/7/93) FL 14+20/2 FLC 0+2 FAC 6+1/2 Others 3/1
Scarborough (Loaned on 11/8/94) FL 10+4/1 FLC 4/1
Bury (Loaned on 20/3/95) FL 1+2
York C (£80,000 on 19/2/97) FL 71+19/21 FLC 4/1 FAC 2+3/3 Others 2/2

Gary Rowett

ROWETT Gary
Born: Bromsgrove, 6 March 1974
Height: 6'0" Weight: 12.10
Signed from Derby last August, Gary made his debut for Birmingham at right back four games into 1998-99, and proved to be a strong, athletic defender whose surging runs were a feature of the team. So impressive was his form for City that his new manager, Trevor Francis, nominated him for England selection. He also deputised superbly as an emergency centre half, due to injuries, and scored his seventh goal with a header at Swindon, which all but secured a play-off spot. An impressive tackler, he has excellent vision, picks out the forwards with good early balls, and ended the campaign with selection for the award-winning PFA First Division side.
Cambridge U (From trainee on 10/9/91) FL 51+12/9 FLC 7/1 FAC 5+2 Others 5/3
Everton (£200,000 on 21/5/94) PL 2+2
Blackpool (Loaned on 23/1/95) FL 17
Derby Co (£300,000 on 20/7/95) P/FL 101+4/3 FLC 8/2 FAC 5+2
Birmingham C (£1,000,000 on 17/8/98) FL 42/5 FLC 4/2 FAC 1 Others 2

ROWLAND Keith
Born: Portadown, 1 September 1971
Height: 5'10" Weight: 10.0
International Honours: NI: 18; B-3; Yth
Keith is a left-sided Queens Park Rangers' player who can play either as a wing back or in a more traditional midfield role. A Northern Ireland international, who claimed his first goal for his country against Finland last October, during the second half of the season he played in a more forward position and scored his first goal for the club at Tranmere Rovers in mid February. This was followed by a few more before the end of the season. In the absence of Rangers' regular penalty taker, Keith took responsibility at Bury and scored.
Bournemouth (From trainee on 2/10/89) FL 65+7/2 FLC 5 FAC 8 Others 3
Coventry C (Loaned on 8/1/93) PL 0+2
West Ham U (£110,000 on 6/8/93) PL 63+17/1 FLC 3+2 FAC 5+1
Queens Park R (Signed on 30/1/98) FL 23+14/3 FLC 1 FAC 1

ROWLANDS Martin Charles
Born: Hammersmith, 8 February 1979
Height: 5'9" Weight: 10.10
Club Honours: Div 3 '99
International Honours: Ei: U21-2
Another Brentford signing from non-league football, joining the club from Farnborough during the summer of 1998, this enthusiastic midfielder had a brilliant first half of the 1998-99 season alongside his "minder" Warren Aspinall in central midfield, and showed he had a good strong right-foot shot, which he used to good effect with screamers against Darlington, Hartlepool, and Chester. As the campaign wore on, and the grounds got heavier, his first season in league football caught up with him, forcing him out of the line up. Having played for the Nationwide League versus the Italian Serie "B", and also called up for the Eire U21 squad, as well as winning a Third Division championship medal, he is sure to come again.
Brentford (£45,000 from Farnborough T on 6/8/98) FL 32+4/4 FLC 4 FAC 3 Others 3/1

ROYCE Simon Ernest
Born: Forest Gate, 9 September 1971
Height: 6'2" Weight: 12.8
Released by Southend during the 1998 close season, Simon started 1998-99 as Charlton's third-choice 'keeper, but when Andy Petterson was loaned to Portsmouth and Sasa Ilic suffered a loss of form, he got his chance. Made his debut against Newcastle at the Valley, and went on to make himself the regular goalie, keeping four consecutive clean sheets during February. He stayed in the side until a training ground injury forced him to miss seven games in the crucial run in to the end of the campaign, but returned against Blackburn, only to sustain a leg injury early on, and having to be substituted at half time. Very agile and good on crosses, he positions himself well, is quick off his line, and if able to keep free from injury could well be the first-choice 'keeper in 1999-2000.

Southend U (£35,000 from Heybridge Swifts on 15/10/91) FL 147+2 FLC 9 FAC 5 Others 6
Charlton Ath (Free on 2/7/98) PL 8

RUDDOCK Neil
Born: Wandsworth, 9 May 1968
Height: 6'2" Weight: 12.12
Club Honours: FLC '95
International Honours: E: 1; B-1; U21-4; Yth
Having joined West Ham from Liverpool during the 1998 close season, his physical presence added steel to the Hammers' defence in 1998-99. Good in the air, where he attacks the ball, and strong in the tackle, it is not surprising that many forwards do not relish coming up against him. Full of conviction, he always wants to win, and had excellent games against Manchester United and Newcastle at Upton Park, stopping Dwight Yorke and Alan Shearer from scoring. Known for possessing a great left foot, and his diagonal passing out of defence, against Chelsea in November he thumped a 20 yarder past the 'keeper, and scored again in April with a header against Derby.
Millwall (From apprentice on 3/3/86) Others 3+1/1
Tottenham H (£50,000 on 14/4/86) FL 7+2 FAC 1+1/1
Millwall (£300,000 on 29/6/88) FL 0+2/1 FLC 2/3 Others 1+1
Southampton (£250,000 on 13/2/89) FL 100+7/9 FLC 14+1/1 FAC 10/3 Others 6
Tottenham H (£750,000 on 29/7/92) PL 38/3 FLC 4 FAC 5
Liverpool (£2,500,000 on 22/7/93) PL 111+4/11 FLC 19+1/1 FAC 11 Others 5+1
Queens Park R (Loaned on 26/3/98) FL 7
West Ham U (£100,000 + on 31/7/98) PL 27/2 FLC 1 FAC 2

Petter Rudi

RUDI Petter
Born: Kristiansund, Norway, 17 September 1973
Height: 6'2" Weight: 12.0
International Honours: Norway: 23
After the disappointment of missing out through injury on Norway's World Cup trip to France, Petter had a good, steady season with Sheffield Wednesday in

1998-99. As a regular and consistent provider and coverer on the left-hand side of midfield, he is not the most robust of players, tackling not being his strongest quality, but it is his attacking flair which gets the crowd roaring, his ungainly "gait" hiding a tremendous amount of skill. On top of this, he started to score a few goals, and also regained his place in the Norwegian international side. All in all he is a quality player who is just coming into his prime.

Sheffield Wed (£800,000 from Molde on 17/10/97) PL 52+4/6 FLC 1 FAC 6/1

RUFUS Richard Raymond
Born: Lewisham, 12 January 1975
Height: 6'1" Weight: 11.10
International Honours: E: U21-6

A tall and extremely quick Charlton central defender, Richard is good in the air and distributes the ball well. He is also a strong and determined tackler who is very calm under pressure. Usually gets forward for corners and set pieces, and scored his first league goal, at Anfield against Liverpool, last September. Was a mainstay of the side throughout a troubled campaign in 1998-99, although he missed seven games with a cracked bone just above his wrist, which he sustained in the home game against Manchester United. An excellent prospect, he reads the game well.

Charlton Ath (From trainee on 1/7/93) P/FL 169+3/1 FLC 11 FAC 8 Others 5/1

RUSH David
Born: Sunderland, 15 May 1971
Height: 5'11" Weight: 11.4

A quality striker who had gone through a nightmare year of bad luck and misfortune when he joined Hartlepool as a trialist early in 1998-99, having previously been with York and non-league Morpeth. Desperately keen to do well, he impressed manager Mick Tait sufficiently that he was awarded a one-year contract when other clubs were also interested in signing him. Unfortunately, his resumed career never really got going. Although he scored regularly for the reserves, he struggled to make a real impact when played in the first team, and was released on a free transfer at the end of the season.

Sunderland (From trainee on 21/7/89) FL 40+19/12 FLC 1+1 FAC 9/1 Others 1+1
Hartlepool U (Loaned on 15/8/91) FL 8/2
Peterborough U (Loaned on 27/10/93) FLC 1/1
Cambridge U (Loaned on 12/9/94) FL 2
Oxford U (£100,000 on 23/9/94) FL 67+25/21 FLC 3+3 FAC 2+3/1 Others 6+1/2
York C (£80,000 on 31/1/97) FL 2+3 Others 1 (Freed in November 1997)
Hartlepool U (Free from Morpeth on 7/9/98) FL 5+5 FAC 0+1 Others 0+1

RUSH Ian James
Born: St Asaph, 20 October 1961
Height: 6'0" Weight: 12.6
Club Honours: Div 1 '82, '83, '84, '86, '90; FLC '81, '82, '83, '84, '95; FAC '86, '89, '92; EC '84; CS '82, '89
International Honours: W: 73; U21-2; Sch

Joined Wrexham from Newcastle during the 1998 close season, amid a certain amount of over-inflated hype which suggested he would be the answer to the club's goalscoring problems. Sadly, it was not to be. Although his guile and positional play continued to impress, the pace of which this "legend" of goalscoring was so renowned was no longer there, and despite his workrate and non-stop running being still evident, the player/coach continued to struggle with injuries. However, ultimately it is in passing on his vast experience to the Racecourse youngsters who must surely benefit from the great man's presence at the club, and it is his capacity as a coach that will be of immense value to the club forwards. With his coaching badges, he assists Joey Jones in charge of the reserves, and enjoys great satisfaction in telling youngsters what to do and then seeing his advice bear fruit. Stop Press: Surprisingly left Wrexham on 8 July.

Chester C (From apprentice on 25/9/79) FL 33+1/14 FAC 5/3
Liverpool (£300,000 on 1/5/80) FL 182/109 FLC 38/21 FAC 22/20 Others 31+1/17 (£3,200,000 to Juventus on 1/7/86)
Liverpool (Loaned on 1/7/86) FL 42/30 FLC 9/4 FAC 3 Others 3/6
Liverpool (£2,800,000 on 23/8/88) F/PL 223+22/90 FLC 30/23 FAC 30+6/19 Others 16+1/7
Leeds U (Free on 24/5/96) PL 34+2/3 FLC 2 FAC 2+2
Newcastle U (Free on 15/8/97) PL 6+4 FLC 2/1 FAC 0+1/1 Others 1
Sheffield U (Loaned on 24/2/98) FL 4
Wrexham (Free on 7/8/98) FL 12+5 FLC 2 FAC 4 Others 0+1

RUSSELL Alexander (Alex) John
Born: Crosby, 17 March 1973
Height: 5'9" Weight: 11.7

A free transfer signing from Rochdale early last August, his pedigree as a former Liverpool player showed through for Cambridge in 1998-99. Something of a dead-ball specialist who can bend free kicks around a defensive wall, the club claiming him to be one of the signings of the season, his influence in midfield was one of the key factors behind United's success, and he was rewarded with the accolade of fans' "Player of the Year". Is the son of the former Southport stalwart, also named Alex.

Rochdale (£4,000 from Burscough on 11/7/94) FL 83+19/14 FLC 5/1 FAC 1+1 Others 2+3
Cambridge U (Free on 4/8/98) FL 36+1/7 FLC 5 FAC 2 Others 2

RUSSELL Craig Stewart
Born: South Shields, 4 February 1974
Height: 5'10" Weight: 12.6
Club Honours: Div 1 '96

After an indifferent 1997-98 season, Craig was brought into the Manchester City squad for the summer friendlies, but once the dust had settled he failed to be selected and was loaned to Tranmere in August. At Prenton Park, he proved a tenacious performer who possessed a direct style of play and a decent turn of speed, appearing at his happiest when at wing back. Back at Maine Road, he

spent time in the reserves before being called up for first round FA Cup-tie at home to Halifax, and scoring two goals. He then enjoyed a run of eight games, when delivering telling crosses from the flank, until it was back to the bench and a loan spell with Port Vale at the end of January. Had an impressive debut against Huddersfield, and scored directly from a free kick at Norwich, but that apart there was nothing more to write home about before he returned to City and reserve football.

Sunderland (From trainee on 1/7/92) P/FL 103+47/31 FLC 7+6/1 FAC 6+3/2 Others 2
Manchester C (£1,000,000 on 14/11/97) FL 22+9/2 FAC 5+1/2
Tranmere Rov (Loaned on 7/8/98) FL 3+1
Port Vale (Loaned on 29/1/99) FL 8/1

RUSSELL Darel Francis Roy
Born: Stepney, 22 October 1980
Height: 5'11" Weight: 11.9
International Honours: E: Yth

Having signed for Norwich as a full professional during the first season of his traineeship, and made his senior debut on the last day of the 1997-98 campaign, 1998-99 was always going to be a big campaign for this talented midfield prospect. However, it was not until mid March that Darel at last created the kind of positive impact he was hoping for when he put together a sequence of mature displays in City's engine room, highlighted by his first senior goal, at Huddersfield. A strong-running player, he is a fine athlete, being able to win his fair share of tackles, as well as enjoying getting forward from midfield in support of the attack. And, as a regular member of the England U18 squad in 1998-99, the youngster was also selected for the World Youth championship squad in Nigeria, but was withdrawn due to his first-team involvement.

Norwich C (From trainee on 29/11/97) FL 8+6/1

RUSSELL Kevin John
Born: Portsmouth, 6 December 1966
Height: 5'9" Weight: 10.12
Club Honours: Div 2 '93
International Honours: E: Yth

A former out-and-out goalscorer, "Rooster" can always be counted on to give his best in a Wrexham shirt. Although occupying a midfield slot in 1998-99, this cult figure continued to join in with the attack at every opportunity, and was always industrious on the left-hand side of midfield, his high workrate being missed when he was out of the side. Although lacking a little in pace, only injury kept him out of the line up on occasion.

Portsmouth (Free from Brighton & Hove A juniors on 9/10/84) FL 3+1/1 FLC 0+1 FAC 0+1 Others 1+1
Wrexham (£10,000 on 17/7/87) FL 84/43 FLC 4/1 FAC 4 Others 8/3
Leicester C (£175,000 on 20/6/89) FL 24+19/10 FLC 0+1 FAC 1 Others 5/2
Peterborough U (Loaned on 6/9/90) FL 7/3
Cardiff C (Loaned on 17/1/91) FL 3
Hereford U (Loaned on 7/11/91) FL 3/1 Others 1/1
Stoke C (Loaned on 2/1/92) FL 5/1

Stoke C (£95,000 on 16/7/92) FL 30+10/5 FLC 3 FAC 2 Others 4+1/1
Burnley (£150,000 on 28/6/93) FL 26+2/6 FLC 4/1 FAC 4 Others 1/1
Bournemouth (£125,000 on 3/3/94) FL 30/1 FLC 3/1 FAC 2/1
Notts Co (£60,000 on 24/2/95) FL 9+2
Wrexham (£60,000 on 21/7/95) FL 110+18/9 FLC 5+1/1 FAC 14+3/4 Others 9

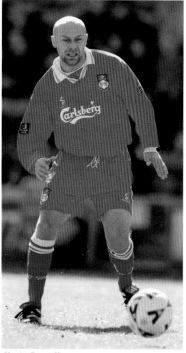

Kevin Russell

RUSSELL Lee Edward
Born: Southampton, 3 September 1969
Height: 5'11" Weight: 12.0
Having suffered badly from injury at Portsmouth in 1997-98, which kept his appearances down to a minimum, Lee failed to make the team at all last season, being allowed to go on loan to Torquay in transfer deadline week. Able to perform equally well as a left-wing back, in midfield, or in the centre of the defence, he quickly got into the swing of things with the Gulls, playing in the final nine games and looking a class act at the back, his distribution being excellent. Released by Pompey during the summer, and rumoured to be joining Torquay on a more permanent basis, he could play a big part in the development of his younger defensive partners.
Portsmouth (From trainee on 12/7/88) FL 103+20/3 FLC 8+2 FAC 4+2 Others 5+2
Bournemouth (Loaned on 9/9/94) FL 3
Torquay U (Loaned on 25/3/99) FL 9

RUSSELL Matthew Lee
Born: Dewsbury, 17 January 1978
Height: 5'11" Weight: 11.5
A talented and versatile player who has come through the ranks at Scarborough, despite the club suffering poor results in

1998-99 Matthew continued to look an outstanding young prospect, whether it was as an attacking midfielder or in the wing-back role. Having had a trial period with West Ham late on in the campaign, with the Boro ultimately relegated to the Conference they will struggle to hold on to one of their most prized possessions.
Scarborough (From trainee on 3/7/96) FL 21+23/3 FLC 0+2 FAC 1+1 Others 1
Doncaster Rov (Loaned on 26/3/98) FL 4/1

RUST Nicholas (Nicky) Charles Irwin
Born: Ely, 25 September 1974
Height: 6'1" Weight: 13.1
International Honours: E: Yth
Nicky was signed at the start of last season, from Brighton via the Bosman ruling, as cover at Barnet for Lee Harrison, and made three reserve appearances before making his ill-fated debut for the Bees in September, against Peterborough. The record books will always remember him for conceding an incredible nine goals during that game, but the score line does not paint an accurate portrait of what exactly happened on that bizarre autumn afternoon, and to comment that the defence was undermanned was a complete understatement. However, he showed great resilience by bouncing back to play in a 1-0 defeat at Cardiff three days later, proving to be a competent 'keeper, and producing a string of saves before being beaten in the latter stages of the game. When his one-month contract expired days after the City match, he departed without ever really illustrating what he was capable of, joining non-league Cambridge City, where he made great strides in the process of rebuilding his reputation as a talented goalie.
Brighton & Hove A (Free from Arsenal juniors on 9/7/93) FL 177 FLC 14 FAC 9 Others 9
Barnet (Free on 6/8/98) FL 2

RUTHERFORD Mark Robin
Born: Birmingham, 25 March 1972
Height: 5'11" Weight: 12.0
Loaned from Shelbourne last September, Shrewsbury's manager, Jake King, tried to sign Mark on a permanent basis after the midfielder had appeared three times as substitute. However, despite it being his second spell at the club, he decided to return to Ireland.
Birmingham C (From trainee on 11/7/90) FL 1+4 (Free during 1992 close season)
Shrewsbury T (Loaned from Shelbourne on 24/2/94) FL 7+7
Shrewsbury T (Loaned from Shelbourne on 7/9/98) FL 0+3

RYAN Darragh Joseph
Born: Cuckfield, 21 May 1980
Height: 5'10" Weight: 10.10
A young Brighton midfielder who recovered from a broken leg sustained in December 1997, Darragh worked hard to regain his fitness, signalling his return to first-team action last March when coming on as a substitute to score only his second league goal in the 3-1 defeat

at Scunthorpe. Ironically, his first was in the corresponding fixture the previous season. A level-headed player, and a good passer of the ball, he never fulfilled his earlier promise prior to being released on a free transfer during the summer.
Brighton & Hove A (From trainee on 25/3/98) FL 4+5/2

RYAN Keith James
Born: Northampton, 25 June 1970
Height: 5'11" Weight: 12.8
Club Honours: FAT '91, '93; GMVC '93
As club captain and a popular central defender at Wycombe, Keith started the first five games of last season, but then suffered the huge disappointment of a medial ligament injury to his knee, this after so much bad luck with injuries in the last three years. After 12 weeks out he returned to the centre of defence, before the new manager, Lawrie Sanchez, agreed to his request for him to return to his favoured central midfield role for the final ten matches. There he enjoyed his best form of the campaign, where his speed, stamina, and strength of tackle, helped the club avoid relegation. Was sometimes asked to revert to his original role of striker when the situation demanded it.
Wycombe W (Signed from Berkhamstead T) FL 150+7/13 FLC 9/2 FAC 8+3/3 Others 13+1/1

RYAN Robert (Robbie) Paul
Born: Dublin, 16 May 1977
Height: 5'10" Weight: 12.0
International Honours: Ei: U21-9; Yth; Sch
A bargain signing from Huddersfield in January 1998, Robbie was brought in to fill Millwall's troublesome left-back slot, and did so with some aplomb during a difficult time for the club, before finding himself vying with Jamie Stuart throughout last season. Unfortunately, his campaign came to an end when he damaged his knee ligaments against Notts County in March, and, hopefully, when he regains full fitness he can get back to full steam. Is a pacy full back who tackles hard, and likes getting forward to help the attack with telling crosses. Continued as a virtual regular in the Republic of Ireland U21 side.
Huddersfield T (Free from Belvedere on 26/7/94) FL 12+3 FLC 2
Millwall (£10,000 on 30/1/98) FL 38+4 FAC 1 Others 2

RYDER Stuart Henry
Born: Sutton Coldfield, 6 November 1973
Height: 6'0" Weight: 12.6
International Honours: E: U21-3
This former England U21 centre back was signed from Walsall immediately before the start of last season as a replacement for Stuart Watkiss, whose career at Mansfield was finished through injury. A stylish defender, who likes to play the ball out of defence, he was in and out of the side throughout the campaign until he was finally left out after a 7-2 thrashing at Cambridge, before being released during the summer.
Walsall (From trainee on 16/7/92) FL 86+15/5 FLC 5+1 FAC 9 Others 7+1
Mansfield T (Free on 30/7/98) FL 18+4/2 Others 1+1

SAAR Mass

Born: Liberia, 6 February 1973
Height: 5'11" Weight: 13.0
International Honours: Liberia: 2

The Liberian international striker joined Reading from Hadjuk Split just before the start of last season, and quickly became a favourite with the fans because of his impressive dribbling skills and ball control. He was quick too, and became a regular in the team until January, despite several call ups for the Liberian team. However, following the 6-0 home defeat by Bristol Rovers, he was only on the fringes of the starting line-up and needs to show the Royals' faithful that he can stay the course.

Reading (£158,000 from Hadjuk Split, via Olimpique Ales, on 17/7/98) FL 18+10/3 FLC 2 FAC 0+1 Others 0+1

SADLIER Richard Thomas

Born: Dublin, 14 January 1979
Height: 6'2" Weight: 12.10
International Honours: Ei: Yth

Another exciting prospect at Millwall, Richard took his opportunity of regular first-team football after an injury to Paul Shaw, grabbing his chance with some aplomb, and putting in some excellent performances. As a hard-working forward, who can also defend very well, it was down to this dual quality that his performance against Walsall in the second leg of the Auto Windscreens Shield was outstanding, and was the main factor between the sides. He is also good in the air, can hold the ball up, tackles well, and has a strong shot with either foot. It was thought that he would not make the Auto Windscreens final at Wembley due to international commitments in Nigeria but, because the Republic of Ireland were eliminated in the final stages, he was back in time to play.

Millwall (Signed from Belvedere on 14/8/96) FL 28+17/8 FLC 3 FAC 1 Others 5+1/2

SAHA Louis

Born: Paris, France, 8 August 1978
Height: 5'10" Weight: 11.12

Louis is a livewire striker who arrived at Newcastle last January on a six-month loan from Metz, and made an immediate debut as a substitute against Chelsea. Unfortunately, he strained his hamstring towards the end of the game and was out of action for a month. Tino Asprilla is one of his heroes, and he has some similar qualities in his ability and willingness to do the unexpected. With an excellent first touch, and surprisingly fleet footed and quick off the mark, on his return to the team he visibly grew in confidence, and improved his game as the season progressed, scoring a stunning goal to win the FA Cup replay at Blackburn. Having come through the same French youth structures as Arsenal's Nicolas Anelka and United team-mate, Didier Domi, he is working hard to develop his game in order to demonstrate his potential, hoping his performances will persuade Ruud Gullit to pay the £2m needed to make his move to Tyneside a permanent one. However, he suffered a serious setback when he fractured a cheekbone in a training ground accident in April, only returning to first-team action as a sub in the final Premiership game of the season.

Newcastle U (Loaned from Metz on 8/1/99) PL 5+6/1 FAC 1/1

SAIB Moussa

Born: Theniet El Had, Algeria, 6 March 1969
Height: 5'9" Weight: 11.8
International Honours: Algeria: 43

An experienced midfield playmaker who is creative going forward, while strong in his defensive duties, Moussa made only three appearances for Tottenham before picking up an injury which was to keep him out for over two months. However, during that time, he clashed with new boss, George Graham, over a club versus country dispute and on failing to reach an agreement he did not appear for first-team action again, amidst rumours of a move from White Hart Lane as the season closed. During his time at the club, the Algerian international showed himself to be an all rounder who was confident with the ball and able to get in excellent crosses to the front men, while able to read the play well in a defensive position.

Tottenham H (£2,300,000 from Valencia, via Auxerre, on 25/2/98) PL 3+10/1

SALAKO John Akin

Born: Nigeria, 11 February 1969
Height: 5'10" Weight: 12.8
Club Honours: FMC '91; Div '94
International Honours: E: 5

Signed on a free from Bolton during the 1998 close season, this nippy left winger, who is an excellent crosser of the ball, began 1998-99 at Fulham well, scoring twice in the first four games. After four more appearances, in all of which he was substituted, he rarely featured in the first team again, apart from the odd game due to Fulham having switched to a 3-5-2 system, and there being no place for an out-and-out winger. A regular in the Football Combination side, where he often played in a wing-back role, John looks to give it his best shot in 1999-2000.

Crystal Palace (From apprentice on 3/11/86) F/PL 172+43/22 FLC 19+5/5 FAC 20/4 Others 11+3/2
Swansea C (Loaned on 14/8/89) FL 13/3 Others 2/1
Coventry C (£1,500,000 on 7/8/95) PL 68+4/4 FLC 9/3 FAC 4/1
Bolton W (Free on 26/3/98) PL 0+7
Fulham (Free on 22/7/98) FL 7+3/1 FLC 2/1 FAC 2+2 Others 1

SALE Mark David

Born: Burton on Trent, 27 February 1972
Height: 6'4" Weight: 14.4

A tall target man, Mark opened his 1998-99 Colchester goals account with an injury-time winner on the opening day at home to Chesterfield. He scored again a month later at Wigan, but that was to be his last United goal of the season. Virtually ever present up front for the first half of the campaign, he then drifted out of the picture as Jason Dozzell took over his role in the side, and after prospective moves to Hartlepool and Macclesfield fell through he went on loan to Plymouth during transfer deadline week. There he proved an instant hit with the Home Park faithful, his ability in the air and his build up play giving the side another dimension to their game. Despite his time there being reduced by suspensions he formed a good partnership with Steve Guinan in their games together.

Stoke C (From trainee on 10/7/90) FL 0+2
Cambridge U (Free on 31/7/91) Free to Rocester in December 1991)
Birmingham C (Free on 26/3/92) FL 11+10 FLC 2/1 Others 3+1/2
Torquay U (£10,000 on 5/3/93) FL 30+14/8 FLC 1 FAC 2/1 Others 3+1
Preston NE (£20,000 on 26/7/94) FL 10+3/7 FLC 1+1 FAC 0+1 Others 4
Mansfield T (£50,000 on 31/7/95) FL 36+9/12 FLC 4/1 FAC 2 Others 1
Colchester U (£23,500 on 10/3/97) FL 69+11/12 FLC 4 FAC 4/1 Others 7+1
Plymouth Arg (Loaned on 25/3/99) FL 8/1

SALMON Michael (Mike) Bernard

Born: Leyland, 14 July 1964
Height: 6'2" Weight: 14.0

Sadly, Mike will be remembered at Oxford for one game in 1998-99, his only one for the club, when the team went down to a 7-1 home defeat at the hands of Birmingham. After being signed on loan from Charlton on a Friday morning he met his new team mates the following day, eager to get some first-team action under his belt, having recovered from a long-term knee injury. However, after a collectively bad display, Mike immediately returned to the Valley, but was unable to break into the side with Sasa Ilic and Simon Royce performing so capably. Still at Athletic, he is now registered on non-contract forms.

Blackburn Rov (From juniors on 16/10/81) FL 1
Chester C (Loaned on 18/10/82) FL 16 FAC 2
Stockport Co (Free on 3/8/83) FL 118 FLC 10 FAC 3 Others 3
Bolton W (Free on 31/7/86) FL 26 FLC 2 FAC 4 Others 4
Wrexham (£18,000 on 7/3/87) FL 100 FLC 4 FAC 4 Others 9
Charlton Ath (£100,000 on 6/7/89) FL 148 FLC 11 FAC 10 Others 6
Oxford U (Loaned on 11/12/98) FL 1

SALT Phillip (Phil) Thomas

Born: Oldham, 2 March 1979
Height: 5'11" Weight: 11.9

Furthering his Oldham career in 1998-99, after making three appearances during the previous campaign, although used mainly from the bench Phil managed three starts before opening his scoring account in the 2-0 FA Cup win against Gillingham at Boundary Park. A graduate of the Latics' youth development programme, he is a skilful right-sided midfielder of some quality, having excellent passing ability, and

is expected to go far in the game. Never gives the ball away without a struggle.
Oldham Ath (From trainee on 1/7/97) FL 4+7 FLC 0+1 FAC 1/1 Others 2

SAMPSON Ian
Born: Wakefield, 14 November 1968
Height: 6'2" Weight: 13.3

A rock-like central defender, and Northampton vice captain, "Sammo" is now the club's longest-serving player. Missed the start of last season through injury, but came back in late August to give some sterling displays in a defence that changed regularly throughout 1998-99. With a liking to move up field for set pieces, Ian is one of the best headers of the ball on Town's books. Valiantly played the latter part of the campaign with an injury, preferring to assist the club in their relegation fight rather than have an operation.
Sunderland (Signed from Goole T on 13/11/90) FL 13+4/1 FLC 1 FAC 0+2 Others 0+1
Northampton T (Loaned on 8/12/93) FL 8
Northampton T (Free on 5/8/94) FL 196+3/14 FLC 13 FAC 6/1 Others 16/2

Ian Sampson

SAMUELS Jerome Livingston
Born: Jamaica, 8 March 1976
Height: 5'11" Weight: 12.2

Recommended to Notts County by former favourite, Michael Johnson, Jerome earned himself an extended trial period after arriving at the club from Jamaica on a monthly contract last November, having earlier played his football in the USA with Lightning SC. A skilful defender who loved to join in with his midfielders, but not quite able to make the transition to senior football, following a subs' appearance in the Auto Windscreens Shield, a 1-0 home defeat against Hull City in December, he was released in February.
Notts Co (Free from Lightning SC on 20/11/98) Others 0+1

SAMWAYS Mark
Born: Doncaster, 11 November 1968
Height: 6'2" Weight: 14.0

Freed by York during the 1998 close season, and then signing for Darlington, this very experienced goalkeeper had to be content with just one Auto Windscreens Shield appearance, at Oldham Athletic, in 1998-99 due to the good form and freedom from injury of first-choice custodian, David Preece. Although still under contract, and a good shot stopper who stands up well, Mark was told that he was free to find another club in the summer if he wished.
Doncaster Rov (From trainee on 20/8/87) FL 121 FLC 3 FAC 4 Others 10
Scunthorpe U (Signed on 26/3/92) FL 180 FLC 10 FAC 16 Others 16
York C (Free on 18/7/97) FL 29 FLC 4 FAC 1
Darlington (Free on 22/7/98) Others 1

SANDFORD Lee Robert
Born: Basingstoke, 22 April 1968
Height: 6'1" Weight: 13.4
Club Honours: AMC '92; Div 2 '93
International Honours: E: Yth

Lee played a prominent role in the Sheffield United defence in 1998-99, having earlier received his Bsc in Sports Science and Coaching. Perhaps lacking in pace, he nevertheless produced a series of reliable performances, playing to his strengths, rarely trying anything fancy, showing good anticipation, doing the simple things right, and always being dangerous in the opposition penalty area at corners and free kicks. Out of contract at the end of the campaign, at the time of going to press he was in negotiations with the club as to his future.
Portsmouth (From apprentice on 4/12/85) FL 66+6/1 FLC 11 FAC 4 Others 2+1
Stoke C (£140,000 on 22/12/89) FL 255+3/8 FLC 19 FAC 16/2 Others 31/4
Sheffield U (£500,000 on 22/7/96) FL 74+6/2 FLC 6+1 FAC 12/1 Others 3+1
Reading (Loaned on 5/9/97) FL 5

SANETTI Francesco
Born: Rome, Italy, 11 January 1979
Height: 6'1" Weight: 13.0

This young Italian striker failed to impress in his few appearances last season with Sheffield Wednesday, albeit all of them made as a substitute. Unfortunately, his performances in the reserve side were not committed enough to put pressure on a goal-starved Wednesday Premiership side, lacking aggression and drive, many put down to him not being able to settle in England. His only first-team goal so far came in the last game of 1997-98, and he really is in need of a major confidence booster. However, he is young enough, and talented enough, once settled, to make his mark in the game.
Sheffield Wed (Free from Genoa on 30/4/98) PL 1+4/1 FLC 0+2

SANTOS Georges
Born: Marseille, France, 15 August 1970
Height: 6'3" Weight: 14.0

Signed from Toulon during the 1998 close season, this tall, seemingly awkward

Frenchman soon became a cult figure at Tranmere, thanks to his enthusiasm and commitment. Perhaps hampered by his lack of English, Georges picked up an early suspension due to being sent off in a summer friendly, and went on to collect 14 bookings before the campaign was over. More ungainly and uncompromising rather than vicious, his rough edges were smoothed out as the campaign progressed. Operating in a number of positions for Rovers, including emergency centre forward and in defence, he was at his most influential in the front of the midfield, where he was ever eager and willing to support the attack, while still able to protect his defence. Picked up seven "Man of the Match" awards, and was rumoured to be a target of several top French clubs.
Tranmere Rov (Free from Toulon on 29/7/98) FL 37/1 FLC 4 FAC 1

SAUNDERS Dean Nicholas
Born: Swansea, 21 June 1964
Height: 5'8" Weight: 10.6
Club Honours: FAC '92; FLC '94
International Honours: W: 69

Dean continued from where he had left off the previous season at Sheffield United, and not surprisingly added to his total of Welsh Caps in 1998-99. Despite his 34 years he played with great enthusiasm and his unselfish running off the ball, his quick thinking and awareness, were always clearly evident. Ten goals in 23 league and cup games were a measure of his value, including the two that salvaged a draw at Darlington during extra time in the Worthington Cup. But, due to a clause in his contract, the club was powerless to prevent his move to Benfica, for £500,000, in December.
Swansea C (From apprentice on 24/6/82) FL 42+7/12 FLC 2+1 FAC 1 Others 1+1
Cardiff C (Loaned on 29/3/85) FL 3+1
Brighton & Hove A (Free on 7/8/85) FL 66+6/21 FLC 4 FAC 7/5 Others 3
Oxford U (£60,000 on 12/3/87) FL 57+2/22 FLC 9+1/8 FAC 2/2 Others 2/1
Derby Co (£1,000,000 on 28/10/88) FL 106/42 FLC 12/10 FAC 6 Others 7/5
Liverpool (£2,900,000 on 19/7/91) F/PL 42/11 FLC 5/2 FAC 8/2 Others 6/10
Aston Villa (£2,300,000 on 10/9/92) F/PL 111+1/37 FLC 15/7 FAC 9/4 Others 8/1 (£2,350,000 to Galatasaray on 1/7/95)
Nottingham F (£1,500,000 on 16/7/96) F/PL 39+4/5 FLC 5+1/2 FAC 2/2
Sheffield U (Free on 5/12/97) FL 42+1/17 FLC 4/3 FAC 6/2 Others 2

SAUNDERS Mark Philip
Born: Reading, 23 July 1971
Height: 5'11" Weight: 11.12

Having been released by Plymouth during the 1998 close season, Mark arrived at Gillingham in time for the summer friendlies, and had the satisfaction of scoring the club's first league goal of 1998-99 in the 1-1 draw at York. Always looking to get forward to help the strikers, he sustained a serious neck injury after only five minutes in the home game against Oldham in November, and it was over two months before he regained his place in the side.

Plymouth Arg (Signed from Tiverton T on 22/8/95) FL 60+12/11 FLC 1+1 FAC 2+3 Others 2
Gillingham (Free on 1/6/98) FL 28+6/5 Others 2+3

SAVAGE David (Dave) Thomas Patrick
Born: Dublin, 30 July 1973
Height: 6'1" Weight: 12.7
International Honours: Ei: 5; U21-5

Having had a disappointing 1997-98 at Millwall, Dave knew he had something to prove during the close season, but following just two substitute appearances early on in 1998-99, he joined Northampton in October. A powerful midfielder, who can operate on either side, and is at his best playing just behind the forwards, he was signed to add bite to a team looking to move up the Second Division table. While his strong running and powerful shooting, soon made him a crowd favourite, and also resurrected his international career with Eire, his five goals in the last five games of the campaign failed to maintain Town's league status.
Brighton & Hove A (Signed from Kilkenny on 5/3/91) Free to Longford T in May 1992)
Millwall (£15,000 on 27/5/94) FL 104+28/6 FLC 11/2 FAC 6+2/2 Others 2/1
Northampton T (£100,000 on 7/10/98) FL 18+9/5 FAC 2 Others 1

SAVAGE Robert (Robbie) William
Born: Wrexham, 18 October 1974
Height: 6'1" Weight: 11.11
Club Honours: FAYC '92
International Honours: W: 13; U21-5; Yth; Sch

Leicester right-footed midfielder or wing back. Full of energy and self confidence, Robbie was destined to make the headlines throughout last season, initially getting into hot water with the Welsh boss, Bobby Gould, over an interview with Sky television prior to the Euro 2000 qualifier with Italy, when his fashion statement was not taken as a joke by his manager. Later, he incurred the wrath of the Tottenham fans at Wembley, and subsequently and unjustly the London press, after he had been struck by Justin Edinburgh, resulting in the latter being dismissed. In fact, he gave an outstanding performance in the final, despite coming under extreme provocation from certain members of the opposition during the closing stages. Two weeks later, he again showed his mettle in the cauldron of White Hart Lane to help the Foxes to a vital league double, in giving another top-class display, and followed that up with a spectacular goal at home to Villa when lobbing Mark Bosnich from 25 yards.
Manchester U (From trainee on 5/7/93)
Crewe Alex (Free on 22/7/94) FL 74+3/10 FLC 5 FAC 5 Others 8/1
Leicester C (£400,000 on 23/7/97) PL 57+12/3 FLC 6+2 FAC 2/1 Others 0+1

SAVILLE Andrew (Andy) Victor
Born: Hull, 12 December 1964
Height: 6'0" Weight: 12.13
International Honours: Div 3 '96

The much-travelled striker was never going to figure in Frank Burrows' long-term plans at Cardiff in 1998-99, despite playing in the

opening three games and scoring City's first home goal, against Peterborough, of the new campaign. With his family still living in Yorkshire, Burrows allowed him to stay on at Hull, following a three-match loan spell with the club in September, in order for him to achieve full fitness prior to joining Scarborough on a short-term contract in March. Although appearing nine times for the Boro, all of them when coming off the bench in the final 13 matches, following the club's relegation to the Conference he was not retained.
Hull C (Signed on 23/9/83) FL 74+27/18 FLC 6/1 FAC 3+2/1 Others 4+2
Walsall (£100,000 on 23/3/89) FL 28+10/5 FLC 2 Others 1+1
Barnsley (£80,000 on 9/3/90) FL 71+11/21 FLC 5+1 FAC 2+1 Others 4/1
Hartlepool U (£60,000 on 13/3/92) FL 37/14 FLC 4/1 FAC 4/5 Others 3/1
Birmingham C (£155,000 on 22/3/93) FL 51+8/17 FLC 4/1 FAC 1 Others 1
Burnley (Loaned on 30/12/94) FL 3+1/1 FAC 1
Preston NE (£100,000 on 29/7/95) FL 56/30 FLC 6 FAC 2 Others 2/1
Wigan Ath (£125,000 on 25/10/96) FL 17+8/4 FLC 0+1 FAC 1 Others 1
Cardiff C (£75,000 on 31/10/97) FL 34+1/12 FLC 1 FAC 4+1/2
Hull C (Loaned on 18/9/98) FL 3
Scarborough (Free on 12/3/99) FL 0+9

SAWYERS Robert (Rob)
Born: Dudley, 20 November 1978
Height: 5'10" Weight: 11.7

1998-99 was a season of progression for Rob, who had only made one appearance for Barnet previously, and he clearly enjoyed an excellent start to the campaign when producing his most efficient performance to date against his former club, Wolves. Utilised in the role of central defender in a defensive quartet, he coped admirably against the midland's outfit to ensure an historic Worthington Cup victory for the Bees. As the season unravelled, his duties on the pitch evolved, and he emerged as a left-sided attacking midfielder, his close control and trickery on the wing making him a natural for the role, despite feeling more comfortable distributing crunching tackles than he did when asked to evade them. Although of slight build, he did not shirk from any challenges on the field, and as an intelligent player with accurate distribution he eventually was fielded back to his favoured position of left back, when the injury to Mike Harle enabled him to wear the number three shirt on a regular basis. Still in the formative stages of a career that holds plenty of promise, he will be striving to use the 1999-2000 season to fulfil his outstanding potential.
Barnet (Free from Wolverhampton W juniors on 22/10/97) FL 22+1 FLC 1 Others 1

SCALES John Robert
Born: Harrogate, 4 July 1966
Height: 6'2" Weight: 13.5
Club Honours: FAC '88; FLC '95, '99
International Honours: E: 3; B-2

Injury yet again wrecked what had promised to be an exciting season for John, who found himself playing under George

Graham after all, the latter having earlier failed in his attempt to bring the ex-Anfield star to Leeds. The agile, athletic central defender looked extremely promising partnered with Sol Campbell at the heart of the Spurs' defence early in 1998-99, complimenting Campbell with tremendous aerial ability and great presence, and despite the re-occurring injuries John worked hard at the club's backroom team in a bid to be fit, managing to get back in time for crunch title deciders against Chelsea and Manchester United in May. Looking to be back to his solid, pacy self, he would have been delighted with his goal in the 3-1 Worthington Cup defeat of his old club Liverpool at Anfield in November. Is expected to be a key figure in the Tottenham squad in 1999-2000, and all at the club will be hoping for an injury-free campaign for him as the club hopefully challenge for honours.
Bristol Rov (Free from Leeds U juniors on 11/7/85) FL 68+4/2 FLC 3 FAC 6 Others 3+1
Wimbledon (£70,000 on 16/7/87) F/PL 235+5/11 FLC 18+1 FAC 20+1 Others 7+1/4
Liverpool (£3,500,000 on 2/9/94) PL 65/2 FLC 10/2 FAC 14 Others 4+1
Tottenham H (£2,600,000 on 11/12/96) PL 26+3 FLC 4/1

SCARLETT Andre Pierre
Born: Wembley, 11 January 1980
Height: 5'4" Weight: 9.6

This pocket sized right-sided midfield dynamo was yet another 18-year-old ex-trainee to make his mark in Luton's colours in 1998-99. In an eventful 25-minute substitution appearance, at home to Oldham in October, Andre exploded on the scene and, within minutes he was on the end of a bad tackle that saw the red card brandished at Latics' Scott McNiven. He then completed an impressive debut by netting Town's second in stoppage time. Protecting his young prospect, handing him just seven more appearances, his manager said of him: "He is a good footballer with a magnificent attitude." Tenacious and skilful, if he is not snapped up first by a bigger club, and continues his promising start, both he and Town will benefit from it.
Luton T (From trainee on 8/7/98) FL 2+4/1 FAC 0+1 Others 0+1

SCHMEICHEL Peter Boleslaw
Born: Gladsaxe, Denmark, 18 November 1963
Height: 6'4" Weight: 16.0
Club Honours: ESC '91; FLC '92; PL '93, '94, '96, '97, '99; FAC '94, '96, '99; CS '93, '94, '96, '97; EC '99
International Honours: Denmark (UEFAC '92): 110

A highly influential goalkeeper with great presence, Peter started last season in excellent fashion, keeping five clean sheets in Manchester United's opening nine games. Although a crucial mistake in the Champions' League against Bayern Munich in September resulted in the Germans' equalising goal, it was due more to a lack of understanding in a revamped defence, rather than a drop in form as many experts

suggested. After suffering a stomach injury in that game, he was sidelined for the next two, and no sooner had he returned to action than he shocked United fans by announcing his intention to leave the club at the end of the campaign. Suggesting that he would like to end his career in Italy, Udinese were the first to show an interest when they offered the Reds £2 million in January. Given a mid-season break by Alex Ferguson after Christmas, he came back from his Caribbean holiday completely recharged, his continuing influence being very much in evidence as United continued their quest for major honours. Playing an inspiring role against Inter Milan in the European Cup quarter final, he then saved a last-minute penalty in the FA Cup semi final against Arsenal, which helped United to Wembley. With Roy Keane suspended from the Champions' League final against Bayern Munich in Barcelona, Peter was given the task of leading the Reds to an historic treble, and although at one stage it looked like ending in disappointment he played a major part as United forced a dramatic victory. When he finally departs Old Trafford in the summer, leaving a void which the club may find impossible to fill, one thing is for sure – his presence will be sadly missed both by his team mates and his vast army of supporters.

Manchester U (£550,000 from Brondby on 12/8/91) P/FL 292 FLC 17 FAC 41 Others 48/1

Peter Schmeichel

Stefan Schnoor

SCHNOOR Stefan
Born: Neumunster, Germany, 18 April 1971
Height: 5'10" Weight: 11.10
Arrived in the 1998 close season at Derby on a free transfer from Hamburg, and made an immediate impression with a goal on his debut in a friendly. A stylish defender, who can play as a sweeper, but whose initial games, including his debut on the opening day at Blackburn, were as a left-sided wing back, Stefan showed that he liked to venture forward to shoot from long range, which brought him a couple of important strikes in the first half of last season. In and out of the side throughout the campaign, this was more to do with tactical switches than with the player himself.

Derby Co (Free from Hamburg, via Neumunster FC, on 13/7/98) PL 20+3/2 FLC 2 FAC 3

SCHOFIELD Daniel (Danny) James
Born: Doncaster, 10 April 1980
Height: 5'10" Weight: 11.3
A teenage signing from non-league Brodsworth last February, Danny did not take long to settle at Huddersfield, earning a surprise call up for Town's final match of the season, at home to Crewe, and enjoying a very astute Football League debut. Showing himself to be able to hold on to the ball under pressure, and possessing a skilful touch and good passing ability, the young striker looked as if he could become a regular player before too long and certainly looks to be one for the future.

Huddersfield T (£2,000 from Brodsworth on 8/2/99) FL 1

SCHOFIELD John David
Born: Barnsley, 16 May 1965
Height: 5'11" Weight: 11.8
Continued where he left off at the heart of the Mansfield defence in 1998-99. After some inconsistent performances in the second half of the season, John became another casualty of the 7-2 defeat at Cambridge, losing his place in the side. A solid and reliable player who can also perform equally well in midfield, he was soon back in contention for a first-team place. Interestingly, he was once again called upon as stand in "goalie" when Ian Bowling broke his arm against Exeter and, in playing in all but two minutes of the second half, did not concede a goal. Was released during the summer.

Lincoln C (Free from Gainsborough Trinity on 10/11/88) FL 221+10/11 FLC 15/2 FAC 5+2 Others 13+1
Doncaster Rov (Free on 18/11/94) FL 107+3/12 FLC 4 FAC 2 Others 3
Mansfield T (£10,000 on 8/8/97) FL 81+5 FLC 4 FAC 4 Others 4

John Schofield

Paul Scholes

SCHOLES Paul
Born: Salford, 16 November 1974
Height: 5'7" Weight: 11.10
Club Honours: PL '96, '97, '99; FAC '96, '99; CS '96, '97
International Honours: E: 17; Yth (UEFAC '93)

A prolific Manchester United goalscorer who can play as an out-and-out striker, or in central midfield, Paul returned to England as one of the great successes of the 1998 World Cup campaign. An ever present during the early stages of last season, he scored important goals in successive games against Barcelona and Bayern Munich in the Champions' League, before hitting the winner against Liverpool in September. With further strikes against Brondby, Blackburn (2), Aston Villa, and Middlesbrough, he was given a mid-season break by Alex Ferguson in January, which helped to recharge his batteries. Coming back refreshed to score United's vital winner against Inter Milan in the San Siro, which took the Reds through to the European Cup semi finals, he then hit a hat trick playing for England against Poland in the European championship's qualifier at Wembley. In peak form as the campaign reached its exciting climax, his yellow-card offence in the European Cup semi final against Juventus ruled him out of the final. Despite his immense disappointment, he remained one of United's key players, and played an inspiring role in the FA Cup final at Wembley, scoring the club's deciding goal, which completed the second leg of an historic treble.
Manchester U (From trainee on 29/1/93) PL 90+39/32 FLC 6+2/5 FAC 8+6/4 Others 20+10/7

SCHWARZER Mark
Born: Sydney, Australia, 6 October 1972
Height: 6'5" Weight: 13.6
International Honours: Australia: 5

The giant Aussie usually acted as aerial traffic controller to everything passing overhead in the Middlesbrough goal area in 1998-99, and seemingly back in favour with his national coach he had every reason to feel content with his contribution, having saved a couple of penalties, kept well over a dozen clean sheets, and won numerous "Man of the Match" awards. However, most pleasing for him though must have been the removal at last of a steel plate inserted after he suffered a broken leg during the previous season. Although on a personal note he will no doubt still be smarting from the Everton and Arsenal results, he is rapidly proving to be a sensational bargain buy from Bradford City a couple of seasons ago, his future now well and truly tied up at Boro, where his contract is not due to expire until 2004.
Bradford C (£350,000 from Kaiserslautern, via Blacktown, Marconi and Dynamo Dresden, on 22/11/96) FL 13 FAC 3
Middlesbrough (£1,500,000 on 26/2/97) F/PL 76 FLC 10 FAC 4

SCIMECA Riccardo
Born: Leamington Spa, 13 June 1975
Height: 6'1" Weight: 12.9
Club Honours: FLC '96
International Honours: E: B-1; U21-9

Having signed a new contract binding himself to Aston Villa for the next four years, Riccardo found himself picked to play up front in the second game of last season, following the sale of Dwight Yorke, and the unavailability of Stan Collymore. However, after the arrival of Paul Merson in September, and left out of the side apart from a few appearances from the subs' bench, Dion Dublin's move from Coventry prompted him to hand in a transfer request. Thankfully, nothing came of it, and on Boxing Day a run of injuries saw him feature in the next 14 games, playing both in defence and midfield, and scoring two goals. Unfortunately, the return of players from injury, together with the signings of both Steve Stone and Colin Calderwood, meant he was hardly called upon from early April. Comfortable on the ball, with excellent skills and tight control, and able to go past defenders as if they didn't exist, he will be back.
Aston Villa (From trainee on 7/7/93) PL 50+23/2 FLC 4+3 FAC 9+1 Others 5+2

SCOTT Andrew (Andy)
Born: Epsom, 2 August 1972
Height: 6'1" Weight: 11.5
Club Honours: Div 3 '99

A left-sided Brentford forward with good control and an excellent crosser of the ball, Andy had a fine start to 1998-99, scoring against Tottenham, both home and away in the Worthington Cup, and twice at Peterborough in the league, as well as creating many goals for his colleagues. Suffered a bad ankle injury at Plymouth in November, forcing his absence for 12 games, and then missed another four in February due to a knee problem. The winner of a Third Division championship medal as the Bees turned their fortunes around, he is one step ahead of his brother, Rob, who plays for Rotherham.

Sheffield U (£50,000 from Sutton U on 1/12/92) P/FL 39+36/6 FLC 5/2 FAC 2+1 Others 3+1/3
Chesterfield (Loaned on 18/10/96) FL 4+1/3
Bury (Loaned on 21/3/97) FL 2+6
Brentford (£75,000 on 21/11/97) FL 55+5/12 FLC 4/2 Others 3/2

SCOTT Christopher (Chris) James
Born: Burnley, 12 February 1980
Height: 5'11" Weight: 12.5

The latest in a Turf Moor dynasty – grandfather Brian Miller, father Derek Scott, and uncle David Miller are all ex-Clarets – Chris had an early introduction to Burnley's first team last season owing to an injury crisis, and took his chance well. A first-year professional, he was used mainly at right back, and never failed to let opposing forwards know he was around although, unfortunately, this led to an excessive number of bookings. If experience can iron out the over exuberance, he will do very well.
Burnley (From trainee on 6/7/98) FL 9+5 FAC 1

SCOTT Gary Craig
Born: Liverpool, 3 February 1978
Height: 5'8" Weight: 11.2

A Rotherham's right back, Gary had a run of seven successive matches last October and November but was unable to maintain his first-team place thereafter, having to be content with reserve-team football. Released during the summer, he likes to get forward, and is still young enough to make himself a good career if he gets the opportunity.
Tranmere Rov (From trainee on 18/10/95)
Rotherham U (Free on 7/8/97) FL 19+1 FAC 2 Others 1

SCOTT Keith James
Born: Westminster, 9 June 1967
Height: 6'3" Weight: 14.3
Club Honours: GMVC '93; FAT '93

An enormously popular, if not legendary, target man at Wycombe, who unfortunately dislocated his elbow within a minute of coming on as a sub at Millwall in the third game of last season, he returned with a vengeance in October, scoring on his return against Macclesfield, and then adding two more in the next game, against Wrexham. It was no coincidence that these were the club's first two wins of 1998-99, and he continued to lead the attack well, scoring four more goals, including the only goal in two games against Chesterfield. While his deadline day transfer to Reading came as a considerable shock to the supporters, it was an offer the cash-strapped manager could not refuse, and Keith left the club after two spells and an impressive record of 97 goals in 201 starts (including his Conference record). With his new club, he soon became the big, bustling centre forward that the Royals had been looking for, and he repaid his faith in them when scoring in each of his first two games.
Lincoln C (Free from Leicester U on 22/3/90) FL 7+9/2 FLC 0+1 Others 1+1
Wycombe W (£30,000 in March 1991 on 1/3/91) FL 15/10 FLC 4/2 FAC 6/1 Others 2/2
Swindon T (£375,000 on 18/11/93) P/FL 43+8/12 FLC 5/3 Others 3/1

Stoke C (£300,000 on 30/12/94) FL 22+3/3 FAC 2/1 Others 0+1
Norwich C (Signed on 11/11/95) FL 10+15/5 FLC 0+2 FAC 0+2
Bournemouth (Loaned on 16/2/96) FL 8/1
Watford (Loaned on 7/2/97) FL 6/2 Others 2
Wycombe W (£55,000 on 27/3/97) FL 60+3/20 FLC 1+1/1 FAC 5/1 Others 1+1
Reading (£250,000 on 24/3/99) FL 5+4/2

SCOTT Kevin Watson
Born: Easington, 17 December 1966
Height: 6'3" Weight: 14.5
Club Honours: FAYC '85; Div 1 '93
A series of knee injuries completely disrupted this dominant Norwich central defender's progress in 1998-99, and restricted to just a handful of appearances at either first or reserve-team levels he was placed on the free transfer list early in 1999. The former Newcastle and Tottenham man spent a month on loan at Darlington after Christmas, playing four games, before returning to Carrow Road for further treatment on his knee. A solid and reliable defender, he is particularly effective in the air, and also has great composure on the ball, always being prepared to play his way out from the back.
Newcastle U (From apprentice on 19/12/84) BL 227/8 FLC 18 FAC 15+1/1 Others 1/1
Tottenham H (£850,000 on 1/2/94) PL 16+2/1 FLC 0+1
Port Vale (Loaned on 13/1/95) FL 17/1
Charlton Ath (Loaned on 20/12/96) FL 4
Norwich C (£250,000 on 21/1/97) FL 31+2 FLC 1+1 FAC 1
Darlington (Loaned on 29/1/99) FL 4

SCOTT Martin
Born: Sheffield, 7 January 1968
Height: 5'9" Weight: 11.7
Club Honours: Div 4 '89; Div 1 '96, '99
Even prior to winning his second Division One championship medal with Sunderland in 1998-99, Martin was informed that he would be surplus to requirements for next term. The decision came as a surprise to the fans who have admired the left back's commitment to the cause over the years, along with his overlapping ability and crossing strengths. He also appeared as a centre back during the campaign, and showed his prowess from the penalty spot in the nerve-wracking Worthington Cup shoot-out victory at Everton. Having captained the side in the absence of Kevin Ball, without question Martin will leave Wearside with the very best wishes of every Sunderland fan. Stop Press: Signed for Bradford on 29 June.
Rotherham U (From apprentice on 10/1/86) FL 93+1/3 FLC 11/2 FAC 7+2 Others 7/2
Bristol C (£200,000 on 5/12/90) FL 171/14 FLC 10/1 FAC 10 Others 8/1
Sunderland (£750,000 on 23/12/94) P/FL 104+2/9 FLC 14/2 FAC 6

SCOTT Philip Campbell
Born: Perth, 14 November 1974
Height: 5'9" Weight: 11.2
Club Honours: S Div 1 '97
International Honours: S: U21-4
Due to be out of contract during the summer, Sheffield Wednesday moved for this hard-working, attacking St Johnstone midfielder

on transfer deadline day last March in exchange for a small fee. Unfortunately, he managed just four subs' appearances before picking up a niggling injury that put him out of action for the rest of 1998-99. However, before that, Philip had shown some of his ability when scoring an excellent goal in the 1-1 Hillsborough draw against Newcastle, and looks to become an exciting addition to the Owls' squad in 1999-2000. A Scottish U21 international, but yet to play for the full side, at first glance he could well put that right.
St Johnstone (Signed from Scone Thistle on 30/7/91) SL 115+17/27 SLC 6+2/2 SC 9+1/4 Others 5/2
Sheffield Wed (£75,000 on 26/3/99) PL 0+4/1

SCOTT Richard Paul
Born: Dudley, 29 September 1974
Height: 5'9" Weight: 12.8
Equally at home on the right side of midfield or at full back, Richard moved from Shrewsbury to Peterborough during the 1998 close season and started the opening game of the new campaign in fine fettle. Disappointingly though, he failed to live up to expectation and lost his place, seeming to lack stamina, before fighting his way back to impress with his "Martin Peters' type" late arrivals into the box. Scored four goals for his new club, three of them being in 1-1 away draws.
Birmingham C (From trainee on 17/5/93) FL 11+1 FLC 3+1 Others 3
Shrewsbury T (Signed on 22/3/95) FL 91+14/18 FLC 6 FAC 8+1/3 Others 8+1/1
Peterborough U (Signed on 20/7/98) FL 19+8/4 FLC 1+1 FAC 1 Others 1+1

SCOTT Robert (Rob)
Born: Epsom, 15 August 1973
Height: 6'1" Weight: 11.10
Unable to regain a regular place at Fulham in 1998-99, having suffered a knee injury in the previous campaign, the bustling, pacy forward spent a month on loan at Carlisle in the early part of the season, working hard to impress the Brunton Park faithful. He deservedly netted three times in his seven appearances, his 25-yard chip against Swansea being especially memorable, and he showed enthusiasm and determination as well as no little skill in his performances. Back at Craven Cottage, Rob was transferred to Rotherham in November, and was just settling in when he suffered a broken shoulder at Cambridge on Boxing Day. Operated on and pinned, it kept him out of action until the last couple of weeks, so he will be looking forward to 1999-2000 where his face up front should be a major asset. His long throw is another attacking option for United.
Sheffield U (£20,000 from Sutton U on 1/8/93) FL 2+4/1 FLC 0+1 Others 2+1
Scarborough (Loaned on 22/3/95) FL 8/3
Northampton T (Loaned on 24/11/95) FL 5 Others 1
Fulham (£30,000 on 10/1/96) FL 65+19/17 FLC 3+5 FAC 3/1 Others 2+2/1
Carlisle U (Loaned on 18/8/98) FL 7/3
Rotherham U (£50,000 on 17/11/98) FL 5+1/1 FAC 2/1 Others 3

SCOWCROFT James (Jamie) Benjamin
Born: Bury St Edmunds, 15 November 1975
Height: 6'1" Weight: 12.2
International Honours: E: U21-5
After missing the start of last season because of a foot injury, when he returned to the side at Port Vale he scored Ipswich's first league goal of 1998-99 when heading home Kieron Dyer's cross. He went on to score in each of the next four games, including a double against eventual promotion rivals, Bradford City. Continuing to develop as a leading target man, winning a good percentage of balls in the air, while being no slouch on the ground either, he was unfortunate to break a collarbone in an accidental collision with the Barnsley goalkeeper in December, and the healing process took longer than originally expected, keeping him out until March. The highlight of his campaign, however, was the hat trick he scored at Crewe – a close-range tap in, a shot from outside the box, and a penalty.
Ipswich T (From trainee on 1/7/94) FL 101+26/30 FLC 13+1/3 FAC 7 Others 5+4/1

SCULLY Anthony (Tony) Derek Thomas
Born: Dublin, 12 June 1976
Height: 5'7" Weight: 11.12
International Honours: Ei: U21-10; Yth; Sch
Tony normally operated on the right wing, but also played on the left-hand side in attack, or as a wing back. A skilful ball winner who links up play well, although a regular choice for Queens Park Rangers at the start of last season he was unable to hold a regular place after the arrival of Gerry Francis. Despite his lack of progress at club level, in February he was selected for the Republic of Ireland's "B" side for the match against the Irish National League.
Crystal Palace (From trainee on 2/12/93) FL 0+3
Bournemouth (Loaned on 14/10/94) FL 6+4 Others 2
Cardiff C (Loaned on 5/1/96) FL 13+1
Manchester C (£80,000 on 12/8/97) FL 1+8
Stoke C (Loaned on 27/1/98) FL 7
Queens Park R (£155,000 on 17/3/98) FL 17+13/2 FLC 4

SEABURY Kevin
Born: Shrewsbury, 24 November 1973
Height: 5'10" Weight: 11.11
A Shrewsbury full back, "Mr Dependable" is now approaching 200 Football League appearances. Able to play as a right-sided wing back, in midfield, or in central defence in emergency, he gets forward well and scored more times in 1998-99 than during the rest of his career. Very popular for his vital tackles and some amazing goal line clearances, he is Shrewsbury through and through, and very popular. Out of contract during the summer, but offered terms of re-engagement by Town, he should be able to make his mark on the game for many years yet.
Shrewsbury T (From trainee on 6/7/92) FL 166+20/7 FLC 8+2/1 FAC 9 Others 8+2

SEAL David
Born: Penrith, Australia, 26 January 1972
Height: 5'11" Weight: 12.4

An out-and-out striker, David found it hard to hold down a first-team place at Northampton in 1998-99, despite being the previous season's top scorer. With seven strikers on the books, first-team spots were at a premium, as were goals, and the Australian front man was unable to find the breaks with his style of play, preferring the ball to be on the ground not in the air. Was released during the summer.

Bristol C (£80,000 from Aalst on 7/10/94) FL 24+27/10 FLC 4+1/3 FAC 1+1 Others 2+1/1
Northampton T (£90,000 on 11/8/97) FL 35+8/12 FLC 2/1 FAC 3+1/1 Others 1+3

SEAMAN David Andrew
Born: Rotherham, 19 September 1963
Height: 6'4" Weight: 14.10
Club Honours: Div 1 '91; PL '98; FAC '93, '98; FLC '93; ECWC '94; CS '98
International Honours: E: 52; B-6; U21-10
Once again, David was a model of consistency behind the ever-green Arsenal back four in 1998-99, keeping a high percentage of clean sheets. Very relaxed and composed, both on and off the field, he plays a big part in the tremendous team spirit which exists at Highbury. With safe hands, and a strong kick from both hand and dead-ball situations, he is still regarded as the number-one goalkeeper in England, despite the worrying back and rib injuries that caused him to miss some games last season. However, on regaining full fitness, he was back to his best for both club and country.

Leeds U (From apprentice on 22/9/81)
Peterborough U (£4,000 on 13/8/82) FL 91 FLC 10 FAC 5
Birmingham C (£100,000 on 5/10/84) FL 75 FLC 4 FAC 5
Queens Park R (£225,000 on 7/8/86) FL 141 FLC 13 FAC 17 Others 4
Arsenal (£1,300,000 on 18/5/90) F/PL 312 FLC 31 FAC 41 Others 37

Damon Searle

SEARLE Damon Peter
Born: Cardiff, 26 October 1971
Height: 5'11" Weight: 10.4
Club Honours: WC '92, '93; Div 3 '93
International Honours: W: B-1; U21-6; Yth; Sch
Out of contract at Stockport in the summer of 1998, the experienced defender, cum midfielder, was a virtual ever present for Carlisle during last season, and proved to be one of the most consistent performers in the squad. Mostly, he wore the number three shirt, but he often looked at his best pushing forward down the left flank or surging through midfield. Although he only scored three times, his free kick against Torquay in April was voted the club's "Goal of the Season."

Cardiff C (From trainee on 20/8/90) FL 232+2/3 FLC 9/1 FAC 13 Others 29
Stockport Co (Free on 28/5/96) FL 34+7 FLC 2+1 FAC 2 Others 1
Carlisle U (Free on 6/7/98) FL 43+2/2 FLC 2 FAC 1 Others 1+1/1

SEARLE Stephen (Stevie)
Born: Lambeth, 7 March 1977
Height: 5'10" Weight: 11.13
Stevie missed Barnet's opening seven games of last season due to an ankle injury, and he eventually appeared as a substitute in the 9-1 home defeat against Peterborough in August. His performance was one of the few positive factors to emerge from the match, and he rapidly established himself as the creative force in the Bees' midfield, being instrumental in the home victories over Hull City and Rotherham in September, with his neat, concise passing style carving open the opposing team's back-lines. His game revolved around finding a team mate with an accurate pass, and later he added a robust edge to that. He also developed a clinical goalscoring technique, his finest being a headed effort against Darlington at Underhill in January, and he added to his tally with strikes against Cardiff and Leyton Orient. Tagged as the latest playmaker to grace Underhill's slope, he is showing signs of becoming just as effective as some of his illustrious predecessors, and is currently being touted as one of the most gifted midfielders in the basement division.

Barnet (Free from Sittingbourne on 1/8/97) FL 59+6/4 FAC 1 Others 4

SEBOK Vilmos
Born: Budapest, Hungary, 13 June 1973
Height: 6'3" Weight: 13.1
International Honours: Hungary: 21
A Hungarian international, Vilmos joined Bristol City last January following long negotiations over contracts and a work permit. Although finding some difficulty in adjusting to the English game, the defender, cum midfielder, showed a steady improvement, despite not being the man marker that fans had expected, and his City career being interrupted by international demands. The highlight of his season was a hat trick for Hungary against Liechtenstein, which saw him become the first City player to score three goals in a full international match whilst at the club.

Bristol C (£200,000 from Upjest Dosza, via Tatabanya and REAC, on 15/1/99) FL 10+2

SEDGEMORE Benjamin (Ben) Redwood
Born: Wolverhampton, 5 August 1975
Height: 5'11" Weight: 12.10
International Honours: E: Sch
This big, talented Macclesfield midfielder, whose enthusiasm is infectious, struggled with a groin strain at the start of last season, finding it difficult to gain a regular starting place with a settled midfield in place. However, his opportunity came in late October against Burnley, when he took possession near the half-way line and strode forward to score a blistering goal with a low drive from 25 yards. Ben's turn of pace is good, and he finds space well, as proven with his second goal of the season at York, in November, when he was left unmarked to head home a pin-point cross from the wing.

Birmingham C (From trainee on 17/5/93)
Northampton T (Loaned on 22/12/94) FL 1
Mansfield T (Loaned on 25/8/95) FL 4+5 Others 1
Peterborough U (Free on 10/1/96) FL 13+4 FAC 1
Mansfield T (Free on 6/9/96) FL 58+9/6 FLC 1 FAC 2+1 Others 2
Macclesfield T (£25,000 on 19/3/98) FL 30+10/2 FLC 2 FAC 4/1 Others 1

SEDGLEY Stephen (Steve) Philip
Born: Enfield, 26 May 1968
Height: 6'1" Weight: 13.13
Club Honours: FAC '87, '91
International Honours: E: U21-11
The Wolves' midfielder, cum defender, had his 1998-99 pre-season campaign disrupted by injury, not starting either of the first two games. He then had a 20-match run, mainly in defence, though he did venture up to score twice at Crystal Palace. January saw him lose his place after some poor displays, but Steve came back keen to prove any doubters wrong, performing more in midfield, and adding some much-needed grit, as well as heading the winner at Queens Park Rangers. He is an experienced man to have around, and captains Wolves on the odd occasion. Is a dead-ball specialist who can be relied on to take accurate free kicks, penalties, and corners, when required.

Coventry C (From apprentice on 2/6/86) FL 81+3/3 FLC 9/2 FAC 2+2 Others 5+1
Tottenham H (£750,000 on 28/7/89) F/PL 147+17/8 FLC 24+3/1 FAC 22+1/1 Others 5+3
Ipswich T (£1,000,000 on 15/6/94) P/FL 105/15 FLC 10/2 FAC 5 Others 5/1
Wolverhampton W (£700,000 on 29/7/97) FL 59+4/3 FLC 5 FAC 6+1

SEDGWICK Christopher (Chris) Edward
Born: Sheffield, 28 April 1980
Height: 5'11" Weight: 10.10
Yet another homegrown Rotherham player, Chris is an exciting old-fashioned type right winger who, at times, had to adopt to a right-wing-back role, but did so with great enthusiasm. He will surely have benefited from his first full season at Football League level in 1998-99, and if he continues to improve he will be a real handful for defences in the not too distant future.

Rotherham U (From trainee on 16/8/97) FL 24+13/3 FLC 0+2 FAC 3+2 Others 0+2

SEDLAN Jason Mark
Born: Peterborough, 5 August 1979
Height: 5'9" Weight: 11.2
Although used very sparingly by Mansfield last season, Jason, having signed professional forms during the summer, showed a maturity beyond his years. This was best demonstrated in his only full outing in the first team against Torquay, when he played his part in subduing former England stalwart, Chris Waddle. Surprisingly released during the summer, he can also be used to good effect further forward in midfield, where his strong, probing runs create problems to opposition defences.
Mansfield T (From trainee on 3/7/98) FL 1+5 Others 0+1

SEGERS Johannes (Hans)
Born: Eindhoven, Holland, 30 October 1961
Height: 5'11" Weight: 12.12
Freed by Wolves, and joining Tottenham as the goalkeeping coach in July 1998, Hans himself may have raised an eyebrow if it had been suggested that he would find himself back in the action in the Premiership, but on 19 September he did exactly that. With both Ian Walker and Espen Baardsen injured, the Dutchman took his place in the first team for the Premiership game at Southampton, and again the following week at home to Brentford in the Worthington Cup second round, second leg. With a wealth of goal-keeping experience, he demonstrated much of the confidence and agility which has been the trademark of his career to date, and seemed to thoroughly enjoy the two opportunities handed to him before being released in the summer.
Nottingham F (£50,000 from PSV Eindhoven on 14/8/84) FL 58 FLC 4 FAC 5
Stoke C (Loaned on 13/2/87) FL 1
Sheffield U (Loaned on 19/11/87) FL 10 Others 1
Dunfermline Ath (Loaned on 1/3/88) SL 4
Wimbledon (£180,000 on 28/9/88) F/PL 265+2 FLC 26 FAC 22 Others 7
Wolverhampton W (Free on 30/8/96) FL 11 FAC 2
Tottenham H (Free on 4/8/98) PL 1 FLC 1

SEGURA Victor Abascal
Born: Zaragoza, Spain, 13 March 1973
Height: 6'0" Weight: 12.3
This former Spanish U21 international did not figure regularly in Bruce Rioch's Norwich line-up during the 1998-99 campaign, although when called upon he never let the side down. His best-ever display in a City shirt came in the local derby win at Ipswich last October, when he repelled everything the Ipswich attack could throw at him, even suffering a punctured lung in the process. Predominantly left footed, he is good in the air, strong in the tackle, and also tries to play the ball forward constructively from defence. Was released during the summer.
Norwich C (Free from Lleida on 2/8/97) FL 24+5 FLC 3 FAC 1

SELLARS Scott
Born: Sheffield, 27 November 1965
Height: 5'8" Weight: 10.0
Club Honours: FMC '87; Div 1 '93, '97
International Honours: E: U21-3

A vital part of the Bolton set-up, wearing the captain's armband on a number of occasions, last season was one of mixed fortunes for Scott. When playing he contributed greatly to the good fortunes of the Wanderers, although injury took it's toll as the campaing progressed, a thigh strain keeping him out during the early stages, whilst an ankle injury meant that he missed the majority of the end of 1998-99. However, when he did play, he turned in the kind of mesmerising, skilful performances for which he is known. A tricky left winger, his undoubted talent, along with his vast experience of the game, suggests that opposing teams are in for a torrid time when he is at the top of his game. And, as the possessor of a supreme left foot (especially in dead-ball situations), his right-foot volley against Port Vale earlier in the season came as something of a surprise. Was surprisingly released during the summer.
Leeds U (From apprentice on 25/7/83) FL 72+4/12 FLC 4/1 FAC 4 Others 2/1
Blackburn Rov (£20,000 on 28/7/86) FL 194+8/35 FLC 12/3 FAC 11/1 Others 20/2
Leeds U (£800,000 on 1/7/92) PL 6+1 FLC 1+1 Others 1
Newcastle U (£700,000 on 9/3/93) F/PL 56+5/5 FLC 6+1/2 FAC 3 Others 4/1
Bolton W (£750,000 on 7/12/95) P/FL 106+5/15 FLC 8+1 FAC 5/1 Others 0+1

SENDA Daniel (Danny) Luke
Born: Harrow, 17 April 1981
Height: 5'10" Weight: 10.0
International Honours: E: Yth
Signed as a youth player from Southampton last summer, with several England youth caps to his name, Danny proved to be extremely quick and nimble at Wycombe, playing in a wide-right midfield attacking role. An injury prevented his season from starting until last October, but he impressed at reserve level, and was rewarded with first-team football when coming on as sub in the 3-0 home win over Oldham at the end of March. He then made five further substitute appearances, and his progress in 1999-2000 is eagerly looked forward to at the club, after signing a two-year contract.
Wycombe W (Signed from Southampton juniors on 26/1/99) FL 0+6

SERRANT Carl
Born: Bradford, 12 September 1975
Height: 6'0" Weight: 11.2
International Honours: E: B-1; U21-2; Yth
Brought to Newcastle from Oldham by Kenny Dalglish during the 1998 close season, the young left back found it very difficult to establish himself in the plans of the new manager, Ruud Gullit. Arriving on Tyneside with a good reputation as a solid and dependable left-sided defender, with the flexibility to be able to play as a conventional full back, a central defender, or a modern wing back, he is good in the air, very quick on the ground, and has represented his country at several levels with some distinction. However, he only made four appearances during the season, one of them as a substitute and the rest at left back, and after conceding the penalty by which Everton beat United at Goodison he

lost his place. Unable to regain it, although injury problems did not help him, he had a spell on loan at Bury in February.
Oldham Ath (From trainee on 22/7/94) FL 84+6/1 FLC 7 FAC 6/1 Others 3
Newcastle U (£500,000 + on 9/7/98) PL 3+1
Bury (Loaned on 18/2/99) FL 15

SERTORI Mark Anthony
Born: Manchester, 1 September 1967
Height: 6'2" Weight: 14.2
Club Honours: GMVC '88
Mark was a colossus at the centre of Halifax's defence in 1998-99, having signed from Scunthorpe United in the summer of 1998, his no-nonsense style of defending making him a big crowd favourite. Although he has yet to appear on the score sheet for the Shaymen, his defending qualities more than made up for that.
Stockport Co (Signed from East Manchester on 7/2/87) FL 3+1 FLC 1
Lincoln C (Free on 1/7/88) FL 43+7/9 FLC 6 FAC 4/1 Others 5/2
Wrexham (£30,000 on 9/2/90) FL 106+4/3 FLC 8+1 FAC 6 Others 9+1
Bury (Free on 22/7/94) FL 4+9/1 FLC 1 FAC 2+1 Others 1+2/1
Scunthorpe U (Free on 22/7/96) FL 82+1/2 FLC 6 FAC 7 Others 4+1
Halifax T (Free on 7/7/98) FL 39+1 FLC 4 FAC 1 Others 2

SHAIL Mark Edward David
Born: Sandviken, Sweden, 15 October 1966
Height: 6'1" Weight: 13.3
International Honours: E: SP-1
Returning to the Bristol City team last October following serious injury problems, Mark's comeback brought an immediate improvement to the centre of the defence, following early season problems which had seen the side concede too many goals. Having been given the captaincy, and leading by example, always producing 100 per-cent effort, further injury problems and the return of Shaun Taylor, forced him on to the bench. However, he ended the campaign partnering Taylor, once again giving the side the solid base that was so badly missing at the start of the season. A long-serving player who was a member of the team that won a memorable FA Cup replay at Anfield in 1994, he is a centre back of real substance, whether it be on the ground or in the air.
Bristol C (£45,000 from Yeovil on 25/3/93) FL 117+10/4 FLC 5+1 FAC 11/1 Others 4

SHARP Kevin Phillip
Born: Ontario, Canada, 19 September 1974
Height: 5'9" Weight: 11.11
Club Honours: FAYC '93; Div 3 '97; AMC '99
International Honours: E: Yth (UEFAYC '93); Sch
A classy and skilful Wigan left back with excellent vision, Kevin played throughout last season on a week-to-week basis. Although not starting in the campaign, his impressive performances in the second half saw him collect the supporters' "Away Player of the Season" award. Scored three goals, including the important strike in the first leg of the area final of the Auto

Windscreens Shield competition, and was delighted to take away a winners medal following the 1-0 victory over Millwall in the Wembley final.

Leeds U (£60,000 from Auxerre on 20/10/92) PL 11+6 Others 0+1
Wigan Ath (£100,000 on 30/11/95) FL 109+15/10 FLC 2+2 FAC 4+1 Others 10+1/1

SHARPE Lee Stuart
Born: Halesowen, 27 May 1971
Height: 6'0" Weight: 12.12
Club Honours: ECWC '91; FLC '92; PL '93, '94, '96; CS '94
International Honours: E: 8; B-1; U21-8
After missing the whole of the previous campaign through a serious knee-ligament injury, Lee came back in 1998-99 to play four games for Leeds, before an inept display in the second leg of the UEFA Cup-tie against Roma saw him loaned first to the Italian side, Sampdoria, and then Bradford during the transfer deadline week. Signed until the end of the season, Lee was hoping to put an end to the most frustrating spell of his career, and opened his goals account in his second game for the Bantams, at home to Grimsby. Able to play on either the right or left of midfield, although associated mainly with the latter, his creativity and eye for a goal was much appreciated at City, where he quickly became a crowd favourite. Stop Press: Completed a cut-price £200,000 move to Bradford from Leeds on 15 June.

Torquay U (From trainee on 31/5/88) FL 9+5/3 Others 2+3
Manchester U (£185,000 on 10/6/88) F/PL 160+33/21 FLC 15+8/9 FAC 22+7/3 Others 18+2/3
Leeds U (£4,500,000 on 14/8/96) PL 28+2/5 FLC 3/1 FAC 0+1 Others 1+2
Bradford C (Loaned on 25/3/99) FL 6+3/2

SHARPS Ian William
Born: Warrington, 23 October 1980
Height: 6'4" Weight: 13.2
Still a trainee, Ian was yet another product of Tranmere's invaluable YTS scheme who became a regular in the Pontins' League team, but was then unlucky to break a bone in his foot during his August 1998 first-team debut. A tall centre back who is strong in the air and difficult to shake off the ball, as well as having vision and accurate distribution skills, he would undoubtedly have had further opportunities towards the end of the season if not for a groin injury. Is definitely one for the future.

Tranmere Rov (Trainee) FL 0+1

SHAW Paul
Born: Burnham, 4 September 1973
Height: 5'11" Weight: 12.4
International Honours: E: Yth
Having had a great first season at Millwall, although 1998-99 started well enough, with Paul forming a great partnership with Neil Harris, first suspension and then a hernia injury saw him sidelined for nearly half the campaign. There was no doubting that the Lions missed him. A tall, quick forward who has a good shot, especially from long range, and who must be the best long-range shooter in the Second Division, he can also play

behind the front two when needed, dependent on the system being used, due to his great workrate. Obviously disappointed not to make the starting line-up for the Auto Windscreens Wembley team, he will be looking for an injury-free 1999-2000.

Arsenal (From trainee on 18/9/91) PL 1+11/2 FAC 0+1
Burnley (Loaned on 23/3/95) FL 8+1/4
Cardiff C (Loaned on 11/8/95) FL 6
Peterborough U (Loaned on 20/10/95) FL 12/5 Others 2
Millwall (£250,000 on 15/9/97) FL 71+3/21 FLC 4/2 FAC 1 Others 5/4

SHAW Richard Edward
Born: Brentford, 11 September 1968
Height: 5'9" Weight: 12.8
Club Honours: FMC '91; Div 1 '94
1998-99 was another solid season for this dependable Coventry defender. A player with no frills, although one who always gives 100 per-cent effort, his future seemed to be in doubt when Jean-Guy Wallemme arrived from France, but after an early uncomfortable spell at right back, he was an ever present, initially alongside Gary Breen, and then Paul Williams. The highlight of his excellent campaign being the marking of the Manchester United goal twins, Dwight Yorke and Andy Cole, in the game at Highfield Road. In winning all of the club's "Player of the Year" awards, a just reward for his outstanding performances, after almost 150 games for City all that is missing is a goal!

Crystal Palace (From apprentice on 4/9/86) F/PL 193+14/3 FLC 28+2 FAC 18 Others 12+1
Hull C (Loaned on 14/12/89) FL 4
Coventry C (£1,000,000 on 17/11/95) PL 125+1 FLC 10 FAC 13

SHEARER Alan
Born: Newcastle, 13 August 1970
Height: 6'0" Weight: 12.6
Club Honours: PL '95
International Honours: E: 51; B-1; U21-11; Yth
Local lad Alan remains the talismanic hero of the Toon Army, particularly as he was appointed Newcastle club captain during last season in succession to Rob Lee, following the latter's lengthy absence through injury. Also made captain of England by Glenn Hoddle, he retained the honour when Kevin Keegan succeeded to the post of England manager. Because of this, and his excellent scoring record in the Premiership, he remains one of the highest profile players in the land, with his performance continually under the closest of scrutiny. And, having suffered a series of serious injuries in recent years, there were regular suggestions that he is no longer the player he was. However, he continues to confound his critics, and his scoring record in a season interrupted again by injury was a goal every other game, his penalty at Forest in March being his 50th counter for Newcastle. Remaining as committed as ever, with a very high will to win, and an important influence in the dressing room, he has a very strong all-round game, mixing stunning goals from a distance with tap-ins

gained through a striker's sharp positional sense. He is also physically very strong and difficult to knock off the ball, and his spring makes him a real danger in the air. After ten games, beginning the previous season, without a Newcastle goal he rediscovered his touch and scored seven in four (including the six in three Premiership) games, plus one for England. Subject of frequent rumours predicting his imminent departure from his hometown club, which he became weary of denying, he suffered his longest ever goal famine in league football when failed to score from September to the end of January, spanning 14 hours and 50 minutes playing time, although he did score in both the Worthington and FA Cups during this period. During this time he also suffered a hamstring tear in his right leg, against Sheffield Wednesday, which sidelined him for a month, before breaking the drought against Villa in a match in which he gave a sterling performance against a highly-regarded defence. Suspended in February for the first time in his career, because of an accumulation of yellow cards, the fans await with keen anticipation the development of a partnership with Duncan Ferguson that has been frustrated to date by untimely injuries to both players. A glimpse of it was provided when Duncan made a substitute appearance in the FA Cup semi-final, in which Alan was for the second consecutive year the winning scorer, this time with a penalty, coolly converted in a cauldron atmosphere, and a fulminating drive from the edge of the penalty area, to take his club back to Wembley. He was honoured to be chosen as the FA Premier League Hall of Fame inductee for season 1994-95.

Southampton (From trainee on 14/4/88) FL 105+13/23 FLC 16+2/11 FAC 11+3/4 Others 8/5
Blackburn Rov (£3,600,000 on 24/7/92) PL 132+6/112 FLC 16/14 FAC 8/2 Others 9/2
Newcastle U (£15,000,000 on 30/7/96) PL 75+3/41 FLC 3/2 FAC 15/11 Others 7/2

Alan Shearer

271

SHEFFIELD Jonathan (Jon)
Born: Bedworth, 1 February 1969
Height: 5'11" Weight: 12.10
Looked likely to be ever present for his second season running at Plymouth in 1998-99, until fracturing his cheekbone in the away fixture at Chester. Prior to this accident, Jon had another sound year as Plymouth's custodian, keeping 17 clean sheets, and proving yet again that he is an excellent shot stopper who is always quick to spot dangers and come off his line.
Norwich C (From apprentice on 16/2/87) FL 1
Aldershot (Loaned on 22/9/89) FL 11 Others 1
Aldershot (Loaned on 21/8/90) FL 15 Others 1
Cambridge U (Free on 18/3/91) FL 56 FLC 3 FAC 4 Others 6
Colchester U (Loaned on 23/12/93) FL 6
Swindon T (Loaned on 28/1/94) PL 2
Hereford U (Loaned on 15/9/94) FL 8 FLC 2
Peterborough U (£150,000 on 20/7/95) FL 62 FLC 8 FAC 6 Others 5
Plymouth Arg (£100,000 on 28/7/97) FL 85 FLC 4 FAC 6 Others 1

SHELDON Gareth Richard
Born: Barnsley, 8 May 1980
Height: 5'11" Weight: 12.0
A very pacy Scunthorpe striker who is at his best when running at opponents, Gareth is still very raw, but showed a great deal of promise when he broke into the first team last March. Signed a professional contract in February, and was a regular part of the United squad in the promotion run-in, scoring the winner in only his second start at Southend on Easter Monday. He then became a hero in the play offs, when coming off the bench to score twice at home to Swansea in extra time, before creating the winner against Leyton Orient at Wembley.
Scunthorpe U (From trainee on 4/2/99) FL 5+7/1 Others 1+2/2

SHELIA Murtaz
Born: Tbilisi, Georgia, 25 March 1969
Height: 6'2" Weight: 13.6
International Honours: Georgia: 27
Started the 1998-99 season at Manchester City still sidelined from his knee-ligament damage obtained in March 1998. However, after making steady progress, he made his comeback in the reserves at home to Sheffield Wednesday at the end of September. He then made the first team, playing three consecutive games against Wigan and Lincoln away, and Reading at home. A strong-tackling centre back, who always gives his best, following the arrival of Andy Morrison his opportunities of appearing again seemed remote and he was put on the transfer list, although still playing in the reserves. Loaned to West Ham United for one month in January, when nothing permanent came out of it he returned to the reserve team before receiving a groin injury which needed an operation. Played for Georgia against Greece in the Euro 2000 game in Athens.
Manchester C (£400,000 from Alana Vladikavkas on 26/11/97) FL 15/2 FAC 2

SHELTON Andrew (Andy) Marc
Born: Sutton Coldfield, 19 June 1980
Height: 5'11" Weight: 12.0
Having progressed through Chester's youth team to the first-team squad in 1997-98, the 19-year-old son of City's assistant manager, Gary, quickly established himself as a regular in 1998-99, his first season as a full-time professional. Used to great effect playing wide on the right, Andy has a good turn of pace, loves to push forward, and scored his first league goal with a header against Darlington at the Deva last December, the only goal of the game.
Chester C (From trainee on 7/7/98) FL 5+20/1 FLC 1 Others 1/1

SHEPHERD Paul David
Born: Leeds, 17 November 1977
Height: 5'11" Weight: 12.0
International Honours: E: Yth
A local-born midfield player who came through Leeds' junior ranks to make his first-team debut in 1996-97, Paul has failed to get a game at the club for the last two seasons, being loaned to the Scottish leaguers, Ayr United in April 1998, and then to Tranmere last February. Pacy, and blessed with the ability to read the game, despite just making one senior appearance from the bench in two months, the full back kept match fit in the Pontins' League side before returning to Elland Road. Able to play in midfield as well, he is still highly thought of.
Leeds U (From trainee on 15/9/95) PL 1
Ayr U (Loaned on 31/3/97) SL 6/1
Tranmere Rov (Loaned on 23/2/99) FL 0+1

SHERIDAN Darren Stephen
Born: Manchester, 8 December 1967
Height: 5'5" Weight: 11.5
The less famous brother of Oldham's Republic of Ireland international, John, he was yet another player who made a public declaration of his intention to leave Barnsley when his contract ran out last summer. An excellent passer of the ball when in possession, he was more of a squad player than a regular starter in 1998-99, and missed part of the season after suffering a broken jaw at Crystal Palace in February. A combative central midfielder, he can also play at left-wing back if required.
Barnsley (£10,000 from Winsford U on 12/8/93) F/PL 149+22/5 FLC 9+4/1 FAC 9+2/1 Others 1+1

SHERIDAN John Joseph
Born: Stretford, 1 October 1964
Height: 5'10" Weight: 12.0
Club Honours: FLC '91; Div 1 '97
International Honours: Ei: 34; B-1; U23-2; U21-2; Yth
As far as Oldham were concerned, John was the find of 1998-99. Having been released by Bolton during the 1998 close season, he was plying his trade with the Conference new boys, Doncaster Rovers, when he was persuaded to come to Boundary Park on non-contract terms, a move that was made permanent a few weeks later when accepting a contract until June 2000. Almost immediately, the vastly experienced midfielder sparkled, his range of passing taking the fans' breath away, and it came as no surprise when he romped home with the club's "Player of the Season" award. He

even scored a couple of goals as a bonus, both against Bristol Rovers – one that ultimately secured a point at the Memorial Ground and the first in a vital 2-1 win at home. Should be a key player at the club in 1999-2000, despite his age.
Leeds U (Free from Manchester C juniors on 2/3/82) FL 225+5/47 FLC 14/3 FAC 11+1/1 Others 11/1
Nottingham F (£650,000 on 3/8/89) FLC 1
Sheffield Wed (£500,000 on 3/11/89) F/PL 187+10/25 FLC 24/3 FAC 17+1/3 Others 4/2
Birmingham C (Loaned on 9/2/96) FL 1+1 FLC 2
Bolton W (£180,000 on 11/3/96) F/PL 24+8/2 FLC 2 FAC 2 (Free to Doncaster Rov in 1998 close season)
Oldham Ath (Free on 20/10/98) FL 30/2 FAC 4

SHERINGHAM Edward (Teddy) Paul
Born: Liam, 2 April 1966
Height: 5'11" Weight: 12.5
Club Honours: Div 2 '88; FMC '92; CS '97; PL '99; FAC '99; EC '99
International Honours: E: 38; U21-1; Yth
A natural goalscorer, who is widely acclaimed as one of the most intelligent strikers in the Premiership, Teddy was arguably the biggest loser at Manchester United as the Dwight Yorke-Andy Cole roadshow motored into action early last October. Confined mostly to the substitutes' bench, he was also blighted by several injury problems during the course of the campaign. An invaluable player to have in reserve, however, he scored his first goal of the season against his old club, Spurs, in the Worthington Cup in December, and netted his 250th in league football against Sheffield Wednesday in April. Prior to that, he was desperately unlucky to have a goalbound effort ruled out against Juventus in the European Cup semi-final at Old Trafford. With the season reaching its exciting climax, it seemed that Teddy would have to sit it out on the bench, patiently awaiting his chance. However, after replacing Roy Keane in the FA Cup final against Newcastle after nine minutes, he scored United's opener, made the second for Paul Scholes, and even carried off the "Man of the Match" award. Four days later, in the Nou Camp Stadium in Barcelona, it was a case of dejavu, as he came off the bench against Bayern Munich in the Champions' League final to score the equaliser before setting up Ole Solskjae for a last-gasp winner. After such a wonderful career, despite being devoid of major honours, Teddy was a winner at last. Played three times for England last year under two managers, Glenn Hoddle and Kevin Keegan.
Millwall (From apprentice on 19/1/84) FL 205+15/93 FLC 16+1/8 FAC 12/5 Others 11+2/5
Aldershot (Loaned on 1/2/85) FL 4+1 Others 1
Nottingham F (£2,000,000 on 23/7/91) FL 42/14 FLC 10/5 FAC 4/2 Others 6/2
Tottenham H (£2,100,000 on 28/8/92) PL 163+3/76 FLC 14/10 FAC 17/13
Manchester U (£3,500,000 on 1/7/97) PL 35+13/11 FLC 1/1 FAC 3+4/4 Others 10+3/3

SHERON Michael (Mike) Nigel
Born: Liverpool, 11 January 1972
Height: 5'10" Weight: 11.13
International Honours: E: U21-16

Starting 1998-99 as Queens Park Rangers' record signing, the striker appeared to have recaptured his scoring touch, with five goals in eight games before pulling a hamstring after just 13 seconds last Boxing Day against Norwich. Following the subsequent substitution, the quickest in the club's history, he was transferred to Barnsley as a ready-made replacement for Ashley Ward, who had moved to Blackburn. However, plagued by the earlier hamstring problem, his appearances were somewhat restricted for a considerable length of time until forming a formidable trio with Bruce Dyer and Craig Hignett. Very skilful, with an eye for goal, he is especially good at playing his colleagues into dangerous areas.

Manchester C (From trainee on 5/7/90) F/PL 82+18/24 FLC 9+1/1 FAC 5+3/3 Others 1
Bury (Loaned on 28/3/91) FL 1+4/1 Others 2
Norwich C (£1,000,000 on 26/8/94) P/FL 19+9/2 FLC 6/3 FAC 4/2
Stoke C (£450,000 on 13/11/95) FL 64+5/34 FLC 4/5 FAC 1 Others 2
Queens Park R (£2,750,000 on 2/7/97) FL 57+6/19 FLC 2+2/1 FAC 2
Barnsley (£1,000,000 on 27/1/99) FL 14+1/2 FAC 1+1

SHERWOOD Timothy (Tim) Alan
Born: St Albans, 6 February 1969
Height: 6'0" Weight: 12.9
Club Honours: PL '95
International Honours: E: 3; B-1; U21-4

Despite making it public that he was unhappy with the direction the side were taking in 1998-99, the Blackburn captain still gave it everything on the field of play, being a committed player who cared about the result. However, the club finally lost patience with him, and he joined Tottenham in February, making his debut at home to Coventry and bringing a much needed creativity to the heart of the midfield. Immediately impressing with his ability to be first to the ball, his strength in the challenge, and his accurate passing ability, Tim found White Hart Lane the ideal platform on which to rebuild his reputation as one of the best midfielders in England. Bagging his first goal in a fine performance in the FA Cup fifth round at Leeds, his form went from strength to strength, and was recognised with a call up to the England team for the Euro 2000 qualifier against Poland, where he gave a fine performance to establish himself as a key figure in new England coach Kevin Keegan's plans. An intelligent player when creating width from the centre, he stabilised Spurs' midfield without stifling its flair. With determination being a part of Tim's make up, it was best demonstrated with a goal late on in the home Premiership game with Aston Villa – when grabbing a goal from a fiery scramble in the six-yard box. Now established as a firm favourite at the club, he is sure to be a key figure in their immediate future.

Watford (From trainee on 7/2/87) FL 23+9/2 FLC 4+1 FAC 9 Others 4+1
Norwich C (£175,000 on 18/7/89) FL 66+5/10 FLC 7/1 FAC 4 Others 5+1/2
Blackburn Rov (£500,000 on 12/2/92) F/PL 239+7/25 FLC 24+1/2 FAC 15+2/4 Others 12
Tottenham H (£3,800,000 on 5/2/99) P/FL 12+2/2 FAC 4/1

SHIELDS Anthony (Tony) Gerald
Born: Londonderry, 4 June 1980
Height: 5'7" Weight: 10.10

A product of Peterborough's highly successful youth policy, who made his league debut as a sub in the final game of 1997-98, Tony signed pro forms during the summer, and following some impressive displays with the reserves, made his first league start last March against Mansfield at London Road. Never shirking a tackle, the diminutive midfielder battled away non stop to eventually hold his place in the side, showing good touches and a fine eye for the telling pass to match his hard work. Is expected to make it big in the game.

Peterborough U (From trainee on 6/7/98) FL 6+4

SHILTON Samuel (Sam) Roger
Born: Nottingham, 21 July 1978
Height: 5'10" Weight: 11.6

The son of Peter, the once great England 'keeper, Sam is a left-sided Coventry midfield player who is tipped for a bright future. A regular in the reserves, he made only two starts for the senior side, at Charlton and at Southend, but also made six appearances from the bench. Although his crosses created two of the goals at Southend, Steve Froggatt's arrival put question marks over Sam's immediate future.

Plymouth Arg (Trainee) FL 1+2 FAC 0+1
Coventry C (£12,500 on 31/10/95) PL 3+4 FLC 1+1 FAC 0+1

SHIPPERLEY Neil Jason
Born: Chatham, 30 October 1974
Height: 6'1" Weight: 13.12
International Honours: E: U21-7

A tall, powerful striker, and the son of Dave who played for Charlton, Gillingham and Reading in the 1970s, Neil started last season for Crystal Palace six games into the campaign, scoring in a 1-1 draw at Stockport, before being surprisingly sold to Nottingham Forest towards the end of September against his manager Terry Venables' wishes. Renewing his acquaintances with Dave Bassett, his former manager at Palace, he proved to be quite a handful for defenders, being good in the air and with the ball at his feet, but forced out through injury in mid season did his game no good at all. However, in scoring just one goal throughout the campaign, in a 3-1 win at Wimbledon, does not tell the true picture of all his efforts as a target man that came to no avail. Stop Press: Was reported to have signed for Barnsley for £700,000 in early July.

Chelsea (From trainee on 24/9/92) PL 26+11/7 FLC 4+2/1 FAC 3/1 Others 2
Watford (Loaned on 7/12/94) FL 5+1/1
Southampton (£1,250,000 on 6/1/95) PL 65+1/11 FLC 5+1/2 FAC 10/5
Crystal Palace (£1,000,000 on 25/10/96) F/PL 49+12/20 FLC 3 FAC 2 Others 3/1
Nottingham F (£1,500,000 on 22/9/98) PL 12+8/1 FAC 1

SHORE James (Jamie) Andrew
Born: Bristol, 1 September 1977
Height: 5'9" Weight: 11.0
International Honours: E: Yth

A former England U16 international, this creative midfielder returned to his home-town club, Bristol Rovers, in the 1998 close season, after spending four years at Norwich. Having sustained a serious knee injury, which meant that he had been out of action for almost 18 months, Jamie scored a spectacular first league goal in an impressive 1-0 victory over Bournemouth on 3 October at the Memorial Stadium. He then followed that up with his second goal, at Notts County, after coming on as a substitute. Sent off twice in his first ten appearances for Rovers, he received a four-match ban, but his first season in league football proved what a very promising player the club had secured.

Norwich C (From trainee on 1/9/94)
Bristol Rov (Free on 28/7/98) FL 18+6/2 FAC 3+1/2 Others 1

SHORT Christian (Chris) Mark
Born: Munster, Germany, 9 May 1970
Height: 5'10" Weight: 12.2
Club Honours: AIC '95

Out of contract at Sheffield United during the summer of 1998, he moved to Stoke in time for the new season, but following a tremendous start, when the fans quickly took the pacy defender to their hearts, Chris' health caused worry to the staff. He seemed to lack stamina, having collapsed after being taken off at Craven Cottage. Given oxygen in the dugout there were real concerns for the future, but a change of diet was prescribed and for a time things improved. Unfortunately, by March, a series of muscle injuries and further health worries had resurfaced, and it must be hoped that this sound right back, who can be used in central defence if required, comes back good as new.

Scarborough (Free from Pickering T on 11/7/88) FL 42+1/1 FLC 5 FAC 1 Others 3+1
Notts Co (£100,000 on 5/9/90) FL 77+17/2 FLC 7 FAC 4+1 Others 8+1/1
Huddersfield T (Loaned on 23/12/94) FL 6 Others 1
Sheffield U ((Signed on 29/12/95) FL 40+4 FLC 3+1 FAC 7 Others 1+1
Stoke C (Free on 2/7/98) FL 19+2 FLC 2

SHORT Craig Jonathan
Born: Bridlington, 25 June 1968
Height: 6'1" Weight: 13.8

A tall, commanding centre half with the ability to bring the ball out of defence like a continental sweeper, Craig enjoyed another consistent season at Everton in 1998-99. Dogged earlier in his career by a lack of confidence, his self belief continued to grow at Goodison, and he was rewarded when he was named captain on several occasions. Unfortunate to suffer a torn calf muscle that stole a large chunk from his campaign, he returned as good as new to organise the club's successful run-in to avoid relegation, prior to signing a long-term deal tying him to Goodison in the summer.

Scarborough (Free from Pickering T on 15/10/87) FL 61+2/7 FLC 6 FAC 2 Others 7/1
Notts Co (£100,000 on 27/7/89) FL 128/6 FLC 6/1 FAC 8/1 Others 16/2
Derby Co (£2,500,000 on 18/9/92) FL 118/9 FLC 11 FAC 7/4 Others 7
Everton (£2,700,000 on 18/7/95) PL 90+9/4 FLC 7 FAC 4 Others 3

SHOWLER Paul
Born: Doncaster, 10 October 1966
Height: 5'7" Weight: 11.6
International Honours: E: SP-2
Despite having made just one subs' appearance for Luton in 1997-98, being plagued by injury, Paul was expected to be back in action early in 1998-99, but unfortunately sustained another injury when under consideration for a return to the first team. Sidelined again, the left-sided midfielder eventually came back in December for three games before dropping out of selection yet again and being released during the summer. Nicknamed "PC", due to him once being a policeman, at his best he attacked the full back to get dangerous crosses in to the front men.
Barnet (Free from Altrincham on 15/8/91) FL 69+2/12 FLC 2 FAC 3+1/1 Others 7
Bradford C (Free on 4/8/93) FL 72+16/15 FLC 8+1/5 FAC 6/2 Others 4+1
Luton T (£50,000 on 19/8/96) FL 23+4/6 FLC 3+1 FAC 3 Others 1+1

SHUTT Carl Steven
Born: Sheffield, 10 October 1961
Height: 5'10" Weight: 12.10
Club Honours: Div 2 '90; Div 1 '92
This greatly experienced striker, turned midfielder, had little opportunity to show his skills at Darlington in 1998-99, his second full season with the club, as he made only eight starts with the same number of games as a substitute. Although he managed to find the net twice, while operating wide on the right, he was released at the end of the campaign.
Sheffield Wed (Free from Spalding on 13/5/85) FL 36+4/16 FLC 3/1 FAC 4+1/4
Bristol C (£55,000 on 30/10/87) FL 39+7/10 FLC 5+2/4 FAC 7+1/4 Others 10+1/4
Leeds U (£50,000 on 23/3/89) F/PL 46+33/17 FLC 6+2/2 FAC 10/1 Others 4+5/4
Birmingham C (£50,000 on 23/8/93) FL 18+8/4 FLC 3
Manchester C (Loaned on 31/12/93) PL 5+1
Bradford C (£75,000 on 11/8/94) FL 60+28/15 FLC 8+2/1 FAC 3+2 Others 5+2/1
Darlington (Signed on 27/3/97) FL 28+25/9 FLC 2+2 FAC 1+1

SHUTTLEWORTH Barry
Born: Accrington, 9 July 1977
Height: 5'8" Weight: 11.0
Released by Rotherham during the 1998 close season, and signing for Blackpool, Barry was soon given a run in the side at left back, when standing in for the injured John Hills, until injuries restricted his appearances in the second half of the campaign. Scored his first ever senior goal in the 1-0 home league win against Notts County.
Bury (From trainee on 5/7/95)
Rotherham U (Free on 1/8/97) FAC 0+1 Others 1
Blackpool (Free on 7/8/98) FL 12+2/1 FLC 2 FAC 1

SIGURDSSON Larus Orri
Born: Akureyri, Iceland, 4 June 1973
Height: 6'0" Weight: 13.11
International Honours: Iceland: 23
Still a regular in the Iceland first team, "Siggie" remained very popular with the Stoke public, and with more protection in a three-man central defence had a good season in 1998-99. Although good in the air, and a mean tackler, his distribution is still the part of the game where he can improve even further. Is the cousin of the former City midfielder, Toddy Orlygsson.
Stoke C (£150,000 from Thor on 21/10/94) FL 194+1/6 FLC 13 FAC 6+1 Others 6

SIMB Jean-Pierre
Born: Paris, France, 4 September 1974
Height: 6'0" Weight: 12.0
Initially signed on non-contract forms from Paris Red Star last March, this French midfielder, cum striker, is arguably unlike any other player to have appeared in Torquay's colours. With a "Paulo Wanchope" like mixture of brilliant close control and unorthodoxy, he proved a big hit with the Plainmoor faithful, but the one-year contract he earned still represents a big gamble in the hurly-burly of Division Three. Made his debut in a 3-0 home win over Hartlepool and, occasionally used from the bench as well as starting, he opened his scoring account against Rotherham.
Torquay U (Free from Paris Red Star on 19/3/99) FL 3+6/1

Amara Simba

SIMBA Amara Sylla
Born: Paris, France, 23 December 1961
Height: 6'1" Weight: 11.8
International Honours: France: 3
Having joined Leyton Orient on a free transfer from Leon in Mexico last October, Amara, a former French international, showed his international class, and became an instant hit with the fans with his ability to control the ball and run at defenders with ease. A quality front man, he has two great feet, is powerful in the air, and at Third Division level what more do you want? Finishing the campaign as leading scorer, he scored on his debut in a 2-0 home win over Exeter, and plundered braces against Chester, Scarborough, Shrewsbury, and Barnet, the last three coming in the space of five games. Out of contract during the summer, at the time of going to press the club had offered him terms of re-engagement.
Leyton Orient (Free from Leon on 7/10/98) FL 19+5/10 FAC 3+2/1 Others 3

SIMONSEN Steven (Steve) Preben
Born: South Shields, 3 April 1979
Height: 6'3" Weight: 13.2
International Honours: E: U21-4; Yth
Having started last season in nine of Tranmere's first 11 games, the promising young 'keeper continued to attract attention from the bigger clubs and eventually moved to nearby Everton towards the end of September. Although he has yet to appear for the Toffees, in time he may become the most expensive number one in the country, the eventual transfer fee possibly reaching £3.3 million dependant on appearances and international honours. With courage, athleticism, uncanny positional ability, and excellent distribution skills, despite the fact that he was unable at times to even claim a regular reserve spot, it is almost certain that he will be challenging Thomas Myhre strongly in 1999-2000. Continued to play for the England U21 side, making three appearances.
Tranmere Rov (From trainee on 9/10/96) FL 35 FLC 4 FAC 3
Everton (£3,300,000 on 23/9/98)

SIMPKINS Michael James
Born: Sheffield, 28 November 1978
Height: 6'1" Weight: 12.0
Michael joined Chesterfield in March 1998 from Sheffield Wednesday, after graduating to the professional ranks as a trainee. Having made steady progress through the reserves in 1998-99, he made his first-team debut in the Spireites' last match of the season, at Wigan, and although a central defender he played in a midfield role on the left – his natural side– and caught the eye with some fine crosses and well-timed tackles.
Sheffield Wed (From trainee on 4/7/97)
Chesterfield (Free on 26/3/98) FL 0+1

SIMPSON Fitzroy
Born: Bradford on Avon, 26 February 1970
Height: 5'8" Weight: 12.0
International Honours: Jamaica: 22
The former Swindon and Manchester City defender coped extremely well with no break from football following last year's World Cup, and played virtually the whole of last season for Portsmouth. A tough-tackling defender, who can also play in midfield, he has pace and stamina, and is not afraid to shoot from distance, scoring an excellent 30-yard free kick in an important home game versus Stockport. Strong in physical and mental ability, he shows a fiery temper at times, which can spoil his natural all-round skills, but he is a maturing footballer who should become a real asset to Pompey.

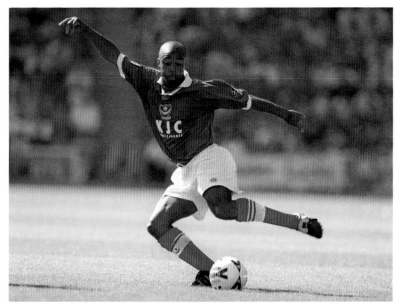

Fitzroy Simpson

Swindon T (From trainee on 6/7/88) FL 78+27/9 FLC 15+2/1 FAC 2+1 Others 3+2
Manchester C (£500,000 on 6/3/92) ßL 58+13/4 FLC 5+1 FAC 4+1
Bristol C (Loaned on 16/9/94) FL 4
Portsmouth (£200,000 on 17/8/95) FL 122+9/10 FLC 10 FAC 8

SIMPSON Michael

Born: Nottingham, 28 February 1974
Height: 5'9" Weight: 10.8
Club Honours: AIC '95
Skilful and industrious midfielder who asked for a transfer after being told by the Wycombe manager, Neil Smillie, at the start of last season, that he did not feature in his plans. As the team results went from bad to worse, Michael was recalled to the side in October, scoring with a wonderful 25-yard kick against Macclesfield, and scored again two games later to become the influential player the fans always knew he was. He was virtually ever present from then on, and played a major contribution in the fight against relegation. The new manager, Lawrie Sanchez, experimented successfully by pushing him up wide right against Burnley at home, and in addition to his impressive wing play he also scored a goal. Accepted a two-year contract near the end of the campaign.
Notts Co (From trainee on 1/7/92) FL 39+10/3 FLC 4+1 FAC 2+1 Others 7+3
Plymouth Arg (Loaned on 4/10/96) FL 10+2
Wycombe W (£50,000 on 5/12/96) FL 57+17/5 FLC 2 FAC 3+2 Others 4

SIMPSON Paul David

Born: Carlisle, 26 July 1966
Height: 5'6" Weight: 11.10
International Honours: E: U21-5; Yth
The left-sided Wolves' midfielder appeared at Barnet in the second match of 1998-99, but then had difficulty even getting on the bench. This was despite scoring twice in two successive reserve outings. Not surprisingly, he went on loan to Walsall during September, the first of two spells there, scoring once and making a good impression. Back at Molineux, Paul was still capable of producing good long-range shooting, as well as getting dangerous centres in. His second start of the season came in February, and it took him just four minutes to score against Port Vale, before setting up two other goals. However, after a short run in the team he was dropped again before returning at Birmingham, and scoring at Bradford on the final day. Was released during the summer.
Manchester C (From apprentice on 4/8/83) FL 99+22/18 FLC 10+1/2 FAC 10+2/4 Others 8+3
Oxford U (£200,000 on 31/10/88) FL 138+6/43 FLC 10/3 FAC 9/2 Others 5/2
Derby Co (£500,000 on 20/2/92) P/FL 134+52/48 FLC 12+3/6 FAC 4+4/1 Others 14+2/2
Sheffield U (Loaned on 6/12/96) FL 2+4
Wolverhampton W (£75,000 on 10/10/97) FL 31+8/6 FLC 1 FAC 2+3
Walsall (Loaned on 17/9/98) FL 4/1
Walsall (Loaned on 11/12/98) FL 6

SIMPSON Phillip (Phil) Mark

Born: Lambeth, 18 October 1969
Height: 5'8" Weight: 11.9
Began 1998-99 as an integral part of Barnet's midfield line-up, but as the season progressed he found his first-team opportunities limited. In fact, the Bees' all-action midfielder started the first three games of the campaign, but gradually became utilised in the role of substitute. Having remarkable close control, which can wrong foot any defender in the Third Division, he showed that he could read the game very well, and managed to record numerous interceptions as a result of anticipating opponent's passes. Placed on the transfer list at his own request in late 1998, Phil eventually enjoyed a loan stint at Farnborough before joining fellow Conference outfit, Yeovil, on a permanent basis in early February. His final appearance for Barnet, as a substitute in the game at Swansea in December, was a fitting farewell because, during the previous campaign, he had scored the "Goal of the Year" with an effort from the half-way line at the Vetch Field, and he left the Underhill faithful with fond memories.
Barnet (Signed from Stevenage Borough on 27/10/95) FL 91+9/7 FLC 8/2 FAC 3+2/1 Others 3+1

SINCLAIR Frank Mohammed

Born: Lambeth, 3 December 1971
Height: 5'9" Weight: 12.9
Club Honours: FAC '97; FLC '98
International Honours: Jamaica: 9
A right-footed Leicester wing back or central defender, signed from Chelsea for a club record fee in August 1998, Frank immediately impressed with his pace and power, though was inclined to pick up a succession of yellow cards, a trait which eventually culminated in an appearance before the disciplinary committee in April. Two of those cards also resulted in one of the red variety at Highfield Road. Scored a high-class goal against Birmingham in the FA Cup, finishing off a passing movement that scythed through the Blues' defence. Made the headlines on the day of the Worthington Cup final by being omitted from the squad for turning up late to the team meeting the previous evening, but returned immediately afterwards to put in a string of competent performances.
Chelsea (From trainee on 17/5/90) F/PL 163+6/7 FLC 17+1/2 FAC 18/1 Others 13/3
West Bromwich A (Loaned on 12/12/91) FL 6/1
Leicester C (£2,000,000 on 14/8/98) PL 30+1/1 FLC 6 FAC 2/1

Frank Sinclair

Trevor Sinclair

SINCLAIR Trevor Lloyd
Born: Dulwich, 2 March 1973
Height: 5'10" Weight: 12.10
International Honours: E: B-1; U21-14; Yth
In 1998-99, Trevor was often asked to play a more versatile wing-back role at West Ham, sometimes at the expense of being further up the pitch where he could use his lightning pace to damage opposing defences. Very consistent – missing just two games due to injury – wherever he was asked to perform, and a player who is on the verge of full international honours, he had a superb game against Spurs in November when he scored twice in a 2-1 home win. He also scored another brace in a 4-0 victory over Middlesbrough on the final day of the campaign, a result which saw the Hammers finish fifth in the Premiership. Able to play through the middle or down either flank, not only has he the pace, which makes him difficult to dispossess when in full flow, but he also has the skill to match; his versatility giving the club quite a few options.
Blackpool (From trainee on 21/8/90) FL 84+28/15 FLC 8 FAC 6+1 Others 8+5/1
Queens Park R (£750,000 on 12/8/93) P/FL 162+5/16 FLC 13/3 FAC 10/2
West Ham U (£2,300,000 + on 30/1/98) PL 50/14 FLC 2 FAC 2

SINNOTT Lee
Born: Pelsall, 12 July 1965
Height: 6'1" Weight: 13.7
International Honours: E: U21-1; Yth
Although he started last season in Oldham's opening four games, Lee soon lost out in the pecking order to Shaun Garnett and Stuart Thom, and ended the campaign on the free transfer list, before being released in the summer. A centre back who attacks the ball at both ends of the park, but now in latter stages of an excellent career, he was still dependable when called upon, and appeared not to have lost his powers of distribution. His experience means that he can read a game from cover to cover.
Walsall (From apprentice on 16/11/82) FL 40/2 FLC 3 FAC 4

Watford (£100,000 on 15/9/83) FL 71+7/2 FLC 6 FAC 11
Bradford C (£130,000 on 23/7/87) FL 173/6 FLC 19 FAC 9 Others 12/1
Crystal Palace (£300,000 on 8/8/91) F/PL 53+2 FLC 9+1 FAC 1 Others 2
Bradford C (£50,000 on 9/12/93) FL 34/1 FLC 2 FAC 2 Others 2
Huddersfield T (£105,000 on 23/12/94) FL 86+1/1 FLC 6 FAC 4 Others 3
Oldham Ath (£30,000 + on 7/7/97) FL 25+6 FLC 3 FAC 1
Bradford C (Loaned on 26/3/98) FL 7

SINTON Andrew (Andy)
Born: Cramlington, 19 March 1966
Height: 5'8" Weight: 11.5
Club Honours: FLC '99
International Honours: E: 12; B-3; Sch
An experienced midfielder who has been a valuable member of the Tottenham squad, Andy likes nothing better than to get forward with the ball at his feet, his highlight of last season being a superb individual goal in the FA Cup fourth-round replay at home to Wimbledon in February. Having won the ball deep into his own half, the pacy winger drove down the left, dropping his shoulder to pass the midfield challenges and, with his eye set firmly on goal, drove a cracking strike high into the top right-hand corner to send Spurs on their way to the 3-0 victory, which set up a fifth-round tie with Leeds. He also held his own when asked to play at left back in support of David Ginola, before being granted a free transfer during the summer. With his high level of personal fitness and enthusiasm, he looks certain to generate interest from a host of clubs. Stop Press: Moved to Wolves on 6 July.
Cambridge U (From apprentice on 13/4/83) FL 90+3/13 FLC 6/1 FAC 3 Others 2/1
Brentford (£25,000 on 13/12/85) FL 149/28 FLC 8/3 FAC 11/1 Others 14/2
Queens Park R (£350,000 on 23/3/89) F/PL 160/22 FLC 14 FAC 13/2 Others 3/1
Sheffield Wed (£2,750,000 on 19/8/93) PL 54+6/3 FLC 13 FAC 5
Tottenham H (£1,500,000 on 23/1/96) PL 66+17/6 FLC 6+3 FAC 4+4/1

SISSON Michael Anthony
Born: Sutton in Ashfield, 24 November 1978
Height: 5'9" Weight: 10.10
Another local youngster who has found his way into the Mansfield first team from the YTS ranks, the midfielder made only one brief appearance in 1998-99, again from the bench, but was not out of place and will surely be called on again before too long. Neat and tidy with his passing game, and strong in the tackle, his workrate allows him to close the opposition down quickly.
Mansfield T (From trainee on 27/1/98) FL 0+2

SKELTON Aaron Matthew
Born: Welwyn Garden City, 22 November 1974
Height: 5'11" Weight: 12.6
Aaron had a season disturbed by injury, when he managed only seven full games for Colchester in the early spring before breaking his leg in a crucial bottom-of-the-table clash at Wycombe last March. It is

surely no coincidence that those seven games were part of United's best unbeaten run of the campaign, when his defensive class helped shore up the rearguard, playing alongside David Greene and Richard Wilkins as part of a three-man back line. Despite being out of contract during the summer, U's fans are hoping to see much more of him during the coming term.
Luton T (From trainee on 16/12/92) FL 5+3 FLC 0+1 FAC 2 Others 2
Colchester U (Free on 3/7/97) FL 44+4/7 FLC 1 FAC 3+1 Others 3+1

SKELTON Gavin Richard
Born: Carlisle, 27 March 1981
Height: 5'9" Weight: 11.0
Still a trainee, Gavin was another young Carlisle prospect who was given an opportunity by the club, when coming off the bench in the Worthington Cup-tie at Tranmere last August. On the night he did a reasonable job in replacing the injured Richard Prokas for nearly an hour, and looks to have a successful career in the game.
Carlisle U (From trainee on 19/5/99) FLC 0+1

SKINNER Craig Richard
Born: Heywood, 21 October 1970
Height: 5'9" Weight: 11.6
Not involved at Wrexham on too many occasions last season, having to compete with Martyn Chalk, Terry Cooke (loan), and Robin Gibson for the right-wing spot. Despite featuring a number of times earlier on he was not helped when undergoing a hernia operation halfway into the term. Although making a good recovery, Craig could not force his way into the side, and with transfer deadline day approaching he accepted a three-year contract at York. An industrious midfielder, injury prevented him from making an immediate impact at Bootham Crescent, but he is sure to feature strongly in 1999-2000 as City look to play their way out of the Third Division.
Blackburn Rov (From trainee on 13/6/89) FL 11+5 FLC 0+1 FAC 1 Others 3/1
Plymouth Arg (Signed on 21/8/92) FL 42+11/4 FLC 4 FAC 5+2/1 Others 3+1
Wrexham (£50,000 on 21/7/95) FL 70+17/10 FLC 3+3/1 FAC 8+1 Others 3+1
York C (£20,000 on 25/3/99) FL 3+2

SLADE Steven (Steve) Anthony
Born: Hackney, 6 October 1975
Height: 6'0" Weight: 11.2
International Honours: E: U21-4
A forward who is happier on the wing, but can also play in the centre of attack, he started last season on Queens Park Rangers' substitutes' bench. However, when coming on, usually late in a game, he often made an impact on the left-hand side of the attack and eventually progressed to the starting line-up. Unfortunately, he soon lost his place and was unable to get back before April. Hard running and good in the air, his excellent movement both on and off the ball creates chances for others.
Tottenham H (From trainee on 1/7/94) PL 1+4 FLC 0+1 FAC 0+2
Queens Park R (£350,000 on 12/7/96) FL 24+35/5 FLC 3+3/1 FAC 1+2
Brentford (Loaned on 13/2/97) FL 4

SMALL Bryan
Born: Birmingham, 15 November 1971
Height: 5'9" Weight: 11.9
International Honours: E: U21-12; Yth
An overlapping left-sided wing back, Bryan joined Stoke on a free transfer from Bury during the 1998 close season, being known to Brian Little from their time at Villa together. The 5-3-2 style and the wing backs saw Stoke take all before them in the first part of the campaign, but the newcomer was one of the players who appeared to lose confidence in January and February when results faltered. Although he has lost a little of his pace, he is still a fine wing back on his day, with strength and tenacity to spare.
Aston Villa (From trainee on 9/7/90) F/PL 31+5 FLC 2 FAC 2+1 Others 4
Birmingham C (Loaned on 9/9/94) FL 3
Bolton W (Free on 20/3/96) F/PL 11+1 FLC 1 FAC 3
Luton T (Loaned on 8/9/97) FL 15
Bradford C (Loaned on 19/12/97) FL 5
Bury (Free on 30/1/98) FL 18/1
Stoke C (Free on 14/7/98) FL 35+2 FLC 2 FAC 2 Others 2

SMART Allan Andrew Colin
Born: Perth, 8 July 1974
Height: 6'2" Weight: 12.10
Club Honours: AMC '97
An orthodox striker signed for a bargain fee from Carlisle in the summer of 1998, Allan soon impressed at Watford in 1998-99 with his honesty and effort, and proved an effective foil to his various striking partners. He scored a memorable first goal for the club at Sunderland, and although his form dipped a little towards the end of the season he passed the 100 league appearances mark. His only serious black mark came when he was sent off at home to Tranmere.
Preston NE (£15,000 from Caledonian Thistle on 22/11/94) FL 17+4/6 FAC 2/1 Others 1+1
Carlisle U (Loaned on 24/11/95) FL 3+1
Northampton T (Loaned on 13/9/96) FL 1
Carlisle U (Signed on 9/10/96) FL 41+3/17 FLC 1/1 FAC 4 Others 4+1
Watford (£75,000 + on 2/7/98) FL 34+1/7 FLC 0+1 FAC 1 Others 0+3/1

SMEETS Jorg
Born: Amsterdam, Holland, 5 November 1970
Height: 5'6" Weight: 10.4
Possessing the smallest feet in the Football League with a shoe size of 4¹/₂, Jorg made just three substitute's appearances for Wigan during last season, his final appearance seeing him miss a penalty against Notts County in a penalty shoot-out in the FA Cup. With opportunities obviously limited, he joined Chester on loan during transfer deadline week and made his debut against Plymouth at the Deva. With a liking to play just behind the forwards, and showing some nice touches, he was unable to show his full potential as injuries limited him to just two further subs' appearances before he returned to the Latics. Jorg returned to Holland after his contract was cancelled by mutual consent at the end of the campaign.
Wigan Ath (£100,000 from Heracles on 3/10/97) FL 10+14/3 FLC 0+1 FAC 1+1 Others 3
Chester C (Loaned on 25/3/99) FL 1+2

SMITH Alan
Born: Wakefield, 28 October 1980
Height: 5'9" Weight: 11.10
International Honours: E: Yth
Every so often, reality surpasses wildest dreams. Just three weeks after his 18th birthday, Alan came on as a substitute for Leeds and with his first touch in senior football, struck in front of the Anfield Kop, to level the scores, in a game which United went on to win 3-1 last November. And all this when he would have been in the Middle East if an U18 tour had not been called off. The fairytale continued. The following week he came off the bench for his home debut and scored again, this time in the 4-1 victory over Charlton. He then went on to maintain his first-team squad place, averaging nearly a goal every other game, including substitute appearances, his skill and ability belying his inexperience. In the home victory over Middlesbrough, a well executed "stepover" dummy completely fooled Gary Pallister and Colin Cooper in the six yard box, which almost resulted in a second goal of the game for him. The media then exploded with suggested potential that he could be someone special. To Leeds' supporters, he bears an uncanny resemblance to ex-hero, Alan "Sniffer" Clarke, with a deadly eye for goal, being able to score with both feet, and having a real aggression and desire, which is unusual in someone of slight stature. Undoubtedly, he is a real prospect for the future.
Leeds U (From trainee on 26/3/98) PL 15+7/7 FAC 2+2/2

Alan Smith

SMITH Alexander (Alex) Philip
Born: Liverpool, 15 February 1976
Height: 5'7" Weight: 11.10
Released by Huddersfield, Alex joined Chester during the 1998 close season, and was to prove to be one of the most talented players to play for the club in recent years,

putting in some tremendous performances on the left of City's midfield and joining the attack at every opportunity. Having the ability to take on players, he will be remembered for his tremendous run from within his own half to set up Mike Conroy's goal in the televised game against Brighton at the Deva. Despite all that, and to the disappointment of the fans, he was transferred to Port Vale on transfer deadline day to help ease the club's precarious financial situation. Having earlier run Vale ragged in a Worthington Cup-tie, he became the club's 43rd player when he came on at Bristol City. And, in adapting well to the higher grade of football, he should be one to watch out for this time round.
Everton (From trainee on 1/7/94)
Swindon T (Free on 12/1/96) FL 17+14/1
Huddersfield T (Free on 6/2/98) FL 4+2
Chester C (Free on 8/7/98) FL 32/2 FLC 4/1 Others 1
Port Vale (£75,000 on 25/3/98) FL 7+1

SMITH Carl Paul
Born: Sheffield, 15 January 1979
Height: 5'7" Weight: 11.4
With only one substitute appearance under his belt prior to last season, Carl was soon in favour with the new manager, Stan Ternent. Mainly a holding player in midfield, he never let the side down but lost his place to new signing Rune Vindheim, and was later loaned out to a Greek club along with Colin Carr-Lawton.
Burnley (From trainee on 2/9/97) FL 5+6 FLC 1

SMITH David
Born: Stonehouse, 29 March 1968
Height: 5'8" Weight: 10.7
Club Honours: AMC '98
International Honours: E: U21-10
A hard and effective worker, who is able to operate on the left flank or in defence, David won the battle with Kingsley Black for his favoured position on Grimsby's left flank in 1998-99, his tally of league goals making him the Mariners' second highest scorer for the season. Without a doubt a valuable contribution, especially in view of the team's difficulties in that department, his pace also caused opponents problems on the break.
Coventry C (From apprentice on 7/7/86) ßL 144+10/19 FLC 17 FAC 6 Others 4+1
Bournemouth (Loaned on 8/1/93) FL 1
Birmingham C (Signed on 12/3/93) FL 35+3/3 FLC 4 FAC 0+1 Others 1
West Bromwich A (£90,000 on 31/1/94) FL 82+20/2 FLC 4+2 FAC 1+3 Others 4+1
Grimsby T (£200,000 on 16/1/98) FL 47+1/6 FLC 2+2 FAC 2 Others 7/1

SMITH David (Dave) Christopher
Born: Liverpool, 26 December 1970
Height: 5'9" Weight: 12.9
A midfield grafter who covered more for others at Oxford, rather than making lots of runs into the box himself, he lost his place on the arrival of Paul Tait, and moved to Stockport last February, having made nearly 200 league appearances for the U's. His introduction at Edgeley Park coincided with an upturn in the side's fortunes, with just two defeats in 12 games, and while not a

recognised goalscorer he was quick to open his County scoring account with a super strike in a 1-1 draw against Port Vale in March. Performing well, his steadying influence provided an excellent link between defence and attack.

Norwich C (From trainee on 4/7/89) F/PL 13+5 FAC 2+1 Others 1+1
Oxford U (£100,000 on 5/7/94) FL 193+5/2 FLC 23+1/1 FAC 9+1 Others 7
Stockport Co (Free on 4/2/99) FL 17/1

SMITH Dean

Born: West Bromwich, 19 March 1971
Height: 6'1" Weight: 12.10

As Leyton Orient's club captain and centre back, he is an excellent choice, being a natural leader, and missed very few games in 1998-99, once again scoring valuable goals – ten to be precise. Strong on the ground and in aerial confrontations, and a difficult player to pass, he can also play further forward in central midfield if required. Always dangerous at set plays, creating confusion in opponents' penalty areas, he was the club's second highest goalscorer during a season that saw the O's reach Wembley to contest the play-off final, losing 1-0 at the hands of Scunthorpe. Having scored one of the penalties that took the side there, although an obvious disappointment, come the new term he will be looking to put the record straight.

Walsall (From trainee on 1/7/89) FL 137+5/2 FLC 10 FAC 4 Others 10
Hereford U (£75,000 on 17/6/94) FL 116+1/19 FLC 10/3 FAC 7 Others 11+1/4
Leyton Orient (£42,500 on 16/6/97) FL 80/18 FLC 8 FAC 7/2 Others 5

SMITH James (Jamie) Jade Anthony

Born: Birmingham, 17 September 1974
Height: 5'7" Weight: 11.4

This highly popular right back became another casualty of the financial difficulties suffered by his club, Crystal Palace, when they loaned him to Fulham last March in an effort to cut the wage bill. Having performed with great consistency at Selhurst throughout 1998-99, Jamie immediately took over the right-wing-back berth at Craven Cottage for the remainder of the campaign. He certainly fitted in well, his sorties down the flank and accurate crosses, having the Fulham fans hoping that a permanent transfer could be secured during the summer. Scored his first goal in the league with a powerful low drive in a 2-2 draw at Walsall, in the penultimate game.

Wolverhampton W (From trainee on 7/6/93) FL 81+6 FLC 10+1 FAC 2 Others 4/1
Crystal Palace (Signed on 22/10/97) P/FL 41+3 FLC 3 FAC 5
Fulham (Loaned on 25/3/99) FL 9/1

SMITH Jason Leslie

Born: Bromsgrove, 6 September 1974
Height: 6'3" Weight: 13.7
International Honours: E: Sch

Signed from non-league Tiverton Town prior to the start of last season, Jason forged a good partnership with Matthew Bound in the centre of Swansea's defence. With each passing game, the Swans appeared to have uncovered another bargain as he became a regular in their Third Division line-up throughout the campaign. Strong in aerial challenges, and deceptively quick on the ground for a big man, he is also a danger at set-piece plays.

Coventry C (Signed from Tiverton T on 5/7/93) (Free to Tiverton T on 15/7/95)
Swansea C (£10,000 on 1/7/98) FL 42/4 FLC 2 FAC 4/1 Others 3/1

SMITH Jeffrey (Jeff)

Born: Middlesbrough, 28 June 1980
Height: 5'10" Weight: 11.1

Although starting just three first-team games, he was the most successful of Hartlepool's seven young first-year professionals signed for 1998-99. A left-sided player, who can play in attack or defence, he made his debut with a brief substitute appearance before getting a couple of senior opportunities at left back due to an injury to Ian Clark. He did not let the club down, but it was apparent that he will need to become more physically stronger if he is to make the grade.

Hartlepool U (From trainee on 3/7/98) FL 2+1 Others 1

SMITH Mark Jonathan

Born: Bristol, 13 September 1979
Height: 5'11" Weight: 11.8

Mark is a Bristol Rovers' central defender with pace, who is at his best as a man marker, while his positional play has improved, along with his distribution from defence. Having experienced first-team football when making his league debut at Gillingham in 1998-99, and winning the "Man of the Match" award for his splendid performance, the match itself was notable for events in injury time, as two of his team mates and two Gillingham players were sent off. Despite not returning to the starting line-up in the last half of the season, he remains a good prospect.

Bristol Rov (From trainee on 9/7/98) FL 11+3 FLC 1 FAC 2+1 Others 2

SMITH Martin Geoffrey

Born: Sunderland, 13 November 1974
Height: 5'11" Weight: 12.6
Club Honours: Div 1 '96
International Honours: E: U21-1; Sch

The left-sided striker is something of an enigma at the Stadium of Light. Undoubtedly one of the most gifted players on Sunderland's books, he played only a walk-on part as the club raced to the First Division title in 1998-99. Yet, when called upon, Martin showed his prowess in front of goal, scoring three in only four league starts, including two against Grimsby in October, one of which, a stunning left-foot volley was arguably the best strike seen to date at the Stadium of Light – the kind of effort few players would even attempt. Having stated that he needs regular first-team football, at the time of going to press he has yet to sign the new two-year deal offered to him by the club, and if he does decide to move on it will definitely be a case of what might have been.

Sunderland (From trainee on 9/9/92) P/FL 90+29/25 FLC 10+6/2 FAC 7+3/1

SMITH Neil James

Born: Lambeth, 30 September 1971
Height: 5'9" Weight: 12.12
Club Honours: FAYC '90; Div 2 '99

There were more skilful players in Fulham's championship side of 1998-99 but none who were more committed than Neil. With so many experienced midfielders in the squad, he could not force his way into the team until October, but he kept putting in good performances with the reserves, and once in the first-team squad he was rarely out of it. Although he could have gone to Wycombe with Matty Lawrence early in the season, he preferred to try to win his place back, which was a big asset to the club. He also played a big part in the FA Cup, his selfless running and good tackling making him one of the stars at Old Trafford.

Tottenham H (From trainee on 24/7/90)
Gillingham (£40,000 on 17/10/91) FL 204+9/10 FLC 14+1/1 FAC 18/2 Others 7+1/2
Fulham (Signed on 4/7/97) FL 62+11/1 FLC 3+1 FAC 6+3/1 Others 1+1

SMITH Paul Antony

Born: Hastings, 25 January 1976
Height: 5'11" Weight: 11.7

A right-sided Lincoln winger with both skill and pace, Paul was a regular member of the Imps' starting line-up until last last January, before suffering a series of niggling injuries which kept him on the sidelines. His injury problems undoubtedly reduced his effectiveness, and he was only to offer glimpses of his best form in the second half of the campaign.

Nottingham F (£50,000 from Hastings T on 13/1/95)
Lincoln C (£30,000 on 17/10/97) FL 37+8/5 FLC 2 FAC 3 Others 2

SMITH Ian Paul

Born: Easington, 22 January 1976
Height: 6'0" Weight: 13.3

Fate has not been kind to this talented winger. Having missed most of Burnley's previous campaign with a succession of injuries, he began 1998-99 as first choice on the left, and showed occasional glimpses of his best before a recurrence of a knee injury in October kept him out for most of the season. Hopes were high that he would be fit for the coming term, and if he could recapture the form of a couple of years ago he should, in Stan Ternent's words, be as good as a new signing for the club.

Burnley (From trainee on 10/7/94) FL 52+22/4 FLC 3+1 FAC 4+1 Others 5

SMITH Paul William

Born: East Ham, 18 September 1971
Height: 5'11" Weight: 13.0

Once again, this time in 1998-99, Paul was Gillingham's most consistent player of the season, and missed just one league game through suspension when he accumulated five bookings, which rather annoyed him! Full of running and skill, and a clean tackler, he also got on the scoresheet on a few occasions. A ball-winning central mid-fielder, most of the team's moves stem from

his area of the pitch, and it would be difficult to imagine the Gills being without him.

Southend U (From trainee on 16/3/90) FL 18+2/1 Others 0+1
Brentford (Free on 6/8/93) FL 159/11 FLC 12/1 FAC 12/3 Others 15/2
Gillingham (Signed on 25/7/97) FL 91/9 FLC 4 FAC 3 Others 7/1

SMITH Peter (Pete) Edward
Born: Skelmersdale, 31 October 1980
Height: 6'0" Weight: 11.0
Still a trainee, but showing much promise in the Exeter youth team, Pete was elevated to the senior side and came off the bench for the final game of 1998-99, a home 2-1 win over Halifax. Hailing from Liverpool, and known as "Forrest Gump", he is a central midfielder who can play equally well either at centre half or as a sweeper, having a great engine, good vision, and neat passing skills. Voted by the staff as Exeter's "Young Player of the Year", he looks to be one to watch out for in 1999-2000.

Exeter C (Trainee) FL 0+1

SMITH Peter John
Born: Stone, 12 July 1969
Height: 6'1" Weight: 12.7
Brighton's right-wing back or winger. An entertaining player to watch who, with his ungainly running style, and long-legged tackling, cuts an instantly recognisable figure in the Third Division, being just as likely to whip in a match-winning cross as he was to mistime a tackle. A player who always gives his all, his enthusiasm will be missed as he was released at the end of 1998-99 after being transfer listed in November.

Brighton & Hove A (Free from Alma Swanley on 8/8/94) FL 122+18/4 FLC 10+2 FAC 6/1 Others 7+1

SMITH Peter Lee
Born: Rhyl, 18 September 1978
Height: 5'10" Weight: 10.8
International Honours: E: Yth; Sch
Another Crewe graduate from the FA School at Lilleshall, and capped by England at school and youth levels, after making his first start for the club in the final match of 1997-98 the skilful young forward was expected to break into the first team on a more regular basis last season. Although he started quite brightly, being involved in the opening four games, he was loaned to Macclesfield at the end of September, spending three months there in a bid to boost Town's strike rate and, at the same time, find his feet. That he did, hammering in a great goal at Preston. Then, with growing confidence, a few days later, he bent the ball inside the post against Burnley before ending his loan period with 13 starts and three goals. Unfortunately, for Macclesfield, their manager, Sammy McIlroy, who was hoping to sign him on a more permanent basis, was told politely that Peter's contract was being renewed, and that he was one for Alex's future, not Town's.

Crewe Alex (From trainee on 12/7/96) FL 1+10 FLC 3 FAC 0+1
Macclesfield T (Loaned on 25/9/98) FL 12/3 Others 1

SMITH Philip Anthony
Born: Wembley, 14 December 1979
Height: 6'1" Weight: 13.12
An up-and-coming youngster who signed a three-year professional contract last season, Phil was one of four goalkeepers that Millwall used last season because of injuries to Tony Roberts, Nigel Spink, and then Ben Roberts. Made his debut at Gillingham in December, in a difficult match which saw the Lions finish the game with nine men, and made a string of fine saves during the 1-1 draw before going on to make a further four appearances during the campaign. A good shot stopper, who stands up well, he will only get better when being in the same company as Nigel Spink and Ben Roberts.

Millwall (From trainee on 17/1/98) FL 5

SMITH Richard Geoffrey
Born: Lutterworth, 3 October 1970
Height: 6'0" Weight: 13.12
Undoubtedly the Grimsby success story of last season, when coming back from an appalling achilles heel injury which had kept him out of the game for 16 months, this classy central defender was able to return to the game showing that he had lost none of his ability. Together with Peter Handyside, Richard formed one of the most effective central defensive partnerships in the First Division, and it was this tightness at the back that enabled the Mariners to consolidate their league status. Another welcome sight was his ability to throw the ball into danger areas from the byline. Unfortunately, what appeared to be a recurrence of achilles heel trouble kept him out of the side during the run in, and it was hoped that the problem would be resolved during the summer.

Leicester C (From trainee on 15/12/88) F/PL 82+16/1 FLC 6/1 Others 12
Cambridge U (Loaned on 6/9/89) FL 4 FLC 1
Grimsby T (Loaned on 8/9/95) FL 8
Grimsby T (£50,000 on 11/3/96) FL 51+3 FLC 6 FAC 1

SMITH Gareth Shaun
Born: Leeds, 9 April 1971
Height: 5'10" Weight: 11.0
As one of Crewe's longest-serving players, he is someone who you can rely upon and, as the side's regular penalty taker, he despatched another three in 1998-99 as Alex successfully fought their way clear of the relegation zone. He also scored in the 3-1 home win over Portsmouth, a victory that ensured that the club would be playing First Division football again in 1999-2000. As the regular occupant of the left-back spot, and the captain, he has now played over 350 games for the club since arriving from non-league Emley back in 1991, and was an ever present last season. Always dangerous from set pieces, he gets forward well, has a good recovery rate, and is strong in the tackle.

Halifax T (From trainee on 1/7/89) FL 6+1 Others 1 (Free to Emley in May 1991)
Crewe Alex (Free on 31/12/91) FL 265+19/34 FLC 12+1/2 FAC 13+2/3 Others 19+2/3

SMITH Thomas (Tommy) William
Born: Hemel Hempstead, 22 May 1980
Height: 5'8" Weight: 11.4
International Honours: E: Yth
A Watford striker in his first full season with the club in 1998-99, Tommy is blessed with good control and an excellent turn of pace. Having pressed his first-team claims with a reserve hat trick against Norwich in December, he had the unusual distinction of scoring his first league goal before he had started a game, when coming on as a sub against Queens Park Rangers. His full debut, against Swindon, soon followed.

Watford (From trainee on 21/10/97) FL 3+6/2 FAC 0+1

SNEEKES Richard
Born: Amsterdam, Holland, 30 October 1968
Height: 5'11" Weight: 12.2
Richard played well within himself for most of the 1998-99 season, occupying a more deeper position at West Bromwich than normal, hence his lack of goals! However, he still managed to put in some excellent performances in the engine room, and was always seeking to create openings for his strikers. Mainly a right-sided player, he did most of his work in the centre of the field, spraying passes out to his wide men, and was still a big favourite with the fans.

Bolton W (£200,000 from Fortuna Sittard, via Ajax and Volendam, on 12/8/94) P/FL 51+4/7 FLC 11+1/3 FAC 2/1
West Bromwich A (£385,000 on 11/3/96) FL 127+13/25 FLC 9/1 FAC 4/2

SNIJDERS Mark Werner
Born: Alkmaar, Holland, 12 March 1972
Height: 6'2" Weight: 13.12
Port Vale central defender who was limited in 1998-99 to just a handful of appearances through a combination of injuries and being out of favour. He began the season in the team, but scored a spectacular own goal in the Worthington Cup at Chester before being dropped after a 3-0 home defeat by West Bromwich. Although an excellent passer of the ball, he is not a fan of the more physical nature of the English game compared to his native Dutch version.

Port Vale (Free from AZ Alkmaar on 8/9/97) FL 28+6/2 FLC 2 FAC 2

SODJE Efetobore (Efe)
Born: Greenwich, 5 October 1972
Height: 6'1" Weight: 12.0
Club Honours: GMVC '96
This big Macclesfield central defender, who wears a bandanna at the request of his mother who believes it will bring him luck, has a great turn of pace, is a tenacious tackler, and likes to get up for set pieces. He scored three times last season in such a manner, at Preston, and at home to Blackpool and Oldham, and attracted a host of scouts, with an offer from Bristol Rovers in December being rejected. A target of referees in 1998-99, at the time of going to press Town were looking for ways and means of holding on to him when his contract expires, before he became available

under the Bosman ruling during the summer. Stop Press: Was called up by Nigeria in early June for a three-nation tournament involving Croatia and South Korea.

Macclesfield T (£30,000 from Stevenage Borough on 11/7/97) FL 83/6 FLC 6 FAC 6/1 Others 1

Efe Sodje

SOLANO Nolberto (Nol) Albino
Born: Lima, Peru, 12 December 1974
Height: 5'8" Weight: 10.8
International Honours: Peru: 29

The first Peruvian to play in English football, signing for Newcastle from Boca Juniors at the start of last season, Nol is a subtly skilful player who is able to perform as an attacking wing back or as an orthodox winger on either flank, although he favours the right. His good, close control makes him a tricky man to face, and he skates over the ground surprisingly quickly. He also has a keen eye for goal, allied to a powerful shot, having scored over 50 times for Sporting Cristal in seven seasons, many of them direct from set pieces, for which he developed a reputation in South America. Contributing some important goals for Newcastle during the season, he is a regular for Peru, having first been capped at the age of 19. However, he agreed with the national manager that journeys back and forth between Europe and South America were overtaxing, so he would only play for his country in competitive games during the Premiership season. Quickly establishing a regular place in the United side, his contribution grew as the campaign progressed, and he came increasingly to terms with both life in the Premiership and the English weather. He had particularly good matches in the wins at Leeds, and at home to Derby, whilst his stunning free kick goal at home to Manchester United demonstrated

that his set-piece reputation was well deserved. He enjoys music and plays Peruvian Tumba drums and trumpet.

Newcastle U (£2,763,958 from Boca Juniors, via Cristal Alianza Lima, Sporting and Deportivo Municipal, on 17/8/98) PL 24+5/6 FLC 1 FAC 7 Others 1+1

SOLEY Stephen (Steve)
Born: Widnes, 22 April 1971
Height: 5'11" Weight: 12.8
International Honours: E: SP-1

A former bricklayer who was spotted by a Portsmouth scout playing and scoring for Leek Town, Steve arrived at Fratton Park during the 1998 close season, but started just once during 1998-99, in a difficult game at home to Birmingham, and came on as substitute in 11 others. An attacking midfielder, and occasionally striker, he performed well at reserve-team level, but needs to be stronger to show his pace and strengths. In order to further his experience, he was loaned out to Macclesfield in March to make up a depleted squad, and appeared in nine of their final 11 fixtures before going back to Pompey.

Portsmouth (£30,000 from Leek T on 22/7/98) FL 1+7 FLC 0+4
Macclesfield T (Loaned on 19/3/99) FL 5+5

SOLSKJAER Ole Gunnar
Born: Kristiansund, Norway, 26 February 1973
Height: 5'10" Weight: 11.10
Club Honours: PL '97, '99; FAC '99; EC '99
International Honours: Norway: 22

A well-balanced striker, with a powerful shot in either foot, Ole's career at Manchester United appeared to be coming to an end last August when the club accepted a £5.5 million offer from Spurs for his services. When the deal fell through, Alex Ferguson was delighted to see him stay. Two weeks later, he was staking his claim for a regular place in the side, when he netted two goals in United's 4-1 win over Charlton in the Premiership at Old Trafford. Reduced to only fleeting appearances thereafter, Norwegian coach, Nils Johan Semb, warned him that he was risking his international future for refusing to give up his Old Trafford dream. His prolific goalscoring record, however, continued to dominate the headlines, with 17 strikes in 17 games, including four in ten minutes against Nottingham Forest in February, the record for a substitute, and the winner against Liverpool in the FA Cup fourth round. Although he openly admitted that he would have left any other club had it not been United, he calmly awaited his chance. And what better stage than the Nou Camp Stadium in Barcelona on European Cup final night than to show your true worth. With only seconds remaining, and United heading for an extra-time showdown against Bayern Munich, Ole forced home a dramatic winner to write himself into Old Trafford folklore.

Manchester U (£1,500,000 from Molde on 29/7/96) PL 49+25/36 FLC 3/3 FAC 5+8/3 Others 12+11/4

SOLTVEDT Trond Egil
Born: Voss, Norway, 15 February 1967
Height: 6'1" Weight: 12.8
International Honours: Norway: 4

In 1998-99, the Norwegian midfield player won over the fans and the manager at Coventry, following several gutsy performances and some vital goals, three of them coming as a substitute. His great strength is as a ball winner in midfield, but he also likes to get forward at every opportunity, and his winning goal in the vital home game against Charlton came after he popped up on the edge of the box when a corner was not properly cleared and, with the help of a deflection, smashed the ball home. Is highly rated by manager Gordon Strachan for his incredible energy levels and willingness to work, and although he struggled to hold his place at times this was probably due to some inconsistent away performances when his slight lack of pace was exposed.

Coventry C (£500,000 from Rosenborg, via Viking Stavanger and Brann, on 24/7/97) PL 47+10/3 FLC 1+4/1 FAC 5+2

SONG Bahanag Rigobert
Born: Nkanglicock, Cameroon, 1 July 1976
Height: 5'9" Weight: 11.10
International Honours: Cameroon: 31

A class acquisition from the French club, Metz, last January, Rigobert proved to be a snip for Liverpool, the 22-year-old Cameroon skipper – sent off in two World Cups – immediately shoring up the Reds' defence almost single-handedly on his introduction against Coventry. He tackles hard, has a neat turn of pace, is powerful in the air, confident on the ball, and relishes the challenge of a physical encounter. Despite playing in the losing game against the Sky Blues, and being substituted by Steve McManaman near the end, Rigobert was awarded the "Man of the Match" accolade for a breathtaking debut. Alas, one man does not make a team, but his ability will do much to establish Liverpool amongst the title favourites this coming term.

Liverpool (£2,720,000 from Salernitana, via Tonnerre and Metz, on 29/1/99) PL 10+3

SONNER Daniel (Danny) James
Born: Wigan, 9 January 1972
Height: 5'11" Weight: 12.8
International Honours: NI: 3; B-4

Signed for Sheffield Wednesday at a cut-price fee from Ipswich by Danny Wilson last October, he went straight into the side, much to everyone's surprise, and immediately made a good impression in a strong-tackling midfield role. Scored his first goal for the club at Blackburn and soon became an integral part of the team, so much so that he was selected for Northern Ireland "B". Having played once for the full Irish side whilst with Ipswich, he once again pushed himself into the Irish squad with his forceful displays at Wednesday, where his form made him a contender for the Premier's bargain buy of the season. Defence-splitting passes and a good right-foot shot are among his other attributes.

Burnley (Free from Wigan Ath juniors on 6/8/90) FL 1+5 FLC 0+1/1 Others 0+2 (Free to Preussen Koln during 1993 close season)
Bury (Loaned on 21/11/92) FL 5/3 FAC 3 Others 1/1
Ipswich T (Free on 12/6/96) FL 28+28/3 FLC 6+4/1 FAC 1+1 Others 0+1
Sheffield Wed (£75,000 on 15/10/98) PL 24+2/3 FAC 2+1

SORENSEN Thomas
Born: Denmark, 12 June 1976
Height: 6'4" Weight: 13.10
Club Honours: Div 1 '99
The giant Danish U21 international goalkeeper was Sunderland's rock-solid last line of defence in their First Division championship success of 1998-99. Signed from Odense BK in the summer of 1998, Thomas is regarded as the eventual long-term successor to Peter Schmeichel in the Danish national side, and was indeed elevated to the first-team squad last term. Having kept a new club record of 30 clean sheets last season, missing only one league game after suffering a bad concussion whilst making a typically brave save at the feet of Bradford striker, Lee Mills, in March, Thomas established himself as the latest in a long line of cult-hero goalkeepers at Sunderland. A commanding figure in the penalty area, whose handling is excellent, he was the hero in the penalty shoot-out victory in the Worthington Cup at Everton, and was voted Nationwide "Player of the Month" for December.
Sunderland (£500,000 + from Odense BK on 6/8/98) FL 45 FLC 9 FAC 2

SORVEL Neil Simon
Born: Whiston, 2 March 1973
Height: 6'0" Weight: 12.9
Club Honours: GMVC '95, '97; FAT '96
Neil had a shaky start to last season, not being guaranteed a regular place in the Macclesfield Second Division squad, and he put in a transfer request early on. However, he got his chance in late October through squad injuries, and turned into a midfield dynamo with tough tackles, mazy runs, and good distribution. His shots on target also improved. He nodded in at York, tapped home against Luton, volleyed spectacularly from 25 yards at Northampton, and added a fourth from ten yards at Luton, before withdrawing his transfer request to become one of the first names on the team sheet.
Crewe Alex (From trainee on 31/7/91) FL 5+4 FAC 1+1 Others 4
Macclesfield (Free on 21/8/92) FL 79+7/7 FLC 4+1 FAC 5 Others 0+1

SOUTER Ryan John
Born: Bradford, 5 February 1978
Height: 5'10" Weight: 12.0
A player whom Neil Warnock previously had on trial whilst manager at Plymouth, Ryan gave up a full-time job as a postman and part-time football with Weston super Mare to sign for Bury early last January. Able to play left back, centre half, or as a left-sided midfielder, he proved to be a versatile player who quickly made a very good impression at Gigg Lane. Having been

named as a substitute for five games, immediately after signing for the Shakers, but only appearing in one of those games – coming on for the last eight minutes of Bury's 2-1 defeat at Portsmouth – following that, he played 18 games in the Pontins League team, mainly at centre half, and scored two goals.
Bury (£6,000 from Weston super Mare on 8/1/99) FL 0+1

SOUTHALL Neville
Born: Llandudno, 16 September 1958
Height: 6'1" Weight: 14.0
Club Honours: FAC '84, '95; CS '84, '85, '95; Div 1 '85, '87; ECW '85
International Honours: W: 92
Freed by Stoke during the summer of 1998, this vastly experienced goalkeeper went outside the Football League with Doncaster before coming back with Torquay last December. No superlatives can adequately describe the contribution made by him, as time and again he produced match-saving performances before walking away with the Gulls' "Player of the Year" award after only 27 appearances. Originally signed on a match-to-match basis after an injury to Ken Veysey, he has expressed a desire to remain at Plainmoor to help the club to promotion in its centenery season.
Bury (£6,000 from Winsford U on 14/6/80) FL 39 FAC 5
Everton (£150,000 on 13/7/81) F/PL 578 FLC 65 FAC 70 Others 37
Port Vale (Loaned on 27/1/83) FL 9
Southend U (Loaned on 24/12/97) FL 9
Stoke C (Free on 27/2/98) FL 12 (Free to Doncaster Rov on 23/7/98)
Torquay U (Free on 10/12/98) FL 25 Others 2

SOUTHALL Leslie Nicholas (Nicky)
Born: Stockton, 28 January 1972
Height: 5'10" Weight: 12.12
It was not until last November that Nicky gained a regular place in the Gillingham team in the left-sided wing-back slot. For somebody that was not familiar to the position, he took to it like a duck to water, and was undoubtably one of the success stories of the season. He also got forward to score four crucial goals during the campaign, none better than the individual solo effort in the 3-1 home victory over York in January. Nicknamed "Trigger" by his team mates, he was out of contract during the summer.
Hartlepool U (Free from Darlington juniors on 21/2/91) FL118+20/24 FLC 6+1/3 FAC 4+4 Others 6+2
Grimsby T (£40,000 on 12/7/95) FL 55+17/6 FLC 3+3/1 FAC 4+3/2
Gillingham (Free on 9/12/97) FL 56+9/6 FLC 0+1 FAC 1 Others 8

SOUTHGATE Gareth
Born: Watford, 3 September 1970
Height: 6'0" Weight: 12.8
Club Honours: Div 1 '94; FLC '96
International Honours: E: 31
1998-99 was yet another consistent season for Gareth at Aston Villa, as he continued to captain the side successfully, especially when they led the Premiership for a considerable period of time. With the

exception of just one game, he played a major role in the centre of the Villa defence, first in guiding Gareth Barry through his first full campaign, and then having to hold the unit together following Ugo Ehiogu's absence due to injury. After scoring his first ever goal for England, against Luxembourg, in October, he was surprisingly demoted to the subs' bench for the Czech and Poland matches, but he never let it get to him and he just got on with the job in hand. Never one to allow a striker to bustle him out of his stride, comfortable on the ball, while looking to make the right pass, and always making himself available to his team mates, he signed a five-year contract in October which should effectively keep him at Villa Park for the rest of his career.
Crystal Palace (From trainee on 17/1/89) F/PL 148+4/15 FLC 23+1/7 FAC 9 Others 6
Aston Villa (£2,500,000 on 1/7/95) PL 129/3 FLC 10/1 FAC 12 Others 13

SPARROW Paul
Born: Wandsworth, 24 March 1975
Height: 6'1" Weight: 11.4
Club Honours: Div 3 '96
Signed from Preston during the 1998 close season, Paul suffered a torrid start to his Rochdale career in 1998-99, and lost his place at right back after only three games. However, injuries to Dean Stokes and Andy Barlow gave him the chance to return on the left flank, and this coincided with Dale's change to a wing-back system more suited to his attacking instincts, which saw him responding with goals in two of the next four games. Was released during the summer.
Crystal Palace (From trainee on 13/7/93) FL 1 FLC 0+1
Preston NE (Signed on 8/3/96) FL 20 FAC 1 Others 1
Rochdale (Free on 2/7/98) FL 21+4/2 FLC 1 FAC 4 Others 1+1

SPEAKMAN Robert
Born: Swansea, 5 December 1980
Height: 5'11" Weight: 11.6
A prolific scorer at youth and reserve-team level, as well as being an England youth international, Robert made his league debut for Exeter when coming off the bench against Leyton Orient at St James' Park last April. Only 18, and an out-and-out goalgetter who works hard and has a knack for taking chances, he will be looking to make more first-team starts in the coming season. Is still a trainee.
Exeter C (Trainee) FL 0+1

SPEDDING Duncan
Born: Camberley, 7 September 1977
Height: 6'1" Weight: 11.1
Playing as a left-sided midfielder or defender, having joined Northampton during the 1998 close season from Southampton, Duncan pleased the supporters of his new club with some clever football, relying on his ball skills rather than speed. Unfortunately, the injury bug hit him in late September, causing him to miss two months of football with a leg injury before he returned in September. However, from

then on he was in and out of the side, while competing for a place in the 28-man squad.

Southampton (From trainee on 24/5/96) PL 4+3 FLC 0+1

Northampton T (£60,000 on 14/7/98) FL 15+9/1 FLC 2+2 Others 1

SPEED Gary Andrew
Born: Mancot, 8 September 1969
Height: 5'10" Weight: 12.10
Club Honours: Div 2 '90, Div 1 '92; CS '92
International Honours: W: 52; U21-3; Yth

The Welsh international captain, Gary is a midfielder with pace, control, and notable heading ability. Although a regular in the Newcastle team in 1998-99, he did not initially make the impact anticipated when he moved to Tyneside for a large fee. However, following David Batty's transfer to Leeds, he moved from the wide position he was filling to a central role where he clearly felt more at home. There, he became increasingly influential, developing a fine partnership with Dietmar Hamann, which was a critical factor in Newcastle's improving form as the campaign progressed. Playing in a more disciplined way, he did much of the midfield anchoring work, covering back when needed, but breaking forward whenever the opportunity arose to contribute some important goals. Highlighted were the pair which helped win the match against Derby, and his threatening run into the penalty box which caused Sol Campbell to handle and concede a critical penalty in the FA Cup semi-final. Although suffering the first suspension of his career, following an accumulation of five yellow cards during the season, he captained United when Alan Shearer, Rob Lee, and Steve Howey were not playing.

Leeds U (From trainee on 13/6/88) F/PL 231+17/39 FLC 25+1/11 FAC 21/5 Others 14+3/2

Everton (£3,500,000 on 1/7/96) PL 58/15 FLC 5/1 FAC 2/1

Newcastle U (£5,500,000 on 6/2/98) PL 47+4/5 FLC 1+1 FAC 10/2 Others 2

SPENCER John
Born: Glasgow, 11 September 1970
Height: 5'6" Weight: 11.7
International Honours: S: 14; U21-3; Yth; Sch

A small, lively, bustling forward with a good finish, who joined Everton from Queens Park Rangers the previous season, John failed to find the net in a first-team game for the club, and returned to his native Scotland when signing for Motherwell last January, following an extended loan period which began at the end of October. Although he kicked off 1998-99 in Walter Smith's starting line-up at Goodison, it soon became apparent he did not figure in the Toffees' long-term plans, and having made a big impact at Motherwell the Scots were delighted when he joined them permanently.

Glasgow R (From juniors on 11/9/86) SL 7+6/2 SLC 2 Others 1+1/1

Morton (Loaned on 4/3/89) FL 4/1

Chelsea (£450,000 on 1/8/92) PL 75+28/36 FLC 5+4/2 FAC16+4/4 Others 4+1/1

Queens Park R (£2,500,000 on 22/11/96) FL 47+1/22 FLC 1 FAC 6/2

Everton (£1,500,000 on 9/3/98) PL 5+4

SPINK Dean Peter
Born: Birmingham, 22 January 1967
Height: 6'0" Weight: 14.8
Club Honours: Div 3 '94

Similar to his time with Shrewsbury, Dean has become something of a "two for the price of one" asset to Wrexham. Originally bought to bolster the attacking options at the Racecourse, he began last season struggling to make the first team, which was followed by injury to his heel, resulting in him missing the whole of November. However, at the beginning of December, he was installed in the heart of the defence, where his form was a revelation, with several "Man of the Match" performances alongside Brian Carey, his strong build and presence much to the fore. Despite this, he was still willing to revert to his attacking position when required by manager, Brian Flynn, winning the admiration of the fans as a strong character who takes some handling, with strength, verve, and courage. A handful both up front and back in central defence, he won the "Player of the Season" award.

Aston Villa (£30,000 from Halesowen T on 1/7/89)

Scarborough (Loaned on 20/11/89) FL 3/2 Others 1

Bury (Loaned on 1/2/90) FL 6/1

Shrewsbury T (£75,000 on 15/3/90) FL 244+29/53 FLC 22+2/1 FAC 18+2/6 Others 19+2/3

Wrexham (£65,000 on 15/7/97) FL 59+11/9 FLC 2+1/1 FAC 5+2 Others 6+1

SPINK Nigel Philip
Born: Chelmsford, 8 August 1958
Height: 6'2" Weight: 14.6
Club Honours: EC '82; ESC '82; FLC '94
International Honours: E: 1; B-2

Although Nigel's Millwall appearances were dogged by injury and his wife's worrying illness in 1998-99, his experience was invaluable to the others 'keepers in the club when he was unable to play. Now in his 40s, he is still an excellent goalie who commands his box, is a great shot stopper (which he proved beyond doubt against Bournemouth in the Auto Windscreens shoot-out), and still has great enthusiasm for the game. His encouragement to those in front of him is of great value, as players are more confident when knowing that they have such an experienced man behind them.

Aston Villa (£4,000 from Chelmsford C on 1/1/77) F/PL 357+4 FLC 45 FAC 28 Others 25+1

West Bromwich A (Free on 31/1/96) FL 19 FLC 3 Others 2

Millwall (£50,000 on 26/9/97) FL 43 FLC 2 FAC 2 Others 5

SPOONER Nicholas (Nicky) Michael
Born: Manchester, 5 June 1971
Height: 5'10" Weight: 11.9

A gutsy Bolton centre back who, having struggled with injuries throughout his career, and unable to find a first-team opportunity at the Reebok, was loaned out to Oldham at the end of last October, but returned home early after making just two appearances. Following that, he was released by Wanderers on 23 March, and moved to America to play his football with Charleston Battery.

Bolton W (From trainee on 12/7/89) FL 22+1/2 FLC 2 FAC 3 Others 0+1

Oldham Ath (Loaned on 30/10/98) FL 2

SPRING Matthew John
Born: Harlow, 17 November 1979
Height: 5'11" Weight: 11.5

Having made an impressive first-team debut for Luton in 1997-98, and having been handed the club's "Young Player of the Year" award, he was rewarded with a regular place in the side in 1998-99, missing just two games. A tenacious midfielder with a biting tackle, good vision, and an ability to read the game well for a youngster. Matthew also added three goals to his CV, his first for the club at senior level, A 25-yard lob over the stranded York goalie being possibly the pick of the bunch. The club is expecting great things from this youngster.

Luton T (From trainee on 2/7/97) FL 51+6/3 FLC 7 FAC 2+1

Matthew Spring

SRNICEK Pavel (Pav)
Born: Ostrava, Czechoslovakia, 10 March 1968
Height: 6'2" Weight: 14.9
Club Honours: Div 1 '93
International Honours: Czechoslovakia: 23

Signed on a free transfer from Banik Ostrava last November, having been released by Newcastle United during the 1998 close season, Pavel was given the first-team jersey in preference to Kevin Pressman. Although playing reasonably well in goal for the Owls, he appeared suspect on crosses, but his form was still good enough for him to reclaim his place in the Czech Republic's international side. Losing his place at Wednesday while serving a ban for a sending-off offence

against Derby was Pavel's low point of the campaign, but he was quickly reinstated at Kevin Pressman's expense as soon as he was available again. A fine shot-stopping 'keeper, his agility and reflexes make him a real crowd pleaser.

Newcastle U (£350,000 from Banik Ostrava on 5/2/91) F/PL 148+1 FLC 10+1 FAC 11 Others 17 (Free to Banik Ostrava during 1998 close season)
Sheffield Wed (Free on 12/11/98) PL 24 FAC 2

STALLARD Mark
Born: Derby, 24 October 1974
Height: 6'0" Weight: 13.6
After his 18 goal haul for Wycombe in 1997-98, much was expected in 1998-99 from Mark, one of the deadliest strikers at that level. In a struggling team, he managed just three goals in the first 14 games, before suffering a medial ligament injury, ironically, in the side's first win of the season. Ruled out for 12 weeks, he returned at the end of January, as a sub, but started only one more game before leaving for Notts County in March after he was unwilling to commit himself to a new contract. He quickly became quite a favourite with the County fans, scoring some vital goals at the end of the season to help the club avoid relegation. With good vision, Mark is a nippy player, quick over short distances, and often scores goals from close range, being confident with both his left and right foot.

Derby Co (From trainee on 6/11/91) FL 19+8/2 FLC 2+1/2 FAC 2+1 Others 3/2
Fulham (Loaned on 23/9/94) FL 4/3
Bradford C (£110,000 on 12/1/96) FL 33+10/10 FLC 2/1 FAC 0+1 Others 3/2
Preston NE (Loaned on 14/2/97) FL 4/1
Wycombe W (£100,000 on 7/3/97) FL 67+3/23 FLC 5+1/1 Others 2/1
Notts Co (£10,000 on 3/3/99) FL 13+1/4

STAM Jakob (Jaap)
Born: Kampen, Holland, 17 July 1972
Height: 6'3" Weight: 14.0
Club Honours: EC '99; FAC '99; PL '99
International Honours: Holland: 25
Signed from PSV Eindhoven to shore up Manchester United's defence in time for their assault on the 1998-99 Premiership title, and having spent the summer starring for Holland in the World Cup finals, this wonderfully balanced central defender, who is supreme in the air, strong in the tackle, with great recovery skills to match, had a real baptism of fire when making his debut in United's 3-0 defeat against Arsenal in the Charity Shield at Wembley last August. Following that, Jaap picked up a thigh injury against Leicester on his Premiership debut before coming back to silence his critics with a succession of truly outstanding performances. Marshalling the United defence superbly throughout a star-studded campaign, he fully justified his massive fee, missing only 11 games in all competitions. Although he was suspended for the sixth round FA Cup-tie against Chelsea at Old Trafford in March, he returned for the replay, and was hugely instrumental in leading United through one of the most memorable seasons in their history, during which they won the European Cup, the FA

Cup, and the Premiership. Now regarded as one of the best central defenders in the world, he netted his only goal of the season in United's 6-2 win at Leicester in January. Finished the campaign being recognised by his fellow professionals as the best in his position in the Premiership.

Manchester U (£10,750,000 from PSV Eindhoven, via Zwolle, Cambuur and Willem II, on 17/7/98) PL 30/1 FAC 6+1 Others 14

STAMP Darryn Michael
Born: Beverley, 21 September 1978
Height: 6'2" Weight: 12.0
A tall, slim striker, Darryn has pleasing ball skills, and looks good when running at opposing defenders, but had a frustrating season at Scunthorpe in 1998-99. Having scored three crucial goals before the end of September, a knee-ligament injury ruled him out for two months around the turn of the year, and on coming back he spent much of the rest of the campaign on the substitutes' bench.

Scunthorpe U (Signed from Hessle on 7/7/97) FL 9+26/5 FLC 0+2 FAC 2 Others 0+1

STAMP Neville
Born: Reading, 7 July 1981
Height: 5'10" Weight: 10.5
Neville made his Reading first-team debut in the final game of last season, as a half-time substitute at Oldham, but it was deserved recognition for a talented local youngster who had worked his way through the club's junior and reserve teams. His best position proved to be at left back, where he is strong in the tackle, brave in the air, and can distribute the ball accurately. Is a skilled exponent of dead-ball kicks.

Reading (Trainee) FL 0+1

Phil Stamp

STAMP Philip (Phil) Lawrence
Born: Middlesbrough, 12 December 1975
Height: 5'10" Weight: 13.5
International Honours: E: Yth
Another local lad to emerge with credit on coming through the Middlesbrough system, Phil continued to be on the verge of breaking onto centre stage in the big league in 1998-99, but still has to overcome the plague of injuries that have beset him lately. A fully fit "Stampy" is strong and fast, and a tough handful for any side to compete with, being a vigorous and aggressive midfielder with a liking for popping up unexpectedly and banging one in. Needless to say, a great future is predicted for this honest and hard-grafting young player.

Middlesbrough (From trainee on 4/2/93) P/FL 48+27/5 FLC 12+2/1 FAC 5+4/1 Others 5+1

STAMPS Scott
Born: Birmingham, 20 March 1975
Height: 5'10" Weight: 11.10
A left-sided Colchester full back or wing back who had another campaign disrupted by various injury problems in 1998-99, a run of regular appearances at the start of the season ground to a halt after the FA Cup disaster at Bedlington, before he was then tried as a left-sided forward for a brief spell around Christmas. Injury then struck, and Scott made only two more appearances, both as substitute, before being released in the summer.

Torquay U (From trainee on 6/7/93) FL 80+6/5 FLC 5 FAC 2 Others 2+1/1
Colchester U (£10,000 on 26/3/97) FL 52+4/1 FLC 4 FAC 3+1 Others 1+1

STANNARD James (Jim) David
Born: Harold Hill, 6 October 1962
Height: 6'2" Weight: 16.2
On the coaching staff at Gillingham, and a regular in the club's Combination side, Jim was called upon last November when the first-choice goalie, Vince Bartram, injured himself in the warm up at home to Oldham Athletic. Did not let the side down in either of his two league games, the second being in front of 26,500 at Manchester City. Positionally sound, although not so agile as in previous years, the big man still reacts well. Was out of contract during the summer.

Fulham (Signed from Ford U on 5/6/80) FL 41 FLC 3 FAC 1
Southend U (Loaned on 17/9/84) FL 6
Charlton Ath (Loaned on 1/2/85) FL 1
Southend U (£12,000 on 28/3/85) FL 103 FLC 6 FAC 4 Others 5
Fulham (£50,000 on 14/8/87) FL 348/1 FLC 22 FAC 13 Others 18
Gillingham (Free on 4/8/95) FL 106 FLC 8 FAC 10 Others 2

STANSFIELD James Edward
Born: Dewsbury, 18 September 1978
Height: 6'2" Weight: 13.0
Freed by Huddersfield during the 1998 close season, the young centre back entered the first-team fray in the New Year, his only other Halifax senior appearance coming against Cheltenham in the James Thomson Championship Shield. Following an impres-

sive number of matches, James continued where he left off, and is looked upon as a bright prospect for the future.

Huddersfield T (From trainee on 21/7/97)
Halifax T (Free on 7/7/98) FL 12/1 Others 2

STANT Phillip (Phil) Richard
Born: Bolton, 13 October 1962
Height: 6'0" Weight: 13.4
Club Honours: Div 3 '93; WC '93

The veteran striker's main role in 1998-99 was as Lincoln's assistant manager, and he took sole charge of coaching following the dismissal of Shane Westley in November. Despite making a handful of first-team appearances as a second-half substitute, he failed to add to his league goal tally, but showed, however, that he could still hit the target when finishing as leading scorer for City's reserves, knocking in 11 goals in the Pontin's League.

Reading (Signed from Camberley on 19/8/82) FL 3+1/2
Hereford U (Free from Army on 25/11/86) FL 83+6/38 FLC 3/2 FAC 3/2 Others 11/7
Notts Co (£175,000 on 18/7/89) FL 14+8/6 FLC 2/1 FAC 0+1 Others 3+2
Blackpool (Loaned on 5/9/90) FL 12/5
Lincoln C (Loaned on 22/11/90) FL 4
Huddersfield T (Loaned on 3/1/91) FL 5/1
Fulham (£60,000 on 8/2/91) FL 19/5 Others 1
Mansfield T (£50,000 on 1/8/91) FL 56+1/32 FLC 4/1 FAC 2 Others 2
Cardiff C (£100,000 on 4/12/92) FL 77+2/34 FLC 2/2 FAC 6+1/4 Others 10/3
Mansfield T (Loaned on 12/8/93) FL 4/1 FLC 1/1
Bury (£90,000 on 27/1/95) FL 49+13/23 FLC 5+1/4 FAC 1 Others 5
Northampton T (Loaned on 22/11/96) FL 4+1/2
Lincoln C (£30,000 on 26/12/96) FL 39+7/18 FLC 2/1 FAC 2+3 Others 1+1

STANTON Nathan
Born: Nottingham, 6 May 1981
Height: 5'9" Weight: 11.3
International Honours: E: Yth

The former England U16 international defender continued to make great progress in the Scunthorpe reserve side, winning a two-year professional contract last March. Filling in for a few first-team matches, Nathan never letting the side down, his terrific pace and tackling standing out.

Scunthorpe U (From trainee on 19/3/99) FL 3+2

STATHAM Brian
Born: Zimbabwe, 21 May 1969
Height: 5'8" Weight: 11.7
Club Honours: Div 3 '92
International Honours: E: U21-3

A tenacious midfielder, who can also play at the back despite his lack of inches, his only first-team appearance for Gillingham last season was as a seventh-minute substitute in the Auto Windscreens victory at Swansea in January. Apart from that, he had a loan spell with Woking earlier on, and with it being obvious that he was not in Tony Pulis' plans he moved to another Conference side, Stevenage, on loan in February.

Tottenham H (From trainee on 3/8/87) FL 20+4 FLC 2 FAC 0+1
Reading (Loaned on 28/3/91) FL 8
Bournemouth (Loaned on 20/11/91) FL 2 Others 1
Brentford (£70,000 on 16/1/92) FL 148+18/1 FLC 12 FAC 6 Others 22

Gillingham (£10,000 on 22/8/97) FL 16+4 FAC 2 Others 1+1

STAUNTON Stephen (Steve)
Born: Drogheda, Ireland, 19 January 1969
Height: 6'1" Weight: 12.12
Club Honours: FAC '89; Div 1 '90; FLC '94, '96
International Honours: Ei: 78; U21-4; Yth

A former Red, Liverpool secured Steve's services from Aston Villa on a free transfer as a result of the Bosman ruling during the 1998 close season. Liverpool supporters had wished that he had never been sold in the first place, and while it took him a little while to settle in amongst new players in 1998-99, the fans were soon left thinking that he had never been away. His fierce tackling, his excellent runs and deep crosses, and his positional sense all added weight to the belief that he should never have left Anfield first time round. Continuing to be selected for his country, in a spectacular October, the Irishman won "Man of the Match" accolades against Everton and Fulham.

Liverpool (£20,000 from Dundalk on 2/9/86) FL 55+10 FLC 6+2/4 FAC 14+2/1 Others 1/1
Bradford C (Loaned on 13/11/87) FL 7+1 FLC 2 Others 1
Aston Villa (£1,100,000 on 7/8/91) F/PL 205+3/16 FLC 17+2/1 FAC 19+1/1 Others 15+1
Liverpool (Free on 3/7/98) PL 31 FLC 2 FAC 1 Others 5+1

STEELE Lee Anthony
Born: Liverpool, 7 December 1973
Height: 5'8" Weight: 12.7

A distinctive predator with an amazing appetite for work, despite his size Lee is almost impossible to knock off the ball, and often ploughed a lone furrow up front for Shrewsbury in 1998-99, but never gave up. With the ball sticking to his feet as he left defenders in his wake, and having a great

eye for the net given a chance, he scored 13 league goals for the second successive season. A crowd pleaser, he could play in a higher standard.

Shrewsbury T (£30,000 + from Northwich Vic on 23/7/97) FL 70+6/26 FLC 3/3 FAC 1+1 Others 2

STEFANOVIC Dejan
Born: Yugoslavia, 28 October 1974
Height: 6'2" Weight: 12.10
International Honours: Yugoslavia: 10

Unfortunately, Dejan's 1998-99 season got off to a poor start at Sheffield Wednesday because he could not obtain a new work permit, having not fulfilled the criteria of appearances made in 1997-98. However, the club kept on appealing to the authorities and eventually managed to obtain one. But, because it took so long to arrive, he was unable to stake a claim for a regular place in the side, especially in his preferred central defensive role. Although appearing to be laid back, at his best he is a classy defender, who is calm and composed in possession, and has excellent passing ability. Due to limited games played, he was released during the summer.

Sheffield Wed (£2,000,000 from Red Star Belgrade on 22/12/95) PL 59+7/4 FLC 2 FAC 4/1

STEIN Mark Earl Sean
Born: Capetown, South Africa, 29 January 1966
Height: 5'6" Weight: 11.10
Club Honours: FLC '88; AMC '92; Div 2 '93
International Honours: E: Yth

Mark had a tremendous 1998-99, finishing as Bournemouth's leading scorer with 25 league and cup goals, having joined the Cherries permanently in the 1998 close season after spending a three-month loan period at Dean Court during 1997-98. Despite being 33, he is quick and extremely sharp in the box, and an excellent finisher.

Mark Stein (left)

As well as his striking abilities, he is also a tireless runner who will drop back to help out the midfield if needed, his contributions being one of the main reasons for the side remaining in play-off contention right up until the last game. Was recognised by his peers on selection for the PFA award-winning Second Division side.

Luton T (From juniors on 31/1/84) FL 41+13/19 FLC 4+1 FAC 9/3 Others 3/1
Aldershot (Loaned on 29/1/86) FL 2/1
Queens Park R (£300,000 on 26/8/88) FL 20+13/4 FLC 4/2 FAC 2+1/1 Others 4
Oxford U (Signed on 15/9/89) FL 72+10/18 FLC 4 FAC 2+1 Others 3
Stoke C (£100,000 on 15/9/91) FL 94/50 FLC 8/8 FAC 4 Others 17/10
Chelsea (£1,500,000 on 28/10/93) PL 46+4/21 FLC 0+1 FAC 9/2 Others 2+1/2
Stoke C (Loaned on 22/11/96) FL 11/4
Ipswich T (Loaned on 22/8/97) FL 6+1/2 FLC 3+1/1
Bournemouth (Signed on 4/3/98) FL 54/19 FLC 5/5 FAC 4/1 Others 6/4

STEINER Robert Herman
Born: Finsprong, Sweden, 20 June 1973
Height: 6'2" Weight: 13.5
International Honours: Sweden: 3

Although the club's joint leading scorer in 1997-98, Rob only made one cup appearance for Bradford in 1998-99, being loaned out to Dundee United in September, Queens Park Rangers in November and early March, and Walsall in transfer deadline week. Having returned from Dundee early after suffering an ankle injury, the central striker was deemed fit enough to sign for the Loftus Road club, but arrived back at Valley Parade following an extended period with the ankle damaged once more. Back at Queens Park Rangers in March, he scored the winner against Oxford before ending his time there with another goal, this time against Swindon. At Walsall, he headed the winner against Wrexham at the Bescot three days after his debut at Blackpool, and gave the club just the late season promotion boost it needed up front with further goals against Macclesfield and Fulham.

Bradford C (Loaned from Norrkoping on 31/10/96) FL 14+1/3 FAC 1/1
Bradford C (£500,000 from Norrkoping on 31/7/97) FL 26+11/10 FLC 3/1 FAC 1
Queens Park R (Loaned on 6/11/98) FL 1+7/1
Queens Park R (Loaned on 2/3/99) FL 4/2
Walsall (Loaned on 25/3/99) FL 10/3

STENSAAS Stale
Born: Trondheim, Norway, 7 July 1971
Height: 5'11" Weight: 12.1
Club Honours: SPD '98

A Glasgow Rangers' signing from Rosenborg during the 1997 close season, the experienced Norwegian full back was loaned to Nottingham Forest at the end of last January in an effort to help shore up a defence that the forwards could build upon. An all-action player who obviously liked to get forward, he looked useful at times, especially with his shooting ability, but it was difficult to impress in a side that was constantly on the rack and destined for the drop to the First Division almost from day one.

Glasgow R (£1,750,000 from Rosenborg, via Nidelv and Othilienborg, on 29/5/97) SL 18+4/1 SLC 3/1 SC 2 Others 3+1
Nottingham F (Loaned on 29/1/99) PL 6+1

STEPHENSON Paul
Born: Wallsend, 2 January 1968
Height: 5'10" Weight: 12.12
International Honours: E: Yth

An experienced winger who has not had the best of times since joining Hartlepool, Paul looked good in the summer build up, but early in 1998-99 he picked up a knee injury which required a cartilage operation, and although a regular in mid season he struggled to find his best form. After being substituted against Darlington in February he had a transfer request turned down, and in the latter weeks of the season he was often a non-playing substitute. Taking into account all the disappointments he ended the campaign on a high, coming on as a second-half substitute in the last game to score a goal which earned a welcome 1-1 draw at Southend.

Newcastle U (From apprentice on 2/1/86) FL 58+3/1 FLC 3+1 FAC 2 Others 2
Millwall (£300,000 on 10/11/88) FL 81+17/6 FLC 3/1 FAC 9/2 Others 8/1
Gillingham (Loaned on 21/11/92) FL 12/2 Others 2
Brentford (£30,000 on 4/3/93) FL 70/2 FLC 6/1 FAC 1+1 Others 5
York C (Signed on 7/8/95) FL 91+6/8 FLC 9+2 FAC 5 Others 2+2/1
Hartlepool U (Free on 20/3/98) FL 27+3/2 FLC 0+1 FAC 2 Others 2

STEVENS Ian David
Born: Malta, 21 October 1966
Height: 5'10" Weight: 12.6
Club Honours: AMC '89

On his day, Ian is the most dangerous forward at Brunton Park, his haul of ten league and Cup goals in 1998-99 being sufficient for him to head the Carlisle scoring chart. However, most of those efforts came in the early months of the campaign, and a seeming loss of confidence led to the sort of drought that is a striker's nightmare. He did manage to score the vital equaliser in the 3-3 draw with Darlington in late April but, by then, he was more frequently occupying the subs' bench prior to leaving on a free at the end of the term.

Preston NE (From apprentice on 22/11/84) FL 9+2/2 Others 1
Stockport Co (Free on 27/10/86) FL FAC 0+1 Others 0+1 (Free to Lancaster C on 27/11/86)
Bolton W (Free on 25/3/87) FL 26+21/7 FLC 1+2 FAC 4/2 Others 3+1
Bury (Free on 3/7/91) FL 100+10/38 FLC 3+1 FAC 2+2 Others 7+1/2
Shrewsbury T (£20,000 on 11/8/94) FL 94+17/37 FLC 2+1 FAC 4+2/2 Others 10+2/12
Carlisle U (£100,000 on 13/5/97) FL 64+14/26 FLC 2 FAC 2/1 Others 3/2

STEVENS Keith Henry
Born: Merton, 21 June 1964
Height: 6'0" Weight: 12.12
Club Honours: FLT '83; Div 2 '88

A Lions' legend, Keith was appointed player/manager of Millwall, his only club, in succession to Billy Bonds at the age of

33 in May 1998. As the second longest serving Lions' player of all time (to Barry Kitchener), he had experienced all the joys and despairs of a footballer's life since making his league debut for the club as a 16-year-old youngster back in 1981. During the course of his career, he appeared as both a combative midfielder and at full back, before settling at centre back in recent years, his reputation as a fierce competitor often overshadowing his undoubted playing ability. Having suffered a serious cruciate knee ligament injury which threatened his career, an attempt to make a comeback in early 1997 ended in heartbreak. Typically, he refused to concede defeat, and in the latter part of the 1997-98 campaign made four league appearances in addition to playing regularly at reserve level. Brought on to the coaching staff, and taking charge of the reserve side, in his first season as player/manager he consolidated Millwall's top-ten position in the Second Division with some very good young talent. He even stepped into the breach a couple of times to show that he was still a great competitor. Apart from all that, the pinnacle of his season must have been to lead Millwall out at Wembley in the Auto Windscreens Shield final.

Millwall (From apprentice on 23/6/81) FL 452+10/9 FLC 36/1 FAC 28 Others 30+1

STEWART William Paul Marcus
Born: Bristol, 7 November 1972
Height: 5'10" Weight: 11.0
International Honours: E: Sch

The potent Huddersfield striker enjoyed a tremendous season in 1998-99, showing genuine quality throughout a relatively injury-free campaign. Full of confidence, and producing a tremendous workrate, he found the net on a regular basis. In fact, only the woodwork against Portsmouth denied him from scoring the goal of the season with a terrific volley. Always involved in most of the attacks, the unselfish front man had matched his 1997-98 total by Boxing Day, having benefited from a great understanding with Wayne Allison, and a career first hat trick, against Crystal Palace. His excellent skills saw him score his 50th goal for the Terriers in just 124 appearances, and his 25th of the season in the derby dual at Bradford.

Bristol Rov (From trainee on 18/7/91) FL 137+34/57 FLC 11/5 FAC 7+1/3 Others 16+1/14
Huddersfield T (£1,200,000 + on 2/7/96) FL 100+4/45 FLC 12/6 FAC 8/3

STIMAC Igor
Born: Metkovic, Croatia, 6 September 1967
Height: 6'2" Weight: 13.0
International Honours: Croatia: 38

Derby's Croatian international central defender whose leadership qualities are as highly prized as are his tackling and distribution. These attributes made him a natural choice for team captain in 1998-99, but his season was, once again, curtailed due to a series of injuries to both ankle and back, and his absence towards the end of the

campaign was made more noticeable by a series of heavy defeats. A firm favourite at Pride Park, although intending to retire from international football after being a part of the Croatian side which reached the semi finals of France 98, he has changed his mind and will attempt to play a leading role in Euro 2000. Was placed on the transfer list at the end of May.

Derby Co (£1,570,000 from Hadjuk Split, via Cibalia Vinkovic, on 31/10/95) F/PL 84/3 FLC 2 FAC 7

STIMSON Mark Nicholas
Born: Plaistow, 27 December 1967
Height: 5'11" Weight: 12.6

Started last season as a regular in Southend's back four, his strong tackling and distribution being put to good use, then came the seemingly seasonal injury, and although returning to full fitness he dropped out of favour and joined Leyton Orient on a free transfer just before transfer deadline day. Signed as cover for Matt Lockwood, and only called upon a couple of times, he never let his colleagues down before being released in the summer.

Tottenham H (From apprentice on 15/7/85) FL 1+1
Leyton Orient (Loaned on 15/3/88) FL 10
Gillingham (Loaned on 19/1/89) FL 18
Newcastle U (£200,000 on 16/6/89) FL 82+4/2 FLC 5 FAC 7/1 Others 6
Portsmouth (Loaned on 10/12/92) FL 3+1
Portsmouth (£100,000 on 23/7/93) FL 57+1/2 FLC 9/1 FAC 3 Others 3
Barnet (Loaned on 21/9/95) FL 5 Others 1
Southend U (£25,000 on 15/3/96) FL 51+5 FLC 4 FAC 1 Others 1
Leyton Orient (Free on 12/3/99) FL 2 Others 1+1

STOCKDALE Robert (Robbie) Keith
Born: Redcar, 30 November 1979
Height: 5'11" Weight: 11.3

An exciting young Middlesbrough full back who has made the transition from obscurity to the Premiership, and has no intent to lose his place now. Injuries to senior squad members in 1998-99 initially left the door open for him, and he took the opportunities afforded by dint of many super performances, and although more comfortable at the back than when going forward as a wing back, he nevertheless filled that role with equal aplomb. Finishing the season with a steady run of consecutive appearances it is a fair bet that he will continue in the coming campaign where he left off.

Middlesbrough (From trainee on 2/7/98) P/FL 18+2 FLC 3 FAC 1

STOCKLEY Samuel (Sam) Joshua
Born: Tiverton, 5 September 1977
Height: 6'0" Weight: 12.0

As Barnet's swashbuckling right back, Sam was again a regular fixture in the Bees' back line, and attracted attention from a number of scouts during 1998-99. His scintillating pace, coupled with an attentive outlook on the game, indicated that he was an extremely valuable component in the squad during a tumultuous season. Briefly

sidelined with a slight injury in the home match against Rotherham in September, he only missed the next two games before recovering full fitness, and improved as the campaign progressed, his most inspirational display coming against Plymouth, when his surging runs down the right flank were at their most effective. Already established as a seasoned pro with over 100 games under his belt, but still in the formative stages of his career, one aspect he will be striving to improve on during 1999-2000 is his goalscoring ration, as he has not found the net for Barnet since arriving at Underhill in December 1996.

Southampton (From trainee on 1/7/96)
Barnet (Free on 31/12/96) FL 101+2 FLC 6 FAC 2 Others 5

STOCKWELL Michael (Micky) Thomas
Born: Chelmsford, 14 February 1965
Height: 5'9" Weight: 11.4
Club Honours: Div 2 '92

Micky once again, in 1998-99, showed how hard work and enthusiasm are still vital ingredients in the game, as he continued to provide the width on the right-hand side of Ipswich's midfield, and as one of the senior players was a fine example for the youngsters to follow. Pencilled in to fill the wing-back role when Mauricio Taricco left, he injured an ankle in the very next game, which kept him out until mid March. Scored twice during the season, both goals being headers! – against Exeter in the Worthington Cup, and Wolverhampton in the league.

Ipswich T (From apprentice on 17/12/82) F/PL 443+28/33 FLC 40+4/5 FAC 27+3/2 Others 22+4/2

STOKER Gareth
Born: Bishop Auckland, 22 February 1973
Height: 5'9" Weight: 11.4

Cardiff's midfield hard man had been unable to regain his place in the Bluebird's side after injury and was happy to sign for Rochdale on loan last February, making his debut in the excellent victory away to Scunthorpe. He was signed on a permanent contract at the end of his loan, and was an important cog in Dale's engine room for the rest of the season. Netted his first goal for his new club in the excellent draw away to leaders, Cambridge.

Hull C (Free from Leeds U juniors on 13/9/91) FL 24+6/2 FLC 3 FAC 2+1 Others 0+2 (Released during 1993 close season)
Hereford U (Signed from Bishop Auckland on 16/3/95) FL 65+5/6 FLC 5+1 FAC 3+1/1 Others 6+1/1
Cardiff C (£80,000 on 29/1/97) FL 29+8/4 FLC 1+1 FAC 1+3 Others 2+1
Rochdale (Free on 16/2/99) FL 11+1/1 Others 2

STOKES Dean Anthony
Born: Birmingham, 23 May 1970
Height: 5'9" Weight: 11.2

Dean, who had once played junior football in Rochdale, made an immediate favourable impression in the Dale side after joining from Port Vale during the 1998 close season, despite the side only winning twice in the first nine games. He then suffered a long-term injury which kept him out of the team until February, and even then he was unable

to reclaim the left-back spot from Andy Barlow until making his next league start in the final game. Strong tackling is his forte.

Port Vale (Signed from Halesowen T on 15/1/93) FL 53+7 FLC 1+1 FAC 4 Others 5+3
Rochdale (Free on 15/7/98) FL 10+1 FLC 2 Others 1

STOKOE Graham Lloyd
Born: Newcastle, 17 December 1975
Height: 6'0" Weight: 12.4

Released by Stoke, this skilful midfielder joined Hartlepool as a trialist during the 1998 close season, thus returning to the club which had given him his Football league debut when on loan during 1995-96. Although he impressed enough to be given a one-year contract, his time at Victoria Park was spoiled by injury and illness as he struggled to reach match fitness, and while looking his best as Pool played a passing game, getting several first-team opportunities, he was not really successful overall, and was freed during the summer.

Stoke C (Free from Newcastle U juniors on 7/7/94) FL 0+2
Hartlepool U (Loaned on 23/2/96) FL 8
Hartlepool U (Free on 24/8/98) FL 15+5 FAC 1+1 Others 1

STONE Steven (Steve) Brian
Born: Gateshead, 20 August 1971
Height: 5'8" Weight: 12.7
Club Honours: Div 1 '98
International Honours: E: 9

One of the most popular of Nottingham Forest players of recent years, Steve is a wholehearted, right-sided midfield player who gives it everything and more, whether it be as a wing back, in central midfield, or out wide. The former England man started 1998-99 by scoring in two of the first three games of the season, a 1-0 win at home against Coventry, and a 2-1 victory at Southampton, but from then on it all went wrong for both him and the club. Just one more Premiership win, followed by an 8-1 mauling by Manchester United at the City Ground, and a few games later, in mid March, he had transferred to Aston Villa. At Villa Park, he featured in every remaining game, playing on the right-hand side of midfield, and linked well with Steve Watson to provide the strikers with accurate crosses into the area. As an excellent all-rounder he gave Villa the width they had been missing, and was quickly taken to heart by the fans. A player's player, he is committed and passionate about the game he loves.

Nottingham F (From trainee on 20/5/89) F/PL 189+4/23 FLC 14+1/2 FAC 9 Others 12/2
Aston Villa (£5,500,000 on 12/3/99) PL 9+1

STONEMAN Paul
Born: Tynemouth, 26 February 1973
Height: 6'1" Weight: 13.6

Once with Blackpool, Paul was a commanding figure at the heart of the Halifax defence in 1998-99, despite being shown the red card at Torquay and missing four subsequent matches. A good ball winner, who is always likely to get on the score sheet as he has a tremendous shot, he captained the club in the absence of Kevin Hulme.

Blackpool (From trainee on 26/7/91) FL 38+5 FLC 5 FAC 3 Others 3
Colchester U (Loaned on 23/12/94) FL 3/1
Halifax T (Free on 12/7/95) FL 40/5 FLC 4 FAC 1 Others 1

STONES Craig

Born: Scunthorpe, 31 May 1980
Height: 5'11" Weight: 11.2

Craig's third season as a member of Lincoln's first-team squad proved something of a disappointment in 1998-99 as he failed to build on the success that saw him make his league debut as a 16-year old. During the campaign he was mainly restricted to reserve football, either as a right-wing back or in central midfield, his only league appearance being when he came on as a substitute in the 4-0 defeat at Gillingham.

Lincoln C (From trainee on 1/7/97) FL 10+8 FAC 1+2 Others 2

STORER Stuart John

Born: Rugby, 16 January 1967
Height: 5'11" Weight: 12.13
Club Honours: AMC '89

Suffering from the effects of a summer hernia operation, Stuart then had his 1998-99 season at Brighton further plagued by minor injuries. A winger who converted to playing right-wing back, sadly these injuries have taken a toll on his pace, although his effort can never be faulted. An ever-popular player, who empathised with the fans' battle to keep the club going, he was released by Micky Adams at the end of the campaign.

Mansfield T (Juniors) FL 0+1 (Freed in March 1984)
Birmingham C (Free from VS Rugby on 10/1/85) FL 5+3 FLC 1
Everton (Signed on 6/3/87)
Wigan Ath (Loaned on 23/7/87) FL 9+3 FLC 4
Bolton W (£25,000 on 24/12/87) FL 95+28/12 FLC 9+2 FAC 7+3/2 Others 16+5/1
Exeter C (£25,000 on 25/3/93) FL 75+2/8 FLC 4/1 FAC 4+1/1 Others 6
Brighton & Hove A (£15,000 on 2/3/95) FL 114+28/11 FLC 6+2/1 FAC 5+1/1 Others 5/1

STOWELL Michael (Mike)

Born: Portsmouth, 19 April 1965
Height: 6'2" Weight: 14.2

The departure of Hans Segers meant that Mike was clearly the first-choice goalkeeper at Molineux in 1998-99, and he celebrated by not conceding a goal in Wolves' opening four league fixtures. Like most players in his position there were times when he made costly errors, and there were other occasions when it could be said that he saved the day! However, most of his performances were steady rather than spectacular, and in April he equalled and then passed the club record of 420 appearances by a goalkeeper, belonging to the legendary Bert Williams.

Preston NE (Free from Leyland Motors on 14/2/85)
Everton (Free on 12/12/85) Others 1
Chester C (Loaned on 3/9/87) FL 14 Others 2
York C (Loaned on 24/12/87) FL 6
Manchester C (Loaned on 2/2/88) FL 14 FAC 1
Port Vale (Loaned on 21/10/88) FL 7 Others 1
Wolverhampton W (Loaned on 17/3/89) FL 7

Preston NE (Loaned on 8/2/90) FL 2
Wolverhampton W (£250,000 on 28/6/90) FL 359 FLC 27 FAC 21 Others 11

STRACHAN Gavin David

Born: Aberdeen, 23 December 1978
Height: 5'11" Weight: 11.7
International Honours: S: U21-6; Yth

After appearing to break through to Coventry's first-team squad in the previous season, Gavin failed to consolidate that position in 1998-99, and appeared only once, as a substitute at Southend, before leaving for Dundee on a three-month loan in the New Year, and impressing in the Scottish game. A combative midfielder, who can also get forward to link up play well, he played three times for the Scottish U21 side until losing his place. Is the son of the City manager, Gordon.

Coventry C (From trainee on 28/11/96) PL 2+7 FLC 0+1 FAC 2+2

STREET Kevin

Born: Crewe, 25 November 1977
Height: 5'10" Weight: 10.8

Another young striker who has come through the Crewe youth academy, and who was looking to build on progress made in 1997-98, Kevin started the opening game of last season but was mainly consigned to the bench thereafter, apart from injuries. A hard-working youngster, who enjoys getting involved, and is able to play right across the line, he came off the bench after 59 minutes of the home game against Norwich, with Alex 2-0 down, to score twice – a tremendous first-time volley, and an injury-time angled shot – to give the side all three points. Will be looking for more of the same in 1999-2000, hopefully, as a regular.

Crewe Alex (From trainee on 4/7/96) FL 19+36/6 FLC 1+1 FAC 0+1

STRODDER Gary John

Born: Cleckheaton, 1 April 1965
Height: 6'1" Weight: 13.3
Club Honours: Div 3 '98

A former captain of Notts County who lost his place in the side in 1998-99 after being suspended, Gary is a consummate professional. Always amongst the fittest of players, his tough and no-nonsense approach endearing him to the supporters, it was a great surprise when he was allowed to leave Meadow Lane in February. Loaned to Rotherham in January, the central defender played just three games before moving to Hartlepool on a permanent basis, having made his debut against the same side at the start of his loan spell. At Hartlepool, he became Chris Turner's first signing in an attempt to bolster a squad which desperately needed strengthening to have any chance of holding on to its Nationwide status. An unqualified success, he was the star of several games in the closing weeks, and although his best days may be behind him he looks to play a major role in helping to transform Pool into a successful unit.

Lincoln C (From apprentice on 8/4/83) FL 122+10/6 FLC 7+1 FAC 2+1 Others 5+1
West Ham U (Signed on 20/3/87) FL 59+6/2 FLC 8 FAC 4+2 Others 2

West Bromwich A (£190,000 on 22/8/90) FL 123+17/8 FLC 8+1 FAC 7/1 Others 10
Notts Co (£145,000 on 14/7/95) FL 116+5/10 FLC 9 FAC 10+1 Others 7
Rotherham U (Loaned on 29/1/99) FL 3
Hartlepool U (£25,000 on 25/2/99) FL 13

STRONG Gregory (Greg)

Born: Bolton, 5 September 1975
Height: 6'2" Weight: 11.12
International Honours: E: Yth; Sch

A powerful (excuse the pun!) central defender, Gregg found senior opportunities hard to come by at Bolton last season, making just four league starts, despite scoring his first goal for the club in the 2-2 home draw with Sheffield United in August. With competition for places against the likes of Mark Fish, Gudni Bergsson, Andy Todd, and Paul Warhurst preventing him from getting the first-team action, which he desperately craved, he joined Stoke on loan just prior to the transfer deadline. There, he maintained his proud record of scoring for sides on his debut, with a late winner against Wigan, and slotted in well to Brian Little's style of play at City.

Wigan Ath (From trainee on 1/10/92) FL 28+7/3 FLC 5 FAC 1 Others 3+1
Bolton W (Signed on 10/9/95) P/FL 4+2/1 FLC 5+1
Blackpool (Loaned on 21/11/97) FL 11/1 Others 1
Stoke C (Loaned on 24/3/99) FL 5/1

Graham Stuart

STUART Graham Charles

Born: Tooting, 24 October 1970
Height: 5'9" Weight: 11.10
Club Honours: FAC '95
International Honours: E: U21-5; Yth

Ever present for Sheffield United to the end of last November, playing in midfield and as a striker, he was successful in both roles as his goalscoring and assists tally showed. However, linked with a return to Everton, which came to nothing, his final appearance for United was the "replayed" FA Cup-tie at

Arsenal, where he was injured in the first few minutes of the game, and signed for Charlton just before the transfer deadline. Immediately thrust into first-team action at the Valley against one of his former clubs, Chelsea, he showed himself to be a hard-working player who liked to get forward, and scored three goals in his next five games, including a penalty against another of his former clubs, Everton, at Goodison Park. Immediately set up an understanding with Mark Kinsella in the Charlton midfield which should endure.

Chelsea (From trainee on 15/6/89) F/PL 70+17/14 FLC 11/2 FAC 5+2/1 Others 3+2/1
Everton (£850,000 on 19/8/93) PL 116+20/23 FLC 9/3 FAC 10+3/5 Others 2+1/1
Sheffield U (£850,000 on 28/11/97) FL 52+1/11 FLC 4 FAC 10+1/1 Others 0+1
Charlton Ath (£1,100,000 on 25/3/99) PL 9/3

STUART Jamie Christopher
Born: Southwark, 15 October 1976
Height: 5'10" Weight: 11.0
International Honours: E: U21-4; Yth

Jamie arrived at Millwall during the 1998 close season from Charlton, having been banned from the game after testing positive for an illegal substance. The local-born youngster has clearly learned from the experience, and was grateful for the chance to resurrect his career with the club he supported as a boy. Although he vied for the left-back position with Robbie Ryan throughout 1998-99, on a few outings he played in the centre of defence, where he acquitted himself well. Despite not being tall, he can get up to the ball very well, reads the game intelligently, can tackle hard, and delivers clinical crosses that put many a defence under great pressure. Because of an injury to Ryan he made the left-back position his own, with the trip to Wembley for the Auto Windscreens Shield final being a great bonus.

Charlton Ath (From trainee on 18/1/95) FL 49+1/3 FLC 8+1 FAC 3 Others 0+1
Millwall (Free on 25/9/98) FL 33+2 FLC 2 FAC 1 Others 6

STUART Mark Richard
Born: Chiswick, 15 December 1966
Height: 5'10" Weight: 11.10
International Honours: E: Sch

Rochdale's tricky winger had a good run in the side at the start of last season, with Dale using both Mark and Izzy Diaz down the flanks. Unfortunately, an injury cost him his place, and while he was out the club adopted a wing-back system that left little room for wingers. Four of his last five full games were in the FA Cup, three of them in the number nine shirt, as loan players Miquel de Souza and Michael Holt were ineligible. Then, after three months as a virtually permanent substitute he went on loan to Southport, still stuck on 99 career goals, before being released in the summer.

Charlton Ath (From juniors on 3/7/84) FL 89+18/28 FLC 7+3/2 FAC 1/1 Others 9+1
Plymouth Arg (£150,000 on 4/11/88) FL 55+2/11 FLC 4 FAC 3 Others 2/1
Ipswich T (Loaned on 22/3/90) FL 5/2
Bradford C (£80,000 on 3/8/90) FL 22+7/5 FLC 6/1 FAC 0+1 Others 1+1

Huddersfield T (Free on 30/10/92) FL 9+6/3 FAC 2 Others 4/1
Rochdale (Free on 5/7/93) FL 166+36/41 FLC 9+1/1 FAC 10/1 Others 6+4/2

Mark Stuart

STURGESS Paul Christopher
Born: Dartford, 4 August 1975
Height: 5'11" Weight: 12.5

A left back signed initially from Millwall on a month's loan to replace Graeme Atkinson last September, this period was extended to two months before his contract was taken over by Brighton, in order that he could play in the first round FA Cup-tie against Leyton Orient. Despite excelling when able to get forward, and possessing a thunderbolt shot from distance, Paul lost his place towards the end of the season, and was subsequently released by the manager, Micky Adams.

Charlton Ath (From trainee on 1/7/93) FL 43+8 FLC 4+1 FAC 1 Others 5
Millwall (Free on 3/7/97) FL 12+2 FLC 4 FAC 1 Others 0+1
Brighton & Hove A (Free on 15/9/98) FL 28+2 FAC 1 Others 1

STURRIDGE Dean Constantine
Born: Birmingham, 26 July 1973
Height: 5'8" Weight: 12.1

A fast, direct, and predominantly right-footed Derby striker who formed part of an unconventional strike force with Paulo Wanchope, 1998-99 was a relatively injury-free season for Dean. However, having earlier signed another contract with County, after transfer rumours in the summer, it proved, ultimately, to be a disappointing one in terms of goals scored. Although the potential is still there to be seen, he suffered a hamstring injury in the spring which allowed Jim Smith to try out other options up front. The subject of transfer talk throughout the season, despite stating he was happy to remain at Pride Park, he was placed on the transfer list,

along with Igor Stimac and Paulo Wanchope, at the end of May.

Derby Co (From trainee on 1/7/91) P/FL 125+26/46 FLC 8+1/3 FAC 7/2 Others 2+1
Torquay U (Loaned on 16/12/94) FL 10/5

STURRIDGE Simon Andrew
Born: Birmingham, 9 December 1969
Height: 5'6" Weight: 11.8
Club Honours: AMC '91

After almost two and a half years out of contention with serious injuries to both knees, Simon returned to regular football with Stoke last season, making occasional appearances in the first team and reserves. Unfortunately, troubles were not far away, and a cracked anklebone interrupted his progress. Despite a dearth of goals from the first-choice strike force, Brian Little allowed him to go on loan to Blackpool, managed by Nigel Worthington, and Simon was soon on the goal list for the Seasiders before being released by City during the summer.

Birmingham C (From trainee on 8/7/88) FL 129+21/30 FLC 10+4/1 FAC 8/2 Others 14/5
Stoke C (£75,000 on 24/9/93) FL 43+28/14 FLC 2+2 FAC 3+4/1 Others 8+3
Blackpool (Loaned on 9/3/99) FL 5/1

SUGDEN Ryan Stephen
Born: Bradford, 26 December 1980
Height: 6'1" Weight: 11.10

A lot of exciting youngsters have come through Oldham's youth development system, but none like this one. Tall and quick, with a terrific shot to match, and great in the air, the Latics' management are raving about this lad – who scored 38 goals in 39 reserve matches last season – saying that if anyone has a chance to make the grade, it has to be him. Coming off the bench at Walsall to make his senior bow at the beginning of May, and then given another subs' opportunity in the final game, at home to Reading, merely paved the way for him to explode onto the 1999-2000 stage.

Oldham Ath (From trainee on 25/11/98) FL 0+2

SULLIVAN Neil
Born: Sutton, 24 February 1970
Height: 6'0" Weight: 12.1
International Honours: S: 8

This tall, commanding goalkeeper brought up through the ranks in Wimbledon's youth team is now firmly established as Scotland's number one. As "Don's" "Player of the Year" for 1998-99, Neil gave some outstanding performances throughout the season, perhaps the most memorable being the superb displays in the home games against Manchester United and Liverpool. The latter included a wonderful save from a Michael Owen penalty, and he would also have gained a lot of personal satisfaction from his clean sheet in Scotland's 1-0 victory over Germany. A good organiser of the defence, and an agile shot stopper, his inspirational form was obviously observed by some of the bigger clubs in the country, and there has been much speculation about his future. Certainly, at 29, he has matured into one of the Premiership's top 'keepers.

Wimbledon (From trainee on 26/7/88) F/PL 143+1 FLC 13 FAC 23
Crystal Palace (Loaned on 1/5/92) FL 1

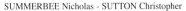

Neil Sullivan

SUMMERBEE Nicholas (Nicky) John
Born: Altrincham, 26 August 1971
Height: 5'11" Weight: 12.8
Club Honours: Div 1 '99
International Honours: E: B-1; U21-3
A First Division championship medal was
just reward for Nicky, who created an
endless string of opportunities for
Sunderland's forwards in 1998-99. In some
ways an unsung hero at the Stadium of
Light, the right winger has the ability to
cross a ball from seemingly impossible
positions, and in tandem with fellow winger,
Allan Johnston, gave First Division full
backs a torrid time last term. And, with his
Premiership experience, he should prove a
valuable member of the current squad.
Having spent most of the campaign providing for others, it was perhaps fitting that he
should set Sunderland on the way to the title
with the opening goal in the 3-1 win at
Barnsley in April. From a footballing
family, he is the son of the former England
star, Mike.
Swindon T (From trainee on 20/7/89) F/PL
89+23/6 FLC 9+1/3 FAC 2+4 Others 7/1
Manchester C (£1,500,000 on 24/6/94) P/FL
119+12/6 FLC 11+2/2 FAC 12/2
Sunderland (£1,000,000 on 14/11/97) FL 58+3/6
FLC 5+1 FAC 2+1 Others 3/1

SUMMERBELL Mark
Born: Durham, 30 October 1976
Height: 5'9" Weight: 11.9
Another bright, well thought of
Middlesbrough starlet, oozing confidence
and ability, Mark is a hard-tackling, hard-
working midfield powerhouse in the mould
of Robbie Mustoe, whose place he took on a
number of occasions in 1998-99. Having
scored some important goals for the Boro in
previous seasons, he is well poised to grab
and hold onto a Premier League place when
the inevitable opportunity arises.
Middlesbrough (From trainee on 1/7/95) F/PL
14+11 FLC 1+2/2

SUTCH Daryl
Born: Lowestoft, 11 September 1971
Height: 6'0" Weight: 12.0
International Honours: E: U21-4; Yth
Norwich City's longest-serving player,
Daryl turned in yet another season of highly
consistent displays in 1998-99. As ever, he
filled a number of roles for his manager,
starting games in both full-back positions
and on the right-hand side of midfield, but it
was his stint as an emergency goalkeeper at
Huddersfield in late March which earned
him the greatest praise. Taking over in goal
after Andy Marshall received a red card
after just nine minutes, he made some

Nicky Summerbee

spectacular saves and catches to deny the
Town frontmen until a soft own goal from
Paul Hughes finally sneaked past him five
minutes from time. He reads the game well
and has good pace, attributes that are well
suited to his full-back role, and his well-
deserved testimonial season was due to
culminate in a high profile pre-season
friendly against Borussia Moenchengladbach
during the past summer.
Norwich C (From trainee on 6/7/90) F/PL
166+35/7 FLC 15+3 FAC 7+3 Others 2+3

SUTTON Christopher (Chris) Roy
Born: Nottingham, 10 March 1973
Height: 6'3" Weight: 13.5
Club Honours: PL '95
International Honours: E: 1; B-2; U21-13
Having had such an excellent season for
Blackburn in 1997-98, 1998-99 turned into a
desperate one for Chris, who started with
ankle problems caused by stress fractures,
and then underwent surgery in September in
an effort to sort the matter out. Next, an
October return to action was aborted and he
was again forced out, this time until
December, before that comeback also
proved premature. He eventually returned in
February, only to be sidelined by a groin
injury, and despite making an attempt to
play through the pain barrier the club
eventually decided to rest him for an
extended period. Given the captaincy after
Tim Sherwood left for Tottenham, the
skilful striker was undoubtedly the club's
prime asset and inspiration, being able to
hold the ball and spread play, but after
spending not one game in full fitness he
even had to turn down a call up for Kevin
Keegan's England team. A player who on
his day can look the complete footballer,
1999-2000 cannot come quick enough. Stop
Press: Commanded the third highest

289

transfer, behind Alan Shearer and Dwight Yorke, between British clubs when signing for Chelsea on 5 July, a £10 million fee doing the trick.

Norwich C (From trainee on 2/7/91) F/PL 89+13/35 FLC 8+1/3 FAC 10/5 Others 6
Blackburn Rov (£5,000,000 on 13/7/94) PL 125+5/47 FLC 11+1/7 FAC 9/4 Others 7+3/1

SVENSSON Mathias (Matt)

Born: Boras, Sweden, 24 September 1974
Height: 6'0" Weight: 12.4
International Honours: Sweden: 2

Having been transferred to Tirol Innsbruck from Portsmouth during the 1998 close season, the hard-running, bustling striker was not expected to be back in England for quite a while, if at all. However, Terry Venables, the new Crystal Palace manager and former boss of Matt at Pompey, had other ideas and brought him to Selhurst Park at the end of last September. Standing out due to his blond hair, the Swede scored in the 5-1 home win over Norwich, his second start, before a broken ankle followed by a ruptured spleen saw his season halted after just eight games.

Portsmouth (£200,000 from Elfsborg on 6/12/96) FL 34+11/10 FLC 1/1 FAC 3+2/1 (£100,000 to Tirol Innsbruck on 15/7/98)
Crystal Palace (£100,000 on 29/9/98) FL 6+2/1

SWAILES Christopher (Chris) William

Born: Gateshead, 19 October 1970
Height: 6'2" Weight: 12.11

The former Ipswich central defender experienced an amazing turnaround in fortunes at Bury during 1998-99. In 1997-98 he had largely been frozen out of the first-team picture but, following the sale of Paul Butler to Sunderland in summer 1998, he was given a regular place in the Shakers' defence, and grabbed the opportunity with both hands. The scorer of three goals, the only black side to his campaign was a dismissal for two bookable offences at home to West Bromwich in December. In fact, he served three separate one-match suspensions due to his dismissal and tally of bookings – the only three games he missed all season. Was voted "Player of the Season" by the club's supporters.

Ipswich T (From trainee on 23/5/89)
Peterborough U (£10,000 on 28/3/91) Free to Boston in August 1991)
Doncaster Rov (Free from Bridlington T on 27/10/93) FL 49 FLC 2/1 FAC 1 Others 2
Ipswich T (£225,000 on 23/3/95) P/FL 34+3/1 FLC 3 Others 2
Bury (£200,000 on 14/11/97) FL 55+1/4 FLC 5 FAC 2

SWAILES Daniel (Danny)

Born: Bolton, 1 April 1979
Height: 6'3" Weight: 13.0

The former Bury apprentice, and now in his second year as a professional at Gigg Lane, Danny was on the fringe of the Shakers' first-team squad for cup matches last season. Named as a substitute against Crystal Palace in both legs of the Worthington Cup-tie, he made his debut in the first leg, playing for almost 70 minutes, and appeared as a late sub at Selhurst Park. He made his full debut

in the FA Cup third round against Stockport, when he deputised for his namesake (no relation) Chris Swailes. Was later sent on loan to Gainsborough Trinity.

Bury (From trainee on 9/7/97) FLC 0+2 FAC 1

SWALES Stephen (Steve) Colin

Born: Whitby, 26 December 1973
Height: 5'8" Weight: 10.6

Having at one stage been linked with Arsenal and Wimbledon, Steve appeared to fall out of favour at Reading following the arrival of manager, Tommy Burns, and was released from his contract last December. Homesick for his Yorkshire roots he contacted Hull City, and was soon joining their fight for Football League survival. With injuries to Neil Mann and Greg Rioch, he was drafted in to the left-wing-back role (his favoured side), although later being used on the right flank.

Scarborough (From trainee on 3/8/92) FL 51+3/1 FAC 5 Others 3
Reading (£70,000 on 13/7/95) FL 33+10/1 FLC 6+1 FAC 6
Hull C (Free on 7/12/98) FL 20+2 Others 1

SWAN Iain

Born: Glasgow, 16 October 1979
Height: 6'3" Weight: 12.6

Another Oldham youngster, Iain came through the trainee ranks to sign pro forms at the end of 1996, and then waited patiently in the wings, despite a bout of homesickness, until given his senior debut at Wycombe last March. A giant centre back, he showed great aerial ability on his debut, and looked a real old-fashioned stopper type when giving nothing away and settling well. Reckoned by the staff to be one to look out for.

Oldham Ath (From trainee on 12/11/96) FL 1 FAC 0+1

SWAN Peter Harold

Born: Leeds, 28 September 1966
Height: 6'2" Weight: 15.9
Club Honours: AMC '93

Rejoining Burnley, and his old manager, Stan Ternent, last August after just a season away from Turf Moor at Bury, Peter soon slotted into central defence, but a sending off at Reading brought suspension after only five games. Thereafter, it was a stop-start season for him, achilles and knee injuries keeping him out for long spells. His later appearances often saw him using his considerable physical presence to disturb opposing defences rather than bolster his own, a role for which he was probably best employed as a substitute. Was out of contract during the summer.

Leeds U (From trainee on 6/8/84) FL 43+6/11 FLC 3/2 FAC 3 Others 1+2
Hull C (£200,000 on 23/3/89) FL 76+4/24 FLC 2+3/1 FAC 2 Others 1
Port Vale (£300,000 on 16/8/91) FL 105+6/5 FLC 6 FAC 9/1 Others 12/1
Plymouth Arg (£300,000 on 22/7/94) FL 24+3/2 FLC 2/1 FAC 2
Burnley (£200,000 on 4/8/95) FL 47+2/7 FLC 2 FAC 3 Others 6
Bury (£50,000 on 8/8/97) FL 26+11/6 FLC 1+1 FAC 1
Burnley (Free on 28/8/98) FL 11+6

Terry Sweeney

SWEENEY Terry Neil

Born: Paisley, 26 January 1979
Height: 5'6" Weight: 10.10

A versatile youngster with an eye for goal, and a professional at Luton since March 1997 without a first-team opportunity, he was released last October and signed for Plymouth on a month-to-month contract following a successful trial. Able to play in a number of positions, either right or left of midfield, and with a good attitude, he scored a spectacular winner in the second round of the FA Cup to set up a tie with Derby. Out of action with injury for most of the last quarter, he moved on during the summer.

Luton T (From trainee on 26/3/97)
Plymouth Arg (Free on 16/10/98) FL 6+7/1 FAC 1+2/1 Others 1

SYMONS Christopher (Kit) Jeremiah

Born: Basingstoke, 8 March 1971
Height: 6'2" Weight: 13.7
Club Honours: Div 2 '99
International Honours: W: 31; B-1; U21-2; Yth

Signed from Manchester City during the 1998 close season, Kit, along with the skipper, Chris Coleman, missed just one game all season, and this was the rock on which Fulham's Second Division championship success was based. Only 32 league goals were conceded, while the Welsh international central defender found time to net 11 league goals at the other end. As a superb reader of the game, his experience with bigger clubs will be invaluable in Fulham's Division One campaign. It was a big surprise that Kit didn't make the PFA award-winning Division Two team but, maybe the voters felt there were likely to be too many Fulham players selected.

Portsmouth (From trainee on 30/12/88) FL 161/10 FLC 19 FAC 10 Others 13+1/1
Manchester C (£1,600,000 on 17/8/95) P/FL 124/4 FLC 6 FAC 9
Fulham (Free on 30/7/98) FL 45/11 FLC 5 FAC 7

TAAFFE Steven Lee
Born: Stoke, 10 September 1979
Height: 5'6" Weight: 9.0
A dimiFnutive Stoke striker with an appetite for goals and taking up good positions at the heart of the opponents area, chances were still only rare in 1998-99, but manager Brian Little knew that, if needed, Steven would not let the side down. Competitive and mobile, he could still make his mark in the game.
Stoke C (From trainee on 8/8/96) FL 1+5

Steven Taaffe

TAGGART Gerald (Gerry) Paul
Born: Belfast, 18 October 1970
Height: 6'1" Weight: 13.12
Club Honours: Div 1 '97
International Honours: NI: 45; U23-2; Yth; Sch
The left-footed central defender signed for Leicester on a free transfer under the Bosman ruling from Bolton Wanderers in July 1998, having previously played for Manchester City and Barnsley. Battled throughout last season to win a regular place in the starting line-up, including playing with a broken toe, and in October was rewarded with selection for the Worthington Cup final at Wembley. Always looked to be a rugged defender, with a surprisingly good touch on the ball, Gerry scored against Chesterfield in the opening round of the Worthington Cup, then later set up a classic Neil Lennon goal against Charlton with a cultured break from defence, followed by a neat interchange of passes with his Irish international colleague. Badly sprained his ankle in training late in the campaign, just as he looked to have established himself in the starting line-up. Not given the chance to add to his international tally of caps during 1998-99, but cannot be far short of a recall.
Manchester C (From trainee on 1/7/89) FL 10+2/1 Others 1
Barnsley (£75,000 on 10/1/90) FL 209+3/16 FLC 15/1 FAC 14/2 Others 6/1
Bolton W (£1,500,000 on 1/8/95) F/PL 68+1/4 FLC 8/1 FAC 4
Leicester C (Free on 23/7/98) PL 9+6 FLC 5+1/1 FAC 1+1

TAIT Paul Ronald
Born: Sutton Coldfield, 31 July 1971
Height: 6'1" Weight: 10.10
Club Honours: Div 2 '95; AMC '95
Unable to get into the team at Birmingham, Paul signed for Oxford on a free last January and missed only two games after his arrival. A consistent, competitive midfielder, he was always involved in the action, covering the ground well and working hard in both penalty areas, but failed to find the net. Has struggled against injury throughout his career.
Birmingham C (From trainee on 2/8/88) FL 135+35/14 FLC 13+2 FAC 6+2 Others 13+5/4
Northampton T (Loaned on 24/12/97) FL 2+1
Oxford U (Free on 15/1/99) FL 17 FAC 2

TALBOT Stewart Dean
Born: Birmingham, 14 June 1973
Height: 5'11" Weight: 13.7
As a midfield player with Port Vale, Stewart normally occupies a central role but his adaptability also saw him play wide on the right, and even at right back in an emergency in 1998-99. And able to get from box to box, he became a permanent fixture in the line-up thanks to his "never-say-die" attitude. Not bad in the air, his best game probably coming in the remarkable 4-3

Paul Tait

victory at Norwich, his season ended three games early when he suffered a double fracture of the right leg following an horrendous tackle, and is expected to be out of the game for eight months.

Port Vale (Signed from Moor Green on 10/8/94) FL 106+25/10 FLC 4+3 FAC 4+1 Others 2+3/1

TALIA Francesco (Frank)
Born: Melbourne Australia, 20 July 1972
Height: 6'1" Weight: 13.6
Club Honours: Div 2 '96

With Fraser Digby moving on during the 1998 close season, Swindon's Australian 'keeper proved himself a consistent replacement in 1998-99, and put pen to paper in a new three-year deal. Extremely agile, and a good shot stopper who comes out well for crosses and commands the area well, he missed just four games during a campaign where just one or two further bad results would have seen Town in relegation trouble, his good form keeping Jimmy Glass in the background.

Blackburn Rov (Free from Sunshine George Cross on 28/8/92)
Hartlepool U (Loaned on 29/12/92) FL 14 Others 1
Swindon T (£150,000 on 8/9/95) FL 76 FLC 7 FAC 2

TALLON Gerrit (Gary) Thomas
Born: Drogheda, 5 September 1973
Height: 5'9" Weight: 12.1

In his first full season at Mansfield after arriving initially on trial during the previous term, this skilful left-sided midfielder put in some excellent performances, missing only the odd match in 1998-99 only to injury or, more usually, suspension. His enthusiasm and commitment could not be faulted and was appreciated on the terraces, before his campaign was ended prematurely by injury which caused him to miss the last four matches. Out of contract during the summer, he likes to get down the line where he can find the front men with excellent crosses.

Blackburn Rov (£30,000 from Drogheda on 27/11/91)
Kilmarnock (Free on 20/6/96) SL 4 SLC 1 SC 1
Chester C (Loaned on 26/3/97) FL 1
Mansfield T (Free on 1/12/97) FL 57+5/2 FLC 2 FAC 2 Others 4

TANKARD Allen John
Born: Islington, 21 May 1969
Height: 5'10" Weight: 12.10
International Honours: E: Yth

Had an excellent season in 1998-99 as Port Vale's left back, and also had a successful spell in midfield when he kept scoring. Hardly missing a game, after popping up with an equaliser at Watford he was switched to a midfield role and particularly impressed new manager, Brian Horton. He scored three more goals, including a very important winner against Oxford, but by that time he had been restored to the back four for the run-in. Has now topped 500 games in his career.

Southampton (From apprentice on 27/5/87) FL 5 Others 2
Wigan Ath (Free on 4/7/88) FL 205+4/4 FLC 15/1 FAC 13 Others 20
Port Vale (£87,500 on 26/7/93) FL 202+5/6 FLC 18 FAC 14/1 Others 8+1

Allen Tankard

TANNER Adam David
Born: Maldon,, 25 October 1973
Height: 6'0" Weight: 12.1

Adam continued to be a valuable member of the Ipswich first-team squad in 1998-99, being well capable of playing in midfield, central defence, or as a wing back, without being able to establish himself as a regular. Although his versatility made him an ideal person to have on the substitutes' bench, that was sometimes a handicap when not being considered for the starting line-up. However, the arrival of Jean-Manuel Thetis and the emergence of Titus Bramble saw the competition for places in the defence become even keener, and its clean sheet record meant that changes were only made because of injuries or suspensions. Missed the closing stages of the season because of a cartilage operation.

Ipswich T (From trainee on 13/7/92) P/FL 49+24/7 FLC 2+2 FAC 5+2 Others 3+1/1

TARICCO Mauricio Ricardo
Born: Buenos Aires Argentine, 10 March 1973
Height: 5'9" Weight: 11.7

Ipswich began last season with the formation that had proved popular in the previous campaign, which meant that Mauricio continued to excite the locals in the right-wing-back position, defending soundly and joining the attack at every opportunity. He opened the scoring in the home Worthington Cup game with a fine shot from the edge of the box, and his goal against Crystal Palace when he picked up the ball just inside the Palace half, ran past a couple of defenders, cut into the box, and smashed it into the roof of the net, would have won him the "Goal of the Season" trophy had he still been at the club. After making his 150th appearance for Town, against Wolverhampton in November, and

helping secure the victory that took them into second place, he was stretchered off in the last minute with an ankle injury, and it was to prove to have been his last in an Ipswich shirt as the next day the club announced that they had accepted an offer from Tottenham. A keen follower of the internet – he uses it to keep in touch with his family in Argentina – he received over 500 messages from Ipswich fans asking him to stay, before signing for Spurs in December. Quickly settling in at White Hart Lane, looking confident with the ball at his feet, and strong in the challenge, once in the side he missed very few games, and looks good for 1999-2000, especially under the new George Graham regime.

Ipswich T (£175,000 from Argentinos on 9/9/94) FL 134+3/4 FLC 18/3 FAC 8 Others 7
Tottenham H (£1,800,000 on 4/12/98) PL 12+1 FAC 2+1

TATE Christopher (Chris) Douglas
Born: York, 27 December 1977
Height: 6'0" Weight: 11.10

A talented young Scarborough striker, 1998-99 was, for him, a season of two halves. Struggling with injuries during the first part of the campaign, he did not start a league match until the home fixture with Exeter in January, but then fairly exploded onto the scene with a flurry of goals, including a brilliant hat trick in a 3-0 win at Carlisle. Stop Press: Although his goals failed to keep Boro in the league, following their relegation to the Conference he became Halifax's record signing when moving to the Shay on 10 June for £150,000.

Sunderland (Free from York C juniors on 17/7/96)
Scarborough (Free on 5/8/97) FL 21+9/13 FLC 0+1 FAC 0+1 Others 2+1

Chris Tate

Craig Taylor

TAYLOR Craig

Born: Plymouth, 24 January 1974
Height: 6'1" Weight: 13.2
The brother of Bristol City's Shaun, having recovered from injury problems, and in an effort to get match fit, Craig enjoyed a spell on loan at Plymouth last October. Strong in the air and determined in the tackle, the young central defender also proved to be comfortable on the ball and a handful in the opposition's penalty area, scoring a superb header in the home game against Brentford. Back at Swindon he was soon in the team on a regular basis, becoming one of Jimmy Quinn's automatic selections.
Swindon T (£25,000 from Dorchester T on 15/4/97) FL 46+7/2 FAC 3
Plymouth Arg (Loaned on 16/10/98) FL 6/1

TAYLOR Gareth Keith

Born: Weston super Mare, 25 February 1973
Height: 6'2" Weight: 13.8
International Honours: W: 8; U21-7
Arrived at Manchester City late last November from Sheffield United, having had a good scoring record in 1997-98 before losing his touch when hampered by injury. Settling in quickly, his style being to compete for aerial possession and lay off the ball for oncoming strikers, he made his debut away at Luton and played 22 league and cup games, before being relegated to the substitutes' bench. After scoring his first goal for City in his eighth game, the winner at home against Stoke, in the 33 games involved in he struck just four times, and missed an important penalty in the home defeat by Oldham. Lack of goals aside, his

sheer physical presence always creates problems for the opposition which, in turn, relieves the other strikers.
Bristol Rov (Free from Southampton juniors on 29/7/91) FL 31+16/16 FLC 3+1 FAC 1+1 Others 5
Crystal Palace (£750,000 on 27/9/95) FL 18+2/1 FAC 2/1
Sheffield U (Signed on 8/3/96) FL 56+28/24 FLC 8+3/2 FAC 5+2 Others 1+1
Manchester C (£400,000 on 26/11/98) FL 20+6/4 FAC 3 Others 1+3

Ian Taylor

TAYLOR Ian Kenneth

Born: Birmingham, 4 June 1968
Height: 6'1" Weight: 12.4
Club Honours: AMC '93; FLC '96
Although Ian persistently featured in the Aston Villa side in 1998-99, and the fact that he was well worthy of his place, it was admirable due to him carrying a lingering knee injury throughout the whole campaign. Even as early as the third game he was missing, and it was thought that he required surgery. However, he continued to play, apart from the odd game here and there, before missing the FA Cup game against Hull after suffering a groin strain and later picking up a strained thigh muscle at home to Coventry. Disappointed not to have scored more goals, he is totally committed to Villa, having publicly announced that he wants to spend the rest of his career at the club. Extremely versatile, and able to play in midfield or up front, he is a tenacious tackler, is composed on the ground, is good in the air, and loves to drive forward in pursuit of a goal or two. Hopefully, he will have had the knee problem sorted in the close season and be back in good shape for the coming term.
Port Vale (£15,000 from Moor Green on 13/7/92) FL 83/28 FLC 4/2 FAC 6/1 Others 13/4
Sheffield Wed (£1,000,000 on 12/7/94) PL 9+5/1 FLC 2+2/1
Aston Villa (£1,000,000 on 21/12/94) PL 136+10/16 FLC 9+1/2 FAC 8+1/1 Others 11+1/3

TAYLOR John Patrick

Born: Norwich,, 24 October 1964
Height: 6'2" Weight: 13.12
Club Honours: Div 3 '91
Now in his second spell at Cambridge, "Shaggy" can claim to be the most popular United player ever, having been accorded the accolade of "King of the Abbey", the best player for United in the last 25 years. The award came in the same week in December that saw him break Alan Biley's career goalscoring record of 81 goals, and he followed this up by breaking the latter's league scoring record of 74 goals, in April. He finished the campaign as second leading scorer to Martin Butler, and all this as well as being coach to the reserve team. Intelligent and great in the air, and one of the club's senior professionals, there is every likelihood of him scoring more goals and achieving the target for Cambridge United.
Colchester U (From juniors on 17/12/82)
Cambridge U (Signed from Sudbury T on 24/8/88) FL 139+21/46 FLC 9+2/2 FAC 21/10 Others 12+2/2
Bristol Rov (Signed on 28/3/92) FL 91+4/44 FLC 4/1 FAC 3 Others 5
Bradford C (£300,000 on 5/7/94) FL 35+1/11 FLC 4/2 FAC 2 Others 3
Luton T (£200,000 on 23/3/95) FL 27+10/3 FLC 2 Others 1/1
Lincoln C (Loaned on 27/9/96) FL 5/2
Colchester U (Loaned on 8/11/96) FL 8/5 Others 1
Cambridge U (Free on 10/1/97) FL 67+28/31 FLC 3+3/1 FAC 4+2 Others 1+1/1

TAYLOR Maik Stefan

Born: Hildeshein, Germany, 4 September 1971
Height: 6'4" Weight: 14.2
Club Honours: Div 2 '99
International Honours: NI: 4; B-1; U21-1

The fact that Fulham conceded just 43 goals in 57 league, Worthington Cup, and FA Cup matches in 1998-99 was partly down to a strong defence, but the man behind them played a big part too. Early on in the season, Maik had his critics as a number of free kicks and long shots found a way past him, but he improved dramatically midway through, and made many brilliant and vital saves in the unbeaten run of 15 games which clinched the Second Division championship. Just two games were drawn, with only six goals conceded, and this resulted in Maik gaining his first Northern Ireland caps, along with a well-deserved place in the PFA Division Two side. Not only is he a good shot stopper, but he commands his area, talks to his defenders, and is confident when coming for crosses.

Barnet (Free from Farnborough on 7/6/95) FL 70 FLC 6 FAC 6 Others 2
Southampton (£500,000 on 1/1/97) PL 18
Fulham (£800,000 + on 17/11/97) FL 74 FLC 5 FAC 9 Others 3

TAYLOR Martin

Born: Ashington, 9 November 1979
Height: 6'4" Weight: 15.0
International Honours: E: Yth

With suitable irony this Blackburn player was nicknamed "Tiny". As the centre half from the previous year's FA Youth Cup final side, he probably did not expect a debut playing centre forward for the last few minutes in the EUFA Cup-tie in Lyons in 1998-99, but his surprisingly quick feet, control, and lightness of foot, marks him as a natural footballer. His league debut came in the relegation battle at Coventry where, opposed to Dion Dublin, he was impressive in a stout-hearted defending display. Despite his height, his headwork is probably the area of the game that needs most attention, and his durability has yet to be proved, but he appears to be a remarkable natural talent.

Blackburn Rov (From trainee on 13/8/97) PL 1+2 Others 0+1

TAYLOR Martin James

Born: Tamworth, 9 December 1966
Height: 6'0" Weight: 14.6

1998-99 was an even more impressive season for the first-choice Wycombe 'keeper, and he earned second place in the "Player of the Year" award. The highlights were many, including two games against Chesterfield, the first in the FA Cup when he ensured a 1-0 win with a stunning reflex save which put the famous Bank's save from Pele in the shade, while the league game at Chesterfield even had the Spireite manager, John Duncan, singing his praises. The historic win at Manchester City was largely due to his inspired goalkeeping, and he was at his best when the defence was under great pressure, seeming to be an unpenetrable barrier. Unusually for Martin, he missed two consecutive games on two occasions last season, due to back and hamstring strains.

Derby Co (Signed from Mile Oak Rov on 2/7/86) F/PL 97 FLC 7 FAC 5 Others 11
Carlisle U (Loaned on 23/9/87) FL 10 FLC 1 FAC 1 Others 2
Scunthorpe U (Loaned on 17/12/87) FL 8

Crewe Alex (Loaned on 20/9/96) FL 6
Wycombe W (Free on 27/3/97) FL 93 FLC 5 FAC 5 Others 3

TAYLOR Robert Anthony

Born: Norwich, 30 April 1971
Height: 6'1" Weight: 13.8

Signed for a then club record fee from Brentford last August, Robert took time to settle and win over the Gillingham fans in 1998-99. By his own admission, he was unfit due to injury, having missed all of the Bees' pre-season training because of it, and despite labouring on his confidence was drained. Gradually, however, he got himself fit, and with the signing of his former team mate, Carl Asaba, he began to show his real ability around the penalty area. In February, he scored all of Gills' goals in a 5-0 victory (all five in 34 minutes), and became the first player from the club to score five in a game since 1957. Voted the supporters' "Player of the Year" and "Away Player of the Year", it was quite a remarkable story for a player who in the space of nine months went from villian to super hero!

Norwich C (From trainee on 26/3/90)
Leyton Orient (Loaned on 28/3/91) FL 0+3/1
Birmingham C (Signed on 31/8/91)
Leyton Orient (Free on 21/10/91) FL 54+19/20 FLC 1+1 FAC 2+1 Others 2+1
Brentford (£100,000 on 24/3/94) FL 172+1/56 FLC 16/6 FAC 10/8 Others 14/4
Gillingham (£500,000 on 6/8/98) FL 43/16 FLC 1 FAC 1 Others 7/5

TAYLOR Robert (Bob)

Born: Horden, 3 February 1967
Height: 5'10" Weight: 12.12

One of the game's genuine nice guys, Bob joined Bolton in July 1998 from West Bromwich Albion, having completed two highly successful loan periods with the club during the previous season. That free transfer proved to be a genuine bargain as he proceeded to form successful partnerships with first Arnar Gunnlaugsson, then Dean Holdsworth, and finally Eidur Gudjohnsen as 1998-99 progressed. Already a crowd favourite from his loan spell (helped no doubt by scoring in the 1-1 draw with the local enemy, Manchester United, at Old Trafford) the stiker enjoyed a fine season in which he found the net with some regularity, regardless of who his partner happened to be at the time. His 110 per-cent commitment to the cause ensured that even when he did not get on the scoresheet he would have played a major part in the game, and there is no doubt that he still has a good few seasons of upper league football left in him yet. The season's highlight came in the second leg of the First Division play-off semi-final, when his two goals in the 4-3 defeat at Ipswich ultimately sent Bolton to Wembley for the final against Watford.

Leeds U (Free from Horden Colliery on 27/3/86) FL 33+9/9 FLC 5+1/3 FAC 1 Others 4+1/1
Bristol C (£175,000 on 23/3/89) FL 96+10/50 FLC 6+1/2 FAC 9+1/5 Others 3/1
West Bromwich A (£300,000 on 31/1/92) FL 211+27/96 FLC 16/6 FAC 6+2/3 Others 16+3/8
Bolton W (Free on 8/1/98) P/FL 42+8/18 FLC 3+3/1 FAC 1 Others 3/2

TAYLOR Scott James

Born: Chertsey, 5 May 1976
Height: 5'10" Weight: 11.4

Rumoured to be a Tranmere target for some time, the club finally got its man from Bolton last October, and what a bargain he turned out to be. He immediately slotted into the first team in a striking position, and proved himself to be hard working and assured in every respect, his transfer being partly funded by the gate receipts from the third round Worthington Cup-tie at home to Newcastle. Scott amply repaid the supporters' faith with his willingness to track back, his valuable decoy runs, cool finishing, inventive distribution, impressive control, and the ability to hold up the ball while his colleagues regrouped. In doing all of that, he contributed nine invaluable league goals.

Millwall (£15,000 from Staines on 8/2/95) FL 13+15 FLC 0+2/2 FAC 1+1
Bolton W (£150,000 on 29/3/96) P/FL 2+10/1 FLC 0+4/1 FAC 1/1
Rotherham U (Loaned on 12/12/97) FL 10/3 Others 1
Blackpool (Loaned on 26/3/98) FL 3+2/1
Tranmere Rov (£50,000 on 9/10/98) FL 31+5/9 FAC 1

TAYLOR Shaun

Born: Plymouth, 26 February 1963
Height: 6'1" Weight: 13.0
Club Honours: Div 4 '90; Div 2 '96

The strong central defender came back into the Bristol City team last Easter after a long absence due to injury, having been missed more than the club could have realised when they planned for their first season back in Division One. Lifted the fans in his come-back game against Port Vale, by winning the ball both in the air and on the ground, and generally giving the side a solid look which had been missing since his injury. Re-instated as team captain, Shaun led by example, just as he has done throughout his long career. Out of contract during the summer, City made an offer of re-engagement.

Exeter C (Free from Bideford T on 10/12/86) FL 200/16 FLC 12 FAC 9 Others 12
Swindon T (£200,000 on 26/7/91) F/PL 212/30 FLC 22+1/2 FAC 14 Others 10/1
Bristol C (£50,000 + on 6/9/96) FL 80/3 FLC 4/2 FAC 5/1 Others 5

TEBILY Olivier

Born: Ivory Coast, 19 December 1975
Height: 6'1" Weight: 13.4
International Honours: Ivory Coast: 1

Signed during transfer deadline week last March from the French Second Division club, Chateauroux, the French U21 international, who also has a full cap for the Ivory Coast, made his first appearance for Sheffield United as a substitute in midfield before reverting to his role as a central defender. Having showed good pace, distribution, and anticipation, in his early outings, the club has high hopes for the 23-year-old, who has had little time as yet to adjust to the English game, nor to learn English! Stop Press: Signed for Glasgow Celtic for £1.25 million on 8 July.

Sheffield U (£175,000 from Chateauroux on 24/3/99) FL 7+1

TELFER Paul Norman
Born: Edinburgh, 21 October 1971
Height: 5'9" Weight: 11.6
International Honours: S: B-2; U21-3
Another steady season from the hard-working and dependable Scottish mid-fielder, Paul appeared on Coventry's right flank for most of 1998-99, although moving inside to successfully "mind" Gary McAllister later in the campaign. Although his disciplinary record was poor, clocking up 12 bookings before the end of March and being called in front of the FA, he is not, however, a dirty player, and many of his bookings were careless trips caused by his keenness to win the ball. Goals, as ever, were in short supply, but he did score with a fierce volley from the edge of the box against Forest, and with a stunning drive in the final game, at home to Leeds. His aggressive play often belies his excellent distribution.
Luton T (From trainee on 7/11/88) FL 136+8/19 FLC 5 FAC 14/2 Others 2/1
Coventry C (£1,500,000 on 11/7/95) PL 125+5/6 FLC 12/2 FAC 11+3/4

TERRY John George
Born: Barking, 7 December 1980
Height: 6'0" Weight: 12.4
Following that old maxim of "Go West, Young Man", John travelled across London and found himself playing in the Chelsea first team before his 18th birthday. He came on as substitute in his accustomed central defensive position against Aston Villa in the Worthington Cup, and to underline his versatility his next two appearances were in central midfield and at right back – against Southampton and the FA Cup-tie at Oldham (his full debut), respectively. Going on to give assured performances as a right back in potentially tricky cup ties at Oxford and Valerenga, he is highly regarded by the backroom staff at Chelsea, his main attributes being alertness and an ability to read the game. He is also outstanding in the air, strong in the tackle, and has a reputation in junior football for notching vital goals.
Chelsea (From trainee on 18/3/98) PL 0+2 FLC 0+1 FAC 2+1 Others 1

THACKERAY Andrew (Andy) John
Born: Huddersfield, 13 February 1968
Height: 5'9" Weight: 11.0
Club Honours: FAYC '86
Another Halifax player with plenty of Football League experience, Andy, a consistent defender who pushes forward whenever possible, made the right-back position his own until suffering a knee injury last March. Sorely missed, on his return to the side in April he celebrated with a crucial goal away at Mansfield before being released during the summer. Was the club's PFA representative and fulfilled his role well.
Manchester C (From juniors on 15/2/86)
Huddersfield T (Free on 1/8/86) FL 2 Others 0+1
Newport Co (£5,000 on 27/3/87) FL 53+1/4 FLC 3+1 FAC 1 Others 2+1/1
Wrexham (£5,000 on 20/7/88) FL 139+13/14 FLC 10/1 FAC 6 Others 13+2

Rochdale (£15,000 on 15/7/92) FL 161+4/13 FLC 8+1 FAC 7+1/1 Others 10+3/2
Halifax T (Free on 7/8/97) FL 37+1/5 FLC 4 FAC 1 Others 1

THATCHER Benjamin (Ben) David
Born: Swindon, 30 November 1975
Height: 5'10" Weight: 12.7
International Honours: E: U21-4; Yth
After having a rough time of it with injuries at Wimbledon in 1997-98, he spent the summer fully recovering before coming back into the team in the fifth game last season, and was then rarely out of it, again proving to be well worth the transfer fee paid by the Dons in 1996. A good, strong tackler, and the saviour on many occasions, seemingly appearing from nowhere to save the day, he is an extremely competitive player who is equally confident playing at left back or as a central defender. Completed his best ever season for the Dons in 1998-99, performing to a consistently high level, and showing a more mature approach on the pitch. The ex-Millwall defender always gave 100 per-cent commitment, and tamed the more physical side of his game to show a skilful player in the making.
Millwall (From trainee on 8/6/92) FL 87+3/1 FLC 6 FAC 7 Others 1
Wimbledon (£1,840,00 on 5/7/96) PL 63+3 FLC 10 FAC 5

THETIS Jean-Manuel (Manu)
Born: France, 5 November 1971
Height: 6'3" Weight: 14.12
A giant of a defender who joined Ipswich from Seville last September, he did not take long to endear himself to the fans. Right footed, and able to play in central defence or as a right-wing back, with a deceptive turn of pace for a man of his stature, he fell foul of the referees who seemed to book him by reputation, and there were occasions when he appeared to be shown the yellow card for the most innocuous tackles. A keen attacker, who likes to get forward as often as possible, Manu ended the season with three goals to his credit, the best of which was the overhead kick which gleaned the points at West Bromwich.
Ipswich T (£50,000 from Seville on 11/9/98) FL 29+2/2 FLC 2/1 FAC 2 Others 1+1

THIRLWELL Paul
Born: Washington, 13 February 1979
Height: 5'11" Weight: 11.4
Sunderland boss Peter Reid stated last season that in this locally-born youngster he had found the "new Paul Bracewell". Certainly, the diminutive, but tigerish midfielder showed in his handful of first-team appearances that he had the temperament and the ability to make the step-up from the reserves to the first team. Made his debut against York in the Worthington Cup in August, and looked comfortable in the midfield holding role, tackling and providing short, accurate passes for those around him. Paul's highlight of the season was his excellent display in the superb 3-0 win away at Bolton in November, and he looks to have a very bright future.
Sunderland (From trainee on 14/4/97) FL 1+1 FLC 2+1

THOGERSEN Thomas
Born: Copenhagen, Denmark, 2 April 1968
Height: 6'2" Weight: 12.10
Signed from Brondby during the 1998 close season, Alan Ball introduced this big Dane into Portsmouth's midfield, and he quickly became an automatic choice as a right-wing back, starting 19 league games. Whilst he is strong, physical, and menacing, he has not adapted to the English game when playing a tactical role, but, given time, his pace and defending skills should improve to make him an established defender.
Portsmouth (£100,000 from Brondby, via Frem, on 5/8/98) FL 29+5 FLC 2 FAC 0+1

THOM Stuart Paul
Born: Dewsbury, 27 December 1976
Height: 6'2" Weight: 11.12
Unable to get a game at Nottingham Forest in 1998-99, Stuart was allowed to move to Oldham in October, and immediately set up in partnership with Shaun Garnett at the heart of the Latics' defence. Only absent through falling foul of referees and the odd injury, the strong central defender showed himself to be extremely forceful in aerial battles, and totally committed to the cause. He could also play the ball away on occasion, having two good feet, something you would automatically expect of a man who learned his trade at Forest.
Nottingham F (From trainee on 11/1/94)
Mansfield T (Loaned on 24/12/97) FL 5 Others 2
Oldham Ath (£45,000 on 21/10/98) FL 19+6/2 FAC 1 Others 1

THOMAS Anthony (Tony)
Born: Liverpool, 12 July 1971
Height: 5'11" Weight: 13.0
Club Honours: AMC '90
Powerfully built, and a good competitive tackler, he is also an attacking right back with the ability to deliver damaging crosses into the opposition penalty area. However, he featured in only two minutes of Everton's 1998-99 season, coming off the bench at Nottingham Forest before being sold for £150,000 to Scottish Premier Division's Motherwell in December.
Tranmere Rov (From trainee on 1/2/89) FL 254+3/12 FLC 23+1/1 FAC 7 Others 26/1
Everton (£400,000 + on 7/8/97) PL 6+2 FLC 1 FAC 1

THOMAS David (Dai) John
Born: Caerphilly, 26 September 1975
Height: 5'10" Weight: 12.7
Club Honours: Div 2 '98
International Honours: W: U21-2
Having signed from Watford at the start of 1998-99, Dai spent a disappointing personal season on the fringe of the Cardiff first team. He still scored a few goals, and was crucially on target against Shrewsbury, Hull City (2) and Halifax Town in Third Division victories. An aggressive, strong-running front man, he has pledged to spend the summer training in order to return fitter and slimmer than ever, and could prove to be a useful squal member for 1999-2000.
Swansea C (From trainee on 25/7/94) FL 36+20/10 FLC 2 FAC 0+1 Others 5+3/3

Watford (£100,000 on 17/7/97) FL 8+8/3 FAC 1+3
Cardiff C (£50,000 on 20/8/98) FL 16+8/4 FAC 0+2 Others 1

THOMAS Geoffrey (Geoff) Robert
Born: Manchester, 5 August 1964
Height: 6'1" Weight: 13.2
Club Honours: FMC '91; Div 1 '98
International Honours: E: 9; B-3
Handed a one-year contract by Nottingham Forest, following their return to the Premiership, Geoff started at Arsenal on the opening day of 1998-99 and scored the club's first goal of the new season in a 2-1 defeat. He than played in the next four matches but, on suffering ligament damage to his left knee, having already recovered from similar problems to his other knee, his campaign came to a halt. A very competitive left-sided midfielder who never gives up, he was beginning to show good form, but it is difficult to see where his career goes from here. At his best a hard-working dynamo of a player with a super left foot, his career has been beset by hard luck in the shape of injuries.
Rochdale (Free from Littleborough on 13/8/82) FL 10+1/1 Others 0+1
Crewe Alex (Free on 22/3/84) FL 120+5/20 FLC 8 FAC 2 Others 2+1
Crystal Palace (£50,000 on 8/6/87) F/PL 192+3/26 FLC 24/3 FAC 13+1/2 Others 15+1/4
Wolverhampton W (£800,000 on 18/6/93) FL 36+10/8 FLC 1 FAC 1 Others 6
Nottingham F (Free on 18/7/97) P/FL 18+7/4 FLC 2/1

Geoff Thomas

THOMAS Glen Andrew
Born: Hackney, 6 October 1967
Height: 6'1" Weight: 13.12
An experienced central defender signed from Brighton's landlords, Gillingham, on a

free transfer during the summer of 1998, groin problems limited his appearance for Albion in 1998-99, and he had every defender's worst nightmare at Brentford by conceding an own goal, then providing the back pass which led to the home side's second shortly afterwards, before being substituted at half time. Retired through injury in October, and is now running a gift shop in Bow.
Fulham (From apprentice on 9/10/85) FL 246+5/6 FLC 21 FAC 8 Others 14+1
Peterborough U (Free on 4/11/94) FL 6+2 FAC 0+1 Others 2
Gillingham (£30,000 on 15/1/96) FL 20+8 FAC 1 Others 1
Brighton & Hove A (Free on 6/7/98) FL 2+1 FLC 1+1

THOMAS Martin Russell
Born: Lymington, 12 September 1973
Height: 5'8" Weight: 12.6
A summer signing from Fulham, Martin made an encouraging start for Swansea in 1998-99, scoring on his debut against Exeter. A good competitor in midfield, having the ability to get forward in support of his strikers, and to cover for his defence, he scored the match winner against West Ham in an FA Cup replay at Vetch Field, beating Shaka Hislop with a vicious volley. A medial knee-ligament injury, plus surgery to a long-standing hernia problem, unfortunately saw him sidelined until the last month of the campaign.
Southampton (From trainee on 19/6/92)
Leyton Orient (Free on 24/3/94) FL 5/2
Fulham (Free on 21/7/94) FL 59+31/8 FLC 6+1 FAC 4/1 Others 7+1/2
Swansea C (Free on 30/7/98) FL 26+4/3 FLC 2 FAC 4/2 Others 2

THOMAS Mitchell Anthony
Born: Luton, 2 October 1964
Height: 6'2" Weight: 13.0
International Honours: E: B-1; U21-3; Yth
Struggling with back and groin problems, the new player/coach only played sporadically for Luton in 1998-99 before coming on strong to appear in the last 16 matches of the campaign, prior to being released in the summer. Ungainly but effective, his long legs often getting the ball clear when opponents felt they had passed him, at his best he was sound and reliable in Town's defence, while further forward his ability to knock-on balls from set pieces often set the forwards up.
Luton T (From apprentice on 27/8/82) FL 106+1/1 FLC 5 FAC 18
Tottenham H (£233,000 on 7/7/86) FL 136+21/6 FLC 28+1/1 FAC 12/1
West Ham U (£525,000 on 7/8/91) FL 37+1/3 FLC 5 FAC 4 Others 2
Luton T (Free on 12/11/93) FL 170+15/5 FLC 12+1 FAC 6 Others 5+1

THOMAS Roderick (Rod) Clive
Born: Brent, 10 October 1970
Height: 5'5" Weight: 11.0
Club Honours: FAYC '89; Div 3 '95; AMC '97
International Honours: E: U21-1; Yth; Sch
A skilful ball player who started last season well for Chester after an indifferent 1997-98, Rod scored three goals in six league

appearances before being sold to Brighton in October to ease City's financial position. With the fee being paid for by the Albion supporters, he became known as the "People's Player", and his arrival coincided with the club's revival. Making an immediate impact, when scoring the opening goal on his debut in the 3-2 away win at Cambridge, the Seagulls' strikers, particularly Richie Barker, benefited from his mazy wing play and endless supply of crosses. Having suffered an ankle-ligament injury whilst training in January, just before he was due to make his comeback from a hamstring injury sustained a fortnight earlier, he returned to first-team action on the last day of the campaign.
Watford (From trainee on 3/5/88) FL 63+21/9 FLC 3+2 FAC 0+1 Others 3+1
Gillingham (Loaned on 27/3/92) FL 8/1 Others 1
Carlisle U (Free on 12/7/93) FL 124+22/16 FLC 11+1/3 FAC 9+4 Others 22+4/9
Chester C (Free on 4/7/97) FL 28+16/7 FLC 3+2 FAC 2
Brighton & Hove A (£25,000 on 8/10/98) FL 11+1/3

THOMAS Stephen (Steve)
Born: Hartlepool, 23 June 1979
Height: 5'10" Weight: 12.0
International Honours: W: Yth
In 1998-99, having completed his second season as a full-time professional at Wrexham, although born in the north east Steve had qualifications to play for Wales, and appeared for his country at youth level. Made his Football League debut when coming on as substitute against Stoke City at the Racecourse last September, and scored the winning goal in the FAW Premier Cup (the competition sponsored by BBC, Wales) against Caernarfon Town of the League of Wales. In the opinion of many, he was on the verge of a first-team breakthrough when he fractured his ankle in an early December Pontins League reserve match, but forced his way back into contention with a number of strong performances in the reserves to again be involved with the senior squad by the end of term. Unfortunately, on making his first start for the club in the final match of the season, at Bournemouth, he broke his ankle in a 24th-minute challenge. Hopefully, he will figure strongly before the year 2000.
Wrexham (From trainee on 4/7/97) FL 1+4

THOMAS Wayne
Born: Walsall, 28 August 1978
Height: 5'9" Weight: 12.10
This skilful Walsall midfielder who specialises in the telling long ball, and is more than comfortable in possession, played just one full game last season in the 3-3 draw against Bristol Rovers, but coolly netted a penalty in the Auto Windscreens shoot-out against Cambridge. A player with a future, Wayne will be back to hold down a more regular place in 1999-2000.
Walsall (From trainee on 25/7/96) FL18+19 FLC 0+1 FAC 2 Others 1+4/1

THOMAS Wayne Junior Robert
Born: Gloucester, 17 May 1979
Height: 5'11" Weight: 11.12

The young and powerful Torquay central defender finally came of age in a difficult season for the club in 1998-99, and his displays at the back caught the eye of many of the bigger clubs. In running Neville Southall close for the "Player of the Year" award, if he can improve his distribution expect him to make it to the very top. Missed just three games throughout the campaign, and scored his first-ever league goal at Barnet.

Torquay U (From trainee on 4/7/97) FL 51+32/2 FLC 2+1/1 FAC 3 Others 3+4

THOMPSON Alan

Born: Newcastle, 22 December 1973
Height: 6'0" Weight: 12.8
Club Honours: Div 1 '97
International Honours: E: U21-2; Yth
Signed during the 1998 close season from Bolton, Alan was John Gregory's first signing for Aston Villa, and was brought to the club to give the left side more quality, being very much a left-footed player. Unfortunately, he was yet another Villa man who suffered from injuries during the campaign, being forced to miss six games at the end of December with an ankle injury and, following that, a pulled hamstring, sustained at Villa Park against Southampton was thought serious enough to have finished his campaign early. However, he bounced back to make an earlier than expected return, when appearing on the subs' bench on a couple of occasions. A dead-ball specialist, despite missing two penalties early on in the campaign, he has a lot of power and strikes the ball well, and when playing he appeared mainly in the centre of midfield if the wing-back formation was in operation, but was switched to the left-hand side when the 4-4-2 system was in use. In summary, it was obviously a disappointing season for "Thommo", and he will be looking to remain injury free in 1999-2000.

Newcastle U (From trainee on 11/3/91) FL 13+3 FAC 1 Others 3
Bolton W (£250,000 on 22/7/93) P/FL 143+14/34 FLC 24+1/5 FAC 6+2/2 Others 7+1/1
Aston Villa (£4,500,000 on 12/6/98) PL 20+5/2 FLC 0+1 Others 3

THOMPSON Andrew (Andy) Richard

Born: Cannock, 9 November 1967
Height: 5'5" Weight: 10.1
Club Honours: Div 4 '88, Div 3 '89; AMC '88
A compact and reliable performer in his favourite left-back role, Andy continued to turn in sound and consistent displays for Tranmere all last season. Is a controller rather than a playmaker, but he would run all day in the team's cause if he had to. Remained mostly injury free, and would probably have been an ever present had it not been for a mid-season suspension, following an unaccustomed red card at Bristol City. He may be small in stature, but is as tenacious as they come, and loves the opportunity to sneak in a crafty goal when he goes up front for set pieces. Scored once, and picked up a "Man of the Match" award during 1998-99.

West Bromwich A (From apprentice on 16/11/85) FL 18+6/1 FLC 0+1 FAC 2 Others 1+1
Wolverhampton W (£35,000 on 21/11/86) FL 356+20/43 FLC 22 FAC 20/1 Others 33/1
Tranmere Rov (Free on 21/7/97) FL 81/4 FLC 9 FAC 4

THOMPSON David Anthony

Born: Birkenhead, 12 September 1977
Height: 5'7" Weight: 10.0
Club Honours: FAYC '96
International Honours: E: U21-2; Yth
David showed up as a possible star for the future towards the end of 1997-98, but was left on the Liverpool subs' bench for much of the early part of last season. However, during November he came into his own with some fine displays, winning two "Man of the Match" awards. Against Leeds at Anfield, despite his side losing 1-3, and being booked for a foul on Jimmy Floyd Hasselbaink, he performed brilliantly, playing on the right side of midfield and getting through a prodigious amount of hard work, while creating several openings for his side. However, at present, the youngster is one for the future, with more experienced players getting the nod ahead of him.

Liverpool (From trainee on 8/11/94) PL 5+16/2 FLC 2 Others 2
Swindon T (Loaned on 21/11/97) FL 10

THOMPSON Glyn William

Born: Telford, 24 February 1981
Height: 6'1" Weight: 12.4
As a young goalkeeper at Shrewsbury who had come through the trainee ranks to sign professional forms last December, even before making his senior debut in the final game of the season he had reportedly attracted Premiership scouts, based on his excellent progress in reserve and youth-team matches. If true, the assessment is correct, and he impressed all at the game when keeping a clean sheet in a 3-1 win at Torquay. Tall, and well built, Glyn is definitely one for the future.

Shrewsbury T (From trainee on 14/12/98) FL 1

THOMPSON Neil

Born: Beverley, 2 October 1963
Height: 5'10" Weight: 13.8
Club Honours: GMVC '87; Div 2 '92
International Honours: E: SP-4
A vastly experienced left back who took over the mantle of caretaker manager at York upon the dismissal of Alan Little in March 1999, Neil led by example in the closing weeks as the club once again walked the relegation tightrope. Netted seven goals, including a last-minute winner against Millwall, while others of note were a thunderous free kick at Luton Town, and a superb strike at Sunderland in the Worthington Cup.

Hull C (Free from Nottingham F juniors on 28/11/81) FL 29+2
Scarborough (Free on 1/8/83) FL 87/15 FLC 8/1 FAC 4 Others 9/1
Ipswich T (£100,000 on 9/6/89) F/PL 199+7/19 FLC 14+1/1 FAC 17/1 Others 8/2
Barnsley (Free on 14/6/96) F/PL 27/5 FLC 4 FAC 1
Oldham Ath (Loaned on 24/12/97) FL 8
York C (Free on 2/3/98) FL 36/8 FLC 2/1

THOMPSON Philip Paul

Born: 1 April 1981,
Height: 5'11" Weight: 12.0
Another of Blackpool's promising youngsters who were blooded in 1997-98, the strongly-built central defender signed professional forms during the 1998 close season and quickly made his mark, scoring twice at Bloomfield Road in his first four games in 1998-99. Both were important strikes, the first coming in a 2-2 fight back versus Gillingham, and the second being a headed winner in the game against Northampton. Phil looks as though he could become a real crowd pleaser.

Blackpool (From trainee on 4/9/98) FL 19+4/2 FLC 2

THOMPSON Steven (Steve) James

Born: Oldham, 2 November 1964
Height: 5'10" Weight: 13.5
Club Honours: AMC '89
A vastly experienced Rotherham midfielder with a tremendous ability to spray out accurate passes, Steve lost his place at Rotherham in mid season 1998-99, but returned with a major impact. Generally, when he was on top form so was the team. The penalty expert with a 100 per-cent record from the spot, he also scored with some superbly struck free kicks. Out of contract during the summer, he has the knowledge and approach to continue in the game after his playing days are over.

Bolton W (From apprentice on 4/11/82) FL 329+6/49 FLC 27/2 FAC 21/4 Others 39/2
Luton T (£180,000 on 13/8/91) FL 5 FLC 2
Leicester C (Signed on 22/10/91) ßL 121+6/18 FLC 6/2 FAC 8/1 Others 11+3/4
Burnley (£200,000 on 24/2/95) FL 44+5/1 FLC 2 Others 1+1
Rotherham U (Free on 24/7/97) FL 60+12/8 FLC 3 FAC 4+2 Others 3+1

Steve Thompson

THOMSON Andrew (Andy)

Born: Motherwell, 1 April 1971
Height: 5'10" Weight: 10.13
Andy joined Oxford in the summer of 1998 from Southend, and after a shaky first few games in 1998-99, mainly from the bench, he scored three goals in seven games, but

then only scored another four during the rest of the campaign, as the team struggled collectively for goals. A tireless, hard-working player who is constantly looking for the net, he was often just out of luck, hitting the woodwork or shooting just wide on many occasions, despite showing some good striking instincts. Hopefully, United fans will see the net bulge more from him this season.

Queen of the South (Free from Jerviston BC on 28/7/89) SL 163+12/93 SLC 8/3 SC 7+2/5 Others 9/8
Southend U (£250,000 on 4/7/94) FL 87+35/28 FLC 4+1 FAC 3+2 Others 1+2
Oxford U (Free on 21/7/98) FL 25+13/7 FLC 1 FAC 0+1

THOMSON Andrew (Andy) John
Born: Swindon, 28 March 1974
Height: 6'3" Weight: 14.12
This tall, powerful, tough-tackling per-former proved resolute for Portsmouth last season, especially when away from home, either filling in for Andy Awford in defence or any player in midfield. Allowed to join Bristol Rovers in January, he could not have dreamt of a more impressive debut, being part of the side which thumped in six goals at Reading, all of them coming in the second half. Adding physical strength to Rovers' defence, and posing a real threat in opponents' penalty areas, he was suitably rewarded with a fine headed goal against the Second Division champions elect, Fulham.

Swindon T (From trainee on 1/5/93) P/FL 21+1 FLC 5/1 Others 3
Portsmouth (£75,000 on 29/12/95) FL 85+8/3 FLC 4 FAC 6+1
Bristol Rov (£60,000 on 15/1/99) FL 21/1

THOMSON Steven (Steve)
Born: Glasgow, 23 January 1978
Height: 5'8" Weight: 10.4
International Honours: S: Yth
A Scottish youth international, and a professional at Crystal Palace since 1995, Steve was finally given his opportunity in an Inter Toto Cup game prior to the start of 1998-99. He obviously impressed the new manager, Terry Venables, who then gave him a first-team league debut for Palace at home to Bury in September. Definitely one for the future, despite being sent off in the last minute at Sheffield United after coming on as a sub, he finished the campaign in style, and looks to continue his progress during the coming season. Is a strong, ball-winning central midfielder who is building a reputation among supporters for his hard tackling.

Crystal Palace (From trainee on 9/12/95) FL 11+5

THORNE Peter Lee
Born: Manchester, 21 June 1973
Height: 6'0" Weight: 13.6
Club Honours: Div 2 '96
Back and ankle injuries disrupted a fine season at Stoke in 1998-99 for this regular scorer, and he was sorely missed when on the treatment table, the side lacking much when he was out. Won over the fans with a fine game against Lincoln City, when he

scored twice to ensure City's first home win after a run of five Britannia Stadium defeats.

Blackburn Rov (From trainee on 20/6/91) Others 0+1
Wigan Ath (Loaned on 11/3/94) FL 10+1
Swindon T (£225,000 on 18/1/95) FL 66+11/27 FLC 5+1/4 FAC 4+2 Others 1+1/1
Stoke C (£350,000 + on 25/7/97) FL 66+4/21 FLC 6/5 FAC 2+1 Others 1/1

THORNLEY Benjamin (Ben) Lindsay
Born: Bury, 21 April 1975
Height: 5'9" Weight: 11.12
Club Honours: FAYC '92
International Honours: E: U21-3; Sch
Signed from Manchester United during the 1998 close season, Ben was no stranger to the McAlpine, having been on loan at Huddersfield some two-and-a-half years earlier. An exciting winger, with excellent close control, and good awareness to pass a telling ball, the early part of 1998-99 saw him terrorise several defences with fantastic pace and pin-point crossing. Linking well with those around him, he also showed that he knew where the net was, scoring with a cracking last-minute volley against Wolves, and a wonderful long-range effort against Queens Park Rangers. Having suffered a broken foot at Norwich in October, he returned in January to win the "Man of the Match" award in the FA Cup win over Wrexham but, although still scoring the odd goal here and there, he struggled to regain his earlier flow. Is sure to be back to his best in the coming season.

Manchester U (From trainee on 29/1/93) PL 1+8 FLC 4 FAC 1
Stockport Co (Loaned on 6/11/95) FL 8+2/1 Others 1
Huddersfield T (Loaned on 22/2/96) FL 12/2
Huddersfield T (£175,000 + on 3/7/98) FL 32+3/4 FLC 4 FAC 3/1

Ben Thornley

THORPE Anthony (Tony) Lee
Born: Leicester, 10 April 1974
Height: 5'9" Weight: 12.6
Signed from Fulham during the 1998 close season, much was expected from the £1 million striker, as Bristol City looked to get 1998-99 underway successfully. Unfortunately, Tony was unable to hold down a place in the side, appearing mainly in midfield, having started the campaign on the bench and appearing only spasmodically prior to going to Reading on loan in February. However, scoring just one goal in six games was not a great success, and he returned to Ashton Gate before moving back, again on loan, to his former club, Luton, in transfer deadline week. Immediately striking a rapport at Town, he scored four in the last four games as Town moved clear of the relegation zone. A player with quick reactions in the area who is not afraid to run at defenders, he needs to be utilised correctly, and it will be interesting to see whether the City coach, Benny Lennartsson, is able to get the best out of him in 1999-2000.

Luton T (Free from Leicester C juniors on 18/8/92) FL 93+27/50 FLC 5+4/5 FAC 4+3/2 Others 4+3/3
Fulham (£800,000 on 26/2/98) FL 5+8/3 Others 1+1
Bristol C (£1,000,000 on 23/6/98) FL 9+7/2 FLC 1+1/1
Reading (Loaned on 5/2/99) FL 6/1
Luton T (Loaned on 25/3/99) FL 7+1/4

THORPE Jeffrey (Jeff) Roger
Born: Whitehaven, 17 November 1972
Height: 5'10" Weight: 12.8
Club Honours: Div 3 '95
Now something of an old war horse, with almost a decade at Carlisle, Jeff's career has been badly blighted by injury in recent years. That he is playing at all is testament to his grit and determination, qualities that are still evident in his performances on the park. A player who can operate in a number of positions, but more at home on the left-hand side, once again his appearances were restricted during the last campaign.

Carlisle U (From trainee on 2/7/91) FL 100+63/6 FLC 8+3 FAC 4+3 Others 8+8/1

THORPE Lee Anthony
Born: Wolverhampton, 14 December 1975
Height: 6'1" Weight: 12.4
Lee finished as Lincoln's leading goalscorer in 1998-99 for the second successive season, after a late burst saw him net six goals in five matches. His second goal at Colchester was a candidate for "Goal of the Season", and he was only denied a hat trick in that match by a harsh refereeing decision. Earlier in the campaign, the aggressive goalscorer, who was often used on the right-hand side of midfield instead of his preferred striking role, found the going tough, lacking confidence in front of goal.

Blackpool (From trainee on 18/7/94) FL 2+10 FLC 0+1 FAC 1 Others 1
Lincoln C (Free on 4/8/97) FL 79+3/22 FLC 2+1 FAC 7/1 Others 2+1/1

TIATTO Daniele (Danny) Amadio
Born: Melbourne, Australia, 22 May 1973
Height: 5'7" Weight: 12.0
International Honours: Australia: 9
Having drifted to Stoke City on loan from FC Baden, and playing a few games in 1997-98, Manchester City's Joe Royle kept an eye on him and signed him on a permanent basis in the summer of 1998. Good when coming forward, and working well on the overlaps, Danny made his City debut at home to Walsall, and had a fine game on the left-hand side. He then scored a spectacular bicycle-kick goal at Derby in a thrilling 1-1 draw in the Worthington Cup. Not an unduly strong player, he still picked up five yellow and two red cards, and following the middle of December he failed to feature in the first team, except for coming off the bench occasionally. Can be used at left back or as a wide-sided midfielder.
Stoke C (Loaned from FC Baden on 25/11/97) FL 11+4/1
Manchester C (£300,000 on 15/7/98) FL 8+9 FLC 1/1 FAC 0+1 Others 1

TIERNEY Francis (Fran)
Born: Liverpool, 10 September 1975
Height: 5'10" Weight: 11.0
International Honours: E: Yth
Fran arrived at Notts County in July 1998 having not figured at first-team level for some time. An injury hampered his debut even further, and it was December before he came into action for the first team, but once in the side he became a regular member of the squad. Developed by Dario Grady at Crewe, the skilful midfielder appeared on both flanks for County where he contributed quality crosses and set-piece free kicks, and scored on his full debut in a 3-1 home win against Northampton. Having notched another goal in a 4-2 win over York, he grabbed the winner in a 1-0 victory at Lincoln, and looks set to become an integral member of the Magpies as they look to battle their way out of Division Two in 1999-2000.
Crewe Alex (From trainee on 22/3/93) FL 57+30/10 FLC 6 FAC 1+4 Others 5+6/3
Notts Co (Free on 2/7/98) FL 13+7/3 FAC 1+2 Others 1

TILER Carl
Born: Sheffield, 11 February 1970
Height: 6'3" Weight: 13.10
International Honours: E: U21-13
Not figuring too much in Everton's plans for 1998-99, this tall, strong central defender joined Charlton last September, making his debut at Nottingham Forest. Dominant in the air, and with good distribution, Carl is also dangerous at corners and set pieces, and scored with a header against West Ham at the Valley. Despite some suspect performances when he first came into the side, he settled down well to become an integral part of either a four or five-man defence, as the team continuously fought against the threat of relegation.
Barnsley (From trainee on 2/8/88) FL 67+4/3 FLC 4 FAC 4+1 Others 3+1
Nottingham F (£1,400,000 on 30/5/91) F/PL 67+2/1 FLC 10+1 FAC 6 Others 1

Swindon T (Loaned on 18/11/94) FL 2
Aston Villa (£750,000 on 28/10/95) PL 10+2/1 FLC 1 FAC 2
Sheffield U (£650,000 on 26/3/97) FL 23/2 FLC 5 Others 3
Everton (£500,000 on 28/11/97) PL 21/1 FLC 1 FAC 1
Charlton Ath (£700,000 on 30/9/98) PL 27/1 FAC 1

TILLSON Andrew (Andy)
Born: Huntingdon, 30 June 1966
Height: 6'2" Weight: 12.10
As Bristol Rovers' central defender and captain, Andy missed the opening weeks of last season due to injury, and after regaining his place he performed consistently before being very unfortunate to suffer a recurrence of tendonitis. Following an absence of five months out of the team, he returned to rapturous praise from both supporters and team mates when scoring the match-winning goal on 20 February against Luton Town to mark his 200th league appearance for the Pirates. Had a trial with Walsall just prior to the transfer deadline, but declined a loan opportunity to regain his place at the heart of Rovers' defence.
Grimsby T (Free from Kettering T on 14/7/88) FL 104+1/5 FLC 8 FAC 10 Others 5
Queens Park R (£400,000 on 21/12/90) FL 27+2/2 FLC 2 Others 1
Grimsby T (Loaned on 15/9/92) FL 4 Others 1
Bristol Rov (£370,000 on 7/11/92) FL 207+3/10 FLC 12/1 FAC 10 Others 18+1/2

TINDALL Jason
Born: Mile End, 15 November 1977
Height: 6'1" Weight: 11.10
Jason was signed in the 1998 close season from Charlton where he was captain of the league-winning reserve side. Although he found it difficult to find a regular place in the Bournemouth side in 1998-99, his season being disrupted by injury, he did, however, manage seven starts and 13 substitute appearances. Predominantly a central midfield player, who has also played in the back four, he will be looking forward to more first-team opportunities in 1999-2000.
Charlton Ath (From trainee on 18/7/96)
Bournemouth (Free on 3/7/98) FL 6+11/1 FLC 1+2

TINKLER Eric
Born: Capetown, South Africa, 30 July 1970
Height: 6'2" Weight: 12.8
International Honours: South Africa: 29
An injury that hampered Eric throughout the 1997-98 season was finally diagnosed and operated upon, but unfortunately kept him out of the Barnsley team until last October. Coming back to play in his best position as a ball-winning midfielder sitting in front of the back line, he again proved a good tackler who was able to break up many opposition attacks before they were able to develop. Always a danger at the other end with his height at corner, and long-range shooting, he scored in home wins against Huddersfield and Crewe.
Barnsley (£650,000 from Cagliari on 23/7/97) P/FL 42+8/4 FLC 4 FAC 5

TINKLER Mark Roland
Born: Bishop Auckland, 24 October 1974
Height: 5'11" Weight: 13.3
Club Honours: FAYC '93
International Honours: E: Yth (UEFAC '93); Sch
A skilful and hard-working player who operated in either the centre of defence or in midfield for York in 1998-99, Mark scored only twice, but these were vital efforts which enabled City to win both at Walsall and Macclesfield. Although his season was marred by the fact that he was sent off three times, on a positive front he continued to show an ability to read the game, allied to strength and purpose.
Leeds U (From trainee on 29/11/91) PL 14+11 FLC 1 Others 0+1
York C (£100,000 on 25/3/97) FL 88+2/7 FLC 6 FAC 5 Others 2

TINNION Brian
Born: Stanley, 23 February 1968
Height: 6'0" Weight: 13.0
Unfortunately, Brian's season at Bristol City in 1998-99 was affected by injuries, which kept him out of the side for some time. Despite that, he still showed that he had the ability to produce the "killer" long ball which opened up defences and put team mates in on goal, and was seen at his best when linking with Mickey Bell, and later Jim Brennan. When "on song", the midfielder is a vital part of the team, having helped bring the best out of Brennan, just as he did previously with Bell, and before that, Darren Barnard and Martin Scott.
Newcastle U (From apprentice on 26/2/86) FL 30+2/2 FLC 5 Others 1+1
Bradford C (£150,000 on 9/3/89) FL 137+8/22 FLC 12/1 FAC 9/4 Others 7+1/2
Bristol C (£180,000 on 23/3/93) FL 217+11/18 FLC 16 FAC 13+2/3 Others 6+2

TINSON Darren Lee
Born: Birmingham, 15 November 1969
Height: 6'0" Weight: 13.12
Club Honours: GMVC '97
Darren, formerly employed as an anaesthetist's assistant before turning to full-time football with Macclesfield, visited his former work place twice last season, having a hernia operation in the summer and keyhole surgery on a knee cartilage in November. Quick to recover, and back in two weeks, unfortunately, this return was too quick and he was out again after two games, this time for a month. Physically very strong, with a good turn of speed, he is a right back who comes forward quickly to overlap with the winger, but can easily revert to central defence, and played well in there for four games when injury depleted players for that position.
Macclesfield T (£10,000 from Northwich Vic on 14/2/96) FL 81 FLC 6 FAC 4 Others 1

TIPTON Matthew John
Born: Conway, 29 June 1980
Height: 5'10" Weight: 11.7
International Honours: W: U21-3; Yth
Another homegrown player, Matthew built on his full appearance at Oldham in 1997-98 to grab an occasional first-team place last

season, and 17 starts, plus 16 from the bench, was a fair reward for his endeavours. A quick and pacy forward, who has scored a lot of goals in youth and reserve games, he is two footed, chases half chances, and opened his scoring account for Latics with a 35-yard screamer in a 3-2 win at home to Wrexham, before following it up with a close-range effort in a 1-1 home draw against Burnley in April. Having played alongside Liverpool's Michael Owen at Welsh youth level, he has now graduated to U21 status, and big things are expected of him in the millennium campaign.

Oldham Ath (From trainee on 1/7/97) FL 16+15/2 FAC 2+2 Others 0+2

TISTIMETANU Ivan

Born: Moldova, 27 April 1974
Height: 5'10" Weight: 11.2
International Honours: Moldova: 23

A Moldovan international who, like Vilmos Sebok, was subject to lengthy transfer negotiations before finally joining Bristol City last December, he was heralded as a full back, cum central defender, before being introduced into the side by Benny Lennartsson in midfield. City fans immediately warmed to his total commitment to the cause, and he was just beginning to become a vital part of the team as a ball winner and provider when he suffered a serious injury at the Hawthorns, in February, being forced to miss the remainder of the season. Although facing a long break from the game, Ivan now knows what to expect in the coming campaign.

Bristol C (£225,000 from FC Zimbru Chisinau on 24/12/98) FL 8 FAC 1

TODD Andrew (Andy) Jonathan

Born: Nottingham, 22 February 1979
Height: 6'0" Weight: 11.3

Andy, a promising young striker who found his way to Nottingham Forest from non-league Eastwood Town in February 1996, in failing to make an appearance for the senior side, and on a monthly contract, was allowed to sign for struggling Scarborough early last February. Unfortunate to make his Football League debut a day later, when coming off the bench for the last 30 minutes of a 5-1 shellacking at the hands of Cambridge, he appeared regularly in the Pontins' League without making further progress.

Nottingham F (Signed from Eastwood T on 29/2/96)
Scarborough (Free on 5/2/99) FL 0+1

TODD Andrew (Andy) John James

Born: Derby, 21 September 1974
Height: 5'10" Weight: 11.10
Club Honours: Div 1 '97

After an excellent season in the Premiership in 1997-98, Andy had a slightly tougher time of it last year. He began the season reprising his role at the heart of the defence before various niggling injuries kept him out of the side for the mid-season spell, until he returned in time for the 3-1 home defeat by Crewe in February. A versatile player who can play in defence or midfield, he will be

looking to shake off last season's disappointments to retain a permanent place at the heart of the Trotters' defence.

Middlesbrough (From trainee on 6/3/92) FL 7+1 FLC 1+1 Others 5
Swindon T (Loaned on 27/2/95) FL 13
Bolton W (£250,000 on 1/8/95) P/FL 56+16/2 FLC 10+5/1 FAC 1 Others 3

TODD Lee

Born: Hartlepool, 7 March 1972
Height: 5'6" Weight: 11.2

Signed from Southampton immediately prior to the start of 1998-99, the left back had an horrendous season with injuries. In only his second game he suffered a groin injury, which forced him to miss 11 matches, then, after another eight games, he pulled a hamstring and was absent for another 14 games. Has mainly played at right back, but always looks comfortable wherever he is asked to perform. An effervescent character, Lee might be small in stature but has a big heart and gives it everything, being a tremendous asset for City.

Stockport Co (Free from Hartlepool U juniors on 23/7/90) FL 214+11/2 FLC 24+2 FAC 17/2 Others 33+1
Southampton (£500,000 on 28/7/97) PL 9+1 FLC 1
Bradford C (£250,000 + on 6/8/98) FL 14+1 FLC 2

TOLSON Neil

Born: Walsall, 25 October 1973
Height: 6'2" Weight: 12.4

Although playing a secondary role for most of 1998-99 up front for York, on his day he can be a dangerous forward who can trouble most defences. Hit four goals, including winners against Bristol Rovers and Lincoln, plus one in a 3-3 away draw to eventual Second Division champions, Fulham. Surprisingly released in the summer, he is good in the air, quick off the mark, and has the ingredients to trouble defences, especially in the Third Division.

Walsall (From trainee on 17/12/91) FL 3+6/1 FAC 0+1/1 Others 1+2
Oldham Ath (£150,000 on 24/3/92) PL 0+3
Bradford C (Signed on 2/12/93) FL 32+31/12 FLC 1+4/1 FAC 3+1/1 Others 2+2/3
Chester C (Loaned on 6/1/95) FL 3+1
York C (Free on 15/7/96) FL 66+18/18 FLC 7+2/3 FAC 6+1/2 Others 0+2/1

TOMLINSON Graeme Murdoch

Born: Watford, 10 December 1975
Height: 5'10" Weight: 12.7

Released by Manchester United in the 1998 close season, Macclesfield manager, Sammy McIlroy, was quick to use his United connections to secure the free signing of Graeme. His early form showed a good awareness around the box, close control, and an ability to get round defenders, but he was then out of the team for a month with a back injury sustained in September, and his goalscoring prowess was not to be seen until November, when he scored with a curling finish against Slough in the FA Cup. The following week, he saved the club's blushes by snatching a late equaliser against Walsall, and two weeks later, again in the FA Cup, he bagged a glorious hat trick against

Cambridge, before scoring another a week later against Luton to make it six goals in six games. Disappointingly, the goals dried up, and he was rested during February and March. However, brought back in mid April, he completed his goal tally with another brace.

Bradford C (Trainee) FL 12+5/6 FAC 0+1
Manchester U (£100,000 on 12/7/94) FLC 0+2
Luton T (Loaned on 22/3/96) FL 1+6
Bournemouth (Loaned on 8/8/97) FL 6+1/1
Millwall (Loaned on 26/3/98) FL 2+1/1
Macclesfield T (Free on 9/7/98) FL 15+13/4 FLC 1+1 FAC 4/4 Others 1

TORPEY Stephen (Steve) David James

Born: Islington, 8 December 1970
Height: 6'3" Weight: 14.6
Club Honours: AMC '94

Highly rated by Bristol City coach, Benny Lennartsson, who pointed to his excellent workrate, ability to hold play up in forward positions, and aerial power when defending against set pieces, the fans saw it differently and criticised him for a lack of goals. Loaned to Notts County early on in 1998-99, in order to get match fit after coming back from injury, he failed to make a huge impact, although he scored twice in his eight games. Despite being good in the air and battling well, he returned to Bristol after his loan spell expired, eventually getting his place back on a regular basis while missing just three games in the final 23 of the campaign, and was almost back to his best at the final whistle. Stop Press: The subject of enquiries from Reading and Northampton, Steve signed for Liverpool on 13 May.

Millwall (From trainee on 14/2/89) FL 3+4 FLC 0+1
Bradford C (£70,000 on 21/11/90) FL 86+10/22 FLC 6 FAC 2+1 Others 8/6
Swansea C (£80,000 on 3/8/93) FL 151+11/44 FLC 9+2/2 FAC 10/5 Others 18+3/6
Bristol C (£400,000 on 8/8/97) FL 38+12/11 FLC 2 FAC 2 Others 2
Notts Co (Loaned on 7/8/98) FL 4+2/1 FLC 1+1/1

TOSH Paul James

Born: Arbroath, 18 October 1973
Height: 6'0" Weight: 11.12

Signed on loan from Hibs last February, he duly scored the only goal of the game at Barnet in his first appearance for Exeter. At home in midfield or up front, he would have undoubtedly stayed longer if his club had not recalled him. Proved himself to be a very strong character who could upset defenders with his strength and presence in the penalty box, and was lethal with either foot from dead-ball situations.

Arbroath (From juniors on 13/7/91) SL 29+14/13 SLC 1+1 SC 1+2 Others 2+1/1
Dundee (Signed on 4/8/93) SL 75+32/10 SLC 9+3/4 SC 2+6/1 Others 8/2
Hibernian (Signed on 20/3/97) SL 11+11/2 SLC 0+1
Exeter C (Loaned on 26/2/99) FL 8+2/2

TOWN David Edward

Born: Bournemouth, 9 December 1976
Height: 5'8" Weight: 11.13

David made just one start and 12 substitute appearances for Bournemouth throughout 1998-99 and, at the end of the season, he decided to further his career with a different

club, having been at Dean Court since his junior days. Joining the Conference side, Rushden and Diamonds, he is a quick and lively striker who pursues half chances in and around the box, and will always run at defenders when the opportunity presents itself.

Bournemouth (From trainee on 11/4/95) FL 18+38/2 FLC 0+8 Others 0+2

TOWNSEND Andrew (Andy) David
Born: Maidstone, 23 July 1963
Height: 5'11" Weight: 13.6
Club Honours: FLC '94, '96
International Honours: Ei: 70; B-1
The veteran Middlesbrough skipper continued to belie his advancing years in 1998-99 when displaying the vigour of thriving youth as he controlled the vital midfield area. "My enthusiasm for the game is as strong as ever, and as long as the legs keep moving, my ambition will be as strong as the next man's", he said recently. Andy was a natural to take over the captaincy after Nigel Pearson, being in the same mould, and having captained every team he has played for, including his national side, he was able to forewarn his charges about the bitter fight for Premiership survival that lay ahead. During a hectic season he was almost an ever present, scored a very important goal, collected many "Man of the Match" awards, and was the perfect role model to all of the other players, whom he led by example throughout.

Southampton (£35,000 from Weymouth on 15/1/85) FL 77+6/5 FLC 7+1 FAC 2+3 Others 3+2
Norwich C (£300,000 on 31/8/88) FL 66+5/8 FLC 3+1 FAC 10/2 Others 3
Chelsea (£1,200,000 on 5/7/90) ßL 110/12 FLC 17/7 FAC 7 Others 4
Aston Villa (£2,100,000 on 26/7/93) PL 133+1/8 FLC 20/2 FAC 10/1 Others 10/1
Middlesbrough (£500,000 on 29/8/97) P/FL 70+2/3 FLC 7 FAC 4/1

TRACEY Richard Shaun
Born: Dewsbury, 9 July 1979
Height: 5'11" Weight: 11.0
A speedy striker whose chances at Rotherham were limited last season, making just one first-team start, he welcomed a move to Carlisle last March, and made his debut for the club as a substitute at Halifax. Thereafter, he started most games, netting three times, notably in the 3-3 draw with Darlington when his persistence also won the club a penalty. He looks to have potential, and has been offered terms for the new season.

Sheffield U (From trainee on 4/6/97)
Rotherham U (Free on 24/2/98) FL 0+3 FAC 1+1
Carlisle U (Free on 12/3/99) FL 10+1/3

TRACEY Simon Peter
Born: Woolwich, 9 December 1967
Height: 6'0" Weight: 13.12
Starting last season as, so often, second-choice goalkeeper at Sheffield United to Alan Kelly, Simon got his chance due to the latter's injury, giving some impressive displays as a shot stopper, and should not shoulder the blame for the lack of clean sheets. Also missing games through injury,

although returning in November, only to be ousted by Kelly, he played throughout March but once again lost his place when the latter was fit again.

Wimbledon (From apprentice on 3/2/86) FL 1 Others 1
Sheffield U (£7,500 on 19/10/88) F/PL 203+3 FLC 11 FAC 14 Others 10
Manchester C (Loaned on 27/10/94) PL 3
Norwich C (Loaned on 31/12/94) PL 1 FAC 2
Wimbledon (Loaned on 2/11/95) PL 1

TRAMEZZANI Paolo
Born: Castelnovo, Italy, 30 July 1970
Height: 6'1" Weight: 12.6
After joining Tottenham from Piacenza in the summer of 1998, this experienced defender was to have little impact at Tottenham in 1998-99, making only seven appearances before picking up an injury which, along with a widely reported public dispute with the new manager, George Graham, kept him out of the Spurs' line-up for the remainder of the campaign. Reportedly not figuring in Graham's plans at the club, Paolo was expected to leave during the past summer.

Tottenham H (£1,350,000 from Piacenza, via Lucchese, Inter Milan, Venezia and Cesena, on 13/7/98) PL 6 FLC 1

TRAVIS Simon Christopher
Born: Preston, 22 March 1977
Height: 5'7" Weight: 10.0
Having arrived at Stockport as a full back from Holywell Town in 1997, his pace and control of the ball persuaded Gary Megson to employ him as a wide player in the 1997-98 season. His performances and promise won him another year's contract, but he was unable to make an impression on the first team last season, starting just once. Has the speed to become a good wide player, and with time on his side he can work on the final delivery which is missing from his game at the moment.

Torquay U (Trainee) FL 4+4 FLC 1 FAC 1 (Freed on 5/1/96)
Stockport Co (£10,000 from Holywell T on 14/8/97) FL 4+18/2 FLC 0+2 FAC 0+2

TREES Robert (Rob) Victor
Born: Manchester, 18 December 1977
Height: 5'11" Weight: 12.2
An all-action utility player, Rob was given a second opportunity in professional football when Bristol Rovers, who had him on trial 12 months earlier, offered him a two-year contract during the 1998 close season. A former Manchester United professional, he had drifted into non-league football with Stalybridge, and then Witton Albion, before the move to the West Country. In just his third league match, at Gillingham, he was used as an emergency goalkeeper for the last few minutes after the dismissal of Lee Jones. He himself was sent off for two bookable offences against Bournemouth on 3 October at the Memorial Stadium, as Rovers finished the match with only nine players. A confident attacking player, who always preferred the central midfield role, he showed his adaptability in playing at right and left back, or out wide.

Manchester U (From trainee on 5/7/96) (Free to Stalybridge Celtic during 1997 close season)
Bristol Rov (Free from Witton A on 22/6/98) FL 33+3 FLC 1+1 FAC 6 Others 1

TRETTON Andrew David
Born: Derby, 9 October 1976
Height: 6'0" Weight: 12.9
Injured in 1997-98, his start in 1998-99 was curtailed until November, and then a few games were needed for Shrewsbury's central defender to get steam up. Assured in the air and on the ground, Andrew looks like a player with much more experience than his 50 odd games, and once match fit was an automatic choice in the middle, alongside Brian Gayle. A full season will bring out the best in him.

Derby Co (From trainee on 18/10/93)
Shrewsbury T (Free on 12/12/97) FL 36+1/1 FAC 1 Others 1

TROLLOPE Paul Jonathan
Born: Swindon, 3 June 1972
Height: 6'0" Weight: 12.6
Club Honours: Div 2 '99
International Honours: W: 5; B-1
For two thirds of last season, Fulham had such a strong set of midfielders that Paul was rarely in contention for other than a place on the subs' bench. However, at his best when playing on the left-hand side of a midfield three, the opportunity came his way when Paul Bracewell was injured early in February, and he went on to pick up a Second Division championship medal. Playing in ten successive games which yielded 28 points, and scoring twice, he showed by far the best form of his time at the club, and with three years left on his contract he should be an integral part of Fulham's drive towards the Premiership. Is the son of John, who holds the Swindon appearance record. Represented the Welsh "B" side that played Northern Ireland.

Swindon T (From trainee on 23/12/89)
Torquay U (Free on 26/3/92) FL 103+3/16 FLC 9+1/1 FAC 7 Others 8+1
Derby Co (£100,000 on 16/12/94) F/PL 47+18/5 FLC 3+2/1 FAC 3+1
Grimsby T (Loaned on 30/8/96) FL 6+1/1
Crystal Palace (Loaned on 11/10/96) FL 0+9
Fulham (£600,000 on 28/11/97) FL 36+8/5 FLC 1+1 FAC 3+3 Others 4/1

TROUGHT Michael (Mike) John
Born: Bristol, 19 October 1980
Height: 6'2" Weight: 13.0
A former trainee, Mike made his first-team debut on 8 December for Bristol Rovers as a central defender in an exciting Auto Windscreens Shield-tie at Walsall. Stalemate after extra time, it entered a penalty shoot-out which the Saddlers won 5-4 following 16 penalty attempts. It was a fine debut for the teenager in a young Rovers' team, and along with his team mates he drew a lot of credit from manager, Ian Holloway. He then made his league debut four days later at Manchester City in front of 24,000 supporters, but was unfortunately injured after half an hour. A composed player on the ball, the youngster will add stiff competition to Rovers' squad, and has

already attracted the attention of the Welsh U21 selectors.

Bristol Rov (From trainee on 18/3/99) FL 6+3 FAC 3+1 Others 1

TSKHADADZE Kakhaber

Born: Rustavi, Georgia, 7 September 1968
Height: 6'2" Weight: 12.7
International Honours: CIS/Georgia: 28

Having earlier expected to be leaving Manchester City, the Georgian made an excellent start to last season in City's centre-back position, giving strong performances, and scoring two goals from corners in the first three games. Unfortunately, cruel luck caught up with him in the game at Fulham, where he received a nasty injury early on in the game, which transpired to be a ruptured cruciate ligament, thus ending his playing time for the campaign. Recovering well, by January he was doing light training work, but following a set back in February he went to Germany to see a specialist, and is aiming now to be ready for the start of the 1999-2000 season.

Manchester C (£300,000 from Alana Vladikavkaz, via Dynamo Tbilisi, Sundsvall, Moscow Spartak and Eintracht Frankfurt, on 6/2/98) FL 12/2 FLC 1/1

TUCK Stuart Gary

Born: Brighton, 1 October 1974
Height: 5'11" Weight: 12.0

A locally-born Brighton defender who underwent a major groin operation during the 1998 close season, Stuart played in the first three matches before being forced to retire in October aged 24, having been with the club for seven years. Now studying to become a taxi driver, his tough-tackling, no-nonsense style at full back will be greatly missed.

Brighton & Hove A (From trainee on 9/7/93) FL 78+15/1 FLC 7 FAC 2 Others 6+1

TULLY Stephen (Steve) Richard

Born: Paignton, 10 February 1980
Height: 5'9" Weight: 11.0

Having made his Torquay first-team debut in 1997-98, Steve signed a pro contract during the 1998 close season, and became a regular at right-wing back after Andy Gurney's departure to Reading. A no-nonsense tackler, who also took up good goalscoring positions, netting twice in home draws against Leyton Orient and Darlington, he is sure to add to that total in the near future. In maintaining his improvement he is most certainly one for the future.

Torquay U (From trainee on 18/5/98) FL 35+11/2 FLC 0+1 FAC 0+1 Others 3

TURLEY William (Billy) Lee

Born: Wolverhampton, 15 July 1973
Height: 6'4" Weight: 14.10

This tall and commanding Northampton goalkeeper waited two seasons for a regular first-team place, finally taking over the number-one jersey in 1998-99 from Andy Woodman, and allowing the latter to be sold on to Brentford. Billy's run came at the same time that the defence in front of him was going through changes, and it was something of a "baptism of fire". However,

he settled down well to have some outstanding games, including the 0-0 draw at Manchester City, where he made some heroic saves.

Northampton T (Free from Evesham on 10/7/95) FL 28 FAC 2 Others 4
Leyton Orient (Loaned on 5/2/98) FL 14

TURNER Andrew (Andy) Peter

Born: Woolwich, 23 March 1975
Height: 5'10" Weight: 11.12
International Honours: Ei: U21-7. E: Yth; Sch

Out of favour at Portsmouth, Andy was yet another of Terry Venables' former players to arrive at Crystal Palace last season, signing on a free in late October. However, two subs' appearances later, and following the departure of Venables, he was on the move again, this time to Wolves during transfer deadline week. There is no doubt that when fit, he is both quick and skilful down the left flank, and a great crosser, but he was none of those at Molineux, being released in the summer and expected to sign for Rotherham.

Tottenham H (From trainee on 8/4/92) PL 8+12/3 FLC 0+2/1 FAC 0+1
Wycombe W (Loaned on 26/8/94) FL 3+1
Doncaster Rov (Loaned on 10/10/94) FL 4/1 Others 1/1
Huddersfield T (Loaned on 28/11/95) FL 2+3/1
Southend U (Loaned on 28/3/96) FL 4+2
Portsmouth (£250,000 on 4/9/96) FL 34+6/3 FLC 2+2 FAC 1
Crystal Palace (Free on 27/10/98) FL 0+2
Wolverhampton W (Free on 25/3/99)

TURNER Michael Christopher

Born: Liverpool, 2 April 1976
Height: 6'2" Weight: 13.5

Signed from Bilston Town last December, before picking up an extended two-year deal, he enjoyed an exciting debut in the league for Barnsley when coming on as substitute at Ipswich – making the opening goal and scoring the second. Although finding the rigours of full-time training hard, he was willing to listen and learn, in becoming a dependable back up to the more experienced strikers.

Barnsley (Signed from Bilston T on 4/12/98) FL 2+11/1

TUTILL Stephen (Steve) Alan

Born: York, 1 October 19695'10"
Height: 5'10" Weight: 12.6
International Honours: E: Sch

Named the supporters "Player of the Year" at the end of his first full season at Darlington, after ten years at York, his wholehearted displays at the centre of the defence, with his tremendous aerial power and hard tackling, certainly endeared him to the Feethams fans in 1998-99. Is still looking for his first goal for the Quakers, despite being a constant danger at set pieces.

York C (From trainee on 27/1/88) FL 293+8/6 FLC 21 FAC 18+1 Others 22+3/1
Darlington (Free on 20/2/98) FL 40+3 FLC 1 FAC 3 Others 2

TUTTLE David Philip

Born: Reading, 6 February 1972
Height: 6'1" Weight: 12.10
Club Honours: FAYC '90
International Honours: E: Yth

A strong-tackling central defender who, despite a poor start to last season with Crystal Palace, came back to give some fine performances at a time the club were going through troubled times. Scored twice, against Watford and Bradford, and was sent off against Grimsby, his last match at Selhurst Park before going on loan to Charlton in transfer deadline week, in order to cut the high wage bill. Having returned from injuries that would have seen many players off, it was amazing to see him coming out of bone-crunching tackles with the ball. Also gives nothing away in the air.

Tottenham H (From trainee on 8/2/90) F/PL 10+3 FLC 3+1 Others 1/1
Peterborough U (Loaned on 21/1/93) FL 7
Sheffield U (£350,000 on 1/8/93) P/FL 63/1 FLC 2 FAC 3
Crystal Palace (Signed on 8/3/96) F/PL 73+7/5 FLC 6 FAC 2 Others 5

TWEED Steven (Steve)

Born: Edinburgh, 8 August 1972
Height: 6'3" Weight: 13.2
International Honours: S: B-2; U21-3

The tall central defender failed to win a place in the Stoke side following Brian Little's arrival, and a move back to his native Scotland looked likely. Finally, after a long off-on saga, Steven signed for Dundee last December, £150,000 changing hands.

Hibernian (Free from Hutchison Vale BC on 25/8/90. Freed during 1996 close season) SL 105+3/3 SLC 9/1 SC 9/1
Stoke C (Free from Ionikos on 8/8/97) FL 35+4 FLC 5+1 FAC 1 Others 1

TWISS Michael John

Born: Salford, 26 December 1977
Height: 5'11" Weight: 12.8

As Steve Bruce's first signing, Michael joined Sheffield United on a one-year loan from Manchester United in time for the start of 1998-99. Strangely, he was never given an extended run in the side, most of his appearances coming from the bench, but when played both in midfield and up front he showed both commitment and promise. The high point of his season was scoring the last-minute winner against Huddersfield.

Manchester U (From trainee on 5/7/96) FAC 0+1
Sheffield U (Loaned on 6/8/98) FL 2+10/1 FAC 2+3

TYLER Mark Richard

Born: Norwich, 2 April 1977
Height: 6'0" Weight: 12.9
International Honours: E: Yth

Having been an ever present in Peterborough's goal in 1997-98, Mark started last season as the first-choice 'keeper but, unfortunately, had an injury-hit campaign which saw him forced to give way first to Bart Griemink, and then to young Daniel Connor, before he came back strongly to appear in the final 11 games. Ever reliable, and still only a youngster in goalkeeping terms, the former England youth international again proved to be a very agile and good shot stopper. He also showed improved kicking ability, and is definitely one for the future.

Peterborough U (From trainee on 7/12/94) FL 80+1 FLC 5 FAC 4 Others 9

UHLENBEEK Gustav (Gus) Reinier
Born: Paramaribo, Surinam, 20 August 1970
Height: 5'10" Weight: 12.6
Club Honours: Div 2 '99
Signed by Fulham from Ipswich under the Bosman ruling in the summer of 1998, Gus had a mixed season in 1998-99, despite winning a Third Division championship medal, having as many starts for the reserves as for the first team, but never failing to excite when he did play. Very much an attack-minded player, his terrific pace in the right-wing-back berth took him into great positions, although his final ball sometimes let him down. Scored a lovely goal at Wrexham, and with a slightly less cavalier approach in the final third of the field could claim back his place in the side.
Ipswich T (£100,000 from Top Ost, via Ajax and Cambuur, on 11/8/95) FL 77+12/4 FLC 5+3 FAC 4+3 Others 7+1
Fulham (Free on 22/7/98) FL 11+12/1 FLC 3 FAC 3+2 Others 1

ULLATHORNE Robert
Born: Wakefield, 11 October 1971
Height: 5'8" Weight: 11.3
International Honours: E: Yth
The left-sided wing back or central defender enjoyed an outstanding season for Leicester in 1998-99, regularly displaying top form either on the left of a back four or in the centre of a back three. Also moved into midfield when necessary, where he gave a great performance to man mark David Ginola in the Worthington Cup final, as well as troubling Ian Walker with a rasping low drive. In fact, Rob was voted "Man of the Match" at Wembley, until the journalists were asked to reconsider their decision in the light of the late Tottenham winner. He also managed to find the net from an acute angle in the FA Cup victory over Birmingham. Unfortunately, his campaign came to a premature end when he suffered a double fracture of his right leg in a collision with his own 'keeper, Kasey Keller, at Chelsea. Out of contract during the summer, at the time of going to press he had yet to sign a new contract.
Norwich C (From trainee on 6/7/90) F/PL 86+8/7 FLC 10+2/1 FAC 7+1 Others 1 (Free to Osasuna during 1996 close season)
Leicester C (£600,000 on 18/2/97) PL 28+3/1 FLC 8+1 FAC 2/1

UNGER Lars
Born: Eutin, Germany, 30 September 1972
Height: 6'2" Weight: 13.9
Having joined Southend on loan from the German Bundesliga last February, Lars showed why he had been capped at German U21 level when giving some polished midfield displays, although finding it hard to adapt to the pace of the Third Division at first. A hard worker with good vision, his

height caused opposition defences problems at set pieces, and while hoping to use his time at Roots Hall as a springboard to better things, at the time of writing it was unknown where he would be plying his trade in 1999-2000.
Southend U (Loaned from Fortuna Dusseldorf, via Werder Bremen, on 11/2/99) FL 14

UNSWORTH David Gerald
Born: Chorley, 16 October 1973
Height: 6'1" Weight: 14.2
Club Honours: FAC '95; CS '95
International Honours: E: 1; U21-7; Yth
A powerful, pacy left-sided central defencer, David returned to his spiritual home in the summer of 1998 – after one of the more bizarre transfers in Premiership history. Transferring the claret and blue of West Ham for Aston Villa in July, he soon realised that his old Everton employers also coveted his signature, and after pleading with the Villa hierarchy he was allowed to move back to Merseyside for the same £3 million fee Villa had paid the Hammers, without kicking a ball! He immediately displayed the defensive assurance and strength which won him so many admirers at Upton Park, and even enjoyed a successful spell in midfield at the height of a Toffees' injury crisis. That period included a superlative FA Cup strike at Newcastle from 20 yards, as he again settled comfortably back into life at Goodison.
Everton (From trainee on 25/6/92) F/PL 108+8/11 FLC 5+2 FAC 7 Others 4/1
West Ham U (£1,000,000 + on 18/8/97) PL 32/2 FLC 5 FAC 4
Aston Villa (£3,000,000 on 28/7/98)
Everton (£3,000,000 on 22/8/98) PL 33+1/1 FLC 3 FAC 3/1

Lee Unsworth

UNSWORTH Lee Peter
Born: Eccles, 25 February 1973
Height: 5'11" Weight: 11.8
An extremely versatile defender who has operated in a number of positions for Crewe, despite not being an automatic choice, Lee

missed just eight of the opening 34 games of last season before disappearing from view due to injury and the good form of others. Is sound in the air, likes to get forward, and has excellent powers of recovery which often allows him to get back in time to make vital tackles. Although useful with flick ons from set pieces, he has yet to score a league goal for Alex.
Crewe Alex (Signed from Ashton U on 20/2/95) FL 90+28 FLC 8+1/1 FAC 5+1/1 Others 8+2

UPSON Matthew James
Born: Stowmarket, 18 April 1979
Height: 6'1" Weight: 11.4
International Honours: E: U21-5; Yth
An intelligent young Arsenal centre back who turned in some tremendous performances with the England U21 team last season, scoring two goals in the process. Although he is now in his third season at Highbury, he has still not managed to break into the first team on a regular basis, mainly due to the continued good form of experienced defenders such as Tony Adams, Martin Keown, and Steve Bould. He has, however, benefited tremendously from training with those men, and playing alongside them when the occasion arises. With excellent distribution skills, which see him mixing up the play well between long and short balls, he is also very strong in the air, and reads the game well. Playing regularly in the reserves, he is undoubtedly one of the brightest young central defenders in the country, and has developed his game immensely since arriving at the club. It is surely only a matter of time before he becomes a first-team regular.
Luton T (From trainee on 24/4/96) FL 0+1 Others 1
Arsenal (£1,000,000 on 14/5/97) PL 5+5 FLC 4 FAC 2 Others 1

VAESEN Nico Jos-Theodor
Born: Ghent, Belgium, 28 September 1969
Height: 6'3" Weight: 12.8
Huddersfield's new number one was snapped up from Eendracht Aalst in the summer of 1998 for a bargain, having originally been on trial the previous season. The modest Belgian's first term proved to be nothing short of spectacular, starting with him being sent off after only nine minutes against Bury, an act repeated later on in the season against West Bromwich. Once settled in, however, the confident import began to show great handling and saving ability, and was soon having the McAlpine faithful crowing over his super displays. Due to Town's erratic away performances, he constantly made the headlines with some outstanding rearguard work, even saving three penalties on his travels. Nico oozed quality against Bolton in March at the McAlpine, with a ten-out-of-ten performance in one of the best matches seen at the stadium, and all this in front of his native television cameras. Rumoured to be on the verge of a call up to the Belgium squad, and on the wanted list of the Premier league clubs, Huddersfield were quick to extend his contract for a further two years. Scooped all

the club's "Player of the Year" awards in recognition of his fine work between the sticks.

Huddersfield T (£80,000 from Eendracht Aalst on 10/7/98) FL 43 FLC 4 FAC 5

Nico Vaesen

VAN BLERK Jason
Born: Sydney, Australia, 16 March 1968
Height: 6'1" Weight: 13.0
International Honours: Australia: 22

A hard-tackling, resolute, and competent West Bromwich left back who was moved forward into a midfield position by manager Denis Smith during the final six weeks of last season – and did well alongside Richard Sneekes and Sean Flynn, and behind Kevin Kilbane. Unfortunately, he was yellow carded several times during the campaign, and missed a few games through suspension. Although released during the summer, he is known for an exciting turn of pace, good control, and well-judged crossing when getting down the line.

Millwall (£300,000 from Go Ahead Eagles on 8/9/94) FL 68+5/2 FLC 5 FAC 6+1 Others 1+1
Manchester C (Free on 9/8/97) FL 10+9 FLC 0+1 FAC 0+1
West Bromwich A (£250,000 on 13/3/98) FL 38 FLC 2

VAN DER GOUW Raimond (Rai)
Born: Oldenzaal, Holland, 24 March 1963
Height: 6'3" Weight: 13.10
Club Honours: EC '99; FAC '99

A highly experienced Manchester United goalkeeper with a safe pair of hands, Rai continued to show his value to United when deputising for Peter Schmeichel at various stages of last season. A first-team regular for the Worthington Cup campaign, who also made appearances in the Premiership and Champions' League, he is an important member of the squad, and continues to show outstanding form when called into short-term action. As the goalkeeping coach at

Old Trafford, and responsible for the club's future in that department, with his contract up for grabs in the summer it will be interesting to see where he fits in now that Schmeichel is leaving. Won European Cup and FA Cup winners medals as a non-playing sub.

Manchester U (Signed from Vitesse Arnhem, via Go Ahead Eagles, on 12/7/96) PL 10+1 FLC 6 Others 2

VAN DER KWAAK Peter
Born: Haarlem, Holland, 12 October 1968
Height: 6'4" Weight: 13.13

The tall Dutch goalkeeper signed for Reading on a free transfer under the Bosman ruling from Ajax immediately prior to 1998-99, before going straight into the first team for the opening game. Surprisingly, he made a couple of elementary errors in the 3-0 defeat at Wrexham, and only stayed in the side for three more matches before being relegated to the reserves. His only other involvement was as a non-playing substitute goalie in the FA Cup-tie against Stoke.

Reading (Free from Ajax on 7/8/98) P/FL 3 FLC 1

VAN DER LAAN Robertus (Robin) Petrus
Born: Schiedam, Holland, 5 September 1968
Height: 6'0" Weight: 13.8
Club Honours: AMC '93

Signed from Derby during the 1998 close season, the hard-tackling, attacking midfielder was just settling at Barnsley in 1998-99 when an injury to his toe put him out of action for three months. Always looking to be struggling with his fitness after that, and only spasmodically featuring in the first team, he missed a huge chunk of the campaign before coming back at the close. At his best, he likes nothing better than driving forward to encourage the front men, and as an imposing figure at set pieces he often creates chances for others.

Port Vale (£80,000 from Wageningen on 21/2/91) FL 154+22/24 FLC 11+1/1 FAC 9+1/1 Others 11+1/1
Derby Co (£675,000 on 2/8/95) F/PL 61+4/8 FLC 6+2 FAC 3+1/3
Wolverhampton W (Loaned on 11/10/96) FL 7
Barnsley (£325,000 + on 17/7/98) FL 13+4/1 FLC 2/1 FAC 0+1

VAN HEUSDEN Arjan
Born: Alphen, Holland, 11 December 1972
Height: 6'3" Weight: 14.7

A free transfer summer signing from Port Vale, "Ice" assumed the number-one goalkeeping role on his arrival at Cambridge, and held it through to early October. A hand injury sustained against Brighton on 9 October resulted in him missing the next 12 fixtures, before he returned for the Boxing Day game against Rotherham. However, another hand injury at the end of March saw him miss the remainder of the campaign, but he will be able to look back on the season with great fondness, having started it with an incredible opening-day save at Torquay, and there are high hopes that he will perform in the same way in 1999-2000.

Port Vale (£4,500 from Noordwijk on 15/8/94) FL 27 FLC 4 Others 2
Oxford U (Loaned on 26/9/97) FL 11 FLC 2
Cambridge U (Free on 4/8/98) FL 27 FLC 4 Others 3

VAN HOOIJDONK Pierre
Born: Steenbergen, Holland, 29 November 1969
Height: 6'4" Weight: 13.12
Club Honours: SC '95; Div 1 '98
International Honours: Holland: 15

Having scooped Nottingham Forest's "Player of the Year" award for his huge efforts in getting the club promotion to the Premiership, the big Dutch striker went missing at the start of 1998-99, claiming that by selling its best assets before the season had started showed a lack of commitment, and were not the signs of an ambitious club just about to enter one of the most competitive leagues in the world. While there was much sympathy with his view there was no sympathy with his actions. Staying on "strike" until November, he finally swallowed his pride and returned to the City Ground. Coming back into the side for a 1-0 home defeat at the hands of Wimbledon was hardly the right tonic but, following a subs' appearance, he got off the mark with three goals in the next five games, and later scored the winner at Everton, just one of six victories attained by Forest throughout a campaign which ultimately saw them relegated. His pace and control, and the ability to run at defenders from outside the box, allied to good aerial power, will always make him a threat, but will his temperament continue to let him down.Stop Press: Returned to Holland on 29 June when transferred to Vitesse for £3.5 million.

Glasgow C (£1,200,000 from NAC Breda on 7/1/95) SL 66+3/44 SLC 5+1/3 SC 10/9 Others 5+2
Nottingham F (£4,500,000 on 11/3/97) F/PL 68+3/36 FLC 4+1/4 FAC 0+1/1

VARTY John William (Will)
Born: Workington,, 1 October 1976
Height: 6'0" Weight: 12.4
Club Honours: AMC '97

Will is another Carlisle player who will not look back too fondly on the last campaign, making just a handful of appearances after being an automatic choice previously. A surprise move on loan to Rotherham in March saw him performing well in central defence, where his cool inflappability made him a vital member of a back line that conceded far less goals following his arrival. Has quick feet.

Carlisle U (From trainee on 10/7/95) FL 79+3/1 FLC 8+1 FAC 3 Others 9+1
Rotherham U (Loaned on 12/3/99) FL 14 Others 2

VASSELL Darius
Born: Birmingham, 13 June 1980
Height: 5'7" Weight: 12.0
International Honours: E: U21-1; Yth

Another youngster to have progressed through the Aston Villa youth academy to reach the first team in 1998-99, Darius

featured on the subs' bench in over half of the games during the season, and although being called up as a sub on a number of occasions has yet to start. His most memorable moment would have undoubtedly been in the first round of the UEFA Cup game against Stromgodset, when he came off the bench to replace Darren Byfield and scored two of Villa's three goals. Fast and skilful on the ball, with plenty of trickery, he likes to run at defenders, either down the middle or out wide on the left, to get in shots on goal. Very much a forward player for the future, his good form was recognised by his selection for the England U18 side in matches against the Republic of Ireland and Italy, before going on to make his debut for the U21s.

Aston Villa (From trainee on 14/4/98) PL 0+6 FLC 0+1 FAC 0+1 Others 0+3/2

VAUGHAN Anthony (Tony) John
Born: Manchester, 11 October 1975
Height: 6'1" Weight: 11.2
International Honours: E: Yth; Sch
Tony started last season as a central defender, and was a Manchester City ever present up to the home game against Preston North End in mid October, complementing Gerard Wiekens well. However, after being sent off at Millwall for a strong tackle on a home player his playing sequence was broken when he missed the next three games. Came back into the side at home to Colchester, before having another run of 17 league and cup games disjointed in mid December, missing two games through injury. A solid defender who is quick in retreating back to cover, he can slot in very well either in the middle or as a left-sided defender. It was noticeable that his game strengthened in the last quarter of the campaign, as he looked more comfortable on the ball and the team continued to move towards promotion.

Ipswich T (From trainee on 1/7/94) P/FL 56+11/3 FLC 4+2 FAC 2 Others 4
Manchester C (£1,350,000 on 9/7/97) FL 54+3/2 FLC 6 FAC 3 Others 3+1

VAUGHAN John
Born: Isleworth, 26 June 1964
Height: 5'10" Weight: 13.1
Club Honours: Div 3 '91, '96
An experienced 'keeper who began last season as Lincoln's first choice, before losing his place in September after suffering a back injury, he returned to the team on Boxing Day and stayed until the end of the campaign. In all he kept 11 clean sheets, and his form after the New Year was his best since signing for City in August 1996.

West Ham U (From apprentice on 30/6/82)
Charlton Ath (Loaned on 11/3/85) FL 6
Bristol Rov (Loaned on 5/9/85) FL 6
Wrexham (Loaned on 3/10/85) FL 4
Bristol C (Loaned on 4/3/86) FL 2
Fulham (£12,500 on 21/8/86) FL 44 FLC 4 FAC 4 Others 3
Bristol C (Loaned on 21/1/88) FL 3
Cambridge U (Free on 6/6/88) FL 178 FLC 13 FAC 24 Others 16
Charlton Ath (Free on 5/8/93) FL 5+1 FAC 2 Others 1+1
Preston NE (Free on 26/7/94) FL 65+1 FLC 2 FAC 2 Others 5

Lincoln C (Free on 14/8/96) FL 60 FLC 5 FAC 1 Others 3
Colchester U (Loaned on 3/2/97) FL 5 Others 1

VEGA Ramon
Born: Zurich, Switzerland, 14 June 1971
Height: 6'3" Weight: 13.0
Club Honours: FLC '99
International Honours: Switzerland: 19
Versatile Tottenham defender who prefers to play on the left, but whose tremendous aerial ability and pace lends itself to a central role when required. Ramon made an encouraging start to last season, looking confident and in control in Spurs' back four, but as results became poor and team performances indifferent, he became somewhat of a scapegoat for the disappointed crowd. However, with his determination being both a physical and mental attribute, it did not take him long to re-establish himself as a stalwart of a much improved defence. Physically a defender built in the George Graham mould, the Swiss international responded well to his new manager, and despite a lengthy lay off mid term due to injury he was a key figure as results began to turn in Tottenham's favour. Along with his defensive capabilities, he has a keen eye for goal from set pieces, and again netted three fine goals with powerful, direct headers which have become his trademark. With his clear commitment to the team, and a genuine enthusiasm in every game he plays, he has become an integral member of the squad, having the raw skill which Graham is renowned for nurturing.

Tottenham H (£3,750,000 from Cagliari, via Trimbach and Grasshoppers, on 11/1/97) PL 43+6/6 FLC 7/1 FAC 7

VENUS Mark
Born: Hartlepool, 6 April 1967
Height: 6'0" Weight: 13.11
Club Honours: Div 3 '89
Mark's contribution to Ipswich's successful season in 1998-99 was immense, being a key figure on the left-hand side of the three-man central defence which helped equal a club record of 26 clean sheets during the campaign, and weighing in with nine goals to make him the club's third highest scorer. He was helped in this respect by being the regular penalty taker, scoring six out of the eight he took. In favouring his left foot, his distribution out of defence created a number of goals and, dangerous from free kicks, he also scored some memorable goals, the best of which was against Watford when his rising drive from the right of the "D" gave neither the wall nor the 'keeper any chance as it powered into the roof of the net. Mark's abilities were recognised by his inclusion in the PFA First Division select.

Hartlepool U (From juniors on 22/3/85) FL 4 Others 0+1
Leicester C (Free on 6/9/85) FL 58+3/1 FLC 3 FAC 2 Others 2+1
Wolverhampton W (£40,000 on 23/3/88) FL 271+16/7 FLC 17+1/1 FAC 15+1 Others 17/2
Ipswich T (£150,000 on 29/7/97) FL 56+2/10 FLC 9/1 FAC 3 Others 4

VERNAZZA Paulo Andrea Pietro
Born: Islington, 1 November 1979
Height: 6'0" Weight: 11.10
International Honours: E: Yth
A very talented Arsenal midfield player who is another product of the successful youth squad at Highbury, Paulo is strong and powerful, with good natural skill, and always produces a high workrate from box to box. As a good header of the ball, and possessing fine judgement with both short and long balls, he should score more goals from the positions he creates, something that should improve with experience. His only first-team game last season was in the Champions' League away leg at Panathinaikos, where he performed with great calmness and credit. Most definitely a player with a bright future, part of his development in 1998-99 was a three-month loan spell at Ipswich.

Arsenal (From trainee on 18/11/97) PL 1 FLC 1 Others 1
Ipswich T (Loaned on 2/10/98) FL 2

VEYSEY Kenneth (Ken) James
Born: Hackney, 8 June 1967
Height: 5'11" Weight: 12.7
1998-99 was an unlucky season for this talented shot stopper. Having taken over as Torquay's regular 'keeper, following Matt Gregg's departure to Crystal Palace in October, he then suffered an injury which led to Neville Southall's arrival. Unable to win his place back in the side, although there was talk of him being offered a coaching role at the club, he was told that he would be released during the summer.

Torquay U (Signed from Dawlish T on 19/11/87) FL 72 FLC 2 FAC 10 Others 9
Oxford U (£110,000 on 29/10/90) FL 57 FLC 2 FAC 4 Others 4
Reading (Free on 17/8/93)
Exeter C (Free on 14/10/93) FL 11+1 Others 3 (Free to Dorchester T on 17/9/94)
Torquay U (Free on 11/8/97) FL 37 FLC 1 FAC 4 Others 3

VIALLI Gianluca (Luca)
Born: Cremona, Italy, 9 July 1964
Height: 5'11" Weight: 13.6
Club Honours: FAC '97; FLC '98; ECWC '98
International Honours: Italy: 59
In the aftermath of Ruud Gullit's controversial departure, Luca made a sensational start to his managerial career by winning three trophies in his first five months, and signing world-class players Marcel Desailly, Brian Laudrup, Albert Ferrer, and Pierluigi Casiraghi, but his most profound acquisition may turn out to be fitness coach, Antonio Pintus, who was lured from Juventus. Despite the cup triumphs, his ultimate goal was always the Premiership, and his objective was to ally highly-skilled players with a high level of fitness to cope with the demands of a successful campaign. And, if it is the duty of a player/manager to lead from the front, then he did so admirably during Chelsea's spirited defence of the Worthington League Cup in 1998-99. In the third round he scored a superb hat trick as the Blues inflicted Aston Villa's first defeat

of the season with a 4-1 victory, and in the following round he scored twice in Chelsea's 5-0 triumph at Highbury – Arsenal's heaviest home defeat for 73 years. His sixth followed in the quarter-final defeat at Wimbledon, and he finished as the competition's top scorer. Two FA Cup goals at Oldham and one at Valerenga constituted his nine for the season in cup competitions. He used himself sparingly in the Premiership, preferring to direct operations from the bench, and only started during the January-February injury crisis when Tore Andre Flo, Gus Poyet, and Pierluigi Casiraghi were missing. A cult hero with the fans and "style guru", he came back to score the Blues' final goal of the season – his first in the league – against Derby, and plans to have one more season as a player before bringing the curtain down on his illustrious career at the end of 1999-2000. At the turn of the year, Chelsea were favourites to lift the title (their first since 1954-55), but points dropped in unfortunate home draws undermined their challenge, despite losing just three league matches. Nevertheless, it was a superb campaign, despite not winning any silverware, and Luca will proudly lead "the chaps" (as he calls the squad!) into the Champions' League, the first Chelsea manager to do so.

Chelsea (Free from Juventus, via Sampdoria and Cremonese, on 10/7/96) PL 46+12/21 FLC 6+1/6 FAC 4+4/6 Others 13+1/7

VICKERS Stephen (Steve)
Born: Bishop Auckland, 13 October 1967
Height: 6'1" Weight: 12.12
Club Honours: AMC '90; Div 1 '95
Like so many great Middlesbrough players, Steve grew up and learned his football around that hotbed of local soccer, Bishop Auckland, although his actual route to the club was via Tranmere Rovers. Now in his sixth year with Boro, he is a competent stopper who demonstrated well the art of blending talent with experience, and continued to take enormous pleasure at getting forward for corners and set pieces in 1998-99. A strong tackler, and no-nonsense clearance maker, he unfortunately suffered from one or two injuries, along with some over zealous refereeing decisions during the campaign, but always came back strongly.

Tranmere Rov (Signed from Spennymoor U on 11/9/85) FL 310+1/11 FLC 20+1/5 FAC 19/3 Others 36/1
Middlesbrough (£700,000 on 3/12/93) P/FL 187+8/8 FLC 23+1/2 FAC 15/1 Others 2

VIEIRA Patrick
Born: Dakar, Senegal, 23 June 1976
Height: 6'4" Weight: 13.0
Club Honours: PL '98; FAC '98; CS '98
International Honours: France: 11
A tall, powerful French international with wonderful distribution skills, Patrick has developed into one of the most talented midfield players in the country. In 1998-99 he continued to benefit tremendously from playing alongside fellow international, Manu Petit, at Arsenal, where power and commitment turned them into one of the strongest midfield duos in the Premiership. With an extremely powerful shot, and a

player who can score exciting goals from long range, his discipline is one area that needs to be worked on, although many of his bookings came about as a result of clumsiness as opposed to malice. Has an abundance of energy and enthusiasm, and with time on his side he could develop into one of the finest midfield players in the world. Was one of three Arsenal players selected by his fellow professionals for the PFA award-winning Premiership side.

Arsenal (£3,500,000 from AC Milan, via Cannes, on 14/8/96) PL 95+3/7 FLC 5 FAC 16+1/1 Others 7

VINCENT Jamie Roy
Born: Wimbledon, 18 June 1975
Height: 5'10" Weight: 11.8
Leaving Bournemouth bound for Huddersfield on transfer deadline day last March, Jamie had been the Cherries' first choice left back in 1998-99, producing consistently high performances. A solid defender who will support the front players when necessary, especially at set pieces, he provided the basis for a number of Bournemouth's winning performances. Quick to get forward at Town, immediately showing himself to be comfortable on the ball, and possessing good touch when giving a string of impressive performances for his new team, he was selected by his fellow professionals for the PFA award-winning Second Division side.

Crystal Palace (From trainee on 13/7/93) FL 19+6 FLC 2+1/1 FAC 1
Bournemouth (Loaned on 18/11/94) FL 8
Bournemouth (£25,000 + on 30/8/96) FL 102+3/5 FLC 7+1 FAC 8 Others 9/1
Huddersfield T (£440,000 + on 25/3/99) FL 7

VINDHEIM Rune
Born: Hoyanguer, Norway, 15 May 1972
Height: 5'11" Weight: 12.4
Although primarily a defender, the Norwegian made his Burnley debut in midfield, in front of 30,000 at Main Road, following his arrival from SK Brann last October. A spectacular baptism into English football saw him score in each of the next two games, but he often looked short of the pace and stamina required at Second Division level and faded from the scene when the Clarets' injury crisis eased.

Burnley (Free from SK Brann on 2/10/98) FL 8/2 FAC 1 Others 1

VINNICOMBE Christopher (Chris)
Born: Exeter, 20 October 1970
Height: 5'9" Weight: 10.12
Club Honours: SPD '91
International Honours: E: U21-12
Out of contract at Burnley in the summer of 1998, Wycombe signed up the nippy left back to fill a position which had been a problem for some years. He was actually used as a left-wing back before losing his place after five games to Alan Beeton, but soon returned, and was ever present, bar two games, for the rest of last season. His performance improved notably under the new manager, Lawrie Sanchez, when he was asked to revert to the left-back role, and he became one of the most consistent players in the side. Is excellent when bringing the ball

out of defence, passes accurately, and is able to cross with his trusty left, or cut inside if required.

Exeter C (From trainee on 1/7/89) FL 35+4/1 FLC 5/1 Others 2
Glasgow R (£150,000 on 3/11/89) SL 14+9/1 SLC 1+2 Others
Burnley (£200,000 on 30/6/94) FL 90+5/3 FLC 9 FAC 2 Others 7+1/1
Wycombe W (Free on 6/8/98) FL 39+2 FLC 4 FAC 3 Others 1

VIVAS Nelson David
Born: Buenos Aires, Argentina, 18 October 1969
Height: 5'6" Weight: 10.6
International Honours: Argentina: 16
Arriving at Highbury in August 1998 from Lugano, Nelson became the first Argentinian player to be signed by Arsenal. Superb in the air for a small man, he is a strong utility player who can perform effectively, either in midfield or in defence. After making his first-team debut at Sheffield Wednesday last September, he played on both the left and right side of the back four, and in midfield, and capped a superb performance by scoring in the 2-1 victory at Derby in the third round of the Worthington Cup. A regular in the Argentine international team since making his debut in 1994, he played four times in the 1998 World Cup finals, which included the game against England. Should become a regular in the Arsenal starting line-up, as senior players eventually move on.

Arsenal (£1,600,000 from Lugano on 5/8/98) PL 10+13 FLC 2/1 FAC 4+2 Others 2+3

VIVEASH Adrian Lee
Born: Swindon, 30 September 1969
Height: 6'2" Weight: 12.13
In what was his fourth season at Walsall, Adrian had to battle for a regular place at the heart of the defence in 1998-99 in the face of keen competition from Richard Green and Ian Roper, but missed only nine games all season. An ever present from January onwards, once again he was a towering presence in the air, while firm in the tackle.

Swindon T (From trainee on 14/7/88) FL 51+3/2 FLC 6+1 FAC 0+1 Others 2
Reading (Loaned on 4/1/93) FL 5 Others 1/1
Reading (Loaned on 20/1/95) FL 6
Barnsley (Loaned on 10/8/95) FL 2/1
Walsall (Free on 16/10/95) FL 159/12 FLC 10 FAC 13/2 Others 13/1

VLACHOS Michail
Born: Athens, Greece, 20 September 1967
Height: 5'11" Weight: 12.10
International Honours: Greece: 10
A Greek international, and Alan Ball's first permanent signing for Portsmouth, who can play as left-wing back or as he did for most of last season, in midfield. Possessing tremendous ability in the air, and gifted with both feet as well as being strong in the tackle, he has not fully adapted to the English game as illustrated by eight yellow and two red cards in 1998-99, along with spasmodic injury problems. Good in a man-to-man marking role, he should be a great asset if Pompey can achieve a settled side in 1999-2000.

Portsmouth (Signed from AEK Athens on 30/1/98) FL 44+1 FLC 1/1 FAC 2

WADDLE Christopher (Chris) Roland
Born: Felling, 14 December 1960
Height: 6'2" Weight: 13.3
International Honours: E: 62; U21-1
After leaving Burnley, where he was the player/manager, during the summer of 1998, the former England star joined Torquay on a non-contract basis at the end of September, and showed touches of his old class. However, the long travelling involved in commuting from his home, soon led to a mutual parting of the ways following just seven appearances. Stop Press: Was appointed Sheffield Wednesday's reserve team coach during the summer.
Newcastle U (£1,000 from Tow Law on 28/7/80) FL 169+1/46 FLC 8/2 FAC 12/4
Tottenham H (£590,000 on 1/7/85) FL 137+1/33 FLC 21/4 FAC 14/5 Others 4
Sheffield Wed (£1,000,000 on 1/7/92) PL 94+15/10 FLC 19 FAC 12+1/3 Others 3+1/1
Falkirk (Free on 13/9/96) SL 3/1
Bradford C (Free on 12/10/96) FL 25/6 FAC 3/1
Sunderland (£75,000 on 20/3/97) PL 7/1
Burnley (Free on 17/7/97) FL 26+5/1 FLC 2+1 FAC 2
Torquay U (Free on 24/9/98) FL 7

WAINWRIGHT Neil
Born: Warrington, 4 November 1977
Height: 6'0" Weight: 11.5
A tall left winger who joined Sunderland in July 1998 from Wrexham, Neil found first-team opportunities in 1998-99 limited – hardly surprising as the man in front of him was Scottish international, Allan Johnston. With good first touch and a confident approach, he made his debut in the Worthington Cup against York in August, and impressed with his willingness to take defenders on and shoot from distance. Was signed as a player for the future.
Wrexham (From trainee on 3/7/96) FL 7+4/3 FAC 1 Others 1
Sunderland (£100,000 + on 9/7/98) FL 0+2 FLC 2+1

WALKER Andrew William
Born: Bexley, 30 September 1981
Height: 6'0" Weight: 11.10
Still a first-year YTS goalkeeper, Andy became the youngest ever Colchester senior custodian when making his debut at Blackpool in the final game of last season, following Carl Emberson's broken finger and Tamer Fernandes's release. Not the most auspicious start, as Blackpool scored in the first minute, but the youngster was blameless and went on to produce a fine display which bodes well for the future safe keeping of the green jersey. Is another one to watch out for.
Colchester U (Trainee) FL 1

WALKER Desmond (Des) Sinclair
Born: Hackney, 26 November 1965
Height: 5'11" Weight: 11.13
Club Honours: FLC '89, '90; FMC '89, '92
International Honours: E: 59; U21-7
What more can be said about this top-class, pacy Sheffield Wednesday central defender who, despite advancing years, shows no signs of slowing down. A footballing defender, Des began an excellent partnership in 1998-99 with the equally skilful Brazilian stopper, Emerson, a partnership which augurs well for Wednesday's future well-being if the pair can stay together. Still good enough to be recalled for England international duties, despite last playing in 1993-94, the fans are willing him on to score his first goal for the club, having netted just once in a career that encompasses over 600 games. A manager's dream player – carrying injuries and missing very few games – where would Wednesday be without his superb positional play, last-ditch tackling, and timely interceptions.
Nottingham F (From apprentice on 2/12/83) FL 259+5/1 FLC 40 FAC 27 Others 14 (£1,500,000 to Sampdoria on 1/8/92)
Sheffield Wed (£2,700,000 on 22/7/93) PL 227 FLC 19 FAC 18

WALKER Ian Michael
Born: Watford, 31 October 1971
Height: 6'2" Weight: 13.1
Club Honours: FAYC '90; FLC '99
International Honours: E: 3; B-1; U21-9; Yth
After a disappointing start to last season which saw him dropped from the Tottenham side, having conceded six goals to Wimbledon and Sheffield Wednesday in the opening two games of 1998-99, the goalie finally reclaimed his place in December against Manchester United. Returning to form just at the right time, Ian later went on to concede only six goals in 17 consecutive games, commencing at Hillsbrough on 9 January through to the final of the Worthington Cup on 21 March. This fine run of form saw his new manager, George Graham, calling for him to be given another chance at international level, having lost his place as England number two to the in-form Nigel Martyn, who plays for one of Graham's former clubs – Leeds. As the son of a former pro goalie, Mike, who more recently managed Norwich, he has always been extremely agile and athletic, and the campaign saw him regain his confidence and grow in ability to organise his defence. Looking far more confident, and actively asserting that confidence over his back four, he was called into the England side as cover for an injured David Seaman for the Euro 2000 qualifier against Poland at Wembley. Although not being named in the final squad, he would have been delighted to be back on the international scene, and Tottenham fans will look forward to a continuation of that form when he faces the top names in Europe in the 1999-2000 UEFA Cup.
Tottenham H (From trainee on 4/12/89) F/PL 216+1 FLC 20 FAC 23 Others 2
Oxford U (Loaned on 31/8/90) FL 2 FLC 1

WALKER James (Jimmy) Barry
Born: Sutton in Ashfield, 9 July 1973
Height: 5'11" Weight: 13.5
In his sixth season at Walsall, Jimmy was an ever present for the second term in succession, and was voted the club's 1998-99 "Player of the Season". Agile and fearless, and renowned for his hefty clearances, he saved no fewer than six penalties in the shoot outs that took Walsall to the final of the Auto Windscreens Shield, and was one of the main reasons for the club's automatic promotion to the First Division as runners up to Fulham.
Notts Co (From trainee on 9/7/91)
Walsall (Free on 4/8/93) FL 188+1 FLC 12 FAC 17 Others 16

WALKER John
Born: Glasgow, 12 December 1973
Height: 5'7" Weight: 10.0
International Honours: S: Yth
Finally free of the injuries which have dogged him for the past couple of seasons this very talented Mansfield midfielder played a full part in the Stags' successes in 1998-99, despite half of his appearances being from the subs' bench. John passes the ball well, has good awareness, and cannot be faulted for his 100 per-cent commitment to the Club's cause. Was surprisingly released during the summer.
Glasgow R (From Clydebank BC on 29/8/90)
Clydebank (Signed on 31/7/93) SL 18+9/2 Others 4+3
Grimsby T (Signed on 19/9/95) FL 1+2/1
Mansfield T (£50,000 on 6/9/96) FL 51+23/4 FLC 0+1 FAC 4 Others 2+1

WALKER Justin Matthew
Born: Nottingham, 6 September 1975
Height: 5'11" Weight: 12.12
International Honours: E: Yth; Sch
A key player in the Scunthorpe midfield, Justin was the driving force of the team in 1998-99, showing strong tackling, good passing, and a tremendous workrate. A regular throughout the season, he only missed out through suspension, including a three-match ban for a sending off against Leyton Orient in March. Out of contract during the summer, it was reported that the Iron had offered him terms of re-engagement.
Nottingham F (From juniors on 10/9/92)
Scunthorpe U (Signed on 26/3/97) FL 86+4/2 FLC 6 FAC 5 Others 6/1

WALKER Keith Cameron
Born: Edinburgh, 17 April 1966
Height: 6'0" Weight: 12.8
After missing the start of last season with an injury picked up at a summer training camp, the strong-tackling central defender returned for the Swansea versus Leyton Orient game at the end of August. A few days later, after leaving the Vetch Field on crutches to visit the hospital for a scan to discover whether he had a second stress fracture on his leg, he fell and broke a bone in his ankle. Despite the break healing, tendonitis problems forced him to have further surgery, thus delaying his return to first-team duty, and then, following a couple of reserve games, a swollen ankle further delayed his comeback. Has the ability to find the forwards with excellent long passes out of defence.
Stirling A (Signed from ICI in 1984) SL 82+9/17 SLC 5/3 SC 5/2

St Mirren (Signed during 1987 close season) SL 41+2/6 SLC 3 SC 1 Others 3
Swansea C (£80,000 on 23/11/89) FL 262+8/9 FLC 10 FAC 21/1 Others 26

WALKER Richard Martin
Born: Birmingham, 8 November 1977
Height: 6'0" Weight: 12.0
With too many strikers ahead of him at Aston Villa, Richard joined Cambridge on loan last December for the remainder of the season. A pacy player, most of his appearances were as substitute, but he was rewarded for his efforts with two important goals in the latter part of the campaign. With a superb first touch, the youngster showed a marked improvement once he found a place in the starting line-up, and returned to Villa to improve the physical side of his game, where his progress will continue to be monitored by United.
Aston Villa (From trainee on 13/12/95) PL 0+1
Cambridge U (Loaned on 31/12/98) FL 7+14/3 Others 1+2/1

WALLACE Raymond (Ray) George
Born: Greenwich, 2 October 1969
Height: 5'6" Weight: 11.4
International Honours: E: U21-4
Despite being a hard-tackling, competitive central midfielder, "Razor" found it difficult to win or hold down a place in a Stoke team, who on occasions missed his involvement in the heart of their midfield in 1998-99. Always committed, Ray never let the side down when called on, before being released during the summer. Is one of three footballing brothers, Rod and Danny being the other two.
Southampton (From trainee on 21/4/88) FL 33+2 FLC 8 FAC 2 Others 2
Leeds U (£100,000 on 8/7/91) F/PL 5+2
Swansea C (Loaned on 20/3/92) FL 2
Reading (Loaned on 11/3/94) FL 3
Stoke C (Free on 11/8/94) FL 152+27/15 FLC 13+1 FAC 5+1 Others 12/1
Hull C (Loaned on 16/12/94) FL 7

WALLEMME Jean-Guy
Born: Naubeuge, France, 10 August 1967
Height: 6'1" Weight: 12.12
A central defender, Jean-Guy was a member of Lens' French championship winning side in 1998, before joining Coventry in the summer of that year, making only six starts. Although he was "Man of the Match" in two of those games, he looked ill at ease with the English game, and his encounter with Alan Shearer saw the England man score twice in a 5-1 win. Then, when his family failed to settle, and no French speaking school was found for his son, he returned to France to play for Sochaux on 5 January 1999.
Coventry C (£700,000 from RC Lens on 2/7/98) PL 4+2 FLC 2

WALLING Dean Anthony
Born: Leeds, 17 April 1969
Height: 6'0" Weight: 11.10
Club Honours: Div 3 '95; AMC '97
International Honours: St Kitts & Nevis
The Lincoln central defender spent much of last season on the injury list after undergoing a hernia operation in the

summer which took longer than expected to heal. Finally making his comeback in the youth team in February, after several reserve matches he returned to first-team action when he came off the subs' bench at Wigan in April. Dean made a further two appearances as a sub, coming on as a makeshift striker, and won a further three caps for the St Kitts and Nevis national team when he appeared for them in the Caribbean Cup. Stop Press: Signed for non-league Doncaster on 29 May.
Rochdale (Free from Leeds U juniors on 30/7/87) FL 43+22/8 FAC 3 FAC 0+1 Others 1+1 (Free to Kitchener (Toronto), during 1990 close season)
Carlisle U (Free from Guiseley, via Franklin (Toronto), on 1/7/91) FL 230+6/21 FLC 18/3 FAC 14+1/1 Others 35/5
Lincoln C (£75,000 on 30/9/97) FL 35+3/5 FAC 4/3

WALLWORK Ronald (Ronnie)
Born: Manchester, 10 September 1977
Height: 5'10" Weight: 12.9
Club Honours: FAYC '95
International Honours: E: Yth
A highly talented Manchester United forward who is a brilliant striker of the ball, especially with his left foot, Ronnie was hoping to claim a regular place amongst United's elite in 1998-99, after coming to the fore during the previous season's campaign. However, having played in the Worthington Cup against Nottingham Forest in November, he moved to Royal Antwerp in December on loan as part of United's link with the Belgium club, and playing in the centre of defence he was instrumental in helping them to top the Second Division in February. On current form, he is certain to remain a major part of Alex Ferguson's long-term plans.
Manchester U (From trainee on 17/3/95) PL 0+1 FLC 0+2
Carlisle U (Loaned on 22/12/97) FL 10/1 Others 2
Stockport Co (Loaned on 18/3/98) FL 7

WALSCHAERTS Wim
Born: Antwerp, Belgium, 5 November 1972
Height: 5'10" Weight: 12.4
Signed on a free transfer in the summer of 1998 from Belgian side, KFC Tielen, this Belgium midfielder, who can also play in the right-wing-back position when required, joined Leyton Orient as an unknown quantity. However, he soon settled into the English style of play, and contributed a couple of goals in the FA Cup, against Brighton and Kingstonian, before scoring his first league goal against Darlington in January. Prior to being sent off in the penultimate game, at Peterborough, and thus being forced to miss the play offs, he had shown himself to be a player of tremendous energy and stamina, who tackled and passed the ball well, and hardy enough to miss just three games all season.
Leyton Orient (Free from KFC Tielen on 30/7/98) FL 44/3 FLC 4 FAC 5/2

WALSH Daniel (Danny) Gareth
Born: Pontefract, 23 September 1979
Height: 5'11" Weight: 12.1
Another product of the Oldham youth

development system, Danny is an agile, pacy forward with an eye for goal, who was given a senior opportunity at Boundary Park last season when coming off the bench against Burnley in April. Still only a youngster, he deserved the chance after scoring 21 goals for the reserves. Gets into good positions in the box and is always looking to unsettle defenders.
Oldham Ath (From trainee on 7/7/98) FL 0+1

WALSH Gary
Born: Wigan, 21 March 1968
Height: 6'3" Weight: 15.10
Club Honours: ECWC '91; ESC '91; FAC '94
International Honours: E: U21-2
Last year's "Player of the Year", Gary had another terrific season for Bradford in 1998-99. They say goalkeepers get better with age, and that is certainly the case with Gary, his agility and domination of the area being outstanding. In not missing a game throughout the season, he pulled off many excellent saves to keep City in the promotion race, and is idolised by all the fans, young and old.
Manchester U (From juniors on 25/4/85) F/PL 49+1 FLC 7 Others 6
Airdrie (Loaned on 11/8/88) SL 3 SLC 1
Oldham Ath (Loaned on 19/11/93) PL 6
Middlesbrough (£500,000 on 11/8/95) PL 44 FLC 9 FAC 4
Bradford C (£500,000 + on 26/9/97) FL 81 FLC 5 FAC 3

WALSH Michael Shane
Born: Rotherham, 5 August 1977
Height: 6'0" Weight: 13.2
A highly-rated defender who joined Port Vale prior to last season from Scunthorpe, Michael began the campaign at right back, and displayed such excellent form that it prompted talk of a call up to the England U21 squad. Unfortunately, he then picked up a hamstring injury that kept him out for two months, and six games after his return a knee problem meant another lay off. His stop-start campaign ended in March when he underwent an operation on his ankle ligaments. A long-throw expert who can also play centre half, he scored one goal, at Norwich.
Scunthorpe U (From trainee on 3/7/95) FL 94+9/1 FLC 4 FAC 9 Others 5
Port Vale (£100,000 on 30/7/98) FL 18+1/1 FLC 1+1 FAC 1

WALSH Steven (Steve)
Born: Preston, 3 November 1964
Height: 6'3" Weight: 14.9
Club Honours: AMC '85; FLC '97
As the left-footed Leicester defender and club captain, Steve has long achieved cult status on the Filbert Street terraces, where he has now moved into the club's top five of all time in terms of appearances. Still regularly troubled by a catalogue of injuries throughout 1998-99, particularly a rib injury sustained in the early weeks, and a sprained ankle towards the end, he still led his troops magnificently all the way to Wembley once again. He even found the time to pop up as an emergency striker during an injury crisis, but generally settled for commanding the

team from the defensive line. Goals were scarcer last season, but the occasionally vital one enabled him to add to his tally as the club's most prolific defender ever, notably a trade-mark far post header from a Steve Guppy free kick against Southampton.

Wigan Ath (From juniors on 11/9/82) FL 123+3/4 FLC 7 FAC 6 Others 10+2
Leicester C (£100,000 on 24/6/86) F/PL 347+10/53 FLC 37/3 FAC 13/1 Others 23/4

WALTERS Mark Everton
Born: Birmingham, 2 June 1964
Height: 5'10" Weight: 12.8
Club Honours: FAYC '80; ESC '82; SPD '89, '90, '91; SLC '89, '91; FAC '92; FLC '95
International Honours: E: 1; B-1; U21-9; Yth; Sch

As a former England international, no one can question the natural ability of Swindon's left winger, cum midfield maestro. For the first half of last season, Mark was showing his skill and bagging a number of important goals, but after Christmas the ex-Liverpool star went off the boil and found it hard to get involved in games, particularly away from home. However, his ability to turn a game with one piece of genius means that he will remain a first-choice player while retaining this ability. Skilful and speedy, with good balance, and a player who can go both ways, he commits defenders when running at them.

Aston Villa (From apprentice on 18/5/82) FL 168+13/39 FLC 20+1/6 FAC 11+1/1 Others 7+3/2
Glasgow R (£500,000 on 31/12/87) SL 101+5/32 SLC 13/11 SC 14/6 Others 10/2
Liverpool (£1,250,000 on 13/8/91) F/PL 58+36/14 FLC 10+2/4 FAC 6+3 Others 8+1/1
Stoke C (Loaned on 24/3/94) FL 9/2
Wolverhampton W (Loaned on 9/9/94) FL 11/3
Southampton (Free on 18/1/96) PL 4+1 FAC 4
Swindon T (Free on 31/7/96) FL 80+19/23 FLC 7+1/1 FAC 3+1/2

WALTON David (Dave) Lee
Born: Bedlington, 10 April 1973
Height: 6'2" Weight: 14.8
Club Honours: Div 3 '94

A commanding centre back, and one of the first names on the team sheet, Dave was a regular for Crewe last season, missing games only through injury – a facial one at Sheffield United being particularly nasty – and was again outstanding at the heart of the defence, his commitment to the cause shining through. And, with Alex bottom of the First Division table with just four games to go, his defensive partnership with Steve Macauley was one of the reasons the club won three and drew one to avoid the drop by just one point. Scored his first goal for the Railwaymen in a 1-1 draw at Palace.

Sheffield U (Free from Ashington on 13/3/92)
Shrewsbury T (Signed on 5/11/93) FL 127+1/10 FLC 7 FAC 10/1 Others 11/1
Crewe Alex (£500,000 + on 20/10/97) FL 65/1 FLC 4 FAC 1

WALTON Mark Andrew
Born: Merthyr Tydfil, 1 June 1969
Height: 6'4" Weight: 15.8
International Honours: W: U21-1

An experienced goalkeeper signed in the summer of 1998 from Fulham, Mark turned in some impressive displays initially before becoming the focus for the Brighton fans' frustration as the team struggled. Beginning to look short on confidence, he was replaced by Mark Ormerod, but returned to the side for Jeff Wood's first game in charge, when the latter had flu. After suffering a hernia problem, which required surgery in February, he came back into the reserve side near the end of the season.

Luton T (From juniors on 21/2/87)
Colchester U (£15,000 on 5/11/87) FL 40 FLC 3 FAC 8 Others 5
Norwich C (£75,000 on 15/8/89) FL 22 FLC 1 FAC 5
Wrexham (Loaned on 27/8/93) FL 6
Dundee U (Free on 27/1/94)
Bolton W (Free on 2/3/94) FL 3 (Free to Wroxham on 9/9/94)
Fulham (Free from Fakenham T on 12/8/96) FL 40 FLC 5 Others 3
Gillingham (Loaned on 6/2/98) FL 1
Brighton & Hove A (£20,000 on 15/7/98) FL 19 FLC 2

WANCHOPE Pablo (Paulo) Cesar
Born: Costa Rica, 31 July 1976
Height: 6'4" Weight: 12.6
International Honours: Costa Rica: 20

An instantly recognisable and completely unorthodox striker whose physical presence alone can upset the best laid defensive plans of opponents, Paulo was a first choice for Derby throughout last season, as well as being part of the Costa Rica team crowned CONCACAF champions. Though not as prolific in terms of goals scored, his overall play showed a consistent improvement, and he demonstrated a useful ability to hold on to the ball to relieve pressure on defenders. Derby fans were united in hoping he signed a contract extending his stay beyond next season – perhaps in the role in which he played, behind the front two, as the campaign drew to a close – but, at the end of May, along with Igor Stimac and Dean Sturridge, he was surprisingly placed on the transfer list.

Derby Co (£600,000 from CS Heridiano on 27/3/97) PL 65+7/23 FLC 6+1/5 FAC 4

WANLESS Paul Steven
Born: Banbury, 14 December 1973
Height: 6'1" Weight: 13.12

Once again a very important player in Cambridge's midfield, this time in 1998-99, always showing commitment, never shirking a tackle, and doing everything a captain should do – lead by example. As a ball winner, and a box-to-box player, he also gets forward to score goals, last season being no exception, scoring eight – three coming in four games. Although falling short of winning the Third Division title by four points, under Paul's leadership United gained promotion as runners up.

Oxford U (From trainee on 3/12/91) FL 12+20 FLC 0+3/1 Others 2+2
Lincoln C (Free on 7/7/95) FL 7+1 Others 2
Cambridge U (Free on 8/3/96) FL 128+3/20 FLC 8 FAC 7 Others 3

WARBURTON Raymond (Ray)
Born: Rotherham, 7 October 1967
Height: 6'0" Weight: 12.13

"Razor" started last season as Northampton's club captain, and centre half, turning in his usual competent displays. He played a large part in the Worthington Cup win over West Ham, and was inspirational in the club's first league win over Bristol Rovers. Following that, he went into hospital for a hernia operation, and while convalescing was transferred to non-league Rushden and Diamonds, along with Carl Heggs, much to the surprise of many Town supporters.

Rotherham U (From apprentice on 5/10/85) FL 3+1 FAC 2 Others 2
York C (Free on 8/8/89) FL 86+4/9 FLC 8/1 FAC 6/1 Others 7
Northampton T (£35,000 on 4/2/94) FL 186/12 FLC 10 FAC 7/1 Others 17/3

WARD Ashley Stuart
Born: Manchester, 24 November 1970
Height: 6'2" Weight: 13.10

Although missing Barnsley's first game last season through injury and making a slow start it was not long before he was back to his best as one of the leading target men outside the Premiership. A good team player, strong in the air, and able to lay the ball off well, his goal output was excellent from both head and feet. However, with Blackburn looking to supplement their strike force in order to maintain Premiership status, Ashley moved to Ewood Park on the last day of December, and quickly proved to be the only striker on the club's books who was capable of playing every game. A non-stop runner, he often had the unenviable task of getting on the end of long balls out of defence, but despite lacking that extra pace he compensated by endeavour and enthusiasm, being never less than a handful for the opposition, to finish the campaign as Rovers' leading marksman.

Manchester C (From trainee on 5/8/89) FL 0+1 FAC 0+2
Wrexham (Loaned on 10/1/91) FL 4/2 Others 1
Leicester C (£80,000 on 30/7/91) FL 2+8 FLC 2+1 FAC 0+1 Others 0+1
Blackpool (Loaned on 21/11/92) FL 2/1
Crewe Alex (£80,000 on 1/12/92) FL 58+3/25 FLC 4/2 FAC 2/4 Others 7/5
Norwich C (£500,000 on 8/12/94) P/FL 53/18 FLC 6/3 FAC 1
Derby Co (£1,000,000 on 19/3/96) F/PL 32+8/9 FLC 1+1 FAC 2/1
Barnsley (£1,300,000 + on 5/9/97) P/FL 45+1/20 FLC 9/4 FAC 6/1
Blackburn Rov (£4,250,000 + on 31/12/98) PL 17/5 FAC 2+1

WARD Darren
Born: Worksop, 11 May 1974
Height: 6'2" Weight: 14.2
Club Honours: Div 3 '98
International Honours: W: B-1; U21-2

The appointment of specialist goalkeeper, Steve Sutton, proved to be of enormous benefit to Darren at Notts County in 1998-99, a season in which he showed substantial development. His improvement was recognised by both his club manager and Bobby Gould, who promoted him to the Welsh senior squad. Keeping 11 clean sheets, including three in a row towards the end of the campaign, he missed very few games, and his progress could yet see him

Darren Ward

become a full Welsh international and no doubt at some point a Premier League 'keeper. Represented Wales in the "B" game against Northern Ireland.
Mansfield T (From trainee on 27/7/92) FL 81 FLC 5 FAC 5 Others 6
Notts Co (£160,000 on 11/7/95) FL 171 FLC 12 FAC 16 Others 9

WARD Darren Philip
Born: Brentford, 13 September 1978
Height: 6'0" Weight: 12.6
A strapping Watford central defender who spent much of last season regaining his confidence and sharpness after sustaining a broken leg in February 1998, Darren finally returned to the first team in March, making his first league appearance for two years, at Sheffield United. A player who likes the ball at his feet, and is a good passer, he is still only 21.
Watford (From trainee on 13/2/97) FL 9 FAC 1 Others 0+1

WARD Gavin John
Born: Sutton Coldfield, 30 June 1970
Height: 6'3" Weight: 14.12
Club Honours: Div 3 '93; WC '93
Following Paul Crichton's recall by West Bromwich after only one game, Burnley turned to Bolton to sign Gavin on loan, and he stayed as first-choice 'keeper for three months, coping well behind an often shaky and inexperienced defence, proving capable on crosses as well as shot stopping, and

saving Burnley from embarrassment on more than one occasion. Lack of funds ruled out a permanent signing, and he returned to Bolton in November, subsequently signing for Stoke in February. Having taken Carl Muggletons's place in the side immediately, bringing much-needed competition, unfortunately, after just a handful of games he was sidelined.
Shrewsbury T (Free from Aston Villa juniors on 26/9/88)
West Bromwich A (Free on 18/9/89)
Cardiff C (Free on 5/10/89) FL 58+1 FAC 1 Others 7
Leicester C (£175,000 on 16/7/93) F/PL 38 FLC 3 FAC 0+1 Others 4
Bradford C (£175,000 on 13/7/95) FL 36 FLC 6 FAC 3 Others 2
Bolton W (£300,000 on 29/3/96) F/PL 19+3 FLC 2 FAC 4
Burnley (Loaned on 14/8/98) FL 17
Stoke C (Free on 25/2/99) FL 6

WARD Mitchum (Mitch) David
Born: Sheffield, 19 June 1971
Height: 5'8" Weight: 11.7
A versatile performer capable of operating on the left and right of defence, Mitch's Everton career has been hounded by injury. Rarely sidelined at Sheffield United, since a move to Goodison late in 1997 he has been plagued by a succession of problems. After getting his first chance to impress the new manager, Walter Smith, as a substitute in the Merseyside derby last October, he earned his first start of the season a week

later – and sustained an ankle injury. Despite being admired by the Blues' coaching staff for his attitude and reliability, dogged by a persistent heel injury on top of previous knee trouble, he was released during the summer.
Sheffield U (From trainee on 1/7/89) F/PL 135+19/11 FLC 8+3/2 FAC 7+2/2 Others 5+1/1
Crewe Alex (Loaned on 1/11/90) FL 4/1 FAC 1/1 Others 2
Everton (£850,000 on 25/11/97) PL 12+2 FLC 1 FAC 2

WARD Peter
Born: Durham, 15 October 1964
Height: 5'11" Weight: 11.10
1998-99 was a frustrating season for Peter. As the free-kick specialist and cog in the Wrexham midfield engine room, he featured strongly early on before a knee injury which required an operation on a cartilage in January, saw him miss the second half of the campaign. Although not as prominent as in previous terms, his patient passing style was missed in the latter stages, to say nothing of his free kicks. Was released during the summer.
Huddersfield T (Signed from Chester le Street on 7/1/87) FL 24+13/2 FLC 1+1 FAC 2 Others 1
Rochdale (Free on 20/7/89) FL 83+1/10 FLC 5 FAC 7/1 Others 5
Stockport Co (Signed on 6/6/91) FL 140+2/10 FLC 8/1 FAC 7 Others 26/6
Wrexham (£50,000 on 19/7/95) FL 117+3/15 FLC 7 FAC 20/1 Others 2+1/1

WARHURST Paul
Born: Stockport,, 26 September 1969
Height: 6'1" Weight: 13.6
Club Honours: PL '95
International Honours: E: U21-8

Football's "Mr Bionic", Paul has suffered injuries that would force a vast majority of footballers out of the game for good. A vastly experienced player who established himself with firstly Sheffield Wednesday, and then Blackburn, he started last season with a transfer request owing to his wife wanting to return to the north. Crystal Palace then granted him a loan spell at Bolton in November, when the Trotters were experiencing something of a defensive crisis, and he formed a formidable central defensive partnership with Jon Newsome, who was at the club on loan himself. Bolton did not lose in the period that Paul played for the club, and although the club did not sign both players (as the vast majority of the Reebok faithful would have liked), they managed to secure the services of Paul. Ironically, it was in the 3-0 home win over Palace that he made his full debut for the club. A highly versatile and skilled player, who can play in just about every outfield position, although he seems to be most effective at centre half or centre forward, his experience, supreme passing ability, and exceptional footballing brain will serve him well for many seasons to come. Is the son of Roy, an early post-war wing half who turned out for Sheffield United, Birmingham, Manchester City, Crewe, and Oldham.
Manchester C (From trainee on 1/7/88)
Oldham Ath (£10,000 on 27/10/88) FL 60+7/2 FLC 8 FAC 5+4 Others 2
Sheffield Wed (£750,000 on 17/7/91) F/PL 60+6/6 FLC 9/4 FAC 7+1/5 Others 5/3
Blackburn Rov (£2,700,000 on 17/8/93) PL 30+27/4 FLC 6+2 FAC 2+1 Others 4+2
Crystal Palace (£1,250,000 on 31/7/97) P/FL 27/4 FLC 2 FAC 1
Bolton W (£800,000 on 25/11/98) FL 17+3 Others 0+2

WARNE Paul
Born: Norwich, 8 May 1973
Height: 5'9" Weight: 11.2

Although very quick around the penalty box, Paul found his first-team opportunities limited at Wigan last season, and after scoring against Rotherham in the Auto Windscreens Shield he joined the Yorkshire club in January, initially on loan, before the arrangement was made more permanent. The striker soon became a Millmoor favourite, with his willing running and blistering start – scoring five goals in his first four games, including two on his debut – and went on to forge an excellent partnership with Leo Fortune-West, for whom he laid on several goals. Should be a key figure in 1999-2000.
Wigan Ath (£25,000 from Wroxham on 30/7/97) FL 11+25/3 FLC 0+1 FAC 1 Others 1+2/1
Rotherham U (Free on 15/1/99) FL 19/8 Others 2

WARNER Michael (Mickey) James
Born: Harrogate, 17 January 1974
Height: 5'9" Weight: 10.10

A right-sided wing back, and a great favourite with the Northampton crowd, first-team appearances in 1998-99 were few and far between for Mickey, but he always gave 100 per cent. In his first full game for Town last season, at home to Gillingham, he was voted "Man of the Match", and he starred in the Worthington Cup against Tottenham, when he came on as substitute, twice sending shots goalwards, only to see them stop in the mud inches from the goal line! Was released during the summer.
Northampton T (Free from Tamworth on 10/7/95) FL 9+19 FLC 0+2 FAC 0+3 Others 2+3

WARNER Philip
Born: Southampton, 2 February 1979
Height: 5'10" Weight: 11.7

This young Southampton central defender or full back, having been a product of the junior ranks at the Dell, had several opportunities at the start of last season deputising for various players, but did not feature in the first team after playing in the 1-1 draw at Arsenal in October. Despite being given a torrid time at Highbury by Marc Overmars, before being withdrawn after 34 minutes, he is very quick, a good jumper, and it is expected that we will see a lot more of him in the future.
Southampton (From trainee on 23/5/97) PL 5+1 FLC 1

WARNER Vance
Born: Leeds, 3 September 1974
Height: Weight:
International Honours: E: Yth

This speedy Rotherham defender, with a strong tackle, was hampered by a string of injuries last season which meant he missed half the campaign and did not play again after the end of February. Prior to that, he had got the team off to a great start by hitting the first goal of 1998-99, his one and only for United. Fully fit this coming term, he must be a serious contender for a regular place again.
Nottingham F (From trainee on 14/9/91) F/PL 4+1 FLC 1+1
Grimsby T (Loaned on 2/2/96) FL 3
Rotherham U (Signed on 29/8/97) FL 44/1 FLC 1 FAC 6 Others 1

WARREN Christer Simon
Born: Dorchester, 10 October 1974
Height: 5'10" Weight: 11.10

Christer played in a variety of positions for Bournemouth in 1998-99, making 32 starts and nine substitute appearances, and although performing mainly on the left-hand side of midfield or up front, he also deputised at left back following the sale of Jamie Vincent to Huddersfield. Quick, and not afraid to run at defenders, he looks comfortable in whatever position he plays.
Southampton (£40,000 from Cheltenham T on 31/3/95) PL 1+7 FLC 1
Brighton & Hove A (Loaned on 11/10/96) FL 3
Fulham (Loaned on 6/3/97) FL 8+3/1
Bournemouth (£50,000 on 8/10/97) FL 55+7/11 FLC 0+3 FAC 7 Others 6

WARREN Mark Wayne
Born: Clapton, 12 November 1974
Height: 6'0" Weight: 12.2
International Honours: E: Yth

As Leyton Orient's longest-serving player, Mark started 1998-99 in the first-team squad before a combination of good form by others and suspension saw him failing to hold down a regular place in the side from then on. Loaned out to Oxford at the end of December, and impressing enough in four games for United to want to sign him, he returned to Orient due to lack of funds at the Manor Ground. On his return to Brisbane Road, and on telling the manager, Tommy Taylor, that he would be leaving the club during the summer under the Bosman ruling, he was sold to Notts County without delay. Recruited to add extra pace to the County rearguard, he quickly established himself as a favourite with the fans, who admired his quick-tackling, no-nonsense defending, allied to great power of speedy recover. Captaining the side in the latter stages of the season, and playing on through injury to help his club to safety, he could prove to be one of the manager's better bargain buys.
Leyton Orient (From trainee on 6/7/92) FL 134+18/5 FLC 8+1/2 FAC 5+1 Others 10+4/1
Oxford U (Loaned on 24/12/98) FL 4
Notts Co (Signed on 28/1/99) FL 18

WARRINGTON Andrew (Andy) Clifford
Born: Sheffield, 10 June 1976
Height: 6'3" Weight: 12.13

Started last season as first-choice 'keeper for York, before mistakes in the first two games caused him to lose confidence, and subsequently his place. Returned in November, only to break a bone in his hand in a FA Cup win over Enfield, he then came back for another spell of first-team duty in March and did well in a vital win at Lincoln before being released in the summer. Tall and well built, Andy will continue to improve with experience.
York C (From trainee on 11/6/94) FL 61 FLC 7 FAC 4 Others 4

WASSALL Darren Paul
Born: Birmingham, 27 June 1968
Height: 6'0" Weight: 12.10
Club Honours: FMC '92

Made his first appearance in a Birmingham shirt for 13 months last December, following three achilles tendon operations, and then suffered a stress fracture before having the heel raised on his right boot by 15mm on coming back into action. A strong central defender, and man marker with pace and good tackling technique, he finally got himself match fit to get back in the first-team squad in time for the play-off charge.
Nottingham F (From apprentice on 1/6/86) FL 17+10 FLC 6+2 FAC 3+1 Others 4+2/1
Hereford U (Loaned on 23/10/87) FL 5 FAC 1 Others 1
Bury (Loaned on 2/3/89) FL 7/1
Derby Co (£600,000 on 15/6/92) FL 90+8 FLC 9 FAC 4 Others 11
Manchester C (Loaned on 11/9/96) FL 14+1 FLC 2
Birmingham C (£100,000 on 26/3/97) FL 22+3 FLC 5

WATERMAN David (Dave) Graham
Born: Guernsey,, 16 May 1977
Height: 5'10" Weight: 13.2
International Honours: NI: U21-9
In a story-book apprenticeship, Dave has come through the ranks to become a strong, physical, good all rounder, and an excellent prospect for Portsmouth, who rewarded him this summer with a new three-year contract. An excellent man-to-man marker who, given a long run in the first team, will show his true potential, hopefully in 1999-2000. Apart from a five-match run in November, Dave's only other first-team starts in 1998-99 were when filling in for suspended or injured players, something he performed extremely well whenever asked, particularly against Leeds United in the FA Cup in January. Continued to represent the Northern Ireland U21 side.
Portsmouth (From trainee on 4/7/95) FL 21+8 FLC 1 FAC 3

WATKIN Stephen (Steve)
Born: Wrexham, 16 June 1971
Height: 5'10" Weight: 11.10
Club Honours: WC '95
International Honours: W: B-2; Sch
With a change in management at Swansea prior to the start of last season, a different style of play saw Steve show his true qualities when being able to hold the ball up to shield it from the opposition. With a renewed confidence, he also regained his eye for goal, forging an excellent partnership with Julian Alsop, as both players vied to reach the top of the goalscoring stakes for the Swans.
Wrexham (From juniors on 24/7/89) FL 167+33/55 FLC 11+3/4 FAC 16+6/12 Others 17+5/4
Swansea C (£108,000 on 26/9/97) FL 64+11/20 FLC 2 FAC 4+1 Others 2

WATSON Alexander (Alex) Francis
Born: Liverpool, 5 April 1968
Height: 6'1" Weight: 13.0
Club Honours: CS '88
International Honours: E: Yth
A damaged knee ligament at Scunthorpe last September ruined the season for Torquay's popular player/coach and, although making a brief comeback in the New Year, the injury flared up again, forcing him to sit out the rest of the campaign. The loss of such an experienced central defender, obviously had a serious effect on United's fortunes, and it is to be hoped that he will be fighting fit come the start of 1999-2000.
Liverpool (From apprentice on 18/5/85) FL 3+1 FLC 1+1 FAC 1+1 Others 1
Derby Co (Loaned on 30/8/90) FL 5
Bournemouth (£150,000 on 18/1/91) FL 145+6/5 FLC 14/1 FAC 12/1 Others 5

Gillingham (Loaned on 11/9/95) FL 10/1
Torquay U (£50,000 on 23/11/95) FL 129/4 FLC 8 FAC 6 Others 6/1

WATSON Andrew (Andy) Anthony
Born: Leeds, 1 April 1967
Height: 5'9" Weight: 12.6
Club Honours: WC '91
Andy's injury problems from the end of the previous season at Walsall continued in 1998-99 and again he did not have much luck. However, he did have a purple patch early in the New Year when getting the goal that earned a point against Manchester City, and then netting a delightful curling shot at York that proved to be a matchwinner. Released during the summer, he is a striker who has good movement in the box, dragging defenders out of position, and looks to get back into goalscoring form this coming term, injuries allowing.
Halifax T (Free from Harrogate T on 23/8/88) FL 75+8/15 FLC 5+1/2 FAC 6/1 Others 7/1
Swansea C (£40,000 on 31/7/90) FL 9+5/1 FLC 0+1 Others 1+1
Carlisle U (£30,000 on 19/9/91) FL 55+1/22 FLC 4/5 FAC 3 Others 1/1
Blackpool (£55,000 on 5/2/93) FL 88+27/43 FLC 6/5 FAC 3+2 Others 7+1/1
Walsall (£60,000 on 5/9/96) FL 57+27/15 FLC 6+1/4 FAC 4+5/3 Others 7/2

WATSON David (Dave)
Born: Liverpool, 20 November 1961
Height: 6'0" Weight: 12.4
Club Honours: FLC '85; Div 2 '86; Div 1 '87, CS '87, '95; FAC '95
International Honours: E: 12; U21-7 (UEFAC '84)
An Everton institution, Dave's enduring excellence throughout another difficult time at Goodison led to the club shop stocking T-shirts bearing the legend "If only everything in life was as reliable as . . . Dave Watson." He began 1998-99 as first-team coach, hoping to make the handful of appearances which would take him beyond 500 for the club, before being surprisingly recalled to the starting line-up after just four games, and passing the 500 mark in September. From then on, Walter Smith found it increasingly difficult to leave the defensive inspiration on the sidelines, and he ended the campaign with the captain's armband back in his possession, a new one-year playing contract in his pocket – with the likelihood of yet another season to come in the Premiership. Powerful, alert and uncompromising in the tackle, his keen mind makes up for the half-yard of pace he may have lost in recent years, and although unable to coax his 37-year-old legs through two games in a week these days he is still more than capable of adding to his Goodison legend in 1999-2000.
Liverpool (From juniors on 25/5/79)
Norwich C (£100,000 on 29/11/80) FL 212/11 FLC 21/3 FAC 18/1
Everton (£900,000 on 22/8/86) F/PL 414+3/24 FLC 39/7 FAC 47/5 Others 16+1/3

WATSON David (Dave) Neil
Born: Barnsley, 10 November 1973
Height: 6'0" Weight: 12.12
International Honours: E: U21-5; Yth

Dave Watson

Started last season as Barnsley's first-choice goalie, and continued to show the form that made him one of the most underrated custodians in the league, in keeping four clean sheets from eight games. However, only a month into 1998-99 he developed cartilage problems which were to rule him out for the rest of the campaign. An excellent shot stopper who has improved his ability to command the penalty area, he will be desperate to get back into first-team action in 1999-2000.

Barnsley (From trainee on 4/7/92) F/PL 178 FLC 16 FAC 11 Others 1

WATSON Gordon William George
Born: Sidcup, 20 March 1971
Height: 5'11" Weight: 12.9
International Honours: E: U21-2
"Flash" missed the whole of 1997-98, being out of the game for 18 months after breaking his leg in just his third game for the club in February 1997. At one time, the talented striker feared his career was over, but made his comeback in September, and was then involved in the next 15 games. He opened his scoring account when coming on as substitute in the 83rd minute against Barnsley, and struck both goals in the 2-1 win. Still not back to full fitness, but playing regularly in the reserves, this hard-working target man, who chases lost causes, and who is excellent in the air, could be a key man for City in 1999-2000 if he takes up their offer of re-engagement.

Charlton Ath (From trainee on 5/4/89) FL 20+11/7 FLC 2/1 FAC 0+1 Others 1+1
Sheffield Wed (£250,000 on 20/2/91) F/PL 29+37/15 FLC 6+5/3 FAC 5+2/2 Others 2+2/1
Southampton (£1,200,000 on 17/3/95) PL 37+15/8 FLC 6+3/5 FAC 5+1/1
Bradford C (£550,000 on 17/1/97) FL 8+13/5 FLC 1+3

WATSON Kevin Edward
Born: Hackney, 3 January 1974
Height: 6'0" Weight: 12.6
Although not a favoured midfielder under Steve McMahon at Swindon in 1998-99, the new manager, Jimmy Quinn, gave him his chance and by mid term he had notched up a handful of games. Although he showed some quality touches, ultimately it was not enough. His inability to get his foot in and score goals meant he was more often than not on the bench, before being released in the summer. Skilful, with a lovely touch on the ball, and a creative passer, he will need to find a side that appreciates his abilities.

Tottenham H (From trainee on 15/5/92) PL 4+1 FLC 1+1/1 FAC 0+1
Brentford (Loaned on 24/3/94) FL 2+1
Bristol C (Loaned on 2/12/94) FL 1+1
Barnet (Loaned on 16/2/95) FL 13
Swindon T (Free on 15/7/96) FL 39+24/1 FLC 2+2 FAC 1+2

WATSON Mark Stewart
Born: Vancouver, Canada, 8 September 1970
Height: 6'0" Weight: 12.6
International Honours: Canada: 48
Previously with the Swedish team, Osters IFV, Mark had an impressive first season for Oxford after joining them last December following a successful trial

spell, and after starting at Stockport he was ever present. A central defender who is quick and reads the game well, and formed a good partnership with Phil Gilchrist, he has been capped over 50 times for Canada, his latest cap coming this season against Northern Ireland. Earlier in his career, the Canadian had spent two seasons with Watford before going back to Canada following an injury.

Watford (Signed from Vancouver 86ers on 19/11/93) FL 18 FAC 1+2 (Freed during 1995 close season)
Oxford U (Free from Osters IFV on 17/12/98) FL 23 FAC 3

WATSON Paul Douglas
Born: Hastings, 4 January 1975
Height: 5'8" Weight: 10.10
Club Honours: Div 3 '99
A compact left-sided full back who can play on either flank if required, he was selected for the first ten games of the 1998-99 season for Brentford before losing his place to the comebacking Ijah Anderson. Made only a few appearances thereafter, before asking for a transfer which was granted. Recognised for his ability to get plenty of movement on free kicks and corners, his early performances ensured that he won a Third Division championship medal as the Bees were promoted at the first time of asking.

Gillingham (Signed on 8/12/92) FL 57+5/2 FLC 4 FAC 6 Others 5+3
Fulham (£13,000 on 30/7/96) FL 48+2/4 FLC 3/1 FAC 2 Others 2
Brentford (£50,000 on 12/12/97) FL 37 FLC 2 FAC 2 Others 0+1

WATSON Stephen (Steve) Craig
Born: North Shields, 1 April 1974
Height: 6'0" Weight: 12.7
International Honours: E: B-1; U21-12; Yth
As one of the Premiership's most consistent full backs, it came as a great surprise to the Newcastle fans when he was transferred to Aston Villa last October after appearing to be in good form in all of United's opening eight games of 1998-99. The club explained that as Ruud Gullit was well stocked with full backs, he could not refuse the offer, especially as he could use the fee to help rebuild the side. Calm under pressure, skilled on the ball, and a player who can be relied upon to give 100 per-cent effort, his versatility allows him to play in any position, although he admits to favouring the right side of defence. When he arrived at Villa Steve knew he had a battle to win a regular place, but once he had achieved it, apart from being stretchered off against Coventry with a badly-sprained ankle and missing a couple of games, there was no stopping him. Prior to the signing of Steve Stone, he was always encouraged by manager John Gregory to push forward down the right flank, but since the arrival of the latter, the two have linked up well to provide even more chances for the forwards.

Newcastle U (From trainee on 6/4/91) F/PL 179+16/12 FLC 10+6/1 FAC 13+4 Others 3
Aston Villa (£4,000,000 on 15/10/98) PL 26+1 FLC 1 FAC 2

WATT Michael
Born: Aberdeen, 27 November 1970
Height: 6'1" Weight: 12.6
Club Honours: SLC '96
International Honours: S: B-1; U21-12; Sch
Having left Aberdeen at the end of 1997-98, following an unsuccessful loan period at Blackburn, Michael impressed the Norwich coaching staff during an initial trial spell, earning himself a one-year contract in the process. He immediately placed Andy Marshall under pressure for a first-team place, and was rewarded when he came off the bench to replace the injured Marshall at Barnsley in September. His capable displays earned him an extended run in the first-team through December and January, starting eight games in that time, showing excellent positional skills and good handling techniques before being released in the summer.

Aberdeen (From Cove R on 28/11/87) SL 79 SLC 5 SC 7 Others 4
Norwich C (Free on 10/8/98) FL 7+1 FAC 1

WATTS Julian
Born: Sheffield, 17 March 1971
Height: 6'3" Weight: 13.7
Club Honours: FLC '97
After signing from Leicester during the 1998 close season, Julian never really fitted into the Bristol City side and, following several heavy defeats, he was dropped, going on loan to Lincoln in mid December after being told by the coach, Benny Lennartsson, that he did not figure in his future plans. At his best a central defender with good ability in the air, and pace to spare, although he had a poor debut for City in the heavy defeat at Wycombe he performed well in his only other league appearance when replacing the injured Kevin Austin at Burnley, before returning to Ashton Gate when his one-month loan period came to an end. Loaned to Blackpool during transfer deadline week, he appeared in nine of the last ten games.

Rotherham U (Signed from Frecheville CA on 10/7/90) FL 17+3/1 FLC 1 FAC 4 Others 2
Sheffield Wed (£80,000 on 13/3/92) PL 12+4/1 FLC 1 Others 1
Shrewsbury T (Loaned on 18/12/92) FL 9 Others 1
Leicester C (£210,000 on 29/3/96) P/FL 31+7/1 FLC 6+1 FAC 2+1 Others 4
Crewe Alex (Loaned on 29/8/97) FL 5
Huddersfield T (Loaned on 5/2/98) FL 8
Bristol C (Free on 6/7/98) FL 16+1/1 FLC 3+1
Lincoln C (Loaned on 18/12/98) FL 2 Others 1
Blackpool (Loaned on 25/3/99) FL 9

WATTS Steven (Steve)
Born: Lambeth, 11 July 1976
Height: 6'1" Weight: 13.7
Having joined Leyton Orient from Fisher Athletic last October, after entering a competition in the Sun newspaper for "wannabe strikers" who wanted to be offered a professional contract, far from it being a publicity stunt, Steve was duly awarded his contract and became a vital part of the first team, whilst also scoring six goals in only ten starts. Already rumoured to have been watched by First Division sides, and definitely one to watch for in 1999-

Nicky Weaver

2000, he` is big, strong, quick, and powerful in the air. Is reckoned by those in the know to be a natural goalscorer.
Leyton Orient (Signed from Fisher on 14/10/98) FL 10+18/6 Others 4

WAUGH Warren Anthony
Born: London, 9 October 1980
Height: 6'1" Weight: 13.5
Still a trainee, Warren made his debut for Exeter as a sub against Swansea last January. A prolific scorer at youth level, being big and strong, quick around the box, and with an eye for the goal, Warren is highly thought of at Exeter and will no doubt be making in-roads towards more appearances this coming term.
Exeter C (Trainee) FL 0+7 Others 0+1

WEATHERSTONE Simon
Born: Reading, 26 January 1980
Height: 5'10" Weight: 11.12
A young Oxford striker, Simon missed a large part of last season with a blood disorder which laid him low for several months, and after starting with four substitute appearances he scored what turned out to be one of two goals for the season in the Worthington Cup-tie at Luton. His other goal earned the team a point at

Tranmere. Yet to score at the Manor Ground, he twice went close against Norwich, both times hitting the woodwork, and the signs are that he will have an extended run in 1999-2000 after ending the campaign in the side.
Oxford U (From trainee on 27/3/97) FL 6+18/2 FLC 0+2/1

WEAVER Luke Dennis Spencer
Born: Woolwich, 26 June 1979
Height: 6'2" Weight: 13.2
International Honours: E: Yth; Sch
With Thomas Sorensen and Andy Marriott ahead of him in the goalkeeping pecking order at Sunderland in 1998-99, Luke was loaned out to the struggling Third Division side, Scarborough, in December in an effort to further his experience. That he proved to be an extremely competent young custodian was no real surprise, having earlier played for England at both schools and youth level, and he impressed in the 1-0 home derby win over Halifax on his debut. Unfortunately, following a run of six league games, he suffered a knee injury and returned to the Stadium of Light.
Leyton Orient (From trainee on 26/6/96) FL 9 FAC 1 Others 1
Sunderland (£250,000 on 9/1/98)
Scarborough (Loaned on 10/12/98) FL 6

WEAVER Nicholas (Nicky) James
Born: Sheffield, 2 March 1979
Height: 6'3" Weight: 13.6
Signed from Mansfield, Nicky played for Manchester City at the end of the 1997-98 season in a friendly against the Jamaican World Cup team, and immediately impressed the loyal fans with a talented display of agility and safe handling in City's goal. Started last season in the first game at home against Blackpool, and never looked back, only missing three games out of 32 due to a leg strain which was slow in repairing. Excelling with his adventurous style, he was tested well at Derby in the Worthington Cup 1-1 draw by top class players, and worked hard at his understanding with the back players in passing out of defence. As one of the few 'keepers who can clear his lines by strong kicking with both feet, and seldom having to resort to panic, his good form saw him called up for two England U21 games, although he did not make the team. Rewarded with a new four-year contract in February, his time will certainly come, especially if the FA Cup-tie at Wimbledon, where he commanded the goal area on a difficult pitch, is anything to go by.
Mansfield T (Trainee) FL 1
Manchester C (£200,000 on 2/5/97) FL 45 FLC 3 FAC 4 Others 3

WEIR David Gillespie
Born: Falkirk, 10 May 1970
Height: 6'2" Weight: 13.7
Club Honours: S Div 1 '94; B&Q '94
International Honours: S: 13; Sch
Signed from Hearts last February, this versatile defender who is at home in the centre or at wing back, used his skills to good effect in Everton's successful fight to avoid relegation from the Premiership. In his first few weeks at Goodison he played everywhere but in his most natural central defensive position, and acquitted himself well. He eventually settled in at right-wing back, ending the campaign as a fixture in the Blues' starting line-up. Tall and strong in the tackle, a good reader of the game, and an excellent passer out of defence, he proved a shrewd acquisition for the squad. Played six times for Scotland during the season.
Falkirk (From Celtic BC on 1/8/92) SL 133/8 SLC 5 SC 6 Others 5
Heart of Midlothian (Signed on 29/7/96) SL 92/8 SLC 10/2 SC 9/2 Others 6
Everton (£250,000 on 17/2/99) PL 11+3 FAC 1

WELCH Keith James
Born: Bolton, 3 October 1968
Height: 6'2" Weight: 13.7
The long-serving Bristol City goalkeeper suffered last season when playing behind a defence experiencing major difficulties from the very first match. Despite producing a brilliant performance in the game at Sunderland, his appearances were severely restricted following the arrival of new coach, Benny Lennartsson. Played very few games of any sort, after losing his place to Steve Phillips, and out of contract during the summer Keith was expected to be elsewhere in 1999-2000.

Rochdale (Free from Bolton W juniors on 3/3/87) FL 205 FLC 12 FAC 10 Others 12
Bristol C (£200,000 on 25/7/91) FL 271 FLC 20 FAC 13 Others 14

WELLER Paul Anthony
Born: Brighton, 6 March 1975
Height: 5'8" Weight: 11.2
Trials with West Ham having come to nothing, Paul was involved in protracted contract negotiations with Burnley at the start of last season before finally committing himself to the Clarets' cause. However, 1998-99 was virtually a lost campaign for the young right-sided midfielder, as he was laid low with a stomach problem requiring three operations. Hopefully, he will be back in time for the start of the coming term.
Burnley (From trainee on 30/11/93) FL 79+17/5 FLC 5+2 FAC 4+2/1 Others 6

WEST Dean
Born: Morley, 5 December 1972
Height: 5'10" Weight: 12.2
Club Honours: Div 2 '97
The popular Bury wing back made his comeback at Huddersfield last January after a 17-month lay off, due to a succession of groin injuries. Marking his return with a goal, for a while he adopted a midfield role but by March had reverted back to his right-back position and signed 1998-99 off by scoring twice in the closing three games of the campaign. Manager Neil Warnock described his return from injury as "like signing a new player", and he spent the rest of the season trying to persuade this versatile and popular performer to sign a new contract.
Lincoln C (From trainee on 17/8/91) FL 93+26/20 FLC 11/1 FAC 6/1 Others 5+2/1
Bury (Signed on 29/9/95) FL 100+10/8 FLC 6 FAC 3 Others 2+1

WESTCOTT John Peter James
Born: Eastbourne, 31 May 1979
Height: 5'6" Weight: 10.4
Having broken back into first-team reckoning at Brighton last season when Rod Thomas was injured, before suffering ankle-ligament damage himself whilst playing for the reserves, the young winger finished up in plaster with his campaign effectively ended in January, although he did return to reserve action towards the end of 1998-99. Always willing to run at defenders, sadly, he never lived up to his early promise and despite having a year left on his contract, manager Micky Adams made him available for a free transfer.
Brighton & Hove A (From trainee on 10/7/97) FL 19+19 FLC 0+2 FAC 1 Others 0+1

WESTHEAD Mark Lee
Born: Blackpool, 19 July 1975
Height: 6'2" Weight: 14.8
Signed in the summer of 1998 after impressing on a goalkeeping course at nearby Bisham Abbey Sports Centre, Mark came to Wycombe from non-league Telford, after being at Bolton, Stalybridge Celtic, Sligo Rovers, and Kidderminster Harriers. Given an early chance to make his senior debut in football when first-choice 'keeper Martin Taylor was injured last September, he produced a sound display in the 1-1 draw at Burnley, and impressed even more in the next game at Middlesbrough, in the Worthington Cup. Paul Gascoigne even sought out Mark after the game to congratulate him on one particular save he made from him. He then had a further two-match spell in January, again because of an injury to Taylor, and again proved to be a more than capable deputy, being a particularly good shot stopper and safe in the air. Signed a new two-year contract in March.
Bolton W (Free from Blackpool Mechanics on 23/11/94) (Free to Sligo Rov during 1997 close season)
Wycombe W (Free from Telford U on 6/8/98) FL 2 FLC 1 Others 1

WESTWOOD Ashley Michael
Born: Bridgnorth, 31 August 1976
Height: 6'0" Weight: 12.8
Club Honours: FAYC '95
International Honours: E: Yth
A 1998 summer signing from Crewe Alexandra, Ashley proved that he could play anywhere in Bradford's defence in 1998-99, although performing mainly at centre back. Despite missing the start of the new campaign with an ankle injury suffered during pre-season training, he made his full debut, ironically against his former club, Crewe, and unluckily picked up ankle-ligament damage. Absent for the next 14 games, he came back for three more appearances before being forced out with another ankle injury. He then came back strongly, however, to keep John Dreyer and Andy O'Brien out, his ability to read the game and tackle with the best of them proving to be just what City needed to strengthen the defence.
Manchester U (From trainee on 1/7/94)
Crewe Alex (£40,000 on 26/7/95) FL 93+5/9 FLC 8 FAC 9/2 Others 10
Bradford C (£150,000 on 20/7/98) FL 17+2/2 FAC 1+1

WESTWOOD Christopher (Chris) John
Born: Dudley, 13 February 1977
Height: 6'0" Weight: 12.2
Released by Wolves in the 1998 close season, this central defender was out of football for most of 1998-99, recovering from a stress fracture operation, and although he had been training with Telford United he was still short of match fitness when signed by Pool shortly before the transfer deadline. A player well known to manager Chris Turner from his Wolves' days, he was seen as a squad member for the future, and gave a good account of himself in his few appearances towards the end of the campaign.
Wolverhampton W (From trainee on 3/7/95) FL 3+1/1 FLC 1+1 (Released during 1998 close season)
Hartlepool U (Signed from Telford U on 24/3/99) FL 3+1

Chris Westwood

WETHERALL David

Born: Sheffield, 14 March 1971
Height: 6'3" Weight: 13.12
International Honours: E: Sch

Big, strong, and excellent in the air in both penalty areas, unfortunately, David was overlooked for much of last season, despite being a Leeds' regular for the past four campaigns. In fact, the victory at Newcastle on Boxing Day, when he and Jonathan Woodgate outplayed Alan Shearer and Duncan Ferguson, was only his second game of the campaign. However, owing to long-term injuries to Robert Molenaar and Martin Hiden, he played a more prominent part in the first team after that, even scoring in the FA Cup victory at Portsmouth with a text-book header. A solid Premier League defender, and 100 per-cent Leeds United, in the replay at Tottenham he clashed heads with Les Ferdinand in a sickening looking incident which resulted in a hospital stay for both of them. Stop Press: Broke Bradford's transfer record when signing for £2 million on 30 June.

Sheffield Wed (From trainee on 1/7/89)
Leeds U (£125,000 on 15/7/91) F/PL 188+14/12 FLC 19+1/2 FAC 21+3/4 Others 4

WHALLEY Gareth

Born: Manchester, 19 December 1973
Height: 5'10" Weight: 11.12

Having joined his ex-team mate, Ashley Westwood, in the summer of 1998 from Crewe, Gareth showed himself to be a tremendously skilful Bradford midfielder, his crisp passing game and composure on the ball being a joy to watch. Having played for the Republic of Ireland against an Irish League XI in a 3-2 win, he was then called up for the Republic squad, and proved worthy of the opportunity. At club level, he missed just one game all season, and his partnership with Stuart McCall in the centre of City's midfield was as good as any in the First Division. Always wanting the ball, and always looking to get forward, he can also defend if he has to, and can be used at full back with absolute confidence if needed.

Crewe Alex (From trainee on 29/7/92) FL 174+6/9 FLC 10+1/1 FAC 15+1/4 Others 24/3
Bradford C (£600,000 on 24/7/98) FL 45/2 FLC 5 FAC 2

WHELAN Noel

Born: Leeds, 30 December 1974
Height: 6'2" Weight: 12.3
Club Honours: FAYC '93
International Honours: E: U21-2; Yth (UEFAC '93)

When Noel was involved in off-the-field antics last August it looked like a re-run of his old problems, however, it later transpired he was the innocent party and he quickly buckled down to reproduce the form of the previous season. His silky skills and deft ball control thrilled Coventry fans, while his maturity shone through after the departure of Dion Dublin in October, and despite being played largely as an out-and-out striker he responded with seven goals in 14 games in mid season. Although he reverted

to a midfield role later on in the campaign, he will be remembered for scoring some memorable goals, including a stunning drive to clinch the win at Blackburn, the cheeky finish to end Liverpool's hopes at Highfield Road, and the sublime shot for the equaliser against Charlton.

Leeds U (From trainee on 5/3/93) PL 28+20/7 FLC 3+2/1 FAC 2 Others 3
Coventry C (£2,000,000 on 16/12/95) PL 107+1/30 FLC 6/1 FAC 14/5

Noel Whelan

WHELAN Philip (Phil) James

Born: Stockport, 7 March 1972
Height: 6'4" Weight: 14.7
International Honours: E: U21-3

After missing most of the previous season with injury, Phil was keen to make up for lost time at Oxford in 1998-99, and although starting well enough with a goal in his first game of the campaign – a Worthington Cup-tie with Luton – that was to turn out to be his only goal of the campaign. Then, not featuring in Malcolm Shotton's plans, following the signing of the two Marks, Watson and Warren, he fell out of favour before his season was rescued with a deadline day loan transfer to Rotherham. Starting well, scoring on his debut in a 4-0 win over Scarborough, he quickly showed his strength at the heart of the defence, and at the same time he was a constant danger in opposition penalty areas. Has a great left foot.

Ipswich T (From juniors on 2/7/90) F/PL 76+6/2 FLC 6+1 FAC 3+1 Others 1
Middlesbrough (£300,000 on 3/4/95) PL 18+4/1 FLC 5 FAC 3
Oxford U (£150,000 on 15/7/97) FL 20+3 FLC 2/1 FAC 2
Rotherham U (Loaned on 12/3/99) FL 13/4

WHELAN Spencer Randall

Born: Liverpool, 17 September 1971
Height: 6'2" Weight: 12.8

Signed from troubled Chester last November, injury had prevented Spencer having the benefit of pre-season training,

and by his own admission there is better to come. With competition at Shrewsbury strong in central defence he only had one extended run and as his form improved he suffered injury which knocked him back. A full, injury-free campaign should see him being more effective, and watch out for him at set pieces.

Chester C (Free from Liverpool juniors on 3/4/90) FL 196+19/8 FLC 11+1/2 FAC 9+3 Others 5+2
Shrewsbury T (Signed on 6/11/98) FL 8+1 Others 1

WHITBREAD Adrian Richard

Born: Epping, 22 October 1971
Height: 6'1" Weight: 12.12

Portsmouth captain who survived and led the club through another stormy season in 1998-99, while rising above many difficult periods. He would have fulfilled all 46 matches, but for a knee injury from which he returned extremely quickly and determined. A very dependable, solid centre half, who is effective and a good communicator, his only faults, if you could call them faults, would be five yellow cards and not enough shots on goal himself.

Leyton Orient (From trainee on 13/11/89) FL 125/2 FLC 10+1 FAC 11/1 Others 8
Swindon T (£500,000 on 29/7/93) P/FL 35+1/1 FAC 2
West Ham U (£650,000 on 17/8/94) PL 3+7 FLC 2+1 FAC 1
Portsmouth (Loaned on 9/11/95) FL 13
Portsmouth (£250,000 on 24/10/96) FL 95/1 FLC 6/1 FAC 3

WHITE Alan

Born: Darlington, 22 March 1976
Height: 6'1" Weight: 13.2

Although a promising central defender, Alan made almost as many appearances from the bench than he did starts for Luton in 1998-99, but towards the end of the campaign he was looking more like it, finishing in a flurry to play the final four matches. He also scored his customary seasonal goal, in a 2-2 draw at Colchester. Injuries permitting, he should be one of the players Town will look to rely on in the immediate future, and his strength in the air, good feet, and tackling ability is sure to be seen to good advantage in 1999-2000.

Middlesbrough (From trainee on 8/7/94) Others 1
Luton T (£40,000 on 22/9/97) FL 44+17/2 FLC 1+3 FAC 2 Others 4

WHITE Devon Winston

Born: Nottingham, 2 March 1964
Height: 6'3" Weight: 14.0
Club Honours: Div 3 '90; AIC '95

A vastly experienced Shrewsbury striker in the twilight of his career, Devon was injured for over six months of last season, and as a strong target man with a proven goalscoring record he was sorely missed. Certainly, 1998-99 was a campaign that he will want to forget, as strikers thrive on goals. Released during the summer, it remains to be seen if he can regain his form after such a long lay off.

Lincoln C (From Arnold FC on 14/12/84) FL 21+8/4 Others 2+1/2 (Free to Boston U in October 1986)
Bristol Rov (Free on 21/8/87) FL 190+12/53 FLC 9/2 FAC 10/3 Others 19/2

Cambridge U (£100,000 on 28/3/92) FL 15+7/4 FLC 4/1 FAC 1 Others 1/1
Queens Park R (£100,000 on 26/1/93) PL 16+10/9 FLC 1+1
Notts Co (£110,000 on 23/12/94) FL 34+6/15 FLC 4/6 FAC 2+1/2 Others 4/1
Watford (£100,000 on 16/2/96) FL 28+10/7 FLC 4 FAC 2/1 Others 1
Notts Co (£20,000 on 14/3/97) FL 11+4/2 FLC 3/1
Shrewsbury T (£35,000 on 23/9/97) FL 37+6/10 FLC 1+1 FAC 2 Others 1

WHITE Jason Gregory
Born: Meriden, 19 October 1971
Height: 6'0" Weight: 12.10
Unfortunately, for him, 1998-99 was blighted by injuries, and his longest spell of games for Rotherham came at the start of the campaign when he made eight successive appearances. A strong, battling striker, Jason was often used as a substitute in the closing stages of the season, and he will have been disappointed with his scoring record.
Derby Co (From trainee on 4/7/90)
Scunthorpe U (Free on 6/9/91) FL 44+24/16 FLC 2 FAC 3+3/1 Others 4+4/1
Darlington (Loaned on 20/8/93) FL 4/1
Scarborough (Free on 10/12/93) FL 60+3/20 FLC 2+1 FAC 5/1 Others 1
Northampton T (£35,000 on 15/6/95) FL 55+22/18 FLC 1+4 FAC 3 Others 5+2
Rotherham U (£25,000 on 9/9/97) FL 44+9/17 FLC 2 FAC 3+1/1 Others 1

WHITEHALL Steven (Steve) Christopher
Born: Bromborough, 8 December 1966
Height: 5'10" Weight: 11.5
Signed from Mansfield during the 1998 close season, with a reputation as a goalscorer, Steve struggled throughout 1998-99 with a niggling ankle injury and, consequently, was unable to do himself justice with just a handful of goals in 43 appearances for Oldham. A poor return on previous campaigns, when he has top scored for Rochdale and Mansfield, hopefully, the strong-running striker will get an injury-free 1999-2000 so that he can show Latics' fans what he is made of.
Rochdale (£20,000 from Southport on 23/7/91) FL 212+26/75 FLC 10+3/4 FAC 13+2/3 Others 15+1/10
Mansfield T (£20,000 on 8/8/97) FL 42+1/24 FLC 2 FAC 2/1 Others 2/1
Oldham Ath (£50,000 on 10/7/98) FL 28+8/4 FLC 0+2 FAC 4 Others 1

WHITEHEAD Philip (Phil) Matthew
Born: Halifax, 17 December 1969
Height: 6'3" Weight: 15.10
Phil was an ever present in the Oxford goal in 1998-99 until his move to West Bromwich in November. Unfortunately, he was a player the club had to sell to stay afloat, being rated by many as one of the top 'keepers in the division, and he continued to be number one at Albion after replacing Alan Miller. Dominating the penalty box, and a good shot stopper, he had the dubious distinction of conceding almost as many goals at Sunderland as the home 'keeper did during the complete season after two big losses there for his two clubs – seven with Oxford and three for Albion. Despite that, he has excellent hands, and is utterly reliable.
Halifax T (From trainee on 1/7/88) FL 42 FLC 2 FAC 4 Others 4

Barnsley (£60,000 on 9/3/90) FL 16
Halifax T (Loaned on 7/3/91) FL 9
Scunthorpe U (Loaned on 29/11/91) FL 8 Others 2
Scunthorpe U (Loaned on 4/9/92) FL 8 FLC 2
Bradford C (Loaned on 19/11/92) FL 6 Others 4
Oxford U (£75,000 on 1/11/93) FL 207 FLC 15 FAC 13 Others 3
West Bromwich A (£250,000 on 1/12/98) FL 26 FAC 1

WHITEHEAD Stuart David
Born: Bromsgrove, 17 July 1976
Height: 5'11" Weight: 12.4
Unable to settle at Bolton, Stuart moved to Carlisle during the 1998 close season to become one of the successes of the club's generally disappointing 1998-99 campaign, being deservedly voted as "Player of the Season" by United fans. A sound, if unspectacular footballer, he reads the game very well and formed a solid partnership at the heart of the defence with David Brightwell. Possessing most of the qualities of a class defender, he looks to be destined for a successful career in that role.
Bolton W (Signed from Bromsgrove Rov on 18/9/95)
Carlisle U (Free on 31/7/98) FL 36+1 FLC 2 FAC 1 Others 2

WHITLEY James (Jim)
Born: Zambia, 14 April 1975
Height: 5'9" Weight: 11.0
International Honours: NI: 2; B-1
Started last season for Manchester City as a used substitute in the first home match, against Blackpool, before playing four full games. In between, he came on as a substitute in the Worthington Cup at home against Notts County, scoring the last goal in the team's 7-1 romp. Considered a regular in the team at the end of October, from November was only used as a substitute on seven occasions, prior to being pitched in for a full game in the FA Cup at Wimbledon. A skilful midfielder, his plus is that he is establishing himself in the Northern Ireland national team.
Manchester C (From juniors on 1/8/94) FL 27+10 FLC 3+1/1 FAC 2+1 Others 0+1

WHITLEY Jeffrey (Jeff)
Born: Zambia, 28 January 1979
Height: 5'8" Weight: 11.2
International Honours: NI: 3; B-2; U21-9
Jeff was hoping to establish himself in the Manchester City first team in 1998-99 after his 17 appearances in 1997-98. However, he only managed one league and one Auto Windscreens Shield game, and an occasional substitute appearance. Continued playing a defensive roll in the reserves, before spending two months on loan at Wrexham from January to March. At the Racecourse Ground, he contributed to Wrexham's good run in the Auto Windscreens Shield, which saw them reach the Northern Section final. Still on the fringe of the Northern Ireland U21 squad, playing in the 1-1 draw against Finland in Ballymena, the young midfielder went back to Maine Road, only to be placed on the transfer list. Scored on his debut for Wrexham, the club's first win

of the season, and created a good impression with his energetic displays.
Manchester C (From trainee on 19/2/96) FL 27+21/3 FLC 1+1 FAC 1 Others 4
Wrexham (Loaned on 14/1/99) FL 9/2

WHITLOW Michael (Mike) William
Born: Northwich, 13 January 1968
Height: 6'0" Weight: 12.12
Club Honours: Div 2 '90, Div 1 '92; FLC '97
Currently in his second spell with Bolton (he originally started his career as a trainee with the club), after a distinguished playing career with Leeds and Leicester, Mike is a valuable member of the squad and occupied the left-back berth for much of last season despite fierce competition from Jimmy Phillips and Robbie Elliott, until ligament damage forced him out of the team's run-in at the end of the campaign. A steady and reliable performer, he is a solid full back with a no-nonsense style, and carries out his job with a minimum of fuss, his experience of the game being invaluable to Wanderers. Although yet to score his first goal for the club, his favoured marauding runs upfield should soon rectify that particular statistic.
Leeds U (£10,000 from Witton A on 11/11/88) FL 62+15/4 FLC 4+1 FAC 1+4 Others 9
Leicester C (£250,000 on 27/3/92) F/PL 141+6/8 FLC 12/1 FAC 6 Others 14
Bolton W (£500,000 + on 19/9/97) P/FL 40+1 FLC 6+1 FAC 2

WHITNEY Jonathan (Jon) David
Born: Nantwich, 23 December 1970
Height: 5'10" Weight: 13.8
A fearless defender, Jon became one of a number of Hull City's pre-Christmas signings, moving along with Jason Perry from Lincoln. Having dropped down to the reserves at Sincil Bank, he jumped at the chance of joining the Tigers, even though they were at the bottom of the Football League. His no-nonsense, but thoroughly professional approach played a vital part in stabilising City's previously leaky backline and ultimate move up the table. Most often used as the left-sided of three centre halves, his highlight was a point-earning, long-range goal at Peterborough.
Huddersfield T (£10,000 from Winsford, via Wigan Ath YTS and Skelmersdale, on 21/10/93) FL 17+1 FLC 0+1 Others 4/1
Wigan Ath (Loaned on 17/3/95) FL 12
Lincoln C (£20,000 on 31/10/95) FL 98+3/8 FLC 9/1 FAC 6+1/2 Others 1
Hull C (Signed on 18/12/98) FL 21/1 Others 1

WHITTAKER Stuart
Born: Liverpool, 2 January 1975
Height: 5'7" Weight: 10.2
In 1998-99, this tricky little Macclesfield left winger carried on where he left off in 1997-98, picking up the ball on the halfway line, jinking the defenders, turning his man, and then outpacing him to the byline before crossing whilst still on the run. As the supplier on numerous occasions for Town's limited goals during the season, he often swapped to the right during the game to confuse the opposition, particularly when the defender had worked out Stuart's tactics. Unfortunately, his campaign finished in February with a severe groin strain and, sent

for a scan in late April to determine the extent of the damage, he may well have had an operation during the summer.
Bolton W (Free from Liverpool juniors on 14/5/93) FL 2+1 FLC 0+1
Wigan Ath (Loaned on 30/8/96) FL 2+1
Macclesfield T (Free on 8/8/97) FL 47+11/5 FLC 4 FAC 5+1/2 Others 2

WHITTINGHAM Guy
Born: Evesham, 10 November 1964
Height: 5'9" Weight: 12.2
An experienced but unorthodox striker, who still has pace, workrate, and great ball skills at the age of 34, Guy started 1998-99 at Sheffield Wednesday, appearing just three times in the opening 11 fixtures before spending the rest of the campaign on loan at Wolves (November), Portsmouth (January), and Watford (March). Strangely, at his earlier loan spell at Molyneux the manager left following his first game – this time it was Mark McGhee – and although he scored at Bristol City, he was unable to add to that in another eight matches. At Portsmouth, however, he was welcomed back with open arms, having started his career at Fratton Park, and immediately got to work in lifting the club away from the foot of the First Division table, scoring seven goals in nine outings, including a hat trick at home to Port Vale. Then it was on to Watford for the much travelled front man, where he failed to make an impression in five games. A free agent during the summer, it will be interesting to see where he ends up next.
Portsmouth (Free from Yeovil on 9/6/89) FL 149+11/88 FLC 7+2/3 FAC 7+3/10 Others 9/3
Aston Villa (£1,200,000 on 1/8/93) PL 17+8/5 FLC 4+1/1 Others 2+1
Wolverhampton W (Loaned on 28/2/94) FL 13/8 FAC 1
Sheffield Wed (£700,000 on 21/12/94) PL 90+23/22 FLC 7+2/2 FAC 7+1/1
Wolverhampton W (Loaned on 2/11/98) FL 9+1/1
Portsmouth (Loaned on 28/1/99) FL 9/7
Watford (Loaned on 18/3/99) FL 4+1

WHITTLE Justin Phillip
Born: Derby,, 18 March 1971
Height: 6'1" Weight: 12.12
Having become surplus to requirements with the arrival of Brian Little at Stoke, new Hull boss, Warren Joyce, made the former Royal Engineer his main transfer target to help lift the club off the Football League's bottom rung, signing his man last November. Although the fee was the most the Tigers had paid since they recruited David Norton for £80,000 in 1991, it proved to be money well spent. A succession of supremely peerless performances earned the right-footed centre back the tag of City's best signing for many years, and his dominance was recognised by a wider audience as he won Match Magazine's award of "Third Division Player of the Month" for March. Sorely missed when absent, and captaining the Tigers when David D'Auria was missing, Justin's vital contribution to City's Football League survival saw him become the overwhelming winner of the "Player of the Season" trophy.

Glasgow C (Free from Army during 1994 close season)
Stoke C (Free on 20/10/94) FL 66+13/1 FLC 3+4 FAC 2 Others 2
Hull C (£65,000 on 27/11/98) FL 24/1 FAC 2

WHITWORTH Neil Anthony
Born: Wigan, 12 April 1972
Height: 6'2" Weight: 12.6
International Honours: E: Yth
A veritable season of two halves for the big centre back who joined Hull City from Kilmarnock last July, his strength, bravery, and character holding the defence together in the first half of the campaign, and although the club sank to the foot of Division Three it could have been much worse but for his determined efforts. Unfortunately, he picked up a very troublesome achilles tendon problem in November, which sidelined him for the rest of the season. The former Manchester United defender eventually underwent surgery and was looking forward to playing some games in Scandinavia during the summer so that he would be back to full fitness in time for 1999-2000.
Wigan Ath (Trainee) FL 1+1
Manchester U (£45,000 on 1/7/90) FL 1
Preston NE (Loaned on 16/1/92) FL 6
Barnsley (Loaned on 20/2/92) FL 11
Rotherham U (Loaned on 8/10/93) FL 8/1 Others 2
Blackpool (Loaned on 10/12/93) FL 3
Kilmarnock (£265,000 on 2/9/94) SL 74+1/3 SLC 3 SC 4 Others 1
Wigan Ath (Loaned on 11/3/98) FL 1+3
Hull C (Free on 16/7/98) FL 18/2 FLC 4 FAC 1

WHYTE David Antony
Born: Greenwich, 20 April 1971
Height: 5'9" Weight: 11.10
Club Honours: Div 1 '94
Although possessing a lot of skill, David struggled to shine in a poor Southend team in 1998-99, and ultimately lost his place in November before an injury put paid to any hopes of a return to first team action prior to the end of the season. A tricky forward who caused defences problems, he appeared to suffer from the lack of a good supporting player in the United front line.
Crystal Palace (Free from Greenwich Borough on 15/2/89) FL 17+10/4 FLC 5+2/2 FAC 0+1 Others 0+3/1
Crystal Palace (Free from Greenwich Borough on 15/2/89) FL 17+10/4 FLC 5+2/2 FAC 0+1 Others 0+3/1
Charlton Ath (Loaned on 26/3/92) FL 7+1/2
Charlton Ath (£450,000 on 5/7/94) FL 65+20/28 FLC 5+2/4 FAC 3+1/1 Others 0+2
Reading (Free on 19/9/97)
Ipswich T (Free on 31/10/97) FL 2
Bristol Rov (Free on 22/1/98) FL 0+4 Others 0+1
Southend U (Free on 13/3/98) FL 17+9/3 FLC 3 FAC 1

WICKS Matthew Jonathan
Born: Reading, 8 September 1978
Height: 6'2" Weight: 13.5
International Honours: E: Yth
As the son of the former Chelsea star of the 1970s, Steve, this strapping young central defender, who was once a trainee at Manchester United, signed professional forms for Arsenal before

being transferred to Crewe during the 1998 close season, having failed to make his mark at Highbury. Made his league debut when starting against Bradford at Gresty Road last August, but six appearances later he was allowed to join Peterborough at the beginning of March, and appeared in the final 11 games of the season. So well did he perform that the club released a more experienced player to make way for him. A ball-playing youngster whose only fault seems to be in holding on to the ball too long, United are sure that with experience he will develop into a top-class player.
Arsenal (Free from Manchester U juniors on 23/1/96)
Crewe Alex (£100,000 on 15/6/98) FL 4+2/1
Peterborough U (Free on 3/3/99) FL 11

WIDDRINGTON Thomas (Tommy)
Born: Newcastle, 1 October 1971
Height: 5'9" Weight: 11.12
Not one of his better seasons, Tommy found himself in and out of the Grimsby team in 1998-99 as the manager, Alan Buckley, preferred Stacy Coldicott in the number six shirt. As his senior appearances became less frequent, and it became apparent that he did not figure in Buckley's long-term plans, he joined Port Vale on loan in transfer deadline week, remaining until the end of the term. Quietly effective, the defensive midfielder helped to tighten up the middle of the park in the successful battle against relegation, and scored one goal from the penalty spot against Watford before big sent off in the final game, at Bury. Very versatile, he can be used with confidence as a tough-tackling full back, or even as a sweeper. Stop Press: Was released during the summer and signed for Port Vale on 18 June.
Southampton (From trainee on 10/5/90) F/PL 67+8/3 FLC 3+1 FAC 11
Wigan Ath (Loaned on 12/9/91) FL 5+1 FLC 2
Grimsby T (£300,000 on 11/7/96) FL 72+17/8 FLC 10+3 FAC 3+1 Others 1
Port Vale (Loaned on 24/3/99) FL 9/1

WIEKENS Gerard
Born: Tolhuiswyk, Holland, 25 February 1973
Height: 6'0" Weight: 13.4
One of the most improved players in the Football League, Gerard was an ever present for Manchester City in 1998-99 until the York away game in mid December, where he went down with flu. Back in the team, and missing two games with groin strains, his calm reading of the game was a feature in the central midfield position. His great asset is that he can tackle precisely in order to win the ball and set up an attack with telling passes. Scored two important goals giving 1-0 wins at Wrexham and at Stoke City, which cemented the excellent run of results from Christmas through to the end of the campaign. Able to perform equally well in central defence or midfield, he is a typically Dutch kind of player, being quick, skilful, and technically correct.
Manchester C (£500,000 from SC Veendam on 28/7/97) FL 77+2/7 FLC 6 FAC 5 Others 3

WIJNHARD Clyde
Born: Surinam, 9 November 1973
Height: 5'11" Weight: 12.4
Signed from Willem 11 as Leeds prepared for the 1998-99 campaign, Clyde was a direct replacement for Rangers-bound Rod Wallace. He began brightly, scoring twice in his first six games, but in many ways found it hard to settle into English football. Also, his arrival coincided with the emergence of both Harry Kewell and Alan Smith, which resulted in him spending more time on the bench rather than in the starting line-up. As regular scorer for the club's reserves, he was always part of the first-team squad.
Leeds U (£1,500,000 from Willem 11, via Ajax, Groningen and RKC Waelwijk, on 22/7/98) PL 11+7/3 FLC 1 FAC 1+1/1 Others 1+3

WILBRAHAM Aaron Thomas
Born: Knutsford, 21 October 1979
Height: 6'3" Weight: 12.4
A tall, tricky Stockport striker who filled out physically to become an ideal understudy to Brett Angell in 1998-99, Aaron defies his awkward appearance with fine ball control and the ability to beat tight markers with a range of skills. The one thing missing from his game at the moment is finding the net regularly, but if he can add this attribute to his game he will make a fearsome forward.
Stockport Co (From trainee on 29/8/97) FL 14+19/1 FLC 0+1

WILCOX Jason Malcolm
Born: Farnworth, 15 July 1971
Height: 5'11" Weight: 11.10
Club Honours: PL '95
International Honours: E: 2; B-2
A close-season hernia operation at Blackburn resulted in Jason being hardly fit for the start of 1998-99, and, ultimately, he had to have the same operation again in October, which cost him a month and a half's football. Earlier, a shortage of strikers in September caused Roy Hodgson to play him up front, where he surprised with his strong, angled running, his strength and his enthusiasm. By the end of January, the new manager, Brian Kidd, utilised him as a midfield player, and his effort and energy in the games with Leeds and Sunderland, when the side were down to ten men, was remarkable. As other players fell out with injuries Jason was appointed the on-field captain, and contributed vital goals at Coventry and Southampton when the club most needed them. He also added another England cap to his previous one. Strangely, despite Kidd's belief that he is the best left-sided English attacker, his best displays during the campaign were not in that position.
Blackburn Rov (From trainee on 13/6/89) F/PL 226+23/31 FLC 16+1/1 FAC 18+2/2 Others 7

WILCOX Russell (Russ) Hemsworth
Born: 25 March 1964,
Height: 6'0" Weight: 12.12
Club Honours: Div 4 '87; Div 3 '96
International Honours: E: SP-3
The experienced, strong central defender was an ever present in the Scunthorpe

defence up until breaking a bone in his foot just before last Christmas. Although being on the sidelines for two months, and unable to win back a regular place, spending a number of matches on the substitutes' bench, his experience proved a great help for the younger players in the squad.
Doncaster Rov (Apprentice) FL 1
Northampton T (£15,000 from Frickley Ath on 30/6/86) FL 137+1/9 FLC 6 FAC 10 Others 8/1
Hull C (£120,000 on 6/8/90) FL 92+8/7 FLC 5 FAC 5/1 Others 5+1
Doncaster Rov (£60,000 on 30/7/93) FL 81/6 FLC 5/2 FAC 3 Others 3
Preston NE (£60,000 on 22/9/95) FL 62/1 FLC 4 FAC 3/1 Others 2
Scunthorpe U (£15,000 on 8/7/97) FL 54+5/3 FLC 4+1 FAC 6/2 Others 6

Russ Wilcox

WILDE Adam Matthew
Born: Southampton, 22 May 1979
Height: 5'10" Weight: 11.8
1998-99 was a disappointing season for Adam, and he only managed one first-team appearance for Cambridge, against Scunthorpe in September, after which he moved to non-league football, playing for Cambridge City and Kettering. Primarily an attacking left-sided winger, he also played as an emergency full back when needed.
Cambridge U (From trainee on 21/2/97) FL 1+3

WILDER Christopher (Chris) John
Born: Stocksbridge, 23 September 1967
Height: 5'11" Weight: 12.8
1998-99 was a disappointing season for Chris, rarely featuring in Sheffield United manager Steve Bruce's plans before being loaned to Northampton in November. A solid and dependable defender, either at full back or in the centre of the defence, he had a disastrous spell with the Cobblers, playing just 45 minutes at Colchester until injury struck. Still going nowhere fast at Bramall Lane, he went out on loan to Lincoln in transfer deadline week as cover for injuries. Although he made a steady if unspectacular debut against York, there was only one other start prior to the end of the campaign, and he was released during the summer.
Southampton (From apprentice on 26/9/85)
Sheffield U (Free on 20/8/86) FL 89+4/1 FLC 8+1 FAC 7 Others 3
Walsall (Loaned on 2/11/89) FL 4 FAC 1 Others 2
Charlton Ath (Loaned on 12/10/90) FL 1
Charlton Ath (Loaned on 28/11/91) FL 2
Leyton Orient (Loaned on 27/2/92) FL 16/1 Others 1
Rotherham U (£50,000 on 30/7/92) FL 129+3/11 FLC 11 FAC 6+2/1 Others 6+1
Notts Co (£150,000 on 2/1/96) FL 46 FLC 2 FAC4 Others 1
Bradford C (£150,000 on 27/3/97) FL 35+7 FLC 2 FAC 1
Sheffield U (£150,000 on 25/3/98) FL 11+1 FLC 0+1 Others 1
Northampton T (Loaned on 6/11/98) FL 1
Lincoln C (Loaned on 25/3/99) FL 2+1

WILDING Peter John
Born: Shrewsbury, 28 November 1968
Height: 6'1" Weight: 12.12
Why did Peter have to wait until he was 29 to make his Football League debut for Shrewsbury, Town's fans asked. The no-nonsense, committed central defender who operated in a sweeping role most of last season again proved very determined and versatile. He even deputised in goal for part of a game. It is hardly surprising that he is a crowd favourite and an automatic choice for all the hard work he gets through every game.
Shrewsbury T (£10,000 from Telford on 10/6/97) FL 75+1/1 FLC 4 FAC 3 Others 2/1

WILES Ian Robert
Born: Woodford, 28 April 1980
Height: 6'0" Weight: 11.9
A first-year Colchester professional, left-sided centre half or full back, Ian had a very impressive pre-season and was rewarded with a first-team debut as substitute at Wrexham last August, where he acquitted himself admirably against the likes of Ian Rush. Never made the first team later on, and unfortunately broke his arm during a reserves win at Ipswich to finish his campaign before Easter, but is expected to make a greater impact in 1999-2000.
Colchester U (From trainee on 8/7/98) FL 0+1

WILKINS Ian John
Born: Lincoln, 3 April 1980
Height: 6'0" Weight: 12.7
A central defender in his first full season as a pro at Lincoln in 1998-99 after coming

through the ranks, he was loaned out to Dr Martens League club, Grantham Town, in October, before returning to become more involved in the City first-team squad. However, he made only two appearances in the Auto Windscreens Shield, and failed to add to his Nationwide League experience.

Lincoln C (From trainee on 28/3/98) FL 1+1 Others 1+1

WILKINS Richard John

Born: Lambeth, 28 May 1965
Height: 6'0" Weight: 12.3
Club Honours: Div 3 '91

An inspirational club and first-team captain at Colchester in 1998-99, "Wilky" suffered a succession of injuries throughout the season, restricting him to only half of the games, and often playing when below full fitness to plug the gaps caused by other injuries. Richard again showed his versatility by playing as a centre half, full back, and in midfield throughout the campaign, as well as weighing in with two goals, including the winner against Wigan. Now approaching the veteran stage, "Captain Fantastic" still has a lot of offer the U's.

Colchester U (Free from Haverhill Rov on 20/11/86) FL 150+2/22 FLC 6 FAC 7+2/4 Others 9+3/3
Cambridge U (£65,000 on 25/7/90) FL 79+2/7 FLC 6 FAC 8+1 Others 9
Hereford U (Free on 20/7/94) FL 76+1/5 FLC 6 FAC 6 Others 8/2
Colchester U (£30,000 on 3/7/96) FL 102+1/9 FLC 5 FAC 3/1 Others 8

WILKINSON John Colbridge

Born: Exeter, 24 August 1979
Height: 5'9" Weight: 11.0

John's first season as a professional at Exeter in 1998-99 brought him only a handful of starts, although he made more than a dozen appearances as a substitute. This was due, no doubt, to the abundance of midfield players at the club with whom he was competing for a first-team place. However, able to play wide on the right or left, skilful on the ball, with good vision, and a great shot, he has bags of time on his side, and will be looking to make a good impression this coming season. Scored his first ever league goal, against Scunthorpe, in October.

Exeter C (From trainee on 9/7/98) FL 6+13/2 FAC 1+1 Others 0+2

WILKINSON Paul

Born: Louth, 30 October 1964
Height: 6'1" Weight: 12.4
Club Honours: CS '86; Div 1 '87, '95
International Honours: E: U21-4

Released by Millwall during the summer of 1998, the tall, experienced striker's season at Northampton did not start until late September after fracturing his jaw in a pre-season friendly. Unfortunately, injury struck again in December, when he needed an operation on his ankle, and he did not reach fitness again until very late in the season. Signed as a target man, Paul is just short of 200 first-class goals in domestic football.

Grimsby T (From apprentice on 8/11/82) FL 69+2/27 FLC 10/5 FAC 4+2/1

Everton (£250,000 on 28/3/85) FL 19+12?7 FLC 3+1/7 FAC 3/1 Others 6+2/1
Nottingham F (£200,000 on 26/3/87) FL 32+2/5 FLC 3/1 FAC 4+1/1/2 Others 1
Watford (£300,000 on 16/8/88) FL 133+1/52 FLC 4/1 FAC 8+1 Others 8/3
Middlesbrough (£550,000 on 16/8/91) F/PL 161+5/49 FLC 16/8 FAC 14/5 Others 5+1/4
Oldham Ath (Loaned on 26/10/95) FL 4/1 Others 1/1
Watford (Loaned on 1/12/95) FL 4
Luton T (Loaned on 28/3/96) FL 3
Barnsley (Free on 19/7/96) F/PL 48+1/9 FLC 4/2 FAC 2
Millwall (£150,000 on 18/9/97) FL 22+8/3 FLC 1 FAC 1 Others 1
Northampton T (Free on 13/7/98) FL 12+3/1 FLC 2+1 FAC 2

WILKINSON Stephen (Steve) John

Born: Lincoln, 1 September 1968
Height: 6'0" Weight: 11.12
Club Honours: Div 3 '96

This mobile forward, who played much of his football in midfield in 1998-99, was sidelined by a lower back injury in October, but capped an excellent performance against Wigan in December with Chesterfield's equalising goal. Upon being substituted that day, Steve left the field to warm applause, rather than suffering the type of negative reaction that he has had to bear on previous occasions. Almost in celebration, he scored a wonder goal against Luton in March, winning the ball in his own half and weaving 70 yards before crashing a shot in from outside the box.

Leicester C (From apprentice on 6/9/86) FL 5+4/1 FAC 1
Crewe Alex (Loaned on 8/9/88) FL 3+2/2
Mansfield T (£80,000 on 2/10/89) FL 214+18/83 FLC 13+1/4 FAC 10/2 Others 17/1
Preston NE (£90,000 on 15/6/95) FL 44+8/13 FLC 4/4 FAC 3/1 Others 3
Chesterfield (£70,000 + on 4/7/97) FL 42+11/12 FLC 3 FAC 3+1 Others 3/1

WILLIAMS Adrian

Born: Reading, 16 August 1971
Height: 6'2" Weight: 13.2
Club Honours: Div 2 '94
International Honours: W: 12

The solid central defender appeared for Wales (versus Italy) before he made it to the Wolves' team in 1998-99, his first club appearance coming in the tenth match, at Bournemouth on 15 September. He later scored for Wales as they beat Denmark 2-1, but was injured during his stay with the squad, rupturing a disc in his neck, and would not be in contention until the closing phase of the season. Powerful and commanding at the back, he can also be used effectively in midfield or up front where his physique often allows him to get into dangerous areas.

Reading (From trainee on 4/3/89) FL 191+5/14 FLC 16/1 FAC 16/2 Others 14/2
Wolverhampton W (£750,000 on 3/7/96) FL 26 FLC 3 FAC 2+2 Others 2/1

WILLIAMS Andrew (Andy) Phillip

Born: Bristol, 8 October 1977
Height: 5'10" Weight: 10.10
International Honours: W: 2; U21-7

A very fast and tricky young Southampton winger who can play on either flank, Andy

featured only once last season when he came on as a sub in the home game against Aston Villa in November. Perhaps, after last year's progress, and having made his full international debut for Wales, it was a disappointing campaign for him, but it is more than possible that his manager is keeping him under wraps for the future and decided not to throw him into the frenetic relegation battles once too often! Played five times for the Welsh U21 side in 1998-99.

Southampton (From trainee on 24/5/96) PL 3+18 FLC 1+2 FAC 0+1

WILLIAMS Anthony (Tony) Simon

Born: Bridgend, 20 September 1977
Height: 6'1" Weight: 13.5
International Honours: W: U21-14; Yth

This Welsh U21 international 'keeper was brought in on loan from Blackburn by Macclesfield's Sammy McIlroy last October, and acquitted himself well in his four games. Although he did not keep a clean sheet, he pulled off some superb saves with his telling presence in the box, while his punched clearances, and a superb save from a spot kick at Blackpool were memorable. Unfortunately, his one-month loan was not renewed as more outfield players were required for the squad, and he returned to Ewood before joining Bristol Rovers on loan in transfer deadline week. A very promising goalie, Tony again impressed, making nine league appearances and shining for the Pirates in his final game, against Manchester City, which was televised live on Sky.

Blackburn Rov (From trainee on 4/7/96)
Macclesfield T (Loaned on 16/10/98) FL 4
Bristol Rov (Loaned on 24/3/99) FL 9

WILLIAMS Darren

Born: Middlesbrough, 28 April 1977
Height: 5'10" Weight: 11.12
Club Honours: Div 1 '99
International Honours: E: B-1; U21-2

Despite picking up a First Division championship medal with Sunderland in 1998-99, Darren lost his regular first-team berth due to the successful Paul Butler/Alan Melville partnership at the heart of the Wearsider's defence. Nevertheless, the young man remained very much a part of the England U21 set up, and is, without doubt, a player with a big future. With pace, aerial strength, and the ability to play in a variety of positions with good effect be it centre half or wide midfield, he will have one of the strongest claims for a regular place in the Premiership side.

York C (From trainee on 21/6/95) FL 16+4 FLC 4+1 FAC 1 Others 3/1
Sunderland (£50,000 on 18/10/96) F/PL 61+11/4 FLC 7/1 FAC 3+1 Others 3

WILLIAMS Eifion Wyn

Born: Anglesey, 15 November 1975
Height: 5'11" Weight: 11.12
International Honours: W: B-1

Last March, Torquay's Wes Saunders paid Barry Town a club record for this striker, who had been such a prolific scorer in the League of Wales (including a goal in the Champions' League against Dynamo Kiev),

and his signing paid instant dividends with a magnificent hat trick against Hartlepool (only the second United player to score three on his debut). If a striking partner can be found for him, expect many Third Division defences to suffer at his hands in the coming season. Represented the Welsh "B" side in the match against Northern Ireland, and scored after coming off the bench.
Torquay U (£70,000 from Barry T on 25/3/99) FL 7/5

WILLIAMS Gareth James
Born: Isle of Wight, 12 March 1967
Height: 5'11" Weight: 12.2
Signed from Scarborough, it was a case of third time lucky for Gareth as, after two previous loan spells at Hull, he became a permanent Tiger last November. Joining the club on the same day as Justin Whittle was recruited from Stoke City – they both live in the Derby area – "Griper's" versatility was a major boost to City's survival hopes. His touch and speed of thought soon assisted David Brown in the front line, although later he was more often used in the left-wing-back berth where his experience came to the fore.
Aston Villa (£30,000 from Gosport Borough on 9/1/88) FL 6+6 FLC 0+1 FAC 2 Others 0+1
Barnsley (£200,000 on 6/8/91) FL 23+11/6 FLC 1 FAC 1+1 Others 1+1
Hull C (Loaned on 17/9/92) FL 4
Hull C (Loaned on 6/1/94) FL 16/2
Wolverhampton W (Free on 23/8/94)
Bournemouth (Free on 6/9/94) FL 0+1
Northampton T (Free on 27/9/94) FL 38+12/1 FLC 2 FAC 2 Others 5+1
Scarborough (Free on 9/8/96) FL 102+3/27 FLC 8/1 FAC 6/1 Others 4
Hull C (Free on 27/11/98) FL 24+1/1 Others 1/1

WILLIAMS David Geraint (George)
Born: Treorchy, 5 January 1962
Height: 5'7" Weight: 12.6
Club Honours: Div 2 '87
International Honours: W: 13; U21-2; Yth
A vastly experienced midfield general, who has played in the top divisions and internationally, George was brought to Colchester in the summer of 1998 on a free from Ipswich to add his years of experience to a young squad as they stepped up a level. Despite his none-too-tender age, he had an impressive first half to the season, putting in many solid displays in a holding role in front of the central defenders, and showing great vision and passing ability. Struggling a bit more as the pitches turned heavier, he suffered a knee injury which kept him out of the last few games, but not before he had made his 650th league appearance at Manchester City in October. Out of contract during the summer, at the time of going to press it was known that the club had made him an offer of re-engagement.
Bristol Rov (From apprentice on 12/1/80) FL 138+3/8 FLC 14 FAC 9+2/2 Others 5
Derby Co (£40,000 on 29/3/85) FL 276+1/9 FLC 26+1/1 FAC 17 Others 11
Ipswich T (£650,000 on 1/7/92) P/FL 217/3 FLC 24+1 FAC 18 Others 4
Colchester U (Free on 30/7/98) FL 38+1 FLC 2 FAC 1 Others 1

WILLIAMS James
Born: Liverpool, 15 July 1982
Height: 5'7" Weight: 10.8
A 16-year-old first-year trainee at Swindon, James made his full league debut in the final game of last season, having already appeared as a sub at West Bromwich Albion and against Grimsby at home, weeks earlier. Although he is an extremely promising right back with plenty of pace to get down the flank, his tender age will almost certainly see him protected this coming term, but he is most definitely a player to watch out for.
Swindon T (Trainee) FL 1+2

John Williams

WILLIAMS John Nelson
Born: Birmingham, 11 May 1968
Height: 6'1" Weight: 13.12
A striker with both pace and power, Exeter let him go at the end of 1997-98, and he became a cult hero with the Cardiff fans after signing for the club prior to the start of 1998-99. "Willo" could be frustrating – brilliant one minute and not so good the next. But, oh those good moments. He was, at times, magnificent and scored 18 goals during the campaign. The best of the lot was a cracking match winner at Southend United when he took possession surrounded by home players, ran across the edge of the penalty area, and unleashed a fierce shot which swerved round the 'keeper and into the corner. John loved playing for City, his passion plain to see every time he pulled on the Bluebirds' shirt.
Swansea C (£5,000 from Cradley T on 19/8/91) FL 36+3/11 FLC 2+1 FAC 3 Others 1
Coventry C (£250,000 on 1/7/92) PL 66+14/11 FLC 4 FAC 2
Notts Co (Loaned on 7/10/94) FL 3+2/2
Stoke C (Loaned on 23/12/94) FL 1+3
Swansea C (Loaned on 3/2/95) FL 6+1/2
Wycombe W (£150,000 on 15/9/95) FL 34+14/8 FLC 4+1/2 FAC 5/4 Others 2
Hereford U (Free on 14/2/97) FL 8+3/3
Walsall (Free on 21/7/97) FL 0+1
Exeter C (Free on 29/8/97) FL 16+20/4
Cardiff C (Free on 3/8/98) FL 25+18/12 FLC 2/1 FAC 5/3 Others 1

WILLIAMS Lee
Born: Birmingham, 3 February 1973
Height: 5'7" Weight: 11.13
International Honours: E: Yth
In and out of the Mansfield side in 1998-99, a third of his appearances being from the subs' bench, Lee can play equally well in midfield or at wing back, from where he gets well forward and is a good crosser of the ball. His form, perhaps, suffered by not having a settled position in the side.
Aston Villa (From trainee on 26/1/91)
Shrewsbury T (Loaned on 8/11/92) FL 2+1 FAC 1+1/1 Others 2
Peterborough U (Signed on 23/3/94) FL 83+8/1 FLC 4+1 FAC 5+1/1 Others 7 (Free to Shamrock Rov during 1996 close season)
Tranmere Rov (Free on 26/2/97)
Mansfield T (Free on 27/3/97) FL 67+21/5 FLC 2 FAC 2+1 Others 2+1

WILLIAMS Marc Lloyd
Born: Bangor, 8 February 1973
Height: 5'11" Weight: 12.0
International Honours: W: B-1
A prolific scorer for non-league Bangor City, having earlier played in the Football League with Stockport, Marc signed for Halifax after scoring 12 goals for the reserves, and netted twice on his full debut, at Scunthorpe. Following selection for Wales "B" against Northern Ireland at Wrexham, the lively go-ahead forward joined York in March, and quickly made an impact with his energetic style. Scoring four crucial goals in City's battle against relegation, he hit both goals in the win at Lincoln, and one each in the games against Blackpool and Northampton in the final weeks of the season.
Stockport Co (£10,000 from Bangor on 23/3/95) FL 12+6/1 FLC 1+2 Others 0+1 (Free to Altrincham during 1996 close season)
Halifax T (Signed from Bangor on 3/9/98) FL 18+6/6 FLC 0+1 FAC 1 Others 2/2
York C (£30,000 on 19/3/99) FL 11/4

WILLIAMS Mark
Born: Bangor, 10 December 1973
Height: 5'11" Weight: 13.6
A striker with Shrewsbury for more than two years now, Mark has suffered badly with injury, and has never quite realised his potential, playing just one game in the Worthington Cup in 1998-99. There were those who thought that his height and strength would have been useful at times, but the management felt otherwise and he was released in the summer.
Shrewsbury T (From trainee on 6/7/92) FL 0+3 (Freed on 8/3/93)
Shrewsbury T (Signed from Telford on 2/7/97) FL 0+5 FLC 0+1

WILLIAMS Mark Stuart
Born: Stalybridge, 28 September 1970
Height: 6'0" Weight: 13.0
Club Honours: Div 3 '94
International Honours: NI-4; B-1
Chesterfield's rock-like centre-half perform-ed consistently to his best in 1998-99, being rewarded with a call up to the Northern Ireland "B" squad in January, playing the full 90 minutes against Wales "B", and earning praise from his national manager,

Lawrie McMenemy. Having been in discussions with the club for half the season over a new contract, it appears likely that a Bosman move might be in the pipeline, particularly after Mark became the first Chesterfield player to make a full international debut, when starting the match against Germany in March.

Shrewsbury T (Free from Newtown on 27/3/92) FL 96+6/3 FLC 7+1 FAC 6 Others 6/1
Chesterfield (£50,000 on 7/8/95) FL 168/12 FLC 10 FAC 13/1 Others 7/1

WILLIAMS Mark Thomas
Born: Liverpool, 10 November 1978
Height: 6'1" Weight: 13.0
The former Tranmere junior joined Rochdale last September, his arrival coinciding with an upturn in the side's fortunes, which saw them beaten only twice in 14 games. The right back's powerful shooting also became a useful weapon in Dale's armoury, and he netted his first senior goal in the 1-0 defeat of Halifax. However, he was left out after the cup defeat at Rotherham, and although reappearing in the victory over Brentford asked for a move when further first-team opportunities did not materialise, ironically signing for Rotherham in March. At Millmoor, Mark quickly showed himself to be at home either in the centre of defence or in the right-back slot and, with youth on his side, should develop into an accomplished player with a bright future.

Rochdale (Signed from Barrow on 18/9/98) FL 11+3/1 FAC 4
Rotherham U (Free on 5/3/99) FL 10+1 Others 0+2

WILLIAMS Martin Keith
Born: Luton, 12 July 1973
Height: 5'9" Weight: 11.12
Martin had an excellent first half to last season, and was Reading's leading goalscorer with 11 from 31 games before a knee injury sidelined him from February onwards. His speed and bravery brought him the majority of his goals, but he was also a reliable penalty taker. Supporters will hope that a full recovery from the subsequent operation will see him back to his mercurial best for the 1999-2000 campaign.

Luton T (Free from Leicester C juniors on 13/9/91) FL 12+28/2 FLC 1 FAC 0+1 Others 2+1
Colchester U (Loaned on 9/3/95) FL 3
Reading (Free on 13/7/95) FL 77+22/21 FLC 8+5/2 FAC 4+1

WILLIAMS Michael (Mike) Anthony
Born: Bradford, 21 November 1969
Height: 5'10" Weight: 11.6
In the Burnley side at the beginning of last season, Mike was one of four players discarded after the home defeat by York, and never played for the club again before moving to Oxford in transfer deadline week. At the Manor Ground he made just two brief appearances, both as a substitution for forwards, and struggling for fitness he was released in the summer. Having suffered with injuries for several seasons, this strong-running midfielder, who can also play at the back or up front, needs a fresh start.

Sheffield Wed (Free from Maltby MW on 13/2/91) F/PL 16+7/1 FLC 3+2 Others 1
Halifax T (Loaned on 18/12/92) FL 9/1
Huddersfield T (Loaned on 18/10/96) FL 2
Peterborough U (Loaned on 27/3/97) FL 6
Burnley (Free on 18/7/97) FL 15+1/1 FLC 3 FAC 2 Others 1
Oxford U (Free on 25/3/99) FL 0+2

WILLIAMS Paul Darren
Born: Burton, 26 March 1971
Height: 6'0" Weight: 13.0
International Honours: E: U21-6
The Coventry central defender had looked

Martin Williams

surplus to requirements when 1998-99 started, his disciplinary record for 1997-98 had been poor, while Gary Breen's form and the arrival of Jean-Guy Wallemme was ominous for the big-hearted Paul. After a shaky game against Chelsea on the opening day, he did not appear again until the game at Southend where he suffered concussion after colliding with David Burrows. His next opportunity came at half time at Blackburn in November and he grabbed it with both hands, becoming an automatic choice for the rest of the campaign and giving some outstanding displays without reverting to the strong arm tactics of before. The partnership with Richard Shaw peaked in the Manchester United home game when neither Dwight Yorke nor Andy Cole got a shot on target and were largely nullified.
Derby Co (trainee on 13/7/89) FL 153+7/26 FLC 10+2/2 FAC 8/3 Others 14+1/2
Lincoln C (Loaned on 9/11/89) FL 3 FAC 2 Others 1
Coventry C (£975,000 on 6/8/95) PL 96+10/4 FLC 11+1/1 FAC 8

WILLIAMS Paul Richard Curtis
Born: Leicester, 11 September 1969
Height: 5'7" Weight: 11.0
Signed on a free transfer from Plymouth during the 1998 close season, he made few appearances for Gillingham before being loaned out to Bury last November when Neil Warnock was attempting to rectify the problematic left-back role. After a successful month's loan the Shakers agreed an initial fee of £10,000 (rising to £40,000) with the Gills on 10 December, and the following day he scored his first goal for the club in a 3-3 draw with Sheffield United. Reliable, strong in the tackle, and pacy, he played 15 successful games until losing his place to another loan man, Carl Serrant, in February, and being confined to a few substitute outings from then on.
Leicester C (From trainee on 1/7/88)
Stockport Co (Free on 5/7/89) FL 61+9/4 FLC 3 FAC 4 Others 7+5/1
Coventry C (£150,000 on 12/8/93) PL 8+6 FLC 1+1 FAC 3
West Bromwich A (Loaned on 19/11/93) FL 5
Huddersfield T (Loaned on 17/3/95) FL 7
Plymouth Arg (£50,000 on 10/8/95) FL 131/4 FLC 6 FAC 8 Others 7/1
Gillingham (Free on 6/8/98) FL 9+1 FLC 2
Bury (£50,000 on 5/11/98) FL 14+1/1 FAC 1

WILLIAMS Ryan Neil
Born: Sutton in Ashfield, 31 August 1978
Height: 5'5" Weight: 11.4
International Honours: E: Yth
Rumoured to be the target of several top clubs, Tranmere achieved something of a coup when they secured his services from Mansfield in the summer of 1997. Developing his talent gradually in the reserves during the following couple of seasons, Ryan broke into the first team at the end of 1998-99, making two appearances as a sub before starting his first full game against Barnsley at Prenton Park. Stocky, but strong, he is a striker who can also adapt to a deeper supporting role, and hit a purple patch in the reserves towards the end of the campaign, scoring six times in six games.

Skilful and fearless, despite his lack of inches, he never shirks a challenge or holds back when faced with larger opponents.
Mansfield T (Trainee) FL 9+17/3 FLC 2 FAC 0+1
Tranmere Rov (£70,000 + on 8/8/97) FL 2+3

WILLIAMSON John Barry
Born: Derby, 3 March 1981
Height: 6'2" Weight: 12.0
A tall, young defender who made his first Burnley appearance in 1998-99, prior to signing pro forms, as a substitute in the 4-3 win against Macclesfield, a game which triggered the run to Second Division safety. Clearly a part of Stan Ternent's plans, more may be seen of him this coming season.
Burnley (Trainee) FL 0+1

WILLIS Adam Peter
Born: Nuneaton, 21 September 1976
Height: 6'1" Weight: 12.2
Snapped up on a free transfer from Premiership Coventry City after impressing in a couple of trial matches towards the end of 1997-98, Adam was recommended to Swindon by the veteran centre-back, Brian Borrows, who had watched him close-up with the Sky Blues. Making his first-team debut for Town at Tranmere towards the end of last September he put in some good performances, making 11 appearances in the centre of defence, but appeared to need added strength, and went out on loan to Mansfield during transfer deadline week in March. Quickly fitting into the Stag's defence, the tall defender played a significant part in helping the team to five clean sheets in the final ten matches. Likes to play the ball out of defence if he can.
Coventry C (From trainee on 1/7/95)
Swindon T (Free on 21/4/98) FL 11
Mansfield T (Loaned on 25/3/99) FL 10

WILLIS Roger Christopher
Born: Sheffield, 17 June 1967
Height: 6'1" Weight: 12.0
Club Honours: GMVC '91
International Honours: E: SP-1
"Harry" endured something of a poor season in 1998-99, being unable to force himself into regular first-team contention after a succession of minor injuries continued to dog his progress. A move to Gillingham was tentatively discussed in February, but this fell through, leaving him to battle for a place after returning to full fitness in March. His pace would have been an asset up front, but he was never quite able to make up for the ground lost to a persistent back injury.
Grimsby T (Signed from Dunkirk on 20/7/89) FL 1+8 FLC 0+1
Barnet (£10,000 on 1/8/90) FL 39+5/13 FLC 2 FAC 5+1/3 Others 1+4/1
Watford (£175,000 on 6/10/92) FL 30+6/2 FAC 1
Birmingham C (£150,000 on 31/12/93) FL 12+7/5 FAC 0+1
Southend U (Signed on 16/9/94) FL 30+1/7 FAC 1 Others 1
Peterborough U (Free on 13/8/96) FL 34+6/6 FLC 3 FAC 5+1 Others 5
Chesterfield (£100,000 on 11/7/97) FL 26+25/8 FLC 7/2 FAC 1+1/1 Others 1+1

WILLMOTT Christopher Alan
Born: Bedford, 30 September 1977
Height: 6'2" Weight: 11.12
A Luton central defender, who can also play at full back, and a former trainee, Chris, it is claimed, is being tracked by representatives from several Premiership clubs who have declared an interest. Similar in style to Arsenal's Matthew Upson, he is a reliable, steady player, and very strong in the tackle. He also has much skill and looks to pass rather than "lump" the ball upfield. Making his first-team debut at home to Blackpool towards the end of last February, three games later he was a regular, starting the final 12 fixtures of the campaign. Injuries permitting, he will continue to impress in 1999-2000. He is another Town player with a big future in front of him. Stop Press: Was reported to have signed for Wimbledon in early July.
Luton T (From trainee on 1/5/96) FL 13+1

WILLS David John
Born: Ashton under Lyne, 9 March 1979
Height: 5'5" Weight: 9.10
Having joined Halifax from Manchester City early on in 1998-99, and following his debut against York City in the Auto Windscreens Shield, David was told he would be making his full league debut at right back against Carlisle United due to Andy Thackeray's knee injury. Unfortunately, however, the day before the game he broke his leg in a training ground accident.
Manchester C (From trainee on 6/3/97)
Halifax T (Free on 9/12/98) Others 1

WILLS Kevin Michael
Born: Torquay, 15 October 1980
Height: 5'8" Weight: 10.7
The first of the Plymouth youngsters to be given his chance in 1998-99, Kevin made two brief substitute appearances in September, and completely undaunted by his elevation had a cracking attempt in the game against Darlington which nearly salvaged a point for Argyle. Unfortunate to suffer a back injury in a youth match at Swansea, which put him out of the running, he can play in midfield or up front, having an eye for a goal, and can also put his foot in. With a good attitude, he is one to watch out for.
Plymouth Arg (Trainee) FL 0+2

WILNIS Fabian
Born: Surinam, 23 August 1970
Height: 5'8" Weight: 12.6
This skilful defender came to Ipswich from De Graafschap last January as the replacement for Mauricio Taricco. Although the wing-back role was new to him, having played a more traditional full-back role in Holland, Fabian seemed ideally suited to it, with his good turn of speed and ability to cross the ball – it was from his cross that Kieron Dyer headed the last-minute goal which took the play-off semi final with Bolton into extra time. Scored his first goal for the club in the 6-0 win at

Swindon, when he broke down the right, cut in, and shot past the 'keeper.

Ipswich T (£200,000 from De Graafschap, via NAC Breda, on 6/1/99) FL 17+1/1 FAC 1 Others 2

WILSON Che Christian Aaron Clay
Born: Ely, 17 January 1979
Height: 5'9" Weight: 11.3
Another homegrown product given his chance in Norwich's senior line-up during 1998-99, a season when youth was given its head. An accomplished and stylish defender, who can play anywhere across the defensive line, although usually utilised at full-back, he is an excellent passer of the ball. Occasionally, he has played in midfield, but his ability to read the game and anticipate danger mark him down as a natural defender. Given his debut in December at Swindon, Che, named after Cuban revolutionary leader, Che Guevara, retained his place in the squad for the rest of the campaign.
Norwich C (From trainee on 3/7/97) FL 14+3

WILSON Clive Euclid Aklana
Born: Manchester, 13 November 1961
Height: 5'7" Weight: 11.4
Club Honours: Div 2 '89
One of the most experienced players at Tottenham, and naturally a defender, Clive made just the one appearance in 1998-99, the 3-1 Worthington Cup fourth round victory over Liverpool in November. However, even in that one appearance he still showed a level of personal fitness and enthusiasm that not only was a credit to him, but would be valuable to a top club in the lower divisions. Offered a free transfer during the summer, he still has all the qualities to continue his playing career for a couple more seasons before thinking of another role in football. A true professional and gentleman, he will be missed by the Tottenham faithful and fondly remembered for his contributions as a left-wing back with a good recovery rate.
Manchester C (From juniors on 8/12/79) FL 96+2/9 FLC 10/2 FAC 2 Others 5
Chester C (Loaned on 16/9/82) FL 21/2
Chelsea (£250,000 on 19/3/87) FL 68+13/5 FLC 3+3 FAC 4 Others 10+2
Manchester C (Loaned on 19/3/87) FL 11
Queens Park R (£450,000 on 4/7/90) F/PL 170+2/12 FLC 16/1 FAC 8/1 Others 2+1
Tottenham H (Free on 12/6/95) PL 67+3/1 FLC 7+1 FAC 7+1/1

WILSON Kevin James
Born: Banbury, 18 April 1961
Height: 5'8" Weight: 11.4
Club Honours: Div 2 '89; FMC '90
International Honours: NI: 42
As Northampton's assistant manager, Kevin was not considered for a first-team spot last season until the last few games, despite scoring regularly for the reserves. Had taken over the running of the second team midway through the campaign after Garry Thomson moved on to Bristol Rovers in a similar capacity. Although reaching the veteran stage for a striker, he still plays with enthusiasm and commitment, and his experience makes him ideal for the deep-lying forward position. Is just a handful off 200 first-class goals in domestic football.
Derby Co (£20,000 from Banbury U on 21/12/79) FL 106+16/30 FLC 8+3/8 FAC 8/3
Ipswich T (£100,000 on 5/1/85) FL 94+4/34 FLC 8/8 FAC 10/3 Others 7/4
Chelsea (£335,000 on 25/6/87) FL 124+28/42 FLC 10+2/4 FAC 7+1/1 Others 14+5/8
Notts Co (£225,000 on 27/3/92) FL 58+11/3 FLC 3+1 FAC 2 Others 5+1
Bradford C (Loaned on 13/1/94) FL 5
Walsall (Free on 4/8/94) FL 124+1/38 FLC 8/3 FAC 13/7 Others 6/1
Northampton T (Free on 28/7/97) FL 9+8/1 FAC 0+1

WILSON Mark Antony
Born: Scunthorpe, 9 February 1979
Height: 5'11" Weight: 13.0
Club Honours: E: Yth; Sch
A young Manchester United player with excellent presence and neat skills to match, having played in the Football League when on loan at Wrexham in 1997-98, Mark made his introduction to first-team football with United in the Worthington Cup last October, playing against Bury, before retaining his place for the tie against Nottingham Forest in November. Predominantly a central midfielder, who can play further forward if required, being direct and possessing a powerful shot, he is a young man with great promise and United fans have not heard the last of him.
Manchester U (From trainee on 16/2/96) FLC 2 Others 0+1
Wrexham (Loaned on 23/2/98) FL 12+1/4

WILSON Paul Robert
Born: Forest Gate, 26 September 1964
Height: 5'9" Weight: 12.6
Club Honours: GMVC '91
Paul experienced an emotional 1998-99

Paul Wilson

campaign with Barnet, and it proved that even though he was in his testimonial season he was still an essential part of the line-up. He began in his trade-mark style of delivering committed and passionate displays in the middle of the park, but by the middle of September he found himself relegated to the role of a bit-part player, and enjoyed a brief loan spell with Aldershot in October before returning to Underhill to inspire the Bees to a victory over high-flying Scunthorpe. The importance of his inclusion can never be underestimated, and he adds that touch of experience and steel to an otherwise youthful side, never shirking a challenge, an attribute that makes him the best tackler on the club's books. Also, his distribution is measured, and he rarely ever sends a pass astray. However, his strongest asset is possibly a combination of composure and clinical accuracy from the penalty spot, which resulted in two successfully converted efforts during the term. Although his antics on the pitch rarely ever grab the headlines, he has evolved into one of the most popular players in the club's history because of his tenacity and resolute spirit in the face of adversity. Was due to be out of contract during the summer.

Barnet (Signed from Barking on 1/3/88) FL 232+12/23 FLC 12+1/1 FAC 22+1 Others 9+4/1

WILSON Stephen (Steve) Lee
Born: Hull, 24 April 1974
Height: 5'10" Weight: 10.12
Due to young Matthew Baker's injury, Steve became Hull City's only senior 'keeper during the first half of a troubled season in 1998-99, and his confidence appeared to suffer as the team's fortunes nosedived. Following the arrival of Andy Oakes in December, he was pulled out of the firing line, but responded magnificently whenever called upon. His manager, Warren Joyce, demonstrated his confidence in the current longest-serving Tiger with the offer of a new two-year contract in March.

Hull C (From trainee on 13/7/92) FL 153+1 FLC 13 FAC 11 Others 10+1

WILSON Stuart Kevin
Born: Leicester, 16 September 1977
Height: 5'8" Weight: 9.12
A promising young Leicester midfielder, Stuart still appears a little lightweight, but has pace to trouble defenders at any level. Mostly used from the bench in 1998-99, though he did start to find the net in the Worthington Cup win away to Chesterfield, his only league start came as part of a makeshift front partnership in the home drubbing by Manchester United. May eventually prove to be an effective right winger or a nippy central striker feeding off a target man, but must look to force his way into more regular contention during the coming season.

Leicester C (From trainee on 4/7/96) PL 1+21/3 FLC 1+5/1 FAC 0+4

WILSTERMAN Brian Hank
Born: Surinam, 19 November 1966
Height: 6'1" Weight: 13.8
Despite having had a good run in the Oxford

team for three months in 1998-99, Brian, a centre back, could never claim to be a regular and was released in the summer. However, he always gave wholehearted performances, scoring twice – home and away – against Norwich, although the game against the Canaries at the end of the season had been his first appearance in 12 games. Is a strong tackler.

Oxford U (£200,000 from Beerschot on 28/2/97) FL 28+14/2 FLC 2 FAC 1

WINDASS Dean
Born: Hull, 1 April 1969
Height: 5'10" Weight: 12.6
Having become Oxford's record signing when he joined the club from Aberdeen in the summer of 1998, despite starting the season as a midfielder, just behind the strikers, he soon became the top marksman and moved up front to good effect. Adept at free kicks, he also took penalties, quickly becoming one of the leading strikers in the division with 18 goals – including two against Chelsea in the FA Cup – a run which saw him score in five successive games. Keen to move to a successful side in the north, and with United in need of funds, Dean moved to Bradford in March, in a deal that realised Oxford £1 million following City's promotion. Took a few games to settle, and scored three goals, including two in a 2-0 win at Bury, but he had several near misses with shots that hit the woodwork. Hardworking, and able to play in a number of positions, he looks forward to Premiership football in 1999-2000.

Hull C (Free from North Ferriby on 24/10/91) FL 173+3/57 FLC 11/4 FAC 7 Others 12/3
Aberdeen (£700,000 on 1/12/95) SL 60+13/21 SLC 5+2/6 SC 7/3 Others 6/1
Oxford U (£475,000 on 6/8/98) FL 33/15 FLC 2 FAC 3/3
Bradford C (£950,000 + on 5/3/99) FL 6+6/3

WINSTANLEY Mark Andrew
Born: St Helens, 22 January 1968
Height: 6'1" Weight: 12.7
Club Honours: AMC '89
Starting last season with an appearance for Burnley in the first game, before being sent out on loan to Shrewsbury in mid September, the vastly experienced central defender played eight times, immediately making an excellent impression when tightening up the defence, his arrival helping lift Town from the foot of the table. His class and experience was clear to see as he settled easily into Third Division football, and it was a disappointment that the club were not able to sign him permanently. After being loaned to Scunthorpe in December, but sent home before playing, he signed for Preston in transfer deadline week to act as defensive cover, although not called upon.

Bolton W (From trainee on 22/7/86) FL 215+5/3 FLC 19+1 FAC 19 Others 26/3
Burnley (Signed on 5/8/94) FL 151+1/5 FLC 13 FAC 8 Others 8+1
Shrewsbury T (Loaned on 17/9/98) FL 8
Preston NE (Free on 22/3/99)

WINTERBURN Nigel
Born: Nuneaton, 11 December 1963
Height: 5'9" Weight: 11.4

Club Honours: Div 1 '89, '91; PL '98; FAC '93, '98; FLC '93; ECWC '94; CS '99
International Honours: E: 2; B-3; U21-1; Yth
Despite the passing of the years, Nigel remains as enthusiastic and as committed as ever. A fierce tackling left-sided wing back, he continued to be an automatic choice in the Arsenal back-four in 1998-99. With strength and speed, he gets forward into overlap positions, and is a good thrower and crosser of the ball. In late November, he sustained a hamstring injury, which caused him to miss a number of games, and while re-occurrences of the injury were worrying, his ongoing form earned him a recall to the England international squad for the match against France. Is a wonderful servant of Arsenal who is appreciated by the fans. Out of contract in the summer, he is almost certain to have signed up again in time for the new term.

Birmingham C (From apprentice on 14/8/81)
Wimbledon (Free on 22/9/83) FL 164+1/8 FLC 13 FAC 12 Others 2
Arsenal (£407,000 on 26/5/87) F/PL 410+2/8 FLC 48/3 FAC 47 Others 40

WISE Dennis Frank
Born: Kensington, 16 December 1966
Height: 5'6" Weight: 10.10
Club Honours: FAC '88, '97; FLC '98; ECWC '98
International Honours: E: 12; B-3; U21-1
To cap an incredible 1998 when he skippered the Blues to three major cup triumphs within six months, "Wisey" was voted "Player of the Year" by the Chelsea faithful for the first time. The fact that he beat off opposition from a host of world-class overseas stars is a measure of the high esteem in which he is held by Chelsea supporters. His all-action style makes him the "heartbeat" of the team's fluent midfield but, as in previous seasons, his poor disciplinary record cost him dearly, with suspensions reducing his appearances. A dismissal in a pre-season match against Atletico Madrid brought him a three-match ban and, after vowing to change his ways, he was sent off against Aston Villa in a third-round Worthington Cup-tie! That transgression resulted in a four-match suspension, but worse was to follow, when, in his second match back, he was dismissed at Goodison Park for two bookable offences, thus limiting his Premiership starts, pre-Christmas, to just seven. An incident-free six-match spell followed before disaster struck again! He notched a smartly-taken equaliser against Oxford in the FA Cup fourth round replay at the Bridge in February – incredibly, being Chelsea's first English goalscorer of the season! The skipper's joy was short lived, however, when he was sent off in the second half for a second handball offence – his fourth dismissal of the campaign, and another lengthy suspension. To prove that trouble followed Dennis around, he was wrongly accused of biting Real Mallorca defender, Marcelino Elena, in the European Cup-Winners' Cup semi final. These mis-

demeanours have obscured the fact that this extrovert character is one of the most improved players in the country over the past few years, his performances improving with the arrival of the foreign contingent. The four trophies gained in two years makes him Chelsea's most successful captain in the club's history with the Premiership needed to complete the set, and how close the Blues came until a couple of unfortunate draws after Easter scuppered their chances. He now has the honour of becoming the first skipper to lead the club in the Champions' League – that is if he can keep out of trouble!

Wimbledon (Free from Southampton juniors on 28/3/85) FL 127+8/27 FLC 14 FAC 11/3 Others 5
Chelsea (£1,600,000 on 3/7/90) F/PL 258+8/46 FLC 29/6 FAC 30/7 Others 28/4

WITTER Anthony (Tony) Junior
Born: London, 12 August 1965
Height: 6'1" Weight: 13.0

A tall, fast, and mobile central defender, having been released by Millwall during the summer, Tony joined Northampton at the start of last season during an injury crisis, and gave a good account of himself when he played. Signed as a "cover" player on non-contract forms, he moved on to Torquay early in November, performing impressively in six games before leaving for non-league Welling United following a disagreement over a permanent contract. It was a huge bonus for Scunthorpe when they captured him in mid February, despite him being sent off on his debut, and he quickly settled down as a regular member of the defence until a knee cartilage injury suffered against Cardiff on 1 May ruled him out of action for the rest of the campaign.

Crystal Palace (£10,000 from Grays Ath on 24/10/90)
Queens Park R (£125,000 on 19/8/91) PL 1
Plymouth Arg (Loaned on 9/1/92) FL 3/1
Reading (Loaned on 11/2/94) FL 4
Millwall (£100,000 on 14/10/94) FL 99+3/2 FLC 8 FAC 8
Northampton T (Free on 14/8/98) FL 1+3 FLC 0+1
Torquay U (Free on 5/11/98) FL 4 FAC 2 (Free to Welling U on 5/12/98)
Scunthorpe U (Free on 12/2/99) FL 14

WOAN Ian Simon
Born: Heswall, 14 December 1967
Height: 5'10" Weight: 12.4
Club Honours: Div 1 '98

Unfortunately, Ian did not have a good return to the Premiership with Nottingham Forest in 1998-99, suffering back and knee problems for most of the campaign, and appeared just twice from the bench. A talented left-sided player, who is a superb crosser of the ball, with the ability to strike from distance, he has now been at Forest for over nine years, but has rarely had a more depressing season. With a wide range of passing skills, and able to pick his team mates out without thinking, how the team could have done with his experience.

Nottingham F (£80,000 from Runcorn on 14/3/90) F/PL 188+22/31 FLC 15+3/1 FAC 20+1/6 Others 13/2

WOOD Steven (Steve) Ronald
Born: Oldham, 23 June 1963
Height: 5'9" Weight: 10.10

The veteran Macclesfield midfielder was given a one-year contract at the start of last season and told not to expect a regular starting place in Town's Division Two team. However, in failing to read the script, he commanded a start in all matches up until mid October, showing that despite his age he still had plenty of stamina left, and scored three much-needed goals into the bargain. Despite that, in the New Year he was back on the bench after younger midfielders regained fitness, and became known as "Super Sub Stevie Wood" as he tried to turn the game and lift spirits when he came on. Regaining his starting place in April before injury took its toll, his campaign finished two weeks early.

Macclesfield T (Free from Ashton U on 22/7/93) FL 72+13/17 FLC 6/1 FAC 5/2 Others 2

WOODGATE Jonathan Simon
Born: Middlesbrough, 22 January 1980
Height: 6'2" Weight: 13.0
Club Honours: FAYC '97
International Honours: E: 1; Yth

Of all the talented youngsters breaking through the ranks at Leeds, none benefited more from the arrival of David O'Leary as manager in 1998-99 than this 19-year old. "Woody", a centre back of skill and composure, and very much in the mould of O'Leary himself, was singled out by the former manager, George Graham, as the most likely of the club's crop of youngsters to make an impact in the first team. Ironically, despite having to wait until David O'Leary's second game in charge, at Nottingham Forest in October, for his full debut, from then on he was virtually ever present, and even played at right back on occasions, notably when doing a man-marking job on David Ginola in the FA Cup-ties. He also showed his value at set pieces, with goals against Sheffield Wednesday, and at Charlton. Is able to combine defensive skills with the ability to break forward like a midfielder, and be just as comfortable, playing with a confidence that belies his relative inexperience. Very highly thought of at Elland Road, he was also selected for "squad training" with England prior to the game with Poland in March, before being named in Kevin Keegan's England squad for

Jonathan Woodgate

the friendly with Hungary in Budapest on 25 April, an occasion he unfortunately had to withdraw from due to injury. Made his England debut on 9 June when playing against Bulgaria.

Leeds U (From trainee on 13/5/97) PL 25/2 FLC 2 FAC 5 Others 1

WOODHOUSE Curtis

Born: Beverley, 17 April 1980
Height: 5'8" Weight: 11.0
International Honours: E: U21-3; Yth

Regularly chosen for the England U18 squad, and playing against the Republic of Ireland last August after a few appearances for Sheffield United, Curtis was sidelined by a knee injury before regaining his place in October and producing some tremendous performances in midfield. A non-stop worker who tackled, challenged, produced some decisive passing and last ditch defending, and still found time to score, it was no surprise when he was named as Blades' "Player of the Year". Signed a new contract in March until 2002, prior to winning his first England U21 cap towards the end of the season.

Sheffield U (From trainee on 31/12/97) FL 35+7/3 FLC 1+2 FAC 6

WOODMAN Andrew (Andy) John

Born: Camberwell, 11 August 1971
Height: 6'3" Weight: 13.7
Club Honours: Div 3 '99

A tall Brentford shot stopper, Andy was a surprise arrival at Griffin Park from Northampton last January, and had a very shaky start, conceding a number of goals. However, he gradually gained in confidence, keeping six clean sheets in nine games, and began to win over the Bees' fans as the side moved closer to the Third Division championship, which they ultimately won. Earlier in the season, while at Northampton, he was "Man of the Match" in the two Worthington Cup games against West Ham, before saving a penalty from Tottenham's David Ginola in the same competition.

Crystal Palace (From trainee on 1/7/89)
Exeter C (Free on 4/7/94) FL 6 FLC 1 FAC 1 Others 2
Northampton T (Free on 10/3/95) FL 163 FLC 13 FAC 8 Others 13
Brentford (Signed on 22/1/99) FL 22

WOODS Matthew (Mattie) James

Born: Gosport, 9 September 1976
Height: 6'1" Weight: 12.13

After appearing in both midfield and defence during 1997-98, Mattie had probably his best season for Chester in 1998-99, when playing in the centre of defence. Developing a good partnership with Andy Crosby, and turning in some solid performances, he also enjoyed getting forward to yet again show that he had a tremendous shot.

Everton (From trainee on 1/7/95)
Chester C (Free on 12/8/96) FL 74+19/4 FLC 4+3/1 FAC 4 Others 3+1

WOODS Neil Stephen

Born: York, 30 July 1966
Height: 6'0" Weight: 12.11

Released by Grimsby during the 1998 summer, Neil, a York-born lad, joined his hometown club in time for the beginning of 1998-99. Started the season in the senior side, helping the club to wins over Burnley and Wycombe, but then struggled to make an impact, and did not figure in the second half of the campaign. Freed during the summer, he is adept at holding play up to destabilise defenders with his quick movements in and around the box, and looks to be on that kind of form in time for the start of the coming season at a new club.

Doncaster Rov (From apprentice on 31/8/83) FL 55+10/16 FLC 4/1 FAC 5/2 Others 5+2/3
Glasgow R (£120,000 on 22/12/86) SL 0+3
Ipswich T (£120,000 on 3/8/87) FL 15+12/5 Others 4/1
Bradford C (Signed on 1/3/90) FL 13+1/2
Grimsby T (£82,000 on 23/8/90) FL 175+51/42 FLC 11+3/2 FAC 8+2/3 Others 8/1
Wigan Ath (Loaned on 6/11/97) FL 1
Scunthorpe U (Loaned on 19/1/98) FL 2
Mansfield T (Loaned on 16/2/98) FL 5+1
York C (Free on 1/7/98) FL 5+3 FLC 1 FAC 1

WOODS Stephen (Steve) John

Born: Davenham, 15 December 1976
Height: 5'11" Weight: 11.13

Having been out to Plymouth on loan at the end of the previous season, and with many at the club believing his career at Stoke was over, Brian Little gave Steve a chance in the side in 1998-99, which he grabbed with both hands. His early form was outstanding, and it was no surprise that the manager released two central defenders to raise a little cash. Commanding in defence, his place kicking was a feature of his game, and despite losing confidence as the side's form collapsed he showed over 20 plus games that he has much to offer, before surprisingly being freed in the summer.

Stoke C (From trainee on 3/8/95) FL 33+1 FLC 2 FAC 2 Others 2
Plymouth Arg (Loaned on 26/3/98) FL 4+1

WOODTHORPE Colin John

Born: Ellesmere Port, 13 January 1969
Height: 5'11" Weight: 11.8

Having made a nightmare start to last season, giving away two goals in a first round Worthington Cup-tie against Hull City, typically, the Stockport left back bounced back and produced some sterling displays to turn around his dip in form. Strong in the challenge, his wholehearted style of play meant that he picked up more than his share of bookings, though he is a committed player rather than a malicious one. Switched into a central, then a left-sided midfield role after Christmas, Colin demonstrated his versatility and willingness when making a number of "Man of the Match" performances and scoring vital goals, including the winner against local rivals, Bolton. Signed for Stockport on 11 May.

Chester C (From trainee on 23/8/86) FL 154+1/6 FLC 10 FAC 8+1 Others 18/1
Norwich C (£175,000 on 17/7/90) ßL 36+7/1 FLC 0+2 FAC 6 Others 1+1

Aberdeen (£400,000 on 20/7/94) SL 43+5/1 SLC 5+1/1 SC 4 Others 5+2
Stockport Co (£200,000 on 29/7/97) FL 66+3/3 FLC 6/1 FAC 2/1

WOODWARD Andrew (Andy) Stephen

Born: Stockport, 23 September 1973
Height: 5'11" Weight: 13.6
Club Honours: Div 2 '97

Bury's "Mr Reliable", who has waited patiently for his opportunity over past seasons, enjoyed a particularly consistent season in 1998-99, whether playing at right back or as a central defender. With a strong physique, he is a powerful header of the ball and eager to attack – although when he scored on Boxing Day against his former club, Crewe, it was his first league goal of his career. The low point of his season will undoubtedly have been a dismissal at Birmingham in September, but he went on to enjoy a very steady campaign.

Crewe Alex (From trainee on 29/7/92) FL 9+11 FLC 2 Others 0+3
Bury (Signed on 13/3/95) FL 81+20/1 FLC 5+2 FAC 3 Others 5

WOOLLISCROFT Ashley David

Born: Stoke, 28 December 1979
Height: 5'10" Weight: 11.2

Having come through Stoke's trainee ranks to turn pro early in 1997, after a full season in the reserves Ashley was called into the squad for the last two games of 1998-99, and made his debut at half time in the final game, at home to promoted Walsall. A defender with promise, who is strong in the tackle and one for the future, he looks to kick start his career this coming term.

Stoke C (From trainee on 10/2/97) FL 0+1

WOOZLEY David (Dave) James

Born: Ascot, 6 December 1979
Height: 6'0" Weight: 12.10

Although turning professional with Crystal Palace in November 1997 after coming through the club's trainee ranks, it was not until the last few games of a troubled 1998-99 campaign that he came into the first team. Given his chance by the manager, Steve Coppell, to replace the ageing Andy Linighan in March, playing in a 1-0 home win over Bradford, the youngster was outstanding in the centre of the defence, showing a strong left foot and ability both in the air and on the ground. Watch out for him in 1999-2000.

Crystal Palace (From trainee on 17/11/97) FL 7

WORRALL Benjamin (Ben) Joseph

Born: Swindon, 7 December 1975
Height: 5'7" Weight: 11.6
International Honours: E: Yth

Started last season in Scarborough's opening day line-up in a 2-1 defeat at home to Southend, and ended it in a 1-1 home draw against Peterborough, a result which sent the club spiralling into the Conference. In between, this diminutive, tenacious midfielder always gave 100 per-cent effort to the cause, despite missing a large chunk of the action following a groin injury in January. Will be looking for

better fortunes in 1999-2000, wherever he is playing his football.
Swindon T (From trainee on 8/7/94) FL 1+2
Scarborough (Free on 2/8/96) FL 45+22/3 FLC 3+3 FAC 2 Others 2+1

WORTHINGTON Martin Paul
Born: Torquay, 25 January 1981
Height: 6'0" Weight: 12.4
A young second-year YTS midfielder or striker at Torquay, Martin made a brief subs' appearance against Halifax last March, and over the season impressed the Plainmoor staff with his all-round game. Seen as a youngster who could go some way, he was due to be rewarded with a full contract for the coming campaign.
Torquay U (Trainee) FL 0+1

WOTTON Paul Anthony
Born: Plymouth, 17 August 1977
Height: 5'11" Weight: 12.0
Having developed into an accomplished young player at Plymouth, Paul's preferred position is in central defence, despite him appearing in various other positions during 1998-99. With pace, good feet, and distribution to match, often carrying the ball upfield, he took on extra responsibilities as Argyle's penalty king, scoring twice in 3-2 victories. Obviously a reflection of his confidence, and the fact that he has become more established at Home Park, he missed just ten games throughout the campaign. Continued to improve his aerial strength.
Plymouth Arg (From trainee on 10/7/95) FL 73+14/3 FLC 4 FAC 9/1 Others 4+1/2

WRACK Darren
Born: Cleethorpes, 5 May 1976
Height: 5'9" Weight: 12.10
Released by Grimsby during the 1998 close season, Darren signed for Walsall in time for 1998-99, and was one of several players to make his debut in the opening day win at Gillingham. Three weeks later, he netted a header and a penalty in the last two minutes to win the game against Burnley, and his speedy runs down the right flank and eye for goal were major factors in Walsall's promotion season. With the pressure on in the last two months he netted match winners against Luton, Bournemouth, and Lincoln, and scored the opening goal in the promotion clincher against Oldham. Like Jimmy Walker an ever present, his 14 goals during the campaign told its own story for a player who had scored just twice in the previous four. Was selected by his fellow professionals for the PFA award-winning Second Division side.
Derby Co (From trainee on 12/7/94) FL 4+22/1 FLC 0+3 FAC 0+2
Grimsby T (£100,000 + on 19/7/96) FL 5+8/1 Others 0+1
Shrewsbury T (Loaned on 17/2/97) FL 3+1 Others 1
Walsall (Free on 6/8/98) FL 46/13 FLC 2 FAC 2 Others 6/1

WRAIGHT Gary Paul
Born: Epping, 5 March 1979
Height: 5'7" Weight: 11.11
In his first full season in the senior team at Wycombe in 1998-99, Gary started the

Darren Wrack

game at Fulham, where he was rather unlucky to be sent off for two bookable offences, but employed as a right-wing back, he impressed most in the 2-2 draw at Walsall on Boxing Day. Is probably the nearest thing to a wing back at Adams Park, looking particularly good going forward, being able to whip dangerous crosses in without having to beat his man.
Wycombe W (From trainee on 1/7/97) FL 7 FLC 0+2 FAC 1 Others 0+2

WREH Christopher (Chris)
Born: Liberia, 14 May 1975
Height: 5'8" Weight: 11.13
Club Honours: PL '98; FAC '98; CS '98
International Honours: Liberia: 16
Into his second season with Arsenal in 1998-99, he continued to develop into a good team player, being a quick and confident target man with a good touch and eye for goal. Despite displaying tremendous enthusiasm, both on and off the field, his only goal during the campaign came in the Charity Shield, and unable to produce the form he displayed during the run in to the championship the previous season, he was released in February on loan to AEK Athens.
Arsenal (£300,000 from Guincamp, via Monaco, on 14/8/97) PL 10+18/3 FLC 3+2 FAC 2+4/1 Others 3+2/1

WRIGHT Alan Geoffrey
Born: Ashton under Lyne, 28 September 1971
Height: 5'4" Weight: 9.9
Club Honours: FLC '96
International Honours: E: U21-2; Yth; Sch

As in 1997-98, Alan was consistency personified for Aston Villa in the left-wing-back slot last season, and ended the campaign as the club's only ever present. Encouraged by his manager, John Gregory, to push forward, his solid, all-round performances helped the club to hit the top of the Premiership and stay there for some while before sliding away to finish fifth. Despite being one of the smallest defenders around, that has never really held him up, and he continues to show all the qualities of a winger – excellent control and good crossing ability – allied to a quick recovery rate, which enables him to pick up all but the fastest of attackers. Is a player Villa can rely on for a good few years yet.

Blackpool (From trainee on 13/4/89) FL 91+7 FLC 10+2 FAC 8 Others 11+2
Blackburn Rov (£400,000 on 25/10/91) F/PL 67+7/1 FLC 8 FAC 5+1 Others 3
Aston Villa (£1,000,000 on 10/3/95) PL 157+2/3 FLC 12 FAC 14 Others 14

WRIGHT Andrew (Andy)
Born: Bristol, 12 September 1979
Height: 6'0" Weight: 11.4

Freed by Sunderland after playing in their youth side, this tall young striker was brought in as a first year pro for the newly-formed Macclesfield reserve team, and quickly established himself as a prolific goalscorer for the team. Given his first-team chance, when he had a seven-minute run out in the Auto Windscreens first-round defeat against Wrexham, that was it at senior level, and he was released during the summer.

Macclesfield T (Free from Sunderland juniors on 16/7/98) Others 0+1

WRIGHT Andrew (Andy) James
Born: Leeds, 21 October 1978
Height: 5'6" Weight: 9.11
Club Honours: FAYC '97

The young left winger was spotted playing for Leeds' reserve team, before being given the chance to make his Football League debut by joining Reading for a month's loan last December. He played in an Auto Windscreens Shield-tie against Bournemouth, then came on as a 79th-minute substitute against Millwall, but did not really have time to shine. His only other game for the Royals was again as substitute, this time at home to Oldham. By coincidence, both league games in which he played were 1-1 draws.

Leeds U (From trainee on 26/10/95)
Reading (Loaned on 8/12/98) FL 0+2 Others 1

WRIGHT Anthony (Tony) Allan
Born: Swansea, 1 September 1979
Height: 5'8" Weight: 11.8
International Honours: W: B-1; U21-3; Yth

Much was expected of Oxford's young Welsh U21 player, but he failed to move forward as was hoped, and was released at the end of the 1998-99 season. A slight midfield player, he did have two small runs

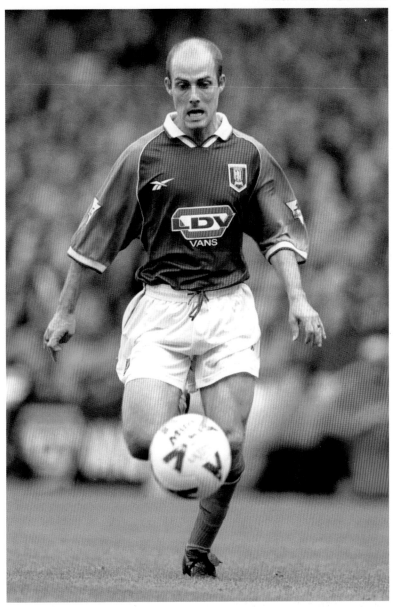

Alan Wright

in the side (totalling seven games), but never took hold of the game as was expected. However, he is still young and will surely find success elsewhere.

Oxford U (From trainee on 10/12/97) FL 4+3 FAC 1

WRIGHT Darren
Born: Warrington, 7 September 1979
Height: 5'8" Weight: 11.2

Having just completed his first year as a full-time professional for Chester after breaking through from the youth team, Darren prefers to play as a central striker but can also play on either wing. A youngster who also represented Cheshire and England

in athletics, and looks to go to the top as a footballer, he scored his first league goal against Rochdale at the Deva.

Chester C (From trainee on 8/7/98) FL 9+14/1 FLC 1+1 FAC 1 Others 0+1

WRIGHT David
Born: Warrington, 1 May 1980
Height: 5'11" Weight: 10.8
International Honours: E: Yth

Having been blooded by Crewe in 1997-98, David made three early appearances last season before replacing Marcus Bignot at right back and starting the final 18 games of a campaign. Selected for the England youth

team, he is a talented youngster who is adept at the tackling game as well as getting forward, and opened his scoring account in the 5-1 win at West Bromwich. His excellent performances during a difficult time at the club has most definitely marked him as one for the future.

Crewe Alex (From trainee on 18/6/97) FL 20+3/1 FLC 0+1

WRIGHT Ian Edward
Born: Woolwich, 3 November 1963
Height: 5'10" Weight: 11.8
Club Honours: PL '98; FMC '91; FLC '93; FAC '93, '98
International Honours: E: 33; B-3

The dynamic striker joined West Ham from Arsenal during the 1998 close season after an illustrious career at Highbury, and quickly became a crowd favourite for his enthusiasm and, of course, his goals. After scoring on his debut, at Sheffield Wednesday, he cracked in two of the spectacular variety against Wimbledon, and had a superb game up at St James' Park where two of the best put paid to Newcastle in a 3-0 win. He then gave a great performance for England against the Czechs, who were beaten 2-0 at Wembley. However, all good things come to an end, and a bad cartilage injury sustained in January forced him out of action for three months, which was a huge set back for the Hammers' European hopes. Bounced back in April to score against Spurs with an exquisite lob over the 'keeper's head, and finished the campaign as the club's leading scorer. Despite his age, there is still plenty of gas left in the tank.

Crystal Palace (Free from Greenwich Borough on 2/8/85) FL 206+19/89 FLC 19/9 FAC 9+2/3 Others 19+3/16
Arsenal (£2,500,000 on 24/9/91) F/PL 212+9/128 FLC 29/29 FAC 16/12 Others 22/16
West Ham U (£750,000 on 27/7/98) PL 20+2/9 FLC 2 FAC 1

WRIGHT Jermaine Malaki
Born: Greenwich, 21 October 1975
Height: 5'9" Weight: 11.9
International Honours: E: Yth

Began 1998-99 hoping to gain a regular place in the Crewe First Division side, having arrived at the club from Wolves the previous February, and following some good performances in the pre-season friendlies he duly started in the first team, missing just two games throughout a difficult campaign. Very mobile and fast, and a player who likes to run at defenders, he was converted from an out-and-out attacking role to that of a midfielder, which proved to be a great success. Able to play out wide or in central midfield, he opened his scoring account with a goal in a 1-1 draw at Stockport before going on to score four more times, all important goals, and all in games that were won. His speed gives the team plenty of options, especially when he comes from deep positions.

Millwall (From trainee on 27/11/92)
Wolverhampton W (£60,000 on 29/12/94) FL 4+16 FLC 1+3/1 Others 0+1

Doncaster Rov (Loaned on 1/3/96) FL 13
Crewe Alex (£25,000 on 19/2/98) FL 47+2/5 FLC 5 FAC 1

WRIGHT Mark Stephen
Born: Chorley, 4 September 1981
Height: 5'9" Weight: 9.10

This left-sided striker made his Preston debut in 1998-99, when appearing as a substitute in the FA Cup second-round tie versus Walsall, and repeated this feat at Burnley in the Auto Windscreens match three days later. North End's injury problems in February saw him making his full debut, almost scoring twice in the league win over Oldham before being subbed early in the second half. Turning pro in April, great things are expected from this direct, powerful shooting 17-year-old youngster.

Preston NE (From trainee on 16/4/99) FL 1 FAC 0+1 Others 0+1

WRIGHT Nicholas (Nick) John
Born: Ilkeston, 15 October 1975
Height: 5'10" Weight: 11.7

A right-sided midfielder signed from Carlisle in the summer of 1998, he proved to be hard working, willing, and skilful at Watford in 1998-99. Resembling Ray Parlour both in looks and playing style, and with a similar eye for goal, his first for Watford came against Crewe, while his best was probably a cracker at Queens Park Rangers. Can always be found in the thick of the action.

Derby Co (From trainee on 12/7/94)
Carlisle U (£35,000 on 28/11/97) FL 25/5 Others 2/2
Watford (£100,000 on 6/7/98) FL 31+2/6 FAC 0+1 Others 3/1

WRIGHT Richard Ian
Born: Ipswich, 5 November 1977
Height: 6'2" Weight: 13.0
International Honours: E: U21-14; Yth; Sch

A club record equalling 26 clean sheets in 1998-99 tells its own tale – another tremendous season for Ipswich's ever-present goalkeeper – and, although he would say that it was not all due to him, he played a large part in the effort. His finest hour was possibly the home game against West Bromwich, who virtually played Town off the park in the first half. Richard found himself facing the prolific Lee Hughes, and denied him a hat-trick of chances with brilliant saves. Needless to say, tactics were changed at half time, Town going on to win 2-0! Performances against Tranmere and Bristol City must also be mentioned. Tuesday 3rd November was a day not to be forgotten. He was at the hospital in the afternoon to witness the birth of his son, Harry, and back at Portman Road in the evening to thwart Wolves and keep another clean sheet. He also won further England U21 caps, keeping four clean sheets out of five games, and captaining the side in Bulgaria, but the highlights were his call ups to the full England squad for the games against the Czech Republic and France. Was recognised by his fellow professionals with selection to the PFA award-winning First Division side.

Ipswich T (From trainee on 2/1/95) P/FL 158 FLC 17 FAC 10 Others 8

WRIGHT Stephen
Born: Bellshill, 27 August 1971
Height: 5'10" Weight: 12.2
International Honours: S: 2; B-2; U21-14

Signed from Glasgow Rangers on a free transfer during the 1998 close season, having previously been loaned to Wolves, Stephen played in Bradford's first three games before getting a knock on his knee and missing the next four. He then played another six until being forced to have an operation on his right knee for a slight tear to his medial ligament. Recovering well, he came back to play another 14 games before suffering a thigh injury that saw him miss a further ten. Hoping for an injury-free 1999-2000, he is a very strong right back who does not shirk a tackle, which is probably the reason he had so many ankle injuries. Composed under pressure, he still has hopes of resuming his Scottish international career, and it will be interesting to see whether he takes up City's offer of re-engagement.

Aberdeen (Free from Eastercraigs on 28/11/87) SL 141+7/1 SLC 11+1 SC 13 Others 3
Glasgow R (Signed on 5/7/95) SL 7 SLC 5 Others 6+1
Wolverhampton W (Loaned on 20/3/98) FL 3
Bradford C (Free on 30/7/98) FL 21+1 FLC 3 FAC 2

WRIGHT Thomas (Tommy) James
Born: Belfast, 29 August 1963
Height: 6'1" Weight: 14.5
Club Honours: Div 1 '93
International Honours: NI: 30; U23-1

Having shared the 'keeper's job with Martyn Margetson in 1997-98, the rise of Nicky Weaver as the number-one goal-keeper at Manchester City saw Tommy make just three starts up to the end of March, two back-to-back home wins against Chesterfield and Derby County in late September, due to the latter being out with a groin injury. In the Derby Worthington Cup game at Maine Road he excelled himself with a fine performance, keeping the County stars down to the one goal that decided the two-legged fixture. He then played against Mansfield in the Auto Windscreens Shield game at Maine Road. Somewhat surprisingly, after a 14-month gap he was included in the Northern Ireland squad for two European championship games against Finland and Moldova, but did not play. In March, Tommy went on a one-month loan to Wrexham, subject to an instant recall if needed, kept a clean sheet on his debut at Stoke, and showed himself to be a good handler of the ball who gave defenders assurance at the back.

Newcastle U (£30,000 from Linfield on 27/1/88) F/PL 72+1 FLC 6 FAC 4 Others 1
Hull C (Loaned on 14/2/91) FL 6
Nottingham F (£450,000 on 24/9/93) P/FL 11 FLC 2
Reading (Loaned on 4/10/96) FL 17
Manchester C (Loaned on 17/1/97) FL 5
Manchester C (£450,000 on 3/3/97) FL 27 FLC 1 FAC 2 Others 1
Wrexham (Loaned on 26/2/99) FL 16

YATES Dean Richard
Born: Leicester, 26 October 1967
Height: 6'2" Weight: 12.6
Club Honours: AIC '95
International Honours: E: U21-5

An experienced left-sided central defender signed on a free transfer from Derby in the summer of 1998, Dean lost his Watford first-team place in October because of a knee injury which needed surgery and kept him out for the rest of the season. Obviously a blow, the Hornets missed his control and vision, normally associated with a continental sweeper, and his coolness under pressure.

Notts Co (From apprentice on 14/6/85) FL 312+2/33 FLC 24 FAC 20 Others 36/4
Derby Co (£350,000 on 26/1/95) F/PL 65+3/3 FLC 3 FAC 3
Watford (Free on 16/7/98) FL 9/1 FLC 1

Dean Yates

YATES Stephen (Steve)
Born: Bristol, 29 January 1970
Height: 5'11" Weight: 12.2
Club Honours: Div 3 '90

A central or right-sided defender who has been with Queens Park Rangers for six years, Steve began last season in the first team before receiving a knee injury in the game at Molineux at the end of September. He tried a comeback in the reserves during December, but suffering a recurrence of the problem did not complete the match and failed to make it back to the first team before the end of the campaign. Released during the summer, at his best he is a tough-tackling player who works hard for his team mates, and is good in the air.

Bristol Rov (From trainee on 1/7/88) FL 196+1 FLC 9 FAC 11 Others 21
Queens Park R (£650,000 on 16/8/93) P/FL 122+12/2 FLC 8 FAC 7

YORKE Dwight
Born: Canaan, Tobago, 3 November 1971
Height: 5'10" Weight: 12.4
Club Honours: FLC '96; FAC '99; PL '99; EC '99
International Honours: Trinidad & Tobago

A natural athlete with great balance and a wonderful left foot, Dwight's dream move to Manchester United finally reached fruition last August, when he joined the Reds for £12.6 million. Although a few eyebrows were raised at the size of the fee, he quickly established himself as one of the bargain transfers of the season, and even before he pulled on the famous red shirt the plaudits were flowing thick and fast, with former United ace, Denis Law, stating that he could become one of United's greatest-ever goalscorers, whilst George Best even suggested he could become a more important signing to United than Eric Cantona. If that was not praise enough, he soon began to show the United faithful that he was up to the task of replacing their former idol. After making a goalless debut against West Ham in August he went on a bonanza, netting the first of 17 Premiership goals in the corresponding fixture against Charlton. A sensational overhead strike against Barcelona at Old Trafford in September, again had the expert's comparing him to Eric Cantona. From then until the end of the campaign it was goals all the way, with doubles against Charlton, Nottingham Forest, and Chelsea, and a much-lauded hat-trick against Leicester at Filbert Street. The only month in which he failed to find the net was December, but from January to March, he netted nine goals in six consecutive games. Without a goal in eight matches, he scored one of United's three against Juventus in March, which took them through to the European Cup final. Although he missed out to David Ginola in both the PFA and Football Writers' "Footballer of the Year" awards, he was selected for the PFA award-winning Premiership side, while his talents were recognised in Tobago, in March, when he was given the keys of the capital – the country's highest honour. Having won European Cup, FA Cup, and Premiership winners medals, all in his first season at the club, it should not be too long before Alex Ferguson gives him the keys to the kingdom of Old Trafford.

Aston Villa (£120,000 from Signal Hill on 19/12/89) F/PL 195+36/75 FLC 20+2/8 FAC 22+2/13 Others 10/3
Manchester U (£12,600,000 on 22/8/98) PL 32/18 FAC 5+3/3 Others 11/8

YOUDS Edward (Eddie) Paul
Born: Liverpool, 3 May 1970
Height: 6'2" Weight: 14.2

The commanding Charlton central defender started last season as first choice alongside either Richard Rufus or Steve Brown. However, when Carl Tiler was signed in September, Athletic played with three centre halves for a fair proportion of the games, and Eddie did well. Continuing to make his presence felt in the opposing penalty area, he found the net on three occasions, including a goal against Queens Park Rangers in the Worthington Cup, before losing his place towards the end of the campaign through injury. At his best, is good in the air, and a ferocious tackler, who excels at free kicks and corners.

Everton (From trainee on 10/6/88) FL 5+3 FLC 0+1 Others 1
Cardiff C (Loaned on 8/2/90) FL 0+1 FAC 0+1
Wrexham (Loaned on 8/2/90) FL 20/2
Ipswich T (£250,000 on 15/11/91) F/PL 38+12/1 FLC 1+2 FAC 5+1
Bradford C (£175,000 on 2/1/95) FL 85/8 FLC 7/2 FAC 3 Others 4
Charlton Ath (£550,000 on 26/3/98) P/FL 29+1/2 FLC 3/1 FAC 1 Others 3

Luke Young

YOUNG Luke Paul
Born: Harlow, 19 July 1979
Height: 6'0" Weight: 12.4
Club Honours: FLC '99
International Honours: E: U21-1; Yth

Joining Tottenham as a trainee in July 1995, and signing professional terms in July 1997, Luke broke through into the first team last November at West Ham. Looking extremely confident and relaxed on the ball, the young left back fitted naturally into the side, possessing great pace, while showing himself to be a fine crosser of the ball. And, with George Graham's reputation for nurturing a strong youth policy, he looks set for great things at White Hart Lane if he maintains his opening high standards. Is a tremendous prospect for the future. Made his debut for the England U21 side that played against Hungary.

Tottenham H (From trainee on 3/7/97) PL 14+1 FLC 1+1 FAC 3+2

YOUNG Neil Anthony
Born: Harlow, 31 August 1973
Height: 5'9" Weight: 12.0
1998-99 was yet another good season for Neil, who was one of Bournemouth's most consistent performers at right back, while missing just two games throughout the season. An athletic full back who is quick to support the front players and can deliver a telling cross, he also undertakes his defensive role with ability and confidence.
Tottenham H (From trainee on 17/8/91)
Bournemouth (Free on 11/10/94) FL 203+2/3 FLC 12 FAC 13 Others 14

YOUNG Scott
Born: Pontypridd, 14 January 1976
Height: 6'2" Weight: 12.6
International Honours: W: B-1; U21-5
The solid Cardiff central defender whose 1998-99 season was disrupted by injury, played on despite a hernia problem, but eventually had to have an operation and missed the end of the campaign. Certainly figuring in City's plans for 1999-2000, in Division Two, he had his operation early to ensure he would be ready for the start of 1999-2000.
Cardiff C (From trainee on 4/7/94) FL 151+14/5 FLC 9+1 FAC 12 Others 12+3/1

YOUNGS Thomas (Tom) Anthony John
Born: Bury St Edmunds, 31 August 1979
Height: 5'9" Weight: 10.4
This highly-rated Cambridge teenager who, because of studies, bypassed the YTS system to earn a contract at the age of 17, has yet to burst on the scene as first expected. Despite being a talented forward, with great pace and enthusiasm to match, he possibly needs building up physically before he is given an extended first-team run. More of a taker than a maker of chances in the reserves, where he looks to pick up bits and pieces around the box, Tom has yet to score for the seniors.
Cambridge U (From juniors on 3/7/97) FL 7+7 Others 1+2

ZABEK Lee Kevin
Born: Bristol, 13 October 1978
Height: 6'0" Weight: 12.0
A combative central midfield ball winner, Lee played in the opening four matches of last season, but failed to hold down a regular place in Bristol Rovers' starting line-up after that. A throat problem hindered his early form, but he did score his only goal of the campaign on 15 December in the 5-0 victory second round FA Cup replay against Exeter City at the Memorial Stadium. A series of injuries, and competition from new signings, restricted his opportunities in the second half of the term.
Bristol Rov (From trainee on 28/7/97) FL 18+7/1 FLC 2 FAC 1+1/1 Others 4

ZAGORAKIS Theodoros (Theo)
Born: Kavala Greece, 27 October 1971
Height: 5'9" Weight: 11.6
International Honours: Greece: 38
A right-footed Leicester midfielder and captain of the Greek national team, Theo was a regular squad member for City in 1998-99, operating either as a starter or coming on from the bench in the latter stages. Despite being clearly talented, he has found the pace of the

Premiership more hectic than football back home, but scored with a terrific swerving long-range effort at home to Manchester United that got rather overlooked due to the final result, and displayed outstanding skill to set up a goal for Tony Cottee at Villa Park. Having replaced Robbie Savage in the closing minute at Wembley, he was denied the chance to make an impression in extra time by Tottenham's last-gasp winner.
Leicester C (£750,000 from PAOK Salonika on 6/2/98) PL 28+5/2 FLC 3+2 FAC 1+1 Others 2/1

Theo Zagorakis

ZAHANA-ONI Landry
Born: Ivory Coast, 8 August 1976
Height: 5'10" Weight: 10.8
Having been released by the Scottish side, Stirling Albion, during the 1998 close season Landry came south to play non-league football at Bromley, and it was there that he was watched for quite some time by Luton's scouts, before Lennie Lawrence decided on bringing him to Kenilworth Road last January. A 22-year-old striker, cum winger, he became the latest player to fill the problematic left-sided forward role, being substituted after 45 minutes in Town's 3-1 victory at home to Wycombe, when he seemed to be struggling just a bit. Although making just three more starts before the campaign came to a close, the skilful Ivory Coast man is likely to get a second chance, having agreed an 18-month contract with the club.
Stirling A (Signed from Ancenis RC on 2/10/97) SL 24+4/5 SC 2 (Freed during 1998 close season)
Luton T (£35,000 from Bromley on 5/1/99) FL 4+4

ZHIYI Fan
Born: Shanghai, China, 6 November 1969
Height: 6'2" Weight: 12.1
International Honours: China: 9
Reckoned by supporters to be the best of Crystal Palace's foreigners, the captain of the Chinese international team was brought to Selhurst Park, along with Jihai, by Terry Venables last September. After making his first-team debut in the Worthington Cup defeat at Bury, two games later he scored a brilliant goal in a 2-1 home win over the same team, and although he lost quite a chunk of the season due to international duty and injury he came back strongly. Capable of playing on the left side of midfield or up front, he has great vision, especially with the long ball, and always looks to shoot on sight of goal.
Crystal Palace (£500,000 from Shanghai on 10/9/98) FL 28+1/2 FLC 2/1 FAC 1

ZOLA Gianfranco (Franco)
Born: Sardinia Italy, 5 July 1966
Height: 5'6" Weight: 10.10
Club Honours: FAC '97; FLC '98; ECWC '98; ESC '98
International Honours: Italy: 35
Following the disappointment of his exclusion from Italy's World Cup squad, and by his own admission a slightly sub-standard season, Franco's form in the early part of 1998-99 was, as we say down at the Bridge, imponente – awesome! He scored in consecutive Premiership matches against Nottingham Forest, Blackburn (a trademark free kick), and Middlesbrough (an impudent lob over the stranded goalkeeper) as the Blues overcame a sluggish start and put together a 21-match unbeaten league run. Fortunately for Chelsea, Franco was the one front-line goalscorer who remained fit and available throughout the whole season as they lost Brian Laudrup, Pierluigi Casiraghi, Gus Poyet, and Tore-Andre Flo – either temporarily or permanently – though a variety of reasons and, as a consequence, Luca Vialli was forced to rely heavily on his twinkling ball skills as the goals continued to flow. Two at Filbert Street in a 4-2 victory, along with a beautifully taken equaliser at Old Trafford put Chelsea in the Premiership pole position, and yet more classic free kicks against Aston Villa and Southampton maintained their lead. Although a sequence of drawn games ruined the team's chances of winning the title, Franco had returned to the form of two seasons previously when he was voted FWA "Footballer of the Year", a delicate lob against Leicester and a brace against Everton virtually assuring Chelsea of a Champions' League spot for the first time as the Premiership's third-placed side. Having celebrated his 33rd birthday during the 1999 close season he, like Vialli, may retire at the end of the 1999-2000 campaign, but, in the meantime, is pleased to have another crack at the European Champions' League, his last attempt being with Napoli in 1991. He has gone on record as saying that he wished to go out in a blaze of glory, and when that dreaded day of retirement eventually arrives, the little Italian will take his place as one of the great Chelsea heroes in the club's history, his contribution since his move from Parma being immense.
Chelsea (£4,500,000 from Parma, via Napoli, Torres and Nuorese, on 15/11/96) PL 80+7/29 FLC 4 FAC 14/5 Others 14+1/5

ZWIJNENBERG Clemens
Born: Enschede, Holland, 18 May 1970
Height: 6'0" Weight: 13.8
This Dutch defender was just one of a number of European players arriving at Bristol City on trial in 1998-99. Originally rejected by John Ward, after returning home he was brought back to the club for a loan spell, during which he failed to make any impact and was released before his time was up. Clemens found it difficult adapting to the English game, where the demands are much different to those experienced on the continent.
Bristol C (Loaned from Aalborg, via Twente Enschede and Feyenoord, on 15/9/98) FL 1+2 FLC 1

Where Did They Go?

Below is a list of all players who were recorded in the 1998-99 Factfile but failed to make the current book, which includes only men who appear in a senior game in 1998-99. They are listed alphabetically, and show their leaving dates as well as their first port of call if known. Of course, they may well have moved on from the club in question by now, but space does not allow further reference.

* Shows that the player in question is still at the same club, but failed to make an appearance in 1998-99 for any number of reasons, the most common being long-term injury. Where a player has been released during the 1999 close season we have recorded him by his leaving date, not an *.

+ Players retained by the club relegated to the Conference.

Name	Club	Date	Destination
ADAMS Kieran	Barnet	3/99	Billericay
ADAMS Micky	Brentford	12/97	Retired
AGNEW Paul	Swansea C	11/97	Wisbech T
ALDERSON Richard	York C	6/98	Whitby T
ALDRIDGE John	Tranmere Rov	5/98	Retired
ALLEN Martin	Portsmouth	5/98	Retired
ALLEN Paul	Millwall	6/98	Purfleet
ALLON Joe	Hartlepool U	2/98	Retired
ALVES Paulo	West Ham U	1/98	Sporting Lisbon (Portugal)
ANDERSSON Anders	Blackburn Rov	10/98	Aalborg (Denmark)
ANDRADE Jose	Stoke C	2/98	(Portugal)
ARCHDEACON Owen	Carlisle U	11/97	Greenock Morton
ASANOVIC Aljosa	Derby Co	12/98	Napoli (Italy)
ASPRILLA Tino	Newcastle U	1/98	Parma (Italy)
ATKIN Paul	Scarborough	6/98	Gainsborough Trinity
AUNGER Geoff	Stockport Co	1/98	(Canada)
BAILEY Dennis	Lincoln C	5/98	Farnborough T
BAIRD Ian	Brighton & Hove A	12/97	(Hong Kong)
BANKOLE Ademola	Crewe Alex	7/98	Queens Park R
BARNWELL-EDINBORO Jamie	Cambridge U	6/98	Stevenage Borough
BARRASS Matt	Bury	*	
BARROW Lee	Torquay U	9/97	Barry T
BARROWCLIFF Paul	Brentford	6/98	Chesham U
BARWOOD Danny	Swansea C	*	
BEARDSMORE Russell	Bournemouth	*	
BEENEY Mark	Leeds U	2/99	Retired
BEESTON Carl	Southend U	9/97	Hednesford T
BENNETT Troy	Scarborough	6/98	Gainsborough Trinity
BENSTEAD Graham	Brentford	1/98	Basingstoke T
BETTNEY Chris	Sheffield U	7/99	
BETTS Robert	Doncaster Rov	8/98	Coventry C (YT)
BIBBO Sal	Reading	7/98	
BILLIO Patrizio	Crystal Palace	4/98	(Italy)
BIRCH Paul	Exeter C	6/98	Halesowen T
BLACK Tony	Wigan Ath	11/97	Accrington Stanley
BLAKE Mark	Walsall	6/98	Retired
BLAKE Mark	Fulham	6/98	Cannes (France)
BLAMEY Nathan	Shrewsbury T	9/98	Saltash U
BLANEY Steve	Brentford	5/98	Billericay T
BLONDEAU Patrick	Sheffield Wed	1/98	Bordeaux (France)
BODIN Paul	Reading	4/98	Bath C
BOERE Jeroen	Southend U	7/98	(Japan)
BONETTI Ivano	Crystal Palace	11/97	Genoa (Italy)
BORG John	Doncaster Rov	7/98	Bury
BOSANCIC Jovo	Barnsley	6/98	En Avant Guingamp (France)
BOWER Mark	Bradford C	*	
BOYAK Steve	Hull C	5/98	Glasgow Rangers
BRADLEY Russell	Hartlepool U	6/98	Hednesford T
BRADSHAW Darren	Blackpool	10/97	Rushden & Diamonds
BRAITHWAITE Leon	Exeter C	1/98	St Patricks Ath (Ireland)
BRIEN Tony	Hull C	1/98	Retired
BROLIN Thomas	Crystal Palace	5/98	Retired
BROOKES Darren	Doncaster Rov	+	
BROWN Andrew	Hull C	9/97	Clydebank
BROWN Linton	Swansea C	3/98	Emley
BROWN Simon	Tottenham H	7/99	
BRUNO Pasquale	Wigan Ath	3/98	
BRYDON Lee	Darlington	6/98	Bishop Auckland
BUTLER Lee	Wigan Ath	7/98	Dunfermline Ath
BUXTON Nicky	Scarborough	9/98	Spennymoor U
BYRNE Paul	Southend U	10/97	Glenavon (N. Ireland)
BYWATER Stephen	Rochdale	8/98	West Ham U
CARR Franz	West Bromwich A	3/98	Retired
CARTER Mark	Rochdale	6/98	Ashton U
CAVACO Luis	Stockport Co	6/98	(Portugal)
CAWLEY Pete	Colchester U	6/98	Braintree T
CHAMBERS Leroy	Macclesfield T	8/98	Altrincham
CHANDLER Dean	Lincoln C	6/98	Chesham U
CHANNING Justin	Leyton Orient	6/98	Slough T
CHAPMAN Ian	Gillingham	6/98	Retired
CHAPPLE Shaun	Swansea C	10/97	Merthyr Tydfil
CHARLES Lee	Queens Park R	6/98	Hayes
CLARK Dean	Brentford	*	
CLARKE Matt	Sheffield Wed	*	
CLARKE Steve	Chelsea	10/98	Retired
CLOUGH Nigel	Manchester C	10/98	Burton A
COCKERILL Glenn	Brentford	5/98	Retired
COLGAN Nick	Chelsea	7/98	Bournemouth
COLKIN Lee	Northampton T	3/98	Hednesford T
CONLON Paul	Doncaster Rov	1/98	Chester le Street
CONWAY Paul	Northampton T	6/98	(USA)
COOK Aaron	Portsmouth	12/98	Crystal Palace
COOPER Mark	Leyton Orient	1/98	Rushden & Diamonds
CORBET Jim	Gillingham	5/98	Blackburn Rov
COULBAULT Regis	Southend U	6/98	(France)
COWANS Gordon	Burnley	5/98	Retired
CROCI Laurent	Carlisle U	11/97	(France)
CUNNINGHAM Harvey	Doncaster Rov	+	
CUNNINGTON Shaun	Notts Co	6/98	Kidderminster Hrs
CYRUS Andy	Exeter C	6/98	Dulwich Hamlet
DALE Carl	Cardiff C	6/98	Yeovil T
DARRAS Frederic	Swindon T	1/98	Paris Red Star (France)
DAVEY Simon	Preston NE	7/99	
DAVIES Glen	Hartlepool U	6/98	Worthing
DAVIS Craig	Doncaster Rov	5/98	Grantham T
DAY Chris	Watford	*	
DEBENHAM Robert	Doncaster Rov	7/98	Bury
DEMPSEY Mark	Shrewsbury T	6/98	Barry T
DENNIS Kevin	Brentford	7/99	
DENYS Ryan	Brentford	5/99	
DE VITO Claudio	Barnet	10/98	Moor Green
DEVLIN Mark	Exeter C	7/98	
DIBBLE Andy	Middlesbrough	6/98	Altrincham
DICKINSON Patrick	Hull C	6/98	
DIUK Wayne	Notts Co	12/98	
DIXON Ben	Blackpool	6/98	(Singapore)
DOBSON Ryan	Chester C	6/98	Bridgnorth T

DOBSON Warren	Hartlepool U	6/98	Spennymoor U
DONCEL-VARCACEL Antonio	Hull C	6/98	(Spain)
DONNELLY Mark	Doncaster Rov	7/98	Bury
DONOWA Louie	Walsall	12/97	Ayr U
DOWELL Wayne	Doncaster Rov	9/97	Accrington Stanley
DOYLE Maurice	Millwall	8/98	Telford U
DRUCE Mark	Rotherham U	6/98	Hereford U
DRYSDALE Jason	Northampton T	3/98	Forest Green Rov
DUCROSS Andy	Coventry C	7/99	
DUNN Iain	Chesterfield	9/98	Gainsborough Trinity
EDEY Cec	Macclesfield T	6/98	Hyde U
EDWARDS Paul	Doncaster Rov	5/98	
ELLIOTT Andy	Hartlepool U	6/98	Dunstan FB
EMERSON	Middlesbrough	1/98	Tenerife (Spain)
ENES Robbie	Portsmouth	6/98	(Australia)
ESDAILLE Darren	Doncaster Rov	6/98	Hyde U
ESDAILLE David	Doncaster Rov	6/98	Retired
EYDELIE Jean-Jacques	Walsall	5/98	(Switzerland)
FEATHERSTONE James	Scunthorpe U	1/99	Emley
FENSOME Andy	Rochdale	6/98	Barrow
FEUER Ian	Luton T	3/98	(USA)
FEWINGS Paul	Hull C	6/98	Hereford U
FINLEY Gary	Doncaster Rov	10/97	Hyde U
FOLLAND Bob	Oxford U	*	
FOSTER Colin	Cambridge U	6/98	Retired
FOSTER Martin	Leeds U	7/98	Greenock Morton
GALL Benny	Shrewsbury T	3/98	(Denmark)
GARDINER Mark	Macclesfield T	12/97	Northwich Victoria
GAVIN Mark	Hartlepool U	11/97	Retired
GAYLE Mark	Crewe Alex	6/98	Rushden & Diamonds
GENTILE Marco	Burnley	10/97	Volendam (Holland)
GEORGE Danny	Doncaster Rov	+	
GERMAINE Gary	West Bromwich A	6/98	(USA)
GHAZGHAZI Sufyan	Exeter C	6/98	Dorchester T
GIALLANZA Gaetano	Bolton W	6/98	Nantes (France)
GILBERT Dave	West Bromwich A	6/98	Grantham T
GILES Martin	Chester C	6/98	
GINTY Rory	Crystal Palace	6/98	
GISLASON Valur	Arsenal	2/98	Stromgodest (Norway)
GUIMMARA Willie	Darlington	10/97	(Canada)
GLEGHORN Nigel	Burnley	6/98	Altrincham
GLOVER Dean	Port Vale	6/98	Kidderminster Hrs
GODDARD-CRAWLEY Richard	Brentford	3/98	Woking
GOMM Richard	Torquay U	7/98	
GOODWIN Shaun	Rotherham U	4/98	Doncaster Rov
GORE Ian	Doncaster Rov	3/98	
GOUCK Andy	Rochdale	6/98	Southport
GRAHAM Mark	Queens Park R	7/99	
GRAVES Wayne	Scunthorpe U	*	
GRAY Alan	Carlisle U	5/98	Workington
GRAY Andy	Millwall	5/99	Retired
GRIDELET Phil	Southend U	6/98	Stevenage Borough
GRIEVES Danny	Watford	7/99	
GULLIT Ruud	Chelsea	2/98	Retired
GUNN Bryan	Norwich C	7/98	Hibernian
HADDOW Paul	Blackpool	6/98	Morecambe
HADLEY Stewart	Mansfield T	1/98	Kidderminster Hrs
HALLIDAY Stephen	Hartlepool U	7/98	Motherwell
HAMMOND Andy	Doncaster Rov	6/99	Maltby Main
HAMPSHIRE Steve	Chelsea	*	
HARE Matty	Exeter C	6/98	Sligo Rov (Ireland)
HARRINGTON Justin	Bournemouth	6/98	Porthleven
HARRIOTT Marvin	Cardiff C	12/97	Cambridge C
HARRIS Jamie	Swansea C	6/98	
HARRIS Mark	Cardiff C	6/98	Kingstonian
HARRISON Tommy	Carlisle U	1/98	Berwick R
HARVEY Richard	Luton T	6/98	Aylesbury U
HATHAWAY Ian	Colchester U	9/98	Aldershot T
HAWTHORNE Mark	Doncaster Rov	6/98	Grantham T
HAYES Adi	Cambridge U	6/98	Kettering T
HAYWARD Anthony	Rotherham U	6/98	Hednesford T
HELLIWELL Ian	Burnley	6/98	Ilkeston T
HENDRY Colin	Blackburn Rov	8/98	Glasgow Rangers
HENRIKSEN Tony	Southend U	11/98	Rushden & Diamonds
HEY Tony	Birmingham C	*	
HIGGINBOTTOM Danny	Manchester U	*	
HIGGS Shane	Bristol Rov	6/98	Worcester C
HILL Andy	Port Vale	6/98	Retired
HILTON Damian	Brighton & Hove A	6/98	Kings Lynn
HILTON David	Darlington	11/97	Ayr U
HILTON Maurice	Doncaster Rovers	5/98	Grantham T
HODGE Steve	Leyton Orient	8/97	Retired
HOGG Graeme	Brentford	6/98	Retired
HOGGETH Gary	Doncaster Rov	7/98	Bury
HOLCROFT Peter	Swindon T	7/99	
HOLSGROVE Paul	Stoke C	6/98	Hibernian
HONE Mark	Lincoln C	6/98	Kettering T
HOWARTH Lee	Barnet	6/98	Stevenage Borough
HUGHES David	Aston Villa	*	
HUMPHREY John	Brighton & Hove A	1/98	Chesham U
HURDLE Gus	Brentford	2/98	Whyteleafe
HURST Chris	Huddersfield T	9/98	Emley
HUXFORD Richard	Burnley	2/98	Dunfermline Ath
HYDE Paul	Leyton Orient	12/98	Hendon
ILLMAN Neil	Exeter C	2/98	Northwich Victoria
INGHAM Gary	Doncaster Rov	11/97	Leek T
IRELAND Simon	Doncaster Rov	3/98	Boreham Wood
IRONSIDE Ian	Oldham Ath	6/98	Retired
IRVING Richard	Macclesfield T	2/98	Runcorn
ISMAEL Valerien	Crystal Palace	10/98	RC Lens (France)
JACKSON Kirk	Chesterfield	6/98	Grantham T
JAMES Julian	Luton T	7/99	
JENKINS Iain	Chester C	3/98	Dundee U
JOBSON Richard	Manchester C	*	
JOHANSEN Martin	Coventry C	7/98	Lyngby (Denmark)
JOHANSEN Stig	Southampton	8/98	Helsingborg (Sweden)
JOHNSON Gavin	Wigan Ath	6/98	Dunfermline Ath
JONES Rob	Liverpool	7/99	
KALOGERACOS Vas	Stockport Co	2/98	(Australia)
KEAN Robert	Luton T	3/98	Stevenage Borough
KEEBLE Chris	Ipswich T	*	
KELLY Garry	Leeds U	*	
KELLY Paddy	Newcastle U	7/99	
KELLY Ray	Manchester C	12/98	Bohemians (Ireland)
KERNAGHAN Alan	Manchester C	9/97	St Johnstone
KINKLADZE Giorgiou	Manchester C	5/98	Ajax (Holland)
KIWOMYA Andy	Notts Co	2/98	Halifax T
KLINSMAN Jurgen	Tottenham H	5/98	Retired
KYRATZOGLOU Alex	Oldham Ath	11/97	
LAMA Bernard	West Ham U	5/98	Paris St Germain (France)
LARKIN Jim	Walsall	7/98	(Canada)
LARSEN Stig	Hartlepool U	3/98	(Norway)
LAWS Brian	Scunthorpe U	5/98	Retired
LEWIS Ben	Southend U	6/98	Heybridge Swifts
LEWIS Neil	Peterborough U	*	
LINGER Paul	Brighton & Hove A	6/98	Welling U
LINIGHAN Brian	Bury	*	
LJUNG Per-Ola	Watford	2/98	
LLOYD Kevin	Cardiff C	6/98	
LOVELL Stuart	Reading	6/98	Hibernian
LOWE Kenny	Darlington	11/97	Gateshead
LOWNDES Nathan	Watford	8/98	St Johnstone
LOWTHORPE Adam	Hull C	6/98	Gainsborough Trinity
MABBUTT Gary	Tottenham H	6/98	Retired
McAREE Rod	Fulham	3/98	Woking
MACARI Paul	Stoke C	6/98	
McCLAIR Brian	Manchester U	6/98	Motherwell
McDONALD Alan	Swindon T	7/99	

Name	Club	Date	Destination
MacDONALD Dave	Barnet	6/98	Welling U
McDONALD Paul	Brighton & Hove A	1/98	Dunfermline Ath
McDONALD Rod	Chester C	6/98	Winsford U
McELHATTON Mike	Scarborough	6/98	Rushden & Diamonds
McGHEE David	Brentford	1/99	Retired
McGOLDRICK Eddie	Manchester C	6/98	Retired
McGRATH Paul	Sheffield U	2/98	Retired
McINTYRE Kevin	Tranmere Rov	12/98	Doncaster Rov
McKAY Matty	Everton	*	
McKINLAY Tosh	Stoke C	2/98	Glasgow Celtic
McMAHON Gerry	Stoke C	2/98	St Johnstone
McMAHON Steve	Swindon T	5/98	Retired
McNALLY Mark	Stoke C	6/98	Dundee U
McNALLY Ross	Brighton & Hove A	6/98	
McPHERSON Malcolm	Brentford	6/98	Dorchester T
McROBERT Lee	Millwall	6/98	Hastings T
MAHER Shaun	Fulham	9/98	
MAHONEY-JOHNSON Michael	Queens Park R	*	
MAHORN Paul	Port Vale	8/98	Stevenage Borough
MAINWARING Carl	Swansea C	5/99	
MAKEL Lee	Huddersfield T	3/98	Heart of Midlothian
MARSH Mike	Southend U	2/98	Barrow
MARTIN Kevin	Scarborough	6/98	
MARTIN Lee	Bristol Rov	7/98	
MASON Andy	Macclesfield T	6/98	Kettering T
MASSEY Stuart	Oxford U	6/98	Retired
MASTERS Neil	Gillingham	7/99	
MAUTONE Steve	Reading	7/99	
MAXFIELD Scott	Hull C	6/98	Doncaster Rov
MAYRLEB Christian	Sheffield Wed	6/98	FK Austria-Wien (Austria)
MEDLIN Nicky	Exeter C	6/98	Dorchester T
MELVANG Lars	Watford	3/98	
MESSER Gary	Doncaster Rov	9/98	Bury
MIDWOOD Michael	Huddersfield T	10/97	Emley
MIKE Adie	Doncaster Rov	5/98	Leek T
MILDENHALL Steve	Swindon T	*	
MILLIGAN Ross	Carlisle U	6/98	Gretna
MILNER Andy	Chester C	11/97	Morecambe
MILNER Jonathan	Mansfield T	*	
MILOSEVIV Savo	Aston Villa	7/98	Real Zaragossa (Spain)
MILTON Simon	Ipswich T	6/98	Braintree T
MINETT Jason	Exeter C	6/98	Doncaster Rov
MISSE-MISSE Jean Jacques	Chesterfield	4/98	(France)
MITCHELL Jamie	Scarborough	6/98	Gainsborough Trinity
MITCHELL Neil	Macclesfield T	1/98	Morecambe
MITCHELL Paul	Notts Co	6/98	
MITCHELL Paul	Torquay U	2/98	Barry T
MOLBY Jan	Swansea C	10/97	Retired
MOLDOVAN Viorel	Coventry C	7/98	Fenerbahce (Turkey)
MONCRIEFFE Prince	Doncaster Rov	6/98	Hyde U
MOORE Mark	Cambridge U	5/98	
MOREIRA Fabio	Middlesbrough	6/98	
MOREIRA Joao	Swansea C	3/98	(Portugal)
MORENO Jamie	Middlesbrough	3/98	Washington UDC (USA)
MORLEY Trevor	Reading	5/98	SK Brann Bergen (Norway)
MORRIS Mark	Brighton & Hove A	12/97	Hastings T
MOYES David	Preston NE	3/98	Retired
MUNROE Karl	Swansea C	5/99	
MUNTASSER Jehad	Bristol C	*	
MURRAY Rob	Bournemouth	6/98	Dorchester T
MUSTAFA Tarkan	Barnet	9/98	Kingstonian
MUTCH Andy	Stockport Co	6/98	Barrow
MYALL Stuart	Brentford	1/98	Hastings T
NASH Marc	Hartlepool U	8/98	
NASH Martin	Stockport Co	6/98	(Canada)
NAYLOR Dominic	Leyton Orient	6/98	Stevenage Borough
NAYLOR Martyn	Shrewsbury T	1/99	Telford U
N'DIAYE Pepe	Southend U	6/98	(France)
NEAL Ashley	Peterborough U	12/98	Radcliffe Borough
NEIL Jimmy	Scunthorpe U	12/98	Gainsborough Trinity
NELSON Fernando	Aston Villa	7/98	Porto (Portugal)
NEWELL Justin	Torquay U	9/98	
NICOL Steve	Sheffield Wed	6/98	Doncaster Rov
NIELSEN John	Southend U	5/98	(Denmark)
NIELSEN Martin	Huddersfield T	5/98	FC Copenhagen (Denmark)
NOLAN Ian	Sheffield Wed	*	
NOTTINGHAM Steven	Scunthorpe U	1/99	Stamford AFC
NURSE David	Millwall	8/98	Grantham T
NWADIKE Emeka	Shrewsbury T	6/98	Grantham T
NZAMBA Guy	Southend U	*	
O'CONNELL Brendan	Wigan Ath	9/98	Retired
O'CONNOR Derek	Huddersfield T	6/98	Bradford PA
O'CONNOR Mark	Gillingham	10/97	Retired
O'HAGAN Danny	Plymouth Arg	1/98	Dorchester T
OMIGIE Joe	Brentford	1/98	Welling U
ORD Richard	Sunderland	7/98	Queens Park R
ORMONDROYD Ian	Scunthorpe U	6/98	Retired
OTTO Ricky	Birmingham C	12/97	Retired
PAATELAINEN Mixu	Wolverhampton W	9/98	Hibernian
PAGAL Jean	Carlisle U	3/98	
PAPACONSTANTINOU Loukas	Darlington	2/98	(Canada)
PARMENTER Steve	Bristol Rov	3/98	Yeovil T
PARRIS George	Southend U	9/97	St Leonards Stamcroft
PASCOLO Marco	Nottingham F	7/98	(Switzerland)
PATTERSON Darren	Luton T	7/98	Dundee U
PATTIMORE Michael	Swindon T	6/98	
PATTON Aaron	Wycombe W	5/99	
PEAKE Trevor	Luton T	3/99	Retired
PEARSON Nigel	Middlesbrough	5/98	Retired
PEDERSEN Jan	Hartlepool U	2/98	SK Brann Bergen (Norway)
PEDERSEN Per	Blackburn Rov	8/98	Strasbourg (France)
PEDERSEN Tore	Blackburn Rov	10/98	Eintracht Frankfurt (Germany)
PEEL Nathan	Macclesfield T	1/98	Winsford U
PELL Robert	Rotherham U	6/98	Grantham T
PEMBERTON John	Crewe Alex	8/98	Retired
PEMBRIDGE Mark	Sheffield Wed	7/98	Benfica (Portugal)
PENDER John	Rochdale	7/99	
PEREZ Lionel	Sunderland	7/98	Newcastle U
PERKINS Chris	Southend U	*	
PETTINGER Paul	Rotherham U	*	
PHELAN Terry	Everton	*	
PHILLISKIRK Tony	Cardiff C	8/98	Oldham Ath
PIPER Lenny	Gillingham	6/98	St Albans C
PITCHER Darren	Crystal Palace	3/98	Purfleet
PLATT David	Arsenal	7/98	Retired
PLUCK Colin	Watford	*	
PLUMMER Dwayne	Bristol C	10/98	Stevenage Borough
POBORSKY Karel	Manchester U	12/98	Benfica (Portugal)
POPE Steven	Crewe Alex	5/98	Kidderminster Hrs
PORIC Adem	Notts Co	5/98	
POUNTNEY Craig	Shrewsbury T	7/99	
POWER Phil	Macclesfield T	6/98	Altrincham
PRUDHOE Mark	Bradford C	*	
PUGH David	Bury	6/98	Retired
PUTTNAM David	Swansea C	9/97	Gresley Rov
QUIGLEY Michael	Hull C	6/98	Altrincham
RAMASUT Tom	Bristol Rov	7/98	Merthyr Tydfil
RAMSAY John	Doncaster Rov	12/97	Blyth Spartans
RANDALL Adrian	Bury	6/98	Salisbury C
RANDALL Dean	Notts Co	6/98	Ilkeston T
RATCLIFFE Simon	Gillingham	9/98	Retired
RAVANELLI Fabrizio	Middlesbrough	9/97	Marseilles (France)
REED John	Blackpool	8/98	Gainsborough Trinity
REGIS Dave	Scunthorpe U	3/98	Retired
REINA Ricky	Brentford	4/98	Dover Ath
RESCH Franz	Darlington	6/98	(Austria)
RHODES Andy	Scarborough	2/98	Halifax T

Name	Club	Date	Destination
RICHARDSON Craig	Leyton Orient	6/98	
RICHARDSON Lloyd	Oldham Ath	6/98	Hyde U
RIEPER Marc	West Ham U	9/97	Glasgow Celtic
RIMMER Stuart	Chester C	6/98	Retired
ROBERTSON David	Leeds U	*	
ROBERTSON Graham	Millwall	8/98	Raith Rov
ROBERTSON John	Lincoln C	6/98	Northwich Victoria
ROBINSON Paul	Newcastle U	*	
ROBSON Glenn	Rochdale	8/98	Harrogate T
ROCASTLE David	Chelsea	3/98	Retired
ROCKETT Jason	Scarborough	7/99	
RODGER Graham	Grimsby T	6/98	
RODOSTHENOUS Michael	Cambridge U	11/97	
ROGERS Darren	Walsall	10/97	Stevenage Borough
ROGERS Lee	Chesterfield	6/98	Gainsborough Trinity
ROLLO Jimmy	Cardiff C	6/98	Forest Green Rov
ROONEY Mark	Watford	6/98	Aylesbury U
ROSE Colin	Macclesfield T	3/98	Runcorn
ROSLER Uwe	Manchester C	5/98	Kaiserslautern (Germany)
ROWBOTHAM Jason	Plymouth Arg	*	
RUSH Matthew	Oldham Ath	9/98	Retired
SAMUELS Dean	Barnet	9/98	Stevenage Borough
SANDERS Steve	Doncaster Rov	3/98	Boreham Wood
SANDWITH Kevin	Carlisle U	9/98	Barrow
SAN JUAN Jesus	Wolverhampton W	12/97	Real Zaragoza (Spain)
SAUL Eric	Brighton & Hove A	6/98	
SCHREUDER Dick	Stoke C	6/98	Helmond Sport (Holland)
SCOTT Andy	Rochdale	6/98	Stalybridge Celtic
SEAGRAVES Mark	Swindon T	6/98	Barrow
SEDLOSKI Goce	Sheffield Wed	2/99	Croatia Zagreb (Croatia)
SELLEY Ian	Fulham	*	
SEPP Dennis	Bradford C	6/98	HSC 91 (Holland)
SHAKESPEARE Craig	Scunthorpe U	3/98	Telford U
SHAW Simon	Darlington	6/98	Doncaster Rov
SHELTON Gary	Chester C	5/98	Retired
SHIRTLIFF Peter	Barnsley	7/98	Retired
SIMPSON Colin	Leyton Orient	7/99	
SIMPSON Karl	Norwich C	6/98	Witney T
SIMPSON Robbie	Portsmouth	*	
SINCLAIR Ronnie	Chester C	10/98	Retired
SISSOKO Habib	Preston NE	4/98	(France)
SKINNER Justin	Bristol Rov	3/98	Hibernian
SLATER Robbie	Wolverhampton W	8/98	Retired
SLATER Stuart	Watford	7/99	
SMITH Craig	Derby Co	3/98	Burton A
SMITH David	Doncaster Rov	+	
SMITH Mike	Doncaster Rov	5/98	Barrow
SMITH Tommy	Cambridge U	9/98	
SNODIN Ian	Scarborough	6/98	Doncaster Rov
SOBIECH Jorg	Stoke C	4/98	Twente Enschede (Holland)
SOLBAKKEN Stale	Wimbledon	3/98	Aalborg BK (Denmark)
SOLIS Mauricio	Derby Co	8/98	
SPENCER Simon	Brentford	1/98	Yeovil T
SQUIRES Jamie	Preston NE	3/98	Dunfermline Ath
STARBUCK Phil	Plymouth Arg	6/98	Cambridge C
STEVENS Gary	Tranmere Rov	6/98	Retired
STEVENS Mark	Oxford U	2/98	Bath C
STEVENS Shaun	Notts Co	10/97	
STEWART Paul	Stoke C	8/98	Workington
STREETER Terry	Brighton & Hove A	7/99	
SUNDGOT Ole	Bradford C	11/97	Molde (Norway)
SUTHERLAND Colin	Scarborough	6/98	Doncaster Rov
TALBOYS Steve	Watford	1/98	Kingstonian
TAYLOR Lee	Shrewsbury T	6/98	Hayes
TAYLOR Mark	Shrewsbury T	6/98	Hereford U
TEATHER Paul	Manchester U	*	
TEDALDI Domenico	Doncaster Rov	5/98	Bury (YT)
TEN HEUVEL Laurens	Barnsley	6/98	
TERRIER David	Newcastle U	6/98	(France)
THOLOT Didier	Walsall	5/98	Sion (Switzerland)
THOMAS James	Blackburn Rov	*	
THOMAS Michael	Liverpool	7/98	Benfica (Portugal)
THOMAS Scott	Manchester C	6/98	
THOMPSON Niall	Brentford	9/98	
THOMSEN Claus	Everton	3/98	AB Bagsvaerd (Denmark)
THOMSON Scott	Hull C	6/98	Airdrieonians
THORN Andy	Tranmere Rov	6/98	Retired
THORNLEY Rod	Doncaster Rov	11/97	Warrington T
THORP Hamilton	Portsmouth	5/98	(Australia)
THORP Michael	Reading	6/98	Slough T
THORPE Andy	Doncaster Rov	10/97	Chorley
TISDALE Paul	Bristol C	8/98	Panionis (Greece)
TOMASSON Jon	Newcastle U	6/98	Feyenoord (Holland)
TOWNLEY Leon	Brentford	*	
TREVITT Simon	Hull C	6/98	Guiseley
TUCKER Dexter	Hull C	*	
TURNBULL Lee	Darlington	6/98	Gainsborough Trinity
UTLEY Darren	Doncaster Rov	3/98	Stocksbridge PS
VALERY Patrick	Blackburn Rov	7/98	Bastia (France)
VAN DER VELDEN Carel	Scarborough	7/98	Rushden & Diamonds
VAN DULLEMEN Raymond	Northampton T	6/98	Tonegido (Holland)
VAN GOBBEL Ulrich	Southampton	9/77	Feyenoord (Holland)
VEART Carl	Millwall	7/98	
VERITY Daniel	Bradford C	7/99	
VICKERS Ashley	Peterborough U	8/98	St Albans C
VONK Michel	Sheffield U	7/98	Maastricht VV (Holland)
WADDOCK Gary	Luton T	6/98	Retired
WALKER Andy	Sheffield U	7/98	Ayr U
WALLACE Rod	Leeds U	7/98	Glasgow Rangers
WARD Nic	Shrewsbury T	1/98	Newtown
WARNER Tony	Liverpool	11/98	Glasgow Celtic
WARREN Lee	Doncaster Rov	+	
WATKISS Stuart	Mansfield T	11/98	Retired
WDOWCZYK Dariusz	Reading	6/98	Polonia Warsaw (Poland)
WEBBER Damien	Millwall	6/98	Worthing
WEST Colin	Leyton Orient	2/98	Rushden & Diamonds
WHARTON Paul	Hull C	6/98	Farsley Celtic
WHITE David	Sheffield U	7/98	Retired
WHITE Steve	Cardiff C	6/98	Bath C
WHITE Tom	Bristol Rov	*	
WHITEHOUSE Dane	Sheffield U	7/99	
WHITTON Steve	Colchester U	5/98	Retired
WHYTE Derek	Middlesbrough	12/97	Aberdeen
WILLEMS Ron	Derby Co	8/98	
WILLIAMS Dean	Doncaster Rov	12/97	Gateshead
WILLIAMS Michael	Leyton Orient	6/98	
WILLIAMS Paul	Southend U	6/98	Canvey Island
WILLIAMS Scott	Wrexham	7/98	Bangor C
WILLIAMSON Danny	Everton	*	
WILLIAMSON Davey	Cambridge U	3/98	Kingstonian
WILSON Padi	Doncaster Rov	5/98	Hyde U
WILSON Paul	Cambridge U	6/98	Rushden & Diamonds
WOODS Chris	Burnley	8/98	Retired
WOOLSEY Jeff	Brighton & Hove A	6/98	Dagenham & Redbridge
WORMULL Simon	Brighton & Hove A	9/98	Dover Ath
WORTHINGTON Nigel	Blackpool	7/99	Retired
WRIGHT Ian	Hull C	6/98	Hereford U
WRIGHT Mark	Liverpool	9/98	Retired
WRIGHT Tommy	Oldham Ath	11/97	St Johnstone
XAUSA Davide	Stoke C	3/98	St Johnstone
ZABICA Robert	Bradford C	2/98	(Australia)
ZOETEBIER Ed	Sunderland	1/98	Feyenoord (Holland)
ZOHAR Itzy	Crystal Palace	1/98	Maccabi Haifa (Israel)
ZOIS Peter	Cardiff C	2/98	

FA Carling Premiership and Nationwide League Clubs
Summary of Appearances and Goals for 1998-99

KEY TO TABLES: P/FL = Premier/Football League. FLC = Football League Cup. FAC = FA Cup. Others = Other first team appearances.
Left hand figures in each column list number of full appearances + appearances as substitute. Right hand figures list number of goals scored.

ARSENAL (PREM: 2nd)

	P/FL App	Goals	FLC App	Goals	FAC App	Goals	Others App	Goals
Adams	26	1			5		5	1
Anelka	34 + 1	17			5		6	2
Bergkamp	28 + 1	12	1		6	3	4	1
Black							0 + 1	
Boa Morte	2 + 6		2		1	1	2 + 2	1
Bould	14 + 5				3 + 1		2 + 2	
Caballero	0 + 1		0 + 1		0 + 1			
Crowe			0 + 1					
Diawara	2 + 10				1 + 2			
Dixon	36				5		6	
Garde	6 + 4		2		2 + 2		3 + 2	
Grimandi	3 + 5		2		1 + 1		1 + 2	
Grondin	1		2				1	
Hughes	4 + 10	1	2		2 + 2		2 + 3	1
Kanu	5 + 7	6			0 + 5	1		
Keown	34	1			4		6	1
Ljungberg	10 + 6	1	2		2 + 1			
Manninger	6		2		2			
Mendes	0 + 1		1 + 1		1		1	1
Overmars	37	6			6 + 1	4	5	2
Parlour	35	6			7		5	
Petit	26 + 1	4			3	2	4	
Riza			0 + 1					
Seaman	32				5		7	
Upson	0 + 5		2		1		1	
Vernazza							1	
Vieira	34	3			5	1	4	
Vivas	10 + 13		2	1	4 + 2		2 + 3	
Winterburn	30				6		6	
Wreh	3 + 9		2				3 + 1	1

ASTON VILLA (PREM: 6th)

	P/FL App	Goals	FLC App	Goals	FAC App	Goals	Others App	Goals
Barry	27 + 5	2			2		3	
Bosnich	15						2	
Byfield			1				1	
Calderwood	8							
Charles	10 + 1	1	1		0 + 1		4	1
Collymore	11 + 9	1			1	2	3	4
Delaney	0 + 2							
Draper	13 + 10	2	1	1	1		3 + 1	
Dublin	24	11						
Ehiogu	23 + 2	2	1		2		3	
Ferraresi							0 + 1	
Grayson	4 + 11		1		0 + 1		2 + 1	
Hendrie	31 + 1	3			2		3	
Jaszczun			0 + 1					
Joachim	29 + 7	14	1		2	1	4	1
Lescott			0 + 1					
Merson	21 + 5	5			1			
Oakes	23		1		2		2	
Rachel	0 + 1							
Scimeca	16 + 2	2	1		2		1 + 2	
Southgate	38	1			2		4	
Stone	9 + 1							
Taylor	31 + 2	4	1				2 + 1	
Thompson	20 + 5	2	0 + 1				3	
Vassell	0 + 6		0 + 1		0 + 1		0 + 3	2
Watson	26 + 1				2			
Wright	38		1		2		4	
Yorke	1							

BARNET (DIV 3: 16th)

	P/FL App	Goals	FLC App	Goals	FAC App	Goals	Others App	Goals
Alsford	9	1			1		1	
Arber	35	2					1	
Barnes	3 + 9							
Basham	32	1	1					
Charlery	40 + 2	16	1 + 1		1			
Currie	33 + 5	4	2	1	1	1	1	
Dearden	1							
Devine	10 + 10	1	1				1	
Doolan	40 + 2	2	1 + 1		1		1	
Ford	15	1	2		1		1	
Gledhill	0 + 1							
Goodhind	15	1			1			
Hackett	3 + 4							
Harle	11		0 + 1		1			
Harrison	43		2		1		1	
Heald	19	2						
King	17 + 5	6			0 + 1		1	
McGleish	25 + 11	9	2	1	1		0 + 1	
Manuel	3 + 9	1	0 + 1				1	
Onwere	14 + 5	2	2				0 + 1	
Rust	2							
Sawyers	21 + 1		1					
Searle	33 + 2	2					1	
Simpson	11 + 2		2		0 + 1		1	
Stockley	40 + 1		2		1		1	
Wilson	31	2	1		1		0 + 1	

BARNSLEY (DIV 1: 13th)

	P/FL App	Goals	FLC App	Goals	FAC App	Goals	Others App	Goals
Appleby	33 + 1		2		3 + 1			
Bagshaw	0 + 1		0 + 1					
Barnard	26	4	6	1	1			
Blackmore	4 + 3				1			
Bullock M	20 + 12	2	5		0 + 5	2		
Bullock T	32		2		5			
Burton	3							
De Zeeuw	38	4	6		5			
Dyer	28	7			2	1		
Eaden	38 + 2	1	4	1	5			
Fjortoft	9 + 10	3	5 + 1	4				
Goodman	5 + 3				2			
Hendrie	6 + 3	1	0 + 3		2			
Hignett	24	9			5	5		
Hristov	2 + 1							
Jones	28 + 1	3	2		3 + 1			
Krizan	1		1					
Leese	8		2					
Liddell	3 + 5		1 + 1					
McClare	23 + 7	3	4 + 1		5	1		
Marcelle	2 + 7		0 + 2		1			
Markstedt	2		0 + 1					
Moore	4 + 1							
Morgan	18 + 1		3		1			
Moses	33 + 1		5		5			
Parkin	0 + 2							
Piri	2							
Richardson	24 + 2		4		2 + 1			
Rose	2 + 2				1 + 2			
Sheridan	15 + 10	1	2 + 3		2	1		
Sheron	14 + 1	2			1 + 1			
Tinkler	21 + 4	3	2		3			
Turner	2 + 11	1						
Van der Laan	13 + 4	1	2	1	0 + 1			
Ward	17	12	6	3				

BARNSLEY cont.

	P/FL App	Goals	FLC App	Goals	FAC App	Goals	Others App	Goals
Watson	6		2					

BIRMINGHAM CITY (DIV 1: 4th)

	P/FL App	Goals	FLC App	Goals	FAC App	Goals	Others App	Goals
Ablett	23 + 3		4		1			
Adebola	33 + 6	13	4	2	1	1	1 + 1	1
Bass	9 + 2							
Bennett	10		4					
Bradbury	6 + 1						1 + 1	
Charlton	27 + 1		3					
Forinton	0 + 3	1	1 + 1					
Forster	8 + 25	5	2 + 2	1	0 + 1			
Furlong	24 + 5	13	1		1		2	
Gill	3							
Grainger	30 + 10	4	2 + 1		0 + 1		2	
Holdsworth	8	1					2	
Holland	7 + 7		1 + 4				1 + 1	
Hughes	20 + 8	3	1 + 1		0 + 1		1	
Hyde	13							
Johnson A	0 + 4		0 + 2					
Johnson M	43 + 2	4	4	2	1		2	
McCarthy	35 + 8		5		1		2	
Marsden	20	2	5	3				
Marsh	6 + 1				1			
Ndlovu	37 + 6	11	4	2	1		1 + 1	
O'Connor	35 + 2	4	4		1		2	
Poole	36		1		1		2	
Purse	11 + 9		2 + 1		1		0 + 1	
Robinson	20 + 11		2		1	1	1	
Rowett	42	5	4	2	1		2	
Wassall	0 + 3							

BLACKBURN ROVERS (PREM: 19th)

	P/FL App	Goals	FLC App	Goals	FAC App	Goals	Others App	Goals
Blake	9 + 2	3			1 + 2			
Broomes	8 + 5				4			
Carsley	7 + 1							
Croft	10 + 2		1		2 + 2			
Dahlin	2 + 3						0 + 1	
Dailly	14 + 3		2				2	
Davidson	34	1	2 + 1		2		1 + 1	
Davies	9 + 12	1	3		2	1	1	
Duff	18 + 10	1	3		3 + 1		1	
Dunn	10 + 5	1	1 + 1		2 + 1			
Fettis	2							
Filan	26		2		4			
Flitcroft	8	2					2	1
Flowers	10 + 1		1		0 + 1		2	
Gallacher	13 + 3	5	1		1			
Gillespie	13 + 3	1			4	1		
Henchoz	34		3		2		2	
Jansen	10 + 1	3						
Johnson	14 + 7	1	3				0 + 1	
Kenna	22 + 1		3		3	1	1	
Konde					0 + 1			
McAteer	13	1						
McKinlay	14 + 2		1		1		1	
Marcolin	5 + 5	1	2		3			
Peacock	27 + 3	1	2		3		2	
Perez	4 + 1	1			1		2	1
Sherwood	19	3	2	1	3		2	
Sutton	17	3	1	1	1		1	
Taylor	1 + 2						0 + 1	
Ward	17	5			2 + 1		2	
Wilcox	28 + 2	3			3	1	2	

BLACKPOOL (DIV 2: 14th)

	P/FL App	P/FL Goals	FLC App	FLC Goals	FAC App	FAC Goals	Others App	Others Goals
Aldridge	19+3	7	2	2	1	1		
Banks	35		4		1			
Bardsley	29		3				1	
Barnes K	2+2							
Barnes P	1						1	
Bent	21+18	1	2+1	1	0+1		1	
Blunt	1+1				1	1	1	
Brabin	5+2		2+1					
Bryan	37+4	1	2		1		1	
Bushell	31	3	4		1			
Butler	20		2		1			
Caig	10							
Carlisle	34+5	1	2+1				1	
Clarkson	44	9	4		1		1	
Coid	0+1							
Conroy	7+1		2	1			0+1	
Couzens	6							
Garvey	6+9	1						
Hills	27+1	1	2		1		1	
Hughes	31+2	1	4				1	
Jarrett	2				0+1		1	
Lawson	9	3						
Longworth							1	
Malkin	24+5	1	3+1	1				
Nowland	13+24	3	0+1					
Ormerod	30+10	8	2		1	1		
Patterson	7							
Robinson	2+3		0+1		1			
Rogan	9+5							
Shuttleworth	12+2	1	2		1			
Sturridge	5	1						
Thompson	18+4	2	2					
Watts	9							

BOLTON WANDERERS (DIV 1: 6th)

	P/FL App	P/FL Goals	FLC App	FLC Goals	FAC App	FAC Goals	Others App	Others Goals
Aljofree	1+3		1					
Banks	9						3	
Bergsson	15+2		3		1		0+2	
Blake	11+1	6	2+1	3				
Branagan	3		1					
Cox	42+2	4	5		1		3	
Elliott	14+8		1	1			3	
Fish	36	1	5		1		3	
Frandsen	44	8	4	1	1		3	1
Fullarton	1							
Gardner	19+11	2	2+1	1	0+1		3	
Gudjohnsen	8+6	5	0+1				3	
Gunnlaugsson	22+5	13	6	1	0+1			
Hansen	1+7						0+3	
Holdsworth	22+10	12	3+1		1			
Jaaskelainen	34		5		1			
Jensen	44	2	6	2	1		3	
Johansen	40+3	7	4+1	1	1		3	1
Newsome	6							
Phillips	14+1		3+1	1				
Sellars	22+3	2	2		1	1	0+1	
Strong	4+1	1	4					
Taylor R	32+6	15	3+3	1	1		3	2
Taylor S			0+1					
Todd	18+2		3				3	
Warhurst	17+3						0+2	
Whitlow	27+1		3+1		1			

BOURNEMOUTH (DIV 2: 7th)

	P/FL App	P/FL Goals	FLC App	FLC Goals	FAC App	FAC Goals	Others App	Others Goals
Bailey	30+2		5		4		3	
Berthe	12+3	2	4		1		0+1	
Boli	5+1		0+1		0+2		0+1	
Cox	46	5	5		3		3	1
Day	0+2							

BOURNEMOUTH cont.

	P/FL App	P/FL Goals	FLC App	FLC Goals	FAC App	FAC Goals	Others App	Others Goals
Dean	1+8							
Fletcher C	0+1							
Fletcher S	38+1	7	4	1	3		3	2
Griffin	1+5							
Hayter	16+4	2						
Howe	45	2	5	1	4	2	3	
Huck	6+2							
Hughes	43+1	2	5		4		3	
Jenkins	0+1							
Lovell	1+6							
O'Neill	18+6	3	2+2		1+3	1	1+2	
Ovendale	46		5		4		3	
Rawlinson	5+2							
Robinson	42	14	4	1	4	1	3	1
Rodriguez	0+5						0+2	
Stein	43	15	5	5	4	1	3	4
Tindall	6+11	1	1+2					
Town	1+9		0+3					
Vincent	31+1	2	5		4		3	
Warren	26+6	5	0+3		4		2	
Young	44	1	5		4		3	

BRADFORD CITY (DIV 1: 2nd)

	P/FL App	P/FL Goals	FLC App	FLC Goals	FAC App	FAC Goals	Others App	Others Goals
Beagrie	43	12	5	3	2			
Blake	35+4	16	3	1	2			
Bolland	2		2					
Dreyer	19+2		3+2					
Edinho	1+2		0+1					
Grant	1+4		1+1					
Jacobs	42+2	3	3		2			
Lawrence	33+2	2	2+1		2	1		
McCall	43	3	3		2			
Mills	44	23	4		2	1		
Moore	44	3	5	1	2			
O'Brien	19+12		3		1			
Pepper	5+4	1	2	1				
Ramage	0+3		0+1					
Rankin	15+12	4	2	1	0+1			
Sharpe	6+3	2						
Steiner			1					
Todd	14+1		2					
Walsh	46		5		2			
Watson	5+13	4	1+3					
Westwood	17+2	2			1+1			
Whalley	45	2	5					
Windass	6+6	3						
Wright	21+1		3		2			

BRENTFORD (DIV 3: 1st)

	P/FL App	P/FL Goals	FLC App	FLC Goals	FAC App	FAC Goals	Others App	Others Goals
Anderson	35+3	1	3		1+1		2	
Aspinall	17+2	2	4		1+1		1	
Bates	27	1	4	1	3	1	2	
Boxall	37+1	1	4		2		2	
Broughton	1							
Bryan	9+11	4			0+2		1+1	
Coyne	7		1					
Cullip	2		2					
Dearden	7		1		1		2	
Evans	14	3						
Folan	19+10	4	0+1		3	2	2	
Fortune-West	2+9				0+1		2+1	1
Freeman	16+6	6	4	1	3	2	1	
Hebel	6+9				2+1		1	
Hreidarsson	33	4			2		3	1
Jenkins	0+1							
Mahon	29	4					3	
Oatway	7+17		1+2	1	2		0+1	
Owusu	42+4	22	0+4	2	3		2+1	
Partridge	12+2	7						

BRENTFORD cont.

	P/FL App	P/FL Goals	FLC App	FLC Goals	FAC App	FAC Goals	Others App	Others Goals
Pearcey	17		3		2		1	
Powell	33	2	3				0+1	
Quinn	34+9	2	4		3	1	3	1
Rapley	3+9	3	0+4	1	0+1			
Rowlands	32+4	4	4		3		3	1
Scott	31+3	7	4	2			2	2
Watson	12		2		2		0+1	
Woodman	22							

BRIGHTON & HOVE ALBION (DIV 3: 17th)

	P/FL App	P/FL Goals	FLC App	FLC Goals	FAC App	FAC Goals	Others App	Others Goals
Allan	21+1	1	1				0+1	
Andrews	0+1							
Ansah	3+8						0+1	
Armstrong	21+7	2			1			
Arnott	27	2			1		1	
Atkinson	7		1					
Barker	33+10	10	1+1	1	1	1		
Bennett	37+1		2		1		1	
Browne S	2+1							
Browne T	13				1		1	
Culverhouse	35				1		1	
Davies	2+6							
Davis	0+1							
Doherty	3							
Hart	42+2	12	1+1		1			
Hinshelwood	3+1							
Hobson	12+1		1					
Ifejiagwa	2	1						
Johnson	30+4	2	1		1			
King	3							
McArthur	3							
McPherson	10							
Mayo	21+4	1	2		0+1	1	0+1	
Mills	1+1							
Minton	35	9	2				1	
Moralee	22+9	3	2		0+1	1	1	1
Nicholls	4	1						
Ormerod	27				1		1	
Ryan	3+2	1						
Smith	8+6		2					
Storer	14+9		1+1	1	1		1	
Sturgess	28+2				1		1	
Thomas G	2+1		1+1					
Thomas R	11+1	3						
Tuck	2		1					
Walton	19		2					
Westcott	0+4							

BRISTOL CITY (DIV 1: 24th)

	P/FL App	P/FL Goals	FLC App	FLC Goals	FAC App	FAC Goals	Others App	Others Goals
Akinbiyi	44	19	4	4	1			
Andersen B	10							
Andersen S	26+13	10	2+1	1	1			
Bell	33	5	3		1			
Brennan	29	1	2					
Brown	14							
Carey	40+1		3		1			
Cramb	4+9		1+1					
Doherty	15+8	1	2		1			
Dyche	4+2		1+1					
Edwards C	3							
Edwards R	19+4		1+2					
Goodridge	15+15	2	3		0+1			
Heaney	2+1							
Hewlett	8+2	1	2		1			
Hill	0+3							
Howells	8	1						
Hutchings	16+5	2	2+1	1	0+1			
Jordan	1							
Langan	1							

BRISTOL CITY cont.

	P/FL App	P/FL Goals	FLC App	FLC Goals	FAC App	FAC Goals	Others App	Others Goals
Locke	26+2	3	3		1			
Meechan	0+1							
Murray	27+5	3	2+2		1			
Phillips	15				1			
Pinamonte	1	1						
Sebok	10+2							
Shail	21+3				1			
Taylor	8							
Thorpe	9+7	2	1+1	1				
Tinnion	32+3	2	4					
Tistimetanu	8				1			
Torpey	19+2	3			1			
Watts	16+1	1	3+1					
Welch	21		4					
Zwijnenberg	1+2		1					

BRISTOL ROVERS (DIV 2: 13th)

	P/FL App	P/FL Goals	FLC App	FLC Goals	FAC App	FAC Goals	Others App	Others Goals
Andreasson	4+1		2					
Andrews	3							
Basford	6+3							
Bennett	1+3	1						
Challis	38		2		6		1	
Collett	3							
Cureton	46	25	1+1	1	6	2	1	
Ellington	1+9	1						
Foster	41+2	1	2		6		1	
Hayles	17	9	2	1				
Hillier	13							
Holloway	33+4		2		4			
Ipoua	15+9	3	1+1		3+1		1	
Johnston	1							
Jones	32		2		6		1	
Kuipers	1							
Lee	10+1	1			3	1		
Leoni	25+5		0+1		4	1	1	
Low	5+3				0+1			
McKeever	5+2							
Meaker	17+3	2	2		4+1			
Penrice	10+16	1	0+1		2+3	1		
Pethick	9							
Phillips	2							
Pritchard	11+1				2+1		0+1	
Roberts	32+5	16	2		5	7	1	
Shore	18+6	2			3+1	2	1	
Smith	11+3		1		2+1			
Thomson	21							
Tillson	18+1	2						
Trees	33+3		1+1		6		1	
Trought	6+3				3+1		1	
Williams	9							
Zabek	9+2		2		1+1	1	1	

BURNLEY (DIV 2: 15th)

	P/FL App	P/FL Goals	FLC App	FLC Goals	FAC App	FAC Goals	Others App	Others Goals
Armstrong	40	1						
Blatherwick	3		2					
Branch	14+6	1						
Brass	33+1		2		1		1	
Carr-Lawton	2+2		0+2				1	
Cook	12	1						
Cooke	36	9	1	1			1	
Cowan	12	1						
Crichton	29						1	
Davis	19	3						
Devenney							0+1	
Eastwood	6+7	1			1		1	
Ford	11+1				1		1	
Henderson	0+7	1	0+2				0+1	
Hewlett	2						1	
Heywood	11+2				1		1	

BURNLEY cont.

	P/FL App	P/FL Goals	FLC App	FLC Goals	FAC App	FAC Goals	Others App	Others Goals
Howey	3		2					
Jepson	3+12	1	2					
Johnrose	9+3	1						
Kval					1			
Little	32+2	5	2		1			
Maylett	0+17						1	
Mellon	20	2						
Moore	10+2		1+1					
Morgan	17		2		1			
O'Kane	8							
Parks			2					
Payton	39+1	20	1	1	1	2		
Pickering	21	1						
Reid	30+1	3			1		1	
Robertson	19+5	1	0+1					
Scott	9+5				1			
Smith C	5+5		1					
Smith P	11+1		2					
Swan	11+6							
Vindheim	8	2			1		1	
Ward	17							
Weller	1		1					
Williams	2		1					
Williamson	0+1							
Winstanley	1							

BURY (DIV 1: 22nd)

	P/FL App	P/FL Goals	FLC App	FLC Goals	FAC App	FAC Goals	Others App	Others Goals
Armstrong	0+2		0+2	1				
Avdiu	0+6	1						
Baldry	0+5							
Barnes	6+2							
Barrick	16+4	1	5					
Billy	35+2				1			
Bullock	12	1						
Daws	46	2	5	1	1			
D'Jaffo	35+2	8	4+1	1	1			
Ellis	3+13	2	2+2					
Forrest	0+1				0+1			
Foster	6+1							
Grobbelaar	1							
Hall	7							
James	10+7	2	0+1					
Jemson	6+8		0+2		0+1			
Johnrose	26+1	2	5	2	1			
Kiely	45		5		1			
Lilley	5	1						
Littlejohn	11+9	1			1			
Lucketti	43	1	5		1			
Matthews	12+4	2	3+2	3				
Patterson	9+4		4					
Preece	19+20	3	4+1		0+1			
Redmond	26		4					
Rigby	1+1		0+1					
Serrant	15							
Souter	0+1							
Swailes C	43	3	5					
Swailes D			0+2		1			
West	18+5	3			1			
Williams	14+1	1			1			
Woodward	36+1	1	4		1			

CAMBRIDGE UNITED (DIV 3: 2nd)

	P/FL App	P/FL Goals	FLC App	FLC Goals	FAC App	FAC Goals	Others App	Others Goals
Andrews	1+1							
Ashbee	25+6	4	2		2		2+1	
Benjamin	37+5	10	5	4	2	1	3	2
Bruce	2+2							
Butler	46	17	5	2	2	1	2+1	1
Campbell	45	4	5		2	1	3	
Chenery	44		5		2		3	

CAMBRIDGE UNITED cont.

	P/FL App	P/FL Goals	FLC App	FLC Goals	FAC App	FAC Goals	Others App	Others Goals
Duncan	45	1	5		2		3	
Eustace	15+1							
Joseph	28+1		4		0+1		3	
Kyd	5+7		2+1		1		2	
McAvoy	1							
McCammon	1+1							
MacKenzie	3+1	1						
McMahon	1+2							
McNeil	4+2		1		2			
Marshall	19		1		2			
Mustoe	28+6	3	3		0+1		2	
Preece	5+9	1	0+1				1	
Russell	36+1	7	5		2		2	
Taylor	29+11	17	3+1	1	1+1		1+1	1
Van Heusden	27		4				3	
Walker	7+14	3					1+2	1
Wanless	45	8	5		2		2	
Wilde	1							
Youngs	6+4						0+2	

CARDIFF CITY (DIV 3: 3rd)

	P/FL App	P/FL Goals	FLC App	FLC Goals	FAC App	FAC Goals	Others App	Others Goals
Allen	3+1						1	
Bonner	21+4	1	2				1	
Bowen	10+7	2			0+1			
Brazier	11							
Cadette					0+1		0+1	
Carpenter	41+1	1	2		4			
Delaney	28		2		5	1		
Earnshaw	1+4	1	0+1		0+1			
Eckhardt	31+4	5	0+2	1	3	1	1	
Ford	25				5			
Fowler	32+5	3	1		5	3		
Hallworth	41		2		5		1	
Hill	14+12	2			1+2		1	
Jarman	2+4	1					1	
Kelly	5							
Legg	18+6	2			0+3			
Middleton	20+15	4			5	2	1	
Mitchell	46		2		5		1	
Nugent	40+1	15	1+1		5	3		
O'Sullivan	38+4	2	1+1		5		1	
Penney	1		0+1					
Phillips	2		2					
Roberts	0+4		2		0+2		0+1	
Saville	2	1	1					
Thomas	16+8	4			0+2		1	
Williams	25+18	12	2	1	5	3	1	
Young	33	1	2		2			

CARLISLE UNITED (DIV 3: 23rd)

	P/FL App	P/FL Goals	FLC App	FLC Goals	FAC App	FAC Goals	Others App	Others Goals
Anthony	21+5		1				1+1	
Bagshaw	5+4							
Barr	21+2		2				1	
Bass	8+1							
Boertien	8	1						
Bowman	24	1			1		1	
Bridge-Wilkinson	4+3							
Brightwell	41	4	2		1		1	
Caig	37		2				2	
Clark	35+1				1		2	
Couzens	10+5		0+1				1	
Dobie	26+7	6	1+1				2	
Douglas	0+1				1			
Finney	22+11	6	1+1				2	
Glass	3	1						
Hopper	17+6		0+1		1		2	
Knight	6							
Kubicki	7		2					
McAlindon	3+13		1					

CARLISLE UNITED cont.

	P/FL App	Goals	FLC App	Goals	FAC App	Goals	Others App	Goals
McGregor	9+ 1	3					1	
Mendes	5+ 1	1						
Ormerod	5						1+1	
Paterson	18+ 1	1	2				0+1	
Prokas	33+ 1		1		1		2	
Scott	7	3						
Searle	43+ 2	2	2		1		1+1	1
Skelton			0+1					
Stevens	31 +10	9	2		1	1		
Thorpe	6+ 7		1		0+1			
Tracey	10+ 1	3						
Varty	5+ 1		0+1					
Whitehead	36+ 1		2		1		2	

CHARLTON ATHLETIC (PREM: 18th)

	P/FL App	Goals	FLC App	Goals	FAC App	Goals	Others App	Goals
Allen			0+1					
Barnes	2 +10							
Barness	0+ 3							
Bowen	2+ 4							
Bright	1+ 5	1	0+1		0+1			
Brown	13+ 5		0+2					
Holmes					0+1			
Hunt	32+ 2	7	2		1			
Ilic	23		2		1			
Jones K	13+ 9	1	3					
Jones S	7 +18	1	1+1					
Kinsella	38	3	1		1			
Konchesky	1+ 1							
Lisbie	0+ 1		0+1					
Mendonca	19+ 6	8	3					
Mills	36	2	3		1			
Mortimer	10+ 7	1	2+1	1				
Newton	13+ 3		1+1	1	0+1			
Parker	0+ 4		0+1		1			
Petterson	7+ 3		1					
Powell	38		3		1			
Pringle	15+ 3	3						
Redfearn	29+ 1	3	2	1	1			
Robinson	27+ 3	2	3		1			
Royce	8							
Rufus	27	1	3		1			
Stuart	9	3						
Tiler	27	1			1			
Youds	21+ 1	2	3	1	1			

CHELSEA (PREM: 3rd)

	P/FL App	Goals	FLC App	Goals	FAC App	Goals	Others App	Goals
Babayaro	26+ 2	3	3		4+1		7+1	1
Casiraghi	10	1					3+2	
Clement			0+2					
De Goey	35				6		8	
Desailly	30+ 1				6		8	1
Di Matteo	26+ 4	2	1+1		4+2	1	8	
Duberry	18+ 7		3		2		3	
Ferrer	30		0+1		2		8	
Flo	18 +12	10	2+1	1	2+1		4+5	2
Forssell	4+ 6	1			1+2	2		
Goldbaek	13 +10	5	2		2+4			
Harley			0+1					
Hitchcock	2+ 1							
Kharine	1		3				1	
Lambourde	12+ 5		2+1		2		2+1	1
Laudrup	5+ 2						3+1	1
Leboeuf	33	4	2	1	4	1	7	1
Le Saux	30+ 1				6		9	
Morris	14+ 4	1	2		5		1+1	
Myers	1				0+2		0+1	
Newton	1+ 6				0+1		0+1	
Nicholls	0+ 9		2		0+3		0+2	
Percassi			0+1					

CHELSEA cont.

	P/FL App	Goals	FLC App	Goals	FAC App	Goals	Others App	Goals
Petrescu	23+ 9	4	3		4		4+2	
Poyet	21+ 7	11	3	2			3+4	1
Terry	0+ 2		0+1		2+1		1	
Vialli	9	1	3	6	3	2	5	1
Wise	21+ 1		2		5	1	8	1
Zola	35+ 2	13			6	1	6	1

CHESTER CITY (DIV 3: 14th)

	P/FL App	Goals	FLC App	Goals	FAC App	Goals	Others App	Goals
Aiston	11						1	
Alsford	9+ 1	1						
Beckett	24+ 4	11	1	2				
Bennett	5+ 2	1	1+1					
Brown	23		3					
Carson	1+ 1							
Conroy	11+ 4	3						
Crosby	41	4	3		1		1	
Cross	33+ 2	1	4		1		1	
Cutler	23		1		1		1	
Davidson	40	1	4		1			
Fisher	7+ 1							
Flitcroft	42	6	4		1		1	
Jones	2+ 6		0+1		0+1			
Lancaster	8+ 3				0+1		0+1	
Moss	5+ 2							
Murphy	41+ 1	12	4		1		1	
Priest	35	4	3		1			
Reid	16+ 6	1	2		1		1	
Richardson	41+ 2	3	3		1		1	
Shelton	5 +18	1	1				1	1
Smeets	1+ 2							
Smith	32	2	4	1			1	
Thomas	3+ 3	3	1+2					
Woods	41+ 2	1	4		1		1	
Wright	6 +12	1	1+1		1			

CHESTERFIELD (DIV 2: 9th)

	P/FL App	Goals	FLC App	Goals	FAC App	Goals	Others App	Goals
Beaumont	35+ 4	2	3+1				2	
Blatherwick	9+ 5	1					2	
Breckin	44		2	4			2	
Carss	2+ 2							
Curtis	24	3	2		1		1	
Ebdon	39+ 1	1	1		1+1		1	
Eustace					0+1			
Hewitt	40	2	3		1		1	1
Holland	32+ 1	3	4	2	1			
Howard	34+ 3	9	4	1	1		2	
Jules	19+ 4		2+1		1		1+1	
Leaning	2		2					
Lee	14+ 8	1			0+1		0+2	
Lenagh	6+ 4	1					1	
Lomas	5+ 2		1				0+2	
Mercer	44		2		1		2	
Morris	0+ 1							
Nicholson	23+ 1						1	
Pearce	0+ 1							
Perkins	32+ 2	1	4		1		1	1
Reeves	37+ 3	10	3	1	1		2	
Simpkins	0+ 1							
Wilkinson	18+ 5	6	2		0+1		2	1
Williams	40	3	3		1		1	1
Willis	7 +10		4				0+1	

COLCHESTER UNITED (DIV 2: 18th)

	P/FL App	Goals	FLC App	Goals	FAC App	Goals	Others App	Goals
Abrahams	13 +14	2	2	1				
Adcock	0+ 6		0+1		0+1	1		
Allen	4	1						
Aspinall	15	3						
Betts	22+ 6	2	2				1	
Branston	0+ 1							

COLCHESTER UNITED cont.

	P/FL App	Goals	FLC App	Goals	FAC App	Goals	Others App	Goals
Buckle	39+ 4	2	2		1		1	
Dozzell	23+ 6	4			1		0+1	
Dublin	2							
Duguid	23 +10	4	0+1		0+1			
Dunne	32+ 4		0+1		1		1	
Emberson	37		2		1		1	
Fernandes	8							
Forbes	8+ 7	2	0+1		1		1	
Fumaca	1+ 5							
Germain	1+ 5							
Greene	42	8	2		1		1	
Gregory D	43+ 1	11	2	2	1		1	1
Gregory N	29+ 9	4	2				1	
Haydon	7+ 6	1	2		0+1			
Launders	1							
Lock	14+ 9	1			1		0+1	
Lua Lua	6+ 7	1						
Okafor	0+ 1							
Opara	0+ 1							
Pounewatchy	15	1						
Rainford	0+ 1							
Richard	10							
Sale	21 +10	2	2		1		1	
Skelton	7+ 2							
Stamps	19+ 2		2		1		0+1	
Walker	1							
Wiles	0+ 1							
Wilkins	25+ 1	2						
Williams	38+ 1				1		1	

COVENTRY CITY (PREM: 15th)

	P/FL App	Goals	FLC App	Goals	FAC App	Goals	Others App	Goals
Aloisi	7+ 9	5			0+2			
Boateng	29+ 4	4	3	1	3	1		
Boland			1					
Breen	21+ 4		2		1			
Brightwell			1					
Burrows	23		2		3			
Clement	6+ 6		1+1		1+1			
Dublin	10	3	2	1				
Edworthy	16+ 6				1			
Froggatt	23	1			3	2		
Gioacchini	0+ 3							
Hall M	2+ 3		1					
Hall P	2+ 7		2	1				
Haworth	1							
Hedman	36		3		3			
Huckerby	31+ 3	9	2		3	3		
Jackson	0+ 3							
Konjic	3+ 1							
McAllister	29	3	1		3	1		
McSheffrey	0+ 1							
Nilsson	28				2			
Ogrizovic	2							
Quinn	6+ 1		1					
Shaw	36+ 1	3			3			
Shilton	1+ 4		1+1		0+1			
Soltvedt	21+ 6	2	0+3	1	2+1			
Strachan			0+1					
Telfer	30+ 2	2	2		0+3	1		
Wallemme	4+ 2		2					
Whelan	31	10	2	1	3	2		
Williams	20+ 2		1+1		2			

CREWE ALEXANDRA (DIV 1: 18th)

	P/FL App	Goals	FLC App	Goals	FAC App	Goals	Others App	Goals
Anthrobus	16+ 5	3	1+1					
Bignot	26		5		1			
Charnock	40+ 4	2	5		1			
Collins	5+ 1	1	1					
Foran	4+ 2				1			

CREWE ALEXANDRA cont.

	P/FL App Goals	FLC App Goals	FAC App Goals	Others App Goals
Foster	0+1	0+1		
Jack	37+2 9	2 2	1	
Johnson	42 4	3	1 1	
Kearton	46	5	1	
Lightfoot	19+3 2	2		
Little	27+10 10	5 2	1	
Lovelock		0+1		
Lunt	6+12 1	0+3	0+1	
Macauley	12+8 1			
Murphy	16 1			
Newell	1+3			
Rivers	38+5 7	4 3	1	
Smith P	0+4	3	0+1	
Smith S	46 4	5	1	
Street	4+19 2	1+1	0+1	
Unsworth	15+9	3	1	
Walton	38	4		
Wicks	4+2 1			
Wright D	20 1	0+1		
Wright J	44 5	5	1	

CRYSTAL PALACE (DIV 1: 14th)

	P/FL App Goals	FLC App Goals	FAC App Goals	Others App Goals
Amsalem	6+4	1+1		
Austin	17+3 1	4		
Bent	3+9	0+2	0+1	
Bradbury	19+3 4		1 1	
Burton-Godwin	18+5 1	1		
Carlisle	2+4			
Crowe	8			
Curcic	4+11 4	2		
Del Rio	1+1	0+1		
Digby	18	3		
Dyer	5+1 2	2+1		
Edworthy	1+2	0+1		
Evans	0+4			
Foster	30+2 2		1	
Frampton	4+2			
Fullarton	7			
Graham	0+1			
Harris	0+1			
Hibburt	0+2			
Hreidarsson	6+1	3 1		
Jansen	18 7	4	0+1	
Jihai	22+1	1	1	
Linighan	19+1	1+2	0+1	
Lombardo	19 3	4 2		
McKenzie	10+6 1			
Martin	2+1			
Miller	28	1	1	
Moore	23 3		1	
Morrison	27+10 12	1+2 1	1	
Mullins	38+2 5	4	1	
Padovano	0+2			
Petric	18 1			
Rizzo	13+6 1	1		
Rodger	18 1	2	1	
Shipperley	3 1	1		
Smith	25+1 1	3	1	
Svensson	6+2 1			
Thomson	11+5			
Turner	0+2			
Tuttle	17+5 2	2	1	
Warhurst	5 1	1		
Woozley	7			
Zhiyi	28+1 2	2 1	1	

DARLINGTON (DIV 3: 11th)

	P/FL App Goals	FLC App Goals	FAC App Goals	Others App Goals
Atkinson	42+1 1	2	2 1	2
Barnard	29+4 1	2	3 1	2

DARLINGTON cont.

	P/FL App Goals	FLC App Goals	FAC App Goals	Others App Goals
Bennett	26+3 4		3 1	1
Brumwell	24+13	0+1	1+1	2
Campbell	6+3 1			1
Carruthers	11 2			
Carter	1 1		0+1	
Costa	0+3 1			0+1
De Vos	12 2	2 1		
Dorner	9+13 3	2	1+2 1	1
Duffield	10+4 2			
Ellison	3+17			0+2
Gabbiadini	40 24	2	3	1+1 1
Gaughan	12+11 2	2	3	1
Heckinbottom	10			
Himsworth	14 1			
Hope	8	1		
Kilty	0+2			
Kubicki	2+1			0+1
Leah	7 1		1+1	1
Liddle	44 3	2	3	2
Naylor	32+10 9	2	3	2
Oliver	33+3 1		1+1	1+2
Pepper	5+1	2		
Preece	46	2	3	1
Reed	25+4 2		2	0+1
Roberts	10+14 5	0+2 1	1	1
Samways				1
Scott	4			
Shutt	8+6 2	0+2		
Tutill	33+3		3	2

DERBY COUNTY (PREM: 8th)

	P/FL App Goals	FLC App Goals	FAC App Goals	Others App Goals
Baiano	17+5 4	3	3 2	
Beck	6+1 1			
Boertien	0+1			
Bohinen	29+3		3	
Borbokis	3+1			
Bridge-Wilkinson	0+1			
Burton	14+7 9	1	5 3	
Carbonari	28+1 5		4	
Carsley	20+2 1	2+1	5	
Christie	0+2			
Dailly	1			
Delap	21+2	3 1	0+1	
Dorigo	17+1 1	1	3 2	
Elliott	7+4	1+1	1+1	
Eranio	18+7 2	2	4 1	
Harper	6+21 1	0+3	0+3 1	
Hoult	23		3	
Hunt	0+6 1		0+3	
Kozluk	3+4	1	1+1	
Launders	0+1			
Laursen	37	3	4	
Murray	0+4			
Poom	15+2	3	2	
Powell	30+3	3	1+1	
Prior	33+1 1	2	4	
Robinson	0+1			
Schnoor	20+3 2	2	3	
Stimac	14	1	3	
Sturridge	23+6 5	3 1	4	
Wanchope	33+2 9	2+1 1	2	

EVERTON (PREM: 14th)

	P/FL App Goals	FLC App Goals	FAC App Goals	Others App Goals
Bakayoko	17+6 4	2 1	1+2 2	
Ball	36+1 3	3+1	3	
Barmby	20+4 3	1+1	4 1	
Bilic	4		1	
Branch	1+6		0+2	
Cadamarteri	11+19 4	3+1	3+1	

EVERTON cont.

	P/FL App Goals	FLC App Goals	FAC App Goals	Others App Goals
Campbell	8 9			
Cleland	16+2	2+1	1	
Collins	19+1 1	2+2 1		
Dacourt	28+2 2	4 1	2	
Degn	0+4			
Dunne	15+1	2	2	
Farley	0+1			
Farrelly	0+1			
Ferguson	13 4	4 1		
Gemmill	7 1			
Gerrard		1		
Grant	13+3	1+1	3+1	
Hutchison	29+4 3	3+1 1	4	
Jeffers	11+4 6		2 1	
Jevons	0+1			
Madar	2	0+1		
Materazzi	26+1 1	4 1	2	
Milligan	0+3			
Myhre	38	3	4	
O'Kane	2		1+2	
Oster	6+3	1+1	2+2 1	
Short	22	2		
Spencer	2+1			
Thomas	0+1			
Tiler	2	1		
Unsworth	33+1 1	3	3 1	
Ward	4+2	1	2	
Watson	22	1 1	3	
Weir	11+3		1	

EXETER CITY (DIV 3: 12th)

	P/FL App Goals	FLC App Goals	FAC App Goals	Others App Goals
Baddeley	23		2	
Bayes	41	2	4	2
Blake	4+3		1	
Breslan	24+10 4	2	1+2	2
Clark	8+2	2	2+1	2 1
Crowe	3+6	1		
Curran	30+4 4	2	3	2
Flack	38+6 11	1+1	4 2	2 2
Fry	27+5 2	0+2	2+1	1
Gale	21+6	2	1	1+1
Gardner	23+4	0+1	3+1 1	1
Gittens	44 2	2	3 1	2
Holloway	27+7 1	0+1	1	1
McConnell	15+7 5		0+2	
Potter	5			
Power	40	2	4	2
Quailey	8+4 2			2 1
Rees	44 1	2	4	1
Richardson	39+1 2	2 2	4 1	1
Rowbotham	28+4 6	2	4 2	
Smith	0+1			
Speakman	0+1			
Tosh	8+2 2			
Waugh	0+7			0+1
Wilkinson	6+12 2		1+1	0+2

FULHAM (DIV 2: 1st)

	P/FL App Goals	FLC App Goals	FAC App Goals	Others App Goals
Albert	12+1 2			
Arendse				1
Beardsley	11+2 3	4+1 1		
Betsy	1+6	0+1	0+1	1
Bracewell	25+1 1	4	5	
Brazier	1+1		2+1	1
Brevett	45 1	5	5	
Brooker	0+1			0+1
Coleman	45 4	5 1	7	
Collins	18+3 2	4	3+1	1
Cornwall	1+3 1	1		

FULHAM cont.

	P/FL App	P/FL Goals	FLC App	FLC Goals	FAC App	FAC Goals	Others App	Others Goals
Davis	1+5		1+1		1			
Finnan	21+1	2			4		1	
Hayles	26+4	8			4	1		
Hayward	42	3	4+1		6+1	2		
Horsfield	26+2	15			5+1	2		
Keller	0+1						1	
Lawrence	1		0+1					
Lehmann	16+10	2	5	2	2+2	1	1	
McAnespie	1+2							
Moody	2+5	4	0+1					
Morgan	32+2	5	5	1	3	2		
Neilson	3+1	1	0+1		2		1	
Peschisolido	19+14	7	1+1	1	5	2		
Salako	7+3	1	2	1	2+2		1	
Scott	2+1							
Smith J	9	1						
Smith N	20+9	1	0+1		3+3			
Symons	45	11	5		7			
Taylor	46		5		7			
Trollope	17+3	2	1+1		1+3		1	1
Uhlenbeek	11+12	1	3		3+2		1	

GILLINGHAM (DIV 2: 4th)

	P/FL App	P/FL Goals	FLC App	FLC Goals	FAC App	FAC Goals	Others App	Others Goals
Asaba	40+1	20			1		7	2
Ashby	38	1	2		1		4	
Bartram	44		2				7	
Brown	2+2						0+1	
Browning	1+3							
Bryant	16+7		1+1		0+1		3	
Butler	4+3		1					
Butters	23	3					7	
Carr	22+8	2	2		1		3+1	
Dobson	2							
Edge	1+7				1		2	
Elliott	4+1							
Galloway	19+6	3	1		0+1		5	
Hessenthaler	36+3	7	2		1		5	2
Hodge	7+27	1	2		0+1		2+4	
Lisbie	4+3	4						
Nosworthy	0+3						0+1	
Patterson	42	2			1		4	
Pennock	39+1	1	1		1		6	1
Pinnock	0+4		1+1				0+2	
Rolling	1							
Saunders	28+6	5					2+3	
Smith	45	6	2		1		6	1
Southall	34+8	4	0+1		1		7	
Stannard	2				1			
Statham							0+1	
Taylor	43	16	1		1		7	5
Williams	9+1		2					

GRIMSBY TOWN (DIV 1: 11th)

	P/FL App	P/FL Goals	FLC App	FLC Goals	FAC App	FAC Goals	Others App	Others Goals
Ashcroft	21+6	3	2	1				
Black	29+13	4	4		0+1			
Bloomer	0+4							
Buckley	0+2							
Burnett	15+5	2	2+1					
Butterfield	9+3		1+1					
Chapman	0+1							
Clare	7+15		0+2	1				
Coldicott	35+2	3	2		1			
Croudson	2							
Davison	35		5		1			
Dobbin	0+4		0+1					
Donovan	27+1		5		1			
Gallimore	43		5		1			
Groves	46	14	5	1	1			
Handyside	30+1	2	2+1		1			

GRIMSBY TOWN cont.

	P/FL App	P/FL Goals	FLC App	FLC Goals	FAC App	FAC Goals	Others App	Others Goals
Lester	26+7	4	5		1			
Lever	15+9		1		0+1			
Livingstone	15+8		3+2		1			
Love	9							
McDermott	37		5		1	1		
Nogan	30+8	2	3+1	1	1			
Smith D	30+1	5	2+2		1			
Smith R	29+1		5		1			
Widdrington	16+10	1	3+2		0+1			

HALIFAX TOWN (DIV 3: 10th)

	P/FL App	P/FL Goals	FLC App	FLC Goals	FAC App	FAC Goals	Others App	Others Goals
Bradshaw	41	4	3		1		1	1
Brown	32+8		3		1		0+1	
Butler	33	1	2		1		1	
Carter	9+1						1	
Duerden	1+1		0+1					
Etherington	4						1	
Grant	0+3						0+1	
Guinan	12	2						
Hanson	19+12	2	4	2			2	1
Horsfield	10	7	4	1				
Hulme	30	4	4				2	
Jackson	16	3						
Lucas	29+7		3		1		2	1
Martin	37		4		1		1	
Murphy J	21+2	1			1		1	
Murphy S	10+2		2		0+1		0+1	
Newton	8+6	1					0+1	
O'Regan	15+4	2	2+1					
Overson			0+1					
Paterson	19+5	10	1+1	1	1			
Power	14+4	4						
Sertori	39+1		4		1		2	
Stansfield	12	1					2	
Stoneman	40	5	4		1		1	
Thackeray	37+1	5	4		1		1	
Williams	18+6	6	0+1		1		2	2
Wills							1	

HARTLEPOOL UNITED (DIV 3: 22nd)

	P/FL App	P/FL Goals	FLC App	FLC Goals	FAC App	FAC Goals	Others App	Others Goals
Baker	3+10	2					0+1	
Barron	38	1	2		1		3	
Beardsley	22	2					2	
Beech	16	9	2					
Brightwell	8+9	1	0+1		1+1		0+1	1
Clark	36+3	2	2		2		3	
Davies	2+1							
Di Lella	18+5	2	1		2		1	
Dunwell	0+1							
Elliott	5							
Evans	0+1							
Freestone	9+1	3						
Heckinbottom	5	1						
Hollund	41		2		2		3	
Howard	25+3	5	1+1		2	2	2	1
Hughes	6+2							
Hutt	2+2				0+1		1	
Ingram	37+1	4	2		2		3	
Irvine	10+8	1	1+1		0+1		0+2	
Jones	12	1						
Knowles	46		2		2		3	
Lee	23+1	3	2		1		2	
McDonald	5		1					
McGuckin	8							
McKinnon	7							
Midgley	26+3	7	2		2	1	3	
Miller	29+5	4	2		2	1	3	2
Miotto	5							
Pemberton	0+4		0+1					

HARTLEPOOL UNITED cont.

	P/FL App	P/FL Goals	FLC App	FLC Goals	FAC App	FAC Goals	Others App	Others Goals
Rush	5+5				0+1		0+1	
Smith	2+1						1	
Stephenson	24+3	2	0+1		2		2	
Stokoe	15+5				1+1		1	
Strodder	13							
Westwood	3+1							

HUDDERSFIELD TOWN (DIV 1: 10th)

	P/FL App	P/FL Goals	FLC App	FLC Goals	FAC App	FAC Goals	Others App	Others Goals
Allison	44	9	3	2	4	2		
Armstrong	13	1						
Baldry	8+5				1+1			
Barnes	2+13	1	0+3		1+1			
Beech	13+4	2			2	2		
Beresford	13+6	2	0+2		1+1			
Browning	2+4		1+2					
Collins	22+1		4		3			
Cowan	5				2			
Dalton	7+2	3	3+1	1				
Dyson	10+4	1			2			
Edmondson	1+2				2+1			
Edwards	45	2	4		5			
Facey	5+15	3			0+2			
Francis	3							
Gray	28+6	1	2+1		5			
Hamilton	10	1						
Heary	3							
Hessey	7+3				1			
Horne	20	1	4					
Jackson	5							
Jenkins	36	1	4		3			
Johnson	36	4	4	1	5			
Lawson	2+4	2						
Mattis	0+2							
Morrison	12		3					
Phillips	15+8	1			5			
Richardson	13+2							
Schofield	1							
Stewart	43	22	4	2	5	2		
Thornley	32+3	4	4		3	1		
Vaesen	43		4		5			
Vincent	7							

HULL CITY (DIV 3: 21st)

	P/FL App	P/FL Goals	FLC App	FLC Goals	FAC App	FAC Goals	Others App	Others Goals
Alcide	17	3						
Bolder	0+1							
Bonner	1	1						
Brabin	21	4						
Brown	38+4	11	4	3	3		2	
Darby	4+4							
D'Auria	42	4	4		2		2	1
Dewhurst	4+4				1	1		
Dudley	4+3	2						
Edwards	28+2		2+1		3		2	
Ellington	3+3		1+1		0+2		0+1	
Faulconbridge	4+6				1		1+1	
French	9+6		2+1		1		0+1	
Gage	2+1		1		0+1			
Gibson	4							
Greaves	18+7		2		3		0+1	
Harrison	8							
Hateley	8+4	3	0+1					
Hawes	18+1		4		1+1		0+1	
Hocking	24+2	1	4		3		2	
Joyce	28+1	2			2		1	
McGinty	22+10	4	4	1	2+1	1	2	
Mann	16+4	1	3+1		1			
Morley	1+11		1+1		2	1	0+1	
Oakes	19						1	
Peacock	13+1	2	3+1		0+1		2	

HULL CITY cont.

	P/FL App Goals	FLC App Goals	FAC App Goals	Others App Goals
Perry	7+1			2
Rioch	10+3	1 1	2 1	1
Saville	3			
Swales	20+2			1
Whitney	21 1			1
Whittle	24 1		2	
Whitworth	18 2	4	1	
Williams	24+1 1			1 1
Wilson	23	4	3	1

IPSWICH TOWN (DIV 1: 3rd)

	P/FL App Goals	FLC App Goals	FAC App Goals	Others App Goals
Abou	5 1			
Bramble	2+2		0+1	
Brown	0+1			
Clapham	45+1 3	3+1	2	2
Cundy	1+3			
Dyer	36+1 5	4	2	2 2
Harewood	5+1 1			
Hodges	0+4			
Holland	46 5	4 2	2	2 2
Holster	1+9	0+1	0+1	
Hunt	2+4			
Johnson	41+1 13	4 1	2	2
Kennedy	6+1		1	
Logan	0+2			
Magilton	19 3			2
Mason		0+1 1		
Mathie	2+6 1	1+1 1		
Mowbray	40 2	2	2	2
Naylor	10+20 5	1+1	1+1	0+2
Petta	26+6 2	4	2	1
Scowcroft	29+3 13	2 1		2
Sonner	0+4	0+2		
Stockwell	23+7 2	4 1	1	0+2
Tanner	13+6	1+1	0+1	
Taricco	16 1	4 1		
Thetis	29+2 2	2 1	2	1+1
Venus	44 9	4	2	2
Vernazza	2			
Wilnis	17+1 1		1	2
Wright	46	4	2	2

LEEDS UNITED (PREM: 4th)

	P/FL App Goals	FLC App Goals	FAC App Goals	Others App Goals
Batty	10			
Bowyer	35 9	2	4	4
Granville	7+2	1	3	0+1
Haaland	24+5 1		3+1	2+1
Halle	14+3 2	1	2+1	2
Harte	34+1 4	1	5 2	3
Hasselbaink	36 18	2	5 1	4 1
Hiden	14 1			4
Hopkin	32+2 4	2	5	4
Jones	3+5		0+1	
Kewell	36+2 6	2 2	5 1	4
Knarvik			0+1	
Korsten	4+3 2		2+1	
Lilley	0+2			0+1
McPhail	11+6	1		2
Martyn	34	1	5	4
Molenaar	17 2	2		4
Radebe	29	1	3	3
Ribeiro	7+6 1	1	1 1	1+1
Robinson	4+1	1		
Sharpe	2+2			1+2
Smith	15+7 7		2+2 2	4
Wetherall	14+7		4 1	4
Wijnhard	11+7 3	1	1+1 1	1+3
Woodgate	25 2	2	5	1

LEICESTER CITY (PREM: 10th)

	P/FL App Goals	FLC App Goals	FAC App Goals	Others App Goals
Arphexad	2+2	1		
Campbell	1+11	1+1	1	
Cottee	29+2 10	5 5	1 1	
Elliott	37 3	8	2	
Fenton	3+6	1+1 1		
Gunnlaugsson	5+4			
Guppy	38 4	8	2 1	
Heskey	29+1 6	8 3	2	
Impey	17+1		1	
Izzet	31 5	5 1	2	
Kaamark	15+4	1+1		
Keller	36	7	2	
Lennon	37 1	8 1	2	
Marshall	6+4 3	0+1	0+1	
Miller	1+3			
Oakes	2+1			
Parker	2+5	3+1 1	0+2	
Savage	29+5 1	5+2		
Sinclair	30+1 1	6	2 1	
Taggart	9+6	5+1 1	1+1	
Ullathorne	25	7+1	2 1	
Walsh	17+5 3	5	1	
Wilson	1+8	1+4 1		
Zagorakis	16+3 1	3+2	1+1	

LEYTON ORIENT (DIV 3: 6th)

	P/FL App Goals	FLC App Goals	FAC App Goals	Others App Goals
Ampadu	26+3 1	4	2+1	
Baker	0+4	0+1		1
Barrett	20			3
Beall	21+2 2		5	3
Brown				1
Canham	2+6			1
Capleton		1		
Clark	40 4	2	5	3
Curran	0+1		0+1	0+1
Downer	0+1			1
Finney	2+3			
Griffiths	21+3 8	3+1	3 1	
Harris	1+1 1			
Hicks	29	3	3	1+1
Inglethorpe	15+8 4	1 1	2+2	1+2
Joseph M	34	2	4+1	1
Joseph R	13+11	1+1	0+1	1
Ling	44 4	4	5	3
Lockwood	36+1 3	2	4	3
McCormick	1+3	2		
McDougald	3+5		1+1	
MacKenzie	26	3	5	1
Martin	1	2		1
Maskell	8+7	2	0+2	1+2
Morrison	7+16 3	1+3	1	1+1
Omoyinmi	3+1 1			
Raynor	1+4	1+1		
Reinelt	2+5	0+4 1		
Richards	28+1 7	1 1	2 3	3
Simba	19+5 10		3+2 1	3
Smith	37 9	4	5 1	3
Stimson	2			1+1
Walschaerts	44 3	4	5 2	
Warren	10	1+1 1	0+1	1
Watts	10+18 6			4

LINCOLN CITY (DIV 2: 23rd)

	P/FL App Goals	FLC App Goals	FAC App Goals	Others App Goals
Alcide	20+3 1	2	2+1 1	1
Austin	38+1 1	2	2	2
Barnett	29		1	3
Battersby	35+4 7	2 1	2	2 1
Bimson	30+1 2		3	3 1
Brabin	3+1			1

LINCOLN CITY cont.

	P/FL App Goals	FLC App Goals	FAC App Goals	Others App Goals
Brown	21+1 1	2	2	1+1
Fenn	0+4			1
Finnigan	36+1 1	2	3 1	1
Fleming	40+3	2	3	2
Fortune-West	7+2 1	2		
Gain	0+4			1
Gordon	21+6 5			2+1
Grobbelaar	2			
Hartfield	3 1			
Holmes	37 6		3 1	2 1
Miller	26+6 2		2	2 1
Oatway	3			
Peacock	3+7			
Perry	10+2	2	1	
Phillips	9			
Philpott	15+9	0+1	0+1	1+2
Richardson	13		2	1
Smith	22+6 2	2	3	1
Stant	0+3		0+1	0+1
Stones	0+1		0+1	1
Thorpe	35+3 8	0+1	3 1	1+1 1
Vaughan	31	2	1	2
Walling	0+3			
Watts	2			1
Whitney	13	2 2	0+1	
Wilder	2+1			
Wilkins				1+1

LIVERPOOL (PREM: 7th)

	P/FL App Goals	FLC App Goals	FAC App Goals	Others App Goals
Babb	24+1		1	3+1
Berger	30+2 7	1	2	6 2
Bjornebye	20+3	2	2	4
Carragher	34 1	2	2	6
Dundee	0+3	0+1		0+1
Ferri	0+2			
Fowler	23+2 14	2 1	1+1 1	5+1 2
Friedel	12	2		1+1
Gerrard	4+8			1
Harkness	4+2	0+1	1+1	1+1
Heggem	27+2 2	1	1	4+1
Ince	34 6	2 1	2 1	3 1
James	26		2	5
Kvarme	2+5			1
Leonhardsen	7+2 1	1		1+2
McAteer	6+7	2	1+1	3+2
McManaman	25+3 4			3 1
Matteo	16+4 1		1	1+1
Murphy	0+1	1+1		0+1
Owen	30 18	2 1	2	5+1 2
Redknapp	33+1 8		2	4 2
Riedle	16+18 5	0+1	1	2+2 1
Song	10+3			
Staunton	31	2	1	5+1
Thompson	4+10 1			2

LUTON TOWN (DIV 2: 12th)

	P/FL App Goals	FLC App Goals	FAC App Goals	Others App Goals
Abbey	2			1
Alexander	28+1 4	7 2	2	1
Bacque	2+5	1+2		1
Boyce	1			1
Cox	3+5	1+1		
Davies	2			
Davis K	44	7	2	
Davis S	20 6	7 2	2 2	
Doherty	5+15 6	0+1	1+1	0+1
Douglas	42 9	6 2	1+1	
Dyche	14 1			1
Evers	27 3	7 1	2	1
Fotiadis	8+13 2	1+2 1		1

LUTON TOWN cont.

	P/FL App	P/FL Goals	FLC App	FLC Goals	FAC App	FAC Goals	Others App	Others Goals
Fraser	5 + 3						1	
George	6 + 6		0 + 2					
Gray	32 + 3	8	6	3	2	2		
Harrison	14						1	
Johnson	42		7		1	1	1	
Kandol	2 + 2						0 + 1	
McGowan	27 + 4		7		2			
McIndoe	17 + 5		2 + 1		0 + 2		1	
McKinnon	29 + 1	2	4 + 1		2			
McLaren	14 + 9		1 + 3	1	2		1	
Marshall	3 + 1	1	3					
Nyamah			0 + 1		1			
Scarlett	2 + 4	1			0 + 1		0 + 1	
Showler	2 + 1							
Spring	45	3	7		1 + 1			
Thomas	26 + 6		3					
Thorpe	7 + 1	4						
White	18 +15	1	0 + 3		1		1	
Willmott	13 + 1							
Zahana-Ooni	4 + 4							

MACCLESFIELD TOWN (DIV 2: 24th)

	P/FL App	P/FL Goals	FLC App	FLC Goals	FAC App	FAC Goals	Others App	Others Goals
Askey	31 + 7	4	4	2	4	1		
Bailey	5 + 5	1						
Barclay	3 + 6	1	1 + 2					
Brown G	5							
Brown S	1 + 1		1 + 1					
Davenport	0 + 1				0 + 1			
Davies	9 + 3	2			1			
Durkan	23 + 3	3	1 + 2		0 + 2		0 + 1	
Griffiths	4	1	0 + 1		0 + 1	1		
Hitchen	35		1 + 1		4			
Holt	3 + 1	1						
Howarth	11 + 8		1		1 + 2		1	
Ingram	23 + 6		2		2 + 1		1	
Landon	10 + 4	2						
Lomax	0 + 1							
Lonergan					0 + 2		0 + 1	
McDonald	23	2	4					
Matias	21 + 1	2			1			
Payne	32 + 6	2	4		3		1	
Price	42		4		4		1	
Sedgemore	25 +10	2	2		4	1	1	
Smith	12	3					1	
Sodje	42	3	4		4	1		
Soley	5 + 5							
Sorvel	38 + 3	4	2 + 1		3			
Tinson	37		4		2		1	
Tomlinson	15 +13	4	1 + 1		4	4	1	
Whittaker	18 + 9	1	4		3 + 1		1	
Williams	4							
Wood	29 +13	4	4	1	4		1	
Wright							0 + 1	

MANCHESTER CITY (DIV 2: 3rd)

	P/FL App	P/FL Goals	FLC App	FLC Goals	FAC App	FAC Goals	Others App	Others Goals
Allsop	3 +21	4	0 + 3	1			1 + 1	1
Bailey							0 + 1	
Bishop	21 + 4				1 + 1		0 + 1	
Bradbury	11 + 2	3	4	1				
Branch	4							
Brown	26 + 5	2	0 + 1		2 + 1	1	4	
Conlon			0 + 1					
Cooke	21	7					3	
Crooks	32 + 2	1			3		3	
Dickov	22 +13	10	3 + 1	2	2 + 2	1	3	2
Edghill	38		4		2		3	
Fenton	15		3				1	
Goater	41 + 2	17	3	2	4		3	1
Greenacre	1							

MANCHESTER CITY cont.

	P/FL App	P/FL Goals	FLC App	FLC Goals	FAC App	FAC Goals	Others App	Others Goals
Heaney							1	
Horlock	36 + 1	9	3		3		3	1
Mason	18 + 1		3	1	2			
Morrison	21 + 1	4			4		1	
Pollock	24 + 2	1	4		3 + 1		1 + 1	
Rimmer							1	
Robins	0 + 2							
Russell	5 + 2	1			3 + 1	2		
Shelia	3							
Taylor	20 + 6	4			3		1 + 3	
Tiatto	8 + 9		1	1	0 + 1		1	
Tskhadadze	2		1	1				
Vaughan	35 + 3	1	4		3		3 + 1	
Weaver	45		3		4		3	
Whitley Jeff	1 + 7	1	0 + 1				4	
Whitley Jim	10 + 8		3 + 1	1	1		0 + 1	
Wiekens	42	2	4		4		3	
Wright	1		1				1	

MANCHESTER UNITED (PREM: 1st)

	P/FL App	P/FL Goals	FLC App	FLC Goals	FAC App	FAC Goals	Others App	Others Goals
Beckham	33 + 1	6	0 + 1		7	1	13	2
Berg	10 + 6		3		5		3 + 2	
Blomqvist	20 + 5	1	0 + 1		3 + 2		6 + 1	
Brown	11 + 3	2	0 + 1		2		3 + 1	
Butt	22 + 9	2	2		5		5 + 4	
Clegg			3					
Cole	26 + 6	17			6 + 1	2	11	5
Cruyff	0 + 5	2	2				0 + 4	
Curtis	1 + 3		3					
Giggs	20 + 4	3	1		5 + 1	2	10	5
Greening	0 + 3		3		0 + 1			
Irwin	26 + 3	2			6	1	13	
Johnsen	19 + 3	3	1		3 + 2		7 + 2	
Keane	33 + 2	2			7		13	3
May	4 + 2		2		1			
Mulryne			2					
Neville G	34		1		7		13	
Neville P	19 + 9		2		4 + 3		4 + 3	1
Nevland			0 + 1	1				
Notman			0 + 1					
Schmeichel	34				8		14	
Scholes	24 + 7	6	0 + 1		3 + 3	1	11 + 2	4
Sheringham	7 +10	2	1	1	1 + 3	1	2 + 3	1
Solskjaer	9 +10	12	3	3	4 + 4	1	1 + 6	2
Stam	30	1			6 + 1		14	
Van der Gouw	4 + 1		3					
Wallwork			0 + 1					
Wilson			2				0 + 1	
Yorke	32	18			5 + 3	3	11	8

MANSFIELD TOWN (DIV 3: 8th)

	P/FL App	P/FL Goals	FLC App	FLC Goals	FAC App	FAC Goals	Others App	Others Goals
Adamson	2							
Allardyce	6							
Bowling	37		2		2		2	
Carruthers	0 + 5							
Cherry	1							
Christie	18 +24	8	2	1	0 + 2		2	
Clarke	24 + 9	5	2	1	2	1		
Ford	39 + 3	2	2		2		2	
Hackett	24 + 2		2		2		1	
Harper	45	6	2		2		2	
Hassell	1 + 2							
Kerr	30 + 5	2	0 + 1		0 + 1		1	
L'Helgoualch	3 + 1	1						
Linighan	10							
Lormor	35 + 6	11	0 + 1		2	2	2	
Naylor	6							
Peacock	42 + 3	17	2		2		2	2
Peters	37	1	2	1	2		2	

MANSFIELD TOWN cont.

	P/FL App	P/FL Goals	FLC App	FLC Goals	FAC App	FAC Goals	Others App	Others Goals
Rose	0 + 1							
Ryder	18 + 4	2					1 + 1	
Schofield	37 + 5		2		2		2	
Sedlan	1 + 4						0 + 1	
Sisson	0 + 1							
Tallon	31 + 5	1	2		2		2	
Walker	18 +19	1	0 + 1		2		1	
Williams	31 +13	2	2		0 + 1		0 + 1	
Willis	10							

MIDDLESBROUGH (PREM: 9th)

	P/FL App	P/FL Goals	FLC App	FLC Goals	FAC App	FAC Goals	Others App	Others Goals
Armstrong	0 + 6	1						
Baker	1 + 1							
Beck	13 +14	5	2		0 + 1			
Beresford	4		3					
Blackmore			1					
Branca	0 + 1							
Campbell	1 + 7		1 + 2					
Cooper	31 + 1	1	1		1			
Cummins	1							
Deane	24 + 2	6	0 + 1		1			
Festa	25	2	2	1				
Fleming	12 + 2	1	1		1			
Gascoigne	25 + 1	3	2		1			
Gavin	2							
Gordon	38	3	2		1			
Harrison	3 + 1		1 + 1					
Kinder	0 + 5		1 + 1					
Maddison	10 +11		1		1			
Merson	3							
Moore	3 + 1		1					
Mustoe	32 + 1	4	1		1			
O'Neill	4 + 2							
Ormerod			0 + 1					
Pallister	26				1			
Ricard	32 + 4	15	3	3	1			
Schwarzer	34				1			
Stamp	5 +11	2	3		0 + 1			
Stockdale	17 + 2		3					
Summerbell	7 + 4		0 + 2	1				
Townsend	35	1	1		1		1	1
Vickers	30 + 1	1	3					

MILLWALL (DIV 2: 10th)

	P/FL App	P/FL Goals	FLC App	FLC Goals	FAC App	FAC Goals	Others App	Others Goals
Bircham	20 + 8		0 + 1		1		1 + 1	
Bowry	22 + 3		2		1		4	
Bubb	1 + 2							
Bull	1							
Cahill	34 + 2	6	0 + 1		1		5	1
Carter	16		2		0 + 1			
Cook	1 + 1							
Dolan	9	1					3	
Fitzgerald	32		2		1		2	
Grant	4 +12	3					0 + 1	
Harris	37 + 2	15			0 + 1		6	3
Hicks	0 + 1							
Hockton	1 + 7	1					0 + 2	1
Ifill	12 + 3	1					2 + 1	
Lavin	38		2		1		7	1
Law	5		2					
McDougald	0 + 1							
McLeary	2							
Neill	33 + 2	6	2		1		5 + 1	
Nethercott	35 + 2	2			1		7	
Newman	22 + 2		2				4	
Odunsi	2 + 1						0 + 1	
Reid	25		0 + 1				6	
Roberts A	8							
Roberts B	11						4	

MILLWALL cont.

	P/FL App Goals	FLC App Goals	FAC App Goals	Others App Goals
Roche	3			1
Ryan	22 + 4		1	2
Sadlier	18 +13 5	2	1	5 + 1 2
Savage	0 + 2			
Shaw	31 + 3 10	2 1	1	3 3
Smith	5			
Spink	22	2	1	3
Stevens	1 + 2			1
Stuart	33 + 2	2	1	6

NEWCASTLE UNITED (PREM: 13th)

	P/FL App Goals	FLC App Goals	FAC App Goals	Others App Goals
Albert	3 + 3			0 + 1
Andersson	11 + 4 2		1	1
Barnes	0 + 1			
Barton	17 + 7	1	5	
Batty	6 + 2	2		1
Beharall	4			
Brady	3 + 6		2 + 1	
Charvet	30 + 1 1	1	5	2
Dabizas	25 + 5 3	2	6	2 1
Dalglish	6 + 5 1	2 1		
Domi	14		4	
Ferguson	7 2		0 + 2	
Georgiadis	7 + 3	1	0 + 2 1	
Gillespie	5 + 2	0 + 1		
Given	31	2	6	2
Glass	18 + 4 3	2	2 + 2	2
Griffin	14	1	3	1
Guivarc'h	2 + 2 1			
Hamann	22 + 1 4	1	7 1	
Harper	7 + 1		1 + 1	
Howey	14		4	
Hughes	12 + 2	1	1 + 1	
Ketsbaia	14 +12 5		6 3	2
Lee	20 + 6		3	1
McClen	1			
Maric	9 + 1		1 + 2	
Pearce	12	2		2
Pistone	2 + 1			
Saha	5 + 6 1		1 1	
Serrant	3 + 1			
Shearer	29 + 1 14	2 1	6 5	2 1
Solano	24 + 5 6	1	7	1 + 1
Speed	34 + 4 4	1 + 1	6 1	2
Watson	7		1	

NORTHAMPTON TOWN (DIV 2: 22nd)

	P/FL App Goals	FLC App Goals	FAC App Goals	Others App Goals
Bishop	4	2		
Clarke	2 + 2			
Clarkson	3 + 2	1 + 1		
Corazzin	36 + 3 16	4 + 1	2	1 1
Dobson	8 + 3	0 + 1		
Frain	40 + 1	4	2	1
Francis				
Freestone	17 +15 2	4 3	0 + 2	1 1
Gibb	30 +11	5	2	
Heggs	8 + 5 1	2 + 1 2		
Hendon	7			
Hill	22 + 5	5	2	0 + 1
Hodgson	7 + 1 1	1	1	
Hope	17 + 2			1
Howard	12			
Howey	25 6			1
Hughes			0 + 1	
Hunt	24 +11 2	2 + 2	1 + 1	0 + 1
Hunter	15 + 3 1	2	1	
Lee	9 +10 1		1	
Matthew	1	1		
Parrish	33 1	3 1	1	

NORTHAMPTON TOWN cont.

	P/FL App Goals	FLC App Goals	FAC App Goals	Others App Goals
Peer	21 + 5 1	3		1
Sampson	42 1	3	2 1	1
Savage	18 + 9 5		2	1
Seal	5 + 1		1	
Spedding	15 + 9 1	2 + 2		1
Turley	25		2	1
Warburton	12 1	4		
Warner	5 + 4	0 + 2	0 + 1	1
Wilder	1			
Wilkinson	12 + 3 1	2 + 1	2	
Wilson	8 1			
Witter	1 + 3	0 + 1		
Woodman	18	5		

NORWICH CITY (DIV 1: 9th)

	P/FL App Goals	FLC App Goals	FAC App Goals	Others App Goals
Adams	15 + 3 3	2	1	
Anselin	7 1			
Bellamy	38 + 2 17	5 2		
Brannan	10 + 1 1	1		
Carey	7 + 3	1		
Coote	2 + 4	0 + 1		
Dalglish	3 + 2			
Eadie	21 + 1 3	5	1	
Fleming	35 + 2 3	5	0 + 1	
Forbes	7 + 8	0 + 2	0 + 1	
Fuglestad	22 + 2	1	1	
Grant	31 + 2	4	1	
Green	2			
Hughes	2 + 2 1			
Jackson	36 + 1 1	3	1	
Kenton	22 1	5		
Llewellyn	21 +10 2	2 + 1	1	
Mackay	24 + 3 1	1 + 1	1	
Marshall A	37	5		
Marshall L	38 + 6 3	5	1	
Milligan	1 + 1	0 + 1		
Mulryne	6 + 1 2			
O'Neill	14 + 4	2 + 1 1		
Roberts	40 + 5 19	3 + 2 3	1 1	
Russell	8 + 5 1			
Scott		0 + 1		
Segura	2 + 2	1		
Sutch	34 + 2	4	1	
Watt	7 + 1		1	
Wilson	14 + 3			

NOTTINGHAM FOREST (PREM: 20th)

	P/FL App Goals	FLC App Goals	FAC App Goals	Others App Goals
Allou	0 + 2			
Armstrong	20 + 2	4 1		
Bart-Williams	20 + 4 3	2	1	
Beasant	26	3	1	
Bonalair	24 + 4 1	3		
Burns		0 + 1		
Chettle	32 + 2 2	3	1	
Crossley	12	1 + 1		
Darcheville	14 + 2 2	1 + 2		
Dawson		1		
Doig	1 + 1			
Edwards	7 + 5			
Freedman	20 +11 9	4 3	1	
Gemmill	18 + 2	2	1	
Gough	7			
Gray	3 + 5	2 + 1	0 + 1	
Harewood	11 +12 1	2 + 2 2	0 + 1	
Harkes	3			
Hjelde	16 + 1 1	2	1	
Hodges	3 + 2			
Johnson	25 + 3	2 1	1	
Louis-Jean	15 + 1	2 + 1	1	

NOTTINGHAM FOREST cont.

	P/FL App Goals	FLC App Goals	FAC App Goals	Others App Goals
Lyttle	5 + 5	1 + 1	1	
Mattsson	5 + 1			
Melton	1			
Palmer	13			
Porfirio	3 + 6 1			
Quashie	12 + 4	2	0 + 1	
Rogers	34 4	4		
Shipperley	12 + 8 1		1	
Stensaas	6 + 1			
Stone	26 3	3 2	1	
Thomas	5 1			
Van Hooijdonk	19 + 2 6	0 + 1		
Woan	0 + 2			

NOTTS COUNTY (DIV 2: 16th)

	P/FL App Goals	FLC App Goals	FAC App Goals	Others App Goals
Beadle	13 + 1 3			
Billy	3 + 3	2		
Bolland	12 + 1			
Creaney	13 + 3 3			
Devlin	5			
Dudley	0 + 4	0 + 1		
Dyer	19 +10	0 + 2	3 + 1	
Fairclough	16 1	2	1	
Farrell	7 + 4 3	1	1	
Finnan	12 + 1			
Foley	2			1
Garcia	10 + 9 2		3 + 2	1
Gibson	1			
Goram	1			
Grant	6 1			
Hendon	32 6	1	6	
Henshaw		0 + 1		1
Holmes	3 + 5			
Hughes	21 + 9 3	1	3	1
Jackson	3 + 7		3 + 1	1
Jones	23 + 5 2	2	5 6	1
Liburd	27 + 8 1	1 + 1	3 + 3	
Matthews	4 + 1			
Murray	32 + 3 3	2	6 1	
Owers	36 + 3 3	2	6 1	
Parkin	1			
Pearce	31 + 2 1	1	6	1
Pennant			0 + 1	0 + 1
Quayle	2 + 3		0 + 2	0 + 1
Rabat				1
Rapley	10 + 6 2			
Redmile	39 + 2 1	2	6	
Richardson	23 7		6	
Robson	0 + 2	1 + 1		
Samuels				0 + 1
Stallard	13 + 1 4			
Strodder	8 + 3 1	1	1 + 1	1
Tierney	13 + 7 3		1 + 2	1
Torpey	4 + 2 1	1 + 1 1		
Ward	43	2	6	1
Warren	18			

OLDHAM ATHLETIC (DIV 2: 20th)

	P/FL App Goals	FLC App Goals	FAC App Goals	Others App Goals
Allott	32 + 9 7	2 1	1 + 2	0 + 1
Beavers	7 2			
Clitheroe	1 + 1			
Duxbury	41 6	2	4 1	1
Garnett	36 + 1 2		4	1
Graham	11 3	2	2	
Gray	4			
Hodgson	0 + 1			
Holt	39 + 4 4	2	3 + 1	1
Hotte	0 + 1			
Innes	8 + 5 1			

	P/FL App	P/FL Goals	FLC App	FLC Goals	FAC App	FAC Goals	Others App	Others Goals
OLDHAM ATHLETIC cont.								
Kelly	45		2		4		1	
Littlejohn	11+ 5	2	2	1				
McGinlay	4+ 3	1			1+1	2	1	
McLean	5							
McNiven D	1+ 5							
McNiven S	33+ 4	1	2		4	1	1	
Mardon	12	3						
Miskelly	1							
Orlygsson	19+ 3		2					
Reid	40	1	2	1	4		1	
Rickers	44+ 1	4	2		4		1	
Ritchie	0+ 1				0+1			
Salt	3+ 6		0+1		1	1	1	
Sheridan	30	2			4			
Sinnott	14+ 4		2		1			
Spooner	2							
Sugden	0+ 2							
Swan	1				0+1			
Thom	19+ 6	2			1		1	
Tipton	15+13	2			2+2		0+1	
Walsh	0+ 1							
Whitehall	28+ 8	4	0+2		4		1	
OXFORD UNITED (DIV 1: 23rd)								
Banger	22+10	5	2		3			
Beauchamp	31+ 6	4	2		1+1			
Cook	9+10	1	0+1		2			
Davis	3							
Francis	12+ 6	1			0+2			
Gerrard	16							
Gilchrist	39	2	2		2	1		
Gray	40		1		2			
Hill	1+ 8		0+1					
Jackson	1				3			
Lundin	7							
Marsh	20+ 1	2	2					
Murphy	33+10	4	2	2	3	2		
Powell	40+ 4	3	0+1		3			
Remy	10+ 2	1			1+2			
Robinson	44		2		3			
Rose	1+ 3		1					
Salmon	1							
Smith	19+ 3		1+1		0+1			
Tait	17				2			
Thomson	25+13	7	1		0+1			
Warren	4							
Watson	23				3			
Weatherstone	4+ 8	1	0+2	1				
Whelan	14+ 1		1	1				
Whitehead	21		2					
Williams	0+ 2							
Wilsterman	12+ 5	2	1		1			
Windass	33	15	2		3	3		
Wright	4+ 2				1			
PETERBOROUGH UNITED (DIV 3: 9th)								
Allardyce	3							
Andrews	8+ 2	5						
Bodley	24		2		1			
Broughton	14+11	7					1+1	1
Butler	13+ 1	2			1		1	1
Carruthers	13+ 1	2	2	1			1	
Castle	26	4	1+1		1		1	
Chapple	1						1	
Cleaver	0+ 2				0+1			
Connor	2							
Davies	43	4	2		1		2	
De Souza	4							
Drury	39+ 1		2		1		2	
PETERBOROUGH UNITED cont.								
Edwards	41	2	2		1		2	1
Etherington	21+ 8	3	0+1		0+1		2	
Farrell	28+ 9	4	0+1		1		1	
Forbes	1+ 2							
Gill	22+ 4		2				0+1	
Grazioli	21+13	15	1				0+2	
Green	3+ 4	1						
Griemink	17		1					
Hanlon	0+ 4	1					1	
Hann	0+ 4						1	
Hooper	36+ 2	2	2		0+1		1	
Houghton	7+ 1	1	1					
Inman	1+ 2	1	0+1					
Koogi	0+ 1							
Legg	5							
Linton	8				1			
Lyttle			0+1					
McKenzie	14	8					1	1
McMenamin	4+ 1							
Martin	0+ 4							
Payne	8+ 1							
Quinn	7	5	2					
Rennie	9						1	
Rowe	0+ 7				1			
Scott	19+ 8	4	1+1		1		1+1	
Shields	6+ 3							
Tyler	27		1		1		2	
Wicks	11							
PLYMOUTH ARGYLE (DIV 3: 13th)								
Adams							0+1	
Ashton	22+ 4		0+1		4		1	
Barlow	45	5	2		5		1	
Barrett	0+ 1							
Bastow	21+ 8	2			3		1	
Beswetherick	18+ 4				4		1	
Branston	7	2					1	
Collins	40	2	1		1			
Crittenden	1+ 1							
Crowe	3+ 8	1						
Dungey	7				1		1	
Edmondson	4							
Flash	4+ 1		1					
Ford	0+ 1							
Forinton	8+ 1	3						
Gibbs	27	3	2					
Gill							0+1	
Gritton	0+ 2							
Guinan	11	7						
Hargreaves	30+ 2	2	2		4			
Heathcote	43	3	2		5	1	1	
Jean	21+ 8	3	2	1	4		1	
McCall	14+ 3		1+1		2+1			
McCarthy	14+ 2	3	2	2	5			
McGovern	0+ 2							
Marker	4							
Marshall	25+ 3	12			1+2			
Mauge	31+ 1	3	2		3		1	
Phillips	8+ 7	1			3+2		1	
Power	7+ 9		1+1				0+1	
Sale	8	1						
Sheffield	39		2		4			
Sweeney	6+ 7	1			1+2	1	1	
Taylor	6	1						
Wills	0+ 2							
Wotton	32+ 4	1	2		5	1		
PORTSMOUTH (DIV 1: 19th)								
Aloisi	22	14	4	3				
Andreassen	0+ 2				1			
Awford	35	1	4					
Claridge	39	9	2+1		2	1		
Durnin	16+10	7	3+1					
Flahavan	13		2					
Hillier	11+ 5		1	1				
Igoe	39+ 1	5	2+1		2			
Kizeridis	2+ 2		2					
Knight	20		2+1		2			
McLoughlin	41	7	4	3	2			
Miglioranzi	4+ 3							
Nightingale	6+13	3			1+1	1		
Peron	37+ 1	1	2		2			
Perrett	12+ 3		2					
Pethick	4+ 6		1					
Petterson	13							
Phillips	2+15	1	0+2		0+1			
Robinson	27+ 2	1	0+1		2			
Simpson	38+ 3	1	4		2			
Soley	1+ 7		0+4					
Thogersen	29+ 5		2		0+1			
Thomson	14		2		1			
Vlachos	29+ 1		1	1	2			
Waterman	10				2			
Whitbread	33		4	1	1			
Whittingham	9	7						
PORT VALE (DIV 1: 21st)								
Ainsworth	15	5	2	1				
Allen	2+ 3	1						
Aspin	28+ 2		1		1			
Barker	23+ 4	2						
Barnett	26+ 1				1			
Beadle	18+ 5	6	2		1			
Beesley	33+ 2	3			1			
Bent	10+ 5							
Berntsen	1							
Bogie	31+ 4	2	2		1			
Brammer	9							
Brisco	1				1			
Burns	2+ 2							
Butler	4							
Carragher	8+ 2		2					
Clarke	2+ 4							
Corden	4+12		1		0+1			
Eyre	8+ 3							
Foyle	32+ 3	9	1+1					
Gardner	14+ 1	1						
Griffiths	3	1						
Horlaville	1+ 1				0+1			
Jansson	5+ 2		1					
Koordes	13+ 2		0+1					
Lee	7+ 4	2						
Lyttle	7							
McGill	0+ 3							
McGlinchey	10+ 5	1	0+1		1			
McQuade	0+ 3		0+1					
Mean	1							
Musselwhite	38		2					
Naylor	14+ 8	4	1+1	2	1			
O'Callaghan	4				0+1			
Pilkington	8				1			
Pounewatchy	2							
Rougier	8+ 5							
Russell	8	1						
Smith	7+ 1							
Snijders	6+ 4		2					
Talbot	29+ 4		2					

PORT VALE cont.

	P/FL App	P/FL Goals	FLC App	FLC Goals	FAC App	FAC Goals	Others App	Others Goals
Tankard	37	4	2		1			
Walsh	18+1	1	1+1		1			
Widdrington	9	1						

PRESTON NORTH END (DIV 2: 5th)

	P/FL App	P/FL Goals	FLC App	FLC Goals	FAC App	FAC Goals	Others App	Others Goals
Alexander	10						2	
Appleton	13+12	2	2		1+1		2+1	
Basham	15+12	10						
Byfield	3+2	1					1	
Cartwright	14+13	4	0+1		3		3	
Clement	4							
Darby	12+8	1			0+1	1	2+1	1
Eyres	33+1	8	2		1		2	1
Gray	5							
Gregan	40+1	3	2		3		3	
Harris	9+25	6			2+1	1	2+2	
Harrison	6						1	
Holt	0+3		0+1					
Jackson	44	8	2		2		4	
Kidd	27+1	3	1		3		1	
King							0+1	
Lucas	31				3		4	
Ludden	26+6		1		2		2	
McGregor	1+3							
Macken	30+12	8	2		1+1		4	1
McKenna	31+5		1		1+1	1	2	
Moilanen	15		2					
Murdock	28+5	1	1		2		4	
Nogan	39+3	18	2		3	3	1+2	
Parkinson	27	1	2		3		2	1
Rankine	42	3	2		3	1	2	
Wright	1				0+1		0+1	

QUEENS PARK RANGERS (DIV 1: 20th)

	P/FL App	P/FL Goals	FLC App	FLC Goals	FAC App	FAC Goals	Others App	Others Goals
Baraclough	41+2	1	4		1			
Breacker	18	1						
Darlington	4							
Dowie	7+12	1	0+1		0+1			
Gallen	41+3	8	4		1			
Graham	0+2							
Harper	15		4					
Heinola	23		3		1			
Jeanne	7+3							
Jones	1+1							
Kiwomya	12+4	6	0+1		0+1			
Kulcsar	17	1	0+2					
Langley	7+1	1						
Linighan	4+3							
Maddix	37	4	4	1				
Miklosko	31				1			
Morrow	24				1			
Murray	32+7	1	4		1			
Peacock	41+1	8	4		1			
Perry	1							
Plummer	8+2							
Ready	40+1	2	4		1			
Rose	27+2		1		1			
Rowland	16+14	3	1		1			
Scully	10+13	2	4					
Sheron	21+2	8	2+2	1				
Slade	10+10	1	2+2	1	1			
Steiner	5+7	3						
Yates	6		3					

READING (DIV 2: 11th)

	P/FL App	P/FL Goals	FLC App	FLC Goals	FAC App	FAC Goals	Others App	Others Goals
Asaba	0+1		0+2	1				
Barras	4+2	1						
Bernal	18+4				1			
Booty	7+1		4					

READING cont.

	P/FL App	P/FL Goals	FLC App	FLC Goals	FAC App	FAC Goals	Others App	Others Goals
Bowen	1	1						
Brayson	13+15		0+1		1		1	
Brebner	36+3	9	3	1	1			
Caskey	42	7	3+1	2	1		1	
Casper	32		1		1		1	
Clement	11	1					1	
Crawford	9+2		1		1		1	
Davies	1							
Evers	0+1							
Fleck	2+2	1	1					
Glasgow	28+4	1	2		1		1	
Gray	25+2	2	4					
Gurney	5+3							
Hadland			1					
Hammond	1		1					
Hodges	0+1							
Houghton	13+5		2+1					
Howie	42		2		1		1	
Hunter	2+1							
Kromheer	11		1					
Lambert	1							
Legg	2		1					
McIntyre	22+10	6	1				1	
McKeever	6+1	2						
McLaren	7	1						
McPherson	13+2		2		1			
Maybury	8							
Murty	8+1							
Parkinson	42	5	3					
Polston	4							
Primus	31		3		1		1	
Reilly	4+2		2					
Roach	3+2				0+1		0+1	
Saar	18+10	3	2		0+1		0+1	
Scott	5+4	2						
Stamp	0+1							
Thorpe	6	1						
Van der Kwaak	3		1					
Williams	20+6	11	2+2		1			
Wright	0+2						1	

ROCHDALE (DIV 3: 19th)

	P/FL App	P/FL Goals	FLC App	FLC Goals	FAC App	FAC Goals	Others App	Others Goals
Bailey	12+7	1	1+1				1	
Barlow	25+4	1			0+1		2	
Bayliss	22+3	1	2		0+2		2+1	
Bryson	31+8		1		4	2		
Carden	24+1				3		3	
De Souza	5							
Diaz	12+2	2	1		1+2			
Edwards	45		2		3+1		3	
Farrell	36+2		2		2+1		3	
Gray	0+3							
Hicks	1							
Hill	33		1		2		4	1
Holt	17+7	7					3	1
Johnson	13+3		2		1			
Jones	11+9		1		1+2		1+1	1
Key					1			
Lancashire	7+4	3	1+1				0+1	
Leonard	2+6		1					
Lydiate	14	1						
Monington	37	3			4	1	3	1
Morris	25	7					3	1
Painter	35+5	6	1		4		1+2	
Peake	36+2	5	2		4		3	
Priestley	1							
Sparrow	21+4	2	1		4		1+1	
Stoker	11+1	1					2	
Stokes	10+1		2				1	

ROCHDALE cont.

	P/FL App	P/FL Goals	FLC App	FLC Goals	FAC App	FAC Goals	Others App	Others Goals
Stuart	9+10				4			
Williams	11+3	1			4			

ROTHERHAM UNITED (DIV 3: 5th)

	P/FL App	P/FL Goals	FLC App	FLC Goals	FAC App	FAC Goals	Others App	Others Goals
Beech	24		2					
Berry	11+7	2			3+2	1	1	
Bos	1+1							
Clark	1							
Dillon	25+1	1	2		4		3	
Fortune-West	20	12					2	
Garner	40	4	2		5	2	1	
Glover	18+1	10	2		4+1	2	1	
Hudson	19+7	5	0+2		3	1	1	
Hurst	31+1	2			5	1	3	
Ingledow	15+6	2			5		1	
Jackson	2	1						
Knill	35+1	2	2		1		3	
Martindale	6+4	2	0+2					
Monkhouse	0+5	1			0+1		1	
Pollitt	46		2		5		3	
Raven	11	3						
Richardson	4+1		1		4			
Roscoe	27+11	5	2		4		2	
Scott G	13				1			
Scott R	5+1	1			2	1	3	
Sedgwick	24+9	3	0+1		3+2		0+2	
Strodder	3							
Thompson	28+5	5	2		1+2		2+1	
Tracey	0+3				1+1			
Varty	14						2	
Warne	19	8					2	
Warner	23	1	1		3		1	
Whelan	13	4						
White	18+8	5	2		1+1			
Williams	10+1						0+2	

SCARBOROUGH (DIV 3: 24th)

	P/FL App	P/FL Goals	FLC App	FLC Goals	FAC App	FAC Goals	Others App	Others Goals
Atkinson G	15	1						
Atkinson P	23+4		2		2		1	
Brodie	43	12	2		2			
Bullimore	33+2	1	1		2		1	
Campbell	3+8		2		0+1			
Carr	5+5							
Dabelsteen	5	1						
Elliott	20		2					
Goodlad	1							
Greenacre	10+2	2					1	
Hodges	1							
Hoyland	44	3	2		2		1	
Jackson	19+1		2					
Jones	8+1							
Kay	23+1				2			
Lydiate	26+1	1	2		2		1	
McAuley	6+1							
McNaughton	22+9	1			1		1	
Marinkov	22	4	2		1			
Milbourne	2+14		1+1				0+1	
Morris					0+1			
Mountfield	5+1							
Naisbett	2						1	
Parks	15							
Porter	11+2							
Radigan	4+5		0+2					
Rainford	0+2						1	
Rennison	15	1					1	
Renshaw	0+1							
Roberts	18	3						
Robinson	17+12	3	1		1			
Russell	20+17	3	0+1		1+1		1	

SCARBOROUGH cont

	P/FL App	Goals	FLC App	Goals	FAC App	Goals	Others App	Goals
Saville	0+9							
Tate	18+7	12	0+1				1	
Todd	0+1							
Weaver	6							
Williams	17	2	2		2	1		
Worrall	25+6		1+1		2			

SCUNTHORPE UNITED (DIV 3: 4th)

	P/FL App	Goals	FLC App	Goals	FAC App	Goals	Others App	Goals
Atkinson	0+1							
Bull	4+20		0+1		0+1		0+2	
Calvo-Garcia	42+1	9	2		3		4	1
Clarke	22		2		2		2	
Dawson	24				4		4	1
Evans	24				1		2	
Eyre	41	15	2		2	2	3	
Fickling	28+1		2		2		2	
Forrester	46	20	2	1	3	2	4	
Gayle	36+1	4	2		1		4	
Harsley	32+2		2		2+1	1	3	
Hope	46	5	2		3		4	
Housham	11+5				1+1	1	1+3	
Logan	38+3	6			3		3	
McAuley	16+1		2		3			
Marshall	5+14	1	0+1		1+2			
Sheldon	5+6	1					1+2	2
Stamp	5+20	4	0+1		2		0+1	
Stanton	3+1							
Walker	40+1	1	2				4	1
Wilcox	24+4	1	2		2		3	
Witter	14							

SHEFFIELD UNITED (DIV 1: 8th)

	P/FL App	Goals	FLC App	Goals	FAC App	Goals	Others App	Goals
Borbokis	19	2	4	1	3	1		
Bruce	10		1					
Campbell	11	3						
Cullen	0+2							
Dellas	9+8	3	2					
Derry	23+3				4			
Devlin	23+10	5	0+3		4	1		
Donis	5+2	1						
Ford	27+3		2	1	1+4			
Goram	7		2					
Hamilton D	6							
Hamilton I	27+3	2	4	1	2			
Henry	3+3				2+1			
Holdsworth	16	1			4	2		
Hunt	12+1	2						
Jacobsen	8+4				0+1			
Katchouro	8+8	6						
Kelly	22		2		5			
Kozluk	10							
Marcelo	26+9	16	1+1		5	4		
Marker	17+1	3	3		1			
Morris	14+6	6			2+3	2		
Nilsen	14+3		3					
O'Connor	2				1			
Quinn	41+3	1	3		5			
Sandford	34+1		3+1		5			
Saunders	19	7	4	3				
Stuart	25	6	4		4+1	1		
Taylor	7+5	1	3+1	1				
Tebily	7+1							
Tracey	17+1							
Twiss	2+10	1			2+3			
Wilder	4		0+1					
Woodhouse	31+2	3	1+2		5			

SHEFFIELD WEDNESDAY (PREM: 12th)

	P/FL App	Goals	FLC App	Goals	FAC App	Goals	Others App	Goals
Agogo	0+1				0+1			
Alexandersson	31+1	3	0+1		3			
Atherton	38	2	2		3			
Barrett	0+5		0+1					
Booth	34	6	2		1+1			
Briscoe	5+11	1	1		0+2			
Carbone	31	8	2		3	1		
Cobian	7+2	1						
Cresswell	1+6	1						
Di Canio	5+1	3	2					
Emerson	38	1	2		3	1		
Haslam	2							
Hinchcliffe	32	3	2		2			
Humphreys	10+9	1			2	2		
Hyde	0+1							
Jonk	38	2	2		3			
McKeever	1+2							
Magilton	1+5							
Morrison	0+1							
Newsome	2+3		1		0+1			
Oakes	0+1							
Pressman	14+1		2		1			
Quinn	1							
Rudi	33+1	6	1		3	1		
Sanetti	0+3		0+2					
Scott	0+4	1						
Sonner	24+2	3			2+1			
Srnicek	24				2			
Stefanovic	8+3				2	1		
Walker	37		2		3			
Whittingham	1+1		0+1					

SHREWSBURY TOWN (DIV 3: 15th)

	P/FL App	Goals	FLC App	Goals	FAC App	Goals	Others App	Goals
Beavers	2						1	
Berkley	41	8			1		1	
Brown	15+19	2			1		0+1	
Cooksey	2						1	
Craven	6+4		2					
Drysdale	2							
Edwards	43		2		1			
Evans	32	6	2	3	1		1	
Gayle	43	1	2		1			
Hanmer	46		2		1		1	
Hayfield	1+1							
Herbert	6+2		1					
Jagielka	13+18	1	1+1		1		0+1	
Jobling	41		2	1			1	
Jones	0+1							
Kerrigan	32+5	10	1		1			
Preece	16+4	2	1					
Rutherford	0+3							
Seabury	44	5	2		1		1	
Steele	33+5	13	1		0+1		1	
Thompson	1							
Tretton	22+1				1		1	
Whelan	8+1						1	
White	7+4		1+1					
Wilding	42		2		1		1	
Williams			0+1					
Winstanley	8							

SOUTHAMPTON (PREM: 17th)

	P/FL App	Goals	FLC App	Goals	FAC App	Goals	Others App	Goals
Basham	0+4	1	0+1					
Beattie	22+13	5	1+1	1	2			
Benali	19+4		2					
Beresford	1+3							
Bradley	0+3							
Bridge	15+8							
Colleter	16	1			2			

SOUTHAMPTON cont.

	P/FL App	Goals	FLC App	Goals	FAC App	Goals	Others App	Goals
Dodd	27+1	1	2		2			
Dryden	4							
Gibbens	2+2		2					
Hiley	27+2				1			
Hirst	0+2							
Howells	8+1	1	1		1			
Hughes D	6+3							
Hughes M	32	1	2		1+1			
Jones	31		2		2			
Kachloul	18+4	5	2		2			
Le Tissier	20+10	7	2		0+1			
Lundekvam	30+3		1+1		2			
Marsden	14	2						
Marshall	2							
Monk	4				0+1			
Monkou	22				2			
Moss	7							
Oakley	21+1	2			2			
Ostenstad	27+7	7	2		2	1		
Pahars	4+2	3						
Palmer	18+1		2		1			
Ripley	16+6		1		0+1			
Warner	5		1					
Williams	0+1							

SOUTHEND UNITED (DIV 3: 18th)

	P/FL App	Goals	FLC App	Goals	FAC App	Goals	Others App	Goals
Beard	36+1		1		1		1	
Booty	18+2							
Burns	26+5	5	3				1	
Campbell	9+3	2						
Capleton	14							
Clarke	14+10	3	3	1	1			
Coleman	41+1	4	4		1		1	
Conlon	28+6	7			1		1	
Coyne	0+1							
De Souza	2		1+1					
Dublin	6+3		1+1				1	
Fitzpatrick	7+16		1+2		0+1			
Gooding	19+4		2				1	
Hails	11	1	4					
Harris	1							
Hodges	10		1					
Houghton	26+1	3					1	
Hunter	5		2					
Iorfa	0+2							
Jones	5+12		1+1		0+1		0+1	
Livett	19+4	1	1		1		1	
McGavin	4+7							
Maher	34	4	4		1		1	1
Margetson	32		4		1		1	
Morley	26+1		2		0+1			
Newman	36	7	4	1	1		1	
Patterson	5							
Rapley	9	4						
Roach	7+1	1						
Roget	11+3		1					
Stimson	17		4		1			
Unger	14							
Whyte	14+4	2	3		1			

STOCKPORT COUNTY (DIV 1: 16th)

	P/FL App	Goals	FLC App	Goals	FAC App	Goals	Others App	Goals
Alsaker	1							
Angell	42	17	2		2	1		
Bennett	3+4							
Branch	10+4	3	1					
Byrne C	11	2	2	1				
Byrne D	2							
Connelly	33+2	1	1		2			
Cook	23+1		1+1		1			

STOCKPORT COUNTY cont.

	P/FL App	P/FL Goals	FLC App	FLC Goals	FAC App	FAC Goals	Others App	Others Goals
Cooper	27+11	1	1+1					
Dinning	35+6	5	2		2			
Ellis	16	6						
Flynn	46	1	2		2			
Gannon	28+10		1+1		1+1			
Grant	1+12	1			0+1			
Gray	3							
Hughes	7							
McInnes	13				2			
McIntosh	41	3	1		2			
Mannion	0+1							
Matthews	19+4	2			1+1			
Moore	32+6	3	2	1	2			
Nash	43		2		2			
Phillips	7+2		1		1			
Smith	17	1						
Travis	1+8		0+1		0+1			
Wilbraham	8+18		0+1					
Woodthorpe	37	2	2		2	1		

STOKE CITY (DIV 2: 8th)

	P/FL App	P/FL Goals	FLC App	FLC Goals	FAC App	FAC Goals	Others App	Others Goals
Clarke	2							
Collins	4							
Connor	2+1	2						
Crowe	19+19	8	1				1	1
Forsyth	13+5	2			2		1+1	
Fraser	0+1							
Heath	7+3						2	
Kavanagh G	36	11	2	1	2		2	1
Kavanagh J	8							
Keen	43+1	2	1		2		1+1	
Lightbourne	28+8	7	1		1	1	1	
MacKenzie	3+3						0+1	
Mohan	15							
Muggleton	40		2		2		2	
O'Connor	4						0+1	
Oldfield	43+3	6	2		2		1	
Petty	9+2				1		1	
Pickering	0+1		1					
Robinson	39+1	1	2		2			
Short	19+2		2					
Sigurdsson	38	4	1		2		2	
Small	35+2		2		2		2	
Strong	5	1						
Sturridge	1+2		0+1		0+1		1	
Taaffe	1+2							
Thorne	33+1	9	2	1	2		1	1
Tweed	0+1		0+1				1	
Wallace	11+20	3	0+1		0+1		1	
Ward	6							
Whittle	9+5	1	1					
Woods	33		2		2		2	
Woolliscroft	0+1							

SUNDERLAND (DIV 1: 1st)

	P/FL App	P/FL Goals	FLC App	FLC Goals	FAC App	FAC Goals	Others App	Others Goals
Aiston	0+1		0+1					
Ball	42	2	4		1			
Bridges	13+17	8	5+2	4				
Butler	44	2	6+1		2			
Clark	26+1	3	3+1		2			
Craddock	3+3		3+2					
Dichio	16+20	10	4+1	2	1+1			
Gray	36+1	2	5		2			
Harrison			1					
Holloway	1+5							
Johnston	40	7	6+1	1	1			
Lumsdon			0+1					
McCann	5+6		1	1	1+1	1		
Makin	37+1		7					

SUNDERLAND cont.

	P/FL App	P/FL Goals	FLC App	FLC Goals	FAC App	FAC Goals	Others App	Others Goals
Maley		1						
Marriott	1							
Melville	44	2	6		2			
Mullin	8+1	2	4+1					
Phillips	26	23	5	2	1			
Proctor			0+1					
Quinn	36+3	18	4+1	3	2			
Rae	12+3	2	2		1			
Scott	14+2	2	6	1	1			
Smith	4+4	3	4+2	1	0+1			
Sorensen	45		9		2			
Summerbee	36	3	5+1		0+1			
Thirlwell	1+1		2+1					
Wainwright	0+2		2+1					
Williams	16+9		4		1			

SWANSEA CITY (DIV 3: 7th)

	P/FL App	P/FL Goals	FLC App	FLC Goals	FAC App	FAC Goals	Others App	Others Goals
Alsop	37+4	10	2		4+1	1	4	
Appleby	36+3	3			2+1	1	1+2	1
Bird	8+21	3	0+1		1+1		2+2	3
Bound	45		2		5		4	1
Casey	5+5	1	1+1					
Clode	2						1	
Coates	30+3		2		3		3+1	
Cusack	42+1	1	2	1	5		3	
Davies	0+1							
Freestone	38		2		5		4	
Gregg	5							
Howard	38+1	1	2		5		3	
Jenkins	6+5		0+1		0+1		2	
Jones J	3							
Jones S	31+1	2			5		3	
Lacey	7+5				1		1	
Newhouse	5+1				1		0+1	
O'Gorman	2+3		1					
O'Leary	17+2	2			1		1+2	
Phillips	0+1							
Price	25+3	4	2		2	1	2+1	
Roberts	15+17	3	0+2		3		3+1	
Smith	42	4	2		4	1	3	1
Thomas	26+4	3	2		4	2	2	
Walker	2							
Watkin	40+3	17			4		2	

SWINDON TOWN (DIV 1: 17th)

	P/FL App	P/FL Goals	FLC App	FLC Goals	FAC App	FAC Goals	Others App	Others Goals
Borrows	40		2		1			
Bradley	6+1							
Bullock	17+5	1	2		1			
Campagna	0+2							
Collins	2+2							
Cowe	2+3				0+2			
Cuervo	2+4		0+1					
Davies	6							
Davis	21+4				1			
Fenn	4							
Glass	3		1					
Gooden	36+2	1	2		2			
Griffin	1+4	1						
Hall	39+2	1	2		2			
Hay	16+11	6	1+1		1			
Howe	20+3	3			2			
Hulbert	7+9				2			
Kerslake	12+2							
Leitch	23+1				1			
Linton	7+1							
McAreavey	0+1							
McHugh			0+1					
Ndah	40+1	11	2	1	2			
Onuora	40+3	20	2		1+1			

SWINDON TOWN cont

	P/FL App	P/FL Goals	FLC App	FLC Goals	FAC App	FAC Goals	Others App	Others Goals
Reeves	23+1	2	2	1				
Robinson	25+4		2		1			
Talia	43		1		2			
Taylor	18+3				2			
Walters	31+7	10	2		1+1	1		
Watson	9+9		1+1		0+1			
Williams	1+2							
Willis	11							

TORQUAY UNITED (DIV 3: 20th)

	P/FL App	P/FL Goals	FLC App	FLC Goals	FAC App	FAC Goals	Others App	Others Goals
Aggrey	22+3				2		1	
Bedeau	28+8	8	2	1	1+1		0+2	
Clayton	15		1		1			
Donaldson	7+5	1						
Forrester	1+4							
Gregg	11		1					
Gurney	20	1			2			
Hadley	0+2							
Hapgood	11+6		0+1		0+1		0+1	
Harries	5							
Healy	16+3	2					2	
Herrera	39+1		2		2		2	
Hill	22+13	5	2		2		2	
Jermyn	0+1							
Leadbitter	37	1	1		1		1+1	
Lee	6+1	2					2	1
McFarlane	5+10	3	0+1				0+1	
McGorry	31+3	1	2		2		2	
Monk	6							
Neil	6+1							
Nichols	5+1							
Partridge	29	13	2		2	1	2	1
Platts	7+1							
Robinson	29	1	2		2		1	
Russell	9							
Simb	3+6	1						
Southall	25						2	
Thomas	44	1	2	1	1		2	
Tully	31+6	2	0+1				2	
Veysey	10		1		2			
Waddle	7							
Watson	8		2				1	
Williams	7	5						
Witter	4				2			
Worthington	0+1							

TOTTENHAM HOTSPUR (PREM: 11th)

	P/FL App	P/FL Goals	FLC App	FLC Goals	FAC App	FAC Goals	Others App	Others Goals
Allen	0+5		1+2					
Anderton	31+1	3	7		7	2		
Armstrong	24+10	7	5	5	3+2			
Baardsen	12		3					
Berti	4							
Calderwood	11+1		5					
Campbell	37	6	8	2	7			
Carr	37		8	1	7			
Clemence	9+9		2+1		0+1			
Dominguez	2+11	2	0+2	1				
Edinburgh	14+2		5		4+1			
Ferdinand	22+2	5	2+2		6+1			
Fox	17+3	3	1+2		2	1		
Freund	17		3		6			
Ginola	30	3	8	1	6	3		
Gower			0+2					
Iverson	22+5	9	6	2	5+2	2		
King	0+1							
Nielsen	24+4	3	7	3	2+2	3		
Nilsen	3							
Saib	0+4							
Scales	7		2	1				

	P/FL App	P/FL Goals	FLC App	FLC Goals	FAC App	FAC Goals	Others App	Others Goals
TOTTENHAM HOTSPUR cont.								
Segers	1		1					
Sherwood	12+2	2			4	1		
Sinton	12+10		3+3		2+4	1		
Taricco	12+1				2+1			
Tramezzani	6		1					
Vega	13+3	2	5	1	4			
Walker	25		4		7			
Wilson			0+1					
Young	14+1		1+1		3+2			
TRANMERE ROVERS (DIV 1: 15th)								
Achterberg	24		1					
Allen	41	5	2		1			
Challinor	29+5	2	1+1		1			
Coyne	17				1			
Frail	5		1					
Gibson	0+1							
Hill	33	4	5					
Hinds	1+1							
Irons	43+1	15	5	3	1			
Jones G	15+11	5	3+2		1			
Jones L	18+12	2	1+3	1	0+1			
Kelly	16+11	4	2	2				
Koumas	11+12	3	3+1	1				
McGreal	36		5		1			
Mahon	34+5	6	2+1	1				
Mellon	21+3	1	4		1			
Morgan	4+2		1					
Morrissey	5+19		1+2		0+1			
O'Brien	18+5	2	2+1					
Parkinson	20+9	2	4+1	1	0+1			
Russell	3+1							
Santos	37	1	4		1			
Sharps	0+1							
Shepherd	0+1							
Simonsen	5		4					
Taylor	31+5	9			1			
Thompson	37	1	4		1			
Williams	2+3							
WALSALL (DIV 2: 2nd)								
Brissett	27+8	2	2		1		3+2	
Carter	0+1							
Cramb	4	4					2	
Davis	0+1							
Dyer	0+1		0+1					
Evans	6+5				1		1+3	
Eyjolfsson	0+10	1					0+1	1
Gadsby	3+3						0+2	
Garrault					0+1		1	
Green	22+8	1	2		2		1	
Henry	8							
Keates	38+5	2	2		2		6	1
Keister	2		1					
Lambert	4+2							
Larusson	33+3	3			2		6	1
Marsh	43	2	2		2		5	
Mavrak	12+1	2					3	
Otta	6+2	3			2		1	1
Platt	6+1	1					0+3	
Pointon	43		2		2		6	
Porter	14+1		2		0+1		0+1	
Rammell	39	18	2	1	2		5	1
Ricketts	2+6		0+1					
Roper	29+3	1	0+1		2	1	6	
Simpson	10	1						
Steiner	10	3						
Thomas	1+11						0+4	
Viveash	40		2				5	

	P/FL App	P/FL Goals	FLC App	FLC Goals	FAC App	FAC Goals	Others App	Others Goals
WALSALL cont.								
Walker	46		2		2		6	
Watson	12+9	3	1+1		0+2		3	1
Wrack	46	13	2		2		6	1
WATFORD (DIV 2: 5th)								
Bazeley	36+4	2	1+1		1		3	
Bonnot	1+3							
Chamberlain	46		2		1		3	
Daley	6+6	1	1+1					
Easton	7		2					
Gibbs	9+1						1	
Gudmundsson	6+7	2						
Hazan	8+15	2	1+1				0+3	
Hyde	43+1	2	2		1		3	
Iroha	8+2				1			
Johnson	40	4			1	1	3	
Kennedy	46	6	2		1	1	3	
Lee	1	1	1		1			
Millen	10+1	1	1+1					
Mooney	20+16	9	1				3	
Ngonge	13+9	4	1	1			3	1
Noel-Williams	19+7	10			1			
Page	37+2				1		3	
Palmer	40+1	2	2		1		3	
Perpetuini	1							
Robinson	26+3		1+1		1		2	
Rosenthal	1+4		2		0+1			
Smart	34+1	7	0+1		1		0+3	1
Smith	3+5	2						
Ward	1							
Whittingham	4+1							
Wright	31+2	6			0+1		3	1
Yates	9	1	1					
WEST BROMWICH ALBION (DIV 1: 12th)								
Angel	4+18	1	0+1		0+1			
Bortolazzi	25+10	2			1			
Burgess	15+5		0+1					
Carbon	38+1	2	2		1			
Crichton			1					
De Freitas	22+15	7			0+1			
Evans	17+3	2	2	1				
Flynn	33+5	2	2		0+1			
Gabbidon	2							
Holmes	17				1			
Hughes	42	31	2	1	1			
Kilbane	44	6	2		1			
McDermott	20							
Mardon	12+6		2					
Maresca	9+13	2						
Miller	20		1					
Murphy	30+7	4	2		1			
Oliver	0+1		0+1					
Potter	19+3		0+1		1			
Quailey	1+1		0+1					
Quinn	39+4	6	2		1			
Raven	6+1							
Richards	0+1							
Sneekes	35+5	4	2		2			
Van Blerk	30		2					
Whitehead	26				1			
WEST HAM UNITED (PREM: 5th)								
Abou	2+1		1		0+1			
Berkovic	28+2	3	1		1+1			
Breacker	2+1		0+1		1			
Cole	2+6				0+1			
Coyne	0+1							
Di Canio	12+1	4						

	P/FL App	P/FL Goals	FLC App	FLC Goals	FAC App	FAC Goals	Others App	Others Goals
WEST HAM UNITED cont.								
Dicks	9		1		2	1		
Ferdinand	31		1		1			
Foe	13							
Forrest	1+1							
Hall					0+1			
Hartson	16+1	4	1		2			
Hislop	37		2		2			
Hodges	0+1							
Holligan	0+1							
Impey	6+2		1					
Keller	17+4	5	1					
Kitson	13+4	3						
Lampard	38	5	2	1	1			
Lazaridis	11+4		1		2			
Lomas	30	1			2			
Margas	3							
Minto	14+1							
Moncur	6+8		1					
Omoyinmi	0+3		0+1		1+1			
Pearce	33	2	2		1			
Potts	11+8		2		1			
Ruddock	27	2	1		2			
Sinclair	36	7	2		2			
Wright	20+2	9	2		1			
WIGAN ATHLETIC (DIV 2: 6th)								
Balmer	36	1	1		3		7	1
Barlow	39+2	19	2	1	2	1	8+1	5
Bradshaw	39	6	3		2		6	
Carroll	43		4		3		9	
Fitzhenry	1							
Green	32+5		4		3		4+1	
Greenall	40	6	2		3	1	9	
Griffiths	20		4	1	1		1	
Haworth	19+1	10			1	1	5	3
Jenkinson	3+4		3		0+1		0+1	
Jones	8+12	3	2				2+2	1
Kilford	16+7		2		3		3+1	1
Lee	20+16	6	4	1	1+2		2+4	1
Liddell	28	10					7	
Lowe	5+11	1	3		1+1	2	1+1	
McGibbon	35+1	5	3		2		9	
Martinez	3+7		2		0+1		1	
Nixon	3							
O'Neill	35+1		1		3		7	3
Porter	6+10	1	0+2		1		3+3	
Rogers	42	2	4		2		6	1
Sharp	25+6	2	0+1		1		8	1
Smeets	0+1		0+1		0+1			
Warne	8+3	1	0+1		1		1	1
WIMBLEDON (PREM: 16th)								
Ainsworth	5+3							
Ardley	16+7		5	3	3			
Blackwell	27+1		4		2			
Castledine	1							
Cort	6+10	3	2+1		0+3	1		
Cunningham	35		6+1		2			
Earle	35	5	5	1	3	1		
Ekoku	11+11	6	4+1	3	2			
Euell	31+2	10	5+2		3			
Fear	0+2		1					
Francis								
Gayle	31+4	10	4	1	1			
Goodman	0+1							
Hartson	12+2	2						
Heald			2					
Hughes C	8+6		0+1		0+3			
Hughes M	28+2	2	4	1	2			

WIMBLEDON cont.

	P/FL App	Goals	FLC App	Goals	FAC App	Goals	Others App	Goals
Jupp	3+ 3		2		1			
Kennedy	7+10		4+1	1	2			
Kimble	22+ 4		1+2		2			
Leaburn	14+ 8		3+4	1	3			
McAllister			1					
Perry	34		7		2			
Roberts	23+ 5	2	3+1		2+1			
Sullivan	38		5		3			
Thatcher	31		7		2			

WOLVERHAMPTON WANDERERS (DIV 1: 7th)

	P/FL App	Goals	FLC App	Goals	FAC App	Goals	Others App	Goals
Atkins	15		0+1		2			
Bull	11+ 4	3	2	3				
Connolly	18+14	6	2		0+1			
Corica	20 +11	2	1+1		1			
Curle	44	4	3		2			
Emblen	30+ 3	2	2+1		2			
Ferguson	2+ 2		0+2	1				
Flo	18+ 1	5			1	1		
Foley	2+ 3	2						
Froggatt	8		2+1					
Gilkes	25+ 5		0+1		2			
Gomez	17+ 2	2	2		1			
Green	1							
Jones	0+ 2		0+2					
Keane	30+ 3	11	4	3	2	2		
Muscat	37	4	4		2			
Naylor	17+ 6	1	4					
Niestroj	2+ 3							
Osborn	36+ 1	2	4	1	1			
Richards	40+ 1	3	4		1			
Robinson	29+ 5	7	1		2			

WOLVERHAMPTON WANDERERS cont.

	P/FL App	Goals	FLC App	Goals	FAC App	Goals	Others App	Goals
Sedgley	41+ 3	3	3		0+1			
Simpson	8+ 3	2	1		0+1			
Stowell	46		4		2			
Whittingham	9+ 1	1						
Williams			1					

WREXHAM (DIV 2: 17th)

	P/FL App	Goals	FLC App	Goals	FAC App	Goals	Others App	Goals
Barrett	8+ 2							
Brace	15+ 2		1					
Brammer	31+ 3	2	1+1		5	1	6	1
Carey	36	2	2		3		5	
Cartwright	30		2		5		6	
Chalk	19+ 9		1		4+1		5	
Connolly	43+ 1	11	2	1	5	5	5	1
Cooke	10						1	
Edwards	4+ 5	1					1+4	2
Elliott	8+ 1						1	
Gibson	3+ 4	1			0+1		2+3	
Griffiths	4	3					1	1
Hardy	31+ 2		1		4		4	
Humes	10+ 2	1	1					
McGregor	43	1	2		5		6	
Morrell	4+ 3						0+1	
Owen	35	3	2		2+1		5+1	1
Ridler	35+ 1	1	1		4		5+1	1
Rishworth	0+ 4							
Roberts N	11 +11	3	1	1	3	1	2+1	2
Roberts S							0+1	
Rush	12+ 5	2	2		4		0+1	
Russell	25+ 6	2	1+1		4+1	1	6	
Skinner	12	2	0+2					
Spink	26+ 8	3	0+1		4+1		5+1	

WREXHAM cont.

	P/FL App	Goals	FLC App	Goals	FAC App	Goals	Others App	Goals
Thomas	1+ 4							
Ward	25	2	2		3		0+1	
Whitley	9	2						
Wright	16							

WYCOMBE WANDERERS (DIV 2: 19th)

	P/FL App	Goals	FLC App	Goals	FAC App	Goals	Others App	Goals
Baird	25+ 3	6	0+2		3	1	1	
Bates	9							
Beeton	11+ 5		2		0+1			
Brown	34+ 4	3	3	2	2		2	
Bulman	5+ 6	1	1+1		0+2			
Carroll	27+ 5	6	2+1		2	1	2	
Cornforth	9+ 4	1	4				0+1	
Cousins	34	2	4		3		1	
Devine	11+ 1	8						
Emblen	28+ 7	2	2		2+1		1	
Forsyth	4							
Harkin	1+ 1		0+1					
Holsgrove	0+ 1							
Kavanagh	14+ 4		4				1	
Lawrence	34	2			3		2	
Lee	2+ 1							
McCarthy	26+ 3	1	2+1		3		1	
McGavin	1+ 4		1				0+1	
McSporran	11 +15	4					1+1	1
Mohan	25	2	3		2		1	
Read	11+ 5	1	2	1	0+1	1	1	
Robson	1+ 3							
Ryan	26+ 2	1	2				1	1
Scott	23+ 2	6	0+1		3	1	1	
Senda	0+ 6							
Simpson	31+ 2	4			3		2	
Stallard	12+ 3	2	4	1				
Taylor	44		3		3		1	
Vinnicombe	39+ 2		4		3		1	
Westhead	2		1				1	
Wraight	6		0+2		1			

YORK CITY (DIV 2: 21st)

	P/FL App	Goals	FLC App	Goals	FAC App	Goals	Others App	Goals
Agnew	19+ 1	2	1		3			
Barras	24				1		1	
Bullock					1			
Carruthers	3+ 3							
Connelly	28	4	2		3		1	
Cresswell	36	16	2		3	3		
Dawson	7+ 4	1						
Fairclough	11							
Garratt	33+ 5	1	1+1		3		0+1	
Hall	26+ 1	1	2				1	
Himsworth	12+ 1				1+1		1	
Hocking	4+ 2							
Jones	44+ 1	2	2		3		1	
Jordan	27+ 5	5			3	2	1	
McMillan	33		2		2		1	
Mimms	35		1		1		1	
Pouton	24+ 3	1	2					
Prendergast	1+ 2		0+1		0+1			
Reed	8+ 4		1+1					
Rennison					0+1			
Rowe	24 +15	7	1		0+3		1	1
Skinner	3+ 2							
Thompson	24	6	2	1				
Tinkler	36+ 1	2	2		3		1	
Tolson	17 +11	3	0+1		2+1		0+1	1
Warrington	11		1		2			
Williams	11	4			2			
Woods	5+ 3		1		1			

Steve Brown (Wycombe Wanderers)

PFA AWARDS 1999

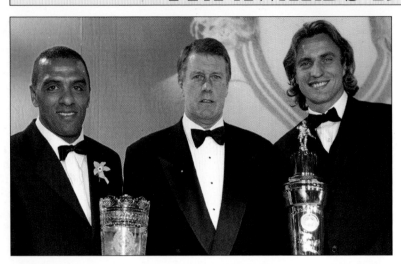

Player of the Year
DAVID GINOLA

Young Player of the Year
NICOLAS ANELKA

Special Merit Award
TONY FORD

DIVISIONAL AWARDS

FA Carling Premiership

Nigel Martyn	Leeds United
Gary Neville	Manchester United
Denis Irwin	Manchester United
Sol Campbell	Tottenham Hotspur
Jaap Stam	Manchester United
David Ginola	Tottenham Hotspur
Emmanuel Petit	Arsenal
Patrick Vieira	Arsenal
David Beckham	Manchester United
Dwight Yorke	Manchester United
Nicolas Anelka	Arsenal

Nationwide League Division 1

Richard Wright	Ipswich Town
Gary Rowett	Birmingham City
Michael Gray	Sunderland
Darren Moore	Bradford City
Paul Butler*	Sunderland
Mark Venus*	Ipswich Town
Kieron Dyer	Ipswich Town
Per Frandsen	Bolton Wanderers
Allan Johnston	Sunderland
Lee Clark	Sunderland
Lee Hughes	West Bromwich Albion
Niall Quinn	Sunderland

Nationwide League Division 2

Maik Taylor	Fulham
Steve Finnan	Fulham
Rufus Brevett*	Fulham
Jamie Vincent*	AFC Bournemouth
Chris Coleman	Fulham
Steve Davis	Burnley
Sean Gregan	Preston North End
Graham Kavanagh	Stoke City
Darren Wrack	Walsall
Steve Robinson	AFC Bournemouth
Mark Stein	AFC Bournemouth
Geoff Horsfield	Fulham

Nationwide League Division 3

Jon Hallworth	Cardiff City
Mark Delaney	Cardiff City
Paul Gibbs	Plymouth Argyle
Chris Hope	Scunthorpe United
Hermann Hreidarsson	Brentford
Jason Fowler	Cardiff City
Paul Evans	Shrewsbury Town
Jeff Minton	Brighton & Hove Albion
Simon Davis*	Peterborough United
Matt Etherington*	Peterborough United
Jamie Forrester	Scunthorpe United
Martin Butler	Cambridge United

*Players tied for position